Fodor's 2003

France

The Guide
for All Budgets

Completely
Updated

Where to Stay, Eat,
and Explore

On and Off
the Beaten Path

When to Go,
What to Pack

Maps, Travel Tips,
and Web Sites

Fodor's Travel Publications • New York, Toronto, London, Sydney, Auckland
www.fodors.com

Fodor's France 2003

EDITOR: Robert I. C. Fisher

Editorial Contributors: Simon Hewitt, Rosa Jackson, Nicola Keegan, Christopher Mooney, George Semler
Editorial Production: Tom Holton
Maps: David Lindroth, *cartographer;* Rebecca Baer and Robert Blake, *map editors*
Design: Fabrizio La Rocca, *creative director;* Guido Caroti, *art director;* Jolie Novak, *senior picture editor;* Melanie Marin, *photo editor*
Cover Design: Pentagram
Production/Manufacturing: Yexenia (Jessie) Markland
Cover Photo (Women in Lavender Field, Provence): Robb Kendrick/ Aurora

Copyright

ISBN 1–4000–1044–6

ISSN 0532–5692

Important Tip

Although all prices, opening times, and other details in this book are based on information supplied to us at press time, changes occur all the time in the travel world, and Fodor's cannot accept responsibility for facts that become outdated or for inadvertent errors or omissions. So **always confirm information when it matters,** especially if you're making a detour to visit a specific place.

Special Sales

Fodor's Travel Publications are available at special discounts for bulk purchases for sales promotions or premiums. Special editions, including personalized covers, excerpts of existing guides, and corporate imprints, can be created in large quantities for special needs. For more information, contact your local bookseller or write to Special Markets, Fodor's Travel Publications, 280 Park Avenue, New York, NY 10017. Inquiries from Canada should be directed to your local Canadian bookseller or sent to Random House of Canada, Ltd., Marketing Department, 2775 Matheson Boulevard East, Mississauga, Ontario L4W 4P7. Inquiries from the United Kingdom should be sent to Fodor's Travel Publications, 20 Vauxhall Bridge Road, London SW1V 2SA, England.

PRINTED IN THE UNITED STATES OF AMERICA

10 9 8 7 6 5 4 3 2 1

CONTENTS

Maps

ON THE ROAD WITH FODOR'S

TAKING A TRIP COMPLETELY TAKES YOU OUT OF YOURSELF. Concerns of life at home are quickly driven away by more immediate thoughts—about, say, what marvels will beguile the next day or where you'll have dinner. That's where Fodor's comes in. We make sure that you have all the right choices and that you don't knowingly miss out on something that's around the next bend just because you didn't know it was there. Always mindful that it's often the things that you didn't come to France expecting to see that end up meaning the most, we guide you to sights large and small all over the country. You might set out to explore the Loire Valley château at Chenonceaux but back at home you find yourself unable to forget that idyllic afternoon spent learning the difference between Sauvignon and Cabernet Franc in the wine cellars of nearby Montlouis or sharing a sunset with the swans at the Domaine des Hauts-de-Loire. With Fodor's at your side, serendipitous discoveries are never far away.

Our success in showing you every corner of France is a credit to our extraordinary writers. While there's no substitute for travel advice from a good friend who knows your style, our contributors are the next best thing—the kind of people you would poll for travel advice if you knew them.

About Our Writers

Nancy Coons is based in a 300-year-old farmhouse in Lorraine and covers much of northeastern France while satisfying her long-distance love affair with the luscious south of the country. Author of Fodor's *Provence and the Côte d'Azur*, as well as two of Fodor's color-photograph guide books—*Escape to Provence* and *Escape to the Riviera*—she has become adept at describing the golden light of Arles from under the iron-gray skies back home.

Simon Hewitt headed to Paris straight from studying French and art history at Oxford. It was a return to base: His grandmother was French, as are his wife and daughter. He moved to Versailles a few years ago to gain a different perspective on life in and around the French capital. When not contemplating the Sun King's bicep-flexing Baroque, his thoughts often turn to cricket—he is captain of the French national team. For this edition, he updated our Paris Exploring section as well as the chapters on the Ile de France, the Loire Valley, Brittany, Normandy, and Bordeaux.

Rosa Jackson's love affair with French pastries began at age four, when she spent her first year in Paris before returning to the Canadian north. Early experiments with eclairs and croissants led her to enroll in the Paris Cordon Bleu, where she learned that even great chefs make mistakes. A food writer for the past ten years, a Parisian since 1995, and now updater of our Paris Dining section, Rosa has eaten in hundreds of Paris restaurants—and always has room for dessert.

Nicola Keegan was born in Ireland and raised in Iowa. But after spending one year at the Sorbonne, she knew Paris was going to be her home forever. Now famous for crossing the city on foot even in the worst storms, and her uncanny knowledge of where to purchase absolute necessities from truffle oil to that perfect pair of gold-hued boots, she brings all her hard earned "savoir faire" to the Smart Travel Tips and Paris Shopping sections and has also updated our chapters on the North and Alsace, Lorraine, and Franche-Comté.

Christopher Mooney originally came to Paris to study French philosophy, smoke Gîtanes cigarettes, and hang out in cafés. Twelve years later he's still there, but his taste for Gallic thought and tobacco has given way to an unslakeable thirst for fine Burgundy vintages. For this edition, this passionate writer (his pet computer often doubles as an additional pillow when he's traveling on the road) devoted his efforts to finding the best Parisian hotels and also updated our chapters on Burgundy, the Massif Central, Provence, and the Côte d'Azur.

George Semler lives over the border in Spain, but he has skied, hiked, fly-fished, and explored every side of the Pyrénées. He's acquainted with every trout—of Spanish *and* French persuasion—as well as each wild mushroom and Romanesque chapel. For this edition, he updated our chapters on Lyon and the Alps, the Midi-Pyrénées, Basque Country, and Corsica. Author of *Fodor's Barcelona to Bilbao*, he also writes for a variety of publications including *Saveur* and *Forbes FYI*.

Robert I. C. Fisher, New York City–based editor of *Fodor's France 2003*, succeeded in getting one foot in the caviar when he was sent to the French capital to write up the Hôtel Lambert—the noted Ile St-Louis residence of Baron and Baroness Guy de Rothschild—for the April 1988 issue of *Town & Country.* His recent trips to the Loire Valley have greatly expanded this edition's coverage of that beautiful realm.

Special thanks to **Satu Hummasti**—sterling formatter of our Smart Travel Tips section—and **Yan Baczkowski,** who so helpfully and delightfully lent us the aid and auspices of the French Government Tourist Office.

Rest assured that you're in good hands and that no property mentioned in the book has paid to be included—each has been selected strictly on its merits, as the best of its type in its price range.

How to Use This Book

Up front is Smart Travel Tips A to Z, arranged alphabetically by topic and loaded with tips plus Web sites and contact information for the companies and organizations we recommend. Our introductory chapter, Destination: France, helps get you in the mood for your trip. Subsequent chapters are arranged regionally. The Paris chapter begins with Exploring information, with a section for each neighborhood (each recommending a walking tour and listing sights alphabetically). All regional chapters are divided geographically; within each area, towns are covered in logical geographical order. To help you decide what you'll have time to visit in the days available, all chapters begin with our writers' favorite itineraries. The A to Z section that ends every chapter covers getting there and getting around and provides more helpful contacts and resources. At the end of the book you'll find the Background and Essentials chapter, which includes a wonderful essay about food as well as a dateline of French history.

Icons and Symbols

★ Our special recommendations
✕ Restaurant
🏨 Lodging establishment
✕🏨 Lodging establishment whose restaurant warrants a special trip
🦆 Good for kids (rubber duck)
☞ Sends you to another section of the guide for more information
✉ Address
☎ Telephone number
⏲ Opening and closing times
🎟 Admission prices (those we give apply to adults; substantially reduced fees are almost always available for children, students, and senior citizens)

Numbers in white and black circles ③ ❸ that appear on the maps, in the margins, and within the tours correspond to one another.

Don't Forget to Write

Your experiences—positive and negative—matter to us. If we have missed or misstated something, we want to hear about it. We follow up on all suggestions. Contact the France editor at editors@fodors.com or c/o Fodor's at 280 Park Avenue, New York, New York 10017. And have a fabulous trip!

Karen Cure
Editorial Director

France

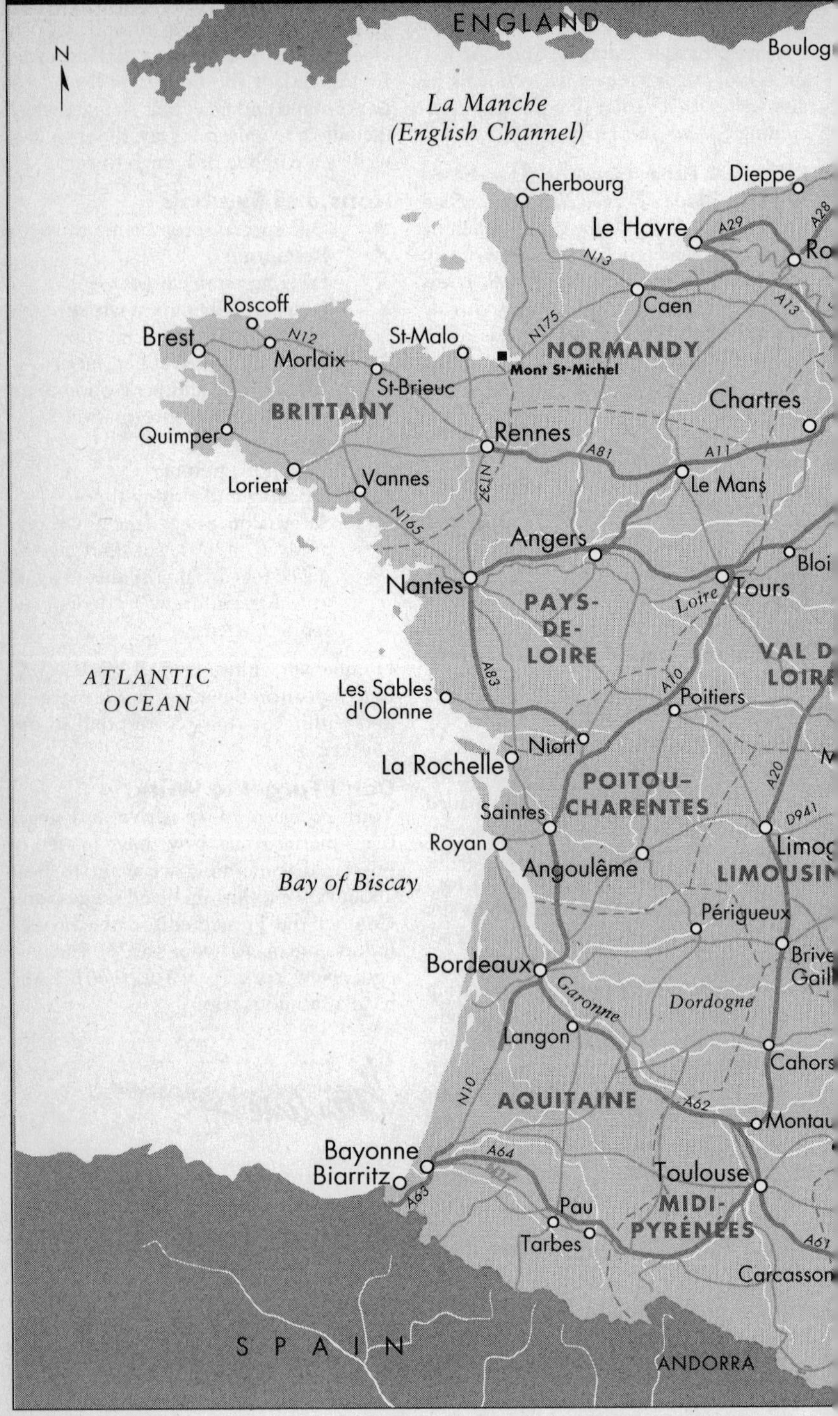
N
ENGLAND
La Manche
(English Channel)
Cherbourg
Dieppe
Le Havre
A29
A28
N13
Caen
A13
Roscoff
Brest
N12
Morlaix
St-Malo
Mont St-Michel
N175
NORMANDY
St-Brieuc
BRITTANY
Chartres
Quimper
Rennes
A81
A11
Lorient
Vannes
N137
Le Mans
N165
Angers
Nantes
Tours
Loire
PAYS-
DE-
LOIRE
ATLANTIC
OCEAN
A83
A10
Les Sables
d'Olonne
Poitiers
Niort
La Rochelle
POITOU-
CHARENTES
A20
Saintes
D941
Royan
Angoulême
Bay of Biscay
Périgueux
Bordeaux
Garonne
Dordogne
Langon
Cahors
N10
AQUITAINE
A62
Bayonne
Biarritz
A64
A63
Toulouse
MIDI-
PYRÉNÉES
Pau
Tarbes
A61
S P A I N
ANDORRA

Calais
A26
A16
BELGIUM
Lille
Arras
Cambrai
St. Quentin
A16
A26
Beauvais
CHAMPAGNE
ARDENNES
Reims
ILE-DE-
FRANCE
A4
Paris
A26
Châlons-en-
Champagne
LUXEMBOURG
Metz
A4
LORRAINE
Rhine
Nancy
Strasbourg
Sens
A5
Troyes
A6
GERMANY
A35
A31
Colmar
ALSACE
Mulhouse
Belfort
Auxerre
A6
Dijon
A36
Besançon
Bourges
Beaune
Nevers
BURGUNDY
FRANCHE-
COMTÉ
SWITZERLAND
Saône
A71
Mâcon
Bourg-en-
Bresse
A40
A72
Clermont-
Ferrand
Lyon
Rhône
ALPES
Chambéry
Rhône
A7
A49
Le Puy
Aurillac
RHÔNE
VALLEY
Grenoble
ITALY
A75
Montélimar
Gap
Millau
PROVENCE
Sisteron
Avignon
A51
CÔTE D'AZUR
Nîmes
Nice
MONACO
Monte Carlo
Montpellier
Aix-en-Provence
Cannes
A8
Marseille
Narbonne
Toulon
A9
Perpignan
0
50 mi
0
75 km
Mediterranean Sea
Corsica
Corsica
Bastia
Calvi
Corte
Ajaccio
N198
Bonifacio

ESSENTIAL INFORMATION

Half the fun of traveling is looking forward to your trip—but when you look forward, don't just daydream. There are plans to be made, things to learn about, serious work to be done. The following information will give you helpful pointers on many of the questions that arise when planning your trip and also when you are on the road. In addition, the organizations listed in this section will supplement the information in this guidebook. Note that additional essential information is provided in the A to Z sections found at the end of each regional chapter of this book. Many trips begin by first contacting the French tourist bureau: consult the French Government Tourist Offices listed under Visitor Information, *below*. Happy landings!

ADDRESSES

Addresses in France are fairly straightforward: there is the number and the street name. However, you may see an address with a number plus "bis," for instance, 20 bis rue Vavin: This indicates the next entrance or door down from 20 rue Vavin. In small towns a street number may not be given, as the site will be the dominant (or only) building on the block or square. In rural areas, however, a site may list only a route name, a number near the site, or sometimes just the name of the small village in which it is located.

In Paris a site's location in one of the city's 20 arrondissements is noted by its mailing code or, simply, the last one or two digits of that code (for example, Paris 75010 or 10^e^, both of which indicate that the address is in the 10th arrondissement; Paris 75005 or 5e, for another example, indicates the address is in the 5th arrondissement). Because of its large size, Paris's 16th arrondissement has two numbers assigned to it: 75016 and 75116. Note that in France you enter a building on the *rez-de-chaussée* (RC or 0), as the ground floor is known, and you have to go up one floor to reach the first floor, or *premier étage*.

AIR TRAVEL

As one of the premier destinations in the world, Paris is serviced by many international carriers and a surprising number of U.S.–based airlines. **Air France** is the French flag carrier and offers numerous flights (often several per day) between Paris's Charles de Gaulle airport and New York City's JFK airport; Newark, New Jersey; Washington, D.C.'s Reagan airport; as well as the cities of Miami; Chicago; Houston; San Francisco; Los Angeles; Toronto; Montréal; and Mexico City. American-based carriers are usually less expensive but offer, on the whole, fewer nonstop flights. **Delta Airlines** is a popular U.S.–France carrier; departures for Paris leave Atlanta, Cincinnati, and New York City's JFK, although Delta's regional flights link airports throughout the southeastern United States and the Midwest with its main international hub in Atlanta. Travelers in the northeast and southwest of the United States often use **Continental Airlines,** whose nonstop Paris flights generally depart from Newark and Houston; in peak season they often offer daily departures. Another popular carrier is **United Airlines,** with nonstop flights to Paris from Chicago, Washington, D.C., and San Francisco. **American Airlines** also offers daily nonstop flights to Paris's Orly Airport from numerous cities, including New York City's JFK, Boston, Miami, Chicago, and Dallas/Fort Worth. **Northwest** offers a daily departure to Paris from its hub in Detroit; connections from Seattle, Minneapolis, and numerous other airports link up to Detroit. In Canada, Air France and **Air Canada** are the leading choices for departures from Toronto and Montréal; in peak season, departures are often daily. From London, Air France, **British Airways, British Midland,** and **Air U.K.** are the leading carriers, with up to 15 flights daily in peak season. In addition, direct routes link Manchester, Edinburgh, and Southampton with Paris. **Ryan Air,** an Irish charter company that connects Paris, London, and Dublin, is getting raves for its cheaper-than-cheap flights. In order to assure their incredible prices they do not use the main airports that service all the major airlines but the smaller airports located a little bit farther out of Paris. In France, Ryan Air flights land at Le Bourget airport, about 45 minutes from Paris; they have a bus waiting to take you into the city for the minimal charge of €15, making the entire trip quite a bargain. Options are more limited for travelers to Paris from Australia and New Zealand, who usually wind up taking British Airways and **Qantas** flights to London, then connections to Paris.

There is also the quick and efficient option of using train transport via the Eurostar Express through the Channel Tunnel (☞ The Channel Tunnel and Train Travel to and from Paris, *below*).

BOOKING

When you book **look for nonstop flights** and **remember that "direct" flights stop at least once.** Try to avoid connecting flights, which require a change of plane. Two airlines may operate a connecting flight jointly, so ask if your airline operates every segment of the trip; you may find that the carrier you prefer flies you only part of the way. To find more booking tips and to check prices and make on-line flight reservations, log on to www.fodors.com.

CARRIERS

➤ MAJOR AIRLINES: **Air Canada** (☎ 800/776–3000 in the U.S. and Canada). **Air France** (☎ 800/237–2747 in the U.S.; 08–02–80–28–02 in France, www.airfrance.com). **American Airlines** (☎ 800/433–7300 in the U.S.; 01–69–32–73–07 in France, WEB www.aa.com). **British Airways** (☎ 800/247–9297 in the U.S.; 0345/222111 in the U.K.; 08–25–82–54–00 in France, WEB www.britishairways.com). **Continental** (☎ 800/231–0856 in the U.S.; 01–42–99–09–09 in France, WEB www.continental.com). **Delta** (☎ 800/241–4141 in the U.S.; 01–47–68–92–92 in France, WEB www.delta.com). **Northwest** (☎ 800/225–2525 in the U.S.; 01–42–66–90–00 in France, WEB www.klm.com). **Qantas** (☎ 800/227–4500 in the U.S.; 08–03–84–68–46 in France, WEB www.qantas.com). **United** (☎ 800/538–2929 in the U.S.; 08–01–72–72–72 in France, WEB www.unitedairlines.com). **US Airways** (☎ 800/428–4322 in the U.S.; 01–49–10–29–00 in France, WEB www.usairways.com).

➤ DOMESTIC AIRLINES: **Air France** (☞ *below*). **Air Liberté** (☎ 08–03–80–58–05, WEB www.air-liberte.fr).

➤ U.K. TO FRANCE: **Air France** (☎ 020/8742–6600 in the U.K.; 08–02–80–28–02 in France, WEB www.airfrance.com). **Air U.K.** (☎ 0345/666–777 in the U.K.; 01–44–56–18–08 in France). **British Airways** (☎ 0345/222–111 in the U.K.; 08–02–80–29–02 in France, WEB www.britishairways.com). **British Midland** (☎ 020/8754–7321; 0345/554–554 in the U.K.; 01–48–62–55–65 in France, WEB www.flybmi.com). **Easyjet** (☎ 0990/292–929 in the U.K.; 04–93–21–48–33 in France, WEB www.easyjet.com) runs scheduled services to Nice from Luton. **Ryan Air** (☎ 0990/292–929 in the U.K.; 04–93–21–48–33 in France, WEB www.ryanair.com).

CHECK-IN & BOARDING

Always **ask your carrier about its check-in policy.** Plan to arrive at the airport about two hours before your scheduled departure time for domestic flights and 2½ to 3 hours before international flights. Assuming that not everyone with a ticket will show up, airlines routinely overbook planes. When everyone does, airlines ask for volunteers to give up their seats. In return, these volunteers usually get a certificate for a free flight and are rebooked on the next flight out. If there are not enough volunteers, the airline must choose who will be denied boarding. The first to get bumped are passengers who checked in late and those flying on discounted tickets, so **get to the gate and check in as early as possible,** especially during peak periods.

Always **bring a government-issued photo I.D. to the airport;** even when it's not required, a passport is best.

CUTTING COSTS

The least expensive airfares to France must usually be purchased in advance and are nonrefundable. It's smart to **call a number of airlines and check the Internet;** when you are quoted a good price, **book it on the spot**—the same fare may not be available the next day. Always **check different routings** and look into using alternate airports. Also, price off-peak flights, which may be significantly less expensive than others. Travel agents, especially low-fare specialists (☞ Discounts and Deals, *below*), are helpful.

Consolidators are another good source. They buy tickets for scheduled international flights at reduced rates from the airlines, then sell them at prices that beat the best fare available directly from the airlines, usually without restrictions. Sometimes you can even get your money back if you need to return the ticket. Carefully read the fine print detailing penalties for changes and cancellations, and **confirm your consolidator reservation with the airline.**

When you **fly as a courier,** you trade your checked-luggage space for a ticket deeply subsidized by a courier service. There are restrictions on when you can book and how long you can stay. Some courier companies list with membership organizations, such as the Air Courier Association and the International Association of Air Travel Couriers; these require you to become a member before you can book a flight.

➤ CONSOLIDATORS: **Cheap Tickets** (☎ 800/377–1000 or 888/922–8849, WEB www.cheaptickets.com). **Discount Airline Ticket Service** (☎ 800/576–1600). **Unitravel** (☎ 800/325–2222, WEB www.unitravel.com). **Up & Away Travel** (☎ 212/889–2345, WEB www.upandaway.com). **World Travel Network** (☎ 800/409–6753).

➤ COURIERS: **Air Courier Association** (✉ 15000 W. 6th Ave., Suite 203, Golden, CO 80401, ☎ 800/282–1202, WEB www.aircourier.org). **International Association of Air Travel Couriers** (✉ 220 S. Dixie Hwy. #3, Box 1349, Lake Worth, FL 33460, ☎ 561/582–8320, FAX 561/582–1581, WEB www.courier.org). **Now Voyager Travel** (✉ 74 Varick St., Suite 307, New York, NY 10013 ☎ 212/431–1616, FAX 212/219–1753 or 212/334–5243).

➤ DISCOUNT PASSES: **Air France** (☞ Major Carriers, *above*).

ENJOYING THE FLIGHT

State your seat preference when purchasing your ticket, and then repeat it when you confirm and when you check in. For more legroom, you can request one of the few emergency-aisle seats at check-in, if you are capable of lifting at least 50 pounds—a Federal Aviation Administration requirement of passengers in these seats. Seats behind a bulkhead also offer more legroom, but they don't have underseat storage. Don't sit in the row in front of the emergency aisle or in front of a bulkhead, where seats may not recline.

Ask the airline whether a snack or meal is served on the flight. If you have dietary concerns, **request special meals when booking.** These can be vegetarian, low-cholesterol, or kosher, for example. It's a good idea to pack some healthy snacks and a small (plastic) bottle of water in your carry-on bag. On long flights, try to maintain a normal routine, to help fight jet lag. At night, **get some sleep.** By day, **eat light meals, drink water** (not alcohol), and **move around the cabin** to stretch your legs. For additional jet-lag tips consult *Fodor's FYI: Travel Fit & Healthy* (available at bookstores everywhere).

FLYING TIMES

Flying time to Paris is 7½ hours from New York, nine hours from Chicago, 11 hours from Los Angeles, and one hour from London. Flying time between Paris and Nice is one hour.

HOW TO COMPLAIN

If your baggage goes astray or your flight goes awry, complain right away. Most carriers require that you **file a claim immediately.** The Aviation Consumer Protection Division of the Department of Transportation publishes *Fly-Rights,* which discusses airlines and consumer issues and is available on-line. At PassengerRights.com, a Web site, you can compose a letter of complaint and distribute it electronically.

➤ AIRLINE COMPLAINTS: U.S. Department of Transportation **Aviation Consumer Protection Division** (✉ C-75, Room 4107, Washington, DC 20590, ☎ 202/366–2220, WEB www.dot.gov/airconsumer). **Federal Aviation Administration Consumer Hotline** (☎ 800/322–7873).

AIRPORTS

There are two major gateway airports to France, both just outside the capital: Orly, 16 km (10 mi) south of Paris, and Charles de Gaulle—also known as Roissy—26 km (16 mi) northeast of the city. Orly has two terminals: Orly Ouest (domestic flights) and Orly Sud (international, regular, and charter flights). Roissy has three terminals: Aérogare 1 (foreign flights), Aérogare 2 (Air France flights), and Aérogare T-9 (charter flights). Terminal information should be noted on your ticket. The three Orly terminals are connected with a free shuttle service, called the *navette*. At Roissy there's a TGV station (from Terminal 2) where you can connect to trains going all over the country. Many airlines have less frequent flights to Lyon, Nice, Marseille, Bordeaux, and Toulouse. Or you can fly to Paris and get a connecting flight to other destinations in France.

➤ AIRPORT INFORMATION: **Charles de Gaulle/Roissy** (☎ 01–48–62–22–80 in English, WEB www.adp.fr). **Orly** (☎ 01–49–75–15–15, WEB www.adp.fr).

AIRPORT TRANSFERS: PARIS

Always allot at an extra hour to the commute (via car, bus, or train) to the Paris airports when departing from the capital since horrendous traffic tie-ups within the airports proper can seriously add to the time it takes to get to the ticket counter. Once you arrive at the airport from Paris, you'll often need to take the inter-airport bus to shuttle you from one terminal to another, and if there is traffic congestion, a serious case of nail-biting can result.

Charles de Gaulle/Roissy: From Charles de Gaulle airport, **the least expensive way to get into Paris is on the RER-B line,** the suburban express train. Each terminal has an exit where the free RER shuttle bus (a white and yellow bus with the letters ADP in gray) will pass every 7–15 minutes to take you on the short ride to the nearby RER station: Terminal 2A (exit A8), Terminal 2C (exit C8), Terminal 2B (exit B6), Terminal 2D (exit D6), Terminal 2F (exit 2.08). Trains to central Paris (Les Halles, St-Michel, Luxembourg) depart every 15 minutes. The fare (including métro connection) is €7.62, and journey time is about 30 minutes.

The **Air France shuttle service** is a comfortable option to get to and from the city—you don't need to have flown the carrier to use this. Line one goes from the airport to Paris's Charles de Gaulle Etoile and Porte Maillot from 5:45 AM to 11 PM. It leaves every 12 minutes and costs €10, which you can pay on board. Passengers arriving in Terminal 1 need to take exit 34; Terminal 2A and 2C, exit 5; Terminal 2B and 2D, exit 6; Terminal 2F, exit 0.07. Line Four goes to Montparnasse and the Gare de Lyon from 7 AM to 9 PM. Buses run every 30 minutes and cost €11.50. Passengers arriving in Terminal 1 need to look for exit 34, Terminal 2A and 2C need to take either exit 2 or 2C, Terminal 2B and 2D exit 2 or 2B, and Terminal 2F exit 0.07.

Another option is to take **Roissybus,** operated by the Paris Transit Authority, which runs between Charles de Gaulle and the Opéra every 20 minutes from 5:45 AM to 11 PM; the cost is €8.08. Note that you have to hail the bus you want—it will not stop automatically—and that rush-hour traffic can make for a slow ride.

Taxis are your least desirable mode of transportation into the city. If you are traveling at peak tourist times, you may have to stand in a very long line with a lot of other disgruntled European travelers (most of whom smoke). Journey times, and as a consequence, prices, are therefore unpredictable. At best, the journey takes 30 minutes but it can take as long as one hour.

Orly: From Orly Airport **the most economical way to get into Paris is to**

take the RER-C or Orlyrail line; catch the free shuttle bus from the terminal to the train station. Trains to Paris leave every 15 minutes. Passengers arriving in either the South or West Terminal need to use exit G. The fare is €5.20, and journey time is about 35 minutes. Another option is to **take the monorail service, Orlyval,** which runs between the Antony RER-B station and Orly Airport every four to eight minutes. The fare to downtown Paris is €8.70.

You can also **take an Air France bus** from Orly to Les Invalides on the Left Bank and Montparnasse; these run every 12 minutes from 6 AM to 11:30 PM (you need not have flown on Air France to use this service). The fare is €7.50, and journey time is between 30 and 45 minutes, depending on traffic. The Paris Transit Authority's **Orlybus is yet another option**; buses leave every 15 minutes for the Denfert-Rochereau métro station; the cost is €5.65.

➤ TAXIS & SHUTTLES: **Air France Bus** (☎ 01–41–56–89–00 recorded information in English, WEB www.cars-airfrance.com). **Airport Shuttle** (☎ 01–30–11–11–90; 888/426–2705 toll free from the U.S., FAX 01–30–11–11–99, WEB www.airportshuttle.fr).

DUTY-FREE SHOPPING

Duty-free shopping at French airports is no longer available for those traveling *within* the boundaries of the European Community. You can purchase whatever you want at airport stores, of course, but only travelers *leaving* European territory will benefit from the duty-free prices.

BARGE AND YACHT TRAVEL

Canal and river trips are popular in France, particularly along the picturesque waterways in Brittany, Burgundy, and the Midi. For further information, contact a travel agent; ask for a "Tourisme Fluvial" brochure at any French tourist office; or get in touch with one of the companies that organize barge trips. It's also possible to rent a barge or crewed sailboat to travel around the coast of France, particularly along the Côte d'Azur.

➤ DOMESTIC BARGE COMPANIES: **Bourgogne Voies Navigables** (✉ 1 quai de la République, 89000 Auxerre, ☎ 03–86–72–92–10, WEB www.tourisme-yonne.com). **Connoisseur Cruisers** (✉ Halye Nautique, Ile Sauzay, 70100 Gray, ☎ 03–84–64–95–20, WEB www.connoisseur.fr).

➤ INTERNATIONAL BARGE COMPANIES: **Abercrombie & Kent** (✉ 1520 Kensington Rd, Oak Brook, IL 60521, ☎ 630/954–2944 or 800/323–7308, FAX 630/954–3324). **Étoile de Champagne** (✉ 88 Broad St., Boston, MA 02110, ☎ 800/280–1492, FAX 617/426–4689). **European Waterways** (✉ 140 E. 56th St., Suite 4C, New York, NY 10022, ☎ 212/688–9489 or 800/217–4447, FAX 212/688–3778 or 800/296–4554). **French Country Waterways** (✉ Box 2195, Duxbury, MA 02331, ☎ 781/934–2454 or 800/222–1236, FAX 781/934–9048). **KD River Cruises of Europe** (✉ 2500 Westchester Ave., Purchase, NY 10577, ☎ 914/696–3600 or 800/346–6525, FAX 914/696–0833, WEB www.rivercruises.com). **Kemwel's Premier Selections** (✉ 106 Calvert St., Harrison, NY 10528, ☎ 914/835–5555 or 800/234–4000, FAX 914/835–5449).

BEACHES

Along the miles of French coast you'll find broad-brimmed hats, parasols, and opaque sunglasses—their modesty and discretion charmingly contradictory in view of (and we mean full view of) the frankly bare flesh that bobbles up and down the same miles of seashore. And not just the famous *seins nus* (topless women), but the bellies of gastronome *pépés* (grandfathers) as well. Naked children crouch over sand châteaux, their unself-consciousness a reflection of their elders' own. For the French the summer beach holiday is a sacred ritual, a counterbalance to the winter ski trip.

To avoid the July–August stampede, **go in June or September.** Ironic as it may be, France's most famous coastline has the country's worst beaches: sand along the Côte d'Azur is in shorter supply than pebbles. By far the finest French beaches are those facing north (toward the Channel) and west (toward the Atlantic). Many are so vast that you can spread out even at the most popular resorts (like

Biarritz, Royan, Dinard, or Le Touquet). Brittany's beaches are the most picturesque, though the water can be chilly, even in summer.

If you're planning to devote a lot of time to beaches and haven't tackled the French coast before, get to **know the distinction between private and public.** France's waterfront is carved up into private frontage, often roped off and advertised by color-coordinated awnings, parasols, and mattresses. These private beaches frequently offer full restaurant and bar service and rent mattresses, umbrellas, and lounge chairs by the day and half-day. Dressing rooms and showers are included; some even rent private cabanas. Prices can run from €9 a day to €18.45 or more. Interspersed between these commercial beaches is plenty of public space.

BIKE TRAVEL

The French are great bicycling enthusiasts—witness the Tour de France—and there are many good bicycling routes in France. For about €7.70 a day (€10.75 for a 10-speed touring bike) you can **rent a bike from one of 30 train stations throughout the country;** you need to show your passport and leave a deposit of €152 or a Visa or MasterCard. Mountain bikes (known as VTT, or Vélos Touts Terrains) can be rented from many shops as well as from some train stations. Tourist offices supply details on the more than 200 local shops that rent bikes, and the SNCF has a brochure entitled the "Guide du Train et du Vélo," available at any train station. Bikes may be taken as accompanied luggage from any station in France; most trains in rural areas do not charge for bikes (but inquire at the SNCF ticket agencies about which ones do). Free bike space works on a first-come, first-served basis; you must take your bike to the designated compartment for loading yourself, so plan accordingly.

For information about good bike routes, contact the Fédération Française de Cyclotourisme. The yellow Michelin maps (1:200,000 scale) are fine for roads, but for off-road bicycling you may want to get one of the Institut Géographique National's detailed, large-scale maps. Try their blue series (1:25,000) or orange series (1:50,000).

➤ BIKE MAPS: **Institut Géographique National** (IGN; ✉ 107 rue La Boétie, 75008 Paris, ☎ 01–42–56–06–68, WEB www.ign.fr).

➤ BIKE RENTALS: **SNCF** (☞ Train Travel, *below*).

➤ BIKE ROUTES: **Fédération Française du Cyclisme** (✉ 5 rue de Rome, 93561 Rosny-sous-Bois cedex, ☎ 01–49–35–69–00, WEB www.ffc.fr).

➤ BIKE TOURS: **Backroads** (✉ 801 Cedar St., Berkeley, CA 94710-1800, ☎ 510/527–1555 or 800/462–2848, FAX 510/527–1444, WEB www.backroads.com). **Butterfield & Robinson** (✉ 70 Bond St., Toronto, Ontario M5B 1X3, ☎ 416/864–1354 or 800/678–1147, FAX 416/864–0541, WEB www.butterfield.com). **Chateaux Bike Tours** (✉ Box 5706, Denver, CO 80217, ☎ 303/393–6910 or 800/678–2453, FAX 303/393–6801). **Discover France Biking** (✉ 1603 E. Gardenia Ave., Phoenix, AZ 85020, ☎ 800/960–2221, FAX 602/944–5934, WEB www.discoverfrance.com). **Europeds** (✉ 761 Lighthouse Ave., Monterey, CA 93940, ☎ 800/321–9552, FAX 831/655–4501). **RMF** (✉ 1342 Birchcliff Dr., Oakville, Ontario, L6M2A4, ☎ 905/825–0796 or 800/530–5957, FAX 905/825–4177). **VBT (Vermont Biking Tours)** (✉ Box 711, Bristol, Vermont 05443, ☎ 800/245–3868, WEB www.vbt.com).

BIKES IN FLIGHT

Most airlines accommodate bikes as luggage, provided they are dismantled and boxed. Airlines sell bike boxes, which are often free at bike shops, for about $5 (it's at least $100 for bike bags). International travelers can sometimes substitute a bike for a piece of checked luggage at no charge; otherwise, the cost is about $100. Domestic and Canadian airlines charge $25–$50.

BOAT AND FERRY TRAVEL

BETWEEN THE U.K. AND FRANCE

A number of ferry and hovercraft routes link the United Kingdom and France. Driving distances from the French ports to Paris are as follows:

from Calais, 290 km (180 mi); from Boulogne, 243 km (151 mi); from Dieppe, 193 km (120 mi); from Dunkerque, 257 km (160 mi). The fastest routes to Paris from each port are via the N43, A26, and A1 from Calais and the Channel Tunnel; via the N1 from Boulogne; via the N15 from Le Havre; via the D915 and N1 from Dieppe; and via the A25 and A1 from Dunkerque.

➤ DOVER–CALAIS: **Hoverspeed** (✉ International Hoverport, Marine Parade, Dover CT17 9TG, ☎ 01304/240241, WEB www.hoverspeed.com) operates up to 15 crossings a day by hovercraft and catamaran. The crossings take 35 minutes (hovercraft) or 55 minutes (catamaran). **P&O European Ferries** (✉ Channel House, Channel View Rd., Dover, Kent CT17 9TJ, ☎ 020/8575–8555, WEB www.poportsmouth.com) has up to 25 sailings a day; the crossing takes about 75 minutes. **Seafrance** (✉ 23 rue Louis le Grand Paris, France 75002, ☎ 01–44–94–40–40, WEB www.seafrance.net) operates up to 15 sailings a day; the crossing takes about 90 minutes.

➤ FOLKESTONE–BOULOGNE: **Hoverspeed** (☞ Dover–Calais, *above*) is the sole operator on this route, with 10 35-minute crossings a day.

➤ NEWHAVEN–DIEPPE: **Seafrance** (☞ Dover–Calais, *above*) has as many as four sailings a day, and the crossing takes four hours.

➤ PORTSMOUTH–LE HAVRE: **P&O European Ferries** (☞ Dover–Calais, *above*) has up to three sailings a day, and the crossing takes 5½ hours by day, 7½ by night.

FARES & SCHEDULES

Note that sample fares are difficult to assess because of the number of variables involved, including; destination, season, and number of people traveling. Sample fare (high season): Dover–Calais, round-trip (within five days): one person, €36.65; two adults plus car, €220 (this price doubles if the visit exceeds five days). Schedules and tickets are available at any travel agency throughout France or via the Internet. You can pay by traveler's checks, major credit cards, and cash.

BUS TRAVEL

France's excellent train service means that long-distance buses are rare; **regional buses are found mainly where train service is spotty.** Excursions and bus tours are organized by the SNCF and other tour companies. Ask for a brochure at any major travel agent or contact the French Tourism Office (☞ Visitor Information, *below*). Bus tours from the United Kingdom generally depart from London for Paris, the Atlantic Coast, Chamonix and the Alps, Grenoble, Lyon, and the Côte d'Azur. Note that **reservations are necessary on most long-distance buses.**

There is no central bus network servicing France because train service here is considered the best in the world, and if you are traveling off-season or have researched the best rates, train service can be just as economical as bus travel, if not more so. What a bus service saves in money, it often loses in both comfort and time. The largest international operator is Eurolines France, whose main terminal is in the Parisian suburb of Bagnolet (a half-hour métro ride from central Paris, at the end of métro Line 3). Eurolines runs many international routes, including a route from London to Paris, usually departing at 9 AM, arriving at 6 PM; noon, arriving at 9 PM; and 10 PM, arriving at 7 AM. Fares are £60 round-trip (under-25 youth pass £56), £35 one-way. Other Eurolines routes include: Amsterdam (seven hours, €65); Barcelona (15 hours, €160); and Berlin (10 hours, €145). There are also international-only arrivals and departures from Avignon, Bordeaux, Lille, Lyon, Toulouse, and Tours. Local bus information to the rare rural areas where trains do not have access can be obtained from the SNCF.

➤ FROM THE U.K.: **Eurolines** (✉ 28 av. Général-de-Gaulle, Bagnolet, ☎ 08–36–69–52–52 in France; 020/7730–3499 in the U.K., WEB www.eurolines.fr).

➤ WITHIN FRANCE: **Paris Vision** (✉ 1 rue d'Auber, 75009 Paris, ☎ 01–47–42–27–40; WEB www.parisvision.com). **SNCF** (✉ 88 rue St-Lazare, 75009 Paris, ☎ 08–36–35–35–39 in English, WEB www.sncf.fr).

BUSINESS HOURS

BANKS AND OFFICES

Generally, **banks are open weekdays, from 9:30 to 4:30** (note that the Banque de France closes at 3:30), and some banks are also open on Saturday. Most take a one-hour, or even a 90-minute, lunch break, except for those in Paris. In general, government offices and businesses are open 9–5. For information about post office hours, *see* Mail & Shipping, *below.*

GAS STATIONS

Gas stations in cities and towns are generally open 8–8, Monday–Saturday, with the exception of those stations located in the major *portes,* or entryways into each city, which are open 24 hours a day, seven days a week, as are those along the highways.

MUSEUMS AND SIGHTS

The usual opening times for museums and other sights are from 9:30 to 5 or 6. Many close for lunch (noon–2). Most are closed one day a week (generally Monday or Tuesday) and on national holidays: **check museum hours before you go.**

PHARMACIES

Pharmacies are generally open Monday–Saturday 8:30–8; on the door of every pharmacy is a list of those closest that are open on Sunday or 24 hours.

SHOPS

Large stores in big towns are open from 9 or 9:30 until 7 or 8. Smaller shops often open earlier (8 AM) and close later (8 PM) but take a lengthy lunch break (1–4), particularly in the south of France. Corner groceries frequently stay open until around 10 PM. Some Paris stores are beginning to stay open on Sunday, although it's still uncommon.

CAMERAS AND PHOTOGRAPHY

If you need to get your camera repaired, your best bet in Paris and other major cities is to go to a FNAC (a book, record, and electronics store). You should be able to find a small camera repair shop in most small towns. Note that you may have to wait some time to get your camera fixed. The *Kodak Guide to Shooting Great Travel Pictures* (available at bookstores everywhere) is loaded with tips.

➤ PHOTO HELP: **Kodak Information Center** (☎ 800/242–2424).

EQUIPMENT PRECAUTIONS

Don't pack film and equipment in checked luggage, where it is much more susceptible to damage. X-ray machines used to view checked luggage are becoming much more powerful and therefore are much more likely to ruin your film. Try to **ask for hand inspection of film,** which becomes clouded after repeated exposure to airport X-ray machines, and **keep videotapes and computer disks away from metal detectors.** Always **keep film, tape, and computer disks out of the sun.** Carry an extra supply of batteries, and **be prepared to turn on your camera, camcorder, or laptop** to prove to airport security personnel that the device is real.

FILM AND DEVELOPING

In Paris and most major cities, the easiest place to get film developed and printed is a FNAC store. If you're in a smaller town and want your film developed, look for a store with a Kodak sign outside its door. Keep in mind that **it's expensive to develop and print film in France**—around $20 per 36-exposure roll.

VIDEOS

France uses SECAM, which is a different system from that used either in the United States (NTSC) or in the United Kingdom (PAL). Therefore, you won't be able to play the videotapes you bring from home on French equipment. In addition, you probably won't be able to use SECAM videotapes in your camera, so it's a good idea to **bring extra videotapes from home.**

CAR RENTAL

Though renting a car in France is expensive—about twice as much as in the United States—as is gas (€.90–€1.25 per liter), it can pay off if you're traveling with two or more people. In addition, renting a car gives you the freedom that trains cannot. Rates in Paris begin at about

$70 a day and $200 per week for an economy car with air-conditioning, manual transmission, and unlimited mileage. The price doesn't usually take into account the 19.6% VAT tax or, if you pick it up from the airport, the airport tax. You won't need a car in the capital, so **wait to pick up your rental until the day you leave Paris.**

➤ MAJOR AGENCIES: **Alamo** (☏ 800/522–9696; WEB www.alamo.com). **Avis** (☏ 800/331–1084; 800/879–2847 in Canada; 0870/606–0100 in the U.K.; 02/9353–9000 in Australia; 09/526–2847 in New Zealand; WEB www.avis.com). **Budget** (☏ 800/527–0700; 0870/156–5656 in the U.K.; WEB www.budget.com). **Dollar** (☏ 800/800–6000; 0124/622–0111 in the U.K., where it's affiliated with Sixt; 02/9223–1444 in Australia; WEB www.dollar.com). **Hertz** (☏ 800/654–3001; 800/263–0600 in Canada; 020/8897–2072 in the U.K.; 02/9669–2444 in Australia; 09/256–8690 in New Zealand; WEB www.hertz.com). **National Car Rental** (☏ 800/227–7368; 020/8680–4800 in the U.K.; WEB www.nationalcar.com).

CUTTING COSTS

Renting a car through local French agencies has a number of serious disadvantages, notably price, as they simply cannot compete with the larger international companies. These giants combine bilingual service, the security of name recognition, extensive services (such as 24-hour hot lines), and automatic vehicles. However, SNAC—a France-based agency—can be useful if you are interested in luxury cars (convertible BMWs) or large family vans (Renault Espace, for example). Note that the big international agencies like Hertz and Avis offer better prices to those clients who make reservations in their home countries before they arrive in France; if you need to rent a car while in France, it even pays to call home and have a friend take care of it for you from there. So, to get the best deal, **reserve a car before you leave home.**

To get the best deal, **book through a travel agent who will shop around.** Remember to ask about required deposits, cancellation penalties, and drop-off charges if you're planning to pick up the car in one city and leave it in another. If you're traveling during a holiday period, also make sure that a confirmed reservation guarantees you a car.

Do **look into wholesalers,** companies that do not own fleets but rent in bulk from those that do and often offer better rates than traditional car-rental operations. Payment must be made before you leave home. Also **look into long-term leasing**; Renault rents new cars for a minimum of 17 days.

➤ LOCAL AGENCIES: **ACAR** (✉ 99 bd. Auguste-Blanqui, Bercy/Tolbiac, 75013, Paris, ☏ 01–45–88–28–38). **Locabest** (✉ 104 bd. Magenta, République, 75010 Paris, ☏ 01–44–72–08–05). **Rent-A-Car** (✉ 79 rue de Bercy, Bercy /Tolbiac, 75012 Paris, ☏ 01–43–45–98–99).

➤ WHOLESALERS: **Auto Europe** (☏ 207/842–2000 or 800/223–5555, FAX 800/235–6321, WEB www.autoeurope.com). **Europe by Car** (☏ 212/581–3040 or 800/223–1516, FAX 212/246–1458, WEB www.europebycar.com). **DER Travel Services** (✉ 9501 W. Devon Ave., Rosemont, IL 60018, ☏ 800/782–2424, FAX 800/282–7474 for information; 800/860–9944 for brochures, WEB www.der.com). **Kemwel Holiday Autos** (☏ 800/678–0678, FAX 914/825–3160, WEB www.kemwel.com).

INSURANCE

When driving a rented car, you are generally responsible for any damage to or loss of the vehicle. Before you rent, see what coverage your personal auto-insurance policy and credit cards provide. Before you buy collision coverage, check your existing policies—you may already be covered. However, collision policies that car-rental companies sell for European rentals usually do not include stolen-vehicle coverage.

REQUIREMENTS AND RESTRICTIONS

In France you must be 21 to rent a car, though rates may be higher if you're under 25. Your own driver's license is acceptable (☞ Rules of the Road *in* Car Travel, *below*).

SURCHARGES

Before you pick up a car in one city and leave it in another, **ask about**

drop-off charges or one-way service fees, which can be substantial. Note, too, that some rental agencies charge extra if you return the car before the time specified in your contract. To avoid a hefty refueling fee, **fill the tank just before you turn in the car,** but be aware that gas stations near the rental outlet may overcharge.

CAR TRAVEL

In France **you may use your own driver's license,** but you must be able to prove you have third-party insurance. You don't need an International Driver's Permit unless you are planning on a long-term stay; if needed, you can obtain one from the American and Canadian automobile associations, and, in the United Kingdom, from the Automobile Association or Royal Automobile Club. You must be 18 years old to drive, but there is no top age limit (if your faculties are intact).

EMERGENCY SERVICES

If your car breaks down on an expressway, **go to a roadside emergency telephone.** If you have a breakdown anywhere else, find the nearest garage or contact the police. There are also 24-hour assistance hot lines valid throughout France (available through rental agencies and supplied to you when you rent the car), but do not hesitate to call the police in case of any roadside emergency, for they are quick and reliable, and the phone call is free. There are special phones just for this purpose on all highways—just pick up the phone and dial 17. The French equivalent of the AAA is the Club Automobile de l'Ile de France, but it only takes care of its members and is of little use to international travelers.

➤ CONTACTS: Police (☎ 17).

FROM THE U.K.

If you're driving from the United Kingdom to the Continent, you have a choice of either the Channel Tunnel or ferry services. Reservations are essential at peak times and are always a good idea, especially when going via the Chunnel. Cars don't drive in the Chunnel but are loaded onto trains (☞ Boat and Ferry Travel, *above,* and Channel Tunnel and Train Travel, *below.*)

GASOLINE

Gas is expensive, especially on expressways and in rural areas. When possible, **buy gas before you get on the expressway** and keep an eye on pump prices as you go. These vary enormously—anything from €1 to €1.40 per liter. The cheapest gas can be found at *hypermarchés* (large supermarkets). Credit cards are accepted in every gas station. It's possible to go for miles in the country without passing a gas station—**don't let your tank get too low in rural areas.**

PARKING

Parking is a nightmare in Paris and often difficult in other large towns. Meters and ticket machines (pay and display) are common: make sure you **have a supply of the appropriate change in euros** (€.75–€1). If you're planning on spending a lot of time in Paris with a car, **it might be a good idea to buy a parking card** (*carte de stationnement*) for €15, available at any café posting the red TABAC sign. This card works like a credit card in the parking meters, allowing you to avoid the inconvenience of finding exact change. Whether you are paying with coins or with a parking card, you'll receive a green receipt from the machine. Be sure to make it clearly visible to the meter patrol by putting it inside the front window on the passenger side.

Note that in August, parking is free in certain residential areas; however, **only parking meters showing a dense yellow circle indicate a free parking zone;** if you do not see the circle, pay. Parking tickets are expensive, and there is no shortage of the blue-uniformed parking police. Parking lots, indicated by a blue sign with a white P are usually underground and are generally expensive. In smaller towns, parking may be permitted on one side of the street only—alternating every two weeks—so pay attention to signs.

ROADS

For the fastest roads between two points, **look for roads marked A for autoroute.** A *péage* (toll) must be paid on most expressways: The rate varies but can be steep. The N (*route na-*

tionale) roads—which are sometimes divided highways—and D (*route départementale*) roads are usually also wide and fast. Don't be daunted by smaller (C and V) roads, either.

There are excellent links between Paris and most French cities, but poor ones between the provinces (the principal exceptions are A26 from Calais to Reims, A62 between Bordeaux and Toulouse, and A9/A8 the length of the Mediterranean coast).

Though routes are numbered, **the French generally guide themselves from city to city and town to town by destination name.** When reading a map, keep one eye on the next big city toward your destination as well as the next small town; most snap decisions will have to be based on town names, not road numbers.

When traveling in and out of Paris, note that there are two major rings that run parallel to each other and encircle the city: the *périphérique intérieur,* the inside ring, also known as the *grands boulevards* (not to be confused with the major avenue layout in the center of Paris's Right Bank); and the *périphérique extérieur,* the outside ring, which is a major highway. From this ring there are *portes* (gates) that connect to the major highways of France. The names of these highways function on the same principal as the Paris métro, with the final destination determining which direction you take. These directions are indicated by major cities, and the major highways connect to Paris at these points. For instance, heading north, look for Porte de la Chapelle (direction Lille and Charles de Gaulle Airport); east, for Porte de Bagnolet (direction Metz and Nancy); south, for Porte d'Orléans (direction Lyon and Bordeaux); and west, for Porte d'Auteuil (direction Rouen and Chartres) or Porte de St-Cloud. Other portes include Porte de la Villette; Porte de Pantin; Porte de Bercy (A4 to Reims); Porte d'Italie; and Porte de Maillot (A14 to Rouen).

The major expressways into Paris are the A1, from the north/Great Britain; the A13, from Rouen, Normandy, and northwestern France; the A6, from Lyon, the French Alps, the Riviera, and Italy; the A10, from France's southwest and the Pyrénées; and the A4, from Nancy and Strasbourg in eastern France.

ROAD MAPS

If you plan to drive through France, **get a yellow Michelin map** for each region you'll be visiting. The maps are available from most bookshops and magazine stores.

RULES OF THE ROAD

Drive on the right and **yield to drivers coming from streets to the right.** However, this rule does not necessarily apply at traffic circles, where you should watch out for just about everyone. You must **wear your seat belt,** and children under 12 may not travel in the front seat. Speed limits are 130 kph (80 mph) on expressways (*autoroutes*), 110 kph (70 mph) on divided highways (*routes nationales*), 90 kph (55 mph) on other roads (*routes*), 50 kph (30 mph) in cities and towns (*villes et villages*). French drivers break these limits, and police dish out hefty on-the-spot fines with equal abandon. Do not expect to find traffic lights in the center of the road, as French lights are usually on the right- and left-hand sides.

Some important traffic terms and signs to note: SORTIE (exit); SENS UNIQUE (one-way); STATIONNEMENT INTERDITE (no parking); and CUL DE SAC (dead end). Blue rectangular signs indicate a highway; green rectangular signs indicate a major direction; triangles carry illustrations of a particular traffic hazard; speed limits are indicated in a circle with the maximum limit circled in red.

➤ AUTO CLUBS: **American Automobile Association** (☎ 800/564–6222). **Australian Automobile Association** (☎ 02/6247–7311). **Canadian Automobile Association** (CAA; ☎ 613/247–0117). **Club Automobile de l'Ile de France** (☎ 01–40–55–43–00). **New Zealand Automobile Association** (☎ 09/377–4660). **Royal Automobile Club** (RAC, ☎ 0990/722–722 for membership; 0345/121–345 for insurance). **U.K. Automobile Association** (AA; ☎ 0990/500–600).

THE CHANNEL TUNNEL

Short of flying, the "Chunnel" is the fastest way to cross the English Channel: 35 minutes from Folkestone to Calais, 60 minutes from motorway to motorway, or three hours from London's Waterloo Station to Paris's Gare du Nord.

➤ Car Transport: **Eurotunnel** (☏ 0870/535–3535 in the U.K., 070/223210 in Belgium, 03–21–00–61–00 in France, WEB ww2.eurotunnel.com).

➤ Passenger Service: **Eurostar** (☏ 1233/617575 or 0870/518–6186, in the U.K., WEB www.eurostar.co.uk) **InterCity Europe** (☏ 0870/584–8848 for credit-card bookings). **Rail Europe** (☏ 800/942–4866 or 800/274–8724; 0870/584–8848 U.K. credit-card bookings; WEB www.raileurope.com).

CHILDREN IN FRANCE

Be sure to plan ahead and **involve your youngsters** as you outline your trip. When packing, include things to keep them busy en route. On sightseeing days try to schedule activities of special interest to your children.

Getting around Paris and other major cities with a stroller can be a challenge, so **take your lightest folding stroller.** Many museums require you to check strollers at the entrance. In Paris few métro stations have escalators; you're better off taking the bus in off-peak hours. *Fodor's Around Paris with Kids* (available in bookstores everywhere) can help you plan your days together. For general advice on traveling with children, consult *Fodor's FYI: Travel with Your Baby* (available in bookstores everywhere).

➤ Family-Friendly Tour Operators: **Grandtravel** (✉ 6900 Wisconsin Ave., Suite 706, Chevy Chase, MD 20815, ☏ 301/986–0790 or 800/247–7651) for people traveling with grandchildren ages 7–17. **Families Welcome!/Great Destinations** (✉ 92 N. Main St., Ashland, OR 97520, ☏ 541/482–6121 or 800/326–0724, FAX 541/482–0660). **A Touch of France** (✉ 660 King Rd., Fords, NJ 08863, ☏ 800/738–5240).

➤ Local Information: **CIDJ** (Centre d'Information et de Documentation pour la Jeunesse; ✉ 101 quai Branly, 75015 Paris, ☏ 01–44–49–12–00, WEB www.cidj.asso.fr).

CAR TRAVEL

If you're renting a car, don't forget to **arrange for a car seat** when you reserve. Playgrounds can be found off many highways. Most rest-stop bathrooms have changing tables.

FOOD

The best restaurants in France do not welcome small children; except for the traditional family Sunday-noon dinner, fine dining is considered an adult pastime. Aim for more modest *auberges* (country inns), and if there's a choice, **consider having your meal in the café or bar** rather than in the linen-and-goblet filled dining room. In cities, brasseries and cafés offer a casual option and the flexible meal times that children often require. If you get desperate, France has its share of McDonald's, Pizza Huts, and other fast-food restaurants. Very few mainstream restaurants have high chairs, but some do serve children's portions *(menu enfant)*, usually spaghetti or the ubiquitous *steak-frîtes,* a mountain of fries with a thin steak or fat patty of ground beef, usually cooked extremely rare. If you're queasy about this, ask for it *bien cuit* (well done) or *à point* (medium). If your children go to bed early, **opt for your hot meal at noon** (there are cheaper prix-fixe menus then, too) and consider having a sandwich, quiche, a *croque monsieur* (a grilled egg-and-cheese sandwich), or pizza at a café or brasserie in the early evening; full-service restaurants usually do not serve before 7 PM.

LODGING

If you're planning to stay in hotels, it is essential to book ahead. Many small hotels have only one or two rooms that sleep four (triples are much more common); if there are more of you, you'll have to book two neighboring rooms or a suite. Larger hotels often provide cribs free to guests with young children, which is not usually the case at inns and smaller hotels. Older children are charged at adult rates unless the hotel offers a special family rate. Be sure to **ask about the cutoff age for children's discounts** when booking.

Some hotel chains offer discounts for families and programs for children. Club Med is particularly family friendly: it has a "Baby Club" (from age four months) at its resort in Chamonix, and "Mini Clubs" (for ages 4–6 or 4–8, depending on the resort) and "Kids Clubs" (for ages eight and up during school holidays) at all its resort villages in France except at Val d'Isère. Some clubs are only French-speaking. The Novotel chain allows up to two children under 15 to stay free in their parents' room. Sofitel hotels offer a free second room for children during July and August and over the Christmas period.

Another option: **consider a gîte, a short-term apartment or house rental,** or a home exchange (☞ Lodging, *below*).

➤ BEST CHOICES: **Club Med** (✉ 40 W. 57th St., New York, NY 10019, ☎ 800/258–2633, WEB www.clubmed.com). **Novotel** (☎ 800/221–4542, WEB www.novotel.com). **Sofitel** (☎ 800/221–4542, WEB www.sofitel.com).

SIGHTS AND ATTRACTIONS

Places that are especially appealing to children are indicated by a rubber-duckie icon (🐤) in the margin. There are plenty of diversions for the young, and **almost all museums and movie theaters have discounted rates.**

SUPPLIES AND EQUIPMENT

Supermarkets carry several major brands of diapers (*couches*), universally referred to as Pampers (pawm-*paires*). Junior sizes are hard to come by, as the French toilet-train early. Baby formula is available in grocery stores or pharmacies. There are two types of formulas: *lait prémier age,* for infants 0–4 months, and *lait deuxieme age,* for four months or older. French formulas come in powder form and need to be mixed with a pure, low-mineral-content bottled water such as Evian or Volvic (the French *never* mix baby formula with tap water). American formulas do not exist in France. If you're looking for treats for your little ones, some items to keep in mind are: *coloriage* (coloring books), *crayons de couleur* (crayons), *pate à modeler* (modeling clay), and *feutres* (magic markers).

TRANSPORTATION

SNCF allows children under four to travel free (provided they don't occupy a seat) or for €7.70 for a seat, and children 4–12 to travel at half fare with an accompanying adult. The Carte "Enfant Plus" (€54) allows children under 12 and as many as four accompanying adults to make an unlimited number of trips at as much as half the cost (though you are only guaranteed at least 25% off on all trains). This card is worth your while only if you are planning on traveling extensively in France—it is valid for one year.

When traveling by train with children, you may want to travel first class, as there is more space and it is considerably calmer and cleaner than second-class space. Another option is to request an "*espace famille*" ("family space") in second class (when you make reservations), which consists of two sets of seats facing each other. For more information, *see* Train Travel, *below.*

COMPUTERS ON THE ROAD

If you use a major Internet provider, getting on line in France shouldn't be difficult. Some hotels even have in-room modem lines. You may, however, need an adapter for your computer for the European-style plugs (☞ Electricity, *below*). As always, if you're traveling with a laptop, carry a spare battery and adapter. Never plug your computer into any socket before asking about surge protection. IBM sells a pen-size modem tester that plugs into a telephone jack to check if the line is safe to use.

➤ ACCESS NUMBERS IN PARIS: **AOL** (☎ 01–41–45–81–00). **Compuserve** (☎ 08–03–00–60–00, 08–03–00–80–00, or 08–03–00–90–00).

CONSUMER PROTECTION

Whenever shopping or buying travel services in France, **pay with a major credit card,** if possible, so you can cancel payment or get reimbursed if there's a problem. If you're doing business with a particular company for the first time, **contact your local Better Business Bureau and the attorney general's offices** in your state and (for U.S. businesses) the company's home state as well. Have any complaints been filed? Finally, if you're buying a package or tour, always **consider travel insurance** that includes default coverage (☞ Insurance, *below*).

➤ BBBs: **Council of Better Business Bureaus** (✉ 4200 Wilson Blvd., Suite 800, Arlington, VA 22203, ☎ 703/276–0100, FAX 703/525–8277, WEB www.bbb.org).

CUSTOMS AND DUTIES

When shopping, **keep receipts** for all purchases. Upon reentering the country, **be ready to show customs officials what you've bought.** If you feel a duty is incorrect or object to the way your clearance was handled, note the inspector's badge number and ask to see a supervisor. If the problem isn't resolved, write to the appropriate authorities, beginning with the port director at your point of entry.

IN AUSTRALIA

Australian residents who are 18 or older may bring home $A400 worth of souvenirs and gifts (including jewelry), 250 cigarettes or 250 grams of tobacco, and 1,125 milliliters of alcohol (including wine, beer, and spirits). Residents under 18 may bring back $A200 worth of goods. Prohibited items include meat products. Seeds, plants, and fruits need to be declared upon arrival.

➤ INFORMATION: **Australian Customs Service** (Regional Director: ✉ Box 8, Sydney, NSW 2001, ☎ 02/9213–2000 or 1300/363263, FAX 02/9213–4043, WEB www.customs.gov.au).

IN CANADA

Canadian residents who have been out of Canada for at least seven days may bring in C$750 worth of goods duty-free. If you've been away fewer than seven days but more than 48 hours, the duty-free allowance drops to C$200. If your trip lasts 24 to 48 hours, the allowance is C$50. You may not pool allowances with family members. Goods claimed under the C$750 exemption may follow you by mail; those claimed under the lesser exemptions must accompany you. Alcohol and tobacco products may be included in the seven-day and 48-hour exemptions but not in the 24-hour exemption. If you meet the age requirements of the province or territory through which you reenter Canada, you may bring in, duty-free, 1.5 liters of wine *or* 1.14 liters (40 imperial ounces) of liquor *or* 24 12-ounce cans or bottles of beer or ale. If you are 19 or older you may bring in, duty-free, 200 cigarettes and 50 cigars. Check ahead of time with the Canada Customs and Revenue Agency or the Department of Agriculture for policies regarding meat products, seeds, plants, and fruits. You may send an unlimited number of gifts (only one gift per recipient, however) worth up to C$60 each duty-free to Canada. Label the package UNSOLICITED GIFT—VALUE UNDER $60. Alcohol and tobacco are excluded.

➤ INFORMATION: **Revenue Canada** (✉ 2265 St. Laurent Blvd. S, Ottawa, Ontario K1G 4K3, ☎ 613/993–0534; 800/461–9999 in Canada, WEB www.ccra-adrc.gc.ca/).

IN FRANCE

There are two levels of duty-free allowance for travelers entering France: one for goods obtained (tax paid) within another European Union (EU) country and the other for goods obtained anywhere outside the EU or for goods purchased in a duty-free shop within the EU.

In the first category, you may import duty-free: 300 cigarettes or 150 cigarillos or 75 cigars or 400 grams of tobacco; 5 liters of table wine and (1) 1½ liters of alcohol over 22% volume (most spirits), (2) 3 liters of alcohol under 22% by volume (fortified or sparkling wine), or (3) 3 more liters of table wine, 90 milliliters of perfume, 375 milliliters of toilet water, and other goods to the value of €365 (€95 for those under 15).

In the second category, you may import duty-free: 200 cigarettes or 100 cigarillos or 50 cigars or 250 grams of tobacco (these allowances are doubled if you live outside Europe); 2 liters of wine and (1) 1 liter of alcohol over 22% volume (most spirits), (2) 2 liters of alcohol under 22% volume (fortified or sparkling wine), or (3) 2 more liters of table wine, 60 milliliters of perfume, 250 milliliters of toilet water, and other goods to the value of €45 (€25 for those under 15).

➤ INFORMATION: **Direction des Douanes** (✉ 16 rue Yves Toudic, Paris 10^e, ☎ 01–40–40–39–00).

IN NEW ZEALAND

All homeward-bound residents may bring back NZ$700 worth of souvenirs and gifts; passengers may not pool their allowances, and children can claim only the concession on goods intended for their own use. For those 17 or older, the duty-free allowance also includes 4.5 liters of wine or beer; one 1,125-ml bottle of spirits; and either 200 cigarettes, 250 grams of tobacco, 50 cigars, *or* a combination of the three up to 250 grams. Meat products, seeds, plants, and fruits must be declared upon arrival to the Agricultural Services Department.

➤ INFORMATION: **New Zealand Customs** (Head office: ✉ The Customhouse, 17–21 Whitmore St., Box 2218, Wellington, ☎ 09/300–5399 or 0800/428–786, WEB www.customs.govt.nz).

IN THE U.K.

If you are a U.K. resident and your journey was wholly within the European Union, you probably won't have to pass through customs when you return to the United Kingdom. If you plan to bring back large quantities of alcohol or tobacco, check EU limits beforehand. In most cases, if you bring back more than 200 cigars, 800 cigarettes, 10 liters of spirits, and/or 90 liters of wine, you have to declare the goods upon return. From countries outside the European Union, you may bring home, duty-free, 200 cigarettes or 50 cigars; 1 liter of spirits or 2 liters of fortified or sparkling wine or liqueurs; 2 liters of still table wine; 60 ml of perfume; 250 ml of toilet water; plus £145 worth of other goods, including gifts and souvenirs. Prohibited items include meat products, seeds, plants, and fruits.

➤ INFORMATION: **HM Customs and Excise** (✉ Portcullis House, 21 Cowbridge Rd. E, Cardiff CF11 9SS, ☎ 029/2038–6423 or 0845/010–9000, WEB www.hmce.gov.uk).

IN THE U.S.

U.S. residents who have been out of the country for at least 48 hours may bring home, for personal use, $400 worth of foreign goods duty-free, as long as they haven't used the $400 allowance or any part of it in the past 30 days. This exemption may include 1 liter of alcohol (for travelers 21 and older), 200 cigarettes, and 100 non-Cuban cigars. Family members from the same household who are traveling together may pool their $400 personal exemptions. For fewer than 48 hours, the duty-free allowance drops to $200, which may include 50 cigarettes, 10 non-Cuban cigars, and 150 milliliters of alcohol (or perfume containing alcohol). The $200 allowance cannot be combined with other individuals' exemptions, and if you exceed it, the full value of all the goods will be taxed. Antiques, which the U.S. Customs Service defines as objects more than 100 years old, enter duty-free, as do original works of art done entirely by hand, including paintings, drawings, and sculptures.

You may also send packages home duty-free, with a limit of one parcel per addressee per day (except alcohol or tobacco products or perfume worth more than $5). You can mail up to $200 worth of goods for personal use; label the package PERSONAL USE and attach a list of its contents and their retail value. If the package contains your used personal belongings, mark it PERSONAL GOODS RETURNED to avoid paying duties. You may send up to $100 worth of goods as a gift; mark the package UNSOLICITED GIFT. Mailed items do not affect your duty-free allowance on your return.

➤ INFORMATION: **U.S. Customs Service** (✉ 1300 Pennsylvania Ave. NW, Washington, DC 20229, WEB www.customs.gov; inquiries ☎ 202/354–1000; complaints c/o ✉ 1300 Pennsylvania Ave. NW, Room 5.4D, Washington, DC 20229; registration of equipment, c/o ✉ Resource Management, ☎ 202/927–0540).

DINING

All establishments must post their menus outside, so study them carefully before deciding to enter. Most restaurants have two basic types of menu: à la carte and fixed-price (prix-fixe or *un menu*). The prix-fixe menu is usually the best value, though choices are more limited. Most menus begin with a first course (*une entrée*), often subdivided into cold and hot starters, followed by fish and poultry, then meat; it's rare today that anyone orders something from all three. The restaurants we review in this book are the cream of the crop in each price category.

A few pointers on French dining etiquette: diners in France don't negotiate their orders much, so don't expect serene smiles when you ask for sauce on the side. Order your coffee after dessert, not with it. When you're ready for the check, ask for it: no professional waiter would dare put a bill on your table while you're still enjoying the last sip of coffee. And don't ask for a doggy bag; it's just not done. The French usually drink wine or mineral water—not soda or coffee—with their food. You may ask for a carafe of tap water, but not always: in general, diners order mineral water if they don't order wine.

MEALS AND SPECIALTIES

What's the difference between a bistro and a brasserie? Can you order food at a café? Can you go to a restaurant just for a snack? The following definitions should help.

A **restaurant** traditionally serves a three-course meal (first, main, and dessert) at both lunch and dinner. Although this category includes the most formal, three-star establishments, it also applies to humble neighborhood spots. Don't expect to grab a quick snack. In general, restaurants are what you choose when you want a complete meal and when you have the time to linger over it.

Many say that **bistros** served the world's first fast food. After the fall of Napoléon, the Russian soldiers who occupied Paris were known to bang on zinc-top café bars, crying "*bistro*"—"quickly" in Russian. In the past, bistros were simple places with minimal decor and service. Although nowadays many are quite upscale, with beautiful interiors and chic clientele, most remain cozy establishments serving straightforward, frequently gutsy cooking.

Brasseries—ideal places for quick, one-dish meals—originated when Alsatians fleeing German occupiers after the Franco-Prussian War came to Paris and opened restaurants serving specialties from home. Pork-based dishes, *choucroute* (sauerkraut), and beer (*brasserie* also means brewery) were—and still are—mainstays here. The typical brasserie is convivial and keeps late hours. Some are open 24 hours a day—a good thing to know since many restaurants stop serving at 10:30 PM.

Like bistros and brasseries, **cafés** come in a confusing variety. Often informal neighborhood hangouts, cafés may also be veritable showplaces attracting chic, well-heeled crowds. At most cafés the regulars congregate at the bar, where coffee and drinks are cheaper than at tables. At lunch tables are set, and a limited menu is served. Sandwiches, usually with *jambon* (ham), *fromage* (cheese, often Gruyère or Camembert), or *mixte* (ham and cheese), are served throughout the day. *Casse croûtes* (snacks) are also offered. Cafés are for lingering, for people-watching, and for daydreaming. If none of these options fit the bill, head to the nearest **traiteur** (deli) for picnic fixings.

See the Menu Guide at the end of the book for guidance with menu items that appear frequently on French menus and throughout the reviews in this book.

MEALTIMES

Breakfast is usually served from 7:30 to 10, lunch from noon to 2, and dinner from 8 to 10. Restaurants in Paris usually serve dinner until 10:30 PM. Unless otherwise noted, the restaurants listed in this guide are open daily for lunch and dinner.

PAYING

By French law, prices must include tax and tip (*service compris* or *prix nets*), but pocket change left on the table in basic places, or an additional 5% in better restaurants, is always appreciated. Beware of bills stamped SERVICE NOT INCLUDED in English or restaurants slyly using American-style credit-card slips, hoping that you'll be confused and add the habitual 15% tip.

RESERVATIONS AND DRESS

Reservations are always a good idea; we mention them only when they're essential or not accepted. Book as far ahead as you can, and reconfirm as soon as you arrive. (Large parties should always call ahead to check the reservations policy.) We mention dress only when men are required to wear a jacket or a jacket and tie.

DISABILITIES AND ACCESSIBILITY

Though the French government is doing much to ensure that public facilities provide for visitors with disabilities, it still has a long way to go.

➤ LOCAL RESOURCES: **Association des Paralysés de France** (✉ 17 bd. Auguste-Blanqui, 75013 Paris, ☎ 01–40–78–69–00, WEB www.apf-asso.com) for a list of Paris hotels. **Comité Nationale Français de Liaison pour la Réadaptation des Handicapés** (✉ 236-B rue de Tolbiac, 75013 Paris, ☎ 01–53–80–66–66, WEB www.handitel.org).

LODGING

Only some hotels—particularly more modern ones—are equipped with ramps, elevators, and special toilet facilities. Lists of regional hotels include a symbol to indicate which hotels have rooms accessible to people using wheelchairs.

RESERVATIONS

When discussing accessibility with an operator or reservations agent, **ask hard questions.** Are there any stairs, inside *or* out? Are there grab bars next to the toilet *and* in the shower/tub? How wide is the doorway to the room? To the bathroom? For the most extensive facilities meeting the latest legal specifications, **opt for newer accommodations.**

SIGHTS AND ATTRACTIONS

Only some monuments and museums—especially those constructed within the past decade—are equipped with ramps, elevators, and special toilet facilities.

TRANSPORTATION

The SNCF has special accommodations in the first-class compartments (for the usual second-class rate) on non-TGV and mainline rail services that have been reserved exclusively for people using wheelchairs; arrangements can be made for those passengers to be escorted on and off trains and assisted in making connections (this service must be requested in advance at 08–00–05–47–53).

Unfortunately, at this time very few métro stations in Paris and only some RER stations are wheelchair accessible. For information about accessibility, **get the RER and métro access guide,** available at most stations and from the Paris Transit Authority.

The Airhop shuttle company runs adapted vehicles to and from the airports; Orly–Paris costs €29 and Charles de Gaulle–Paris costs €40; this service is available Monday through Friday only. Reservations (in French) must be made in advance. Note that you must pay €2 for every 15 minutes there is a delay.

➤ COMPLAINTS: **Aviation Consumer Protection Division** (☞ Air Travel, *above*) for airline-related problems. **Civil Rights Office** (✉ U.S. Department of Transportation, Departmental Office of Civil Rights, S-30, 400 7th St. SW, Room 10215, Washington, DC 20590, ☎ 202/366–4648, FAX 202/366–3571, WEB www.dot.gov/ost/docr/index.htm) for problems with surface transportation. **Disability Rights Section** (✉ NYAV, U.S. Department of Justice, Civil Rights Division, 950 Pennsylvania Ave. NW, Washington, DC 20530; ☎ ADA information line 202/514–0301, 800/514–0301, 202/514–0383 TTY, 800/514–0383 TTY, WEB www.usdoj.gov/crt/ada/adahom1.htm).

➤ LOCAL RESOURCES: **Airhop** (☎ 01–41–29–01–29). **Paris Transit Authority** (RATP) kiosk (✉ 54 Quai de la Rapée, 75599 Cedex 12, ☎ 08–36–68–77–14, WEB www.ratp.fr).

TRAVEL AGENCIES

In the United States the Americans with Disabilities Act requires that travel firms serve the needs of all travelers. Some agencies specialize in working with people with disabilities.

➤ TRAVELERS WITH MOBILITY PROBLEMS: **Access Adventures** (✉ 206 Chestnut Ridge Rd., Scottsville, NY 14624, ☎ 716/889–9096, dltravel@prodigy.net), run by a former physical-rehabilitation counselor. **Care-Vacations** (✉ 5-5110 50th Ave., Leduc, Alberta T9E 6V4, Canada, ☎ 780/986–6404 or 877/478–7827, FAX 780/986–8332, WEB www.carevacations.

com), for group tours and cruise vacations. **Flying Wheels Travel** (✉ 143 W. Bridge St., Box 382, Owatonna, MN 55060, ☎ 507/451–5005 or 800/535–6790, FAX 507/451–1685, WEB www.flyingwheelstravel.com).

ELECTRICITY

To use your U.S.-purchased electric-powered equipment, **bring a converter and adapter.** The electrical current in France is 220 volts, 50 cycles alternating current (AC); wall outlets take wall outlets take continental-type plugs, with two round prongs.

If your appliances are dual-voltage, you'll need only an adapter. Don't use 110-volt outlets marked FOR SHAVERS ONLY for high-wattage appliances such as blow-dryers. Most laptops operate equally well on 110 and 220 volts and so require only an adapter.

EMBASSIES

If you need assistance in an emergency, you can go to your country's embassy. Proof of identity and citizenship are generally required to enter. If your passport has been stolen, get a police report then contact your embassy for assistance.

➤ AUSTRALIA: **Australian Embassy** (✉ 4 rue Jean-Rey, Paris, 15e, Invalides/Eiffel Tower, ☎ 01–40–59–33–00, métro: Bir Hakeim. ⏲ Weekdays 9:15–12:15).

➤ CANADA: **Canadian Embassy** (✉ 35 av. Montaigne, Paris, 8e,Champs-Élysées, ☎ 01–44–43–29–00, métro: Franklin-D.-Roosevelt. ⏲ Weekdays 8:30–11).

➤ NEW ZEALAND: **New Zealand Embassy** (✉ 7 ter rue Léonardo da Vinci, Paris, 16e, Trocadero, métro: Victor Hugo, ☎ 01–45–00–24–11. ⏲ Weekdays 9–1).

➤ UNITED KINGDOM: **British Embassy** (✉ 35 rue du Faubourg-St-Honoré, Paris, 8e, Louvre/Tuileries, ☎ 01–44–51–31–00, métro: Madeleine. ⏲ Weekdays 9:30–12:30 and 2:30–5; ✉ 24 av. du Prado, Marseille, ☎ 04–91–15–72–10. ⏲ Weekdays 9–noon and 2–5).

➤ UNITED STATES: **U.S. Embassy** (✉ 2 rue St-Florentin, Paris, 1er, Louvre/Tuileries, ☎ 01–43–12–22–22 in English; 01–43–12–23–47 in emergencies, métro: Concorde. ⏲ Weekdays 9–3; ✉ 12 bd. Paul Peytral, Marseille, ☎ 04–91–54–92–00. ⏲ Weekdays 8:30–12:30 and 1:30–5:30 (until 4:30 Fri.).

EMERGENCIES

The World Health Organization recently ranked the French medical system as the best in the world, so the first thing to do in an emergency is to remain calm—you are definitely in good hands. France's emergency services are conveniently streamlined and universal, so no matter where you are in the country you can dial the same phone numbers, listed below. Every town and village has a *médecin de garde* (on-duty doctor) for flus, sprains, tetanus shots, and similar problems. To find out who's on call on any given evening, call any *généraliste* (general practitioner), and a recording will refer you. If you need an X-ray or emergency treatment, call an ambulance, and you'll be whisked to the hospital of your choice—or the nearest one. Note that outside Paris it's very difficult to find English-speaking doctors.

Pharmacies in France can be very helpful with minor health problems and remedies. In case of fire, hotels are required to post emergency exit maps with multilingual instructions on the inside door of every room. On the street the French phrases that may be needed in an emergency are: *Au secours!* (Help!), *urgence* (emergency), *samu* (ambulance), *pompiers* (firemen), *poste de station* (police station), *médecin* (doctor), and *hôpital* (hospital).

See also Emergencies *in* A to Z sections *in* some of the regional chapters for information on local hospitals.

➤ CONTACTS: **Ambulance** (☎ 15). **Fire Department** (☎ 18). **Police** (☎ 17).

ENGLISH-LANGUAGE MEDIA

BOOKS

Paris has many bookstores selling English-language books (☞ Shopping *in* Chapter 2), and you can probably find at least one bookstore in other major cities with English-language books. However, in most smaller towns you won't have much luck.

NEWSPAPERS AND MAGAZINES

Besides a large variety of French newspapers and magazines, all kinds of English-language newspapers and magazines can be found at newsstands in larger cities and even in smaller towns, including: the *International Herald Tribune, USA Today,* the *New York Times,* the *European Financial Times,* the *London Times, Newsweek, The Economist, Vogue,* and *Elle.* In Paris you'll find a number of free English-language magazines with all kinds of listings, including events, bars, restaurants, shops, films, and museums: Look for *Time Out Paris, FUSAC,* the *Paris Free Voice,* and *Irish Eyes.*

RADIO AND TELEVISION

Turn on the television, and you'll notice many American shows dubbed into French (Canal Jimmy, Channel 8, shows American shows in their original, undubbed format). France has both national stations (TF1, France 2, France 3, La Cinq/Arte, and M6) and cable stations (most notably Canal+, France's version of HBO). Every morning at 7:05 AM, ABC News (from the night before) is aired on Channel 4. You can also find CNN, BBC World, and BBC Prime on cable.

You'll find all kinds of music on French radio stations: some focus on one type of music, while others play different kinds of music, from rock to jazz to classical, depending on the time of day.

ETIQUETTE AND BEHAVIOR

SMOKING

The French are smokers—there's no way around it. And they're notorious for disregarding the few no-smoking laws that do exist, with little retribution. Even in restaurants, cafés, and train and métro stations that have no-smoking sections, you'll see people smoking. Even if you ask people to move or not to smoke, don't expect them to respond or respect your request. Your best bet for finding an environment as smoke-free as possible is to stick to the larger cafés and restaurants, where there is a greater likelihood of clearly defined smoking and no-smoking areas, or if you're lucky enough to enjoy good weather, to simply sit at an outside table.

SNCF trains have cars designated for smoking and no-smoking (specify when you make reservations), and these are some of the few places where the laws are respected. Some hotels, too, have designated no-smoking rooms; ask for these when reserving.

GAY AND LESBIAN TRAVEL

The largest gay and lesbian communities in France are in Paris. A number of informative newspapers and magazines that cover the Parisian gay and lesbian scene are available at stores and kiosks in the city: ***Gai Guide, Gai Pied Hebdo, Lesbia,*** and ***Têtu.***

➤ GAY- AND LESBIAN-FRIENDLY TRAVEL AGENCIES: **Different Roads Travel** (✉ 8383 Wilshire Blvd., Suite 902, Beverly Hills, CA 90211, ☎ 323/651–5557 or 800/429–8747, FAX 323/651–3678, lgernert@tzell.com). **Kennedy Travel** (✉ 314 Jericho Turnpike, Floral Park, NY 11001, ☎ 516/352–4888 or 800/237–7433, FAX 516/354–8849, WEB www.kennedytravel.com). **Now, Voyager** (✉ 4406 18th St., San Francisco, CA 94114, ☎ 415/626–1169 or 800/255–6951, FAX 415/626–8626, WEB www.nowvoyager.com). **Skylink Travel and Tour** (✉ 1006 Mendocino Ave., Santa Rosa, CA 95401, ☎ 707/546–9888 or 800/225–5759, FAX 707/546–9891), serving lesbian travelers.

➤ ORGANIZATIONS: **Act Up Paris** (✉ 45 rue Sedaine, 11e, ☎ 01–48–06–13–89).

Association des Médecins Gais (☎ 01–48–05–81–71). **Centre Gai et Lesbien** (✉ 3 rue Keller, 11e, ☎ 01–43–57–21–47).

GUIDEBOOKS

Plan well and you won't be sorry. Guidebooks are excellent tools—and you can take them with you. Fodor's regional gold guides: *Fodor's Provence and the Côte d'Azur* and *Fodor's Paris.* Or study color-photo-illustrated *Fodor's Exploring France, Exploring Paris, Exploring Provence,* and *Exploring Brittany,* thorough on culture and history; *Escape to Provence* and *Escape to the Riviera,* highlighting unique experiences; and pocket-size *Citypack Paris,* with a supersize map. All are available at on-line retailers and bookstores everywhere.

HEALTH

For information about emergencies and hospitals, *see* Emergencies, *above*.

HIKING AND WALKING

France has many good places to hike and an extensive network of mapped-out *Grandes Randonnées* (GRs, or long trails) that range from easy to challenging. For details on hiking in France and guides to GRs in specific areas, contact the Club Alpin Français or the Fédération Française de la Randonnée Pédestre, which also publishes good topographical maps. The IGN maps sold in many bookshops are also invaluable (☞ Bike Travel, *above*).

➤ HIKING ORGANIZATIONS: **Club Alpin Français** (✉ 24 av. Laumière, 75019 Paris, ☎ 01–53–72–87–00, WEB www.clubalpin.com). **Fédération Française de la Randonnée Pédestre** (✉ 14 rue de Riquet, 75019 Paris, ☎ 01–44–89–93–93, WEB www.ffrp.asso.fr).

➤ HIKING AND WALKING TOURS: **Abercrombie & Kent** (☞ Barge Travel, *above*). **BCT Scenic Walking** (✉ 703 Palomar Airport Rd, Suite 200, Carlsbad, CA 92009-1042, ☎ 760/431–7306, FAX 760/431–7782). **Butterfield & Robinson** (☞ Bike Travel, *above*). **Classic Adventures** (☞ Bike Travel, *above*). **Country Walkers** (✉ Box 180, Waterbury, VT 05676-0180, ☎ 802/244–1387 or 800/464–9255, FAX 802/244–5661). **Mountain Travel-Sobek** (✉ 6420 Fairmount Ave., El Cerrito, CA 94530, ☎ 510/527–8100 or 800/227–2384, FAX 510/525–7710). **Wilderness Travel** (✉ 1102 9th St., Berkeley, CA 94710, ☎ 510/558–2488 or 800/368–2794, FAX 510/558–2489, WEB www.wildernesstravel.com).

HOLIDAYS

With 11 national *jours feriés* (holidays) and five weeks of paid vacation, the French have their share of repose. In May there is a holiday nearly every week, so be prepared for stores, banks, and museums to shut their doors for days at a time. Be sure to **call museums, restaurants, and hotels in advance to make sure they will be open.**

Note that these dates are for the calendar year 2003: January 1 (New Year's Day); April 20/21 (Easter Sunday/Monday); May 1 (Labor Day); May 8 (V.E. Day); May 29 (Ascension); June 9/10 (Pentecost Sunday/Monday); July 14 (Bastille Day); August 15 (Assumption); November 1 (All Saints); November 11 (Armistice); December 25 (Christmas).

INSURANCE

The most useful travel-insurance plan is a comprehensive policy that includes coverage for trip cancellation and interruption, default, trip delay, and medical expenses (with a waiver for preexisting conditions). Without insurance you will lose all or most of your money if you cancel your trip, regardless of the reason. Default insurance covers you if your tour operator, airline, or cruise line goes out of business. Trip-delay covers expenses that arise because of bad weather or mechanical delays. Study the fine print when comparing policies.

If you're traveling internationally, a key component of travel insurance is coverage for medical bills incurred if you get sick on the road. Such expenses are not generally covered by Medicare or private policies. U.K. residents can buy a travel-insurance policy valid for most vacations taken during the year in which it's purchased (but check preexisting-condition coverage). Australian citizens need extra medical coverage when traveling abroad.

Always **buy travel policies directly from the insurance company**; if you buy them from a cruise line, airline, or tour operator that goes out of business, you probably will not be covered for the agency or operator's default, a major risk. Before making any purchase, **review your existing health and home-owner's policies** to find out what they cover away from home.

➤ TRAVEL INSURERS: In the U.S.: **Access America** (✉ 6600 W. Broad St., Richmond, VA 23230, ☎ 804/285–3300 or 800/284–8300, FAX 804/673–1586, WEB www.accessamerica.com). **Travel Guard International** (✉ 1145 Clark St., Stevens Point, WI 54481, ☎ 715/345–0505 or 800/

826–1300, FAX 800/955–8785, WEB www.travelguard.com).

➤ INSURANCE INFORMATION: In the U.K.: **Association of British Insurers** (✉ 51–55 Gresham St., London EC2V 7HQ, ☎ 020/7600–3333, FAX 020/7696–8999, WEB www.abi.org.uk). In Canada: **Voyager Insurance** (✉ 44 Peel Center Dr., Brampton, Ontario L6T 4M8, ☎ 905/791–8700, 800/668–4342 in Canada). In Australia: **Insurance Council of Australia** (✉ Level 3, 56 Pitt St., Sydney NSW 2000, ☎ 03/9614–1077, FAX 03/9614–7924). In New Zealand: **Insurance Council of New Zealand** (✉ Box 474, Wellington, ☎ 04/472–5230, FAX 04/473–3011, WEB www.icnz.org.nz).

LANGUAGE

Although many French people, especially in major tourist areas, speak some English, it's important to remember you are going to France and that people speak French. However, generally at least one person in most hotels can explain things to you in English (unless you are in a very rural area). Be patient, and speak English slowly.

The French may appear prickly at first to English-speaking visitors. But it usually helps if you **make an effort to speak a little French.** So even if your own French is terrible, try to master a few words. A simple, friendly *bonjour* (hello) will do, as will asking if the person you are greeting speaks English ("*Parlez-vous anglais?*"). *See* the French Vocabulary and Menu Guide at the back of the book for more suggestions.

LANGUAGES FOR TRAVELERS

Fodor's French for Travelers (☎ 800/733–3000 in the U.S.; 800/668–4247 in Canada; $7 for phrase book, $16.95 for audio set plus $5.50 for shipping) is a comprehensive guide.

LODGING

The lodgings we list are the cream of the crop in each price category. We always list the facilities available—but we don't specify whether they cost extra: when pricing accommodations, always ask what's included and what costs extra. Properties indicated by a ✕🏨 are lodging establishments whose restaurant warrants a special trip.

Assume that hotels operate on the **European Plan** (EP, with no meals). Although middle-range hotels sometimes offer a free breakfast, those at both the high and low ends of the scale generally do not. On occasion, hotels (generally in the rural countryside) offer rates that include full- or half-board; inquire when making your reservation.

APARTMENT AND HOUSE RENTALS

If you want a home base that's roomy enough for a family or group and comes with cooking facilities, **consider a furnished rental.** Renting an apartment or a *gîte rural*—a furnished house in the country—for a week or month can also save you money.

The national rental network, the Fédération Nationale des Gîtes de France, rents rural homes with regional flavor. Gîtes are nearly always maintained by on-site owners, who greet you on your arrival and provide information on groceries, doctors, and nearby attractions. A nationwide catalog (€16) is available from the Fédération Nationale des Gîtes de France, listing gîtes ruraux for rent. Called "Nouveaux Gîtes Ruraux," the catalog only lists the newest additions to the network, because a comprehensive nationwide listing of all gîtes would make an unwieldy volume. If you know the region you want to visit, contact the departmental branch directly and order a photo catalog that lists every property. If you specify which dates you plan to visit, the office will narrow down the choice to rentals available for those days.

Individual tourist offices often publish lists of *locations meublés* (furnished rentals); these are often inspected by the tourist office and rated by comfort standards. Usually they are booked directly through the individual owner, which generally requires some knowledge of French. Rentals that are not classified or rated by the tourist office should be undertaken with trepidation, as they can fall well below your minimum standard of comfort.

Vacation rentals in France always book from Saturday to Saturday (with some offering weekend rates off-season). Most do not include bed linens and towels but make them available for an additional fee. Always check on policies on pets and children and specify if you need an enclosed garden for toddlers, a washing machine, a fireplace, etc. If you plan to have overnight guests during your stay, let the owner know; there may be additional charges. Insurance restrictions prohibit loading in guests beyond the specified capacity.

➤ INTERNATIONAL AGENTS: **At Home Abroad** (✉ 405 E. 56th St., Suite 6H, New York, NY 10022, ☎ 212/421–9165, 212/752–1591, WEB member.aol.com/athomabrod/index.html). **Drawbridge to Europe** (✉ 102 Granite St., Ashland, OR 97520, ☎ 541/482–7778 or 888/268–1148, FAX 541/482–7779, WEB www.drawbridgetoeurope.com). **Hideaways International** (✉ 767 Islington St., Portsmouth, NH 03801, ☎ 603/430–4433 or 800/843–4433, FAX 603/430–4444, WEB www.hideaways.com; membership $129). **Hometours International** (✉ Box 11503, Knoxville, TN 37939, ☎ 865/690–8484 or 800/367–4668, WEB thor.he.net/~hometour/). **Interhome** (✉ 1990 N.E. 163rd St., Suite 110, North Miami Beach, FL 33162, ☎ 305/940–2299 or 800/882–6864, FAX 305/940–2911, WEB www.interhome.com). **Vacation Home Rentals Worldwide** (✉ 235 Kensington Ave., Norwood, NJ 07648, ☎ 201/767–9393 or 800/633–3284, FAX 201/767–5510, WEB www.vhrww.com). **Villanet** (✉ 1251 N.W. 116th St., Seattle, WA 98177, ☎ 206/417–3444 or 800/964–1891, FAX 206/417–1832, WEB www.rentavilla.com). **Villas and Apartments Abroad** (✉ 1270 Ave. of the Americas, 15th floor, New York, NY 10020, ☎ 212/897–5045 or 800/433–3020, FAX 212/897–5039, WEB www.vaanyc.com). **Villas International** (✉ 950 Northgate Dr., Suite 206, San Rafael, CA 94903, ☎ 415/499–9490 or 800/221–2260, FAX 415/499–9491, WEB www.villasintl.com).

➤ LOCAL AGENTS: **Fédération Nationale des Gîtes de France** (✉ 59 rue St-Lazare, 75009 Paris, ☎ 01–49–70–75–75, FAX 01–42–81–28–53, WEB www.gitesdefrance.fr). **French Government Tourist Office** (☞ Visitor Information, *below*).

BED-AND-BREAKFASTS

Chambres d'hôtes (bed and breakfasts) can mean simple lodging, usually in the hosts' home, with breakfast, but can also mean a beautiful room in an 18th-century château with gourmet food and a harpsichord in the living room. Chambres d'hôtes are most common in rural France, though they are becoming more so in Paris and other major cities. Check with local tourist offices or contact Gîtes de France, a national organization that lists B&Bs all over the country, or private reservation agencies. Often table d'hôte dinners (meals cooked by and eaten with the owners) can be arranged for an extra, fairly nominal fee. Note that your hosts at B&Bs, unlike those at hotels, are more likely to speak only speak French.

➤ RESERVATION SERVICES: **Gîtes de France** (✉ 59 rue St-Lazare, 75439 Cedex 09 Paris, ☎ 01–49–70–75–75, FAX 01–42–81–28–53, WEB www.gitesdefrance.fr). **Paris Bed & Breakfast** (☎ 800/872–2632).

CAMPING

French campsites have a good reputation for organization and amenities but are crowded in July and August. Many campsites welcome reservations, and in summer it makes sense to book in advance. The Fédération Française de Camping et de Caravaning publishes a guide to France's campsites (€15.25, plus shipping).

➤ CAMPSITE GUIDE: **Fédération Française de Camping et de Caravaning** (✉ 78 rue de Rivoli, 75004 Paris, ☎ 01–42–72–84–08, WEB www.motorpressefrance.fr).

HOSTELS

No matter what your age, you can **save on lodging costs by staying at hostels.** In some 5,000 locations in more than 70 countries around the world, Hostelling International (HI), the umbrella group for a number of national youth-hostel associations, offers single-sex, dorm-style beds and, at many hostels, rooms for couples and family accommodations. Membership in any HI national hostel association, open to travelers of all ages, allows you to stay in HI-affiliated hostels at member rates; one-year membership is about $25 for adults (C$26.75 in Canada, £13 in the United Kingdom, $30 in Australia, and $30 in New Zealand); hostels run about $10–$30 per night. Members have priority if the hostel is full; they're also eligible for discounts around the world, even on rail and bus travel in some countries.

Paris's major public hostels are run by the Féderation Unie des Auberges de Jeunesse (FUAJ)—for about €20, a bed, sheets, shower, and breakfast are provided, with beds usually three to four to a room. Maisons Internationales des Jeunes Étudiants (MIJE) have the plushest hostels, sometimes in historic mansions. Private hostels have accommodations that run from pleasant, if spartan, double rooms to dormlike arrangements.

➤ ORGANIZATIONS: **Féderation Unie des Auberges de Jeunesse (FUAJ/Hostelling International)** (FUAJ Beaubourg: ✉ 9 rue Brantôme, 3e, Paris, ☎ 01–48–04–70–40, WEB www.fuaj.org; Centre National: ✉ 27 rue Pajol, 18e, Paris, ☎ 01–44–89–87–27, WEB www.fuaj.org). **Hostelling International—American Youth Hostels** (✉ 733 15th St. NW, Suite 840, Washington, DC 20005, ☎ 202/783–6161, FAX 202/783–6171, WEB www.hiayh.org). **Hostelling International—Canada** (✉ 400–205 Catherine St., Ottawa, Ontario K2P 1C3, ☎ 613/237–7884, FAX 613/237–7868, WEB www.hostellingintl.ca). **Youth Hostel Association of England and Wales** (✉ Trevelyan House, Dimple Rd., Matlock, Derbyshire DE4 3YH, ☎ 0870/870–8808, FAX 0169/592–702, WEB www.yha.org.uk). **Australian Youth Hostel Association** (✉ 10 Mallett St., Camperdown, NSW 2050, ☎ 02/9565–1699, FAX 02/9565–1325, WEB www.yha.com.au). **Youth Hostels Association of New Zealand** (✉ Box 436, Christchurch, ☎ 03/379–9970, FAX 03/365–4476, WEB www.yha.org.nz).

HOTELS

Hotels in France are officially classified from one star to four-star deluxe, and stars appear on a shield on the facade of most hotels. The grading system is based on a notoriously complicated evaluation of amenities and services. At the bottom end of the scale are one-star hotels, where you might have to share a bathroom and do without an elevator. You can expect two- and three-star hotels to have private bathrooms, elevators, and in-room televisions. At the high end are luxurious four-star hotels, which have excellent amenities, and prices to match. The ratings are sometimes misleading, however, since many hotels prefer to be understarred for tax reasons.

Rates are always by room, not per person. Prices must, by law, be posted at the hotel entrance and should include taxes and service. You might try negotiating rates if you're planning on staying for a week or longer or are coming off season.

Assume all hotel rooms have air-conditioning, telephones, TV, and private bath unless otherwise noted. You should always **check what bathroom facilities the price includes.** When making your reservation, state your preference for shower (*douche*) or tub (*baignoire*)—the latter always costs more. Also when booking, **ask for a *grand lit* if you want a double bed.**

If you're counting on air-conditioning you should **make sure, in advance, that your hotel room is *climatisé*** (air-conditioned). If you throw open the windows, **don't expect screens** *(moustiquaires)*. Nowhere in Europe are they standard equipment.

The quality of accommodations, particularly in older properties and even in luxury hotels, can vary greatly from room to room; **if you don't like the room you're given, ask to see another.**

Breakfast is not always included in the price, but you're sometimes expected to have it and are occasionally charged for it regardless. Make sure to **inform the hotel if you are not going to be breakfasting there**; you may want to find the nearest café anyway. Occasionally, smaller rural hotels with restaurants expect you to have your evening meal at the hotel.

It's always a good idea to **make hotel reservations in Paris and other major**

tourist destinations as far in advance as possible, especially in late spring, summer, or fall. Faxing is the easiest way to contact the hotel (the staff is probably more likely to read English than to understand it spoken over the phone long-distance), though calling also works, while larger, more modern hotels now correspond using their e-mail address (always found on their Web site). But whether by fax, phone, or e-mail, you should specify the exact dates you want to stay at the hotel (don't forget to notify your hotel of a possible late check-in to prevent your room from being given away); the size of the room you want and how many people will be sleeping there; the type of accommodations you want (two twins, double, etc.); and what kind of bathroom (private with shower or bath, or both). You might also ask if a deposit (or your credit-card number) is required, and if so, what happens if you cancel. Request that the hotel fax you back so you have a written confirmation of your reservation.

If you arrive without a reservation, the tourist offices in major train stations and most towns can probably help you find a room.

Many hotels in France are small, often independently owned or family-run establishments. Some are affiliated with hotel groups, such as Logis de France, which can be relied on for comfort, character, and regional cuisine (look for its distinctive yellow-and-green sign). A Logis de France paperback guide is widely available in bookshops or from Logis de France. Two prestigious international groups with numerous converted châteaux and manor houses among its members are Relais & Châteaux and Small Luxury Hotels of the World; booklets listing members are available from these organizations. France also has some hotel chains. Examples in the upper price bracket are Frantel, Novotel, and Sofitel as well as Inter-Continental, Marriott, Hilton, Hyatt, Westin, and Sheraton. The Best Western, Campanile, Climat de France, Ibis, and Timhotel chains are more moderate. Typically, chains offer a consistently acceptable standard of modern features (modern bathrooms, TVs, etc.) but tend to lack atmosphere, with some exceptions (Best Western, for instance, tries to maintain the local character of the hotels it takes over).

➤ TOLL-FREE NUMBERS: **Best Western** (☎ 800/528–1234, WEB www.bestwestern.com). **Choice** (☎ 800/424–6423, WEB www.hotelchoice.com). **Clarion** (☎ 800/252–7466, WEB www.choicehotels.com). **Comfort** (☎ 800/424–6423, WEB www.comfortinn.com). **Forte** (☎ 800/225–5843, WEB www.forte-hotels.com). **Holiday Inn** (☎ 800/465–4329, WEB www.sixcontinentshotels.com). **Hyatt Hotels & Resorts** (☎ 800/233–1234, WEB www.hyatt.com). **Inter-Continental** (☎ 800/327–0200, WEB www.intercontinental.com). **Le Meridien** (☎ 800/543–4300, WEB www.lemeridien-hotels.com). **Nikko Hotels International** (☎ 800/645–5687, WEB www.nikkohotels.com). **Quality Inn** (☎ 800/424–6423, WEB www.choicehotels.com). **Ramada** (☎ 800/228–2828, WEB www.ramada.com). **Renaissance Hotels & Resorts** (☎ 800/468–3571, WEB www.renaissancehotels.com). **Sheraton** (☎ 800/325–3535, WEB www.starwood.com). **Sleep Inn** (☎ 800/753–3746, WEB www.sleepinn.com). **Westin Hotels & Resorts** (☎ 800/228–3000, WEB www.westin.com).

MAIL AND SHIPPING

Post offices, or PTT, are found in every town and are recognizable by a yellow LA POSTE sign. They are usually open weekdays 8–7, Saturday 8–noon, but the **main Paris post office** (✉ 52 rue du Louvre, 1er) is open 24 hours, seven days a week.

OVERNIGHT SERVICES

Sending overnight mail from major cities in France is relatively easy. Besides DHL, Federal Express, and UPS, the French post office has overnight mail service, called Chronopost.

➤ MAJOR SERVICES: **DHL** (✉ 6 rue des Colonnes, 2e, Opéra/Grands Boulevards, Paris, ☎ 01–55–35–30–30; ✉ 59 rue Iéna, 16e, Trocadero, Paris, ☎ 01–45–01–91–00; WEB www.dhl.com). **Federal Express** (✉ 63 bd. Haussmann, 8e, Champs-Élysées, Paris, ☎ 01–40–06–90–16; ✉ 2 rue 29 Juillet, 1er, Louvre/Tuileries, Paris, ☎ 01–49–26–04–66; 08–00–12–38–

00 for information about pickups all over France, WEB www.fedex.com). UPS (✉ 34 bd. Malesherbes, 8e, Champs-Élysées, Paris; ✉ 107 rue Réaumur, 2e, Beaubourg/Les Halles, Paris, ☎ 08–00–87–78–77 for information all over France, WEB www.ups.com).

POSTAL RATES

Letters and postcards to the United States and Canada cost €.67 (about 60 cents) for 20 grams. Letters and postcards to the United Kingdom cost €.46 (about 33 pence) for up to 20 grams. Letters and postcards within France cost €.46. Stamps can be bought in post offices and in cafés displaying a red TABAC sign outside. It takes, on the average, five days for a letter to reach the United States, 5–6 days to Australia, 4–5 days to Canada, and three days to any location in Europe.

RECEIVING MAIL

If you're uncertain where you'll be staying, **have mail sent to the local post office,** addressed as "poste restante," or to American Express, but remember that during peak seasons American Express may refuse to accept mail. The French postal service has a €.45 per item service charge.

MONEY MATTERS

Prices throughout this guide are given for adults. Substantially reduced fees are almost always available for children, students, and senior citizens. For information on taxes, *see* Taxes, *below.*

The following prices are for Paris; other cities and areas are often cheaper (with the notable exception of the Côte d'Azur). Keep in mind that it's less expensive to eat or drink standing at a café or bar counter than to sit at a table. Two prices are listed, *au comptoir* (at the counter) and *à salle* (at a table; sometimes orders cost even more if you're seated at a terrace table). Coffee in a bar: €.90–€1 (standing), €1.50–€4.75 (seated); beer in a bar: €2.30 (standing), €3–€6 (seated); Coca-Cola: €1.25–€3 a can; ham sandwich: €2.30–€4.75; 2 km (1-mi) taxi ride: €5.40; movie-theater seat: €9 (15%–33% cheaper on Monday and Wednesday); foreign newspaper: €2.30–€3.

ATMS

Fairly common in Paris and other big towns as well as in airports and train stations, **ATMs are one of the easiest ways to get euros.** Don't, however, count on finding ATMs in smaller towns and rural areas. Banks usually offer excellent wholesale exchange rates through ATMs.

To get cash at ATMs in France, **your PIN must be four digits long.** Note that the machine will give you two chances to enter your correct PIN number; if you make a mistake on the third try, your card will be held, and you'll have to return to the bank the next morning to retrieve it. You may have better luck with ATMs with a credit or debit card that is also a Visa or MasterCard, rather than just your bank card. Note, too, that you may be charged by your bank for using ATMs overseas; inquire at your bank about charges. Before you go, it's a good idea to **get a list of ATM locations that you can use** in France from your bank.

CREDIT CARDS

France is a credit-card society. Credit cards are used for just about everything, from the automatic gas pumps (now starting to pop up all over the country), to the tolls on highways, payment machines in underground parking lots, stamps at the post office, and even the most minor purchases in the larger department stores. A restaurant or shop would either have to be extremely small or brand new not to have some credit-card or debit-card capability. However, some of the smaller restaurants and stores do have a credit-card minimum, usually around €15, which normally should be clearly indicated; to be safe, ask before you order. Do not forget to take your credit-card receipt, as fraudulent use of credit-card numbers taken from receipts is on the rise.

Throughout this guide the following abbreviations are used: **AE,** American Express; **DC,** Diners Club; **MC,** MasterCard; and **V,** Visa.

➤ REPORTING LOST CARDS: **American Express** (☎ 336/939–1111 or 336/668–5309), call collect. **Diners Club** (☎ 303/799–1504), call collect. **MasterCard** (☎ 0800/90–1387). **Visa**

(☎ 0800/90–1179; 410/581–9994 collect).

CURRENCY

On January 1st, 2002, the new single European Union (EU) currency, the euro (€), became the official currency of the 12 countries participating in the European Monetary Union (with the notable exceptions of Great Britain, Denmark, and Sweden). The first thing you will notice is that the euro system has quite a lot of coins, eight to be exact: 1 and 2 euros, plus 1, 2, 5, 10, 20, and 50 cents. All coins display their value on one side, while the other side is adorned with the national symbol of the issuing country. There are seven colorful notes: 5, 10, 20, 50, 100, 200, and 500 euros. Notes have illustrations of the principal architectural styles from antiquity onward on one side and a map of Europe on the other, and are the same in all countries. The first thing you must do when you change your money is memorize the coins as soon as you can (notes are much easier to grasp, as they start off at €5) and you'll undoubtedly find yourself quickly weighted down with all those coins. This was the first complaint most Europeans had about this new system, and this, in turn, led to the second complaint: euro coins, with their high nickel content, pose a problem for people with an allergic sensitivity to the mineral (if you're one of them, try to handle the coins as little as possible, and if you do come in contact with them, rinse your hands as soon as you can).

The advent of the euro makes any whirlwind grand European tour all the easier. From France, you'll glide across the borders of Austria, Germany, Italy, Spain, Holland, Ireland, Greece, Belgium, Finland, Luxembourg, and Portugal with no pressing need to run to the local exchange booth to change yet another currency before you even had the time to become familiar with the last. You'll be able to do what drives many tourists crazy—to assess the value of a purchase (for example, to realize that eating a three-course meal in a small restaurant in Lisbon is cheaper than the ham sandwich you bought on the Champs Élysées). Along with the facility of movement from country to country, the euro has another benefit in that it was created as a direct competitor with the U.S. dollar and is, therefore, of nearly equal value. At press time (summer 2002), one euro equals .97 U.S.$—a definite plus for those who both hated yet felt compelled to convert prices into dollars.

Such are the ground rules when it comes to the euro and the old EU currencies. But you still have to **pay close attention to where you change your U.S. dollars and all other currencies that are not part of the EU community**—shop around for the best exchange rates (and also check the rates before leaving home) when it comes to non-EU currencies such as the dollar, the Japanese yen, and the British pound. The rates of conversion between the euro and other local currencies have been irrevocably fixed: 1 euro = 1.95 German marks; 1.39 Canadian dollars; 0.78 Irish punts; 13.76 Austrian schillings; 1.79 Australian dollars; 2.14 New Zealand dollars; 1,936.26 Italian liras; 40.33 Belgian francs; 166.38 Spanish pesetas; 2.20 Dutch guilders; 200.48 Portuguese escudos; 40.33 Luxembourg francs; 5.94 Finnish markkas; and 0.62 English pounds.

CURRENCY EXCHANGE

These days, the **easiest way to get euros is through ATMs**; you can find them in airports, train stations, and throughout the city. ATM rates are excellent because they are based on wholesale rates offered only by major banks. It's a good idea, however, to bring some euros with you from home and always to have some cash and traveler's checks as backup. For the best deal when exchanging currencies not within the Monetary Union purview (the U.S. dollar, the yen, and the English pound are examples), compare rates at banks (which usually have the most favorable rates) and booths and look for exchange booths that clearly state "no commission." At exchange booths always confirm the rate with the teller before exchanging money. You won't do as well at exchange booths in airports or rail and bus stations, in hotels, in restaurants, or in stores. Of all the banks in Paris, the Banque of France has the best rates. To avoid lines at airport exchange booths, **get an initial amount of euros before you leave home.**

➤ EXCHANGE SERVICES: **International Currency Express** (☏ 888/278–6628 for orders). **Thomas Cook Currency Services** (☏ 800/287–7362 for telephone orders and retail locations, WEB www.us.thomascook.com).

TRAVELER'S CHECKS

Do you need traveler's checks? It depends on where you're headed. If you're going to rural areas and small towns, go with cash; traveler's checks are best used in cities. Lost or stolen checks can usually be replaced within 24 hours. To ensure a speedy refund, buy your own traveler's checks—don't let someone else pay for them: irregularities like this can cause delays. The person who bought the checks should make the call to request a refund.

PASSPORTS AND VISAS

When traveling internationally, **carry your passport** even if you don't need one (it's always the best form of I.D.) and **make two photocopies of the data page** (one for someone at home and another for you, carried separately from your passport). If you lose your passport, promptly call the nearest embassy or consulate and the local police.

U.S. passport applications for children under age 14 require consent from both parents or legal guardians; both parents must appear together to sign the application. If only one parent appears, he or she must submit a written statement from the other parent authorizing passport issuance for the child. A parent with sole authority must present evidence of it when applying; acceptable documentation includes the child's certified birth certificate listing only the applying parent, a court order specifically permitting this parent's travel with the child, or a death certificate for the non-applying parent. Application forms and instructions are available on the Web site of the U.S. State Department's Bureau of Consular Affairs (www.travel.state.gov).

ENTERING FRANCE

All Australian, Canadian, New Zealand, U.K., and U.S. citizens, even infants, need only a valid passport to enter France for stays of up to 90 days.

PASSPORT OFFICES

The best time to apply for a passport or to renew is in fall and winter. Before any trip, check your passport's expiration date and, if necessary, renew it as soon as possible.

➤ AUSTRALIAN CITIZENS: **Australian State Passport Office** (☏ 131–232, WEB www.passports.gov.au).

➤ CANADIAN CITIZENS: **Passport Office** (to mail in applications: ✉ Department of Foreign Affairs and International Trade, Ottawa, Ontario K1A 0G3, ☏ 819/994–3500 or 800/567–6868, WEB www.dfait-maeci.gc.ca/passport).

➤ NEW ZEALAND CITIZENS: **New Zealand Passport Office** (☏ 04/474–8100 or 0800/22–5050, WEB www.passports.govt.nz).

➤ U.K. CITIZENS: **London Passport Office** (☏ 0870/521–0410, WEB www.passport.gov.uk) for fees and documentation requirements and to request an emergency passport.

➤ U.S. CITIZENS: **National Passport Information Center** (☏ 900/225–5674; calls are 35¢ per min for automated service, $1.05 per min for operator service, WEB www.travel.state.gov/npicinfo.html).

PUBLIC TRANSPORTATION

For information about public transportation in France, *see* A to Z sections *in* individual chapters.

REST ROOMS

Although most cafés reserve the right to limit use of their bathroom facilities to paying customers, most French are willing to ignore the frustrated glare of the waiter in an emergency. Bathrooms are often downstairs, are usually unisex (which means you may have to walk by urinals in use), are often just holes in the ground with porcelain pads on either side for your feet, and to top it all off, you'll probably have to pay a fee of 30 cents. They are not the cleanest places in the world, especially for children, so it is in your best interest to be prepared and always carry a small box of tissues with you. In cities, your best bets may be fast-food chains, large department stores, and hotel lobbies. Do not be alarmed if you don't see any light switches—once the bathroom door is shut and locked, the lights will go on. You can also find pay-per-use toilet units on Parisian streets; these require 50 cents (small children, however, should not use these alone, as the self-sanitizing system works with weight-related sensors that might not sense the presence of a child). There are bathrooms in the larger métro stations and in all train stations for a cost of 20–50 cents. Highway rest stops also have bathrooms, which are equipped with changing tables for babies and even showers during summer months.

SAFETY

Beware of petty theft—purse snatching, pickpocketing, and pilfering from automobiles—throughout France, particularly in Paris and along the Côte d'Azur. Use common sense: avoid pulling out a lot of money in public; wear a handbag with long straps that you can sling across your body, bandolier style, with a zippered compartment for your money and passport. It's also a good idea to wear a money belt. When withdrawing money from cash machines, be especially aware of your surroundings and anyone standing uncomfortably close. If you feel uneasy, press the cancel button (*annuler*) and walk to an area where you feel more comfortable. Incidents of credit-card fraud are on the rise in France, especially in urban areas; be sure to collect your receipts, as these have recently been used by thieves to charge over the Internet, where a PIN number is not mandatory. Men should keep their wallets up front. Car break-ins, especially in isolated parking lots where hikers set off for the day, are on the rise. It makes sense to **take valuables with you or leave your luggage at your hotel.**

Avoid walking alone in dark, unknown areas at night and be careful on public transportation; if you are uncomfortable on the métro or bus, change cars or seats, getting as close as possible to the driver. Note one cultural difference; a friendly smile or steady eye contact is often seen as an invitation to further contact; so, unfortunately, you should avoid being overly friendly with strangers—unless you feel perfectly safe.

SENIOR-CITIZEN TRAVEL

Older travelers (60 and older) can take advantage of many discounts, such as reduced admissions of 20%–50% to museums and movie theaters. For rail travel in France, the Carte Senior entitles travelers 60 years or older to discounts (☞ Train Travel, *below*).

To qualify for age-related discounts, **mention your senior-citizen status up front** when booking hotel reservations (not when checking out) and before you're seated in restaurants (not when paying the bill). When renting a car, ask about promotional car-rental discounts, which can be cheaper than senior-citizen rates.

➤ EDUCATIONAL PROGRAMS: **Elderhostel** (✉ 11 Ave. de Lafayette, Boston, MA 02111-1746, ☎ 877/426–8056, FAX 877/426–2166, WEB www.elderhostel.org). **Interhostel** (✉ University of New Hampshire, 6 Garrison Ave., Durham, NH 03824, ☎ 603/862–1147 or 800/733–9753, FAX 603/862–1113, WEB www.learn.unh.edu).

STUDENTS IN FRANCE

Studying in France is the perfect way to shake up your perception of the world, make international friends, and improve your language skills. You may choose to study through a U.S.–sponsored program, usually through an American university, or enroll in a program sponsored by a French organization. Do your homework: programs vary greatly in expense, academic quality, exposure to language, amount of contact with locals, and living conditions. Working through your local university is the easiest way to find out about study-abroad programs in France. Most universities have staff members who distribute information on programs at European universities, and they might be able to put you in touch with program participants.

Student bargains can be found almost everywhere—on train and plane fares, and for movie and museum tickets. Note, however, that you must be 26 or under.

➤ I.D.S AND SERVICES: **Council Travel** (✉ 205 E. 42nd St., 15th floor, New York, NY 10017, ☎ 212/822–2700 or 888/226–8624, FAX 212/822–2719, WEB www.counciltravel.com). **Travel Cuts** (✉ 187 College St., Toronto, Ontario M5T 1P7, Canada, ☎ 416/979–2406 or 888/838–2887, FAX 416/979–8167, WEB www.travelcuts.com).

➤ RESOURCES: **American Institute for Foreign Study** (✉ 102 Greenwich Ave., Greenwich, CT 06830, ☎ 203/869–9090 or 800/727–2437, FAX 203/863–6180). **American Council of International Studies** (ACIS; ✉ 19 Bay State Rd., Boston, MA 02215, ☎ 617/236–2051 or 800/888–2247). **Council on International Educational Exchange** (CIEE; ✉ 205 E. 42nd St., 15th floor, New York, NY 10017, ☎ 212/822–2600 or 888/268–6245, FAX 212/822–2699). **Institute of International Education** (IIE; ✉ 809 UN Plaza, New York, NY 10017, ☎ 212/984–5413). **World Learning** (✉ Kipling Rd., Box 676, Brattleboro, VT 05302, ☎ 802/257–7751 or 800/336–1616, FAX 802/258–3248).

TAXES

All taxes must be included in posted prices in France. The initials TTC (*toutes taxes comprises*—taxes included) sometimes appear on price lists but, strictly speaking, they are superfluous. By law, **restaurant and hotel prices must include 19.6% taxes and a service charge.** If they show up as extra charges on your bill, complain.

VALUE-ADDED TAX

A number of shops offer VAT refunds to foreign shoppers. You are entitled to a export refund of the 19.6% tax, depending on the item purchased, but it is often applicable only if your purchases in the same store reach a minimum of €430 (for U.K. and EU residents) or €184 (others, including U.S. and Canadian residents). In most instances, you need to fill out a form, which must then be tendered to a customs official at your last port of departure. Remember to **ask for the refund, as some stores—especially larger ones—offer the service only upon request.** and note that VAT refunds can't be processed after you arrive back home. In the end, you often wind up getting a credit on your charge card.

A refund service can save you some hassle, for a fee. Global Refund, one of many such outfitters, is a Europe-wide service with 130,000 affiliated stores and more than 700 refund counters—located at every major airport and border crossing. Its refund form is called a Shopping Cheque. The service issues refunds in the form of cash, check, or credit-card adjustment, minus a processing fee. If you don't have time to wait at the refund counter, you can mail in the form instead.

➤ V.A.T. REFUNDS: **Global Refund** (✉ 99 Main St., Suite 307, Nyack, NY 10960, ☎ 800/566–9828, FAX 845/348–1549, WEB www.globalrefund.com).

TELEPHONES

AREA AND COUNTRY CODES

The country code for France is 33. The first two digits of French numbers are a prefix determined by zone: Paris and Ile-de-France, 01; the northwest, 02; the northeast, 03; the southeast, 04; and the southwest, 05. Numbers that begin with 06 are for mobile phones (and are notoriously expensive). Pay close attention to the numbers beginning with 08; 08 followed by 00 is a toll-free number but 08–36 numbers are very costly, at least €.35 per minute.

CALLING FRANCE

Note that **when dialing France from abroad, drop the initial 0 from the number.** For instance, to call a telephone number in Paris from the United States, dial 011–33 plus the phone number minus the initial 0 (phone numbers in this book are listed with the full 10 digits, which you use to make local calls). To call France from the United Kingdom, dial 00–33, then dial the number in France minus the initial 0.

DIRECTORY AND OPERATOR ASSISTANCE

To find a number **in France, dial 12 for information.** For international inquiries, dial 00–33 plus the country code.

Another source of information is the Minitel, an online network similar to the Internet. You can find one—they look like a small computer terminal—in most post offices. Available free is an online phone book covering the entire country. To find information, hit the *appel* (call) key, then, when prompted, type the name you are looking for and hit *envoi* (return). It is also useful for tracking down services: choose *activité* (activity), tap in *piscine* (swimming pool), then Chartres, for example, and it will give you a list of all the pools in Chartres. Go to other lines or pages by hitting the *suite* (next) key. Newer models will connect automatically when you hit the book-icon key. To disconnect, hit *fin* (end).

INTERNATIONAL CALLS

To make a direct international call out of France, dial 00 and wait for the tone, then dial the country code (1 for the United States and Canada, 44 for the United Kingdom, 61 for Australia, and 64 for New Zealand) and the area code (minus any initial 0) and number.

Telephone rates have decreased recently in France due to the fact that the French Telecom monopoly finally has some stringent competition. As in most countries, the highest rates fall between 8 AM and 7 PM; you can expect to pay €.23 per minute for a call to the U.S., Canada, or some of the closer European countries such as Great Britain, Belgium, Italy, and Germany. Rates are slashed by almost half when you make that same call between 7 PM and 8 AM, at just €.12 per minute, making it definitely worth the wait. There should be very little to compel you to call home with the help of international directory assistance, as it costs a hefty €6 per call; If this doesn't dissuade you, dial 00–33 plus the code of the country you'd like to call and a bilingual operator will come on line. Try not to make calls directly from your hotel either, unless you're using a phone card; they charge heavily for local calls and slap a service charge on for international calls. Your best bet is to buy a French phone card, a *télécarte,* which can be used from any phone and will end up saving you a bundle.

LOCAL CALLS

To make calls in the same city or town, or in the same region, dial the full 10-digit number.

LONG-DISTANCE CALLS

To call any region in France from another region, just dial the full 10-digit number.

LONG-DISTANCE SERVICES

AT&T, MCI, and Sprint access codes make calling long distance relatively convenient, but you may find the local access number blocked in many hotel rooms. First, ask the hotel operator to connect you. If the hotel operator balks, ask for an international operator, or dial the international operator yourself. One way to improve your odds of getting connected to your long-distance carrier is to travel with more than one company's calling card (a hotel may block Sprint, for example, but not MCI). If all else fails, call from a pay phone.

➤ ACCESS CODES: **AT&T Direct** (☎ 08–00–99–00–11; 08–00–99–01–11; 800/874–4000 for information). **MCI WorldPhone** (☎ 08–00–99–00–19; 800/444–4444 for information). **Sprint International Access** (☎ 08–00–99–87; 800/793–1153 for information).

PHONE CARDS

The rare French person who doesn't have a mobile phone uses ***télécartes*** (phone cards), which you can buy just about anywhere, from post offices, tabacs, métro stations, magazine kiosks, small grocery stores, or any France Telecom office. These phone cards will save you money because the international rates they offer have been negotiated and are the best you will find. They will also save you time, as it is virtually impossible to find a phone that will take coins nowadays. There are two télécartes available; *une pétite* that costs €7.50 for fifty units or *une grande* that costs €15.20 for 120 units. Scratch the card to uncover your personal PIN, dial the toll-free number and the number you wish to reach (be it local or international) and the operator will tell you the exact amount of time you have to chat.

PUBLIC PHONES

Telephone booths can be found in airports, post offices, train stations, on the street, and often in cafés. At press time, prices were falling, and a local call made between 8 AM and 7 PM cost €.034 per minute. Low rates of €.018 per minute apply weekdays between 7 PM and 8 AM, all day Saturday and Sunday, and all national holidays. You may still be able to find one of the rare pay phones left in France that operate with coins in a café, but do not count on it. If you do find a coin-operated phone, simply lift the receiver, place your coin(s) in the appropriate slots, then dial. There will be three long beeps indicating when you are running out of time, so put coins in immediately or you will abruptly be cut off.

TIME

The time difference between New York and Paris is six hours (so when it's 1 PM in New York, it's 7 PM in Paris). The time difference between London and Paris is one hour; between Sydney and Paris, 8–9 hours; and between Auckland and Paris, 12 hours. France, like the rest of Europe, uses the 24-hour (or "military") clock, which means that after noon you continue counting forward: 13h00 is 1 PM, 14h00 is 2 PM, 22h30 is 10:30 PM.

TIPPING

The French have a clear idea of when they should be tipped. Bills in bars and restaurants include a service charge, but **it is customary to round out your bill with some small change** unless you're dissatisfied. The amount varies: anywhere from €.20, if you've merely bought a beer, to €2 after a meal. Tip taxi drivers and hairdressers about 10%. Give ushers in theaters and movie theaters (€.15 or €.30). In some theaters and hotels, coat-check attendants may expect nothing (if there is a sign saying POURBOIRE INTERDIT—tips forbidden); otherwise give them €.30–€.75. Washroom attendants usually get €.30, though the sum is often posted.

If you stay in a hotel for more than two or three days, it is customary to leave something for the chambermaid—about €1.50 per day. In expensive hotels you may well call on the services of a baggage porter (bellboy) and hotel porter and possibly the telephone receptionist. All expect a tip: plan on about €1.50 per item for the baggage porter, but the other tips will depend on how much you've used their services—common sense must guide you here. In hotels that provide room service, give €.75 to the waiter (this does not apply to breakfast served in your room). If the chambermaid does some pressing or laundering for you, give her €.75 on top of the charge made. If the concierge has been very helpful, it is customary to leave a tip of €10–20, depending on the type of hotel and the level of service.

Gas-station attendants get nothing for gas or oil but €.75 or €1.50 for checking tires. Train and airport porters get a fixed €1–€1.50 per bag, but you're better off getting your own baggage cart if you can (a €1 coin—refundable—is necessary in train stations only). Museum guides should get €.75–€1.50 after a guided tour, and it is standard practice to tip tour guides (and bus drivers) €1.50 or more after an excursion, depending on its length.

TOURS AND PACKAGES

Because everything is prearranged on a prepackaged tour or independent vacation, you'll spend less time planning—and often get it all at a good price.

BOOKING WITH AN AGENT

Travel agents are excellent resources. But it's a good idea to collect brochures from several agencies as some agents' suggestions may be influenced by relationships with tour and package firms that reward them for volume sales. If you have a special interest, **find an agent with expertise in that area**; ASTA (☞ Travel Agencies, *below*) has a database of specialists worldwide.

Make sure your travel agent knows the accommodations and other services of the place they're recommending. Ask about the hotel's location, room size, beds, and such facilities as a pool, room service, or programs for children, if you care about these. Has your agent been there in person or sent others whom you can contact?

Do some homework on your own, too: local tourism boards can provide information about lesser-known and small-niche operators, some of which may only sell direct.

BUYER BEWARE

Each year consumers are stranded or lose their money when tour operators—even large ones with excellent reputations—go out of business. So **check out the operator.** Ask several travel agents about its reputation, and try to **book with a company that has a consumer-protection program** (Look for information in the company's brochure). In the United States, members of the National Tour Association and the United States Tour Operators Association are required to set aside funds to cover your payments and travel arrangements in the event the company defaults. It's also a good idea to choose a company that participates in the American Society of Travel Agents' Tour Operator Program (TOP), in which case ASTA will act as mediator in any disputes between you and your tour operator.

Remember that the more your package or tour includes, the better you can predict the ultimate cost of your vacation. Make sure you know exactly what is covered, and **beware of hidden costs.** Are taxes, tips, and transfers included? Entertainment and excursions? These can add up.

➤ TOUR-OPERATOR RECOMMENDATIONS: **American Society of Travel Agents** (☞ Travel Agencies, *below*). **National Tour Association** (NTA; ✉ 546 E. Main St., Lexington, KY 40508, ☎ 859/226–4444 or 800/682–8886, WEB www.ntaonline.com). **United States Tour Operators Association** (USTOA; ✉ 342 Madison Ave., Suite 1522, New York, NY 10173, ☎ 212/599–6599 or 800/468–7862, FAX 212/599–6744, WEB www.ustoa.com).

THEME TOURS

The following tour companies specialize in trips to France. The French Government Tourist Office (☞ Visitor Information, *below*) publishes brochures on theme trips in France including "In the Footsteps of the Painters of Light in Provence" and "France for the Jewish Traveler." Also *see* Barge and Boat Travel, Bike Travel, *and* Children in France, *above,* for more information about theme tours.

➤ FOOD AND WINE: **DuVine Adventures** (✉ 635 Boston Ave., Suite 2, Boston, MA 02144, ☎ 781/395–7440 or 888/396–5383, FAX 781/395–8472, WEB www.duvine.com). **European Culinary Adventures** (✉ 5 Ledgewood Way, Suite 6, Peabody, MA 01960, ☎ 978/535–5738 or 800/852–2625). **France In Your Glass** (✉ 814 35th Ave., Seattle, WA 98122, ☎ 206/325–4324 or 800/578–0903, FAX 206/325–1727 or 800/578–7069, WEB www.inyourglass.com). Le Cordon Bleu (✉ 8 rue Léon Delhomme, 75015 Paris, ☎ 01–53–68–22–50, FAX 01–48–56–03–77, WEB www.cordonbleu.net). **Ritz-Escoffier** (✉ 15 pl. Vendôme, 75001 Paris, ☎ 800/966–5758, WEB www.ritzparis.com), in Paris's Ritz hotel. **La Varenne** (✉ Box 25574, Washington, DC 20007, ☎ 202/337–0073 or 800/537–6486, FAX 703/823–5438, WEB www.lavarenne.com).

➤ MUSIC: **Dailey-Thorp Travel** (✉ 330 W. 58th St., #610, New York, NY 10019-1817, ☎ 212/307–1555 or 800/998–4677, FAX 212/974–1420).

TRAIN TRAVEL

The SNCF, France's national rail service, is fast, punctual, comfortable, and comprehensive. Traveling across France, you have various options: local trains, overnight trains with sleeping accommodations, and the high-speed TGV, the *Trains à Grande Vitesse* (very fast trains).

TGVs average 255 kph (160 mph) on the Lyon/southeast line and 300 kph (190 mph) on the Lille and Bordeaux/southwest lines and are the best and the fastest domestic trains. They operate between Paris and Lille/Calais, Paris and Brussels, Paris and Amsterdam, Paris and Lyon/Switzerland/the Côte d'Azur, Paris and Angers/Nantes, and Paris and Tours/Poitiers/Bordeaux. As with other main-line trains, a small supplement may be assessed at peak hours.

It's possible to get from one end of France to the other without traveling overnight, especially on TGVs. Otherwise, you have a choice between high-price *wagons-lit* (sleeping cars) and affordable *couchettes* (bunks, six to a compartment in second class, four to a compartment in first, with sheets and pillow provided, priced at around €15).

Try to **get to the station half an hour before departure** to ensure you'll have a good seat. Before boarding, you must **punch your ticket (but not Eurailpass) in one of the orange machines** at the entrance to the platforms, or else the ticket collector will fine you €15 on the spot.

In Paris there are six international rail stations: Gare du Nord (northern France, northern Europe, and England via Calais or Boulogne); Gare St-Lazare (Normandy and England via Dieppe); Gare de l'Est (Strasbourg, Luxembourg, Basel, and central Europe); Gare de Lyon (Lyon, Marseille, the Côte d'Azur, Geneva, and Italy); and Gare d'Austerlitz (Loire Valley, southwest France, and Spain). Note that Gare Montparnasse has taken over as the main terminus for trains bound for southwest France.

BETWEEN THE U.K. AND FRANCE

Short of flying, taking the "Chunnel" is the fastest way to cross the English Channel: 3 hours from London's central Waterloo Station to Paris's central Gare du Nord, 35 minutes from Folkestone to Calais, and 60 minutes from motorway to motorway. There is a vast range of prices for Eurostar—round-trip tickets range from €520 for first class to €105.35 for second class depending on when you travel. It's a good idea to **make a reservation if you're traveling with your car on a Chunnel train**; cars without reservations, if they can get on at all, are charged 20% extra.

British Rail also has four daily departures from London's Victoria Station, all linking with the Dover–Calais/Boulogne ferry services through to Paris. There is also an overnight service on the Newhaven–Dieppe ferry. Journey time is about eight hours. Credit-card bookings are accepted by phone or in person at a British Rail travel center.

➤ CAR TRANSPORT: **Le Shuttle** (☏ 0990/353–535 in the U.K.; 03–21–00–61–00; 01–43–18–62–22 in France, WEB www.eurotunnel.com.fr).

➤ PASSENGER SERVICE: In the U.K.: **Eurostar** (☏ 0990/186–186, WEB www.eurostar.com). **InterCity Europe** (✉ Victoria Station, London, ☏ 0990/848–848 for credit-card bookings). In the U.S.: **BritRail Travel** (☏ 800/677–8585). **Rail Europe** (☏ 800/942–4866, WEB www.raileurope.com).

CLASSES

There are two classes on French trains: first and second. The main differences between them—other than the 50% markup—are seating and atmosphere: each row in first class has only three seats, which are larger and more comfortable, and the atmosphere is clean and quiet; each row in second class has four seats, which are smaller and provide less leg room, and during peak summer hours you may find your car overcrowded and loud.

CUTTING COSTS

To save money, **look into rail passes.** But be aware that if you don't plan to cover many miles, you may come out ahead by buying individual tickets.

There are two kinds of rail passes: those you must purchase at home before you leave for France, including the France Rail Pass, the EurailPass, and the EuroPass, and those available in France from SNCF. Eurail- and EuroPasses are available through travel agents and a few authorized organizations. SNCF rail passes are available at any train station in France.

If you plan to travel outside of Paris by train, **consider purchasing a France Rail Pass,** which allows three days of unlimited train travel in a one-month period. If you travel solo, first class will run you $240, while second class is $210: you can add up to six days on this pass for $30 a day. For two people traveling together on a Saver

Pass, the cost is $196, while in second class it is $171; additional days (up to 6) cost $25 each. Other options include the France Rail 'n Drive Pass (combining rail and rental car), France Rail 'n Fly Pass (rail travel and one air-travel journey within France), and the France Fly Rail 'n Drive Pass (a rail, air, and rental-car program all in one).

France is one of 17 countries in which **you can use EurailPasses,** which provide unlimited first-class rail travel in all of the participating countries for the duration of the pass. If you plan to rack up the miles, get a standard pass. These are available for 15 days ($572), 21 days ($740), one month ($918), two months ($1,298), and three months ($1,606). If your plans call for only limited train travel, **look into a Europass,** which costs less money than a EurailPass. Unlike with the EurailPasses, however, you get a limited number of travel days, in a limited number of countries, during a specified time period. For example, a two-month Europass ($360–$710) allows between 5 and 15 days of rail travel but costs around $200 less than the least expensive EurailPass. Keep in mind, however, that the Europass is good only in France, Germany, Italy, Spain, and Switzerland, and the number of countries you can visit is further limited by the type of pass you buy.

In addition to standard EurailPasses, **ask about special rail-pass plans.** Among these are the Eurail Youthpass (for those under age 26), the Eurail Saver Pass (which gives a discount for two or more people traveling together), a Eurail Flexipass (which allows a certain number of travel days within a set period), the Euraildrive Pass, and the Europass Drive (train and rental car).

Whichever of the above passes you choose, remember that **you must purchase your Eurail and Euro passes at home before leaving for France.**

Another option is to **purchase one of the discount rail passes available only for sale in France** from SNCF. When traveling together, **two people (who don't have to be a couple) can save money with the Prix Découverte à Deux.** You'll get a 25% discount during "*périodes bleus*" (blue periods: weekdays and not on or near any holidays). Note that you have to be with the person you said you would be traveling with.

You can **get a reduced fare if you're a senior citizen (over 60).** There are two options: for the Prix Découverte Senior, all you have to do is show a valid ID with your age and you're entitled to up to a 25% reduction in fares in first and second class. The second, the Carte Senior, is better if you're planning on spending a lot of time traveling; it costs €44.20, is valid for one year, and entitles you to up to a 50% reduction on most trains with a guaranteed minimum reduction of 25%. It also entitles you to a 30% discount on trips outside of France.

With the Carte Enfant Plus, for €53.35 **children under 12 and up to four accompanying adults can get up to 50% off on most trains for an unlimited number of trips.** This card is perfect if you're planning on spending a lot of time traveling in France with your children, as it's valid for one year. You can also opt for the Prix Découverte Enfant Plus: when you buy your ticket, simply show a valid ID with your child's age and you can get a significant discount for your child and a 25% reduction for up to four accompanying adults.

If you purchase an individual ticket from SNCF in France and you're under 26, you automatically get a 25% reduction (a valid ID, such as an ISIC card or your passport, is necessary). If you're going to be using the train quite a bit during your stay in France and **if you're under 26, consider buying the Carte 12–25** (€41.15), which offers unlimited 50% reductions for one year (provided that there's space available at that price; otherwise you'll just get the standard 25% discount).

If you don't benefit from any of these reductions and **if you plan on traveling at least 200 km (132 mi) round-trip and don't mind staying over a Saturday night, look into the Prix Découverte Séjour.** This ticket gives you a 25% reduction.

Don't assume that your rail pass guarantees you a seat on the train you wish to ride. You need to **book seats ahead even if you're using a rail pass.**

➤ Rail Pass Agents: **CIT Tours Corp.** (✉ 15 W. 44th St., 10th floor, New York, NY 10036, ☎ 800/248–7245 for rail; 800/248–8687 for tours and hotels). **DER Travel Services** (✉ 9501 W. Devon Ave., Rosemont, IL 60018, ☎ 800/782–2424). **Rail Europe** (☞ *above*).

FARES, SCHEDULES, AND RESERVATIONS

You can **call for train information from any station or reserve tickets in any station.** Train schedules are available at stations or on the multilingual computerized schedule information network found at many stations. You can also make reservations and buy your ticket at the computer. Go to the Grandes Lignes counter for travel within France and to the Billets Internationaux desk if you're heading out of the country. Note that calling the SNCF's 08 number costs money (you are charged per minute, and you often have to wait for minutes at a time), so it's better to go to the nearest station.

You must **always make a seat reservation for the TGV**—easily obtained at the ticket window or from an automatic machine. Seat reservations are reassuring but seldom necessary on other main-line French trains, except in summer and at certain busy holiday times. You also need a reservation for sleeping accommodations.

➤ Train Information: **BritRail Travel** (☎ 800/677–8585 in the U.S.; 020/7834–2345 in the U.K.). **Eurostar** (☎ 08–36–35–35–39 in France; 0345/881881 in the U.K., WEB www.eurostar.com). **InterCity Europe** (✉ Victoria Station, London, ☎ 020/7834–2345; 020/7828–0892; 0990/848–848 for credit-card bookings). **Rail Europe** (☎ 800/942–4866 in the U.S., WEB www.raileurope.com). **SNCF** (✉ 88 rue St-Lazare, 75009 Paris, ☎ 08–36–35–35–35, WEB www.sncf.fr/indexe.htm).

LUGGAGE DELIVERY SERVICE

With an advance arrangement, SNCF will pick up and deliver your luggage at a given time. For instance, if you're planning on spending a weekend in Nice, SNCF will pick up your luggage at your hotel in Paris in the morning before check out and deliver it to your hotel in Nice, where it will be awaiting your arrival. The cost is €15 for the first bag, and €9.25 for two additional bags, with a maximum of three bags per person.

➤ Contact: **SNCF Luggage Delivery Service** (☎ 08–03–84–58–45; WEB www.sncf.fr).

TRAVEL AGENCIES

A good travel agent puts your needs first. Look for an agency that has been in business at least five years, emphasizes customer service, and has someone on staff who specializes in your destination. In addition, **make sure the agency belongs to a professional trade organization.** The American Society of Travel Agents (ASTA), with more than 24,000 members in some 140 countries, is the largest and most influential in the field. Operating under the motto "Without a travel agent, you're on your own," it maintains and enforces a strict code of ethics and will step in to help mediate any agent-client disputes if necessary. ASTA also maintains a Web site that includes a directory of agents. (If a travel agency is also acting as your tour operator, *see* Buyer Beware *in* Tours and Packages, *above.*)

In France there are a number of good local agencies with offices in Paris as well as in other major cities. Nouvelles Frontiéres has offices in France as well as the United States.

➤ Local Agent Referrals: **American Society of Travel Agents** (ASTA; ☎ 800/965–2782 for 24-hr hot line, FAX 703/739–3268, WEB www.astanet.com). **Association of British Travel Agents** (✉ 68–71 Newman St., London W1T 3AH, ☎ 020/7637–2444, FAX 020/7637–0713, WEB www.abtanet.com). **Association of Canadian Travel Agents** (✉ 130 Albert St., Suite 1705, Ottawa, Ontario K1P 5G4, ☎ 613/237–3657, FAX 613/237–7502, WEB www.acta.ca). **Australian Federation of Travel Agents** (✉ Level 3, 309 Pitt St., Sydney, NSW 2000, ☎ 02/9264–3299, FAX 02/9264–1085, WEB www.afta.com.au). **Travel Agents' Association of New Zealand** (✉ Box 1888, Wellington 6001, ☎ 04/499–0104,

FAX 04/499–0827, WEB www.taanz.org.nz).

➤ LOCAL AGENCIES: **Access Voyages** (✉ 6 rue Pierre Lescot, 1e, métro: Châtelet–Les Halles, ☎ 01–44–76–84–50). **American Express** (✉ 11 rue Scribe, 8e, ☎ 01–47–77–77–07; ✉ 38 av. de Wagram, 8e, ☎ 01–42–27–58–80). **Nouvelles Frontières** (✉ 5 av. de l'Opéra, 1er, métro: Pyramides, ☎ 08–03–33–33–33; ✉ 14 av. de Verdun, 06000 Nice; ✉ 12 E. 33rd St. New York, NY 10016, FAX 212/779–1007). **Soltours** (✉ 48 rue de Rivoli, 4e, métro: Hôtel-de-Ville, ☎ 01–42–71–24–34).

VISITOR INFORMATION

➤ FRANCE TOURISM INFORMATION: **France On-Call** (☎ 410/286–8310, weekdays 9–7, WEB www.francetourism.com). **Chicago** (✉ 676 N. Michigan Ave., Chicago, IL 60611, fgto@mcs.net). **Los Angeles** (✉ 9454 Wilshire Blvd., Suite 715, Beverly Hills, CA 90212, fgto@gte.net). **New York City** (✉ 444 Madison Ave., 16th floor, New York, NY 10022, info@francetourism.com). **Canada** (✉ 1981 Ave. McGill College, Suite 490, Montréal, Québec H3A 2W9). **U.K.** (✉ 178 Piccadilly, London W1V OAL, ☎ 171/6399–3500, FAX 171/6493–6594).

➤ LOCAL TOURIST OFFICES: *See* the A to Z sections *in* individual chapters for local tourist office telephone numbers and addresses.

➤ U.S. GOVERNMENT ADVISORIES: **U.S. Department of State** (✉ Overseas Citizens Services Office, Room 4811 N.S., 2201 C St. NW, Washington, DC 20520, ☎ 202/647–5225 for interactive hot line or 888/407–4747, WEB travel.state.gov/travel/html); enclose a business-size SASE.

WEB SITES

Do check out the World Wide Web when planning your trip. You'll find everything from weather forecasts to virtual tours of famous cities. Be sure to **visit Fodors.com** (www.fodors.com), a complete travel-planning site. You can research prices and book plane tickets, hotel rooms, rental cars, vacation packages, and more. In addition, you can post your pressing questions in the Travel Talk section and, in the site's Rants & Raves section, read comments about some of the restaurants and hotels in this book—and chime in yourself. Other planning tools include a currency converter and weather reports, and there are loads of links to other travel resources.

➤ RECOMMENDED WEB SITES: Tourism in France, with links to 3,500 tourist offices (www.tourisme.fr). **Bordeaux Tourist Office** (WEB www.bordeaux-tourisme.com). **Eurail** (WEB www.eurail.com). **Eurostar** (WEB www.eurostar.com). **French Embassy** (WEB www.france.diplomatie.fr). **French Government Tourist Office** (WEB www.francetourism.com). **French Ministry of Culture** (WEB www.culture.fr). **Louvre Museum** (WEB mistral.culture.fr/louvre/louvrea.htm). **Lyon Tourist Office** (WEB www.lyon-france.com). **Monaco Tourist Office** (WEB www.monaco.mc/usa). **Paris Tourist Office** (WEB www.paris.org). **Provence Tourist Office** (WEB www.visitprovence.com). **Rail Europe** (WEB www.raileurope.com). **Riviera Tourist Office** (WEB www.crt-riviera.fr). **SNCF** (WEB www.sncf.fr/indexe.htm). **Strasbourg Tourism Office** (WEB www.strasbourg.com).

WHEN TO GO

June and September are the best months to be in France, as both are free of the midsummer crowds. June offers the advantage of long daylight hours, while cheaper prices and frequently warm weather (often lasting well into October) make September attractive. Try to avoid the second half of July and all of August, when almost everyone in France goes on vacation. Huge crowds jam the roads and beaches, and prices are jacked up in resorts. Don't travel on or around July 14 and August 1, 15, and 31. July and August in southern France can be stifling. Paris can be stuffy and uncomfortable in August, made worse by pollution, which has hit record highs recently. However, the city is pleasantly deserted. Many restaurants, theaters, and small shops close, but enough stay open these days to make a low-key, unhurried visit a pleasure.

The ski season in the Alps and Pyrénées lasts from Christmas to Easter; if you can, avoid February, when school holidays mean crowds. Anytime between March and November will offer you a good chance to soak up the sun on the Côte d'Azur. If Paris and the Loire are among your priorities, remember that the weather is unappealing before Easter. If you're dreaming of Paris in the springtime, May is your best bet, not rainy April. But the capital remains a joy during midwinter, with plenty of things to see and do.

CLIMATE

What follows are average daily maximum and minimum temperatures for Paris and Nice.

➤ FORECASTS: **Weather Channel Connection** (☎ 900/932–8437), 95¢ per minute from a Touch-Tone phone.

NICE

Jan.	55F	13C	May	68F	20C	Sept.	77F	25C
	39	4		55	13		61	16
Feb.	55F	13C	June	75F	24C	Oct.	70F	21C
	41	5		61	16		54	12
Mar.	59F	15C	July	81F	27C	Nov.	63F	17C
	45	7		64	18		46	8
Apr.	64F	18C	Aug.	81F	27C	Dec.	55F	13C
	46	8		64	18		41	5

PARIS

Jan.	43F	6C	May	68F	20C	Sept.	70F	21C
	34	1		49	10		53	12
Feb.	45F	7C	June	73F	23C	Oct.	60F	16C
	34	1		55	13		46	8
Mar.	54F	12C	July	76F	25C	Nov.	50F	10C
	39	4		58	15		40	5
Apr.	60F	16C	Aug.	75F	24C	Dec.	44F	7C
	43	6		58	15		36	2

FESTIVALS AND SEASONAL EVENTS

France is a festival year-round, with special events taking place throughout the country. In Paris check the listings in *Pariscope* (which includes *Time Out,* a section with reviews in English of the week's main events), *L'Officiel des Spectacles,* or *Figaroscope* to find out what's going on around town. The *International Herald Tribune* also lists special events in its weekend edition but not in great detail. The most complete listing of festivals comes in a small pamphlet published by the French Government Tourist Office, or you can consult the official Web site of the *Maison De France* which has a list (over 3,000 strong) of current festivals, seminars, antique fairs, concerts, and temporary exhibits at www.franceguide.com.

➤ JAN.: The **International Circus Festival,** featuring top acts from around the world, and the **Monte Carlo Motor Rally,** one of the motoring world's most venerable races, take place in Monaco. Wine-producing villages throughout France celebrate **St. Vincent's Day** with festivities on January 22 in honor of their patron saint. The **Tournament St-Vincent,** a colorful Burgundy wine festival, takes place on the third weekend in Meursault in 2003; more than 200,000 wine lovers are expected to attend. Angoulême hosts the world's biggest and most popular comic-book festival, the **Fête de la Bande Dessinée,** from January 24 to January 27.

➤ FEB.: The **Carnival de Nice** is a period of parades and revelry in the weeks leading up to Lent. Other cities and villages also have their own smaller versions. **The Carnival de Dunkerque,** on the weekend before Shrove Tuesday, is the most rambunctious street carnival in northern France. The **Festival de Film Fantastique** is the international horror film festival, which takes place in Gerardmer.

➤ MAR.: The **Salon de Mars,** an art and antiques fair, and the **Salon du Livre,** France's biggest book festival, take place in Paris. **La Foire à la Brocante et au Jambon** is an important, high-quality antiques fair held every year in Chatou, a beautiful village outside Paris.

➤ APR.: The **Monte Carlo Open Tennis Championships** get under way at the Monte Carlo Country Club.

➤ MAY: The **Cannes Film Festival** sees two weeks of star-studded events. Classical-music festivals get under way throughout the country. The **Foire de Paris** is a giant fair with food and agricultural products from all over France; it takes place at the Porte de Versailles in Paris. At the end of the month are the **French Open Tennis Championships,** at Roland Garros Stadium, in Paris.

➤ JUNE: From now until September you will find **son-et-lumière** (sound-and-light) shows—historical pageants featuring special lighting effects—at many French châteaux and churches in the Loire. Throughout France, there's dancing in the streets during the **Fête de la Musique,** a free live-music festival on June 21 that lasts all night. Strasbourg's **Fête de la Musique** features concerts in the Cathédrale Notre-Dame and various halls. This is a popular time for horse races: the **Prix du Président de la République** is run at the Hippodrome de Vincennes, the **Grand Steeplechase de Paris** is at the Auteuil Racecourse, and the **Grand Prix de Paris** is at Longchamp Racecourse. The **24 Heures du Mans,** the famous 24-hour car race, is held in Le Mans. The **Paris Air Show** is a display of planes at Le Bourget Airport, near Paris. On the last weekend in June the **Fête du Cinéma** allows you to take in as many movies as you can for the price of a single ticket. **The International Wine and Liquor Fare** will be held in Bordeaux from June 18 to June 22.

➤ JULY: The **summer arts festival season** gets into full swing, particularly in Provence. Avignon offers a month of top-notch theater, Aix-en-Provence specializes in opera and Carpentras in religious music, Nice holds a big jazz festival, and Arles mounts a major photography festival. Northern France's spectacular **Fête de Gayant** (Festival of the Giant, in local patois) is held in Douai on the first Sunday after July 5. The **Tour de France,** the world's most famous bicycle race, dominates national attention for three weeks before crossing the finish line on the Champs-Élysées on the last Sunday of the month. The **Festival de l'Art Lyrique** brings more than 1 million music lovers to Aix-en-Provence to hear music spanning several centuries. On **Bastille Day** (July 14) all of France commemorates the storming of the Bastille in 1789—the start of the French Revolution. Look out for fireworks, free concerts, and street festivities beginning the evening of July 13, with the **Bal des Pompiers** (Firemen's Ball) organized by local firemen.

➤ AUG.: On **Assumption** (August 15) many towns, notably Chartres and Lisieux, hold religious festivals and processions dedicated to the Virgin Mary. On the first Sunday following August 15, the **Festival de la Force Basque,** in St-Palais, brings together participants from eight villages to compete in contests of strength. The most famous annual religious festival in Brittany is the ***pardon*** in Ste-Anne-la-Palud, near Quimper, on the last Sunday of August. If you want to drive yourself insane, you can always visit the **International Mime Festival,** held in early August, when the city of Perigueux, in Dordogne, is overtaken by those white-face Marcel Marceau wanna-bes. The **Festival Interceltique** takes place in Lorient, Brittany, from August 2 to August 11, with a street fair commemorating contemporary expressions of Celtic art, music, and dance.

➤ SEPT.: The **vendanges** (grape harvests) begin, and festivals take place in the country's wine regions. The **Grande Braderie** turns Lille into one giant street fair on the month's first weekend. The **Fête de Musique de Besançon et Franche-Comté** consists of a series of chamber-music concerts in and around Besançon during the month. The **Fête d'Automne,** a major arts and film festival, opens in Paris and continues until December. The **Rencontres Polyphoniques,** in Calvi, is an excellent chance to hear authentic Corsican music. The **Journée du Patrimoine,** on the Sunday nearest September 21, opens the doors of many official and private buildings usually closed to the public. The

American Film Festival, in Deauville, is one of the most important international events (second to Cannes) for American film. The **Biennale des Antiquaires** is held in the Carrousel du Louvre in Paris this month with more than 120 antiques dealers from Europe and the United States; the next one will be in 2004. The **International Car Salon** takes place in the Porte de Versailles from September 28 to October 13 with one of the most impressive car selections in the world (second only to Tokyo).

➤ OCT.: The **Prix de l'Arc de Triomphe,** horse racing's most prestigious flat race, is held at the Longchamp Racecourse, in Paris, on the first Sunday of the month. A giant contemporary art exhibition called **FIAC** takes place in Paris early in the month. The weeklong **Paris Indoor Open** attracts the world's top tennis players at the end of the month.

➤ NOV.: **Les Trois Glorieuses,** Burgundy's biggest wine festival, includes the year's most important wine auction and related merriment, which occurs in several Burgundy locations. The **Festiventu,** in Calvi (Corsica), is a celebration of wind-related activities ranging from windsurfing to woodwinds. Nationwide **Armistice Day** ceremonies on November 11 commemorate veterans of World Wars I and II; in Paris there's a military parade down the Champs-Élysées. On the third Thursday in November France—especially Paris—celebrates the arrival of the **Beaujolais Nouveau.** The **Salon des Caves Particulières** is a giant wine fair held in Paris at the end of the month. November is also the **Mois de la Photo,** with open photography exhibits in most galleries throughout France.

➤ DEC.: On the 24th, a Christmas celebration known as the **Shepherds' Festival,** featuring midnight Mass and picturesque "living crèches," occurs in Les Baux, Provence. From the end of November through the New Year, Strasbourg mounts its famous **Christmas Market,** with echoes of German Gemütlichkeit. **Christmas in Paris** spells celebrations, especially for children, from late December to early January. A giant crèche and a full-size ice-skating rink are set up on the square in front of the Hôtel de Ville.

1 DESTINATION: FRANCE

À la Française

What's Where

Pleasures and Pastimes

Fodor's Choice

Great Itineraries

À LA FRANÇAISE

THERE IS AN OLD FAMILIAR SAYING: "Everyone has two countries, his or her own—and France." For France is the Land of Cockaigne, where every man and woman does what he or she pleases, where you can allow your personal idiosyncracies full play and apologize for them with complete acceptability by the simple remark, *Je suis comme ça.* I am like that. It's all that need be said. In France, every man has a right to be like himself. He needn't conform to the model of another.

It is this freedom that, millennia ago, made France the cultural—and hoopla—capital of the world; and it is that freedom that given us Notre-Dame, Chartres, Versailles, and the Tour Eiffel; writers like Molière, Hugo, Balzac, and Proust; composers like Berlioz and Debussy; and painters like Georges de la Tour, Fragonard, Monet, Cézanne, and Matisse. Only when Picasso came to Paris from Spain did he become Picasso; Only when Van Gogh traveled to Provence from Holland did he become Van Gogh. Clearly, there are few other countries that can contribute so much to the spiritual development of the individual. If environment can add to a person's stature, the environment of France can be counted upon to do it, by virtue of the influence she brings to bear upon everyone sensitive to beauty, measure, and intellectual stimulation. In addition to the roll-call listed above, the best witnesses to that are the many American and British expatriates who came to admire, and remained to praise.

For them, France is neither too hot nor too cold, neither too wet nor too dry, neither too flat nor too crammed with inconvenient mountains. At any rate, that is what the French say. They think that countries should be hexagonal in shape and about 600 miles across. Spain is too square, Norway is frayed at the edges, l'Angleterre (which is what they usually call Great Britain) is awkwardly surrounded by cold water, Switzerland is landlocked and too small, and the United States is too large.

Appropriately for them, France sits squarely in the middle of Western Europe; according to Francophiles, it might just as well be the center of the universe. The country has been the locus of European intellectual life ever since the founding of the Sorbonne in Paris in the 13th century. During the next few centuries, the entire Western world began to adopt the French language and aspects of French culture. Then, with the French Revolution of 1789 and Napoléon's frolic over the European continent, France established itself as a world political, as well as cultural, power—a fact the proud French have not forgotten, and are always eager to remind you about.

In more recent years, the tables have turned, and foreign cultures have been invading France. And here "foreign" means American. For decades now, young French people have emulated Americans in the way they dress, the music they listen to, and even in their manner of speaking. Levi's go for $80 a pair and can be seen gracing the legs of any slick twenty something, buskers sing Bob Dylan tunes in the streets, and teenagers hang out in the local MacDo (MacDonald's to the French), not in the corner café. And though they curse American movies to the death, the French love-hate relationship with Yankee films has let Hollywood win over the big screen.

But the French also fear the movement toward what they call *mondialisation* (globalization), which to many is a synonym for Americanization. The older generation in particular sees the infiltration of American fads and the country's integration into the European Union (EU) as eroding traditional French ways of life. Many grumble about the universality of the English language, which is commanding World Wide Chats across the Internet and is the common parlance in international business deals. The Académie Française, tireless preserver of French culture, even set about to strike English words (like "le weekend" and "le parking") from the French vocabulary and establish 66% French music quotas for radio stations. The proposed changes stuck like wet Velcro when a cultural minister accidentally slipped an English word into his announcement speech. But even with the trend toward mondialisation, French culture remains, well, distinctly French. Paris is still the world center of the ultra stylish, and its cafés continue to be the breeding ground for smoking, coffee-drinking, armchair intellectuals. And in the French provinces, with their pastoral landscapes, stunning architecture, and delicious cuisine, there remains a determination to keep Old World charm uncompromised.

It is also important to remember, however, that there is not just one France: the country's geography is as diverse as the people who inhabit it. The Riviera attracts an international jet-set crowd to its famous strips of sand. In the south you'll find an influx of recent immigrants and a myriad of cultures to match, a phenomenon that has met hostility from the steadily expanding Front National, France's ultra right party. In Provence, the soil yields many gifts, and sunny pride blends with Spanish influence and Roman history to create an intriguing culture. In the southwest, along the Spanish border, the Basque people struggle to preserve their culture and their unique language, Euskera, in the face of trends toward centralization. Alsace-Lorraine, on the eastern edge of France, is almost as German as it is French. And in Brittany, one of the last regions to be incorporated into France, people still occasionally speak Breton and celebrate their Celtic heritage.

To really see France, you obviously must travel outside of Paris. In the small villages of the Loire Valley, Burgundy, and the Ile-de-France, you'll be surprised at how relaxed the pace is and at how much care goes into preparing a meal (and how much time is spent enjoying it). Venture off the Eurail pass trail, and head to the Pyrénées at the Spanish border and the Alps at France's eastern edge to ski or mountain-bike. Or head north through rolling farmland where you might not be awed by dramatic vistas, but where you will find plenty of locals willing to listen to your fumbling French and show you what "la belle vie française" is all about.

You'll discover your fellow villagers are kind, patient, and friendly, behaving with natural dignity and good manners, like most of the other French people you'll meet—except Parisians during the rush hour (if you've had to circle the Arc de Triomphe twelve times before being able to exit L'Etoile, you can't blame them). Visitors to France, whether they stay a week or a year, will have a better time if they "go native" as far as they find it practicable—and when and where they don't, they should be philosophically aware of the drawbacks of trying to behave as in dear old Grosse Pointe, Michigan, or the U.K.

Let's look at the French timetable. Most of the French are up early, gulping a café au lait and getting to work by 8. By 10, Parisian executives are fuming because their London contacts haven't yet answered the phone (it's only 9 in England). There is no coffee break. At noon, they are hungry. Work stops for two hours on occasion. Small shops close. *Le déjeuner* (called*le dîner* in the country) is a sacred rite. Fast-food outlets have multiplied, but the norm is a proper meal, taking an hour and a half; a surprising number manage to get home for it. However, the increasing number of women at work means that 6 lunches out of 10 are eaten at restaurants or canteens—substantial, freshly cooked affairs, eaten with serious critical attention. The French grew rich in the '60s: back in 1920, they each ate nearly three pounds of bread a day—now it is just under a pound, with a corresponding increase in the consumption of meat, fish, and cheese. Less wine is drunk, but more of it is of higher quality.

The typical restaurant in your nearest market town (pop. 6,000) has only one menu: copious hors d'oeuvres, a fish dish or a light meat dish, a more serious meat dish, vegetables in season, a good cheese board, fruit or ice cream. It's always full by 12:30. A couple from San Francisco who stayed in a rented cottage in that village were hardly ever able to use it. They used to get up at 9 and were hopelessly out of phase with the commercial travelers (up at 6) who form the restaurant's main clientele. You can't start your lunch there at 1:30 or 2, and there are no doggy bags in France. When you are in the Midi, an early start and a siesta prove convenient (many of the shops don't reopen until 3:30). However, the couple in question happily developed the picnic habit: France is God's own country for picnicking, if only you get to the *charcuterie* and the *boulangerie* and the *pâtisserie* well before they close at noon.

Back to work for another four-hour stretch. No tea or coffee break. Are the French mighty toilers? Yes and no. In the '90s, the average industrial worker put in 1,872 hours of work per year in the United States, 1,750 in Great Britain, but only 1,650 in France. Five weeks' paid vacation is the official minimum, and there are many public holidays. The French have become addicts of leisure in the past two decades. One family in 10 has a second house in the country, where they go on weekends and vacations, causing astounding traffic jams as they flee the cities.

If he finishes his day's work at 6 or 6:30, will our average Frenchman call in at his favorite café for a chat and an aperitif on his way home? Probably not, nowadays. In the past, the cafэwas used as a sort of extra living room for meeting friends or professional contacts, or even for writing novels if you were Jean-Paul Sartre or Simone de Beauvoir. But today an average of two hours and 50 minutes is spent watching television at home, which reduces the time available for social life. This is sad. The number of cafés has diminished. Fortunately, there are still a lot left, and how convenient they are for the visitor! On the terrace of a French café you can bask in the sun or enjoy the shade of a multicolor parasol, sipping a cool beer and keeping an eye on life's passing show. A small black coffee entitles you to spend an hour or two—no hurry.

When one talks about the apéritif hour you are not only talking about cafés but about friendliness. Some people—notably Americans—complain that the French are inhospitable and standoffish. The fact is that they are great respecters of privacy. If the Englishman's home is his castle, the Frenchman's apartment or house is his lair. People simply do not pop into one another's lairs, drinking casual cups of coffee and borrowing half a pound of sugar. They need a neutral place in which to socialize. Britons come somewhere between typical French people and the American middleclass. According to Paul Fussell (*Caste Marks*, 1983):"Among the [American] middles there's a convention that erecting a fence or even a tall hedge is an affront."

IT'S DIFFERENT in France. People in the Midi, for instance, just love to talk, and even to listen. But village neighbors will prove timid about entering your house. If they want to ask you something, they will wait until you meet, or stay on the doorstep, or phone (from 50 yards away). They penetrate your house, and you penetrate theirs, when specifically invited. That is how they behave among themselves, too. It's not because we are foreigners.

So when do we talk? There are benches everywhere, in the sun and in the shade. The villagers—and visitors—sit there for hours, chatting. The locals really are interested in you, your habits and tastes, the number and ages of your children, your work, where you come from, and so forth, and are longing to impart a discreet selection of their own personal details. Of course you*may* be invited home. There are no rules about this sort of thing. And if there were, the French would take pleasure in breaking them.

When talking with the French, there are conventions that should be observed if you don't want to be thought a barbarian by people who are unaware of Anglo-Saxon attitudes. You must say "*Bonjour*" followed by *Monsieur, Madame, Mademoiselle, Messieurs, Mesdames,* or *Messieurs-dames* much more often than you would think necessary (on entering a small shop, for instance) and "*Au revoir, Monsieur*" (etc.). Hands are shaken frequently (by colleagues at work, morning and evening, and by the most casual acquaintances). *Bon appétit* can replace *au revoir* shortly before mealtimes. On going through a door, a certain amount of *après-vous*-ing is normal, with *pardon* if you go through first, turning your back. Getting on first-name terms is a sign of much greater intimacy than in England or the United States. Rush-hour Parisian life is more brutal, of course, and, as elsewhere in the world, the driving seat of a car exerts a malign influence. In England or the States, a headlight flash sometimes means "After you"; in France, it means either "After me" or "I am a criminal and I expect you are, too, so watch it, chum, the cops are round the corner."

BACK HOME FROM the café, our typical Frenchman eats *le dîner* (called *le souper* in the country) around 8, rich and poor. It's a lighter meal than at midday, with soup replacing hors d'oeuvres. The movies, after a sharp fall as television established itself in every home, have resisted well. Except in Paris, films are dubbed into French, a practice deplored by intellectuals. Almost all employed people now have a two-day weekend, usually Saturday and Sunday, but Sunday and Monday for many shop workers. Schoolchildren have Wednesday free, but may attend Saturday morning, instead. In recent years, the French have revolutionized their leisure habits: jogging, swimming, soccer, gymnastics, tennis, and vigorous bicycling (for fun, not transport) are practiced, mainly on weekends, by large numbers of all social classes.

The great Sunday ritual takes place at noon or soon after. Four out of 10 will visit friends or relations. Sixty percent of families do more cooking on Sundays than on other days. This is also a big day for restaurants that feature a special Sunday menu. Half the French end their Sunday lunch with a fresh fruit tart or some sort of gâteau, which is why the pastry shops are open in the morning and why you see Frenchmen carefully carrying flat cardboard boxes.

An essay such as this has to contain rash generalizations. Is there an average French person? Obviously not. There are the rich and the poor, for example. The poor, in France, like champagne, oysters, and foie gras, but they get them less often than do the rich. The same is true of other aspects of life. The gulf between one class and another is not one of tastes and aspirations; rich and poor are in broad agreement on what constitutes a pleasant life. The poor are simply further away from it than are the rich. The surge of prosperity in the '60s brought improvements to French life, with some drawbacks, but basic traditions die hard. The young ape foreign fashions, with a fast-food/motorcycle/mid-Atlantic pop noise/comic-strip culture, but they grow out of it. Official morality has changed. Contraception used to be forbidden; Paris was famed for its elegant brothels, but women had to go to London for diaphragms and to Switzerland for abortions. All that has gone. In 1988, the rise of AIDS caused a quickly smothered quarrel among bishops about the sinfulness of condoms, which are readily available. *Le topless* is seen on most beaches, and total nakedness on some. But the family remains a powerful, cohesive unit.

In the end, there are those who love France and those who don't. It's a matter of taste and character. The former find it easy to slip into the French way of life for a week or a month or permanently. The latter are better off in Paris or on the Riviera. But really, the French are canny operators when it comes to enjoying *la douceur de vivre,* the sweetness of life. If you follow their example while in France, you can't go far wrong. (One way to go wrong would be to quote almost any paragraph from this essay to them; at any rate, it will start a vigorously French argument.)

WHAT'S WHERE

Paris

Paris is one of the most written about, raved about, and spat upon cities in the entire world. Droves of people have come for hundreds of years looking to inject their lives with beauty, glamour, culture, scandal, and romance. They have sung about Paris, painted her, found themselves, lost their religion, and learned how to eat well and smoke too much. Gargoyles leering down from medieval walls, the smell of freshly baked croissants, the pulse of jazz through overcrowded streets, and that first sip of wine to start off the evening are all part of the Parisian obsession with the physical world. Paris voluptuaries explore the city during the late-night but when daybreaks, Paris puts her face on. Fashionable 85-year-old matrons parade their freshly coifed Pekingese pooches past boutique windows, spruced-up facades of medieval buildings, and artfully arranged *pâtisserie* (pastry shop) displays. Cafés fill up, and the strong, dark coffee starts to pour, wiring up the professionals seated at little bitty tables packed along the sidewalks. All the while, tourists sweep through town, trying to see in a week what locals haven't seen in a lifetime. The **Eiffel Tower,** needless to say, gives you an overview; the **Louvre,** a good look at the art of the past (with a peek, too, at architecture's present and future). Say a prayer at **Notre-Dame,** buy a dress you'll love forever, and eat an unforgettable meal anywhere at all. Open your eyes—there's something beautiful or amusing at every step; dawdle around the **Latin Quarter,** climb up to **Montmartre** for a peek at **Sacré-Coeur,** spend a morning at the *marché aux puces* (flea market), and sail down the Seine on the **Bateaux Mouches.** *Oui,* Paris is a fete.

Ile-de-France

Kings, clerics, paupers, and ordinary Parisians have long taken refuge from urban life in Ile-de-France, the green surround of Paris. Most have been content to spend a day in the country, which is lushly forested and is landed by meandering rivers, while others have left behind spectacular secular and religious monuments. Noble occupants spared no expense in outfitting the **Château de Chantilly** with formal gardens, fountains, a lagoon, and all the other trappings that were standard amenities during the 16th-century château-building craze. Biggest and most ostentatious of these palaces, the **Château de Versailles** is pompous proof that French monarchs lost their heads long before Louis XVI and Marie-Antoinette, the last occupants, walked to the guillotine. Other palatial piles include **Fontainebleau, Vaux-le-Vicomte,** and Napoléon's **Malmaison.** All this worldly froth fades in the stained-glass luster of **Chartres Cathedral,** so sublime its soft limestone hulk has brought the faithful to their knees for centuries. Then skip over the centuries to discover Monet's **Giverny,** Van Gogh's **Auvers,** and Uncle Walt's **Disneyland Paris.**

The Loire Valley

Sometimes owned by England, and fought over for centuries, this stretch of the Loire southwest of Paris resounds today with the noise of contented tourists, music festivals, and son-et-lumière spectacles at its extraordinary châteaux. This is France at its purest and most elegant—just wait until you hear the diamond-sheen of the French spoken hereabouts. Stylish château-hotels and lovely country auberges tempt the traveler at nearly every bend in the river. The roll-call of châteaux is legendary. At the **Château de Chenonceau,** Catherine de Medici built a white pleasure palace to hover over the river Cher. At the **Château de Chambord** it's easy to imagine the days when King François I arrived with a retinue so large it took 12,000 horses to transport them. At magical **Château de Ussé,** Charles Perrault was inspired to write the fairy tale we know as "Sleeping Beauty." Elsewhere, **Fontevraud** allures as the largest medieval abbey in France, while storybook **Chinon** has block after block of houses built during the days of Joan of Arc, who went on to capture the city of **Orléans.**

Brittany

"Finistère," or "land's end," is what a part of Brittany is called, and the name suits the entire region. A long arm of rocky land stretching into the Atlantic, Brittany lives to the rhythm of tides and winds, with its own language and legends. The people are Bretons first, rather than French, Celtic rather than Latin, and proud of their difference. They are also proud of their land—with reason. Here you'll find time-defying monuments and customs in awe-inspiring landscapes, such as those at **Pont-Aven,** which once inspired Gauguin. The prehistoric standing stones of **Carnac** are a gateway to the gorgeous sandy peninsula of the **Côte Sauvage,** where birds and flowers abound. The craftspeople in **Quimper** carry on a centuries-old practice of hand-painting delicate-looking faience wares. Tides bathe the foot of **St-Malo**'s impressive fortifications, still haunted by phantom pirates. A trip across the waters to the aptly named **Belle-Ile,** or "beautiful island," will take you to heaths of yellow broom, fine beaches, and quaint towns. When you are finally tired, treat yourself to the freshest of oysters at **Cancale.** Like them, Brittany is a rare gift from the sea.

Normandy

Normandy is a land of fashionable resorts and austere abbeys, warriors and prolific painters, saints and sinners. At **Bayeux,** the town's famous tapestry provides a scene-by-scene look at the Norman invasion of England in 1066 and stars William the Conqueror. Not far away, **Mont-St-Michel** may be the sublimest sight in France, perching dramatically atop its rocky shoreline roost. In **Rouen,** famed for its cathedral immortalized by Monet in paint, medieval rue du Gros-Horloge leads to the spot where Joan of Arc was burned at the stake in 1431 (but not before she changed the course of the Hundred Years' War). Off to the west at **Omaha Beach,** vast expanses of windswept dunes pay quiet homage to the 10,000 Allied soldiers who lost their lives during 1944's D-Day. Elsewhere lovely seascapes and lush fields allure. Pretty **Honfleur** made Impressionists long to paint the sea and sky. **Étretat** invites a day of ambling along limestone

falaises (cliffs). Chic **Deauville** and **Trouville** beckon you to stroll along their seafront boardwalks. Of course, indulge in the region's cuisine, ruled and inspired by local cream, butter, eggs, and apples, along with fine lamb sweetened by the salty grasses on which the animals graze. Heady apple brandy, like the calvados made at the Grandval Calvados Distillery in **Cambremer,** in Pays d'Auge, is often downed with a meal to make a *trou normand* (Norman hole)—or room for more rich food.

The North and Champagne

"Brother, come quickly, I'm drinking stars," exclaimed Dom Pérignon upon first sipping the bubbling beverage that he invented through luck and alchemy. The blind 17th-century monk put **Hautvillers** and an entire region on the world map; he also ensured that vineyards around **Épernay** and elsewhere in the vicinity produce some of the world's finest wine grapes. In towns like **Reims**—once important enough to host the coronation of French kings, with many an amiable monument and spectacular cathedral as proof of its stature—it's perfectly clear what adds extra sparkle to these parts. Besides fine food and drink, there's plenty in the north to capture your attention—the lively city of **Lille** (just an hour from Paris by TGV), the long stretches of empty sand along the Channel coast, and the haunting cemeteries that evoke crucial battles of World War I. The new Channel Tunnel, like the traditional ferries, arrives at **Calais**; Head inland to admire the palace of **Compiègne,** the mighty castle of **Pierrefonds,** and the awesome cathedrals of **Beauvais, Amiens, Noyon,** and **Laon.** Away to the northeast lie the game-filled forests of the **Ardennes.**

Alsace, Lorraine, and Franche-Comté

"Let them speak German," said Napoléon of the Alsatians, "as long as they think in French." The emperor would be pleased to know that after centuries of conquest and liberation, Alsace and its neighbor Lorraine are now resolutely and proudly French. Yet there are enough imports from beyond the Rhine to make the region fascinating. **Strasbourg,** capital of Alsace and the cosmopolitan home of the European Parliament, has sophisticated restaurants and fine museums as well as a lacy-spired cathedral, an old quarter known as La Petite France, beer gardens, and winstubs. **Nancy,** capital of Lorraine, adds another element to the region's cultural mix: Much of the elegant, easygoing city was laid out with pomp and grandeur by Stanislas Leszczynski, dethroned king of Poland; it was also a center of Art Nouveau architecture in the late 19th century. The **Route du Vin,** running through the green foothills of the **Vosges mountains,** leads to half-timbered, impossibly picturesque wine villages such as **Riquewihr.** Farther south, the verdant folds of **Franche-Comté** roll seamlessly into yet another world, that of neighboring Switzerland. In the **Jura,** you can visit pretty little towns and buy wooden toys, clocks, and pipes, and even ski.

Burgundy

Farms, pastures, and fall foliage make Burgundy enticingly, romantically rural. But it's also evident that whether building, ruling, worshiping, dining, or drinking, Burgundians have never embraced life on anything less than a grand scale. From magnificent palaces like the one in the city of **Dijon** and châteaux like the one at **Tanlay,** dukes more powerful than kings once ruled vast tracts of Western Europe. They left behind mighty medieval cathedrals in **Sens** and **Auxerre,** and religious orders built the other Burgundian architectural masterpieces—the Romanesque basilica at **Vézelay** and even more impressive abbeys, such as the Abbaye de **Cluny,** the largest church in the world until the construction of St. Peter's in Rome. Most likely to evoke a reverential hush, though, is a first sip of one of Burgundy's treasured wines. Follow the **Côte d'Or,** perhaps the world's most famous wine route, out of Dijon, a gastronomic hub and cultural center and then visit the Marché aux Vins in the wine capital of **Beaune** (with its fabulous Roger van der Weyden altarpiece). As you sample the bounty of the highly anticipated annual *vendange* (harvest), you'll be introduced to wines so fine that, as the novelist, playwright, and observer of French life Alexandre Dumas once counseled, they should only be drunk on bended knee.

Lyon and the Alps

If the very mention of **Lyon** teases the taste buds, give credit to this sophisticated city's chefs—masters who can render even a plate of fruit ethereal. Savor their creations, then enjoy the city's visual delights—Lyon's covered passageways, known as *traboules,* lead to treasure-filled museums and a first-class opera house. Near at hand, seek out more *sportif* amusements: a sail from canal-lined, bridge-bedecked **Annecy** across its breezy and gorgeous lake, perhaps, or a gambol through meadows near **Chamonix,** a resort with a reputation for winter pleasures overshadowed only by its Alpine peaks. Discover the **wine villages of the Beaujolais** and the **Dombes lakes,** then venture down the Rhône to **Vienne** for Roman ruins and Renaissance facades. Pass through **Grenoble** with its fine museum en route to the Alps.

The Massif Central

"Early to bed, early to rise" is the rule of thumb in this craggy, rural heartland at the center of France. You'll want to rise early to venture into the spectacular gorges or tackle the slopes of the highest of the region's 80 dormant volcanoes, the **Puy-de-Dôme.** The same dictum applies at elegant and in famous **Vichy,** a long-favored place to take the waters and get back on the straight and narrow (a path from which the spa town strayed during World War II, when Nazi sympathizers ran their puppet government from here). Early risers in **Bourges,** a medieval city gloriously bypassed by time, have a special reward in store—the sight of the brilliantly hued stained-glass windows of the 13th-century Cathédrale St-Étienne achieving their fullest luster in the morning light. This is also the gateway city to the Loire Valley approached from the south. Also on the to-see list are the **Parc des Volcans,** the museums and cathedral in **Clermont-Ferrand,** and wonderful medieval towns and villages like **Salers, Ste-Foy,** and high-perched **Rocamadour.**

Provence

Even the cattle and flamingos wallowing in the salty coastal marshes of the **Camargue** enjoy the sun-drenched good life that Provence provides so generously. In this smiling landscape and in soft-hued, elegant cities, where life still proceeds at an old-fashioned pace, you'll find no end of pleasures. Elegant **Aix-en-Provence** has museums, fountains, and the beautiful Cours Mirabeau boulevard. **Arles** and **Avignon** have bewitched Roman legionnaires, popes, and Vincent van Gogh. The tarnished, exotic, and newly chic port of **Marseille** continues to intrigue sailors and travelers with its hint of mystery. And dusty **Nîmes** headlines the Pont du Gard aqueduct and the beautiful Maison Carrée temple. But the region works its charms most potently in rural places, aided in no small part by cypress trees and vineyards, warm breezes scented with wild rosemary and thyme, and by a cooling glass of pastis. In heavenly lavender fields at the foot of **Mont Ventoux** and in ocher-colored villages—few more enticing than pretty **St-Rémy-de-Provence,** where sunlight really does dapple lanes of plane trees and where you don't have to look hard to find the bounty for a simple and fragrant feast.

The Côte d'Azur

Invisible celebrities, pebbly beaches, backed-up traffic, hordes of sunburned bathers—why do people come? Because the medieval hilltop villages (**St-Paul-de-Vence, Mougins, Vence, and Èze**), the fields of fragrant flowers that supply the Grasse perfume factories, the wonderful museums, and the lovely, limpid light are still as magnetic as ever. Stylish boutiques, great art, splendid food, exciting nightlife, and spectacular views of crystal bays and cliff-side villas don't hurt either. Nor do the lively, cobbled streets of **Nice**'s Old Town or the pretty, pastel colors of **St-Tropez.** If only once in your lifetime you want to sip champagne from a slipper or slink up to a roulette table and go for broke, **Monte Carlo** and **Antibes** are the places to do so. Or you may want to sample the small pleasures of this fabled coast: a session amid scantily but stylishly attired sunbathers on the beach in **Cannes**; an excursion up to medieval **St-Paul-de-Vence** to see a stunning collection of modern art; or just a flutter with glamour in an enchanted seaside retreat such as **Beaulieu.**

Corsica

For centuries great powers have fought over this strategically placed piece of Mediterranean real estate, leaving behind both architectural and cultural relics that set this stunning island (about 160 km/100 mi southeast of Monaco) apart from the rest of France. In **Piana** and other ancient stone villages, news from across the sea still seems far removed—delightfully so. Corsica's capital, **Ajaccio,** hometown of the greatest empire builder of them all,

Napoléon Bonaparte, is now a port for launching pleasure craft, not naval fleets. Today's spoils are granite peaks, pine forests, and crystalline waters—those around **Bonifacio,** where Ulysses was besieged, are especially inviting. Visit **Bastia**'s Old Town; explore the mountains along the **Scala di Santa Regina**; see **Corte**'s citadel; hear folk songs in **Pigna**; and splurge at the Grand Hôtel de Cala Rossa in the walled town of **Porto-Vecchio.**

The Midi-Pyrénées and the Languedoc-Roussillon

In the vast stretches of southwest France, the strong sun makes fields of flowers glow and renders the brick buildings of Toulouse-Lautrec's native **Albi** and lively, cosmopolitan, Spanish-flavored **Toulouse** a rosy pink. It reflects upon the walled, storybook town of **Carcassonne** and hilltop **Cordes** (so safely high it's known as Cordes-sur-Ciel or "Cordes in the Sky"), medieval villages with long histories of defending the region. It brightens the cloisters at **Moissac** and **St-Guilhem-le-Désert,** and beckons you to climb the Pyrénées' peaks. Along the scenic way, you'll be sure to build up your appetite for the trout, foie gras, and cassoulet, three of the region's many culinary specialties. Forging onward, you'll discover relaxing spa towns and wonderful views enliven the Pyrénées' twisting roads on the way from red-hued and ravishing **Roussillon** to **Ceret.** And when you see picturesque **Collioure**'s stunning Mediterranean setting you'll know why artists such as Matisse and Derain were so inspired.

Basque Country, the Béarn, and the Hautes Pyrénées

At its southwesternmost corner, France eases with grace and dignity toward Spain, separated from it in many ways only by the Pyrénées. Basque country, south from **Bayonne** to the border with Spain, along the coast and in the Pyrénées, is a world of its own. Come here to discover the ancient and mysterious Basque culture, and dine on the incomparable cuisine. Napoléon III and his Spanish wife, Empress Eugénie, put the resort towns of **Eugénie-les-Bains** and **Biarritz** on the map. **Ainhoa, Ste-Engrâce,** and many other towns and villages have a distinctly Basque look and temperament. To the east is Béarn and its capital, the elegant city of **Pau.** The Hautes Pyrénées, the most central and the highest part of the range, hold, among other treasures, two of the region's most famous natural phenomena, the **Cirque de Gavarnie** and the **Brèche de Roland.** The peaks of the Pyrénées are breathtaking, and are spectacular for hiking. When you come back down, the incomparable local cuisine and the wine produced on the vineyard-clad lower slopes taste all the better.

Bordeaux, Dordogne, and Poitou-Charentes

Since prehistoric times, this hinterland near the Atlantic coast has had its appeal, as is apparent when you see the cave paintings at the **Grotte de Lascaux.** In the Middle Ages the French and British fought over the area, leaving behind many castles and cathedrals. The continued allure of the rural landscape lies in the opportunity for pleasurable idleness. Float along the waters of Green Venice, as the **Marais Poitevin** near Coulon is known, or explore the fabled vineyards around **Cognac** and **Bordeaux,** perhaps ambling through an estate that rolls right up to the walls of **St-Émilion,** the loveliest of many villages producing wines that are sure to add a memorable note to any day. Come in May to Bordeaux, the regional capital, for the music festival, or anytime to sip splendid wines while you indulge in oysters, truffles, foie gras, and caviar.

PLEASURES AND PASTIMES

Art

It is through the eyes of France's artists that many first get to know the country. No wonder people from across the globe come to find Gauguin's bobbing boats at Pont-Aven, Monet's bridge at Giverny, and the gaslit Moulin Rouge of Toulouse-Lautrec—not framed in gilt and hung in a museum but alive in all their three-dimensional glory. In Arles you can stand on the spot where van Gogh painted and compare his perspective to a placard with his finished work; in Paris you can climb into the garret-atelier where Delacroix created his epic canvases, or wander the redolent streets of Montmartre, once haunted by Renoir, Utrillo, and Modigliani. And, of course, the museums and châteaux hang heavy with masterworks, many of them bringing a telling local insight into French history, culture, and joie de vivre.

Cathedrals

Their extraordinary permanence, their everlasting relevance even in a secular world, and their transcending beauty make the Gothic and Romanesque cathedrals of France a lightning rod if you are in search of the essence of French culture. The product of a peculiarly Gallic mix of mysticism, exquisite taste, and high technology, France's cathedrals provide a thorough grounding in the history of architecture (some say there was nothing new in the art of building between France's Gothic arch and Frank Lloyd Wright's cantilevered slab). Each cathedral imparts its own monumental experience—knee-weakening grandeur, a mighty resonance that touches a chord of awe, and humility in the unbeliever. Even cynics will find satisfaction in the cathedrals' social history—the anonymity of the architects, the solidarity of the artisans, and the astonishing bravery of experiments in suspended stone.

Châteaux

From the humblest feudal ruin to the most delicate Renaissance spires to the grandest of Sun King spreads, the castles, manor houses, and châteaux of France evoke the history of Europe as no museum can. Standing on castellated ramparts overlooking undulating valleys, it is easy to slip into the role of a feudal lord scrambling to protect his patchwork of holdings from the centralized stronghold of kings and dukes. The lovely landscape takes on a strategic air and you find yourself role-playing thus, whether swanning aristocratically over Japanese bridges in the château park or curling a revolutionary lip at the splendid excesses of Versailles. These are, after all, the castles that inspired "Sleeping Beauty," "Beauty and the Beast," and "Snow White," and their fairy-tale magic—rich with history and Disney-free—still holds true.

Cities

Besides being home to the most sophisticated city in the world, France has more to offer than just Paris. Other French cities offer the best of Paris without the staggering crowds, noise, pollution, and traffic. Lille, Lyon, Dijon, Bordeaux, Rennes, Marseille, and Strasbourg all have strong regional identities (and cuisines), as well as historic *vieilles villes* (old towns), sidewalk cafés, vast farmers' markets, and fine old parks. As for the arts, France's ministry of culture ensures that even the country's farthest outreaches have top-notch orchestras, stellar operas, and excellent museums.

Dining

Few countries match France's reputation for good food or offer as many fine restaurants. Eating in France can be a memorable experience, from the simplest picnic lunch of baguette, Camembert, and local *jambon* (ham) *sur l'herbe* (on the grass) to the most magnificent haute cuisine in formal splendor. Don't feel guilty if you spend as much of your day in restaurants as in museums and cathedrals: dining is the heart and soul of French culture. Give yourself over to the leisurely meal; two hours for a three-course menu is par, and you may, after relaxing into the routine, feel pressed at less than three.

L'Esprit Sportif

Though the physically inclined would consider walking across Scotland or bicycling across Holland, they often misconstrue France as a sedentary site where one plods from museum to château to restaurant. But it's possible to have a more active approach: imagine pedaling past barges on the Saône River or along slender poplar son a *route départmentale* (provincial road); hiking through the dramatic gorges in the Massif Central or over Alpine meadows in the Savoie; or sailing the historic ports of Honfleur or Cap d'Antibes. Experiencing this side of France will take you off the beaten path and into the countryside (and away from those rest stops on the auto route). As you bike along French country roads or along the extensive network of *Grands Randonnées* (Lengthy Trails) crisscrossing the country, you will have time to tune into the landscape—to study crumbling garden walls, smell the honeysuckle, and chat with a farmer in his *potager*(vegetable garden). Moreover, picnics are more sublime after a day of strenuous activity, and you can gorge without guilt on three-hour dinners when you reach your auberge.

Shopping

Although it is somewhat disconcerting to see Gap stores gracing almost every major street corner in Paris and other urban areas in France, if you take the time to peruse smaller specialty shops, you can find rare original gifts—be it an antique brooch from the 1930s or a modern vase crafted from Parisian rooftop tile zinc. It is true that the traditional gifts of silk scarves, perfume, and wine can often be purchased for less in the shopping mall back home, but you can make an interesting twist by purchasing a vintage Hermès scarf, or a unique perfume from an artisan perfumer. Take the time to explore, and you will find that France still remains one of the shopping capitals of the world.

For other unique gift ideas, it's always interesting to look to the past: Flea markets and *brocantes* (secondhand shops) sell art-deco brooches, tiny eau-de-vie glasses, and evocative old copies of *Paris Match*. And there's always the chance of finding a stray bit of Quimper faience. Another good bet is purchasing regional specialties, though your exports must be legal—madeleines, say, or nougat—as those savory sausages and glass jars of foie gras may be confiscated by customs.

People in France like to bargain when they have a good feeling with the salesperson, even if the prices are clearly marked; it's one of the great pleasures of shopping in a country rich in small local businesses (in fact, the only places people don't bargain are in your typical large shopping center or big-name business). Bargaining is traditional in outdoor and flea markets, antiques stores, small jewelry shops, and art galleries, for example. If you're thinking of buying several items, or if you're simply in love with something a little bit too expensive, you've nothing to lose by cheerfully suggesting to the proprietor, "*Vous me faites un prix?*"("How about a discount?"). The small business man will immediately size you up, and you'll have some good-natured fun.

Wine

From the chipped carafe of a coarse *vin de pays* on a local café table to the Gevrey-Chambertin decanted with surgical concentration by a linen-swathed sommelier to the perfect glass sampled at family-tended vineyard in Burgundy, wine is indispensable to the French experience. Intricately interlaced with the progress of a well-planned menu (the magical combination of certain foods with the right wines is referred to as a *bon mariage,* or a good marriage), wine can dominate your memory of a fine meal.

FODOR'S CHOICE

Châteaux We Love

Balleroy, Brittany. Unlike many another château that grew willy-nilly over the centuries, this Baroque-era jewel is all of a piece, and one of architect François Mansart's most elegant accomplishments.

Chenonceau, Loire Valley. The most romantic of them all, with arched galleries spanning the Cher, this palace owes its gardens to Catherine de' Medici.

Hautefort, Périgord. Part medieval, part Renaissance, vast Hautefort raises an eclectic skyline above its gardens and is full of 17th-century furnishings.

Pierrefonds, Champagne. This huge château, begun in the 12th century, was restored in the 1860s by the fairy-tale imagination of Viollet-le-Duc and the money of Napoléon III.

Ussé, Loire Valley. Motorists often come to a screeching halt when they spot this many-turreted wonder on the straight-arrow road that brings them directly to the door. Perrault, the 17th-century author of "Sleeping Beauty," was inspired to write the tale when he stayed here.

Vaux-le-Vicomte, Ile-de-France. Louis XIV was so jealous on seeing Nicolas Fouquet's new château that he jailed him on the spot and started work on Versailles to show who was boss. The sumptuous gardens and interior remain unchanged.

Versailles, Ile-de-France. The world's grandest palace has it all: paintings, murals, gold-leafed furniture, the Hall of Mirrors, a landscaped park, a phony village, a giant canal, artful fountains, and shady glades.

Churches and Abbeys

Abbaye de St-Michel de Cuxa, Prades. With its 10th-century pre-Romanesque arches and its elegant crypt, this abbey is one of the gems of the eastern Pyrénées.

Basilique, Vézelay. This great pilgrim church, part Romanesque, part Gothic, gazes serenely over the rolling hills of Burgundy. Marvel at the miniature figures on the carved capitals in the nave.

Cathédrale, Chartres. Take your binoculars to survey the world's finest collection of medieval stained-glass windows. The mighty, asymmetric spires dominate the flat grainlands for miles around.

Cathédrale Notre-Dame, Amiens. The colossal cathedral was built in 44 years during the 13th century; note the rose window and humorous carved misericords.

Cathédrale Notre-Dame, Laon. The hilltop setting—known as the Crowned Mountain—is the most spectacular of any French cathedral, bristling with elegant, openwork towers.

Cathédrale St-Étienne, Bourges. Look for the towers of the cathedral as you approach on N151; inside, note its stained glass and the slender columns rising to an extraordinaryheight.

Église St-Joseph, Le Havre. Concrete construction at its most spartan yet spectacular is represented in Auguste Perret's 1950s tour de force: part silo, part movie theater, part rocket.

Mont-St-Michel, Normandy. From its silhouette against the horizon to the abbey and gardens at the peak of the rock, you'll never forget this awe-inspiring sight.

Notre-Dame de l'Espérance, Mézières. All the windows of this elegant 15th-century church are filled with modern stained glass—the mix is sensational.

Notre-Dame-du-Haut, Ronchamp. Some say that this free-form chapel is Le Corbusier's masterpiece—utterly individual, yet imbued with peace and calm.

Dazzling Dining

Alain Ducasse, Paris. Ducasse's reputation is so hot you can practically smell it burning in the kitchen—but some still consider him France's finest chef. $$$$

Boyer, Reims, Champagne. Chef Gérard Boyer's innovative cuisine and his extensive wine list draw sophisticated diners (and lodgers) to this opulent restaurant in a 19th-century château. $$$$

Les Élysées du Vernet, Paris. A remarkable harmonic alignment of staff, decor, and kitchen make this tops in Paris: superb, sophisticated cooking, a glass roof designed by Eiffel himself, and roses given to departing guests—what more can you ask for? $$$$

La Ferme de Mon Père, Megève, Alps. The talk of foodies everywhere, Marc Veyrat creates peasant-luxe dishes that showcase the best of Haute Savoie cuisine and his Farmhouse Chic decor is an eye-knocker. $$$$

Le Grand Véfour, Paris. Back when Napoléon dined here, this was the most beautiful restaurant in Paris. Guess what? It still is. $$$$

Les Loges, Lyon. With dazzlers like roast wild boar with rosemary raisins and poached red pears on his bill of fare, it's little wonder their creator, Nicolas Le Bec, was named Gault-Millau Chef of the Year 2002. Modern art and a medieval hearth make for a stunning setting. $$$$

La Terrasse at Juana, Juan-les-Pins, Côte d'Azur. Chef Christian Morisset, with his delicious and exquisitely presented seafood dishes, is on his way to becoming one of France's top chefs. $$$$

Lapérouse, Paris. Dine with the ghosts of Émile Zola, George Sand, and Victor Hugo—all former regulars—here in this boiserie-graced townhouse, then fast forward to the future with one bite of lobster flavored with Szechuan pepper and lemon vinaigrette. $$$–$$$$

Les Feuillants, Céret, Languedoc-Roussillon. The cuisine at this restaurant, one of the best in the area, is yet another manifestation of the town's superb artistic endowment. $$$

La Régalade, Paris. Yves Camdeborde is the chef of the moment these days in Paris, staking his claim as the leading priest who marries bistro and nouvelle cookery. You'll forget about the dull room once you taste his soup of lentils and puréed chestnuts poured over a mound of fois gras. $$$

L'Assiette Gourmande, Honfleur, Normandy. The harbor-front setting gives a hint that seafood is a strong point, but all of Gérard Bonnefoy's food is to die for—including the delectable desserts. $$–$$$

La Corde, Toulouse, Midi-Pyrénées. It's worth finding this doyen of Toulouse restaurants, hidden in a small 15th-century tower in the courtyard of a 16th-century mansion. *$$–$$$*

Le Pamphlet, Paris. Basque and Béarn delights of southwestern France make this Marais bistro popular—what many Parisians love is the provincial feel, with a beamed ceiling, old-fashioned lamps, and a selection of faience that seems to have been borrowed from *grandmère. $$–$$$*

L'Ami Fritz, Obernai, Alsace. With a fire lighted stone-and-beam cellar and *toile-de-jouy* accents, this place is as succulent as the local specialties and wine served up by the chef. *$$*

L'Ardoise, Paris. This minuscule storefront, painted white and decorated with enlargements of old sepia postcards of Paris, is the very model of contemporary bistros making waves in Paris. Who can resist the crab flan in a creamy parsley emulsion? *$$*

Pigeons Blancs, Cognac. Chef Jacques Tachet's cooking would be worth a detour even if the handful of rooms weren't charming and reasonable. His three-course carte du jour is a find. *$$*

Chez Yvonne, Strasbourg, Alsace. This chic yet cozy *winstub* (inn) serves classic Alsatian fare and local wines to hip locals and heads of state. *$*

Les Pipos, Paris Bursting with laughter and chatter, this place has everything you could ask for in a Latin Quarter bistro. *$*

Memorable Hotels

Costes, Paris. For off-duty celebrities and models, this is the place to be seen trying not to be seen—but everyone will enjoy the palatial Napoléon III–style digs created by superstar decorator Jacques Garcia. *$$$$*

La Cour des Loges, Lyon. Any hotel that can please both Carl XVI Gustaf of Sweden and the Rolling Stones has to be something—and this is: Spectacularly renovated around a glassed-in Renaissance courtyard, this former Jesuit convent is now an extravaganza of glowing fireplaces, baroque credenzas, and antique Lyon silks. *$$$$*

Pavillon de la Reine, Paris. King Henri IV wouldn't blink an eye upon pulling up to the entryway here—it hasn't changed a bit since it was built on gorgeous place des Vosges in the 17th century. *$$$$*

Les Prés d'Eugénie, Eugénie-les-Bains, Basque Coast. Founded in the late 1970s by the father of nouvelle cooking, Michel Guérard, this landmark of Basque luxe is still going strong—needless to say, the breakfast here nearly outdoes dinner at most other places. *$$$$*

Relais Christine, Paris. In St-Germain-des-Pres—the loveliest quartier for tourists in Paris—this luxurious hotel occupies 16th-century abbey cloisters and oozes romantic ambience. *$$$$*

Château de la Bordaisière, Montlouis, Loire Valley. Not one but two princes de Broglie welcome you to this unforgettably idyllic and sumptuous neo-Renaissance retreat—if you want to taste *la vie de château* at its best, head here. *$$$–$$$$*

Château des Reaux, Bourgueil, Loire Valley. With its red-and-white chessboard facade, swans in the moat, and the Comtesse de Bouillé in residence, this 17th-century castle is relentlessly, exquisitely picturesque. *$$$–$$$$*

Le Maquis, Porticcio. The evocatively named Maquis, by the sea, ranks as one of Corsica's finest *hôtels de charme. $$$–$$$$*

Nord-Pinus, Arles, Provence. The adventurer and mail-order genius J. Peterman would feel right at home in this quintessentially Mediterranean hotel on place du Forum; Hemingway certainly did. *$$$–$$$$*

L'Oustau de la Baumanière, Baux-de-Provence. This veritable museum of Provençal tradition—names like Churchill, Picasso, and Elizabeth Taylor litter the guest book—has been given a nouvelle face-lift (as one bite of lobster cooked in Châteauneuf-du-Pape served up in the famed restaurant will prove). *$$$–$$$$*

Le Vieux Logis, Les Eyzies-de-Tayac, Bordeaux. A stay at this old stone house, which has a pool and a garden, in the Dordogne is unforgettable; so are the chef's five-course meals. *$$$–$$$$*

Le Vieux Manoir, Amboise, Loire Valley. The Boston-born restorer of this charming manor house could probably teach Edith Wharton a thing or two about French style. *$$$–$$$$*

Belles Rives, Juan-les-Pins, Côte d'Azur. Roaring Twenties millionaires loved this

Neoclassic-Moderne landmark on the Riviera, now finding a whole new generation of fans. *$$$*

Colombe d'Or, St-Paul-de-Vence, Côte d'Azur. Yes, those are works by Klee, Picasso, Braque, and Utrillo hanging on the wall. Some will quibble that the food has gone downhill, but there is only one Colombe d'Or. *$$$*

Ithurria, Ainhoa, Atlantic Pyrénées. Once a staging post on the fabled medieval pilgrims' route to Santiago de Compostela, this is a perfect stopover if you are doing a modern version of the pilgrims' journey. *$$$*

Caron de Beaumarchais, Paris. The theme of this intimate hotel in the heart of the Marais is the work of Caron de Beaumarchais, who wrote *The Marriage of Figaro* in 1778. Rooms reflect the taste of 18th-century French nobility. *$$*

L'Hostellerie du Vieux Cordes, Cordes. This old house around a wisteria-draped courtyard is an enchanting place to stay and eat in the opulent crimson dining rooms. *$$*

La Maison Rose, Eugénie-les-Bains, Basque Coast. Michel and Christine Guérard's newest hotel is set in a super-stylish 18th-century farmhouse adorned with old paintings and Pays Basque handicrafts, and comes complete with a spa. *$$*

Les Templiers, Collioure. No visit is complete without a stay at this warm and welcoming hotel filled with more than 2,500 original works of art. *$$*

La Treille Muscate, Cliousclat. In this charming village halfway between Lyon and Avignon is this gem of a hotel with individually styled rooms and a delightful, inexpensive restaurant serving regional cuisine. *$$*

Clos d'Ussé, Rigny-Ussé, Loire Valley. The whole Duchemin family runs this adorable inn set at the foot of the Chateau d'Ussé—the "Sleeping Beauty" castle—with wife Muriel in charge of this deescrumptious restaurant. *$*

Esméralda, Paris This quirky, cozy, eccentric place was once any *Vogue* editor's best-kept secret—now it's everyone's favorite Left Bank *hôtel de charme*. The lobby is right out of a Flaubert novel. *$*

Where Art Comes First

Fondation Maeght, St-Paul-de-Vence. A small gem of a museum of modern art, it blends its stunning holdings with stylish presentation.

Louvre, Paris. No matter how many times you've visited, be sure to come again; I. M. Pei's pyramid and the newly opened exhibit rooms are stunning.

Musée d'Art Modern, Céret. This modern art museum has one of the best collections of French and Catalan artist sever assembled outside a major metropolis.

Musée des Arts Décoratifs, Lyon. You can see the well-displayed furniture, silverware, ceramics, and artifacts of early Lyonnais life in a satisfying couple of hours.

Musée des Beaux-Arts, Lille. This fine-arts museum in Lille is one of the largest French museums outside of Paris.

Musée Condé, Chantilly. The château houses a remarkable collection of illuminated manuscripts, tapestries, furniture, paintings, Fouquet miniatures, and stained glass.

Musée Fesch, Ajaccio. Wonderful Italian Old Masters make up the museum's collection.

Musée Ingres, Montauban. Drawings and paintings by the great French classicist and works from his own collection are housed in this museum in the former Bishop's Palace.

Musée Matisse, Le Cateau. The Palais Fénelonis now home to paintings, sculpture, and drawings by the town's native son.

Musée de l'Oeuvre Notre-Dame, Strasbourg. This museum is much more than just a collection of weathered statues rescued from the cathedral; an effort has been made to create a churchlike atmosphere.

Palais de la Berbie, Albi. The world's greatest collection of works by Henri de Toulouse-Lautrec is housed in this former fortress with gardens designed by André Le Nôtre.

GREAT ITINERARIES

France from North to South

So, you want to taste France, gaze at its beauty, and inhale its special joie de vivre—

all in a one-week to 10-day trip. Let's assume at least that you've seen Paris, and you're ready to venture into the countryside. Here are some itineraries to help you plan your trip. Or create your own route using the suggested itineraries in each chapter. First, zoom from Paris to the heart of historic Burgundy, its rolling green hills traced with hedgerows and etched with vineyards. From here, plunge into the arid beauty of Provence and toward the spectacular coastline of the Côte d'Azur.

6 or 9 Days.

Burgundy Wine Country *(2 to 3 days).* Base yourself in the market town of Beaune and visit its famous Hospices and surrounding vineyards. Make a day trip to the ancient hill town of Vézelay, with its incomparable basilica, stopping in Autun to explore Roman ruins and its celebrated Romanesque cathedral. For more vineyards, follow the Côte d'Or from Beaune to Dijon. Or make a beeline to Dijon, with its charming Old Town and fine museums. From here it's a two-hour drive to Lyon, where you can feast on this city's famous earthy cuisine. Another three hours' push takes you deep into the heart of Provence. ☞ *Northwest Burgundy and Wine Country* in *Chapter 9* and *Lyon* in *Chapter 10.*

Arles *(2 or 3 days).* Arles is the atmospheric, sun-drenched southern town that inspired van Gogh and Gauguin. Make a day trip into grand old Avignon, home to the 14th-century rebel popes, to view their imposing palace. And make a pilgrimage to the Pont du Gard, the famous triple-tiered Roman aqueduct west of Avignon. From here two hours' drive will bring you to the glittering Côte d'Azur. ☞ *Arles, Avignon, and Pont du Gard* in *Chapter 12.*

Antibes *(2 or 3 days).* This historic and atmospheric port town is well positioned for day trips. First head west to glamorous Cannes. The next day head east into Nice, with its exotic Old Town and its bounty of modern art. There are ports to explore in Ville franche and St-Jean-Cap-Ferrat, east of Nice. Allow time for a walk out onto the tropical paradise–peninsula of Cap d'Antibes, or for an hour or two lolling on the coast's famous pebble beaches. ☞ *Cannes, Nice, Villefranche-sur-Mer, St-Jean-Cap-Ferrat,* and *Cap d'Antibes* in *Chapter 12.*

By Public Transportation

The high-speed TGV travels from Paris through Burgundy and Lyon then zips through the south to Marseille. Train connections to Beaune from the TGV are easy; getting to Autun from Beaune takes up to two hours, with a change at Chagny. Vézelay can be reached by bus excursion from Dijon or Beaune. Rail connections are easy between Arles and Avignon; you'll need a bus from Avignon to get to the Pont du Gard. Antibes, Cannes, and Nice are easily reached by the scenic rail line, as are most of the resorts and ports along the coast. To squeeze the most daytime out of your trip, take a night train or a plane from Nice back to Paris.

The Good Life

Great châteaux, fine porcelain, superb wine, brandy, truffles, and foie gras sum up France for many. Beginning in château country, head south and west, through Cognac country into wine country around Bordeaux. Then lose yourself in the Dordogne, a landscape of rolling hills peppered with medieval villages, fortresses, and prehistoric caves.

7–10 Days.

Loire Valley Châteaux *(3 or 4 days).* Base yourself at the crossroads of Blois, starting with its multi-era château. Then head for the huge château in Chambord. Amboise's château echoes with history, and the neighboring manor Clos Lucé was Leonardo da Vinci's final home—or instead of this "town" château, head west to the tiny village of Rigny-Ussé for the "Sleeping Beauty" castle of Ussé. Heading south east, finish up at Chenonceau—the most magical one of all—then return to the transportation hub city of Tours. ☞ *The Loire Valley* in *Chapter 4.*

Cognac Country *(1 or 2 days).* Cognac's very air is saturated with evaporations of its heady product, enough to grow mushrooms on its black stone walls; Hennessy and Martell give tasting tours. In neighboring Jarnac you can visit Hine and Courvoisier—and François Mitterrand's grave. ☞ *Charente* in *Chapter 17.*

Bordeaux Wine Country *(2 days).* Pay homage to the great names of Médoc, north of the city of Bordeaux, though the hallowed villages of Margaux, St-Julien, Pauillac, and St-Estèphe aren't much to look at. East of Bordeaux, via the prettier Pomerol vineyards, the village of St-Emilion is everything you'd want a wine town to be, with ramparts and medieval streets. ☞ *Bordeaux* in *Chapter 17.*

Dordogne and Périgord *(2 or 3 days).* Follow the famous Dordogne River east to the half-timber market town of Bergerac. Wind through the green, wooded countryside into the region where humans' earliest ancestors left their mark, in the caves in Les Eyzies-de-Tayac and the famous Grotte de Lascaux. Be sure to sample the region's culinary specialties: truffles, foie gras, and preserved duck. Then travel south to the stunning and sky-high village of Rocamadour. ☞ *Dordogne and Poitou-Charentes* in *Chapter 17.*

By Public Transportation

It's easy to get to Blois and Chenonceaux by rail, but you'll need to take a bus to visit other Loire châteaux. Forays farther into Bordeaux country and the Dordogne are difficult by train, involving complex and frequent changes (Limoges is a big railway hub). Further exploration requires a rental car or sometimes sketchy bus routes.

A Child's-Eye View

Lead your children (and yourself) wide-eyed through the wonders of Europe, instilling some sense of France's cultural legacy. Make your way through Normandy and Brittany, with enough wonders and evocative topics, from William the Conqueror to D-Day, to inspire any child to put down his computer game and gawk. Short daily drives forestall mutiny, and you'll be in crêperie country, satisfying for casual meals.

7 days.

Versailles *(1 day).* Here's an opportunity for a history lesson: With its obscene baroque extravagance, no other monument so succinctly illustrates what inspired the rage of the French Revolution. Louis XIV's eye-popping château of Versailles pleases the secret monarch in most of us. ☞ *Southwest from Versailles to Chartres* in *Chapter 3.*

Honfleur *(1 day).* From this picture-book seaport lined with skinny half-timber row houses and salt-dampened cobblestones, the first French explorers set sail for Canada in the 15th century. ☞ *Upper Normandy* in *Chapter 6.*

Bayeux *(2 days).* William the Conqueror's extraordinary invasion of England in 1066 was launched from the shores of Normandy. The famous Bayeux tapestry, showcased in a state-of-the-art museum, spins the tale of the Battle of Hastings. From this home base you can introduce the family to the modern saga of 1944's Allied landings with a visit to the Museum of the Battle of Normandy, then make a pilgrimage to Omaha Beach. ☞ *Lower Normandy* in *Chapter 6.*

Mont-St-Michel *(1 day).* Rising majestically in a shroud of sea mist over vacillating tidal flats, this mystical peninsula is Gothic in every sense of the word. Though its tiny, steep streets are crammed with visitors and tourist traps, no other sight gives you a stronger sense of the worldly power of medieval monasticism than Mont-St-Michel. ☞ *Lower Normandy* in *Chapter 6.*

St-Malo *(1 day).* Even in winter you'll want to brave the Channel winds to beach comb the shores of this onetime pirate base. In summer, of course, it's mobbed with sun seekers who stroll the old streets, restored to quaintness after World War II. ☞ *Northeast Brittany and the Channel Coast* in *Chapter 5.*

Chartres *(1 day).* Making a beeline on the autoroute back to Paris, stop in Chartres to view the loveliest of all of France's cathedrals. ☞ *Southwest from Versailles to Chartres* in *Chapter 3.*

By Public Transportation

Coordinating a sightseeing tour like this with a limited local train schedule isn't easy, and connections to Mont-St-Michel are especially complicated. Versailles, Chartres, and St-Malo are easy to reach, and Bayeux and Honfleur are doable, if inconvenient. But you'll spend a lot of vacation time waiting along train tracks.

Vintage Sampler

Tasting wines in a cool, mossy cave redolent of cork gives vintages new dimensions, and you'll meet vintners of every stripe, from gnarled-fingered grandpas in blue aprons to ascoted gentry in cashmere. Along the way, taste the widely varied wines of eastern France, from Champagne to Alsace to the little-known whites of the Jura, then on to Burgundy, Beaujolais, and the Côtes du Rhône. Take it easy on the *dégustations* (tastings) if you're driving.

6–9 Days.

Reims *(2 days)*. At the heart of the green panorama of Champagne country lies Reims, with its magnificent cathedral. There's no shortage of downtown sources of bubbly, but you'll probably also want to venture south down the *Route du Vin* (Wine Road) to Épernay, home to Moët et Chandon. Just northwest is the old-fashioned village of Hautvillers, which claims Dom Pérignon as its native son. ☞ *Champagne and the Ardennes* in *Chapter 7*.

Ribeauvillé *(2 days)*. Head east to Franco-Germanic Strasbourg and south down Alsace's Route du Vin. At the foot of forested Vosges foothills, the tiny wine village of Ribeauvillé sums up the spirit of Alsace. Here you'll taste sharp, fruity Rieslings and late-harvest Gewürztraminers as sweet as sauternes. Picture-perfect Riquewihr and Colmar are a stone's throw away. ☞ *Alsace* in *Chapter 8*.

Arbois *(1 day)*. South of Alsace, follow the Doubs River through the citadel town of Besançon to Arbois. This is the center for the production of the Jura region's obscure and eccentric *vin jaune*: sharp, dry, and sherrylike. Venture to the other-worldly hilltop village of Château-Chalon for some of the finest of the genre. ☞ *Franche-Comté* in *Chapter 8*.

Beaune *(2 days)*. Press westward to Beaune, Burgundy's wine-market town (☞ France from North to South itinerary, *above*). Wine shops abound in the center, but you'll want to cruise along the famous Côte d'Or. ☞ *Wine Country* in *Chapter 9*.

Villefranche-sur-Saône *(1 day)*. Head south along the west bank of the Saône. South of Mâcon, home of the last and lightest of the Burgundies, veer westward and follow the winding southbound Route du Vin through Beaujolais country. Cruise through the famous villages that produce this fruity, Gamay-based red. If you're traveling in autumn, look for the sharp young Beaujolais nouveau: the market-town of Villefranche-sur-Saône celebrates annually with carnival-like festivities. ☞ *Wine Country* in *Chapter 9* and *Beaujolais and La Dombes,* and *The Rhône Valley* in *Chapter 10*.

Châteauneuf-du-Pape *(2 days)*. At Lyon you'll merge into the Rhône Valley. Just north of Valence cross the river at Tournon and pay homage to the vineyards at Tain-l'Hermitage. Press on south past Orange to the famous wine region and village of Châteauneuf-du-Pape, named for the Avignon popes who weekended here. You could continue from here into the region of the "sun wines" of the Côtes de Provence and Languedoc, but you might never get home. ☞ *Lyon and the Rhône Valley* in *Chapter 10,* and *Avignon and the Vaucluse* in *Chapter 11*.

By Public Transportation

An abbreviated version of this journey can be worked out via train, leaving out the inaccessible vineyards and villages (which serve as lovely scenery through the train window). Start in Reims, move directly on to Colmar (substituting the atmospheric wine-market center for Ribeauvillé); take the train onward to Beaune. From Beaune the train makes stops along the northbound Côte d'Or route, but the best vineyards are hard to reach on foot. To get closer to the sources, look into package excursions or rent a car.

2 PARIS

Brilliantly radiating 2,000 years of history and culture, the City of Light intrigues, astonishes, provokes, and overwhelms. Its combined wealth of architectural beauty, artistic expression, and culinary delight gets under your skin—and does it know it! As drop-dead arrogant as the Arc de Triomphe, as disarmingly quaint as a lace-curtain bistro, Paris seduces newcomers with its debonair air—and this siren song invites long, unhurried explorations of its picture-perfect streets.

Updated by Simon Hewitt, Rosa Jackson, Christopher Mooney, and Nicola Keegan

Introduction by Nancy Coons

IF THERE'S A PROBLEM WITH A TRIP TO PARIS, it's the embarrassment of riches that faces you. No matter which aspect of Paris you choose—touristy, historic, fashion-conscious, pretentious-bourgeois, thrifty, or the legendary bohemian arty Paris of undying attraction—one thing is certain: you will carve out your own Paris, one that is vivid, exciting, ultimately unforgettable. Wherever you head, your itinerary will prove to be a voyage of discovery. But choosing the Paris of your dreams is a bit like choosing a perfume or cologne. Do you want something young and dashing, or elegant and worldly? How about sporty, or perhaps strictly glamorous? No matter: they are all here—be it perfumes, famous museums, legendary churches, or romantic cafés. Whether you spend three days or three months in this city, it will always have something new to offer you, which may explain why the most assiduous explorers of Paris are the Parisians themselves.

Veterans know that Paris is a city of vast, noble perspectives and intimate, ramshackle streets, of formal *espaces vertes* (green open spaces) and quiet squares. This combination of the pompous and the private is one of the secrets of its perennial pull. Another is its size: Paris is relatively small as capitals go, with distances between many of its major sights and museums invariably walkable.

For the first-timer there will always be several must-dos at the top of the list, but getting to know Paris will never be quite as simple as a quick look at Notre-Dame, the Louvre, and the Eiffel Tower. You'll discover that around every corner, down every *ruelle* (little street) lies a resonance-in-waiting. You can stand on the rue du Faubourg St-Honoré at the very spot where Edmond Rostand set Ragueneau's pastry shop in *Cyrano de Bergerac.* You can read the letters of Madame de Sévigné in her actual *hôtel particulier,* or private mansion, now the Musée Carnavalet. You can hear the words of Racine resound in the ringing, hair-raising diction of the Comédie Française. You can breathe in the fumes of hubris before the extravagant onyx tomb Napoléon designed for himself. You can try to resist genuflecting in the Panthéon, where religion bowed before France's great post-Revolution statesmen. You can gaze through the gates at the school where Voltaire honed his wit, and you can lay a garland on Oscar Wilde's poignant grave at Père-Lachaise Cemetery.

If this is your first trip, there's no harm in taking a guided tour of the city—a perfectly good introduction that will help you get your bearings and provide you with a general impression before you return to explore the sights that particularly interest you. To help track down those, this chapter's exploration of Paris is divided into eight neighborhood walks. Each *quartier,* or neighborhood, has its own personality, which is best discovered by footpower. Ultimately, your route will be marked by your preferences, your curiosity, and your state of fatigue. You can wander for hours without getting bored—though not, perhaps, without getting lost. By the time you have quartered the city, you should not only be culturally replete but downright exhausted—and hungry, too. Again, take your cue from Parisians and think out your next move in a sidewalk café. So you've heard stories of a friend who paid $5 for a coffee at a café. That's a bad deal—for only a coffee. But bear in mind that what you're paying for is time—to watch the intricate dramas of Parisian street life unfold in front of you. Hemingway knew the rules; after all, he would have remained just another unknown sportswriter if the waiters in the cafés had hovered around him impatiently.

Pleasures and Pastimes

Cafés

Some would say Paris is all about people-watching; and there's no better place to indulge in this pursuit than at a sidewalk café. Favored locales include place St-Michel, boulevard du Montparnasse, and place St-Germain-des-Prés, on the Left Bank; and place de l'Opéra, the Champs-Élysées, and Les Halles, on the Right Bank. But you may enjoy seeking out your own (less expensive) local haunts.

Churches

Paris is rich in churches of two architectural styles: the 15th- to 16th-century overlap of Flamboyant Gothic and Renaissance (at St-Gervais, St-Étienne du Mont, St-Eustache, and St-Séverin), and 17th-century Baroque, with domes and two-tiered facades (at Les Invalides, Val de Grâce, and St-Paul–St-Louis). But the city's most enduring religious symbols are from the medieval age (Sainte-Chapelle and the cathedral of Notre-Dame) and the 19th-century (Sacré-Coeur and La Madeleine).

Dining

As for dining, well . . . the French wrote the book. Paris is one of the world's great food capitals and a bastion of classic French cuisine. Nonetheless, if you're coming from New York, London, or Los Angeles, where innovative restaurants abound, you may find the French capital a little staid. In fact, a battle is currently being waged between the traditionalists and a remarkable new generation of chefs who are set on modernizing food preparation—forever changing the French culinary landscape in the process. In the end, fads and trends may come and go, but the pragmatic Parisian will always know that this is the city that sets the standards.

Museums

You'll find Leonardos, Monets, and Toulouse-Lautrecs tossed into one bright bouquet when you go museum hopping in Paris. Alongside the superstars—the Louvre, the Musée d'Orsay, and the newly renovated Centre Pompidou—are such delights as the Musée National du Moyen Age (displaying medieval works of art in the famous Hôtel de Cluny), the regal Louis Quinze splendor of the Musée Nissim de Camondo, and single-artist museums dedicated to the works of Picasso, Rodin, Dalí, and Maillol.

Shopping

Whether you decide to bargain at a flea market or go snob shopping on place Vendôme, buying opportunities in Paris are endless and geared to every taste. You can spend an afternoon browsing through bookstalls along the Seine, shopping for one of Hermès's famous *foulards* (scarves), touring high-gloss department stores, or bargaining over prices in the sprawling flea markets on the outskirts of town. Everywhere you turn, tastefully displayed wares—luscious chocolates, exquisite clothing, gleaming copper pots—entice the eye and fire the imagination.

EXPLORING PARIS

Revised and updated by Simon Hewitt

As world capitals go, Paris is surprisingly compact. With the exceptions of the Bois de Boulogne and Montmartre, you can easily walk from one major sight to the next. The city is divided in two by the River Seine, with two islands (Ile de la Cité and Ile St-Louis) in the middle. Each bank of the Seine has its own personality; the Rive Droite (Right Bank), with its spacious boulevards and formal buildings, generally has a more genteel feel than the carefree Rive Gauche (Left Bank), to the south. The east–west axis from Châtelet to the Arc de Triomphe, via the rue de Rivoli and the Champs-Élysées, is the Right Bank's principal thoroughfare for sightseeing and shopping.

The city is divided into 20 *arrondissements* (districts). The last one or two digits of a city zip code (e.g., 75002) will tell you the arrondissement (in this case, the 2e, or 2nd). Although the best method of getting to know Paris is on foot, public transportation—particularly the métro system—is excellent. Buy the *Plan de Paris* booklet, a city map and guide with a street-name index that also shows métro stations. Note that all métro stations have detailed neighborhood maps displayed just inside the entrance.

This chapter is divided into eight Paris neighborhood walks. A few monuments and museums close for lunch between noon and 2, and many are closed on either Monday or Tuesday: Check before you set off.

Numbers in the text correspond to numbers in the margin and on the Paris and Montmartre maps.

Great Itineraries

A visit to Paris will never be quite as simple as a quick look at a few landmarks. Each *quartier* (neighborhood) has its own treasures, and you should be ready to explore—an enticing prospect in this most elegant of cities. Outlined here are the main areas on which to concentrate, depending on the length of your stay. Bear in mind that the amount of time spent visiting monuments—and museums in particular—is not something you can predict with any certainty, nor would you want to. Just to see the city's larger museums, let alone its smaller ones, would probably take a whole week.

IF YOU HAVE 3 DAYS

On your first day begin at the beginning: the Ile de la Cité, settled more than 2,000 years ago and home to the cathedral of Notre-Dame. Take a cue from Victor Hugo and climb the 387 steps of one of its towers to the former haunts of its mythic hunchback, Quasimodo—you'll be rewarded by a great view of Paris framed by the stone gargoyles created by Viollet-le-Duc. Then head several blocks over to marvel at the Sainte-Chapelle, a jewel box of Gothic art shimmering with hundreds of stained-glass panels. After visiting the nearby Conciergerie—the last abode of Queen Marie-Antoinette—walk over the Pont Neuf, which spans the Seine, and turn left to reach the greatest museum in the world—the Louvre (keep in mind it's closed Tuesday), famed showcase for the *Winged Victory,* the *Venus de Milo,* and the haunting, ironic smile of the *Mona Lisa.* After a lengthy visit, exit into the calm, green Tuileries Gardens, immortalized by the Impressionists, then head west to the city's heart, place de la Concorde. Walk up the leafy lower reaches of the Champs-Élysées, heading over to the Seine and its most gorgeous bridge—the Pont Alexandre III—just in time for *l'heure bleue,* or dusk.

On day two you're ready to tackle picture-postcard Paris. Start at the Eiffel Tower, then take in some culture at the Palais de Chaillot museums, or the nearby Musée Guimet (for great Asian art) and the Musée d'Art Moderne de la Ville de Paris (for fine modern art). At the place de l'Alma opt for a ride on the Bateaux Mouches up and down the Seine. Head along avenue Montaigne—Dior is here along with numerous other temples of fashion—to the Champs-Élysées and up left to the Arc de Triomphe. On day three explore the Faubourg St-Honoré, Paris's legendary center of luxe, where world-class shopping and two of Paris's most beautiful urban set pieces—place Vendôme and the Palais Royal—await. Continue north to hit the Grand Boulevards, famed for their sidewalk cafés, the glittering Opéra Garnier—still haunted by the Phantom?—and then enjoy a tranquil afternoon in the chic and rich residential neighborhood around Parc Monceau, with a stop at the art-filled mansion of the Musée Nissim de Camondo.

IF YOU HAVE 5 DAYS

Follow the three-day itinerary above, then on your fourth day begin at the Musée d'Orsay, where many of the most famous Impressionist paintings in the world are on view. Pay your respects to Napoléon, at the nearby church of the Invalides, and then to the great sculptor Rodin, at the Musée Rodin, housed in one of the prettiest hôtels particuliers in the city. Head east along the boulevard St-Germain to the picturesque place Furstenberg to visit Atelier Delacroix, the haunt of another great artist. South a few blocks is the Jardin du Luxembourg, perfect for a sylvan time-out. End at Paris's extraordinary Musée National du Moyen-Age, which graces the time-stained Hôtel de Cluny. On your fifth day begin on the Ile St-Louis—the little island sitting next to the larger Ile de la Cité in the Seine. Although there are no major sights to see here, you'll find a charming neighborhood that has more than a touch of the time machine to it. Cross over the Seine to the Marais—one of the city's most venerable quarters, studded with great Baroque and Rococo mansions, many of which are now museums, including the Musée Picasso. Nearby is another mecca for modern-art lovers, the Centre Beaubourg, while those with more traditional tastes will make a beeline for the Musée Carnavalet, or the Paris History Museum, and the magnificent 17th-century square place des Vosges.

IF YOU HAVE 7 DAYS

On your sixth day take a vacation from your Paris vacation by heading out for a day trip to Versailles, built in bicep-flexing Baroque splendor. Don't forget to explore its vast park in order to take in the intimate and charming Petit Trianon and Hameau, which was Marie-Antoinette's toy farm. On your seventh day get up at dawn and hurry up to the Butte (mound) of Montmartre, which graces a dramatic rise over the city. Get here to see the sun rise over the entire city from your perch on place du Parvis, in front of the basilica of the Sacré-Coeur. Track the spirit of Toulouse-Lautrec through the streets and to the Musée de Montmartre. For your last afternoon, descend back down into the city to either attack some of the city's "other" museums (the Cognacq-Jay and the Maillol), to explore Montparnasse, or to envy some "permanent" Parisians ensconced in noble marble splendor at Père-Lachaise Cemetery. As an alternative, you can spend your last day on a excursion out to the majestic château in Fontainebleau, the tranquil artists' village of Auvers-sur-Oise, or the sublime Gothic cathedral in Chartres.

The Historic Heart: From Notre-Dame to the Place de la Concorde

No matter how you first approach Paris—historically, geographically, emotionally—it is the River Seine that summons all and that harbors two celebrated islands, the Ile de la Cité and the Ile St-Louis, both at the very center of the city. Of the two, it is the Ile de la Cité that forms the historic ground zero of Paris. It was here that the earliest inhabitants of Paris, the Gaulish tribe of the Parisii, settled in about 250 BC, calling their home Lutetia, meaning "settlement surrounded by water." Today it is famed for the great, brooding cathedral of Notre-Dame, the haunted Conciergerie, and the dazzling Sainte-Chapelle. If Notre-Dame represents Church, another major attraction of this walk—the Louvre—symbolizes State. A succession of French rulers was responsible for filling this immense, symmetrical structure with the world's greatest paintings and works of art, now the largest museum in the world, as well as one of the easiest to get lost in. Beyond the Louvre lie the graceful Tuileries Gardens, the grand place de la Concorde—the very hub of the city—and the Belle Epoque splendor of the Grand Palais and the Pont Alexandre III. All in all, this area comprises some of the most historic and beautiful sights to see in Paris.

A Good Walk

Place du Parvis—the square regarded by the French as *kilomètre zero,* the spot from which all distances to and from the city are officially measured—makes a fitting setting for **Notre-Dame de Paris** ①, familiar and yet regal, like the gracious lady (as the priests will tell you) whose name it bears. Explore the interior, then toil up the steps to the towers for a grand view of the heart of Paris. Head behind the cathedral to the Pont de l'Archevêché for the best view of the cathedral, then cross over to the quai de la Tournelle (where Leslie Caron and Gene Kelly so memorably pas-de-deux-ed in *An American in Paris*) for a waterside vista.

Walk along the Seine embankment until the Pont au Double, cross over the Seine once again to place du Parvis, then head across the square and along rue de la Cité to rue de Lutèce, where you should make a left and walk to boulevard du Palais and the imposing **Palais de Justice** ②, the 19th-century Law Courts, which harbors the medieval **Sainte-Chapelle** ③—a vision in shimmering stained glass—and the **Conciergerie** ④, the prison where Marie-Antoinette awaited her appointment with Madame Guillotine. At the end of quai de l'Horloge is the charming **place Dauphine** ⑤. Opposite, on the other side of the Pont Neuf, is **square du Vert-Galant** ⑥, with its proud equestrian statue of Henri IV. On the quay side of the square, *vedettes* (glass-top motorboats) start their tours along the Seine.

Cross the **Pont Neuf** ⑦—the New Bridge, confusingly so called given that it is actually the oldest bridge in Paris—to the Rive Droite and make a left turn toward the **Louvre** ⑧, the vast museum on the quai du Louvre, entering through the grand East Front and heading through the Cour Carrée to the I. M. Pei glass-pyramid entry. After viewing some of the greatest artworks in the world, exit through the **Carrousel du Louvre** ⑨ complex, a posh underground shopping mall, to the manicured lawns of the **Jardin des Tuileries** ⑩, or Tuileries Gardens. Standing sentinel is the **Musée du Jeu de Paume** ⑪, host to outstanding exhibits of contemporary art. At the far end lies one of the world's grandest squares, **place de la Concorde** ⑫, centered by a grand Egyptian obelisk with a gilded top. Continue up the Champs-Élysées to avenue Winston-Churchill to the **Grand Palais** ⑬, whose back half houses the **Palais de la Découverte** ⑭, with Paris's planetarium and exhibits on science and technology. For a romantic finale, head back over to the Seine and the floridly beautiful **Pont Alexandre-III** ⑮.

TIMING

Allowing for toiling up towers, dancing down quays, and musing at *Mona Lisa,* this walk will take a full day—enabling you to reach Pont Alexandre-III just before sundown. Of course, if you want to do full justice to the vast collections of the Louvre, you could easily spend a week there and still not see everything. If you return to ogle the museum, visit in the mornings, when it is less crowded (note that it is closed Tuesday).

Readers have raved about Paris's **Carté Musées et Monuments** (Museums and Monuments Pass), which offers unlimited access to more than 65 museums and monuments over a one-, three-, or five-consecutive day period; the cost, respectively, is €13, €26, and €39. Considering that most Paris museums cost between €4 and €6, you have to be serious about museum-going to make this pay off, but there is one incredible plus: you get to jump to the head of the line by displaying it—quite a feat when there are 600 people lined up to get into the Musé d'Orsay. Since most museums don't charge for kids under 18, a family of four need only buy 2 passes. The Pass is available at Paris's tourist offices, métro stations, and at all participating museums. Information: www.intermusees.com.

Sights to See

9 **Carrousel du Louvre.** Part of the early '90s Louvre renovation program, this subterranean shopping complex is centered on an inverted glass pyramid (overlooked by the regional Ile-de-France tourist office) and contains a wide range of stores, spaces for fashion shows, an auditorium, and a huge parking garage. At lunchtime, museum visitors rush to the mall-style food court, where fast food goes international. Note that you can get into or exit from the museum (and avoid some lines) by entering through the mall. ✉ *Entrances on rue de Rivoli or by Arc du Carrousel, Louvre/Tuileries. Métro: Palais-Royal.*

4 **Conciergerie.** Bringing a tear to the eyes of ancien régime devotees, this is the famous prison in which dukes and duchesses, lords and ladies, and, most famously, Queen Marie-Antoinette were imprisoned during the Revolution before being carted off to the guillotine. Originally part of a royal palace, the turreted medieval building still holds Marie-Antoinette's cell; a chapel, embellished with the initials M. A., occupies the true site of her confinement. Out of one of these windows, Toni (the queen's nickname) saw a notorious scene of the Revolution: her best friend, the Comtesse de Lamballe—lover of the arts and daughter of the richest duke in France—torn to pieces by a wild mob, her dismembered limbs then displayed on pikes. Elsewhere are the courtyard and fountain where victims of the Terror spent their final days playing piquet, writing letters to their loved ones, and waiting for the dreaded climb up the staircase to the Chamber of the Revolutionary Council to hear its final verdict. ✉ *1 quai de l'Horloge, Ile de la Cité,* ☎ *01–53–73–78–50,* WEB *www.monum.fr.* 🎟 *€5.50; joint ticket with Sainte-Chapelle €7.60.* ⏲ *Spring–fall, daily 9:30–6:30; winter, daily 10–5. Métro: Cité.*

13 **Grand Palais** (Grand Palace). With its curved glass roof, the Grand Palais is unmistakable when approached from either the Seine or the Champs-Élysées, and forms an attractive duo with the **Petit Palais,** on the other side of avenue Winston-Churchill. Although undergoing renovation until late 2003, it also houses the Palais de la Découverte—home to the city planetarium—which can be visited. ✉ *Av. Winston-Churchill, Champs-Élysées,* ☎ *01–42–65–12–73.* ⏲ *Tues.–Sun. 10–5:40. Métro: Champs-Élysées–Clemenceau.*

10 **Jardin des Tuileries** (Tuileries Gardens). Immortalized in Impressionist canvases by Monet and Pissarro, the Tuileries Gardens are typically French: formal and neatly patterned, with rows of trees, gravel paths, flower beds, and a host of statuary from various eras. This is a delightful place from which to survey the surrounding cityscape. *Métro: Concorde, Tuileries.*

★ 8 **Louvre.** Leonardo da Vinci's *Mona Lisa* and *Virgin and St. Anne,* Veronese's *Marriage at Cana,* Giorgione's *Concert Champêtre,* Delacroix's *Liberty Guiding the People,* Whistler's *Mother (Arrangement in Black and White)* . . . you get the picture. This is the world's greatest (and, in fact, largest) art museum. Today, after two decades of renovations, the Louvre is now a coherent, unified structure, and search parties no longer need to be sent in to bring you out. Begun by Philippe-Auguste in the 13th century as a fortress, it was not until the reign of pleasure-loving François I, 300 years later, that the Louvre of today gradually began to take shape. Through the years Henri IV (1589–1610), Louis XIII (1610–43), Louis XIV (1643–1715), Napoléon I (1804–14), and Napoléon III (1852–70) all contributed to its construction. The recent history of the Louvre centers on I. M. Pei's glass pyramid, unveiled in March 1989, and numerous renovations.

The number one attraction is the Most Famous Painting in the World: Leonardo da Vinci's enigmatic ***Mona Lisa*** (*La Joconde,* to the French), painted in 1503–06. The portrait of the wife of one Francesco del Giocondo, a 15th-century Florentine millionaire, Leonardo's masterpiece is now believed to have been painted as a memorial after the lady's death. To those who recall Théophile Gautier's words calling her "a sphinx of beauty," the portrait is a bit of a disappointment. Once you get in front of the videotaping tourists, you, too, may find yourself asking, "Is this it?" when faced with this 30 by 18 inch painting of an eyebrowless woman with yellowing skin and an annoyingly smug smile. In fact, most art historians award the beauty prize instead to Leonardo's *Virgin and St. Anne,* hanging nearby. Also in this room you will find other legendary works of the High Renaissance, including Raphael's *La Belle Jardinière.*

The Louvre is packed with legendary collections, which are divided into seven sections: Asian antiquities; Egyptian antiquities; Greek and Roman antiquities; sculpture; paintings, prints, and drawings; furniture; and objets d'art. Don't try to see it all at once; try, instead, to make repeat visits—the admission is nearly half price on Sunday and after 3 PM on other days. (Unless you plan on going to a number of museums every day, the one-, three-, and five-day tourist museum passes probably aren't worth your money, since you could easily spend a whole day at the Louvre alone.) Some other highlights of the painting collection are Jan van Eyck's magnificent *The Madonna and Chancellor Rolin,* painted in the early 15th century; *The Lacemaker,* by Jan Vermeer (1632–75); *The Embarkation for Cythera,* by Antoine Watteau (1684–1721); *The Oath of the Horatii,* by Jacques-Louis David (1748–1825); *The Raft of the Medusa,* by Théodore Géricault (1791–1824); and *La Grande Odalisque,* by Jean-Auguste-Dominique Ingres (1780–1867).

The French crown jewels (in the objets d'art section of the Richelieu Wing) include the mind-boggling 186-carat Regent diamond. The Nike, or *Winged Victory of Samothrace,* seems poised for flight at the top of the stairs (remember Audrey Hepburn's high-cheekboned take on this statue in *Funny Face*?), and other much-loved pieces of sculpture are Michelangelo's two *Slaves,* intended for the tomb of Pope Julius II. These can be admired in the Denon Wing, where a new medieval and Renaissance sculpture section is housed partly in the former imperial stables. In 1997 new rooms for Persian, Arab, Greek, and Egyptian art were opened, followed in 1999 by rooms for Italian and Spanish painting and French furniture and objets d'art from the period 1815–48. For fans of the Napoléon III style—the apotheosis of 19th-century opulence—be sure to see the galleries that once housed the Ministry of Finance. To get into the Louvre, you may have to wait in two long lines: one outside the Pyramide entrance portal and another downstairs at the ticket booths. You can avoid the first by entering through the Carrousel du Louvre, but you can't avoid the second. Your ticket will get you into any and all the wings as many times as you like during one day. ✉ *Palais du Louvre (other than the main en-*

trance at the Pei pyramid, you can also enter through the East Front, from the Porte des Lions overlooking the Seine, and through the Carrousel du Louvre mall on rue de Rivoli), Louvre/Tuileries, ☎ *01–40–20–51–51,* WEB *www.louvre.fr.* 🎫 *€7.50; €5 after 3* PM *and on Sun.; free 1st Sun. of month.* ⏲ *Thurs.–Sun. 9–6, Mon. and Wed. 9* AM*–9:45* PM*. Some sections open limited days. Métro: Palais-Royal.*

⓫ **Musée du Jeu de Paume.** At the entrance to the Tuileries Gardens, this museum is an ultramodern white-walled showcase for excellent temporary exhibits of bold contemporary art. Its adjoining sister museum, the **Musé de l'Orangerie**—home to Claude Monet's largest *Water Lilies*—is closed for renovation until 2003. ✉ *1 pl. de la Concorde, Louvre/Tuileries,* ☎ *01–42–60–69–69.* 🎫 *€5.80.* ⏲ *Tues. noon–9:30, Wed.–Fri. noon–7, weekends 10–7. Métro: Concorde.*

★ ❶ **Notre-Dame.** Looming above the large, pedestrian place du Parvis is la cathédrale de Notre-Dame, the most enduring symbol of Paris. Begun in 1163, completed in 1345, badly damaged during the Revolution, and restored by Viollet-le-Duc in the 19th century, Notre-Dame may not be France's oldest or largest cathedral, but in terms of beauty and architectural harmony, it has few peers—as you can see by studying the facade from the open square. Many historical events happened here, including Napoléon's self-coronation as emperor in May 1804. The doorways seem like hands joined in prayer, and the sculpted kings form a noble procession, while the rose window gleams, to wax poetic, like the eye of divinity. Above, the gallery breaks the guipure of the stone vaults, and between the two high towers the flêche soars from the crossing of the transept. The chancel and altar were consecrated in 1182, but the magnificent sculptures surrounding the main doors were not put into position until 1240.

The facade divides neatly into three levels. At the first-floor level are the three main entrances, or portals: the Portal of the Virgin, on the left; the Portal of the Last Judgment, in the center; and the Portal of St. Anne, on the right. All three are surmounted by magnificent carvings—most of them 19th-century copies of the originals—of figures, foliage, and biblical scenes. Above these are the restored statues of the kings of Israel, the Galerie des Rois. Above the gallery is the great rose window and, above that, the Grande Galerie, at the base of the twin towers. The south tower houses the great bell of Notre-Dame, as tolled by Quasimodo, Victor Hugo's fictional hunchback. The 387-step climb to the top of the towers is worth the effort for a close-up of the famous gargoyles—most added in the 19th century by Viollet-le-Duc—as they frame an expansive view of the city. If some find both towers a bit top heavy, that's because they were designed to be topped by two needlelike spires, which were never built. The cathedral interior, with its vast proportions, soaring nave, and soft multicolor light dimly filtering through the stained-glass windows, inspires awe—visit early in the morning, when the cathedral is at its lightest and least crowded. To put the cathedral in its proper medieval context, explore the adorable **Medieval Cloître Quarter,** set just to the north of the cathedral—famous folk from Helöise and Abelard to Ludwig Bemelmans (creator of *Madeline*) have called this tiny warren of crooked streets home. At the intersection of rue des Ursins and rue des Chantres, where a medieval palace, tiny flower garden, and quayside steps form a cul-de-sac, time seems to be holding its breath. ✉ *Pl. du Parvis, Ile de la Cité,* WEB *www.monum.fr.* 🎫 *Towers €5.50.* ⏲ *Cathedral 8* AM*–7* PM*; towers summer, daily 9:30–7:30; winter, daily 10–5. Métro: Cité.*

⓮ **Palais de la Découverte** (Palace of Discovery). A planetarium, working models, and scientific and technological exhibits on such topics as optics, biology, nuclear physics, and electricity make up this science museum behind the Grand Palais. ✉ *Av. Franklin-D.-Roosevelt, Champs-Élysées,* ☎ *01–56–43–20–21.* 🎫 *€5.35, €3.05 extra for planetarium.* ⏲ *Tues.–Sat. 9:30–6, Sun. 10–7. Métro: Champs-Élysées–Clemenceau.*

❷ **Palais de Justice** (Law Courts). In about 1860 the city law courts were built by Baron Haussmann in his characteristically weighty Neoclassical style. You can wander around the buildings, watch the bustle of the lawyers, or attend a court hearing. But the real interest here is the medieval part of the complex, spared by Haussmann: La Conciergerie and Sainte-Chapelle. ✉ *Bd. du Palais, Ile de la Cité. Métro: Cité.*

⓬ **Place de la Concorde.** This majestic square at the foot of the Champs-Élysées was laid out in the 1770s, but there was nothing in the way of peace or concord about its early years. Between 1793 and 1795 more than a thousand victims, including Louis XVI and Marie-Antoinette, were sent into oblivion at the guillotine, prompting Madame Roland's famous cry, "Liberty, what crimes are committed in thy name." The top of the 107-ft **Obelisk**—a present from the viceroy of Egypt in 1833—was regilded in 1998. *Métro: Concorde.*

❺ **Place Dauphine.** The Surrealists loved place Dauphine, which they called "*le sexe de Paris*" because of its location—at the far-western end of the Ile de la Cité—and suggestive V-shape. Its origins were much more proper: built by Henri IV, it was named in homage to his successor, the dauphin, who grew up to become Louis XIII. The triangular square is lined with some charming 17th-century houses that the writer André Maurois felt represented the very quintessence of Paris and France. Take a seat on a park bench, enjoy a picnic, and see if you agree. *Métro: Cité.*

⓯ **Pont Alexandre-III** (Alexander III Bridge). No other bridge over the Seine epitomizes the fin-de-siècle frivolity of the Belle Epoque (or Paris itself) like the exuberant, bronze-lamp-lined Pont Alexandre-III. An urban masterstroke that seems as much created of cake frosting and sugar sculptures as stone and iron, it was built, like the Grand and Petit Palais nearby, for the 1900 world's fair and inaugurated by the ill-fated czar Nicholas II, and ingratiatingly named in honor of his father. *Métro: Invalides.*

❼ **Pont Neuf** (New Bridge). Crossing the Ile de la Cité, just behind square du Vert-Galant, is the oldest bridge in Paris, confusingly called the New Bridge, or Pont Neuf. It was completed in 1607 and was the first bridge in the city to be built without houses lining either side. *Métro: Pont-Neuf.*

★ ❸ **Sainte-Chapelle** (Holy Chapel). Not to be missed and one of the most magical sights in European medieval art, this chapel was built by Louis IX (1226–70; later canonized as St. Louis) in the 1240s to house what he believed to be Christ's Crown of Thorns, purchased from Emperor Baldwin of Constantinople. A dark lower chapel is a gloomy prelude to the shimmering upper one, whose walls consist of little else but dazzling 13th-century stained glass. Think of it as an enormous magic lantern, illuminating 1,130 figures from the Bible, to create—as one writer put it—"the most marvelous colored and moving air ever held within four walls." ✉ *4 bd. du Palais, Ile de la Cité,* ☎ *01–43–54–30–09 for concert information,* WEB *www.monum.fr.* 🎫 *€5.50; joint ticket with Conciergerie €7.60.* ⏲ *Apr.–Sept., daily 9:30–6:30; Oct.–Mar., daily 10–5. Métro: Cité.*

Paris

Arc de Triomphe . . . **22**
Archives Nationales **59**
Atelier Brancusi **56**
Atelier Delacroix . . . **79**
Bateaux Mouches . . . **20**
Bois de Boulogne **24**
Bourse **45**
Bourse du Commerce **34**
Carrousel du Louvre **9**
Centre Pompidou . . . **55**
Champs–Élysées **21**
Cimetière du Père–Lachaise **49**
Comédie Française **31**
Conciergerie **4**
Cour du Commerce St-André **82**
La Défense **23**
École Nationale des Beaux-Arts **80**
Église de La Madeleine **26**
Forum des Halles . . . **36**
Grand Palais **13**
Hôtel Drouot **44**
Hôtel des Invalides . . **74**
Hôtel de Lauzun **66**
Hôtel de Sully **52**
Ile St-Louis **65**
Institut de France . . . **81**
Institut du Monde Arabe **71**
Jardin du Luxembourg **83**
Jardin des Tuileries . . **10**
Louvre **8**
Louvre des Antiquaires **30**
Musée d'Art et d'Histoire du Judaïsme **57**
Musée d'Art Moderne de la Ville de Paris **19**
Musée Bricard **60**
Musée Carnavalet **63**
Musée Cernuschi . . . **39**
Musée de la Chasse et de la Nature **58**
Musée Cognacq-Jay **62**
Musée Guimet **18**
Musée Jacquemart–André **41**
Musée du Jeu de Paume **11**
Musée Maillol **76**
Musée National du Moyen-Age **68**
Musée Nissim de Camondo **40**
Musée d'Orsay **72**
Musée Picasso **61**
Musée Rodin **75**

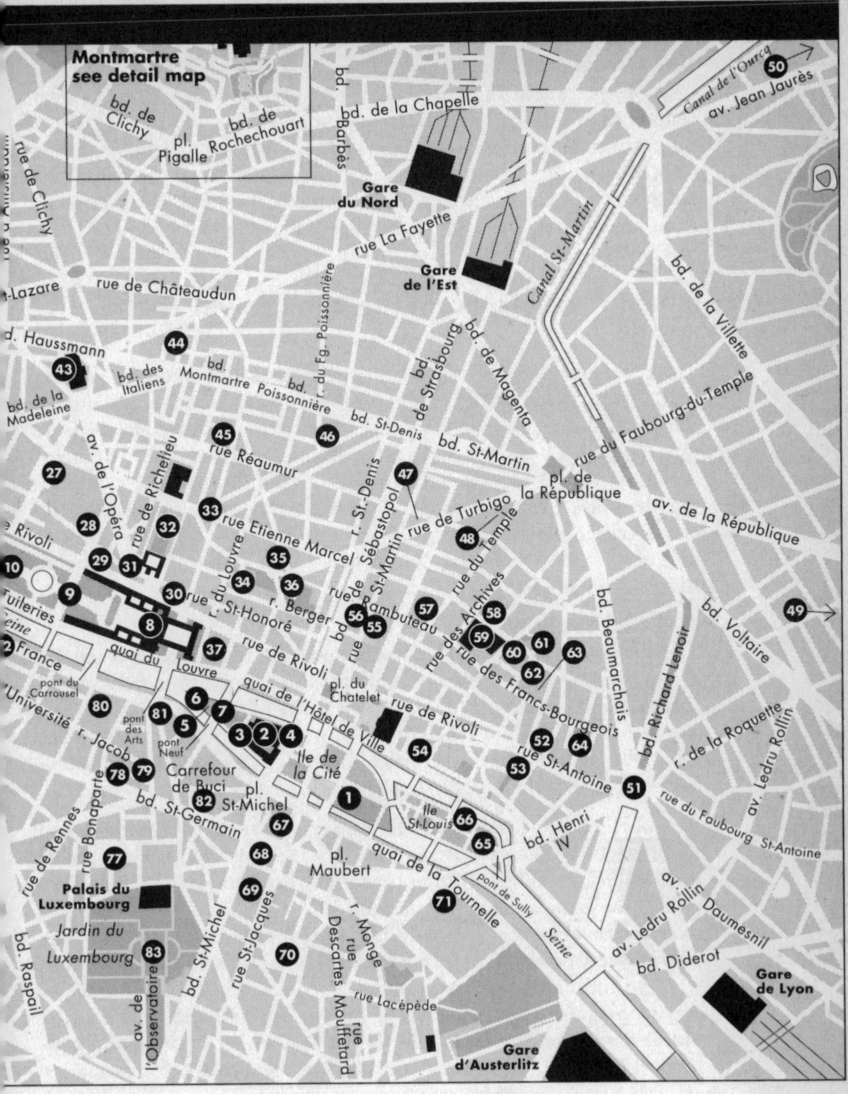

Notre-Dame 1
Notre-Dame de Bonne-Nouvelle 46
Opéra Garnier 43
Palais Bourbon 73
Palais de Chaillot . . . 17
Palais de la Découverte 14
Palais de Justice 2
Palais de l'Élysée . . . 25
Palais-Royal 32
Panthéon 70
Parc Monceau 38
Parc de La Villette . . . 50
Place de la Bastille 51
Place de la Concorde 12
Place Dauphine 5
Place Vendôme 27
Place des Victoires 33
Place des Vosges . . . 64
Pont Alexandre-III . . . 15
Pont Neuf 7
Sainte-Chapelle 3
Square du Vert-Galant 6
St-Augustin 42
Ste-Élisabeth 48
St-Eustache 35
St-Germain-des-Prés 78
St-Germain l'Auxerrois 37
St-Gervais—St-Protais 54
St-Nicolas des Champs 47
St-Paul—St-Louis 53
St-Roch 28
St-Séverin 67
St-Sulpice 77
Sorbonne 69
Tour Eiffel (Eiffel Tower) 16
Union Centrale des Artes Décoratifs 29

❻ **Square du Vert-Galant.** The equestrian statue of the Vert-Galant himself—amorous adventurer Henri IV—surveys this leafy square at the western end of the Ile de la Cité. Henri, king of France from 1589 until his assassination in 1610, is probably best remembered for his cynical remark that *"Paris vaut bien une messe"* ("Paris is worth a mass"), a reference to his readiness to renounce Protestantism to gain the throne of predominantly Catholic France. A fine spot to linger on a sunny afternoon, the square is also the departure point for the glass-top *vedettes* (tour boats) on the Seine (at the bottom of the steps to the right). *Métro: Pont-Neuf.*

Monuments and Marvels: From the Eiffel Tower to the Arc de Triomphe

The Eiffel Tower lords it over southwest Paris, and wherever you are on this walk, you can see it looming ahead. Water is the second theme: fountains playing beneath place du Trocadéro and tours along the Seine on a Bateau Mouche. Museums are the third: the area around Trocadéro is full of them. And style is the fourth, but not just because the buildings here are overwhelmingly elegant—but because this is also the center of haute couture, with the top names in world fashion all congregated around avenue Montaigne, only a brief walk from the Champs-Élysées, to the north.

A Good Walk

The verdant expanse of the Champ de Mars, once used as a parade ground by the École Militaire (still in use as a military academy and therefore not open to the public), then as site of the world exhibitions, provides a thrilling approach to the iron symbol of Paris, the **Tour Eiffel** ⑯. As you get nearer, the Eiffel Tower's colossal bulk (it's far bigger and sturdier than pictures suggest) becomes increasingly evident.

Across the Seine from the Eiffel Tower, above stylish gardens and fountains on the heights of place du Trocadéro, is the Art Deco **Palais de Chaillot** ⑰, a cultural center containing three museums: an anthropology museum, a maritime museum, and a museum of French architecture. The area around place du Trocadéro is a feast for museum lovers. The **Musée Guimet** ⑱, on place d'Iéna, contains three floors of Indo-Chinese and Far Eastern art that were reopened in 2001 after extensive renovation. Farther down the avenue du Président-Wilson is the **Musée d'Art Moderne de la Ville de Paris** ⑲, which has temporary exhibits as well as a permanent collection of modern art.

Continue down to bustling place de l'Alma, where a giant golden torch appears to be saluting the memory of Diana, Princess of Wales, who died in a car crash in the tunnel below in 1997. Down the sloping side road just beyond the Pont de l'Alma (Alma Bridge) is the embarkation point of the **Bateaux Mouches** ⑳ and their tours of Paris by water. Stylish avenue Montaigne, lined with some of the leading Paris fashion houses, runs up from place de l'Alma toward the **Champs-Élysées** ㉑. Local charm is not a feature of this sector of western Paris, though renovation has gone some way toward restoring the avenue's legendary elegance, particularly as you head up the grand promenade to that icon of Paris, the **Arc de Triomphe** ㉒. Through the arch to the west lies the city's own Manhattan-on-the-Seine—the skyscraper complex of **La Défense** ㉓. For a more tranquil respite, head southwest from the Arc down Avenue Foch—one of Paris's most fashionable addresses—to the sylvan glades of Paris's largest park, the **Bois de Boulogne** ㉔.

TIMING

You can probably cover this walk in a couple of hours, but if you wish to ascend the Eiffel Tower, take a trip along the Seine, or visit any of the myriad museums along the way, you'd be best off allowing most of the day.

Sights to See

★ 22 **Arc de Triomphe.** This huge arch, standing 164 ft high, was planned by Napoléon but not finished until 1836, 20 years after the end of his rule. It is decorated with some magnificent sculptures by François Rude, such as the *Departure of the Volunteers,* better known as *La Marseillaise,* to the right of the arch when viewed from the Champs-Élysées. A small museum halfway up the arch is devoted to its history. France's Unknown Soldier is buried beneath the archway; the flame is rekindled every evening at 6:30. ✉ *Pl. Charles-de-Gaulle, Champs-Élysées,* ☎ *01–55–37–73–77,* WEB *www.monum.fr.* €7. ⏲ *Spring–autumn, daily 9:30 AM–11 PM; winter, daily 10 AM–10:30 PM. Métro, RER: Charles-de-Gaulle–Étoile.*

20 **Bateaux Mouches.** These popular motorboats set off on their hour-long tours of Paris waters regularly (every half hour in summer). ✉ *Pl. de l'Alma, Trocadéro/Eiffel Tower,* ☎ *01–40–76–99–99,* WEB *www.bateaux-mouches.fr.* €7. *Métro: Alma-Marceau.*

24 **Bois de Boulogne.** Class and style have been associated with this 2,200-acre wood—known to Parisians as simply *Le Bois*—ever since it was landscaped into an upper-class playground by Baron Haussmann in the 1850s. Today the park is a happy escape for rowers, joggers, strollers, riders, and picnickers. Crowds head here for the racetracks of **Longchamp** and **Auteuil,** along with the **Roland Garros** stadium (where the French Open tennis tournament is held in late May). After dark, ladies of the night festoon some sections. *Main entrance at bottom of av. Foch, Bois de Boulogne. Métro: Porte Maillot, Porte Dauphine, Porte d'Auteuil; Bus 244.*

21 **Champs-Élysées.** The 2-km (1-mi) Champs-Élysées was originally laid out in the 1660s by landscape gardener André Le Nôtre as parkland sweeping away from the Tuileries. In an attempt to reestablish this thoroughfare as one of the world's most beautiful avenues, the city has planted extra trees, broadened sidewalks, refurbished Art Nouveau newsstands, and clamped down on garish storefronts. Site of most French national celebrations, the Champs-Élysées is the last leg of the Tour de France bicycle race, on the third or fourth Sunday in July, and the site of vast ceremonies on Bastille Day (July 14) and Armistice Day (November 11). *Métro: George-V, Champs-Élysées–Clemenceau, Franklin-D.-Roosevelt.*

23 **La Défense.** This is the skyscraper district of Paris, just west of the city (thankfully), across the Seine from Neuilly. Crowning the main plaza is the **Grande Arche de La Défense,** an enormous open cube of a building where tubular glass elevators whisk you 360 ft to the top. ✉ *Parvis de La Défense, La Défense,* ☎ *01–49–07–27–57.* €7. ⏲ *Daily 10–7. Métro, RER: Grande Arche de La Défense.*

19 **Musée d'Art Moderne de la Ville de Paris** (City Museum of Modern Art). Both temporary exhibits and a permanent collection of top-quality 20th-century art can be found at this museum. It takes over, chronologically speaking, where the Musée d'Orsay leaves off: Among the earliest works are Fauve paintings by Vlaminck and Derain, followed by Picasso's early experiments in Cubism. ✉ *11 av. du Président-Wilson, Trocadéro/Eiffel Tower,* ☎ *01–53–67–40–00.* *Free.* ⏲ *Tues.–Fri. 10–5:30, weekends 10–6:45. Métro: Iéna.*

18 **Musée Guimet.** This museum was founded by Lyonnais industrialist Émile Guimet, who traveled around the world in the late 19th century amassing Indo-Chinese and Far Eastern objets d'art, plus a fabled collection of Cambodian art. After a massive renovation, the museum reopened in 2001. ✉ *6 pl. d'Iéna, Trocadéro/Eiffel Tower,* ☎ *01–56–52–53–00,* WEB *www.museeguimet.fr.* 🎫 *€5.50.* ⏲ *Wed.–Mon. 9:45–6. Métro: Iéna.*

17 **Palais de Chaillot** (Chaillot Palace). This honey-color, Art Deco culture center facing the Seine, perched atop tumbling gardens with sculpture and fountains, was built in the 1930s and houses three museums: the **Musée de l'Homme** (Museum of Mankind) with an array of prehistoric artifacts; the **Musée de la Marine** (Maritime Museum), with its salty collection of model ships, marine paintings, and naval paraphernalia; and the **Musée des Monuments Français** (Museum of French Monuments), closed for renovation until sometime in 2003. ✉ *Pl. du Trocadéro, Trocadéro/Eiffel Tower,* ☎ *01–44–05–72–72 Museum of Mankind; 01–53–65–69–69 Maritime Museum,* WEB *www.mnhn.fr.* 🎫 *Museum of Mankind €4.60; Maritime Museum €6.* ⏲ *Museum of Mankind Wed.–Mon. 9:45–5:15; Maritime Museum Wed.–Mon. 10–6. Métro: Trocadéro.*

★ 16 **Tour Eiffel** (Eiffel Tower). Known to the French as La Tour Eiffel (pronounced ef-*el*), Paris's most famous landmark was built by Gustave Eiffel for the World Exhibition of 1889, the centennial of the French Revolution, and was still in good shape to celebrate its own 100th birthday. Such was Eiffel's engineering wizardry that even in the strongest winds his tower never sways more than 4½ inches. Since its colossal bulk exudes a feeling of mighty permanence, you may have trouble believing that it nearly became 7,000 tons of scrap iron when its concession expired in 1909. At first many Parisians hated the structure, and only its potential use as a radio antenna saved the day (it still bristles with a forest of radio and television transmitters). Today it is the beloved symbol of Paris. If you're full of energy, stride up the stairs as far as the third deck. If you want to go to the top, you'll have to take the elevator. The shimmering nocturnal illumination, installed for the millennium celebrations at the start of 2000, is breathtaking—every girder highlighted in glorious detail. Installed atop the tower is a powerful, revolving light that sends a beam across the Paris sky, turning the Tour Eiffel into a giant lighthouse. ✉ *Quai Branly, Trocadéro/Eiffel Tower,* ☎ *01–44–11–23–23,* WEB *www.tour-eiffel.fr.* 🎫 *By elevator: 2nd floor, €3.70; 3rd floor, €6.90; 4th floor, €9.90. On foot: 2nd and 3rd floors only, €3.05.* ⏲ *July–Aug., daily 9 AM–midnight; Sept.–June, daily 9 AM–11 PM. Métro: Bir-Hakeim; RER: Champ-de-Mars.*

Le Style, C'est Paris: The Faubourg St-Honoré

The Faubourg St-Honoré, north of the Champs-Élysées and the Tuileries, is synonymous with style—as you will see as you progress from the President's Palace, past a wealth of art galleries, to the monumental Madeleine church and on to stately place Vendôme; on this ritzy square, famous boutiques sit side by side with famous banks—but then elegance and finance have never been an unusual combination. Famous dressmakers, renowned jewelers, exclusive perfume shops, and the Hôtel Ritz made this *faubourg* (district) a symbol of luxury throughout the world. Leading names in modern fashion are found farther east on place des Victoires, close to what was for centuries the gastronomic heart of Paris: Les Halles (pronounced lay-*al*), once the city's main market. In 1969 Les Halles was closed and replaced by a park and a modern shopping mall, the Forum des Halles. The brash modernity of the

Forum stands in contrast to the august church of St-Eustache nearby. Similarly, the incongruous black-and-white columns, an in-situ artwork created by Minimalist artist Daniel Buren in the 1980s, in the classical courtyard of Richelieu's neighboring Palais-Royal present a further case of daring modernity—or architectural vandalism, depending on your point of view.

A Good Walk

Start in front of the most important home in France: the **Palais de l'Élysée** ㉕, or Presidential Palace. Crash barriers and gold-braided guards keep visitors at bay; in fact, there's more to see in the plethora of art galleries and luxury fashion boutiques lining rue du Faubourg–St-Honoré as you head east. Pass the British Embassy and turn left onto rue Boissy-d'Anglas; then cut right through an archway into Village Royal, a restored courtyard with several trendy boutiques. It leads to rue Royale, a classy street lined with jewelry stores. Looming to the left is the **Église de la Madeleine** ㉖, a sturdy Neoclassical edifice.

Take boulevard de la Madeleine, to the right as you face the church, then the first right down rue Duphot to Notre-Dame de l'Assomption, noted for its huge dome and solemn interior. Continue left on rue St-Honoré to rue de Castiglione and then head left to **place Vendôme** ㉗, one of the world's most soigné squares. Return to rue St-Honoré and follow it to the mighty church of **St-Roch** ㉘.

Take the next right onto rue des Pyramides and cross the place des Pyramides, with its gilded statue of Joan of Arc on horseback, to the northwest wing of the Louvre, site of the **Union Centrale des Arts Décoratifs** ㉙, with three separate museums dedicated to fashion, publicity, and the decorative arts. Stay on arcaded rue de Rivoli to the place du Palais-Royal. On the far side of the square is the **Louvre des Antiquaires** ㉚, a chic shopping mall housing upscale antiques stores. Just beyond Jean-Michel Othaniel's aluminum and psychedelic glass entrance canopy to the Palais-Royal Métro station, erected in 2000, is the **Comédie Française** ㉛, the time-honored house for performances of classical French drama. To the right of the theater is the unobtrusive entrance to the **Palais-Royal** ㉜; its courtyard is an unexpected oasis in the heart of the city. Cross through the Palais-Royal gardens and turn right into rue des Petits-Champs to reach circular **place des Victoires** ㉝: that's Louis XIV riding the plunging steed in the center of the square. Head south down rue Croix-des-Petits-Champs, past the nondescript Banque de France on your right, and take the second street on the left to the circular **Bourse du Commerce** ㉞, or Commercial Exchange. Alongside it is the 100-ft-high fluted Colonne de Ruggieri.

You don't need to scale Ruggieri's column to spot the bulky outline of the church of **St-Eustache** ㉟, a curious architectural hybrid of Gothic and Classical. The vast site next to St-Eustache is now occupied by a garden, the Jardin des Halles, and the modern **Forum des Halles** ㊱ shopping mall. Rue Berger leads from allée de St-Jean-de-Perse to the Square des Innocents, with its handsome Renaissance fountain. Head south along rue St-Denis from the far end of Square des Innocents to place du Châtelet, with its theaters, fountain, and the Tour St-Jacques, the tower looming up to your left. Turn right along the Seine to reach **St-Germain l'Auxerrois** ㊲, opposite the Louvre, once the French royal family's parish church.

TIMING

With brief visits to churches and monuments, this walk should take from three to four hours. On a nice day you may want to linger in the gardens of the Palais-Royal, and on a cold day you may want to indulge in an unbelievably thick hot chocolate at the Angélina tearoom.

Sights to See

34 **Bourse du Commerce** (Commercial Exchange). The 18th-century circular, shallow-dome Commercial Exchange, near Les Halles, began life as a corn exchange; Victor Hugo waggishly likened it to a jockey's cap without the peak. ✉ *Rue de Viarmes, Beaubourg/Les Halles. Métro or RER: Les Halles.*

31 **Comédie Française.** This theater is the most celebrated venue for performances of classical French drama. The building itself dates from 1790, but the Comédie Française company was created by that most theatrical of French monarchs, Louis XIV, back in 1680. If you understand French and have a taste for the mannered, declamatory style of French acting—it's a far cry from method acting—you'll appreciate an evening here. ✉ *Pl. Colette, Louvre/Tuileries,* ☎ *01–44–58–15–15. Métro: Palais-Royal.*

26 **Église de La Madeleine** (Church of La Madeleine). With its rows of uncompromising columns, this sturdy Neoclassical edifice—designed in 1814 but not consecrated until 1842—looks more like a Greek temple than a Christian church. In fact, La Madeleine, as it is known, was nearly selected as Paris's first train station (the site of the Gare St-Lazare, just up the road, was chosen instead). Inside, the walls are richly and harmoniously decorated; gold glints through the murk. The portico's majestic Corinthian colonnade supports a gigantic pediment with a frieze of the Last Judgment. ✉ *Pl. de la Madeleine, Opéra/Grands Boulevards.* ⏲ *Mon.–Sat. 7:30–7, Sun. 8–7. Métro: Madeleine.*

36 **Forum des Halles.** Les Halles, the iron-and-glass halls that made up the central Paris food market, were closed in 1969 and replaced in the late '70s by the Forum des Halles, a mundane shopping mall. Nothing remains of either the market or the rambunctious atmosphere that led 19th-century novelist Émile Zola to dub Les Halles *le ventre de Paris* ("the belly of Paris"), although rue Montorgueil, behind St-Eustache, retains something of its original bustle. For really stylish shopping, wend your way northeast several blocks to rue Dussoubs and rue St-Denis to the 19th-century covered gallery the **Passage du Grand-Cerf,** filled with crafts shops offering innovative selections of jewelry, paintings, and ceramics. ✉ *Main entrance on rue Pierre-Lescot, Beaubourg/Les Halles. Métro: Les Halles; RER: Châtelet–Les Halles.*

NEED A BREAK?

Founded in 1903, **Angélina** (✉ 226 rue de Rivoli, Louvre/Tuileries, ☎ 01–42–60–82–00) is an elegant *salon de thé* (tearoom) famous for its *chocolat africain,* a jug of hot chocolate served with whipped cream (irresistible even in summer).

30 **Louvre des Antiquaires.** This "shopping mall" of superelegant antiques dealers, off place du Palais-Royal opposite the Louvre, is a minimuseum in itself. Its stylish glass-walled corridors—lined with Louis XVI *boiseries* (antique wood paneling), Charles Dix bureaus, and the pretty sort of bibelots that would have gladdened the heart of Marie-Antoinette—deserve a browse whether you intend to buy or not. Don't wear your flip-flops in here. ✉ *Main entrance: Pl. du Palais-Royal, Louvre/Tuileries.* ⏲ *Tues.–Sun. 11–7. Métro: Palais-Royal.*

25 **Palais de l'Élysée** (Élysée Palace). Madame de Pompadour, Napoléon, Joséphine, the Duke of Wellington, and Queen Victoria all stayed at this "palace," today the official home of the French president. It was originally constructed as a private mansion in 1718 and has housed

presidents only since 1873. You can catch a glimpse of the palace forecourt and facade through the Faubourg St-Honoré gateway. ✉ *55 rue du Faubourg St-Honoré, Champs-Élysées.* ⏲ *Not open to public. Métro: Miromesnil.*

32 **Palais-Royal** (Royal Palace). One of the most Parisian sights in all of Paris, the Palais-Royal is especially loved for its gardens, where children play, lovers whisper, and senior citizens crumble bread for the sparrows, seemingly oblivious to the ghosts of history that haunt this place. The buildings of this former palace—royal only in that all-powerful Cardinal Richelieu (1585–1642) magnanimously bequeathed them to Louis XIII—date from the 1630s. In front of one of its shop fronts Camille Desmoulins gave the first speech calling for the French Revolution in 1789. Today the Palais-Royal is occupied by the French Ministry of Culture and private apartments (Colette and Cocteau were two lucky former owners), and its buildings are not open to the public. You can, however, visit its colonnaded courtyard and classical gardens, a tranquil oasis prized by Parisians. Around the exterior of the complex are famous arcades—notably the Galerie Valois—whose elegant shops have been attracting customers since the days when Thomas Jefferson used to come here for some retail therapy. ✉ *Pl. du Palais-Royal, Louvre/Tuileries. Métro: Palais-Royal.*

27 **Place Vendôme.** Snobbish and self-important, this famous square is also gorgeous; property laws have kept away cafés and other such banal establishments, leaving the plaza stately and refined, the perfect home for the rich and famous (Chopin lived and died at No. 12; today's celebs camp out at the Hôtel Ritz, while a lucky few, including the family of the sultan of Brunei, actually own houses here). Mansart's rhythmic, perfectly proportioned example of 17th-century urban architecture still shines in all its golden-stone splendor. Napoléon had the square's central column made from the melted bronze of 1,200 cannons captured at the Battle of Austerlitz in 1805. There he is, perched vigilantly at the top. If you're feeling properly soigné, repair to Hemingway's Bar at the Hôtel Ritz and raise a glass to "Papa" (☞ Close-Up Box, "Hemingway's Paris," below). *Métro: Opéra.*

33 **Place des Victoires.** This circular square, now home to many of the city's top fashion boutiques, was laid out in 1685 by Jules Hardouin-Mansart in honor of the military victories (*victoires*) of Louis XIV. The Sun King gallops along on a bronze horse in the center. *Métro: Sentier.*

35 **St-Eustache.** This huge church was built as the people's Right Bank reply to Notre-Dame, though St-Eustache dates from a couple of hundred years later. The church is a curious architectural hybrid: with the exception of the feeble west front, added between 1754 and 1788, construction lasted from 1532 to 1637, spanning the decline of the Gothic style and the emergence of the Renaissance. ✉ *2 rue du Jour, Beaubourg/Les Halles,* ☎ *01–46–27–89–21 for concert information.* ⏲ *Daily 8–7. Métro: Les Halles; RER: Châtelet–Les Halles.*

37 **St-Germain l'Auxerrois.** Until 1789, St-Germain was used by the French royal family as its parish church, in the days when the adjacent Louvre was a palace rather than a museum. The facade reveals the influence of 15th-century Flamboyant Gothic style, although the fluted columns around the choir, the area surrounding the altar, demonstrate the triumph of Classicism. ✉ *Pl. du Louvre, Louvre/Tuileries. Métro: Louvre-Rivoli.*

28 **St-Roch.** Designed by Lemercier in 1653 but completed only in the 1730s, this huge church is almost as long as Notre-Dame (138 yards) thanks

Close-Up

HEMINGWAY'S PARIS

"THERE IS NEVER ANY ENDING to Paris," wrote Ernest Hemingway, the legendary author. For the "Lost Generation" after World War I, his aperçu rang particularly true. Disillusioned by America's Depression and Prohibition, lured by favorable exchange rates and a booming artistic scene, many American writers, composers, and painters moved to Paris in the 1920s and 1930s. Heading this impressive list—F. Scott Fitzgerald, Gertrude Stein, Ezra Pound, e. e. cummings, Janet Flanner, and John dos Passos are just a few of the famous figures—was "Papa," who came to epitomize the flamboyant lifestyle of Gertrude Stein's "Lost Generation." He used her phrase—itself an lament made by one French bartender to bemoan the years, and chances, lost to the world war—to preface *The Sun Also Rises,* but he may or may not have liked it. "The hell with her lost-generation talk and all the dirty, easy labels" he wrote elsewhere.

Hemingway arrived in Paris with his first wife, Hadley, in December 1921, and made for the Left Bank—the Hôtel Jacob et d'Angleterre, to be exact (still operating at 44 rue Jacob). To celebrate their arrival, the couple went to the Café de la Paix for a meal they nearly couldn't afford. In 1922 the couple moved to 74 rue du Cardinal-Lemoine (his writing studio was around the corner on the top floor of 39 rue Descartes), then in early 1924 the couple and their baby son settled at 113 rue Notre-Dame des Champs. Nearby, he settled in at La Closerie des Lilas café to write much of *The Sun Also Rises*. The Closerie was "the nearest good café we had"—around the corner from Hemingway's "old friend," the 1853 statue of Marshal Michel ("Mike") Ney. This proved for Heminway to be a time "when we were very young and very happy," as he wrote in *A Moveable Feast.*

Not happy long. In 1926 Hemingway left Hadley and next year wedded his mistress Pauline Pfeiffer across town at St-Honoré-d'Eylau, then moved to 6 rue Férou, near the Musée du Luxembourg, whose collection of Cézanne landscapes (now in the Musée d'Orsay) he revered. Hemingway once proclaimed that "unless you have geography, background, you have nothing." You can follow the steps of Jake and Bill in *The Sun Also Rises* as they "circle" the Ile St-Louis before the "steep walking . . . all the way up to the Place de la Contrescarpe," then right along rue du Pot-de-Fer to the "rigid north and south" of rue St-Jacques and on to boulevard du Montparnasse.

For gossip and books, Papa would visit Shakespeare & Co. at 12 rue de l'Odéon, owned by Sylvia Beach, an early buddy (the bookstore can now be found at 37 rue de la Bûcherie). Hemingway would later imply that his sallies across the Seine to the upmarket Right Bank reflected a need for upmarket cocktails, but the youthful Hemingway's first port of call was invariably the Guaranty Trust Company on 1 rue des Italiens, for money and mail. It was then on to, when flush, the bar of the Hôtel Crillon, or, when poor, either the Caves Mura, at 19 rue d'Antin, or Harry's Bar, still in brisk business at 5 rue Daunou. Hemingway's legendary association with the Hôtel Ritz, where he now has his own bar named for him, dates from the Liberation in 1944, when he strode in at the head of his platoon and "liberated" the joint by ordering 73 dry martinis. Here Hemingway asked Mary Welsh to become his fourth wife, and also righted the world with Jean-Paul Sartre, George Orwell, and Marlene Dietrich. It is only fitting that Paris—a city that loves naming streets after adopted sons—has given Papa a plaque of his own, heralding short Rue Ernest-Hemingway in the outer confines of the 15th arrondissement.

to Hardouin-Mansart's domed Lady Chapel at the far end. ✉ *Rue St-Honoré, Louvre/Tuileries. Métro: Tuileries.*

㉙ **Union Centrale des Arts Décoratifs** (Decorative Arts Center). A must for lovers of fashion and the decorative arts, this northwestern wing of the Louvre building houses three high-style museums: the **Musée de la Mode,** devoted to costumes and accessories dating from the 16th century to today; the **Musée des Arts Décoratifs,** with furniture, tapestries, glassware, paintings, and other necessities of life from the Middle Ages through Napoléon's time and beyond—a highlight here are the sumptuous period-style rooms; and the **Musée de la Publicité,** with temporary exhibits of advertisements and posters. ✉ *107 rue de Rivoli, Louvre/Tuileries,* ☎ *01–44–55–57–50,* WEB *www.ucad.fr.* 🎫 *€5.35.* ⏲ *Tues.–Sun. 11–6. Métro: Palais-Royal.*

Urban Kaleidoscope: The Grand Boulevards

The French have a word for it: *flâner*—to stroll, promenade, dawdle. Back in the 19th century, the Parisian made this a newly fashionable activity, thanks to the magisterial boulevards Baron Haussmann—the regional prefect who oversaw the reconstruction of the city in the 1850s and 1860s—had designed and laid out. The focal point of this walk is the uninterrupted avenue that runs in almost a straight line from St-Augustin, the city's grandest Second Empire church, to place de la République, whose very name symbolizes the ultimate downfall of the imperial regime. The avenue's name changes six times along the way, which is why Parisians refer to it as the *Grands Boulevards* (plural). The makeup of the neighborhoods along the Grand Boulevards changes steadily as you head east from the posh 8ᵉ arrondissement toward working-class east Paris. The *grands magasins* (department stores) at the start of the walk epitomize upscale Paris shopping and stand on boulevard Haussmann. The opulent Opéra Garnier, just past the grands magasins, is the architectural showpiece of the period (often termed *Second Empire* and corresponding to the rule of Napoléon III). While the hurly-burly traffic and neon signs of today have done much to dampen the charm of the grands boulevards, look hard and you can still spot aspects of street life that once inspired dozens of Impressionist paintings.

A Good Walk

Take the métro to Monceau and step through gilt-top iron gates to enter the enchantingly idyllic **Parc Monceau** ㊳ by the domed Chartres Pavilion. At the middle of the park, head left to avenue Velasquez—lined by some of the most regal mansions in the city—past the **Musée Cernuschi** ㊴, with its distinguished collection of Chinese art from Neolithic pottery to contemporary paintings, to boulevard Malesherbes. Turn right on boulevard Malesherbes and right again on rue de Monceau to reach the **Musée Nissim de Camondo** ㊵, whose aristocratic interior reflects the upscale tone of this haughty part of Paris. More splendor awaits at the **Musée Jacquemart-André** ㊶, a grand 19th-century residence stuffed with antiques and Old Master paintings, which you can find by continuing down rue de Monceau and turning left onto rue de Courcelles, then left again onto boulevard Haussmann.

Continue eastward along the boulevard and cross the square to find the innovative iron-and-stone church of **St-Augustin** ㊷. Cross the square in front and turn left along boulevard Haussmann to Square Louis-XVI, the original burial spot of Louis XVI and Marie-Antoinette—a mausoleum in their honor stands here now. Some 300 yards farther down boulevard Haussmann you'll find the grands magasins, Paris's most renowned department stores. First come the cupolas of Au Printemps, then Galeries Lafayette. Opposite looms the massive bulk of the **Opéra Garnier** ㊸, the most sumptuous theater in the world.

Boulevard des Capucines, lined with cinemas and restaurants, heads east from in front of the Opera, becoming boulevard des Italiens before colliding with boulevard Haussmann. A left here down rue Drouot will take you to the **Hôtel Drouot** ㊹, Paris's central auction house. Rue Rossini leads from Drouot to rue de la Grange-Batelière. Halfway along on the right is the Passage Jouffroy, one of the many covered galleries that honeycomb the center of Paris. Head down to boulevard Montmartre and cross to passage des Panoramas, leading to rue St-Marc. Turn right, then left down rue Vivienne to find the foursquare, colonnaded **Bourse** ㊺, the Paris Stock Exchange.

Head east along rue Réaumur, once the heart of the French newspaper industry—stationery shops still abound—and cross rue Montmartre. Take the second left up rue de Cléry, a narrow street that is the exclusive domain of fabric wholesalers. Continue up rue de Cléry as far as rue des Degrés—not a street at all but a 14-step stairway—then look for the crooked church tower of **Notre-Dame de Bonne-Nouvelle** ㊻, hemmed in by rickety housing. The porticoed entrance is around the corner on rue de la Lune, which leads back to the Grand Boulevards, by now going under the name of boulevard de Bonne-Nouvelle.

The Porte St-Denis, a triumphal arch, looms up ahead, and a little farther on is the smaller but similar Porte St-Martin. From here take rue St-Martin south past the Musée des Arts et Métiers, a technology museum housed partly in the former church of St-Martin. Then cross rue Réaumur to the high, narrow, late-Gothic church of **St-Nicolas des Champs** ㊼. Head left on rue de Turbigo, past the cloister ruins and Renaissance gateway that embellish the far side of St-Nicolas. Some 400 yards along on the right is the Baroque church of **Ste-Élisabeth** ㊽; shortly after, you'll reach place de la République. It's a short métro ride from here to either the city's most famous cemetery, the **Cimetière du Père-Lachaise** ㊾, or to the **Parc de La Villette** ㊿, with its postmodern science and music museums.

TIMING

The distance between Parc Monceau and place de la République is almost 6 km (4 mi), which will probably take you four hours to walk, including coffee breaks and window-shopping. Allot a few additional hours, if not a whole morning or afternoon, to visit the Père Lachaise Cemetery or the Parc de La Villette. Or return to these on another day.

Sights to See

㊺ **Bourse** (Stock Exchange). The Paris Stock Exchange, a serene, colonnaded 19th-century building, is a far cry from Wall Street. Take your passport if you want to tour it. ✉ *Rue Vivienne, Opéra/Grands Boulevards.* *€4.60.* ⏲ *Guided tours only (in French), weekdays every ½ hr 1:15–3:45. Métro: Bourse.*

㊾ **Cimetière du Père-Lachaise** (Père-Lachaise Cemetery). Cemeteries may not be your idea of the ultimate attraction, but this is the largest and most interesting in Paris. It forms a veritable necropolis, with cobbled avenues and tombs competing in pomposity and originality. Leading incumbents include Jim Morrison, Frédéric Chopin, Marcel Proust, Edith Piaf, and Gertrude Stein. Get a map at the entrance and track them down. ✉ *Entrances on rue des Rondeaux, bd. de Ménilmontant, rue de la Réunion, Père-Lachaise.* ⏲ *Apr.–Sept., daily 8–6; Oct.–Mar., daily 8–5. Métro: Gambetta, Philippe-Auguste, Père-Lachaise.*

44 **Hôtel Drouot.** Paris's central auction house has everything from stamps and toy soldiers to Renoirs and 18th-century commodes. The 16 salesrooms make for fascinating browsing, and there's no obligation to bid. In the next few years, however, chances are the real action will move to the new Parisian venues of Sotheby's and Christie's. ✉ *9 rue Drouot, Opéra/Grands Boulevards,* ☎ *01–48–00–20–00,* WEB *www.gazette-drouot.com.* ⊙ *Mid-Sept.–mid-July, viewings Mon.–Sat. 11–noon and 2–6, with auctions starting at 2. Métro: Richelieu-Drouot.*

39 **Musée Cernuschi.** The collection includes Chinese art from Neolithic pottery (3rd century BC) to funeral statuary, painted 8th-century silks, and contemporary paintings, as well as ancient Persian bronze objects. The museum is closed for renovation through 2004. ✉ *7 av. Velasquez, Parc Monceau,* ☎ *01–45–63–50–75,* WEB *www.paris-france.org/musees.* 🎫 *Free.* ⊙ *Tues.–Sun. 10–5:40. Métro: Monceau.*

★ 41 **Musée Jacquemart-André.** Sometimes compared to New York City's Frick Collection, this was one of the grandest private residences of 19th-century Paris. Built between 1869 and 1875, it found Hollywood fame when used as Gaston Lachaille's mansion in the 1958 musical *Gigi.* Edouard André and his painter-wife, Nélie Jacquemart, the house's actual owners, were very cultured, so art from the Italian Renaissance and 18th-century France compete for attention here. Top works include Uccello's *St. George Slaying the Dragon* and Rembrandt's *Pilgrims of Emmaus.* ✉ *158 bd. Haussmann, Parc Monceau,* ☎ *01–42–89–04–91,* WEB *www.musee-jacquemart-andre.com.* 🎫 *€8.* ⊙ *Daily 10–6. Métro: St-Philippe-du-Roule.*

★ 40 **Musée Nissim de Camondo.** The elegant decadence of the last days of the ancien régime is fully reflected in the lavish interior of this aristocratic Parisian mansion. Built in the style of Louis XVI by the super-rich Camondo family in the late 19th century, it was then furnished with the choicest pieces of Louis Quinze and Louis Seize furniture, porcelain, and tapestries. Paris's most splendid mansion, this is a must-do if you are a connoisseur of the decorative arts. ✉ *63 rue de Monceau, Parc Monceau,* ☎ *01–53–89–06–50,* WEB *www.ucad.fr.* 🎫 *€4.60.* ⊙ *Wed.–Sun. 10–5. Métro: Villiers.*

46 **Notre-Dame de Bonne-Nouvelle.** This wide, soberly Neoclassical church, built in 1823–29, is tucked away off the Grand Boulevards. ✉ *Rue de la Lune, Opéra/Grands Boulevards. Métro: Bonne-Nouvelle.*

★ 43 **Opéra Garnier.** Haunt of *Phantom of the Opera,* setting for Degas's famous ballet paintings, and still the most opulent theater in the world, the Paris Opéra was begun in 1862 by Charles Garnier at the behest of Napoléon III. But it was not completed until 1875, five years after the emperor's abdication. Awash with Algerian colored marbles and gilt putti, it is said to typify Second Empire architecture: a pompous hodgepodge of styles with about as much subtlety as a Wagnerian cymbal crash. The composer Debussy famously compared it to a Turkish bathhouse, but lovers of pomp and splendor will adore it. To see the theater and lobby, you don't actually have to attend a performance: after paying an entry fee, you can stroll around at leisure and view the auditorium and the Grand Foyer, whose grandeur reminds everyone that this was a theater for Parisians who attended the opera primarily to see and be seen. The **Musée de l'Opéra,** containing a few paintings and theatrical mementos, is unremarkable. Although technically the official home of the Paris Ballet, this auditorium usually mounts one or two full-scale operas a season (although most operas are presented at the drearily modern Opéra de la Bastille). ✉ *Pl. de l'Opéra, Opéra/Grands Boulevards,*

☎ *01–40–01–22–63,* WEB *www.opera-de-paris.fr.* *€5, guided tours in English at 3* PM, *€9.20.* *Daily 10–5. Métro: Opéra.*

NEED A BREAK? Few cafés in Paris are grander than the Belle Epoque **Café de la Paix** (✉ 5 pl. de l'Opéra, Opéra/Grands Boulevards, ☎ 01–40–07–30–10).

38 **Parc Monceau.** The most picturesque gardens on the Right Bank were laid out as a private park in 1778 and retain some of the fanciful elements then in vogue, including mock ruins and a faux pyramid. ✉ *Entrances on bd. de Courcelles, av. Velasquez, av. Ruysdaël, av. van Dyck, Parc Monceau. Métro: Monceau.*

50 **Parc de La Villette.** Usually known simply as La Villette, this ambitiously landscaped, futuristic park has several attractions, including the **Cité de la Musique.** This giant postmodern musical academy also houses the **Musée de la Musique** (Museum of Musical Instruments). At the **Géode** cinema, which looks like a huge silver golf ball, films are shown on an enormous 180-degree curved screen. The science museum, the **Cité des Sciences et de l'Industrie,** contains dozens of interactive exhibits (though most displays are in French only). *Science Museum:* ✉ *30 av. Corentin-Cariou, La Villette,* ☎ *01–40–05–80–00,* WEB *www.cite-sciences.fr, www.cite-musique.fr.* *Museum of Musical Instruments €6.10; Science Museum €7.60.* *Museum of Musical Instruments Tues.–Sat. noon–6, Sun. 10–6; Science Museum Tues.–Sun. 10–6. Métro: Porte de La Villette, Porte de Pantin.*

42 **St-Augustin.** This domed church was dexterously constructed in the 1860s within the confines of an awkward V-shape site. It represented a breakthrough in ecclesiastical engineering because the use of metal pillars and girders obviated the need for exterior buttressing. ✉ *Pl. St-Augustin, Opéra/Grands Boulevards. Métro: St-Augustin.*

48 **Ste-Élisabeth.** This studied essay in Baroque (1628–46) has brightly restored wall paintings and a wide, semicircular apse around the choir. ✉ *Rue du Temple, République. Métro: Temple.*

47 **St-Nicolas des Champs.** The rounded arches and fluted Doric columns in the chancel of this church date from 1560 to 1587, a full century later than the pointed-arch nave (1420–80). ✉ *Rue St-Martin, Opéra/Grands Boulebards. Métro: Arts-et-Métiers.*

The Changing Face: The Marais and the Bastille

The Marais is one of the city's most historic and sought-after residential districts. Except for the architecturally whimsical Pompidou Center, the tone here is set by the gracious architecture of the 17th and 18th centuries (the Marais was spared the attentions of Haussmann, the man who rebuilt so much of Paris in the mid-19th century). Today most of the Marais's spectacular *hôtels particuliers*—loosely translated as "mansions," the onetime residences of aristocratic families—have been restored; many are now museums, including the noted Musée Picasso and Musée Carnavalet. There are trendy boutiques and cafés among the kosher shops in what used to be a predominantly Jewish neighborhood around rue des Rosiers, and there's an impressive Jewish Museum on nearby rue du Temple.

On the eastern edge of the Marais is place de la Bastille, site of the infamous prison stormed on July 14, 1789, an event that came to symbolize the beginning of the French Revolution. Largely in commemoration of the bicentennial of the Revolution, the Bastille area was renovated and became one of the trendiest sections of Paris.

Galleries, shops, theaters, cafés, restaurants, and bars now fill formerly decrepit buildings and alleys.

A Good Walk

Make your starting point **place de la Bastille** (51), easily accessible by the métro. Today the square is dominated by the Colonne de Juillet, the curving glass facade of the modern **Opéra de la Bastille.**

Walk down rue St-Antoine to the **Hôtel de Sully** (52), now housing the Caisse Nationale des Monuments Historiques (National Treasury of Historic Monuments), at No. 62. Cross the road and pause at the mighty Baroque church of **St-Paul–St-Louis** (53). Take the left-hand side door out of the church into narrow passage St-Paul; then turn right onto rue St-Paul, past the grid of courtyards that make up the Village St-Paul antiques-shops complex. Wend your way through the small streets to the quai de l'Hôtel-de-Ville.

Turn right on quai de l'Hôtel-de-Ville; *bouquinistes* (booksellers) line the Seine to your left. Pause by the Pont Louis-Philippe to admire the dome of the Panthéon floating above the skyline; then take the next right up picturesque rue des Barres to **St-Gervais–St-Protais** (54). Beyond the church stands the Hôtel de Ville, the city hall. From the Hôtel de Ville, cross rue de Rivoli and go up rue du Temple. On your right you'll pass one of the city's most popular department stores, the Bazar de l'Hôtel de Ville, or BHV, as it is known.

Take rue de la Verrerie, the first street on your left. Cross rue du Renard and take the second right past the ornate 16th-century church of St-Merri. Rue St-Martin, which is lined with stores, restaurants, and galleries, leads to the **Centre Pompidou** (55). In front of the Pompidou Center is the **Atelier Brancusi** (56), the reconstituted studio of sculptor Constantin Brancusi. The adjacent Square Igor-Stravinsky merits a stop for its unusual modern fountain.

Cross rue Beaubourg behind the Pompidou Center to rue Rambuteau, then take the first left onto rue du Temple. The stimulating **Musée d'Art et d'Histoire du Judaïsme** (57) opened in the Hôtel de St-Aignan, at No. 71, in 1998. Farther up the street, at No. 79, pause to admire the Hôtel de Montmor, a large-windowed Baroque mansion. Take a right onto rue des Haudriettes. Just to the left at the next corner is the **Musée de la Chasse et de la Nature** (58), the Museum of Hunting and Nature, housed in one of the Marais's most stately mansions. Head right on rue des Archives, crossing rue des Haudriettes, and admire the medieval gateway with two fairy-tale towers, now part of the **Archives Nationales** (59), the archives museum, entered from rue des Francs-Bourgeois around to the left.

Continue past the Crédit Municipal (the city's grandiose pawnbroking concern), the Dôme du Marais restaurant (housed in a circular 18th-century chamber originally used for auctions), and the church of Notre-Dame des Blancs-Manteaux. A corner turret signals rue Vieille-du-Temple: turn left past the palatial Hôtel de Rohan (now part of the Archives Nationales), then right onto rue de la Perle to the **Musée Bricard** (60), occupying a mansion as impressive as the assembly of locks and keys within. From here it is a step down rue de Thorigny (opposite) to the imposing 17th-century Hôtel Salé, now the **Musée Picasso** (61).

Backtrack along rue de Thorigny and cross place de Thorigny to rue Elzévir. Halfway along is the **Musée Cognacq-Jay** (62), a must if you love 18th-century furniture, porcelain, and paintings. Turn left at the end of the street onto rue des Francs-Bourgeois, then right into rue Pavée, past the cheerfully askew facade of the city history library, to reach rue des Rosiers, with its excellent Jewish bakeries and falafel shops. Double back to rue des Francs-Bourgeois and turn right, then left to find rue de Sévigné and the **Musée Carnavalet** ⑥③, the Paris history museum, in perhaps the prettiest edifice in the Marais. A short walk along rue des Francs-Bourgeois takes you to one of Paris's most historic squares, the **place des Vosges** ⑥④, lined with pink brick and covered arcades.

TIMING

This walk will comfortably take a morning or an afternoon. If you choose to spend an hour or two in any of the museums along the way, allow a full day. Be prepared to wait in line at the Picasso Museum. Note that some of the museums don't open until the afternoon.

Sights to See

59 **Archives Nationales** (National Archives). If you're a serious history buff, you'll be fascinated by the thousands of intricate historical documents, dating from the Merovingian period to the 20th century, at the National Archives. Architecture buffs will also enjoy this place, as it occupies the **Hôtel de Soubise,** one of the grandest of all 18th-century Parisian mansions, whose salons were among the first to show the Rococo style in full bloom. ✉ *60 rue des Francs-Bourgeois, Le Marais,* ☎ *01–40–27–62–18.* 🎫 *€3.05.* ⏲ *Mon. and Wed.–Fri. 10–5:45, weekends 1:45–5:45. Métro: Rambuteau.*

56 **Atelier Brancusi** (Brancusi Studio). Romanian-born sculptor Constantin Brancusi settled in Paris in 1898 at age 22. This light, airy museum in front of the Pompidou Center contains four glass-fronted rooms that re-create Brancusi's studio, crammed with smooth, stylized works from all periods of his career. ✉ *Place Georges-Pompidou, Beaubourg/Les Halles,* ☎ *01–44–78–12–33.* 🎫 *€5.50.* ⏲ *Weekends 1–7. Métro: Rambuteau.*

★ 55 **Centre Pompidou.** The futuristic, funnel-top Pompidou Center—known to Parisians as Beaubourg, after the surrounding district—was built in the mid-1970s and named in honor of former French president Georges Pompidou (1911–74). After being deluged with vast crowds, the center was closed in 1997 for top-to-bottom renovation, reopening at the start of 2000. You approach the center across **place Georges-Pompidou,** a sloping piazza, where you'll find (if you look carefully enough) the **Atelier Brancusi.** The center is most famous for its **Musée National d'Art Moderne** (Modern Art Museum), recently extended to cover two stories: one devoted to figurative works from Fauvism and Cubism onward; the other to postwar abstract art and recent video-based creations. Also look for rotating exhibits of contemporary art. In addition, there are a public reference library, a language laboratory, an industrial design center, a movie theater, a café, Georges (Paris's chic-est rooftop restaurant), a gift shop, and the famous escalator that snakes up the outside to offer a sweeping panorama of central and western Paris. ✉ *Pl. Georges-Pompidou, Beaubourg/Les Halles,* ☎ *01–44–78–12–33,* WEB *www.centrepompidou.fr.* 🎫 *€5.50.* ⏲ *Wed.–Mon. 11–9. Métro: Rambuteau.*

52 **Hôtel de Sully.** This late-Renaissance mansion, begun in 1624, has a stately garden and a majestic courtyard with statues, richly carved pediments, and dormer windows. It is the headquarters of the **Caisse Nationale des Monuments Historiques** (National Treasury of Historic Monuments), responsible for administering France's historic monuments. Guided visits to Paris sites and buildings begin here, though all are conducted in French. ✉ *62 rue St-Antoine, Le Marais,* ☎ *01–44–61–20–00,* WEB *www.monum.fr. Métro: St-Paul.*

57 **Musée d'Art et d'Histoire du Judaïsme** (Museum of Jewish Art and History). With its clifflike courtyard ringed by giant pilasters, Pierre Le Muet's Hôtel St-Aignan—completed in 1650—is one of the most awesome sights in the Marais. It opened as a museum in 1998 after a 20-year, $35 million restoration. The interior has been remodeled to the point of blandness, but the displays—including silverware, clothing, and furniture—are carefully presented. ✉ *71 rue du Temple, Le Marais,* ☎ *01–53–01–86–60.* 🎫 *€6.10.* ⏲ *Sun.–Fri. 11–6. Métro: Rambuteau.*

60 **Musée Bricard.** This museum—also called the Musée de la Serrure (Lock Museum)—is housed in a sober Baroque mansion designed in 1685 by the architect of Les Invalides, Libéral Bruand, for himself. If you've a taste for fine craftsmanship, you will appreciate the intricacy and ingenuity of many of the locks displayed here. ✉ *1 rue de la Perle, Le Marais,* ☎ *01–42–77–79–62.* 🎫 *€4.60.* ⏲ *Tues.–Fri. 10–noon and 2–5, Mon. 2–5. Métro: St-Paul.*

★ 63 **Musée Carnavalet.** Two adjacent mansions in the heart of the Marais house the Carnavalet Museum, or the Paris History Museum, with material dating from the city's origins to the present. The museum is full of maps and plans, furniture, and busts and portraits of Parisian worthies down the ages. Lovers of the decorative arts will enjoy the period rooms here, especially those devoted to that most French of French styles, the 18th-century Rococo. Most entertaining, however, are the re-creations of Marcel Proust's cork-lined bedroom, the late-19th-century Fouquet jewelry shop, and a room from that Art Nouveau monument, the Café de Paris. ✉ *23 rue de Sévigné, Le Marais,* ☎ *01–44–59–58–58,* WEB *www.paris-france.org/musees.* 🎫 *Free.* ⏲ *Tues.–Sun. 10–5:30. Métro: St-Paul.*

NEED A BREAK?

Marais Plus (✉ 20 rue des Francs-Bourgeois, Le Marais, ☎ 01–48–87–01–40), on the corner of rue Elzévir and rue des Francs-Bourgeois, is a delightful, artsy gift shop with a cozy *salon de thé* at the rear.

58 **Musée de la Chasse et de la Nature** (Museum of Hunting and Nature). This museum is housed in the grandly elegant Hôtel de Guénégaud, designed around 1650 by François Mansart. There is a series of immense 17th- and 18th-century still lifes (notably by Desportes and Oudry) and a wide panoply of swords, guns, muskets, and taxidermy. ✉ *60 rue des Archives, Le Marais,* ☎ *01–42–72–86–42.* 🎫 *€4.60.* ⏲ *Wed.–Mon. 11–6. Métro: Rambuteau.*

62 **Musée Cognacq-Jay.** Prized by connoisseurs, this museum is devoted to the arts of the 18th century and contains outstanding furniture, porcelain, and paintings (notably by Watteau, Boucher, and Tiepolo). ✉ *8 rue Elzévir, Le Marais,* ☎ *01–40–27–07–21,* WEB *www.paris-france.org/musees.* 🎫 *Free.* ⏲ *Tues.–Sun. 10–5:40. Métro: St-Paul.*

★ 61 **Musée Picasso.** Housed in the 17th-century Hôtel Salé, this museum contains the paintings, sculptures, drawings, prints, ceramics, and assorted works of art given to the government by Picasso's heirs after the painter's death in 1973 in lieu of death duties. There are works from every period of Picasso's life, as well as pieces by Cézanne, Miró, Renoir, Braque, Degas, and Matisse. Unfortunately, this museum can get as crowded as a railway station on peak-season weekends—little wonder it's looking so shopworn these days. ✉ *5 rue de Thorigny, Le Marais,* ☎ *01–42–71–25–21.* 🎫 *€5.50, Sun. €4.* ⏲ *Wed.–Mon. 9:30–5:30. Métro: St-Sébastien.*

Opéra de la Bastille. The state-of-the-art Bastille Opera was erected on the south side of place de la Bastille. Designed by Argentine-born

Carlos Ott, it opened on July 14, 1989, in commemoration of the bicentennial of the French Revolution. The steep-climbing auditorium seats more than 3,000 and has earned more plaudits than the curving glass facade, which most people compare to a hideous convention center. ✉ *Pl. de la Bastille, Bastille/Nation,* ☎ *01–40–01–19–70,* WEB *www.opera-de-paris.fr.* 🎫 *Guided tours €9.50. Métro: Bastille.*

51 **Place de la Bastille.** Nothing remains of the infamous Bastille prison destroyed at the beginning of the French Revolution. In the midst of the large traffic circle is the **Colonne de Juillet** (July Column), commemorating the overthrow of Charles X in July 1830. As part of the countrywide celebrations for July 1989, the bicentennial of the French Revolution, the Opéra de la Bastille was erected, inspiring substantial redevelopment on the surrounding streets, especially along rue de Lappe and rue de la Roquette. What was formerly a humdrum neighborhood rapidly gained art galleries, clubs, and bars. *Métro: Bastille.*

★ 64 **Place des Vosges.** Laid out by Henri IV at the start of the 17th century and originally known as place Royale, this square is one of the prettiest in Paris, thanks to its redbrick and white-stone trim. For several decades, nobles flocked here to flaunt money and prestige, but as soon as Versailles became the hot ticket, everybody decamped to Louis XIV's new palace. The two larger buildings on either side were originally the king's and queen's pavilions, while today's pretty park (to drink in the view, get a seat at one of the cafés set under the arcades surrounding the square) was originally a jousting ground. The statue in the center is of Louis XIII. At No. 6 is the **Maison de Victor Hugo** (Victor Hugo's home), where the workaholic French author, famed for *Les Misérables* and *The Hunchback of Notre-Dame,* lived between 1832 and 1848. ✉ *Maison de Victor Hugo, 6 pl. des Vosges, Le Marais,* ☎ *01–42–72–10–16,* WEB *www.paris-france.org/musees.* 🎫 *Free.* ⏲ *Tues.–Sun. 10–5:45. Métro: St-Paul, Chemin-Vert.*

54 **St-Gervais–St-Protais.** This imposing church near the Hôtel de Ville is named after two Roman soldiers martyred by the emperor Nero in the 1st century AD. The church, a riot of Flamboyant style, went up between 1494 and 1598, making it one of the last Gothic constructions in the country; the facade, however, is an essay in 17th-century Classicism. ✉ *Pl. St-Gervais, Le Marais,* ☎ *01–47–26–78–38 for concert information.* ⏲ *Tues.–Sun. 6:30 AM–8 PM. Métro: Hôtel-de-Ville.*

53 **St-Paul–St-Louis.** The leading Baroque church in the Marais, with its elegant dome soaring 180 ft above the crossing, was begun in 1627 by the Jesuits and partly modeled on their Gesù church in Rome. Look for Delacroix's dramatic *Christ on the Mount of Olives* high up in the transept. ✉ *Rue St-Antoine, Le Marais. Métro: St-Paul.*

Across the Seine: The Ile St-Louis and the Latin Quarter

Set behind the Ile de la Cité is one of the most romantic corners of Paris—tiny Ile St-Louis, where clocks seem to have been stopped sometime in the 18th century. South of the Ile St-Louis on the Left Bank of the Seine is the bohemian Quartier Latin (Latin Quarter), with its warren of steep, sloping streets, populated largely by Sorbonne students and academics. The name *Latin Quarter* comes from the old university tradition of studying and speaking in Latin, a tradition that disappeared during the Revolution. The university began as a theology school in the Middle Ages and later became the headquarters of the University of Paris; in 1968 the student revolution here had an explosive effect on French politics, resulting in major reforms in the education system. Most of the district's appeal is less emphatic: Roman ruins, tumbling street markets, the two oldest trees in Paris, and chance glimpses of Notre-Dame all await your discovery.

A Good Walk

Four bridges link the **Ile St-Louis** 65, the smaller of the city's two islands, to the mainland. Rue St-Louis-en-l'Ile runs the length of the island, bisecting it. Walk down this street and admire the strange, pierced spire of St-Louis-en-l'Ile, and stop off for an ice cream at Berthillon, at No. 31. In spring and summer walk to the northern edge of the island to quai d'Anjou to visit the historic and opulent **Hôtel de Lauzun** 66 (open weekends only from Easter to October).

Head toward the west end of the island, which gloriously overlooks Notre-Dame, and cross the Pont St-Louis. Just across the bridge on the left, at the eastern tip of the Ile de la Cité, is the Mémorial de la Déportation, a starkly moving modern crypt dedicated to the French people who died in Nazi concentration camps. Head through the gardens to the left of Notre-Dame and take the Pont au Double across the Seine to Square René-Viviani. Behind the square are the church of St-Julien-le-Pauvre, built at the same time as Notre-Dame, and the tiny, elegant streets of the Maubert district. Turn left out of St-Julien, then make the first right, and cross rue St-Jacques to the elegantly proportioned church of **St-Séverin** 67. The surrounding streets are for pedestrians only. Take rue St-Séverin, a right on rue Xavier-Privas, and a left on rue de la Huchette to reach place St-Michel. Gabriel Davioud's grandiose 1860 fountain, depicting St. Michael slaying the dragon, is a popular meeting spot at the nerve center of the Left Bank.

Turn left up boulevard St-Michel and cross boulevard St-Germain. To your left, behind some forbidding railings, lurks a garden with ruins that date from Roman times. These belong to the **Musée National du Moyen-Age** 68, the National Museum of the Middle Ages. The entrance is down rue Sommerard, the next street on the left. Cross place Paul-Painlevé in front of the museum up toward the **Sorbonne** 69, fronted by a small plaza where the Left Bank's student population congregates after classes. Continue uphill until you are confronted, up rue Soufflot on your left, by the menacing domed bulk of the **Panthéon** 70. On the far left corner of place du Panthéon is St-Étienne-du-Mont, a church whose facade is a mishmash of architectural styles. Head along rue Clovis to reach rue du Cardinal-Lemoine, which leads into rue des Fosses-St-Bernard, and head back toward the Seine and the glass-facade **Institut du Monde Arabe** 71, a center devoted to Arab culture. End your walk here with a cup of mint tea in the lovely rooftop café, which allures with a grand view overlooking Paris.

TIMING

This walk can be fitted into a morning or afternoon or serve as the basis for a leisurely day's exploring—given that several sites, notably the Musée National du Moyen-Age, deserve a lengthy visit.

Sights to See

66 **Hôtel de Lauzun.** A very rare view inside an Ile St-Louis mansion, a visit here permits you to see opulent salons that were among the first examples of the 17th-century Baroque style in Paris. Later, the visionary poet Charles Baudelaire (1821–67) had his apartment here, where he kept a cache of stuffed snakes and crocodiles and where he wrote a large chunk of *Les Fleurs du Mal* (*The Flowers of Evil*). In 1848 poet Théophile Gautier moved in, making it the meeting place of the Club des Haschischines (Hashish Eaters' Club); novelist Alexandre Dumas and painter Eugène Delacroix were both members. Now the building is used for more decorous receptions by the mayor of Paris and is open

to the public on weekends from Easter to October. ✉ *17 quai d'Anjou, Ile St-Louis,* ☎ *01–43–54–27–14.* 🎫 *€4.* 🕐 *Easter–Oct., weekends 10–5:30. Métro: Pont-Marie.*

★ 65 **Ile St-Louis.** One of the more fabled addresses in Paris, this tiny island has long harbored the rich and famous, including Chopin, Daumier, Helena Rubenstein, Chagall, and the Rothschilds, who still occupy the island's grandest house. In fact, the entire island displays striking architectural unity, stemming from the efforts of a group of early 17th-century property speculators led by Christophe Marie. The group commissioned leading Baroque architect Louis Le Vau (1612–70) to erect a series of imposing town houses. Other than some elegant facades and the island's highly picturesque quays along the Seine, there are no major sights here—just follow your nose and soak in the atmosphere. The island has remained in the heart of Parisians as it has remained in the heart of every tourist who has come upon it by accident and found a tiny universe unto itself. It is reputed that until the 1800s some island residents never crossed the bridges to Paris proper—and once you discover the island's quiet charm, you may understand why. *Métro: Pont-Marie.*

NEED A BREAK? Cafés all over sell Berthillon, the haute couture of ice cream, but the **Berthillon** (✉ 31 rue St-Louis-en-l'Ile, Ile St-Louis, ☎ 01–43–54–31–61) shop itself is the place to go. More than 30 flavors are served; expect to wait in line. The shop is open Wednesday–Sunday.

71 **Institut du Monde Arabe** (Institute of the Arab World). Jean Nouvel's striking 1988 glass-and-steel edifice adroitly fuses Arabic and European styles. Note the 240 shutterlike apertures that open and close to regulate light exposure. Inside, the institute tries to do for Arab culture what the Pompidou Center does for modern art, with the help of a sound-and-image center, a vast library and documentation center, and an art museum. The top-floor café provides a good view of Paris. ✉ *1 rue des Fossés-St-Bernard, Latin Quarter,* ☎ *01–40–51–38–38.* 🎫 *€3.80.* 🕐 *Tues.–Sun. 10–6. Métro: Cardinal-Lemoine.*

★ 68 **Musée National du Moyen-Age** (National Museum of the Middle Ages). This museum is housed in the 15th-century Hôtel de Cluny, erstwhile residence of the abbots of Cluny, the great—but now largely destroyed—abbey in Burgundy. A stunning selection of tapestries, including the world-famous *Dame à la Licorne* (*Lady and the Unicorn*) series, headlines its exhibition of medieval decorative arts. Alongside the mansion are the city's Roman baths and the *Boatmen's Pillar,* Paris's oldest sculpture. ✉ *6 pl. Paul-Painlevé, Latin Quarter,* ☎ *01–53–73–78–00,* WEB *www.musee-moyenage.fr.* 🎫 *€5.50, Sun. €4.* 🕐 *Wed.–Mon. 9:15–5:45. Métro: Cluny–La Sorbonne.*

70 **Panthéon.** Originally commissioned as a church by Louis XV as a mark of gratitude for his recovery from a grave illness in 1744, the Panthéon is now a monument to France's most glorious historical figures, including Voltaire, Zola, Rousseau, and dozens of French statesmen, military heroes, and other thinkers. Germain Soufflot's building was not begun until 1764, and was not completed until 1790, during the French Revolution, whereupon its windows were blocked and it was transformed into the national shrine it is today. A giant pendulum, suspended on a 220-ft steel wire, commemorates Léon Foucault's 1851 experiment to prove the earth's rotation. ✉ *Pl. du Panthéon, Latin Quarter,* ☎ *01–44–32–18–00,* WEB *www.monum.fr.* 🎫 *€6.* 🕐 *Summer, daily 9:30–6:30; winter, daily 10–6:15. Métro: Cardinal-Lemoine; RER: Luxembourg.*

(67) **St-Séverin.** This unusually wide, Flamboyant Gothic church dominates a Left Bank neighborhood filled with squares and pedestrian streets. Note the splendidly deviant spiraling column in the forest of pillars behind the altar. ✉ *Rue des Prêtres St-Séverin, Latin Quarter.* ⏲ *Weekdays 11–5:30, Sat. 11–10. Métro: St-Michel.*

(69) **Sorbonne.** Named after Robert de Sorbon, a medieval canon who founded a college of theology here in 1253, this is one of the oldest universities in Europe. The church and university buildings were restored by Cardinal Richelieu in the 17th century, and the maze of amphitheaters, lecture rooms, and laboratories, along with the surrounding courtyards and narrow streets, retains a hallowed air. You can visit the main courtyard on rue de la Sorbonne and peek into the main lecture hall, a major meeting point during the tumultuous student upheavals of 1968. The square is dominated by the noble university church with cupola and Corinthian columns. Inside is the white-marble tomb of that ultimate crafty cleric, Cardinal Richelieu himself. ✉ *Rue de la Sorbonne, Latin Quarter. Métro: Cluny–La Sorbonne.*

Toujours la Politesse: From Orsay to St-Germain

This walk covers the Left Bank, from the Musée d'Orsay in the stately 7e arrondissement to the chic and colorful area around St-Germain-des-Prés in the 6e. The Musée d'Orsay, in a daringly converted Belle Epoque rail station on the Seine, houses one of the world's most spectacular arrays of Impressionist paintings. Farther along the river, the 18th-century Palais Bourbon—now home to the National Assembly—sets the tone for the 7e arrondissement. This is Edith Wharton territory—select, discreet *vieille France,* where all the aristocrats live in gorgeous, sprawling, old-fashioned apartments or *maisons particulières* (*very* private town houses). Embassies—and the Hôtel Matignon, residence of the French prime minister—line the surrounding streets, their majestic scale in total keeping with the Hôtel des Invalides, whose gold-leaf dome climbs heavenward above the regal tomb of Napoléon. The Rodin Museum—set in a gorgeous 18th-century mansion—is only a short walk away. This remains a district where manners maketh the man.

To the east, away from the splendor of the 7e, the boulevard St-Michel slices the Left Bank in two: on one side, the Latin Quarter; on the other, the Faubourg St-Germain, named for St-Germain-des-Prés, the oldest church in Paris. Ask Parisians and tourists alike and many venture that this is their favorite district in Paris, stuffed as it is with friendly cafés, soigné boutiques, and adorably quaint streets. The venerable church tower has long acted as a beacon for intellectuals, most famously during the 1950s when Albert Camus, Jean-Paul Sartre, and Simone de Beauvoir ate and drank existentialism in the neighborhood cafés. Today most of the philosophizing is done by tourists, yet a wealth of bookshops, art stores, and antiques galleries ensures that St-Germain, as the area is commonly known, retains its highbrow and very posh appeal. In the southern part of this district is the city's most colorful park, the Jardin du Luxembourg.

A Good Walk

Start at the **Musée d'Orsay** (72), famed for its collection of art from 1848 to 1914. A good meeting point is the pedestrian square outside the museum, where huge bronze statues of an elephant and a rhinoceros disprove the idea that the French take their art *too* seriously. Head west along rue de Lille to the **Palais Bourbon** (73), home of the Assemblée Nationale (French Parliament).

Rue de l'Université leads from the Assemblée to the grassy Esplanade des Invalides and an encounter with the **Hôtel des Invalides** (74), founded by Louis XIV to house invalid, or wounded, war veterans. The most impressive dome in Paris towers over the church at the Invalides—the Église du Dôme. From the church, double back along boulevard des Invalides and take rue de Varenne to the Hôtel Biron, better known as the **Musée Rodin** (75), where you can see a fine collection of Auguste Rodin's emotionally charged statues. The quiet, distinguished 18th-century streets between the Rodin Museum and the Parliament are filled with embassies and ministries.

Continue on to rue du Bac, turn left, then take a right onto rue de Grenelle, to the **Musée Maillol** (76), dedicated to the work of sculptor Aristide Maillol. Continue on rue de Grenelle past Edme Bouchardon's monumental 1730s Fontaine des Quatre Saisons (Four Seasons Fountain) to the carrefour de la Croix-Rouge, with its mighty bronze Centaur by the contemporary sculptor César. Take rue du Vieux-Colombier to place St-Sulpice, a spacious square whose north side is lined with cafés. Looming over the square is the enormous church of **St-Sulpice** (77).

Exit the church, head back across the square, and turn right on rue Bonaparte to reach **St-Germain-des-Prés** (78), Paris's oldest church. Across the cobbled place St-Germain-des-Prés is the café Les Deux Magots, one of the principal haunts of the intelligentsia after World War II. Two doors down boulevard St-Germain is the Café de Flore, another popular spot with the likes of Jean-Paul Sartre and Simone de Beauvoir. Follow rue de l'Abbaye, alongside the far side of the church, to rue de Furstenberg. The street opens out into place Furstenberg—a relentlessly picturesque square—where you'll find Eugène Delacroix's studio, the **Atelier Delacroix** (79). Take a left on rue Jacob and turn right down rue Bonaparte to the **École Nationale des Beaux-Arts** (80), whose students can often be seen painting and sketching on the nearby quays and bridges.

Continue down to the Seine and turn right along the quay, past the **Institut de France** (81). With its distinctive dome, curved facade, and commanding position overlooking the Pont des Arts—a footbridge affording delightful views of the Louvre and Ile de la Cité—the institute is one of the city's most impressive waterside sights. Continue along quai de Conti past the Hôtel des Monnaies, the former national mint. Head up rue Dauphine. Just 150 yards up, it's linked by the open-air passage Dauphine to rue Mazarine, which leads left to the carrefour de Buci, where you can find one of the best food markets in Paris. Where rue Dauphine crosses rue St-André-des-Arts, make a left for about a half a block to find the enchanting **Cour de Commerce St-André** (82), an alleyway lined with cafés and the hidden Cour du Rohan courtyard. Follow the Cour de Commerce St-André up to busy place de l'Odéon. Cross boulevard St-Germain and climb rue de l'Odéon to the colonnaded Théâtre de l'Odéon. Behind the theater lies the spacious **Jardin du Luxembourg** (83), one of the most stylish parks in the city.

TIMING

This walk could take from four hours to a couple of days, depending on how long you spend in the plethora of museums along the way. Aim for an early start—that way you can hit the Musée d'Orsay early, when crowds are smaller, then get to the rue de Buci street market when it's in full swing, in the late afternoon (the stalls are generally closed for lunch until 3 PM). Note that the Hôtel des Invalides is open daily, but Orsay is closed Monday. You might consider returning to one or more museums on another day or night—Orsay is open late on Thursday evening.

Sights to See

79 **Atelier Delacroix** (Delacroix's Studio). The studio of artist Eugène Delacroix (1798–1863) contains only a small collection of his sketches and drawings. But if you want to pay homage to France's foremost Romantic painter, you'll want to visit this museum. Speaking of pictures, don't forget to take some photographs here of **place Furstenberg,** one of the loveliest corners of 19th-century Paris still preserved. ✉ *6 rue Furstenberg, St-Germain-des-Prés,* ☎ *01–44–41–86–50.* *€3.80.* *Wed.–Mon. 9:30–5. Métro: St-Germain-des-Prés.*

★ 82 **Cour du Commerce St-André.** Like an 18th-century engraving come to life, this exquisite, cobblestoned street-arcade is one of Paris's loveliest sights. While it has been tatted up with some faux cafés, its shop signs, awnings, and outdoor tables make it a most festive tableau, where Napoléon himself still wouldn't look too out of place taking his coffee (as he did back when). Halfway up the alley is Paris's oldest café, **Le Procope** (☎ 01–40–46–79–00), opened in 1686. Just opposite Procope is that hidden treasure, the **Cour de Rohan,** a series of three cloistered courtyards that found Hollywood immortality when Cecil Beaton picked it as the locale for Gigi's home, "Chez Mamita," in the 1958 Oscar-winning Best Picture, *Gigi.* ✉ *Linking bd. St-Germain and rue St-André-des-Arts, St-Germain-des-Prés. Métro: Odéon.*

80 **École Nationale des Beaux-Arts** (National Fine Arts College). In three large mansions near the Seine, this school—today the breeding ground for painters, sculptors, and architects—was once the site of a convent, founded in 1608. Wander into the courtyard and galleries of the school to see the casts and copies of the statues stored here for safekeeping during the Revolution. ✉ *14 rue Bonaparte, St-Germain-des-Prés.* *Daily 1–7. Métro: St-Germain-des-Prés.*

NEED A BREAK? The popular **La Palette** café (✉ 43 rue de Seine, St-Germain-des-Prés, ☎ 01–43–26–68–15), on the corner of rue de Seine and rue Callot, has long been a favorite haunt of Beaux-Arts students.

★ 74 **Hôtel des Invalides.** Famed as the final resting place of Napoléon, Les Invalides, as it is widely known, is an outstanding monumental Baroque ensemble, designed by Libéral Bruand in the 1670s at the behest of Louis XIV to house wounded, or invalid, soldiers. Although no more than a handful of old-timers live at the Invalides these days, the army link remains in the form of the **Musée de l'Armée,** a military museum. The **Musée des Plans-Reliefs,** also housed here, contains a fascinating collection of old scale models of French towns. The 17th-century **Église St-Louis des Invalides** is the Invalides's original church. More impressive is Jules Hardouin-Mansart's **Église du Dôme,** built onto the end of the church of St-Louis but blocked off from it in 1793. The showpiece here is that grandiose monument to glory and hubris, **Napoléon's Tomb.** ✉ *Pl. des Invalides, Invalides,* ☎ *01–44–42–37–72,* WEB *www.invalides.org.* *€6.* *Apr.–Sept., daily 10–6; Oct.–Mar., daily 10–4:30. Métro: Latour-Maubourg.*

81 **Institut de France** (French Institute). Built to the designs of Louis Le Vau from 1662 to 1674, the institute's curved, dome-top facade is one of the Left Bank's most impressive waterside sights. It also houses one of France's most revered cultural institutions, the Académie Française, created by Cardinal Richelieu in 1635. Unfortunately, the interior is closed to the general public. ✉ *Pl. de l'Institut, St-Germain-des-Prés. Métro: Pont-Neuf.*

83 **Jardin du Luxembourg** (Luxembourg Gardens). One of the prettiest of Paris's few large parks, the Luxembourg Gardens have fountains,

ponds, trim hedges, precisely planted rows of trees, and gravel walks typical of the French fondness for formal landscaping. The 17th-century **Palais de Luxembourg** (Luxembourg Palace), overlooking the gardens, houses the French senate (not open to the public); an adjacent wing of the palace houses the **Musée de Luxembourg,** only open for special temporary exhibitions. The palace, like the gardens, was built for Marie de' Medici, widow of Henri IV. *Métro: Odéon; RER: Luxembourg.*

76 **Musée Maillol.** Drawings, paintings, tapestries, and, above all, bronzes by Art Deco sculptor Aristide Maillol (1861–1944)—whose sleek, stylized nudes adorn the Tuileries—can be admired at this handsome town house, lovingly restored by his former muse, Dina Vierny. ✉ *61 rue de Grenelle, St-Germain-des-Prés,* ☎ *01–42–22–59–58.* 💶 *€6.10.* ⏲ *Wed.–Mon. 11–6. Métro: Rue du Bac.*

★ 72 **Musée d'Orsay.** In a spectacularly converted Belle Epoque train station, the Orsay Museum—devoted to the arts (mainly French) spanning the period 1848–1914—is one of the city's most popular, thanks to the presence of the world's greatest collection of Impressionist and Postimpressionist paintings. Here you'll find Manet's *Déjeuner sur l'Herbe* (*Lunch on the Grass*), the painting that scandalized Paris in 1863 when it was shown at the Salon des Refusés, an exhibit organized by artists refused permission to show their work at the academy's official annual salon, as well as the artist's provocative nude, *Olympia.* There is a dazzling rainbow of masterpieces by Renoir (including his beloved *Le Moulin de la Galette*), Sisley, Pissarro, and Monet. The Postimpressionists—Cézanne, van Gogh, Gauguin, and Toulouse-Lautrec—are on the top floor. On the ground floor you'll find the work of Manet, the powerful realism of Courbet, and the delicate nuances of Degas. If you prefer more academic paintings, look for Puvis de Chavannes's larger-than-life classical canvases. And if you're excited by more modern developments, look for the early 20th-century Fauves (meaning "wild beasts," the name given them by an outraged critic in 1905)—particularly Matisse, Derain, and Vlaminck. Thought-provoking sculptures also lurk at every turn. Check out the restaurant here, set in a magnificent hall that was the waiting room of the former station. ✉ *1 rue de Bellechasse, St-Germain-des-Prés,* ☎ *01–40–49–48–14,* WEB *www.musee-orsay.fr.* 💶 *€6.90, Sun. €5.05.* ⏲ *Tues.–Wed. and Fri.–Sat. 10–6, Thurs. 10–9:45, Sun. 9–6. Métro: Solférino; RER: Musée d'Orsay.*

NEED A BREAK? Find respite from the overwhelming collection of art in the **Musée d'Orsay Café** behind one of the giant station clocks, close to the Impressionist galleries on the top floor.

★ 75 **Musée Rodin.** The exquisite 18th-century Hôtel Biron makes a gracious stage for the sculpture of Auguste Rodin (1840–1917). You'll doubtless recognize the seated *Le Penseur* (*The Thinker*), with his elbow resting on his knee, and the passionate *Le Baiser* (*The Kiss*). From the upper rooms, which contain some fine if murky paintings by Rodin's friend Eugène Carrière (1849–1906) and some fine sculptures by Rodin's mistress, Camille Claudel (1864–1943), you can see the large garden behind the house. Don't skip the garden: it is exceptional not only for its rosebushes and sculpture, but also its view of the Invalides dome with the Eiffel Tower behind. ✉ *77 rue de Varenne, Invalides,* ☎ *01–44–18–61–10.* 💶 *€5, Sun. €3; gardens only €1.* ⏲ *Easter–Oct., Tues.–Sun. 9:30–5:45; Nov.–Easter, Tues.–Sun. 9:30–4:45. Métro: Varenne.*

73 **Palais Bourbon.** The most prominent feature of the home of the Assemblée Nationale (French Parliament) is its colonnaded facade, commissioned by Napoléon. ✉ *Pl. du Palais-Bourbon, Invalides.* ⏲ *During temporary exhibits only. Métro: Assemblée Nationale.*

78 **St-Germain-des-Prés.** Paris's oldest church was first built to shelter a relic of the true cross brought back from Spain in AD 542. The chancel was enlarged and the church then consecrated by Pope Alexander III in 1163; the tall, sturdy tower—a Left Bank landmark—dates from this period. The church stages superb organ concerts and recitals. ✉ *Pl. St-Germain, St-Germain-des-Prés.* ⏲ *Weekdays 8–7:30, weekends 8–9. Métro: St-Germain-des-Prés.*

77 **St-Sulpice.** Dubbed the "Cathedral of the Left Bank," this enormous 17th-century church is of note for the powerful Delacroix frescoes in the first chapel on the right. The 18th-century facade was never finished, and its unequal towers add a playful touch to an otherwise sober design. ✉ *Pl. St-Sulpice, St-Germain-des-Prés. Métro: St-Sulpice.*

Montmartre: The Citadel of Paris

On a dramatic rise above the city is Montmartre, site of the Sacré-Coeur Basilica and home to a once-thriving artist community. This was the quartier that Toulouse-Lautrec and Renoir immortalized with a flash of their brush and a tube of their paint. Although the great painters have long departed, and the fabled nightlife of Old Montmartre has fizzled down to some glitzy nightclubs and skin shows, Montmartre still exudes history and Gallic charm. Windmills once dotted Montmartre (often referred to by Parisians as *La Butte,* meaning "mound"). They were set up here not just because the hill was a good place to catch the wind—at more than 300 ft it's the highest point in the city—but because Montmartre was covered with wheat fields and quarries right up to the end of the 19th century. Today only two of the original 20 windmills remain. Visiting Montmartre means negotiating a lot of steep streets and flights of steps. The crown atop this urban peak, the Sacré-Coeur Basilica, is something of an architectural oddity, with a silhouette that looks more like that of a mosque than a cathedral. No matter: when viewed from afar at dusk or sunrise, it looks like Paris's "sculpted cloud."

A Good Walk

Begin at place Blanche, landmarked by the **Moulin Rouge** (84), the windmill turned dance hall immortalized by Toulouse-Lautrec. Just along boulevard de Clichy is the **Musée de l'Erotisme** (85). Wind your way up rue Lepic to the **Moulin de la Galette** (86), atop its leafy hillock opposite rue Tholozé, once a path over the hill. Turn right down rue Tholozé, past Studio 28, the first cinema built expressly for experimental films. Continue down rue Tholozé to rue des Abbesses and turn left toward the triangular **place des Abbesses** (87). Follow rue Ravignan as it climbs north, via place Émile-Goudeau, an enchanting little cobbled square, to the **Bateau-Lavoir** (88), or Boat Wash House, at its northern edge. Painters Picasso and Braque had studios in the original building; this drab concrete edifice was built in its place. Continue up the hill via rue de la Mire to place Jean-Baptiste Clément, where Amedeo Modigliani had a studio.

The upper reaches of rue Lepic lead to rue Norvins, formerly rue des Moulins. At the end of the street to the left is stylish avenue Junot. Continue right past the bars and tourist shops until you reach **place du Tertre** (89). Around the corner on rue Poulbot, the **Espace Dalí** (90) houses works by Salvador Dalí, who once had a studio in the area. Return to place du Tertre. Looming behind is the scaly white dome of the Basilique du **Sacré-Coeur** ⑨①. The cavernous interior is worth visiting for its golden mosaics; climb to the top of the dome for the view of Paris. Walk back toward place du Tertre. Turn right onto rue du Mont-Cenis and left onto rue Cortot, site of the **Musée de Montmartre** ⑨②, which, like the Bateau-Lavoir, once sheltered an illustrious group of painters, writers, and assorted cabaret artists. Another famous Montmartre landmark is at No. 22: the bar-cabaret **Au Lapin Agile** ⑨③. Opposite the Lapin Agile is the tiny Cimetière St-Vincent, where painter Maurice Utrillo is buried.

TIMING

Reserve a morning or afternoon (late afternoon if you want to catch Au Lapin Agile open in the early evening) for this walk: many of the streets are steep and slow. Include half an hour each at Sacré-Coeur and the museums (the Dalí museum is open daily, but the Montmartre museum is closed Monday). From Easter through September Montmartre is besieged by tourists. Two hints for avoiding the worst of the rush: come on a gray day, when Montmartre's sullen-tone facades suffer less than most others in the city; or visit during the afternoon and return to place du Tertre (maybe via the funicular) by the early evening, when the tourist buses will have departed.

Sights to See

★ 93 **Au Lapin Agile.** One of the most picturesque spots in Paris, this legendary bar-cabaret (open nights only) is a miraculous survivor from the 19th century. It got its curious name—the Nimble Rabbit—when the owner, André Gill, hung up a sign (now in the Musée du Vieux Montmartre) of a laughing rabbit jumping out of a saucepan clutching a bottle of wine. Founded in 1860, this adorable maison-cottage was a favorite subject of painter Maurice Utrillo. Once owned by Aristide Bruant (immortalized in many Toulouse-Lautrec posters), it became the home-away-from-home for Braque, Modigliani, Apollinaire, and Vlaminck. The most famous habitué, however, was Picasso, who once paid for a meal with one of his paintings, then promptly went out and painted another, which he named after this place (it now hangs in New York's Metropolitan Museum, which purchased it for $50 million). Note: the best time to spot famous ghosts is the wee hours of the morning. ✉ *22 rue des Saules, Montmartre,* ☎ *01–46–06–85–87,* WEB *www.au-lapin-agile.com.* €20. ⏲ *Tues.–Sat. 9 PM–2 AM. Métro: Lamarck-Caulaincourt.*

88 **Bateau-Lavoir** (Boat Wash House). Montmartre poet Max Jacob coined the name for the original building on this site (which burned down in 1970), saying it resembled a boat and that the warren of artists' studios within was perpetually paint-splattered and in need of a good hosing down. It was here that Pablo Picasso and Georges Braque made their first bold stabs at the concept of Cubism. The new building also contains art studios, but is the epitome of poured-concrete drabness. ✉ *13 pl. Émile-Goudeau, Montmartre. Métro: Abbesses.*

90 **Espace Dalí** (Dalí Center). Some of Salvador Dalí's less familiar works are among the 25 sculptures and 300 etchings and lithographs housed in this museum, whose atmosphere is meant to approximate the experience of Surrealism. ✉ *11 rue Poulbot, Montmartre,* ☎ *01–42–64–40–10.* €6. ⏲ *Daily 10–6:30. Métro: Abbesses.*

86 **Moulin de la Galette** (Wafer Windmill). This is one of two remaining windmills in Montmartre. It was once the focal point of an open-air cabaret (made famous in a painting by Renoir). Rumor has it that in 1814 the miller Debray, who had struggled in vain to defend the windmill from invading Cossacks, was then strung up on its sails and spun

Montmartre

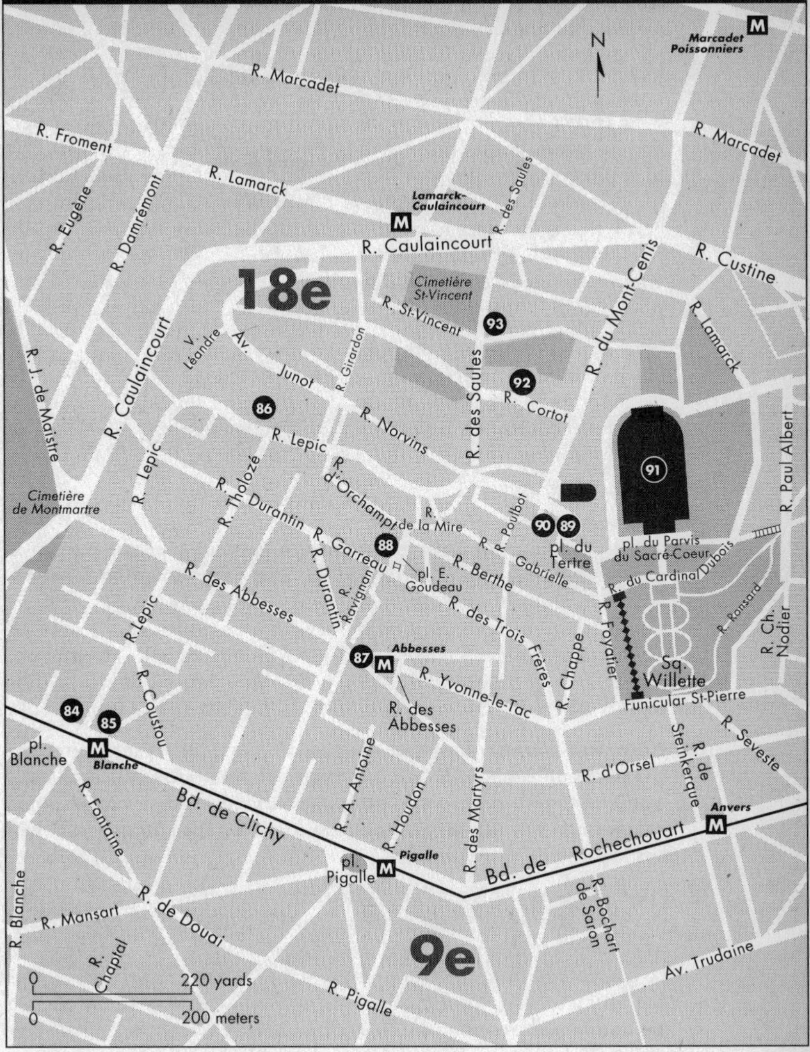

Au Lapin Agile **93**

Bateau-Lavoir **88**

Espace Dalí **90**

Moulin de la Galette **86**

Moulin Rouge **84**

Musée de l'Erotisme. **85**

Musée de Montmartre **92**

Place des Abbesses. **87**

Place du Tertre **89**

Sacré-Coeur. **91**

to death by the invaders. Unfortunately, it is privately owned and can only be admired from the street below. ✉ *Rue Tholozé, Montmartre. Métro: Abbesses.*

84 **Moulin Rouge** (Red Windmill). This world-famous cabaret was built in 1885 as a windmill, then transformed into a dance hall in 1900. Those wild, early days were immortalized by Toulouse-Lautrec in his posters and paintings. It still trades shamelessly on the notion of Paris as a city of sin: if you fancy a gaudy Vegas-style night out—sorry, admirers of the ravishing 2001 Baz Luhrman film won't find any of that charm here—this is the place to go. ✉ *82 bd. de Clichy, Montmartre,* ☎ *01–53–09–82–82,* WEB *www.moulin-rouge.com.* *€80–€125.* ⏲ *Shows nightly at 9 and 11. Métro: Blanche.*

85 **Musée de l'Erotisme** (Erotic Art Museum). Opened in 1997, this museum claims to offer "a prestigious showcase for every kind of erotic fantasy." Its 2,000 works of art—some might question that term—range from Peruvian potteries, African carvings, and Indian miniatures to Nepalese bronzes, Chinese ivories, and Japanese prints. ✉ *72 bd. de Clichy, Montmartre,* ☎ *01–42–58–28–73.* *€6.20.* ⏲ *Daily 10 AM–2 AM. Métro: Blanche.*

92 **Musée de Montmartre** (Montmartre Museum). In its turn-of-the-20th-century heyday, Montmartre's historical museum was home to an illustrious group of painters, writers, and assorted cabaret artists. Foremost among them were Renoir and Maurice Utrillo. The museum also provides a view of the tiny **vineyard**—the only one in Paris—on neighboring rue des Saules. A token 125 gallons of wine are still produced here every year. ✉ *12 rue Cortot, Montmartre,* ☎ *01–46–06–61–11.* *€3.80.* ⏲ *Tues.–Sun. 11–6. Métro: Lamarck-Caulaincourt.*

87 **Place des Abbesses.** This triangular square is typical of the picturesque, slightly countrified style that has made Montmartre famous. The entrance to the Abbesses métro station, a curving, sensuous mass of delicate iron, is one of only two original Art Nouveau entrance canopies left in Paris. *Métro: Abbesses.*

89 **Place du Tertre.** This tumbling square (*tertre* means "hillock") regains its village atmosphere only in the winter, when the branches of the plane trees sketch traceries against the sky. At any other time of year you'll be confronted by crowds of tourists and a swarm of third-rate artists clamoring to do your portrait (if one of them whips up an unsolicited portrait, you are not obliged to buy it). **La Mère Catherine,** on one corner of the square, was a favorite with the Russian Cossacks who occupied Paris in 1814. They couldn't have suspected that by banging on the table and yelling "*bistro*" (Russian for "quickly"), they were inventing a new breed of French restaurant. *Métro: Abbesses.*

NEED A BREAK?

Patachou (✉ 9 pl. du Tertre, Montmartre, ☎ 01–42–51–06–06), serving exquisite if expensive cakes and teas, sounds the one classy note on place du Tertre.

★ 91 **Sacré-Coeur.** Often compared to a "sculpted cloud" atop Montmartre, the Sacred Heart Basilica was erected as a sort of national guilt offering in expiation for the blood shed during the Paris Commune and Franco-Prussian War in 1870–71, and was largely financed by French Catholics fearful of an anticlerical backlash under the new republican regime. The basilica was not consecrated until 1919. Stylistically, the Sacré-Coeur borrows elements from Romanesque and Byzantine models. The gloomy, cavernous interior is worth visiting for its golden mosaics; climb to the top of the dome for the view of Paris. ✉ *Pl. du Parvis-du-Sacré-Coeur, Montmartre. Métro: Anvers.*

DINING

Revised and updated by Rosa Jackson

Whether you get knee-deep in white truffles at Les Ambassadeurs or merely discover pistachioed sausage (the poor man's caviar) at a classic corner bistro, you'll discover that food in Paris is an obsession, an art, a subject of endless debate. From the edible genius of haute cuisine wizard Alain Ducasse—whose turbot with "marmalade" of asparagus will make you purr—to brilliant bistro chef Yves Camdeborde's red mullet with chestnuts and cèpes, dining in Paris can easily leave you in a pleasurable stupor. And when it all seems a bit overwhelming, you can slip away to a casual little place for an earthy, bubbling cassoulet, have a midnight feast of the world's silkiest oysters, or even opt out of Gaul altogether for superb pasta, couscous, or an herb-bright Vietnamese stir-fry. Once you know where to go, Paris is a city where perfection awaits at all levels of the food chain.

Generally, restaurants are open from noon to about 2 and from 7:30 or 8 to 10 or 10:30. It's best to make reservations, particularly in summer, although the reviews only state when reservations are absolutely essential. If you want no-smoking seating, make this clear; the mandatory no-smoking area is sometimes limited to a very few tables. Brasseries have longer hours and often serve all day and late into the evening; some are open 24 hours. Assume a restaurant is open every day unless otherwise indicated. Surprisingly, many prestigious restaurants close on Saturday as well as Sunday. July and August are the most common months for annual closings, although Paris in August is no longer the wasteland it once was. For help with the vocabulary of French cooking, see the Menu Guide at the end of this book. Although prices include tax and tip by law, pocket change left on the table in simple places, or an additional 5% in better restaurants, is appreciated. Places where a jacket and tie are de rigueur are noted. Otherwise, use common sense—jeans and T-shirts are not suitable in Paris restaurants, nor are shorts or running clothes, except in the most casual bistros and cafés.

CATEGORY	COST*
$$$$	over €38
$$$	€23–€38
$$	€12–€22
$	under €12

**per person for a main course only, including tax (19.6%) and service; note that if a restaurant offers only prix-fixe (set-price) meals, it is given a price category that reflects the full prix-fixe price.*

1er Arrondissement (Louvre/Les Halles)

CONTEMPORARY

$$$–$$$$ ✕ **Cabaret.** The food—poached egg with sea-urchin coral, seared tuna with Thai spices, beef carpaccio—isn't substantial enough to give you indigestion, but you might find other reasons to recline on the beds of this hyper-trendy new restaurant after your meal. Lunch is served in the cool white dining room but dinner in the funky basement is where it's at—superstar decorator Jacques Garcia has gone all out with phosphorescent floors, silk cushions, an "African bar," and the aforementioned beds, each with a built-in table. ✉ *2 place du Palais Royal, Louvre/Tuileries,* ☎ *01–58–62–56–25. AE, DC, MC, V. Closed Sun. Métro: Palais-Royal.*

Paris Dining

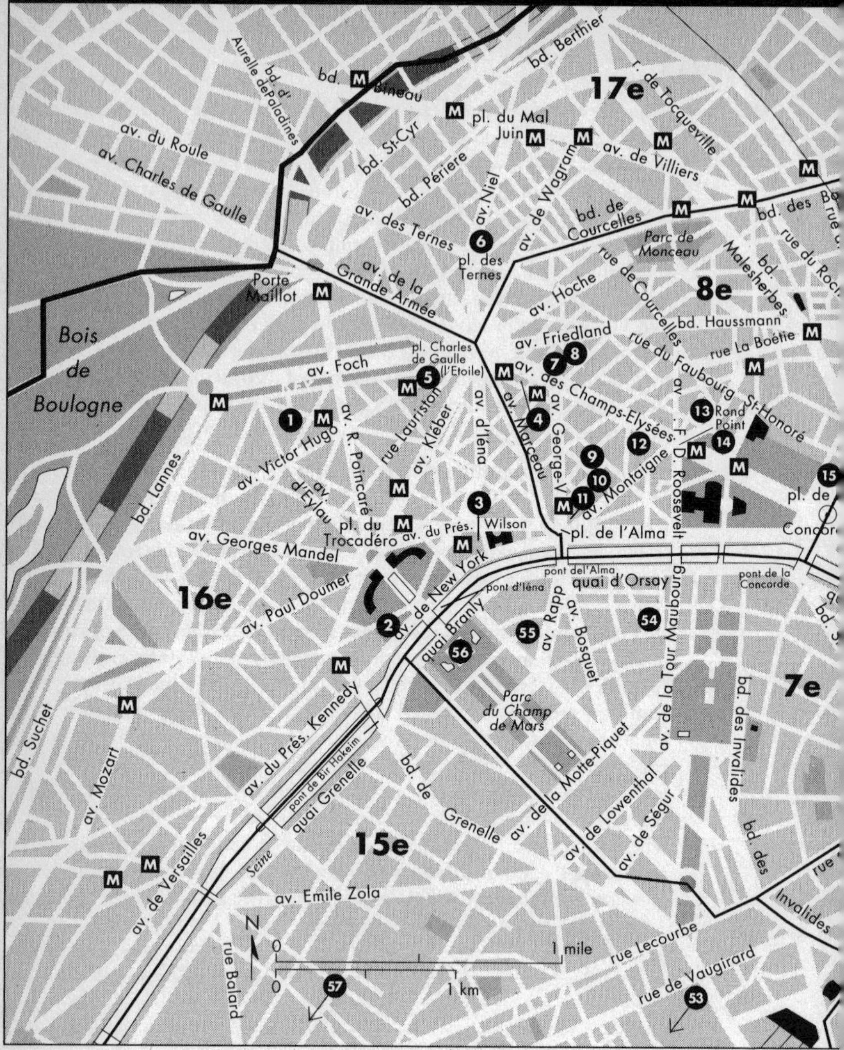

Alain Ducasse 10
Les Ambassadeurs . . 15
L'Ardoise. 16
Astier 35
L'Astrance 2
Bofinger 39
L'As du Fallafel 37
Au Bon Accueil 55
Au Bourguignon du Marais 40
Le Bouillon Racine . . 45
Brasserie de l'Ile St-Louis 41
Cabaret 18
Le Café des Délices 49
Chartier 27
Chez Dumonet-Josephine 52
Chez Georges 24
Chez Michel 29
Chez Omar 33
Chez Savy. 14
La Coupole 51
Les Élysées du Vernet. 4
Georges 32
Ghislaine Arabian . . . 1
Le Grand Colbert . . . 35
Le Grand Véfour. . . . 19
Grizzli Café 31
Guy Savoy 6
Le Hangar 30
Hélène Darroze 48
Jamin 3
Jules Verne 56
Le Kitch. 35
Korova 12
Lapérouse 47
Maison Blanche 11
Market 13
Le Moulin à Vins. . . . 28
Nobu 9
L'Os à Moelle 57
Le Pamphlet 34
Petrossian 54

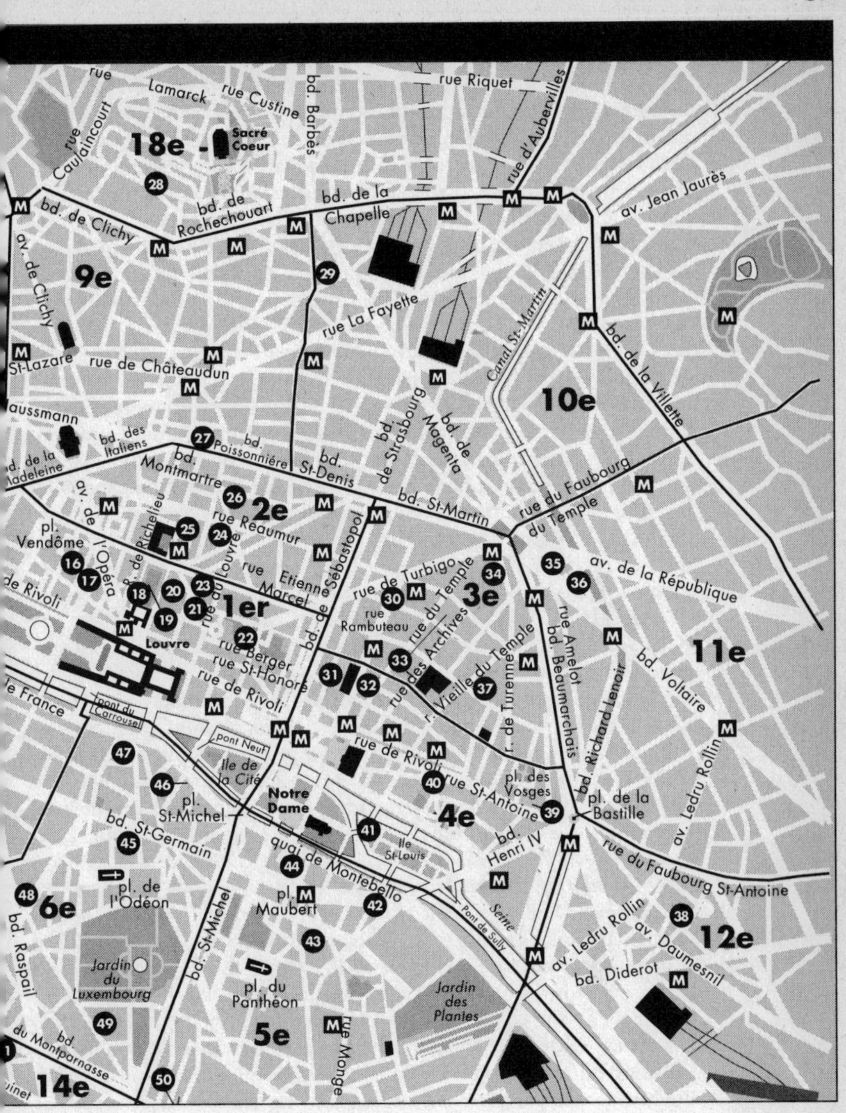

rre Gagnaire 7
s Pipos 43
unier 5
Régalade 53
Reminet 44
staurant du
lais-Royal 20
Safran 17
Souletin 23
Square
ousseau 38
illevent 8

Le Terroir 50
La Tour d'Argent 42
La Tour du
Montlhéry 22
Willi's Wine Bar . . . 21
Le Vaudeville 26
Ze Kitchen
Galerie 46

FRENCH

$$$$ ✕ **Le Grand Véfour.** Victor Hugo could stride in and still recognize this place—in his day, as now, a contender for the prize of most beautiful restaurant in Paris. Originally built in 1784, set in the arcades of the Palais-Royal, it has welcomed everyone from Napoléon to Colette to Jean Cocteau—nearly every seat bears a plaque commemorating a famous patron. The mirrored ceiling and Restauration-era glass paintings of goddesses beguile the foodies as well as the fashionable who gather here to enjoy chef Guy Martin's delights. He hails from Savoie, so you'll find lake fish and mountain cheeses on the menu alongside such luxurious dishes as foie gras–stuffed raviolis. ✉ *17 rue Beaujolais, Louvre/Tuileries,* ☎ *01–42–96–56–27. Jacket and tie. AE, DC, MC, V. Closed weekends and Aug. No dinner Fri. Métro: Palais-Royal.*

$$$ ★ ✕ **Restaurant du Palais-Royal.** Tucked away in the northeast corner of the magnificent Palais-Royal garden, this bistro offers traditional cuisine and—very prime real estate—a lovely terrace. Sole and scallops are beautifully prepared, but juicy steak with fat, symmetrically stacked *frites* is also a favorite of the expense-account lunchers who love this place. Don't miss the mango-in-summer, hazelnut-in-winter *mille-feuille.* Be sure to book in advance, especially during the summer, when the terrace tables are hotly sought after. ✉ *Jardins du Palais-Royal, 110 Galerie Valois, Louvre/Tuileries,* ☎ *01–40–20–00–27. AE, MC, V. Closed weekends. Métro: Palais-Royal.*

$$–$$$ ✕ **Le Safran.** If food scares have made you eye steak-frites with suspicion, this is the place to treat yourself to a reassuringly organic bistro meal. Passionate chef Caroll Sinclair works according to what she finds in the market—creamy shellfish and spinach soup brightened by fresh coriander, red mullet stuffed with cèpe mushrooms, and *gigot de sept heures* (leg of lamb cooked for seven hours) are some signature dishes. Cool it all off with dessert such as black grapes with caramelized pineapple or a saffron crème brûlée. ✉ *29 rue d'Argenteuil, Louvre/Tuileries,* ☎ *01–42–61–25–30. MC, V. Closed 2 wks in Sept. Métro: Tuileries, Pyramides.*

$$ ★ ✕ **L'Ardoise.** This minuscule storefront, painted white and decorated with enlargements of old sepia postcards of Paris, is the very model of contemporary bistros making waves in Paris. This one's claim to fame is chef Pierre Jay, who trained at La Tour d'Argent. His first-rate three-course menu for €28 (you can also order à la carte at no extra cost) is adorned with such original dishes as crab flan in a creamy parsley emulsion and fresh cod with grilled chorizo chips, served on a tempting bed of mashed potatoes. Just as enticing are the desserts, such as a superb *feuillantine au citron*—caramelized pastry leaves filled with lemon cream and lemon segments. With friendly service and a small but well-chosen wine list, L'Ardoise would be perfect if it weren't often crowded and noisy. ✉ *28 rue du Mont Thabor, Beaubourg/Les Halles,* ☎ *01–42–96–28–18. Reservations essential. MC, V. Closed Mon.–Tues. Métro: Concorde.*

$$ ✕ **La Tour du Montlhéry.** When the centuries-old Les Halles marketplace became a soulless shopping mall, many neighborhood bistros closed or went upscale. The Montlhéry managed to hang on to the old-market feel, with its sagging wood-beam ceilings, red-check tablecloths, and exposed brick walls lined with imaginative portraits. If you don't mind passing under hanging samples of your future meal (sausages, etc.) on your way into the dining room, then you can enjoy the simple grilled food served by jovial waiters. ✉ *5 rue des Prouvaires, Beaubourg/Les Halles,* ☎ *01–42–36–21–82. Reservations essential. MC, V. Closed weekends and July 14–Aug. 15. Métro: Les Halles.*

$$ ✕ **Willi's Wine Bar.** Don't be fooled by the name—this English-owned spot is no modest watering hole but rather a stylish haunt for Parisian

and foreign gourmands. The often original menu changes daily to reflect the market's offerings, and might include chicken-liver terrine, cod with pesto and eggplant, and crème brûlée or a bitter chocolate *terrine* (pudding). Owner Mark Williamson has a passion for Rhône Valley wines, reflected in the extensive list, and for Spanish sherries. ✉ *13 rue des Petits-Champs, Louvre/Tuileries,* ☎ *01–42–61–05–09. MC, V. Closed Sun. Métro: Bourse.*

2e Arrondissement (La Bourse/Opéra)

FRENCH

$$–$$$ ✕ **Chez Georges.** When you ask sophisticated Parisians—think bankers, aristocrats, or antiques dealers—to name their favorite bistro, many would choose Georges. The traditional bistro fare is good—herring, sole, kidneys, steaks, and *frites* (fries)—and the atmosphere is better. A wood-paneled entry leads you to an elegant and unpretentious dining room where one long, white-clothed stretch of tables lines the mirrored walls and attentive waiters sweep efficiently along its entire length. ✉ *1 rue du Mail, Louvre/Tuileries,* ☎ *01–42–60–07–11. AE, DC, MC, V. Closed Sun. and 3 wks in Aug. Métro: Sentier.*

$$ ✕ **Le Souletin.** Sandwiched between the fashion and financial districts on either side of place des Victoires, this polished bistro attracts a potentially intimidating crowd of designer suits, but the welcome is jovial and the food reassuringly rustic. Specializing in the gutsy cuisine of the Basque country, Le Souletin serves such regional dishes as *axua*—a veal, tomato, and pepper stew spiced with dried Espelette pepper—and smooth white-bean soup with nibbles of panfried foie gras. Sorbets, so often an afterthought, are exceptionally fruity here. ✉ *6 rue La Vrillière, Louvre/Tuileries,* ☎ *01–42–61–43–78. MC, V. Closed Sun. No lunch Sat. Métro: Bourse.*

$$ ✕ **Le Vaudeville.** One of Jean-Paul Bucher's seven Flo brasseries, Le Vaudeville is filled with journalists, bankers, and locals *d'un certain âge* who come for its good-value assortment of prix-fixe menus. Shellfish, house-smoked salmon, and desserts such as profiteroles are particularly enticing. Enjoy the handsome 1930s decor—almost the entire interior of this intimate dining room is done in real or faux marble—and lively dining until 2 AM daily. ✉ *29 rue Vivienne, Opéra/Grands Boulevards,* ☎ *01–40–20–04–62. AE, DC, MC, V. Métro: Bourse.*

3e Arrondissement (Beaubourg/Marais)

FRENCH

$$–$$$ ★ ✕ **Le Pamphlet.** Chef Alain Carrere's modern and very affordable take on the hearty cooking of the Basque and Béarn regions of southwestern France has made this Marais bistro popular with an artsy crowd. Beyond the delicious, homey food, what many Parisians love is the provincial feel, with a beamed ceiling and faïence that seems to have been borrowed from *grandmère.* The market-fresh menu runs from first courses such as sea bream and salmon tartare with oyster sauce to a juicy pork chop with béarnaise and hand-cut *frites.* Finish up with a slice of sheep's cheese. ✉ *38 rue Debelleyme, Le Marais,* ☎ *01–42–72–39–24. Reservations essential. MC, V. Closed Sun., first 2 wks of Jan., and Aug. 8–23. No lunch Sat. Métro: St-Sébastien–Froissart.*

$$ ✕ **Le Hangar.** For years Le Hangar hasn't changed its winning formula, serving food that's far more refined than this too-bright room (hidden down a gloomy impasse) or the prices might suggest. A meal here begins with a little pot of tapenade and ends with *mignardines* (luscious mini-pastries), an haute-cuisine touch. Pan-fried foie gras on a cushion of olive-oil mash is about as good as it gets in Paris, and the chocolate soufflé makes a suitably extravagant ending. ✉ *12 impasse Berthaud, Le Marais,* ☎ *01–42–74–55–44. Reservations essential. No credit cards. Closed Sun. No lunch Mon. Métro: Rambuteau.*

NORTH AFRICAN

$–$$ ✕ **Chez Omar.** Popular with a high-voltage fashion crowd—yes, that is Vivienne Westwood having dinner with Alexander McQueen—this is the place to come for couscous with all the trimmings. Order it with grilled skewered lamb, spicy *merguez* sausage, a lamb shank, or chicken—portions are generous—and wash it down with robust Algerian or Moroccan wine. Proprietor Omar Guerida speaks English and is famously friendly. Since he doesn't take reservations, arrive early or be prepared for a mouthwatering wait. ✉ *47 rue de Bretagne, République,* ☏ *01–42–72–36–26. Reservations not accepted. No credit cards. No lunch Sun. Métro: Filles du Calvaire.*

4e Arrondissement (Beaubourg/Marais/Ile St-Louis)

CONTEMPORARY

$$–$$$ ★ ✕ **Georges.** Decorated in white and gray, with angular chairs and giant metallic shells, Georges stands in stark contrast to its graceful view of Paris from the top floor of the Centre Georges Pompidou. Staff are as sleek as the furniture, and at night the terrace has distinct snob appeal: come snappily dressed or suffer the consequences (you may be relegated to something resembling a dentist's waiting room). The menu headlines predictable Costes comfort food such as macaroni with morel mushrooms, but, sadly, most dishes are considerably less dazzling than the view. Exception: desserts by star pâtissier Stéphane Secco, whose YSL (as in Yves St-Laurent, darling) bitter chocolate cake is an event. ✉ *Centre Pompidou, 6th floor, rue Rambuteau, Beaubourg/Les Halles,* ☏ *01–44–78–47–99. AE, DC, MC, V. Closed Tues. Métro: Rambuteau.*

FRENCH

$$ ✕ **Au Bourguignon du Marais.** The handsome, contemporary look of this Marais bistro and wine bar is the perfect backdrop for the good traditional fare and excellent Burgundies served by the glass and bottle. Always on the menu are Burgundian classics such as *jambon persillé* (ham in parsleyed aspic jelly), escargots, and *oeufs en meurette* (eggs poached in a red wine sauce). ✉ *19 rue de Jouy, Beaubourg/Les Halles,* ☏ *01–48–87–15–40. AE, MC, V. No dinner Sun. Métro: St-Paul.*

$$ ✕ **Bofinger.** One of the oldest, most beautiful, and most popular brasseries in Paris has generally improved since brasserie maestro Jean-Paul Bucher (of the Flo group) took over. Settle in to one of the tables dressed in crisp white linen under the gorgeous Art Nouveau glass cupola—this part of the dining room is no-smoking—and enjoy classic brasserie fare, such as oysters, grilled sole, or lamb fillet. The prix fixe includes a decent half bottle of red or white wine (Provençal on our last visit). ✉ *5–7 rue de la Bastille, Bastille/Nation,* ☏ *01–42–72–87–82. AE, DC, MC, V. Métro: Bastille.*

$–$$ ✕ **Brasserie de l'Ile St-Louis.** Set on picturesque Ile St-Louis and opened in 1870—when Germany took over Alsace-Lorraine and its chefs decamped to the capital—this outpost of Alsatian cuisine remains a cozy cocoon filled with stuffed animal heads, antique fixtures fashioned from barrels, and folk-art paintings. The food is gemütlich, too: *coq-au-Riesling,* omelets with Muenster cheese, onion tarts, and *choucroutes garni* (sauerkraut studded with ham, bacon, and pork loin—one variant is made with smoked haddock). Pots of cumin seeds (for sprinkling on Muenster cheese) accompany the salt and pepper shakers on the communal tables and in warm weather, the crowds move out to the terrace overlooking the Seine and Notre-Dame. ✉ *55 quai de Bourbon, Ile St-Louis,* ☏ *01–43–54–02–59. MC, V. Métro: Pont Marie.*

$–$$ ★ ✕ **Grizzli Café.** The closing of this 19th-century bistro in 2001 for renovations sent shudders down the spines of its many French and foreign devotees. The result is, well, not disastrous—much of the historic main-floor dining room has been preserved, while the upstairs has been modernized (though the new owners wisely hung on to its bizarre bear tableau). The chef has fortunately stayed on, but some of the hearty classics have vanished to make way for pastas and salads. All-day serving hours are good news—too bad about the thumping music, which sadly makes the place feel like just another trendy Marais bar. ✉ *7 rue St-Martin, Le Marais,* ☎ *01–48–87–77–56. AE, DC, MC, V. Métro: Châtelet.*

MIDDLE EASTERN

$ ✕ **L'As du Fallafel.** Look no farther than the fantastic falafel stands on rue de Rosiers for some of the cheapest and tastiest meals in Paris, with the laurel crown usually awarded to this place. A falafel costs €3.50, but shell out a little extra money for the "spécial" with grilled eggplant, cabbage, hummus, tahini, and hot sauce. Though take-out is popular, you might find that it's quicker, easier and more entertaining to eat off a plastic plate in the buzzy dining room. ✉ *34 rue des Rosiers, Le Marais,* ☎ *01–48–87–63–60. MC, V. Closed Fri. dusk–Sat. dusk. Métro: St-Paul.*

5ᵉ Arrondissement (Latin Quarter)

FRENCH

$$$$ ★ ✕ **La Tour d'Argent.** Beyond the pretty wonderful food (the current chef is Jean-François Sicallac), many factors conspire to make a meal here memorable: the extraordinary wine cellar, considerate service, and of course that privileged view across the Seine and beyond. If the price of dinner makes you pause, you can't go wrong with the €60 lunch—you'll even be entitled to succulent slices of one of the restaurant's numbered ducks (the great duck slaughter began in 1919). Try to splurge a little on the wine—for about €80 you can taste a rare vintage Burgundy. The lunch crowd is remarkably casual, while evenings are a more formal affair. ✉ *15 quai de la Tournelle, Latin Quarter,* ☎ *01–43–54–23–31. Reservations essential. AE, DC, MC, V. Closed Mon. Métro: Cardinal Lemoine.*

$$$–$$$$ ★ ✕ **Lapérouse.** Emile Zola, George Sand, and Victor Hugo were regulars, and ladies are said to have mercilessly tested the authenticity of their diamonds on the restaurant's mirrors, which still bear the scratches today—all this makes it hard not to fall in love with this 17th-century Seine-side town house. Chef Alain Hacquard seems to have found the right track with a daring (for Paris) spice-infused menu: his lobster, Dublin Bay prawn, and crayfish bisque is flavored with Szechuan pepper and a lemon vinaigrette. For the ultimate romantic meal, reserve a private salon where anything could happen (and probably has). ✉ *51 quai des Grands Augustins, Latin Quarter,* ☎ *01–43–26–68–04. Reservations essential. AE, DC, MC, V. Closed Sun., 3 wks in July, 1 wk in Aug. No lunch Sat. Métro: St-Michel.*

$$ ★ ✕ **Le Reminet.** Chandeliers and mirrors add an unexpected note of elegance at this relaxed and unusually good bistro set in a narrow salon with stone walls. The menu changes regularly and displays the young chef's talent with dishes like a salad of scallops, greens, and sesame seeds, and roasted guinea hen with buttered Savoy cabbage. If it's available, try the luscious caramelized pear with cream. ✉ *3 rue des Grands-Degrés, Latin Quarter,* ☎ *01–44–07–04–24. MC, V. Closed Tues.–Wed., 2 wks in Aug., and 3 wks in Feb. Métro: Maubert-Mutualité.*

$ ✕ **Les Pipos.** The tourist-trap restaurants along romantic rue de la Montagne Ste-Genevieve are enough to make you despair—and then you stumble across this corner bistro, bursting with chatter and laughter. Slang for students of the famous École Polytechnique nearby, Les Pipos is everything you could ask of a Latin Quarter bistro: the space is cramped, the food is substantial (the cheese comes from the Lyon market), and conversation flows as freely as the wine. ✉ *2 rue de L'École*

Polytechnique, Latin Quarter, ☎ *01–43–54–11–40. No credit cards. Closed Sun. Métro: Maubert Mutualité.*

6e Arrondissement (St-Germain-des-Prés/Latin Quarter)

BELGIAN

$–$$ ★ ✕ **Le Bouillon Racine.** Originally a *bouillon*—a Parisian soup kitchen popular at the turn of the 20th century—this two-story restaurant is now a lushly renovated Belle Epoque oasis featuring a sophisticated Belgian menu. *Waterzooi* (Belgian stewed chicken and vegetables) and roast cod with white beans are excellent main dishes. For a finale, opt for the mocha-beer mousse with malt sauce. There are more than 50 beers available, and you can also drop into the new annex next door for a quick snack. ✉ *3 rue Racine, St-Germain-des-Prés,* ☎ *01–44–32–15–60. Reservations essential. AE, MC, V. Métro: Odéon.*

CONTEMPORARY

$$ ★ ✕ **Le Café des Délices.** There is a lot to like about this new contemporary bistro, from the warm and spacious decor, with little pots of spices on each table, to the polished service and lip-smacking food. Drop in for the bargain €13 lunch, or indulge in à la carte dishes such sea bream on white beans cooked with anchovy, lemon, coriander, and chile pepper. Tongue-in-cheek comfort-food desserts tease with ingredients such as Chupa Chups (lollipops) and sugary cereal. ✉ *87 rue d'Assas, Montparnasse,* ☎ *01–43–54–70–00. AE, MC, V. Closed weekends. Métro: Vavin.*

$$ ★ ✕ **Ze Kitchen Galerie.** Baby bistros grow up so fast—now they are even spawning their own offshoots. William Ledeuil made his name at the popular Les Bookinistes (a Guy Savoy baby) before opening this pared-down contemporary bistro nearby in late 2001. If the name isn't exactly inspired, the cooking shows unbridled creativity: expect dishes such as a chicken wing, broccoli, and artichoke soup with lemongrass, or pork ribs with curry jus and white beans. All in all, one of the most mouthtickling kitchens in the city. ✉ *4 quai des Grands-Augustins, Latin Quarter,* ☎ *01–44–32–00–32. AE, DC, MC, V. Closed Sun. No lunch Sat. Métro: St-Michel.*

FRENCH

$$–$$$ ✕ **Chez Dumonet–Josephine.** Stylish and convivial, this venerable bistro with amber walls, moleskin banquettes, and frosted-glass lamps is popular with theater people and politicians. Generous portions of classic French cuisine are served; typical are the very good boeuf bourguignon and the roasted saddle of lamb with artichokes. The wine list is excellent but expensive. ✉ *117 rue du Cherche-Midi, St-Germain-des-Prés,* ☎ *01–45–48–52–40. AE, MC, V. Closed weekends, Aug. and 1 wk in Feb. Métro: Duroc.*

$$$–$$$$ ✕ **Hélène Darroze.** Hélène Darroze has been crowned the newest female culinary star in Paris, thanks to the creative flair she has given the classics of southwestern French cooking, from the lands around Albi and Toulouse. You know it's not going to be *la même chanson*—the same old song—as soon as you see the contemporary Tse & Tse tableware, and her intriguingly modern touch comes through in such dishes as a sublime duck foie gras confit served with chutney of exotic fruits, or a blowout of roast wild duck stuffed with foie gras and truffles. Be warned, however, that portions are small and service can be downright unprofessional. Few can resist the *île flottante* meringue in a rose water–flavored crème anglaise. Recently made over, the downstairs bistro offers similar food in smaller, tapas-style portions, but you can still expect to pay €53–€61 per person with wine. ✉ *4 rue d'Assas, St-Germain-des-Prés,* ☎ *01–42–22–00–11. AE, DC, MC, V.*

Closed Sun.–Mon. Métro: Sèvres Babylone.

7e Arrondissement (Invalides/Eiffel Tower)

CONTEMPORARY

$$$–$$$$ ★ ✕ **Petrossian.** If you think even serious food should be playful, you'll be delighted by this deceptively plain-looking restaurant. Left Bank politicos and intellectuals gather here for one of the most entertaining dining experiences in Paris—Philippe Conticini serves many of his dishes in straight-sided glasses rather than on plates, to be scooped out with a small spoon. Petrossian is a legendary name in the smoked fish and caviar game, so why not splurge? After a pause for "drinkable perfumes," end with a symphony of desserts. ✉ *18 bd. de La-Tour-Maubourg, Invalides/Eiffel Tower,* ☎ *01–44–11–32–32. AE, DC, MC, V. Closed Sun. and Mon. Métro: La-Tour-Maubourg, Invalides.*

FRENCH

$$$$ ★ ✕ **Jules Verne.** Top-flight chef Alain Reix's cuisine—not to mention a location at 400 ft up on the second level of the Eiffel Tower—makes a table at the Jules Verne one of the hardest dinner reservations to get in Paris. Sautéed baby squid with duck foie gras and veal filet mignon cooked with preserved lemon and dried fruits are examples of Reix's cooking. A mere €48 will buy you the Jules Verne experience at lunch, though the food doesn't live up to the à la carte offerings. A table is easier to snag at lunch—arrive early for a prime seat near the window to enjoy the views of Paris—the restaurant itself is a tired hybrid of *Star Trek* and '70s disco. ✉ *Eiffel Tower, Invalides/Eiffel Tower,* ☎ *01–45–55–61–44. Reservations essential. Jacket and tie. AE, DC, MC, V. Métro: Bir-Hakeim.*

$$–$$$ ✕ **Au Bon Accueil.** To see what well-heeled Parisians like to eat these days, book a table at this extremely popular bistro as soon as you get to town. The excellent, reasonably priced *cuisine du marché* has made it a hit: typical of the winter fare is roast suckling pig with thyme and endives. ✉ *14 rue de Montessuy, Invalides/Eiffel Tower,* ☎ *01–47–05–46–11. Reservations essential. MC, V. Closed weekends, 2 wks in Aug. Métro, RER: Pont de l'Alma.*

8e Arrondissement (Champs-Élysées/Louvre)

CONTEMPORARY

$$$–$$$$ ★ ✕ **Market.** Following hot on the heels of Nobu, New York chef Jean-Georges Vongerichten (of New York's Vong, Mercer Kitchen, Jean-Georges fame) set up shop in Paris in late 2001. Put together with deceptively simple raw materials—burnt pine and stone offset with African masks—the dining room makes a stylish and relaxed, if sometimes noisy, setting for well-travelled dishes such as pizza with raw tuna and wasabi cream, Thai-style chicken-coconut soup with galanga, and duck fillet with sesame jus and tamarind confit. ✉ *15 av. Matignon, Champs-Élysées,* ☎ *01–56–43–40–90. AE, MC, V. Métro: Franklin-D.-Roosevelt.*

$$–$$$ ✕ **Korova.** Named after the Milk Bar in the film *Clockwork Orange* (*korova* is Russian for "cow"), this funky "diner" attracts the area's moooovers and shakers. Four curvy rooms are done up in white, pearl gray, and watery green: groovy music and soft lighting complete the space-age picture. Korova has a jet-set menu that hops from hot dogs (with lobster and mayonnaise) to vintage canned sardines. A meal will set you back at least €46 a head, but you could always drop in from 8 AM for breakfast or after 11 PM for a drink to watch the city's fashion victims in action. ✉ *33 rue Marbeuf, Champs-Élysées,* ☎ *01–53–89–93–93. AE, DC, MC, V. No lunch Sat. and Sun. Métro: Franklin-D.-Roosevelt.*

$$–$$$ ★ ✕ **Maison Blanche.** The twin Pourcel brothers preside over this "White House," which trumpets a show-off view across Paris from the top floor of the Théâtre du Champs-Élysées. The formerly gray decor has gone fashionably white and the food offers a refreshing taste of the south: hot and iced tomatoes on a pumpkin purée with fresh truffles, scallop carpaccio with sea urchin coral, and Swiss chard ravioli with tomato confit. Soothe frayed urban nerves with comforting desserts such as a caramel popsicle with pecan cake. ✉ *15 av. Montaigne, Champs-Élysées,* ☎ *01–53–89–93–93. AE, DC, MC, V. Closed Sun. No lunch Sat. Métro: Franklin-D.-Roosevelt.*

FRENCH

$$$$ ★ ✕ **Alain Ducasse.** You may need to set a steel trap outside his door to actually catch Alain Ducasse in this kitchen—he now has restaurants around the globe (and never cooks on weekends)—but it would probably be worth the wait. The rosy rococo salons in the Plaza Athenée hotel were updated by decorator Patrick Jouin, who draped metallic organza over the chandeliers and, in a symbolic move, made time stand still by stopping the clock. Overlooking the prettiest courtyard in Paris, this makes for a setting as delicious as Ducasse's roast lamb garnished with "crumbs" of dried fruit. The menu changes constantly, but the Dublin Bay prawns—at a cool €115—are popular with his jet-set customers. ✉ *Hotel Plaza-Athénée, 27 av. Montaigne, Champs-Élysées,* ☎ *01–53–67–66–65. AE, DC, MC, V. Closed weekends, Christmas wk, 2 wks in July, 3 wks in Aug. No lunch Mon.–Wed. Métro: Alma-Marceau.*

$$$$ ★ ✕ **Les Ambassadeurs.** Looking as if Madame de Pompadour might stroll in the door at any moment, Les Ambassadeurs offers a world of ancien régime splendor. Chef Dominique Bouchet likes to mix luxe with more down-to-earth flavors: potato pancakes topped with smoked salmon, caviar-flecked scallops wrapped in bacon with tomato and basil, duck with rutabaga, turbot with cauliflower. The €62 lunch menu is well worth the splurge—especially in summer, when you can while away the rest of the afternoon on the gorgeous terrace. There is even a breakfast—talk about luxury—served from 7 to 10:30 AM. Jacket and tie are required at dinner. ✉ *Hôtel Crillon, 10 pl. de la Concorde, Louvre/Tuileries,* ☎ *01–44–71–16–16. AE, DC, MC, V. Métro: Concorde.*

$$$$ ★ ✕ **Les Élysées du Vernet.** This may be the most perfect choice for a *classique* blowout in Paris today, thanks to its remarkable harmonic alignment of staff, decor, and kitchen. One taste of chef's Alain Solivères's *Parmentier de sanglier au panais* (shepherd's pie of roasted boar with garlic parsnips) will tell you why he's a hero in food circles. Service is impeccable and the intimate dining room, under a magnificently beautiful turn-of-the-20th-century *verrière* (glass ceiling) designed by Gustave Eiffel himself, is the kind of place where you want to linger and dream. ✉ *Hôtel Vernet, 25 rue Vernet, Champs-Élysées,* ☎ *01–44–31–98–98. Reservations essential. AE, DC, MC, V. Closed weekends, Aug., and 2 wks in Dec. Métro: George V.*

$$$$ ★ ✕ **Pierre Gagnaire.** Legendary chef Pierre Gagnaire's cooking is at once intellectual and poetic—in a single dish at least three or four often unexpected tastes come together in a sensational experience. Just taking in the menu requires concentration, so complex are descriptions such as "suckling lamb from Aveyron: sweetbreads, saddle and rack; green papaya and turnip velouté thickened with Tarbais beans." The businesslike gray-and-wood dining room feels refreshingly informal, but uneven service and a scanty wine list are unfortunate drawbacks at this price. ✉ *6 rue de Balzac, Champs-Élysées,* ☎ *01–58–36–12–50. Reservations essential. AE, DC, MC, V. Closed Sat. and mid-July–mid-Aug. No lunch Sun. Métro: Charles-de-Gaulle–Étoile.*

$$$–$$$$ ★ ✕ **Taillevent.** Once the most traditional of all Paris luxury restaurants, this grande dame has been subtly modernized since the arrival of chef Michel Del Burgo. He has judiciously revised the menu here, adding creations that sometimes eerily resemble dishes served in modern bistros. Classics such as the *boudin de homard*—an airy sausage-shaped lobster soufflé—offer continuity with the fabled past. Service is flawless, the 19th-century paneled salons *luxe,* the well-priced wine list probably one of the top 10 in the world—all in all, a meal here is usually an event. ✉ *15 rue Lamennais, Champs-Élysées,* ☏ *01–44–95–15–01. Reservations essential a month in advance. Jacket and tie. AE, DC, MC, V. Closed weekends and Aug. Métro: Charles-de-Gaulle–Étoile.*

$$ ★ ✕ **Chez Savy.** Just off the glitzy avenue Montaigne, Chez Savy exists in its own circa-1930s dimension, oblivious to the area's galloping fashionization. The Art Deco cream-and-burgundy interior looks blissfully intact (avoid the back room unless you're in a large group) and the waiters show not a trace of attitude, even offering to change a wine bottle that's just a touch too chilled. Fill up on rib-sticking specialties from the Auvergne in central France—lentil salad with bacon, beautifully charred lamb with feather-light shoestring frites, poached peach with sorbet—order a celebratory bottle of Mercurey, and feel smug that you've found this place. ✉ *23 rue Bayard, Champs-Élysées,* ☏ *01–47–23–46–98. AE, MC, V. Closed weekends and Aug. Métro: Franklin-D.-Roosevelt.*

JAPANESE

$$–$$$ ★ ✕ **Nobu.** The Parisian branch of Nobu opened just in time for the fall 2001 fashion shows and has been drawing an insouciant crowd ever since. This is one place where *branché* Parisians go as much for the cuisine as the scene: bye-bye boring salmon and tuna, *bienvenue* eel sashimi, soft-crab sushi, beef toban yaki, and Peruvian-inspired sole with black bean sauce. Nobu is definitely the only restaurant in Paris where waiters kneel to take your order—and, even more shocking, the dining room is no-smoking. ✉ *15 rue Marbeuf, Champs-Élysées,* ☏ *01–56–89–53–53. AE, DC, MC, V. Métro: Franklin-D.-Roosevelt.*

9e Arrondissement (Opéra/Pigalle-Clichy)

FRENCH

$ ✕ **Chartier.** People come here more for the bonhomie than the food, which is often stunningly ordinary. This cavernous 1896 restaurant enjoys a huge following among budget-minded students, solitary bachelors, and tourists. You may find yourself sharing a table with strangers as you study the long, old-fashioned menu of such favorites as hard-boiled eggs with mayonnaise, steak tartare, and roast chicken with fries. ✉ *7 rue du Faubourg-Montmartre, Opéra/Grands Boulevards,* ☏ *01–47–70–86–29. Reservations not accepted. AE, DC, MC, V. Métro: Montmartre.*

10e Arrondissement (République/Gare du Nord)

FRENCH

$$$ ★ ✕ **Chez Michel.** Effusive chef Thierry Breton pulls in a stylish crowd of Parisians and tourists with his wonderful market-inspired cooking, despite the out-of-the-way location in a pretty neighborhood near Gare du Nord. The prix-fixe-only menu changes constantly, but you'll almost invariably find the Breton specialties *kig ha farz* (a robust pork stew with a bread stuffing) and *kouing aman* (the butteriest cake imaginable). In winter, don't miss Breton's succulent game dishes such as the surprisingly mild-tasting boar chops, served in a cast-iron pot with tiny potatoes and roasted garlic. ✉ *10 rue Belzunce, République,* ☏

01–44–53–06–20. *Reservations essential. MC, V. Closed Sun.–Mon. and Aug. Métro: Gare du Nord.*

11e Arrondissement (Bastille/République)

FRENCH

$$ ★ ✕ **Astier.** The prix-fixe menu (there's no à la carte) at this popular, old-fashioned restaurant must be one of the best values in town. Among the beautifully prepared seasonal dishes are baked eggs topped with truffled foie gras, fricassee of *joue de boeuf* (beef cheeks), rabbit in mustard sauce with fresh tagliatelle, and plum *clafoutis* (a fruit flan). This is a great place to come if you're feeling cheesy, since it's locally famous for having one of the best *plateaux de fromages* (cheese plates) in Paris. ✉ *44 rue Jean-Pierre Timbaud, République,* ☎ *01–43–57–16–35. Reservations essential. MC, V. Closed weekends, Aug., Christmas wk, Easter wk. Métro: Parmentier.*

$ ✕ **Le Kitch.** Fighting the good fight against ennui, this whimsically casual place attracts graphic designers, couturiers-in-training, and other denizens of its arty neighborhood. There's more than a touch of Pee-Wee's Playhouse here—faux-stucco walls, plastic children's furniture, and naïf paintings of cats make this a cute boutique restaurant. Happily, once you taste the dishes here, you won't need to call the chef The Mad Batter: the food here is snappy, if not stylish, and tasty enough to give a satisfied buzz to the room. ✉ *10 rue Oberkampf, Père Lachaise,* ☎ *01–40–21–94–14. No credit cards. No lunch Sat. and Sun. Métro: Oberkampf.*

12e Arrondissement (Bastille/Nation)

FRENCH

$$ ★ ✕ **Le Square Trousseau.** This beautiful Belle Epoque bistro is a favorite of the fashion set, led by Jean-Paul Gaultier, who has his headquarters nearby. You might see a supermodel—Claudia Schiffer often comes in when in town—while dining on the homemade foie gras, slow-cooked lamb, or tender baby chicken with mustard and bread-crumb crust. Some dishes are more successful than others, but atmosphere is never lacking and staff are cheerful. ✉ *1 rue Antoine Vollon, Bastille/Nation,* ☎ *01–43–43–06–00. AE, MC, V. Closed Sun.–Mon., and Christmas wk. Métro: Ledru-Rollin.*

13e Arrondissement (Les Gobelins)

FRENCH

$$–$$$ ✕ **Le Terroir.** A jolly crowd of regulars makes this little bistro festive. Based on first-rate ingredients from all over France, the menu is solidly classical—salads with chicken livers or fresh marinated anchovies, calves' liver or monkfish with saffron, and pears marinated in wine for dessert, for instance. ✉ *11 bd. Arago, St-Germain-des-Prés,* ☎ *01–47–07–36–99. AE, MC, V. Closed weekends, Easter wk, 3 wks in Aug., Christmas wk. Métro: Les Gobelins.*

14e Arrondissement (Montparnasse)

FRENCH

$$$ ★ ✕ **La Régalade.** To satisfy the hungry hordes who trek to the edge of town for his inspired seasonal cooking, Yves Camdeborde does three dinner sittings—and you still have to book at least two weeks ahead. The crowded, no-frills room evokes the provinces, but the food is worthy of a luxury restaurant: tempting dishes on a winter menu might include paper-thin Dublin Bay prawn carpaccio, juicy roast capon with chestnuts, fresh duck foie gras panfried in spice-bread crumbs, and a bitter, adult dessert of grapefruit in Campari jelly. Portions are small, but the country pâté that begins each meal will take the edge off your appetite. ✉ *49 av. Jean-Moulin, Montparnasse,* ☎

01–45–45–68–58, Reservations essential 2 wks. in advance. MC, V. Closed Sun.–Mon. and Aug. No lunch Sat. Métro: Alésia.

$$–$$$ ✕ **La Coupole.** This world-renowned, cavernous spot practically defines the term brasserie—and its Art Deco murals are famous, too. La Coupole might have lost its intellectual aura since the Flo group's restoration—that giant rotating sculpture was one of the "improvements"—but it has been popular since the days when Jean-Paul Sartre and Simone de Beauvoir were regulars. Today it attracts a mix of bourgeois families, tourists, and elderly lone diners treating themselves to a dozen oysters. Expect the usual brasserie menu, including perhaps the largest shellfish platter in Paris. ✉ *102 bd. du Montparnasse, Montparnasse,* ☏ *01–43–20–14–20. AE, DC, MC, V. Métro: Vavin.*

15e Arrondissement (Motte-Picquet/Balard)

FRENCH

$$–$$$ ★ ✕ **L'Os à Moelle.** This small, popular bistro has a very good-value six-course dinner menu (there's no à la carte) that changes daily; portions are generous. A sample meal might include white-bean soup, sautéed foie gras, *rouget* (red mullet fish), lamb with potato puree, cheese with a small salad, and a delicious roasted pear with cinnamon ice cream. At lunch, there is a shorter, equally good prix-fixe. ✉ *3 rue Vasco-de-Gama, Invalides/Eiffel Tower,* ☏ *01–45–57–27–27. Reservations essential. MC, V. Closed Sun.–Mon. and Aug. Métro: Balard.*

16e Arrondissement (Trocadéro/Bois de Boulogne)

FRENCH

$$$–$$$$ ★ ✕ **Ghislaine Arabian.** After a two-and-a-half year absence from the Paris restaurant scene, the former chef of Ledoyen is back with a vengeance. Ghislaine Arabian's small, contemporary dining room reflects her sparkling personality, with gold leaf on the walls and a frieze of women's faces sculpted from Murano glass. Her cooking, as always, is inspired by her northern French roots: try the classic shrimp croquettes with fried parsley and perhaps roasted pigeon with Flemish-style red-cabbage confit (the menu changes seasonally). Whatever you do, save room for her frozen parfait of chicory and spice bread with white beer sabayon. ✉ *16 av. Bugeaud, Trocadéro,* ☏ *01–56–28–16–16. Reservations essential. AE, DC, MC, V. Closed Sun. No lunch Sat. or Mon. Metro: Victor-Hugo.*

$$$–$$$$ ★ ✕ **Jamin.** At this intimate if rather frilly restaurant, where Joël Robuchon made his name, you can find excellent haute cuisine at almost half the price of other restaurants of its kind: there is a lunch prix-fixe at just €47 and a €76 menu at lunch and dinner. Benoît Guichard, Robuchon's second for many years, is a subtle and accomplished chef and a particularly brilliant *saucier* (sauce maker). The menu changes regularly, but Guichard favors such dishes as sea bass with pistachios in fennel sauce and braised beef with cumin-scented carrots. ✉ *32 rue de Longchamp, Trocadéro,* ☏ *01–45–53–00–07. Reservations essential. AE, DC, MC, V. Closed weekends and 3 wks in Aug. Métro: Iéna.*

$$–$$$ ★ ✕ **L'Astrance.** *Le Point* has called L'Astrance "a miracle," while *Le Figaro*'s respected critic François Simon has described it as "perfect." What's all the fuss about? Well, this split-level gray dining room is probably the best place in Paris to part with your hard-earned euros for a special-occasion meal: you get the quality of haute cuisine without the pomposity or the crushing price tag. For a mere €28.20 at lunch you might feast on a ballotine of quail and foie gras, spiced mackerel fillet on Asian-style spinach, and orange soufflé with marjoram ice cream. Don't forget to reserve a month in advance. ✉ *4 rue Beethoven, Trocadéro,* ☏ *01–40–50–84–40. Reservations essential. AE, DC, MC, V. Métro: Passy.*

SEAFOOD

$$$–$$$$ ★ ✕ **Prunier.** Founded in 1925, this seafood restaurant is one of the best, and surely the prettiest, in Paris—even more so following recent renovations (though the wood-paneled upstairs dining room does look a bit sauna-like). Now a New York–style caviar house, Maison Prunier doesn't offer much in the way of cooking—a world-weary set from the blasé 16th comes here to feast on Aquitaine caviar (for a cool €100 a tablespoon), chilled oysters with hot, spiced sausages (a Bordeaux specialty), and the so-chic "Christian Dior jellied egg." ✉ *16 av. Victor-Hugo, Champs-Élysées,* ☎ *01–44–17–35–85. Jacket and tie. AE, DC, MC, V. Closed Sun. and Aug. Métro: Étoile.*

17ᵉ Arrondissement (Monceau/Champs-Élysées)

FRENCH

$$$$ ★ ✕ **Guy Savoy.** Redecorated by Jean-Michel Wilmotte, who dressed up the space with dark African wood, rich leather (like the inside of a Rolls-Royce), and cream-color marble, Guy Savoy's luxury restaurant has stepped gracefully into the 21st century. Come here for a perfectly measured, contemporary haute-cuisine experience, since Savoy's several bistros have not lured him away from his kitchen. The artichoke soup with black truffles, sea bass with spices, and veal kidneys in mustard-spiked jus reveal the magnitude of his talent. Half-portions allow you to graze your way through the menu, and reasonably priced wines are available. Best of all, the atmosphere is joyful—Savoy senses that having fun is just as important as eating well. ✉ *18 rue Troyon, Champs-Élysées,* ☎ *01–43–80–40–61. AE, MC, V. Closed Sun., Mon., mid-July–mid-Aug., Christmas wk. No lunch Sat. Métro: Charles-de-Gaulle–Étoile.*

18ᵉ Arrondissement (Montmartre)

FRENCH

$ ✕ **Le Moulin à Vins.** The atmosphere at this popular wine bar–bistro is sepia-toned, since both the place itself and surrounding neighborhood evoke premodern Paris. It's perfect for a lunch of salad or a cold-meat-and-cheese plate while touring Montmartre. In the evening it's much livelier, when devoted regulars—a great mix that runs from bikers to bankers—come for the daily short list of hot dishes. ✉ *6 rue Burq, Montmartre,* ☎ *01–45–52–81–27. AE, MC, V. Closed Sun.–Mon. and 3 wks in Aug. No lunch Tues., Fri., or Sat. Métro: Abbesses.*

Cafés and Salons de Thé

Along with air, water, and wine (Parisians eat fewer and fewer three-course meals), the café remains one of the basic necessities of life in Paris; following is a small selection of cafés and *salons de thé* (tearooms) to whet your appetite. **Au Père Tranquille** (✉ 16 rue Pierre Lescot, Beaubourg/Les Halles, 1ᵉʳ, ☎ 01–45–08–00–34, métro: Les Halles) is one of the best places in Paris for people-watching. **Café Beaubourg** (✉ 43 rue St-Merri, Beaubourg/Les Halles, 4ᵉ, ☎ 01–48–87–63–96, métro: Hôtel-de-Ville), near the Pompidou Center, is a slick, modern spot. **Café Marly** (✉ Cour Napoléon du Louvre, 93 rue de Rivoli, Louvre/Tuileries, 1ᵉʳ, ☎ 01–49–26–06–60, métro: Palais-Royal), overlooking the main courtyard of the Louvre, is perfect for an afternoon break or a nightcap, though the food could be better. **La Crémaillère** (✉ 15 pl. du Tertre, Montmartre, 18ᵉ, ☎ 01–46–06–58–59, métro: Anvers) is a veritable monument to fin-de-siècle art in Montmartre. **Le Flore en l'Ile** (✉ 42 quai d'Orléans, Ile St-Louis, 4ᵉ, ☎ 01–43–29–88–27, métro: Pont-Marie) is set on the Ile St-Louis and has a magnificent view of the Seine. **Ladurée** (✉ 16 rue Royale, Opéra/Grands Boulevards, 8ᵉ, ☎ 01–42–60–21–79, métro: Madeleine) is pretty enough to bring a tear to Proust's eye—this salon de thé has barely changed since

1862. You'll dote on the signature lemon-and-caramel macaroons (another ravishing outpost is at 75 av. des Champs-Élysées). **Ma Bourgogne** (✉ 19 pl. des Vosges, Le Marais, 4e, ☎ 01–42–78–44–64, métro: St-Paul) is a calm oasis for a coffee or a light lunch away from the noisy streets. **Mariage Frères** (✉ 30 rue du Bourg-Tibourg, Le Marais, 4e, ☎ 01–42–72–28–11, métro: Hôtel-de-Ville) is an outstanding tea shop serving 500 kinds of tea, along with delicious tarts. **Salon de Thé du Palais Royal** (✉ Jardins du Palais Royal, 110 Galérie de Valois, Louvre/Tuileries, 1er, ☎ 01–40–20–00–27, métro: Palais-Royal) serves tea on a terrace overlooking the gardens of the Palais Royal. **Le Vieux Colombier** (✉ 65 rue de Rennes, St-Germain-des-Pres, 7e, ☎ 01–45–48–53–81, métro: St-Sulpice) is just around the corner from St-Sulpice and the Vieux Colombier Theater.

LODGING

Revised and updated by Christopher Mooney

Winding staircases, flower-filled window boxes, concierges who seem to have stepped from a 19th-century novel—all of these can still be found in Paris hotels. So do grand rooms with marble baths, Belle Epoque lobbies, and polished staff at your beck and call. In Paris there are beckoning hotels for every taste and budget.

Criteria when selecting the hotels reviewed below were quality, location, and character. Fewer hotels are listed in outlying arrondissements (the 10e to the 20e) because these are farther from the major sights. Generally, there are more hotels offering luxury on the Right Bank—or, at any rate, formality—than there are on the Left Bank, where hotels are frequently smaller and richer in old-fashioned ambience. In Paris's oldest quarters hotel rooms are generally much smaller than their American counterparts. Although air-conditioning has become de rigueur in middle- to higher-price hotels, it is generally not a prerequisite for comfort (Paris's hot-weather season doesn't usually last long).

Despite the huge choice of hotels, you should always reserve well in advance, especially if you're determined to stay in a specific place. You can do this by telephoning, faxing, or e-mailing ahead, then asking for confirmation of your reservation, detailing the duration of your stay, the price, the location and type of your room (single or double, twin beds or double), and the bathroom (shower—*douche*—or bath—*baignoire*—private or shared).

Almost all Paris hotels charge extra for breakfast, with prices ranging from €4.61 to more than €30 per person in luxury establishments. For anything more than the standard Continental breakfast of café au lait and croissants, the price will be higher. You may be better off finding the nearest café. A nominal *séjour* (lodging) tax of €1.07 per person per night is charged to pay for promotion of tourism in Paris.

Assume that hotel rooms have air-conditioning, TV, telephones, and private bath unless otherwise noted. Internet, when listed in facilities, means in-room data-ports and/or public-area computer provides computer access.

CATEGORY	COST*
$$$$	over €270
$$$	€150–€270
$$	€90–€150
$	under €90

**All prices are for a standard double room in high season, including 19.6% tax and service.*

1er Arrondissement (Louvre/Les Halles)

$$$$ ★ **Costes.** The darling of the fashion and media sets, Jean-Louis and Gilbert Costes's sumptuous hotel conjures up the palaces of Napoléon III. Salons are swathed in rich garnet and bronze tones and contain a luxurious mélange of patterned fabrics, heavy swags, and enough brocade and fringe to blanket the Champs-Élysées. The seductive, go-for-Baroque bar, with its labyrinth of little rooms and secluded nooks, is *the* place to be seen trying not to be seen in Paris. You can't get more chic than this. ✉ *239 rue St-Honoré, Louvre/Tuileries, 75001,* ☎ *01–42–44–50–50,* FAX *01–42–44–50–01,* WEB *www.hotelcostes.com. 85 rooms. Restaurant, bar, cable TV, in-room safes, minibars, Internet, room service, indoor pool, sauna, gym, laundry service. AE, DC, MC, V. Métro: Tuileries.*

$$$$ ★ **Meurice.** One of the finest hotels in the world has become even finer—thanks to the millions of the Sultan of Brunei. The restaurant—a fabled extravaganza of cream boiseries and glittering chandeliers—and the elaborately gilded 18th-century Rococo salons have been entirely restored, while the guest rooms, adorned with Persian carpets, marble mantelpieces, and ormolu clocks, are now more opulent and soigné than ever, if that's possible (book well in advance for a room or a suite overlooking the Tuileries Gardens). ✉ *228 rue de Rivoli, Louvre/Tuileries, 75001,* ☎ *01–44–58–10–10,* FAX *01–44–58–10–15,* WEB *www.meuricehotel.com. 160 rooms, 36 suites. 2 restaurants, bar, in-room safes, cable TV, minibars, Internet, no-smoking rooms, room service, sauna, laundry service, business services. AE, DC, MC, V. Métro: Tuileries, Concorde.*

$$$$ **Ritz.** This legendary place has been regilded at a cost of $150 million by owner Mohammed al-Fayed (whose son Dodi, with Diana, Princess of Wales, set out on their fatal car ride after dining here in August 1997). Of course, there are really two Ritzes. The first is the gilded place Vendôme wing—this is where Gary Cooper serenaded Audrey Hepburn in *Love in the Afternoon* and showcases the legendary suites named after former residents, such as Marcel Proust and Coco Chanel. The newer wing remains surprisingly (disappointingly?) intimate. Don't miss the famous Hemingway Bar or the basement health club—a veritable Louis XIV temple of sweat. ✉ *15 pl. Vendôme, Louvre/Tuileries, 75001,* ☎ *01–43–16–30–30,* FAX *01–43–16–36–68,* WEB *www.parisritz.com. 142 rooms, 45 suites. 3 restaurants, 2 bars, in-room safes, room service, minibars, cable TV, Internet, indoor pool, hair salon, health club, shops, laundry service, parking (fee). AE, DC, MC, V. Métro: Opéra.*

$$$$ ★ **Vendôme.** This hotel has the best guest-to-staff ratio in Paris and every luxury perk imaginable. Rooms are in sumptuous, Second Empire style and bathrooms are over the top. Best of all, besides a videophone for checking out visitors at the door, is the fully automated bedside console that controls the lights, curtains, and electronic do-not-disturb sign. ✉ *1 pl. Vendôme, Louvres/Tuileries, 75001,* ☎ *01–42–60–32–84,* FAX *01–49–27–97–89. 19 rooms, 10 suites. Restaurant, bar, cable TV, minibars, Internet, room service, laundry service. AE, DC, MC, V. Métro: Concorde, Opéra.*

$$–$$$ **Britannique.** Open since 1870, the Britannique blends courteous English service with old-fashioned French elegance. It has retained its handsome winding staircase and has well-appointed, soundproof rooms in chic, warm tones. ✉ *20 av. Victoria, Beaubourg/Les Halles, 75001,* ☎ *01–42–33–74–59,* FAX *01–42–33–82–65. 40 rooms. Bar, no air-conditioning, cable TV, minibars, Internet, no-smoking rooms. AE, DC, MC, V. Métro: Châtelet.*

$$–$$$ **Régina.** In the handsome place des Pyramides, this 100-year-old Art Nouveau gem oozes old-fashioned grandeur in both its public spaces

and guest rooms. There is a sublime Belle Epoque lounge, and there are fine antiques throughout. Request a room on rue de Rivoli facing the Louvre and the Tuileries Gardens. ✉ *2 rue des Pyramides, Louvre/Tuileries, 75001,* ☎ *01–42–60–31–10,* FAX *01–40–15–95–16,* WEB *www.regina-hotel.com. 129 rooms, 15 suites. Restaurant, bar, cable TV, minibars, in-room safes, no-smoking rooms, room service, laundry service. AE, DC, MC, V. Métro: Tuileries.*

$ ★ **Louvre Forum.** This hotel is a find. Smack in the center of town, it has a friendly feel and clean, comfortable, well-equipped rooms (minibars, satellite TV). ✉ *25 rue du Bouloi, Louvre/Tuileries, 75001,* ☎ *01–42–36–54–19,* FAX *01–42–33–66–31. 27 rooms. Bar, minibars. AE, DC, MC, V. Métro: Louvre.*

$ **Tiquetonne.** Just off marché Montorgueil and a short hoof from Les Halles, this is one of the least expensive hotels in the city center. The rooms aren't much to look at, but they're always clean, and some are downright spacious. Book a room on one of the top two floors facing the quiet, pedestrian rue Tiquetonne, not the loud, car-strangled rue Turbigo. ✉ *6 rue Tiquetonne, Beaubourg/Les Halles, 75002,* ☎ *01–42–36–94–58,* FAX *01–42–36–02–94. 47 rooms. AE, MC, V. Métro: Etienne Marcel or Châtelet.*

2e Arrondissement (La Bourse/Les Halles)

$$$ **Hôtel de Noailles.** With a nod to the work of postmodern designers like Putman and Starck, this new-wave inn (part of the Tulip Inn group) is a star among Paris's new crop of well-priced, style-driven boutique hotels. Though not to everyone's taste, rooms are imaginatively decorated with funky furnishings and contemporary details. ✉ *9 rue de Michodière, Opéra/Grands Boulevards, 75002,* ☎ *01–47–42–92–90,* FAX *01–49–24–92–71. 58 rooms. Bar, cable TV, minibars, health club, no-smoking rooms, laundry service. AE, DC, MC, V. Métro: Opéra.*

$$$ **Victoires Opéra.** This terrific hotel is an oasis of calm amid the colorful bustle of Montorgueil, a very popular pedestrian-only market street near Les Halles, the Centre Pompidou, and the Marais. It was recently renovated and renamed (formerly the Besançon), and its rooms are spacious by central Paris standards and decorated in a tastefully restrained modern style. ✉ *56 rue Montorgueil, Beaubourg/Les Halles, 75002,* ☎ *01–42–36–41–08,* FAX *01–45–08–08–79. 20 rooms. In-room safes, cable TV, minibars, Internet, room service, baby-sitting, laundry service. AE, DC, MC, V. Métro: Étienne-Marcel, Les Halles.*

3e Arrondissement (Beaubourg/Marais)

$$$$ ★ **Pavillon de la Reine.** On place des Vosges and fronted by a magnificent drive-in entryway, this lovely mansion, reconstructed from original plans, is filled with Louis XII–style fireplaces and antiques. Lucky guests can book a duplex with French windows overlooking the first of two flower-filled courtyards behind the historic Queen's Pavilion. Breakfast is served in the vaulted cellar, *digestifs* in front of the main salon's gargantuan fireplace. ✉ *28 pl. des Vosges, Le Marais, 75003,* ☎ *01–40–29–19–19; 800/447–7462 in the U.S.,* FAX *01–40–29–19–20. 30 rooms, 25 suites. Bar, cable TV, minibars, Internet, room service, laundry service, free parking. AE, DC, MC, V. Métro: Bastille, St-Paul.*

4e Arrondissement (Marais/Ile St-Louis)

$$–$$$ **Hôtel du Jeu de Paume.** The showpiece of this lovely 17th-century hotel on the Ile St-Louis is the stone-walled, vaulted lobby-cum–breakfast room. It stands on an erstwhile court where French aristocrats once played *jeu de paume*, an early version of tennis using palm fronds. The bright rooms are nicely done up in butter yellow, with rustic antiques, bric-a-brac and objets d'art, beamed ceilings, and damask upholstery. The little garden is a haven of sun-drenched tranquillity. ✉ *54 rue St-*

Paris Lodging

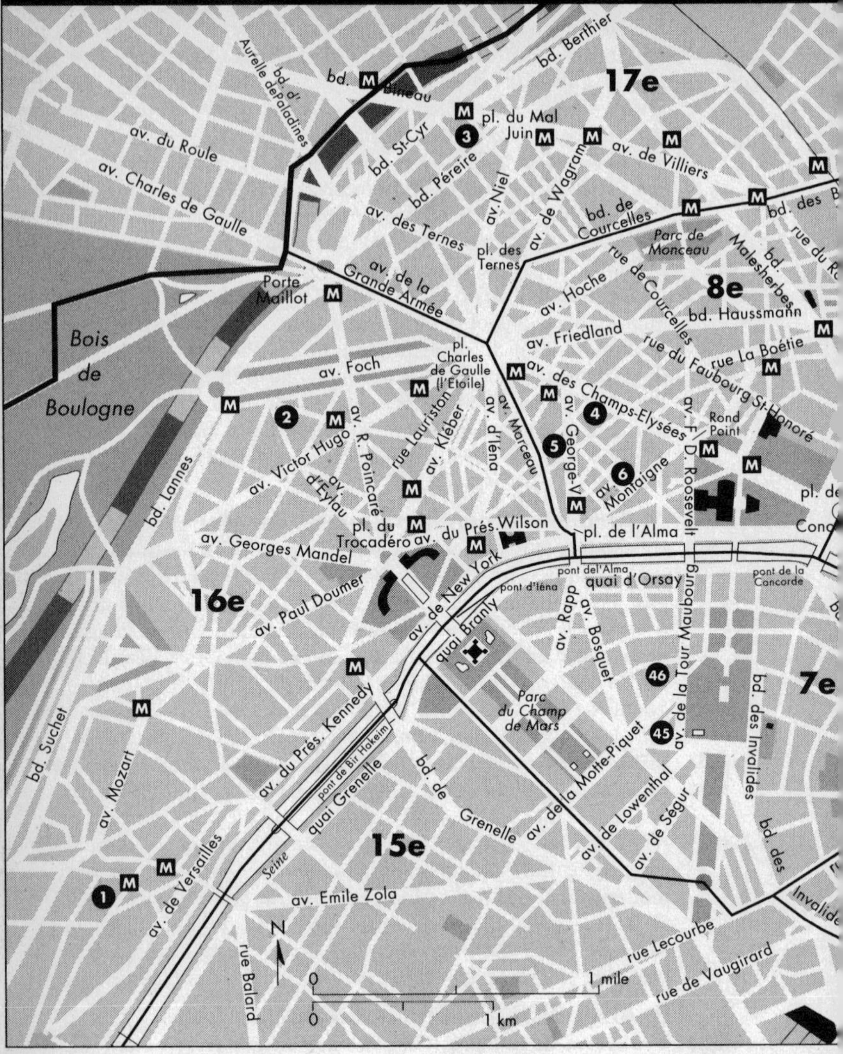

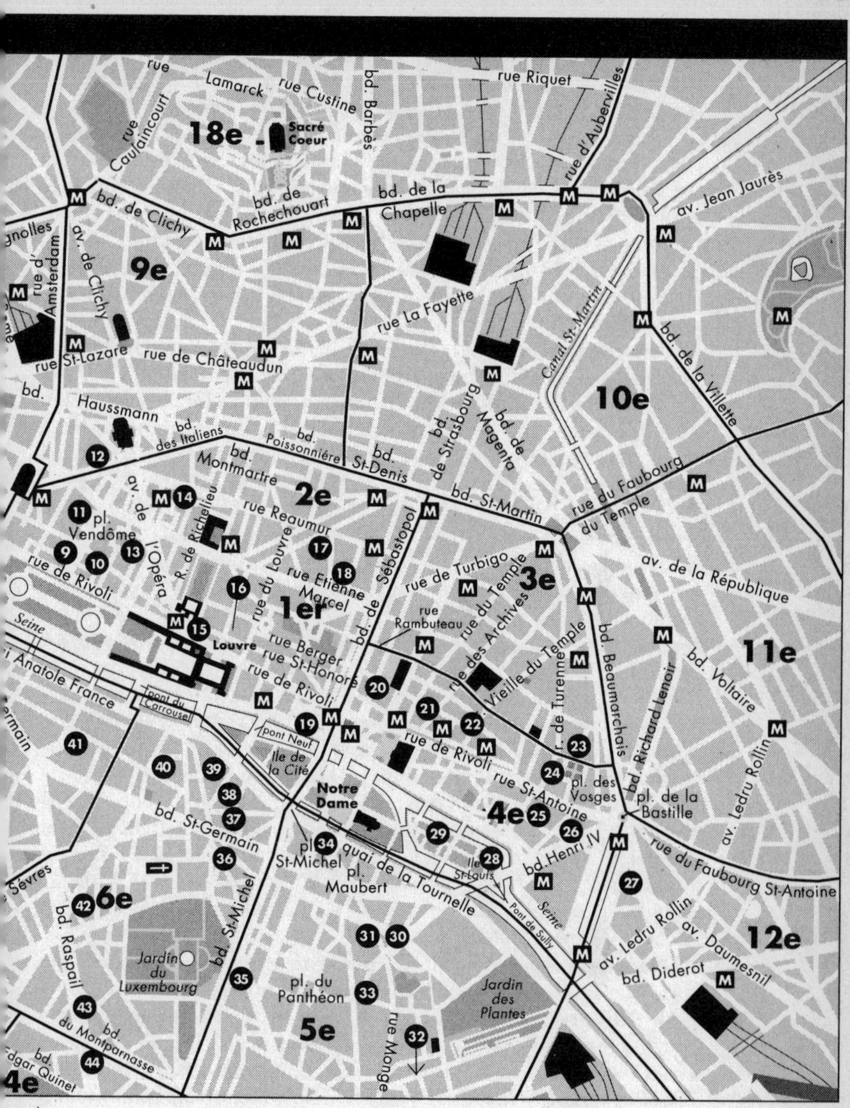

spail-
ontparnasse 44
gina 15
lais Christine 38
lais St-Germain . . . 36
z. 11
int James Paris 2
uetonne. 18
Tourville 43
ndôme. 13
toires Opéra 17

Louis-en-l'Ile, Ile-St-Louis, 75004, ☎ 01-43-26-14-18, FAX 01-40-46-02-76, WEB www.jeudepaumehotel.com. 30 rooms, 1 junior suite. Bar, no air-conditioning, cable TV, minibars, Internet, health club, baby-sitting, laundry service. AE, DC, MC, V. Métro: Pont-Marie.*

$$ **Bretonnerie.** This small hotel is in a 17th-century *hôtel particulier* (town house) on a tiny street in the Marais, a few minutes' walk from the Pompidou Center. Rooms are done in Louis XIII style, complete with upholstered walls; they vary considerably in size from spacious to cramped. ✉ *22 rue Ste-Croix-de-la-Bretonnerie, Le Marais, 75004, ☎ 01-48-87-77-63, FAX 01-42-77-26-78. 27 rooms, 3 suites. No air-conditioning, Internet, in-room safes, cable TV, parking (fee). MC, V. Métro: Hôtel de Ville.*

$$ ★ **Caron de Beaumarchais.** The theme of this intimate jewel is the work of Caron de Beaumarchais, who wrote *The Marriage of Figaro* in 1778. Rooms faithfully reflect the taste of 18th-century French nobility. The second- and fifth-floor rooms with balconies are the largest; those on the sixth floor have beguiling views across Right Bank rooftops. ✉ *12 rue Vieille-du-Temple, Le Marais, 75004, ☎ 01-42-72-34-12, FAX 01-42-72-34-63. 19 rooms. Cable TV, minibars, Internet, laundry service. AE, DC, MC, V. Métro: Hôtel de Ville.*

$$ **Deux-Iles.** This converted 17th-century mansion on the Ile St-Louis has long won plaudits for charm and comfort. The delightfully old-fashioned rooms, blessed with exposed beams, are small but airy; ask for one overlooking the little garden courtyard. In winter a roaring fire warms the lounge. ✉ *59 rue St-Louis-en-l'Ile, Ile-St-Louis, 75004, ☎ 01-43-26-13-35, FAX 01-43-29-60-25. 17 rooms. Cable TV, minibars, Internet, in-room safes, baby-sitting. AE, MC, V. Métro: Pont-Marie.*

$$ **Hôtel du 7e Art.** The theme of this hip Marais hotel ("Seventh Art" is what the French call filmmaking) is Hollywood from the '40s to the '60s. Rooms are small and spartan but clean, quiet, and equipped with cable TV. There's no elevator, but there is an invitingly kitschy bar. The clientele is young, trendy, and primarily American. ✉ *20 rue St-Paul, Le Marais, 75004, ☎ 01-44-54-85-00, FAX 01-42-77-69-10. 23 rooms. Bar, no air-conditioning, cable TV, in-room safes, gym. AE, DC, MC, V. Métro: St-Paul.*

$$ **Place des Vosges.** A loyal, eclectic clientele swears by this small, historic Marais hotel on a delightful street just off place des Vosges. The Louis XIII–style reception area and rooms with oak-beamed ceilings, rough-hewn stone, and a mix of rustic finds from secondhand shops evoke old Marais. ✉ *12 rue de Birague, Le Marais, 75004, ☎ 01-42-72-60-46, FAX 01-42-72-02-64. 16 rooms. Bar, no air-conditioning, cable TV, minibars, in-room safes, gym. AE, DC, MC, V. Métro: Bastille.*

$–$$ **Axial Beaubourg.** A solid bet in the Marais, this hotel in a 16th-century building has beamed ceilings in the lobby and in the six first-floor rooms. Most have pleasant if functional decor, and all have satellite TV. The Pompidou Center and the Picasso Museum are five minutes away. ✉ *11 rue du Temple, Beaubourg/Les Halles, 75004, ☎ 01-42-72-72-22, FAX 01-42-72-03-53. 39 rooms. Cable TV, minibars, Internet, in-room safes, no-smoking rooms. AE, DC, MC, V. Métro: Hôtel de Ville.*

$ **Castex.** This Marais hotel in a Revolution-era building is a bargain hunter's dream. Rooms are low on frills but squeaky clean and up to date, the owners are extremely friendly, and the prices are rock bottom, which means the hotel is often booked months ahead. There's no elevator, and the only TV is in the ground-floor salon. ✉ *5 rue Castex, Le Marais, 75004, ☎ 01-42-72-31-52, FAX 01-42-72-57-91. 29 rooms, 23 with shower. No air-conditioning, no room TVs, Internet. MC, V. Métro: Bastille.*

5e Arrondissement (Latin Quarter)

$$ **Jardin du Luxembourg.** Blessed with a charming staff and a stylish look, this hotel is one of the most sought after in the Latin Quarter. Rooms are a bit small (common for this neighborhood) but intelligently furnished for optimal space and warmly decorated in ocher, rust, and indigo à la Provençal. Ask for one with a balcony overlooking the street; the best, No. 25, has a peekaboo view of the Eiffel Tower. ✉ *5 impasse Royer-Collard, Latin Quarter, 75005,* ☎ *01–40–46–08–88,* FAX *01–40–46–02–28. 27 rooms. In-room safes, sauna, no-smoking rooms. AE, DC, MC, V. Métro: Luxembourg.*

$–$$ **Grandes Écoles.** This delightfully intimate place looks and feels like a country cottage dropped smack in the middle of the Latin Quarter. It's off the street and occupies three buildings in a beautiful leafy garden. Parquet floors, Louis-Philippe furnishings, lace bedspreads, and the absence of TV all add to the rustic ambience. ✉ *75 rue du Cardinal Lemoine, Latin Quarter, 75005,* ☎ *01–43–26–79–23,* FAX *01–43–25–28–15. 51 rooms. No air-conditioning, parking (fee). MC, V. Métro: Cardinal Lemoine.*

$ ★ **Esméralda.** Once any *Vogue* editor's best-kept secret, this place used to be the ultimate Left Bank *hôtel de charme.* Set in a fusty 17th-century building across from Notre-Dame, it has long been cherished for its quirky, cozy, eccentric charm. Some closet-size rooms are nearly overpowered by gaudy imitation antiques or 1970s fabrics, while others could be cleaner. The tiny lobby—adorned with silk flowers, daub and wood moldings, and snoozing cats—is right out of a Flaubert novel. ✉ *4 rue St-Julien-le-Pauvre, Latin Quarter, 75005,* ☎ *01–43–54–19–20,* FAX *01–40–51–00–68. 15 rooms with bath, 4 without. No air-conditioning, no room TV. No credit cards. Métro: St-Michel.*

$ ★ **Familia.** The hospitable owners, the Gaucheron family, bend over backward for you—that is, if they have the time. As this is one of Paris's most popular budget options, they are often rushed off their feet. About half the rooms feature romantic sepia frescoes of celebrated Paris scenes; others are appointed with exquisite Louis XV–style furnishings or have nice mahogany pieces. Book a month ahead for one with a walk-out balcony on the second or fifth floor. ✉ *11 rue des Écoles, Latin Quarter, 75005,* ☎ *01–43–54–55–27,* FAX *01–43–29–61–77. 30 rooms. No air-conditioning, cable TV, minibars. AE, MC, V. Métro: Cardinal Lemoine.*

$ ★ **Minerve.** Fans of the Gaucheron family—and they are legion—will be delighted to learn that the Minerve is now part of the Familia fold. Just next door to the Familia, and twice as big, the hotel has been completely refurbished in the inimitable Gaucheron style: flowers and breakfast tables on the balconies, frescoes in the spacious lobby, tapestries on the walls, and cherry-wood furniture in the rooms. It's less intimate than the Familia—but just as charming. ✉ *13 rue des Écoles, Latin Quarter, 75005,* ☎ *01–43–26–26–04,* FAX *01–44–07–01–96. 54 rooms. No air-conditioning, Internet. AE, MC, V. Métro: Cardinal Lemoine.*

6e Arrondissement (St-Germain/Montparnasse)

$$$$ **Relais Christine.** On a quiet street between the Seine and boulevard St-Germain, this luxurious and popular hotel, occupying 16th-century abbey cloisters, oozes romantic ambience. Rooms are spacious (particularly the duplexes on the upper floors) and well appointed in old Parisian style; the best have exposed beams and overlook the garden. ✉ *3 rue Christine, St-Germain-des-Prés, 75006,* ☎ *01–40–51–60–80; 800/447–7462 in the U.S.,* FAX *01–40–51–60–81. 31 rooms, 18 suites. Bar, cable TV, minibars, no-smoking rooms, room service, baby-sitting, laundry service, meeting rooms, free parking. AE, DC, MC, V. Métro: Odéon.*

$$$–$$$$ ★ **Hôtel d'Aubusson.** This 17th-century mansion, once setting to Paris's first literary salon, is now one of the finest *petites hôtels de luxe* in the city, with original Aubusson tapestries, Versailles-style parquet floors, a chiseled stone fireplace, and restored antiques. Even the smallest rooms are good-size by Paris standards, and all are decked out in rich burgundies, greens, or blues. The 10 best rooms have canopied beds and ceiling beams. In summer, you can have your breakfast or pre-dinner drink in the paved courtyard. ✉ *33 rue Dauphine, St-Germain-des-Prés, 75006,* ☎ *01–43–29–43–43,* FAX *01–43–29–12–62,* WEB *www.hoteldaubusson.com. 49 rooms with bath. Bar, in-room safes, cable TV, minibars, room service, baby-sitting, laundry service. AE, MC, V. Métro: Odéon.*

$$$–$$$$ ★ **Relais St-Germain.** The interior-designer owners of this outstanding hotel have exquisite taste and a superb respect for tradition and detail. Moreover, the rooms are at least twice the size of those in other hotels in the area for the same price. Much of the furniture was selected with a knowledgeable eye from the city's *brocantes* (secondhand dealers), and every room has unique treasures. Breakfast is included. ✉ *9 carrefour de l'Odéon, St-Germain-des-Prés, 75006,* ☎ *01–43–29–12–05,* FAX *01–46–33–45–30. 21 rooms, 1 suite. Bar, Internet, in-room safes, cable TV, minibars, room service, baby-sitting, laundry service. AE, DC, MC, V. Métro: Odéon.*

$$$ **Grand Hotel de l'Univers.** In the very heart of Paris's festive, vacation-friendly St-Germain-des-Prés quarter, this hotel is on a quiet side street, yet only steps away from numerous restaurants. The house dates back to the 15th century, which explains the dimensions of some rooms; if snug, they are so delightfully decorated ("La Bonbonniere" is a *toile-de-Jouy* wonder) that you won't notice. For breakfast, you're treated to a medieval, Louis XI–style vaulted cellar which only Walt Disney's Imagineers could top. The staff is lovely—no wonder so many guests return again and again. ✉ *6 rue Gregoire-de-Tours, St-Germain-des-Prés, 75006,* ☎ *01–43–29–37–00,* FAX *01–40–51–06–45. 34 rooms. Bar, cable TV, minibars. AE, DC, MC, V. Métro: Odéon.*

$$$ **Hôtel de L'Abbaye.** This delightful hotel near St-Sulpice was transformed from an erstwhile convent. The blend of stylishly rustic antiques and earthy apricot and ocher tones makes for a calm, cozy atmosphere. The first-floor rooms open onto the garden; most of those on the upper floors have oak beams and sitting alcoves. Breakfast is included. ✉ *10 rue Cassette, St-Germain-des-Prés, 75006,* ☎ *01–45–44–38–11,* FAX *01–45–48–07–86. 42 rooms, 4 suites. Bar, cable TV, minibars, room service, baby-sitting, laundry service. AE, MC, V. Métro: St-Sulpice.*

$$ **Atelier Montparnasse.** This Art Deco–inspired gem of a hotel was designed with style and comfort in mind. Rooms are tastefully decorated and spacious, and all the bathrooms delight with mosaic reproductions of famous French paintings. One of the rooms sleeps three. The hotel is within walking distance of the Luxembourg Gardens and St-Germain-des-Prés. ✉ *49 rue Vavin, Montparnasse, 75006,* ☎ *01–46–33–60–00,* FAX *01–40–51–04–21. 17 rooms. Bar, no air-conditioning, room service, baby-sitting, laundry service. AE, DC, MC, V. Métro: Vavin.*

$$ **Bonaparte.** The congenial staff only makes staying in this intimate place more of a treat. Old-fashioned upholsteries, 19th-century furnishings, and paintings create a quaint feel in the relatively spacious rooms. And the location in the heart of St-Germain is nothing short of fabulous. ✉ *61 rue Bonaparte, St-Germain-des-Prés, 75006,* ☎ *01–43–26–97–37,* FAX *01–46–33–57–67. 29 rooms. In-room safes, cable TV, refrigerator, laundry service. MC, V. Métro: St-Germain-des-Prés.*

7e Arrondissement (Invalides/St-Germain)

$$$$ ★ **Pont Royal.** Once a favorite watering hole of everyone in the literary world from T. S. Eliot to Gabriel Garcia Marquez, this sumptu-

ously refurbished hotel now attracts more businessmen than writers—for now, the only recognizable authors you'll see are the ones whose photographs line the the lobby. You can't find a more comfortable hotel, however, or a better location, a quiet street just off boulevard St-Germain. The luxe restaurant has become the new favorite of Antoine Gallimard, whose publishing house is just up the street—so perhaps this will soon become, once again, Paris's "hôtel littéraire." ✉ *7 rue de Montalembert, St-Germain-des-Prés, 75007,* ☎ *01–42–84–70–00,* FAX *01–42–84–71–00,* WEB *www.hotel-pont-royal.com/hpr. 65 rooms, 10 suites, with bath. Restaurant (lunch only), bar, cable TV, minibars, Internet, in-room safes, concierge, business center, baby-sitting, room service, health club, parking (fee). AE, DC, MC, V. Métro: Rue de Bac.*

$$$–$$$$ ★ **Le Tourville.** Here is a rare find: an intimate, upscale hotel at an affordable price. Each room has crisp, virgin-white damask upholstery set against pastel or ocher walls, a smattering of antiques, original artwork, and fabulous old mirrors. The staff couldn't be more helpful. ✉ *16 av. de Tourville, Invalides/Eiffel Tower, 75007,* ☎ *01–47–05–62–62; 800/528–3549 in the U.S.,* FAX *01–47–05–43–90,* WEB *www.hoteltourville.com. 27 rooms, 3 junior suites. Bar, cable TV, minibars, laundry service. AE, DC, MC, V. Métro: École Militaire.*

$$ **Latour Maubourg.** In the residential heart of the ritzy seventh, a stone's throw from the Invalides, this hotel with a friendly staff has been inked into many a traveler's journal. Decor is homey and unpretentious, and with just 10 rooms, the accent is on intimacy and personalized service. ✉ *150 rue de Grenelle, Invalides/Eiffel Tower, 75007,* ☎ *01–47–05–16–16,* FAX *01–47–05–16–14,* WEB *www.latour-maubourg.fr. 9 rooms, 1 suite. No air-conditioning in some rooms, in-room data ports, cable TV, minibars. MC, V. Métro: Latour Maubourg.*

8e Arrondissement (Champs-Élysées)

$$$$ ★ **Crillon.** Home away from home for movie stars and off-duty celebrities, this is one of Paris's most famous hotels. The Crillon is in two 18th-century palaces on the grand place de la Concorde—rooms are predictably lavish, with Rococo and Directoire furnishings and crystal-and-gilt wall sconces. The sheer quantity of marble downstairs—especially in Les Ambassadeurs restaurant—is staggering. ✉ *10 pl. de la Concorde, Champs-Élysées, 75008,* ☎ *01–44–71–15–00; 800/888–4747 in the U.S.,* FAX *01–44–71–15–02,* WEB *www.crillon-paris.com. 115 rooms, 45 suites. 2 restaurants, 2 bars, Internet, in-room safes, cable TV, minibars, no-smoking rooms, room service, gym, baby-sitting, laundry service. AE, DC, MC, V. Métro: Concorde.*

$$$$ **George V.** General Eisenhower's headquarters during the liberation of Paris is now owned by a Saudi prince (who gets first dibs on the $8,500-a-night Royal Suite) and managed by the Four Seasons group. The original Art Deco detailings and 17th-century tapestries have been restored, the bas-reliefs regilt, and the marble mosaic floors reconstructed stone by stone. New additions include private health club facilities and the superluxe Le Cinq restaurant. ✉ *31 av. George V, Champs-Élysées, 75008,* ☎ *01–49–52–70–00,* FAX *01–49–52–70–10,* WEB *www.fourseasons.com. 184 rooms, 61 suites. Restaurant, bar, Internet, in-room safes, cable TV, minibars, no-smoking rooms, room service, indoor pool, hair salon, health club, laundry service, business services. AE, DC, MC, V. Métro: George V.*

$$$$ **Hyatt Regency Paris–Madeleine.** This stunning Haussmann-esque building near the Opéra Garnier feels more like a boutique hotel than an international business chain, thanks to stylized details like cherry paneling and mismatched bedside tables. Book a room on the seventh or eighth floor facing boulevard Malesherbes for a view of the Eiffel Tower. ✉ *24 bd. Malesherbes, Opéra/Grands Boulevards, 75008,* ☎ *01–55–27–12–34; 800/223–1234 in the U.S.,* FAX *01–55–27–12–35. 81*

rooms, 5 suites. Restaurant, bar, Internet, in-room safes, minibars, cable TV, no-smoking floor, room service, sauna, gym, laundry service, business services. AE, DC, MC, V. Métro: St-Augustin.

$$$$ ★ **Pershing Hall.** Formerly an American Legion Hall, Pershing Hall is the new must-see, must-stay address in Paris. Designed by Andrée Putman, the grande dame of French interior architecture, this boutique hotel exudes an almost masculine minimalism, with hefty American elm doors, Limoges porcelain pulley-lights, square wash-basins in the dark marbled bathrooms, and, in the central courtyard, a spectacular jungle garden carpeting a six-story-tall wall. The stylish lounge bar has become a hot nightspot, and the restaurant has a hot new star on the food scene, chef Erwan Louaisil. ✉ *49 rue Pierre Charron, Champs-Élysées, 75008,* ☎ *01–58–36–58–00,* FAX *01–58–36–58–01,* WEB *www.pershinghall.com. 20 rooms, 6 suites. Restaurant, bar, in-room safes, cable TV, minibars, Internet, health club, baby-sitting, room service, parking (fee). AE, DC, MC, V. Métro: George-V, Franklin-D.-Roosevelt.*

$$$$ ★ **Plaza-Athenée.** With Alain Ducasse in the kitchens and a brand-new, very contempo bar off the Louis XVI lobby, the landmark Plaza Athenée has suddenly become hip. The avenue Montaigne palace, entirely refurbished, is once again attracting a Blahnik-heeled crowd, partly because of its glamorous allure—after all, this was the favorite Paris hotel of Grace Kelly and Jackie Kennedy—and partly because it's only a croissant lob from the top couture and luxury shops in the city. The geranium-filled, vine-drunk courtyard—with its signature red awnings—is a sublime spot for a summer cocktail. There are—count them—460 staff members. ✉ *25 av. Montaigne, Champs-Élysées, 75008,* ☎ *01–53–67–66–65; 866/732–1106 in the U.S.,* FAX *01–53–67–66–66,* WEB *www.plaza-athenee-paris.com. 121 rooms, 66 suites, with bath. 2 restaurants, 2 bars, in-room safes, cable TV, minibars, Internet, no-smoking rooms, room service, health club, baby-sitting, laundry service. AE, DC, MC, V. Métro: Alma-Marceau.*

9e Arrondissement (Opéra)

$$$$ **Grand Hôtel Inter-Continental.** Open since 1862, Paris's biggest luxury hotel has a facade that seems as long as the Louvre's. The grand salon's Art Deco dome and the restaurant's painted ceilings are registered landmarks. The Art Deco rooms are spacious and light (ask for one on an upper floor). Its famed Café de la Paix is one of the city's great people-watching spots. ✉ *2 rue Scribe, Opéra/Grands Boulevards, 75009,* ☎ *01–40–07–32–32; 800/327–0200 in the U.S.,* FAX *01–42–66–12–51. 475 rooms, 39 suites. 3 restaurants, 2 bars, in-room safes, in-room VCRs, cable TV, minibars, Internet, no-smoking rooms, room service, health club, laundry service, business services. AE, DC, MC, V. Métro: Opéra.*

12e Arrondissement (Bastille/Gare de Lyon)

$$$$ **Le Pavillon Bastille.** The transformation of this 19th-century *hôtel particulier* (across from the Opéra Bastille) into a mod, colorful, high-design hotel garnered both architectural awards and a fiercely loyal, hip clientele. ✉ *65 rue de Lyon, Bastille/Nation, 75012,* ☎ *01–43–43–65–65; 800/233–2552 in the U.S.,* FAX *01–43–43–96–52. 24 rooms, 1 suite. Bar, in-room safes, cable TV, minibars, room service. AE, DC, MC, V. Métro: Bastille.*

14e Arrondissement (Montparnasse)

$–$$ **Raspail-Montparnasse.** Rooms in this hotel are named after the artists who in the '20s and '30s made Montparnasse the art capital of the world. All are decorated in pastels and contemporary blond-wood furniture. Most are at the low end of this price category; five have spectacular panoramic views of Montparnasse and the Eiffel Tower. ✉ *203 bd. Raspail, Montparnasse, 75014,* ☎ *01–43–20–62–86,* FAX *01–43–20–50–79,* WEB *www.globe-market.com./h75014raspail.htm. 38 rooms.*

Bar, in-room safes, cable TV, minibars, Internet. AE, DC, MC, V. Métro: Vavin.

$ **Parc Montsouris.** This modest hotel in a 1930s villa is on a quiet residential street next to the lovely Parc Montsouris. Attractive oak pieces and high-quality French fabrics embellish the small but clean rooms; satellite TV is another plus. Those with shower are very inexpensive; suites sleep four. ✉ *4 rue du Parc-Montsouris, Montparnasse, 75014,* ☎ *01–45–89–09–72,* FAX *01–45–80–92–72. 28 rooms, 7 suites. Cable TV, minibars, Internet, no smoking rooms, laundry service. AE, MC, V. Métro: Montparnasse-Bienvenue.*

16e Arrondissement (Arc de Triomphe/Le Bois)

$$$$ **Saint James Paris.** Touted as the "only château-hôtel" in Paris, this gracious late-19th-century Neoclassical mansion is surrounded by a lush private park. The lavish Art Deco interior was created by designer Andrée Putman. Ten rooms on the third floor open onto a winter garden. The restaurant is reserved for guests; in warm weather meals are served in the garden. ✉ *43 av. Bugeaud, Porte Dauphine, 75016,* ☎ *01–44–05–81–81; 800/447–7462 in the U.S.,* FAX *01–44–05–81–82. 20 rooms, 28 suites. Restaurant, bar, in-room safes, cable TV, minibars, Internet, no-smoking rooms, room service, health club, baby-sitting, laundry service, free parking. AE, DC, MC, V. Métro: Porte Dauphine.*

$ **Queen's Hôtel.** One of only a handful of hotels in the tony residential district near the Bois de Boulogne, Queen's is a small, comfortable hotel with a high standard of service. Each room focuses on a different 20th-century French artist. The rooms with baths have Jacuzzis. ✉ *4 rue Bastien-Lepage, Bois de Boulogne, 75016,* ☎ *01–42–88–89–85,* FAX *01–40–50–67–52,* WEB *www.queens-hotel.fr. 21 rooms. In-room safes, cable TV, minibars, no-smoking rooms. AE, DC, MC, V. Métro: Michel-Ange–Auteuil.*

17e Arrondissement (Monceau/Clichy)

$–$$ **Étoile-Péreire.** Behind a quiet, leafy courtyard in this chic residential district is this unique, intimate hotel, consisting of two parts: a fin-de-siècle building on the street and a 1920s annex overlooking an interior courtyard. Rooms and duplexes are done in deep shades of rose or blue with crisp, white damask upholstery; only suites have air-conditioning. ✉ *146 bd. Péreire, Parc Monceau, 75017,* ☎ *01–42–67–60–00,* FAX *01–42–67–02–90. 21 rooms, 5 duplex suites. Bar, no air-conditioning in some rooms, in-room safes, no-smoking rooms, cable TV, minibars, laundry service. AE, DC, MC, V. Métro: Péreire.*

NIGHTLIFE AND THE ARTS

Revised and updated by Christopher Mooney

With a heritage that includes the cancan, the Folies-Bergère, the Moulin Rouge, Mistinguett, and Josephine Baker, Paris is one city where no one has ever had to ask, "Is there any place exciting to go to tonight?" Today the city's nightlife and arts scenes are still filled with pleasures. Hear a chansonnier belt out Piaf, take in a *Victor/Victoria* show, catch a Molière play at the Comédie Française, or perhaps spot Madonna at the Buddha Bar. Information about what's going on in the city can be found in the weekly magazines (published every Wednesday) *Pariscope* (which has an English section), *L'Officiel des Spectacles, Zurban,* and *Figaroscope* (a supplement to *Le Figaro* newspaper). The **Paris Tourist Office** has a 24-hour hot line in English (☎ 08–36–68–31–12) and a Web site (WEB www.paris-touristoffice.com) listing events.

The best place to buy tickets is at the venue itself; try to purchase in advance, as many of the more popular performances sell out. Also try your hotel or a travel agency, such as **Opéra Théâtre** (✉ 7 rue de Clichy, Montmartre, 9e, ☎ 01–40–06–01–00, métro: Trinité). Tickets for most concerts can be bought at **FNAC** (especially ✉ 1–5 rue Pierre Lescot, Forum des Halles, 3rd level down, Beaubourg/Les Halles, 1er, ☎ 01–49–87–50–50, métro: Châtelet–Les Halles). The **Virgin Megastore** (✉ 52 av. des Champs-Élysées, Champs-Élysées, 8e, ☎ 08–03–02–30–24, métro: Franklin-D.-Roosevelt) also sells theater and concert tickets. Half-price tickets for many same-day theater performances are available at the **Kiosques Théâtre** (✉ across from 15 pl. de la Madeleine, Opéra/Grands Boulevards, métro: Madeleine; ✉ outside Gare Montparnasse on pl. Raoul Dautry, Montparnasse, 15e, métro: Montparnasse-Bienvenüe); both are open Tuesday–Saturday 12:30–8 and Sunday 12:30–4. Expect to pay a €2.46 commission per ticket and to wait in line.

The Arts

Classical Music

Classical- and world-music concerts are held at the **Cité de la Musique** (✉ 221 av. Jean-Jaurès, Parc de la Villette, 19e, ☎ 01–44–84–44–84, métro: Porte de Pantin). The **Salle Pleyel** (✉ 252 rue du Faubourg–St-Honoré, Champs-Élysées, 8e, ☎ 08–25–00–02–52, métro: Ternes) is Paris's principal home of classical music. The **Théâtre des Champs-Élysées** (✉ 15 av. Montaîgne, Champs-Élysées, 8e, ☎ 01–49–52–50–50, métro: Alma-Marceau), an Art Deco temple, hosts concerts and ballet. Paris has a never-ending stream of inexpensive lunchtime and evening concerts in churches, some scheduled as part of the **Festival d'Art Sacré** (☎ 01–44–70–64–10 for information) between mid-November and Christmas. **Churches** with classical concerts (often free) include: Notre-Dame, Sainte-Chapelle, St-Eustache, St-Germain-des-Prés, St-Julien-Le-Pauvre, St-Louis-en-l'Ile, and St-Roch.

Dance

The **Opéra Garnier** (✉ Pl. de l'Opéra, Opéra/Grands Boulevards, 9e, ☎ 08–36–69–78–68, WEB www.opera-de-paris.fr, métro: Opéra) is home to the reputable Paris Ballet. The **Opéra de la Bastille** (✉ Pl. de la Bastille, Bastille, 12e, ☎ 08–36–69–78–68, WEB www.opera-de-paris.fr, métro: Bastille) occasionally hosts major dance troupes, often modern and avant-garde in tenor. Both here and at the Opéra Garnier venue, ballet production ticket prices usually range from about €4.61 to 60. At the **Théâtre de la Bastille** (✉ 76 rue de la Roquette, Bastille, 11e, ☎ 01–43–57–42–14, métro: Bastille), innovative modern dance companies perform. At its two houses, the **Théâtre de la Ville** (✉ 2 pl. du Châtelet, Beaubourg/Les Halles, 4e, ☎ 01–42–74–22–77 for both, métro: Châtelet; ✉ 31 rue des Abbesses, Montmartre, 18e, métro: Abbesses) presents the leading stars of contemporary dance.

Film

Parisians are far more addicted to the cinema as an art form than even Londoners or New Yorkers, as evidenced by the number of movie theaters in the city. Many theaters, especially in principal tourist areas such as the Champs-Élysées, St-Germain-des-Prés, Les Halles, and the boulevard des Italiens near the Opéra, show first-run films in English. Check the weekly guides for a movie of your choice. Look for the initials *v.o.*, which mean *version originale,* that is, not dubbed. Cinema admission runs from €5.38 to €8.46; many theaters reduce rates slightly on Monday and for some morning shows. Most theaters will post two show times: the first is the *séance*, when commercials, previews, and sometimes short films start, and the second is the actual feature presentation time, which is usually 10–20 minutes later. Paris has many small cinemas showing classic and independent films, especially in the Latin Quarter. Screenings are often organized around retrospectives (check "Festivals" in weekly guides). One of the best venues for classic French and international films (Wednesday–Saturday) is the **Cinémathèque**

Française (✉ 42 bd. de Bonne-Nouvelle, Opéra/Grands Boulevards, ☎ 01–56–26–01–01, métro: Bonne-Nouvelle; ✉ Palais de Chaillot, 7 av. Albert de Mun, Trocadéro, ☎ 01–56–26–01–01, métro: Trocadéro). The **Balzac** (✉ 1 rue Balzac, Champs-Élysées, 8e, ☎ 01–45–61–10–60, métro: George V) frequently hosts talks by directors before screenings.

Opera

Getting tickets to the opera can be difficult on short notice, so it's a good idea to plan ahead. For the season's schedule, contact the **Opéra de la Bastille** (✉ 120 rue de Lyon, Bastille, 75012) in advance. Bookings by mail begin roughly two months before the date of performance. Buying from scalpers is not recommended, as they have been known to sell counterfeit tickets. The **Opéra de la Bastille** (✉ Pl. de la Bastille, Bastille, 12e, ☎ 08–36–69–78–68, WEB www.opera-de-paris.fr, métro: Bastille), a modern auditorium, has taken over the role as Paris's main opera house from the Opéra Garnier. However, nothing beats seeing a grand production of a Verdi or Mozart opera within the splendor of the Opéra Garnier, and the good news is that this historic house still hosts a limited number of Opéra National de Paris productions every season. Note that if a *Don Giovanni* is presented, it is only mounted for a minirun of one to two weeks, not in a repertory schedule throughout the season. At both the Bastille and Garnier houses, opera tickets range from about €6.92 to €103; cheaper seats in the Garnier house are sometimes view-obstructed. The **Opéra Comique** (✉ 5 rue Favart, Opéra/Grands Boulevards, 2e, ☎ 01–42–44–45–46, métro: Richelieu-Drouot) is a lofty old hall where comic operas are often performed. Better known as the Théâtre du Châtelet, the **Théâtre Musical de Paris** (✉ Pl. du Châtelet, Beaubourg/Les Halles, 1er, ☎ 01–40–28–28–40, métro: Châtelet) has built up a strong reputation for opera and other productions.

Theater

A number of theaters line the Grand Boulevards between Opéra and République, but there is no Paris equivalent of Broadway or the West End. Shows are mostly in French. **Bouffes du Nord** (✉ 37 bis bd. de la Chapelle, La-Chapelle/Stalingrad, 10e, ☎ 01–46–07–34–50, métro: La Chapelle) is the wonderfully atmospheric theater that is home to English director Peter Brook. The **Comédie-Française** (✉ Pl. Colette, Louvre/Tuileries, 1er, ☎ 01–44–58–15–15, métro: Palais-Royal) is a distinguished venue that stages classical French drama. The **Théâtre de la Huchette** (✉ 23 rue de la Huchette, Latin Quarter, 5e, ☎ 01–43–26–38–99, métro: St-Michel), a tiny Left Bank theater, has been staging Ionesco's *The Bald Soprano* every night since 1950. **Théâtre de l'Odéon** (✉ Pl. de l'Odéon, St-Germain-des-Prés, 6e, ☎ 01–44–41–36–36, métro: Odéon) has made pan-European theater its primary focus.

Nightlife

The City of Light truly lights up after dark. So, if you want to paint the town *rouge* after dutifully pounding the parquet in museums all day, there's a dazzling array of options to discover. The hottest spots are around Ménilmontant, the Bastille, and the Marais. The Left Bank is definitely a lot less happening. The Champs-Élysées is making a comeback, though the clientele remains predominantly foreign. Take note: the last métro runs between 12:30 AM and 1 AM (you can take a taxi, but they can be hard to find, especially on weekend nights).

Bars and Clubs

The famous brasserie **Alcazar** (✉ 62 rue Mazarine, St-Germain-des-Prés, 6e, ☎ 01–53–10–19–99, métro: Odéon) has a stylish bar on the first floor and live DJs from Wednesday to Saturday. It helps to be famous—or look like a model—to get into **Les Bains** (✉ 7 rue du Bourg-l'Abbé, République,

3e, ☎ 01–48–87–01–80, métro: Étienne-Marcel), a forever-trendy club (closed Monday). **Batofar** (✉ 11 quai François Mauriac, République, 11e, ☎ 01–56–29–10–00, métro: Bibliothèque) is an old lighthouse tug, now refitted to include a bar, a club, and a concert venue that's become one of the hippest spots in town. **Buddha Bar** (✉ 8 rue Boissy d'Anglas, Champs-Élysées, 8e, ☎ 01–53–05–90–00, métro: Concorde) is a knockout showplace, complete with its towering gold-painted Buddha contemplating enough Dragon Empress screens and colorful chinoiserie for five old MGM movies. Madonna used to make the scene here, along with a lot of other glitterati, several years ago when the bar opened. **Café Charbon** (✉ 109 rue Oberkampf, Oberkampf, 11e, ☎ 01–43–57–55–13, métro: St-Maur, Parmentier) is a beautifully restored 19th-century café with a trendsetting crowd. **Le Comptoir** (✉ 5 rue Monsieur-Le-Prince, St-Germain-des-Prés, 6e, ☎ 01–43–29–12–05, métro: Odéon) is a traditional wine bar serving burgundy and Bordeaux by the glass. **L'Élysée Montmartre** (✉ 72 bd. de Rochechouart, Montmartre, 18e, ☎ 01–55–07–06–00, métro: Anvers) on Saturday hosts the hottest club nights in Paris (during the week it's a concert hall). **La Fabrique** (✉ 53 rue du Faubourg St-Antoine, Bastille/Nation, 11e, ☎ 01–43–07–67–07, métro: Bastille) brews its own beer (look out for the huge copper vats by the entrance) and really gets going after 9 PM, when a DJ hits the turntables. **Finnegan's Wake** (✉ 9 rue des Boulangers, Latin Quarter, 5e, ☎ 01–46–34–23–65, métro: Jussieu) attracts a mixed Franco-British clientele with its Guinness on tap and Irish music. If you ever get homesick to hear English, Paris has quite a few other pubs, including the Auld Alliance, Connolly's Corner, and the Cricketeer. **Le Fumoir** (✉ 6 rue Amiral de Coligny, Louvre/Tuileries, 1er, ☎ 01–42–92–00–24, métro: Louvre), a fashionable spot for cocktails, has a large bar, a library, and comfy leather couches. **Polo Room** (✉ 3 rue Lord Byron, Champs-Élysées, 8e, ☎ 01–40–74–07–78, métro: George V) is the very first martini bar in Paris; there are polo photos on the wall, regular live jazz concerts, and DJs every Friday and Saturday night. **Wax** (✉ 15 rue Daval, Bastille/Nation, 11e, ☎ 01–40–21–16–16, métro: Bastille) is worth a visit simply for its decor—check out the orange-and-pink walls and the molded plastic banquettes by the window; DJs spin techno and house every evening.

GAY AND LESBIAN BARS AND CLUBS

Gay and lesbian bars and clubs are mostly concentrated in the Marais and include some of the most happening addresses in the city. **Le Dépôt** (✉ 10 rue aux Ours, République, 3e, ☎ 01–44–54–96–96, métro: Etienne Marcel) is a bar, club, and backroom for men. The mostly male crowd at **L'Open Café** (✉ 17 rue des Archives, Le Marais, 4e, ☎ 01–42–72–26–18, métro: Hôtel-de-Ville) comes for the sunny decor and convivial ambience. **Le Pulp!** (✉ 25 bd. Poissonnière, Opéra/Grands Boulevards, 2e, ☎ 01–40–26–01–93, métro: Grands Boulevards) is one of the few lesbian-only nightclubs in Paris (Thursday–Saturday). **Queen** (✉ 102 av. des Champs-Élysées, Champs-Élysées, 8e, ☎ 01–53–89–08–90, métro: George-V) is one of the hottest nightspots in Paris: although it's predominantly gay, everyone else lines up to get in, too.

HOTEL BARS

Paris's hotel bars are highly popular nostalgic spots as well as quiet, elegant places to talk. **Bristol** (✉ 112 rue du Faubourg–St-Honoré, Champs-Élysées, 8e, ☎ 01–53–43–43–42, métro: Miromesnil). **Lutétia** (✉ 45 bd. Raspail, Montparnasse, 6e, ☎ 01–49–54–46–09, métro: Sèvres-Babylone). **Ritz Hemingway Bar** (✉ 15 pl. Vendôme, Louvre/Tuileries, 1er, ☎ 01–43–16–33–65, métro: Opéra).

Cabaret

Paris's cabarets are household names, though mostly just tourists go to them these days. Prices range from €30.76 (simple admission plus one drink) to more than €123 (dinner plus show). **Crazy Horse** (✉ 12 av. George-V, Champs-Élysées, 8e, ☎ 01–47–23–32–32, métro: Alma-Marceau) is one of the best-known cabarets, with pretty dancers and raunchy routines. **Au Lapin Agile** (✉ 22 rue des Saules, Montmartre, 18e, ☎ 01–46–06–85–87, métro: Lamarck-Caulaincourt), the fabled artists' hangout in Montmartre, considers itself the doyen of cabarets and is a miraculous survivor from the early 20th century; prices here are lower than elsewhere, but then it is more a large bar than a full-blown cabaret. **Lido** (✉ 116 bis av. des Champs-Élysées, Champs-Élysées, 8e, ☎ 01–40–76–56–10, métro: George-V) stars the famous Bluebell Girls; the owners claim that no show in Las Vegas can rival it for special effects. That old favorite at the foot of Montmartre, **Moulin Rouge** (✉ 82 bd. de Clichy, Montmartre, 18e, ☎ 01–53–09–82–82, métro: Blanche), mingles the Doriss Girls, the cancan, and a horse in an extravagant spectacle. **Paradis Latin** (✉ 28 rue du Cardinal Lemoine, Latin Quarter, 5e, ☎ 01–43–25–28–28, métro: Cardinal Lemoine) is the liveliest and trendiest cabaret on the Left Bank.

Jazz Clubs

For nightly schedules consult the specialty magazines *Jazz Hot, Jazzman,* or *Jazz Magazine.* Nothing gets going till 10 PM or 11 PM; entry prices vary widely from about €6.15 to more than €15.38. At the Méridien Hotel, near Porte Maillot, the **Lionel Hampton Jazz Club** (✉ 81 bd. Gouvion-St-Cyr, Porte Maillot, 17e, ☎ 01–40–68–30–42, métro: Porte Maillot) hosts a roster of international jazz players. **New Morning** (✉ 7 rue des Petites-Écuries, Opéra/Grands Boulevards, 10e, ☎ 01–45–23–51–41, métro: Château-d'Eau) is a premier spot for serious fans of avant-garde jazz, as well as folk and world music. The greatest names in French and international jazz have been playing at **Le Petit Journal** (✉ 71 bd. St-Michel, Latin Quarter, 5e, ☎ 01–43–26–28–59, RER: Luxembourg) for decades; it now specializes in Dixieland jazz (it's closed Sunday).

Rock, Pop, and World Music Venues

Upcoming concerts are posted on boards in FNAC and Virgin Megastores. **L'Élysée Montmartre** is one of the prime venues for emerging French and international rock groups. **L'Olympia** (✉ 28 bd. des Capucines, Opéra/Grands Boulevards, 9e, ☎ 01–47–42–25–49, métro: Madeleine), a legendary venue once favored by Jacques Brel and Edith Piaf, still plays host to leading French vocalists. **Palais Omnisports de Paris-Bercy** (✉ 8 bd. de Bercy, Bercy & Tolbiac, 12e, ☎ 08–25–30–00–31, métro: Bercy) is the largest venue in Paris, where the top international stars perform. **Zenith** (✉ Parc de la Villette, 19e, ☎ 01–42–08–60–00, métro: Porte-de-Pantin) stages large rock shows.

OUTDOOR ACTIVITIES AND SPORTS

Participant Sports

Bicycling

Paris has been making valiant efforts to become more bicycle-friendly. More than 150 km (104 mi) of bicycle lanes now cross the city, notably along rue de Rivoli and boulevard St-Germain. Certain roads are banned to cars altogether on Sunday (including the banks of the Seine along quai de la Tournelle from 9 to 5 mid-March to late fall and the roads alongside the Canal St-Martin from noon to 6 year-round). Paris's two large parks, the Bois de Boulogne and the Bois de Vincennes (métro: Porte Dorée, Château de Vincennes) are also good places for biking. Bikes can be rented from the following: **Pariscyclo** (✉ Rond Point de Jardin d'Acclimatation, Bois de Boulogne, 16e, ☎ 01–47–47–76–50, métro: Les Sablons); **Paris à Vélo, C'est Sympa** (✉ 37 bd.

Bourdon, Bastille/Nation, 4ᵉ, ☎ 01–48–87–60–01, métro: Bastille); and **Paris Vélo Rent a Bike** (✉ 2 rue Fer à Moulin, Latin Quarter, 5ᵉ, ☎ 01–43–37–59–22, métro: Censier-Daubenton).

Health Clubs and Swimming Pools

A number of hotels, gyms, and clubs in the city offer one-day or short-term memberships. **Club Jean de Beauvais** (✉ 5 rue Jean-de-Beauvais, Latin Quarter, 5ᵉ, ☎ 01–46–33–16–80, métro: Maubert-Mutualité) has an entire floor of exercise equipment and classes, as well as a sauna and *hammam* (€30 per day). **Club Quartier Latin** (✉ 19 rue de Pontoise, Latin Quarter, 5ᵉ, ☎ 01–55–42–77–88, métro: Maubert Mutualité) has a 30-meter skylighted pool, a climbing wall, squash courts, and exercise equipment (€13 per day and €11 per 40 minutes of squash). **Espace Vit'Halles** (✉ 48 rue Rambuteau, Beaubourg/Les Halles, 3ᵉ, ☎ 01–42–77–21–71, métro: Rambuteau) has a broad range of aerobics classes (€15.38 a class) and exercise machines, plus a sauna and a steam bath. **Pilates Studio** (✉ 39 rue du Temple, Le Marais, 4ᵉ, ☎ 01–42–72–91–74, métro: Hôtel de Ville) may be based in a three-room apartment, but it attracts numerous celebrities, such as actress Kristin Scott Thomas. A one-hour private class costs €35; group classes without the machines are €19. The **Piscine des Halles** (✉ entrance on pl. de la Rotonde, in Forum des Halles, Beaubourg/Les Halles, 1ᵉʳ, ☎ 01–42–36–98–44) is a 50-meter public pool; admission is €3.85, call for hours. The **Ritz Health Club** (✉ Hotel Ritz, pl. Vendôme, Opéra/Grands Boulevards, 1ᵉʳ, ☎ 01–43–16–30–60, métro: Opéra), as fancy as the hotel, has a swimming pool, sauna, steam room, Jacuzzi, exercise machines, and aerobics classes (all for €122 on weekdays, €153 on weekends). **Sofitel Paris Vitatop Club** (✉ 8 rue Louis-Armand, Montparnasse, 15ᵉ, ☎ 01–45–54–79–00, métro: Balard) has a 15-meter pool, a sauna, a steam room, and a Jacuzzi, plus a stunning view of the Paris skyline (€30 per day and free to hotel guests).

Spectator Sports

Information on upcoming events can be found in the weekly guide *Pariscope,* on posters around the city, or by calling the ticket agencies of **FNAC** (☎ 08–03–80–88–03). You'll find a popular ticket outlet in the **Virgin Megastore** (☎ 08–03–02–30–24). A wide range of sporting events takes place at the **Palais Omnisports de Paris-Bercy** (✉ 8 bd. de Bercy, Bercy/Tolbiac, 12ᵉ, ☎ 08–03–03–00–31, métro: Bercy). Details of events are also on their Web site: WEB www.bercy.com. The **Parc des Princes** (✉ 24 rue du Cdt. Guilbaud, Auteuil, 16ᵉ, ☎ 01–42–88–02–76, métro: Porte d'Auteuil) is the site of the home matches of the city's soccer team, Paris St-Germain. **Roland-Garros** (✉ 2 av. Gordon Bennett, Bois-de-Boulogne, 16ᵉ, ☎ 01–47–43–48–00, métro: Porte d'Auteuil) is the venue for the French Open tennis tournament during the last week of May and first week of June. **Stade de France** (✉ St-Denis, ☎ 01–55–93–00–00, WEB www.stade-de-france.com, RER: La Plaine–Stade de France) is home to the French national soccer and rugby teams.

SHOPPING

Revised and updated by Nicola Keegan

In the most beautiful city in the world, it's no surprise to discover that the local greengrocer displays his tomatoes as artistically as Cartier does its rubies. The capital of style, Paris has an endless panoply of delights to tempt shop-till-you-droppers, from grand couturiers like Dior to the funkiest flea markets. Today every neighborhood seems to reflect a unique attitude and style: designer extravagance and haute couture characterize avenue Montaigne and rue Faubourg St-Honoré; classic sophistication pervades St-Germain; avant-garde style dresses up the Marais; while a hip feel suffuses the area around Les Halles.

Sharon Stone takes two suites at the Ritz, one for herself and one for the luggage she's going to fill, J–Lo was recently photographed hysterically flying along the exclusive rue St-Honoré, changing outfits at each shop, while Madonna and Gwyneth sat cheek to cheek during fashion week, agog with all there is to want. But big luxury names, big luxury money aside; there is something for everyone and bargains are just not as elusive here as they were of old. Why not try on that little black dress from the 1950s hanging in the window with your name written all over it? Or snag that kitsch-but-cute coffee mug with the famous laughing cow on it for your favorite morning grouch? For you bargain hunters, some words to remember: *soldes,* sale; *fripes,* secondhand clothing; *dépôt vent,* secondhand shop; and *dégriffé,* designer labels, often from last year's collection, for sale at a deep discount. Happy hunting.

If you're from outside the European Union, age 15 and over, and stay in France and/or the European Union for less than six months, you can benefit from Value Added Tax (VAT) reimbursements, known in France as TVA, while the sum remitted to non-EU folk is known as the *détaxe.* To qualify, non-EU residents must spend at least €185 in a single store on a single day. Refunds vary from 13% to 19.6% and are mailed to you by check or credited to your charge card.

Shopping by Neighborhood

Avenue Montaigne

Shopping doesn't come much more chic than on avenue Montaigne, with its graceful town mansions housing some of the top names in international fashion: **Chanel, Dior, Céline, Valentino, Krizia, Ungaro, Prada, Dolce & Gabbana,** and many more. Neighboring rue François 1er and avenue George V are also lined with many designer boutiques: **Versace, Yves St-Laurent, Givenchy,** and **Balenciaga.**

Champs-Élysées

Cafés and movie theaters keep the once-chic Champs-Élysées active 24 hours a day, but the invasion of exchange banks, car showrooms, and fast-food chains has lowered the tone. Four glitzy 20th-century arcade malls—**Galerie du Lido, Le Rond-Point, Le Claridge,** and **Élysées 26**—capture most of the retail action, not to mention the **Gap** and the **Disney Store.** The opening of a new Peter Marino–designed **Louis Vuitton** boutique and the cosmetic wonder store **Sephora** have reintroduced a touch of elegance.

The Faubourg St-Honoré

This chic shopping and residential area is also quite a political hub. It is home to the Élysée Palace as well as the official residences of the American and British ambassadors. The Paris branches of **Sotheby's** and **Christie's** and renowned antiques galleries such as **Didier Aaron** add artistic flavor. Boutiques include **Hermès, Lanvin, Gucci, Chloé,** and **Christian Lacroix.**

Left Bank

After decades of clustering on the Right Bank's venerable shopping avenues, the high-fashion houses have stormed the Rive Gauche. The first to arrive were **Sonia Rykiel** and **Yves St-Laurent** in the late '60s. Some of the more recent arrivals include **Christian Dior, Giorgio Armani,** and **Louis Vuitton.** Rue des St-Pères and rue de Grenelle are lined with designer names.

Louvre–Palais Royal

The elegant and eclectic shops clustered in the 18th-century arcades of the Palais-Royal sell such items as antiques, toy soldiers, cosmetics, jewelry, and vintage designer dresses. The glossy, marble **Carrousel du**

Louvre mall, beneath the Louvre Museum, is lighted by an immense inverted glass pyramid. Shops are accompanied by a lively international food court, and all are open on Sunday—still a rare convenience in Paris.

Le Marais

Between the pre-Revolution mansions and tiny kosher food shops that characterize this area are scores of trendy gift and clothing stores, with couturier **Azzedine Alaïa** heading the list of chic boutiques. The Marais is one of the few neighborhoods where shops are open on Sunday.

Opéra to La Madeleine

Two major department stores—**Au Printemps** and **Galeries Lafayette**—dominate boulevard Haussmann, behind Paris's ornate 19th-century Opéra Garnier. Place de la Madeleine tempts many with its two luxurious food stores, **Fauchon** and **Hédiard.**

Place Vendôme and Rue de la Paix

The magnificent 17th-century place Vendôme, home of the Ritz Hotel, and rue de la Paix, leading north from Vendôme, are where you can find the world's most elegant jewelers: **Cartier, Boucheron, Bulgari,** and **Van Cleef and Arpels.** The most exclusive, however, is the discreet **Jar's.**

Rue St-Honoré

A fashionable set makes its way to rue St-Honoré to shop at Paris's trendiest boutique, **Colette.** The street is lined with numerous designer names, while on nearby rue Cambon you'll find the wonderfully elegant **Maria Luisa** and the main **Chanel** boutique.

Department Stores

Paris's top department stores offer both convenience and style. Most are open Monday through Saturday from 9:30 AM to 7 PM, and some are open until 10 PM one weekday evening.

Au Bon Marché (✉ 24 rue de Sèvres, St-Germain-des-Prés, 7e, ☎ 01–44–39–80–00, métro: Sèvres-Babylone), the only department store on the Left Bank, is an excellent hunting ground for housewares, men's clothes, and gifts. On the Right Bank, **Bazar de l'Hôtel de Ville** (✉ 52–64 rue de Rivoli, Beaubourg/Les Halles, 4e, ☎ 01–42–74–90–00, métro: Hôtel de Ville), better known as BHV, has minimal fashion offerings but is noteworthy for its enormous basement hardware store. **La Samaritaine** (✉ 19 rue de la Monnaie, Louvre/Tuileries, 1er, ☎ 01–40–41–20–20, métro: Pont-Neuf or Châtelet) has the Toupary restaurant with magnificent views of the Seine. The Grand Boulevards is home to two major department stores: **Au Printemps** (✉ 64 bd. Haussmann, Opéra/Grands Boulevards, 9e, ☎ 01–42–82–50–00, métro: Havre-Caumartin, Opéra, or Auber) has the widest array of merchandise; **Galeries Lafayette** (✉ 40 bd. Haussmann, Opéra/Grands Boulevards, 9e, ☎ 01–42–82–34–56, métro: Chaussée d'Antin, Opéra, or Havre-Caumartin) is famous for its high-style departments.

Budget

Monoprix is the French dime store par excellance—with scores of branches throughout the city—and stocks inexpensive everyday items like toothpaste, groceries, toys, and paper. It also carries inexpensive children's clothes and makeup of surprisingly good quality.

Markets

The **Marché aux Puces,** on Paris's northern boundary (métro: Porte de Clignancourt), which takes place Saturday through Monday, is a century-old labyrinth of alleyways packed with antiques dealers' booths and junk stalls spreading for more than a square mile; arrive early.

The lively atmosphere that reigns in most of Paris's open-air food markets makes them a sight worth seeing even if you don't want or need to buy anything. Every neighborhood has one, though many are open only a few days each week. Sunday morning till 1 PM is usually a good time to go; Monday the markets are likely to be closed. Many of the better-known markets are in areas you'd visit for sightseeing: **boulevard Raspail** (✉ between rue de Rennes and rue du Cherche-Midi, Latin Quarter, 6e, métro: Rennes), with a Sunday organic market; **rue de Buci** (✉ Latin Quarter, 6e, métro: Odéon), closed Sunday afternoon and Monday; **rue Mouffetard** (✉ Latin Quarter, 5e, métro: Monge), best on weekends, near the Jardin des Plantes; **rue Montorgueuil** (✉ Beaubourg/Les Halles, 1er, métro: Châtelet–Les Halles), closed Monday; **boulevard Richard Lenoir** (✉ Bastille/Nation, 11e, métro: Bastille); and **rue Lepic** (✉ Montmartre, 18e, métro: Blanche or Abbesses), best on weekends.

Shopping Arcades

Paris's 19th-century commercial arcades, called *passages* or *galeries* are the forerunners of the modern mall. Glass roofs, decorative pillars, and mosaic floors give the passages character. The major arcades are on the Right Bank in central Paris. **Galerie Vivienne** (✉ 4 rue des Petits-Champs, Opéra/Grands Boulevards, 2e, métro: Bourse) is home to a range of interesting shops, an excellent tearoom, and a quality wine shop. **Passage du Grand-Cerf** (✉ entrances on rue Dussoubs, rue St-Denis, Beaubourg/Les Halles, 4e, métro: Étienne-Marcel) is a pretty, glass-roofed gallery filled with crafts shops offering an innovative selection of jewelry, paintings, and ceramics. **Passage Jouffroy** (✉ 12 bd. Montmartre, Montmartre, 2e, métro: Montmartre) is full of shops selling toys, postcards, antique canes, and perfumes. **Passage des Panoramas** (✉ 11 bd. Montmartre, Montmartre, 2e, métro: Montmartre), built in 1800, is the oldest of them all. The elegant **Galerie Véro-Dodat** (✉ 19 rue Jean-Jacques Rousseau, Louvre/Tuileries, 1er, métro: Louvre) has shops selling old-fashioned toys, contemporary art, and stringed instruments. It is best known, however, for its antiques stores.

Specialty Stores

Accessories, Cosmetics, and Perfumes

By Terry (✉ Galerie Véro-Dodat, Louvre/Tuileries, 1er, ☎ 01–44–76–00–76, métro: Louvre, Palais-Royal) is the brainchild of Yves Saint Laurent's former director of makeup, Terry de Gunzberg; it offers her own brand of "ready-to-wear" cosmetics as well as a personalized cosmetics service. **E. Goyard** (✉ 233 rue St-Honoré, Louvre/Tuileries, 1er, ☎ 01–42–60–57–04, métro: Tuileries) has been making the finest luggage since 1853; clients in the past included Arthur Conan Doyle, Gregory Peck, and the Duke and Duchess of Windsor, and today Karl Lagerfeld and Madonna are both Goyard fans. **Christian Louboutin** (✉ 19 rue Jean-Jacques Rousseau, Louvre/Tuileries, 1er, ☎ 01–42–36–05–31, métro: Louvre) is famous for his wacky but elegant shoes, trademark blood-red soles, and impressive client list (Caroline of Monaco, Catherine Deneuve, Elizabeth Taylor). **Philippe Model** (✉ 33 pl. du Marché St-Honoré, Louvre/Tuileries, 1er, ☎ 01–42–96–89–02, métro: Tuileries) started off making hats favored by fashionable society ladies and has since added shoes and housewares in two adjacent shops. **Sabbia Rosa** (✉ 73 rue des Sts-Pères, St-Germain-des-Prés, 6e, ☎ 01–45–48–88–37, métro: St-Germain-des-Prés) sells French lingerie favored by celebrities like Catherine Deneuve and Claudia Schiffer. **Les Salons du Palais Royal Shiseido** (✉ Jardins du Palais-Royal, 142 Galerie de Valois, 25 rue de Valois, Louvre/Tuileries, 1er, ☎ 01–49–27–09–09, métro: Palais-Royal) is a magical place with marble floors and purple walls that exclusively sells the scents Serge Lutens dreams up for the Japanese cosmetics firm.

Bookstores (English-Language)

The scenic open-air bookstalls along the Seine sell secondhand books (mostly in French), prints, and souvenirs. Numerous French-language bookstores—specializing in a wide range of topics, including art, film, literature, and philosophy—are found in the Latin Quarter and around St-Germain-des-Prés. For English-language books try these stores: **Brentano's** (✉ 37 av. de l'Opéra, Opéra/Grands Boulevards, 2e, ☎ 01–42–61–52–50, métro: Opéra) is stocked with everything from classics to children's titles. **Galignani** (✉ 224 rue de Rivoli, Louvre/Tuileries, 1er, ☎ 01–42–60–76–07, métro: Tuileries) is especially known for its extensive collection of art and coffee-table books. **Shakespeare and Company** (✉ 37 rue de la Bûcherie, 5e, Latin Quarter, ☎ 01–43–26–96–50, métro St-Michel), the sentimental Left Bank favorite, is named after the publishing house that first edited James Joyce's *Ulysses.* Nowadays, it specializes in expatriate literature. The staff tends to be rather pretentious, but the shelves of secondhand books hold real bargains. Poets give readings upstairs on Monday at 8 PM; there are also tea-party talks on Sunday at 4 PM. **Village Voice** (✉ 6 rue Princesse, St-Germain-des-Prés, 6e, ☎ 01–46–33–36–47, métro: Mabillon) hosts regular literary readings.

Clothing

MENSWEAR

Berluti (✉ 26 rue Marbeuf, Champs-Élysées, 8e, ☎ 01–53–93–97–97, métro: Franklin-D.-Roosevelt) has been making the most exclusive men's shoes for more than a century. **Charvet** (✉ 28 pl. Vendôme, Opéra/Grands Boulevards, 1er, ☎ 01–42–60–30–70, métro: Opéra) is the Parisian equivalent of a Savile Row tailor. **Le Printemps de l'Homme** (✉ 61 rue Caumartin, Opéra/Grands Boulevards, 9e, ☎ 01–42–82–50–00, métro: Havre-Caumartin) has six floors of designer suits, sportswear, coats, ties, and accessories.

WOMENSWEAR

It doesn't matter, say the French, that fewer and fewer of their top couture houses are still headed by compatriots. It's the chic elegance, the classic ambience, the je ne sais quoi, that remains undeniably Gallic. Here are some meccas for Paris chic. **Azzedine Alaïa** (✉ 7 rue de Moussy, Le Marais, 4e, ☎ 01–42–72–19–19, métro: Hôtel-de-Ville) is the undisputed "king of cling" and a supermodel favorite. **Colette** (✉ 213 rue St-Honoré, Louvre/Tuileries, 1er, ☎ 01–55–35–33–90, métro: Tuileries) is the most fashionable, most hip, and most hyped store in Paris (and possibly the world). The ground floor, which stocks design objects, gadgets, and makeup, is generally packed with fashion victims and the simply curious. Upstairs are handpicked fashions, accessories, magazines and books, all of which ooze trendiness. **Maria Luisa** (✉ 2 rue Cambon, Louvre/Tuileries, 8e, ☎ 01–47–03–96–15, métro: Concorde) is a boudoir-like boutique that has become a legend in its own time; it stocks the likes of Martin Margiela, Jean-Paul Gaultier, Helmut Lang, and Olivier Theyskens. **Sonia Rykiel** (✉ 175 bd. St-Germain, St-Germain-des-Prés, 6e, ☎ 01–49–54–60–60, métro: St-Germain-des-Prés; ✉ 70 rue du Faubourg St-Honoré, Louvre/Tuileries, 8e, ☎ 01–42–65–20–81, métro: Concorde) is the queen of French fashion. Since the '60s she has been designing stylish knit separates and has made black her color of preference. **Ungaro** (✉ 2 avenue Montaigne, Champs-Élysées, 8e, ☎ 01–53–57–00–22, métro: Alma-Marceau) is once again a hot fashion ticket, with a new generation of devotees, including Jennifer Lopez and Whitney Houston; the boutique is cozy, with sofas, big cushions, and Asian touches.

Anouschka (✉ 6 av. Coq, Opéra/Grands Boulevards, 9e, ☎ 01–48–74–37–00, métro: St-Lazare–Trinité) has set up shop in her apartment (open Monday–Saturday noon–7) and has rack upon rack of vintage clothing, dating from as far back as the 1920s. **Antik Batik** (✉ 18 rue de Turenne, Le Marais, 4e, ☎ 01–48–87–95–95, métro: St-Paul) sells hippie-chic and ethnic-inspired clothing, bags, and shoes, which has made the label a hit with in-the-know Parisians and supermodels. **Chacok** (✉ 18 rue de Grenelle, St-Germain-des-Prés, 7e, ☎ 01–42–22–69–99, métro: Sèvres-Babylone) is the label for fashion-savvy Parisians, who adore colorful, sunny, and feminine fashions. **Didier Ludot** (✉ Jardins du Palais-Royal, 24 galerie Montpensier, Louvre/Tuileries, 1er, ☎ 01–42–96–06–56, métro: Palais-Royal) is one of the world's most famous vintage clothing dealers; check out the wonderful old Chanel suits, Balenciaga dresses, and Hermès scarves, and bring lots of money. **Isabel Marant** (✉ 16 rue de Charonne, Bastille/Nation, 11e, ☎ 01–49–29–71–55, métro: Ledru-Rollin) is one of the Paris press's favorite designers. French fashionistas flock to her Bastille boutique for her youthful and feminine designs. **Ventilo** (✉ 27 bis rue du Louvre, Louvre/Tuileries, 2e, ☎ 01–44–76–83–00, métro: Louvre) sells ethnic-inspired fashions to savvy Parisians; on the third floor are housewares and a café serving what is perhaps the best chocolate cake in the world.

Food and Wine

Les Caves Augé (✉ 116 bd. Haussmann, Opéra/Grands Boulevards, 8e, ☎ 01–45–22–16–97, métro: St-Augustin) has been one of the best wine shops in Paris since 1850. **L'Epicerie** (✉ 51 rue St-Louis-en-Ile, Ile St-Louis, 4e, ☎ 01–43–25–20–14, métro: Pont-Marie) sells 90 types of jam, 70 kinds of mustard, numerous olive oils, and flavored sugars. **La Maison du Chocolat** (✉ 56 rue Pierre-Charron, Champs-Élysées, 8e, ☎ 01–47–23–38–25, métro: Franklin-D.-Roosevelt; ✉ 8 bd. de la Madeleine, Opéra/Grands Boulevards, 9e, ☎ 01–47–42–86–52, métro: Madeleine; ✉ 225 rue du Faubourg–St-Honoré, Champs-Élysées, 8e, ☎ 01–42–27–39–44, métro: Ternes) is the place for chocolate; take home some or go to the tearoom at rue Pierre Charron or Madeleine.

Housewares and Gifts

R. & Y. Augousti (✉ 103 rue du Bac, St-Germain-des-Prés, 7e, ☎ 01–42–22–22–21, métro: Sèvres-Babylone) makes '30s-inspired furniture and home objects from natural materials like coconut, bamboo, fish skin, palm wood, and parchment. **Christophe Delcourt** (✉ 76 bis rue Vieille-du-Temple, Le Marais, 3e, ☎ 01–42–78–44–97, métro: Rambuteau–St-Paul) attracts fashion designers and French film stars, who go mad for his lamps based on old-fashioned drawing tools, pared-down waxed-steel furniture, and sleek wooden tables. **Diptyque** (✉ 34 bd. St-Germain, St-Germain-des-Prés, 5e, ☎ 01–43–26–45–27, métro: Maubert-Mutualité) sells the best scented candles in Paris. **Van der Straeten** (✉ 11 rue Ferdinand Duval, Le Marais, 4e, ☎ 01–42–78–99–99, métro: St-Paul) is the lofty gallery-cum-showroom of the talented Hervé van der Straeten, who creates poetic jewelry, as well as rather Baroque and often wacky furniture.

PARIS A TO Z

To research prices, get advice from other travelers, and book travel arrangements, visit www.fodors.com.

AIR TRAVEL TO AND FROM PARIS

CARRIERS

Major carriers fly daily from the United States; Air France, British Airways, British Midland, and Air U.K. fly regularly from London.

AIRPORTS AND TRANSFERS

Paris is served by two international airports: Charles de Gaulle, also known as Roissy, 26 km (16 mi) northeast; and Orly, 16 km (10 mi) south. For telephone numbers, ☞ Airports *in* Smart Travel Tips, Chapter 17.

From Charles de Gaulle, the RER-B, the suburban commuter train, beneath Terminal 2, has trains to central Paris (Les Halles, St-Michel, Luxembourg) every 15 minutes; the fare is €7.60, and the journey lasts 30 minutes. Note that you have to carry your luggage up from and down to the platform and that trains can be crowded during rush hour. Buses operated by Air France (you need not have flown with the airline) run every 15 minutes between Roissy and western Paris (Porte Maillot and the Arc de Triomphe). The fare is €10, and the trip lasts about 40 minutes, though rush-hour traffic may make it longer. Additionally, the Roissybus, operated by the RATP, runs directly between Roissy and rue Scribe by the Opéra every 15 minutes and costs €8.05. Taxis are readily available; the fare will be around €30–€40, depending on traffic. Aeroports Limousine Service can meet you on arrival in a private car and drive you to your destination; reservations should be made two or three days in advance; MasterCard and Visa are accepted—readers report inordinate delays, however. The following minibus services can also meet you on arrival: Airport Shuttle, Paris Airports Service, and Parishuttle.

The RER-C line is one way to get to Paris from Orly Airport; there's a free shuttle bus from the terminal building to the train station, and trains leave every 15 minutes. The fare is €5.10 (métro included), and the train journey takes about 45 minutes. The Orlyval service is a shuttle train that runs direct from each Orly terminal to the Antony RER-B station every seven minutes; a one-way ticket for the entire trip into Paris is €8.65. Buses operated by Air France (you need not have flown with the airline) run every 12 minutes between Orly Airport and the Air France air terminal at Les Invalides, on the Left Bank; the fare is €7.50, and the trip can take from 30 minutes to an hour, depending on traffic. RATP also runs the Orlybus between the Denfert-Rochereau métro station and Orly every 15 minutes, and the trip costs €5.60. A 20-minute taxi ride costs about €20–€30. With reservations, Aeroports Limousine Service can pick you up at Orly, but readers report delays.

➤ TAXIS AND SHUTTLES: **Aeroports Limousine Service** (☎ 01–40–71–84–62). **Airport Shuttle** (☎ 01–42–38–55–72; 1–888/426–2705 in the U.S.). **Paris Airports Service** (☎ 01–49–62–78–78). **Parishuttle** (☎ 01–43–90–91–91).

BUS TRAVEL TO AND FROM PARIS

Long-distance bus journeys within France are uncommon, which may be why Paris has no central bus depot. *See* Bus Travel *in* Smart Travel Tips A to Z for information on traveling to and from Paris by bus.

BUS TRAVEL WITHIN PARIS

Paris buses are marked with the route number and destination in front and with major stopping places along the sides. The brown bus shelters, topped by red-and-yellow circular signs, contain timetables and route maps. You can use your métro ticket on buses; if you have individual tickets (as opposed to weekly or monthly tickets), state your destination and be prepared to punch one or more tickets in the red-and-gray machines on board.

FARES AND SCHEDULES

Most routes operate from 6 AM to 8:30 PM; some continue until midnight. Ten *Noctambus,* or night buses, operate hourly (1 AM–6 AM) between Châtelet and various nearby suburbs.

CAR RENTAL

Cars can be rented at both airports, as well as at locations throughout the city, including the ones listed below.

➤ Local Agencies: **Avis** (✉ 60 rue de Ponthieu, Champs-Élysées, 8e, ☎ 01–43–59–03–83, métro: St-Philippe du Roule). **Citer** (✉ 18 rue de Dunkerque, Gare du Nord, 10e, ☎ 01–53–20–06–52, métro: Gare du Nord). **Europcar** (✉ 60 bd. Diderot, Bastille/Nation, 12e, ☎ 08–03–35–23–52, métro: Gare de Lyon). **Hertz** (✉ 193 rue de Bercy, Bercy/Tolbiac, 12e, ☎ 01–43–44–06–00, métro: Gare de Lyon).

CAR TRAVEL

In a country as highly centralized as France, it's no surprise that expressways converge on the capital from every direction: A1 from the north (225 km/140 mi from Lille); A13 from Normandy (225 km/140 mi from Caen); A4 from the east (500 km/310 mi from Strasbourg); A10 from the southwest (580 km/360 mi from Bordeaux); and A7 from the Alps and the Riviera (465 km/290 mi from Lyon). Each connects with the *périphérique*, the beltway, whose exits into the city are named (as *portes*), not numbered.

CHILDREN IN PARIS

BABY-SITTING

Baby-sitting services can provide English-speaking baby-sitters on just a few hours' notice. The hourly rate is approximately $6 (three-hour minimum) plus an agency fee of around $10.

➤ Agencies: **Ababa** (✉ 8 av. du Maine, Montparnasse, 15e, ☎ 01–45–49–46–46). **Allo Maman Poule** (✉ 7 Villa Murat, Passy/Auteuil, 16e, ☎ 01–45–20–96–96). **Baby Sitting Services** (✉ 4 rue Nationale, Boulogne-Billancourt 92100, ☎ 01–46–21–33–16).

EMBASSIES AND CONSULATES

➤ Australia: (✉ 4 rue Jean-Rey, Trocadéro/Eiffel Tower, 15e, ☎ 01–40–59–33–00, métro: Bir Hakeim).

➤ Canada: (✉ 35 av. Montaigne, Champs-Élysées, 8e, ☎ 01–44–43–29–00, métro: Franklin-D.-Roosevelt).

➤ New Zealand: (✉ 7 ter rue Léonardo da Vinci, Champs-Élysées, 16e, ☎ 01–45–00–24–11, métro: Victor-Hugo).

➤ United Kingdom: (✉ 35 rue du Faubourg–St-Honoré, Champs-Élysées, 8e, ☎ 01–44–51–31–00, métro: Concorde).

➤ United States: (✉ 2 av. Gabriel, Champs-Élysées, 8e, ☎ 01–43–12–22–22, métro: Concorde).

EMERGENCIES

A 24-hour emergency service is available at American Hospital. Hertford British Hospital also has all-night emergency service. Pharmacie Les Champs is open 24 hours a day, 365 days a year; Pharmacie Européenne is also open around the clock.

➤ Doctors and Dentists: **Dentist** (☎ 01–43–37–51–00). **Doctor** (☎ 01–43–37–77–77).

➤ Emergency Services: **Ambulance** (☎ 15 or 01–45–67–50–50). **Police** (☎ 17).

➤ Hospitals: **American Hospital** (✉ 63 bd. Victor-Hugo, Neuilly, ☎ 01–46–41–25–25). **Hertford British Hospital** (✉ 3 rue Barbès, Levallois-Perret, ☎ 01–47–58–13–12).

➤ 24-Hour Pharmacies: **Pharmacie Européenne** (✉ 6 pl. de Clichy, Montmartre, 9e, ☎ 01–48–74–65–18, métro: Place de Clichy). **Pharmacie Les Champs** (✉ 84 av. des Champs-Élysées, Champs-Élysées, 8e, ☎ 01–45–62–02–41, métro: George-V).

Paris Métro

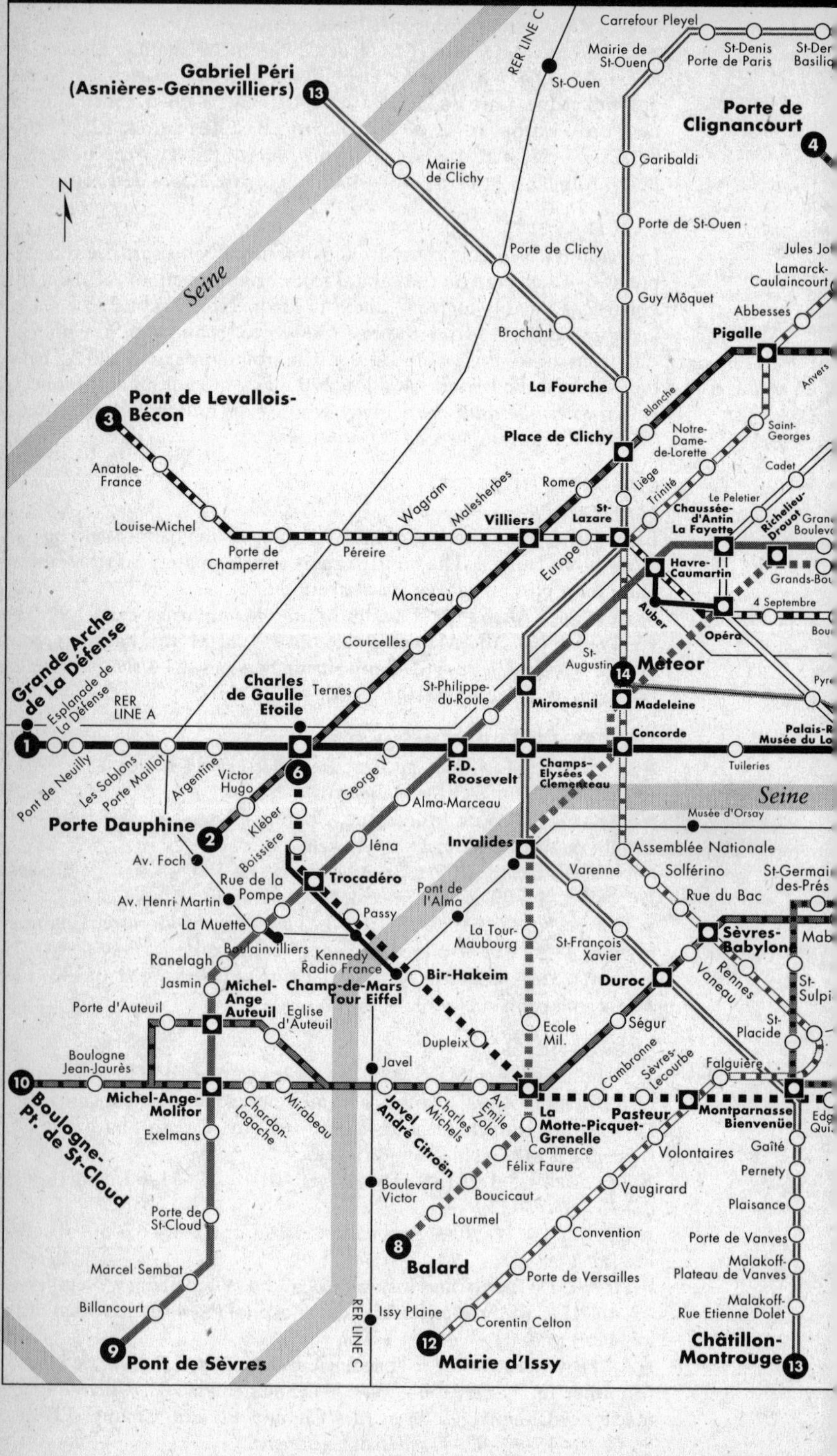

RER LINE C
Carrefour Pleyel
Mairie de St-Ouen
St-Denis Porte de Paris
St-Ouen
Gabriel Péri (Asnières-Gennevilliers)
13
Porte de Clignancourt
4
Mairie de Clichy
Garibaldi
N
Porte de St-Ouen
Porte de Clichy
Jules Jo
Lamarck-Caulaincourt
Seine
Guy Môquet
Abbesses
Brochant
Pigalle
La Fourche
Anvers
Pont de Levallois-Bécon
3
Blanche
Place de Clichy
Notre-Dame-de-Lorette
Saint-Georges
Anatole-France
Cadet
Rome
Liège
Trinité
Le Peletier
Wagram
Malesherbes
St-Lazare
Chaussée-d'Antin La Fayette
Richelieu-Drouot
Louise-Michel
Villiers
Porte de Champerret
Péreire
Europe
Havre-Caumartin
Grands-Bo
Monceau
Auber
4 Septembre
Opéra
Courcelles
St-Augustin
14
Méteor
Grande Arche de La Défense
Esplanade de La Défense
RER LINE A
Charles de Gaulle Etoile
Ternes
St-Philippe-du-Roule
Miromesnil
Madeleine
Concorde
Palais-R Musée du Lo
1
Pont de Neuilly
Les Sablons
Porte Maillot
Argentine
Victor Hugo
6
George V
F.D. Roosevelt
Champs-Elysées Clemenceau
Tuileries
Seine
Alma-Marceau
Musée d'Orsay
Porte Dauphine
2
Kléber
Boissière
Iéna
Invalides
Assemblée Nationale
Av. Foch
Trocadéro
Varenne
Solférino
St-Germain-des-Prés
Rue de la Pompe
Pont de l'Alma
Rue du Bac
Av. Henri Martin
Passy
La Tour-Maubourg
St-François Xavier
Sèvres-Babylone
La Muette
Boulainvilliers
Kennedy Radio France
Bir-Hakeim
Rennes
Vaneau
Ranelagh
Champ-de-Mars Tour Eiffel
Duroc
St-Sulpice
Jasmin
Michel-Ange Auteuil
Eglise d'Auteuil
Ecole Mil.
Ségur
St-Placide
Porte d'Auteuil
Dupleix
Cambronne
Sèvres-Lecourbe
Falguière
Boulogne Jean-Jaurès
Javel
10
Michel-Ange-Molitor
Chardon-Lagache
Mirabeau
Javel André Citroën
Charles Michels
Av. Emile Zola
La Motte-Picquet-Grenelle
Pasteur
Montparnasse Bienvenüe
Edg Qui
Boulogne-Pt. de St-Cloud
Exelmans
Commerce
Volontaires
Gaîté
Félix Faure
Pernety
Boulevard Victor
Boucicaut
Vaugirard
Porte de St-Cloud
Plaisance
Lourmel
Convention
Porte de Vanves
8
Balard
Marcel Sembat
Malakoff-Plateau de Vanves
Porte de Versailles
Billancourt
Malakoff-Rue Etienne Dolet
Issy Plaine
Corentin Celton
12
Châtillon-Montrouge
13
9
Pont de Sèvres
Mairie d'Issy

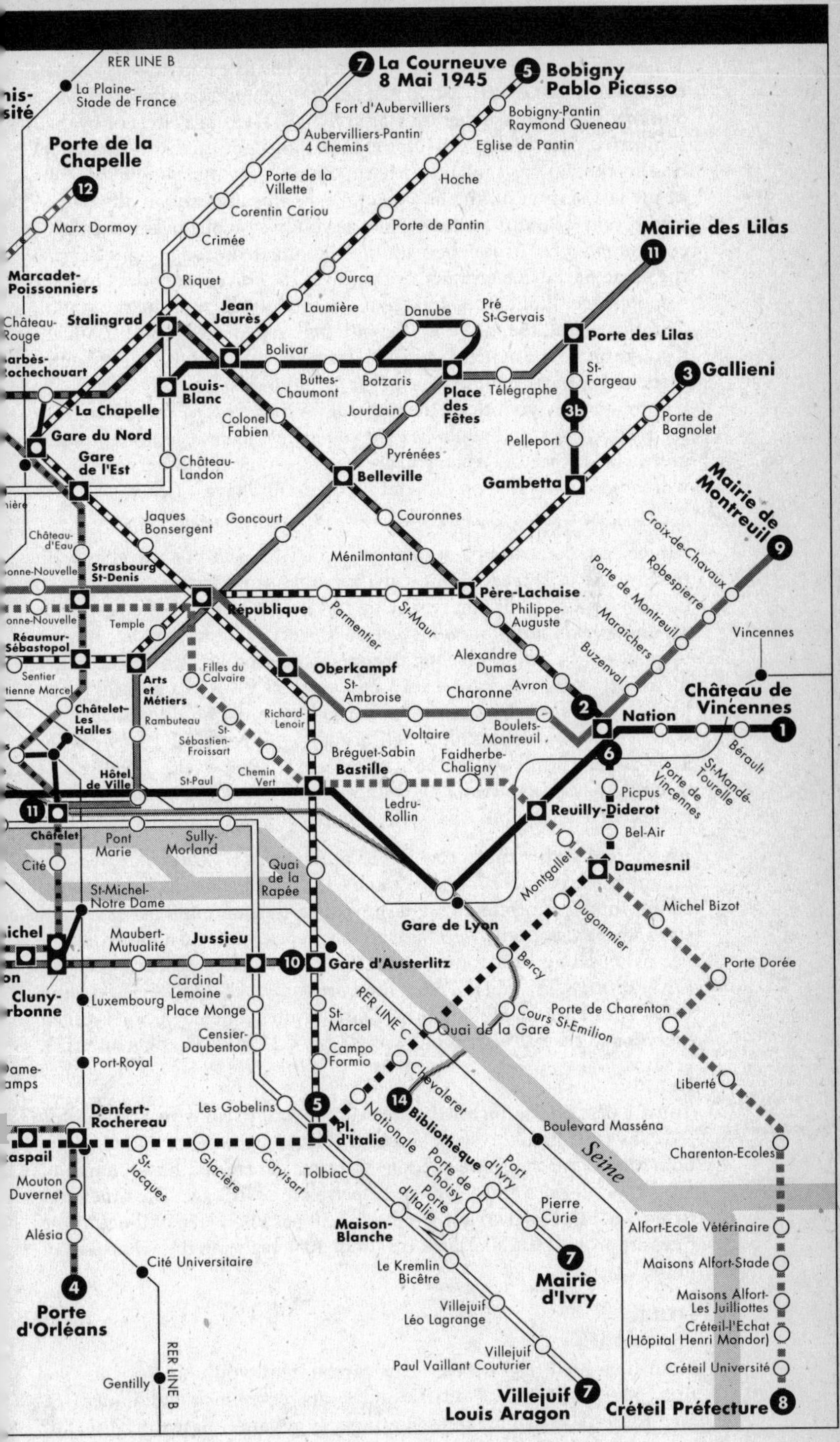

RER LINE B
La Plaine-Stade de France
7 La Courneuve 8 Mai 1945
5 Bobigny Pablo Picasso
Fort d'Aubervilliers
Aubervilliers-Pantin 4 Chemins
Bobigny-Pantin Raymond Queneau
Eglise de Pantin
Porte de la Chapelle
12
Porte de la Villette
Hoche
Corentin Cariou
Marx Dormoy
Crimée
Porte de Pantin
Mairie des Lilas
11
Riquet
Ourcq
Marcadet-Poissonniers
Laumière
Danube
Pré St-Gervais
Stalingrad
Jean Jaurès
Porte des Lilas
Bolivar
St-Fargeau
3 Gallieni
Louis-Blanc
Buttes-Chaumont
Botzaris
Place des Fêtes
Télégraphe
La Chapelle
Colonel Fabien
Jourdain
3b
Porte de Bagnolet
Gare du Nord
Pelleport
Gare de l'Est
Château-Landon
Pyrénées
Belleville
Gambetta
Mairie de Montreuil
Jaques Bonsergent
Goncourt
Couronnes
Croix-de-Chavaux
Château-d'Eau
Ménilmontant
9
Robespierre
Strasbourg St-Denis
Porte de Montreuil
République
Parmentier
St-Maur
Père-Lachaise
Philippe-Auguste
Maraîchers
Temple
Vincennes
Réaumur-Sébastopol
Filles du Calvaire
Oberkampf
Alexandre Dumas
Buzenval
Arts et Métiers
St-Ambroise
Charonne
Avron
Château de Vincennes
Châtelet-Les Halles
Rambuteau
Richard-Lenoir
2
Nation
1
St-Sébastien-Froissart
Voltaire
Boulets-Montreuil
6
Bérault
Bréguet-Sabin
Faidherbe-Chaligny
St-Mandé-Tourelle
Hôtel de Ville
St-Paul
Chemin Vert
Bastille
Porte de Vincennes
Picpus
Ledru-Rollin
Reuilly-Diderot
11
Châtelet
Pont Marie
Sully-Morland
Bel-Air
Cité
Quai de la Rapée
Montgallet
Daumesnil
St-Michel-Notre Dame
Dugommier
Michel Bizot
Gare de Lyon
Maubert-Mutualité
Jussieu
Cluny-Sorbonne
Cardinal Lemoine
10
Gare d'Austerlitz
Bercy
Porte Dorée
Luxembourg
Place Monge
RER LINE C
St-Marcel
Cours St-Emilion
Porte de Charenton
Censier-Daubenton
Quai de la Gare
Campo Formio
Port-Royal
Chevaleret
14
Liberté
Les Gobelins
Bibliothèque
5
Nationale
Denfert-Rochereau
Pl. d'Italie
Boulevard Masséna
Raspail
St-Jacques
Glacière
Corvisart
Tolbiac
Port d'Ivry
Charenton-Ecoles
Mouton Duvernet
Porte de Choisy
Seine
Porte d'Italie
Pierre Curie
Alésia
Maison-Blanche
Alfort-Ecole Vétérinaire
Cité Universitaire
7
Le Kremlin Bicêtre
Mairie d'Ivry
Maisons Alfort-Stade
4
Porte d'Orléans
Villejuif Léo Lagrange
Maisons Alfort-Les Juilliottes
Créteil-l'Echat (Hôpital Henri Mondor)
RER LINE B
Villejuif Paul Vaillant Couturier
Créteil Université
Gentilly
Villejuif Louis Aragon
7
Créteil Préfecture
8

MÉTRO TRAVEL

The métro is by far the quickest and most efficient way to get around. Trains run from 5:30 AM until 1:15 AM (and be forewarned—this means the famous "last métro" can pass your station anytime after 12:30 AM). Stations are signaled either by a large yellow M within a circle or by their distinctive curly green Art Nouveau railings and archway entrances bearing the subway's full title (Métropolitain). You must know the name of the last station on the line you take, as this appears on all signs. A connection (you can make as many as you like on one ticket) is called a *correspondance*. At junction stations illuminated orange signs bearing the name of the line terminal appear over the correct corridors for correspondance. Illuminated blue signs marked SORTIE indicate the station exit. In general, the métro is safe, although try to avoid Lines 2 and 13 if you're alone late at night. Access to métro platforms is through an automatic ticket barrier. Slide your ticket in and pick it up and retrieve it as it pops up. Keep your ticket during your journey; you will need it to leave the RER system, and you'll be glad you have it in case you run into any green-clad inspectors when you are leaving—they can be very nasty and will impose a big fine on the spot if you do not have a ticket.

FARES AND SCHEDULES

All métro tickets and passes are valid for RER and bus travel as well; tickets cost €1.30 each, but it makes more sense to buy a *carnet* (10 tickets) for €9.30. If you're staying for a week or more, the best deals are the weekly *coupon jaune* (yellow ticket) or monthly *carte orange* (orange card), sold according to zone. Zones 1 and 2 cover the entire métro network; tickets cost €13.25 a week or €44.35 a month. If you plan to take suburban trains to visit places in the Ile-de-France, consider a four-zoner (Versailles, St-Germain-en-Laye; €22.10 a week) or a six-zoner (Rambouillet, Fontainebleau; €30 a week). Weekly and monthly passes are available from rail and major métro stations; the monthly pass requires a passport-size photograph.

An alternative for métro travel is to purchase two-, three-, or five-day unlimited-travel tickets (*Paris Visite*). Unlike the coupon jaune, good from Monday morning to Sunday evening, the unlimited ticket is valid starting any day of the week and gives you discounts on a limited number of museums and tourist attractions. The prices are, respectively, €13.70, €18.25, and €26.65 for Paris only; €26.65, €37.35, and €45.70 for Paris and the suburbs. The equivalent one-day ticket is called *mobilis* and costs €5 (Paris only) or €8.50–€14.90 (Paris plus suburbs).

TAXIS

You are best off asking hotel or restaurant staff to call you a taxi; cruising cabs are difficult to spot, especially late at night. Note that taxis seldom take more than three people at a time. There is a basic charge of €2.20 for all rides and a €1 charge per piece of luggage. Daytime rates (from 7 AM to 7:30 PM) are around €0.50 per kilometer, and nighttime rates are around €0.80. Rates are about 40% higher in the suburbs than in the city.

TOURS

BOAT TOURS

Hour-long boat trips on the Seine can be fun if you're in Paris for the first time; the cost is €7–€10. Some boats serve lunch and dinner (for an additional cost); make reservations in advance. Bateaux Mouches boats depart daily 11–10 in summer, 11–9 in winter. Bateaux Parisiens boats depart every half hour in summer and every hour in winter, starting at 10 AM; the last boat departs at 10 PM (11 PM in summer). Canauxrama organizes half- and full-day barge tours along the canals of east Paris. Vedettes du Pont-Neuf depart every half hour 10–noon,

1:30–6:30, and 9–10:30 from March to October and every 45 minutes 10:30–noon and 1:30–6:30 from November to February.

➤ FEES AND SCHEDULES: **Bateaux Mouches** (✉ Pont de l'Alma, Trocadéro/Eiffel Tower, 8ᵉ, ☎ 01–40–76–99–99, métro: Alma-Marceau). **Bateaux Parisiens** (✉ Pont d'Iéna, Trocadéro/Eiffel Tower, 7ᵉ, ☎ 01–44–11–33–44, métro: Trocadéro). **Canauxrama** (boats depart from: ✉ 13 quai de la Loire, Gare de l'Est, 19ᵉ, métro: Jaurès; for information: ✉ Bassin de l'Arsenal, opposite 50 bd. de la Bastille, Bastille/Nation, 12ᵉ, métro: Bastille; ☎ 01–42–39–15–00). **Vedettes du Pont-Neuf** (✉ below Sq. du Vert-Galant, Ile de la Cité, 1ᵉʳ, ☎ 01–46–33–98–38, métro: Pont Neuf).

BUS TOURS

Cityrama and Paris Vision both organize a number of different tours, from two hours on a double-decker bus with live or tape-recorded commentary (English is available) to day trips to sights in the Paris region. Tours generally cost about €25. For a more intimate—albeit expensive—tour of the city, Paris Bus runs several minibus excursions per day; the bus can take eight people and can pick up or drop off at hotels; the cost is €45 for a 2½-hour tour, €56 for four hours. For sightseeing at your own pace, Les Cars Rouges run a red double-decker with nine pickup and drop-off points around Paris. Tours start from Trocadéro at 10:20 AM and every 50 minutes until 5. Tickets are good for two days and cost €20.

➤ FEES AND SCHEDULES: **Cityrama** (✉ 4 pl. des Pyramides, Louvre/Tuileries, 1ᵉʳ, ☎ 01–44–55–60–00, métro: Tuileries). **Paris Bus** (✉ 22 rue de la Prévoyance, Bois de Vincennes, 94300 Vincennes, ☎ 01–43–65–55–55, métro: St-Mandé–Tourelle). **Les Cars Rouges** (✉ 17 quai de Grenelle, Trocadéro/Eiffel Tower, 15ᵉ, ☎ 01–53–95–39–53, métro: Bir-Hakeim). **Paris Vision** (✉ 214 rue de Rivoli, Louvre Tuileries, 1ᵉʳ, ☎ 08-00–03–02–14, métro: Tuileries).

PRIVATE GUIDES

Paris Major Limousines arranges private tours of Paris in luxury cars or minibuses (holding up to seven passengers) with English-speaking drivers. The price starts at €220 but varies with time (a minimum of three hours) and number of passengers. Reservations are essential.

➤ CONTACTS: **Paris Major Limousines** (✉ 14 rue de l'Atlas, Buttes-Chaumont, 19ᵉ, ☎ 01–44–52–50–00).

WALKING TOURS

Plenty of guided walking tours of specific areas of Paris are available, often concentrating on a historical or architectural topic. Guides are enthusiastic but not always English-speaking; costs range from €8 to €10), and tours last about two hours. Details are published in the weekly magazines *Pariscope* and *L'Officiel des Spectacles* under "Conférences." Walking tours are also organized by the Caisse Nationale des Monuments Historiques.

➤ FEES AND SCHEDULES: **Caisse Nationale des Monuments Historiques,** Bureau des Visites (✉ Hôtel de Sully, 62 rue St-Antoine, Bastille, 4ᵉ, ☎ 01–44–61–20–00, métro: St-Paul).

TRAIN TRAVEL

Paris has five international train stations: Gare du Nord (northern France, northern Europe, and England via Calais or the Channel Tunnel); Gare St-Lazare (Normandy and England via Dieppe); Gare de l'Est (Strasbourg, Luxembourg, Basel, and central Europe); Gare de Lyon (Lyon, Marseille, the Riviera, Geneva, Italy); and Gare d'Austerlitz (Loire Valley, southwest France, Spain). The Gare Montparnasse is used by the TGV *Atlantique* bound for Nantes or Bordeaux. Call 08–92–35–35–35 for information.

RER trains travel between Paris and the suburbs. When they go through Paris, they act as a sort of supersonic métro—they connect with the métro network at several points—and can be great time-savers. Access to RER platforms is through the same type of automatic ticket barrier (if you've started your journey on the métro, you can use the same ticket), but you'll need to have the same ticket handy to put through another barrier when you leave the system.

➤ TRAIN INFORMATION: **SNCF** (✉ 1 rue Paturle, Montparnasse, ☎ 01–53–90–20–20, WEB www.sncf.fr).

TRANSPORTATION AROUND PARIS

To help you find your way around, buy a *Plan de Paris par Arrondissement,* a city guide available at most kiosks, with separate maps of each district, including the whereabouts of métro stations and an index of street names. Maps of the métro/RER network are available free from any métro station and from many hotels. They are also posted on every platform, as are maps of the bus network. Bus routes are also marked at bus stops and on buses. The extensive public transportation system is the best way to get around. Don't use a car in Paris unless you have to. Parking is difficult—and expensive—and traffic can be awesome. Meters and ticket machines (pay and display) are common; make sure you have a supply of coins.

TRAVEL AGENCIES

➤ LOCAL AGENT REFERRALS: **Air France** (✉ 119 av. des Champs-Élysées, Champs-Élysées, 8e, ☎ 01–42–99–21–01, métro: Charles-de-Gaulle–Étoile). **American Express** (✉ 11 rue Scribe, Opéra/Grands Boulevards, 8e, ☎ 01–47–77–77–07, métro: Opéra; ✉ 38 av. de Wagram, Champs-Élysées, 8e, ☎ 01–42–27–58–80, métro: Charles-de-Gaulle–Étoile). **Nouvelles Frontières** (✉ 5 av. de l'Opéra, Louvre/Tuileries, 1er, ☎ 08–03–33–33–33, métro: Pyramides). **Soltours** (✉ 46 rue de Rivoli, Le Marais, 4e, ☎ 01–42–71–24–34, métro: Hôtel-de-Ville). **Wagons-Lit** (✉ 32 rue du Quatre-Septembre, Opéra/Grands Boulevards, 2e, ☎ 01–42–66–15–80, métro: Opéra).

VISITOR INFORMATION

The Office de Tourisme de Paris is open daily 9–8. It has branches at all main-line train stations except Gare St-Lazare.

➤ TOURIST INFORMATION: **Office de Tourisme de Paris** (Paris Tourist Office; ✉ 127 av. des Champs-Élysées, Champs-Élysées, 75008, ☎ 01–49–52–53–54; 01–49–52–53–56 for recorded information in English, WEB www.paris-touristoffice.com, métro: Charles-de-Gaulle–Étoile).

3 ILE-DE-FRANCE

Epitomizing the whole of France in miniature, the Ile-de-France region is the heartland of the nation. Here Louis XIV willed the construction of Versailles, the world's most vainglorious palace. Nearby, *la vie de château* continues to dazzle at Chantilly, Fontainebleau, and Vaux-le-Vicomte. More spiritual concerns are evident in Chartres Cathedral, the soaring pinnacle of Gothic architecture. Not far away, the painters' villages of Giverny and Auvers were immortalized by Monet and Van Gogh, respectively. What more can one ask? If it's Mickey Mouse on parade, that's here, too, at Disneyland Paris.

Updated by Simon Hewitt

Introduction by Nancy Coons

TO SOME OBSERVERS THE ILE-DE-FRANCE is the most heartwarming of all the French provinces. First, there is the pleasure of imagination satisfied: there is something comfortingly familiar about the look of lanes bordered with silvery poplar trees, the golden haze in the air, the gray stone of a village steeple. And no wonder, for scores of painters have immortalized them. Corot began with the forest of Fontainebleau and the village of Barbizon. Pissarro worked at Pontoise. Sisley's famous riverside canvases were painted at Moret-sur-Loing, near Fontainebleau. Monet painted the Epte River. And van Gogh died in Auvers.

What actually makes the Ile-de-France so attractive? Is it its proximity to the great city of Paris—or that it's so far removed? Had there not been a world-class cultural hub within spitting distance, would Monet have retreated to his Japanese gardens at Giverny? Or Cézanne and van Gogh to bucolic Auvers? Counts and kings to the game-rich forests of Fontainebleau, Rambouillet, and Dampierre? Would medieval castles and palaces have sprouted in the towns of Vincennes and St-Germain-en-Laye? Would abbeys and cathedrals have sprung skyward in Chartres, Senlis, and Royaumont?

If you had asked Louis XIV, he wouldn't have minced words at all: Paris was simply *démodé*—out of fashion. In the 17th century, the new power base was going to be Versailles, once a tiny village in the heart of the Ile-de-France, now a gigantic château from which the Sun King's rays (Louis XIV was known as *le roi soleil*) could radiate, unfettered by rebellious rabble and European arrivistes. Of course, later heirs kept the lines open and restored the grandiose palace as the country retreat it was meant to be—and commuted to Paris, well before the high-speed RER.

That is, indeed, the dream of most Parisians: to have a foot in both worlds. Paris may be small as capital cities go, with just under 2 million inhabitants, but Ile-de-France, the region around Paris, contains more than 10 million people—a sixth of France's entire population. That's why on closer inspection the once rustic villages of Ile-de-France reveal cosseted gardens, stylishly gentrified cottages, and extraordinary country restaurants no peasant farmer could afford to frequent. And that's why Ile-de-France retains a sophisticated air, along with more than a touch of history, not found in any of France's other patches of verdure.

The Ile-de-France is the ancient heartland of France, the core from which the French kings gradually extended their power over the rest of a rebellious, individualistic nation. Since the time when it was first wrested from savage Gauls by Julius Caesar, in 52 BC, the region has played a leading role in French history; its towns and villages intimately entwined with the course of national fact and legend. Charlemagne confirmed his power in France after generations had fought against the Romans near Soissons; Joan of Arc, battling for her king's supremacy, was finally captured at Compiègne. There is Versailles, from which the three Louis gloriously reigned until the Revolution dealt the French monarchy its death blow. And Napoléon ruled for a time from Malmaison and abdicated in the courtyard at Fontainebleau.

The Ile-de-France is not really an *île* (island), of course. This green-forested buffer that wraps Paris is only vaguely surrounded by the three rivers that meander through its periphery. But France's capital city seems to crown this genteel sprawl of an atoll, peppered with pretty villages, anchored by grandiose châteaux. The spokes of railway and freeway that radiate every which way from the Paris ring roads all merge gently into this verdant countryside.

All in all, Ile-de-France strikes a mellow balance, offering a rich and varied cross section of Gallic culture . . . a mini-sampling of everything you expect from France, and all within easy day trips out of Paris. With cathedrals, châteaux, and places immortalized by great painters, what more could you wish for? Well, how about Goofy on parade along Main Street U.S.A.? Pirates of the Caribbean? And Disney's own answer to Versailles, the bubblegum-pink turrets of Sleeping Beauty's Castle? Yes, the much-maligned, now recherché Disneyland Paris has taken root, drawing sellout crowds of Europeans wanting a taste of the American Dream—and of Americans with children in tow, bargaining against a day at the Louvre. It is just another epic vision realized against the green backdrop of Ile-de-France.

Pleasures and Pastimes

Artists' Residences

At Giverny, Claude Monet's house and garden, with its famous lily pond, is a moving visual link to Impressionist painting. In Auvers-sur-Oise, Vincent van Gogh had a final burst of creativity before taking his life. André Derain lived in Chambourcy; Camille Pissarro in Pontoise; Alfred Sisley in Moret-sur-Loing. Earlier, Rousseau, Millet, and Corot paved the way for Impressionism with their penchant for outdoor landscape painting in the village of Barbizon.

Châteaux

Ile-de-France never lost favor with the powerful, partly because its many forests—large chunks of which still stand—harbored sufficient game to ensure hunters' satisfaction, even for bloated, pampered monarchs. First Fontainebleau, in manageable Renaissance proportions, then Versailles, reflected the royal desire to transform hunting lodges into palatial residences. Other châteaux that exude almost comparable grandeur are at Vaux-le-Vicomte and Chantilly. And there are another dozen châteaux almost as grand—led by those of Dampierre, Rambouillet, Maintenon, Maisons-Laffitte, and Thoiry.

Dining

Ile-de-France's fanciest restaurants can be just as pricey as their Parisian counterparts. Little wonder—unlike Normandy's cider, cream, and chicken, or Périgord's truffles and foie gras, Ile-de-France cuisine mirrors that of the big capital. Textbook "local delicacies"—lamb stew, *pâté de Pantin* (pastry filled with meat), or pig's trotters—tend to be obsolete; instead, look for sumptuous game and asparagus in season in the south of the region and the soft, creamy cheese of Meaux and Coulommiers to the east. However, in smaller towns or if you venture off the beaten tourist path, well-priced meals are not hard to find. Reservations are a must at all restaurants in summer.

CATEGORY	COST*
$$$$	over €30
$$$	€20–€30
$$	€12–€20
$	under €12

**per person for a main course only, including tax (19.6%) and service; note that if a restaurant offers only prix fixe (set-price) meals it has been given the price category that reflects the full prix-fixe price*

Lodging

In summer, hotel rooms are at a premium, and making reservations is essential; almost all accommodations in the swankier towns—Ver-

Ile-de-France

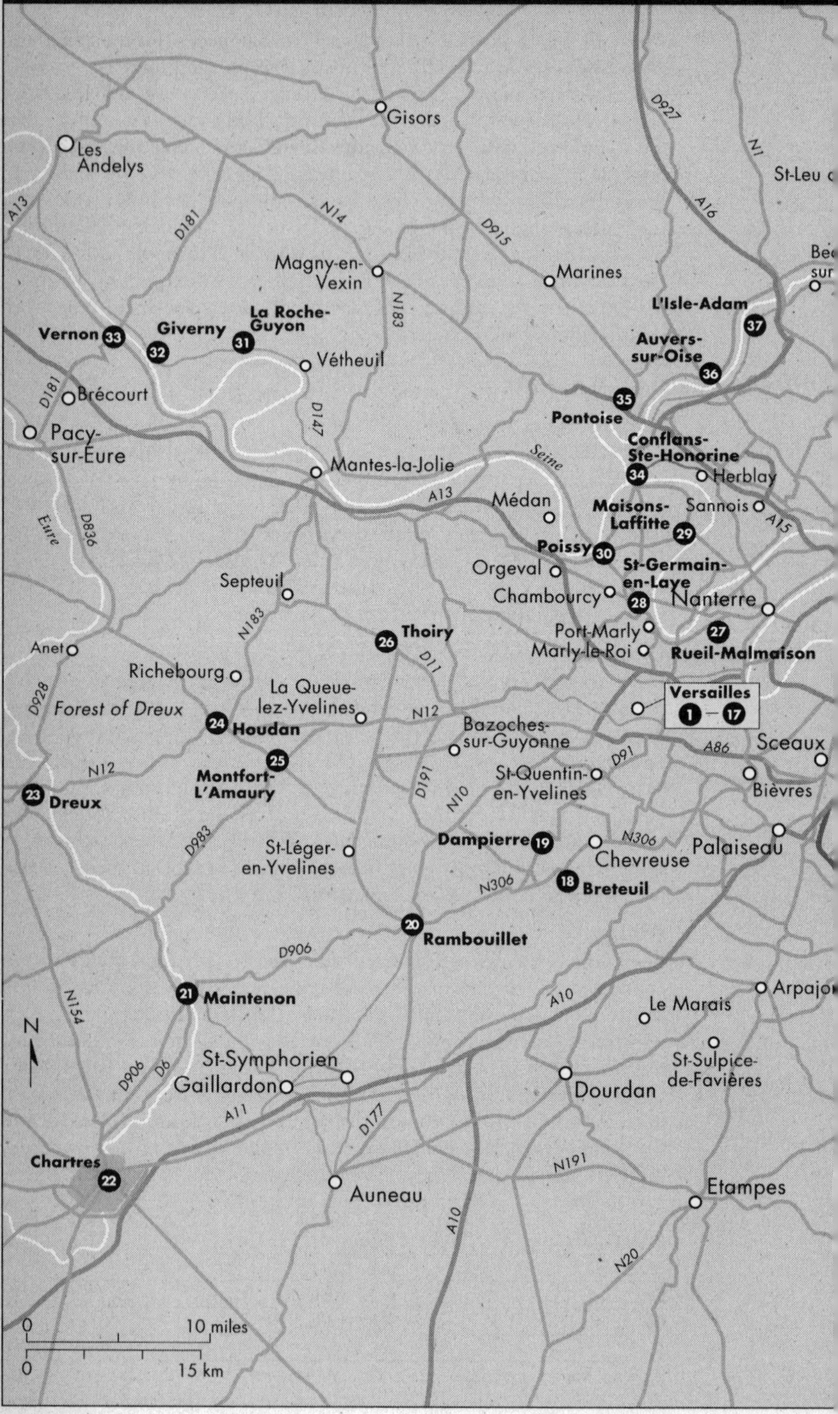

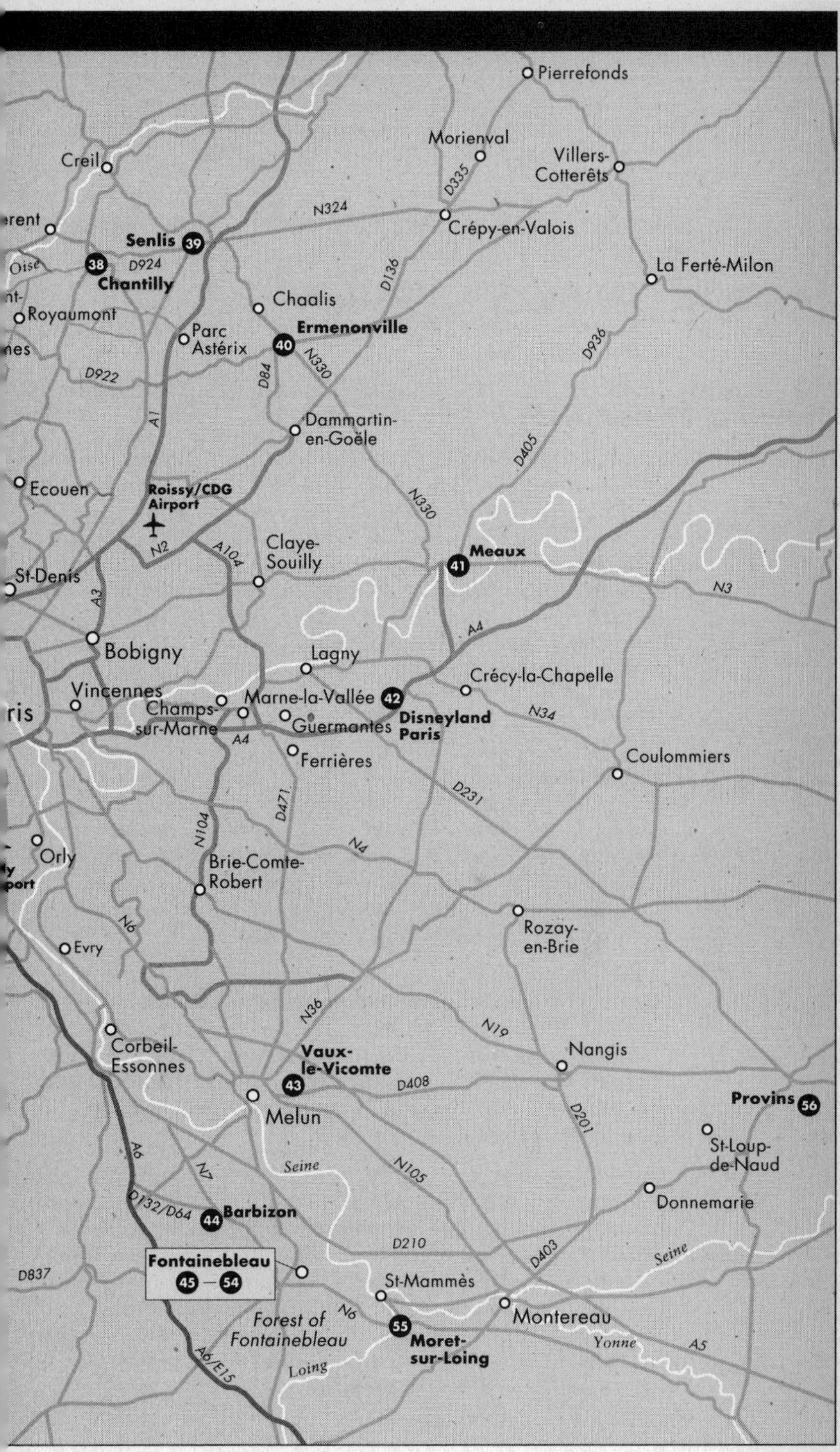
Pierrefonds
Morienval
Villers-Cotterêts
Creil
D335
N324
Crépy-en-Valois
Senlis 39
Chantilly 38
D924
Oise
La Ferté-Milon
D136
Royaumont
Chaalis
Ermenonville 40
Parc Astérix
N330
D936
D922
D84
A1
Dammartin-en-Goële
D405
Ecouen
Roissy/CDG Airport
N330
N2
A104
Claye-Souilly
Meaux 41
St-Denis
N3
A3
A4
Bobigny
Lagny
Crécy-la-Chapelle
Vincennes
Champs-sur-Marne
Marne-la-Vallée 42
Guermantes
Disneyland Paris
N34
A4
Ferrières
Coulommiers
D231
D471
N104
N4
Orly
Brie-Comte-Robert
N6
Rozay-en-Brie
Evry
N36
N19
Corbeil-Essonnes
Vaux-le-Vicomte 43
Nangis
D408
Provins 56
Melun
D201
St-Loup-de-Naud
A6
N7
Seine
N105
D132/D64
Barbizon 44
Donnemarie
D210
Fontainebleau 45 – 54
D403
Seine
D837
St-Mammès
N6
Montereau
Forest of Fontainebleau
55 Moret-sur-Loing
Yonne
A5
Loing
A6/E15

sailles, Rambouillet, and Fontainebleau—are on the costly side. Take nothing for granted; picturesque Senlis, for instance, does not have a single hotel in its historic downtown area. Assume that all hotel rooms have air-conditioning, TV, telephones, and private bath unless otherwise noted. Internet, when listed in facilities, means in-room data-ports and/or public-area computers provide on-line access.

CATEGORY	COST*
$$$$	over €180
$$$	€120–€180
$$	€60–€120
$	under €60

**All prices are for a standard double room in high season, including tax (19.6%) and service charge.*

Exploring Ile-de-France

A great advantage to exploring Ile-de-France is that all its major monuments are within a half-day's drive from Paris. Though small, Ile-de-France is so rich in treasures that a whole day of fascinating exploration may take you no more than 60 km (35 mi) from the capital. The four tours suggested below detail the major points of interest and skip the pedantic: southwest from Paris to Versailles and Chartres; northwest along the Seine to St-Germain and Giverny; north and east along the Oise Valley via Chantilly to Disneyland; and southeast from Vaux-le-Vicomte to Fontainebleau.

Numbers in the text correspond to numbers in the margin and on the Ile-de-France, Versailles, and Fontainebleau maps.

Great Itineraries

With so many legendary sights in the Ile-de-France—each a gratifying human experience rather than a guidebook necessity—you could spend weeks visiting the region. But if you don't have that much time, try one of the following shorter itineraries. Spend from two to eight days exploring the area or take day trips from Paris—most sites are within easy reach of the capital by car or train.

IF YOU HAVE 2 DAYS

Head west from Paris to nearby **St-Germain-en-Laye** ㉘ and visit either the château or the Prieuré Museum. Try to reach 🏨 **Versailles** ①–⑰ for lunch and then visit the château and the park. The next morning spend more time in Versailles or leave early and visit **Rambouillet** ⑳ or **Maintenon** ㉑ on your way to 🏨 **Chartres** ㉒; spend half a day exploring the cathedral and the Old Town.

IF YOU HAVE 5 DAYS

Take the expressway north from Paris to **Senlis** ㊴, visit the Old Town and cathedral, then head to 🏨 **Chantilly** ㊳ for the afternoon. The next morning follow the Oise Valley, stopping briefly in **Auvers-sur-Oise** ㊱ en route to 🏨 **Versailles** ①–⑰. Spend the morning of your third day in Versailles or **Rambouillet** ⑳; try to be in 🏨 **Chartres** ㉒ by early afternoon. Spend the night there and drive to 🏨 **Fontainebleau** ㊺–㊿④ the following morning, perhaps visiting **Barbizon** ㊹ on your way. On day five make sure to visit **Vaux-le-Vicomte** ㊸.

When to Tour Ile-de-France

With its extensive forests, Ile-de-France is especially beautiful in the fall, particularly October. June and July are good months, too, although August can be sultry and crowded. On a Saturday night in summer you can see son-et-lumière shows in Moret-sur-Loing and make candlelight visits to Vaux-le-Vicomte. Be aware when making your travel plans that some places are closed one or two days a week: the châteaux of Versailles and Auvers are closed on Monday; the Prieuré Museum in St-Germain is closed both Monday and Tuesday; and the châteaux of Chantilly and Fontainebleau are closed Tuesday. Disneyland Paris gets really crowded on summer weekends. So does Giverny (Monet's garden), which is at its best May through June and, like Vaux-le-Vicomte, is closed November to March.

SOUTHWEST FROM VERSAILLES TO CHARTRES

Not only is majestic Versailles one of the most unforgettable sights in Ile-de-France, it is also within easy reach of Paris, less than 30 minutes by either train or car (A13 expressway from Porte d'Auteuil). It's also the starting point for a visit to southwestern Ile-de-France, anchored by Chartres to the south and the old town of Dreux to the west.

Versailles

16 km (10 mi) west of Paris via A13.

You'll need no reminding that you're in the world's grandest palace when you arrive at Versailles. Gold, gold, and more gold, multicolor marbles, acres of Charles Le Brun–painted ceilings, and hallways still spirit-warm with the ghosts of Louis XIV, Madame de Pompadour, and Marie-Antoinette remind you that such insensate glory foreshadowed the blood-stained French Revolution. Less a monument than an entire world unto itself, its mere immensity is such that some travelers consider it more an ordeal than a pleasure. That's understandable—even the Bourbon kings needed to escape it, and did so by building one of Europe's largest parks to surround the palace. So take a cue from them and remember: if the grandeur ever becomes too much, the park outside the palace walls is the best place to come back down to earth.

Psychologically and historically, Versailles may be regarded as the result of a childhood shock suffered by the young king Louis XIV. With his mother, Anne of Austria, he was forced to flee Paris and was captured temporarily by a group of nobles, known as the Frondeurs. Louis developed a hatred for Paris and the Parisians who had sided with the conspirators. He lost no time in casting his cantankerous royal eye over Ile-de-France in search of a new power base. Marshy, inhospitable Versailles became the place of his dreams. Down came his father's modest royal hunting lodge and up, up, and along rose a swank new palace.

★ ❶ It's hard to tell which is larger, the monstrously huge **Château de Versailles** that housed a veritable army of 20,000 noblemen, servants, and sycophants who moved in with Louis, or the crowd of 20,000 visitors standing in front of it. You may be able to avoid the crowds (and lines for tours) if you arrive here at 9 AM. The hard part is figuring out where you're supposed to go once you arrive. There are different lines depending on tour, physical ability, and group status. Frequent guided tours in English visit the private royal apartments. More detailed hour-long tours explore the opera house or Marie-Antoinette's private parlors. You can go through the grandest rooms—including the Hall of Mirrors and Marie-Antoinette's stunningly gorgeous bedchamber—without a tour (by means of yet another line). To figure out the system, pick up a brochure at the information office or ticket counter. If you plan on spending the day, keep in mind you can get sandwiches in the town of Versailles (whether you can sneak them past the front-door guards is another question) or opt for luncheon at the La Flotille restaurant by the Grand Canal.

Versailles was a vision dreamed up with avenues broader than the Champs-Élysées and gigantic palace wings decorated in minion-crushing, bicep-flexing Baroque, which the 23-year-old Louis determined on after suffering a blow to his pride during a visit to Vaux-le-Vicomte, the just completed chateau his own finance minister had had the nerve to build in gorgeous, lavishly Baroque style. It's hardly surprising that Louis XIV's successors felt out of sync with their architectural inheritance. Louis XV traded in the heavy, red-and-gilt Baroque style (actually a transplant from Italy) for the newer, lighter pastel-hued Rococo mode. In doing so, he transformed the overwhelming royal apartments into places where normal human lives could be lived. The hapless Louis XVI cowered in the Petit Trianon, in the leafy depths of Versailles's gardens, out of the mighty château's shadow. His queen, Marie-Antoinette, lost her head well before her trip to the guillotine in 1793, pretending to be a peasant shepherdess amid the ersatz rusticity and perfumed flocks of sheep of her Hameau, a faux farm and village she had built just beyond the precincts of the Petit Trianon.

You enter the château—built between 1662 and 1690 by architects Louis Le Vau and Jules Hardouin-Mansart—through the gilt iron gates from huge place d'Armes. On the first floor of the château, dead center across the sprawling cobbled forecourt beyond the Sun King's statue, is **Louis XIV's bedchamber.** The two wings were occupied by the royal children and princes of the blood, while courtiers had to make do in the attics. One of the palace's trademark sights is the sparkling **Galerie des Glaces** (Hall of Mirrors). It was here, after France's capitulation, that Otto von Bismarck proclaimed the unified German Empire in 1871; and here that the Treaty of Versailles, asserting Germany's responsibility for World War I, was signed in 1919. The **Grands Appartements** (state apartments), which flank the Hall of Mirrors, retain much of their original Baroque decoration: gilt stucco, painted ceilings, and marble sculpture. Perhaps the most extravagant is the **Salon d'Apollon** (Apollo Chamber), the former throne room, dedicated to the sun god Apollo, Louis XIV's mythical hero. Equally interesting are the **Petits Appartements** (private apartments), where the royal family and friends lived in relative seclusion.

In the north wing of the château are the solemn white-and-gold **chapelle** (chapel), completed in 1710; the intimate **Opéra Royal** (Opera House), the first oval hall in France, built by Jacques-Ange Gabriel for Louis XV in 1770 and entirely constructed out of wood, then painted over to look like marble; and, connecting the two, the 17th-century **Galeries,** with exhibits retracing the château's history. The south wing contains the bombastic **Galerie des Batailles** (Hall of Battles), lined with gigantic canvases extolling French military glory. The former state rooms and sumptuous debate chamber of the **Aile du Midi** (South Wing) are also open to the public, with infrared headphones (English commentary available) explaining Versailles's parliamentary history. ☎ *01–30–83–78–00,* WEB *www.chateauversailles.fr.* 🎫 *Château €7.50, €5.40 after 3:30: parliament exhibition €4 extra.* ⊙ *May–Sept., Tues.–Sun. 9–6; Oct.–Apr., Tues.–Sun. 9–5 (Galerie des Glaces Tues.–Sun. 9:45–5; Opéra Royal Tues.–Sun. 9:45–3:30). Tours of Opéra Royal and Petits Appartements every 15 mins (€6).*

★ ❷ After the awesome feast of interior pomp, the **Parc de Versailles** (Versailles Park) is an ideal place to catch your breath. The gardens were designed by André Le Nôtre, whose work here represents classical French landscaping at its most formal and sophisticated. The 250-acre grounds include woods, lawns, flower beds, statues, artificial lakes, and foun-

Avenue de Paris 10
Carrés St-Louis 13
Cathédrale St-Louis 12
Château de Versailles 1
Grand Trianon 3
Grandes Écuries 11
Hameau 5
Lycée Hoche 9
Musée Lambinet 7
Notre-Dame . .6
Orangerie . .17
Parc de Versailles 2
Petit Trianon . .4
Pièce d'Eau des Suisses . .16
Place du Marché-Notre-Dame . .8
Potager du Roi 14
Salle du Jeu de Paume 15

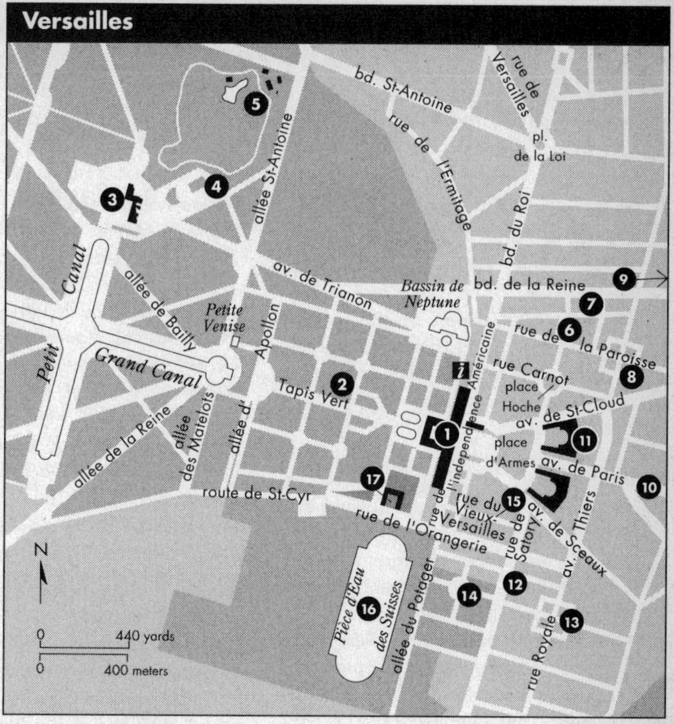

tains galore (for a guided tour of the groves, call ☎ 01–30–83–77–88). An extensive tree-replacement scheme—necessary once a century—was launched in 1998 to recapture the full impact of Le Nôtre's artful vistas; re-plantings became all the more necessary after 10,000 trees were uprooted by a hurricane in 1999. The cost of that damage came to some $35 million, and American donors contributed 40% of that amount. The distances are vast—the Trianons themselves are more than a mile from the château—so you might want to climb aboard a horse-drawn carriage (return trip from the château to Trianon, €6.40, WEB www.calechesversailles.com), or rent a bike from the **Grille de la Reine** near the Trianon Palace Hotel (€4 per hour) or from the **Petite-Venise** building at the top of the Grand Canal (€5 per hour, or €25 for six hours, ☎ 01–39–66–97–66). You can also drive to the Trianons and Canal through the Grille de la Reine (€4.50 per car). The park is at its golden-leafed best in the fall but is also enticing in summer—especially on Sunday afternoons from mid-April through mid-October, when the fountains are in full flow. *Park free (€5 for Sun. fountain displays). Daily 7 AM–8 PM or dusk.*

3 The **Grand Trianon,** built by Hardouin-Mansart in 1687, is a pink-marble pleasure palace occasionally used to entertain visiting heads of state. But most of the time it is open to visitors, who can admire its lavish interior and early 19th-century furnishings. ☎ *01–30–84–75–43. Joint ticket with Petit Trianon €5. Tues.–Sun. noon–5:30.*

★ 4 Art historians go weak in the knees when they see the **Petit Trianon**—although you may wonder what all the hubbub is about. That was precisely the point: a bijou palace, this abode—built by the great Gabriel, architect of Paris's Place de la Concorde, upon command of Madame de Pompadour, Louis XV's amour—was a radical statement, since, for a royal home, its design was so casual and unassuming. Here *le Bien-Aimé*—the

Close-Up

MARIE-ANTOINETTE: QUEEN OF TRIANON

WAS MARIE-ANTOINETTE a luxury-mad butterfly flitting from ball to costume ball? Or was she a misunderstood queen who suffered a loveless marriage and became a prisoner of court etiquette at Versailles? Historians now believe the answer was the latter and point to her private retreats at Versailles as proof. Here, in the northwest part of the royal park, far from the main palace, Marie-Antoinette created a tiny universe of her own: her comparatively dainty mansion called the Petit Trianon and its adjacent "farm," the still extant, still magnificently lovely Hameau ("hamlet"). In a life that took her from royal cradle to throne of France to guillotine, her happiest days were spent at Trianon. For here she could live a life in the "simplest" possible way; here the queen could enter a salon and the game of cards would not stop; here women wore simple gowns of muslin without a single jewel; here she could be called "Toni." In the end, this fairytale realm was so alluring it caused the queen to forget about reality and the monstrous injustices then afflicting France. Toinette only wanted to be "Queen of Trianon," not queen of France. And considering the horrible, chamberpot-pungent, gossip-infested corridors of Versailles, you can almost understand why.

From the first, Maria-Antonia (her actual name), was ostracized as an outsider, *"l'Autrichienne,"* an Austrian. Married to Louis XVI—a kind but witless boob—and shamed by her failure to deliver a royal heir, she grew to hate overcrowded Versailles and soon escaped to the Trianon, built in 1768 in the English "Adamesque" style by Gabriel for Madame de Pompadour. Starting in 1774, Toinette refashioned its interior to make it "modern." The gilt trip of the Rococo was banished. Instead, sober neoclassical *boiseries* (carved wall panels), distinguished Riesener and Carlin bureaus, and walls painted in that most dramatic of new shades—off-white—revealed a sea change in taste. The "return to Nature" was *à la mode,* so flowers were carved into wainscoting to mirror real ones outside (unfortunately, the queen's apple-green taffeta curtains have been replaced by loud crimson silk). Today, her spirit is still present, thanks in part to her bibelots—including the ivory clock fashioned for her by Louis XVI himself—and furniture; her initials still can be seen on the wrought-iron railings of the staircase.

Beyond the Petit Trianon lay the queen's storybook Hameau, a mock-Norman village inspired by the peasant-luxe daydreams caught by Boucher on canvas and by Rousseau in literature. Here Marie-Antoinette lived out her romanticized idyll of "the simple life." With its water mill, genuine lake (Grand Lac), thatched-roof houses built in daub-and-wattle style (a since-destroyed "barn" functioned as a ballroom), pigeon loft, and vegetable plots, this make-believe village was run by Monsieur Valy-Busard, a farmer, and his wife, who often helped the queen—outfitted as a Dresden shepherdess with a Sevres porcelain crook—tend her flock of perfumed sheep. As if to destroy any last link with reality, the queen built nearby a jewel-box theater (also surviving but not open to the public). Here she acted in little plays, sometimes essaying the role of a servant girl. Only the immediate royal family, about seven or so titled friends, and her personal servants were permitted entry; disastrously, the Princes of the Blood, ladies-in-waiting, and the entire officialdom of Versailles society were shut out—a move that only served to infuriate courtiers. This is how fate and destiny closed the circle. It was at Trianon that a page sent by Monsieur de Saint-Priest found Marie-Antoinette on October 5, 1789, to tell her that Paris was marching on Versailles.

Well-Beloved (as the king was called)—and his consort escaped from the pomp (and, truth to tell, filth) at Versailles, abandoning royal duties the better to play with lapdogs, translate poetry, and plan gala balls. *Joint ticket with Grand Trianon €5.* *Tues.–Sun. noon–5:30.*

When La Pompadour died, the house passed to Queen Marie-Antoinette, who refurnished it *à la néo-grecque* (in the Neoclassical style, made fashionable by the rediscovery of Pompeii) while painting its rooms in swooning Redouté pastel hues. Here, across the Petit Lac—which
★ 5 looks more like a wriggly stream—Toinette built her **Hameau** (hamlet), a mock Normandy village where she could live out her romanticized dream of peasant life, pretending to be an idyllic shepherdess tending her flock of perfumed sheep. So enchanting is this little fairytale realm that it is little wonder the ill-fated queen lost sight of reality and didn't hear the rumblings of revolution.

The town of Versailles itself—the capital of France from 1682 to 1789 and again from 1871 to 1879—is easily underestimated, despite its broad, leafy boulevards and majestic buildings. You may feel too tired from exploring the palace and park to spend time visiting the town—but it's worth the effort. Leave the château park by the Bassin de Neptune and turn right onto rue des Réservoirs, past the classical Théâtre Montansier. Up ahead you can make out Louis XIV's equestrian statue in the château courtyard; away in the other direction is the church spire of neighboring Le Chesnay. Rue Carnot, opposite, leads past the stately Écuries de la Reine, once the queen's stables, now a law court, to octagonal place Hoche. Down rue Hoche to the left is the powerful Baroque
6 facade of **Notre-Dame,** built from 1684 to 1686 by Jules Hardouin-Mansart as the parish church for Louis XIV's brand-new town. Around the back of Notre-Dame, on boulevard de la Reine (note the regimented lines of trees), are the elegant Hôtel de Neyret, now used by the Banque de France,
7 and the **Musée Lambinet,** a sumptuous mansion from 1751, furnished with paintings, weapons, fans, and porcelain. *54 bd. de la Reine,* *01–39–50–30–32.* *€5.* *Tues.–Sun. 2–5.*

Take a right onto rue Le Nôtre, then go left and right again into passage de la Geôle, a cobbled alley lined with quaint antiques shops that
8 climbs up to **place du Marché-Notre-Dame,** whose open-air morning market on Tuesday, Friday, and Sunday is famed throughout the region; there are also four 19th-century timber-roof halls with fish, meat, and spice stalls.Cross the square and head up rue de la Paroisse to av-
9 enue de St-Cloud. Around to the left is the **Lycée Hoche,** whose domed, colonnaded chapel was once part of a convent built for Louis XV's queen, Marie Leszczynska, in 1767.

10 Cross avenue de St-Cloud and head along rue Montbauron to **Avenue de Paris**; at 120 yards across, it's wider than the Champs-Élysées, and its buildings are just as grand and more historic. Note the mighty doorway at the **Hôtel de Police** on your left and then, at No. 21, the pretty **Hôtel du Barry.** Cross the avenue and return toward the château, past the **Hôtel des Menus-Plasirs,** where the States General held its first session in May 1789. Just opposite, behind an imposing grille, is the elaborate 19th-century **Préfecture** (the regional government building), confronting the even bigger—but uglier—stone-and-brick **Hôtel de Ville** (Town Hall). Avenue de Paris leads down to place d'Armes, a vast sloping plaza usually filled with tourist buses. Facing the château are
11 the Trojan-size royal stables. One wing of the **Grandes Écuries** (Great Stables), to the right, houses a distinguished parade of royal and imperial carriages in what is known as the **Musée des Carrosses** (Carriage Museum). *1 av. de Paris,* *01–30–83–77–88.* *€3.* *Weekends mid-Mar.–mid-Nov., 2–5:30.*

Cross avenue de Sceaux, pass the imposing chancellery on the corner, and take rue de Satory—a cute pedestrian shopping-street—to the
12 domed **Cathédrale St-Louis,** with its twin-towered facade, built from 1743 to 1754 and enriched with a fine organ and paintings. Turn left down narrow rue du Marché to reach the ramshackle but photogenic
13 **Carrés St-Louis,** a prototype 18th-century housing development.

14 Rue d'Anjou leads down to the 6-acre **Potager du Roi,** the lovingly restored, split-level royal fruit-and-vegetable garden created in 1683 by Jean-Baptiste de La Quintinye. ✉ *Entrance at 4 rue Hardy,* ☎ *01–39–24–62–62.* *€6.20.* ⏲ *Apr.–Oct., daily 10–6.*

From the Potager du Roi, return up rue de Satory and take rue du Vieux-Versailles, just as old—in parts, decrepit—and full of character as its
15 name suggests. The **Salle du Jeu de Paume,** the indoor sports hall (built in 1686) where the Third Estate swore to transform absolutist France into a constitutional monarchy on June 20, 1789, is off to the right. ✉ *1 rue du Jeu-de-Paume,* ☎ *01–30–83–77–88.* ⏲ *June–Sept., Wed. 2–5.*

Rue de l'Indépendence-Américaine leads from the top of rue du Vieux-Versailles up to the château, where Louis XIV, quite uncoincidentally, is clearly visible on his prancing steed. Admire the sculpted porticoes and gilded Sun King emblems on the 17th- and 18th-century state build-
16 ings lining the street. In the other direction, it leads down to the **Pièce d'Eau des Suisses,** a large artificial lake. Opposite the lake is the stately
17 **Orangerie,** erected by Hardouin-Mansart from 1684 to 1686. From November through Easter the Orangerie serves as a hothouse, when it is packed with the orange and palm trees that are artfully arranged in front in summer. Two monumental flights of steps lead up to the château terrace above.

Dining and Lodging

$$$$ ★ ✕ **Les Trois Marches.** Celebrated chef Gérard Vié's take on *cuisine bourgeoise* is one of the luxest around—you'll find it hard to wait for your meal after perusing the menu, studded with delights like turbot *galette* (cake) with onions and *pommes Anna,* cassoulet with Codïza sausages, and a sublime duck simmered with turnips and truffles. The restaurant, within the Trianon Palace Hotel, has a fetching and huge terrace open in pleasant weather. ✉ *1 bd. de la Reine,* ☎ *01–39–50–13–21. Reservations essential. Jacket and tie. AE, DC, MC, V. Closed Aug.*

$$$ ✕ **Café Trianon.** In the Hôtel Trianon, Chef Benoist Bambaud serves traditional French cuisine: salmon, roast bream, confit of canard, and lamb with rosemary. The prix-fixe menus are your best bet. ✉ *1 bd. de la Reine,* ☎ *01–30–84–38–47. AE, DC, MC, V.*

$$ ✕ **Quai No. 1.** Fish and seafood rule supreme amid the sails, barometers, and model ships of this quaintly decked-out restaurant. Lobster and home-smoked salmon are specialties. Eating à la carte isn't too expensive, and there are good-value prix-fixe menus at €16, €19, and €24. ✉ *1 av. de St-Cloud,* ☎ *01–39–50–42–26. MC, V. Closed Mon. No dinner Sun.*

$$$$ ★ **Trianon Palace.** A modern-day Versailles, this deluxe hotel is in a turn-of-the-20th-century creation of imposing size, filled with soaring rooms (including the historic Salle Clemenceau, site of the 1919 Versailles Peace Conference, which brought World War I to an end) and with a huge garden close to the château park. Once faded, the hotel is now aglitter with a health club (alone worth the price of admission—the pool sits beneath a glass pyramid) and Les Trois Marches restaurant, one of France's best. Note that a newer annex, the Pavillon Trianon, has been constructed, but at these prices you should insist on

the full treatment in the main building (and ask for one of the even-numbered rooms, which look out over the woods near the Trianons; odd-numbered rooms overlook the modern annex). ✉ *1 bd. de la Reine, 78000,* ☎ *01–30–84–38–00,* WEB *www.westin.com,* FAX *01–39–49–00–77. 163 rooms, 27 suites. Restaurant, cable TV, minibars, pool, health club, business services, Internet. AE, DC, MC, V.*

$$ **Cheval Rouge.** This unpretentious old hotel, built in 1676, is in a corner of the town market square, close to the château and recommended if you plan to explore the town on foot. Some rooms around the old stable courtyard have their original wood beams. ✉ *18 rue André-Chénier, 78000,* ☎ *01–39–50–03–03,* FAX *01–39–50–61–27,* WEB *www.chevalrouge.fr.st. 38 rooms, 7 with bath, 31 with shower. Bar, no air-conditioning, cable TV, no pets. AE, MC, V.*

$ **Home St-Louis.** This family-run, three-story brick hotel is a good, cheap, quiet bet—close to the cathedral and not too far from the château. ✉ *28 rue St-Louis, 78000,* ☎ *01–39–50–23–55,* FAX *01–39–21–62–45. 25 rooms, 6 with bath, 19 with shower. No air-conditioning. AE, MC, V.*

Nightlife and the Arts

The largest fountain in Versailles' château park, the Bassin de Neptune, becomes a spectacle of rare grandeur during the **Fêtes de Nuit,** a light-and-fireworks show every Saturday evening in July and September (☎ 01–30–83–78–88 for details). The **Mois Molière** (☎ 01–30–97–84–48) in June heralds a program of concerts, drama, and exhibits inspired by the famous playwright. The **Théâtre Montansier** has a full program of plays (☎ 01–39–24–05–06). The **Centre de Musique Baroque** often presents concerts of Baroque music in the château opera and chapel.

Shopping

Aux Colonnes (✉ 14 rue Hoche) is a highly rated *confiserie* (candy shop) with an astounding cornucopia of chocolates and candies; it's closed Monday. **Les Délices du Palais** (✉ 4 rue du Maréchal-Foch) has all the makings for an impromptu picnic (cold cuts, cheese, salads); it's also closed Monday. **Le Gall** (✉ 15 rue Ducis) has a huge choice of cheeses—including one of France's widest selections of goat cheeses; it's closed Sunday afternoon and Monday. **Passage de la Geôle,** which is open Friday–Sunday 9–7 and is close to the town's stupendous market, houses several good antiques shops.

Breteuil

18 *27 km (17 mi) southwest of Versailles, 58 km (35 mi) southwest of Paris, 6 km (4 mi) south of Chevreuse on the N305.*

The elegant, steep-roofed **Château de Breteuil,** built in 1610, houses Swedish porcelain, Gobelin tapestries, the richly inlaid Teschen Table encrusted with pearls and precious stones, and dozens of lifesize wax figures—including onetime guests English king Edward VII and novelist Marcel Proust. The vast wooded park has picnic areas, a playground, a pigeon-loft, a maze, and more waxwork tableaux representing Puss in Boots, Tom Thumb, and other fairy-tale figures from the works of Charles Perrault. ☎ *01–30–52–05–11.* *Château and grounds €9, grounds only €6.* ⏲ *Château Mon.–Sat. 2:30–6, Sun. 11–6; grounds daily 10–6.*

The surrounding **Chevreuse Valley** is a scenic region of hills and woods replete with old churches, abbeys, castles, and houses for the well-heeled. Lovers of 17th-century literature may enjoy exploring the **Chemin de Racine** (Racine Route; WEB www.parc-naturel-chevreuse.org), which begins in the town of Chevreuse, where the poet and dramatist lived in

1661. Out of boredom he would often walk to neighboring Port-Royal; the path he took through the woods in now marked with panels bearing verses of his poetry. Other sights in Chevreuse are the **Château de la Madeleine,** a hilltop castle, and the 13th-century church of **Notre-Dame de la Roche.**

Dampierre

19 *5 km (3 mi) northwest of Breteuil via D906 and D149, 21 km (13 mi) southwest of Versailles via D91.*

The unspoiled village of Dampierre is adorned with one of the most elegant family seats in Ile-de-France. The stone-and-brick **Château de Dampierre,** surrounded by a moat and set well back from the road, was rebuilt in the 1670s by Hardouin-Mansart for the Duc de Luynes. Much of the interior has kept its 17th-century decoration—portraits, wood paneling, furniture, and works of art. But the main staircase, with its trompe-l'oeil murals, and the richly gilded **Salle des Fêtes** (ballroom) date from the 19th century. This second-floor chamber contains a huge wall painting by the celebrated artist Jean-Auguste-Dominique Ingres (1780–1867), a (fairly ridiculous) evocation of the mythical Age d'Or (Golden Age)—fitting, perhaps, since this aristocratic family did many good deeds and was even beloved by locals and farmers during the French Revolution. The large park, fronted by gigantic gates, was planned by Versailles landscape architect André Le Nôtre. ✉ *2 Grande-Rue,* ☎ *01–30–52–53–24.* 🎫 *€9, grounds only €6.* ⏲ *Apr.–mid-Oct., Mon.–Sat. 2–6:30, Sun. 11–noon and 2–6:30.*

Rambouillet

20 *16 km (10 mi) southwest of Dampierre via D91 and D906, 32 km (20 mi) southwest of Versailles, 42 km (26 mi) southwest of Paris.*

Haughty Rambouillet, once favored by kings and dukes, is now home to affluent gentry and, occasionally, the French president. The **Château de Rambouillet** is surrounded by a magnificent 30,000-acre forest that remains a great place for biking and walking. Most of the château dates from the early 18th century, but the brawny **Tour François-I**^er^ (François I Tower), named for the king who died here in 1547, was part of the 14th-century fortified castle that first stood on this site. Highlights include the wood-paneled apartments, especially the **Boudoir de la Comtesse** (Countess's Dressing Room); the marble-wall **Salle de Marbre** (Marble Hall), dating from the Renaissance; and the **Salle de Bains de Napoléon** (Napoléon's Bathroom), adorned with Pompeian-style frescoes. The château's lakeside facade is a sight of unsuspected serenity and, as flowers spill from its balconies, cheerful informality. ☎ *01–34–83–00–25,* WEB *www.monum.fr.* 🎫 *€5.50.* ⏲ *Daily 10–11:30 and 2–5:30.*

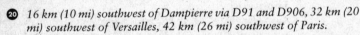

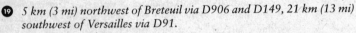

An extensive **park,** with a lake with small islands, stretches behind the château, site of the **Laiterie de la Reine** (Queen's Dairy), built for Marie-Antoinette, who, inspired by the writings of Jean-Jacques Rousseau, came here to escape from the pressures of court life, pretending to be a simple milkmaid. It has a small marble temple and grotto and, nearby, the shell-lined *Chaumière des Coquillages* (Shell Pavilion). The **Bergerie Nationale** (National Sheepfold) is the site of a more serious agricultural venture: The merinos raised here, prized for the quality and yield of their wool, are descendants of sheep imported from Spain by Louis XVI in 1786. A museum alongside tells the tale and evokes shepherd life. The park's exotic, storybook beauty once inspired Jean-Honoré Fragonard to paint one of the greatest landscape paintings of the 18th century, the *Fête at Rambouillet* (now in the Gulbenkian Museum in Lisbon), which tellingly depicts a gilded, courtier-filled barge about to enter a stretch of river torn by raging rapids. "*Apres moi, le deluge,*" indeed. *Dairy and Shell Pavilion €6 (joint ticket with château); Sheepfold €4. Dairy Apr.–Sept., Wed.–Mon. 10–noon and 2–5:30; Oct.–Mar., Wed.–Mon. 10–noon and 2–3:30; Sheepfold mid-Jan.–mid-Dec., Wed.–Sun. 2–5.*

Some 4,000 models, some dating back to 1885, and more than 1,300 ft of track make the **Musée Rambolitrain** a serious model-train museum. It has historic steam engines, old-time stations, and a realistic points and signaling system. *4 pl. Jeanne-d'Arc, 01–34–83–15–93. €3.50. Wed.–Sun. 10–noon and 2–5:30.*

Dining

$$ ✕ **La Poste.** You can bank on traditional, unpretentious cooking at this lively former coaching inn right in the center of town. Service is good, as is the selection of prix-fixe menus €16–€30. Chicken fricassee with crayfish is a specialty, along with game in season. *101 rue du Général-de-Gaulle, 01–34–83–03–01. AE, MC, V. Closed Mon. No dinner Sun. or Thur.*

Maintenon

21 *23 km (14 mi) southwest of Rambouillet via D906, 65 km (41 mi) southwest of Paris.*

Vestiges of Louis XIV, both atmospheric and architectural, make Maintenon an intriguing stopover on the road to Chartres. The **Château de Maintenon** once belonged to Louis XIV's second wife, Françoise Scarron—better known as Madame de Maintenon—whom he married morganatically in 1684 (as social inferiors, neither she nor her children could claim a royal title). She had acquired the château as a young widow 10 years earlier, and her private apartments are the focus of an interior visit. A round brick tower (16th century) and square 12th-century keep give the ensemble a muscular dignity. Mirrored in a canal that contains the waters of the Eure, this remains one of the most picturesque châteaux in France. Inside, lush salons are done up in the Louis XIII style (or rather, in the Second Empire, 19th-century version of them), a homage to royal roots created by the Ducs de Noailles, one of France's most aristocratic families, which has maintained Maintenon as one of its family homes for centuries. *Pl. Aristide Briand, 02–37–23–00–09. €6. Apr.–Oct., Wed.–Mon. 2–6; Nov.–mid-Dec. and late Jan.–Mar., weekends 2–5.*

Looming at the back of the château garden and extending through the village almost from the train station to highway D6 are the unlikely ivy-covered arches of a ruined **aqueduct,** one of the Sun King's most outrageous projects. The original scheme aimed to provide the ornamental lakes in the gardens of Versailles (some 50 km/31 mi away) with water from the River Eure. In 1684, 30,000 men were signed up to construct a three-tiered, 5-km (3-mi) aqueduct as part of the project. Many died in the process, and construction was called off in 1689.

Dining and Lodging

$$$$ ★ ✕ **Château d'Esclimont.** Graced with pointed turrets, *pièces d'eau* (moated pools), and a checkerboard facade, this 19th-century château—built by the de La Rochefoucaulds—is well worth seeking out if you wish to eat and sleep like an aristocrat. This member of the Relais & Châteaux group is replete with luxuriously furnished guest rooms (many are loftily dimensioned, others snug in corner turrets) adorned with reproduction 18th-century French pieces. Carved stone garlands,

cordovan leathers, brocades, and period antiques grace the public salons; the superbly manicured grounds cradle a heated pool. The cuisine is sophisticated: quail, lamb, lobster, and game in season top the menu at the restaurant, La Rochefoucault (dinner reservations are essential, and a jacket and tie are required, as is a very fat wallet). ✉ 2 *rue du Château-d'Esclimont, 28700 St-Symphorien-le-Château (19 km/12 mi southeast of Maintenon: take D116 to village of Gaillardon, keep an eye out for church, then turn left),* ☎ *02–37–31–15–15,* FAX *02–37–31–57–91,* WEB *www.grandes-etapes-francaises.com. 46 rooms, 6 suites. Restaurant, cable TV, minibars, Internet, 2 tennis courts, pool, fishing, helipad. AE, DC, MC, V.*

Chartres

㉒ *19 km (12 mi) southwest of Maintenon via D906, 88 km (55 mi) southwest of Paris.*

As Versailles is the climax of French secular architecture, so Chartres is the religious apogee. All the descriptive prose and poetry that have been lavished on this supreme cathedral can only begin to suggest the glory of its 12th- and 13th-century sculpture and stained glass, the strange sense of the numinous that the whole ensemble imparts even to nonbelievers. Notre-Dame de Chartres is an extraordinary fusion of Romanesque and Gothic elements brought together at a moment when the flame of medieval faith burned brightest. The stone and glass of this cathedral are somehow suffused with that same burning mysticism. Chartres is more than a church—it's a nondenominational spiritual experience.

If you arrive from Maintenon across the edge of the Beauce, one of the richest agrarian plains in France, you can see Chartres's spires rising up from oceans of wheat (at least between early June and late July). In fact, the whole town—with its old houses and picturesque streets—is worth leisurely exploration. Ancient streets tumble down from the cathedral to the river; from rue du Pont-St-Hilaire there is a lovely view of the rooftops below the cathedral. Each year on August 15, pilgrims and tourists flock here for the Procession du Voeu de Louis XIII, a religious procession through the streets commemorating the French monarchy's vow to serve the Virgin Mary.

★ Worship on the site of the **Cathédrale Notre-Dame,** better known as Chartres Cathedral, goes back to before the Gallo-Roman period; the crypt contains a well that was the focus of Druid ceremonies. In the late 9th century Charles II (known as the Bald) presented Chartres with what was believed to be the tunic of the Virgin Mary, a precious relic that attracted hordes of pilgrims. The current cathedral, the sixth church on the spot, dates mainly from the 12th and 13th centuries and was erected after the previous building, dating to the 11th century, burned down in 1194. A well-chronicled outburst of religious fervor followed the discovery that the Virgin Mary's relic had miraculously survived unsinged. Princes and paupers, barons and bourgeois gave their money and their labor to build the new cathedral. Ladies of the manor came to help monks and peasants on the scaffolding in a tremendous resurgence of religious faith that followed the Second Crusade. Just 25 years were needed for Chartres Cathedral to rise again, and it has remained substantially unchanged since.

The lower half of the facade survives from the earlier Romanesque church: this can be seen most clearly in the use of round arches rather than the pointed Gothic type. The **Royal Portal** is richly sculpted with scenes from the life of Christ—these sculpted figures are among the greatest created during the Middle Ages—and the flanking towers are also Romanesque. The taller of the two spires (380 ft versus 350 ft) was built at the start of the 16th century, after its predecessor was destroyed by fire; its fanciful Flamboyant intricacy contrasts sharply with the stumpy solemnity of its Romanesque counterpart (access €4). The **rose window** above the main portal dates from the 13th century, and the three windows below it contain some of the finest examples of 12th-century stained glass in France.

The interior is somber, and your eyes will need time to adjust. The reward is seeing the gemlike richness of the stained glass, with the famous deep Chartres blue predominating. The oldest window is arguably the most beautiful: **Notre-Dame de la Belle Verrière** (Our Lady of the Lovely Window), in the south choir. The cathedral's windows are being gradually cleaned—a lengthy, painstaking process—and the contrast with those still covered in the grime of centuries is staggering. It's worth taking a pair of binoculars along with you to pick out the details. If you wish to know more about stained-glass techniques and the motifs used, visit the small exhibit in the gallery opposite the north porch. For even more detail, try to arrange a tour (in English) with local institution Malcolm Miller, whose knowledge of the cathedral's windows is formidable. (He leads tours twice a day Monday through Saturday; the cost is €5.50. You can reach him at the telephone number below.) The vast black-and-white labyrinth on the floor of the nave is one of the few to have survived from the Middle Ages; the faithful were expected to travel along its entire length (some 300 yards) on their knees. Guided tours of the **Crypte** start from the Maison de la Crypte opposite the south porch. You can also see a 4th-century Gallo-Roman wall and some 12th-century wall paintings. ✉ *16 cloître Notre-Dame,* ☎ *02–37–21–56–33,* WEB *www.ville-chartres.com.* 🎫 *Crypt €2.30.* ⏲ *Cathedral 8:30–7:30; guided tours of crypt Easter–Oct., daily at 11, 2:15, 3:30, 4:30, and 5:15; Nov.–Easter, daily at 11 and 4.*

The **Musée des Beaux-Arts** (Fine Arts Museum) is in a handsome 18th-century building just behind the cathedral that used to serve as the bishop's palace. Its varied collection includes Renaissance enamels, a portrait of Erasmus by Holbein, tapestries, armor, and some fine (mainly French) paintings from the 17th, 18th, and 19th centuries. There's also a room devoted to the forceful 20th-century landscapes of Maurice de Vlaminck, who once lived in the region. ✉ *29 cloître Notre-Dame,* ☎ *02–37–36–41–39.* 🎫 *€2.40.* ⏲ *Wed.–Mon. 10–noon and 2–5.*

The Gothic church of **St-Pierre** (✉ Rue St-Pierre), near the Eure River, has magnificent medieval windows from a period (circa 1300) not represented at the cathedral. The oldest stained glass here, portraying Old Testament worthies, is to the right of the choir and dates from the late 13th century. Exquisite 17th-century stained glass can be admired at the church of **St-Aignan** (✉ Rue des Grenets), around the corner from St-Pierre.

Dining and Lodging

$$$ ✕ **La Vieille Maison.** Just 100 yards from the cathedral, in a pretty 14th-century building with a flower-decked patio, this restaurant is a fine choice for either lunch or dinner. The menu changes regularly, but invariably includes regional specialties such as asparagus, rich duck pâté, and superb homemade foie gras. Prices, though justified, can be steep, but the €26 lunch menu is a good bet. ✉ *5 rue au Lait,* ☎ *02–37–34–10–67. AE, MC, V. Closed Mon. No dinner Sun.*

$$ ★ ✕ **Buisson Ardent.** In an attractive old oak-beam building almost within sight of the cathedral's south portal, this popular restaurant has

inexpensive prix-fixe menus (especially on weekdays) and a choice of imaginative à la carte dishes. Try the papillotte salmon with seafood risotto and the strawberry millefeuille. Service is gratifyingly attentive. ✉ *10 rue au Lait,* ☎ *02–37–34–04–66. MC, V. Closed Wed. No dinner Sun.*

$$$ **Grand Monarque.** The most popular rooms in this 18th-century coaching inn, part of the Best Western chain, are in a separate turn-of-the-20th-century building overlooking a garden. The most atmospheric are tucked away in the attic. The restaurant, which has prix-fixe menus at €28 and €38, offers such delicacies as pheasant pie and roast duck with mushrooms. ✉ *22 pl. des Épars, 28000,* ☎ *02–37–21–00–72,* FAX *02–37–36–34–18,* WEB *www.bw-grand-monarque.com. 55 rooms, 47 with bath, 8 with shower. Restaurant, bar, no air-conditioning in some rooms, cable TV, minibars, Internet. AE, DC, MC, V.*

Shopping

Vitrail (stained glass) being the key to Chartres's fame, you may want to visit the **Galerie du Vitrail** (✉ 17 cloître Notre-Dame, ☎ 02–37–36–10–03, WEB www.galerie-du-vitrail.com), which specializes in the noble art. Pieces range from small plaques to entire windows, and there are books on the subject in English and French.

Dreux

23 *35 km (22 mi) north of Chartres via N154, 74 km (46 mi) west of Paris.*

Dreux, center of an independent province during the Middle Ages, enjoyed an upsurge in prosperity after being united to the French crown in 1556 (shortly after completion of the beefy belfry on the main square). The early 19th century conferred lasting glory on the town in the form of the burial chapel of the royal House of Orléans.

In 1816 the Orléans family, France's ruling house from 1830 to 1848, began the construction of a circular chapel-mausoleum on the hill behind the town center. ★ The **Chapelle Royale St-Louis** is built in sugary but not unappealing neo-Gothic: superficial ornament rather than structural form recalls the medieval style. The magnificent interior can be visited only with a guided tour (in French only, though an English text is provided). No explanations are needed to prompt wonder at either the Sèvres-manufactured "stained glass"—thin layers of glass coated with painted enamel (an extremely rare, fragile, and vivid technique)—or the funereal statuary. Some of the **tombs**—an imploring hand reaching through a window to a loved one or an infant wrapped in a cloak of transparent gauze—may evoke morbid sentimentality, but their technical skill and compositional drama belie any mawkishness. ✉ *2 sq. d'Aumale,* ☎ *02–37–46–07–06.* *€5.50.* ⏲ *Apr.–Nov., Wed.–Mon. 9–11:30 and 2:30–6.*

The church of **St-Pierre,** across the road from the belfry, is an interesting jumble of styles with pretty stained glass and a 17th-century organ loft. It presents a curious silhouette, with its unfinished classical towers cut off midway. ✉ *Pl. Métézeau,* ☎ *02–37–42–06–89.*

Houdan

24 *20 km (12 mi) east of Dreux via N12, 54 km (34 mi) west of Paris.*

Although fast N12 now skirts Houdan, the town grew up as a busy stop on the Paris–Dreux road. It's protected by a mighty 12th-century keep rising from the hilltop above two small rivers, the Opton and the Vesgre. Timber-frame houses along the main street (rue de Paris), including several former inns, recall Houdan's bygone status, as does the ornate church, which retains many of its original 17th- and 18th-century elements, including the pulpit, altarpiece, lectern, pews, and organ case. Houdan was also famed for its poultry market, and a succulent local breed of chicken with a fancy plumed crest—the *poularde de Houdan*—still survives.

Dining

$$ ✕ **La Poularde.** This comfortable restaurant at the foot of the town is named for the local breed of chicken, often served here with truffles or morels. Braised beef and smoked-fish salad are other specialties, and there's a good-value lunch menu. The airy, pastel-shaded dining room turns its back on the highway outside, looking out on a trim lawn instead. ✉ *24 av. de la République,* ☎ *01–30–59–60–50. Reservations essential. MC, V. Closed Wed. and part of Aug. No dinner Tues.*

Montfort-L'Amaury

25 *18 km (11 mi) east of Houdan via N12 and D76, 40 km (25 mi) west of Paris.*

Montfort-L'Amaury, with its 17th-century houses and twisting, narrow streets clustered around an old church, is one of the prettiest towns in Ile-de-France. It has a ruined hilltop castle, remnants of medieval ramparts, and a cloister-lined cemetery. Dominating the town square is the bulky Renaissance tower of the church of **St-Pierre–St-Paul.** Note the gargoyles around the far end and, inside, the 37 splendid Renaissance stained-glass windows.

Composer Maurice Ravel lived in Montfort from 1921 until his death in 1937; he composed his famous *Bolero* in 1928 in his Japanese-style garden. His house, now the **Musée Maurice-Ravel** (Ravel Museum), has been reconstituted with many of his mementos and furnishings (including his piano). ✉ *Le Belvédère, 5 rue Maurice-Ravel,* ☎ *01–34–86–00–89.* *€4.* *Guided visits only, weekends at 10, 11, 2:30, 3:30, and 4:30, Wed.–Fri. 2:30–5 by appointment.*

Dining and Lodging

$–$$ ✕🏨 **Voyageurs.** This small, homey hotel at the bottom of Montfort's cobbled main street is a handy base for exploring Thoiry, Dreux, or Rambouillet. It has rooms with wood beams and a cheerful bar with incongruous but appealing 1950s touches. Chef Loïc Renard serves up asparagus in flaky pastry and crème brûlée with Grand Marnier in the well-priced restaurant (menus €12–€16). ✉ *49 rue de Paris, 78490,* ☎ *01–34–86–00–14,* FAX *01–34–86–14–56,* WEB *www.voyageurs.fr. 7 rooms. Restaurant, bar, no air-conditioning, no pets. MC, V. Closed mid- to late Aug. Restaurant closed Sun. and Mon.*

Thoiry

26 *11 km (7 mi) north of Montfort-L'Amaury via D76 and D11, 44 km (28 mi) west of Paris.*

Thoiry is most famous for its 16th-century château with beautiful gardens, a wild-animal preserve, and a gastronomy museum. The village makes an excellent day trip from Paris, especially if you're traveling with children. The showpiece remains the **Château de Thoiry,** built by Philibert de l'Orme in 1564. This has a handsome Renaissance facade set off by gardens landscaped in the disciplined French fashion by Le Nôtre, in this case with unexpected justification: the château is positioned directly in line with the sun as it sets in the west at the winter solstice (December 21) and as it rises in the east at the summer solstice (June 21). Heightening the effect, the central part of the château appears to be a transparent arch of light because of its huge glass doors and windows. Owners Vicomte Paul de La Panouse and his American wife, Annabelle, have restored the château and park, opening both to the public. The distinguished history of the La Panouse family—a Comte César even fought in the American Revolution—is retraced in the **Musée des Archives** (Archives Museum), where papal bulls and Napoleonic letters mingle with notes from Thomas Jefferson and Benjamin Franklin. The neighboring pantries house a **Musée de la Gastronomie** (Gastronomy Museum), with *pièces montées*—virtuoso banquet showpieces—re-creating the designs of famed 19th-century chef Antoine Carême. Early recipe books, engravings, and old copper pots are also displayed.

Other highlights of the château interior include the grand staircase, the **Escalier d'Honneur,** with its 18th-century Gobelin tapestries; the **Salon Vert** and **Salon Blanc** (Green Salon and White Salon), with their antique painted harpsichord and portraits; and the **Salon de la Tapisserie** (Tapestry Salon), with its monumental Don Quixote tapestry. An authentic, homey, faded charm pervades these rooms, especially when fires crackle in their enormous hearths on damp afternoons. The viscountess is a keen gardener and enjoys experimenting in the less formal **Jardin Anglais** (English Garden) and her late-flowering **Jardin d'Automne** (Autumn Garden). You're allowed to wander at leisure, although it's best not to stray too far from the official footpath through the **Parc Zoologique** (animal preserve). Note that the parts of the reserve that contain the wilder beasts—deer, zebra, camels, hippos, bears, elephants, and lions—can be visited only by car. Tigers can be seen from the safety of a raised footbridge. Nearby is a children's play area with a burrow to wriggle through and a huge netted cobweb to bounce around in. ☎ *01–34–87–52–25,* WEB *www.thoiry.tm.fr.* *Château only, €5.80; park and game preserve, €16.50.* ⏲ *June–Sept., weekdays 10–6, weekends 10–6:30; Oct.–May, daily 10–5:30.*

Dining and Lodging

$$$ ✕ **Domaine du Verbois.** Greek goddesses set the tone here: bedrooms in this stately late-19th-century mansion—set on 6 acres of parkland in Neauphle-le-Château, 11 km (7mi) southeast of Thoiry—are named after them. All have flowered wallpaper, reproduction 18th-century furniture, and Chinese rugs; and each is slightly different, with those on the first floor more spacious than those under the roof. The four-course, €30 set menu in the handsome dining room, with its giltwood mirror and marble chimneypiece, might include salmon with endive or duck with lemon. ✉ *38 av. de la République (11 km/7 mi southeast of Montfort via D11), 78640 Neauphle-le-Château,* ☎ *01–34–89–11–78,* FAX *01–34–89–57–33,* WEB *www.hotelverbois.com. 22 rooms. Restaurant, no air-conditioning, cable TV, some minibars, Internet, baby-sitting. AE, DC, MC, V. Closed 2 wks Aug. No dinner Sun.*

$ ✕ **Auberge de Thoiry.** This hotel-restaurant, just 300 yards from the château along the main street, is more convenient than appealing, although some of its rather small bedrooms have recently been redecorated. But the fine restaurant serves a good *menu touristique* (special tourist menu, a term that doesn't mean you should go running the other way) of robust French dishes. ✉ *38 rue de la Porte-St-Martin, 78770,* ☎ *01–34–87–40–21,* FAX *01–34–87–49–57. 12 rooms. Restaurant, no air-conditioning, no pets. MC, V. Closed Mon.*

NORTHWEST TO GIVERNY ALONG THE SEINE

Renowned for its beauty as it weaves through Paris, the Seine River is no less appealing as it flows gently northwest toward Normandy. The terrace at the château St-Germain-en-Laye, residence of the French kings before Versailles, provides a truly memorable view of the valley, soon to break into a series of chalky cliffs beyond Mantes. Farther on, tucked away on the banks of the Epte (a tributary of the Seine), are Monet's home and fabled garden in Giverny.

Rueil-Malmaison

27 *8 km (5 mi) west of Paris on N13 via La Défense.*

Rueil-Malmaison is a slightly dreary western suburb of Paris, but the memory of the legendary pair Napoléon and Joséphine still haunts its ★ château. Built in 1622, **La Malmaison** was bought by the future empress Joséphine in 1799 as a love nest for Napoléon and herself (they had married three years earlier). After the childless Joséphine was divorced by the heir-hungry emperor in 1809, she retired to La Malmaison and died here on May 29, 1814. The château has 24 rooms furnished with exquisite tables, chairs, and sofas of the Napoleonic period; of special note are the library, game room, and dining room. The walls are adorned with works by artists of the day, such as Jacques-Louis David, Pierre-Paul Prud'hon, and Baron Gérard. Take time to admire the clothes and hats that belonged to Napoléon and Joséphine, particularly the empress's gowns. Their carriage can be seen in one of the garden pavilions, and another pavilion contains a unique collection of snuffboxes donated by Prince George of Greece. The gardens themselves are delightful, especially the regimented rows of tulips in spring. ✉ *15 av. du Château,* ☎ *01–41–29–05–55.* 🎫 *€4.40.* ⏲ *Wed.–Mon. 10–5:45.*

Currently being renovated, the **Bois Préau,** a smaller mansion dating from the 17th century, is close to La Malmaison (and can be visited on the same admission ticket). It was acquired by Joséphine in 1810, after her divorce, but was subsequently reconstructed in the 1850s. Today its 10 rooms, complete with furniture and objects from the Empire period, are devoted mainly to souvenirs of Napoléon's exile on the island of St. Helena. ✉ *Av. de l'Impératrice,* ☎ *01–41–29–05–55.* ⏲ *Closed for renovation at press time.*

St-Germain-en-Laye

28 *4 km (2½ mi) north of Marly-le-Roi via N186 and N13, 9 km (6 mi) west of Rueil-Malmaison, 17 km (11 mi) west of Paris.*

The elegant town of St-Germain-en-Laye, encircled by forest perched behind Le Nôtre's Grande Terrace overlooking the Seine, has lost little of its original cachet, despite the invasion of wealthy former Parisians who commute to work on the RER.

If you're fond of the swashbuckling novels of Alexandre Dumas, then you'll enjoy the **Château de Monte-Cristo** (Monte Cristo Castle), at Port-Marly on the southern fringe of St-Germain (signposted to your left as you arrive from Marly-le-Roi). You may find that its fanciful exterior, where pilasters, cupolas, and stone carvings compete for attention, has crossed the line from opulence to tastelessness, but—as in the novels, *The Count of Monte Cristo* and *The Three Musketeers*—swagger, not subtlety, is what counts. Dumas built the château after his books' surging popularity made him rich in the 1840s. Construction costs and lavish partying meant he went broke just as quickly, and he skedaddled to a Belgian exile in 1849. The château contains pictures, Dumas mementos, and the luxurious Moorish Chamber, with spellbinding, interlacing plasterwork executed by Arab craftsmen (lent by the Bey of Tunis) and restored thanks to a donation from the late Moroccan king Hassan II. ✉ *Av. du Président-Kennedy,* ☎ *01–30–61–61–35,* WEB *www.mairie-marlyleroi.fr.* 🎫 *€5.* ⏲ *Apr.–Oct., Tues.–Fri. 10–12:30 and 2–6, weekends 10–6; Nov.–Mar., Sun. 2–5.*

Next to the St-Germain RER train station is the stone-and-brick ★ **Château de St-Germain,** with its dry moat and intimidating circular towers; it dates from the 16th and 17th centuries. A royal palace has existed here since the early 12th century, when Louis VI—known as Le Gros (the Fat)—exploited St-Germain's defensive potential in his bid to pacify Ile-de-France. A hundred years later Louis IX (St. Louis) added the elegant **Sainte-Chapelle,** the château's oldest remaining section. Charles V (1364–80) built a powerful defensive keep in the mid-14th century, but from the 1540s François I and his successors transformed St-Germain into a palace with more of a domestic than warlike vocation. Louis XIV was born here, and it was here that his father, Louis XIII, died. Until 1682—when the court moved to Versailles—it remained the country's foremost royal residence outside Paris. Since 1867 the château has housed the impressive **Musée des Antiquités Nationales** (Museum of Ancient History), holding a trove of artifacts, figurines, brooches, and weapons from the Stone Age to the 8th century. Behind the château is Andre Le Nôtre's **Grande Terrace,** an enormous, terraced promenade lined by century-old lime trees. Directly overlooking the Seine, it was completed in 1673 and it remains one of the most spectacular of all French garden set pieces. ✉ *Pl. Charles-de-Gaulle,* ☎ *01–39–10–13–00.* 🎫 *€4.* ⏲ *Wed.–Mon. 9–5:15.*

★ The quaint **Musée du Prieuré** (Priory Museum) is devoted to the work of the artist Maurice Denis (1870–1943) and his fellow Symbolists and to Nabis—painters opposed to the naturalism of their 19th-century Impressionist contemporaries. Denis found the calm of the former Jesuit priory, set above tiered gardens with statues and rose bushes, ideally suited to his spiritual themes, which he expressed in stained glass, ceramics, and frescoes as well as oils. ✉ *2 bis rue Maurice-Denis,* ☎ *01–39–73–77–87.* 🎫 *€4.* ⏲ *Wed.–Fri. 10–5:30, weekends 10–6:30.*

Dining and Lodging

$$ ✕ **La Feuillantine.** Friendly service and an imaginative, good-value prix-fixe menu have made this wood-beamed restaurant an often-crowded success. Gizzard salad, salmon with endive, and herbed chicken fricassee with morels are among the specialties. ✉ *10 rue des Louviers,* ☎ *01–34–51–04–24. AE, MC, V.*

$$$–$$$$ ★ ✕🏨 **La Forestière.** Opened in 1928, this hotel, run by Philippe and Isabelle Cazaudehore, is St-Germain's most stylish and a member of the Relais & Châteaux chain. Its forest environs, 18th-century-style furniture, and fine restaurant, the Cazaudehore (closed Monday), contribute to a sense of well-being. ✉ *1 av. du Président-Kennedy, 78100,* ☎ *01–30–61–64–64,* FAX *01–39–73–73–88,* WEB *www.cazaudehore.fr. 25 rooms, 5 suites. Restaurant, no air-conditioning, cable TV, minibars, dogs allowed. AE, DC, MC, V.*

Nightlife and the Arts

The **Fête des Loges** (Loges Festival) is a giant fair and carnival held in the Forest of St-Germain from July to mid-August. Nearly 4 million fans of cotton candy, roller coasters, and Ferris wheels turn up every year.

Maisons-Laffitte

29 *8 km (5 mi) northeast of St-Germain-en-Laye via D157, 16 km (10 mi) northwest of Paris.*

The riverside suburb of Maisons-Laffitte has an unusually high proportion of elegant villas, many of which were built with profits from the town's racetrack by the Seine (with its famous 2,200-yard straight) and training stables; 14 races are held between July and September. The town's ★ steep-roofed, early Baroque **Château de Maisons,** constructed by architect François Mansart from 1634 to 1651, is one of the least known but most elegant châteaux in Ile-de-France. This was not always the case: Sun King Louis XIV came to the housewarming party, and Louis XV, Louis XVI, the 18th-century writer Voltaire, and Napoléon all stayed here. The interior clearly met their exacting standards, thanks to the well-proportioned entrance vestibule with its rich sculpture; the winding **Escalier d'Honneur,** a majestic staircase adorned with paintings and statuary; and the royal apartments above them, with their parquet floors and wall paneling. The **Musée du Cheval de Course** (Racehorse Museum), in the basement, evokes the world of the turf. ✉ *2 av. Carnot,* ☎ *01–39–62–01–49.* €5.50. ⏲ *Wed.–Mon. 10–5.*

Poissy

30 *8 km (4 mi) west of Maisons-Laffitte via D308, 21 km (13 mi) northwest of Paris.*

Three museums and its historic significance as the birthplace of France's saintly king Louis IX help Poissy—the name comes from *poisson* (fish), as you may deduce from the town's ubiquitous emblem—defy its reputation as an unfashionable industrial town.

The remains of the font in which Louis was baptized in 1214 can still be seen in the **Église Notre-Dame,** a medieval church with two striking octagonal towers. The **Musée d'Art et d'Histoire** (Art and History Museum), in a stern brick mansion opposite the church, is packed with tools, sculptures, old postcards, and paintings tracking Poissy's history from its 6th-century origins to its medieval prosperity as a cattle market and vine-growing center to its latter-day position as center for auto plants. ✉ *12 rue St-Louis,* ☎ *01–39–65–06–06.* *Free.* ⏲ *Wed.–Sun. 9:30–noon and 2–5:30.*

Housed behind the turreted facade of the 14th-century royal priory, the **Musée du Jouet** (Toy Museum) has a collection of historical toys, games, automatons, puppets, electric trains, rocking horses, tin soldiers, and dollhouses. ✉ *1 enclos de l'Abbaye,* ☎ *01–39–65–06–06.* €3.05. ⏲ *Tues.–Sun. 9:30–noon and 2–5:30.*

Rising on what look like stilts—in fact, slender concrete pillars—above an extensive lawn that stretched over 15 acres until a (not undistin- ★ guished) school was built alongside in the 1950s, the **Villa Savoye** is considered one of Le Corbusier's most accomplished designs. Industrialist Pierre Savoye and his wife spent weekends here beginning in 1931, but stopped coming in 1938—fed up with the leaky flat roof. The villa appears as an austere white block; this is intentionally misleading—the ground floor, in fact, curves around to the entrance, at the back. An oval funnel emerges from the roof, harboring a solarium. Inside, the visual teasing continues, with a spiral staircase whose vertical emphasis clashes with the gently sloping ramp that serves as the principal transition from floor to floor. Be warned: the villa's delights are hidden in more ways than one, and advance signposting is terrible. Head up from the Toy Museum and turn right at the lights opposite the cemetery: the villa is 700 yards up, at the crest of the hill on the right. ✉ *82 rue de Villiers,* ☎ *01–39–65–01–06,* WEB *www.monum.fr.* 🎫 *€4.* ⏲ *Apr.–Oct., Wed.–Mon. 9:30–12:30 and 1:30–6; Nov.–Mar., Wed.–Mon. 9:30–12:30 and 1:30–4:30.*

En Route As you begin to enter the region of the Ile-de-France the Impressionists made their own, cross the Seine at Vernouillet and follow D190 to **Mantes-la-Jolie,** approaching across the old bridge from Limay, once painted by Corot. Another painter, the Impressionist Maximilien Luce, is the hero of the fine town museum alongside the vast, 12th-century **Église Notre-Dame.** The small, circular windows ringing the east end of the church are an unusual local architectural characteristic—you can also see them 11 km (7 mi) north, at the church in **Vétheuil**—a town immortalized in many a Monet canvas—where the road regains the riverbank beneath impressive chalk cliffs.

La Roche-Guyon

31 *7 km (4 mi) northwest of Vétheuil on D913, 45 km (28 mi) northwest of Poissy via D190 and D147, 69 km (43 mi) northwest of Paris.*

Ruins of a medieval clifftop castle look down on the River Seine and the quaint village of La Roche-Guyon. A steep-climbing stairway, hewn through the rock, links the castle to the classical **château** below, constructed mainly in the 18th century. The château has impressive iron gates incorporating the arms of the owners, the La Rochefoucauld family; its main building is one story higher than ground level, behind an arcaded terrace that towers above the stables and grassy forecourt. An interior highlight is the *Story of Esther* tapestry series. ✉ *1 rue de l'Audience,* ☎ *01–34–79–74–42,* WEB *www.val-doise-tourisme.fr.* 🎫 *€6.15.* ⏲ *Mid-Jan.–mid-Dec., Sat.–Thurs. 10–6.*

Dining

$$–$$$ ✕ **Moulin de Fourges.** Nestled in verdant countryside by the River Epte, 5 km (3 mi) north of La Roche-Guyon, this converted 18th-century water mill has a setting that alone will make you ravenous. Stéphane Lebar's cuisine varies from garlic-stuffed lamb roll to fish from the Mediterranean. ✉ *38 rue du Moulin, Fourges,* ☎ *02–32–52–12–12. Reservations essential. MC, V. Closed Mon. and Nov.–Mar. No dinner Sun. Oct.–Apr. and Tues.–Thurs.*

Giverny

32 *8 km (5 mi) west of La Roche-Guyon on D5, 70 km (44 mi) northwest of Paris.*

The small village of Giverny, just beyond the Epte River, which marks the official boundary of Ile-de-France, has become a place of pilgrimage for art lovers. It was here that Claude Monet lived for 43 years, until his death at the age of 86 in 1926. Although his house is now prized by connoisseurs of 19th-century interior decoration, it is his garden, with its Japanese-inspired water-lily pond and its bridge, that remains the high point for many—a veritable 5-acre, three-dimensional Impressionist painting through which you can stroll. In addition, Monet immortalized the surrounding countryside's haystacks and poplar trees in oils, but these motifs have often been altered beyond recognition—the wheat fields are still there, but the wheat is now rolled up, while Monet's famous rows of poplar trees along the river Epte, near the village of Limetz, about 3 km (2 mi) south of Giverny, are completely overgrown.

★ The **Maison et Jardin Claude-Monet** (Monet House and Garden) has been lovingly restored. Monet was brought up in Normandy and, like many of the Impressionists, was captivated by the soft light of the Seine Valley. After several years in Argenteuil, just north of Paris, he moved downriver to Giverny in 1883 along with his two sons, his mistress, Alice Hoschedé (whom he later married), and her six children. By 1890 a prospering Monet was able to buy the house outright. With its pretty pink walls and green shutters, the house has a warm feeling that may come as a welcome change after the stateliness of the French châteaux. Rooms have been restored to Monet's original designs: the kitchen with its blue tiles, the buttercup-yellow dining room, and Monet's bedroom on the second floor. Reproductions of his works, and some of the Japanese prints he avidly collected, crowd the walls.

Three years after buying his house, Monet purchased another plot of land, across the lane, to continue his gardening experiments, even diverting the Epte to make a pond. The resulting garden, with flowers spilling out across the paths, is as cheerful and natural as the house. The famous Japanese bridge and water-lily pond, flanked by a mighty willow and rhododendrons, are across the lane that runs to the side of the house and can be reached through a tunnel (which goes under a roadway that rather distressingly cuts through the property). Images of the bridge and the water lilies in various seasons appear in much of Monet's later work. Looking across the pond, it's easy to conjure up the grizzled, bearded painter dabbing at his canvases—capturing changes in light and pioneering a breakdown in form that was to have a major influence on 20th-century art. Note that during the height of spring, when the flowers are in full bloom, the place can be packed with tourists—during that period, try to visit during midweek. ✉ *84 rue Claude-Monet,* ☎ *02–32–51–28–21,* WEB *www.giverny.org.* 🎫 *Gardens and home, €5.50; gardens only, €4.* ⏲ *Apr.–Oct., Tues.–Sun. 10–6.*

After touring the painterly grounds of the Monet house, you may wish to see some real paintings at the airy **Musée Américain** (American Museum), along the same road as the Monet House. Endowed by Chicago art patrons Daniel and Judith Terra, it displays works by American Impressionists who were influenced by—and often studied with—Claude Monet. On site are a restaurant and *salon de thé* (tea room), as well as a garden "quoting" some of Monet's plant compositions. ✉ *99 rue Claude-Monet,* ☎ *02–32–51–94–65,* WEB *www.maag.org.* 🎫 *€5.* ⏲ *Apr.–Oct., Tues.–Sun. 10–6.*

Dining and Lodging

$$ ✕ **Baudy.** Back in Monet's day, this pretty-in-pink villa was the hotel of the American painters colony. Today, the dining room and terrace are more modern than historic, but parts of this old *epicerie-buvette* are still so enchanting (notably, the luscious rose gardens and the studio hut where Cézanne once took up residence) that a recent art book was devoted to La Maison Baudy. All this mise-en-scène is quite special, making it easier to forgive the very simple cuisine and busloads of tour groups. ✉ *81 rue Claude-Monet,* ☎ *02–32–21–10–03. MC, V. No dinner Sun. Closed Mon. and Nov.–Mar.*

$$ ✕ **Les Jardins de Giverny.** This restaurant, with a tile-floor dining room overlooking a rose garden, is a few minutes' walk from Monet's house. Enjoy the €20 menu or choose from a repertoire of inventive dishes such as foie gras spiked with calvados, duck in cider, or scallops with wild mushrooms. ✉ *Rue du Roy,* ☎ *02–32–21–60–80. AE, MC, V. Closed Mon., Feb., and 1st ½ Nov. No dinner Sun.–Fri.*

$-$$$ ★ **Giverny B & Bs.** Giverny's dire shortage of hotels is made up by a plethora of enticing, stylish, and affordable bed-and-breakfasts set up in many of the town's homes. Particularly notable are **Le Clos Fleuri,** a Norman manor house set in a lovely garden and run by the Fouche family (✉ 5 rue de la Dime, ☎ FAX 02–32–21–36–51); **La Réserve,** about a mile outside town, an expansive residence surrounded by orchards and with gorgeous, antiques-adorned, and wood-beamed guest apartments, some of which have fireplaces and canopy beds (✉ Rue Blanche-Hoschedé, ☎ 02–32–21–99–09); and the residence of **Marie-Claire Boscher,** which used to be a hotel-restaurant that Monet frequented (✉ 1 rue du Colombier, ☎ FAX 02–32–51–39–70). Log onto the Web site WEB www.giverny.org/hotels for all the details.

$-$$ **La Musardiere.** Just a short stroll from chez Monet, this manor house has a cozy lobby, guest rooms with views overlooking a park, and its own restaurant-crêperie. ✉ *Rue Claude-Monet, 27620 Giverny,* ☎ *02–32–21–03–18,* FAX *02–32–21–60–00. 25 rooms, 5 suites. Restaurant, no air-conditioning, tennis court, pool, no pets. AE, DC, MC, V.*

Vernon

33 *5 km (3 mi) northwest of Giverny on D5, 73 km (46 mi) northwest of Paris.*

The old town of Vernon, on the Seine, has a medieval church, which was often painted by Claude Monet, and several fine medieval timber-frame houses (the best one, on rue Carnot, houses the tourist office).

The church of **Notre-Dame** (✉ Rue Carnot), across from the tourist office, has an arresting rose-window facade that, like the high nave, dates from the 15th century. Rounded Romanesque arches in the choir, however, attest to the building's 12th-century origins. The church is a fine sight when viewed from behind: Monet liked to paint it from across the Seine.

A few minor Monet canvases, along with other late-19th-century paintings, can be admired in the town museum, the **Musée Poulain.** This rambling old mansion is seldom crowded, and the helpful curators are happy to explain local history. ✉ *12 rue du Pont,* ☎ *02–32–21–28–09.* *€2.30.* *Tues.–Fri. 11–1 and 2–6, weekends 2–6.*

Dining and Lodging

$$$ ★ **Château de Brécourt.** This 17th-century stone-and-brick château outside Vernon has high-pitched roofs, an imposing forecourt, and extensive grounds. Guest rooms follow the same exuberant turn-of-the-19th-century lines. Even if you're not staying here, you can dine on the inventive food in the august restaurant, Le Grand Siècle. Dishes such as lobster mousse and veal with truffles make it a popular spot—and it's even easy to get to from Giverny, which is just across the Seine from Vernon. As such châteaux-hotels go, a stay here is a relatively good value. ✉ *7 route de Brécourt (8 km/5 mi southwest of Vernon on D181/D75), 27120 Douains,* ☎ *02–32–52–40–50,* FAX *02–32–52–69–65,* WEB *www.sitedefrance.con/eure/br/brecourt. 25 rooms, 5 suites. Restaurant, minibars, tennis court, pool, jacuzzi, sauna. AE, DC, MC, V.*

THE OISE VALLEY AND EAST TO DISNEYLAND PARIS

This area covers a broad arc, beginning northwest of Paris in Conflans–Ste-Honorine, where the Oise joins the Seine, then heading east along the Oise Valley to Chantilly, and continuing southeast through Meaux. In addition to being the old stamping grounds for several world-famous artists—Pissarro's canvases of Pontoise are among his best-known, while those van Gogh painted in Auvers were his very last—the area is now the domain of Disneyland Paris.

Conflans-Ste-Honorine

34 *28 km (3 mi) northwest of Paris via A15 and D48.*

Conflans is the capital of France's inland waterway network. Barges arrive from as far afield as the ports of Le Havre and Dunkerque, on the Channel coast, and are often moored as many as six abreast along the 1½-km-long (1-mi-long) quayside, near the *conflans* (confluence) of the Rivers Seine and Oise; one, the *Je Sers* (I Serve), is the boatmen's own church (open daily). From the hilltop church of St-Maclou there is a spectacular view of the boats. The **Musée de la Batellerie** (Waterways Museum) explains the historic role of the barges and waterways with the help of pictures and scale models. ✉ *3 pl. Jules-Gévelot,* ☎ *01–39–72–58–05.* 🎫 *€4.* ⏲ *Tues. 1:30–6, Wed.–Fri. 9–noon and 1:30–6, weekends 3–6 (Easter–Sept.) or 2–5 (Oct.–Easter).*

Pontoise

35 *8 km (5 mi) north of Conflans-Ste-Honorine via N184 and N14, 29 km (19 mi) northwest of Paris via A15.*

A pleasant old town on the banks of the Oise, Pontoise is famous for its link with the Impressionists. The small **Musée Pissarro,** high up in the Old Town, pays tribute to one of Pontoise's most illustrious past residents, Impressionist painter Camille Pissarro (1830–1903). The collection of prints and drawings is of interest mainly to specialists, but the view across the valley from the museum gardens will appeal to all. ✉ *17 rue du Château,* ☎ *01–30–38–02–40,* WEB *www.ville-pontoise.fr.* 🎫 *Free.* ⏲ *Wed.–Sun. 2–6.*

The **Musée Tavet-Delacour,** housed in a turreted mansion in the center of Pontoise, stages good exhibitions and has a permanent collection that ranges from street scenes and landscapes by Norbert Goenutte and other local painters to contemporary art and the intriguing abstractions of Otto Freundlich. ✉ *4 rue Lemercier,* ☎ *01–30–38–02–40,* WEB *www.ville-pontoise.fr.* 🎫 *€5.* ⏲ *Wed.–Sun. 10–12:30 and 1:30–6.*

Auvers-sur-Oise

36 *7 km (4 mi) east of Pontoise via D4, 33 km (21 mi) northwest of Paris via N328.*

The tranquil Oise River valley, which runs northeast from Pontoise, retains much of the charm that attracted Camille Pissarro, Paul Cézanne, Camille Corot, Charles-François Daubigny, and Berthe Morisot to Auvers-sur-Oise in the second half of the 19th century. But despite this lofty company, it is the spirit of Vincent van Gogh that haunts every nook and cranny of this pretty riverside village.

Van Gogh moved here from Arles in May 1890 to be nearer his brother, Theo, who lived in Paris. Little has changed here since that summer of 1890, during the last 10 weeks of van Gogh's life, when he painted no fewer than 70 pictures and then shot himself behind the village château. He is buried next to his brother in a simple ivy-covered grave in the village cemetery. The whole village is peppered with plaques marking the spots that inspired his art. The plaques bear reproductions of his paintings, enabling you to compare his final works with the scenes as they are today. After years of indifference and neglect, his last abode has been turned into a shrine. You can also visit the medieval village church, subject of one of van Gogh's most famous paintings, *L'Église d'Auvers,* and admire Osip Zadkine's powerful modern statue of van Gogh in the village park.

The Auberge Ravoux, the inn where van Gogh stayed, is now the **Maison de van Gogh** (van Gogh House). A dingy staircase leads up to the tiny, spartan wood-floor attic where van Gogh stored some of modern art's most famous pictures under his bed. A short film retraces van Gogh's time at Auvers, and there is a well-stocked souvenir shop. Stop for a drink or for lunch in the ground-floor restaurant. ✉ *8 rue de la Sansonne,* ☎ *01–30–36–60–60.* 🎫 *€4.60.* ⏲ *Daily 10–6.*

★ The elegant 17th-century village château, set above split-level gardens, now houses the **Voyage au Temps des Impressionistes** (Journey Through the Impressionist Era). You'll receive a set of infrared headphones (English available), with commentary that guides you past various tableaux illustrating life during the Impressionist years. Although there are no Impressionist originals—500 reproductions pop up on screens interspersed between the tableaux—this is one of France's most imaginative, enjoyable, and innovative museums. Some of the special effects—talking mirrors, computerized cabaret dancing girls, and a simulated train ride past Impressionist landscapes—are worthy of Disney at its best. ✉ *Rue de Léry,* ☎ *01–34–48–48–40,* WEB *www.chateau-auvers.fr.* 🎫 *€10.* ⏲ *May–Oct., Tues.–Sun. 10–8; Nov.–Apr., Tues.–Sun. 11–4:30.*

The landscape artist Charles-François Daubigny, a precursor of the Impressionists, lived in Auvers from 1861 until his death in 1878. You can visit his studio, the **Maison-Atelier de Daubigny,** and admire the remarkable mural and roof paintings by Daubigny and fellow artists Camille Corot and Honoré Daumier. ✉ *61 rue Daubigny,* ☎ *01–34–48–03–03.* 🎫 *€4.30.* ⏲ *Thur.–Sun. 2–6:30.*

You may also want to visit the modest **Musée Daubigny** to admire the drawings, lithographs, and occasional oils by local 19th-century artists, some of which were collected by Daubigny himself. The museum is opposite the Maison de van Gogh, above the tourist office. ✉ *Manoir des Colombières, rue de la Sansonne,* ☎ *01–30–36–80–20.* 🎫 *€3.* ⏲ *Wed.–Sun. 2–6.*

Dining

$$ ★ ✕ **Auberge Ravoux.** For total van Gogh immersion, have lunch in the restaurant he patronized regularly more than 100 years ago and where, in fact, he finally expired. The €30, three-course menu changes regularly, but it's the genius loci that makes eating here special, with glasswork, lace curtains, and wall blandishments carefully modeled on the original designs. A magnificently illustrated book, *Van Gogh's Table* (published by Artisan), by culinary historian Alexandra Leaf and Fred Leeman, recalls Vincent's stay at the Auberge and describes in loving detail the dishes served there at the time. ✉ *52 rue Général-de-Gaulle,* ☎ *01–30–36–60–60. Reservations essential. AE, DC, MC, V. No dinner Sun.–Mon. Closed Jan. and Tues. Oct.–Mar.*

L'Isle-Adam

37 *6 km (4 mi) northeast of Auvers-sur-Oise via D4, 40 km (25 mi) north of Paris via N1.*

Residentially exclusive L'Isle-Adam is one of the most picturesque towns in Ile-de-France. Paris lies just 40 km (25 mi) south, but it could be 100 mi and as many years away. The town has a sandy beach along one stretch of the River Oise (via rue de Beaumont); a curious pagodalike folly, the Pavillon Chinois de Cassan; and an unassuming local museum. The **Musée Louis-Senlecq,** on the main street, often stages painting exhibitions and contains numerous attractive works by local landscapists. ✉ *46 Grande-Rue,* ☎ *01–34–69–45–44,* WEB *www.ville-isle-adam.fr.* *€3.10.* *Wed.–Mon. 2–6.*

Dining and Lodging

$$–$$$ ✕🏨 **Le Cabouillet.** The riverside Cabouillet aptly reflects the quiet charm of L'Isle-Adam, thanks to its pretty views over the Oise. You can savor these from each of its eight cozy rooms or from the chic restaurant (closed Wednesday), where the cooking can be inspired—have the crawfish in Sauternes sauce, if it's on the menu. ✉ *5 quai de l'Oise, 95290,* ☎ *01–34–69–00–90,* FAX *01–34–69–33–88. 8 rooms. Restaurant, no air-conditioning. AE, DC, MC, V. Closed Mon. and late Dec.–early Feb. No dinner Sun.*

Chantilly

38 *10 km (6 mi) northeast of Royaumont via D909, 23 km (14 mi) east of L'Isle-Adam via D4, 37 km (23 mi) north of Paris via N16.*

Celebrated for lace, cream, and the most beautiful medieval manuscript in the world—*Les Très Riches Heures du Duc de Berry*—romantic Chantilly has a host of other attractions: a faux Renaissance château with an eye-popping art collection, splendid Baroque stables, a classy racecourse, and a 16,000-acre forest.

Although its lavish exterior may be 19th-century Renaissance pastiche, ★ the **Château de Chantilly,** sitting snugly behind an artificial lake, houses the outstanding **Musée Condé,** with illuminated medieval manuscripts, tapestries, furniture, and paintings. The most famous room, the **Santuario** (sanctuary), contains two celebrated works by Italian painter Raphael (1483–1520)—the *Three Graces* and the *Orleans Virgin*—plus an exquisite ensemble of 15th-century miniatures by the most illustrious French painter of his time, Jean Fouquet (1420–81). Farther on, in the ***Cabinet des Livres*** (library), is the world-famous book of hours whose title translates as *The Very Rich Hours of the Duc de Berry,* which was illuminated by the Brothers Limbourg with magical pictures of early 15th-century life as lived by one of Burgundy's richest lords (unfortunately, due to their fragility, painted facsimiles of the celebrated calendar illuminations are on display, not the actual pages of the book). Other highlights of this unusual museum are the **Galerie de Psyché** (Psyche Gallery), with 16th-century stained glass and portrait drawings by Flemish artist Jean Clouet II; the **Chapelle,** with sculptures by Jean Goujon and Jacques Sarrazin; and the extensive collection of paintings by 19th-century French artists, headed by Jean-Auguste-Dominique Ingres. In addition, there are grand and petit salons, all stuffed with palace furniture, family portraits, and Sèvres porcelains, making this an absolute must for lovers of the decorative and applied arts. ☎ *03–44–62–62–62,* WEB *www.chateaudechantilly.com.* *€6.40 (including park).* *Mar.–Oct., daily 10–6; Nov.–Feb., Wed.–Mon. 10:30–12:45 and 2–5.*

Le Nôtre's **park** is based on that familiar French royal combination of formality (neatly planned parterres and a mighty, straight-banked canal) and romantic eccentricity (the waterfall and the Hameau, a mock-Norman village that inspired Marie-Antoinette's version at Versailles). The **Aérophile,** the world's largest tethered balloon, floats you 450 ft up for a bird's-eye view; the **Hydrophile,** an electric-powered boat, glides you for 30 mins down the Grand Canal. ☎ *03–44–57–35–35.* *Park only €2.60, with Hydrophile €8, with Aérophile €10, with both €11 (€16.50 joint ticket including château).* *Mar.–Oct., daily 10–6; Nov.–Feb., daily 10:30–12:45 and 2–5.*

★ The palatial 18th-century **Grandes Écuries** by the racetrack, built by Jean Aubert in 1719 to accommodate 240 horses and 500 hounds for stag and boar hunts in the forests nearby, are the grandest stables in France. They're still in use, as the home of the **Musée Vivant du Cheval** (Living Horse Museum), with 30 breeds of horses and ponies housed in straw-lined comfort—in between dressage performances in the courtyard or beneath the awe-inspiring central dome. The 31-room museum has a comprehensive collection of equine paraphernalia: everything from saddles, bridles, and stirrups to rocking horses, anatomy displays, and old postcards. There are explanations in English throughout. *7 rue du Connétable, 03–44–57–40–40, WEB www.musee-vivant-du-cheval.fr. €8. Easter–Sept., Wed.–Mon. 10:30–6:30; Oct.–Easter, Wed.–Fri. and Mon. 2–5, weekends 10:30–5:30.*

Dining and Lodging

$$ **La Ferme de Condé.** At the far end of the racetrack, in a building that originally served as an Anglican chapel, is one of the classiest restaurants in Chantilly. Dishes include roast suckling pig, duck with honey and spices and lobster terrine. A reasonably priced menu makes it a suitable lunch spot. There is a good wine list. *42 av. du Maréchal-Joffre, 03–44–57–32–31. Reservations essential. AE, DC, MC, V.*

$ **Capitainerie.** This self-service restaurant is in the château's vaulted medieval basement, adorned with old kitchen utensils. The buffet is available nonstop from 10:30 through 6:30; you'll find salads, cheeses, and desserts, along with a few hot dishes. *In Château de Chantilly, 03–44–67–40–00. MC, V. Closed Tues.*

$$$–$$$$ **Dolce Chantilly.** This large hotel with a pink facade, 1½ km (1 mi) northeast of the château, is surrounded by forest and overlooks its own 18-hole golf course. The marble-floor reception hall creates a glitzy impression not quite matched by the guest rooms, which are functional, modern, and a bit small. The De Par En Par brasserie, in the golf clubhouse, serves lunch for €15, and the deluxe Carmontelle has formal dining (pastry chef Hugues Lenté is a master at *crème de Chantilly*). *Rte. d'Apremont, 60500 Vineuil–St-Firmin, 03–44–58–47–77, FAX 03–44–58–50–11. 99 rooms, 3 suites. 3 restaurants, cable TV, minibars, Internet, golf course, tennis court, pool, health club, babysitting. AE, DC, MC, V.*

$$ **Campanile.** This functional, modern motel is in quiet Les Huit Curés, just north of Chantilly, on the edge of the forest (which compensates for the lack of interior atmosphere). There's a grill room for straightforward meals, with a buffet for appetizers, cheese, and desserts. You can dine outside on the terrace in summer. *Rte. de Creil (on N16 toward Creil), 60500, 03–44–57–39–24, FAX 03–44–58–10–05. 45 rooms with bath. Grill, bar, no air-conditioning, some pets allowed. AE, DC, MC, V.*

Outdoor Activities and Sports

Since 1834 Chantilly's fabled racetrack, the **Hipprodrome des Princes de Condé** (Route du Pesage, 03–44–62–41–00, WEB www.paristurf.tm.fr/chantil.html), has come into its own each June with two of Europe's most prestigious events: the **Prix du Jockey-Club** (French Derby), on the first Sunday of the month, and the **Prix de Diane** for three-year-old fillies, the Sunday after.

Senlis

39 *10 km (6 mi) east of Chantilly via D924, 45 km (28 mi) north of Paris via A1.*

Senlis is an exceptionally well-preserved medieval town with crooked, mazelike streets dominated by the svelte, soaring spire of its Gothic cathedral. Be sure to also inspect the moss-tile church of St-Pierre, with its stumpy crocketed spire. You can enjoy a 40-minute tour of the Old Town by horse and carriage, which departs from in front of the cathedral, daily April–December (€27 for up to three people).

★ The **Cathédrale Notre-Dame** (✉ Pl. de Parvis), one of France's oldest and narrowest cathedrals, dates from the second half of the 12th century. The superb spire—arguably the most elegant in France—was added around 1240, and the majestic transept, with its ornate rose windows, in the 16th century.

The town's excellent **Musée d'Art** (Art Museum), built atop an ancient Gallo-Roman residence, displays archeological finds ranging from Gallo-Roman votive objects unearthed in the neighboring Halatte Forest to the building's own excavated foundations (uncovered in the basement), including some macabre stone heads bathed in half light. Paintings upstairs include works by Manet's teacher Thomas Couture (who lived in Senlis) and a whimsical fried-egg still life by 19th-century realist Théodule Ribot. ✉ *Palais Épiscopal, pl. du Parvis-Notre-Dame,* ☎ *03–44–53–00–80.* 🎫 *€2.50.* ⏲ *Thurs.–Mon. 9–noon and 1:30–5:30.*

OFF THE BEATEN PATH

PARC ASTÉRIX – A great alternative to Disneyland, and a wonderful day out for young and old, this Gallic theme park, 10 km (6 mi) south of Senlis via A1, opened in 1989 and takes its cue from a French comic-book figure whose adventures are set during the Roman invasion of France 2,000 years ago. Among the 30 rides and six shows that attract thundering herds of families each year are a mock Gallo-Roman village, performing dolphins, splash-happy water slides, and a giant roller-coaster. ☎ *03–44–62–34–04,* WEB *www.parcasterix.fr.* 🎫 *€30.* ⏲ *Apr.–Aug., daily 10–6; Sept.–mid-Oct., Wed. and weekends 10–6.*

Dining and Lodging

$$–$$$ ✕ **Le Bourgeois Gentilhomme.** This pink-and-cream restaurant in old Senlis, named for dapper chef Philippe Bourgeois, serves such interesting dishes as pigeon with cabbage and bacon, fricassee of burbot with mushrooms, and crab lasagna with cress, to name but three. ✉ *3 pl. de la Halle,* ☎ *03–44–53–13–22. AE, DC, MC, V. Closed Mon. and 2 wks in Aug. No lunch Sat., no dinner Sun.*

$–$$ ✕🏨 **Hostellerie de la Porte-Bellon.** This is the closest you'll get to spending a night in the historic center of Senlis. This modest hotel is just a five-minute walk from the cathedral and close to the bus station. ✉ *51 rue Bellon, 60300,* ☎ *03–44–53–03–05,* FAX *03–44–53–29–94. 18 rooms. Restaurant, no air-conditioning, pets allowed. MC, V. Closed mid-Dec.–mid-Jan.*

Ermenonville

40 *13 km (8 mi) southeast of Senlis via N330, 43 km (27 mi) northeast of Paris.*

A ruined abbey and children's amusement park, both nearby, add to the appeal of the village of Ermenonville, best known as the final haunt of the 18th-century French philosopher Jean-Jacques Rousseau. The Cistercian **Abbaye de Chaalis,** just off N330 as you arrive from Senlis, has photogenic 13th-century ruins, a landscaped park, an orangery, and an 18th-century château. Inside is an eclectic collection of Egyptian antiquities and medieval paintings and three rooms displaying manuscripts and other mementos of Jean-Jacques Rousseau. ✉ *Just off N330,* ☎ *03–44–54–04–02.* 🎫 *Abbey and park, €5.50; park only, €2.30.* ⏲ *Mar.–Oct., daily 10:30–12:30 and 2–6; Nov.–Feb., Sun. 10:30–12:30 and 1:30–5:30.*

The **Parc Jean-Jacques Rousseau,** a tranquil oasis in the center of Ermenonville, is famous as the initial resting place of the influential writer, who spent the last three months of his life in Ermenonville in 1778 and was buried on the Ile des Peupliers in the middle of the lake. Rousseau's ideas about natural equality made him a hero of the French Revolution, and in 1794 his body was removed to the Panthéon in Paris.

Dining and Lodging

$$$–$$$$ ✕🏨 **Château d'Ermenonville.** Right out of a storybook, this turreted 18th-century château opposite the Parc Jean-Jacques Rousseau has great style—it's surrounded by a lake, the main courtyard has a sculpted pediment and wrought-iron balconies, and the rooms are furnished with fin-de-siècle opulence. The menu changes regularly at the restaurant, La Table du Poète. ✉ *60950 Ermenonville,* ☎ *03–44–54–00–26,* FAX *03–44–54–01–00. 49 rooms. Restaurant, no air-conditioning, minibars, Internet. AE, DC, MC, V.*

Meaux

41 *24 km (15 mi) southeast of Ermenonville via N330, 40 km (25 mi) east of Paris via N3.*

A sturdy cathedral and a well-preserved bishop's palace embellish Meaux, a dignified old market town on the banks of the Marne River. An excellent Brie is produced locally. Above the Marne sits the **Cathédrale St-Étienne,** which took more than 300 years to complete and is, consequently, a bit of a hodgepodge stylistically. The stonework in the soaring interior becomes increasingly decorative as you approach the west end, culminating in a notable Flamboyant Gothic rose window. The exterior is somewhat eroded and looks sadly battered—or pleasingly authentic, according to taste. A son-et-lumière show replete with medieval costumes is staged outside the cathedral most weekends in June, July, and September. ✉ *Rue St-Étienne,* ☎ *01–60–23–40–00 for details about son-et-lumière show,* WEB *www.feerie.org.* ⏲ *Daily 8–noon and 2–6.*

The former bishop's palace next to the cathedral, overlooking a trimly patterned garden with remains of the town wall, now houses the **Musée Bossuet.** The museum combines French Old Masters with a quirky collection of medals commemorating the Paris Commune and Franco-Prussian War. ✉ *5 pl. Charles-de-Gaulle,* ☎ *01–64–34–84–45.* 🎫 *€2.30, free Wed.* ⏲ *Wed.–Mon. 10–12:15 and 2–6.*

Dining and Lodging

$$–$$$ ✕🏨 **Château des Bondons.** This small 19th-century château, set in a large park just to the northeast of La Ferté-sous-Jarre, a 20-minute drive from Meaux, has been stylishly restored by Jean Busconi and his wife; they've equipped rooms with a mix of English and Louis XV–style furniture, thick carpets, and floral-patterned quilts. The restaurant (closed Monday, Tuesday, and January) opened in 2001, with chef Alban Risse serving up serious cuisine, such as lamb with aubergine and goat cheese. ✉ *47 rue des Bondons, 77260 La Ferté-sous-Jouarre (21 km/13 mi east of Meaux on N3),* ☎ *01–60–22–00–98,* FAX *01–60–22–97–01. 14 rooms. Restaurant, bar, no air-conditioning, cable TV, minibars, Internet. AE, DC, MC, V.*

Disneyland Paris

42 *20 km (13 mi) southwest of Meaux via A140 and A4, 38 km (24 mi) east of Paris via A4.*

Disneyland Paris (originally called Euro Disney) is probably not what you've traveled to France to experience. But if you have a child in tow, the promise of a day here may get you through an afternoon at Versailles or Fontainebleau. If you're a dyed-in-the-wool Disney fan, you'll want to make a beeline for the park to see how it has been molded to appeal to the tastes of Europeans (Disney's "Imagineers" call it their most lovingly detailed park). And if you've never experienced this particular form of Disney showmanship, you may want to put in an appearance if only to see what the fuss is all about. When it opened, few turned up to do so; today the place is jammed with crowds, and Disneyland Paris is here to stay—and grow, with **Walt Disney Studios** slated to open during 2002. The theme park is made up of five "lands": Main Street U.S.A., Frontierland, Adventureland, Fantasyland, and Discoveryland. The central theme of each land is relentlessly echoed in every detail, from attractions to restaurant menus to souvenirs. The park is circled by a railroad, which stops three times along the perimeter.

Main Street U.S.A. goes under the railroad and past shops and restaurants toward the main plaza; Disney parades are held here every afternoon and, during holiday periods, every evening. Top attractions at **Frontierland** are the chilling Phantom Manor, haunted by holographic spooks, and the thrilling runaway mine train of Big Thunder Mountain, a roller-coaster that plunges wildly through floods and avalanches in a setting meant to evoke Utah's Monument Valley. Whiffs of Arabia, Africa, and the West Indies give **Adventureland** its exotic cachet; the spicy meals and snacks served here rank among the best food in the park. Don't miss the Pirates of the Caribbean, an exciting mise-en-scène populated by eerily humanlike, computer-driven figures, or Indiana Jones and the Temple of Doom, a breathtaking ride that recreates some of this luckless hero's most exciting moments.

Fantasyland charms the youngest park goers with familiar cartoon characters from such classic Disney films as *Snow White, Pinocchio, Dumbo,* and *Peter Pan.* The focal point of Fantasyland, and indeed Disneyland Paris, is Le Château de la Belle au Bois Dormant (Sleeping Beauty's Castle), a 140-ft, bubblegum-pink structure topped with 16 blue- and gold-tipped turrets. Its design was allegedly inspired by illustrations from a medieval *Book of Hours*—if so, it was by way of Beverly Hills. The castle's dungeon conceals a 2-ton scaly green dragon that rumbles in its sleep and occasionally rouses to roar—an impressive feat of engineering, producing an answering chorus of shrieks from younger children. **Discoveryland** is a futuristic eyeknocker for high-tech Disney entertainment. Robots on roller skates welcome you on your way to Star Tours, a pitching, plunging, sense-confounding ride based on the *Star Wars* films. In Le Visionarium, a simulated space journey is presented by 9-Eye, a staggeringly realistic robot. Space Mountain pretends to catapult riders through the Milky Way. ☎ *01–60–30–60–30,* WEB *www.disneylandparis.com.* *Apr.–Oct. and Christmas period €36 (€70 for 2-day Passport, €97 for 3-day Passport); Nov.–Mar., except Christmas period, €27 (€52 for 2-day Passport, €73 for 3-day Passport); includes admission to all individual attractions within the park but not meals.* ⏲ *Mid-June–mid-Sept., daily 9 AM–10 PM; mid-Sept.–mid-June, Sun.–Fri. 10–8, Sat. 9–8; Dec. 20–Jan. 1, daily 9–8. AE, DC, MC, V.*

Dining and Lodging

$–$$$ ✕ **Disneyland Restaurants.** Disneyland Paris is peppered with places to eat, ranging from snack bars and fast-food joints to five full-service restaurants—all with a distinguishing theme. In addition, Disney Village and Disney Hotels have restaurants open to the public. But since these are outside the park, it is not recommended that you waste time traveling to them for lunch. Disneyland Paris has relaxed its no-alcohol policy and now serves wine and beer in the park's sit-down restaurants, as well as in the hotels and restaurants outside the park. ☎ *01–60–45–65–40. AE, DC, MC, V accepted at sit-down restaurants.*

$$–$$$$ **Disneyland Hotels.** The resort has 5,000 rooms in six hotels, all a short distance from the park, ranging from the luxurious Disneyland Hotel to the not-so-rustic Camp Davy Crockett. Free transportation to the park is available at every hotel. Packages including Disneyland lodging, entertainment, and admission are available through travel agents in Europe. ✉ *Centre de Réservations, B.P. 100, 77777 Marne-la-Vallée cedex 4,* ☎ *01–60–30–60–30; 407/934–7639 in U.S.,* FAX *01–49–30–71–00. All hotels have at least 1 restaurant, bar, café, Internet, indoor pool, sauna,health club, free parking. AE, DC, MC, V.*

Nightlife and the Arts

Nocturnal entertainment outside the park centers on **Disney Village,** a vast pleasure mall designed by American architect Frank Gehry. Featured are American-style restaurants (crab shack, diner, deli, steak house), including **Billybob's Country Western Saloon** (☎ 01–60–45–70–81). Also in Disney Village is **Buffalo Bill's Wild West Show** (☎ 01–60–45–71–00 for reservations), a two-hour dinner extravaganza with a menu of sausages, spare ribs, and chili; performances by a talented troupe of stunt riders, bronco busters, tribal dancers, and musicians; plus some 50 horses, a dozen buffalo, a bull, and an Annie Oakley–style sharpshooter, with a golden-maned "Buffalo Bill" as emcee. A re-creation of a show that dazzled Parisians 100 years ago, it's corny but great fun if you can manage the appropriate suspension of disbelief. There are two shows nightly, at 6:30 and 9:30; the cost is €49.50.

Outdoor Activities and Sports

A 27-hole **golf course** (☎ 01–60–45–68–04) is open to the public at Disneyland; rental clubs are available, and some special golf packages are available through travel agents.

SOUTHEAST TO FONTAINEBLEAU

Fontainebleau forms the hub of this heavily wooded southeast region of Ile-de-France, but no one will want to bypass the grandeur of Vaux-le-Vicomte, a masterpiece of 17th-century architecture and garden design; or the pretty painters' villages of Barbizon and Moret-sur-Loing.

Vaux-le-Vicomte

★ 43 *56 km (35 mi) southeast of Paris via A6, N104, A5, and N36; 5 km (3 mi) northeast of Melun via N36 and D215; 48 km south (30 mi) of Disneyland Paris via N36.*

The quintessence of French 17th-century splendor, the **Château de Vaux-le-Vicomte** was built between 1656 and 1661 for finance minister Nicolas Fouquet. The construction of this château was monstrous even for those days: entire villages were razed, 18,000 workmen were called in, and architect Louis Le Vau, painter Charles Le Brun, and landscape architect André Le Notre—all biggies of the day—were hired to prove that Fouquet's refined tastes matched his business acumen. The housewarming party was so lavish that star guest Louis XIV, tetchy at the best of times, couldn't contain his envy: he had Fouquet hurled into the slammer and promptly began the building of Versailles to prove just who was top banana.

The high-roofed château, partially surrounded by a moat, is set well back from the road behind iron railings topped with sculpted heads.

A cobbled avenue stretches up to the entrance, and stone steps lead to the vestibule, which seems small given the noble scale of the exterior. Charles Le Brun's captivating decoration includes the ceiling of the **Chambre du Roi** (Royal Bedchamber), depicting *Time Bearing Truth Heavenward,* framed by stuccowork by sculptors François Girardon and André Legendre. Along the frieze you can make out small squirrels, the Fouquet family's emblem—even now squirrels are known as *fouquets* in local dialect. But Le Brun's masterwork is the ceiling in the **Salon des Muses** (Hall of Muses), a brilliant allegorical composition painted in glowing, sensuous colors that some feel even surpasses his work at Versailles. On the ground floor the impressive **Grand Salon** (Great Hall), with its unusual oval form and 16 caryatid pillars symbolizing the months and seasons, has harmony and style despite its unfinished state. In fact, the lack of decoration only points up Le Vau's architectural genius. In the basement, whose cool, dim rooms were used to store food and wine and house the château's staff, you'll find rotating exhibits about the château's past and lifesize wax figures illustrating its history.

There is no mistaking the grandeur of Le Nôtre's carefully restored **gardens,** at their best when the fountains are turned on (the second and fourth Saturdays of each month from April through October 3 PM–6 PM). Also visit the **Musée des Équipages** (Carriage Museum) in the stables, and inspect a host of carriages and coaches in wonderful condition. Get to Vaux by training it to Melun, then taking a local bus. ☎ *01–64–14–41–90,* WEB *www.vaux-le-vicomte.com.* 🎫 *€10, candlelight château visits €13.* ⏲ *Mid-Mar.–Nov. 11, daily 10–6; candlelight visits May–mid-Oct., Sat. 8 PM–midnight.*

Dining

$ ✕ **L'Écureuil.** An imposing barn to the right of the château entrance has been transformed into this self-service cafeteria, where you can enjoy fine steaks (insist yours is cooked enough), coffee, or a snack beneath the ancient rafters of a wood-beam roof. The restaurant is open daily for lunch and tea, and for dinner during candlelight visits. ✉ *Château de Vaux-le-Vicomte,* ☎ *01–60–66–95–66. MC, V.*

Barbizon

44 *17 km (11 mi) southwest of Vaux-le-Vicomte via Melun and D132/D64, 52 km (33 mi) southeast of Paris.*

On the western edge of the 62,000-acre Fontainebleau forest, the village of Barbizon retains its time-stained allure despite the intrusion of art galleries, souvenir shops, and busloads of tourists. The group of landscape painters known as the Barbizon School—Camille Corot, Jean-François Millet, Narcisse Diaz de la Peña, and Théodore Rousseau, among others—lived here from the 1830s on. They paved the way for the Impressionists by their willingness to accept nature on its own terms rather than use it as an idealized base for carefully structured compositions. Sealed to one of the famous sandstone rocks in the forest—which starts, literally, at the far end of the main street—is a bronze medallion by sculptor Henri Chapu, paying homage to Millet and Rousseau.

Corot and company would often repair to the Auberge Ganne after painting to brush up on their social life; the inn is now the **Musée de l'École de Barbizon** (Barbizon School Museum). Here you'll find documents of the village as it was in the 19th century, as well as a few original works. The Barbizon artists painted on every available surface, and even now you can see some originals on the upstairs walls.

Two of the ground-floor rooms have been reconstituted as they were in Ganne's time—note the trompe-l'oeil paintings on the buffet doors. There's also a video on the Barbizon School. ✉ *92 Grande-Rue,* ☎ *01–60–66–22–27.* 🎫 *€4.50 (joint admission with Maison-Atelier Théodore-Rousseau).* ⏲ *Mon. and Wed.–Fri. 10–12:30 and 2–5, weekends 10–5.*

Though there are no actual Millet works, the **Atelier Jean-François Millet** (Millet's Studio) is cluttered with photographs and mementos evoking his career. It was here that Millet painted some of his most renowned pieces, including *The Gleaners.* ✉ *27 Grande-Rue,* ☎ *01–60–66–21–55.* 🎫 *Free.* ⏲ *Wed.–Mon. 9:30–12:30 and 2–5:30.*

By the church, beyond the extraordinary village war memorial featuring a mustached ancient Gaul in a winged helmet, is the **Maison-Atelier Théodore-Rousseau** (Rousseau's House-cum-Studio), in a converted barn. It doubles as the tourist office and exhibition space for temporary shows. ✉ *55 Grande-Rue,* ☎ *01–60–66–22–38.* 🎫 *€4.50 (joint ticket with Barbizon School Museum).* ⏲ *Mon. and Wed.–Fri. 10–12:30 and 2–5, weekends 10–5.*

Dining and Lodging

$–$$ ✕ **Le Relais de Barbizon.** French country specialties are served at this rustic restaurant with a big open fire and a large terrace shaded by lime and chestnut trees. The four-course weekday menu is a good value, but wine here is expensive and cannot be ordered by the *pichet* (pitcher). Reservations are essential on weekends. ✉ *2 av. Général-de-Gaulle,* ☎ *01–60–66–40–28. MC, V. Closed part of Aug. and Wed. No dinner Tues.*

$$–$$$ ★ ✕🏨 **Auberge de l'Ile du Saussay.** Eddie Lebrun's large-windowed, modern hotel just north of Itteville is 24 km (15 mi) south of Orly Airport and handily placed for points both west (Breteuil and Dampierre) and east (Barbizon and Vaux-le-Vicomte). It overlooks a 40-acre lake that was once a medieval peat quarry. All rooms here have contemporary furnishings and a terrace; some look out over the lake, others over the surrounding woods. The dining room serves traditional French cuisine; set menus range from €16 to €35. ✉ *Rte. de Ballancourt, 91760 Itteville (27 km/17 mi west of Breteuil via D11/D83),* ☎ *01–64–93–20–12,* FAX *01–64–93–39–88. 7 rooms, 17 suites. Restaurant, no air-conditioning, minibars, no pets. AE, MC, V. Closed Mon. and Aug.*

$$–$$$ ★ ✕🏨 **Les Alouettes.** This delightful, family-run 19th-century inn is on 2 acres (which the better rooms overlook). The interior is '30s style, but many rooms still have their original oak beams. Lionel Ménard's rustic restaurant (reservations essential; no dinner Sunday from October to March), with its large open terrace, serves traditional French cuisine such as hare with mushrooms and lamb with eggplant. ✉ *4 rue Antoine-Barye, 77630,* ☎ *01–60–66–41–98,* FAX *01–60–66–20–69. 22 rooms. Restaurant, bar, no air-conditioning, cable TV, Internet. AE, DC, MC, V.*

Fontainebleau

9 km (6 mi) southeast of Barbizon via N7, 61 km (38 mi) southeast of Paris via A6 and N7.

Like Chambord, in the Loire Valley, or Compiègne, to the north, Fontainebleau was a favorite spot for royal hunting parties long before the construction of one of France's grandest residences. Although not as celebrated as Versailles, Vaux-le-Vicomte, or Chenonceau, this palace is almost as spectacular as those other sites.

Cour de la Fontaine 50
Cour des Adieux 49
Cour des Offices . .53
Cour Ovale 52
Galerie de Diane 48
Galerie François-I . . .45
Jardin de Diane 54
Napoléon's Apartments . .47
Porte Dauphine . . .51
Salle de Bal 46

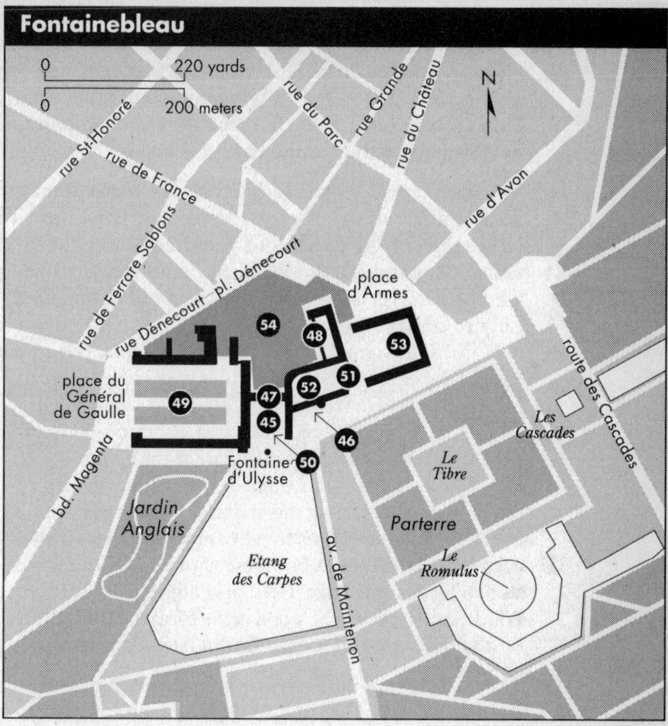

The **Château de Fontainebleau** you see today dates from the 16th century, although additions were made by various royal incumbents through the next 300 years. The palace was begun under the flamboyant Renaissance king François I, the French contemporary of England's Henry VIII. The king hired Italian artists Il Rosso (a pupil of Michelangelo) and Primaticcio to embellish his château. In fact, they did much more: by introducing the pagan allegories and elegant lines of Mannerism to France, they revolutionized French decorative art. Their ex-
45 traordinary frescoes and stuccowork can be admired in the **Galerie**
46 **François-I** (Francis I Gallery) and the jewel of the interior, the **Salle de Bal** (ballroom). Here in the ceremonial ballroom, which is nearly 100 ft long, you can admire the dazzling 16th-century frescoes and gilding. Completed under Henri II, François's successor, it is luxuriantly wood paneled, with a gleaming parquet floor that reflects the patterns on the ceiling. Like the château as a whole, the room exudes a sense of elegance and style—but on a more intimate, human scale than at Versailles: this is Renaissance, not Baroque. Henri II also added the decorative interlaced initials found throughout the château. You might expect to see the royal *H* woven with a C (for Catherine de' Médici, his wife). Instead you'll find a *D*—indicating his mistress, Diane de Poitiers.

47 **Napoléon's apartments** occupied the first floor. You can see a lock of his hair, his Légion d'Honneur medal, his imperial uniform, the hat he wore on his return from Elba in 1815, and one bed in which he definitely did spend a night (almost every town in France boasts a bed in which the emperor supposedly snoozed). The **Salon Jaune** (Yellow Room) of Joséphine is one of the best examples of the Empire style—the Neoclassical style favored by the emperor. There is also a throne room—Napoléon spurned the one at Versailles, a palace he disliked, establishing his imperial seat in the former King's Bedchamber—and

the Queen's Boudoir, also known as the Room of the Six Maries (occupants included ill-fated Marie-Antoinette and Napoléon's second wife, 48 Marie-Louise). The sweeping **Galerie de Diane,** built during the reign of Henri IV (1589–1610), was converted into a library in the 1860s. Other salons have 17th-century tapestries and paintings and frescoes by members of the Fontainebleau School.

Although Louis XIV's architectural fancy was concentrated on Versailles, he commissioned Mansart to design new pavilions and had André Le Nôtre replant the gardens at Fontainebleau, where he and his court returned faithfully in the fall for the hunting season. But it was Napoléon who made a Versailles, as it were, out of Fontainebleau, spending lavishly to restore it to its former glory. He held Pope Pius VII prisoner here in 1812, signed the second church–state concordat here in 1813, and, in the cobbled **Cour des Adieux** (Farewell Courtyard), said goodbye to his Old Guard on April 20, 1814, as he began his brief exile on the Mediterranean island of Elba. The famous **Horseshoe Staircase** that 49 dominates the **Cour des Adieux,** once the Cour du Cheval Blanc (White Horse Courtyard), was built by Androuet du Cerceau for Louis XIII (1610–43); it was down this staircase that Napoléon made his way slowly to take the salute of his loyal troops for the last time. Another court- 50 yard—the **Cour de la Fontaine** (Fountain Courtyard)—was commissioned by Napoléon in 1812 and adjoins the Étang des Carpes (Carp Pond). Across from the pond is the formal Parterre (flower garden) and, on the other side, the leafy Jardin Anglais (English Garden).

51 The **Porte Dauphine** is the most beautiful of the various gateways that connect the complex of buildings; its name commemorates the christening of the dauphin—the heir to the throne, later Louis XIII—under 52 its archway in 1606. The gateway fronts the **Cour Ovale** (Oval Court), 53 shaped like a flattened egg. Opposite the courtyard is the **Cour des Offices** (Offices Court), a large, severe square built at the same time as 54 place des Vosges in Paris (1609). Around the corner is the informal **Jardin de Diane** (Diana's Garden), with peacocks and a statue of the hunting goddess surrounded by mournful hounds. ✉ *Pl. du Général-de-Gaulle,* ☎ *01–60–71–50–70.* 🎫 *€5.50; gardens free.* ⏲ *Wed.–Mon. 9:30–5; gardens Apr.–Sept., daily 9–8:30; Oct.–Mar., daily 9–5.*

Dining and Lodging

$–$$ ✕ **La Route du Beaujolais.** The food is cheap and the welcome cheerful at Giorgio's jolly eatery near the château, where Lyonnais-style cold cuts and bottles of Beaujolais are the mainstays. For something a little more upscale, try the snails or beef fillet with Brie or choose from the wide choice of fish dishes. Prix-fixe meals are priced at €12, €14, and €21. ✉ *3 rue Montebello,* ☎ *01–64–22–27–98. AE, MC, V.*

$$$$ ★ ✕🏨 **Aigle Noir.** This may be Fontainebleau's costliest hotel, but you can't go wrong if you request one of the rooms overlooking either the garden or the château. They have late-18th- or early 19th-century reproduction furniture, creating a Napoleonic ambience. The restaurant, Le Beauharnais, serves subtle, imaginative cuisine—lamb with thyme and gentian, for instance. There's a tranquil garden for alfresco dining in summer. Reservations are essential and jacket and tie are required. ✉ *27 pl. Napoléon-Bonaparte, 77300,* ☎ *01–60–74–60–00,* FAX *01–60–74–60–01,* WEB *www.hotelaiglenoir.fr. 49 rooms, 7 suites. Restaurant, cable TV, minibars, pool, gym, sauna. AE, DC, MC, V.*

$$$ ✕🏨 **Napoléon.** Close to the château, this former post office counts as one of the best local hotels. Pastel-color rooms have modern furniture and marble baths and look out onto terraces or the indoor garden. The restaurant, La Table des Maréchaux, serves satisfying, deftly prepared classics, and the €23 menu is an excellent deal. ✉ *9 rue Grande, 77300,*

☎ *01–60–39–50–50,* FAX *01–64–22–20–87. 58 rooms. Restaurant, no air-conditioning, cable TV, minibars, no pets. AE, DC, MC, V.*

$$$ **Londres.** Established in 1850, the Londres is a small, family-style hotel with Louis XV accents. Some balconies overlook the château and the Cour des Adieux, where Napoléon bade his troops an emotional farewell. The austere 19th-century facade is a registered landmark. ✉ *1 pl. du Général-de-Gaulle, 77300,* ☎ *01–64–22–20–21,* FAX *01–60–72–39–16,* WEB *www.hoteldelondres.com. 11 rooms. Restaurant, bar, no air-conditioning, cable TV, Internet, no pets. AE, DC, MC, V. Closed 1 wk Aug. and mid-Dec.–early Jan.*

Outdoor Activities and Sports

The Forest of Fontainebleau is laced with hiking trails; for more information ask for the *Guide des Sentiers* (trail guide) at the tourist office. Bikes can be rented at the Fontainebleau-Avon train station. The forest is also famed for its fascinating rock formations, where many a novice alpinist first caught the climbing bug; for more information contact the **Club Alpin Français** (✉ 24 av. Laumière, 75019 Paris, ☎ 01–53–72–88–00).

Moret-sur-Loing

55 *10 km (6 mi) southeast of Fontainebleau via N6, 72 km (45 mi) southeast of Paris.*

Close to the confluence of the Seine and Yonne rivers is the village of Moret-sur-Loing. It was immortalized by Impressionist painter Alfred Sisley, who lived here for 20 years at 19 rue Montmartre (not open to the public), around the corner from the church. A narrow bridge, one of the oldest in France, leads across the Loing River (boat trips available) and provides a view of the village walls, rooftops, and church tower. If you've a sweet tooth, take note: Moret is renowned for its barley sugar.

Truculent World War I leader Georges Clemenceau (1841–1929), known as the Tiger, is the subject of a cozy museum at **La Grange-Batelière,** the thatched house in which he used to live. His taste for Asian art and his friendship with Impressionist Claude Monet are evoked here. ✉ *Access via rue du Peintre-Sisley,* ☎ *01–60–70–51–21.* 🎫 *Guided tours only, €5.50.* ⏲ *Easter–mid-Nov., weekends 3–6.*

Nightlife and the Arts

A good time to visit the town is on a Saturday evening in summer (from late June through early September) for the riverside **Festival,** when 600 locals stage son-et-lumière pageants illustrating the town's history. ☎ *01–60–70–41–66.* 🎫 *€12–15.*

Provins

56 *48 km (30 mi) northeast of Moret on N6/D403, 77 km (48 mi) southeast of Paris.*

On the hilltop site of a Roman camp, Provins developed into the third-largest town in France (after Paris and Rouen) in the Middle Ages as capital of the counts of Champagne, acquiring international renown for its fairs and as a rose-growing center. Provins has over 50 protected monuments bearing witness to its opulent past, including the 12th-century Gothic church of **St-Quiriace** with its incongruous 17th-century classical dome. There's plenty to see underground, too—a guided tour of the **Souterrains** takes in a small part of the 6 miles of tunnels that honeycomb the hill on which Provins is built (contact the tourist office Web site for details, www.provins.net).

Climb up to the **Tour César,** a round, ivy-covered 11th-century keep atop a sturdy mound, for a panoramic view of the town and some of the best-preserved medieval ramparts in France. ✉ *7 rue du Palais,* ☎ *01–64–01–40–19.* 🎫 *€3.05.* ⏲ *Apr.–Oct., daily 10–6; Nov.–Mar., daily 2–5.*

The vaulted 13th-century **Grange aux Dimes** (Tithe Barn), originally used as a covered market, houses a collection of waxwork displays evoking the crafts and merchants who brought medieval Provins wealth and fame, and shows a film retracing the town's history. ✉ *Rue St-Jean.* 🎫 *€3.05.* ⏲ *Apr.–Aug., daily 10–6; Sept.–Oct., daily 2–6.*

Dining and Lodging

$$–$$$ ✕🏨 **Aux Vieux-Remparts.** Set, as its name suggests, within the old town walls (or ramparts), this thriving establishment (seven new rooms were added in 2002) has plush-carpeted rooms with contemporary furniture overlooking the leafy inner garden, where you can dine outdoors on balmy summer evenings. Otherwise the delectable talents of young chef Lionel Sarre—ranging from grilled scallops to rose-petal soufflé—are showcased in the adjacent half-timber 16th-century restaurant. ✉ *3 rue Couverte, 77160,* ☎ *01–64–08–94–00,* FAX *01–60–67–77–22,* WEB *www.auxvieuxremparts.com. 32 rooms. Restaurant, bar, no air-conditioning, cable TV, minibars, Internet. AE, DC, MC, V. Closed 3 wks Jan. No lunch Mon.*

Nightlife and the Arts

Reconstituted jousting tournaments and a mock attack on the town walls using medieval war machines are held most weekend afternoons in summer; call the tourist office (☎ 01–64–60–26–26) for details.

ILE-DE-FRANCE A TO Z

To research prices, get advice from other travelers, and book travel arrangements, visit www.fodors.com.

AIRPORTS

Major airports in the Ile-de-France area are Charles de Gaulle, commonly known as Roissy, 25 km (16 mi) northeast of Paris, and Orly, 16 km (10 mi) south. Shuttle buses link Disneyland to the airports at Roissy, 56 km (35 mi) away, and Orly, 50 km (31 mi) distant; buses take 45 minutes and run every 45 minutes from Roissy, every 60 minutes from Orly (less frequently in low season), and cost €13.

➤ AIRPORT INFORMATION: **Charles de Gaulle** (☎ 01–48–62–22–80). **Orly** (☎ 01–49–75–15–15).

BUS TRAVEL

While many of the major sights in this chapter have train lines connecting them on direct routes with Paris, the lesser towns and destinations pose more of a problem. You often need to take a local bus after arriving at a train station (for instance, to get to Senlis from Chantilly Gare SNCF, or Fontainebleau from Avon Gare SNCF, or Vaux-le-Vicomte from Melun Gare SNCF, or Giverny from Vernon Gare SNCF). To reach villages in the Barbizon area, train it to Fontainebleau, then hook up with the local bus lines. Other buses travel outwards from Paris's suburbs—the No. 158A bus, for instance, which goes from Paris's La Défense to such destinations as St-Germain-en-Laye and Rueil-Malmaison.

➤ BUS INFORMATION: **SNCF** (☎ 08–36–35–35–35, WEB http://idf.sncf.fr/GB).

CAR RENTAL

Cars can be rented from agencies in Paris or at Orly or Charles de Gaulle airports.

CAR TRAVEL

A13 links Paris (from the Porte d'Auteuil) to Versailles. You can get to Chartres on A10 from Paris (Porte d'Orléans). For Fontainebleau take A6 from Paris (Porte d'Orléans), or for a more attractive route through the Forest of Sénart and the northern part of the Forest of Fontainebleau, take N6 from Paris (Porte de Charenton) via Melun. A4 runs from Paris (Porte de Bercy) to Disneyland. Although a comprehensive rail network ensures that most towns in Ile-de-France can make comfortable day trips from Paris, the only way to crisscross the region without returning to the capital is by car. There is no shortage of expressways or fast highways, but be prepared for delays close to Paris and during the morning and evening rush hours.

EMERGENCIES

The American Hospital and the British Hospital are closer to Paris, and other regional hospitals are listed by town below.

➤ CONTACTS: **Ambulance** (☎ 15). **American Hospital** in Neuilly (✉ 63 bd. Victor-Hugo, 01–47–45–71–00). **British Hospital** in Levallois-Perret (✉ 3 rue Barbès, ☎ 01–47–58–13–12). **Chartres** (✉ 34 rue du Dr-Maunoury, ☎ 02–37–30–30–30). **Melun** (✉ 2 rue Fréteau-de-Pény, ☎ 01–64–71–60–00). **Le Chesnay** (☎ 01–39–63–91–33). **Versailles** (✉ 177 rue de Versailles).

TOURS

Cityrama, Paris Vision, and American Express organize guided excursions to Giverny (€60) from April through October. Cityrama and Paris Vision run half- and full-day trips to Versailles (€34–72), Chartres, and Fontainebleau/Barbizon/Vaux-le-Vicomte (€47–53), some combined with Versailles (€85–90).

➤ CONTACTS: **American Express** (✉ 11 rue Scribe, Paris, 9e, ☎ 01–47–77–77–07). **Cityrama** (✉ 4 pl. des Pyramides, Paris 1er, ☎ 01–44–55–61–00, WEB www.cityrama.fr). **Paris Vision** (✉ 214 rue de Rivoli, Paris 1er, ☎ 01–47–42–72–31, WEB www.parisvision.com).

PRIVATE GUIDES

Alliance Autos has bilingual guides who can take you on a private tour around the Paris area in a luxury car or minibus for a minimum of four hours for about €80 an hour (call to check details and prices). Paris Bus Service runs minibus excursion to Versailles (€60) and Giverny (€70).

➤ CONTACTS: **Alliance Autos** (✉ 10 bis rue Jeanne-d'Arc, St-Mandé, métro: St-Mandé–Tourelle, ☎ 01–43–28–79–34). **Paris Bus Service** (✉ WEB www.touring-france.com/paris; ☎ contact your hotel for bookings).

TRAIN TRAVEL

Many sights can be reached by train from Paris. Both regional and mainline (Le Mans–bound) trains leave the Gare Montparnasse for Chartres (50–70 minutes); the former also stop at Versailles, Rambouillet, and Maintenon. Gare Montparnasse is also the terminal for trains to Dreux (Granville line) and for the suburban trains that stop at Montfort-L'Amaury, the nearest station to Thoiry (35 minutes).

Some mainline trains from Gare St-Lazare stop at Mantes-la-Jolie (30 minutes) and Vernon (45 minutes) on their way to Rouen and Le Havre. Suburban trains leave the Gare du Nord for L'Isle-Adam (50 minutes). Chantilly is on the main northbound line from Gare du Nord (the trip takes 25 minutes), and Senlis can be reached by bus from

Chantilly; Compiène can also be reached via train from Gare du Nord). Fontainebleau—or, rather, neighboring Avon, 2 km (1½ mi) away (there is frequent bus service)—is 45 minutes from Gare de Lyon. To reach Vaux-le-Vicomte, head first for Melun, then take a local bus; to reach Giverny, rail it to Melun, then use the local bus.

St-Germain-en-Laye is a terminal of the RER-A (commuter train) that tunnels through Paris (main stations at Étoile, Auber, Les Halles, and Gare de Lyon). The RER-A also accesses Poissy and Maisons-Laffitte and, at the other end, the station for Disneyland Paris (called Marne-la-Vallée–Chessy), within 100 yards of the entrance to both the theme park and Disney Village. Journey time is around 40 minutes, and trains operate every 10–30 minutes, depending on the time of day. The handiest of Versailles's three train stations is the one reached by the RER-C line (main stations at Austerlitz, St-Michel, Invalides, and Champ-de-Mars); the trip takes 30–40 minutes. Special *forfait* tickets, combining travel and admission, are available for several regional tourist destinations (including Versailles, Fontainebleau, and Auvers-sur-Oise).

A mainline TGV (Trains à Grande Vitesse) station links Disneyland to Lille, Lyon, Brussels, and London (via Lille and the Channel Tunnel).

➤ TRAIN INFORMATION: **SNCF** (☎ 08–36–35–35–35, WEB idf.sncf.fr/GB). **TGV** (WEB www.tgv.com).

VISITOR INFORMATION

Contact the Espace du Tourisme d'Ile-de-France (open Wednesday–Monday 10–7, www.pidf.com), under the inverted pyramid in the Carrousel du Louvre, for general information on the area. Information on Disneyland is available from the Disneyland Paris reservations office. Local tourist offices are listed below by town.

➤ TOURIST INFORMATION: **Espace du Tourisme d'Ile-de-France** (✉ Place de la Pyramide-Renversée, 99 rue de Rivoli, 75001 Paris, ☎ 08–03–81–80–00). **Disneyland Paris reservations office** (✉ B.P. 100, 77777 Marne-la-Vallée cedex 4, ☎ 01–60–30–60–30; 407/824–4321 in the U.S.). **Barbizon** (✉ 55 Grande-Rue, ☎ 01–60–66–41–87, WEB www.barbizon-france.com). **Chantilly** (✉ 60 av. du Maréchal-Joffre, ☎ 03–44–57–08–58, WEB www.ville-de-chantilly.fr). **Chartres** (✉ Pl. de la Cathédrale, ☎ 02–37–21–50–00, WEB www.ville-chartres.fr). **Fontainebleau** (✉ 4 rue Royale, ☎ 01–60–74–99–99, WEB www.fontinebleau.online.com). **Rambouillet** (✉ 1 pl. de la Libération, ☎ 01–34–83–21–21, WEB www.ot-rambouillet.fr). **St-Germain-en-Laye** (✉ 38 rue au Pain, ☎ 01–34–51–05–12, WEB www.ville-st-germain-en-laye.fr). **Senlis** (✉ Pl. du Parvis Notre-Dame, ☎ 03–44–53–06–40, WEB www.ville-senlis.fr). **Versailles** (✉ 2 bis av. de Paris, ☎ 01–39–24–88–88, WEB www.versailles.tourisme.fr).

4 THE LOIRE VALLEY

Strung like precious gems along the peaceful Loire and its tributaries, the royal and near-royal châteaux of the region are among the most fabled sights in France. From magical Chenonceau—improbably suspended above the River Cher—to mighty Chambord, from the *Sleeping Beauty* abode of Ussé to the famed gardens of Villandry, this parade of châteaux magnificently captures France's golden age of monarchy. In Orléans, a dramatic chapter in the country's history unfolds: it was here that Joan of Arc had her most rousing successes against the English.

Updated by Simon Hewitt

Introduction by Nancy Coons

A **DIAPHANOUS AURA OF SUBTLY SHIFTING LIGHT** plays over the luxuriant countryside of the Loire Valley, a region blessedly mild of climate, richly populated with game, and habitually fertile. Although it had always been viewed as prime real estate, when the dust from the Hundred Years' War began to settle and the bastions of the Plantagenet kings lost some of their utility, the victorious Valois dynasty began to see new possibilities in the territory: an ideal spot for a holiday home, they mused. Sketching, no doubt, on a tavern napkin at Blois, Louis XII dreamed of turrets and gargoyles, a tasteful blend of symmetry and fantasy, while Anne of Bretagne breathed down his neck for more closet space. In no time at all, the neighboring Joneses had kept up, and by the 16th century the area was a showplace of fabulous châteaux *d'agrément,* or pleasure castles—palaces for royalty, yes, but also love nests for mistresses and status statements for arrivistes (Chenonceau was built by a tax collector). There were boxwood gardens endlessly receding toward vanishing points, moats crowned with swans, parades of delicate cone-topped towers, frescoes, and fancywork ceilings. The glories of the Italian Renaissance, observed by the Valois while making war on their neighbor, were brought to bear on these megamonuments with all the elegance and proportions of antiquity.

By the time François I was in charge, extravagance knew no bounds: on a 13,000-acre forest estate, hunting parties at Chambord drew A-list crowds from the far reaches of Europe—and the availability of 430 rooms made weekend entertaining a snap. Queen Claudia hired only the most recherché Italian artisans: Chambord's famous double-helix staircase may, in fact, have been Leonardo da Vinci's design (he was a frequent houseguest when not in residence in a manor on the Amboise grounds). From massive kennels teeming with hunting hounds at Cheverny to luxurious stables at Chaumont-sur-Loire, from endless allées of pollarded lime trees at Villandry to the fairy-tale towers of Ussé—worthy of Sleeping Beauty herself—the Loire Valley became the power base and social center for the New France, allowing the monarchy to go all out in strutting its stuff.

All for good reason. In 1519 Charles V of Spain, at the age of 19, inherited the Holy Roman Empire, leaving François and his New France—as well as England's Henry VIII—out in the cold. It was perhaps no coincidence that in 1519 François, in a grand gesture of face-saving, commenced construction of his ultimate declaration of dominion, the gigantic châteaux of Chambord. After a few skirmishes (the Low Countries, Italy), and no doubt a few power breakfasts, François was cozy enough to entertain the emperor on his lavish Loire estates, and by 1539 he had married Charles V's sister.

Location is everything, as you realize when you think of Hyannisport, Kennebunkport, and Balmoral: homesteads redolent of dynasty, where natural beauty, idyllic views, an invigorating hunt with the boys, and a barefoot stroll in the great outdoors liberate the mind to think great thoughts and make history's decisions. Perhaps this is why French Revolution have-nots sacked so many of the châteaux of the Loire Valley; today most of them have been restored, and are maintained as museums in the public domain. Although these châteaux are testimony to France's most fabled age of kings, their once-restricted pleasures are now shared by the populace. Yet the Revolution and latter-day socialists have not totally erased a lingering gentility in the people of the region, characterized by an air of refined assurance far removed from the shoulder-shrugging, chest-tapping French stereotypes. Here life proceeds at a gentle, pleasant pace, and you'll find a winning concentration of gracious country inns and discerning chefs, a cornucopia of local produce and game, and the famous, flinty wines of Sancerre—all regional blessings still truly fit for a king.

Pleasures and Pastimes

Châteaux

Loire and *château* are almost synonymous; even the word *château*—part fortress, part palace, part mansion—has no English equivalent. More than 20 are described in this chapter, from grandiose Chambord and Saumur to the more intimate Cheverny and Azay-le-Rideau to the rousingly scenic Chenonceau and Ussé. There are genuine castles to admire, too—either preserved in full intimidating glory, such as Langeais, Loches, and Angers, or gloriously ruined, like Chinon. Still, these are but the crème de la crème—indeed, there are almost 400 châteaux in the region.

Dining

The Loire region, known as the Garden of France, produces a cornucopia of fine victuals—from beef, poultry, game, and fish, to butter, cream, wine, fruits, and vegetables (especially asparagus and mushrooms). It sends its early crops to the best Parisian tables, yet keeps more than enough for local use. Loire wines can be extremely good—and varied. Among the best are Savennières, Sancerre and Cheverny, dry whites; Coteaux du Layon and Montlouis, sweet whites; Cabernet d'Anjou, rosé; Bourgueil, Chinon, and Saumur-Champigny, reds; and Vouvray, white—dry, sweet, or sparkling.

CATEGORY	COST*
$$$$	over €30
$$$	€20–€30
$$	€12–€20
$	under €12

**per person for a main course only, including tax (19.6%); note that if a restaurant offers only prix-fixe (set-price) meals, it has been given the price category that reflects the full prix-fixe price*

Lodging

Even before the age of the railway, the Loire Valley drew gawkers from far afield, so there are hundreds of hotels of all types. At the higher end are converted châteaux, but even these are not as pricey as you might think. At the lower end are small, traditional inns in towns and villages, usually offering terrific value for the money. The Loire Valley is a very popular destination, so make reservations well in advance.

Assume all hotel rooms have air-conditioning, telephones, TV, and private bath unless otherwise noted.

CATEGORY	COST*
$$$$	over €180
$$$	€120–€180
$$	€60–€120
$	under €60

**All prices are for a standard double room in high season, including tax (19.6%) and service charge.*

Outdoor Activities

The Loire Valley offers a colorful rainbow of outdoor activities, from bicycling to picnicking to strolling across gently sloping hills or along riverbanks. The short distances between châteaux and other attractions make for pleasant bicycling even if you don't want to spend all day pedaling. Bicycles can be rented at many train stations.

Son-et-Lumière

In summer, concerts, music festivals, fairs, and celebrated son-et-lumière (sound-and-light) extravaganzas are held on the grounds of several châteaux. Dramatic spectacles mounted after dark, these son-et-lumière shows can take the form of historical pageants—with huge casts of people, all in period costume, and caparisoned horses, all floodlighted (some shows dramatically feature the shadows of flickering flames to conjure up the mobs of the French Revolution) and backed by music and commentary, sometimes in English; Amboise is the top (and these days, almost sole) example. Productions are more often shows with spoken commentary and dialogue but no visible figures, as at Chenonceau and Azay-le-Rideau.

Exploring the Loire Valley

Pick up the Loire River halfway along its course from central France to the Atlantic Ocean. Châteaux and vineyards will accompany you throughout a 340-km (210-mi) westbound course from the hilltop wine town of Sancerre to the bustling city of Angers. Lively towns punctuate the route at almost equal distances—Orléans, Blois, Tours, and Saumur—and are useful bases if you're relying on public transportation. But don't let the lack of a car prevent you from visiting and overnighting in the lovely villages of the region because a surprising number can be accessed via train, bus, or comfy taxi. Although you may be rushing around to see as many famous châteaux as possible, try to make time to walk through the poppy-covered hills, picnic along the riverbanks, and sample the local wines. If you want an escape from the usual tourist track, explore the lakes and forests of Sologne or wend your way back along the gentle (but confusingly spelled) Loir Valley.

Great Itineraries

You need two weeks to cover the Loire Valley region in its entirety. But even if you don't have that long, you can still see many of the Loire's finest châteaux in three days by concentrating on the area between Blois and Amboise. Six days will give you time to explore these châteaux in depth, as well as to visit Tours and Angers, two of the region's major cities. In 10 days you can follow the Loire from Orléans to Angers.

Numbers in the text correspond to numbers in the margin and on the Loire Valley, Orléans, and Tours maps.

IF YOU HAVE 3 DAYS

Gateway to the central Loire Valley, **Tours** ①–⑧ is the center hub of Touraine. While there are a few museums to catch and historic Place Plumereau beckons, don't tarry in this big city—begin your tour of some of France's choicest real estate by taking an easy train ride away to **Chenonceau** ⑫, everyone's dream of a Loire Valley castle. If you want your own taste of *la vie de châteaux,* backtrack on the train (or by car, of course) to **Montlouis-sur-Loire** ⑩ and the Broglie princes' gorgeous, neo-Renaissance Château de la Bourdaisière (a hotel but also open to day-trippers), or for a more urban treat, continue on to the north side of the Loire and **Blois** ⑰, where you'll find one of the earliest of the great châteaux. Spend the morning of your second day touring Blois, then move inland through the forest to spend the night at **Chambord** ⑮—such a vast marble pile it seems more a city than a palace. On your third day, return to Blois, then head downstream to **Amboise** ⑪ to take in its massive château and, more delightfully, the Clos-Lucé mansion, the last home of Leonardo da Vinci. If you hustle—and trains can make the journey in around an hour—head instead to the edge of Touraine and spectacular **Chinon** ㉓ for an unforgettable dip into the Middle Ages. Connecting trains from Chinon can get you back to Paris via Tours by night.

The Loire Valley

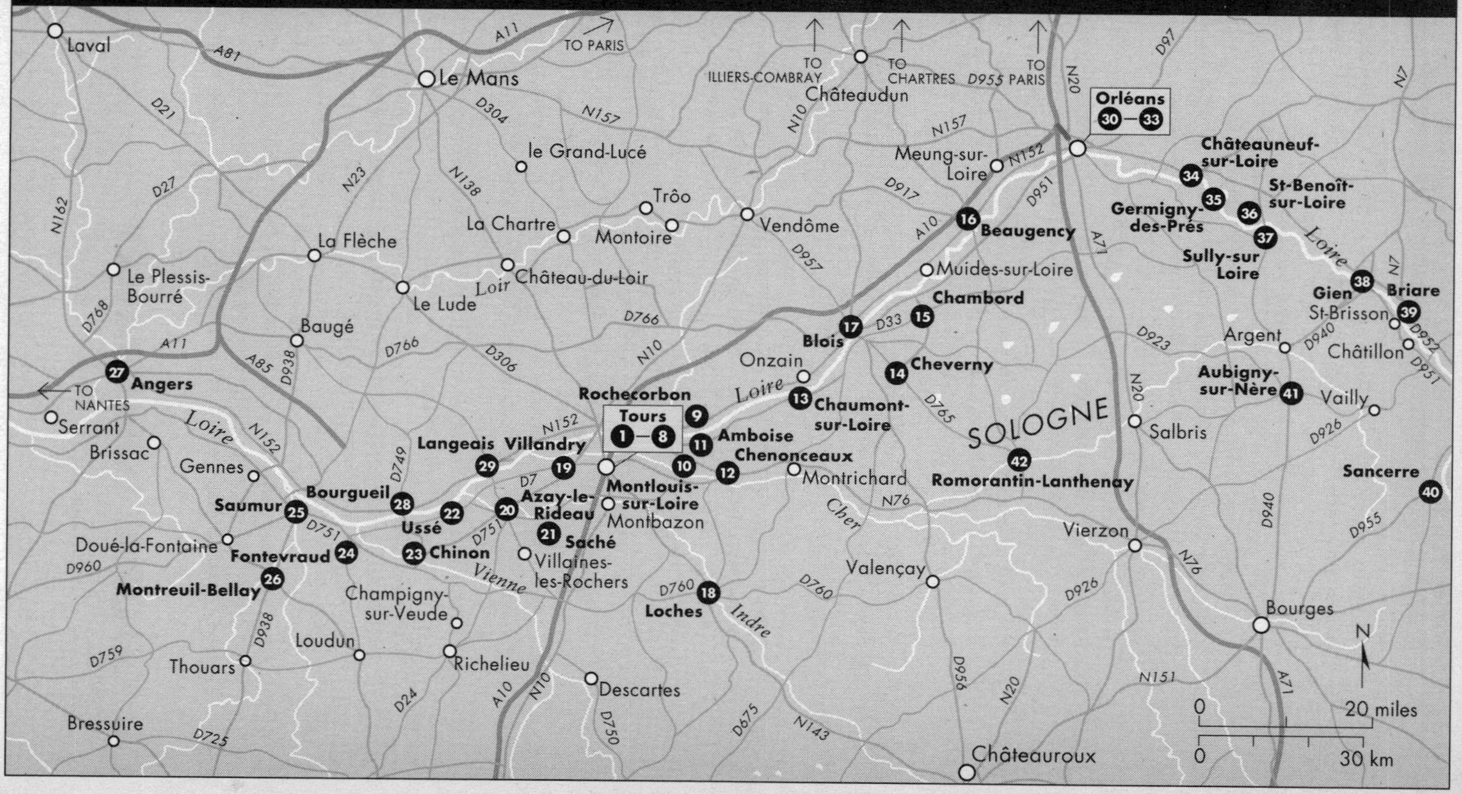

IF YOU HAVE 6 DAYS

Start by following the three-day itinerary. On the fourth day explore enchanting **Chinon** ㉓, then head east to see two of the dreamiest fairy-tale châteaux—the French Renaissance jewel that is **Azay-le-Rideau** ⑳ and, a few miles away (buses are rare, so consider a taxi), **Ussé** ㉒, which inspired Perrault to write *Sleeping Beauty.* On your fifth day, those without a car will need to return to Azay or Chinon, where you can then wend your way to magical **Fontevraud** ㉔, Europe's largest surviving abbey. After marveling at this Romanesque wonder, head to the great river town of **Saumur** ㉕, a posh place with a dramatic clifftop castle and fine train and bus connections.

IF YOU HAVE 10 DAYS

Follow the three- and six-day itineraries. After exploring Saumur on your sixth day, stop off in adjacent **Bourgueil** ㉘ to tour the vineyards or wine caves, making an overnight at the lovely Château de Reaux (save your pennies for this one; it is also open for touring by day-trippers). On your seventh day, a helpful train route can deposit you at the mighty citadel of **Langeais** ㉙, with a sumptuous, tapestried interior. In the afternoon, continue northeast back to Tours, then head out (via bus or taxi if you have no car) to spectacular **Villandry** ⑲, famed for its enormous Renaissance château and garden parterres. On your eighth day, backtrack to Tours and train it to **Orlèans** ㉚–㉝. After exploring this gateway city to the Upper Loire Valley and overnighting here, head out on your ninth morning to explore the region's sights—either the great abbey at **St-Benoît-sur-Loire** ㊱ or the storybook moated castle at **Sully-sur-Loire** ㊲ before ending up in the large town of **Gien** ㊳, famed for its earthenware, for the night. Or, for a dazzling splurge, head south by car or train to the French-Scottish town of **Aubigny-sur-Nère** ㊶ and enjoy a stay at the seignorial hotel, the Château de la Verrerie. On your final morning, visit the hilltop wine town of Sancerre. After lunch, head back to Orléans, Paris, and reality.

When to Tour the Loire Valley

The Loire, the last great European river left undammed, is at its best in May and June, when it still looks like a river; come midsummer, the water level drops, revealing unsightly sandbanks. The valley divides France in two, both geographically and climatically: north of the Loire, France has the moist, temperate climate of northern Europe; southward lies the drier climate of the Mediterranean. It's striking how often the weather can change as you cross the Loire. The valley can be sultry and stuffy in July and August, when most of the son-et-lumière shows take place, which also means that it is crowded at this time. October is a good off-season option, when all is mist and mellow fruitfulness along the Loire and the mysterious pools of the Sologne, and the trees are turning russet and gold. Fall is also the best time to sample regional specialties such as wild mushrooms and game. On Sunday, when most shops are closed, try to avoid the main cities—Orléans, Tours, and Angers.

THE CENTRAL LOIRE VALLEY

Halfway along the route of the Loire—the longest river in France—and just outside the city of Orléans, the river makes a wide, westward bend, gliding languidly through low, rich country known as the Val de Loire—the Loire Valley. In this temperate region—a 225-km (140-mi) stretch between Orléans and Angers—scores of châteaux built of local *tufa* (white limestone) rise from the rocky banks of the Loire and its tributaries: the rivers Cher, Indre, Vienne, and Loir (with no *e*).

The Loire is liquid history. For centuries the river was the area's principal means of transportation and an important barrier against invading armies. Towns arose at strategic bridgeheads, and fortresses—the earliest châteaux—appeared on towering slopes. The Loire Valley was hotly disputed by France and England during the Middle Ages; it belonged to England (under the Anjou Plantagenet family) between 1154 and 1216 and again during the Hundred Years' War (1337–1453). It was the example of Joan of Arc, the Maid of Orléans (so called after the scene of her most stirring victories), that crystallized French efforts to expel the English.

The Loire Valley's golden age came under François I (ruled 1515–47), the flamboyant contemporary of England's Henry VIII. His salamander emblem can be seen in many châteaux, including Chambord, the mightiest one. Although the nation's power base shifted to Paris around 1600, aristocrats continued to erect luxurious palaces along the Loire until the end of the 18th century.

Tours, the capital city of the province of Touraine, is the gateway to the entire region, not only for its central position but because the TGV high-speed train can deposit you there from Paris in little more than an hour. A string of fine châteaux dominates the valley east of Tours—Blois, Chaumont, and Amboise lead the way—but two of the area's most stunning monuments lie inland: romantic Chenonceau, with its arches half-straddling the River Cher, and colossal Chambord, its forest of chimneys and turrets visible above the treetops. By heading westward from Tours, on the other hand, you enter the storybook region par excellence, address to such fairy-tale châteaux as Ussé and Azay-le-Rideau and the more muscular castles of Chinon and Saumur. At Angers you can drive northeast to explore the winding, intimate Loir Valley all the way to Châteaudun, just south of Chartres and the Ile-de-France; or continue along the Loire as far as Nantes, the southern gateway to Brittany.

Tours

240 km (150 mi) southwest of Paris, 112 km (70 mi) southwest of Orléans, 39 km (24 mi) northwest of Loches via N143.

Little remains of Tours's château—one of France's finest cathedrals more than compensates—but the city remains the transportation hub of the Loire Valley. Trains from Tours (and from its adjacent terminal at St-Pierre-de-Corps) run along the river in both directions, and regular bus services radiate from here; in addition, the city is the starting point for organized bus excursions (many with English-speaking guides). The town has mushroomed into a city of a quarter of a million inhabitants, with an ugly modern sprawl of factories, high-rise blocks, and overhead expressway junctions cluttering up the outskirts. But the timber-frame houses in **Le Vieux Tours** (Old Tours), the attractive medieval center around place Plumereau, were smartly restored after extensive damage in World War II. Considering that several of the Loire Valley's most celebrated hotels are just a few minutes outside of Tours (and reachable by train, bus, and taxi), many travelers opt to make the city center a day-trip only.

1 Only two sturdy towers—the Tour Charlemagne and the Tour de l'Horloge (Clock Tower)—remain of the medieval abbey, the **Basilique St-Martin,** that once dominated the heart of the city. Old wall paintings and Romanesque sculptures are on display in the small museum housed in a restored 13th-century chapel that adjoined the abbey cloisters. Here, the life of St. Martin and the history of the abbey, de-

Aquarium 6
Basilique St-Martin 1
Cathédrale St-Gatien 7
Hotêl Goüin et Musée Archéologique .4
Musée des Beaux-Arts 8
Musée du Compagnonnage/ Musée du Vin 5
Musée du Gemmail 3
Place Plumereau 2

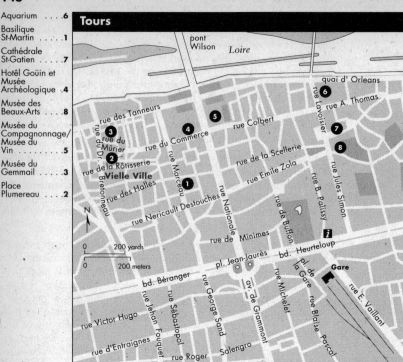

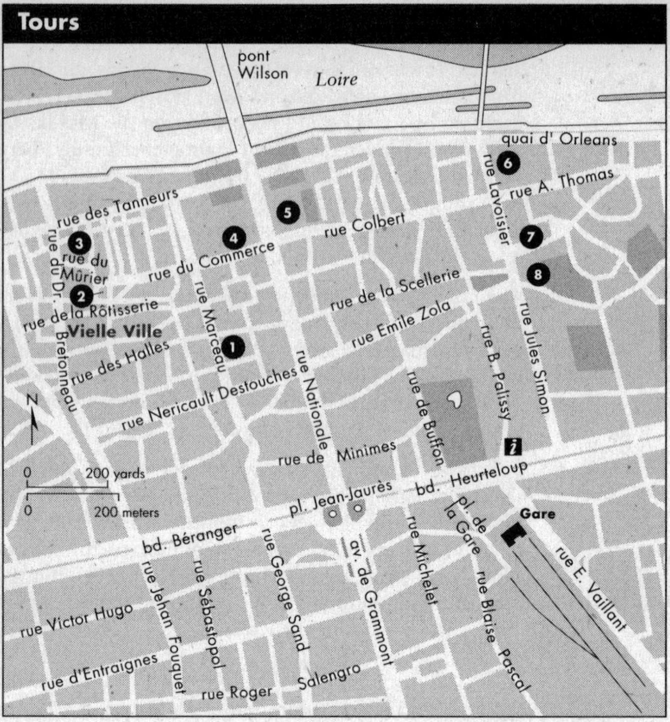

stroyed in 1802 and since replaced by a bombastic neo-Byzantine basilica, are retraced. ✉ *3 rue Rapin,* ☎ *02–47–05–63–87.* 🎫 *Free.* ⏲ *Mid-Mar.–mid-Nov., Wed.–Sun. 9:30–12:30 and 2–5:30.*

North from the Basilique St-Martin to the river is **Le Vieux Tours,** the lovely old medieval quarter. A warren of quaint streets, wood-beamed houses, and grand mansions once home to 15th-century merchants, it is now gentrified with chic apartments and pedestrianized streets—Tours's college students and tourists alike love to sit at the cafés lin-

❷ ing **Place Plumereau,** once the town's *carroi aux chapeaux* (hat market). Lining the square, Nos. 1 through 7 form a magnificent series of half-timbered houses; Note the woodcarvings of royal moneylenders on Nos. 11 and 12. At No. 17 find the back entrance to the medieval-era **Garden of St-Pierre-le-Puellier.** Running off the square are other streets adorned with historic houses, notably rue Briçonnet—No. 16 is the **Maison de Tristan** with a noted medieval staircase. ✉ *Bordered by rues du Commerce, Briçonnet, de la Monnaie, and du Grand Marche.*

❸ The **Musée du Gemmail,** in the imposing 19th-century Hôtel Raimbault, contains an unusual collection of three-dimensional colored-glass window panels. Depicting patterns, figures, and even portraits, the panels are both beautiful and intriguing, since most of the gemlike fragments of glass come from broken bottles. Incidentally, Jean Cocteau coined the word *gemmail* by combining *gemme* (gem) with *émail* (enamel). ✉ *7 rue du Mûrier,* ☎ *02–47–61–01–19,* WEB *www.gemmail.com.* 🎫 *€5.* ⏲ *Apr.–mid-Nov., Tues.–Sun. 10–noon and 2–6:30; mid-Nov.–Dec., weekends 10–noon and 2–6:30.*

❹ The **Hôtel Goüin et Musée Archéologique** is set in Tours's most extravagant example of early Renaissance domestic architecture (too bad its immediate vicinity was among the hardest hit by German bombs), its facade covered with carvings that seemed to have grown like topsy. Inside are assorted oddities ranging from ancient Roman finds to the scientific collection of Dupin de Chenonceau (owner of the great château in the 18th century). ✉ *25 rue du Commerce,* ☎ *02–47–66–22–32.* 🎫 *€3.* ⏲ *Mid-May–Sept., daily 10–7; mid-Mar.–mid-May, daily 10–12:30 and 2–6:30; Oct.–Nov., Jan–mid-Mar., daily 10–12:30 and 2–5:30. Closed Dec.*

❺ The **Musée du Compagnonnage** (Guild Museum) and the **Musée du Vin** (Wine Museum) are both in the cloisters of the 13th-century church of St-Julien. *Compagnonnage* is a sort of apprenticeship–cum–trade union system, and here you see the masterpieces of the candidates for guild membership: virtuoso craft work, some of it eccentric (an Eiffel Tower made of slate, for instance, or a varnished-noodle château). ✉ *8 rue Nationale,* ☎ *02–47–61–07–93.* 🎫 *Musée du Compagnonnage €4, Musée du Vin €2.50; joint ticket €4.60.* ⏲ *Wed.–Mon. 9–noon and 2–6.*

❻ Just alongside Tours's château ruins you will find the **Aquarium** and a painting exhibit center. ✉ *25 av. André-Malraux,* ☎ *02–47–64–29–52.* 🎫 *€5.* ⏲ *Daily 9–noon and 2–6.*

★ ❼ The **Cathédrale St-Gatien,** built between 1239 and 1484, reveals a mixture of architectural styles. The richly sculpted stonework of its majestic, soaring, two-tower facade betrays the Renaissance influence on local château-trained craftsmen. The stained glass dates from the 13th century (if you have binoculars, bring them). Also take a look at the little tomb with kneeling angels built in memory of Charles VIII and Anne of Brittany's two children; and the **Cloître de La Psalette** (cloister), on the south side of the cathedral. ✉ *Rue Lavoisier,* ☎ *02–47–47–05–19.* ⏲ *Daily 8–noon and 2–6.*

❽ The **Musée des Beaux-Arts** (Fine Arts Museum), in what was once the archbishop's palace, has an eclectic selection of treasures: furniture, sculpture, wrought-iron work, and pieces by Rubens, Rembrandt, Boucher, Degas, and Calder. It even displays Fritz the Elephant, stuffed in 1902. ✉ *18 pl. François-Sicard,* ☎ *02–47–05–68–73.* 🎫 *€4.* ⏲ *Wed.–Mon. 9–12:45 and 2–5:45.*

Dining and Lodging

$$ ✕ **Les Tuffeaux.** This restaurant, between the cathedral and the Loire, is the city's best value. Chef Gildas Marsollier wins customers with delicious fennel-perfumed salmon, oysters in an egg sauce seasoned with Roquefort, and remarkable desserts. Gentle lighting and wood-beam and stone-wall decor provide a soothing background. ✉ *19 rue Lavoisier,* ☎ *02–47–47–19–89. MC, V. Closed Sun. No lunch Mon.*

$$$$ ★ ✕🏨 **Jean Bardet.** King of Touranegeaux chefs, Jean Bardet has a propensity for quoting philosophers, is as happy as a rabbit in a garden (as he puts it), and is celebrated for showcasing exotic fruits and vegetables in his signature creations. Specials served up in his plush yellow dining salon on his eight-course, €104 *menu dégustation* (tasting menu) and on the super-expensive à la carte menu might include pigeon with foie gras in cabbage-leaf papillote, baby eel in red wine, oysters poached in Muscadet on a puree of watercress, or roast lobster with duck gizzards (reservations are essential; lunch is not served Saturday, Monday, or Tuesday; there's no dinner Monday from November through March). If you want to enjoy that ultimate luxury—a breakfast masterminded by Bardet—book one of the guest rooms upstairs at this stately Directoire-style mansion; all luxuriously mix-and-match antiques and modern touches in that distinctive Relais & Châteaux way. ✉ *Château de Belmont, 57 rue Groison, 37100,* ☎ *02–*

47–41–41–11, FAX *02–47–51–68–72,* WEB *www.jeanbardet.com. 16 rooms, 5 suites. Restaurant, cable TV, minibars, pool. AE, DC, MC, V. Closed Sun. evening and Mon., Nov.–Mar.*

$$$ ★ **Domaine de la Tortinière.** South of Tours and set atop a vast and sloping lawn, this picture-perfect, toy-sized, neo-Gothic château comes complete with two fairy-tale donjons (towers) and a heated, terraced pool. Guest rooms in the main building, built in 1861, convey quiet, rustic luxury; the conversation pieces are those in the two turrets, while others delight with charmingly beamed ceilings. No. 15, though small, is particularly pleasant and quiet. Most beds are so comfy it's a shame to wake up in them. The rotunda-shape restaurant overlooks the Indre River, and Freddy Lefebvre's cuisine includes roast pigeon in spices and lobster bisque with a pastry top (no dinner Sunday November through March). The picturesque park is covered with cyclamen at times, and includes a path that was once a Roman road. ✉ *10 rte. de Ballan, 37250 Veigné (12 km/7 mi south of Tours),* ☎ *02–47–34–35–00,* FAX *02–47–65–95–70,* WEB *www.tortiniere.com. 29 rooms. Restaurant, no air-conditioning in some rooms, cable TV, minibars, tennis court, pool, no pets. MC, V. Closed mid-Dec.–end of Feb.*

Rochecorbon

❾ *3 km (1 ½ mi) east of Tours on the north bank of the Loire.*

Delightfully, this tiny little town is almost as replete with attractions as its big-city neighbor, Tours. Spread out along the Loire-bank N152 road, with a tiny center set with a church and several fine restaurants, Rochecorbon is noted for its cliffs of quaintly curious troglodyte dwellings—caves-cum-cottages sculpted out of tufa, that milky-white porous stone that lined so many of the Loire Valley cliffs (and was used to built so many great châteaux). If you can't stay at the town's famous hotel, the troglodyte Domaine des Hautes Roches, you can visit ★ the subterranean splendor of the **Manoir des Basses-Rivières,** an adorable mini-estate carved into the river rockface and residence of the 17th-century Marquis de Doisonville. Complete with Trianon-elegant pavilion (emerging from the brute rock) and geranium-bedecked gardens, the main house is threaded by a walkway and medieval staircases that take you through, and over, the cave-like chambers, where wine was once produced by the Marmoutier monks. ✉ *24 quai de la Loire,* ☎ *02–47–52–80–99.* *€4.20.* ⏲ *July–Aug., daily 2–7; Apr.–June, Sept., weekends 2–7.*

Not far from the Manoir des Basses-Rivières are **Les Caves Rupestres,** an abandoned 600-year-old quarry now carved, in a folkloric-modern manner, with 34 wall bas-reliefs detailing the legends of wine in the region, which you can admire with a glass of the grape in your hand. ✉ *Rue Vaufoynard,* ☎ *02–47–52–57–58.* *€5.30.* ⏲ *Apr., weekends 2–6; May–June, Sept.–Oct., daily 2–6; July–Aug., daily 10:30–7.*

Rochecorbon also makes its own wines, and you can explore a vast group of underground galeries at the **Grandes Caves Saint-Roch.** Learn about the extraction of tufa stone, the methods of cave mushroom-growing and silkworm-production, and taste the Blanc-Foussy whites. ✉ *65 quai de la Loire,* ☎ *02–47–52–57–70.* *€3.* ⏲ *Call ahead for details.*

Rochecorbon is the only place from which you can actually take a boat-ride excursion out on the Loire. The hour-long **Bateau-Promenade** glides you along a magnificently tranquil stretch of the river. Although the commentary on the boat is in French, the sights—riverside caves, deserted towers, distant châteaux (like Moncontour, made famous by

Balzac)—make for a most enjoyable outing. ✉ *Observatoire–56 quai de la Loire,* ☎ *02–47–52–68–88.* €8. *July–Aug., daily 3, 4, and 5* PM; *May–June, Sept., weekends 4 and 5* PM.

Dining and Lodging

$$$–$$$$ ★ ✕ **Domaine des Hautes Roches.** *Extraordinaire* is the word for some of luxe-troglodyte rooms at this famous hotel, which stud a towering cliff-face with their elegant sash windows, gas-lantern lamps, and finished marble steps. Don't expect decor à la Fred Flintstone: half the guest-room walls are Ice-Age, but stylish fabrics, Louis Treize chairs, and carved fireplaces are the main allurements. Some prefer rooms in the regular house—no rock-quarry drama, but super-comfortable and exquisitely air-conditioned all the same. The restaurant terrace enchants with wonders like an appetizer panoply of various foie gras, delectable fish and duck, and desserts that are architectonic creations, making this one of the best kitchens in the Loire, if not France. To top it all off, a sapphire pool tempts all during the Loire's *grandes chaleurs.* ✉ *86 quai de la Loire, 37210 Rochecorbon,* ☎ *02–47–52–88–88,* FAX *02–47–52–81–30. 29 rooms, 3 suites. Restaurant, cable TV, minibars, pool. AE, DC, MC, V. Closed end-Jan.–mid-Mar.*

Montlouis-sur-Loire

⑩ *10 km (7 mi) east of Tours on the south bank of the Loire.*

Like Vouvray—its sister town on the north side of the Loire River—Montlouis is noted for its white wines. The outskirts of the town are largely suburban but around the river quais are some historic finds—a church begun in the 12th century, the Renaissance-era Ramée mansion—although on place Courtemanche the **Cave Touristique** will allow you to learn all about the fine vintages produced by the winegrowers of Montlouis. On the eastern border of the town is one of the most alluring, yet least-known, châteaux of the region, **La Bourdaisière.** While open to day-trippers for guided tours, this once-royal retreat and birthplace of noted 17th-century courtesan Gabrielle d'Estreaes is today the enchanted hotel-domain of the princes de Broglie.

Dining and Lodging

$$$–$$$$ ★ ✕ **Château de la Bourdaisière.** Few other hotels so superbly capture the magic of *la vie de château* as this 100-carat jewel. A neo-Renaissance castle atop a picture-perfect hill, this was once the favored retreat of two kings, François I and Henri IV. Today the presiding spirits are just slightly less royal: brothers Princes Philippe-Maurice and Louis-Albert de Broglie, whose aristocratic clan knows more than a few things about high-style hospitality. Inside, ancient family portraits, an immense marble fireplace, and large bouquets designed by Louis-Albert—a famed gardener, who cultivates 400 types of tomatoes in the château's *potager*—allure. Guest rooms range from *François-Premier*—a timber-roof cottage blown up to ballroom dimensions—to more standard-issue salons (garden-view rooms away from the gravel driveway are best). Other rooms are found in an adjoining 17th-century pavilion fitted out with a small eatery that serves up dazzling salads and confections (lunch only, June–September). As you'll find, sitting by the gigantic pool hidden near the Renaissance-style gardens, La Bourdaisière makes a truly exquisite base for exploring the Loire. ✉ *37270 Montlouis-sur-Loire,* ☎ *02–47–45–16–31,* FAX *02–47–45–09–11,* WEB *www.chateaulabourdaisiere.com. 20 rooms. Restaurant, no air-conditioning, no room TV, pool, tennis court, shop, meeting rooms. MC, V. Closed Nov. 15–Mar. 15.*

Amboise

11 *17 km (11 mi) southwest of Chaumont-sur-Loire via D751, 26 km (16 mi) east of Tours.*

Artifacts from the life of Leonardo da Vinci, a château overlooking the Loire, bustling markets, narrow medieval streets, and plenty of hotels and restaurants make Amboise one of the more popular towns along the river. The **Château d'Amboise** became a royal palace in the 15th and 16th centuries. Charles VII stayed here, as did the unfortunate Charles VIII, best remembered for banging his head on a low doorway lintel (you will be shown it) and dying as a result. François I, whose long nose appears in so many château paintings, based his court here, welcoming the Italian Renaissance to France by inviting Leonardo da Vinci to be his guest here. The castle was also the stage for the Amboise Conspiracy, an ill-fated Protestant plot organized against François II; you are shown where the corpses of 1,200 conspirators dangled from the castle walls. The château's interior is, unfortunately, forlorn in the extreme, but don't miss the lovely grounds, adorned with a Flamboyant Gothic gem, the little chapel of St-Hubert with its carvings of the Virgin and Child, Charles VIII, and Anne of Brittany. ☎ *02–47–57–00–98,* WEB *www.chateau-amboise.tm.fr.* 🎫 *€6.50.* ⏲ *Oct.–Mar., daily 9–noon and 2–5; Apr.–June and Sept., daily 9–6; July–Aug., daily 9–7.*

The **Clos Lucé,** a few hundred yards up rue Victor-Hugo from the château, is a handsome Renaissance manor where Leonardo da Vinci (1452–1519) spent the last four years of his life. The basement contains working models, built by IBM engineers using the detailed sketches in the artist's notebooks, of some of Leonardo's extraordinary inventions; by this time, Leonardo had put away his paint box because of arthritis. Mechanisms on display include three-speed gearboxes, a military tank, a clockwork car, and even a flying machine complete with designs for parachutes. Cloux, the house's original name, was given to Anne of Brittany by Charles VIII, who built a chapel for her that is still here. Some of the house's furnishings are authentic to the 16th century, but Leonardo's *Mona Lisa* and *Virgin of the Rocks,* both of which graced the walls here, were bought by his patron, François I, who then moved them to the Louvre. ✉ *2 rue du Clos-Lucé,* ☎ *02–47–57–62–88.* 🎫 *€6.50.* ⏲ *Sept.–June, daily 9–6; July–Aug., daily 9–7.*

Just 3 km (2 mi) south of Amboise on the road to Chenonceaux, the **Pagode de Chanteloup** is an eye-knocking sight—a 140-ft, seven-story Chinese-style lakeside pagoda built for the Duke of Choiseul in 1775. Children will adore puffing their way to the top, although some adults will not fancy the vertigo-inducing views. Sadly, the adjoining park is the worst for wear. ✉ *Rte de Bléré,* ☎ *02–47–57–20–97.* 🎫 *€6.* ⏲ *May–Sept., daily 10–6:30; Oct.–mid-Nov. and mid-Feb.–Apr., daily 10–noon and 2–5.*

Dining and Lodging

$$$ ✕🏨 **Choiseul.** Classical elegance and a formal pink-and-gold restaurant characterize this 18th-century Relais & Châteaux hotel on the bank of the Loire, just below the château. Though rooms are modern, they retain an old and distinctive feel. The highly rated chef, Pascal Bouvier, cooks up such specialties as lobster in pastry and beef with truffles. Prix-fixe menus start at €31 at lunch and €46 at dinner. ✉ *36 quai Charles-Guinot, 37400,* ☎ *02–47–30–45–45,* FAX *02–47–30–46–10,* WEB *www.choiseul.com. 29 rooms, 3 suites. Restaurant, cable TV, minibars, pool. AE, DC, MC, V. Closed Dec.–Feb.*

$ ✕🏨 **Blason.** Two blocks behind Château d'Amboise and a five-minute walk from the town center, this small hotel is enlivened by its enthusiastic owners. The old building has rooms of different shapes and sizes: No. 229, for example, has exposed beams and a cathedral ceiling; No. 109 is comfortably spacious and has a good view of the square. In the restaurant, superior, reasonably priced seasonal fare is served—roast lamb with garlic, and salmon carpaccio with mustard dressing, for instance. ✉ *11 pl. Richelieu, 37400,* ☎ *02–47–23–22–41,* FAX *02–47–57–56–18. 28 rooms. Restaurant, no room phones, no room TV. AE, DC, MC, V. Closed mid-Jan.–mid-Feb.*

$$–$$$ ★ 🏨 **Vieux Manoir.** An adorable manor house, this is the creation of Gloria Belknap—a Boston Brahmin whose immense style Edith Wharton, that noted Francophile, would have cottoned to immediately. Gloria seems to have missed her calling as a decorator extraordinaire: *toile-de-Jouy* screens, gilt-framed paintings, comfy Napoléon III covered-in-jute armchairs, fascinatingly time-worn armoires, and tables adorned with Shaker baskets make this place *House & Garden*–worthy. Each guest room is a delight: a bleached redbrick chimney and red-and-white calico accent one, while ceiling beams and a French provincial four-poster warm another. Larger groups can move into a separate (and proportionately pricier) 17th-century cottage, a cosseting maison filled with antiques, wood beams, and much charm. But you'll probably spend more time in the book-filled library or in the fireplace-warmed main salon—soaking up the wit and wisdom of Gloria and hubby Bob—or in the pretty garden, whose trees and fountain would have tempted Monet to set up his easel. Ask Gloria for great tips and restaurant finds; her garden-conservatory breakfasts are great and included in the room rate. ✉ *13 rue Rabelais, 37400,* ☎ FAX *02–47–30–41–27,* WEB *www.le-vieux-manoir.com. 6 rooms, 1 cottage. No air-conditioning, no room TV. No credit cards.*

Chenonceaux

⓬ *10 km (7 mi) southeast of Amboise via D131 and D140, 32 km (20 mi) east of Tours.*

★ The village of Chenonceaux, on the River Cher, is best known as the site of the **Château de Chenonceau** (without the *x*). Fabled retreat for the likes of Diane de Poitiers, Catherine de' Medici, and Mary, Queen of Scots, it has long been considered the "most romantic" of all the Loire châteaux, thanks in part to its showpiece—a breathtaking *galerie de bal* which spans the River Cher like a bridge (famously used as a escape point for French Resistance fighters during World War II, since all other crossings had been bombed). You could happily spend half a day wandering through the château and grounds. During the peak summer season the château is open—unlike many others—all day. The only drawback is its popularity: if you want to avoid a roomful of schoolchildren, take a stroll on the grounds and come back to the house at lunchtime.

More pleasure-palace than fortress, the château was built in 1520 by Thomas Bohier, a wealthy tax collector, for his wife, Catherine Briçonnet. When he went bankrupt, it passed to François I. Later, Henri II gave it to his mistress, Diane de Poitiers. After his death, Henri's not-so-understanding widow, Catherine de' Medici, expelled Diane to nearby Chaumont and took back the château. Before this time, Diane's five-arched bridge over the River Cher was simply meant as a grand ceremonial entryway leading to a gigantic château, a building never constructed. It was to Catherine, and her architect, Philibert de l'Orme, that historians owe the audacious plan to transform the bridge itself into the most unusual château in France. Two stories were constructed, including an enormous gallery that runs from one end of the château to the other—a grand space that became the stage set for some legendary galas. July and August are the peak months at Chenonceau: only then can you exit at the far end of the gallery to walk along the opposite bank (weekends only), rent a rowboat to spend an hour just drifting in the river where Diane used to enjoy her morning dips, and enjoy an excellent **son-et-lumière,** performed in the illuminated château gardens.

Before you go inside, pick up an English-language leaflet at the gate. Then walk around to the right of the main building to see the harmonious, delicate architecture beyond the formal garden (the southern part belonged to Diane de Poitiers, the northern was Catherine's) with the river gliding under the arches. Inside the château are splendid ceilings, colossal fireplaces, scattered furnishings, and paintings by Rubens, del Sarto, and Correggio. The curatorial staff have delightfully dispensed with velvet ropes and adorned some of the rooms with bouquets designed in 17th-century style. As you tour the salons, be sure to pay your respects to former owner Madame Dupin, tellingly captured in Nattier's charming portrait: thanks to the great affection she inspired among her proletarian neighbors, the château and its treasures survived the Revolution intact. The château's history is illustrated with wax figures in the **Musée des Cires** (Waxwork Museum) in one of the château's outbuildings. A cafeteria, tea room, and the Orangerie restaurant handle the crowds. ☎ *02–47–23–90–07,* WEB *www.chenonceau.com.* 💶 *Château €7.60; Waxwork Museum €3; son-et-lumière €8.* ⏲ *Feb.–May and Oct.–mid-Nov., daily 9–5:30; June–Sept., daily 9–7; Dec.–Jan., daily 9–4:30.*

Dining and Lodging

$$–$$$ ✕🏨 **Bon Laboureur.** In 1882 this ivy-covered inn won Henry James's praise as a simple, rustic place. Since then it has passed through four generations of the Jeudi family, and now, under Antoine, it is an elegantly modern hotel. Rooms in the old house are comfortably traditional; those in the former stables are larger and more contemporary; the biggest and most elegant are in the manor house across the street. Jean-Marie Burnet's stylish cuisine ranges from cream of crayfish with basil to pike-perch with spices and turbot with red pepper and fennel. ✉ *6 rue du Dr-Bretonneau, 37150,* ☎ *02–47–23–90–02,* FAX *02–47–23–82–01. 22 rooms, 5 suites. Restaurant, no air-conditioning, cable TV, minibars, pool, bicycles. AE, DC, MC, V. Closed Jan.–mid-Feb. and mid-Nov.–mid-Dec.*

$$ ★ ✕🏨 **Roseraie.** The Bon Laboureur may be Chenonceaux's most famous hostelry, but this is probably its most charming, thanks in part to the joyful welcome of its English-speaking hosts, Laurent and Sophie Fiorito. But let's not forget the guest rooms, many of which are enchantingly designed with florals, checks, and lace, or the copious meals served in the rustic dining room (where foie gras, duck with fruit and honey, and apple-tart are among the specialties) or the gorgeous pool. Try to get a garden-side room; if car traffic bothers you, avoid those overlooking the main street. ✉ *7 rue du Dr-Bretonneau, 37150,* ☎ *02–47–23–90–09,* FAX *02–47–23–91–59,* WEB *www.charminghotel.com. 17 rooms. Restaurant, no air-conditioning, cable TV, pool. AE, DC, MC, V. Closed mid-Nov.–end Feb.*

$–$$ ✕🏨 **Le Relais Chenonceaux.** The welcome is sunny, the food yummy, the restaurant rustique, and the location—smack dab in the middle of the little town—convenient. The guest rooms upstairs are cozy and quaint, but several a bit too much so, thanks to tilted mansard roofs (they trap hot air in the summer), so ask for a room without one and off the main drag. Big plus here: the friendly staff. ✉ *10 rue du Dr-Bretonneau, 37150,* ☎ *02–47–23–98–11,* FAX *02–47–23–84–07. 8 rooms. Restaurant, no air-conditioning, no room phones. MC, V.*

Chaumont-sur-Loire

13 *21 km (13 mi) northeast of Chenonceaux, 21 km (13 mi) southwest of Blois via D751.*

Set on a bluff that towers over the river, Chaumont is best known for its sturdy castle with its famous stables and magnificent panorama of the Loire. Built between 1465 and 1510, the **Château de Chaumont** (access is up a steep, lengthy ramp, over a double-drawbridge, and through a glorious, twin-towered *châtelet*) was given to Henri II's mistress, Diane de Poitiers, by his wife, Catherine de' Medici, to get her out of the Château de Chenonceau; in one of the bell-tower rooms the queen mother reputedly practiced sorcery, and foresaw the tragic deaths of her three sons in her magic mirror. If Catherine didn't appreciate many of the beauties of Chaumont, neither did the writer Madame de Staël, but then she was exiled here from her beloved Paris by Napoléon. Still, she must have fallen under its spell, because she wrote *De l'Allemagne* (*On Germany*) here, a book that all but created the Romantic movement in France. In the 19th century her descendants, the prince and princess de Broglie, set up shop in a superextravagant way, as you can still see from the stone-and-brick stables, where pure-bred horses (and one elephant) lived like royalty in velvet-lined stalls. The **Festival International des Jardins** held July to October every year in the extensive park showcases the latest in horticultural inventiveness. ☎ *02–54–51–26–26,* WEB *www.chaumont-jardins.com.* €6. *Mid-Mar.–mid-Oct., daily 9:30–6; mid-Oct.–mid-Mar., daily 10–5.*

Dining and Lodging

$$$$ ★ **Domaine des Hauts-de-Loire.** Long a landmark of Loire luxe, this aristocratic yet oh-so-unpretentious outpost is located across the river from Chaumont and some 4 km (2 mi) inland. Set in an 18th-century turreted, vine-covered hunting lodge, it comes with the requisite grand salon furnished with 18th-century antiques, a lovely pool, an adorable swan lake, 180 acres of forest for hikes, and the most blissful air-conditioning in all Touraine. Guest rooms are beige, suave, and tranquil, those in the adjacent carriage houses a mix of old and modern furnishings that harmonize with the spectacular exposed brick walls and gabled ceilings. Thanks to the owners, the Bonnegal family, service here is "just as it should be." The restaurant (closed Monday and no lunch Tuesday off-season) glows with mellow lights, white bouquets, and some of the most truly dazzling food around. ✉ *Rte. de Mesland, 41150 Onzain (across the Loire from Chaumont),* ☎ *02–54–20–72–57,* FAX *02–54–20–77–32,* WEB *www.domainehautsloire.com. 25 rooms, 10 suites. Restaurant, cable TV, minibars, tennis court, pool, helipad. AE, DC, MC, V. Closed Dec.–Feb.*

$ **Ferme de la Quantinière.** This ivy-covered farmhouse southwest of Chaumont was built in 1855. You can enjoy an excellent €21 dinner with English-speaking hosts Annie and Daniel Doyer in their wood-beam, tile-floor dining room, complete with monumental fireplace. Then repair to one of the modernized rooms, priced at around €50 (breakfast included), and enjoy the view over the spacious garden. ✉ *La Quantinière, 41400 Vallières-les-Grandes (8 km/5 mi southwest of Chaumont),* ☎ FAX *02–54–20–99–53,* WEB *www.france-bonjour.com/la-quantiniere. 5 rooms. No air-conditioning, no room TV, no pets. No credit cards, Closed Jan.–Mar.*

Cheverny

⓮ *18 km (12 mi) east of Chaumont, 17 km (11 mi) south of Chambord via D112 and D102.*

Cheverny has become synonymous with its restrained, classical château, although the village is officially named Cour-Cheverny. One of the last in the area to be built, the **Château de Cheverny** was finished in 1634, at a time when the rich and famous had generally stopped building in the Loire Valley. By then, the taste for quaintly shaped châteaux had given way to disciplined Classicism; so here a white, elegantly proportioned, horizontally coursed, single-block facade greets you across manicured lawns. To emphasize the strict symmetry of the plan, a long ruler-straight drive leads to the front door. The Louis XIII interior with its stridently painted and gilded rooms, splendid furniture, and rich tapestries depicting the *Labors of Hercules* is one of the few still intact in the Loire region. Elsewhere, you are free to contemplate the antlers of 2,000 stags in the Trophy Room. Hunting, called "venery" in the leaflets, continues vigorously here, with red coats, bugles, and all. In the château's kennels, hordes of hungry hounds lounge about, dreaming of their next kill. Feeding times—*la soupe aux chiens*—are posted on a notice board, and you are welcome to watch the "ceremony" (delicate sensibilities beware: the dogs line up like statues and are called, one by one, to wolf down their meal from the trainer). You can visit the château grounds by either boat or electric buggy, or get a bird's-eye view from 500 ft up in a charming hot-air balloon; purchase tickets on the spot. ☏ *02–54–79–96–29,* WEB *www.chateau-cheverny.fr.* 🎫 *€5.80.* ⏲ *Mar.–Sept., daily 9–6:30; Oct.–Feb., daily 9:30–noon and 2:15–5.*

Dining and Lodging

$$$$ ★ ✕ **Le Relais.** Top chef Bernard Robin produces succulent nouvelle cuisine in his gleaming kitchens: lobster with dried tomatoes, say, or shepherd's pie with oxtail and truffles. Connoisseurs also savor his simpler fare: carp, game in season, and salmon with beef marrow. The attentive staff brings delicious tidbits to keep you busy between courses. ✉ *1 av. de Chambord, Bracieux (9 km/6 mi northeast of Cour-Cheverny on road to Chambord),* ☏ *02–54–46–41–22. Reservations essential. Jacket and tie. AE, DC, MC, V. Closed Jan. and Wed. Sept.–June. No dinner Tues.*

Chambord

★ ⓯ *16 km (10 mi) northeast of Cheverny via D52 and D112, 19 km (12 mi) east of Blois, 45 km (28 mi) southwest of Orléans.*

The largest of the Loire châteaux, the **Château de Chambord** is the kind of place William Randolph Hearst might have built if he'd had more money. Variously dubbed "megalomaniac" and "an enormous film-set extravaganza," this is one of the most extraordinary structures in Europe. It is set in the middle of a royal game forest, with a cluster of buildings—barely a village—across the road.

A few facts about the château set the scene: the facade is 420 ft long, there are 440 rooms and 365 chimneys, and a wall 32 km (20 mi) long encloses the 13,000-acre forest (you can wander through 3,000 acres of it; the rest is reserved for wild boar and other game). Under François I, building began in 1519, a job that took 12 years and required 1,800 workers. His original grandiose idea was to divert the Loire to form a moat, but someone (perhaps his adviser, Leonardo da Vinci, who some feel may have provided the inspiration behind the entire complex) persuaded him to make do with the River Cosson. François I used the château only for short stays; yet when he came, 12,000 horses were required to transport his luggage, servants, and entourage. Later kings also used Chambord as an occasional retreat, and Louis XIV, the Sun King, had Molière perform here. In the 18th century Louis XV gave the château to Maréchal de Saxe as a reward for his victory over the English and Dutch at Fontenoy (southern Belgium) in 1745. When not indulging himself with wine, women, and song, the marshal stood on the roof to oversee the exercises of his own regiment of 1,000 cavalry. Now, after long neglect—all the original furnishings vanished during the French Revolution—Chambord belongs to the state.

You can wander freely through the vast rooms, filled with exhibits (including a hunting museum)—not all concerned with Chambord, but interesting nonetheless. The enormous double-helix staircase (probably envisioned by Leonardo, who had a thing about spirals) looks like a single staircase, but an entire regiment could march up one spiral while a second came down the other, and they would never meet. Also be sure to visit the roof terrace, whose forest of towers, turrets, cupolas, gables, and chimneys was described by 19th-century novelist Henry James as "more like the spires of a city than the salient points of a single building." The château is sumptuously illuminated at night, and a short son-et-lumière show, delivered successively in French, English, and German, is held on many evenings from mid-May to mid-October; admission is €8. During the entire year there is a full calendar of activities on tap, from performances of 17th-century dressage by Les Ecuries du Maréchal de Saxe to photo-safaris through the game preserve (during deer-rut season) to concerts. ☎ *02–54–50–40–28,* WEB *www.chambord.org.* 🎫 *€7.* ⏲ *Apr.–May and Sept.–Oct., daily 9–6:15; July–Aug., daily 9–6:45; Nov.–Mar., daily 9–5:15.*

Dining and Lodging

$$ ★ ✕🏨 **Grand St-Michel.** Enjoy simple and comfortable quarters in this revamped country house at the edge of the woods, across from the château. A few rooms have spectacular views, the restaurant serves hearty local fare (including game in the fall), and there's a pleasant café-terrace—just the place for reflection while sipping a drink. ✉ *103 pl. St-Michel, 41250,* ☎ *02–54–20–31–31,* FAX *02–54–20–36–40. 39 rooms, 25 with bath. Restaurant, no air-conditioning, tennis court. MC, V. Closed mid-Nov.–mid-Dec.*

Outdoor Activities and Sports

Rent a horse from the former stables, **Les Ecuries du Maréchal de Saxe** (✉ on grounds of Château de Chambord, ☎ 02–54–20–31–01) and ride through the vast national park surrounding the château. From March through October you can hire a boat to explore the château moat and the **Grand Canal** linking it to the River Cosson (☎ 02–54–56–00–43 for details).

Beaugency

⓰ *18 km (12 mi) northeast of Chambord via D111 and D951.*

A clutch of historic towers and buildings around a 14th-century bridge over the Loire lend Beaugency its charm. The buildings in this town on the north bank of the river include the massive 11th-century **donjon** (keep), the Romanesque church of **Notre-Dame,** and the **Tour du Diable** (Devil's Tower), overlooking the river. The **Château Dunois** contains a regional museum with traditional costumes and peasant furniture. ✉ *2 pl. Dunois,* ☎ *02–38–44–55–23.* 🎫 *€3.50.* ⏲ *Guided tours only, Wed.–Mon. at 10, 11, 2, 3, and 4.*

Blois

★ ⑰ *22 km (14 mi) southwest of Beaugency via N152, 13 km (8 mi) northwest of Cour-Cheverny via D765, 54 km (34 mi) southwest of Orléans, 58 km (36 mi) northeast of Tours.*

Perched on a steep hillside overlooking the Loire, site of one of France's most historic châteaux, and birthplace of those delicious Poulain chocolates and gâteaux (check out the bakeries along the main street of rue Denis-Papin and tour the nearby Poulain factory), the bustling old town of Blois is not only an alluring city but a convenient base, well served by train and highway. A signposted route leads you on a walking tour of the **Vieille Ville** (Old Town)—a romantic honeycomb of twisting alleys, cobblestone streets, and half-timber houses—but it is best explored with the help of a map available from the tourist office. The historic highlight is place St-Louis, where you'll find the Maison des Acrobats (note the timbers carved with *jongleurs,* or jugglers), Cathédrale St-Louis, and Hôtel de Villebresme, but unexpected Renaissance-era galleries and staircases lurk in tucked-away courtyards, such as the one in the Hôtel d'Alluye, built by Florimond Robertet, finance minister to three kings and the last patron to commission a painting from Leonardo da Vinci. The best view of the town, with its château and numerous church spires rising sharply above the river, can be had from across the Loire.

The massive **Château de Blois** spans several architectural periods and is among the valley's finest. Your ticket entitles you to a guided tour—given in English when there are enough visitors who don't understand French—but you are more than welcome to roam around without a guide if you visit between mid-March and August. Before you enter, stand in the courtyard to admire four centuries of architecture. On one side stand the 13th-century hall and tower, the latter offering a stunning view of the town and countryside. The Renaissance begins to flower in the Louis XII wing (built between 1498 and 1503), through which you enter, and comes to full bloom in the François I wing (1515–24). The masterpiece here is the openwork spiral staircase, painstakingly restored. The fourth side consists of the Classical Gaston d'Orléans wing (1635–38).

Upstairs in the François I wing is a series of enormous rooms with tremendous fireplaces decorated with the gilded porcupine, emblem of Louis XII, the ermine of Anne of Brittany, and, of course, François I's salamander, breathing fire and surrounded by flickering flames. Many rooms have intricate ceilings and carved, gilt paneling; there is even a sad little picture of Mary, Queen of Scots. In the council room the Duke of Guise was murdered by order of Henri III in 1588. In the **Musée des Beaux-Arts** (Fine Arts Museum), in the Louis XII wing, you'll find royal portraits, including Rubens's puffy portrayal of Maria de' Medici as France Personified. Most evenings May through September, **son-et-lumière** shows are staged (in English on Wednesdays). Call 02–54–78–72–76 for details; admission is €9.50. ☎ *02–54–90–33–33.* 🎫 *€6.* ⏲ *Mid-Mar.–Oct., daily 9–6; Nov.–mid-Mar., daily 9–12:30 and 2–5:30.*

Dining and Lodging

$$$ ★ ✕ **Au Rendez-Vous des Pêcheurs.** This friendly restaurant in an old grocery near the Loire has simple decor but offers excellent value for its creative cooking. Chef Christophe Cosme studied under Bernard Loiseau in Burgundy and brings inventiveness to his seafood specialties (try the crayfish and parsley flan) and desserts. ✉ *27 rue du Foix,* ☎ *02–54–74–67–48. Reservations essential. AE, MC, V. Closed Sun. and Aug. No lunch Mon.*

$$–$$$ ✕ **Espérance.** In a bucolic setting overlooking the Loire, chef Raphaël Guillot serves up inventive cuisine, like fried mangoes with lavender and five different kinds of scallop dishes. ✉ *189 quai Ulysse-Besnard,* ☎ *02–54–78–09–01. AE, MC, V. Closed Mon. and part of Aug. No dinner Sun.*

$$ ✕ **Médicis.** Rooms at this smart little hotel 1 km (½ mi) from the château de Blois are comfortable, air-conditioned, and soundproof; all share a joyous color scheme but are individually decorated. The restaurant alone—done Renaissance-style with a coffered ceiling—makes a stay here worthwhile. Chef-owner Christian Garanger turns his innovative classic dishes into a presentation—*coquilles St-Jacques* (scallops) with bitter *roquette* lettuce, and thin slices of roast hare with a black-currant sauce. The staff is cheerful and there are 250 wines to choose from (the restaurant does not serve dinner Sunday off-season). ✉ *2 allée François-Ier, 41000,* ☎ *02–54–43–94–04,* FAX *02–54–42–04–05. 12 rooms. Restaurant, cable TV, minibars. AE, DC, MC, V. Closed Jan.*

Loches

18 *39 km (24 mi) southeast of Tours.*

A fascinating detour from the main hub of Tours is to follow one of the "spokes" into the southern reaches of Touraine—via car or the handy rail connection—to picturesque, medieval Loches. On a rocky spur just beside the River Indre, the town is dominated by its famous **Citadelle.** Unlike Chinon's, which is a ruined shell, sections of Loches's defensive walls are well preserved and function as part of the town. Inside the **Logis Royaux** (château), on the north end of the citadel, look for the vicious two-man crossbow that could pierce an oak door at 200 yards. There are some interesting pictures, too, including a copy of the well-known portrait showing a disgruntled Charles VII with one of his mistresses, Agnès Sorel, poised as a virtuous Virgin Mary (though semitopless). Her alabaster image decorates her tomb, guarded by angels and lambs. Agnès died in 1450 at age 28, probably poisoned by Charles's son, the future Louis XI. The little chapel was built by Charles VIII for his queen, Anne of Brittany, and is lavishly decorated with sculpted ermine tails, the lady's emblem. But invariably the main attractions here are the notorious **dungeons,** which will delight anyone who revels in prison cells and torture chambers—kids seems to love these scarifying precincts. ✉ *Pl. Charles-VII,* ☎ *02–47–59–01–32.* *€5.10.* ⏲ *Jan.–mid-Mar. and Oct.–Dec., daily 9:30–noon and 2–5; mid-Mar.–June and Sept., daily 9:30–6; July–Aug., daily 9–7.*

Villandry

19 *16 km (10 mi) west of Tours via D7, 35 km (20 mi) northwest of Loches.*

To the west of Tours lies the most glamorous part of the Val de Loire. Here, between the regional capitol and the magnificently historic town of Chinon, breathtaking châteaux dot the Indre Valley as it winds its way to the Veron and the lands watered by the River Vienne. The beauty ★ pageant begins with the **Château de Villandry.** Green-thumbers get weak in the knees at the mere mention of this grand estate near the Cher River, thanks to its painstakingly re-laid 16th-century **gardens,** now the finest example of French Renaissance garden design in France. These were actually designed in 1906 by Dr. Joachim Carvallo and Anne Coleman, his American wife, whose passion resulted in two gigantic terraces planted in styles that combine the French monastic garden with Italianate models depicted in historic du Cerceau etchings. Beyond the water garden and an ornamental garden depicting symbols of chivalric love is the famous *potager,* or vegetable garden. Organized in square patterns, purple cabbages, pumpkins, and pear trees catch the eye at every turn. In total, there are nearly 150,000 plantings, with two seasonal shows presented—the spring one is a veritable "salad." Flower lovers will rejoice in the main *jardin à la française* (French-style garden): framed by a canal, it is a vast carpet of rare and colorful blooms planted *en broderie* (like "embroidery"), set into patterns by box hedges and paths. The aromatic and medicinal garden, its plots neatly labeled in three languages, is especially appealing. Below an avenue of 1,500 precisely pruned lime trees lies an ornamental lake filled with swans: not a ripple is out of place. The château interior itself is magnificent and was restored in the mid-19th century; of particular note are the painted and gilt Moorish ceiling from Toledo and the collection of Spanish pictures. Note that the quietest time to visit is usually during the two-hour French lunch break, while the most photogenic is during the **Nuits des Mille Feux** (Nights of a Thousand Lights, usually held July 5, 6, and 7), when paths and pergolas are illuminated with myriad lanterns. ☎ *02–47–50–02–09,* WEB *www.chateauvillandry.com.* *Château and gardens €7.50, gardens only €5.* *Château June–Sept., daily 9–6; Oct.–mid-Nov. and mid-Feb.–May, daily 9:30–5. Gardens June–Sept., daily 9–7:30; Oct.–May, daily 9–dusk.*

Dining and Lodging

$ **Cheval Rouge.** Most rooms at this fine, old-fashioned hotel are spacious, but ask for one of the quieter ones at the back. The restaurant (closed Monday) is popular with locals, who come for the surprisingly good—considering its touristy location next to the château—classic food and wine. Best bets are the terrine of foie gras, the calf sweetbreads, and the wood-fired-grill fare. ✉ *9 rue de la Mairie, 37510 Villandry,* ☎ *02–47–50–02–07,* FAX *02–47–50–08–77. 18 rooms. Restaurant. MC, V. Closed Feb.–mid-Mar.*

Azay-le-Rideau

20 *5 km (3 mi) southwest of Villandry, 10 km (6 mi) southeast of Langeais via D57, 24 km (15 mi) southwest of Tours.*

In a sylvan dell on the banks of the River Indre, the pleasant village of Azay-le-Rideau is famed for its white-walled Renaissance pleasure palace, called "a faceted diamond set in the Indre Valley" by Honoré ★ de Balzac. The 16th-century **Château d'Azay-le-Rideau** was created as a literal fairy-tale castle. When it was constructed in the Renaissance era (note the Greco-Roman stone detailing), the nouveau-riche treasurer Gilles Berthelot decided he wanted to add tall corner turrets, moat, and machicolations to conjure up the distant seigneurial past when knighthood was in flower and two families, the Azays and the Ridels, ruled this terrain. It was never a serious fortress—it certainly offered no protection to its builder when a financial scandal forced him to flee France shortly after the château's completion in 1529. For centuries the château passed from one private owner to another until it was finally bought by the state in 1905. Though the interior contains an interesting blend of furniture and artwork (one room is a homage to the Marquis de Biencourt, who, in the early 20th century, led the way in renovating château interiors in a sumptuous way–sadly, many of his elegant furnishings were later sold), you may wish to spend most of your time exploring the enchanting site, complete with a moatlike lake. Innovative **son-et-lumière** shows are held on the château grounds from 10:30 PM, May through September. ☎ *02–47–45–42–04,* WEB *www.chateau-france.com/azaylerideau.fr.* *Château €5.50; son-et-lumière €9.50.* *Apr.–Oct., daily 9:30–6; Nov.–Mar., daily 9:30–12:30 and 2–5:30.*

Dining and Lodging

$$–$$$ ✕🏨 **Grand Monarque.** About a 3-minute walk from Azay's great château, this old hotel has been a town landmark for eons. Its fame brings a captive audience, which sometimes results in rather offhand service. However, rooms, which vary in size and style, have character; most are simple, with an antique or two, and many have exposed beams. The restaurant (closed Monday and not serving dinner Sunday) serves good, traditional food; the €16 lunch menu is a particularly good value. Weekend stays must include dinner. ✉ *3 pl. de la République, 37190,* ☎ *02–47–45–40–08,* FAX *02–47–45–46–25,* WEB *www.legrandmonarque.com. 24 rooms. Restaurant, no air-conditioning, cable TV, minibars. AE, MC, V. Closed Dec. and Jan.*

$–$$ ★ ✕🏨 **Biencourt.** Charmingly set on the pedestrian street that leads right to Azay's château gates, this red-shuttered town house in typical Tourangeau style hides a fun find: an authentic, 19th-century schoolhouse within a delightful courtyard-garden, now fitted out with cozily traditional guest rooms (and the stray blackboard and school desk). No matter if you can't land one of the conversation pieces in "La Classe"—the other chambers are fine enough, decorated in pastels as warm as the delightfully helpful owners, the Mariotons. The town has quite a few restaurant selections—if you just don't want to stroll around and pick, ask Cédric and Emmanuelle for the best. ✉ *7 rue Balzac, 37190,* ☎ *02–47–45–20–75,* FAX *02–47–45–91–73. 16 rooms, 12 with bath. No air-conditioning. MC, V. Closed mid-Nov.–end-Feb.*

Outdoor Activities and Sports

Rent bikes from **Leprovost** (✉ 13 rue Carnot, ☎ 02–47–45–40–94) to ride along the Indre; the area around Azay-le-Rideau is among the most tranquil and scenic spots in Touraine.

Shopping

Osier (wicker) products have been made for centuries in Villaines-les-Rochers, 6 km (4 mi) southeast of Azay-le-Rideau via D57. Willow reeds are cultivated in nearby fields and dried in the sun each May, before being transformed into sofas, cat baskets, or babies' rattles. In 1849, when the craft was threatened with extinction, the parish priest persuaded 65 small groups of basket weavers to form France's first agricultural workers' cooperative. The **Coopératif de la Vannerie** (✉ 1 rue de la Cheneillère, ☎ 02–47–45–43–03), which is open Saturday 10–noon and 2–7 and Sunday 2–7, is still going strong and offers a wide choice of wicker goods for sale.

Saché

㉑ *7 km (4 mi) east of Azay-le-Rideau via D17.*

Its town center marked by an Alexander Calder stabile (the great American sculptor created a modern atelier nearby) and the historic Auberge du XIIe Siècle, Saché is best known for its associations with the novelist Honoré de Balzac (1799–1850), who lived and wrote in its **château.** If you've never read Balzac's "Comédie Humaine," you might find little of interest here; but if you have, and do, you'll return to such novels as *Cousin Bette* and *Eugénie Grandet* with fresh enthusiasm and understanding. The present château, built between the 16th and 18th centuries, is more of a comfortable country house than a fortress. Balzac came here—to stay with his friends, the Margonnes—during the 1830s, both to write such works as *Le Pére Goriot* and to escape his creditors. The château houses the substantial **Musée Balzac,** where exhibits range from photographs to original manuscripts to the coffeepot Balzac used to brew the caffeine that helped to keep him writing up to 16 hours a day. A few of the salons have true Second-Empire charm. ☎ *02–47–26–86–50.* ✉ *€3.80.* ⏲ *Daily 9:30–12:30 and 2–5:30.*

Dining

$$–$$$ ★ ✕ **Auberge du XIIe Siècle.** You half expect Balzac to come strolling in the door of this half-timbered, delightfully historic auberge, so little has it changed since the 19th-century. The ample girth of the once Saché resident attested to his great love of food, and he would no doubt enjoy the nouvelle spins on his classic *géline* chicken favorites served here today. The beamed rooms and roaring fireplace are fetching enough—and so is the coffee, a refreshment Balzac drank incessantly (little wonder he created more than 2,000 characters). ✉ *Place de l'Eglise,* ☎ *02–47–26–88–77. MC, V. Closed 3 wks in Jan., 1 wk in June, 1 wk late Aug., and Mon. No dinner Sun., no lunch Tues.*

Ussé

22 *14 km (9 mi) west of Azay-le-Rideau via D17 and D7, 36 km (23 mi) southwest of Tours.*

★ As you approach the **Château d'Ussé** (in the village of Rigny-Ussé), between the Forest of Chinon and the Loire, an astonishing array of delicate towers and turrets greets you. Literature describes this château as the original *Sleeping Beauty* castle; in fact, Charles Perrault—author of this beloved 17th-century tale—spent time here as a guest of the Count of Saumur. Though parts of the castle are from the 1400s, most of it was completed two centuries later. Only Disney could have outdone this white-tufa marvel: the château is a flamboyant mix of Gothic and Renaissance styles—stylish and romantic, built for fun, not for fighting. Its history supports this playful image: it endured no bloodbaths—no political conquests or conflicts—while a tablet in the chapel indicates that even the French Revolution passed it by. After admiring the château's luxurious furnishings and 19th-century French fashion exhibit, climb the spiral stairway to the tower to view the River Indre through the battlements. Here you will also find rooms filled with waxwork effigies detailing the fable of Sleeping Beauty herself—kids will love this. Before you leave, visit the super-elegant 16th-century chapel in the garden; its door is decorated with pleasingly sinister skull-and-crossbones carvings. Fittingly, one 19th-century chatelaine was Claire de Kersaint, who wrote Romantic-era novels; today the castle belongs to Casimir, the Duc de Blacas. Every night the family spotlights the entire castle—a vision that is one of the Loire Valley's dreamiest sights. ☎ *02–47–95–54–05.* ✉ *€9.50.* ⏲ *Mid-Feb.–Mar. and Oct.–mid-Nov., daily 10–noon and 2–5:30; Apr.–May and Sept., daily 9–noon and 2–6:45; June–Aug., daily 9–6:30.*

Dining and Lodging

$$–$$$ ✕🏨 **Castel de Bray et Monts.** In the tiny wine village of Bréhémont, on the south bank of the River Indre halfway between Azay-le-Rideau and Rigny-Ussé, Maxime and Eliane Rochereau have converted a handsome 18th-century manor into an hotel with a difference—Maxime, once a chef at the Paris Ritz, holds weeklong cooking classes. But you don't need to take the course to sample Maxime's cooking (with local fish at the fore), showcased in three prix-fixe menus starting at €30. Other standouts include the magnificent hotel staircase, with its neo-Gothic iron banisters, the shady rose garden, and the duplex bedroom in the converted former chapel. ✉ *10 rue Ridet, 37130 Bréhémont (3 km/1½ mi west of Azay-le-Rideau),* ☎ *02–47–96–70–47,* FAX *02–47–96–57–36,* WEB *www.cooking-class-infrance.com. 9 rooms. Restaurant, no air-conditioning, bicycles. MC, V. Closed mid-Nov.–mid-Feb.*

$ ★ **Clos d'Ussé.** Thank heavens for this delightful inn. The best time to see the great Château d'Ussé is in early morning light or illuminated at night, and the easiest way to do that is to overnight in the village of Rigny-Ussé here at the home of the famille Duchemin. Eric runs the place, Muriel is in charge of the extremely delicious restaurant, *grand-mère* offers a warm smile, while Alexandre, the 7-year-old son, charms everyone. Not surprisingly, families will adore this place, especially as three of the rooms are custom-built for them. Best of all, a one-minute walk from the front door takes you to the château gates. ✉ *Rigny-Ussé,* ☎ FAX *02–47–95–55–47. 8 rooms. Restaurant, no air-conditioning. MC, V. Closed Nov.–Feb.*

Chinon

★ ㉓ *13 km (8 mi) southwest of Rigny-Ussé via D7 and D16, 44 km (28 mi) southwest of Tours.*

The extraordinary town of Chinon—birthplace of author François Rabelais (1494–1553)—is dominated by the towering ruins of its medieval castle, perched high above the River Vienne. Blessed with a unique medieval quarter, the center of town is a storybook warren of narrow, cobbled streets (some are pedestrian-only) lined with half-timber houses; its fairy-tale allure was effectively used to frame Josette Day when she appeared as Beauty in Jean Cocteau's 1949 film *La Belle et la Bête.* The main road of the historic quarter, rue Haute St-Maurice (a continuation of rue Voltaire, which begins at the central place du General du Gaulle) is a virtual open-air museum; other towns may have one or two or three blocks lined with medieval and Renaissance houses, but this street runs, spectacularly, for more than 15 blocks. While there are some unprepossessing museums in town—the **Musée du Vieux Chinon,** in a medieval town house on rue Haute St-Maurice, and the **Maison de la Rivière,** devoted to Chinon's maritime trade and set along the embankment—the medieval quarter remains the must-do, as a walk here unforgettably catapults you back to the days of Rabelais. Because both the village and the château are on steep, cobbled slopes, it's a good idea to wear comfortable walking shoes. For a fun side trip in summer, a steam train chugs from Chinon 15 km (10 mi) south to Richelieu, the town founded and designed by Louis XIV's notorious cardinal (☎ 02–47–58–12–97 for details).

The vast **Château de Chinon,** a veritable fortress with walls 400 yards long, dates from the time of Henry II of England, who died here in 1189 and was buried at Fontevraud. Two centuries later the castle witnessed an important historic moment: Joan of Arc's recognition of the disguised Dauphin, later Charles VII; the castle was also one of the domiciles of Henri II and his warring wife, Eleanor of Aquitaine (Kate Hepburn's 1968 film of *The Lion in Winter* was set, but not filmed, here). In the early 17th century the castle was partially dismantled by Cardinal Richelieu (1585–1642), who used many of its stones to build a new palace 21 km (13 mi) to the south, in Richelieu. At Chinon everything is open to the elements, except the **Logis Royal** (Royal Chambers). Here there is a small museum containing a model of the castle when it was intact, various old tapestries, and precious stones. For a fine view of the region, climb the **Tour Coudray** (Coudray Tower), where in 1307 leading members of the crusading Knights Templar were imprisoned before being taken to Paris, tried, and burned at the stake. The **Tour de l'Horloge** (Clock Tower), whose bell has sounded the hours since 1399, contains the **Musée Jeanne d'Arc** (Joan of Arc Museum). There are sensational views from the ramparts over Chinon and the Vienne Valley. ☎ *02–47–93–13–45.* €4.60. ⏲ *Mid-Mar.–June and*

Sept., daily 9:30–6; July and Aug., daily 9–7; Oct., daily 9–6; Nov.–mid-Mar., daily 9:30–12:30 and 2–5:30.

The **Musée du Vin** (Wine Museum), in a vaulted cellar beneath one of Chinon's fine medieval streets, has a kitschy presentation about vine growing and wine and barrel making, complete with waxwork dummies. English commentary is available, and the admission charge entitles you to a sample of the local product. ✉ *12 rue Voltaire,* ☎ *02–47–93–25–63.* *€3.50.* ⏲ *Apr.–Sept., Fri.–Wed. 10–noon and 2–6.*

Dining and Lodging

$$$ ✕ **Au Plaisir Gourmand.** Jean-Claude Rigollet's tufa-stone 18th-century restaurant by the Vienne River is the finest in Chinon. Specialties served in the Renaissance-style dining room include crayfish salad, snails in garlic, jellied rabbit, *sandre* (pike-perch) with butter sauce, and braised oxtail in red wine. ✉ *2 rue Parmentier,* ☎ *02–47–93–20–48. Reservations recommended. AE, MC, V. Closed Mon., Tues. and mid-Feb.–mid-Mar. No dinner Sun.*

$$$–$$$$ ★ ✕ **Château de Marçay.** This turreted 15th-century hotel is set amid vineyards just south of Chinon. The spacious rooms in the château have beams and a cozy warmth; those in the separate Pavilion are pleasant and less expensive but have little charm. Chef Marc de Passorio serves excellent carpaccio *de canard* (thin slices of marinated cold duck), tournedos of salmon in a Chinon wine sauce, and an extensive cheese board (sample the Ste-Marie chèvre). There's no dinner Sunday in winter. ✉ *Rte. du Château, 37500 Marçay (8 km/5 mi south of Chinon),* ☎ *02–47–93–03–47,* FAX *02–47–93–45–33,* WEB *www.chateaudemarcay.com. 30 rooms, 4 suites. Restaurant, no air-conditioning, cable TV, minibars, tennis court, pool. AE, DC, MC, V. Closed mid-Jan.–early Mar.*

$–$$ **Diderot.** With a facade that seems on sabbatical from an 18th-century François Boucher painting—ivy-covered stone, white shutters, mansard roof, dormer windows, rococo staircase—this is Chinon's prettiest hotel. Inside, a corner bar and cozy stone breakfast room create a warm and welcoming air, one strengthened by the Kazamias family, the hotel's owners, who relocated from Cyprus (and brought a bit of it with them, as the olive and laurel trees planted around the lovely forecourt attest). Guest rooms are standard-issue—avoid those in the separate house on the back street. The hotel is in a nice residential area, about 10 blocks from the medieval quarter. ✉ *4 rue Buffon, 37500,* ☎ *02–47–93–18–87,* FAX *02–47–93–37–10. 24 rooms (including 4 in annex). No air-conditioning, no room TV. AE, DC, MC, V. Mid-Dec.–mid-Jan.*

$–$$ **France.** Right on Chinon's most charming square—a picture postcard come to life with splashing fountain and a bevy of cafés—this sweetly agreeable hotel is set in a 16th-century house just two blocks from the medieval quarter. Many regional notables lived here before the Revolution, when it became the Hôtel Lion d'Or, the first hostelry in the region. Guest rooms are Best Western comfortable and cozy (the hotel is now part of that chain); some overlook two tiny, flowerpot-bedecked courtyards, while some take in views that include Chinon's castle ruins. The ground-floor restaurant (closed Tuesday and no lunch Wednesday) serves Italian cuisine. The hotel staff is most congenial. ✉ *47 pl. du Général-de-Gaulle, 37500,* ☎ *02–47–93–33–91,* FAX *02–47–98–37–03. 27 rooms. Restaurant, air-conditioning in some rooms. AE, DC, MC, V. Closed 2nd ½ Nov.*

Nightlife and the Arts

Chinon stages a **Marché à l'Ancienne** on the third Saturday of August, a free wine-tasting extravaganza with stalls, displays, and costumed locals recalling rural life of a hundred years ago. For details, contact the tourist office.

Fontevraud

24 *20 km (12 mi) northwest of Chinon via D751, 15 km (9 mi) southeast of Saumur.*

A refreshing break from the worldly grandeur of châteaux, the small village of Fontevraud is crowned with the largest abbey in France, a magnificent complex of Romanesque and Renaissance buildings that were of central importance in the history of both England and France. Founded in 1101, the **Abbaye Royale de Fontevraud** had separate churches and living quarters for nuns, monks, lepers, "repentant" female sinners, and the sick. Between 1115 and the French Revolution in 1789, a succession of 39 abbesses—among them a granddaughter of William the Conqueror—directed its operations. The great 12th-century **Église Abbatiale** (Abbey Church), one of the most eclectic architectural structures in France, contains the tombs of Henry II of England, his wife Eleanor of Aquitaine, and their son, Richard Coeur de Lion (the Lion-Hearted). Though their bones were scattered during the Revolution, their effigies still lie *en couchant* in the middle of the immense and shadowy nave. Napoléon turned the abbey church into a prison, and so it remained until 1963, when historical restoration work—still underway—began. The **Salle Capitulaire** (Chapter House), adjacent to the church, with its collection of 16th-century religious wall paintings (prominent abbesses served as models), is unmistakably Renaissance; the paving stones bear the salamander emblem of François I. Next to the long refectory is the famously octagonal **Cuisine** (kitchen), topped by 20 scaly looking stone chimneys led by the **Tour d'Evrault.** ✉ *Pl. des Plantagenêts,* ☎ *02–41–51–71–41,* WEB *www.abbaye-fontevraud.asso.fr.* 🎫 *€5.50.* ⏲ *June–mid-Sept., daily 9–6:30; mid-Sept.–May, daily 9:30–noon and 2–5.*

After touring the Abbaye Royale, head outside the gates of the complex a few blocks to the north to discover one of the Loire Valley's most ★ time-machine streets, **L'Allée Sainte-Catherine.** Bordered by the Fontevraud park, headed by a charming medieval church, and lined with a few scattered houses (which now contain the town tourist office, a gallery that sells medieval illuminated manuscript pages, and the delightful La Licorne restaurant), this street still looks like the 14th century a-borning.

Dining and Lodging

$$$–$$$$ ★ ✕ **La Licorne.** A hanging shop sign adorned with a painted unicorn beckons you to this pretty-as-a-picture town-house restaurant set on Fontevraud's stunningly idyllic allée Sainte-Catherine. Past a flowery garden and table-adorned terrace, tiny salons glow with happy folks feasting on some of the best food in the region: Loire salmon, guineafowl in Layon wine, and lobster with fava beans should make most diners purr with total contentment. ✉ *Allée Sainte-Catherine,* ☎ *02–41–51–72–49. Reservations essential. AE, MC, V. Closed Mon., no dinner Sun., Wed.*

$$–$$$ ★ ✕🏨 **Prieuré St-Lazare.** One of the more unusual hotels in the Loire Valley and set right within the medieval splendor of Fontevraud, this series of outbuildings was once the abbey's lepers' hospice. The entrance gives onto the vast *salle capitulaire* conference room and the cloisters now house an extremely fine restaurant (reservations essential), where such delicacies as swordfish simmered in Saumur-Champigny wine entice. In a snug side wing the erstwhile monks' cells have been trans-

formed into alluring guest rooms, chic and bright in modern checks and fine wood accents. Staying here lets you explore the abbey grounds when its gates are closed to the public—in itself, a truly exceptional treat. ✉ *Abbaye de Fontevraud, 49590 Fontevraud-L'Abbaye,* ☎ *02–41–51–73–16,* FAX *02–41–51–75–50. 52 rooms. Restaurant, no air-conditioning, minibars. AE, MC, V.*

Saumur

★ 25 *15 km (9 mi) northwest of Fontevraud via D947, 65 km (41 mi) west of Tours, 46 km (29 mi) southeast of Angers.*

Ancient Saumur, dominated by its mighty turreted château high above town and river, is one of the largest cities along the Loire and a key transportation hub for Anjou, the province just to the west of Touraine. Saumur is also known for its riding school and flourishing mushroom industry, which produces 100,000 tons per year. The same cool tunnels in which the mushrooms grow provide an ideal storage place for the local *mousseux* (sparkling wines); many vineyards hereabouts are open to the public for tours.

Regional government offices, wealthy wine producers, and the spiffy riding school all help make Saumur's natives some of the Loire's most stylish, nay, snobbish residents—chances are you'll get a blast of old-time French attitude, not just from the preppy ladies but a greater whiff from shopkeepers and waiters. Little seems to have changed over the centuries: Honoré de Balzac famously wrote up the surly side of the Saumurois in his *Eugénie Grandet*. Too bad: the historic center is studded with elegant 19th-century town houses and the magnificent place St-Pierre, lorded over by the vast 14th-century church of St-Pierre and centerpiece of a charming warren of streets, cafés, and ice-cream parlors. Saumur might be best considered as a day trip.

If you arrive in the evening, the sight of the elegant, floodlighted, white 14th-century **Château de Saumur** takes your breath away. Look familiar? Probably because you've seen it in countless reproductions from the famous *Très Riches Heures* (Book of Hours), painted for the Duc de Berry in 1416 (now in the Musée Condé at Chantilly). Inside it's bright and cheerful, with a fairy-tale gateway and plentiful potted flowers. It houses two museums: the **Musée des Arts Décoratifs** (Decorative Arts Museum), with a fine collection of medieval objets d'art and 18th- and 19th-century porcelain, and the **Musée du Cheval** (Equestrian Museum). After climbing the **Tour de Guet** (watchtower) for impressive views of the many-spired town, take time out at the café or the serious restaurant set up on the castle grounds, then take the exit to the carpark and head over to the cliffside promenade to drink in the thrilling vista of the castle on its bluff against the river backdrop. ✉ *Esplanade du Château,* ☎ *02–41–40–24–40,* WEB *www.ville-saumur.fr.* 🎫 *€6.* ⏲ *July–Sept., daily 9–6:30; Oct. and Apr.–June, daily 9–11:30 and 2–6; Nov.–Mar., Wed.–Mon. 9:30–noon and 2–5:30.*

The **Cadre Noir de Saumur** (Riding School) is unique in Europe, with its 400 horses, extensive stables, five Olympic-size riding schools, and 30 miles of specially laid tracks. Try for a morning tour, which includes a chance to admire the horses in training. During the **Carrousel de Samur,** on the last two weekends in July, the horses put on a full gala display for enthusiastic crowds. ✉ *Rue de l'Abbaye,* ☎ *02–41–53–50–60,* WEB *www.cadrenoir.tm.fr.* 🎫 *€6.50.* ⏲ *Guided tours only Apr.–Sept., Tues.–Sat. at 9:30, 11, 2, and 4.*

At the **Musée du Champignon** (Mushroom Museum), on the outskirts of Saumur, take an intriguing subterranean tour through fossil-filled caverns where the edible fungi are grown. ✉ *Rte. de Gennes, St-Hilaire–St-Florent,* ☏ *02–41–50–31–55.* *€6.20.* ⏲ *Mid-Feb.–mid-Sept., daily 10–7.*

Dining and Lodging

$$$ ★ ✕ **Les Ménestrels.** Chef Lucien Von cooks fine fare in a restored 18th-century white-stone mansion up against the castle cliff, on the grounds of the Anne d'Anjou hotel. Specialties include pheasant casserole, fried mushrooms, perch with spring-onion fondue, and beef in local red-wine sauce. ✉ *11 rue Raspail,* ☏ *02–41–67–71–10. AE, DC, MC, V. Closed Sun.*

$$–$$$ **Anne d'Anjou.** On the bank of the Loire, this central hotel has a beautiful courtyard complete with flagstone terrace, half-timber restaurant, and a grand view of Saumur's castle looming directly above. The lobby is staidly traditional, the breakfast wonderful, and the18th-century house (built by rich Protestant merchants) showcases a grand, historically important staircase. Most rooms are simple; if you're lucky, owners Jean-René and Marylyn Camus will point you to their best, No. 102 (€127), with wood-panel paintings and Empire furnishings. Try to get a courtyard room, as those facing the river contend with rushing traffic; some, but not all, of the top-floor rooms are unalluring garrets, so beware. ✉ *32 quai Mayaud, 49400,* ☏ *02–41–67–30–30,* FAX *02–41–67–51–00,* WEB *www.hotel-anneanjou.com. 45 rooms. Restaurant, no air-conditioning. AE, DC, MC, V.*

Outdoor Activities and Sports

If you want to ride through the gentle hills or take a weeklong equestrian tour of the Loire Valley, head to the **Centre Équestre de Saumur** (✉ Petit Souper, St-Hilaire–St-Florent, ☏ 02–41–50–29–90), 3 km (2 mi) northwest of town.

Shopping

Loire wine is not a practical buy—except for instant consumption—but if wine-tasting tours of vineyards inspire you, enterprising wine makers will arrange shipments. For sparkling Saumur wine try **Ackerman** (✉ 19 rue Léopold-Palustre, St-Hilaire, ☏ 02–41–53–30–20). **Veuve Amiot** (✉ 21 rue Jean-Ackerman, St-Hilaire, ☏ 02–41–83–14–14) is a long-established producer of Saumur wines. You can visit the cavernous premises of **Gratien-Meyer** on the east side of Saumur daily from April through September (✉ Rte. de Montsoreau, ☏ 02–41–83–13–32; €2.30; ⏲ daily 9–noon and 2–6).

Just southeast of Saumur, in Dampierre-sur-Loire, stop in at the **Château de Chaintres** (✉ 54 rue de la Croix-de-Chaintre, ☏ 02–41–52–90–54), where gravel-voice Krishna Lester, an English eccentric, produces the region's finest red and enjoys giving lectures about fermentation and vinification.

En Route Along the river east of Saumur (that is, on the way back toward Tours) are some of the Loire's most intriguing troglodyte settlements, in particular the cliff face studded with cave-houses at **Turquant.** The neighboring town of **Montsoreau** is famed for its riverside castle (now a museum devoted to the history of the Loire), although **Candes-St-Martin,** one town over, perches super-picturesquely over the confluence of the Loire and Vienne rivers and huddles within the shadows of its great Gothic church, consecrated to St. Martin of Tours, who died here. Heading eastward from Saumur toward Angers, stop off in the charming village of Brissac-Quincé to admire **Château de Brissac** (www.chateau-brissac.fr), a towering pile (the tallest château in France) of Mannerist, Baroque, and Classical motifs grafted onto a Gothic castle; inside, all is seignorial splendor, with tapestries, Venetian-glass chandeliers, and even a grand theater (whose crimson interior once hosted such eminents as Gounod, Massenet, and Debussy).

Montreuil-Bellay

26 *18 km (11 mi) south of Saumur via N147.*

Many people have a special place in their heart for Montreuil-Bellay, a small riverside town with many 18th- and 19th-century houses, lovely public gardens, and a leafy square next to its castle. The 15th-century **Château de Montreuil-Bellay** has a grandiose exterior—majestic towers and pointed roofs—and a fascinating interior, with fine furniture and tapestries, a fully equipped medieval kitchen, and a chapel adorned with frescoes of angelic musicians. For a memorable view, take a stroll in the gardens; graceful white turrets tower high above the trees and rosebushes, and down below, the little River Thouet winds its lazy way to the Loire. ✉ *Pl. des Ormeaux,* ☎ *02–41–52–33–06.* 🎫 *€7.* 🕐 *Apr.–Oct., Wed.–Mon. 10–noon and 2–5:30.*

Angers

27 *40 km (22 mi) west of Saumur, 51 km (28 mi) northwest of Montreuil-Bellay via D761, 88 km (55 mi) east of Nantes.*

The bustling city of Angers, on the banks of the Maine River, just north of the Loire, is famous for its towering castle filled with the extraordinary Apocalypse Tapestries. But it also has a fine Gothic cathedral, a selection of art galleries, and a network of pleasant, traffic-free streets around place Ste-Croix, with its half-timber houses. The town's principal sights lie within a compact square formed by the three main boulevards and the Maine.

★ The banded black-and-white **Château d'Angers,** built by St. Louis (1228–38), glowers over the town from behind turreted moats, now laid out as gardens and overrun with flowers and deer. As you explore the grounds, note the startling contrast between the thick defensive walls, defended by a drawbridge and 17 massive round towers in a distinctive pattern, and the formal garden, with its delicate white-tufa chapel, erected in the 16th century. For a sweeping view of the city and surrounding countryside, climb one of the castle towers. A well-integrated modern gallery on the castle grounds contains the great **Tenture de l'Apocalypse** (Apocalypse Tapestries), woven in Paris in the 1380s for the Duke of Anjou. Measuring 16 ft high and 120 yards long, its many panels show a series of 70 horrifying and humorous scenes from the Book of Revelation. In one, mountains of fire fall from heaven while boats capsize and men struggle in the water. Another has the beast with seven heads. ✉ *2 prom. du Bout-du-Monde,* ☎ *02–41–87–43–47.* 🎫 *€5.50.* 🕐 *June–mid-Sept., daily 9:30–7; mid-Sept.–May, daily 10–5.*

The **Cathédrale St-Maurice** (✉ Pl. Monseigneur-Chappoulie) is a 12th- and 13th-century Gothic cathedral noted for its curious Romanesque facade and original stained-glass windows; bring binoculars to appreciate both fully.

The **Musée David d'Angers,** in a refurbished glass-roof medieval church, has a collection of dramatic sculptures by Jean-Pierre David (1788–1859), the city's favorite son. ✉ *33 bis rue Toussaint,* ☎ *02–41–87–21–03,* WEB *www.ville-angers.fr.* 🎫 *€2.* 🕐 *Tues.–Sun. 10–noon and 2–6.*

To learn about the heartwarming liqueur made in Angers since 1849, head to the **Distillerie Cointreau** on the east of the city. It has a museum and offers a guided visit of the distillery, which starts with an introductory film, moves through the bottling plant and alembic room, with its gleaming copper-pot stills, and ends with a tasting. ✉ *Carrefour Molière, St-Barthélémy d'Anjou,* ☎ *02–41–31–50–50,* WEB *www.cointreau.com.* 🎟 *€5.50.* ⏲ *Tours daily July and Aug. at 10:30, 3:30, and 4:30; May–June and Sept.–Oct., 10:30 and 3; Nov.–Apr. at 3.*

Dining and Lodging

$$–$$$ ✕ **La Salamandre.** Carefully prepared classic cuisine is served in this restaurant in the Anjou Hotel. Lamb, duck with cranberries, and calamari with crab sauce are just a few of the dishes served amid the Renaissance-style allurements and under stained-glass windows. Opt for one of the reasonably priced prix-fixe menus. ✉ *1 bd. du Maréchal-Foch,* ☎ *02–41–88–99–55. AE, DC, MC, V. Closed Sun.*

$$ ✕ **La Treille.** For traditional, simple fare at affordable prices, try this small two-story mom-and-pop restaurant off place Ste-Croix and across from Maison d'Adam, Angers's finest timber-frame house. The prix-fixe menu may start with a *salade au chèvre chaud* (warm goat-cheese salad), followed by confit of duck and an apple tart. The upstairs dining room draws a lively crowd; downstairs is quieter. ✉ *12 rue Montault,* ☎ *02–41–88–45–51. MC, V. Closed Sun.*

$$–$$$ 🏨 **Anjou.** In business since 1846, the Anjou, now part of the Best Western chain, has a vaguely 18th-century style, including stained-glass windows in the lobby. The spacious rooms have high ceilings, double doors, and modern bathrooms where terry-cloth bathrobes await you. ✉ *1 bd. du Maréchal-Foch, 49000,* ☎ *02–41–88–24–82; 800/528–1324 in the U.S.,* FAX *02–41–87–22–21,* WEB *www.hoteldanjou.fr. 53 rooms, 4 suites. Restaurant, no air-conditioning. AE, DC, MC, V.*

$ 🏨 **Mail.** A stately lime tree stands sentinel outside this 17th-century mansion on a calm street between the Hôtel de Ville and the river. The smallish rooms are decorated in pastel shades with striped wallpaper. ✉ *8 rue des Ursules, 49100,* ☎ *02–41–25–05–05,* FAX *02–41–86–91–20,* WEB *www.destination-anjou.com/mail. 26 rooms. No air-conditioning, no room TV. AE, DC, MC, V.*

Nightlife and the Arts

July and August sees the **Angers L'Eté** (Angers Summer) festival, with concerts at the Cloître Toussaint and Chapelle des Ursules; call 02–41–05–41–48 for details.

Bourgueil

★ ㉘ *65 km (40 mi) east of Angers via 147 and A85, 12 km (8 mi) north of Chinon via N749.*

Connoisseurs like to say that Chinon red wines taste of raspberries, those of Bourgueil—just to the north, past the Veron Valley—smell of violets. If you want to test the veracity of such a judgment, explore the caves and vineyards surrounding the quaint market town of Bourgueil (just down the road in Chevrette is the **Cave Touristic de la Dive Bouteille,** a vast cavern with presentations of regional wines. Headliner here is the **Abbaye de Bourgueil,** where Father Baudry legendarily planted the first Cabernet Franc in the Chinonais in 1089. Aesthetic attractions—although founded by the Benedictines in the 10th century, most structures here date from the far-from-holy 18th-century—are greatly outweighed by those of Fontevraud, but there is a **Musée Arts et Traditions Populaires** to explore in the abbey. ✉ ☎ *02–47–97–72–04.* 🎟 *€4.80.* ⏲ *July–Aug., Wed.–Mon. 2–6; Apr.–June and Sept.–end Oct., weekends 2–6.*

Dining

$$$–$$$$ ★ ✕ **Château des Reaux.** Extravagantly emblazoned with checkered red-and-white brickwork, this historic monument is a must-see for its 15th-century moat, its Renaissance-era fortified entrance, and its fairy-tale, pepper-pot towers (in fact, day-trippers can visit for a fee). But it truly comes into its own when you overnight as guests of the immensely *charmante* Countess Florence de Bouillé, whose family has lived here for more than a century. What with period salons positively dripping with atmosphere (family memorabilia, Louis Quinze sofas, Victorian trictrac tables), storybook-stylish guest rooms, and three swans in residence (wait until you hear their nicknames), this place is an utter delight. ✉ *Chouzé-sur-Loire (5 km/2 mi south of Bourgueil),* ☎ *02–47–95–14–40,* FAX *02–47–95–18–34,* WEB *www.chateaux-france.com/-reaux. 17 rooms. No air-conditioning, no room TV, tennis court. AE, DC, MC, V.*

OFF THE BEATEN PATH

CHÂTEAU DU LUDE – Topped by a flurry of conical turrets and Renaissance chimneys that seems to pay homage to François I's Chambord, this is a "living" chateau with a lucky family still in residence, so the rooms are particularly opulent and inviting. The François I wing, facing the park, combines round fortress towers with dainty Renaissance detail, and contains Flemish and Gobelin tapestries and a chimneypiece with the king's carved salamander emblem. The 18th-century Louis XVI Wing, overlooking the river, displays severe Classical symmetry. Le Lude is 47 km (29 mi) northeast of Saumur. ✉ *Pl. François-de-Nicolay,* ☎ *02–43–94–60–09.* 🎫 *€6; park only, €4.60.* ⏲ *Château Apr.–June and Sept., Thurs.–Tues. 2:30–6; July–Aug., daily 2:30–6; park also open Apr.–Sept., 9:30–noon.*

LE MANS – Best known for its 24-hour automobile race in June (call 02–43–40–24–75 for details), Le Mans (44 km/28 mi north of Le Lude via D307) is a bustling city with Gallo-Roman ramparts, a well-preserved Old Quarter, and a magnificent cathedral—part Gothic, part Romanesque—perched precariously on a hilltop overlooking the River Sarthe.

Langeais

❷❾ *10 km (7 mi) east of Bourgueil via D35 and N152–E60.*

The Renaissance church tower and 16th-century houses of the old town of Langeais are dwarfed by its massive castle. The **Château de Langeais,** built in the 1460s and never altered, contains a superb collection of fireplaces, tapestries, chests, and beds. Outside, tidy gardens nestle behind sturdy walls and battlements. ☎ *02–47–96–72–60.* 🎫 *€6.50.* ⏲ *Apr.–Sept., daily 9–6:30; Oct.–Mar., daily 9–noon and 2–5.*

En Route Heading back to Tours, you can either choose to continue eastward to explore the upper Loire Valley, or turn northeast to return to Paris. If you choose the latter course, make a stop in lovely **Vendôme.** The Loir River splits here into numerous arms, creating a canal-like effect, so take time to stroll along the narrow streets, through the 15th-century Porte St-Georges gateway to the Benedictine abbey church of La Trinité, and climb up to the gardens of the ruined hilltop castle for stunning views of the town. Continue north to **Châteaudun** and admire its majestic château. From here the fast N10 heads a half hour north to Chartres, but if you're a fan of author Marcel Proust you may prefer to make a pilgrimage northwest to **Illiers-Combray** to visit the house where he spent his summers as a boy, which is painstakingly evoked in *Swann's Way* and *The Guermantes' Way* in his grand opus *In Search of Lost Time.*

ORLÉANS AND THE UPPER LOIRE VALLEY

Orléans probably has the biggest inferiority complex this side of Newark, New Jersey. The city pales pitifully in comparison with other cities of central France, so the townfolk cling to the city's finest moment—the coming of *la pucelle d'Orléans* (the Maid of Orleans), Joan of Arc, in 1429 to liberate the city from the English during the Hundred Years' War. There's little left from Joan's time but the city is festooned with everything from her equestrian monument to a Jeanne d'Arc Dry Cleaners. Orléans remains the gateway to the upper Loire Valley, which has some delightful destinations: the hilltop wine town of Sancerre, the ceramics center of Gien, the ancient abbey of St-Benoît, and the extraordinary canal designed by Gustave Eiffel at Briare. Heading back to the central Loire Valley (or south to Bourges), you can can enjoy a grand finale at one of the Loire's most gorgeous hotels—the Comte de Vogüé's Château de la Verrerie (near Aubigny-sur-Nère) and one of the finest restaurants in France, the Lion d'Or, in the moody Sologne region.

Orléans

112 km (70 mi) northeast of Tours, 125 km (78 mi) south of Paris.

Once hallowed by Joan of Arc, Orléans is today a thriving commercial city; sensitive urban renewal has done much to bring it back to life, especially the medieval streets between the Loire and the cathedral. The city has quite a history; as a natural bridgehead over the Loire it was long the focus of hostile confrontations and invasions. In 52 BC Julius Caesar slaughtered its inhabitants and burned it to the ground. Five centuries later Attila and the Huns did much the same. Next came the Normans; then the Valois kings turned it into a secondary capital. The story of the Hundred Years' War, Joan of Arc, and the Siege of Orléans is widely known. In 1429 France had reached the nadir of its long and varied history. The English and their Burgundian allies were carving up the kingdom. Besieged by the English, Orléans was one of the last towns about to yield, when a young peasant girl, Joan of Arc, arrived to rally the troops and save the kingdom. During the Wars of Religion (1562–98), much of the cathedral was destroyed. A century ago ham-fisted town planners razed many of the city's fine old buildings. Both German and Allied bombs helped finish the job during World War II.

30 The **Cathédrale Ste-Croix** is a riot of pinnacles and gargoyles, both Gothic and pseudo-Gothic, embellished with 18th-century wedding-cake towers. After most of the cathedral was destroyed in the 16th century during the Wars of Religion, Henry IV and his successors rebuilt it. Novelist Marcel Proust (1871–1922) called it France's ugliest church, but most find it impressive. Inside are vast quantities of stained glass and 18th-century wood carvings, plus the modern **Chapelle de Jeanne d'Arc** (Joan of Arc Chapel), with plaques in memory of British and American war dead. ✉ *Pl. Ste-Croix.* ⏲ *Daily 9–noon and 2–6.*

31 The modern **Musée des Beaux-Arts** (Fine Arts Museum) is across from the cathedral. Take the elevator to the top of the five-story building; then make your way down to see works by such artists as Tintoretto, Velázquez, Watteau, Boucher, Rodin, and Gauguin. The museum's richest collection is its 17th-century French paintings. ✉ *1 rue Ferdinand-Rabier,* ☎ *02–38–79–21–55.* 🎫 *€3 (joint ticket with History Museum).* ⏲ *Tues.–Sat. 10–12:15 and 1:30–6, Sun. 1:30–6.*

Cathédrale Ste-Croix . . . 30
Maison de Jeanne d'Arc 33
Musée des Beaux-Arts . . 31
Musée Historique . . . 32

Orléans

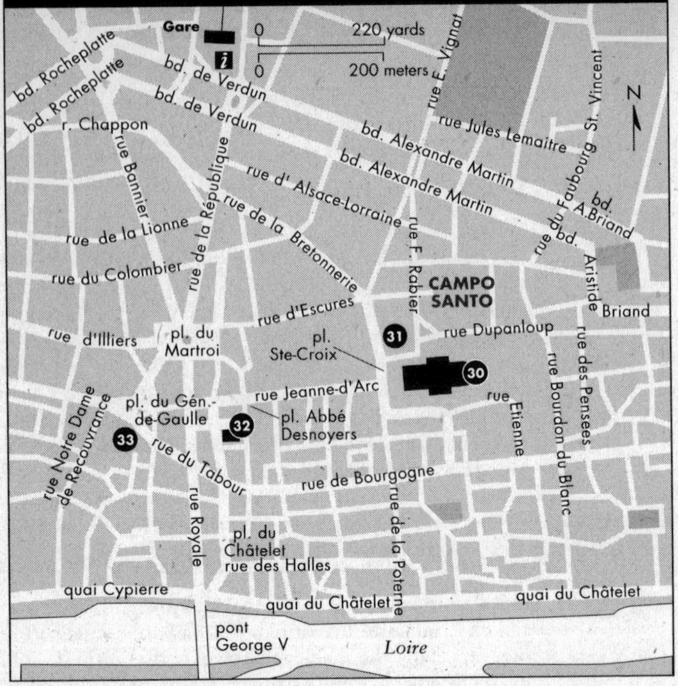

32 The **Musée Historique** (History Museum) is housed in the **Hôtel Cabu,** a Renaissance mansion restored after World War II. It contains works of both "fine" and "popular" art connected with the town's past, including a remarkable collection of pagan bronzes of animals and dancers. These bronzes were hidden from zealous Christian missionaries in the 4th century and discovered in a sandpit near St-Benoît in 1861. ✉ *Square de l'Abbé-Desnoyers,* ☎ *02–38–79–25–60.* 🎫 *€3 (joint ticket with Arts Museum).* ⏲ *July–Aug., Tues.–Sun. 10:30–12:15 and 1:30–6; Sept.–June, Wed. and weekends 1:30–6.*

33 During the 10-day Siege of Orléans in 1429, 17-year-old Joan of Arc stayed on the site of the **Maison de Jeanne d'Arc** (Joan of Arc House). This faithful reconstruction of the house she knew contains exhibits about her life and costumes and weapons of her time. Several dioramas modeled by Lucien Harmey recount the main episodes in her life, from the audience at Chinon to the coronation at Reims, her seizure at Compiègne, and her burning at the stake at Rouen. ✉ *3 pl. du Général-de-Gaulle,* ☎ *02–38–52–99–89.* 🎫 *€2.* ⏲ *May–Oct., Tues.–Sun. 10–12:30 and 1:30–6; Nov.–Apr., Tues.–Sun. 1:30–6.*

Dining and Lodging

$$$ ★ ✕ **Les Antiquaires.** The understated elegance of this cozy, wood-beamed restaurant close to the river, with its red walls, cane-backed chairs, and brass chandeliers, is in telling contrast to Philippe Bardau's penchant for colorfully presented dishes with a Mediterranean flavor: mullet with eggplant, for instance, or sea bass with artichokes and fennel. ✉ *2 rue au Lin,* ☎ *02–38–53–52–35. MC, V. Closed early Jan. and Mon. No dinner Sun.*

$$ ✕🏨 **Rivage.** This small, white-walled hotel south of Orléans makes a pleasant base. Each of the compact rooms has a little balcony with a view of the tree-lined Loiret River; the bathrooms are tiny. The dining

room (no lunch Saturday; no dinner Sunday November through March) opens onto a terrace facing the river. The menu changes with the season—if you're lucky, chef François Tassin's memorable lobster salad with mango, lamb marinated in paprika, and glazed green-apple soufflé with apple marmalade will on tap. Don't miss out on the huge cheeseboard. ✉ *635 rue de la Reine-Blanche, 45160 Olivet (5 km/3 mi south of Orléans),* ☎ *02–38–66–02–93,* FAX *02–38–56–31–11. 17 rooms, 11 with shower, 6 with bath. Restaurant, tennis court. AE, DC, MC, V. Closed late Dec.–mid-Jan.*

Nightlife and the Arts

The two-day **Fête de Jeanne d'Arc** (Joan of Arc Festival), on May 7 and 8, celebrates the heroic Maid of Orléans with a parade and religious procession.

Châteauneuf-sur-Loire

34 *18 km (12 mi) southeast of Orléans via N460.*

The village of Châteauneuf-sur-Loire has a delightful public park with giant tulip trees, magnolias, weeping willows, and rhododendrons, and is especially beautiful in late May and early June. Little streams on their way to the Loire snake their way across the parkland, past benches, shady copses, and scenic picnic spots.

Until the railroad arrived 130 years ago, the Loire was a working river, with boats transporting everything from wheat, salt, wine, and stone to slate, wood, coal, and pottery. The **Musée de la Marine** (Maritime Museum), housed in the former château stables, chronicles that era with documents, old photos and a reconstituted 19th-century fishing boat equipped with ropes, nets, chests, eel pots, and harpoons. The cynosure of all eyes remains an astonishingly elegant **octagonal rotunda**—once centerpiece of the château estate and now the town hall, it gracefully overlooks the river. ✉ *1 pl. Aristide-Briand,* ☎ *02–38–46–84–46.* 🎫 *€3.05.* ⏲ *Apr.–Oct., Wed.–Mon. 10–6; Nov.–Mar., Wed.–Mon. 2–6.*

Germigny-des-Prés

35 *6 km (4 mi) northwest of St-Benoît-sur-Loire via D60, 34 km (21 mi) southeast of Orléans.*

The village of Germigny-des-Prés is famous for its church, one of the oldest in France. Around AD 800, Theodulf, an abbot of St-Benoît, built the tiny **Église de Germigny-des-Prés**—a Byzantine arrangement of round arches on square pillars, with indirect light filtering from smaller arches above the central square. The church was carefully restored to its original condition in the 19th century. Though Theodulf himself brought most of the original mosaics from Italy, only one—covered by plaster and not discovered until 1848—survives. Made of 130,000 cubes of colored glass, it shows the Ark of the Covenant transported by angels with golden halos. The Latin inscription asks us not to forget Theodulf in our prayers. ☎ *02–38–58–27–97.* 🎫 *Free.* ⏲ *Daily 9–noon and 2–5.*

St-Benoît-sur-Loire

36 *6 km (4 mi) southeast of Germigny-des-Prés, 8 km (5 mi) northwest of Sully-sur-Loire via D60, 40 km (30 mi) southeast of Orléans.*

The highlight of St-Benoît-sur-Loire is its ancient abbey, often called the greatest Romanesque church in France. Village signposts refer to it as LA BASILIQUE. St-Benoît (St. Benedict) was the founder of the Benedictine monastic order. In AD 650 a group of monks chose this safe and fertile spot for their new monastery, then returned to Monte Cassino, Italy, to retrieve the bones of St. Benedict with which to bless the site. Despite demands from priests at Monte Cassino for the return of the ★ bones, some of the relics remain here in the 11th-century **Abbaye St-Benoît.** Following the Hundred Years' War in the 14th and 15th centuries, the monastery fell into decline, and the Wars of Religion (1562–98) wrought further damage. During the French Revolution the monks dispersed, and all the buildings were destroyed except the abbey church itself, which became the parish church. Monastic life here began anew in 1944, when the monks rebuilt their monastery and regained the church for their own use. The pillars of the tower porch are noted for their intricately carved capitals, and the choir floor is a gaudy patchwork of multicolor marble. Gregorian chants can be heard daily, at mass or at vespers, and Sunday services attract worshipers and music lovers from all around. Don't forget to explore the church crypt. ☎ *02–38–35–72–43.* 🎫 *Free.* ⏲ *Mass and vespers Sun. 11 AM and 6:15 PM, Mon.–Sat. noon and 6:15 PM. Guided English-language tours of monastic bldgs. can be arranged; inquire at monastery shop.*

Sully-sur-Loire

37 *7 km (5 mi) southeast of St-Benoît-sur-Loire, 24 km (15 mi) northwest of Gien via D951, 48 km (30 mi) southeast of Orléans.*

An imposing castle with a park, moat, and spectacular medieval roof ★ makes Sully-sur-Loire worth visiting. The **Château de Sully** dates from the first half of the 14th century. Other châteaux have Loire-side perches, but few have the picture-perfect allure of this one, fitted out as it is with turrets and machicolated walkways. It also has a sturdy keep with the finest chestnut roof anywhere along the Loire—a vast structure in the form of an overturned boat, erected in 1400. Great families, including the de Sully and Béthune clans, once called this home; their illustrious friends included Voltaire, who enjoyed putting on plays here. The park by the Sange tributary contains a replica of the grotto of Lourdes. ☎ *02–38–36–36–86.* 🎫 *€4.90.* ⏲ *June–Aug., daily 10–6; Sept.–May, daily 10–noon and 2–5.*

Gien

38 *28 km (12 mi) southeast of Sully-sur-Loire, 67 km (42 mi) southeast of Orléans.*

Ceramics and hunting are the twin historical attractions of the pleasant riverside town of Gien. Its redbrick château, completed in 1484, ★ houses the unexpectedly fine **Musée International de la Chasse** (International Hunting Museum). Exhibits trace the various types of hunt—shooting, trapping, fox-hunting with hounds—and the display of firearms ranges from harquebuses to rifles. Vast 18th-century hunting pictures by François Desportes and Jean-Baptiste Oudry line the stately hall under its superb beamed roof. ✉ *Pl. du Château,* ☎ *02–38–67–69–69.* 🎫 *€5.35.* ⏲ *Apr.–Oct., daily 9:30–6:30; Nov.–Mar., daily 9–noon and 2–6.*

At the **Musée de la Faïencerie** (Earthenware Factory Museum), in an old paste store, admire local Gien earthenware (both old and new), with its distinctive deep blue glaze and golden decoration. Call ahead to arrange a tour of the factory; there's also a shop. ✉ *78 pl. de la Victoire,* ☎ *02–38–67–00–05.* 🎫 *€3.* ⏲ *Apr.–Sept., daily 9–noon and 2–6; Oct.–Mar., Sun.–Fri. 2–6, Sat. 9–noon and 2–6.*

Dining and Lodging

$$ ✕🏨 **Rivage.** Jolly Christian Gaillard presides over the finest hotel in Gien. Rooms are large and airy, breakfasts are copious, and the piano bar, with its terrace overlooking the Loire, is the ideal spot to relax before or after a dinner. Fish and herbs are likely to figure in your meal at the restaurant (no lunch Monday, and from November through March no dinner Sunday), unless you opt for the snails or veal kidneys with fresh pasta. Menus start at €24, and there is an extensive wine cellar. *✉ 1 quai de Nice, 45500, ☎ 02–38–37–79–00, FAX 02–38–38–10–21. 16 rooms, 3 suites. Restaurant. AE, DC, MC, V. Closed most of Feb., 2 wks in June.*

Briare

❸❾ *40 km (25 mi) north of Sancerre via D955 and D951, 39 km (24 mi) northeast of La Verrerie.*

The **Pont-Canal de Briare** is one of France's most famous bridges—in fact, a lamp-lined 700-yard aqueduct, held together by a mind-boggling 7 million bolts, built by Gustave Eiffel in 1890 (the year after his Paris tower) to transport the Canal Latéral de la Loire (Loire Side Canal) across the river to join the Canal de Briare. Walk along the span and admire the colorful riverboats along Briare's pretty quay; for those who want to live life along the Loire, there are houseboats available for rent here. (If you're interested in waterways, make a detour 10 km/6 mi north of Briare to admire the abandoned but spectacular 17th-century seven-rise locks at **Rogny-les-Sept-Écluses**).

Just downstream on the opposite bank of the Loire from Briare you'll find the 12th-century castle of **St-Brisson,** whose collection of 13th-century mangonels (giant catapults) is activated by local strongmen every Sunday in summer. The biggest catapult, known as a *couillard,* sends 45-pound rocks spinning as high as the castle roof before crashing 150 yards away. *☎ 02–38–36–71–29.* 🎫 €4. *⏲ Apr.–Oct., Sun. 2–6.*

Sancerre

❹⓿ *200 km (125 mi) south of Paris via A6 and N7, 120 km (75 mi) southeast of Orléans, 46 km (29 mi) northeast of Bourges.*

The hilltop town of Sancerre is a maze of old cobbled streets offering dramatic views of the mountainous vineyards producing lively white wines and flinty, lesser-known rosés and reds. The local setting challenges the Loire's reputation for soft pastures and gentle hills: the vineyards of Sancerre (like the town itself) stand on rugged, towering mounds and are among the most scenic in France. The main square, Nouvelle Place, was once the site of the grain market; here you'll find the tourist office, which has information about a walking tour of town.

From Sancerre visit **Chavignol,** 3 km (2 mi) away, a wine village with a number of producers that have tastings and vintages for sale. Chavignol is also famed for its delicious small, round goat cheese, Crottin de Chavignol, which comes in both hard and soft varieties, depending on the time of year. This famous goat cheese, along with other local cheeses, is celebrated in Sancerre every April during the Fête du Crottin.

Aubigny-sur-Nère

❹❶ *30 km (18 mi) south of Gien via 940.*

Graced with half-timber houses, this town was once the little kingdom of the royal Stuarts of Scotland, who were granted its charter by King

Charles VII in 1423. With the noble Darnley family as presiding spirits, the town had been an obvious rallying point for Mary, Queen of Scots. Centuries later, the town was made the duchy of the royal courtesan, Louise de Kéroualle, by Louis XIV. The town château now displays her famous tapestries and also contains the **Musée de la Vieille Alliance Franco-Ecossaise,** which details the history of the Auld Alliance and the Scot Jacobite refugees who settled here. A Scottish fete is held every July 14th weekend. ✉ *Château d'Aubigny,* ☎ *02–48–81–50–07.* 🎫 *€1.60.* ⏲ *Mid-June–mid-Sept., daily 2:30–7; mid-Sept.–mid-Nov. and Apr.–mid-June, weekends 2:30–6; mid-Nov.–Mar., Sun. 2:30–6.*

Dining and Lodging

$$$$ ★ ✕🏨 **Château de La Verrerie.** Set in the Forêt d'Ivoy next to its own mirror-lake, this turreted abode is the very picture of fairy-tale elegance. Dating from the 15th century and once owned by royal Stuarts, it is now a famously elegant retreat run by Comte Béraud and Comtesse Florence de Vogüé, whose ancestors acquired the place in 1842. Guest rooms are spacious (six have twin beds, six are doubles) with high ceilings, family heirlooms, and sweeping views of the estate. A half-timber 17th-century cottage on the estate has been transformed into **La Maison d'Hélène** restaurant, an excellent spot for light lunches and sumptuous dinners (closed Tuesday, no dinner Wednesday). Don't forget to visit the château's delightful Renaissance chapel, with frescoes dating from 1525. ✉ *18700 Aubigny-sur-Nère (3 mi (1 ½ km) northwest of La Verrerie,* ☎ *02–48–81–51–60 for château; 02–48–58–24–27 for restaurant,* FAX *02–48–58–21–25,* WEB *www.chateauxfrance.com/-verrerie.fr. 12 rooms. Restaurant, no air-conditioning. MC, V. Closed mid-Dec.–mid-Jan.*

Romorantin-Lanthenay

42 *60 km (42 mi) southwest of Aubigny-sur-Nère via 724, 45 km (28 mi) southeast of Blois.*

Silence rules in the flat, wooded Sologne region, famed for its game, mushrooms, asparagus, and hidden lakes. Pretty Romorantin-Lanthenay is the area's main town, which saw its heyday in the early 16th century during the turbulent youth of François I (who in 1517 commissioned Leonardo da Vinci to design a palace for his mother here, though it was never built). Some of the great Renaissance houses, including the Hôtel St-Pol where François had his head shaved by doctors after being hit by a burning log (and thereafter grew a beard, starting the fashion for them), are on rue du Milieu and rue de la Résistance.

Dining and Lodging

$$$–$$$$ ★ ✕🏨 **Grand Hôtel du Lion d'Or.** Along with Jean Bardet in Tours, this restaurant is considered a mandatory pilgrimage spot by Loire Valley gourmands. The Barrat family has owned this former post house for four decades, welcoming guests to fine accommodations and to chef Didier Clément's renowned restaurant. This magician is famous for his prawns with the unusual medieval spice called paradise seed; exotic herbs also enliven other dishes, including a *tabac de cuisine* (half a dozen ground spices) garnishing noisettes of lamb. In the inn, pale greens, blues, and pinks plus old stone and warm wood dominate, along with large beds and marble bathrooms; choose one overlooking the delightful courtyard. ✉ *69 rue Georges-Clemenceau, 41200,* ☎ *02–54–94–15–15,* FAX *02–54–88–24–87. 16 rooms. Restaurant, minibars. AE, DC, MC, V. Closed mid-Feb.–mid-Mar.*

THE LOIRE VALLEY A TO Z

To research prices, get advice from other travelers, and book travel arrangements, visit www.fodors.com.

AIRPORTS

The closest international airports are Paris's Charles-de-Gaulle and Orly (☞ Air Travel *in* Smart Travel Tips A to Z).

BIKE TRAVEL

With its nearly flat terrain, the Loire Valley is custom-built for traveling by bike; however, a single-day expedition visiting three or more châteaux would be difficult, except for professional bicyclists, considering the distances involved. *Vélos tout-terrains* (mountain bikes) are the sturdiest models. When renting, inquire about bike-repair kits. As Tours is the heart of the region, it is the best base.

➤ BIKE RENTALS: **Amster Cycles** (✉ 5 rue du Rempart, Tours, ☎ 02–47–61–22–23).

BUS TRAVEL

Local bus services are extensive and reliable, providing a link between train stations and scenic areas off the river; it is possible to reach many villages and châteaux by bus (although many routes are in place to service school children, meaning service is less frequent in the summer and sometimes all but nonexistent on Sunday). Inquire at tourist offices for information about routes and timetables, available in very handy form. The leading companies are Les Rapides du Val de Loire, originating in Orléans; TLC, serving Chambord and Cheverny from Blois; Touraine Fil Vert, Fil Bleu, and CAT (Compagnies des Autocars de Touraine, which offers buses to Chenonceaux and Amboise from Tours), all of which serve the Touraine region; and Anjou Bus (Anjou region).

➤ BUS INFORMATION: **Les Rapides du Val de Loire** (✉ 1 rue Marcel Proust, Orléans, ☎ 02–38–53–94–75). **TLC (Transports du Loir-et-Cher)** (✉ 9 rue Alexandre-Vézin, Blois, ☎ 02–54–58–55–44). **Touraine Fil Vert** (✉ Pl. du Général Leclerc, Tours, ☎ 02–47–05–30–49). **Fil Bleu** (✉ Pl. Jean Jaurès, Tours, ☎ 02–47–66–70–70). **Anjou Bus** (✉ Pl. de la Poissonnerie, Angers, ☎ 02–41–88–59–25).

CAR RENTAL

➤ LOCAL AGENCIES: **Avis** (✉ 6 rue Jean-Moulin, Blois, ☎ 02–54–74–48–15; ✉ 13 rue Sansonnières, Orléans, ☎ 02–38–62–27–04; ✉ Pl. Gal-Leclerc, Tours, ☎ 02–47–20–53–27). **Europcar** (✉ 81 rue André-Dessaux, on N20 near Orléans at Fleury-les-Aubrais, ☎ 02–33–73–00–40; ✉ 76 rue Bernard-Palissy, Tours, ☎ 02–47–64–47–76). **Hertz** (✉ Chaussée St-Victor [on N7], Blois, ☎ 02–54–74–03–03; ✉ 57 rue Marcel-Tribut, Tours, ☎ 02–47–75–50–00).

CAR TRAVEL

The Loire Valley is an easy drive from Paris. A10 runs from Paris to Orléans—a distance of 125 km (78 mi)—and on to Tours, with exits at Meung, Blois, and Amboise. After Tours, A10 veers south, toward Poitiers and Bordeaux. A11 links Paris to Angers and Saumur via Le Mans. Slower but more scenic routes run from the Channel ports down through Normandy into the Loire region.

The easiest way to visit the Loire châteaux is by car; N152 hugs the riverbank and is excellent for sightseeing. You can rent a car in all the large towns in the region, or at train stations in Orléans, Blois, Tours, or Angers, or in Paris.

EMERGENCIES

➤ CONTACTS: **Ambulance** (☎ 15). **Regional hospitals** (✉ 4 rue Larrey, Angers, ☎ 02–41–35–36–37; ✉ 14 av. de l'Hôpital, Orléans, ☎ 02–38–51–44–44; ✉ 2 bd. Tonnellé, Tours, ☎ 02–47–47–47–47).

TOURS

CHÂTEAU TOURS

Many châteaux insist that you follow one of their tours; try to get a booklet in English before joining, as most are in French. Bus tours of the main châteaux leave daily in summer from Tours, Blois, Angers, Orléans, and Saumur: Ask at the relevant tourist office for latest times and prices (☞ Visitor Information, *below*).

HELICOPTER AND BALLOON TOURS

Jet Systems makes helicopter trips over the Loire Valley on Tuesdays, Thursdays, and weekends from the aerodrome at Dierre, just south of Amboise; cost ranges from €53 (10 minutes) to €221 (50 minutes) per person.

For a more leisurely airborne visit, contact France Montgolfière for details of their balloon trips over the Loire from Chinon; prices run €190–€245.

➤ FEES AND SCHEDULES: **Jet Systems** (☎ 02–47–30–20–21, www.jet-systems.fr). **France Montgolfière** (☎ 02–54–71–75–70, WEB www.franceballons.com).

PRIVATE GUIDES

The tourist offices in Tours and Angers (☞ Visitor Information, *below*) arrange city and regional excursions with personal guides.

WALKING TOURS

A walking tour of Tours sets out from the tourist office (☞ Visitor Information, *below*) every morning at 10 AM from mid-April through October (€6). English-speaking guides show you around Blois on a tour that starts from the château at 4 (€5).

TRAIN TRAVEL

Tours and Angers are both served by the superfast TGV (*Trains à Grande Vitesse*) from Paris (Gare Montparnasse); three TGVs daily reach Vendôme in 40 minutes. There are also TGV trains direct to the Loire Valley from Charles-de-Gaulle Airport: four per day to Angers (2 hours 10 minutes), one per day (around lunchtime) to Blois (1 hour 50 minutes) and Tours (2 hours 20 minutes). Express trains run every two hours from Paris (Gare d'Austerlitz) to Orléans (usually you must change at nearby Les Aubrais) and Blois. Note that trains for Gien leave from Paris's Gare de Lyon (direction Nevers) and that the nearest station to Sancerre is across the Loire at Tracy.

The Loire region's local train network is magnificent, and it's possible to reach many of the châteaux by train. The main line follows the Loire from Orléans to Angers; there are trains every two hours or so, stopping in Blois, Tours, and Saumur; trains stop less frequently in Onzain (for Chaumont), Amboise, and Langeais. There are branch lines with trains from Tours to Loches, Chenonceaux, Azay-le-Rideau, and Chinon, and to Vendôme and Châteaudun. Ask the SNCF for the brochure *Les Châteaux de la Loire en Train* for more detailed information. Be sure to get the very helpful train-schedule brochures, available at main train stations such as Tours and Orléans.

➤ TRAIN INFORMATION: **SNCF** (☎ 08–36–35–35–35, WEB www.sncf.com).

TRAVEL AGENCIES

➤ Local Agent Referrals: **Havas–American Express** (✉ 19 av. des Droits-de-l'Homme, Orléans, ☎ 02–38–22–15–45). **Carlson-Wagonlit** (✉ 9 rue Marceau, Tours, ☎ 02–47–20–40–54).

VISITOR INFORMATION

The Loire region has two area tourist offices, both of which are for written inquiries only. For Chinon and points east, contact the Comité Régional du Tourisme Centre-Val de Loire. For Fontevraud and points west, contact the Comité Régional du Tourisme des Pays-de-Loire. Other main tourist offices are listed below by town.

➤ Tourist Information: **Comité Régional du Tourisme Centre-Val de Loire** (✉ 37 av. de Paris, 45000 Orléans, WEB www.loirevalley-tourism.com). **Comité Régional du Tourisme des Pays-de-Loire** (✉ 2 rue de la Loire, 44200 Nantes).

Amboise (✉ Quai Général-de-Gaulle, ☎ 02–47–57–01–37, WEB www.amboise-valdeloire.com). **Angers** (✉ 7 pl. Kennedy, ☎ 02–41–23–51–11, WEB www.angers-tourisme.com). **Blois** (✉ 3 av. du Dr-Jean-Laigret, ☎ 02–54–90–41–41, WEB www.loiredeschateaux.com). **Fontevraud-L'Abbaye** (✉ Pl. St-Michel, ☎ 02–41–51–79–45). **Gien** (✉ Pl. Jean Jaurès, ☎ 02–38–67–25–28). **Montlouis-sur-Loire** (✉ Pl. F. Mitterand, ☎ 02–47–45–00–16). **Orléans** (✉ 6 rue Albert-Ier, ☎ 02–38–24–05–05, WEB www.ville-orleans.fr). **Rochecorbon** (✉ Pl. du Croissant, Pl. de la Lanterne, ☎ 02–47–52–80–22). **Saumur** (✉ Pl. de la Bilange, ☎ 02–41–40–20–60, WEB www.saumur-tourisme.com). **Tours** (✉ 78 rue Bernard-Palissy, ☎ 02–47–70–37–37, WEB www.tourisme-touraine.com).

5 BRITTANY

Even the French feel they are in a foreign land when they visit Brittany, the triangular patch of northwestern France that juts far out into the Atlantic. Cut off as they are from mainstream culture, the Bretons have closer cultural affinities with the Celts across the Channel than with Parisians. Delights by the score are to be found here—village fêtes, prehistoric megaliths, and picturesque medieval towns among them. Little wonder Brittany remains a favorite vacation destination for Brits—but don't worry about overcrowding: its vast beaches aren't easily crowded, and there are more than enough castles to go around.

Revised and updated by Simon Hewitt

Introduction by Nancy Coons

YOU FEEL IT EVEN BEFORE THE SHARP SALT AIR hits your face from the west—a subliminal rhythm suspended in the mist, a subsonic drone somewhere between a foghorn and a heartbeat, seemingly made up of bagpipes, drums, and the thin, haunting filigree of a tin-whistle tune. This is Brittany, land of the Bretons, where Celtic blood-lines run deep as a Druid's roots into the rocky, sea-swept soil. Wherever you wander—along jagged coastal cliffs, through cobbled seaport streets, into burnished-oak cider pubs—you'll hear this primal pulse of Celtic music. France's most fiercely and determinedly ethnic people, the Bretons delight in celebrating their primeval culture—circle dancing at street fairs, the men and women donning starched lace-bonnet *coiffes* and striped fishermen's shirts at the least sign of a regional celebration. They name their children Erwan and Edwige, carry sacred statues in ceremonial religious processions called *pardons,* pray in Hobbit-scale stone churches decked with elfin, moon-faced gargoyles. And scattered over the mossy hillsides stand Stonehenge-like dolmens and menhirs (prehistoric standing stones), eerie testimony to a primordial culture that predated and has long outlived Frankish France.

Similarities in character, situation, or culture to certain islands across the Channel are by no means coincidental. Indeed, the Celts that migrated to this westernmost outcrop of the French landmass spent much of the Iron Age on the British Isles, where they introduced the indigenes to innovations like the potter's wheel, the rotary millstone, and the compass. This first influx of Continental culture to Great Britain was greeted with typically mixed feelings, and by the 6th century AD the Saxon hordes had sent the Britons packing southward, to the peninsula which became Brittany. So completely did they dominate their new, Cornwall-like peninsula (appropriately named Finistère, from *finis terrae,* or "land's end") that when in 496 they allied themselves with Clovis, the king of the Franks, he felt as if he'd just claimed a little bit of England. Nonetheless the Britons remained independent of France until 1532, only occasionally hiring out as wild and woolly warrior-allies to the Norsemen of Normandy.

Yet the cultural exchange flowed two ways over the Channel. From their days on the British Isles the Britons brought a folklore that shares with England the bittersweet legend of Tristan and Iseult; that weaves mystical tales of the Cornwall/Cornouaille of King Arthur and Merlin. They brought a language that still renders village names unpronounceable: Aber-Wrac'h, Tronoën, Locmariaquer, Poldreuzic, Kerhornaouen. And, too, they brought a way of life with them: half-timber seaside cider bars, their blackened-oak tables softened with prim bits of lace; stone cottages watercolored with hollyhocks, hydrangeas, and foxglove, with damp woolens and rubber boots dripping in flag-stone entryways; chin-bearded fishermen in yellow oilskins heaving the day's catch into weather-beaten boats, terns and seagulls wheeling in their wake. It's a way of life that feels deliciously exotic to the Frenchman and—like the ancient drone of the bagpipes—comfortably, delightfully, even primally familiar to the Anglo-Saxon.

This cozy regional charm extends inland to Rennes, at 200,000 inhabitants the largest city of Bretagne (to use the French name), as well as to Dinan, Vannes, Quimper, and seaside St-Malo. Though many towns took a beating during the the course of the Nazi retreat in 1944, most have been gracefully restored, their sweet whitewashed cottages once again anchoring the soil. And the countryside retains the heather-and-emerald moorscape, framed in forests primeval and bordered by open sea, that first inspired wandering peoples to their pipes.

Pleasures and Pastimes

Beaches

Wherever you go in Brittany, the coast is close by: in winter the frenzied, cliff-bashing Atlantic pounds the shore; in summer the sprawling beaches and bustling harbors are filled with frolicking bathers and boaters. Dozens of islands, many inhabited and within easy reach of the mainland, spangle the coastal waters. The best sandy beaches and a multitude of water sports are found in Dinard, Perros-Guirec, Trégastel-Plage, Douarnenez, Carnac, La Trinité-sur-Mer, and La Baule.

Dining

Not surprisingly, Breton cuisine is dominated by seafood—often lobster. Brittany is the land of *homard à l'armoricaine* (lobster with cream), a name derived from the ancient name for Brittany—Armorici—and not to be confused with Américaine. Other popular meals include smoked ham and lamb, frequently served with green kidney beans. Fried eel is a traditional dish in Nantes. Brittany is particularly famous for its crepes, served with sweet fillings, or as the heartier *galettes*—thicker, buckwheat crepes served as a main course and stuffed with meat, fish, or regional lobster. What's the difference between the two? The dark galette crepe has a deeper flavor best paired with savory fillings—like lobster and mushrooms, or the more traditional ham and cheese. A crepe plain and simple is wafer-thin and made with a lighter batter, reserved traditionally for the sweet—strawberries and cream, apples in brandy, or chocolate, for example. Accompanied by a glass of local cider, they are an ideal light, inexpensive meal; as *crêpes dentelles* (lace crepes) they make a delicious dessert.

CATEGORY	COST*
$$$$	over €30
$$$	€20–€30
$$	€12–€20
$	under €12

**per person for a main course only, including tax (19.6%) and service; note that if a restaurant offers only prix-fixe (set-price) meals, it has been given the price category that reflects the full prix-fixe price.*

Lodging

Brittany has plenty of small, appealing family-run hotels with friendly and personal service, as well as a growing number of luxury hotels and châteaux. Dinard, on the English Channel, and La Baule, on the Atlantic, are the area's two most expensive resorts. In summer, expect crowds, so make reservations far in advance and confirm before arriving. Assume all hotel rooms have air-conditioning, TV, telephones, and private bath unless otherwise noted. Internet, when listed in facilities, means in-room data-ports and/or public-area computer provides computer access

CATEGORY	COST*
$$$$	over €180
$$$	€120–€180
$$	€60–€120
$	under €60

**All prices are for a standard double room in high season, including tax (19.6%) and service charge.*

Exploring Brittany

Brittany can be divided into two basic areas. The first is the northeast, stretching from Rennes—the traditional capital of Brittany—to St-

Malo and along the Channel coast. Here mighty medieval castles survey the land and quaint resort towns line the seacoast. In addition to the cosmopolitan pleasures of Rennes and St-Malo, highlights include the splendid gabled wooden houses of Dinan; Chateaubriand's home at Combourg; and Dinard, the elegant Belle Epoque resort once favored by British aristocrats. The second region is the Atlantic coast between Brest and Nantes, where frenzied surf crashes against the cliffs, alternating with sprawling beaches and bustling harbors. Here is lively Quimper, with its fine cathedral and museum; Pont-Aven, a former artists' colony made famous by Gauguin; the pretty island of Belle-Ile; the prehistoric menhirs of Carnac; the 19th-century resort of La Baule; and the thriving city of Nantes.

Great Itineraries

If you only have three days or so, concentrate on northeast Brittany. With five days you can explore the region in greater depth, including Rennes. With 10 days you can cover the entire region, if you don't spend too much time in any one place. A car is necessary for getting to the small medieval towns and deserted coastline.

Numbers in the text correspond to numbers in the margin and on the Brittany and Nantes maps.

IF YOU HAVE 3 DAYS

Choose either the medieval town of **Dinan** ⑤ or the fortified port of **St-Malo** ⑨—surrounded on four sides by walls and on three by sea—as your base for exploring northeast Brittany. Be sure to visit ancient **Dol-de-Bretagne** ⑦, Chateaubriand's boyhood home at **Combourg** ⑥, or the 16th-century castle in **La Bourbansais,** all pleasant side trips from seaside **Dinard** ⑩. In addition, the magnificent rock island of **Mont-St-Michel** is only 50 km (30 mi) away, in Normandy.

IF YOU HAVE 5 DAYS

Follow the three-day itinerary, then spend your fourth day in **Rennes** ③, the region's capital, yet the least typical of Breton cities. Visit the formidable castles in **Vitré** ② and **Fougères** ① on day five.

IF YOU HAVE 10 DAYS

Make **Rennes** ③ your base for exploring the castles, châteaux, and fortresses in **Vitré** ②, **Fougères** ①, and **Montmuran** ④, making an excursion to the Château de Caradeuc if you have time. On day three stop in **La Bourbansais, Combourg** ⑥, or **Dol-de-Bretagne** ⑦ on your way to **Dinan** ⑤ or **St-Malo** ⑨ for the night. Head west the following day on a scenic tour of the coast and spend the night in **Trébeurden** ⑫, on the tip of the Corniche Bretonne. Start early the next day for quaint **Morlaix** ⑬. Continue west and briefly visit the splendid basilica at **Le Folgoët.** Eat lunch in **Brest** ⑭, a huge, modern port town. By late afternoon plan on being in **Locronan,** where sails used to be made for French fleets. Try to reach picturesque **Douarnenez** ⑯ by evening. On the sixth day head to **Quimper** ⑰, with its lovely riverbank and cathedral. Stop briefly to see the offshore stronghold at **Concarneau** ⑱ and aim to reach **Pont-Aven** ⑲ by the end of the day; then dine on oysters in nearby Riec-sur-Belon. On day seven drive down the Atlantic seaboard to the beaches of Quiberon and catch the ferry to the pretty island of **Belle-Ile-en-Mer** ㉑. On day eight return to the mainland and meander along the coast through the beach resorts of **Carnac** ㉒ and La Trinité-sur-Mer, stopping in the medieval town of **Vannes** ㉔ and exploring the marshy parkland of **La Grande Brière.** Spend the night in seaside **La Baule** ㉕. The following day head to tranquil, prosperous **Nantes** ㉖–㉜.

Brittany

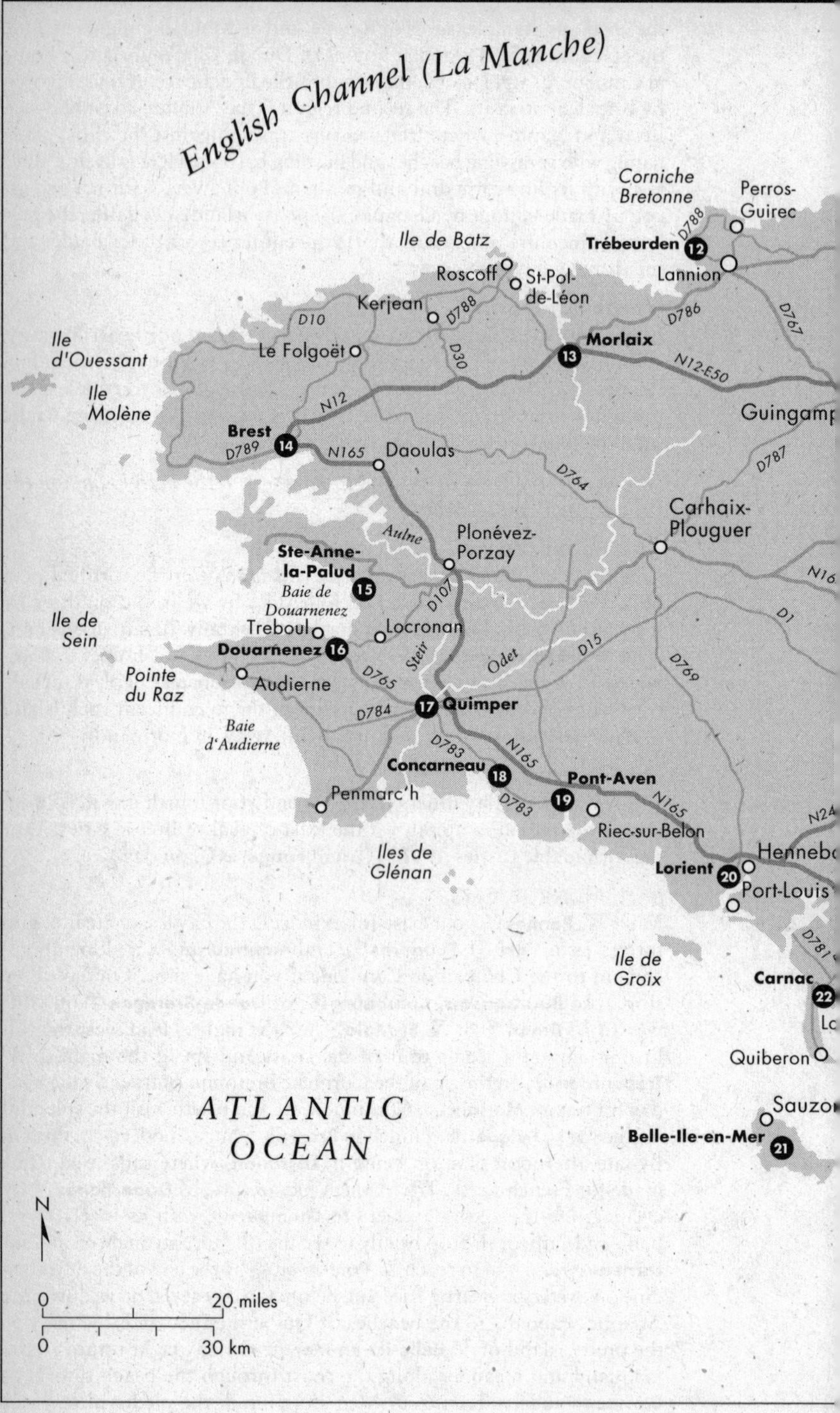
English Channel (La Manche)
Corniche Bretonne
Perros-Guirec
Ile de Batz
Trébeurden 12
D788
Lannion
Roscoff
St-Pol-de-Léon
Kerjean
D788
D10
D786
D767
Ile d'Ouessant
Le Folgoët
D30
Morlaix 13
N12-E50
Ile Molène
N12
Guingamp
Brest 14
D789
N165
Daoulas
D787
D764
Carhaix-Plouguer
Aulne
Plonévez-Porzay
Ste-Anne-la-Palud 15
Baie de Douarnenez
D107
Ile de Sein
Treboul
Locronan
D1
Douarnenez 16
Steir
Odet
D15
D769
Pointe du Raz
Audierne
D765
D784
Quimper 17
Baie d'Audierne
D783
N165
Concarneau 18
Pont-Aven
Penmarc'h
D783
19
N165
Riec-sur-Belon
N24
Iles de Glénan
Lorient 20
Henneb
Port-Louis
D781
Ile de Groix
Carnac
22
Quiberon
ATLANTIC OCEAN
Sauzo
Belle-Ile-en-Mer 21
N
0
20 miles
0
30 km

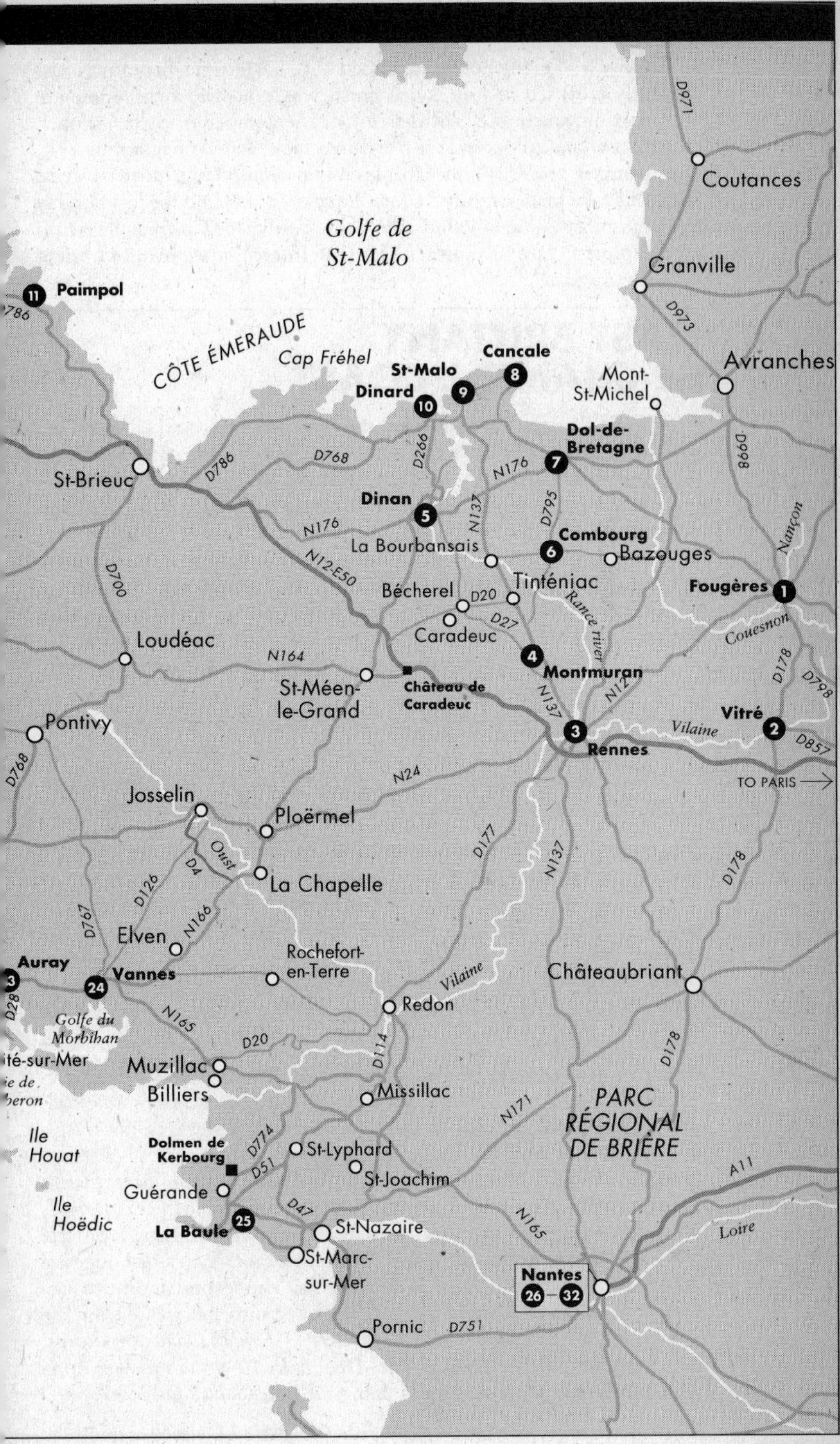

Golfe de St-Malo
CÔTE ÉMERAUDE
Cap Fréhel
Coutances
Granville
Avranches
Mont-St-Michel
Cancale 8
St-Malo 9
Dinard 10
Paimpol 11
St-Brieuc
Dol-de-Bretagne 7
Dinan 5
La Bourbansais
Combourg 6
Bazouges
Tinténiac
Bécherel
Caradeuc
Fougères 1
Couesnon
Nançon
Loudéac
Montmuran 4
St-Méen-le-Grand
Château de Caradeuc
Rance river
Vitré 2
Vilaine
Rennes 3
TO PARIS
Pontivy
Josselin
Ploërmel
Oust
La Chapelle
Elven
Auray
Vannes 24
Golfe du Morbihan
Rochefort-en-Terre
Redon
Vilaine
Châteaubriant
Muzillac
Billiers
Missillac
PARC RÉGIONAL DE BRIÈRE
Ile Houat
Dolmen de Kerbourg
St-Lyphard
St-Joachim
Guérande
Ile Hoëdic
La Baule 25
St-Nazaire
St-Marc-sur-Mer
Nantes 26–32
Loire
Pornic
D971
D973
D998
D786
D768
D266
N176
N137
D795
N12-E50
D700
D20
D27
N164
N12
D178
D798
D857
N24
D177
D768
D126
D4
N166
D767
N165
D20
D114
N171
D774
D51
D47
A11
D751

When to Tour Brittany

The tourist season is short in Brittany. Long, damp winters keep visitors away, and many hotels are closed until Eastertime. Brittany is particularly crowded in July and August, when most French people are on vacation, so choose crowd-free June, September, or early October, when autumnal colors and crisp evenings make for an invigorating visit. Late summer, however, is the most festive time in Brittany: the two biggest pardons take place on July 26 (Ste-Anne d'Auray) and the last Sunday in August (Ste-Anne-la-Palud); the Celtic Festival de Cornouaille is held in Quimper in late July; and the Festival Interceltique invades Lorient in early August.

NORTHEAST BRITTANY AND THE CHANNEL COAST

Northeast Brittany extends from the city of Rennes to the coast. The rolling farmland around Rennes is strewn with mighty castles in Vitré, Fougères, and Dinan—remnants of Brittany's ceaseless efforts to repel invaders during the Middle Ages and a testimony to the wealth derived from pirate and merchant ships. The beautiful Côte d'Émeraude (Emerald Coast) stretches west from Cancale to St-Brieuc, and the dramatic Côte de Granit Rose (Pink Granite Coast) extends from Paimpol to Trébeurden and the Corniche Bretonne. Follow the coastal routes D786 and D34—winding, narrow roads that total less than 100 km (62 mi) but can take five hours to drive; the spectacular views make the journey worthwhile.

Fougères

❶ *320 km (200 mi) west of Paris via A11, A81, and D30; 47 km (29 mi) southeast of Mont-St-Michel, 48 km (30 mi) northeast of Rennes.*

For many centuries Fougères, a traditional cobbling and cider-making center, was a frontier town, valiantly attempting to guard Brittany against attack. One of the reasons for its conspicuous lack of success was the siting of its castle: instead of being high up on the hill, it spreads out down in the valley, though the sinuous River Nançon does make an admirable moat. A number of medieval houses line rue de la Pinterie, which leads directly from the castle up to the undistinguished heart of town.

The 13-tower **Château de Fougères,** one of the largest in Europe, covers more than 5 acres. Although largely in ruins today, it's an excellent example of the military architecture of the Middle Ages, impressive both inside and out. The thick walls—20 ft across in places—were intended to resist 15th-century artillery fire, but the castle nevertheless proved vulnerable to surprise attacks and sieges. Inside the castle walls are three lines of fortification, with the keep at their heart. From the **Tour Mélusine** (Mélusine Tower) are memorable views of Fougères; in the **Tour Raoul** is a small shoe museum. The second and third stories of the **Tour de Coigny** were transformed into a chapel during the 16th century. ✉ *Pl. Symon,* ☎ *02–99–99–79–59,* WEB *www.ot-fougeres.fr.* 🎫 *€3.60.* ⏲ *Feb.–Mar. and Oct.–Dec., daily 10–noon and 2–5; Apr.–mid-June, daily 9:30–noon and 2–6; mid-June–Sept., daily 9–7.*

The town's oldest streets are alongside the castle, clustered around the elegant slate spire of **St-Sulpice** (✉ Rue Le Bouteiller), a Flamboyant Gothic church with several fine altarpieces, and the historic place aux Arbres; fine views can be seen from the Escalier (or steps) de la

Duchesse-Anne. At St-Sulpice note the depiction of the fairy Mélusine, symbol of the de Lusignan family, on its south portal.

In the 1790s Fougères was a center of Royalist resistance to the French Revolution. Much of the action in 19th-century writer Honoré Balzac's bloodcurdling novel *Les Chouans* takes place hereabouts. The church of **St-Léonard** (✉ Rue de la Porte-St-Léonard) overlooks the Nançon Valley. To get there from St-Sulpice, follow the river south. Both the footpath leading to the building and to the church, with its ornate facade and 17th-century tower, have changed little; the park through which the path leads is known today as the **Jardin Public** (Public Garden).

Also inspired by the scenery of Fougères was locally born Emmanuel de La Villéon (1858–1944), a little-known Impressionist painter. More than 100 paintings, pastels, watercolors, and drawings—revealing a serene, underestimated talent—are on display at the **Musée La Villéon.** It is in one of the oldest surviving houses (dating from the 16th century) in Fougères. The artist's work ranges from compassionate studies of toiling peasants to pretty landscapes where soft shades of green melt into hazy blue horizons. To reach it from the Jardin Public, head left past St-Léonard and cross the square into the adjacent rue Nationale. *✉ 51 rue Nationale, ☎ 02–99–99–19–98. Free. Mid-June–mid-Sept., daily 10:30–12:30 and 2–6; mid-Sept.–mid-June, Wed.–Sun. 10–noon and 2–5.*

Dining and Lodging

$$ ✕ **Voyageurs.** This 100-year-old, unpretentious hotel in the city center is a clean and simple address with small, rustic rooms; some have been renovated. Have an aperitif in the bar, where the owner proudly displays a passion for 1950s Americana with his photos of Harley-Davidson motorcycles and an old gas pump. Nothing American about the restaurant (☎ 02–99–99–14–17), where Jean-Pierre Sonnet prepares specialties like foie gras in thin layers of puff pastry, sautéed pigeon with spring vegetables, and monkfish in anchovy cream. Save room for the dessert cart loaded with homemade pastries (the restaurant does not serve lunch Saturday or dinner Sunday). *✉ 10 pl. Gambetta, 35300, ☎ 02–99–99–08–20, FAX 02–99–99–99–04. 37 rooms. Restaurant, no air-conditioning. AE, MC, V. Closed mid-Dec.–early Jan.*

Vitré

❷ *30 km (19 mi) south of Fougères via D798 and D178, 36 km (22 mi) east of Rennes.*

Built high above the Vilaine Valley, Vitré (pronounced vee-*tray*) is one of the age-old gateways to Brittany: there's still a feel of the Middle Ages about its formidable castle, tightly packed half-timber houses, remaining ramparts, and dark, narrow alleys. The castle stands at the west end of town, facing narrow, cobbled streets as picturesque as any in Brittany—rue Poterie, rue d'Embas, and rue Beaudrairie, originally the home of tanners (the name comes from *baudoyers,* or leather workers).

★ Rebuilt in the 14th and 15th centuries to protect Brittany from invasion, the 11th-century **Château de Vitré**—shaped in an imposing triangle with fat, round towers—proved to be one of the province's most successful fortresses: during the Hundred Years' War (1337–1453), the English repeatedly failed to take it, even when they occupied the rest of the town. It's a splendid sight, especially from the vantage point of rue de Fougères across the river valley below. Time, not foreigners, came closest to ravaging the castle, which was heavily though tastefully restored during the past century. The **Hôtel de Ville** (town hall), however, is an unfortunate 1913 accretion to the castle courtyard. Visit the wing to the left of the entrance, beginning with the **Tour St-Laurent** and its museum, which contains 15th- and 16th-century sculptures, Aubusson tapestries, and engravings. Continue along the walls via the **Tour de l'Argenterie** (Silverware Tower)—which contains a macabre collection of stuffed frogs and reptiles preserved in glass jars—to the **Tour de l'Oratoire** (Oratory Tower). ☎ *02–99–75–04–54,* WEB *www.ot.vitre.fr.* 🎫 *€4.* ⏲ *Wed.–Fri. 10–noon and 2–5:30, Sat.–Mon. 2–5:30.*

Fragments of the town's medieval ramparts include the 15th-century **Tour de la Bridolle** (✉ Pl. de la République), five blocks up from the castle. The church of **Notre-Dame** (✉ Pl. Notre-Dame), with its fine, pinnacled south front, was built in the 15th and 16th centuries.

Dining and Lodging

$–$$ ✕🏨 **Le Petit Billot.** Carved-wood paneling and faded pastels give this small family-run hotel a delightful French Provincial air. The staff is friendly, and the restaurant (closed Saturday, no dinner Friday or Sunday) serves good food: try the vegetable terrine with a chopped-tomato sauce or the grilled fresh mackerel. ✉ *5 pl. du Général-Leclerc, 35500,* ☎ *02–99–75–02–10,* FAX *02–99–74–72–96,* WEB *www.petit-billot.com. 21 rooms, 5 with bath. Restaurant. AE, MC, V. Closed last week of Dec. and first week of Jan.*

Rennes

❸ *6 km (22 mi) west of Vitré via D857 and N157, 348 km (216 mi) west of Paris, 107 km (66 mi) north of Nantes.*

Rennes (pronounced *wren*) is the traditional capital of Brittany. It has a different flavor from other towns in the region, mainly because of a terrible fire in 1720 that lasted a week and destroyed half the city. The remaining cobbled streets and 15th-century half-timber houses form an interesting contrast to the Classical feel of the cathedral and Jacques Gabriel's disciplined granite buildings, broad avenues, and spacious squares. Many of the 15th- and 16th-century houses in the streets surrounding the cathedral have been converted into shops, boutiques, restaurants, and *crêperies* (crepe restaurants).

The **Parlement de Bretagne** (✉ Rue Nationale), the palatial original home of the Breton Parliament and now the Rennes law courts, was designed in 1618 by Salomon de Brosse, architect of the Luxembourg Palace in Paris. It was the most important building in Rennes to escape the 1720 flames, but in 1994, following a massive demonstration by Breton fishermen demanding state subsidies, a disastrous fire broke out at the building, which left it just a charred shell. Fortunately, much of the artwork—though damaged—was saved by firefighters, who arrived at the scene after the building was already engulfed in flames. It was a case of the fire bell that cried "fire," once too often; a faulty bell, which rang regularly for no reason, had led the man on duty to ignore the signal. Most of the major restoration was completed in 2001. Call ☎ 02–99–67–11–08 for information on guided tours in English, cost €6.10.

The **Musée des Beaux-Arts** (Fine Arts Museum) contains works by Georges de La Tour, Jean-Baptiste Chardin, Camille Corot, Paul Gauguin, and Maurice Utrillo, to name a few. The museum is particularly strong in French 17th-century paintings and drawings and has an interesting collection of modern French artists. ✉ *20 quai Émile-Zola,* ☎ *02–99–28–55–85,* WEB *www.mbar.org.* 🎫 *€4.* ⏲ *Wed.–Mon. 10–noon and 2–6.*

A late-18th-century building in Classical style that took 57 years to construct, the **Cathédrale St-Pierre** looms above rue de la Monnaie at the west end of the Old Town, bordered by the Rance River. Stop in to admire its richly decorated interior and outstanding 16th-century Flemish altarpiece. ✉ *Pl. St-Pierre.* ⏲ *Mon.–Sat. 8:30–noon and 2–5, Sun. 8:30–noon.*

★ Take a stroll through the lovely **Parc du Thabor** (✉ Pl. St-Melaine), east of the Palais des Musées. It's a large, formal French garden with regimented rows of trees, shrubs, flowers, and a notable view of the church of Notre-Dame-en-St-Melaine.

Dining and Lodging

$ ✕ **Piccadilly Tavern.** Around the corner from the Palais de Justice and next to the municipal theater is this oddly named brasserie. Its huge, sunny terrace is the perfect place to people-watch while downing a half-dozen fresh oysters and an aperitif or, if you're in an adventurous mood, to taste the surprisingly tender grilled ostrich with glazed peaches. ✉ *15 Galeries du Théâtre,* ☎ *02–99–78–17–17. MC, V.*

$$–$$$ ★ ✕🏨 **LeCoq-Gadby.** A 19th-century mansion with huge fireplaces and antiques sets the stage for this cozy retreat. Homey guest rooms have four-poster beds and floral covers, while hydrotherapy facilities, a *hammam* (steam room), a Jacuzzi, and a sauna are all available if you want to be pampered. As for the restaurant, it must be good—French presidents have dined here on such delicacies as *pigeon fermier roti aux chataignes* (pigeon roasted with chestnuts). Book way in advance for this popular hotel and restaurant (which does not serve dinner Sunday). ✉ *156 rue d'Antrain, 35700,* ☎ *02–99–38–05–55,* FAX *02–99–38–53–40,* WEB *www.lecoq-gadby.com. 11 rooms. Restaurant, bar, no air-conditioning, cable TV, minibars, Internet. AE, DC, MC, V.*

$$ 🏨 **Garden.** This picturesque, central hotel has an age-old wooden gallery overlooking the sunny inner courtyard where breakfast is served. Rooms are small but cheerful, with bright colors and antiques. ✉ *3 rue Duhamel, 35000,* ☎ *02–99–65–45–06,* FAX *02–99–65–02–62. 26 rooms. No air-conditioning. AE, MC, V.*

$$ 🏨 **Mercure Centre.** This stately 19th-century hotel is centrally located on a quiet, narrow backstreet close to the cathedral. Rooms overlook the street or a courtyard; all are modern and functional. ✉ *6 rue Lanjuinais, 35000,* ☎ *02–99–79–12–36,* FAX *02–99–79–65–76. 48 rooms. No air-conditioning, cable TV, Internet. AE, DC, MC, V.*

Nightlife and the Arts

Dance the night away at **L'Espace** (✉ 45 bd. de la Tour d'Auvergne, ☎ 02–99–30–21–95). For the night owl, the **Pym's Club** (✉ 27 pl. du Colombier, ☎ 02–99–67–30–00) stays open all night, every night.

Brittany's principal theater is the **Opéra de Rennes** (✉ Pl. de la Mairie, ☎ 02–99–78–48–78). All kinds of performances are staged at the **Théâtre National de Bretagne** (✉ 1 rue St-Hélier, ☎ 02–99–31–12–31). The famous annual international rock-and-roll festival, **Les Transmusicales** (☎ 02–99–31–12–10 for information), happens the second week of December in bars around town and at the Théâtre National de Bretagne. The first week of July sees **Les Tombées de la Nuit,** the Nightfall Festival, featuring Celtic music, dance, and theater performances staged in old historic streets and churches around town (☎ 02–99–67–11–11 for information).

Shopping

A lively **market** is held on place des Lices on Saturday morning.

Montmuran

4 *24 km (15 mi) northwest of Rennes via N137 and D221.*

The **Château de Montmuran** was once ground control to one of France's finest knights, Bertrand du Guesclin (1320–80). Commemorated in countless squares and hostelries across the province, du Guesclin sprang to prominence at the age of 17, when he entered a jousting tournament in disguise and successfully unseated several hoarier knights. He went on to lead the onslaught against the English during the Hundred Years' War. An alley of oak and beech trees leads up to the main 17th-century building, which is surrounded by a moat and flanked by four towers, two built in the 12th century, two in the 14th. You can visit the towers and a small museum devoted to the castle's history. The château also has two pleasant guest rooms, which are open from May to October. Call to reserve. ✉ *Les Iffs,* ☎ *02–99–45–88–88.* €4. ⏲ *June–Sept., daily 2–6.*

OFF THE BEATEN PATH

CHÂTEAU DE CARADEUC – Ambitiously dubbed the Versailles of Brittany, this château, 8 km (5 mi) west of Montmuran just beyond Bécherel, is privately owned and not open to the public. But you can explore the statuary, flower beds, and leafy alleys in the surrounding park—Brittany's largest. ✉ *Rte. de Chateaubriand,* ☎ *02–99–66–77–76.* *€3.* ⏲ *Apr.–June, daily 2–6; July–Aug., daily noon–6; Sept., weekends 2–6; Oct., Sun. 2–6.*

Dinan

★ 5 *29 km (18 mi) northwest of Montmuran via D27 and D68, 24 km (15 mi) south of Dinard.*

Like Montmuran, Dinan has close links with warrior-hero Bertrand du Guesclin, who won a famous victory here in 1359 and promptly married a local girl, Tiphaine Raguenel. When he died in the siege of Châteauneuf-de-Randon in Auvergne (central France) in 1380, his body was dispatched home to Dinan. Owing to the great man's popularity, only his heart completed the journey (it rests in the basilica); the rest of him was confiscated by devoted followers along the way.

On place des Merciers, rue de l'Apport, and rue de la Poissonnerie, note the splendid gabled wooden houses. Rue du Jerzual, which leads down to Dinan's harbor, is also a beautifully preserved medieval street, divided halfway down by the town walls and the massive Porte du Jerzual gateway and lined with boutiques and crafts shops in 15th- and 16th-century houses. A few restaurants brighten the area around the harbor, and boats sail up the Rance River in summer (€22 return, call 02–23–18–15–15 or check www.emeraudelines.com for details), but the abandoned warehouses mostly bear witness to the town's vanished commercial activity. Above the harbor, near Porte St-Malo, is the leafy Promenade des Grands Fossés, the best-preserved section of the town walls, which leads to the castle.

For a superb view of town, climb to the top of the medieval **Tour de l'Horloge** (Clock Tower). ✉ *Rue de l'Horloge.* €1.60. ⏲ *July–Sept., daily 10:45–1:15 and 3–6.*

Du Guesclin's heart lies in the north transept of the **Basilique St-Sauveur** (✉ Pl. St-Sauveur). The church's style ranges from the Romanesque south front to the Flamboyant Gothic facade and Renaissance side chapels. The old trees in the **Jardin Anglais** (English Garden) behind the church provide a nice frame. More spectacular views can be found at the bottom of the garden, which looks down the plummeting Rance Valley to the river below.

The **Château,** at the end of the Promenade des Petits Fossés, has a two-story tower, the **Tour du Coëtquen,** and a 100-ft, 14th-century **donjon** (keep) containing a museum with varied displays of medieval effigies and statues, Breton furniture, and local lace coiffes (headcoverings). ✉ *Porte de Guichet,* ☎ *02–96–39–45–20.* *€3.90.* *Mar.–May and mid-Sept.–mid-Nov., daily 10–11:30 and 2–5:30; June–mid-Sept., daily 10–7:15; mid-Nov.–Feb., Wed.–Mon. 1:30–5:30.*

Dining and Lodging

$ ✕ **Relais des Corsaires.** This riverbank spot is named for the old-time pirates who sporadically plundered Dinan and the Rance Valley. The mid-range prix-fixe menu provides an ample four-course meal of traditional French cuisine, with an emphasis on steak and fish. The welcoming proprietors, Sabine and Christian Boaumond, also have an informal, relaxed seafood restaurant, Au Petit Corsair, where you can compose your own seafood platter from the very fresh choices in the 15th-century building next door. ✉ *7 rue du Quai,* ☎ *02–96–39–40–17. AE, DC, MC, V. Closed Jan.–Feb.*

$$–$$$ ★ **Avaugour.** Set on the town ramparts, this hotel has a sunny flower garden, which the best rooms—all were renovated in 2002—overlook, and where breakfast and afternoon tea are served. Start the day with the full buffet breakfast and a chat with the charming owner, Nicolas Caron, who enjoys speaking English and helping everyone plan day trips. There's a colorful street market opposite the hotel every Thursday. ✉ *1 pl. du Champ, 22100,* ☎ *02–96–39–07–49,* FAX *02–96–85–43–04,* WEB *www.avaugour.hotel.com. 21 rooms, 3 suites. AE, DC, MC, V. No air-conditioning, cable TV, Internet. Closed mid-Nov.–mid-Dec.*

$$ **Arvor.** The cobbled streets of the Old Town are visible from this comfortable 18th-century hotel directly across from the tourist office. It's run by the convivial Brigitte Urvoy and the owner, Monsieur Pierre, who offer clean and simple rooms with friendly service. ✉ *5 rue Auguste-Pavie, 22100,* ☎ *02–96–39–21–22,* FAX *02–96–39–83–09. 23 rooms. No air-conditioning, cable TV. MC, V. Closed Jan.*

Nightlife and the Arts

Every two years (next in 2004), on the third weekend in July, medieval France is re-created with a market, parade, jousting tournament, and street music for **La Fête des Remparts** (Ramparts Festival), one of the largest medieval festivals in Europe.

Shopping

The cobbled, sloping **rue de Jerzual** is lined with medieval houses containing shops selling crafts by local wood-carvers, jewelers, leather workers, glass specialists, and silk painters.

En Route Between Dinan and Combourg is the château **La Bourbansais,** built in the 1580s. Most of the interior furnishings (guided tours only) date from the 18th century, including the fine collection of porcelain and tapestries. Its extensive gardens contain a small zoo, a playground for children, a picnic area (with an on-site restaurant that serves simple sandwiches, steaks, french fries, and salads), and a pack of hunting hounds who perform a popular 20-minute show called *La Meute* from April through September. ✉ *Pleugueneuc,* ☎ *02–99–69–40–07,* WEB *www.labourbansais.com.* *€11.90.* *Apr.–Sept., daily 10–7; Oct.–Mar., daily 2–6.*

Combourg

❻ *24 km (15 mi) southeast of Dinan via D794, 39 km (24 mi) north of Rennes.*

The pretty lakeside village of Combourg is dominated by the boyhood home of Romantic writer Viscount René de Chateaubriand (1768–1848), the thick-walled, four-tower **Château de Combourg.** The castle dates mainly from the 14th and 15th centuries. The Chateaubriand archives and the writer's austere bedroom are in the **Tour du Chat** (Cat's Tower). Chateaubriand was a leading light of Romanticism and the return-to-nature movement—his novel *Atala and René,* about a tragic love affair between a French solider and a Native American maiden, was an international sensation in the mid-19th century. The château grounds—ponds, woods, and cattle-strewn meadowland—are suitably mournful and can seem positively desolate under leaden skies. ☏ *02–99–73–22–95,* WEB *www.combourg.net.* *€3.90, park only €1.30.* *Château open Apr.–Oct., Sun.–Fri. 2–5:30; park open Apr.–Oct., 9–noon and 2–6.*

OFF THE BEATEN PATH

CHÂTEAU DE LA BALLUE – This château, 18 km (11 mi) east of Combourg, dates from 1620 and gleams with original wood paneling and a huge granite staircase. 19th-century writers Alfred de Musset, Honoré Balzac, and Victor Hugo all stayed here, and exhibitions of contemporary art maintain the cultural tradition today. In the garden are sculpture, leafy groves, a labyrinth, and the Temple of Diana. You can stay the night, too, in one of the five large guest rooms (each with a four-poster bed), and dine with the dynamic English-speaking owners Alain Schrotter and Marie-France Barrère. Reserve well in advance and be sure to specify whether you'll be staying for dinner. ✉ *Bazouges-la-Pérouse,* ☏ *02–99–97–47–86,* FAX *02–99–97–47–70.* *€8.* *May–Sept., daily 10:30–5:30.*

Dining

$–$$ ★ ✕ **L'Ecrivain.** Gilles Menier's inventive, light cuisine and good fixed-price menus (starting at €13.50) showcase *milles feuilles de foie gras* (foie gras in layers of thin puff pastry), grilled St. Pierre in fennel vinaigrette, and apple crepe with cider butter. Ask for a table in the intimate wood-paneled dining room, with candles on the tables, rather than in the bustling larger hall, and take your *digestif* in the wood-paneled bar with its oil paintings depicting scenes from Chateaubriand's life. ✉ *1 pl. St-Gilduin,* ☏ *02–99–73–01–61. MC, V. Closed Thurs., 3 wks in Feb., and 2 wks in Oct. No dinner Wed. or Sun.*

Dol-de-Bretagne

❼ *17 km (11 mi) north of Combourg via D795, 56 km (35 mi) north of Rennes.*

The ancient town of Dol-de-Bretagne, which still has its original ramparts, looks out over the Marais de Dol, a marshy plain stretching across to Mont-St-Michel, 21 km (13 mi) northeast. For extensive views of the Marais as well as Mont-Dol—a 200-ft windmill-topped mound 3 km (2 mi) north and the legendary scene of combat between St. Michael and the Devil—walk along the **Promenade des Douves,** on the northern part of the original ramparts. Dol's picturesque main street is **Grande-Rue des Stuarts,** lined with medieval houses; the oldest, the **Maison des Palets,** at No. 17, has a chunky row of Romanesque arches.

The **Cathédrale St-Samson** (✉ Pl. de la Cathédrale) is a damp, soaring, fortresslike bulk of granite dating mainly from the 12th to the 14th centuries. This mighty building shows just how influential the bishopric of Dol was in bygone days. The richly sculpted Great Porch, carved-wood choir stalls, and stained glass in the chancel warrant scrutiny.

The **Cathédraloscope** (Cathedral Museum), opened in 1999 opposite the cathedral, uses models, frescoes, ground plans, and special lighting effects to explain the construction of France's cathedrals, their feats of engineering, and the evolution of the soaring Gothic style that characterizes them. There are also sections on church liturgy and stained glass. ✉ *Pl. de la Cathédrale,* ☎ *02–99–48–35–30,* WEB *www.pays-de-dol.com.* 🎟 *€6.60.* ⏲ *May–Sept., daily 9:30–7:30; Oct.–Dec. and Feb.–Apr., daily 10–6.*

The small, cheerfully managed **Musée Historique** (History Museum), by the cathedral, houses costumes, weapons, and models retracing life in Dol since prehistoric times. The pride of the museum is its assembly of wooden religious statues. If you arrive to find the museum closed, call Monsieur Laick at the number below, and he'll be happy to come and open it for you. ✉ *2 pl. de la Trésorerie,* ☎ *02–99–48–33–46.* 🎟 *€3.* ⏲ *Easter–Sept., daily 9:30–12:30 and 1:30–6.*

Dining and Lodging

$$ ✕🏨 **Bresche Arthur.** With its crisp outlines, white walls, and glassed-in terrace, this hotel doesn't look as historic as it sounds. But it is cozy, and rooms are inexpensive, if functional. People flock here to taste chef-owner Philippe Martel's *filet de sandre à l'anjou rouge* (pike-perch in red wine), *consommé de canard au foie gras* (foie gras in duck consommé), and the *gratin d'agrumes au syrop d'érable* (citrus crumble with maple syrup). The restaurant is closed Monday, and there's no dinner Sunday. ✉ *36 bd. Deminiac, 35120,* ☎ *02–99–48–01–44,* FAX *02–99–48–16–32. 24 rooms. Restaurant. MC, V. Closed Feb.*

$$ ✕🏨 **Domaine des Ormes.** The former country retreat of the bishops of Dol, south of town, serves as the backdrop for this complex which includes a campsite, rental chalets, golf course, artificial lakes, outdoor pool, archery concourse, cricket ground, and modern hotel with spacious rooms and a bilingual staff. Decor throughout is nondescript, but the restaurant's menu is inventive, notably the *blanquette de la mer,* a seafood stew with scallops, shrimp, and monkfish in a light wine sauce. ✉ *35120 Épiniac (7 km/4 mi south of Dol-de-Bretagne),* ☎ *02–99–73–43–33,* FAX *02–99–73–40–84,* WEB *www.lesormes.com. 32 rooms. Restaurant, bar, air-conditioning, cable TV, 9-hole golf course, 2 tennis courts, pool, gym, archery. AE, DC, MC, V. Closed Dec.–Feb.*

Cancale

❽ *22 km (14 mi) northwest of Dol via D155 and D76.*

If you enjoy eating oysters, be sure to get to Cancale, a picturesque fishing village renowned for its offshore *bancs d'huîtres* (oyster beds). You can sample the little brutes at countless stalls or restaurants along the quay. The **Musée de l'Huître et du Coquillage** (Oyster and Shellfish Museum) explains everything you ever wanted to know about farming oysters. ✉ *Les Parcs St-Kerber, Plage de l'Aurore,* ☎ *02–99–89–69–99.* ⏲ *Guided 1-hr tours mid-June–mid-Sept., daily 11 and 3–5; mid-Feb.–mid-June and Oct., daily 3.*

Dining and Lodging

$$$$ ✕🏨 **Château Richeux.** One of three hotels owned by the Roellingers of the Bricourt, the Château Richeux occupies an imposing turn-of-the-20th-century waterfront mansion built on the ruins of the du Guesclin family's 11th-century château, 4 mi (2½ km) south of Cancale. Request one of the rooms with large bay windows, which have stunning views of Mont-St-Michel. Le Coquillage, the hotel's small bistro (closed mid-November through mid-December) majors in local oysters and seafood platters served up in a relaxed, cozy atmosphere. ✉ *Le Point du Jour, St-Méloir des Ondes, 35350,* ☎ *02–99–89–25–25,*

FAX 02–99–89–18–49. 13 rooms. Restaurant, no air-conditioning, cable TV, Internet. AE, DC, MC, V.

$$$–$$$$ ✕ **Maisons de Bricourt.** This large 18th-century stone house where chef Olivier Roellinger grew up has murals, stone fireplaces, and antique tiles that generate a cozily imposing ambience. Seafood seasoned with exotic spices is the specialty. The restaurant is closed Tuesday and Wednesday in winter. If you wish to stay the night, attractive rooms (with views across the bay toward Mont-St-Michel) are available in the annex on rue des Rimains, a short walk away. ✉ *1 rue Du-Guesclin, 35260,* ☎ *02–99–89–64–76,* FAX *02–99–89–88–47,* WEB *www.maisons-de-bricourt.com. 6 rooms. Restaurant, no air-conditioning, cable TV, Internet. AE, DC, MC, V.*

En Route Heading north from Cancale, past the attractive beach of Port-Mer, takes you to the jagged rock formations rising from the sea at the **Pointe de Grouin.** From here follow D201 along the coast to St-Malo.

St-Malo

★ 9 *23 km (14 mi) west of Cancale via coastal D201, 69 km (43 mi) north of Rennes.*

Facing Dinard across the Rance Estuary lies the ancient walled town of St-Malo. The stone ramparts of this onetime pirate base have withstood the Atlantic since the 12th century. They were considerably enlarged and modified in the 18th century and now extend from the castle for more than 1½ km (1 mi) around the Old Town—known as *intra-muros* (within the walls). The views are stupendous, especially at high tide.

The town itself has proved less resistant: a weeklong fire in 1944, kindled by retreating Nazis, wiped out nearly all the old buildings. Restoration work was more painstaking than brilliant, but the narrow streets and granite houses of the Old Town were satisfactorily re-created, enabling St-Malo to regain its role as a busy fishing port, seaside resort, and tourist destination. Battalions of tourists invade this quaint town in summer, so if you want to avoid crowds, don't come here then.

At the edge of the ramparts is the 15th-century **Château,** whose great keep and watchtowers command an impressive view of the harbor and coastline. It houses the **Musée d'Histoire de la Ville** (Town History Museum), devoted to local history, and the **Galerie Quic-en-Grogne,** a museum in a tower, where various episodes and celebrities from St-Malo's past are recalled by way of waxworks. ✉ *Hôtel de Ville,* ☎ *02–99–40–71–57,* WEB *www.ville-saint-malo.fr.* *€4.40.* ⏲ *Tues.–Sun. 10–noon and 2–6.*

Five hundred yards offshore is the **Ile du Grand Bé,** a small island housing the somber military tomb of the great Romantic writer Viscount René de Chateaubriand, who was born in St-Malo. The islet can be reached by a causeway at low tide.

The **Fort National,** also offshore and only accessible by causeway at low tide, is a massive fortress with a dungeon constructed in 1689 by that military-engineering genius Sébastien de Vauban. ☎ *02–99–85–34–33.* *€3.* ⏲ *June–Sept.; call ahead. Times of ½-hr guided tours depend on tides.*

You can pay homage to Jacques Cartier, who set sail from St-Malo in 1535 on a voyage in which he would discover the St. Lawrence River and found Québec, at his tomb in the church of **St-Vincent** (✉ Grand-Rue). His statue looks out over the town ramparts, four blocks away, along with that of swashbuckling corsair Robert Surcouf (hero of many daring 18th-century raids on the British navy), eternally wagging an angry finger over the waves at England.

Dining and Lodging

$$–$$$ ✕ **Chalut.** The reputation of this small restaurant with nautical decor has grown since chef Jean-Philippe Foucat decided to emphasize fresh seafood. The succinct menus change as frequently as the catch of the day. Try the sautéed John Dory in wild-mushroom broth or the fresh lobster in lime. ✉ *8 rue de la Corne-de-Cerf,* ☎ *02–99–56–71–58. AE, MC, V. Closed Mon.–Tues. No dinner Sun. Sept.–June.*

$ ✕ **Café de la Bourse.** Prawns and oysters are downed by the shovelful in this bustling brasserie in the Old Town. Replete with wooden seats, ships' wheels, and posters of grizzled old sea dogs, it's hardly high design. But the large L-shape dining room makes amends with friendly service and a seafood platter for two that includes tanklike crabs flanked by an army of cockles, snails, and periwinkles. ✉ *1 rue de Dinan,* ☎ *02–99–56–47–17. MC, V. Closed Wed. Nov.–Easter.*

$$–$$$ ★ **Elisabeth.** In a town house built into the city wall, the Elisabeth, near the Porte St-Louis, is a little gem of sophistication in touristy St-Malo. Rooms are generally small but tastefully furnished; rates vary with size. ✉ *2 rue des Cordiers, 35400,* ☎ *02–99–56–24–98,* FAX *02–99–56–39–24,* WEB *www.st-malo-hotel-elizabeth.com. 17 rooms. No air-conditioning. AE, DC, MC, V.*

$$ **Bleu Marine-Atlantis.** The view of the sea is magnificent from the hotel's bar, terrace, and breakfast-room. Rooms are airy, with modern furnishings; expect to pay around €10 extra for one with a sea view. ✉ *49 chaussée du Sillon, 35400,* ☎ *02–99–56–09–26,* FAX *02–99–56–41–65,* WEB *www.bleumarine.fr. 55 rooms. Bar, no air-conditioning, cable TV, minibars, sauna. AE, MC, V.*

$ **Jean-Bart.** This clean, quiet hotel next to the ramparts is done in cool blues. Beds are comfortable and bathrooms modern, but the rooms, some with sea views, are somewhat small. ✉ *12 rue de Chartres, 35400,* ☎ *02–99–40–33–88,* FAX *02–99–56–98–89,* WEB *www.hoteljeanbart.multimania.com. 18 rooms. No air-conditioning. MC, V. Closed mid-Nov.–Feb.*

Nightlife and the Arts

Bar de L'Univers (✉ Pl. Chateaubriand) is a nice spot to enjoy sipping a drink in a pirate's-lair setting. **La Belle Époque** (✉ 11 rue de Dinan) is a popular hangout for all ages till the wee hours. **L'Escalier** (✉ La Buzardière, rue de la Tour-du-Bonheur) is the place for dancing the night away.

In summer, performances are held at the **Théâtre Chateaubriand** (✉ 6 rue Groult-de-St-Georges, ☎ 02–99–40–98–05). Bastille Day (July 14) sees the **Fête du Clos Poulet,** a town festival with traditional dancing. July–August brings a monthlong religious music festival, the **Festival de la Musique Sacrée.**

Outdoor Activities and Sports

The **Club Hippique La Cravache** (✉ in St-Coulomb, 8 km/5 mi east of St-Malo on D255, ☎ 02–99–81–65–03) is the source for horses. The harbor and area outside the breakwater are popular sailing spots; boats are available from **Étoile Marine** (✉ 6 av. Louis-Martin, ☎ 02–99–40–48–72).

Shopping

A lively outdoor **market** is held in the streets of Old St-Malo every Tuesday and Friday.

Dinard

10 *13 km (8 mi) west of St-Malo via D168, 71 km (44 mi) north of Rennes.*

Dinard is the most elegant resort town on this stretch of the Brittany coast. Its picture-book perch on the Rance Estuary opposite the walled town of St-Malo lured the English aristocracy here in droves toward the end of the 19th century. What started out as a small fishing port soon became a seaside mecca of lavish Belle Epoque villas, grand hotels, and a bustling casino. A number of modern establishments punctuate the landscape, but the town still retains something of an Edwardian tone. To make the most of Dinard's beauty, head down to the Pointe de la Vicomté, at the town's southern tip, where the cliffs offer panoramic views across the Baie du Prieuré and Rance Estuary, or stroll along the narrow promenade.

The **Promenade Clair de Lune** hugs the seacoast on its way toward the English Channel and passes in front of the small jetty used by boats crossing to St-Malo. It really hits its stride as it rounds the **Pointe du Moulinet** and heads toward the sandy **Plage du Prieuré,** named after a priory that once stood here. River meets sea in a foaming mass of rock-pounding surf: use caution as you walk along the slippery path to the calm shelter of the **Plage de l'Écluse,** an inviting sandy beach bordered by the casino and numerous stylish hotels. The coastal path picks up on the west side of Plage de l'Écluse, ringing the Pointe de la Malouine and the Pointe des Étêtés before arriving at the **Plage de St-Énogat.**

The 24 pools and aquariums at the **Musée de la Mer** (Marine Museum) contain almost every known species of Breton sea creature, and stuffed local birds are also on display. One room is devoted to the polar expeditions of explorer Jean Charcot, one of the first men to chart the Antarctic. ✉ *17 av. George-V,* ☎ *02–99–46–13–90.* *€2.50.* *Mid-May–mid-Sept., daily 10:30–12:30 and 3:30–7:30.*

Dining and Lodging

$$ ✕ **Salle à Manger.** Great chef Jacques Gonthier and his English-speaking wife, Marie-Claire, have chosen a crisp blue-and-yellow color scheme, offset by starched white tablecloths and old furniture. Her unflappable presence makes sure that a casual, unstuffy manner prevails in the small dining room—but that shouldn't stop you from paying reverential attention to the scallops with raisins, grilled swordfish with warm oysters and citrus butter, or pigeon with cumin and rosemary. ✉ *25 bd. Féart,* ☎ *02–99–16-07–95. MC, V. Closed Jan. and Mon. Feb.–May and Oct.–Dec.*

$$ **Printania.** This white-walled, family-run hotel is on the Clair de Lune Promenade. Rooms have regional furnishings and pictures of local scenes; the best ones have a balcony and sea view (ask for Room 101, 102, 211, or 311). ✉ *5 av. George-V, 35800,* ☎ *02–99–46–13–07,* FAX *02–99–46–26–32,* WEB *www.printaniahotel.com. 60 rooms. Restaurant, bar, no air-conditioning. AE, MC, V. Closed mid-Nov.–mid-Mar.*

Nightlife

The main nightlife activity in town is at the **casino** (✉ 4 bd. du Président-Wilson, ☎ 02–99–16–30–30).

Outdoor Activities and Sports

You can go horseback riding at the **Centre Équestre de la Côte d'Emeraude** (✉ Le Val Porée, ☎ 02–99–46–23–57). For windsurfing, wander over to the **Wishbone Club** (✉ Digue de l'Écluse, ☎ 02–99–88–15–20). Boats can be rented from the **Yacht Club** (✉ Promenade Clair de Lune, ☎ 02–99–46–14–32).

En Route Forty kilometers (25 miles) west of Dinard along the coast is the **Cap Fréhel,** where dramatic pink cliffs rise vertically from the sea. The colors are most vivid in the evening, but at any time of day the sight is formidable. Pick your way through the seagulls and cormorants and, if you're not afraid of heights, mosey down past the small restaurant for a vertiginous glimpse of the rocks below. Then climb up to the lighthouse, whose beam can be seen by ships up to 60 miles away. If you've time, check out **Fort de Latte** nearby, a 17th-century fort linked to the mainland by a drawbridge. Then head west, past fine beaches at Pléhérel and Sables-d'Or–les-Pins, to pick up D786 and skirt around the Bay of St-Brieuc.

Paimpol

11 *92 km (57 mi) west of Cap Fréhel via D786, 45 km (28 mi) northwest of St-Brieuc.*

Paimpol is one of the liveliest fishing ports in the area and a good base for exploring this part of the coast. The town is a maze of narrow streets lined with shops, restaurants, and souvenir boutiques. The harbor, where fishermen used to unload their catch from far-off seas, is its main focal point; today most fish is caught in the Channel. From the sharp cliffs you can see the coast's famous pink-granite rocks. For centuries, but no longer, Breton fishermen sailed to Newfoundland each spring to harvest cod—a long and perilous journey. The **Fête des Terres-Neuvas** is a celebration of the traditional return from Newfoundland of the Breton fishing fleets; it is held on the third Sunday in July.

Dining and Lodging

$$–$$$ ★ **Repaire de Kerroc'h.** This delightful hotel overlooks the harbor and has spacious rooms with artfully used odd angles. A favorite, Les Sept Isles, faces the street and has a view of the boats. Chef Yann Trebaol prepares delicious seafood dishes such as the unique *aemer*—a rare, flat shellfish lightly braised in red wine and served with the famous white beans of Paimpol, or if you like beef, try the *boeuf poêlé aux chanterelles,* fillet of beef served with wild mushrooms. Be sure to have breakfast, if just for the seasonal homemade jams. The restaurant is closed Tuesday, except in July and August. ✉ *29 quai Morand, 22500,* ☎ *02–96–20–50–13,* FAX *02–96–22–07–46. 12 rooms, 1 duplex. Restaurant, no air-conditioning. MC, V.*

Trébeurden

12 *42 km (26 mi) west of Paimpol via D786 and D65, 9 km (6 mi) northwest of Lannion.*

A small, pleasant fishing village that is now a summer resort town, Trébeurden makes a good base for exploring the pink-granite cliffs of the Corniche Bretonne, starting with the rocky point at nearby Le Castel. Take a look at the profile of the dramatic rocks off the coast near Trégastel and Perros-Guirec and use your imagination to see La Tête de Mort (Death's Head), La Tortoise, Le Sentinel, and Le Chapeau de Wellington (Wellington's Hat). The scene changes with the sunlight and the sweep and retreat of the tide, whose caprices can strand fishing boats among islands that were, only hours before, hidden beneath the sea.

Five kilometers (3 mi) east of Trébeurden is **Cosmopolis,** whose main claim to fame is the Radôme: a giant white radar dome, its 340-ton antenna captured the first live TV satellite transmission from the U.S. to France in July 1962. Today the sphere houses one of Europe's largest planetariums, a museum retracing the history of telecommunications back to the first telegraph in 1792, and spectacular laser shows that employ 200 projectors to bring the history of satellite communication to life. ✉ *Pleumeur-Bodou,* ☎ *02–96–46–63–80,* WEB *www.telecom.museum.* 🎫 *€7.* ⏲ *Apr. and Sept., Mon.–Fri. 11–6, weekends 2–6; May–June, daily 11–6; July–Aug., daily 11–7.*

Dining and Lodging

$$$–$$$$ ✕🏨 **Manoir Lan Kerellec.** The beauty of the Breton coastline is embraced by this Relais & Châteaux hotel, where guest rooms are far more than just comfortable. The restaurant, whose circular dining room has a delightful model of the *St-Yves* ship suspended from its ceiling, mostly serves seafood, but the roast lamb is also good; it does not serve lunch Tuesday and is closed Monday off-season. ✉ *11 allée Centrale, 22560,* ☎ *02–96–15–47–47,* FAX *02–96–23–66–88. 18 rooms. Restaurant, no air-conditioning, cable TV, Internet, tennis court. AE, DC, MC, V. Closed mid-Nov.–mid-Mar.*

Morlaix

13 *45 km (28 mi) southwest of Trébeurden via D65 and D786, 60 km (37 mi) east of Brest.*

An unforgettable sight is the 19th-century stone railroad viaduct of Morlaix (pronounced mor-*lay*). At 300 yards long and 200 ft high, it spans the entire town. The Old Town's attractive mix of half-timber houses and shops deserves unhurried exploration. At its commercial heart is the pedestrian Grand'Rue, lined with quaint 15th-century houses. Look for the 16th-century, three-story Maison de la Reine Anne (Queen Anne House), on the adjacent rue du Mur—it's adorned with statuettes of saints.

The town's museum, known as the **Musée des Jacobins** because it is in a former Jacobin church (note the early 15th-century rose window at one end), is just off rue d'Aiguillon, parallel to Grand'Rue; it has an eclectic collection ranging from religious statues to archaeological finds and modern paintings. ✉ *Pl. des Jacobins,* ☎ *02–98–88–68–88.* 🎫 *€4.* ⏲ *Apr.–Oct., daily 10–12:30 and 2–6:30; Nov.–Mar., Mon. and Wed.–Fri. 10–noon and 2–5, Sat. 2–5.*

Beer at the **Brasserie des Deux Rivières** (Two Rivers Brewery—named for the two rivers, the Jarlo and the Queffleuth, that flow through Morlaix) is brewed according to traditional English methods. You complete your visit to the brewery—whose long, narrow building was originally a rope factory—with a glass of dark, cask-conditioned *Coreff* ale. ✉ *1 pl. de la Madeleine,* ☎ *02–98–63–41–92.* 🎫 *Free.* ⏲ *July–Aug., tours Mon.–Wed. 10:30, 2, and 3:30. Call ahead to book a tour in English.*

Dining and Lodging

$–$$ ✕🏨 **Europe.** Although rooms here—as in many old French hotels—are in need of renovation, they are large and the hotel is centrally located. In the welcoming, many-mirrored restaurant, chef Brignou prepares sturdy traditional fare with fresh local produce—simple, savory dishes like the authentic *Kigha farz,* a sort of Breton couscous made with ham and spring vegetables in a rich broth over whole wheat grains. ✉ *1 rue d'Aiguillon, 29600,* ☎ *02–98–62–11–99,* FAX *02–98–88–83–38. 60 rooms, 41 with bath. Restaurant, no air-conditioning, cable TV, Internet. AE, DC, MC, V.*

THE ATLANTIC COAST

What Brittany offers in the way of the sea handsomely makes up for its shortage of mountain peaks and passes. Its hundreds of miles of sawtooth coastline reveal the Atlantic Ocean in its every mood and form–

from the peaceful cove where waders poke about hunting seashells to the treacherous bay whose waters swirl over quicksands in unpredictable crosscurrents; from the majestic serenity of the breakers rolling across La Baule's miles of white-sand beaches to the savage fury of the gigantic waves that fling their force against jagged rocks 340 dizzy feet below the cliffs of Pointe du Raz. Brittany's Atlantic coast runs southeast from the down-to-earth port of Brest to the tony city of Nantes, at the mouth of the Loire River. The wild, rugged creeks around the little-visited northwestern tip of Finistère (Land's End) gradually give way to sandy beaches south of Concarneau. Inland, the bent trees and craggy rocks look like they've been bewitched by Merlin in a bad mood.

Brest

14 *75 km (47 mi) southwest of Morlaix, 244 km (151 mi) west of Rennes.*

Brest's enormous, sheltered bay is strategically positioned close to the Atlantic and the English Channel. You need not spend much time here: World War II left the city in ruins. Postwar reconstruction, resulting in long, straight streets of reinforced concrete, has given latter-day Brest the unenviable reputation of being one of France's drabbest cities. Its waterfront, however, offers dramatic views across the bay toward the Plougastel Peninsula, and is worth visiting for its handful of old buildings, its castle, and the **Monument Américain,** a pink-granite tower commemorating the American troops who landed here in 1917. The Pont de Recouvrance, which crosses the Penfeld River, is Europe's longest drawbridge at 95 yards. Boats leave from the Port du Commerce for the islands of Ouessant and Molène.

Begin your visit at one of the town's oldest monuments, the **Tour Tanguy,** next to the bridge. This bulky, round 14th-century tower, once used as a lookout post, contains a museum of local history with scale models of scenes of the Brest of yore. *Square Pierre-Péron, ☎ 02–98–00–88–60. Free. Oct.–May, Wed.–Sun. 2–6; June–Sept., daily 10–noon and 2–7.*

The medieval **Château** across the bridge from the Tour Tanguy houses the **Musée de la Marine** (Naval Museum), containing boat models, sculpture, pictures, and naval instruments. One section is devoted to the castle's 700-year history. The dungeons can also be visited. *☎ 02–98–22–12–39, WEB www.musee-marine.fr. €4.50. Apr.–Sept., Wed.–Mon. 10–6:30; Oct.–Mar., Wed.–Mon. 10–noon and 2–6.*

French, Flemish, and Italian paintings from the 17th to the 20th centuries and the regional Pont-Aven Postimpressionist school make up the collection at the **Musée des Beaux-Arts** (Fine Arts Museum). *✉ 24 rue Traverse, ☎ 02–98–00–87–96. €4. Mon. and Wed.–Sat. 10–11:45 and 2–6, Sun. 2–6.*

The fauna and flora of the world's three ocean climates—temperate, polar, and tropical—are the themes of the exhibits at **Océanopolis,** one of the largest marine complexes in Europe, complete with a battery of pools and aquariums. Arrive at the park as early as you can, as it takes an entire day to do it justice. *✉ Rue Alain-Colas, ☎ 02–98–34–40–40, WEB www.oceanopolis.com. €13.50. Apr.–mid-Sept., Tues.–Sun. 9–7; mid-Sept.–Dec. and Feb.–Mar., Tues.–Sun. 9–5.*

OFF THE BEATEN PATH

LE FOLGOËT – In early September pilgrims come from afar to Le Folgoët, 24 km (15 mi) northeast of Brest, to attend the ceremonial religious procession known as the pardon and to drink from the Fontaine de Salaün, a fountain behind the church, whose water comes from a spring beneath the altar. The splendid church, known as the Basilique, has a sturdy north tower that serves as a beacon for miles around and, inside, a rare, intricately carved granite rood screen separating the choir and nave.

Dining

$–$$ ✕ **Maison de l'Océan.** This giant split-level brasserie by the waterfront mirrors the city of Brest: all earnest bustle with no frills. It serves the freshest seafood, or as they say here, the *top du top*. Try the delicious catch of the day or one of the traditional seafood platters. In the finest French tradition, the service remains hectically unflappable—of course, reservations are a must at this popular spot. ✉ *2 quai de la Douane,* ☎ *02–98–80–44–84. Reservations essential. AE, V.*

Outdoor Activities and Sports

Sailboats are available for rent at the **Eridan Croisie(ac)re** (✉ Port de Plaisance du Moulin Blanc, ☎ 02–98–41–58–33 FAX 02–98–42–24–90, WEB www.eridan.org).

En Route Stop in **Daoulas,** 16 km (10 mi) east of Brest, to admire its still-functioning 12th-century Augustinian abbey, with cloisters and herb garden. Then head south on N165 and D7 to the old weaving town of **Locronan,** 46 km (29 mi) away, and visit the 5th-century **Église St-Ronan** and the adjacent **Chapelle du Penity,** dominating the magnificently preserved ensemble of houses and main square.

Ste-Anne-la-Palud

⓯ *64 km (40 mi) south of Brest.*

It has been said there are as many Breton saints as there are stones in the ground. One of the great attractions of the region is the celebration of a religious festival known as a village ***pardon***: banners and saintly statues are borne in colorful parades, accompanied by hymns, and the entire event is capped by a feast. The seaside village of Ste-Anne-la-Palud has one of the finest and most authentic age-old pardons in Brittany, held on the last Sunday in August.

Dining and Lodging

$$$–$$$$ ✕🏨 **Plage.** This former private house sits nestled in a cove on a quiet strip of sandy beach around the bay—a remote retreat perfect for long, restorative walks. Some of the comfortably furnished rooms face the sea. The hotel, however, has less of a feeling of Brittany than you might want. Alain Leduc's food is consistently good, especially the seafood dishes; reservations are essential, and a jacket is required. ✉ *29550 Ste-Anne-la-Palud,* ☎ *02–98–92–50–12,* FAX *02–98–92–56–54,* WEB *www.relaischateaux.com/laplage. 26 rooms, 4 suites. Restaurant, no air-conditioning, cable TV, minibars, Internet, tennis court, beach, sauna, pool. AE, DC, MC, V. Closed Nov.–Mar.*

Douarnenez

⓰ *10 km (6 mi) west of Locronan via D7, 86 km (54 mi) south of Brest.*

Douarnenez is a quaint old fishing town of quayside paths and zigzagging narrow streets. Boats come in from the Atlantic to unload their catches of mackerel, sardines, and tuna. Just offshore is the Ile Tristan, accessible by foot at low tide (guided tours only, €5.35), and across the Port-Rhu channel is Tréboul, a seaside resort town favored by French families.

One of the three town harbors is fitted out with a unique **Port-Musée** (Port Museum). Along the wharves you can visit the workshops of boatwrights, sail makers, and other old-time craftspeople, then go aboard the historic trawlers, lobster boats, Thames barges, and a former lightship anchored alongside. On the first weekend in May you can sail on an antique fishing boat. ✉ *Place de l'Enfer,* ☎ *02–98–92–65–20.* 🎫 *€3.10.* ⏲ *June–Sept., daily 10–7; Oct. and Apr.–May, Tues.–Sun. 10–12:30 and 2–6.*

Dining and Lodging

$$ ✕🏨 **Manoir de Moëllien.** This lovely 15th-century manor house, filled with precious antiques, is famous for its local seafood dishes. Sample the *terrine de poisson chaud* (warm seafood terrine) or the *duo de truites de mer* (poached sea trout). Rooms have terraces overlooking the garden, which makes for a peaceful country atmosphere. ✉ *29550 Plonévez-Porzay (12 km/7 mi northeast of Douarnenez),* ☎ *02–98–92–50–40,* FAX *02–98–92–55–21. 18 rooms. Restaurant, no air-conditioning, cable TV, some minibars, Internet. AE, DC, MC, V. Closed mid-Nov.–mid-Mar.*

$$ ★ ✕🏨 **Ty Mad.** In the 1920s artists and writers such as Picasso and Breton native Max Jacob frequented this small hotel in a quiet residential area near the beach in Tréboul. Rooms are not large, but the sea views are great. Michel Touchard's fishy menu, served in the glass-enclosed restaurant, includes skate pâté with mint sauce and monkfish flambéed with tarragon. ✉ *Plage St-Jean, 29100,* ☎ *02–98–74–00–53,* FAX *02–98–74–15–16. 19 rooms. Restaurant, no air-conditioning, no TV in some rooms, some pets allowed. MC, V. Closed Oct. –Easter.*

Outdoor Activities and Sports

Sailboats can be rented from **Les Voiles d'Iroise** (✉ 19 quai de Port-Rhu, ☎ 02–98–92–76–25), on the bay.

Quimper

⓱ *28 km (18 mi) southeast of Douarnenez via D765, 72 km (45 mi) south of Brest.*

Lively, commercial Quimper is the ancient capital of the Cornouaille province, founded, it is said, by King Gradlon 1,500 years ago. Quimper (pronounced cam-*pair*) owes its strange name to its site at the confluence (*kemper* in Breton) of the Odet and Steir rivers. Stroll along the banks of the Odet and through the old town, with its cathedral. Then walk along the lively shopping street, rue Kéréon, and down narrow medieval rue du Guéodet (note the house with caryatids), rue St-Mathieu, and rue du Sallé.

The **Cathédrale St-Corentin** (✉ Pl. St-Corentin) is a masterpiece of Gothic architecture and the second-largest cathedral in Brittany (after Dol-de-Bretagne's). Legendary King Gradlon is represented on horseback just below the base of the spires, harmonious mid-19th-century additions to the medieval ensemble. The 15th-century stained glass is luminous. Behind the cathedral is the stately **Jardin de l'Évêché** (Bishop's Garden).

Over 400 works by such masters as Rubens, Corot, and Picasso mingle with pretty landscapes from the local Gauguin-inspired Pont-Aven school in the **Musée des Beaux-Arts** (Fine Arts Museum), next to the cathedral. ✉ *40 pl. St-Corentin,* ☎ *02–98–95–45–20.* 🎫 *€3.85.* ⏲ *July–Aug., daily 9–7; Sept.–June, Wed.–Mon. 10–noon and 2–6.*

Local furniture, ceramics, and folklore top the bill at the **Musée Départemental Breton** (Breton Regional Museum). ✉ *1 rue du Roi-Gradlon,* ☎ *02–98–95–21–60.* 🎫 *€3.80.* ⏲ *June–Sept., daily 9–6; Oct.–May, Tues.–Sun. 9–noon and 2–5.*

In the mid-18th century Quimper sprang to nationwide attention as a pottery manufacturing center when it began producing second-rate imitations of Rouen faïence, or ceramics with blue motifs. Today's more colorful designs, based on floral arrangements and marine fauna, are still often hand-painted. Guided tours are available at the **Musée de la Faïence** (Earthenware Museum). ✉ *14 rue Jean-Baptiste-Bousquet,* ☏ *02–98–90–12–72.* *€4.* *Mid-Apr.–Oct., Mon.–Sat. 10–6.*

Dining

$$ ✕ **Ambroisie.** This cozy little restaurant has soft-yellow walls, huge contemporary paintings, and different settings at every table. Chef Gilbert Guyon's traditional yet nouvelle menu is seasonal; local products are chosen by hand. Try the buckwheat *galette* crepe stuffed with lobster or the pigeon roasted in apple liqueur with whipped potatoes and mushrooms. The homemade desserts, like the *Norvégien* with warm chocolate and nougat ice cream in meringue, are delicious. ✉ *49 rue Élie-Fréron,* ☏ *02–98–95–00–02. Reservations essential. MC, V. Closed early July, 2 wks in Feb., and Nov. No dinner Sun.–Mon.*

Nightlife and the Arts

In late July Quimper hosts the **Festival de Cornouaille** (☏ 02–98–55–53–53), a nine-day Celtic extravaganza. More than 250 artists, dancers, and musicians fill streets already packed with the 4,000 people who come each year to enjoy the traditional street fair.

Shopping

Keep an eye out for such typical Breton products as woven and embroidered cloth, woolen goods, brass and wood objects, puppets, dolls, and locally designed jewelry. When it comes to distinctive Breton folk costumes, Quimper is the best place to look. The streets around the cathedral, especially **rue du Parc,** are full of shops selling woolen goods (notably thick marine sweaters). Faïence and a wide selection of hand-painted pottery can be purchased at the **Faïencerie d'Art Breton** (✉ 16 bis rue du Parc, ☏ 02–98–95–34–13).

Concarneau

⓲ *21 km (13 mi) south of Quimper via D783, 93 km (58 mi) southeast of Brest.*

Concarneau is the third-largest fishing port in France. A busy industrial town, it has a grain of charm and an abundance of tacky souvenir shops. But it is worth visiting to see the fortified islet in the middle of the harbor. The **Ville Close,** which was regarded as impregnable from early medieval times on, is entered by way of a quaint drawbridge. The fortifications were further strengthened by the English under John de Montfort during the War of Succession (1341–64). Three hundred years later Sébastien de Vauban remodeled the ramparts into what you see today: 1 km (½ mi) long, with splendid views across the two harbors on either side. Held here during the second half of August is the **Fête des Filets Bleus** (Blue Net Festival), a weeklong folk celebration in which Bretons in costume swirl and dance to the wail of bagpipes. *Ramparts €1.* *Easter–Sept., daily 10–7:30; Oct.–Easter, daily 10–noon and 2–5.*

The **Musée de la Pêche** (Fishing Museum), close to the island gateway, has aquariums and exhibits on fishing techniques from around the world. ✉ *3 rue Vauban,* ☏ *02–98–97–10–20.* *€6.* *July–Aug., daily 9:30–7:30; Sept.–June, daily 10–noon and 2–6.*

Dining

$$ ✕ **Chez Armande.** Rather than opting for one of the various tourist haunts in the Ville Clos, you might like to wander 300 yards down the waterfront for an excellent fish or seafood meal at Chez Armande. Specialties include *pot-au-feu de la mer au gingembre* (seafood in a clear ginger broth), *St. Pierre à la fricassée de champignons* (John Dory with fresh mushrooms), and *homard rôti en beurre de corail* (roast lobster in coral butter). Try the *tarte de grandmère aux pommes* (grandma's homemade apple pie) for dessert. ✉ *15 bis av. du Dr-Nicolas,* ☎ *02–98–97–00–76. AE, MC, V. Closed Tues.–Wed., mid-Dec.–early Jan., and 2 wks in Feb.*

Pont-Aven

⑲ *14 km (9 mi) east of Concarneau via D783, 91 km (56 mi) northwest of Vannes.*

Pont-Aven is a former artists' colony where Paul Gauguin lived before he headed off to the South Seas. Wanting to break with traditional Western culture and values, the lawyer-turned-painter headed in 1889 to Brittany, a destination almost as foreign to Parisians as Tahiti. Before long, Gauguin took to wearing Breton sweaters, berets, and wooden clogs; in his art he began to leave dewy, sunlit Impressionism behind for a stronger, more linear style. Make sure to visit the museum dedicated to the Pont-Aven School—whose adherents painted Breton landscapes in bold yet dreamy colors—then cool off (in summer) with a boat trip down the estuary, or take a walk in the hills through the pastures to the Trémalo Chapel, where there is a crucifix attributed to Gauguin. While in Brittany, Gauguin painted many of his earliest masterpieces, now given pride of place in great museums around the world. The **Musée Municipal** (Town Museum) has a photography exhibition documenting the Pont-Aven School, and works by its participants. ✉ *Pl. de l'Hôtel-de-Ville,* ☎ *02–98–06–14–43.* 🎫 *€4.* ⏲ *July–Aug., daily 9:30–7:30; Feb.–June and Sept.–Dec., daily 10–12:30 and 2–6.*

Dining and Lodging

$$$ ✕ **La Taupinière.** On the road from Concarneau, 2 mi (3 km) west of Pont-Aven, is this roadside inn with an attractive garden. Chef Guy Guilloux's open kitchen (with the large hearth he uses to grill his famous fish, langoustine, crab, and Breton ham specialties) turns out local delicacies like delicious galette crepes stuffed with turtle and spider crab. Splurge without guilt on the light homemade rhubarb and strawberry compote. ✉ *Croissant St-André,* ☎ *02–98–06–03–12. Reservations essential. Jacket required. AE, MC, V. Closed Mon., Tues. and mid-Sept.–mid-Oct.*

$$$ ✕🏨 **Moulin de Rosmadec.** The Sébilleaus' old water mill sits in the middle of the rushing, rocky Aven River. You can hear the sound of water gently spilling over the stones beneath your window. In the rustic-looking restaurant enjoy such dishes as the *sautée de langoustines* or the grilled fresh Breton lobster. Reservations are essential and a jacket is recommended; the restaurant does not serve dinner Sunday from mid-September to mid-June. ✉ *Pl. Paul-Gauguin, 29930,* ☎ *02–98–06–00–22,* FAX *02–98–06–18–00. 4 rooms. Restaurant, no air-conditioning, some pets allowed. MC, V. Closed Wed. and second half Oct.*

$$ 🏨 **Roz Aven.** Built into a rock face on the bank of the Aven, this efficiently run hotel has simple, clean rooms. You can choose a room in one of three locations: the Ty An Eol thatched cottage, the modern annex, or the *maison bourgeoise* with a river or garden view. Owner Yann Souffez speaks excellent English. He describes the furnishings as Louis

XVI, but, at best, they appear petit-bourgeois. ✉ *11 quai Théodore-Botrel, 29930,* ☎ *02–98–06–13–06,* FAX *02–98–06–03–89,* WEB *www.hotelpontaven.online.fr. 25 rooms. Bar, no air-conditioning, some minibars. AE, MC, V.*

Lorient

20 *36 km (22 mi) southeast of Pont-Aven via D24.*

France's most exotically named town—founded by Colbert in 1666 as a base for the spice-seeking vessels of France's East India Company (Compagnie des Indes) bound for the Orient (thus the name)—was smashed into semi-oblivion during World War II. A handful of Art Deco mansions survived, and you may want to visit the brazen concrete church of Notre-Dame-de-Victoire for its modern frescoes and stained glass. The town is at its liveliest during the Celtic Festival in August.

Lorient is a major fishing port, as you'll deduce from all the activity along the the mile-long quay and from the eye-slapping choice at the Halles de Merville fish market. It's also France's leading Atlantic submarine base. The giant concrete **Base des Sous-Marins Stosskopf,** built by the Nazis during World War II, claims to be the world's largest 20th century fort—with a capacity of over 30 submarines—and its 27-ft-thick roof withstood intensive Allied bombing virtually intact. ✉ *Port de Keroman,* ☎ *02–97–21–07–84.* *€6.* *June and Sept., Mon.–Sat. 2–5; July–Aug., daily 10:30–6.*

Dining and Lodging

$$$–$$$$ ✕ **Château de Locguénolé.** This imposing Neoclassical château is set amid lawns and woods above the Blavet Estuary. Tapestries adorn public spaces and guest rooms; the rooms on the first floor are spacious, with high ceilings and private Jacuzzis; the second-floor rooms have sloped attic ceilings, which give them a cozy feel, but if you want something a bit larger don't be afraid to book a room in the 19th-century manor alongside the main house. Chef Philippe Peudenier's light modern cuisine ranges from grilled John Dory with asparagus in ginger and lemon to roast pigeon with spring vegetable tempura. ✉ *Rte. de Port-Louis, 56700 Kervignac (10 km/6 mi east of Lorient via D194),* ☎ *02–97–76–76–76,* FAX *02–97–76–82–35,* WEB *www.chateau-de-locguenole.fr. 22 rooms, 4 suites. Restaurant, no air-conditioning, cable TV, minibars, Internet, tennis court, indoor/outdoor pool, sauna. AE, DC, MC, V. Closed Jan.–mid-Feb.*

Nightlife and the Arts

The **Festival Interceltique** (☎ 02–97–21–24–29 for information), held in the first half of August, is a jamboree of Celtic culture—music, drama, poetry, dance—with fellow Celts pouring into Lorient from all over northwestern Europe (Cornwall, Wales, Ireland, Scotland, and Galicia) to celebrate.

Outdoor Activities

There's a good beach, **Larmor-Plage,** 5 km (3 mi) south of Lorient. Or you could take a ferry to the rocky **Ile de Groix** or cross the bay to **Port-Louis,** a harbor renowned for tuna fishing and its 17th-century fort and ramparts.

Belle-Ile-en-Mer

21 *45 mins by boat from Quiberon.*

At 18 km (11 mi) long, Belle-Ile is the largest of Brittany's islands. It also lives up to its name: it is undeniably beautiful and much less commercialized than its mainland port city, Quiberon. Because of the cost and inconvenience of reserving car berths on the ferry, cross over to the island as a pedestrian and rent a car—or, if you don't mind the hilly terrain, a bicycle.

Departing from Quiberon—a spa town with pearl-like beaches on the eastern side of the 16-km-long (10-mi-long) Presqu'île de Quiberon (Quiberon Peninsula), a stretch of coastal cliffs and beaches whose dramatic western coast, the Côte Sauvage (Wild Coast), is a mix of crevices and coves lashed by the sea—the ferry lands at **Le Palais,** crushed beneath a monumental Vauban citadelle built in the 1680s. From Le Palais head northwest to **Sauzon,** the prettiest fishing harbor on the island; from here you can see across to the Quiberon Peninsula and the Gulf of Morbihan. Continue on to the **Grotte de l'Apothicairerie,** which derives its name from the local cormorants' nests, said to resemble apothecary bottles. At Port Goulphar is the **Grand Phare** (Great Lighthouse). Built in 1835, it rises 275 ft above sea level and has one of the most powerful beacons in Europe, visible from 120 km (75 mi) across the Atlantic. If the keeper is available and you are feeling well rested, you may be able to climb to the top.

Dining and Lodging

$$$–$$$$ ★ ✕🏨 **Castel Clara.** This modern hotel is perched on a cliff overlooking the surf and the narrow Anse de Goulphar Bay. Ask for a room with a view. In the bright, airy restaurant, chef Christophe Hardouin specializes in seafood, literally caught just offshore. The John Dory baked in sea salt and the grilled sea bream are simple but delicious. ✉ *Port-Goulphar, 56360,* ☎ *02–97–31–84–21,* FAX *02–97–31–51–69. 33 rooms, 8 suites. Restaurant, no air-conditioning, cable TV, minibars, Internet, tennis court, pool, spa. AE, DC, MC, V. Closed mid-Nov.–mid-Feb.*

Carnac

❷❷ *32 km (20 mi) southeast of Lorient, 16 km (10 mi) northeast of Quiberon via D768/D781,*

At the north end of Quiberon Bay, Carnac is known for its expansive beaches and its ancient stone monuments. Dating from around 4500 ★ BC; Carnac's **menhirs** remain as mysterious in origin as their English contemporary, Stonehenge, although religious beliefs and astronomy were doubtless an influence. The 2,395 megalithic monuments that make up the three *Alignements*—Kermario, Kerlescan, and Ménec—form the largest megalithic site in the world and are positioned with astounding astronomical accuracy in semicircles and parallel lines over about 1 km (½ mi). The site, just north of the town, is fenced off for protection, and you can examine the menhirs up close only October through March; in summer you must join a guided tour (some in English, costing €4; call 02–97–52–29–81 for details). More can be learned at the **Archéoscope,** a visitor center where a 30-minute presentation involving slides, a video, and models explains the menhirs' history and significance. ✉ *Alignements du Ménec,* ☎ *02–97–52–07–49.* 🎫 *€6.* ⏲ *Mid-Feb.–mid-Nov., daily 10–5:30, English presentations at 10:30 and 2:30.*

Carnac also has smaller-scale dolmen ensembles and three *tumuli* (mounds or barrows), including the 130-yard-long, 38-ft-high **Tumulus de St-Michel,** topped by a small chapel with views of the rock-strewn countryside. 🎫 *€2.* ⏲ *Easter–Oct.; guided tours of tumulus Apr.–Sept., daily 10, 11, 2, and 3:30.*

Nightlife and the Arts

A cosmopolitan crowd goes dancing at **Les Chandelles** (✉ 24 av. des Druides).

Outdoor Activities and Sports

Horseback-riding tours can be arranged through the **Centre Équestre des Menhirs** (☎ 02–97–55–73–45).

Auray

23 *14 km (12 mi) north of Carnac via D119/D768, 38 km (24 mi) southeast of Lorient.*

The ancient town of Auray grew up along the banks of the Loch River, best admired from the Promenade du Loch overlooking the quayside. Cross the river to explore the old, cobbled streets of the St-Goustan neighborhood. Tied alongside the quay, across the bridge, is the **Goélette St-Sauveur,** an old topsail schooner that once ferried coal from Wales. Today it houses a sailing museum with many unusual nautical artifacts. *Place St-Sauveur,* ☎ *02–97–56–63–38.* €3. *Easter–Sept., daily 10:30–12:30 and 2:30–7.*

Dining

$$$–$$$$ ✕ **Closerie de Kerdrain.** Ebullient chef Fernando Corfmat presides over the kitchen in this large 17th-century Breton manor draped in wisteria. His seasonal menus highlight fresh ingredients prepared in innovative ways: oysters with leeks, sea bass carpaccio with fresh green beans in Parmesan, scallops with hazelnuts, or breast of pigeon roasted in black pepper. The sweet-and-sour lemon pie with a "*salade*" of oranges in mango juice is the perfect way to end the meal. ✉ *20 rue Louis-Billet,* ☎ *02–97–56–61–27,* FAX *02–97–24–15–79. AE, DC, MC, V. Closed Mon. and 3 wks in Dec. No dinner Sun., no lunch Wed.*

Outdoor Activities and Sports

Take a cruise down the Auray River on the **Navix-Vedettes du Golfe** (☎ 02–97–56–59–47); along the way you'll discover the lovely 16th-century Château du Plessis-Kaer and the tiny, tidal fishing port of Bono tucked between the steep banks and the oyster beds of the Pô estuary.

Vannes

★ 24 *16 km (10 mi) east of Auray via N165, 108 km (67 mi) southwest of Rennes.*

Scene of the declaration of unity between France and Brittany in 1532, historic Vannes is one of the few towns in Brittany to have been spared damage during World War II. Be sure to saunter through the Promenade de la Garenne, a colorful park, and admire the magnificent gardens nestled beneath the adjacent ramparts. Also visit the medieval wash houses and the cathedral; browse in the small boutiques and antiques shops in the pedestrian streets around pretty place Henri-IV; check out the Cohue, the medieval market hall now used as an exhibition center; and take a boat trip around the scenic Golfe du Morbihan.

Inside the **Cathédrale St-Pierre** are a 1537 Renaissance chapel, a Flamboyant Gothic transept portal, and a treasury. ✉ *Pl. de la Cathédrale.* *Treasury mid-June–mid-Sept., Mon.–Sat. 2–6.*

The **Musée d'Archéologie** (Archaeology Museum) houses a collection of ancient tools and artifacts dating from the Paleolithic Age to the Middle Ages. ✉ *2 rue Noé,* ☎ *02–97–47–35–86.* €3. *Apr.–Sept., Mon.–Sat. 9:30–noon and 2–6; Oct.–Mar., Mon.–Sat. 2–6.*

Dining and Lodging

$$–$$$ ✕ **Richemont.** Step off the train and right into this popular spot, a haven of refinement where seafood reigns. Chef Régis Mahé prefers a small, seasonal menu with local hand-picked produce and fish so fresh they nearly swim to the plate. For a local specialty with a twist, try the buckwheat galette crepe filled with lobster and pigeon and served with caramelized leeks. Attention chocolate lovers: save room for the warm chocolate tart with homemade salty caramel ice cream. ✉ *24 pl. de la Gare,* ☎ *02–97–42–61–41,* FAX *02–97–54–99–01. MC, V. Closed Sun. and Mon.*

$$$$ ✕🏨 **Domaine de Rochevilaine.** This seaside hotel is surrounded by terraced gardens; all guest rooms have modern furnishings, while some have four-poster beds and private terraces (most, but not all, face the ocean, so be sure to specify). There is a full spectrum of seawater hydrotherapy facilities and spa treatments on tap (reserve when booking a room). Patrice Caillault's cuisine includes *coco de Rennes* (a tender hen roasted whole and sliced steaming at the table), while the noted Breton dessert of caramelized apples in pastry layers with cinnamon ice cream is a house specialty. ✉ *Pointe de Pen-Lan, 56190 Billiers (30 km/19 mi southeast of Vannes, at tip of Pointe de Pen-Lan),* ☎ *02–97–41–61–61,* FAX *02–97–41–44–85,* WEB *www.domainerochevilaine.com. 34 rooms, 3 suites. Restaurant, no air-conditioning, cable TV, minibars, Internet, indoor-outdoor pools, hot tub, sauna. AE, DC, MC, V.*

$$ ✕🏨 **Kyriad.** Set in an old, rustic building in town, this hotel attracts a varied foreign clientele, drawn by the homey guest rooms—clean, bright, and simple, with warm yellow walls—and the friendly and efficient staff. Claude Le Lavisque serves a traditional menu in the rustic Image Sainte-Anne restaurant, with straightforward seasonal specialties like crab in milo pastry, grilled sole, and fisherman's stew. No dinner is served Sunday, November through March. ✉ *8 pl. de la Libération, 56000,* ☎ *02–97–63–27–36,* FAX *02–97–40–97–02,* WEB *www.kyriad.com. 33 rooms. Restaurant, no air-conditioning in some rooms, cable TV, minibars, Internet. AE, DC, MC, V.*

La Baule

25 *72 km (45 mi) southeast of Vannes via N165 and D774.*

One of the most fashionable—and pricey—resorts in France, La Baule has a 5-km (3-mi) seafront promenade lined with hotels. Like Le Touquet and Dinard, it is a 19th-century creation, founded in 1879 to make the most of the excellent sandy beaches that extend around the broad, sheltered bay between Pornichet and Le Pouliguen. A pine forest, planted in 1840, keeps the shifting local sand dunes firmly at bay.

Dining and Lodging

$$ ✕ **Ferme du Grand Clos.** At this lively restaurant in an old farmhouse, just 200 meters from the sea, you have to understand the difference between *crêpe* and *galette* to order correctly since the menus showcase both in all their forms. Or you can opt for the simple, straightforward menu featuring food the owner likes to call *la cuisine de grandmère* (grandmother's cooking). Come early for a table; it's a very friendly and popular place. ✉ *52 av. du Maréchal-de-Lattre-de-Tassigny,* ☎ *02–40–60–03–30. MC, V. Closed Wed. Sept.–June.*

$$–$$$ 🏨 **Concorde.** This blue-shuttered, white-walled establishment numbers among the least expensive good hotels in pricey La Baule. It's calm, comfortable, modernized, and a short block from the beach (ask for a room with a sea view). ✉ *1 bis av. de la Concorde, 44500,* ☎ *02–40–60–23–09,* FAX *02–40–42–72–14,* FAX *www.hotel-la-concorde.com. 47 rooms. No air-conditioning, cable TV. AE, DC, MC, V. Closed Oct.–Mar.*

$$ 🏨 **Hôtel de la Plage.** One of the few hotels on the beach in St-Marc-sur-Mer, this comfortable lodging was the setting for Jacques Tati's classic comedy *Mr. Hulot's Holiday.* It has been updated since and, *hélas,* the swinging door to the dining room is no longer there. But the view of the sea and the sound of the surf remain. The restaurant—reserve a beachfront table in advance—serves seasonal fish specialties like the *choucroute de la mer* (seafood sauerkraut stew). ✉ *37 rue du Commandant-Charcot, 44600 St-Marc-sur-Mer (10 km/6 mi southeast of La Baule),* ☎ *02–40–91–99–01,* FAX *02–40–91–92–00,* WEB *www.hotel-de-la-plage-44.com. 30 rooms. Restaurant, no air-conditioning, cable TV, Internet. MC, V. Closed Jan.*

Nightlife

Occasionally you see high stakes on the tables at La Baule's **casino** (✉ 6 av. Pierre-Loti, ☎ 02–40–11–48–28).

En Route Just north of La Baule is **Guérande,** an appealing 15th-century walled town with towers and moat, surrounded by salt flats. From here follow D51 northeast to the curious **Dolmen de Kerbourg,** a table-shape megalith. Continue to the village of **St-Lyphard** and climb up the church tower for a panoramic view of the regional park known as **La Grande Brière.** With its peat marshes crisscrossed by reed-lined canals, the park is a bird-watcher's delight. The best way to explore it is to take a boat trip organized by the **Maison du Parc Naturel Régional de Brière** (✉ 177 rte. de Fédrun, ☎ 02–40–91–68–68) in St-Joachim—only a few miles east of St-Lyphard as the wild duck flies but, along the highway, a tortuous 19 km (12 mi) waddle via D51 and D50.

Nantes

72 km (45 mi) east of La Baule via N171 and N165, 108 km (67 mi) south of Rennes, 114 km (71 mi) southeast of Vannes.

The tranquil, prosperous city of Nantes seems to get on with its existence without too much concern for what's going on elsewhere in France. Cobbled streets surround its castle and cathedral in the town's medieval sector. Across the broad boulevard, Cours des 50-Otages, is the 19th-century city. Although Nantes is officially part of the Pays de la Loire, its historic ties with Brittany are embodied in its imposing castle.

26 Built by the dukes of Brittany, who had no doubt that Nantes belonged in their domain, the **Château des Ducs de Bretagne** is a massive, well-preserved 15th-century fortress with a moat. François II, the duke responsible for building most of it, led a hedonistic life here, surrounded by ministers, chamberlains, and an army of servants. Numerous monarchs later stayed in the castle, where in 1598 Henri IV signed the famous Edict of Nantes advocating religious tolerance. At press time, work was underway to create an extensive regional history museum in the castle buildings. ✉ *4 pl. Marc-Elder,* ☎ *02–40–41–56–56.* 🎫 *€3.10.* ⏲ *Castle and museums Wed.–Sun. 10–6.*

27 The **Cathédrale St-Pierre–St-Paul** is one of France's last Gothic cathedrals, begun in 1434, well after most other medieval cathedrals had been completed. The facade is ponderous and austere, in contrast to the light, wide, limestone interior, whose vaults rise higher (120 ft) than those of Notre-Dame in Paris. In the transept, notice Michel Colombe's early 16th-century tomb of François II and his wife, Marguerite de Foix; the tomb is one of France's finest examples of funerary sculpture. ✉ *Pl. St-Pierre,* ☎ *02–51–88–95–47.* 🎫 *Crypt €3.* ⏲ *Crypt Mon.–Sat. 10–12:30 and 2–6, Sun. 2–6:30.*

Cathédrale St-Pierre—St-Paul 27
Château des Ducs de Bretagne . . .26
Grand Théâtre 30
Manoir de la Touche 31
Musée des Beaux-Arts . .28
Musée Dobrée 32
Passage Pommeraye .29

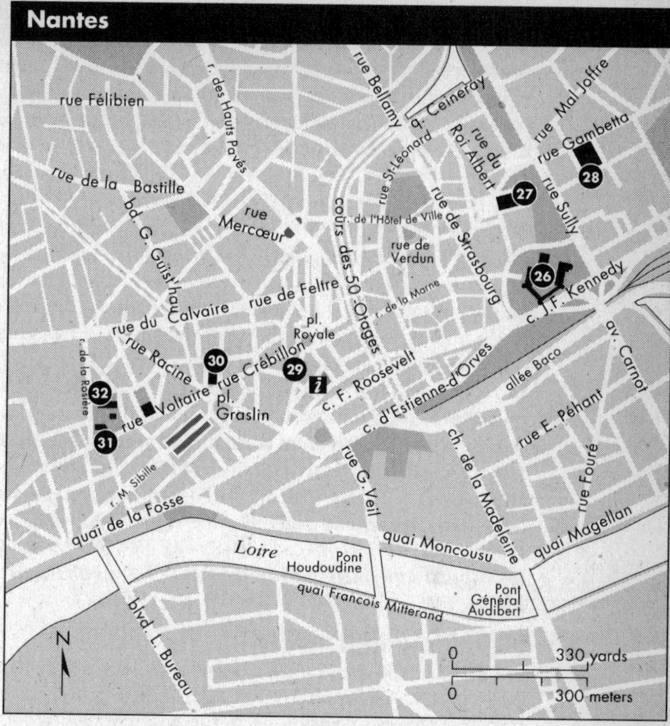

28 A fine collection of paintings from the Renaissance period onward, including works by Jacopo Tintoretto, Georges de La Tour, Jean-Auguste-Dominique Ingres, and Gustave Courbet, is at the **Musée des Beaux-Arts** (Museum of Fine Arts). ✉ *10 rue Georges-Clemenceau,* ☎ *02–40–41–65–65.* 🎫 *€3.10.* ⏲ *Mon., Wed.–Thurs., and weekends 10–6, Fri. 10–8.*

29 Erected in 1843, the **Passage Pommeraye** (✉ Rue Crébillon) is an el-
30 egant shopping gallery in the 19th-century part of town. The **Grand Théâtre** (✉ Pl. Graslin), down the block from the Passage Pommeraye, was built in 1783.

31 The 15th-century **Manoir de la Touche** (✉ Rue Voltaire) was once the
32 abode of the bishops of Nantes. The mock-Romanesque **Musée Dobrée,** offsetting the medieval silhouette of the Manoir de la Touche, across the way, was built by arts connoisseur Thomas Dobrée in the 19th century. Among the treasures within are miniatures, tapestries, medieval manuscripts, and enamels; one room is devoted to the Revolutionary War in Vendée. ✉ *18 rue Voltaire,* ☎ *02–40–71–03–50.* 🎫 *€3.05, free Sun.* ⏲ *Tues.–Sun. 10–noon and 1:30–5:30.*

Dining and Lodging

$$ ✕ **L'Embellie.** Sweet and simple, this spot lures diners with its modern, inventive attitude and friendly service. Chef Yvonnick Briand's "creative regional" cuisine extends to his own smokehouse for salmon and duck, so the foie gras is homemade—he likes to serve it light, atop a mesclun salad. The menu is dependent on Briand's daily trips to markets, so don't hesitate to try any of the fresh fish specials, such as the sea bass steamed in rosemary or other briny delights laced with French West Indian spices. Pineapple *croquant* with rum-laced creole ice cream makes a fitting finale. ✉ *14 rue Armand-Brossard,* ☎ *02–40–48–20–02. AE, MC, V. Closed Sun. and 2nd wk in Aug. No dinner Mon.*

$$ ★ ✕ **Villa Mon Rêve.** This cozy restaurant is in delightful parkland off the D751 outside Nantes. Chef Gérard Ryngel concocts elegantly inventive regional fare (the roast duck in caramel and Muscadet is a good choice), with which you can sample one of more than 50 varieties of Muscadet, the local wine. Request a table on the terrace when you reserve. ✉ *Levêe Divatte, 506 bd. de la Loire, Basse-Goulaine (8 mi/5 mi east of Nantes),* ☎ *02–40–03–55–50,* WEB *www.villa-mon-reve.com. AE, DC, MC, V. Closed part of Feb. and Nov.*

$–$$ ✕ **Cigale.** Miniature palm trees, gleaming woodwork, colorful enamel tiles, and painted ceilings have led to the official recognition of La Cigale brasserie (built in 1895) as a *monument historique.* You can savor its Belle Epoque blandishments without spending a fortune—the prix-fixe lunch menus are a good value. But the banks of fresh oysters and well-stacked dessert cart may tempt you to order à la carte. ✉ *4 Pl. Graslin,* ☎ *02–51–84–94–94. Reservations essential. MC, V.*

$$ **La Pérouse.** Bare parquet floors, plain off-white walls, simple high-tech lighting, and minimal contemporary furnishings make rooms feel spacious; bathrooms are equally modern. The amiable staff speak fluent English. A pedestrian zone full of boutiques and restaurants is right outside the door, and place Royale is just 300 yards away. ✉ *3 allée Dusquesne, 44000,* ☎ *02–40–89–75–00,* FAX *02–40–89–76–00,* WEB *www.hotel-laperouse. 47 rooms. Cable TV, minibars, Internet. AE, DC, MC, V.*

Nightlife and the Arts

For live jazz, the informal **Pub Univers** (✉ 16 rue Jean-Jacques Rousseau) is the spot. **Le Tie Break** (✉ 1 rue des Petites-Écuries) is a popular piano bar. The **Théâtre Graslin** (✉ 1 rue Molière, ☎ 02–40–69–77–18) is Nantes's principal concert hall and opera house.

Outdoor Activities and Sports

You can take a 100-minute cruise along the pretty Erdre River, past a string of gardens and châteaux, with the **Bateaux Nantais.** There are also four-course lunch and dinner cruises that last about 2½ hours (€40–€50). Call ahead to get the schedule for the special activities planned for children—treasure hunts, musical shows, or one of the Halloween dress-up cruises. ✉ *Gare Fluviale pl. Waldeck-Rousseau,* ☎ *02–40–14–51–14.* *€10.* *June–Aug., Mon. and Fri. at 3, weekends at 3 and 5; May and Sept.–Oct., weekends at 3.*

Shopping

The commercial quarter of Nantes stretches from place Royale to place Graslin. Various antiques shops can be found on rue Voltaire. The Devineau family has been selling wax fruit and vegetables at **Devineau** (✉ 2 pl. Ste-Croix) since 1803; for €12, you can take home a basket of purple grapes or a cauliflower, as well as handmade candles and wildflower honey. For chocolate, head to **Gautier-Debotté** (✉ 9 rue de la Fosse); try the local Muscadet grapes dipped in brandy and covered with chocolate.

BRITTANY A TO Z

To research prices, get advice from other travelers, and book travel arrangements, visit www.fodors.com.

AIRPORTS

Rennes, Brest, Nantes, Quimper, Dinard, and Lorient all have domestic airports. Air France (☞ Air Travel *in* Smart Travel Tips A to Z) flies to them all, except Dinard.

BIKE TRAVEL

Bikes can be rented at most major train stations.

BUS TRAVEL

There are many bus routes linking Brittany, serviced by a bewildering number of bus companies. Buses connect the big city of Rennes (often via TIV and Cariane Atlantique Otages) with Nantes, St-Malo, Dinan (via CAT), Dinard (via CAT and TIV), Cancale (via TIV), Mont-St-Michel, Fougères, and Vitré (via TIV)—you can also bus to Mont-St-Michel from Fougères and (via Les Courriers Bretons) from St-Malo. Dinan is linked with Rennes (via TAE); Paimpol with St-Brieuc (via CAT); Morlaix with Roscoff (via Cars du Kreisker); Quimper with Brest (via CAT); Pont-Aven with Brest, Quimper, and Concarneau (via Transports Caoudal); Vannes with Quiberon (via Cariane Atlantique) and Carnac (via Transports Le Bayon). There are many other links, so, as always, check in with the regional tourist office or information window at a big gateway rail or bus station to get printed bus schedules.

➤ Bus Information: **Cariane Atlantique** (☎ 02–97–47–29–64). **Cariane Atlantique Otages–Nantes** (☎ 02–40–20–46–99). **Cars du Kreisker** (☎ 02–98–69–00–93). **CAT** (☎ 02–96–39–21–05). **Les Courriers Bretons** (☎ 02–99–19–70–80). **TIV** (☎ 02–02–99–26–11–11). **Transports Caoudal** (☎ 02–98–90–88–89). **Transports Le Bayon** (☎ 02–97–24–26–20).

CAR RENTAL

➤ Local Agencies: **Avis** (☎ 08–20–05–05–05 national reservations number in Paris; ✉ Pl. Rhin-et-Danube, La Baule, ☎ 02–40–60–36–28; ✉ Aéroport, Dinard, ☎ 02–99–46–25–20; ✉ 20 bis rue de Siam, Brest, ☎ 02–98–44–63–02; ✉ Rue Lourmel, Nantes, ☎ 02–40–89–25–50). **Europcar** (✉ Pl. de la Gare, Rennes, ☎ 02–23–44–02–73). **Hertz** (✉ Rte. de Trégastel, Lannion, ☎ 02–96–05–82–82; ✉ 53 rue de la Gare, St-Brieuc, ☎ 02–96–94–25–89, WEB www.avis.fr).

CAR TRAVEL

Rennes, the gateway to Brittany, is 310 km (195 mi) west of Paris. It can be reached in about three hours via Le Mans and A81 and A11 (A11 continues southwest from Le Mans to Nantes). Rennes is linked by good roads to Morlaix and Brest (E50), Quimper (N24/N165), and Vannes (N24/N166). A car is a good idea if you want to see out-of-the-way places.

EMERGENCIES

➤ Hospitals: **Rennes** (✉ 2 rue Henri-Le-Guilloux, 35000, ☎ 02–99–28–43–21). **Brest** (✉ 5 av. Foch, 29200, ☎ 02–98–22–33–33). **Nantes** (✉ 1 pl. Alexis-Ricordeau, 44000, ☎ 02–40–08–33–33).

OUTDOORS AND SPORTS

For information on various regional activities such as sailing, hiking, camping, fishing, and daily excursions in the Finistére, contact the Regional Tourist Board. For documentation on all local activities and help organizing your stay in the Côtes d'Armor, contact the Armor Tourist Board.

➤ Contacts: **Armor Tourist Board** (✉ 7 Saint Benoit, St. Brieuc, ☎ 02–96–62–72–00, FAX 02–96–33–59–10, WEB www.cotesdarmor.com). **Regional Tourist Board** (✉ 11 rue Théodore-le-Hac, Quimper, ☎ 02–98–76–20–70, FAX 02–98–52–19–19, WEB www.finisteretourisme.com).

TOURS

Information about organized tours of Brittany is available from the very helpful Maison de la Bretagne.

➤ Fees and Schedules: **Maison de la Bretagne** (✉ 203 bd. St-Germain, 75007 Paris, ☎ 01–53–63–11–50, FAX 01–53–63–11–57).

TRAIN TRAVEL

Over 15 high-speed TGVs (*Trains à Grande Vitesse*) depart daily from Paris (Gare Montparnasse) for both Nantes and Rennes, making this region easily accessible. The trip to either city takes about 2¼ hours. There are 8 daily TGVs to Brest (4½ hours) and 10 regional trains to St-Malo. To find out about other regional timetables and fares or to reserve your seat, contact the SNCF Web site.

Most towns in this region are accessible by train, though you need a car to get to some of the more secluded spots. Some trains from Paris stop in Vitré before forking at Rennes on their way to either Brest (via Morlaix) or Quimper (via Vannes). Change at Rennes for Dol-de-Bretagne and St-Malo; at Dol-de-Bretagne for Dinan and Dinard (bus link); at Morlaix for Roscoff; at Rosporden, 19 km (12 mi) south of Quimper, for Concarneau (bus link); and at Auray for Quiberon.
➤ Train Information: **SNCF** (☎ 08–36–35–35–35, WEB www.ter-sncf.com/UK/bretagne).

TRAVEL AGENCIES

➤ Local Agent Referrals: **Havas** (✉ 33 rue Jean-Macé, Brest, ☎ 02–98–80–05–43, WEB www.havasvoyages.com; ✉ 14 rue Ville-Pépin, St-Malo, ☎ 02–99–19–79–90). **Carlson Wagons-lit** (✉ 22 rue du Calvaire, Nantes, ☎ 02–40–08–29–18; ✉ 2 rue Jules-Simon, Rennes, ☎ 02–99–79–45–96).

VISITOR INFORMATION

The principal regional tourist offices are in Brest, Nantes, and Rennes.
➤ Tourist Information: **Brest** (✉ 8 av. Georges-Clemenceau, ☎ 02–98–44–24–96, FAX 02–98–44–53–73). **Nantes** (✉ 2 allée Baco, ☎ 02–51–72–95–30, FAX 02–40–20–44–54, WEB www.cdt44.com). **Rennes** (✉ 11 rue St-Yves, ☎ 02–99–67–11–11, FAX 02–99–67–11–10, WEB www.ville-rennes.fr). **Carnac** (✉ 74 av. des Druides, ☎ 02–97–52–13–52, FAX 02–97–52–86–10, WEB www.ot-carnac.fr). **Concarneau** (✉ Quai d'Aiguillon, ☎ 02–98–97–01–44, FAX 02–98–50–88–81). **Dinan** (✉ 9 rue du Château, ☎ 02–96–87–69–76, FAX 02–96–87–69–77, WEB www.dinan-tourisme.com). **Dinard** (✉ 2 bd. Féart, ☎ 02–99–46–94–12, FAX 02–99–88–21–07, WEB www.ville-dinard.fr). **Dol-de-Bretagne** (✉ 3 Grande-Rue, ☎ 02–99–48–15–37). **Douarnenez** (✉ 2 rue du Dr-Mével, ☎ 02–98–92–13–35, FAX 02–98–92–70–47, WEB www.douarnenez.com). **La Baule** (✉ 8 pl. de la Victoire, ☎ 02–40–24–34–44, FAX 02–40–11–08–10, WEB www.labaule.tm.fr). **Lorient** (✉ Maison de la Mer, quai de Rohan, ☎ 02–97–21–07–84, FAX 02–97–21–99–44, WEB www.lorient-tourisme.com). **Morlaix** (✉ Pl. des Otages, ☎ 02–98–62–14–94). **Quiberon** (✉ 14 rue de Verdun, ☎ 02–97–50–07–84, FAX 02–97–30–58–22, WEB www.quiberon.com). **Quimper** (✉ 7 rue Déesse, ☎ 02–98–53–04–05, FAX 0298533133, WEB www.bretagne-4villes.com). **St-Malo** (✉ Esplanade St-Vincent, ☎ 02–99–56–64–48, FAX 02–99–56–67–00, WEB www.saint-malo-tourisme.com). **Vannes** (✉ 1 rue Thiers, ☎ 02–97–47–24–34, FAX 02–97–47–29–49, WEB www.vannes-bretagne-sud.com). **Vitré** (✉ Pl. St-Yves, ☎ 02–99–75–04–46, FAX 02–99–74–02–01, WEB www.ot-vitre.fr).

6 NORMANDY

Named for the Norsemen who claimed this corner of Gaul and sent a famous conqueror over the Channel in 1066, and eternally tied in our memory to the D-Day landings, Normandy has always played shuttle diplomat in Anglo-French relations. From its half-timber houses to its green apple orchards to its rich dairy cream, it seems to mirror the culture of its English neighbor across the water. Even the island-abbey of Mont-St-Michel is a looking-glass reflection of its over-the-Channel counterpart, St. Michael's Mount, in Cornwall. Other treasures beckon: elegant Deauville, Rouen's great cathedral and museums, the legendary Bayeux Tapestry . . . and those warming glasses of calvados.

Updated by Simon Hewitt

Introduction by Nancy Coons

SAY THE NAME "NORMANDY," and which channel-side scenario comes to mind? Long ships bristling with oars scudding into the darkness toward Hastings? Those very ships were immortalized in the Bayeux Tapestry, which traces step by step the epic tale of William the Conqueror, who in 1066 sailed across the Channel to claim his right to England's throne. Or do you think of iron-gray convoys massing silently along the shore at dawn, lowering tailgates to pour troops of young Allied infantrymen into the line of German machine-gun fire? At Omaha Beach you may marvel at the odds against the handful of soldiers who in June 1944 were able to rise above the waterfront carnage to capture the clifftop battery, paving the way for the Allies' reconquest of Europe.

Or do you think of Joan of Arc—imprisoned by the English yet burned at the Rouen stake by the Church she believed in? In a modern church you may light a candle on the very spot where, in 1431, the Maiden Warrior sizzled into history at the hands of panicky politicians and time-serving clerics: a dark deed that marked a turning point in the Hundred Years' War. Or are you reminded of the dramatic silhouette of Mont-St-Michel looming above the tidal flats, its cobbles echoing with the footfalls of medieval scholars? You may make a latter-day pilgrimage to the famous island-abbey, one of the most evocative monuments in Europe behind its crow's-nest ramparts.

The destinies of England and Normandie (as the French spell it) have been intertwined ever since William, duke of Normandy, insisted that King Edward the Confessor had promised him the succession to the English crown. When a royal council instead anointed the Anglo-Saxon Harold Godwinsson, the irate William stormed across the Channel with 7,000 well-equipped archers, well-mounted knights, and well-paid Frankish mercenaries. They landed at Pevonsey Bary on September 28, 1066, and two weeks later, at Hastings, saw off a ragtag mix of battle-weary English troops hastily reinforced with drafted peasants swinging stones tied to sticks. Harold met his maker, an arrow through his eye. William progressed to London and was crowned King of England on Christmas Day.

There followed nearly 400 years of Norman sovereignty in England. For generations England and Normandy vacillated and blurred, merged, and diverged. Today you'll still feel the strong flow of English culture over the Channel, from the Deauville horse races frequented by high-born ladies in gloves, to silver spoons mounded high with teatime cream; from the bowfront, slope-roof shops along the harbor at Honfleur to the black-and-white row houses of Rouen, which would seem just as much at home in *David Copperfield* as they would in *Madame Bovary.*

And just as in the British Isles, no matter how you concentrate on history and culture, sooner or later you'll find yourself beguiled by the countryside, by Normandy's rolling green hills dotted with dairy cows and half-timber farmhouses. Like the locals, you'll be tempted by seafood fresh off the boat, by sauces rich with crème fraîche, by cheeses redolent of farm and pasture. And perhaps with cheeks pink from the apple-scented country air you'll eventually succumb to the local antidote to northern damp and chill: a mug of tangy hard cider by the crackling fire, and the bracing tonic of Normandy's famous apple brandy, calvados.

Pleasures and Pastimes

The Coast

Normandy has 600 km (375 mi) of coastline bordering the English Channel. There are major ports—Le Havre, Dieppe, and Cherbourg—plus coastal towns with seafaring pasts, like Honfleur, and fishing villages, like Fécamp. Sandwiched between are beaches and fashionable resort towns such as Cabourg, Deauville, and Étretat. Though the waters are chilly, you might be tempted to take a dip on a hot, sunny day.

Dining

The Normans are notoriously heavy eaters. Between the warm-up and the main course traditionally comes the *trou Normand* (Norman gap), a break for calvados—apple brandy (a typically Norman riddle asks, "Did the *trou normand* create calvados, or did calvados create the *trou normand*?"). Norman food isn't light; many dishes are prepared with cream sauces and apple flavoring—hence *à la normande* (with cream sauce or apples); the modern version of the *trou normand* is a tangy apple sorbet floating in calvados, sometimes served between the main course and the cheese plate. Rich local milk makes excellent cheese: Pont-l'Évêque (known since the 13th century) is made in the Pays d'Auge with milk still warm and creamy; Livarot (also produced for centuries) uses milk that has stood a while—don't be put off by its pungent smell. Best known of them all is creamy Camembert, a relative newcomer, invented by a farmer's wife in the late 18th century. Although Normandy is not a wine-growing area, it produces excellent hard cider (the best comes from the Vallée d'Auge), calvados, and its lighter cousin *pommeau,* which is two-thirds apple juice and one-third calvados. Be sure to choose all products, from cheese to apple cider, with the AOC label, which means that they have passed rigorous standards of quality. Local specialties differ from place to place. Rouen is famous for its canard *à la rouennaise* (duck in blood sauce); Caen, for its *tripes à la mode de Caen* (tripe cooked with carrots in a seasoned cider stock); Mont-St-Michel, for *omelettes Mère Poulard* (a secret recipe first made by a local hotel manager in the late 19th century) and *pré-salé* (salt-meadow lamb). Try *andouille de Vire,* a delicate, smoked chitterling sausage served in thin slices like salami. Fish and seafood lovers can feast on oysters, lobster, shrimp, and sole *dieppoise* (sole poached in a sauce with cream and mussels).

CATEGORY	COST*
$$$$	over €30
$$$	€20–€30
$$	€12–€20
$	under €12

**per person for a main course only, including tax (19.6%) and service; note that if a restaurant offers only prix-fixe (set-price) meals, it has been given the price category that reflects the full prix-fixe price*

Lodging

Accommodations to suit every taste can be found in Normandy. The beach-resort season is short—July and August only—but weekends are busy most of the year, and especially during school holidays. In June and September lodging is usually available on short notice, and good discounts are given off-season, particularly for stays of more than one night. If you are traveling in the summer months, reserve your hotel well in advance, request a written confirmation, and inform your hotel of any possible late check-in, or they may give your room away. Assume all hotel rooms have air-conditioning, telephones, TV, and private bath unless otherwise noted. Internet, when listed in facilities, means in-room data-ports and/or public-area computers provide on-line access.

CATEGORY	COST*
$$$$	over €180
$$$	€120–€180
$$	€60–€120
$	under €60

**All prices are for a standard double room in high season, including tax (19.6%) and service charge.*

Exploring Normandy

You won't want to miss medieval Rouen, seaside Honfleur, or magnificent Mont-St-Michel. But if you get away from these popular spots you can lose yourself along the cliff-lined coast and in the green spaces inland, where the closest thing to a crowd is a farmer with his herd of brown-and-white cows. From Rouen northeast to the coast—the area known as Upper Normandy—medieval castles and abbeys stand guard above rolling countryside, while resort and fishing towns line the white cliffs of the Côte d'Alabâtre. Popular seaside resorts and the D-Day landing sites occupy the sandy beaches along the Côte Fleurie; apple orchards and dairy farms sprinkle the countryside of the area known as Lower Normandy. The Cotentin Peninsula to the west juts out into the English Channel. Central Normandy encompasses the peaceful, hilly region of La Suisse Normande, along the scenic Orne River.

Numbers in the text correspond to numbers in the margin and on the Normandy and Rouen maps.

Great Itineraries

With three days you can get a feel for the region. Five days gives you time to meander through the countryside and down the coast. And with nine days, if you don't spend much time in any one place, you can see most of Normandy.

IF YOU HAVE 3 DAYS

Head straight to **Rouen** ⑤–⑮ and spend a day and a half in the region's cultural capital. Then follow the Seine Valley past the abbeys of **Jumièges** ⑯ and the sights of **Caudebec-en-Caux** ⑰ including the Abbaye de St-Wandrille, then head west to **Honfleur** ㉓, the fishing port that caught the Impressionists' eye.

IF YOU HAVE 9 DAYS

Follow the Seine en route from Paris to **Rouen** ⑤–⑮, visiting **Lyons-la-Forêt** ② and **Les Andelys** ③. On the third day wind along the route des Abbayes to the abbeys of **Abbaye de Jumièges** ⑯ and **Caudebec-en-Caux** ⑰. Drive northwest to the fishing town of **Fécamp** ⑲, then head down the Côte d'Alabâtre to the spectacular cliffs of **Étretat** ⑳. Continue south, cross the Pont de Normandie, and spend the night in tony **Honfleur** ㉓. On the next day travel along the Côte Fleurie to the fashionable seaside resorts of **Deauville-Trouville** ㉔ and Belle Epoque **Houlgate** ㉕, reaching **Caen** ㉖, site of some of World War II's fiercest fighting and William the Conqueror's fortress, by mid-afternoon. The following day visit Gold, Juno, and Sword beaches and historic **Arromanches** ㉗, then party in **Bayeux** ㉘ overnight. Visit the storied tapestry and continue your exploration of the **D-Day beaches** ㉙–㉛ before continuing up the Cotentin coast to **Cherbourg** ㉝. On day seven ramble south to the cathedral town of **Coutances** ㉟ and on to seafaring **Granville** ㊱, then continue to the majestic abbey on a rock, **Mont-St-Michel** ㊲. Next morning hurry east to the Suisse Normande's rocky expanse of hills, passing through Clécy before stopping for a picnic lunch at the Roche d'Oëtre, a rock with a spectacular view of the Orne Valley. If time allows, take in William the Conqueror's hilltop castle at **Falaise** ㊳.

When to Tour Normandy

July and August—when French families vacation—are the busiest months, but also the most activity-filled: concerts are presented every evening at Mont-St-Michel, and the region's most important horse races are held in Deauville, culminating with the Gold Cup Polo Championship and the Grand Prix the last Sunday in August. June 6, the anniversary of the Allied invasion, is the most popular time to visit the D-Day beaches. If you're trying to avoid crowds, your best bet is late spring and early autumn, when it is still fairly temperate. May finds the apple trees in full bloom and miles of waving flaxseed fields spotted with tiny butter-yellow flowers. Some of the biggest events of the region take place during these seasons: in Rouen, at the end of May, Joan of Arc is honored at a festival named for her; there is jazz under the apple trees in Coutances; the first week of September in Deauville is the American Film Festival, and the last week sees the nationally acclaimed blues music festival in Lisieux. Winter offers quieter pleasures: the lush Normandy countryside rolling softly under a thick tent of clouds so low you can touch them; the strange desolate poetry of the empty D-Day beaches; intimate evenings in casinos with the fun-loving locals for company, or a good conversation with the less-harried hosts in a quiet country inn; and a last burning snifter of calvados in front of a roaring Norman hearth.

NORMANDY

The French divide Normandy into two: Haute-Normandie and Basse-Normandie. Upper (Haute) Normandy is delineated by the Seine as it meanders northwest from Ile-de-France between chalky cliffs and verdant hills to Rouen—the region's cultural and commercial capital—and on to the port of Le Havre. Pebbly beaches and even more impressive chalk cliffs line the Côte d'Alabâtre from Le Havre to Dieppe. In the 19th century, the dramatic scenery and bathing resorts along the coast attracted and inspired writers and artists like Maupassant, Monet, and Braque. Lower (Basse) Normandy encompasses the sandy Côte Fleurie (Flower Coast), stretching from the the resort towns of Trouville and Deauville to the D-Day landing beaches and the Cotentin Peninsula, jutting out into the English Channel. Inland, lush green meadows and apple orchards form the heart of calvados country west of the pilgrim town of Lisieux. After the World War II D-Day landings, some of the fiercest fighting took place around Caen and Bayeux, as many monuments and memorials testify. To the south, in the prosperous Pays d'Auge, dairy farms produce the region's famous cheeses. The hilly Suisse Normande provides the region's most rugged scenery. Rising to the west is the fabled Mont-St-Michel. Our tour starts along the Seine Valley in Basse Normandie, then heads north to the Channel Coast, which we follow all the way from Dieppe to Mont-St-Michel. Here you can continue into Brittany or return east, cutting back inland to Falaise, Liseux, and Evreux.

Gisors

❶ *64 km (40 mi) northwest of Paris via A15 and D915, 35 km (24 mi) northeast of Vernon.*

Gisors, a peaceful market town in the Vexin region evoked by Impressionist painter Camille Pissarro (who lived just to the north in Er-

Normandy

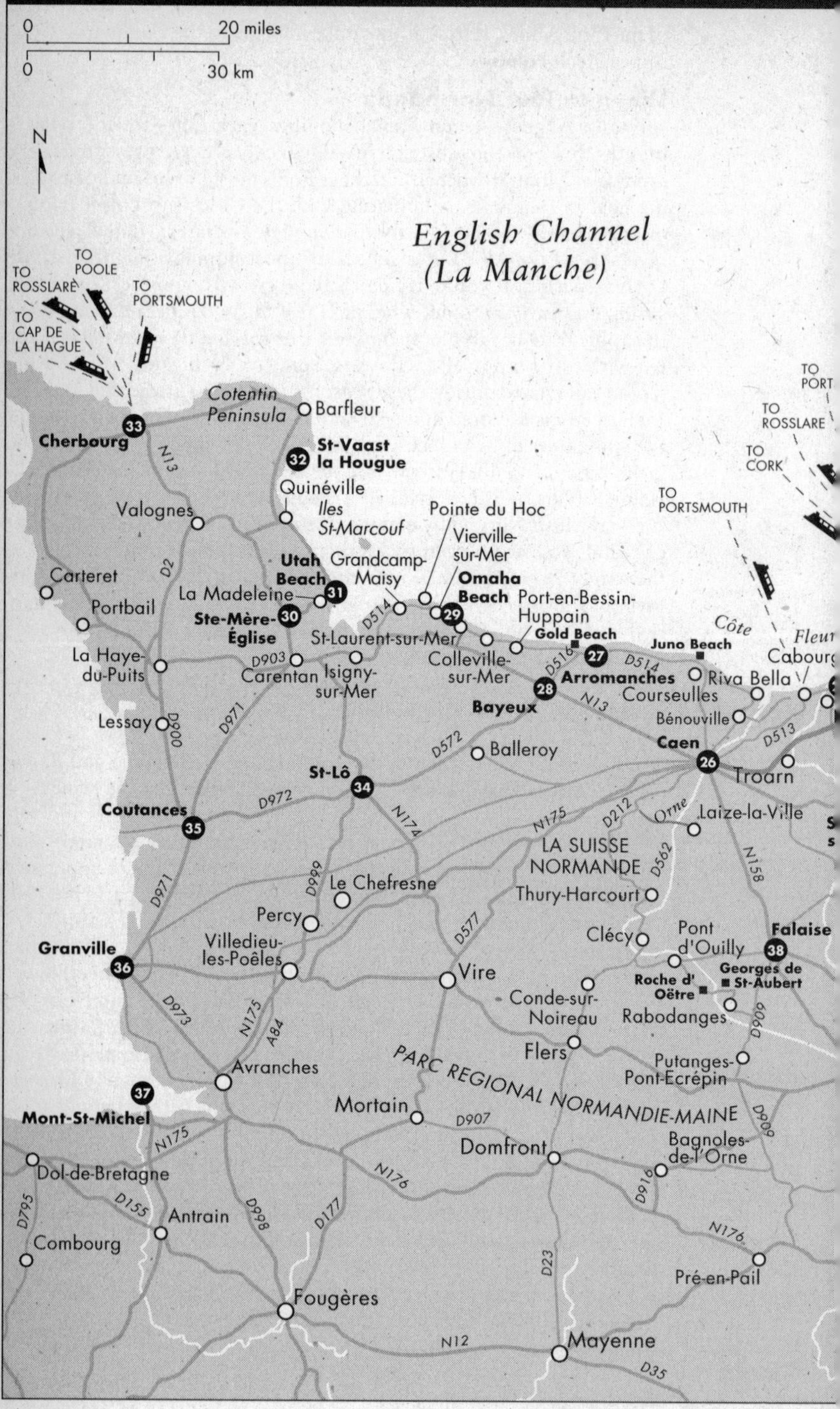
0
20 miles
0
30 km
N
English Channel
(La Manche)
TO POOLE
TO ROSSLARE
TO PORTSMOUTH
TO CAP DE LA HAGUE
TO PORT
TO ROSSLARE
TO CORK
TO PORTSMOUTH
Cotentin Peninsula
Barfleur
Cherbourg
33
St-Vaast la Hougue
32
N13
Quinéville
Iles St-Marcouf
Valognes
Pointe du Hoc
Vierville-sur-Mer
Utah Beach
Grandcamp-Maisy
31
Omaha Beach
Port-en-Bessin-Huppain
D2
Carteret
La Madeleine
Portbail
Ste-Mère-Église
30
D514
29
Côte
Fleur
Gold Beach
Juno Beach
St-Laurent-sur-Mer
La Haye-du-Puits
D903
Carentan
Isigny-sur-Mer
Colleville-sur-Mer
D516
27
D514
Cabourg
Arromanches
Riva Bella
28
Courseulles
Bayeux
N13
Bénouville
Lessay
D900
D971
D572
Balleroy
D513
Caen
26
Troarn
St-Lô
34
D972
Coutances
35
N174
N175
D212
Orne
Laize-la-Ville
LA SUISSE NORMANDE
D562
N158
D971
D999
Le Chefresne
Thury-Harcourt
Percy
Clécy
Pont d'Ouilly
Falaise
38
D577
Granville
36
Villedieu-les-Poêles
Vire
Roche d' Oëtre
Georges de St-Aubert
Conde-sur-Noireau
Rabodanges
D909
D973
N175
A84
Flers
Putanges-Pont-Ecrépin
Avranches
PARC REGIONAL NORMANDIE-MAINE
37
Mortain
D909
Mont-St-Michel
D907
N175
Domfront
Bagnoles-de-l'Orne
Dol-de-Bretagne
N176
D916
D155
D795
Antrain
D998
D177
N176
Combourg
D23
Pré-en-Pail
Fougères
N12
Mayenne
D35

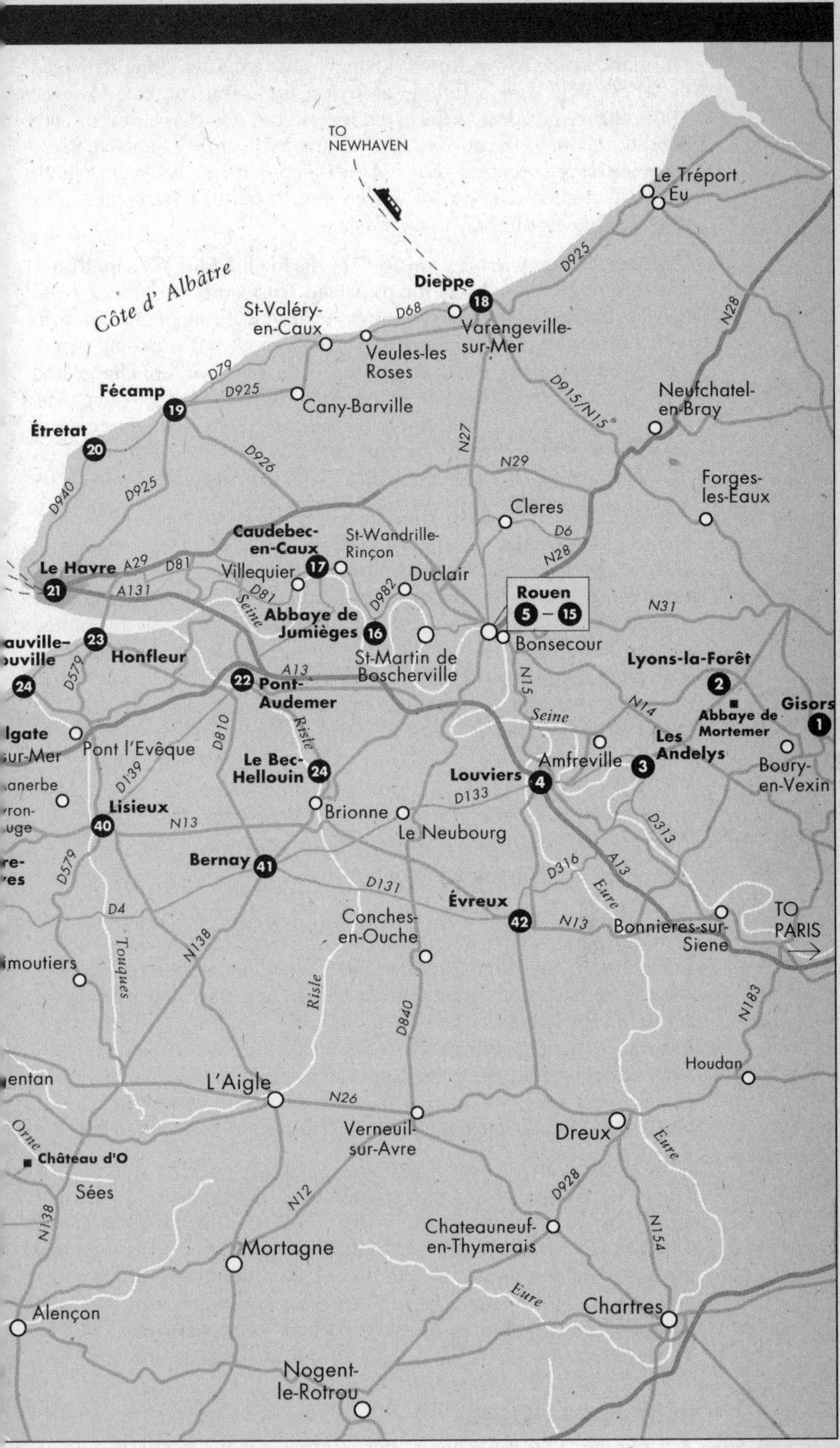

TO NEWHAVEN
Le Tréport
Eu
D925
Côte d' Albâtre
Dieppe
18
St-Valéry-en-Caux
D68
Varengeville-sur-Mer
N28
Veules-les Roses
D79
Fécamp
D925
Cany-Barville
D915/N15
Neufchatel-en-Bray
19
Étretat
20
D926
N27
N29
Forges-les-Eaux
D940
D925
Cleres
Caudebec-en-Caux
St-Wandrille-Rinçon
D6
N28
Le Havre
A29
D81
Villequier
17
Duclair
21
A131
D81
D982
Rouen
5 – 15
Seine
Abbaye de Jumièges
16
N31
Bonsecour
23
Honfleur
St-Martin de Boscherville
Lyons-la-Forêt
D579
A13
N15
2
24
22
Pont-Audemer
Seine
N14
Abbaye de Mortemer
Gisors
1
Risle
Les Andelys
D810
Pont l'Evêque
Amfreville
3
Boury-en-Vexin
Le Bec-Hellouin
24
D139
Louviers
4
D133
Lisieux
Brionne
40
N13
Le Neubourg
D313
D579
Bernay
41
D316
A13
D131
Eure
Évreux
TO PARIS
D4
Conches-en-Ouche
42
N13
Bonnieres-sur-Siene
Touques
N138
N183
Risle
D840
Houdan
L'Aigle
N26
Verneuil-sur-Avre
Dreux
Orne
Eure
Château d'O
Sées
N12
D928
N138
Chateauneuf-en-Thymerais
N154
Mortagne
Eure
Chartres
Alençon
Nogent-le-Rotrou

agny-sur-Epte), has several half-timber houses along the sloping rue de Vienne and a fine hilltop castle standing sentinel at the confines of Normandy. The town church, lovingly restored after being damaged in World War II, is a jumble of styles; the elaborate, two-towered 16th-century facade and florid vaulting in the side chapels clash with the sober choir, consecrated in 1249. The royal fleur-de-lis emblem keeps cropping up unexpectedly—carved on a spiral-patterned pillar, in a modern stained-glass window, or woven into the stone balustrade above the side chapels outside.

The **Château Fort** was begun in 1097 by the English king William Rufus, son of William the Conqueror, to defend Normandy's southeast frontier. The castle has two parts. One is the drumlike ring of curtain walls with a dozen towers, surrounded by a large ditch and enclosing a park of flowers and evergreens. The park is open daily without charge and offers a fine view of the church above the roofs of the Old Town. The other is the 70-ft artificial mound in the middle, the foursquare keep, with a staircase leading to the top—and down to the dungeon. ✉ *Pl. Blanmont,* ☏ *02–32–55–59–36.* 🎫 *€5.* ⏲ *Apr.–Sept., Wed.–Mon. 10–noon and 2–6; Oct.–Nov. and Feb.–Mar., weekends 10–noon and 2–5.*

In the pretty village of Boury-en-Vexin, 8 km (5 mi) southwest of Gisors, the steep-roofed **Château de Boury,** built in 1685 by Jules Hardouin-Mansart, displays the same monumental dignity as the same architect's work at Versailles. The two-tiered facade, with arched ground-floor windows and Ionic pilasters above, surveys a trim lawn with cone-shape topiaries. The château has remained in the same family since it was built, and has a homey, lived-in feel to complement its grand furniture, portraits, and crystal chandeliers. ✉ *Boury-en-Vexin,* ☏ *02–32–55–15–10.* 🎫 *€5.* ⏲ *July–Aug., Wed.–Mon. 2:30–6:30; mid-Apr.–June and Sept.–mid-Oct., weekends 2:30–6:30.*

Lyons-la-Forêt

★ ❷ *34 km (21 mi) northwest of Gisors, 36 km (23 mi) east of Rouen.*

Few villages in France are as pretty as Lyons-la-Forêt, built in a verdant clearing surrounded by a noble beech forest. Lyons has entire streets full of rickety half-timber houses and a venerable market hall built of robust, medieval oak on its main square. In fact, the square is more of a tumbling triangle—all bustle in summer but, come winter, when most hotels and restaurants are shut, as forlorn as the leafless beech trees all around. Lyons is built on two levels, and if you arrive from Gisors, take care not to miss the lower road—a quilt of medieval black-and-white frontages leading to the village church and its life-size wooden statues.

The scenic ruins of the Cistercian **Abbaye de Mortemer** are by a small lake in the heart of the forest, 5 km (3 mi) south of Lyons-la-Forêt. The 100-yard-long church was built at the start of the 13th century but destroyed during the Revolution. Some of the abbey buildings survive, including the large 15th-century pigeon loft that was also used as a prison. A small museum evokes aspects of monastic life. ✉ *Rue de Mortemer, Lisors,* ☏ *02–32–49–54–34.* 🎫 *€6.10.* ⏲ *Easter–Oct., daily 11–6:30; Nov.–Easter, Sun. 2–6.*

Dining and Lodging

$$–$$$ ✕🏨 **Licorne.** This venerable 17th-century inn at the top of the village square has comfortable rooms with rustic wooden furniture. The smaller rooms, Nos. 2, 3, and 9, are also the most reasonably priced. Take a drink in the colorful garden then repair to the dining room (no meals Monday), where a fire crackles in the hearth on cooler evenings.

For a main course, try grilled salmon or guinea fowl with peaches, and for dessert opt for the specialty of the house, *tarte tatin* (an upside-down apple tart with a dollop of crème fraîche). ✉ *Pl. du Marché, 27480,* ☎ *02–32–49–62–02,* FAX *02–32–49–80–09. 19 rooms. Restaurant. AE, DC, MC, V. Closed Dec. 20–Jan. 25.*

Les Andelys

❸ *20 km (13 mi) southwest of Lyons-la-Forêt, 88 km (55 mi) northwest of Paris, 40 km (25 mi) southeast of Rouen.*

In one of the most picturesque loops of the Seine, the small town of Les Andelys, birthplace of France's leading classical painter, Nicolas Poussin, is set against magnificent chalky cliffs. The town is divided between riverside Petit-Andely, with its 13th-century church of St-Sauveur and domed, 18th-century Hôpital St-Jacques, and bustling Grand-Andely, whose Collégiale Notre-Dame gleams with a score of exquisite stained-glass windows created between 1540 and 1560. **Château Gaillard,** a formidable fortress built by England's King Richard the Lion-Hearted in 1196, overlooks Petit Andely from the clifftop, with spectacular views in both directions. Despite its solid defenses, the castle fell to French king Philippe-Auguste in 1204, after a lengthy siege during which it suffered considerable damage; further sections were torn down at the end of the 16th century, and only one of its five main towers remains intact. But the location and the history bring the ruins alive. ✉ *Rue Richard-Coeur-de-Lion,* ☎ *02–32–54–04–16.* *€3.50.* *Apr.–Oct., Thurs.–Mon. 10–noon and 2–5, Wed. 2–5.*

Dining and Lodging

$$$–$$$$ ✕ **Chaîne d'Or.** This charming inn, founded in 1751 within sight of Château Gaillard, has a terrace that overlooks the banks of the Seine (just the place to enjoy your predinner aperitif on warmer days). Rooms are large and bright; for time-burnished charm, request one with a view of the church or courtyard. In the airy, flower-laden restaurant (closed on Sunday and Monday), Christophe Bouche's neo-classical Norman cuisine ranges from grilled lobster with truffles and olives to chicken with vanilla and cinnamon. The dining rooms is elegant, with exposed beams and large bouquets of flowers. ✉ *27 rue Grande, 27700,* ☎ *02–32–54–00–31,* FAX *02–32–54–05–68,* WEB *www.planete-b.fr/la-chaine-d-or. 10 rooms. Restaurant. AE, MC, V. Closed Jan.*

Louviers

❹ *22 km (14 mi) west of Les Andelys via D313, 104 km (65 mi) northwest of Paris.*

Picturesque Louviers owed its medieval prosperity to the weaving of woolen cloth, and a good illustration of this wealthy past is the elaborate stonework of the town church, the Eglise Notre-Dame, whose intricately sculpted porch and gables show just why the late Gothic style of the 15th century is known as *flamboyant.* The Eure River splits scenically into several branches in downtown Louviers, and the pretty valley can be explored just south of the town, with the quaint village of Acquigny and its château park (open Easter–Sept., weekends 2–6) well worth a detour.

Dining and Lodging

$$$–$$$$ ✕ **Hostellerie St-Pierre.** This hotel, just east of Louviers in the Seine Valley, is a great place to stay on your way to Rouen. Room 27 has French windows that open onto a terrace and the best view of the river; its size, like that of most others, is modest; all have comfortingly traditional decor. You have the choice of three prix-fixe menus, ranging from €25 to the epicurean seven-course menu at €55, complete with trou normand. ✉ *6 chemin de la Digue, 27430 St-Pierre-du-Vauvray (5 km/3 mi east of Louviers),* ☎ *02–32–59–93–29,* FAX *02–32–59–41–93. 14 rooms. Restaurant. AE, MC, V. Closed mid-Nov.–mid-Mar.*

En Route From Louviers head east to cross the Seine at St-Pierre-du-Vauvray. Stay on the right bank of the Seine for 8 km (5 mi) to Amfreville; then turn right up steep D508 to what is known as the **Côte des Deux Amants** (Lovers' Mount) for a spectacular view of the Seine Valley and its chalky cliffs. Follow the road to Pont St-Pierre and then head northwest on D138 toward Rouen, pausing in the suburb of **Bonsecours** to check out its 1840s hilltop **Basilique Notre-Dame,** a fine neo-Gothic church overlooking the Seine.

Rouen

★ *32 km (20 mi) north of Louviers, 86 km (53 mi) east of Le Havre, 132 km (82 mi) northwest of Paris.*

"O Rouen, art thou then to be my final abode!" was the agonized cry of Joan of Arc as the English dragged her out to be burned alive on May 30, 1431. The exact spot of the pyre is marked by a concrete and metal cross in front of the Église Jeanne-d'Arc, a modern church on place du Vieux-Marché, just one of the many landmarks that make Rouen a fascinating destination. Although much of the city was destroyed during World War II, a wealth of medieval half-timber houses still lines the cobblestone streets, many of which are pedestrian-only—most famously rue du Gros-Horloge between place du Vieux-Marché and the cathedral, embellished halfway along with a giant Renaissance clock. Rouen is also a busy port—the fifth largest in France—and expects to welcome millions from June 28 to July 6, 2003, when the spectacular **Armada** of galleons and luxury yachts sails again, after a four-year gap, up the Seine to dock in the city center.

Rouen is known as the City of a Hundred Spires, because many of its important edifices are churches. Lording it over them all is the magnificent **Cathédrale Notre-Dame.** If you are familiar with the works of Impressionist artist Claude Monet, you will immediately recognize the cathedral's immense west facade, rendered in an increasingly hazy fashion in his series *Cathédrales de Rouen*—you can enjoy a ringside view and a coffee at the Brasserie Paul, just opposite. The original 12th-century construction was replaced after a devastating fire in 1200; only the left-hand spire, the **Tour St-Romain** (St. Romanus Tower), survived the flames. Construction on the imposing 250-ft steeple on the right, known as the **Tour de Beurre** (Butter Tower), was begun in the 15th century and completed in the 17th, when a group of wealthy citizens donated large sums of money for the privilege of continuing to eat butter during Lent. Interior highlights include the 13th-century choir, with its pointed arcades; vibrant stained glass depicting the crucified Christ (restored after heavy damage during World War II); and massive stone columns topped by some intriguing carved faces. The first flight of the famous **Escalier de la Librairie** (Booksellers' Stairway), attributed to Guillaume Pontifs (also responsible for most of the 15th-century work seen in the cathedral), rises from a tiny balcony just to the left of the transept. ✉ *Pl. de la Cathédrale, St-Maclou,* ☎ *02–32–08–32–40.* ⌚ *Tues.–Sun. 8–6, Mon. 2–6.*

❻ The late-Gothic church of **St-Maclou,** across rue de la République behind the cathedral, bears testimony to the wild excesses of Flamboyant architecture; take time to examine the central and left-hand portals of the main facade, covered with little bronze lion heads and pagan engravings.

Abbaye St-Ouen 8
Aître St-Maclou 7
Cathédrale Notre-Dame . .5
Gros-Horloge 15
Musée des Antiquités 9
Musée des Beaux-Arts . .10
Musée de la Céramique . .12
Musée Le Secq des Tournelles . . .11
St-Maclou 6
Tour Jeanne-d'Arc 14

Rouen

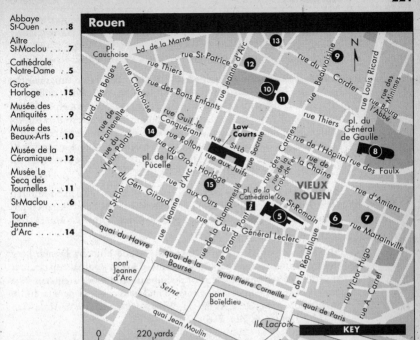

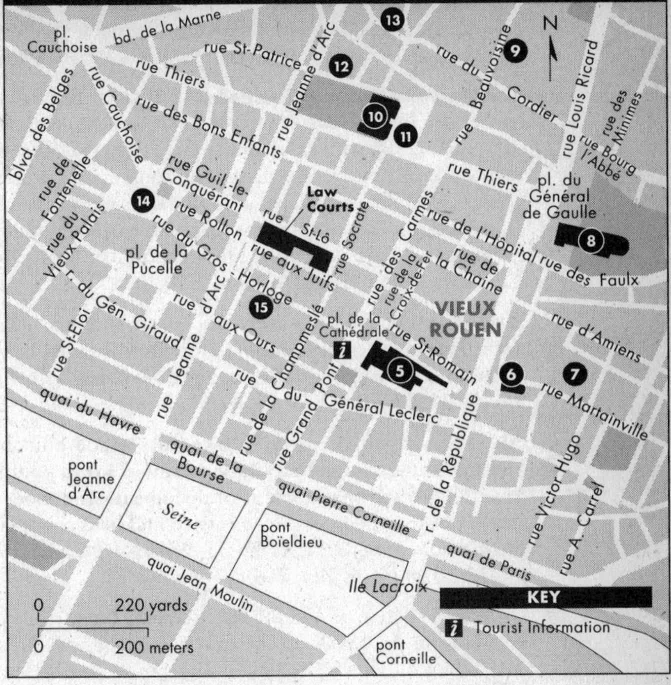

Inside, note the 16th-century organ, with its Renaissance wood carving, and the fine marble columns. ✉ *Pl. St-Maclou, St-Maclou,* ☎ *02–35–71–71–72.* ⌚ *Mon.–Sat. 10–noon and 2–6, Sun. 3–6.*

7 A former ossuary (a charnel house used for the bodies of plague victims), the **Aître St-Maclou** (✉ 186 rue Martainville, St-Maclou) is a reminder of the plague that devastated Europe during the Middle Ages; these days it holds Rouen's Fine Art Academy. French composer Camille Saint-Saëns (1835–1921) is said to have been inspired by the ossuary when he was working on his *Danse Macabre.* The quaint, half-timber courtyard, where you can wander at leisure and maybe visit a picture exhibition, is carved with graphic skulls, bones, and gravediggers' tools.

8 A stupendous example of high Gothic architecture is the **Abbaye St-Ouen** next to the imposing, Neoclassical City Hall. The abbey's stained-glass windows, dating from the 14th to 16th centuries, are the most spectacular grace notes of the spare interior, along with the 19th-century pipe organ, among the finest in France. ✉ *Pl. du Général-de-Gaulle, Hôtel de Ville,* ☎ *02–32–08–13–90.* ⌚ *Mid-Mar.–Oct., Wed.–Mon. 8–12:30 and 2–6; Nov.–mid-Dec. and mid-Jan.–mid-Mar., Wed. and weekends 10–12:30 and 2–4:30.*

9 Gallo-Roman glassware and mosaics, medieval tapestries and enamels, and Moorish ceramics vie for attention at the **Musée des Antiquités,** an extensive antiquities museum housed in a 17th-century former monastery. ✉ *198 rue Beauvoisine, Gare,* ☎ *02–35–71–78–78.* 💳 *€3.* ⌚ *Mon.–Sat. 10–12:15 and 1:30–5:30, Sun. 2–6.*

10 One of Rouen's cultural mainstays is the **Musée des Beaux-Arts** (Fine Arts Museum), which has a scintillating collection of paintings and sculptures from the 16th to the 20th centuries, including works by native son Géricault as well as by David, Rubens, Caravaggio, Velasquez, Poussin, Delacroix, Chassériau, Degas, and Modigliani, not to men-

tion the impressive Impressionist gallery, with Monet, Renoir, and Sisley, and the post-Impressionist School of Rouen headed by Albert Lebourg and Gustave Loiseau. ✉ *Sq. Verdrel, Gare,* ☎ *02–35–52–00–62,* WEB *www.musees-rouen.com.* ✉ *€3.* ⊙ *Wed.–Mon. 10–6.*

11 The **Musée Le Secq des Tournelles** (Wrought-Iron Museum), near the Musée des Beaux-Arts, claims to possess the world's finest collection of wrought iron, with exhibits spanning from the 4th through 19th centuries. The displays, imaginatively housed in a converted medieval church, include many items used in daily life, accessories, and professional instruments of surgeons, barbers, carpenters, clockmakers, and gardeners. ✉ *Rue Jacques-Villon, Gare,* ☎ *02–35–88–42–92.* ✉ *€2.30.* ⊙ *Wed.–Mon. 10–1 and 2–6.*

12 A superb array of local pottery and European porcelain can be admired at the **Musée de la Céramique** (Ceramics Museum), in an elegant mansion near the Musée des Beaux-Arts. ✉ *1 rue Faucon, Gare,* ☎ *02–35–07–31–74.* ✉ *€2.30.* ⊙ *Wed.–Mon. 10–1 and 2–6.*

13 Sole remnant of the early 13th-century castle built by French king Philippe-Auguste, the beefy **Tour Jeanne-d'Arc,** a pointed-top circular tower, houses a small exhibit of documents and models charting the castle's history. Joan of Arc was tried and held prisoner here in 1430. ✉ *Rue Bouvreuil, Gare,* ☎ *02–35–98–55–10.* ✉ *€1.50.* ⊙ *Mon.–Sat. 10–12:30 and 2–6, Sun. 2–6.*

14 Dedicated to Joan of Arc, the **Église Jeanne d'Arc** (Joan of Arc Church) was built in the 1970s on the spot where she was burned to death in 1431. Not all is new, however: the church showcases some remarkable 16th-century stained-glass windows taken from the former Église St-Vincent, bombed out in 1944. The adjacent **Musée Jeanne-d'Arc** evokes St Joan's history with waxworks and documents. ✉ *Place du Vieux-Marché, Vieux-Marché.*

15 The name of the pedestrian rue du Gros-Horloge, Rouen's most popular street, comes from the **Gros-Horloge** itself, a giant Renaissance clock. In 1527 the Rouennais had a splendid arch built especially for it, and today its golden face looks out over the street. You can see the clock's inner workings from the 15th-century belfry. Though the street is crammed with stores, a few old houses, dating from the 16th century, remain. Wander through the surrounding **Vieux Rouen** (Old Town), a warren of tiny streets lined with more than 700 half-timber houses, many artfully transformed into fashionable shops. ✉ *Rue du Gros-Horloge, Vieux-Marché.* ✉ *Clock 10 frs/€1.53.* ⊙ *Wed.–Mon. 10–1 and 2–6.*

Dining and Lodging

$$$ ✕ **La Couronne.** Behind a half-timber facade gushing geraniums, the "oldest inn in France," dating from 1345, is crammed with leather-upholstered chairs and a scattering of sculpture. The traditional Norman cuisine—lobster soufflé, sheep's feet, duck in blood sauce—makes few modern concessions. ✉ *31 pl. du Vieux-Marché, Vieux-Marché,* ☎ *02–35–71–40–90. AE, DC, MC, V.*

$$–$$$ ★ ✕ **Auberge de la Butte.** This 18th-century former post house, in the suburb of Bonsecours, is well worth seeking out (you'll need a car). Veteran chef Pierre Hervé's innovations include roasted *St. Pierre à la vanille,* whole lobster lasagna with West Indian spices, and duck *à la rouennaise.* The magnificent dining room has exposed beams and half-timber walls adorned with paintings and shining copper pots. ✉ *69 rte. de Paris, Bonsecours (3 km/2 mi east of city center),* ☎ *02–35–80–43–11. Jacket and tie. AE, DC, MC, V. Closed Sun.–Mon. and Aug.*

$$ ✕ **La Toque d'Or.** Overlooking the Église Jeanne d'Arc, this large, bustling restaurant has been renowned since time immemorial for Jean-Jacques Báton's Normandy classics like veal with Camembert flamed in calvados, breast of duck glazed in cider, or spicy braised turbot. Try the excellent home-smoked salmon (they'll give you a tour of the smokehouse if you wish) and the Norman apple *tarte soufflée.* ✉ *11 pl. du Vieux-Marché, Vieux-Marché,* ☎ *02–35–71–46–29. AE, DC, V.*

$$–$$$ ✕🏨 **Dieppe.** Dating from 1880, the Dieppe remains up to date thanks to resolute management by five generations of the Guéret family. Staff members also are helpful, and they speak English. The compact rooms are cheerful and modern; street noise can be a problem, however, despite double-glazed windows. The restaurant, Les Quatre Saisons, serves seasonal dishes with an emphasis on fish, such as the sole Michèle (poached in a light wine sauce). ✉ *Pl. Bernard-Tissot, Gare, 76000,* ☎ *02–35–71–96–00; 800/334–7234 for U.S. reservations,* FAX *02–35–89–65–21. 41 rooms. Restaurant, bar, no air-conditioning, cable TV. AE, DC, MC, V.*

$–$$ ✕🏨 **Le Vieux Carré.** Situated in the heart of old Rouen, this cute, central hotel has small, practical, and comfortable rooms, simply furnished with a taste for the exotic: lamps from Egypt, tables from Morocco, and English 1940s armoires. Ask for one of the rooms on the third floor for a view of the cathedral. Breakfast and lunch (but not dinner) are served in the leafy courtyard, weather permitting, or in the cozy little bistro, right off the reception area. Lunches are light and simple, based on creative tourtes—tomato, olive, and Camembert, for example. Brunch is served both Saturday and Sunday until 2 PM. ✉ *34 rue Ganterie, Gare, 76000,* ☎ *02–35–71–67–70,* FAX *02–35–71–19–17. 14 rooms. Restaurant, no air-conditioning, cable TV, Internet. AE, DC, MC, V.*

$$ 🏨 **Cathédrale.** This hotel is in a medieval building on a narrow pedestrian street behind the cathedral. (You can sleep soundly, though: the cathedral bells do not boom out the hour at night.) Rooms are petite, but neat and comfortable. Breakfast is served in the beamed dining room. ✉ *12 rue St-Romain, St-Maclou, 76000,* ☎ *02–35–71–57–95,* FAX *02–35–70–15–54,* WEB *www.hotel-de-la-cathedrale.fr. 25 rooms. No air-conditioning, cable TV, Internet, parking (fee). MC, V.*

$$ 🏨 **Mercure Centre.** In the jumble of streets near the cathedral—a navigational challenge if you arrive by car—this modern chain hotel has small, comfortable rooms done in breezy pastels. The location makes this hotel ideal for exploring the old streets of the city center. ✉ *7 rue de la Croix-de-Fer, St-Maclou, 76000,* ☎ *02–35–52–69–52,* FAX *02–35–89–41–46. 139 rooms. Bar, cable TV. AE, DC, MC, V.*

Nightlife and the Arts

The **Fête Jeanne d'Arc** (Joan of Arc Festival) takes place on the Sunday nearest to May 30, with parades, street plays, concerts, exhibitions, and a medieval market. Evening **concerts** and organ recitals are held at St-Maclou in August and at St-Ouen throughout the year; get details from the Rouen tourist office. Operas, plays, and concerts are staged at the **Théâtre des Arts** (✉ 7 rue du Dr-Rambert, Vieux-Marché, ☎ 02–35–71–41–36). Visit the popular local haunt **Bar de la Crosse** (✉ 53 rue de l'Hôpital, St-Maclou, ☎ 02–35–70–16–68) for an aperitif and a good chat with some friendly Rouennais. At the **Big Ben Pub** (✉ 95 bis rue du Gros-Horloge, Vieux-Marché, ☎ 02–35–88–44–50), relax with a glass of wine on the first floor, listen to music on the second, and on the third witness how the French karaoke (not to be missed).

Abbaye de Jumièges

★ ⓰ *24 km (15 mi) west of Rouen: head west on D982 through St-Martin de Boscherville and then exit left onto D143.*

Imposing ruins are all that is left of the once mighty Benedictine Abbaye de Jumièges, founded in 654 by St-Philbert, plundered by Vikings in 841, then rebuilt by William Longswood, duke of Normandy, around 940, though not consecrated until 1067. The French Revolution forced the evacuation of the remaining 16 monks, whereupon the abbey was auctioned off to a timber merchant, who promptly demolished part of the building to sell the stone. What remains is impressive enough. ✉ *24 rue Guillaume-le-Conquérant,* ☎ *02–35–37–24–02,* WEB *www.monum.fr.* 🎫 *€4.* ⏲ *Apr.–Sept., daily 9:30–7; Oct.–Mar., daily 9:30–1 and 2:30–5:30.*

Caudebec-en-Caux

⓱ *15 km (8 mi) northwest of the Abbaye de Jumièges via D143/D982, 34 km (21 mi) northwest of Rouen.*

The riverside town of Caudebec-en-Caux is dominated by the church spire of Notre-Dame-de-Caudebec, a wonderful medieval church with some of the most vivid 16th-century stained glass in Normandy: don't miss the deep blood-reds of the window showing Pharaoh's army drowning in the Red Sea. The nearby **Musèe de la Marine** charts the history of the Seine Valley with ship models, old photographs, and traditional costumes, and a section on the *mascaret,* the bore or tidal wave that used to power up the estuary during the equinox. *Av. Winston-Churchill,* ☎ *02–32–95–90–13.* 🎫 *€4.* ⏲ *Wed.–Mon. 2–6:30.*

The **Musée Victor-Hugo** in the village of Villequier, 5 km (3 mi) west of Caudebec, occupies the prettily furnished riverside mansion where Hugo's daughter Léopoldine lived with her husband Charles Vacqueyrie. Pictures, letters, drawings, and documents evoke the great poet and his daughter, who, along with her husband, drowned when their boat was overturned by the Seine's notorious *mascaret* (bore) as they returned from Caudebec on September 4, 1843. Léopoldine, who is buried up the hill in the village churchyard, was just 19. ✉ *Rue Ernest-Binet,* ☎ *02–35–56–78–31.* 🎫 *€3.* ⏲ *Daily 10–12:30 and 2–5.*

The Benedictine **Abbaye de St-Wandrille,** 3 km (2 mi) east of Caudebec, is still active today, with 40 monks in residence. Founded in the 7th century, the abbey was sacked by the Normans and rebuilt in the 10th century—although what you see today is an ensemble of styles from the 11th through the early 18th centuries (mainly the latter). You can hear the monks sing their Gregorian chants at morning mass if you arrive early (9:25 weekdays and 10 on Sunday and holidays), or wander at leisure in the gardens. Don't forget to visit the abbey shop down the hill; everything it sells—from floor polish to spiritual aids—is monk-made. ☎ *02–35–96–23–11,* WEB *www.st-wandrille.com.* 🎫 *€3.50.* ⏲ *Guided tour weekdays at 3:30, Sun. at 11:30.*

Dieppe

⓲ *67 km (44 mi) north of Caudebec, 64 km (40 mi) north of Rouen.*

Bustling Dieppe, beneath its clifftop castle, is part fishing and commercial port and part Norman seaside town—though its era in the fashionable spotlight is past, and the ramshackle church of St-Jacques, painted by Pissarro, has seen better days. Still, a new year-round ferry service was launched in 2001 to complement the summer-only jetfoil across the Channel to Newhaven, near Brighton. The seafront promenade, boulevard du Maréchal-Foch, separates an immense lawn from an unspoiled pebble beach where in 1942 many Canadian soldiers were killed during the so-called Jubilee Raid. You might like to continue along the coast from Dieppe to Le Tréport.

The 15th-century **Château-Musée,** overlooking the Channel at the western end of the bay, contains a museum, well known for its collection of ivories. In the 17th century, Dieppe imported vast quantities of elephant tusks from Africa and Asia, and as many as 350 craftsmen settled here to work the ivory; their efforts can be seen in the form of ship models, nautical accessories, religious artifacts, and everyday objects. The museum also has a room devoted to sketches by Georges Braque. ✉ *Rue de Chastes,* ☎ *02–35–84–19–76.* *€2.40,* WEB *www.mairie-dieppe.fr.* ⏲ *Mon. and Wed.–Sat. 10–noon and 2–5, Sun. 10–noon and 2–6.*

Dining and Lodging

$$ ✕ **Auberge du Clos Normand.** This 15th-century inn in the tiny village of Martin-Église, 4 mi (7 km) southeast of Dieppe, is best known for its pretty garden, complete with a stream and flower-strewn balconies. Even the bedrooms—which may seem a little chilly out of season—have flowery wallpaper, in the time-honored rural French tradition. The kitchen, all agleam with copper pots, is at one end of the restaurant (closed Tuesday, no dinner Monday), so you can glimpse the chef at work on his sturdy Norman dishes, with chicken a specialty. ✉ *22 rue Henri-IV, 76370,* ☎ *02–35–04–40–34,* FAX *02–35–04–48–49. 8 rooms. Restaurant, cable TV. AE, MC, V. Closed mid-Nov.–mid-Dec.*

Nightlife and the Arts

At night the **casino** at the Grand Hotel (✉ 3 bd. de Verdun, ☎ 02–35–82–33–60) comes alive with shows and gambling. If you love jazz, come for the **Festival Européen de Jazz Traditionnel** (European Traditional Jazz Festival), held in mid-June in Luneray, 8 km (5 mi) southwest of Dieppe. There is also the spectacular **International Kite Festival**—the skies fill with the most amazing high-flying contraptions during the second week in September. For information contact the Dieppe tourist office.

Outdoor Activities and Sports

Bicycles can be rented at Dieppe's train station for around €8 a day; the flat terrain around the city is great for biking. For information on routes, check with the tourist office.

En Route From Dieppe take the scenic coastal road (D75) to **Varengeville-sur-Mer**; the 20th-century painter Georges Braque (1882–1963)—who, with Picasso, is credited with inventing Cubism—is buried in the graveyard next to its tiny hilltop church. Varengeville also hosts the picturesque **Manoir d'Ango,** and will wow flower-lovers with the nearby **Shamrock Hydrangea Collection** and **Parc Floral des Moustiers** (Moustiers Flower Garden), laid out by Gertrude Jekyll around a house designed by Sir Edward Lutyens in 1898. It has a colorful collection of rare flowers and giant, 100-year-old rhododendrons. ✉ *La Haie des Moustiers,* ☎ *02–35–85–10–02.* *€6.20.* ⏲ *Mid-Mar.–mid-Nov., daily 10–noon and 2–6.*

Fécamp

19 *64 km (40 mi) southwest of Dieppe, 42 km (26 mi) northeast of Le Havre.*

The ancient cod-fishing port of Fécamp was once a major pilgrimage site. The magnificent abbey church, the **Abbaye de La Trinité** (✉ Rue

Leroux) bears witness to Fécamp's religious past. The Benedictine abbey was founded by the Duke of Normandy in the 11th century and became the home of the monastic order of the Précieux Sang de la Trinité (Precious Blood of the Trinity—referring to Christ's blood, which supposedly arrived here in the 7th century in a reliquary from the Holy Land).

Fécamp is also the home of Benedictine liqueur. The **Palais de la Bénédictine** (Benedictine Palace), across from the tourist office, is a florid building dating from 1892 that mixes neo-Gothic and Renaissance styles. Nonetheless, it's one of Normandy's most popular attractions. The interior is just as exhausting as the facade, as paintings, sculptures, ivories, advertising posters, and fake bottles of Benedictine compete for attention with a display of the ingredients used for the liqueur, and a chance to sample it. There's also a shop selling Benedictine products and souvenirs. ✉ *110 rue Alexandre-le-Grand,* ☎ *02–35–10–26–10,* WEB *www.benedictine.fr.* *€5 (including tasting).* ⏲ *Feb.–Dec., daily 10–11:15 and 2–5.*

Dining and Lodging

$ ✕ **L'Escalier.** This delightfully simple little restaurant overlooking the harbor serves traditional Norman cuisine, such as mussels in calvados and homemade fish soup. ✉ *101 quai Bérigny,* ☎ *02–35–28–26–79. Reservations essential. DC, MC, V. Closed 2 wks in Nov.*

$$$ ✕ **Les Hêtres.** Top chef Bertrand Warin runs this restaurant in Ingouville, east of Fécamp. Reservations are essential—as are jacket and tie—for the elegant 17th-century dining room (closed Monday, and no dinner Sunday), where half-timber walls and Louis XIII chairs contrast with sleek, modern furnishings. The five pretty guest rooms, each with old wooden furniture and engravings, are for diners only; the largest has a terrace overlooking the garden. ✉ *Rue des Fleurs, 76460 Ingouville (28 km/17 mi east of Fécamp),* ☎ *02–35–57–09–30,* FAX *02–35–57–09–31. 4 rooms. Restaurant, no air-conditioning, cable TV, Internet. MC, V. Closed Jan.*

$$ ★ ✕ **Auberge de la Rouge.** The Enderlins welcome you to this little inn just south of Fécamp. Rooms are actually good-sized lofts that sleep four. The restaurant (closed Monday; no dinner Sunday) showcases modern classics (the chef trained under Ducasse) and local specialties such as roast turbot, veal and mushrooms in wine, or the special pressed duck in blood sauce. Top it off, if you can, with a local favorite, soufflé *à la Bénédictine.* ✉ *1 rue du Bois-de-Boclion, 76400 St-Léonard (1 km/½ mi south of Fécamp),* ☎ *02–35–28–07–59,* FAX *02–35–28–70–55,* WEB *www.auberge-rouge.com. 8 rooms. Restaurant, minibars. AE, DC, MC, V.*

$$ **Ferme de la Chapelle.** The charm of this former priory lies neither in its simple, comfortable rooms nor in its restaurant with its no-frills menu, but rather in its outstanding location high atop the cliffs overlooking Fécamp. There is a breathtaking, dramatic view over the entire coastline—explore it using a nearby coastal footpath on an invigorating hike. ✉ *Côte de la Vierge, 76400,* ☎ *02–35–10–12–12,* FAX *02–35–10–12–13. 17 rooms, 5 studios. Restaurant.*

Étretat

⑳ *17 km (11 mi) southwest of Fécamp via D940, 88 km (55 mi) northwest of Rouen.*

This town, with its promenade running the length of the pebble beach, is justly famous for the magnificent tall rock formations that extend ★ out into the sea. The **Falaises d'Étretat** are white cliffs that are as famous in France as Dover's are in England—and have been painted by many artists, Claude Monet chief among them. At low tide it's possible to walk through the huge archways formed by the rocks to neighboring beaches. The biggest arch is at the **Falaise d'Aval,** to the south. For a breathtaking view of the whole bay, take the path up to the top of the Falaise d'Aval. From here you can hike for miles across the Manneporte Hills . . . or play a round of golf on one of Europe's windiest and most scenic courses, overlooking **L'Aiguille** (The Needle), a 300-ft spike of rock jutting out of the sea just off the coast. To the north towers the **Falaise d'Amont,** topped by the chapel of Notre-Dame de la Garde.

Dining and Lodging

$ ✕ **Roches Blanches.** The exterior of this family-owned restaurant off the beach is a post–World War II concrete eyesore. But take a table by the window with a view of the cliffs, order Georges Trézeux's superb fresh seafood (try the sea bass roasted in calvados), and you'll be glad you came. Reservations are essential for Sunday lunch. ✉ *Rue de l'Abbé-Cochet,* ☎ *02–35–27–07–34. MC, V. Closed Tues.–Thurs. (Wed. only July–early Sept.), Jan., and Oct.*

$$$–$$$$ ★ ✕🏨 **Donjon.** This charming ivy-covered château, built in 1862 in a park overlooking the town, has lovely sea views. Rooms are individually furnished, spacious, comfortable, and quiet. For a spectacular view, request the Oriental Suite or the Horizon or Marjorie rooms. Jean-Francois Toulain's flamboyant cuisine, ranging from warm hare terrine to scallops and salmon in cider, is dished up in a cozy, romantic restaurant. Rooms are reserved on a half-board basis on weekends. ✉ *Chemin de St-Clair, 76790,* ☎ *02–35–27–08–23,* FAX *02–35–29–92–24,* WEB *www.ledonjon-etretat.fr. 21 rooms. Restaurant, no air-conditioning, cable TV, 11 rooms with minibar, Internet, pool. AE, DC, MC, V.*

$$–$$$ ✕🏨 **Dormy House.** This unpretentious hotel is ideally located halfway up the Étretat cliffs. The rooms are simple and comfortable, but the real beauty is right out your bedroom window, thanks to views of *la mer,* so wonderful they would have Debussy humming in no time. The restaurant specializes in fresh fish and seafood platters, ranging from simple delights such as the sole stew to the full-scale *symphonie* of fish. Of course, request a table near the window for a panoramic view of the coast. ✉ *Rte. du Havre,* ☎ *02–35–27–07–88,* FAX *02–35–29–86–19. 51 rooms. Restaurant, no air-conditioning, internet access, no pets. AE, MC, V. Closed Dec. 30–Jan. 4.*

$–$$ ✕🏨 **La Résidence.** The cheapest rooms in this gorgeous 16th-century house in the heart of Étretat are pretty basic—both the bathroom and the shower are in the hallway—but the most expensive have both an in-room bathroom and a Jacuzzi. The service is friendly; staff are young and energetic. The brasserie-type restaurant on the ground floor, Le Salamandre, is rather cutting-edge for the region; all products are certified organic, farm-raised, and homemade, from the vegetable terrine to the nougat ice cream. In winter a fire crackles in the hearth. ✉ *4 bd. René-Coty, 76790,* ☎ *02–35–27–02–87,* FAX *02–35–27–17–07. 15 rooms. Restaurant, no air-conditioning, minibars, some rooms with Jacuzzi, no pets. AE, MC, V.*

Outdoor Activities and Sports

Don't miss the chance to play on the breathtaking course at the **Golf d'Étretat** (✉ Rte. du Havre, ☎ 02–35–27–04–89), 6,580 yards long (par 72), across the clifftops of the Falaise d'Aval; it's closed Tuesday.

Le Havre

㉑ *28 km (18 mi) southwest of Etretat via D940, 88 km (55 mi) west of Rouen, 200 km (125 mi) northwest of Paris.*

Le Havre, France's second-largest port (after Marseille), was bombarded 146 times during World War II. You may find the rebuilt city, with its uncompromising recourse to reinforced concrete and open spaces, bleak and uninviting; on the other hand, you may admire Auguste Perret's rational planning and audacious modern architecture. The hilly suburb of **Ste-Adresse,** just west of town, is resplendent with Belle Epoque villas and an old fortress. It's also worth a visit for its beach, often painted by Raoul Dufy, and for its fine views of the sea and port, immortalized in a famous Monet masterpiece.

The **Musée André-Malraux,** the city art museum, is an innovative 1960s glass-and-metal structure surrounded by a moat, and includes an attractive sea-view café. Two local artists are showcased here—Raoul Dufy (1877–1953), through a remarkable collection of his brightly colored oils, watercolors, and sketches on the ground floor; and, upstairs, Eugène Boudin (1824–98), a forerunner of Impressionism, whose compelling beach scenes and landscapes tellingly evoke the Normandy coast and skyline. ✉ *2 bd. Clemenceau,* ☎ *02–35–19–62–62.* 🎫 *€3.10.* ⏲ *Wed.–Mon. 11–6.*

★ The other outstanding building in Le Havre, and one of the most impressive 20th-century churches in France, is the **Église St-Joseph,** built to the plans of Auguste Perret in the 1950s. The 350-ft tower powers into the sky like a fat rocket. The interior is just as thrilling. No frills here: the 270-ft octagonal lantern soars above the crossing, filled almost to the top with abstract stained glass that hurls colored light over the bare concrete walls. ✉ *Bd. François-Ier,* ☎ *02–35–42–20–03.*

Dining and Lodging

$$ ✕ **Odyssée.** With the port and fish market within netting distance, seafood is guaranteed to be fresh here. It's a no-frills place—the visual appeal is on your plate, in the pinks and greens of the smoked salmon and avocado sauce that accompany the chef's homemade fish terrine. Although it specializes in fresh fish, the Odyssée has its share of meat dishes—the breast of duck with three-pepper sauce is a winner. ✉ *41 rue du Général-Faidherbe,* ☎ *02–35–21–32–42. AE, MC, V. Closed Mon. and mid-Aug.–early Sept. No dinner Sun., no lunch Sat.*

$$ 🏨 **Bordeaux.** The central location, overlooking the Bassin de Commerce, is this hotel's main plus—along with the welcoming owners. The light, airy rooms have modern furniture; the best have views of the port. As at all other hotels in Le Havre, prices are high for room size. ✉ *147 rue Louis-Brindeau, 76600,* ☎ *02–35–22–69–44,* FAX *02–35–42–09–27. 30 rooms. No air-conditioning, cable TV, 22 rooms with minibar, Internet, parking (fee), no pets. AE, DC, MC, V.*

Pont-Audemer

❷❷ *32 km (20 mi) southwest of St-Wandrille, 50 km (31 mi) west of Rouen.*

Pont-Audemer, on the banks of the Risle River in the heart of calvados country, luckily escaped destruction by warfare and bulldozers. Today many of its buildings are still as they were in the 16th century, when the town made its mark as an important trading center. Stroll along impasse St-Ouen and impasse de l'Épée, narrow streets by the church that are lined with timber-frame medieval houses. The pleasingly dilapidated church of **St-Ouen** has an unfinished single-tower facade and an entertaining clash of modern stained-glass windows and exuberant late medieval stonework. ✉ *Rue de la République,* ☎ *02–32–41–12–88.*

Dining and Lodging

$$$–$$$$ ★ ✕🏨 **Belle-Isle sur Risle.** It's hard not to feel like a personal guest of this private manor—an impression somehow heightened by a few rough edges. The newer, more modern rooms have wall-to-wall carpeting and department-store furniture, but the older ones have wooden floors with rugs and assorted traditional pieces; those on the first floor have balconies. In the restaurant, chef Laurent Matuit turns out tasty foie gras blinis, *coquilles St-Jacques* (scallops) with a coulis (thick sauce) of mushrooms, and light pastry tarts. ✉ *112 rte. de Rouen, 27500,* ☎ *02–32–56–96–22,* FAX *02–32–42–88–96. 15 rooms, 4 suites. Restaurant, tennis court, pool, sauna. MC, V.*

$$–$$$ ✕🏨 **Auberge du Vieux Puits.** Gustave Flaubert, an early admirer of this hotel in a trellised and beamed 17th-century cottage, gave it a few lines in his celebrated novel *Madame Bovary.* The quiet rooms, with heavy wooden pieces and pretty curtains, overlook the courtyard. The restaurant serves rich and innovative first-rate Norman cuisine, such as trout in champagne sauce or duckling stew with sour cherries. Since this place is first and foremost a restaurant (it is closed Monday and Tuesday dinner off-season), you are expected to have dinner here when you stay. ✉ *6 rue Notre-Dame-du-Pré, 27500,* ☎ *02–32–41–01–48,* FAX *02–32–42–37–28. 12 rooms. Restaurant. MC, V. Closed mid-Dec.–late Jan.*

FROM THE SEINE TO MONT-ST-MICHEL

Lower Normandy begins to the west of the Seine Estuary, near the Belle Epoque resort towns of Trouville and Deauville, extending out to the sandy Côte Fleurie (Flower Coast), stretching from the D-Day landing sites of Omaha and Utah beaches and continuing onward to the Cotentin Peninsula, which juts out into the English Channel. After the World War II D-Day landings, some of the fiercest fighting took place around Caen and Bayeux, as many monuments and memorials testify. To the south, in the prosperous Pays d'Auge, dairy farms produce the region's famous cheeses. Rising to the west is the fabled Mont-St-Michel. Inland, heading back toward central France, lush green meadows and apple orchards cover the countryside starting west of the market town of Lisieux—the heart of calvados country.

Honfleur

★ 23 *24 km (15 mi) southeast of Le Havre via A131 and Pont de Normandie, 80 km (50 mi) west of Rouen.*

The colorful port of Honfleur has become increasingly crowded since the elegant Pont de Normandie suspension bridge—providing a direct link with Le Havre and Upper Normandy—opened in 1995 across the Seine. It's the world's largest cable-stayed bridge, supported by two concrete pylons taller than the Eiffel Tower, and designed to resist winds of 160 mph. The town of Honfleur, full of half-timber houses and cobbled streets, was once an important departure point for maritime expeditions, including the first voyages to Canada in the 15th and 16th centuries. The 17th-century harbor is fronted on one side by two-story stone houses with low, sloping roofs and on the other by tall, narrow houses whose wooden facades are topped by slate roofs.

★ Soak up the seafaring atmosphere by strolling around the old harbor and paying a visit to the ravishing wooden church of **Ste-Catherine,** which dominates the harbor's northern side. It was built by townspeople to show their gratitude for the departure of the English at the end of the Hundred Years' War, in 1453. ✉ *Rue des Logettes,* ☎ *02–31–89–11–83.*

Dining and Lodging

$$–$$$ ★ ✕ **Assiette Gourmande.** At one of Honfleur's top restaurants, chef Gérard Bonnefoy offers a seasonal menu. You might find succulent *noix de St-Jacques* (scallops with hazelnut risotto) or roast lamb from the salt marshes. ✉ *2 quai des Passagers,* ☎ *02–31–89–24–88. AE, DC, MC, V. Closed Mon. except July–Aug.*

$ ✕ **Ancrage.** Massive seafood platters top the bill at this delightful old restaurant in a two-story 17th-century building overlooking the harbor. The cuisine is authentically Norman—simple but good. If you want a change, try the succulent calf sweetbreads. ✉ *12 rue Montpensier,* ☎ *02–31–89–00–70,* FAX *02–31–89–92–78. MC, V. Closed Wed., mid-Nov.–early Dec., and last 2 weeks in Mar. No dinner Tues. except July–Aug.*

$$$$ ★ ✕🏨 **Ferme St-Siméon.** The story goes that this 19th-century manor house was the birthplace of Impressionism, and that its park inspired Monet and Sisley. Rooms are opulent, with pastel colors, floral wallpaper, antiques, and period accents. Those in the converted stables are quieter but have less character. Be aware, however, that the high prices have more to do with the hotel's reputation than with the amenities it offers (although thalassotherapy treatment is among them). The sophisticated restaurant specializes in fish; the cheese board does justice to the region. ✉ *Rue Adolphe-Marais, on D513 to Trouville, 14600,* ☎ *02–31–81–78–00,* FAX *02–31–89–48–48,* WEB *www.saint-simeon.com. 31 rooms, 3 suites. Restaurant, no air-conditioning, cable TV, minibar, tennis court, pool, sauna, solarium, no pets. AE, MC, V.*

$$$–$$$$ ★ ✕🏨 **Absinthe.** A 16th-century presbytery with stone walls and beamed ceilings houses a small and charming hotel and the acclaimed restaurant of the same name. Rooms are comfortable but small, except for the attic suite, which has a private living room. Rooms are equipped with large modern bathrooms and Jacuzzis. The elegant and cozy reception area is adorned with an imposing stone fireplace. Chef Antoine Ceffrey is famous for his seasonal seafood and fish dishes such as turbot grilled with leeks. On sunny days request a table on the terrace. ✉ *10 quai de la Quarantaine,* ☎ *02–31–89–39–00,* WEB *www.absinthe.fr. No air-conditioning, cable TV, hot tubs. DC, MC, V. Closed mid-Nov.–mid-Dec. No dinner Mon.*

$$$–$$$$ ✕🏨 **Le Manoir de Butin.** This lovely, ivy covered Anglo-Norman manor is on top of a small wooded hill just 200 meters from the sea. All rooms have a lovely view, are traditionally and tastefully furnished, and have modern marble bathrooms. The room on the first floor has a four-poster bed and its own balcony. The restaurant specializes in seasonal fish dishes such as a light lobster consommé and braised freshwater cod. ✉ *Phare du Butin, 14600,* ☎ *02–31–81–63–00,* FAX *02–31–89–59–23. 9 rooms. No air-conditioning, cable TV, Internet. AE, MC, V. No lunch Wed. and Thurs.*

$$ 🏨 **Hostellerie Lechat.** This typical 18th-century Norman building is in a pretty square just behind the harbor. The well-maintained, spacious rooms have beamed ceilings and are lined with French provincial prints—ask for room with a view of the church. Jean-Luc Blais's trendy Norman cuisine (roast lobster with herb and truffle sauce) is served in the rustic beamed restaurant (closed Wed. and Thur.). ✉ *13 pl. Ste-Catherine, 14600,* ☎ *02–31–14–49–49,* FAX *02–31–89–28–61,* WEB *www.honfleur.com. 23 rooms. Restaurant, bar, no air-conditioning, cable TV, no pets. AE, DC, MC, V. Closed Jan.–mid Feb.*

Nightlife and the Arts

The two-day **Fête des Marins** (Marine Festival) is held on Pentecost Sunday and Monday. On Sunday all the boats in the harbor are decked out in flags and paper roses, and a priest bestows his blessing at high tide. The next day, model boats and local children head a musical procession.

Deauville–Trouville

24 *16 km (10 mi) southwest of Honfleur via D513, 92 km (57 mi) west of Rouen.*

The twin seaside resorts of Deauville and Trouville are separated by the estuary of the River Touques and joined by a bridge. The two towns have distinctly different atmospheres, but it's easy (and common) to shuttle between them. Trouville—whose beaches were immortalized in the 19th-century paintings of Eugene Boudin—is the oldest seaside resort in France. In the days of Louis-Phillipe, it was discovered by artists and the upper crust; by the end of the Second Empire it was the beach à la mode. Then the Duc de Mornay, half brother of Napoléon III, and other aristos who were looking for something more exclusive, built their villas along the deserted beach across the Touques. Thus was launched Deauville, a vigorous grande dame who started kicking up her heels during the Second Empire, kept swinging through the Belle Epoque, and is still frequented by a fair share of millionaires, princes, and French movie stars. Few of them ever go near the water here, since other attractions—casino, theater, music hall, polo, galas, racecourse, marina and regattas, palaces and gardens, and place Vendôme jewelry shops—compete. The Promenade des Planches—the boardwalk extending along the seafront and lined with deck chairs, bars, and striped cabanas—is the place for celebrity-spotting. With high-price hotels, designer boutiques, and one of the smartest gilt-edge casinos in Europe, Deauville's fashionable image still attracts the wealthy throughout the year.

Trouville—a short drive or 5-minute boat trip across the Touques River from its more prestigious neighbor—remains more of a family resort, harboring few pretensions. If you'd like to see a typical French holiday spot rather than look for glamour, Trouville is your best bet. It, too, has a casino and boardwalk, plus an aquarium and bustling fishing port, and a native population that makes it a livelier spot out of season than Deauville.

Dining and Lodging

$$$–$$$$ ✕ 🏨 **Normandy.** Well-heeled Parisians have been attracted to this imposing hotel, with its half-timber facade and underground passage to the casino, since it opened in 1912. Request a room with a sea view, and don't forget to ask about the special thalassotherapy rates with full or half-days of mud baths, salt massages, and soothing heated-seawater swims. Breakfast is served around the indoor pool. Creamy sauces are much in evidence in the mouthwatering Norman dishes served up in the restaurant. ✉ *38 rue Jean-Mermoz, 14800 Deauville,* ☎ *02–31–98–66–22; 800/223–5652 for U.S. reservations,* FAX *02–31–98–66–23. 252 rooms, 28 suites. Restaurant, cable TV, minibars, Internet, pool, sauna, no pets. AE, DC, MC, V.*

$$–$$$ 🏨 **Beach.** Although it lacks character, this hotel, one of the newer ones in town, is handy because of its location behind the casino. Print fabrics add color to the pristine white rooms; most overlook the sea or the harbor. Public rooms are designed for the flow of tour groups, so expect efficiency rather than personal service. ✉ *Quai Albert-I, 14360*

Trouville, ☎ 02–31–98–12–00, FAX 02–31–87–30–29. 110 rooms, 8 suites. Restaurant, no air-conditioning, cable TV, pool. AE, DC, MC, V.

$$ **Continental.** One of Deauville's oldest buildings is now this provincial hotel, four blocks from the sea and within easy walking distance of the town center and downtown Trouville. Rooms are small but simple, pristine, and reasonably priced for Deauville. ✉ *1 rue Désiré-Le-Hoc, 14800 Deauville, ☎ 02–31–88–21–06, FAX 02–31–98–93–67. 42 rooms. No air-conditioning, cable TV, Internet, no pets. AE, DC, MC, V. Closed mid-Nov.–mid-Dec.*

Nightlife and the Arts

One of the biggest cultural events on the Norman calendar is the **American Film Festival,** held in Deauville during the first week of September. Formal attire is required at Deauville's **casino** (✉ 2 rue Edmond-Blanc, ☎ 02–31–14–31–14). Trouville's **casino** (✉ Pl. du Maréchal-Foch, ☎ 02–31–87–75–00) is slightly less highbrow than Deauville's. Night owls enjoy the smoky **Snake Pit Club** (✉ 13 rue Albert-Fracasse, Deauville); it's open until 5 AM. The **Y Club** (✉ 14 bis rue Désiré-le-Hoc, Deauville) is the place to go out dancing.

Outdoor Activities and Sports

At the **Club Nautique de Deauville** (✉ Quai de la Marine, ☎ 02–31–88–38–19), hiring the smallest boat (16 ft) costs €22, while a day on an 80-ft yacht will set you back about €100 per person. Sailing boats large and small can also be rented from the **Club Nautique de Trouville** (✉ Digue des Roches Noires, ☎ 02–31–88–13–59). Deauville becomes Europe's horse capital in August, when breeders jet in from around the world for its yearling auctions and the races at its two attractive **hippodromes** (racetracks). Head for the **Poney Club** (✉ Rue Reynolds-Mahn, ☎ 02–31–98–56–24) for a wonderful horseback ride on the beach (remember the sunsets can be spectacular). They are open weekends and holidays, but be sure to call early to reserve your horse, or a pony for the little one.)

Houlgate

25 *14 km (9 mi) southwest of Deauville via D513, 27 km (17 mi) northeast of Caen.*

Cheerful Houlgate, bursting with wood-beam, striped-brick Belle Epoque villas and thatch-roof houses, paints a pretty picture, with the steep **Falaise des Vaches Noires** (Black Cow Cliffs) providing a rocky backdrop to the town's enormous sandy beach, which extends below the town casino. The town's leisure options include tennis, golf, and crazy golf, helping to make Houlgate a more personable alternative to neighboring Cabourg, evoked (as Balbec) by Marcel Proust in his epic *In Search Of Lost Time*; between the two resort towns is historic **Dives-sur-Mer,** with its oak-beam medieval market hall, rickety square, and chunky Gothic church. William the Conqueror set sail from Dives en route to England in 1066.

Dining and Lodging

$$–$$$ ★ ✕ **1900.** Don't be misled by the tacky glass veranda: A wonderful dining room lurks within, with Art Nouveau lamps and a bronze and mahogany bar almost as old as the regiment of calvados bottles of various sizes that parades across the top. Claire Lemarié is the good-humored *patronne*; her husband, André, is the deft cook with a penchant for fish and seafood (turbot, crayfish and scallops). Service from the young trainees, impeccable in their black-and-white aprons, is discreet and helpful. The kitschy bedrooms are small but comfortable. ✉ *17 rue des Bains, 14510, ☎ 02–31–28–77–77, FAX 02–31–28–08–07, WEB*

www.hotel-1900.fr. 28 rooms. Restaurant, no air-conditioning. MC, V. Closed Jan.

$$$–$$$$ **Pullman Grand Hôtel.** This luxurious white-stucco hotel, on the seafront in Cabourg, has a lively piano bar in summer. Many rooms have balconies overlooking the sea; Proust used to stay in No. 147. In the restaurant, Le Balbec (open November through March, closed Monday and Tuesday), you can dine on traditional French cuisine of a high standard of quality but no great sophistication. ✉ *Promenade Marcel-Proust, 14390 Cabourg,* ☎ *02–31–91–01–79,* FAX *02–31–24–03–20. 68 rooms. Restaurant, piano bar, no air-conditioning, cable TV, minibars, Internet, golf course, 2 tennis courts, horseback riding. AE, DC, MC, V.*

Caen

26 *26 km (16 mi) southwest of Houlgate, 120 km (75 mi) west of Rouen, 150 km (94 mi) north of Le Mans.*

With its abbeys and castle, Caen, a busy commercial city and the capital of Lower Normandy, is very different from the coastal resorts. William of Normandy ruled from Caen in the 11th century before he conquered England. Nine hundred years later, the two-month Battle of Caen in 1944 devastated much of the town in a fire that raged for 11 days. Scenically restored rue Ecuyêre and place St-Sauveur recall the city's former grandeur.

A good place to begin exploring Caen is the **Hôtel d'Escoville,** a stately mansion in the city center built by wealthy merchant Nicolas Le Valois d'Escoville in the 1530s. The building was badly damaged during the war but has since been restored; the austere facade conceals an elaborate inner courtyard, reflecting the Italian influence on early Renaissance Norman architecture. The city **tourist office** is housed here and is an excellent resource. ✉ *Pl. St-Pierre,* ☎ *02–31–27–14–14,* WEB *www.ville-caen.fr.*

Across the square, beneath a 240-foot spire, is the late-Gothic church of **St-Pierre,** a riot of ornamental stonework. Looming on a mound ahead of the church is the **château**—the ruins of William the Conqueror's fortress, built in 1060 and sensitively restored after the war. The castle gardens are a perfect spot for strolling, and the ramparts afford good views of the city. The citadel also contains two museums and the medieval church of St-Georges, used for exhibitions.

The **Musée des Beaux-Arts,** within the castle's walls, is a heavyweight among France's provincial fine-arts museums. Its Old Master collection includes works by Poussin, Perugino, Rembrandt, Titian, Tintoretto, van der Weyden, and Paolo Veronese; there's also a wide range of 20th-century art. ✉ *Entrance by castle gateway,* ☎ *02–31–30–47–70.* 🎫 *€3.90, free Wed.* ⏲ *Wed.–Mon. 9:30–6.*

The **Musée de Normandie** (Normandy Museum), in the mansion built for the castle governor, is dedicated to regional arts, such as ceramics and sculpture, plus some local archaeological finds. ✉ *Entrance by castle gateway,* ☎ *02–31–30–47–50,* WEB *www.ville-caen.fr/mdn.* 🎫 *€1.50, free Wed.* ⏲ *Wed.–Mon. 9:30–12:30 and 2–6.*

★ Caen's finest church, of cathedral proportions, is part of the **Abbaye aux Hommes** (Men's Abbey), built by William the Conqueror of local Caen stone (also used for Canterbury Cathedral, Westminster Abbey and the Tower of London). The abbey was begun in Romanesque style in 1066 and added to in the 18th century; its elegant buildings are now part of City Hall and some rooms are brightened by the town's fine collection of paintings. Note the magnificent yet spare facade of the abbey church of **St-Étienne,** enhanced by two 11th-century towers topped by octagonal spires. Inside, what had been William the Conqueror's tomb was destroyed by 16th-century Huguenots during the Wars of Religion. However, the choir still stands; it was the first to be built in Norman Gothic style, and many subsequent choirs were modeled after it. ✉ *Pl. Louis-Guillouard,* ☎ *02–31–30–42–81.* 🎫 *Church free, abbey tours €2.* ⊙ *Tours daily at 9:30, 11, 2:30, and 4.*

The **Abbaye aux Dames** (Ladies' Abbey) was founded by William the Conqueror's wife, Matilda, in 1063. Once a hospital, the abbey—rebuilt in the 18th century—was restored in the 1980s by the Regional Council, which then promptly requisitioned it for office space; however, its elegant arcaded courtyard and ground-floor reception rooms can be admired during a (free) guided tour. You can also visit the squat **Église de la Trinité** (Trinity Church), a fine example of 11th-century Romanesque architecture, though its original spires were replaced by timid balustrades in the early 18th century. Note the intricate carvings on columns and arches in the chapel; the 11th-century crypt; and, in the choir, the back marble slab commemorating Queen Matilda, buried here in 1083. ✉ *Pl. de la Reine-Mathilde,* ☎ *02–31–06–98–98.* 🎫 *Free.* ⊙ *Guided tours daily at 2:30 and 4.*

★ The **Mémorial,** erected in 1988 in the north side of the city, is a must-see if you're interested in World War II history. The stark, flat facade, with a narrow doorway symbolizing the Allies' breach in the Nazi's supposedly impregnable Atlantic Wall, opens onto an immense foyer containing a café, brasserie, shop, and British Typhoon aircraft suspended overhead. The museum itself is down a spiral ramp, lined with photos and documents charting the Nazi's rise to power in the 1930s. The idea—hardly subtle but visually effective—is to suggest a descent into the hell of the war. The extensive displays range from wartime plastic jewelry to scale models of battleships, with scholarly sections on how the Nazis tracked down radios used by the French Resistance and on the development of the atomic bomb. A room commemorating the Holocaust, with flickering candles and twinkling overhead lights, provides a jarring, somewhat tacky note. The D-Day landings are evoked by a tabletop Allied map of the theater of war and by a split-screen presentation of the D-Day invasion from both the Allied and Nazi standpoints. Four-hour minibus tours of the D-Day beaches are run daily April–September. ✉ *Esplanade Dwight-D.-Eisenhower,* ☎ *02–31–06–06–44,* WEB *www.memorial.fr.* 🎫 *€16.* ⊙ *Feb.–Oct., daily 9–7; Nov.–Dec. and late-Jan., daily 9–6.*

Dining and Lodging

$$$ ★ ✕ **Bourride.** On one of Caen's oldest pedestrian streets near the castle is one of the region's best restaurants. Exuberant, at times irascible chef Michel Bruneau has officiated here since 1972, concocting specialties like steamed sole with hazelnut butter, chitterling fricassee in cider, and baby pigeon in a salted bean crust. The late 17th-century dining room is typically Norman—stone walls, beamed ceilings, and a large fireplace. ✉ *15 rue de Vaugueux,* ☎ *02–31–93–50–76. Reservations essential. Jacket and tie. AE, DC, MC, V. Closed Mon., most of Jan., and 2nd ½ Aug. No dinner Sun.*

$$$ ✕ **La Pommeraie.** Chef-owner José Aparicio's celebrated restaurant is in a 17th-century former priory in the small village of Bénouville, northeast of Caen. Choose from seasonal dishes prepared in the classic Norman manner, like the sole stuffed with wild autumn mushrooms or the pigeon stuffed with marinated cabbage and homemade foie gras. You can stay overnight in one of the 16 cozy rooms at the ad-

joining hotel, Le Manoir d'Hastings. ✉ *18 av. de la Côte-de-Nacre, 14970 Bénouville (10 km/6 mi northeast of Caen),* ☎ *02–31–44–62–43. Reservations essential. Jacket and tie. AE, DC, MC, V. Closed Mon., mid-Nov.–mid-Dec., and mid-Feb. No dinner Sun.*

$$–$$$ **Dauphin.** Despite being in the heart of the city, this hotel, in a former 12th-century priory, is surprisingly quiet. Some of the smallish rooms have exposed beams; those overlooking the street are soundproof; the ones in back look out on the courtyard. Service is friendly and efficient in the hotel and in the excellent though expensive restaurant (closed Saturday and for three weeks in July/August). A 15-room extension is planned for 2003. ✉ *29 rue Gémare, 14000,* ☎ *02–31–86–22–26,* FAX *02–31–86–35–14,* WEB *www.bestwestern.fr. 22 rooms. Restaurant, no air-conditioning, cable TV, minibars, no pets. AE, DC, MC, V. Closed part of Feb.*

Shopping

A ***marché aux puces*** (flea market) is held on Friday morning on place St-Saveur and on Sunday morning on place Courtonne. In June, collectors and dealers flock to Caen's bric-a-brac and **antiques fair.**

Outdoor Activities and Sports

Take a barge trip along the canal that leads from Caen to the sea on the ***Hastings*** (✉ Quai Vendeuvre, ☎ 02–31–34–00–00); there are 4 daily departures; 9 AM, noon, 3 PM, and 7 PM.

En Route Early on June 6, 1944, the British 6th Airborne Division landed by glider and captured the **Pegasus Bridge** (named for the division's emblem, showing Bellerophon astride his winged horse, Pegasus). This proved the first symbolic step toward the liberation of France from Nazi occupation. To see this symbol of the Allied invasion, from Caen take D514 north and turn right at Bénouville. The original bridge—erected in 1935—has been replaced by a similar but slightly wider bridge; but the original can still be seen at the adjacent **Memorial Pegasus** visitor center (open daily Feb.–Nov.). The Café Gondreé by the bridge—the first building recaptured on French soil—is still standing and houses a small museum. A 40-minute son-et-lumière show lights up the bridge and the café at nightfall between June and September.

Five kilometers (3 miles) north of here, just beyond Ouistreham and its **Grand Bunker** museum recalling Hitler's Atlantic Wall, lie the easternmost D-Day landing beaches: **Sword Beach** extends to Luc-sur-Mer; **Juno Beach** to Courseulles; and **Gold Beach** to Arromanches. These flat, sandy beaches, stormed by British (Gold and Sword) and Canadian (Juno) troops, extend beneath pretty resort towns like Lion-sur-Mer, Langrune, and St-Aubin. Inland, slender church spires patrol the vast, flat horizon.

Arromanches-les-Bains

27 *31 km (19 mi) northwest of Caen, 10 km (6 mi) northeast of Bayeux.*

Little remains to mark the furious fighting waged hereabouts after D-Day. In the bay off Arromanches, however, some elements of the floating harbor are still visible. Head up to the terrace alongside Arromanches 360, high above the town on D65, to contemplate the seemingly insignificant hunks of concrete that form a broken offshore semicircle—and try to imagine the extraordinary technical feat involved in towing them across the Channel from England.

The **Musée du Débarquement,** on the seafront, has models, mock-ups, and photographs depicting Operation Overlord—the code name for the invasion of Normandy. Five beachheads (dubbed Utah, Omaha,

Gold, Juno, and Sword) were established along the coast to either side of Arromanches. Preparations started in mid-1943, and British shipyards worked furiously through the following winter and spring building two artificial harbors (called "mulberries"), boats, and landing equipment; the other harbor, moored off Omaha Beach, was destroyed on June 19, 1944, by a violent storm. The British and Canadian troops that landed on Sword, Juno, and Gold on June 6, 1944, quickly pushed inland and joined with parachute regiments previously dropped behind German lines, before encountering fierce resistance at Caen, which did not fall until July 9. ✉ *Pl. du 6-Juin,* ☎ *02–31–22–34–31.* 🎫 *€6.* ⏲ *May–Sept., daily 9–7; Oct.–Dec. and Feb.–Apr., daily 10–12:30 and 1:30–4:30.*

Arromanches 360 is a striking modern movie theater with a 360-degree circular screen—actually nine curved screens synchronized to show an 18-minute film (screenings at 10 past and 20 to the hour) titled *Le Prix de la Liberté* (*The Price of Freedom*). The film, which tells the story of the D-Day landings, is a mix of archival and more recent footage from major sites and cemeteries. Evocative music and sound effects serve as dramatic substitutes for spoken commentary. ✉ *Chemin du Calvaire,* ☎ *02–31–22–30–30.* 🎫 *€4.* ⏲ *June–Aug., daily 9:10–6:40; May and Sept., 10:10–5:40; Oct.–Dec. and Feb.–Apr., daily 10:10–4:40.*

Dining

$–$$ ✕ **Le Bistro d'Arromanches.** This English pub–style bistro has a warm and friendly aura and welcomes children—there is even a room upstairs with games and toys to keep them amused while Mommy and Daddy are enjoying the simple, classic fare. ✉ *23 rue de Maréchal-Joffre,* ☎ *02–31–22–31–32. MC, V. Closed Mon. and mid-Dec.–mid-Jan.*

Bayeux

28 *10 km (6 mi) southwest of Arromanches via D516, 28 km (17 mi) northwest of Caen.*

Bayeux, the first town to be liberated during the Battle of Normandy, was already steeped in history—as home to a Norman-Gothic cathedral, a museum dedicated to the Battle of Normandy, and the world's most celebrated piece of needlework: the Bayeux Tapestry. Bayeux's medieval mise-en-scène makes it a popular base, especially among British travelers, for day trips to other towns in Normandy. The Old World mood is at its most boisterous during the Fêtes Médiévales, a market-cum-carnival held in the streets around the cathedral on the first weekend of July.

★ Really a 225-ft-long embroidered scroll stitched in 1067, the **Bayeux Tapestry,** known in French as the Tapisserie de la Reine Mathilde (Queen Matilda's Tapestry), depicts, in 58 comic-strip-type scenes, the epic story of William of Normandy's conquest of England in 1066. The tapestry was probably commissioned from Saxon embroiderers by the count of Kent—who was also the bishop of Bayeux—to be displayed in his newly built cathedral, the Cathédrale Notre-Dame. Despite its age, the tapestry is in remarkably good condition; the extremely detailed, often homey scenes provide an unequaled record of the clothes, weapons, ships, and lifestyles of the day. It's showcased in the **Musée de la Tapisserie** (Tapestry Museum); for €1 you can rent headphones and listen to an English commentary about the tapestry, scene by scene. ✉ *Centre Guillaume-le-Conquérant, 13 bis rue de Nesmond,* ☎ *02–31–51–25–50.* 🎫 *€6.40 (joint ticket with Musée Baron-Gérard* *and the Hôtel du Doyen). ⏲ May–Aug., daily 9–7; Sept.–Apr., daily 9:30–12:30 and 2–6.*

Housed in the Bishop's Palace beneath the cathedral, and fronted by a majestic plane tree planted in March 1797 and known as the Tree of Liberty, the **Musée Baron-Gérard** contains a fine collection of Bayeux porcelain and lace, ceramics from Rouen, a marvelous collection of apothecary jars from the 17th and 18th centuries, and 16th- to 19th-century furniture and paintings by local artists. ✉ *1 pl. de la Liberté,* ☎ *02–31–92–14–21.* 🎫 *€6.40 (joint ticket with Tapestry Museum and the Hôtel du Doyen.* ⏲ *June–mid-Sept., daily 9–7; mid-Sept.–May, Wed.–Sun., 10–12:30 and 2–6.*

Bayeux's mightiest edifice, the **Cathédrale Notre-Dame,** is a harmonious mixture of Norman and Gothic architecture. Note the portal on the south side of the transept that depicts the assassination of English archbishop Thomas à Becket in Canterbury Cathedral in 1170, following his courageous opposition to King Henry II's attempts to control the church. ✉ *Rue du Bienvenue,* ☎ *02–31–92–01–85.*

Handmade lace is a specialty of Bayeux. The best place to learn about it and to buy some is the **Hôtel du Doyen,** which also houses a display of religious art. ✉ *6 rue Lambert-Leforestier,* ☎ *02–31–92–73–80,* WEB *www.dentelledebayeux.free.fr.* 🎫 *€6.40 (joint ticket with Tapestry Museum and Musée Baron-Gérard).* ⏲ *Daily 9–12:30 and 2–6.*

At the **Musée de la Bataille de Normandie** (Battle of Normandy Museum) detailed exhibits trace the story of the struggle from June 7 to August 22, 1944. This modern museum near the British War Cemetery, sunk partly beneath the level of its surrounding lawns, contains some impressive war paraphernalia, including tanks, uniforms, weapons, and equipment. Waxworks and a film recount the invasion. ✉ *Bd. du Général-Fabian-Ware,* ☎ *02–31–51–46–90,* WEB *www.mairie-bayeux.fr.* 🎫 *€5.40.* ⏲ *May–mid-Sept., daily 9:30–6:30; mid-Sept.–Apr., daily 10–12:30 and 2–6.*

★ Sixteen kilometers (10 miles) southwest of Bayeux stands the **Château de Balleroy.** A connoisseur's connoisseur's favorite, it was built by architect François Mansart in 1626–36 and distills 17th-century elegance as few other houses do. The *cour d'honneur* is marked by two stylish side pavilions—an architectural grace note adapted from Italian Renaissance models—which beautifully frame the small, but very seignorial, central mass of the house. Inside, the *salon d'honneur* is the very picture of Louis XIV decoration, while other rooms were recast in 19th-century chic by Malcolm Forbes, who bought the chateau in 1970. A gallery houses a fascinating **Musée des Ballons** (Balloon Museum), while the companion village was designed by Mansart in one of the first examples of town planning in France. ✉ *Balleroy,* ☎ *02–31–21–60–61,* WEB *www.chateau-balleroy.com.* 🎫 *€7.* ⏲ *Mid-Mar.–June and Sept.–mid-Oct., daily 9–noon and 2–6; July–Aug., daily 10–6.*

Dining and Lodging

$$ ✕ **Amaryllis.** Pascal Marie's small restaurant has three prix-fixe menus, running €11–€28. The three-course dinner, with six selections per course, may include a half-dozen oysters, fillet of sole with a cider-based sauce, and pastries for dessert. Lobster and skate with shallots lurk on the *à la carte.* ✉ *32 rue St-Patrice,* ☎ *02–31–22–47–94. MC, V. Closed Mon., Sun. in winter, and Jan.*

$$$–$$$$ ★ ✕🏨 **Château d'Audrieu.** This family-owned château, with an elegant 18th-century facade, fulfills a Hollywood notion of a palatial property: princely opulence, wall sconces, overstuffed chairs, and antiques. Rooms 50 and 51 have peaked ceilings with exposed-wood beams. The

restaurant (closed Monday, and lunch is served weekends only) has an extensive wine list, and chef Alain Cornet keeps to a classic repertoire of dishes. ✉ *14250 Audrieu (13 km/8 mi southeast of Bayeux off N13),* ☎ *02–31–80–21–52,* FAX *02–31–80–24–73. 25 rooms. Restaurant, bar, no air-conditioning, cable TV, minibars, pool, helipad, no pets. AE, MC, V. Closed mid-Dec.–mid-Feb.*

$$–$$$ ✕🏨 **Grand Hôtel du Luxembourg.** The Luxembourg has small but adequate rooms; all but two face a courtyard garden. It has one of the town's best restaurants, Les Quatre Saisons, with a seasonal menu; depending on the time of year, choose the honey-roasted ham with melted apples, or braised turbot with sage. ✉ *25 rue des Bouchers, 14400,* ☎ *02–31–92–00–04; 800/528–1234 for U.S. reservations,* FAX *02–31–92–54–26. 24 rooms, 3 suites. Restaurant, bar, cable TV, Internet, dance club. AE, DC, MC, V.*

$$ ★ 🏨 **Manoir du Carel.** The narrow slits serving as windows on the tower recall the origins of the Manoir du Carel, set nicely halfway between Bayeux and the sea, which was originally constructed as a fortified manor during the Hundred Years' War. Current owner Jacques Aumond offers comfortable rooms with modern furnishings; public salons have 19th-century accents. The cottage on the grounds has a kitchen plus a fireplace that masks a brick oven where villagers once had their bread baked. ✉ *14400 Maisons (5 km/3 mi northwest of Bayeux),* ☎ *02–31–22–37–00,* FAX *02–31–21–57–00. 3 rooms, 1 cottage. No air-conditioning, no room TV, no pets. No credit cards.*

Outdoor Activities and Sports

Bicycles can be rented from **Family Home** (✉ 39 rue Général-de-Dais, ☎ 02–31–92–15–22) for about €8 a day. Ask the tourist office for information about trails. ★ The **Rassemblement International de Ballons** (International Balloon Festival; ☎ 02–31–21–60–61 for information) takes place in mid-June, 16 km (10 mi) southwest of Bayeux at the early 17th-century **Château de Balleroy** (☞ *see* above).

The D-Day Beaches

★ 29 You won't be disappointed by the rugged terrain and windswept sand of **Omaha Beach,** 16 km (10 mi) northwest of Bayeux. Here you'll find the **Monument du Débarquement** (Monument to the Normandy Landings) and nearby, in Vierville-sur-Mer, the **U.S. National Guard Monument** who fought in both world wars. In Colleville-sur-Mer is the hilltop **American Cemetery and Memorial,** designed by the landscape architect Markley Stevenson. It is a moving tribute to the fallen, with its Wall of the Missing (in the form of a semicircular colonnade), drumlike chapel, and avenues of holly oaks trimmed to resemble open parachutes. The crisply mowed lawns are studded with 9,386 marble tombstones; this is where Stephen Spielberg's fictional hero Captain John Miller was supposed to have been buried in *Saving Private Ryan.* You can look out to sea across the landing beach from a platform on the north side of the cemetery.

★ The most spectacular scenery along the coast is at the **Pointe du Hoc,** 13 km (8 mi) west of St-Laurent. Wildly undulating grassland leads past ruined blockhouses to a clifftop observatory and a German machine-gun post whose intimidating mass of reinforced concrete merits chilly exploration. Despite Spielberg's cinematic genius, it remains hard to imagine just how Colonel Rudder and his 225 men—only 90 survived—managed to scale the jagged cliffs with rope ladders and capture the German defenses in one of the most heroic and dramatic episodes of the war.

Head west around the coast on N13, pause in the town of **Carentan** to admire its modern marina and the mighty octagonal spire of the Église
30 Notre-Dame, and continue northwest to **Sainte-Mère-Église.** At 2:30 AM on June 6, 1944, the 82nd Airborne Division was dropped over Ste-Mère, heralding the start of D-Day operations. Famously, one parachutist got stuck on the church tower (memorably recreated in the 1960 film *The Longest Day*); a dummy is strung up each summer to recall the event, and a stained-glass window inside the church honors American paratroopers. After securing their position at Ste-Mère, U.S. forces pushed north, then west, cutting off the Cotentin Peninsula on June 18 and taking Cherbourg on June 26. German defense proved fiercer farther south, and St-Lô was not liberated until July 19. Ste-Mère's symbolic importance as the first French town to be liberated from the Nazis is commemorated by the Borne 0 (Zero) outside the town hall—a large, domed milestone marking the start of the Voie de la Libertè (Freedom Way), charting the Allies' progress across France.

The **Musée des Troupes Aéroportées** (Airborne Troops Museum), built behind the church in 1964 in the form of an open parachute, houses documents, maps, mementos, and one of the Waco CG4A gliders used to drop troops. ✉ *Pl. du 6-juin-1944,* ☎ *02-33-41-41-35.* *€5.* ⏲ *Apr.–Nov., daily 9–noon and 2–7.*

31 Head east on D67 from Ste-Mère to **Utah Beach,** which, being sheltered from the Atlantic winds by the Cotentin Peninsula and surveyed by lowly sand dunes rather than rocky cliffs, proved easier to attack than Omaha. In **La Madeleine** inspect the modern museum (✉ Plage de La Madeleine, ☎ 02-33-71-53-35) devoted to the battle of Utah Beach; it's open April–June and September–October, daily 9:30–noon and 2–6; and July–August, daily 9:30–6:30. Continue north to the **Dunes de Varreville,** set with a monument to French hero General Leclerc, who landed here. Offshore you can see the fortified **Iles St-Marcouf.** Continue to **Quinéville,** at the far end of Utah Beach, with its **museum** (✉ Rue de la Plage, ☎ 02-33-21-40-44) evoking life during the German Occupation; the museum is open April–May and October, daily 10–noon and 2–6, and June–September, daily 9:30–6:30.

Dining and Lodging

$$$$ ✕ **Chenevière.** This grand 18th-century château, just inland from Port-en-Bessin, to the east of Omaha Beach, has rooms with modern furnishings, floor-to-ceiling windows, and flowered bedspreads. The restaurant (closed Mon., no dinner Tues.) serves cuisine appropriate to its surroundings: Claude Esprabens's roasted scampi with sesame seeds and fresh chanterelles is delicious, as is the warm sliced duck liver with raspberry sauce. ✉ *Les Escures, 14520 Commes,* ☎ *02-31-51-25-25,* FAX *02-31-51-25-20,* WEB *www.lacheneviere.com. 21 rooms. Restaurant, no air-conditioning, cable TV, minibars, Internet. AE, DC, MC, V. Closed Jan.–mid-Feb.*

$$ ✕ **Casino.** You can't get closer to the action. This handsome, postwar, triangular-gabled stone hotel looks directly onto Omaha Beach. The bar is made from an old lifeboat, and it's no surprise that fish and regional cuisine with creamy sauces predominate in Bruno Clemençon's seaview restaurant. ✉ *Rue de la Percée, 14710 Vierville-sur-Mer,* ☎ *02-31-22-41-02,* FAX *02-31-22-41-12. 12 rooms. Restaurant, no air-conditioning. MC, V. Closed mid-Nov.–early Mar.*

St-Vaast-la-Hougue

㉜ *14 km (9 mi) north of Quineville D42/D14.*

The bustling harbor town of St-Vaast-la Hougue has two waterfronts, one facing south toward its famous oyster beds, with Utah Beach beyond, the other to the west out toward the Channel. Between the two is a finger of land tipped by an imposing fort. Just offshore from St-Vaast is the Ile de Tatihou, a small island fortified by Vauban in 1692, along with the tiny Fort de l'Ilet, 200 yards to the south. Tatihou possesses a **Musée Maritime** (www.tatihou.com), where you can admire objects salvaged from local shipwrecks and visit sprawling gardens where marine flora and exotic plants prosper in the temperate climate, along with thousands of seagulls and a hundred different species of migrating birds. Entrance to the museum and gardens is included in the return €6 boat-ticket.

En Route From St-Vaast continue up the coast on D1, stopping first in **Montfarville** to visit its granite church with gaudy ceiling frescoes on the life of Christ by local 19th-century artist Guillaume Fouace, then in **Barfleur,** renowned for its picturesque waterfront. The 230-ft-high lighthouse at nearby **Gatteville-le-Phare,** which is open to the public, is the second-tallest in France, surveying a stretch of coast notorious for its treacherous cross-currents. Head west to **St-Pierre-Église** and its fortified church, again with a painted roof, then go northwest via D210 to **Cap Lévy,** a quaint little cove affording fine views across the bay to Cherbourg.

Cherbourg

㉝ *37 km (23 mi) northwest of St-Vaast-la-Hougue via N13.*

Perhaps best known for Michel Legrand's haunting theme from the 1960s film musical *Les Parapluies de Cherbourg* (*The Umbrellas of Cherbourg*), Cherbourg is no longer the thriving transatlantic port of a Belle Epoque heyday symbolized by the hyperelaborate facade of its 1882 **theater,** one of the few old monuments to survive World War II. Umbrellas are hardly the sunniest of city symbols, but the climate, though gusty, is generally mild, and it's fun to stroll around the grid of narrow lanes (many of them pedestrian-only) between the theater and the ramshackle **Église de la Trinité** by the seafront—especially on Tuesday, Thursday, or Saturday, when the street market is in full action.

It was back in 1686 that Vauban first spotted Cherbourg's potential as a defensive port beneath the rocky 360-ft Montagne du Roule, but it took the completion of a massive breakwater in 1853 before Cherbourg could harbor ocean-going ships. The first transatlantic liner docked in 1869; these days ferries ply the Channel to England (Portsmouth and Poole) and Ireland (Rosslare). You can take a short sea cruise around the bay from Port Chantereyne any afternoon from April through September (call 02–33–93–75–27 for details). Cherbourg is also a major submarine base: more than 90 have been built here since 1899, and one is on display at the **Cité de La Mer** (Marine Center, www.citedelamer.com), scheduled at press time to open in the old maritime rail station during 2002.

Uniforms, photographs, maps, flags, posters, and medals at the **Musée de la Libération** (Liberation Museum), on the hill above the town (excellent sea views), recall Cherbourg's pivotal role at the end of World War II, when it was the Allies' major bridgehead to France after the D-Day landings and the French terminus for the PLUTO sea-bed pipeline that pumped needed fuel under the Channel from the Isle of

Wight. ✉ *Fort du Roule,* ☎ *02–33–20–14–12.* 💶 *€3.* ⏲ *May–Sept., daily 10–6; Oct.–Apr., Tues.–Sun. 9:30–noon and 2–5:30.*

Thirty works by local-born painter François Millet (of *Angélus* renown) can be seen at the **Musée Thomas-Henry,** the city art museum, along with works by Murillo, "Velvet" Brueghel, David, and such talented 19th-century regional artists as Guillaume Fouace and Félix Bahot. Sculpture and ceramics complete the collection. ✉ *Rue Vartel,* ☎ *02–33–23–39–30.* 💶 *€2.30.* ⏲ *Tues.–Sun. 9–noon and 2–6.*

Dining and Lodging

$$ ✕ **Vauban.** Warm, friendly, and family-owned, this spot is headed up by chef Daniel Imbert, who prefers to approach his cuisine with a light, modern touch, avoiding the cream that typifies classic Norman fare. The menu is seasonal, with set menus running €14–€37 and lots of fish and seafood temptations, such as the fresh *bar* (sea bass) with truffles or the coquilles St. Jacques with wild mushrooms. ✉ *22 quai de Caligny,* ☎ *02–33–43–10–11.* FAX *02–33–43–15–18. AE, MC, V. Closed Mon. Sept.–June. No dinner Sun.*

$ ✕ **Faitout.** This cozy, paneled bistro in the shopping district near the Trinité church packs in locals with its friendly service and traditional French cuisine. Stews, steaks, smoked salmon, and mussels are high on the menu. ✉ *25 rue de la Tour-Carree,* ☎ *02–33–04–25–04. MC, V. Closed Sun. No lunch Mon.*

$$ 🏨 **Ambassadeur.** This modernized quayside hotel offers good value, a central location, and an English-speaking staff. The better, and more expensive, rooms have bathtubs rather than showers and look out over the harbor. The Vauban restaurant, right next door, is a calmer dinnertime alternative to the bustling Faitout. ✉ *22 quai de Caligny, 50100,* ☎ *02–33–43–10–00,* FAX *02–33–43–10–01. 40 rooms. No air-conditioning, Internet, no pets. AE, MC, V. Closed Christmas–New Year's.*

St-Lô

34 *78 km (49 mi) southeast of Cherbourg, 36 km (22 mi) southwest of Bayeux.*

St-Lô, perched dramatically on a rocky spur above the Vire Valley, was a key communications center that suffered so badly in World War II that it became known as the "capital of ruins." The medieval **Église Notre-Dame** bears mournful witness to those dark days: its imposing, spire-topped west front was never rebuilt, merely shored up with a wall of greenish stone. Reconstruction elsewhere, though, was wholesale. Some of it was spectacular, like the slender, spiral-staircased tower outside City Hall; the circular theater; or the openwork belfry of the church of Ste-Croix. The city was freed by American troops, and its rebuilding was financed with U.S. support, notably from the city of Baltimore. The **Hôpital Mémorial France–États Unis** (France–United States Memorial Hospital), designed by Paul Nelson and featuring a giant mosaic by Fernand Léger, was named to honor those links.

St-Lô is capital of the Manche *département* and, less prosaically, likes to consider itself France's horse capital. Hundreds of breeders are based in its environs, and the **Haras National** (National Stud) was established here in 1886 (call ☎ 02–33–77–88–77 for details on how to visit on a summer afternoon).

★ The city's fine art museum, the **Musée des Beaux-Arts,** opened in 1989. It's the perfect French provincial museum: airy, seldom busy, not too big, yet full of varied exhibits—including an unexpected masterpiece: *Gombault et Macée,* a set of nine silk-and-wool tapestries woven in Bruges around 1600 that relate a famous tale about a shepherd couple and are exquisitely showcased in a special circular room. Other highlights include brash modern tapestries by Jean Lurçat; paintings by Corot, Boudin, and Géricault; court miniatures by Daniel Saint (1778–1847); and the Art Deco pictures of Slovenian-born Jaro Hilbert (1897–1995), inspired by ancient Egypt. Photographs, models, and documents evoke the city's wartime devastation. ✉ *Centre Culturel, pl. du Champ-de-Mars,* ☎ *02–33–72–52–55.* *€1.52.* ⏲ *Wed.–Mon. 10–noon and 2–6.*

Coutances

35 *27 km (18 mi) southwest of St-Lô via D972.*

If you're interested in church architecture, you'll want to stop off in ★ Coutances. The largely 13th-century **Cathédrale Notre-Dame,** with its famous octagonal lantern rising 135 ft above the nave, is considered the most harmonious Gothic building in Normandy. On the outside, especially the facade, note the obsessive use of turrets, spires, slender shafts, and ultranarrow pointed arches squeezed senseless in their architectural pursuit of vertical takeoff. A further 200 yards down the street is the **Eglise St-Pierre,** topped by a chunky Renaissance pastiche of the cathedral lantern above a richly sculpted interior. The town's tumbling **Jardin des Plantes,** where an army of 12 gardeners tends 47,000 plants, is also worth a visit.

Lodging

$ **Moulin Girard.** For English hospitality, cheerful conversation, and unusual, inexpensive accommodations, head to Roger and Jasmine Albon's wonderful 200-year-old water mill. The main house has three small rooms, and the miller's cottage with exposed beams has a two-bedroom suite—for €75, including breakfast—an ideal choice for a family or two couples. You can have your breakfast on the terrace overlooking the mill stream, or make arrangements for Jasmine to whip up a regional specialty for lunch or dinner. ✉ *50410 Le Chefresne (26 km/16 mi southeast of Coutances; from Villedieu-les-Poêles take a right on D98 as you enter Percy in the direction of Tessy-sur-Vire and then go right on D452 for Le Chefresne),* ☎ FAX *02–33–61–62–06. 3 rooms, 1 suite. No pets. No credit cards.*

Granville

36 *30 km (19 mi) south of Coutances via D971, 107 km (67 mi) southwest of Caen.*

Proud locals like to call Granville the "Monaco of the North." It perches on a rocky outcrop and does have a sea-water therapy center, but the similarities end there. Free of casinos and sequins, Granville instead has a down-to-earth feel. Granite houses cluster around the church in the Old Town, and the harbor below is full of working boats. From the ramparts there are fine views of the English Channel; catamarans breeze over to Jersey and the Iles Chausey daily in summer. Drive a few miles down the coast to find sandy beaches and a view of distant Mont-St-Michel.

Nightlife and the Arts

The rambunctious **Carnaval de Granville** involves four days of parades and festivities, culminating each year on Shrove Tuesday. The **Grand Pardon des Corporations de la Mer,** a *pardon,* or religious festival, devoted to the sea, is celebrated on the last Sunday of July with a military parade, a regatta, and platefuls of shellfish.

Outdoor Activities and Sports

Granville is a center for aquatic sports; inquire about sailboat jaunts at the **Centre Régional de Nautisme de Granville** (✉ Bd. des Amiraux, ☎ 02–33–91–22–60). **Lepesqueux** (✉ 3 rue Clément-Desmaisons, ☎ 02–33–50–18–97) also rents boats and yachts.

Shopping

It is said that every French kitchen worth its salt buys its pans from **Villedieu-les-Poêles,** 28 km (18 mi) east of Granville. The town is famous for its copperware (and its bells), and shops line the main street, rue Carnot, but you can find smaller outlets, with better buys, on the parallel rue du Dr-Harvard. Note that Tuesday is market day, so parking can be a bit of a problem.

Mont-St-Michel

★ 37 *44 km (27 mi) south of Granville via D973, N175, and D43; 123 km (77 mi) southwest of Caen; 67 km (42 mi) north of Rennes; 325 km (202 mi) west of Paris.*

Wrought by nature and centuries of tireless human toil, this sea-surrounded mass of granite adorned with the soul-lifting silhouette of the abbey of Mont-St-Michel may well be your most lasting image of Normandy. The abbey is perched on a 264-ft-high rock a few hundred yards off the coast: it's surrounded by water during the year's highest tides and by desolate sand flats the rest of the time. Be warned: tides in the bay are dangerously unpredictable. The sea can rise up to 45 ft at high tide and rushes in at incredible speed—more than a few ill-prepared tourists over the years have drowned. Also, be warned that there are patches of dangerous quicksand.

Because of its legendary origins and the sheer exploit of its construction, the abbey is known as the *Merveille de l'Occident* (Wonder of the Western World): the granite used to build it was transported from the nearby Isles of Chausey and hauled up to the site. The abbey's construction took more than 500 years, from 1017 to 1521. Legend has it that the Archangel Michael appeared to Aubert, Bishop of Avranches, inspiring him to build an oratory on what was then called Mont Tombe. The original church was completed in 1144, but further buildings were added in the 13th century to accommodate monks as well as the hordes of pilgrims who flocked here even during the Hundred Years' War, when the region was in English hands. The Romanesque choir was rebuilt in Gothic style during the 15th and 16th centuries. The abbey's monastic independence was undermined during the 17th century, when the monks began to flout the strict rules and discipline of their order, drifting into a state of decadence that culminated in their dispersal and the abbey's conversion into a prison, well before the French Revolution. In 1874 the former abbey was handed over to a governmental agency responsible for the preservation of historic monuments. Emmanuel Frémiet's great gilt statute of St. Michael was added to the spire in 1897. Monks now live and work here again, as in medieval times: you can join them for daily mass at 12:15.

A causeway—to be replaced in time by a bridge, allowing the bay waters to circulate freely—links Mont-St-Michel to the mainland. Leave your car in the parking lot (€2.50) along the causeway, outside the main gate. Just inside you'll find the tourist office, to the left, and a pair of old cannons (with cannonballs) to the right. If you're staying the night on Mont-St-Michel, take what you need in a small suitcase; you cannot gain access to your hotel by car.

The climb to the abbey is hard going—by the time you have mounted the celebrated **Escalier de Dentelle** (Lace Staircase) to the gallery around the roof of the abbey church, you will have climbed no fewer than 900 steps—but it's worth it. Stop off halfway up Grande-Rue at the medieval parish church of St-Pierre to admire the richly carved side chapel with its dramatic statue of St. Michael slaying the dragon. The **Grand Degré,** a steep, narrow staircase, leads to the abbey entrance, from which a wider flight of stone steps climbs to the **Saut Gautier Terrace** (named after a prisoner who jumped to his death from it) outside the sober, dignified church. After visiting the arcaded cloisters alongside, which offer vertiginous views of the bay, you can wander at leisure, and probably get lost, among the maze of rooms, staircases, and vaulted halls that make up the abbey. In July and August, evening concerts are held here during the **Heures Musicales** (Musical Hours), and you can a make an eerie lamplight visit (€8) during the **Songes de Nuit** (any night Monday through Saturday, between mid-July and the end of September). The island village, with its steep, narrow streets, is best visited out of season, from September to June. In summer the hordes of tourists and souvenir sellers can be stifling. Give yourself at least half a day here, and follow your nose. The mount is full of nooks, crannies, and little gardens, and there are fine views from along the ramparts. Best of all, when the day-trippers depart, the centuries-old peace and quiet of the mount return, and you can truly appreciate the frightening grandeur of this solitary spot. With this in mind, consider an overnight stay here, even though the hotels have somewhat inflated prices. If possible, time your visit a couple of days after the full moon—then the sunsets over this part of the Atlantic can be of incredible beauty. ☎ *02–33–89–80–00.* ✉ *€6.20,* WEB *www.monum.fr.* ⏲ *May–Sept., daily 9:30–11:30 and 1:30–6; Oct.–Apr., Wed.–Mon. 9:30–4:30.*

Dining and Lodging

$$$–$$$$ ✕🏨 **Mère Poulard.** This legendary hotel consists of adjoining houses with three steep flights of narrow stairs. The restaurant's reputation derives partly from Mère Poulard's famous soufflélike omelet and partly from its convenient location (right by the gateway, so don't expect views from atop the Mont). Room prices start low but ratchet upward according to size; the smallest rooms are bearable for an overnight stay, not longer. Walls throughout are plastered with posters and photographs of illustrious guests. You are usually requested to book two meals with the room. Reservations are essential for the restaurant in summer. ✉ *Grande-Rue, 50116,* ☎ *02–33–60–14–01,* FAX *02–33–48–52–31. 27 rooms. Restaurant, piano bar, no air-conditioning, cable TV, minibars, no pets. AE, DC, MC, V.*

$$$–$$$$ ★ ✕🏨 **Roche Torin.** Run by the Barraux family, this small, ivy-clad manor house on 4 acres of parkland is a delightful alternative to the high cost of staying on Mont-St-Michel. Rooms are pleasantly old-fashioned, and the bathrooms modern. The pleasant restaurant (closed Monday) has an open fireplace and serves superb *pré-salé* (salt-meadow lamb). In summer, aperitifs are served in the garden, with a view of Mont-St-Michel. ✉ *34 rte. de la Roche-Torin, 50220 Courtils (9 km/5 mi from Mont-St-Michel),* ☎ *02–33–70–96–55,* FAX *02–33–48–35–20. 11 rooms, 1 suite. Restaurant, minibars, Internet. MC, V. Closed mid-Nov.–mid-Mar.*

$$–$$$ ✕🏨 **Terrasses Poulard.** Run by the folks who own the noted Mère Poulard hotel, this ensemble of buildings is clustered around a small garden in the middle of the mount. Rooms at this hotel are some of the best—with views of the bay and rustic-style furnishings—and most spacious on the Mont, although many require you to negotiate a

labyrinth of steep stairways first. ✉ *Grande-Rue, opposite parish church, 50116,* ☎ *02–33–60–14–09,* FAX *02–33–60–37–31. 29 rooms. Restaurant, no air-conditioning, cable TV, minibars, billiards, library, no pets. AE, DC, MC, V.*

$$ ✕ **Hôtel du Guesclin.** This hotel is a fine option because of the upkeep by the owners, the courtesy of the staff, the comfy and clean guest rooms, and the discovery that you have two restaurants to choose from. Downstairs try the casual brasserie for simple fare like salads and sandwiches; upstairs the panoramic full-service restaurant has a wonderful view of the bay. ✉ *Grande-Rue, 50116,* ☎ *02–33–60–14–10,* FAX *02–33–60–45–81. 10 rooms. 2 restaurants, no air-conditioning. MC, V.*

$$–$$$ **Auberge St-Pierre.** You are not overwhelmed with choices on Mont-St-Michel when it comes to guest accommodations. However, this inn is a popular spot thanks to the fact that it is in a listed half-timber 15th-century building adjacent to the ramparts and has its own garden restaurant that offers seasonal specialties and interesting half-board rates. If you're lucky, you'll wind up in No. 16, which has a view of the abbey. The hotel annex, La Croix Blanche, has another 9 rooms (shower only). ✉ *Grande-Rue, 50170,* ☎ *02–33–60–14–03,* FAX *02–33–48–59–82,* WEB *www.mont-st-michel-hotel.com. 21 rooms. Restaurant, no air-conditioning, cable TV, Internet, no pets. AE, MC, V.*

En Route From Mont-St-Michel head east on N176/D977 to the attractive hilltop towns of Mortain and Domfront, then north on D962, through Flers and Condé-sur-Noireau, to Clécy, a cute hilltop town on the fringe of **La Suisse Normande** (Norman Switzerland), a rocky expanse of hills and gullies. Stop for a drink at La Potinière café (closed October–April), on the bank of Orne River beneath Clécy, then drive south along the bank to Pont d'Ouilly, whose Hôtel du Commerce serves a good lunch. Take D167 to the Roche d'Oëtre, a rock with spectacular views of the craggy hills that give the region its name, and continue along D301 to the Gorges de St-Aubert, a dramatic river gorge, before taking D21 northeast to Falaise.

Falaise

38 *132 km (82 mi) northeast of Mont-St-Michel, 32 km (20 mi) south of Caen.*

The memory of William the Conqueror, born here in 1027 as the illegitimate child of Duke Robert of Normandy and a local girl called La Belle Arlette, haunts the lively town of Falaise. William can be admired on a rearing bronze steed in the main square, and you can see the fountain where Robert is said to have first laid eyes on the lovely Arlette as she washed her clothes. Although Falaise was badly mauled during the Battle of Normandy, parts of the original town walls remain, as do the impressive medieval churches of St-Gervais, La Trinité, and Notre-Dame de Guibray. The foursquare **Château Guillaume-le-Conquérant** (Castle of William the Conqueror) glowers down from a spur above the town. Little has survived from the original building where William was born—but what remains is old enough. ✉ *Pl. Guillaume-le-Conquérant,* ☎ *02–31–41–61–69.* *€5.* ⏲ *Apr.–Oct., daily 10–6.*

At **Automates Avenue,** 300 clockwork toys and automatons, from the turn of the 20th century to the 1950s, are artfully presented in display windows evoking the streets of Paris. ✉ *Bd. de la Libération,* ☎ *02–31–90–02–43.* *€4.70.* ⏲ *Apr.–Sept., daily 10–12:30 and 1:30–6; Oct.–mid-Jan. and Feb.–Mar., weekends 10–12:30 and 1:30–6.*

Dining

$$ ★ ✕ **Fine Fourchette.** Chef Gilbert Costil attracts local devotees with dishes combining color, flavor, and quantity. Salmon and tuna gazpacho, foie gras with hazelnut dressing, grilled turbot with lemon, and chocolate cake with pistachio cream stand out among his specialties. Madame Costil provides a gracious welcome. ✉ *52 rue Georges-Clemenceau,* ☎ *02–31–90–08–59. AE, MC, V. Closed Wed. and Feb. No dinner Tues.*

OFF THE BEATEN PATH

SÉES AND ALENÇON – The storybook turrets, checkerboard walls, and improbably steep slate roofs of the **Château d'O** rise above a moat patrolled by regal swans near Mortrée, 35 km (22 mi) southeast of Falaise (☎ 02–33–35–34–69, 🎟 €5.40, ⏲ Mar.–Nov., Wed.–Mon. 2–5). Inside, look out for the sculpted ermine emblem of the O family, distinguished both as royal courtiers and for possessing the shortest family name in France. With old houses, a stately town hall, and a majestic bishop's palace, nearby **Sées** exudes faded charm. The 200-ft spires of the **Cathédrale St-Latrium** are visible for miles around; note the exquisite late-13th-century stained glass in the soaring choir and the two rose windows in the transepts.

Historic **Alençon,** 22 km (16 mi) south of Sées via N138, has been a lace-making center since 1665; by the end of the 17th-century *point d'Alençon* (Alençon needlepoint lace) was de rigueur on women's and men's clothing. The Musée des Beaux-Arts et de la Dentelle (Arts and Lace Museum) has a sophisticated collection of lace from Italy, Flanders, and France, along with paintings from the French school that span from the 17th to 20th centuries. (✉ Rue du Capitaine-Charles-Aveline, ☎ 02–33–32–40–07, 🎟 €2.70, ⏲ Tues.–Sun. 10–noon and 2–6).

St-Pierre-sur-Dives

39 *26 km (16 mi) northeast of Falaise on D511.*

St-Pierre-sur-Dives's main claim to fame is the finest medieval barn in Normandy; known as **Les Halles,** it was built in the 11th century, then enlarged in the 16th, and is best visited when the flower and food market is in full swing here on a Monday morning, when a lively cattle auction is held on the square outside. You can also admire the soaring medieval Eglise Abbatiale (abbey church), and visit its chapter house and cloisters; or explore the old tanners' district, with its washhouse and water mill.

En Route For apple brandy, make a detour through the **Pays d'Auge,** north of St-Pierre-sur-Dives. This is the heart of calvados country: you don't need a fixed itinerary, just follow your nose and the minor roads, keeping an eye out for local farmers selling calvados. When you are buying calvados, or any regional product for that matter, always request the AOC label, *appéllation d'origine controlée,* which assures that the product is made from the finest local ingredients. One good distillery to seek out is the Grandval Calvados Distillery, in **Cambremer.**

Lisieux

40 *25 km (16 mi) northeast of St-Pierre-sur-Dives via D511, 82 km (51 mi) southwest of Rouen.*

Lisieux is the main market town of the prosperous Pays d'Auge, an agricultural region famous for cheeses named after such towns as Camembert, Pont l'Évêque, and Livarot. It is also a land of apple orchards whose fruit is used for the finest calvados. Although Lisieux emerged relatively unscathed from World War II, it has few historic monuments beyond the 12th- and 13th-century **Cathédrale St-Pierre.** (The tower to the left of the imposing facade is later than it looks—it's a rare example of 17th-century neo-Gothic reconstruction.) ✉ *Pl. François-Mitterrand,* ☎ *02–31–62–09–82.*

The town's fame stems from St. Theresa (1873–97), who came to Lisieux as a child, joined a convent at 15, and spent the last 10 years of her life as a Carmelite nun. Theresa was canonized in 1925, and in 1954 the **Basilique Ste-Thérèse**—one of the world's largest 20th-century churches, with a huge dome and an interior of colored marble—was built in her honor. From the cathedral walk up avenue Victor-Hugo and branch left onto avenue Jean-XXIII. A **son-et-lumière** show, running through 2,000 years of history, is presented at the basilica Monday–Saturday nights at 9:45 from June to September. The **Procession de la Vierge** (Virgin's Procession) is held on August 15. The **Procession de la Fête Ste-Thérèse** (St. Theresa's Day Parade) is on the last Sunday in September. ✉ *Av. Jean-XXIII,* ☎ *02–31–78–52–62.* 🎫 *Son-et-lumière €6.*

Dining and Lodging

$–$$ ✕🏨 **Grand Hôtel de l'Espérance.** This imposing Art Deco hotel in the center of town has a typically subdued Norman elegance with its exposed beams and small balconies. Rooms are clean, simple, and, despite the location, quiet. The Pays d'Auge restaurant, on the first floor, has a traditional menu with regional specialties like seafood terrine, leg of duck with apple, and sole flamed in calvados. ✉ *16 bd. St-Anne,* ☎ *02–31–62–17–53,* FAX *02–21–62–34–00,* WEB *www.lisieux-hotel.com. 100 rooms. Restaurant, no air-conditioning, cable TV, Internet. AE, DC, MC, V. Closed Nov.–Mar.*

Bernay

41 *32 km (20 mi) southeast of Lisieux via N13/D138.*

It may be off some tourist tracks, but Bernay is well worth seeking out for its narrow, half-timbered streets lined by canals formed by the arms of the Cosnier and Charentonne Rivers; its majestic Romanesque **Eglise Abbatiale** (abbey church), which has been sparklingly restored for use as an exhibit center; and the lovably old-fashioned town museum, with its earnest array of paintings and ceramics.

Eight miles southeast of Bernay lies the early 17th-century **Château de Beaumesnil,** one of the most grandiose constructions in Normandy: a stripey wedding cake of brick and stone whose ski-slope roofs soar above a moat with a Baroque boxwood maze, set within 100 acres of parkland designed by Jean-Baptiste de la Quintinye, Le Nôtre's assistant at Versailles. The interior is famed for its sumptuous library and permanent exhibit on the art of bookbinding. ☎ *02–32–44–40–09,* 🎫 *€5.80,* ⏲ *Apr.–June and Sept., Fri.–Mon. 2–6; July-Aug., Wed.–Mon. 10–noon and 2–6.*

Évreux

42 *59 km (37 mi) east of Bernay via D133/D31, 100 km (62 mi) northwest of Paris via A13 and N13.*

From the 5th century on, Évreux, capital of the Eure *département* (province), was ravaged and burned by a succession of armies—first the Vandals, followed by the Normans, the English, and various French kings. World War II played its part as well. But the town, crisscrossed by the Iton River and known as the City of 100 Bridges, has been embellished with gardens and calm, overgrown footpaths.

Évreux's principal historic site is the **Cathédrale Notre-Dame,** in the heart of town just off rue Corbeau. Unfortunately, it was an easy victim of the many fires and raids that took place over the centuries; all that's left of the original 12th-century construction are the nave arcades. The lower parts of the chancel date from 1260, the chapels from the 14th century. Yet it's an outstanding example of Flamboyant Gothic inside and out. Don't miss the choir triforium and transept, the 14th-century stained-glass windows in the apse, and the entrance to the fourth chapel. ✉ *Pl. Notre-Dame,* ☎ *02–32–33–06–57.*

NORMANDY A TO Z

To research prices, get advice from other travelers, and book travel arrangements, visit www.fodors.com.

AIR TRAVEL

CARRIERS

Air France flies to Caen from Paris. Buzz flies from Rouen to London's Stansted airport.

➤ AIRLINES AND CONTACTS: **Air France** (☎ 08–02–80–28–02 for information, www.air-france.com). **Buzz** (WEB www.buzzaway.com for information).

AIRPORTS

Paris's Charles de Gaulle (Roissy) and Orly airports are the closest intercontinental links with the region. From London there are regular flights to Caen and Deauville on Air France; and from Southampton and the Channel Islands to Cherbourg

➤ AIRPORT INFORMATION: **Caen** (☎ 02–31–71–20–10). **Cherbourg** (☎ 02–33–88–57–60). **Deauville** (☎ 02–31–65–65–65). **Rouen** (☎ 02–35–79–41–00).

BIKE AND MOPED TRAVEL

You can rent bicycles at most major train stations for about €8 per day. Traveling with your bike is free on all regional trains and many national lines; be sure to ask the SNCF which ones when you're booking.

BOAT AND FERRY TRAVEL

A number of ferry companies sail between the United Kingdom and ports in Normandy. Brittany Ferries travels between Caen (Ouistreham) and Portsmouth and between Poole and Cherbourg. The Dieppe-Newhaven route is covered both by boat, with a daily service from Transmanche, and by Hoverspeed, which runs daily in summer, weekends only in winter (and not at all January–mid-February). P&O goes between Le Havre and Portsmouth and between Cherbourg and Portsmouth.

FARES AND SCHEDULES

➤ BOAT AND FERRY INFORMATION: **Brittany Ferries** (☎ 08–03–82–88–28, WEB www.brittany-ferries.com). **Hoverspeed** (☎ 08–20–00–35–55, WEB www.hoverspeed.com). **P&O** (☎ 08–03–01–30–13, WEB www.poportsmouth.com). **Transmanche** (☎ 08–00–65–01–00, WEB www.transmancheferries.com).

BUS TRAVEL

Three main bus systems cover the towns not served by trains. **CNA** (Compagnie Normande Autobus) runs around Upper Normandy from Rouen to the towns along the Côte d'Albatre, including Le Havre. **Autos-Cars Gris** runs buses from Fécamp to Le Havre, stopping in Étretat along the way. **Bus Verts du Calvados** covers the coast from Honfleur to Bayeux; They also run, during July and August, the special D-Day Circuit 44, which allows you to see as many D-Day sights as you can squeeze into one day—these buses depart from the train stations in Bayeux and Caen.

Bus routes connect many towns, including Rouen, Dieppe, Fécamp, Etretat, Le Havre, Caen, Honfleur, Deauville, Trouville, Cabourg, and Arromanches. For Mont-St-Michel, hook up with buses from nearby Pontorson or from Rennes in adjacent Brittany. Tourist offices and train stations in the region will have printed schedules.
➤ BUS INFORMATION: **CNA** (☏ 02–35–52–92–92). **Autos-Cars Gris** (☏ 02–35–28–19–88). **Bus Verts du Calvados** (☏ 02–31–44–77–44).

CAR RENTAL

➤ LOCAL AGENCIES: **Avis** (✉ 44 pl. de la Gare, Caen, ☏ 02–31–84–73–80; ✉ 32 av. de Caen, Rouen, ☏ 02–35–72–64–32). **Europcar** (✉ 6 rue du Docteur-Piasecki, Le Havre, ☏ 02–35–25–21–95).

CAR TRAVEL

From Paris A13 slices its way to Rouen in 1½ hours (toll €4) before forking to Caen (an additional hour, toll €6) or Le Havre (45 minutes on A131). N13 continues from Caen to Cherbourg via Bayeux in another two hours. From Paris, D915, the scenic route, will take you to Dieppe in about three hours.

The Pont de Normandie, between Le Havre and Honfleur, effectively unites Upper and Lower Normandy. A13/N13, linking Rouen to Caen, Bayeux, and Cherbourg, is the backbone of Normandy. At Caen the A84 forks off southwest toward Mont-St-Michel and Rennes.

EMERGENCIES

➤ CONTACTS: **Regional hospitals** (✉ Av. de la Côte-de-Nacre, Caen, ☏ 02–31–06–31–06; ✉ 29 av. Pierre-Mendès-France, Montivilliers, Le Havre, ☏ 02–32–73–32–32; ✉ 1 rue Germont, Rouen, ☏ 02–32–88–89–90).

OUTDOORS AND SPORTS

To find out about hiking trails in the region, contact the Comité Départemental de la Randonnée Pédestre de Seine-Maritime. For information about horseback riding, contact Ligue de Normandie des Sports Équestres. Call the Fédération Française de Canoë–Kayak to find out all there is to know about canoeing and kayaking in the region. For general information about saltwater and freshwater fishing in the region (including the best locations), contact the Conseil Superior de la Pêche.
➤ CANOEING AND KAYAKING: **Fédération Française de Canoë–Kayak** (✉ 87 quai de la Marne BP 58, 94340 Joinville-le-Pont, ☏ 01–48–89–39–89).
➤ FISHING: **Conseil Superior de la Pêche** (✉ 134 av. Malakoff, 75016 Paris, ☏ 01–45–02–20–20).
➤ HIKING: **Comité Départemental de la Randonnée Pédestre de Seine-Maritime** (✉ 18 rue Henri-Ferric, 76210 Gruchet-le-Valasse, ☏ 02–35–31–05–51).
➤ HORSEBACK RIDING: **Ligue de Normandie des Sports Équestres** (✉ 181 rue d'Auge, 14000 Caen, ☏ 02–31–84–61–87).

TOURS

The firm Wellcome arranges personalized driving tours with an English-speaking driver. Viking Voyages specializes in two-day packages by car, with overnight stays in private châteaux, as well as bike trips around the region and the Normandy Antiques tour by car. They can also meet travelers at Orly or Roissy airports.

➤ Fees and Schedules: **Wellcome** (✉ 130 rue Martainville, 76000 Rouen, ☎ 02–35–07–79–79). **Viking Voyages** (✉ 16 rue du Général-Giraud, 14000 Caen, ☎ 02–31–48–58–52, WEB www.viking-voyages.com).

BUS TOURS

Cityrama and Paris-Vision run full-day bus excursions from Paris to Mont-St-Michel for around €130–€150, meals and admission included. This is definitely not for the faint of heart—buses leave Paris at 7:15 AM and return around 10:30 PM. In Caen, Mémorial organizes four-hour English-language daily minibus tours of the D-Day landing beaches; the cost is €60, including entrance fees. Bus Fly runs a number of trips to the D-Day beaches and Mont-St-Michel; a full-day excursion to the D-Day beaches (8:30–6:00) runs about €55.

➤ Fees and Schedules: **Bus Fly** (✉ 25 rue des Cuisiniers, 14400 Bayeux, ☎ 02–31–22–00–08). **Cityrama** (✉ 4 pl. des Pyramides, 75001 Paris, ☎ 01–44–55–61–00). **Mémorial** (☎ 02–31–06–06–44). **Paris-Vision** (✉ 214 rue de Rivoli, 75001 Paris, ☎ 08–00–03–02–14).

TRAIN TRAVEL

From Paris (Gare St-Lazare), separate train lines head to Upper Normandy (Rouen and Le Havre or Dieppe) and Lower Normandy (Caen, Bayeux, and Cherbourg, via Évreux and Lisieux). Taking the train from Paris to Mont-St-Michel is not easy—count on about 3½ hours to get to the closest station (Pontorson), with another 15-minute bus ride to take you to the foot of the abbey (buses are directly in front of the station, with departures every 20 minutes).

Unless you are content to stick to the major towns (Rouen, Le Havre, Dieppe, Caen, Bayeux), visiting Normandy by train may prove frustrating. You can reach several smaller towns (Fécamp, Deauville, Cabourg) on snail-paced branch lines, but the intricacies of what is said to be Europe's most complicated regional timetable will probably have driven you nuts by the time you get there.

➤ Train Information: **SNCF** (☎ 08–36–35–35–35, WEB www.sncf.com).

TRAVEL AGENCIES

➤ Local Agent Referrals: **Havas–American Express** (✉ 57 quai George-V, Le Havre, ☎ 02–32–74–75–76; ✉ 25 Grande-Rue, Alençon, ☎ 02–33–82–59–00; ✉ 80 rue St-Jean, Caen, ☎ 02–31–27–10–50).

VISITOR INFORMATION

Each of Normandy's major *départements*—Caen, Évreux, Rouen, and St-Lô—has its own central tourist office. Other major Norman towns with tourist offices are listed below the département offices by name.

➤ Tourist Information: **Caen** (✉ Pl. du Canada, ☎ 02–31–27–90–30, FAX 02–31–27–90–35, WEB www.ville-caen.fr) for Calvados. **Évreux** (✉ Bd. Georges-Chauvin, ☎ 02–32–31–51–51, FAX 02–32–31–05–98, WEB www.normandy-tourism.org) for Eure. **Rouen** (✉ 6 rue de la Couronne, B.P. 60 Bihorel Cedex, ☎ 02–35–12–10–10, FAX 02–35–59–86–04, WEB www.mairie-rouen.fr) for Seine-Maritime. **St-Lô** (✉ Maison du Département, rte. de Villedieu, ☎ 02–33–05–98–70, WEB www.manchetourism.com) for Manche.

Bayeux (✉ Pont St-Jean, ☎ 02–31–51–28–28, WEB www.bayeux-tourism.com). **Cherbourg** (✉ 2 quai Alexandre-III, ☎ 02–33–93–52–02). **Dieppe** (✉ Pont Jehan-An, ☎ 02–35–84–11–77, WEB www.cherbourg-channel.tm.fr). **Fécamp** (✉ 113 rue Alexandre-le-Grand, ☎ 02–35–28–51–01, WEB www.fecamp.com). **Falaise** (✉ Le Forum, bd. de la Libération, ☎

02–31–90–17–26, WEB www.otsifalaise.fr). Le Havre (✉ 186 bd. Clemenceau, ☎ 02–32–74–04–04, WEB www.ville-lehavre.fr). **Honfleur** (✉ 9 rue de la Ville, ☎ 02–31–89–23–30, WEB www.ville-honfleur.fr). **Lisieux** (✉ 11 rue d'Alençon, ☎ 02–31–62–08–41, WEB www.ville-lisieux.fr). **Mont-St-Michel** (✉ Corps de Garde, ☎ 02–33–60–14–30, WEB www.mont-saintmichel.com).

➤ TOURIST INFORMATION: **Caen** (✉ Pl. du Canada, ☎ 02–31–27–90–30, FAX 02–31–27–90–35) for Calvados. **Évreux** (✉ Bd. Georges-Chauvin, ☎ 02–32–31–51–51, FAX 02–32–31–05–98) for Eure. **Rouen** (✉ 6 rue de la Couronne, B.P. 60 Bihorel Cedex, ☎ 02–35–12–10–10, FAX 02–35–59–86–04) for Seine-Maritime. **St-Lô** (✉ Maison du Département, rte. de Villedieu, ☎ 02–33–05–98–70) for Manche.

Bayeux (✉ Pont St-Jean, ☎ 02–31–51–28–28). **Cherbourg** (✉ 2 quai Alexandre-III, ☎ 02–33–93–52–02). **Dieppe** (✉ Pont Jehan-An, ☎ 02–35–84–11–77). **Fécamp** (✉ 113 rue Alexandre-le-Grand, ☎ 02–35–28–51–01). **Falaise** (✉ Le Forum, bd. de la Libération, ☎ 02–31–90–17–26). **Le Havre** (✉ 186 bd. Clemenceau, ☎ 02–32–74–04–04). **Honfleur** (✉ 9 rue de la Ville, ☎ 02–31–89–23–30). **Lisieux** (✉ 11 rue d'Alençon, ☎ 02–31–62–08–41). **Mont-St-Michel** (✉ Corps de Garde, ☎ 02–33–60–14–30).

7 THE NORTH AND CHAMPAGNE

France's northernmost out-thrust shows its Flemish roots in a Brueghelesque landscape, cozy Old Master interiors, and a violent history worthy of the images of Hieronymus Bosch, from the battle of Agincourt to the battle of the Somme. Add a concentration of six spectacular Gothic cathedrals, fine Flemish art in Lille, the fairy-tale forests of the Ardennes, broad beaches, and Reims—the capital of bubbly—and you'll find that this overlooked region merits exploration.

Revised and updated by Nicola Keegan

Introduction by Nancy Coons

FLAT AS A CREPE AS FAR AS THE EYE CAN SEE and shimmering with hoarfrost, magpies wheeling over gnarl-fingered trees, and white-brick cottages punctuating an otherwise uninterrupted sight line to the horizon: this is the landscape of the north of France, an evocative canvas that conjures up the great 16th-century paintings of Pieter Brueghel and reflects, as no history book can, how closely married this corner of France was—and is—to Flanders. Here, as in Belgium and the Netherlands, the iron grip of the Spanish Inquisition sent thinkers and threshers alike scrambling for cover. Here, also, numerous woolen mills spun the stuff of epic tapestries. And here, as well, the ill humors of the flatland air drove a people and a culture into golden, firelit Vermeer interiors to seek comfort, as did their brethren to the east, in steaming platters of *moules-frites* (mussels and french fries), a mug of amber beer, and a warming swallow of juniper gin.

The landscape recalls images relentlessly epic: Medieval stoneworkers in fingerless gloves raised radically new Gothic arches to improbable heights, running for cover when the naves failed to stand, while in the region's industrial areas the hollow-eyed miners immortalized in Emile Zola's *Germinal* descended into hellish black-coal portals. In Compiègne, Joan of Arc languished in prison after suffering wounds in mounted battle with the English. At Agincourt, Henry V rallied the British to gory victory, temporarily reversing William the Norseman's 349-year-long conquest. And in the Somme, wave upon wave of doughboy infantry slogged through the bomb-torn countryside to gain, lose, and ultimately regain a scrap of land.

Most people give the north of France a wide berth, roaring through the Channel ports at Boulogne and Calais on a beeline for Paris, en route to the south for a sunshine cure. But this underappreciated region, with its chiaroscuro of bleak exteriors and interior warmth, conceals treasures of art, architecture, history, and natural beauty that reward slow and pleasurable study. Just an hour's trip from Paris on the TGV, Lille beckons with its Musée des Beaux-Arts, whose collections of Old Masters are worthy in scale of the capital's. There are no less than six cathedrals, all still standing (though you might want to hover near the exits at Beauvais, whose nave, the tallest in France, makes some engineers nervous) and worth a visit. You may choose to relax on the relatively uncrowded beaches that wrap the coast from Dunkerque to the Bay of the Somme, or to wander through World War I battlefields and cemeteries whose scale is imponderable.

And then you can recover with Champagne. Head southeast toward Reims, and the sky clears, the landscape loosens and undulates, and the hills tantalize with the vineyards that produce the world's antidote to gloom, *à la méthode champenoise*. Between tasting tours at Reims and Epernay, you can contemplate Reims Cathedral, where Clovis was baptized and to which St. Joan dragged a recalcitrant Dauphin to be crowned. Or lose yourself in the dense forests of the Ardennes—Ozark-like highlands concealing châteaux, fortresses, and succulent game. No wonder more and more British are using the Channel Tunnel to visit northern France for day and weekend trips.

Pleasures and Pastimes

Beaches

From Dunkerque to the Bay of the Somme is the Côte d'Opale, one long, sandy beach. It's sometimes short of sun, but not of space or beach sports, like *char à voile* (sand sailing), involving windsurfing boards on wheels that race along the sands at up to 110 kph (70 mph). The climate is bracing, often windy, but there are wonderfully scenic spots along the cliffs south of Calais: Cap Gris Nez and Cap Blanc Nez. Le Touquet is one of France's fanciest coastal resort towns; Le Crotoy, Wimereux, and Hardelot are more family oriented.

Champagne

The world's most famous sparkling wine comes from France's northernmost vineyards, along the towering Marne Valley between Épernay and Château-Thierry and on the slopes of the Montagne de Reims between Épernay and Reims. Champagne firms, in these two towns and in Ay, welcome you into their chalky, mazelike cellars. You can also visit the tomb of Dom Pérignon, the inventor of champagne, in Hautvillers.

Churches and Cathedrals

Northern France contains many of France's most remarkable Gothic cathedrals: Amiens, the largest; Beauvais, the tallest; Noyon, the earliest; Abbeville, the last; Reims, the most regal; and Laon, with the most towers (and the most spectacular hilltop setting). The region's smaller churches are also admirable—the intricate stonework of Rue and L'Épine; the ruined drama of Mont St-Eloi; the modern stained glass of Mézières; and the Baroque brickwork of Asfeld.

Dining

The cuisine of northern France is robust and hearty. In Flanders beer is often used as a base for sauces. French fries and mussels are featured on most menus; vans selling fries and hot dogs are a common sight; and large quantities of mussels and fish, notably herring, are consumed. Smoked ham and, in season, boar and venison are specialties of the Ardennes. In the eastern part of the region, sample creamy cheeses like the soft, square *Maroilles,* with its orange rind, and the spicy, pyramid-shape *boulette d'Avesnes.* To satisfy your sweet tooth, try the macaroons and *bêtises de Cambrai* (minty lollipops) in Flanders. Ham, pigs' feet, gingerbread, and champagne-based mustard are specialties of the Reims area, as is ratafia, a sweet aperitif made from grape juice and brandy. To the north, a glass of *genièvre* (gin flavored with juniper berries, which is sometimes added to black coffee to make a *bistouille*) is the classic way to finish a meal.

CATEGORY	COST*
$$$$	over €30
$$$	€20–€30
$$	€12–€20
$	under €12

**per person for a main course only, including tax (19.6%) and service; note that if a restaurant offers only prix-fixe (set-price) meals, it has been given the price category that reflects the full prix-fixe price.*

Lodging

Northern France is overladen with old, rambling hotels, often simple rather than pretentious; there are also luxurious châteaux with fine restaurants. Top quality is hard to come by, except in major cities such as Lille and Reims, or in Le Touquet, where the Westminster Hotel numbers among the country's best. Assume all hotel rooms have air-conditioning, TV, telephones, and private bath unless otherwise noted. Internet, when listed in facilities, means in-room data-ports and/or public-area computer provides computer access

CATEGORY	COST*
$$$$	over €180
$$$	€120–€180
$$	€60–€120
$	under €60

**All prices are for a standard double room in high season, including tax (19.6%) and service charge.*

War Memorials

Cemeteries and war memorials may not be the most cheerful destinations on your itinerary, but they do have a melancholy, thought-provoking beauty. Northern France was in the frontline of battle during World War I and suffered heavily. The city of Reims was shelled incessantly, and such names as Somme and Vimy Ridge evoke the bloody, deadlocked battles that raged between 1914 and 1918.

Exploring the North and Champagne

The region commonly referred to as northern France stretches from the Somme River up to the Channel Tunnel and includes the vibrant city of Lille, to the northeast. Champagne encompasses Reims and the surrounding vineyards and chalky plains. Picardy, to the south of the region, is traversed by the Aisne and Oise rivers. The hills and forests of the Ardennes lead northeast toward Belgium.

The north of France has a shared history with Flemish-speaking territories. Lille, France's northern metropolis, is the capital of what is known as French Flanders, which stretches northwest from the city to the coastal areas around Dunkerque and Gravelines. West and north of Lille extends the Côte d'Opale, the Channel coastline so named for the color of its sea and sky. To the southeast the grapes of champagne flourish on the steep slopes of the Marne Valley and the Montagne de Reims, really more of a mighty hill than a mountain. Reims is the only city in Champagne—and one of France's richest tourist sites.

Great Itineraries

Count on at least a week to do justice to this vast and varied region, starting at Beauvais, north of Paris, and ending in the Ardennes. Five days will give you time to explore Lille and Arras before heading south to Reims. If you have only three days, just concentrate on the most scenic attractions of Picardy and Champagne.

IF YOU HAVE 3 DAYS

Numbers in the text correspond to numbers in the margin and on the maps for the North; Champagne and the Ardennes; Lille; and Reims.

Start in **Compiègne** ㊳ at its elegant palace, and then head to **Pierrefonds** ㊴ and its storybook castle. By dinnertime be in the hilltop cathedral town of **Laon** ㉝. After touring Laon the next morning, drive to the city that is home to one of France's grandest cathedrals, **Reims** ㊹–52, for the afternoon, the night, and maybe part of the third morning. Make the Champagne vineyards to the south—on the Montagne de Reims, along the Route du Vin, and in the steeply terraced Marne Valley west of **Épernay** ㊶—your final destination.

IF YOU HAVE 5 DAYS

Begin with a day in the vibrant city of **Lille** ⑬–㉔. The next morning take in stately **Arras** ㉘ and the moving war cemeteries nearby en route to princely **Compiègne** ㊳. Devote day three to the medieval splendor of **Pierrefonds** ㊴ and **Laon** ㉝ and day four to **Reims** ㊹–52. Spend your last day touring the Montagne de Reims and the Route du Vin, and then head east from **Épernay** ㊶ to the historic town of **Châlons-en-Champagne** ㊷.

IF YOU HAVE 8 DAYS

Venture along the cliffs from the Channel Tunnel to the historic Upper Town of **Boulogne-sur-Mer** ⑨. If you want to go to the beach, head down the coast to the Victorian-era resort of **Le Touquet** ⑧ and rejoin the itinerary at Amiens. If you prefer history and culture, head inland from Boulogne to **Lille** ⑬–㉔ for the night and following morning. That afternoon go south to **Arras** ㉘. On day four cross the **Somme battlefields,** ending the day in the cathedral city of **Amiens** ②. The next day visit **Beauvais** ①, home to France's tallest cathedral as well as a fine tapestry museum; then go east to **Compiègne** ㊳ and its famous palace. Spend day six at the fairy-tale castle of **Pierrefonds** ㊴ and in **Laon** ㉝. On day seven head northeast into the Ardennes to explore historic **Reims** ㊹–(52). On day eight head to the champagne vineyards south of Reims en route to **Châlons-en-Champagne** ㊷ and the fine hotel-restaurant by the basilica in nearby **L'Épine** ㊸.

When to Tour the North and Champagne

Compared to many other regions of France, the north remains relatively uncrowded in July and August, and the huge Channel beaches have room for everyone. The liveliest time in Lille is the first weekend in September, during its three-day street fair, La Grande Braderie. Other local fairs include the Dunkerque Carnival, in February, and the Giants' Carnival, in Douai in July. Make sure to plan a visit to Reims and Champagne between May and October; the region's ubiquitous vineyards are a dismal, leafless sight the rest of the year. The wooded Ardennes is attractive in fall, when local game highlights area menus.

THE NORTH

Starting with Beauvais and Amiens (both easily accessible by expressway from Paris) and two of France's most splendorous Gothic cathedrals, follow the Somme Valley to the Channel. Unfortunately, the ports of Calais and Dunkerque are among France's uglier towns, but the old sections of Boulogne-sur-Mer have scenic appeal, as do the narrow streets of ancient Montreuil and the posh avenues of fashionable Le Touquet. After wheeling inland to church-and-museum-rich Lille, head south to the World War I battlefields between Arras and Albert, continuing southeast into Picardy and its hilltop castles and cathedrals.

Beauvais

❶ *80 km (50 mi) north of Paris.*

Beauvais and its neighbor Amiens have been rivals since the 13th century, when they locked horns over who could build the bigger cathedral. Beauvais lost—but gloriously.

A work-in-progress preserved for all time, soaring above the characterless modern blocks of the town center, is the tallest cathedral in France: ★ the **Cathédrale St-Pierre.** You may have an attack of vertigo just gazing up at its vaults, 153 ft above the ground. It may be the tallest, but it's not the largest. Paid for by the riches of Beauvais's wool industry, the choir collapsed in 1284, shortly after completion, and was only rebuilt with the addition of extra pillars. This engineering fiasco proved so costly that the transept was not attempted until the 16th century. It was obviously worth the wait: The transept is an outstanding example of Flamboyant Gothic, with ornate rose windows flanked by pinnacles and turrets. It is also still standing—which is more than can be said for the megalomaniacal 450-ft spire erected at the same time. This lasted precisely four years; when it came crashing down, damaging the transept, all remaining funds were hurled at an emergency consolidation program, and Beauvais's dream of having the largest church in Christendom vanished forever. Now the cathedral is starting to lean, and cracks have appeared in the choir vaults because of shifting water levels in the soil. No such problems bedevil the **Basse Oeuvre** (Lower Edifice; closed to the public), which juts out impertinently where the nave should have been. It has been there for 1,000 years. Fittingly donated to the cathedral by the canon Étienne Musique, the oldest surviving **chiming clock** in the world—a 1302 model with a 15th-century painted wooden face and most of its original clockwork—is built into the wall of the cathedral. Perhaps Auguste Verité drew his inspiration from this humbler timepiece when, in 1868, he made a gift to his hometown of the gilded, templelike **astrological clock.** Animated religious figurines surrounded by all sorts of gears and dials emerge for their short program at erratic times, although there is a set schedule for visits with commentary. ✉ *Rue St-Pierre.* ⏲ *May–Oct., daily 9–12:15 and 2–6:15; Nov.–Apr., daily 9–12:15 and 2–5:30.*

From 1664 to 1939 Beauvais was one of France's leading tapestry centers; it reached its zenith in the mid-18th century under the gifted artist Jean-Baptiste Oudry, known for his hunting scenes. Examples from all periods are in the modern **Galerie Nationale de la Tapisserie** (National Museum of Tapestry). ✉ *1 rue St-Pierre,* ☎ *03–44–15–39–10.* 🎟 *€3.95.* ⏲ *Apr.–Sept., Tues.–Sun. 9:30–11:30 and 2–6; Oct.–Mar., Tues.–Sun. 10–11:30 and 2:30–4:30.*

One of the few remaining testaments to Beauvais's glorious past, the old Bishop's Palace is now the **Musée Départemental de l'Oise** (Oise Museum). Don't miss the beautifully proportioned top floor, Thomas Couture's epic canvas of the French Revolution, the 14th-century frescoes of instrument-playing sirens on a section of the palace's vaults, or the 1st-century brass *Guerrier Gaulois* (Gallic Warrior). ✉ *1 rue du Musée,* ☎ *03–44–11–43–83.* 🎟 *€2, free Wed.* ⏲ *Wed.–Mon. 10–noon and 2–6.*

Amiens

❷ *58 km (36 mi) north of Beauvais via N1 or A16.*

Although Amiens showcases some pretty brazen postwar reconstruction, epitomized by Auguste Perret's 340-ft Tour Perret, a soaring concrete stump by the train station, the city is still worth exploring. It has lovely Art Deco buildings in its traffic-free city center, as well as elegant, older stone buildings like the 18th-century Beffroi (belfry) and Neoclassical prefecture. Crowning the city is its great Gothic cathedral, which has survived the ages intact. Nearby is the waterfront quarter of St-Leu—with its small, colorful houses—still rivaling the old city center in Lille as the cutest city district north of Paris.

★ By far the largest church in France, the **Cathédrale Notre-Dame** could enclose Paris's Notre-Dame twice. It may lack the stained glass of Chartres or the sculpture of Reims, but for architectural harmony, engineering proficiency, and sheer size, it is without peer. The soaring, asymmetrical facade of the cathedral has a notable Flamboyant Gothic rose window. Inside, there is no stylistic disunity to mar the perspective, creating an overwhelming sensation of pure space. Construction took place between 1220 and 1264, a remarkably short period in cathedral building spans. One of the highlights of a visit here is hidden from the eye, at least until you lift up some of the 110 choir-stall seats and admire the humorous, skillful misericord (seat) carvings executed between 1508 and 1518. ✉ *Pl. Notre-Dame,* ☎ *03–22–91–72–08.* 🎟 *Free.*

The North and Champagne

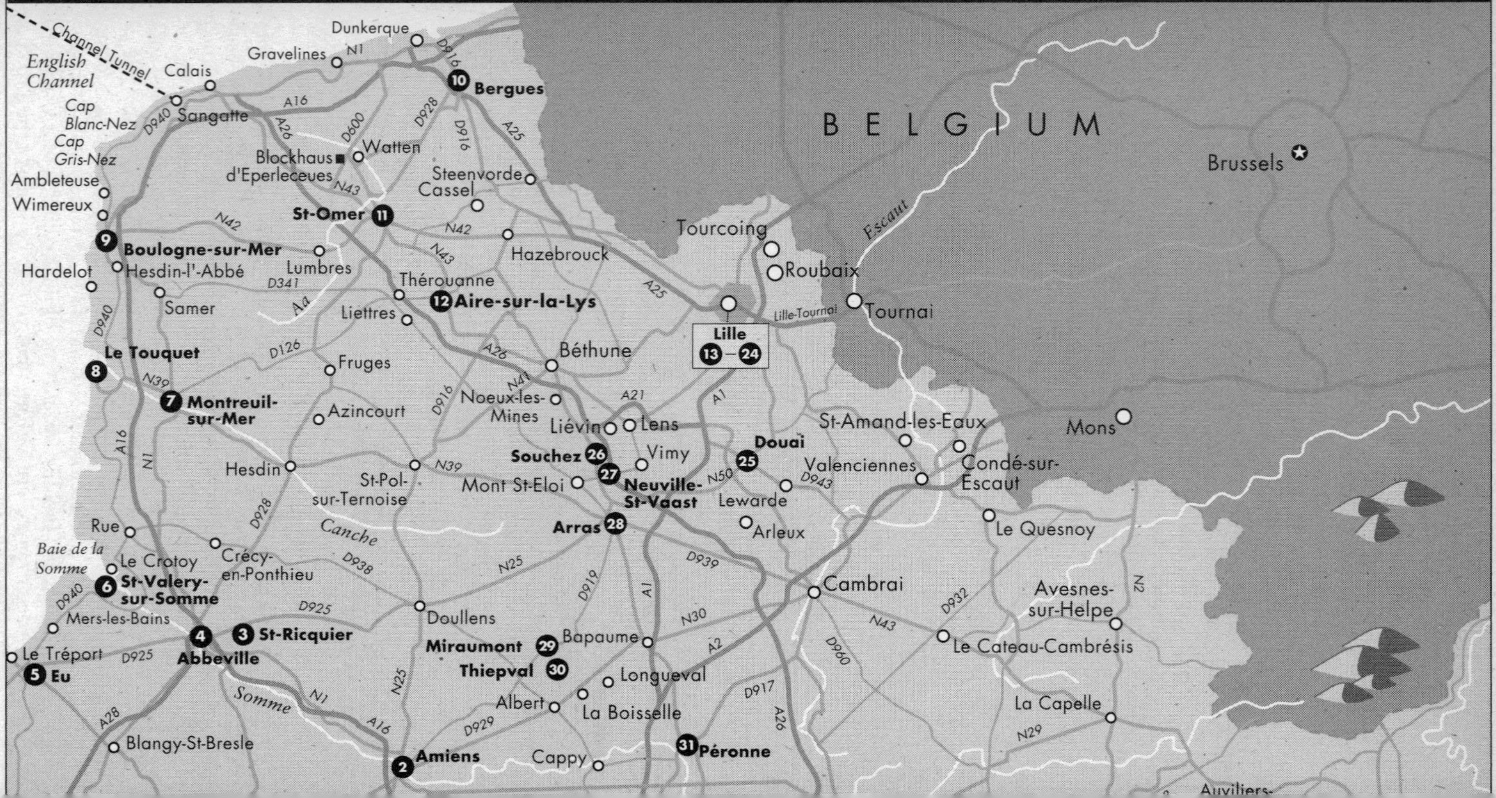

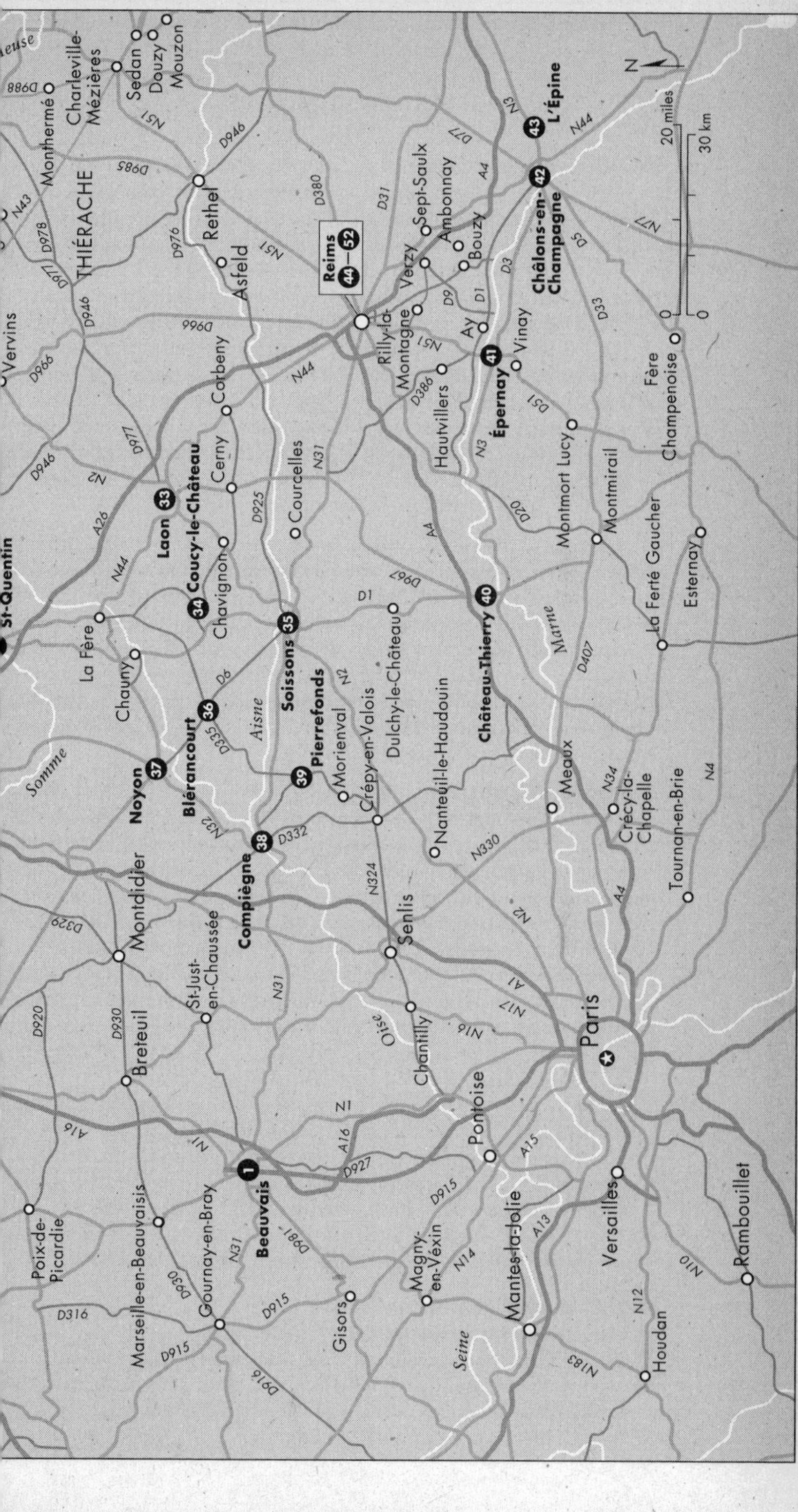
St-Quentin
Vervins
THIÉRACHE
Monthermé
Charleville-Mézières
Sedan
Douzy
Mouzon
Rethel
Asfeld
Reims
44—52
Rilly-la-Montagne
Verzy
Sept-Saulx
Ambonnay
Bouzy
Ay
Hautvillers
Épernay
41
Vinay
Châlons-en-Champagne
42
43
L'Épine
Fère Champenoise
Montmort Lucy
Montmirail
La Ferté Gaucher
Esternay
Laon
33
Coucy-le-Château
34
Corbeny
Cerny
Courcelles
Chavignon
La Fère
Chauny
Soissons
35
Pierrefonds
39
Morienval
Crépy-en-Valois
Dulchy-le-Château
Nanteuil-le-Haudouin
Château-Thierry
40
Meaux
Crécy-la-Chapelle
Tournan-en-Brie
Noyon
37
Blérancourt
36
Compiègne
38
Montdidier
St-Just-en-Chaussée
Senlis
Chantilly
Paris
Breteuil
Poix-de-Picardie
Marseille-en-Beauvaisis
Gournay-en-Bray
Beauvais
1
Pontoise
Gisors
Magny-en-Véxin
Mantes-la-Jolie
Versailles
Rambouillet
Houdan
Meuse
Somme
Aisne
Oise
Marne
Seine
N
0
20 miles
0
30 km
D968
N51
D985
N43
D978
D977
D976
D946
D966
D380
D31
D77
N3
A4
N44
N77
D5
D3
D1
D9
D386
N31
D925
D33
D51
D20
A26
N2
D967
D6
D335
D332
N32
D407
N34
N4
N330
N324
A1
N17
N16
D329
D930
D920
A16
N1
D927
A15
D915
D981
D316
D930
D916
N14
A13
N12
N10
N183

The **Hôtel de Berny,** near the cathedral, is a steep-roof stone-and-brick mansion built in 1633. It's filled with 18th-century furniture, tapestries, and objets d'art. ✉ *34 rue Victor-Hugo,* ☎ *03–22–91–81–12.* *€1.50.* ⏲ *Oct.–mid-Apr., Sun. 10–12:30 and 2–6; mid-Apr.–Sept., Thurs.–Sun. 1–6.*

★ Behind an opulent columned facade, the **Musée de Picardie,** built 1855–67, looks like just another pompous offering from the Second Empire. Initial impressions are hardly challenged by its grand staircase lined with monumental frescoes by local-born Puvis de Chavannes, or its central hall with huge canvases, like Gérôme's 1855 *Siècle d'Auguste* and Maignon's 1892 *Mort de Carpeaux,* with flying muses wresting the dying sculptor from his earthly clay. One step beyond, though, and you're in a rotunda painted top to bottom in modern minimalist fashion by Sol LeWitt in 1992. The basement is filled with subtly lighted archaeological finds and Egyptian artifacts beneath masterly brick vaulting. On the top floor, El Greco leads the Old Masters, along with a humorous set of hunting scenes like Boucher's rococo-framed *Crocodile Hunt,* from 1736. ✉ *48 rue de la République,* ☎ *03–22–97–14–00.* *€3, free Sun.* ⏲ *Tues.–Sun. 10–12:30 and 2–6.*

Jules Verne (1828–1905) lived in Amiens for some 35 years, and his former home has become the **Centre de Documentation Jules Verne** (✉ 2 rue Charles-Dubois, ☎ 03–22–45–37–84). It contains some 15,000 documents about Verne's life as well as original furniture and a reconstruction of the writing studio where he created his science-fiction classics. If you're a true Verne fan, you might want to visit his last resting place in the **Cimetière de la Madeleine** (✉ 2 rue de la Poudrière), where he is melodramatically portrayed pushing up his tombstone as if enacting his own sci-fi resurrection.

Dining and Lodging

$$–$$$ ★ ✕ **Les Marissons.** In the scenic St-Leu section of Amiens, beneath the cathedral, this picturesque waterside restaurant serves creative takes on regional ingredients: burbot with apricots, rabbit with mint and goat cheese, and pigeon with black currants. To avoid pricey dining à la carte, order from the prix-fixe menus. ✉ *68 rue des Marissons,* ☎ *03–22–92–96–66. Jacket and tie. AE, DC, MC, V. Closed Sun. No lunch Sat.*

$$ ✕ **Joséphine.** Despite its unprepossessing facade and drab front room, this good-value restaurant in central Amiens is a reliable choice. It serves solid fare and has decent wines and a back room overlooking a garden courtyard. ✉ *20 rue Sire-Firmin-Leroux,* ☎ *03–22–91–47–38. AE, MC, V. Closed Mon. and 3rd wk in Aug. No dinner Sun.*

$$ 🏨 **Carlton.** This hotel near the train station has a stylish Belle Epoque facade. In contrast, rooms are sober and functional, though light and airy, with spacious bathrooms. Foreign guests are common, and English is spoken. The brasserie-style restaurant, Le Baron, does not serve dinner Sunday. ✉ *42 rue de Noyon, 80000,* ☎ *03–22–97–72–22,* FAX *03–22–97–72–00,* WEB *www.lecarlton.fr. 24 rooms. Restaurant, no air-conditioning, some pets allowed (€6.50 fee). AE, MC, V.*

Nightlife and the Arts

The **Théâtre de Marionnettes** (✉ 31 rue Edouard-David, ☎ 03–22–22–30–90) presents a rare glimpse of the traditional Picardy marionettes, known locally as *Chès Cabotans d'Amiens.* Shows are performed (in French), usually on Friday evening and Sunday afternoon (daily in August), with plot synopses printed in English.

St-Riquier

❸ *37 (23 mi) northwest of Amiens via N1 and D32.*

★ The tumbling village of St-Riquier is dominated by its imposing abbey church. Magnificent **St-Riquier** has a majestic Flamboyant Gothic facade with a superbly sculpted 160-ft tower (illuminated on Friday and Saturday evenings), a 100-yard-long nave, and handsome 17th-century wrought-iron gates at the front of the choir.

Lodging

$$ **Jean de Bruges.** The 1473 abbot's house next to the church has been transformed into a small, stylish hotel owned by the folks who run the neighboring Bernadette-Stubbe wine tavern. Gleaming marble floors, white stonework, cream-color curtains, designer lighting, old carved furniture, and impressive modern art throughout make for stylish accents. Ask for airy Room 2, or Room 8, with a small terrace; all are named for former abbots. The glass-roof breakfast room leads to a patio used for afternoon tea. Unfortunately there's no restaurant—either here or in the village. ✉ *18 pl. de l'Église, 80135,* ☎ *03–22–28–30–30,* FAX *03–22–28–00–69,* WEB *www.somme-tourisme.com.jdb.htm. 9 rooms. No air-conditioning in some rooms, minibars, some pets allowed. AE, MC, V. Closed Jan.*

Abbeville

❹ *9 km (6 mi) southwest of St-Riquier via D925, 43 km (27 mi) northwest of Amiens.*

The historic town of Abbeville was heavily reconstructed after being reduced to rubble in 1940. Its most admirable building is its Gothic church. Begun in 1488, **St-Vulfran** (✉ Rue St-Vulfran) was the last cathedral-size church to be constructed in the Gothic style. According to 19th-century art historian John Ruskin, it was here that Gothic "lay down and died." After decades of restoration, the riotous tracery and ornament of its much-mauled facade have been revived. The tall, elegant nave retains fine medieval stained glass. Work is still in progress on the 17th-century choir.

With typical Gallic flair, the derelict, war-ravaged Gothic church of **St-Sépulcre** was given a new lease on life in 1993, when local artist Alfred Manessier was commissioned to fit it out with 20 windows of nearly psychedelically hued stained glass. The effect is glorious. ✉ *Pl. St-Sépulcre.* *Free.* *June–Sept., daily 2–6.*

The **Musée Boucher de Perthes,** housed in a beefy medieval belfry, contains an eclectic collection of Gallo-Roman items, Vron earthenware, Camille Claudel bronzes, ornithological displays, and Old Master altarpieces. ✉ *24 rue Gonthier-Patin,* ☎ *03–22–24–08–49.* *Free.* *Wed.–Mon. 2–6.*

Dining

$ ✕ **Étoile du Jour.** Abbeville is no great gastronomic shakes, so you might as well check out the town's prettiest restaurant, with its open beams and split-level floors. A hearty steak is your best bet, with the local delicacy, a béchamel-smothered pancake called *ficelle picarde,* served piping hot as an appetizer. ✉ *2 chaussée Marcadé,* ☎ *03–22–24–06–90. MC, V. Closed Mon.*

Eu

❺ *28 km (18 mi) southwest of Abbeville via D925.*

Slightly inland from the English Channel, hilltop Eu is crowed by France's last royal residence: the stone-and-brick Renaissance **Château**

d'Eu, built between 1578 and 1665, was used as a summer palace by France's last king, Louis-Philippe of Orléans, who ruled from 1830 to 1848. In the château, along with the town hall, is the **Musée Louis-Philippe.** It evokes Eu's regal heyday—including two visits by Queen Victoria—but will be closed until 2003 for extensive renovations. ☎ *02–35–50–73–72.*

On the old streets of town, clustered around the stately Gothic **Collégiale** (Collegiate Church), are two outstanding 17th-century buildings, the **Chapelle des Jésuites** (Jesuit Chapel) and the **Hôtel-Dieu** (hospital).

St-Valery-sur-Somme

❻ *31 km (19 mi) northeast of Eu via D940.*

St-Valery-sur-Somme is a pretty fishing harbor (squid and shellfish are specialties) on the Baie de la Somme, with a shady seaside promenade, medieval fortifications, and the remains of St-Valery. The flint-and-sandstone-checkerboard 18th-century **Chapelle des Marins** (Mariners' Chapel), at the far end of the town's bayside promenade (where there are views of the Somme Estuary), houses the tomb of St-Valery. The wide sand flats of the **Baie de Somme** (Bay of the Somme) are a haven for wildlife—especially birds and sheep, which graze peacefully on the salt marshes.

A good overview of the Baie de Somme is provided by the **Chemin de Fer de la Baie de Somme** (steam railway). It chugs around the bay between St-Valery and Le Crotoy on an hour-long trip powered by a 130T locomotive that was used during construction of the Panama Canal. ✉ *Departs from St-Valery-sur-Somme and Le Crotoy train stations,* ☎ *03–22–26–96–96.* 🎫 *€9.25.* ⏲ *Apr.–June and Sept., Wed. and weekends departure 3:30 and return 5:30; July–Aug., Tues.–Sun. departure 3:30 and return 5:30; early Oct.–late Oct., Sun. departure 3:30 and return 5:30.*

The **Maison de l'Oiseau** (Bird Sanctuary), just west of St-Valery on D204 (in the direction of Cayeux-sur-Mer), has a collection of 400 stuffed birds, a video presentation about their local habitats, and occasional special appearances by live and happily obedient birds of prey. ✉ *Carrefour du Hourdel,* ☎ *03–22–26–93–93.* 🎫 *€9.25.* ⏲ *Mid-Feb.–June and Sept.–mid-Nov., daily 10–6; July–Aug., daily 10–7.*

Dining and Lodging

$–$$ ✕ **Parc aux Huîtres.** This large-windowed restaurant in Le Hourdel, on the south side of the bay, is an honest, unpretentious place to have a lunch of fresh seafood, starring oysters (*huîtres*), scallops, turbot, and lobster. Service is brisk and matter of fact: you're treated like a local, and that's a compliment. ✉ *Le Hourdel (8 km/5 mi from St-Valery),* ☎ *03–22–26–61–20. MC, V. Closed Wed. No dinner Tues.*

$$ ✕🏨 **Fiacre.** The Fiacre, an old coaching inn as its name suggests, exudes the unhurried charm of rural France with its whitewashed walls and steep, red-tiled roofs. Rooms are large and plainly furnished in light colors, and most overlook the garden with its pond and rose bushes. The restaurant, recalling an old farm kitchen with its giant hearth and massive oak furniture, has a wide choice of fish dishes (try the turbot with sorrel), game, and lamb from the Somme's salt-marshes. Breakfasts are pleasantly copious by French standards, with a ready supply of succulent homemade pastries. ✉ *Rue des Pommiers, Routhiauville, 80120 Quend (24 km/15 mi north of St-Valery on D940),* ☎ *03–22–23–47–30,* FAX *03–22–27–19–80. 11 rooms. MC, V. Closed mid-Jan.–mid-Feb.*

En Route The small town of **Rue,** 7 km (4 mi) north of St-Valery, is famed for its extravagantly sculpted **Chapelle du St-Esprit,** with lacelike stonework and star-patterned vaulting.

Montreuil-sur-Mer

❼ *38 km (24 mi) northeast of Le Crotoy via D940 and D917, 45 km (28 mi) northeast of St-Valery.*

Despite its seaside-sounding name, Montreuil-sur-Mer is 18 km (11 mi) inland. It was once a port, but the Canche River silted up and left it high and dry. The ancient town has majestic walls and ramparts, as well as a faded charm to which various authors, notably Victor Hugo, succumbed; an episode of *Les Misérables* is set here.

Wherever citadels and city walls loom in France, it's a fair bet that Vauban had a hand in their construction. Montreuil is no exception. First Errard de Bar-le-Duc and then Vauban supplemented the existing 16th-century towers of the **Citadelle.** ✉ *Rue Carnot,* ☎ *03–21–06–10–83.* *€2.50.* ⏲ *Nov.–Sept., Wed.–Mon. 9–11:30 and 2–5:30.*

OFF THE BEATEN PATH **AZINCOURT** – The Battle of Agincourt (Azincourt in French) took place 30 km (19 mi) east of Montreuil in October 1415, when Henry V's longbowmen defeated Charles VI's more numerous and heavily armored French troops. A museum, an orientation map, and a clearly marked 3-km (2-mi) trail recall the event.

Dining and Lodging

$$$–$$$$ ★ ✕ **Château de Montreuil.** At this manor house facing the citadel, rooms are furnished with 18th- and 19th-century antiques. The less expensive rooms in the converted stables are also pleasantly furnished but smaller. Owner Lindsay Germain is English. Her husband, Christian, is an excellent chef: his forte is bringing out the natural flavor in such dishes as lightly sautéed scallops served with *pompadour* potatoes, or lamb chops with a wine-sauce glaze. (The restaurant is closed Monday, September–June; there's no lunch on Tuesday and Thursday.) ✉ *Chaussée des Capucins, 62170,* ☎ *03–21–81–53–04,* FAX *03–21–81–36–43,* WEB *www.chateaudemontreuil.com. 17 rooms. Restaurant, no air-conditioning in some rooms, cable TV, some minibars, some pets allowed (€10 fee). AE, DC, MC, V. Closed mid-Dec.–early Feb.*

Le Touquet

❽ *15 km (9 mi) northwest of Montreuil via N39.*

At the mouth of the Canche Estuary, Le Touquet is an elegant Victorian seaside resort town. First transformed into a sandy pine forest by Alphonse Daloz in the mid-19th century, the town was developed by Yorkshire businessman John White to attract English vacationers. On the Paris end, the newspaper *Le Figaro* baptized it "Paris-Plage" (Paris-Beach) and launched a huge advertising campaign to lure well-to-do Parisians. A cosmopolitan atmosphere remains, and many French people, attracted by the airy, elegant avenues and invigorating climate, have moved here for good (many are retirees). On one side is a fine sandy beach; on the other, the flourishing pine forest. There are also a casino, golf courses, and a racetrack.

Dining and Lodging

$$$–$$$$ ✕ **Flavio.** Fish is the star at this elegant spot near the casino. Chef Guy Delmotte specializes in lobster (for which he charges whale-size prices). The other two prix-fixe menus are more reasonable (wine is included

in the €38 weekday menu). Cut glass and Oriental carpets add a colorful note of dated glamour. ✉ *1 av. du Verger,* ☎ *03–21–05–10–22. Reservations essential. Jacket and tie. AE, DC, MC, V. Closed Jan.–Feb., 2nd ½ Nov., and Mon. Sept.–June.*

$$$–$$$$ ★ ✕🏨 **Westminster.** The Westminster's mammoth redbrick facade looks as if it were built just a few years ago; in fact, it dates from the 1930s and, like the rest of the hotel, has been extensively restored. The enormous double rooms are a good value, and the bridal suite is the last word in thick-carpeted extravagance. The hotel's brasserie, Le Coffee-Shop, is modestly priced (lunch and dinner); the Pavillon restaurant serves inventive French cuisine (it's closed Tuesday and in February). ✉ *Av. du Verger, 62520,* ☎ *03–21–05–48–48,* FAX *03–21–05–45–45,* WEB *www.westminster.fr. 115 rooms. Restaurant, brasserie, bar, no air-conditioning, cable TV, minibars, pool, hot tub, sauna, some pets allowed (€13 fee). AE, DC, MC, V.*

Outdoor Activities and Sports

Aqualud, a water park on the beachfront, has numerous water-sports facilities, half outdoors, half in, including a giant pool with wave machine. ✉ *Bd. Thierry-Sabine,* ☎ *03–21–05–90–96.* 🎫 *€10 for 3 hrs, €13 all day.* ⏲ *Apr.–June and Sept., Wed.–Sun. 10:15–5:45; July–Aug., daily 10:15–6:45; Oct.–Mar., weekends only 10:15–5:45.*

The **Enduro** in February sees thousands of motorbikes converge on Le Touquet for an epic race through the dunes.

Boulogne-sur-Mer

❾ *24 km (15 mi) north of Le Touquet via D940.*

Boulogne-sur-Mer, famous for its smoked herring, is France's largest fishing port. The rebuilt concrete streets around the port are ugly and unpleasant, but the Old Town on the hill is a different world—pretty, well kept, and full of character. Perhaps this is why Napoléon chose Boulogne as his base in 1803 while making his fruitless plans to cross the Channel with 2,000 boats and 180,000 men.

The four main streets of the **Ville Haute** (Upper Town) intersect at **place Godefroy-de-Bouillon.** The square is flanked by the 18th-century rose-brick **Hôtel de Ville,** the 12th- to 13th-century **belfry,** the cloistered **Annonciades** (a former convent, now a library), and the **Hôtel Desandrouins,** Napoléon's imperial palace. Dominating them all is the formidable **Basilique Notre-Dame,** its distinctive elongated dome visible from far out at sea.

Inside the 13th-century ramparts, studded with four gateways and 17 watchtowers, is the polygonal castle, today known as the **Château-Musée.** Built for the counts of Boulogne, the castle dates in part from the 13th-century and houses a fine collection of Egyptian artifacts donated by the celebrated Louvre Egyptologist Auguste Mariette, who was born in Boulogne in 1821. The museum's collection of Greek vases is considered second only to the Louvre's. ✉ *Rue de Bernet,* ☎ *03–21–10–02–20.* 🎫 *€3.50.* ⏲ *Wed.–Mon. 10–12:30 and 2–5, Sun. 10–12:30 and 2:30–5:30.*

★ **Nausicaä,** the Centre National de la Mer (National Marine Center), has a battery of aquariums containing more than 4,000 fish. Highlights include sharks, sea lions, a Plexiglas column of shimmering jellyfish, and playful rays. It also has a coral reef, 3-D films, a swimming pool, a weather center, a library, a large bookstore, and a classy restaurant. ✉ *Bd. Ste-Beuve,* ☎ *03–21–30–99–99.* 🎫 *€10.50.* ⏲ *Sept.–June, daily 9:30–6:30; July–Aug., daily 9:30–8.*

The **Colonne de la Grande Armée,** a 160-ft marble column begun in 1804 to commemorate Napoléon's invasion of England, is north of the town just off the road to Calais. The idea was shelved in 1805, and the column (closed for restoration at press time) was only finished 30 years later under Louis-Philippe. The 263 steps take you to the top and a wide-reaching panoramic view; if the weather is clear, you may be able to make out the distant cliffs of Dover. ✉ *Off A6, the road to Calais,* ☏ *03–21–80–43–69.* *Free.* *Apr.–Sept., Thurs.–Mon. 9–noon and 2–7, Tues.–Wed. 2–7; Oct.–Mar., Thurs.–Mon. 9–noon and 2–5, Tues.–Wed. 2–5.*

Dining and Lodging

$\$\$$–$\$\$\$\$ ✕ **Matelote.** The name of this restaurant, across the way from Nausicaä, means "the Sailor's Wife." Here in the bright yellow interior you can enjoy seafood specialties such as roast fillet of turbot with thyme. ✉ *80 bd. Ste-Beuve,* ☏ *03–21–30–17–97. AE, MC, V. No dinner Sun., Sept.–June.*

$\$\$ ★ ✕ **Epicure.** This intimate, 20-seat restaurant in neighboring Wimereux serves an outstanding three-course (€22) menu that might include duck terrine, salmon with parsley and horseradish butter, and hot pear and chocolate cake. There's a monumental cheese board and an imaginative wine list. Chef Philippe Carrée works alone in the kitchen and is entitled to foibles like refusing diners who turn up "too late"—after 9 PM. Claudette Carrée anxiously surveys the dining room. ✉ *1 rue de la Gare, Wimereux (6 km/4 mi north of Boulogne),* ☏ *03–21–83–21–83. AE, DC, V. Closed Wed. and late Dec.–mid-Jan. No dinner Sun.*

$\$\$–$\$\$\$ ✕ **Cléry.** It was at this hotel that Napoléon decided to abandon his plans to invade England. As you bask on the peaceful grounds of this 18th-century château you may understand why. Rooms vary in price and decor; those in the former stables have been converted into light, airy, and modern spaces. Lunch is offered in the restaurant every day except Saturday. ✉ *Rue du Château, 62360 Hesdin-l'Abbé (8 km/5 mi inland from Boulogne via N1),* ☏ *03–21–83–19–83,* FAX *03–21–87–52–59,* WEB *www.hotelclery-hedin-abbe.com. 22 rooms. Restaurant, no air-conditioning. AE, DC, MC, V. Closed 3 weeks in Jan.*

$–$\$ **Métropole.** This small hotel is handy for hovercraft passengers but, like most of the Ville Basse (Lower Town), no great architectural shakes (it's a rather faceless '50s building). The small garden is pleasant for breakfast in summer, however, and rooms are adequately furnished. ✉ *51 rue Adolphe-Thiers, 62200,* ☏ *03–21–31–54–30,* FAX *03–21–30–45–72,* WEB *www.hotel-metropole-boulonge.com.25 rooms. Cable TV, minibars, some pets allowed (€8 fee). AE, DC, MC, V. Closed late Dec.–early Jan.*

Outdoor Activities and Sports

The coast is a popular spot for speed sailing and sand sailing. For details contact the **Drakkars** club (✉ Base Nautique Sud, 62152 Hardelot-Plage, ☏ 03–21–83–27–93), 14 km (9 mi) south of Boulogne.

En Route Just north of Boulogne are **Wimereux,** a cheerful Belle Epoque resort town, and **Ambleteuse,** with its small seashore fort built by Vauban in the 1680s. Mighty cliffs survey the Channel as D940 continues toward Calais: **Cap Gris-Nez** has a lighthouse and a World War II concrete bunker, **Cap Blanc-Nez** an obelisk war memorial. There's little to warrant a stop at either the entrance to the **Channel Tunnel,** near Coquelles, or in **Calais,** which was flattened in World War II—although its reconstructed 240-ft belfry is visible from far inland. **Gravelines,** at the mouth of the Aa River, warrants a brief stop for Vauban's moated ramparts. **Dunkerque** doesn't: like Calais, it's a working port of little scenic appeal, although it spurts into life with a rambunctious three-day carnival at the beginning of Lent.

Bergues

★ ⑩ *9 km (6 mi) south of Dunkerque via D916.*

One of France's most scenic walled towns, Bergues was first fortified back in the 7th century. Between the 9th and 13th centuries it was sacked seven times, prompting Philip the Bold to rebuild the **ramparts**—more than 5 km (3 mi) of them—in the distinctive shape of an eight. In the 1690s Vauban erected the Baroque **Porte de Cassel** (Cassel Gateway) and perfected the system of moats and canals around the walls, including the triple-ditched, crown-shape **Couronne d'Hondschoote.** Inside the walls, the 160-ft medieval belfry disputes skyline supremacy with the square and pointed towers of the ruined **Abbaye de St-Winoc.**

Nightlife and the Arts

The end of May is the time for Bergues's **beer festival.** The first Sunday of December brings the **Fête St-Nicolas,** a Christmas celebration.

St-Omer

⑪ *23 km (14 mi) southwest of Cassel via D933, 64 km (40 mi) northwest of Lille.*

Hilly St-Omer is not your archetypal northern industrial town. With its yellow-brick buildings it looks different from its neighbors. Its Belle Epoque train station is modeled on a Loire château, and the romantic ruins of the Abbaye de St-Bertin recall the town's medieval preeminence as a religious center.

★ The **Basilique Notre-Dame** (✉ Rue Henri-Dupuis), surrounded by narrow streets at the top of the town, is a homely cathedral-size church. Its lowish vaults and broad windows with geometric tracery bear testimony to the local influence of the English Perpendicular style during the 15th century. Look for the early 18th-century organ case, with its carved angel musicians, the astronomical clock in the north transept, and the majestic **Grand Dieu de Thérouanne,** a 13th-century sculpture of *Christ in Judgment,* gleefully transported here when Charles V razed the rival cathedral of Thérouanne (14 km/9 mi south of St-Omer) in 1553.

The **Hôtel Sandelin,** a 1776 mansion, houses the town museum. Here you'll find period furnishings and paintings and an exceptional collection of porcelain and faïence, with more than 700 pieces of delftware. At press time the museum was undergoing restoration, with a view to reopening at the start of 2003. ✉ *14 rue Carnot,* ☎ *03–21–38–00–94.* 🎫 *Admission details unavailable at press time.*

Vestiges of World War I pepper the north of France, but they pale in comparison with the grisly Nazi specter found in the forest near Watten, 13 km (8 mi) north of St-Omer. The **Blockhaus d'Eperlecques** is a bunker of monstrous size and intent, 80 ft high with concrete walls 20 ft thick. It was erected in 1943 by 35,000 slave laborers as the secret base for the assembly and launch of the V2 rocket bomb, whose destination would have been London. The structure is so secret, in fact, that you can't even see it from the entrance to the site, 100 yards away. Thankfully, it was not secret enough to escape Allied reconnaissance: RAF bombers destroyed the bunker and saved London from being blown to smithereens. Strategic loudspeakers fire out French commentary as you walk around—but the site's message is essentially unspeakable. ✉ *Off D205 west of Watten,* ☎ *03–21–88–44–22.* 🎫 *€6.30.* ⏲ *Mar. and Oct., Sun. 2:15–6; Apr.–June and Sept., daily 2:15–6; July–Aug., daily 10–7.*

★ Another chilling episode of World War II lurks beneath the moss-covered 55,000-ton concrete dome of **La Coupole,** 5 km (3 mi) south of St-Omer. Hitler earmarked this former quarry as a more secure launch site than Eperlecques for his V2 rockets, which were meant to flatten London, 200 km (125 mi)—and only a couple of minutes—away. The rockets were built in central Germany and would have been rail-shipped to St-Omer had the Nazis not started to lose the war. The cupola, built in 1943 by Russian and Polish prisoners to protect the missile chamber, is 75 yards in diameter and 16 ft thick; after the war Allied forces reckoned the amount of dynamite needed to destroy it would have blown up most of St-Omer as well, so they didn't bother. The site lay neglected for more than 50 years until tourist authorities restored it; in fact, they did far more, equipping the huge space beneath the dome with a 45-ft V2 and a battery of movie and TV screens outlining the history of the rocket. Infrared headsets guide you through dank galleries and up to the dome; you end your two-hour visit in the unfinished missile chamber. ✉ *5 mi (3 mi) south of St-Omer between Helfaut and Wizernes,* ☎ *03–21–93–07–07.* 🎫 *€8.50.* ⏲ *Apr.–Oct., daily 9–7; Nov.–Mar., daily 10–6.*

Dining and Lodging

$$–$$$ ✕🏨 **Moulin de Mombreux.** Huge cogs and waterwheels reflect the 18th-century water-mill origins of the Moulin, west of St-Omer in Lumbres. Silver candlesticks and original wood beams lend charm to the dining room, with poached oysters in fennel, lamb in foie gras sauce, and raspberry soufflé often among the chef's selections. The discreet if unoriginal pastel-painted guest rooms are augmented by a spacious breakfast room with large windows and wicker chairs. ✉ *Rte. de Bayenghem, 62380 Lumbres (9 km/6 mi west of St-Omer),* ☎ *03–21–39–62–44,* FAX *03–21–93–61–34,* WEB *www.loisirs-gourmets.com. 24 rooms. Restaurant, no air-conditioning, cable TV, minibars. AE, DC, MC, V.*

Shopping

Founded in 1825 in Arques, 3 km (2 mi) east of St-Omer, the **Verrerie-Cristallerie d'Arques** is France's biggest glassworks, producing 4 million items a day—most famously Cristal d'Arques wineglasses. You can visit the spacious showroom and take a 90-minute tour of the factory (€5.35). ✉ *On N43 just south of Arques,* ☎ *03–21–95–46–96.* ⏲ *Sat.–Mon. 10–6:30.*

En Route Take D77 south from St-Omer to **Thérouanne**—once the leading religious center of northern France, with a population of 20,000 when it was flattened by Charles V in 1553. All that remains are the foundations of the cathedral, in a field to the north of today's unremarkable town. Follow D341 to Estrée-Blanche and then turn left toward **Liettres.** Pop in at the pretty, moated Château de Créminil. The beefier Château de Liettres is farther along the Lacquette Valley; the first written mention of the sport of *criquet* (cricket), in a manuscript now in the Archives Nationales in Paris, refers to a mortal dispute between a player and a spectator here in October 1478—an event commemorated by a brass plaque near the village bridge.

Aire-sur-la-Lys

⓬ *20 km (12 mi) southeast of St-Omer via N43.*

An unspoiled town center and the proximity of A26 have made Aire, once a busy market town and army base, a favored stopover for tourists arriving from England. The grandiose **Hôtel de Ville** (Town Hall), with its sculpted pediment, giant pilasters, and 145-ft cupola-topped belfry, dominates the Grand'Place, the main square. It was built in 1717–

21 as a symbol of the town's resurgence after being partially destroyed by the duke of Marlborough in 1710. The town center contains many other 18th-century Neoclassical buildings—you can get details of a numbered trail from the tourist office, which is housed in a notable survivor from the 17th century: the arcaded stone-and-brick *bailliage* (guard house), on the corner of Grand'Place. The Jesuit **Chapelle St-Jacques**, built in the 1680s, is another survivor from the 17th century.

The 210-ft stone tower of the **Collégiale St-Pierre** (✉ Pl. St-Pierre) dominates the land for miles around. Despite all the pinnacles at the top, this is not a strictly Gothic tower—it was completed only in 1634, and pilasters and rounded arches betray the stylistic influence of the Renaissance. At over 110 yards, the interior is impressively long but has suffered heavily down the ages—most recently from bombs in 1944—and its flaking 19th-century paintwork makes it look messy and disjointed. The highlight is the carved organ case made in 1633.

Dining and Lodging

$–$$ ✕🏨 **Trois Mousquetaires.** English travelers flock to this spacious, timber-frame-and-brick late-19th-century hotel, set on the outskirts of town (well back from N43 behind a large garden). It has the feel of a baronial Scottish mansion, especially when a log fire is blazing in the wood-paneled lobby. Rooms have heavy brass lamps, plush carpeting, and floral-patterned quilts. The restaurant looks out across the fields and serves regional dishes. ✉ *Château du Fort de la Redoute, 62120,* ☎ *03–21–39–01–11,* FAX *03–21–39–50–10,* WEB *www.hostelleriedes3mousquetaires.com. 31 rooms. Restaurant, bar, no air-conditioning, cable TV. AE, DC, MC, V. Closed mid-Dec.–mid-Jan.*

Lille

60 km (37 mi) east of Aire-sur-la-Lys, 220 km (137 mi) north of Paris, 100 km (62 mi) southeast of Calais, 100 km (62 mi) west of Brussels.

For a big city supposedly reeling from the problems of its main industry—textiles—Lille (the name comes from *l'isle,* the island, in the Deûle River, where the city began) is remarkably dynamic and attractive. After experiencing Flemish, Austrian, and Spanish rule, Lille passed into French hands for good in 1668. Lille is a European crossroads—one hour by train from Paris and Brussels, just two from London. The shiny glass towers of the Euralille complex, a high-tech commercial center of dubious aesthetic merit, greet travelers arriving at the TGV station, Lille-Europe.

⓭ The sumptuous church of **St-Maurice** (✉ Rue de Paris), just off place de la Gare, is a large, five-aisle structure built between the 14th and ⓮ 19th centuries. The majestic **Porte de Paris** (✉ Rue de Paris), overlooked by the 340-ft brick tower of the **Hôtel de Ville,** is a cross between a mansion and a triumphal arch. It was built by Simon Vollant in the 1680s in honor of Louis XIV and was originally part of the city walls.

★ ⓯ The **Palais des Beaux-Arts** is the country's largest fine arts museum outside Paris. It houses a noteworthy collection of Dutch and Flemish paintings (Anthony Van Dyck, Peter Paul Rubens, Flemish Primitives, and Dutch landscapists) as well as some charmingly understated still lifes by Chardin, works by the Impressionists, and dramatic canvases by El Greco, Tintoretto, Paolo Veronese, and Goya (including two of his most famous—*Les Jeunes* and the ghastly *Les Vieilles*). A ceramics section displays some fine examples of Lille faïence (earthenware), and there's a superbly lighted display of *plans reliefs* (18th-century scale models of French towns) in the basement, with binoculars provided to help you admire all the intricate detail. ✉ *Pl. de la République,* ☎

Citadelle . . . 23
Hospice Comtesse . . . 20
Maison de Gilles de la Boë . . . 19
Maison Natale du Général de Gaulle . . . 22
Musée d'Art Moderne . . . 24
Notre-Dame de la Treille 21
Palais des Beaux-Arts . . 15
Palais Rihour . 16
Place du Général-de-Gaulle . . . 17
Porte de Paris 14
St-Maurice . . 13
Vieille Bourse 18

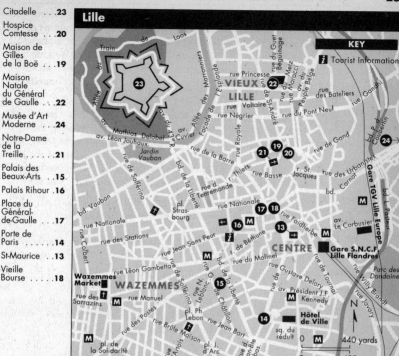

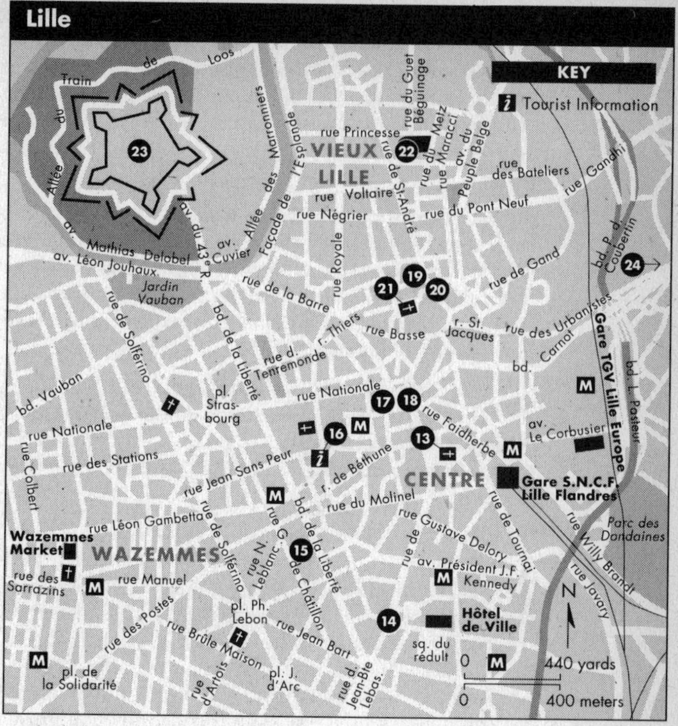

03–20–06–78–00. 🎫 *€4.60.* ⏲ *Wed.–Thurs. and weekends 10–6, Fri. 10–7, Mon. 2–6.*

16 The late-15th-century **Palais Rihour** (Rihour Palace; ✉ Pl. Rihour), built for Philippe le Bon, duke of Burgundy, is famed for its octagonal turret and staircase with intricate swirling-pattern brickwork. The city **tourist office** is housed in the vaulted former guardroom on the ground floor.

17 Lille's most famous square, Grand'Place, is just one block from place Rihour and is now officially called **Place du Général-de-Gaulle.** The *Déesse* (goddess), atop the giant column, clutching a linstock (used to fire a cannon), has dominated the square since 1845; she commemorates Lille's heroic resistance to an Austrian siege in 1792. Other landmarks include the handsome, gabled 1936 facade of *La Voix du Nord* (the main regional newspaper), topped by three gilded statues symbolizing the three historic regions of Flanders, Artois, and Hainaut; and the Furet du Nord, which immodestly claims to be the world's largest bookstore.

18 The elegant **Vieille Bourse** (Old Commercial Exchange), on one side of Grand'Place, was built in 1653 by Julien Destrées as a commercial exchange to rival those of the Low Countries. Note the bronze busts, sculpted medallions, and ornate stonework of its arcaded quadrangle.

19 The Vieux Lille (Old Lille) neighborhood dates mainly from the 17th and 18th centuries; most of its richly sculpted facades, often combining stone facings with pale pink brickwork, have been restored. Perhaps the most ornate building is the **Maison de Gilles de La Boë** (✉ Pl. Louise-de-Bettignies), built in 1636 for a rich grocer.

20 The **Hospice Comtesse** (Countess Hospital), founded as a hospital in 1237 by Jeanne de Constantinople, countess of Flanders, was rebuilt in the 15th century after a fire destroyed most of the original struc-

ture. Local artifacts from the 17th and 18th centuries form the backbone of the museum now housed here, but its star attraction is the **Salle des Malades** (Sick Ward), featuring a majestic wooden ceiling. ✉ *32 rue de la Monnaie,* ☎ *03–28–36–84–00.* 🎫 *€2.30.* ⏲ *Wed.–Fri. 10–12:30 and 2–6, weekends 10–6.*

21 The cathedral of **Notre-Dame de la Treille** (✉ Rue des Trois-Mollettes) stands on the spot of a medieval church dismantled during the Revolution. The present building was begun—in a suitably neo-Gothic style—in 1854. Construction was halted from 1869 to 1893, and by World War I only the choir was finished. The roof vaults were only finished in 1973, and the west front, with its dismal expanses of gray concrete, remained despairingly incomplete until a translucent marble facade was added in 1999.

22 President and General Charles de Gaulle (1890–1970) was born in Lille. His birthplace, the **Maison Natale du Général de Gaulle,** is now a museum. ✉ *9 rue Princesse,* ☎ *03–28–38–12–05.* 🎫 *€2.30.* ⏲ *Wed.–Sun. 10–noon and 2–5.*

23 Lille's gigantic **Citadelle** patrols the northwest of the city from the enchanting Bois de Boulogne Gardens, whose leafy walkways alongside photogenic streams attract hordes of strollers, cyclists, and joggers. The colossal walls of the citadel are immaculately preserved, no doubt because the site is still inhabited by the French military (you can only visit the interior on Sunday afternoon). It was constructed rapidly between 1667 and 1670; of course, that genius of military engineering Sébastien de Vauban got the commission. Some 60 million bricks were baked in record time, and the result is a fortified town in its own right. ☎ *03–20–21–94–21 for tourist office to arrange tours.* 🎫 *€6.15.* ⏲ *Guided tours only Sun. 3–5.*

24 The **Musée d'Art Moderne,** in the eastern suburb of Villeneuve d'Ascq, is a modern, sober brick building ringed by trim lawns alive with boxing bronze hares by Barry Flanagan and a giant Calder mobile. The picture collection ranges from the Cubists, Modigliani, and the Surrealists to Chaissac, Soulages, and postwar abstraction. ✉ *1 allée du Musée,* ☎ *03–20–19–68–68.* 🎫 *€6.50.* ⏲ *Wed.–Mon. 10–6.*

Dining and Lodging

$$$–$$$$ ✕ **Huîtrière.** Behind a magnificent Art Deco fish store lined with local Desvres tiles, this elegant seafood restaurant serves fresh, local seafood, simply prepared in regional (Flemish) style—turbot hollandaise, *waterzoï* (a mild, creamy fish stew), braised eel, scallops, and oysters. The clientele is well heeled and the prices are justifiably high. ✉ *3 rue des Chats-Bossus,* ☎ *03–20–55–43–41, AE, DC, MC, V. Closed mid-July–late Aug. No dinner Sun.*

$$ ✕ **Lion Bossu.** Old bricks and beams distinguish the 17th-century interior of this restaurant in the heart of Old Lille, a cozy, old-fashioned spot serving simple, homey regional food. ✉ *1 rue St-Jacques,* ☎ *03–20–06–06–88. AE, V. Closed Sun. No lunch Mon.*

$ ✕ **Les Brasseurs.** This dark, wood-paneled brasserie beside the Lille-Flandres station brews its own beer. Four types—blond (lager), amber, dark (stout), and white (wheat beer)—are available, and La Palette du Barman lets you sample all for €3.85. *Carbonnade flamande* (Flemish-style beef cooked in a sweet and sour sauce) and *flammekueches* (flattened bread dough topped with bacon and onions) are served. ✉ *18 pl. de la Gare,* ☎ *03–20–06–46–25. AE, V.*

$$–$$$ 🏨 **Bellevue.** The former Hôtel de Bourbon, home to Mozart in 1765, is now an elegant central lodging near Grand'Place. Large, comfortable Art Deco rooms and modern bathrooms are complemented by the sort of deferential service you can no longer take for granted. The leather-lined bar is a good spot in which to rendezvous. ✉ *5 rue Jean-Roisin, 59800,* ☎ *03–20–57–45–64,* FAX *03–20–40–07–93,* WEB *www.grandhotelbellevue.com. 60 rooms. Bar, minibars, some pets allowed (€7.65 fee). AE, DC, MC, V.*

$–$$ **Brueghel.** The Brueghel, named in honor of one of the most famous of Flemish painting dynasties, is a picture of revived Art Deco charm; antiques are scattered throughout the corridors and rooms, many of which retain their original interwar furniture. The mood in the wood-paneled lobby is friendly and welcoming in the best northern French style, and that has made the hotel a favorite among visiting performers at the nearby opera house. The hotel is also handily placed for the Vieille Bourse and Grand'Place, as well as Lille's two train stations, and looks on to the pedestrian piazza around the venerable Gothic church of St-Maurice. ✉ *3 parvis St-Maurice, 59800,* ☎ *03–20–06–06–69,* FAX *03–20–63–25–27,* WEB *www.hotel-brueghel.com. 66 rooms. Bar, no air-conditioning, some Internet, some pets allowed (€5.50 fee). AE, DC, MC, V.*

Nightlife and the Arts

Jazz clubs, piano bars, nightclubs, and all kinds of performances are listed in *Lille by Night,* available at the Lille tourist office. Lille is at its liveliest during the first weekend of September, when the **Grande Braderie** summons folk from miles around to what is theoretically a street market but is better described as one giant beer- and mussel-swilling party.

The **Opéra de Lille** (✉ Pl. du Théâtre, ☎ 03–20–74–32–99) at press time was undergoing extensive renovation expected to continue until the beginning of 2004. The **Orchestre National de Lille** (✉ 30 pl. Mendès-France, ☎ 03–20–12–82–40, WEB www.onlille.com) is a well-respected symphony orchestra. The **Théâtre du Nord** (✉ 4 pl. Général-de-Gaulle, ☎ 03–20–14–24–24, WEB www.theatredunord.com) is one of Lille's most prominent theaters.

En Route En route to Valenciennes, stop in **St-Amand-les-Eaux,** 35 km (23 mi) southeast of Lille on D955, to admire the riotous stonework of its 270-ft 17th-century Baroque abbey tower, topped by a cupola.

Nightlife and the Arts

Giants and processions go together in northern France, most famously during the **Fêtes de Gayant** (Festival of the Giant), which has been held in Douai on the first Sunday after July 5 ever since Flanders and France signed a peace treaty in 1530. A family of five giants, more than 25 ft tall, is borne through the streets. At 11 the city bells ring out, and hundreds of pigeons are released from the Town Hall.

The Artois Battlefields

The most poignant memories of World War I are evoked in the war cemeteries in the countryside between Lens and Arras, all of which are
25 superbly cared for. Take A21 west from **Douai** to Lens and head
26 through Liévin and Angres to **Souchez.** Standing on a windswept hill 500 ft above the Artois plain is Notre-Dame de Lorette, a 30-acre cemetery with endless rows of white crosses, a pseudo-Byzantine church, an ossuary, and a huge tower with a small war museum. From the top there are extensive views of the surrounding countryside.

From Souchez head south on D937, past the beautiful circular ceme-
27 tery of Cabaret Rouge, to **Neuville-St-Vaast,** whose Art Deco church is a stately example of 1920s reconstruction. Just off D937 is gently

sloping **La Targette**, one of the most serene and beautiful of all French war cemeteries. At the nearby crossroads of D937 and D49, opposite a stark war memorial in the form of a giant torch, is the small **Musée de la Guerre 1914–18** (World War I Museum), with a musty collection of posters, documents, costumes, and weapons. From Neuville take D55 to Vimy, where there's a park commemorating the epic Canadian victory during World War I.

Arras

28 *9 km (6 mi) south of Mont-St-Eloi via D341, 178 km (105 mi) north of Paris, 113 km (70 mi) southeast of Calais, 54 km (34 mi) southwest of Lille.*

At first glance you might not guess that Arras, the capital of the historic Artois region between Flanders and Picardy, was badly mauled during World War I. In the Middle Ages Arras was an important trading and tapestry-weaving center, its wealth reflected in two of the finest squares in the country—now home to lively markets on Wednesday and Saturday mornings. Other landmarks include the 18th-century theater, the Palais des États (former regional parliament), the octagonal place Victor-Hugo, and the former home of revolutionary firebrand Maximilien Robespierre. An hour-long audio guided tour of the city is available from the tourist office for a small fee.

Start your visit at the arcaded place des Héros, the smaller of the two main squares, dominated by the richly worked—and much restored—**Hôtel de Ville** (Town Hall). You can take an elevator to the top of its ornate 240-ft **belfry** (€2.15) for a view that stretches as far as the ruined towers of Mont St-Eloi, 10 km (6 mi) northwest, and you can join a guided tour through the **Boves** (€3.05), a maze of underground chalk galleries quarried out back in the 10th century, and then transformed into an underground city by 10,000 British troops during World War I. The tunnels run for miles in all directions—even, it is said, as far as Mont-St-Eloi. The tour lasts about an hour, and you'll need sturdy footwear to negotiate all the steep, damp stairs. ✉ *Pl. des Héros.* ⏲ *May–Sept., Mon.–Sat. 9–6:30, Sun. 10–1 and 2–6:30; Oct.–Apr., Mon.–Sat. 9–noon and 2–6, Sun. 10–12:30 and 3–6:30.*

★ **Grand'Place,** linked to place des Héros by rue de la Taillerie, is a grand, harmonious showcase of 17th- and 18th-century Flemish architecture. The gabled facades recall those in Belgium and Holland and are a reminder of the unifying influence of the Spanish colonizers of the Low Countries during the 17th century—though the oldest house here, the Trois Luppars hotel, at No. 49, actually dates from 1467.

The 19th-century **Cathédrale St-Vaast** (✉ Rue des Teinturiers) is a stately Classical building in cool white stone, every bit as vast as its name (pronounced *va*) almost suggests. It was built between 1775 and 1830 to the designs of Contant d'Ivry; it was half-razed during World War I, although you'd never guess it because the restoration was so diligent.

The **Musée des Beaux-Arts** (Fine Arts Museum), in the massive, regimented 18th-century abbey next to the cathedral, has a rich collection of objects and pictures, including cobalt-blue Arras porcelain; 19th-century landscapes by Camille Dutilleux and other local artists inspired by Camille Corot (also represented), who frequently visited the region; and two smiling 13th-century gilded wooden angels, the *Anges de Saudémont.* ✉ *20 rue Paul-Doumer,* ☎ *03–21–71–26–43.* 🎫 *€4.* ⏲ *Mon. and Wed.–Fri., 10–noon and 2–5, weekends 10–noon and 3–6.*

Dining and Lodging

$$–$$$ ★ ✕ **Faisanderie.** In a former stable, this splendid restaurant serves memorable variations on international fare: *pied de veau* (calves' feet), pike baked with frogs' legs, and cod with local Arleux garlic. A loyal clientele supports its longstanding gastronomic reputation. ✉ *45 Grand'-Place,* ☎ *03–21–48–20–76. Reservations essential. Jacket and tie. AE, DC, MC, V. Closed Aug. and Mon. No dinner Sun.*

$ ✕ **Rapière.** This lively bistro dishes up distinctly local cuisine, including andouillettes (a kind of chitterling sausage) and *poule à la bière* (hen in beer), as well as specialties like *flan aux maroilles* (flan made with regional cheese) and homemade foie gras, all in a casual setting. ✉ *44 Grand'Place,* ☎ *03–21–55–09–92. AE, MC, V. No dinner Sun.*

$$ ★ **Univers.** Once an 18th-century Jesuit monastery, this stylish hotel has a pretty garden, a charming restaurant (no dinner Sunday during January and February), and pale pink brickwork. Although centrally located, it's set well back from the main street and is an oasis of calm. The interior has been modernized but retains rustic provincial furniture. ✉ *3 pl. de la Croix-Rouge, 62000,* ☎ *03–21–71–34–01,* FAX *03–21–71–41–42,* WEB *www.hotel-univers-arras.com. 38 rooms. Restaurant, bar, no air-conditioning, cable TV, Internet. AE, MC, V.*

Outdoor Activities and Sports

Three former mining towns a dozen miles north of Arras have placed sports firmly on their rejuvenation agendas. **Lens** has the top soccer team and the biggest sports stadium in northern France with a seating capacity (41,000) larger than the town's entire population. The Stade Couvert, in neighboring **Liévin,** is France's premier indoor athletics stadium. And, crazy as it may seem in this least mountainous of regions, **Noeux-les-Mines** (✉ Loisinord, rue Léon-Blum, ☎ 03–21–26–84–84) has made a name for itself as France's leading ski center between the Alps and the Channel by transforming its giant *terril* (slag heap) into an artificial ski run.

The Somme Battlefields

32 km (20 mi) south of Arras near Albert.

The Battle of the Somme—a name forever etched into history as the site of one of the bloodiest battle campaigns of World War I—raged south of Arras, near Albert, from July through November 1916, leaving a million dead. During those five futile months, the Allies, including Irish, Canadian, Australian, and South African soldiers, progressed about 8 km (5 mi) along the hills above the Ancre River north of Albert.

From Arras take D919 through gently rolling farmland, to Puisieux, then follow D107 to **Miraumont** and turn right on D50 along the north bank of the Ancre River. Follow signs to the memorial of **Beaumont-Hamel,** where a bronze caribou—emblem of the Newfoundland regiments that fought here—gazes accusingly over trenches and undulating, still shell-shocked terrain. Across the Ancre and up the hill on the other side is the **Tour Ulster** (Ulster Tower), commemorating the troops from Belfast.

29

30 From the village of **Thiepval,** follow signs to the bombastic brick **British War Memorial,** a disjointed triumphal arch that looks as if it were made of giant Lego blocks. Take D73 and then D147 to Bazentin and continue on to Longueval, site of the **Delville Wood Memorial,** set on a long lawn framed by a stately avenue of oaks.

Péronne

31 *23 km (14 mi) southeast of Albert via D938.*

The small, brick town of Péronne was almost entirely razed in 1916. ★ It's now contains, however, a fine World War I museum, the **Historial de la Grande Guerre.** Integrated into a ruined brick castle, this spacious modern museum has a thought-provoking spectrum of exhibits, from TV monitors playing old newsreels to soldiers' uniforms strung out on the floor surrounded by machine guns and a dim roomful of nightmarish war lithographs by Otto Dix. It also has a good gift shop, with books in English, and a café with views of a leafy-banked lake. Walk around to the end, and you'll find the Somme River, strewn with islands, languidly colliding with its tributary, the Cologne. ✉ *Pl. du Château,* ☎ *03–22–83–14–18.* €6.20. ⏲ *May–Sept., daily 10–6; Oct.–Apr., Tues.–Sun. 10–6.*

Dining and Lodging

$–$$ ✕🏨 **Hostellerie des Remparts.** Péronne makes a fine base for exploring the local battlefields and war cemeteries. This small hotel has long been an old-fashioned favorite among traveling salesmen, but redecorated rooms and increasingly inventive cuisine—snail ravioli with mushrooms or fish cooked with chicory and beetroot sauce—suggest the hotel is striving to broaden its appeal. A set menu at lunch runs €14.50, while complete dinners range from €16 to €43. ✉ *23 rue Beaubois, 80200,* ☎ *03–22–84–01–22,* FAX *03–22–84–31–96,* WEB *www.logisdefrance.fr. 16 rooms. Restaurant, no air-conditioning, cable TV, some pets allowed (€6.50 fee). AE, DC, MC, V.*

St-Quentin

32 *28 km (18 mi) southeast of Péronne via N44 and N29.*

Bustling St-Quentin, an industrial town rebuilt with considerable Art Deco panache after World War I (ask about a guided tour at the tourist office), is famed as the birthplace of 18th-century pastelist Maurice Quentin de La Tour—his work can be admired at the town museum.

Appearing to survey the town's sloping, pedestrian-only main square is the riotously sculpted, early 16th-century facade of the **Hôtel de Ville** (Town Hall; ✉ Pl. de l'Hôtel de Ville), complete with arcades and gables and topped by an 18th-century campanile with an attractive peal of bells. The town's cathedral-size hilltop **Basilique** (✉ Pl. de la Basilique) at the top of rue St-André is topped by a 270-ft flèche, reconstructed in 1976. Most of the building, however, is resolutely medieval: the elegant 13th-century choir retains some original stained glass; the soaring nave, rising 112 ft from the ground, was added 200 years later (note the black-and-white labyrinth pattern embedded in the floor); the ornate organ case was designed by Berain in 1690.

Dining and Lodging

$$ ✕🏨 **Le Château de Neuville.** To escape the hustle and bustle of St-Quentin, drive two miles to the neighboring village of Neuville St-Amand, where you will find its peaceful "château." This is in fact a sturdy stone mansion a century old, with white walls, large windows, and prim lines of dark green shutters offering an oasis of calm in its tree-studded park. Rooms are decked out in pastel shades; those in the modern annex have less character but are larger than those in the main block. A real plus is the reliable restaurant. ✉ *Rue du Midi, 02100 Neuville St-Amand (2 km/1 mi southwest of St-Quentin off N44),* ☎ *03–23–68–41–82,* FAX *03–23–68–46–02. 15 rooms. Restaurant, bar, some minibars, Internet. AE, DC, MC, V. Closed 3 wks Aug. No lunch Sat., no dinner Sun.*

OFF THE BEATEN PATH

MUSÉE MATISSE – Artist Henri Matisse (1869–1954) was born in Le Cateau-Cambrésis, 35 km (21 mi) northeast of St-Quentin. The Matisse Museum, housed in the **Palais Fénelon**, contains a number of early oil paintings and sculptures, plus a superb collection of 50 drawings selected by Matisse himself. The museum will be closed for renovation and extension until November 2002. ✉ *Palais Fénelon,* ☎ *03–27–84–13–15.* ⏲ *Wed.–Sun. 10–5.*

Laon

★ 33 *36 km (22 mi) southeast of St-Quentin on A26.*

Thanks to its awesome hilltop site and the forest of towers sprouting from its ancient cathedral, Laon basks in the title of the "crowned mountain." The medieval ramparts, virtually undisturbed by passing traffic, provide a ready-made itinerary for a tour of enchantingly venerable Laon. Panoramic views, sturdy gateways, and intriguing glimpses of the cathedral lurk around every bend. There's even a funicular, which makes frequent trips (except on Sunday in winter) up and down the hillside between the station and the Old Town.

★ The **Cathédrale Notre-Dame,** constructed between 1150 and 1230, is a superb example of early Gothic. The light interior gives the impression of order and immense length, and the first flourishing of Gothic architecture is reflected in the harmony of the four-tiered nave: from the bottom up, observe the wide arcades, the double windows of the *tribune*, the squat windows of the *triforium*, and, finally, the upper windows of the clerestory. The majestic towers can be explored during the guided visits that leave from the tourist office, housed in a 12th-century hospital on the cathedral square. The filigreed elegance of the five towers is audacious and rare. Look for the 16 stone oxen protruding from the tops, a tribute to the stalwart 12th-century beasts that carted up blocks of stone from quarries far below. Medieval stained glass includes the rose window dedicated to the liberal arts in the left transept, and the windows in the flat east end, an unusual feature for France although common in England. ✉ *Pl. du Parvis.* 🎟 *Guided tours €6.* ⏲ *Daily 8:30–6:30; guided tours Apr.–Sept., daily at 3 PM.*

The **Musée de Laon,** the town museum, has some fine antique pottery and work by the local-born Le Nain brothers. But its chief draw is the **Chapelle des Templiers** in the garden—a small, octagonal 12th-century chapel topped by a shallow dome. It houses fragments of the cathedral's gable and the chilling effigy of Guillaume de Harcigny, doctor to the insane king Charles VI, whose death from natural causes in 1393 did not prevent his memorializers from chiseling a skeletal portrait that recalls the Black Death. ✉ *32 rue Georges-Ermant,* ☎ *03–23–20–19–87.* 🎟 *€3.10.* ⏲ *Tues.–Sun. 2–6.*

Dining and Lodging

$–$$ ✕🏨 **Bannière de France.** In business since 1685, this old-fashioned, uneven-floored hostelry is just five minutes from the cathedral. Madame Lefèvre, the German patronne, speaks fluent English. Rooms are cozy and quaint. The restaurant's venerable dining room showcases sturdy cuisine (trout, lemon sole, guinea fowl) and good-value prix-fixe menus. ✉ *11 rue Franklin-Roosevelt, 02000,* ☎ *03–23–23–21–44,* FAX *03–23–23–31–56. 18 rooms, 17 with bath or shower. Restaurant, bar, no air-conditioning, cable TV. AE, DC, MC, V. Closed mid-Dec.–mid-Jan.*

Coucy-le-Château

★ 34 *28 km (18 mi) southwest of Laon via N2 and D5.*

The majestic hilltop fortress, or **château,** in Coucy-le-Château is but a glimmer of its former self—but it still casts a pretty intimidating shadow over the lush, rolling countryside of eastern Picardy. The 30-acre site, ringed with nearly 3 km (2 mi) of walls and no fewer than 31 towers, was developed by all-powerful warlords, the Enguerrands de Coucy, in the 12th century. They also erected the largest keep in Christendom, more than 210 ft high (Barbara Tuchman's *A Distant Mirror* provides fascinating background reading). The fortifications were partially dismantled by Mazarin in 1650 to prevent their use by rebels during the Fronde, later used as an open quarry after the Revolution, and then dynamited by retreating Germans in 1917. You can visit what's left of the keep and the vaulted cellars, and follow a path around the still-imposing town walls. ☎ *03–23–52–71–28.* 🎫 *€4.* ⏲ *Daily 10–12:30, 2–6.*

Dining and Lodging

$ ✕🏨 **Bellevue.** Rooms in this small old hotel just inside the town walls have been unfussily modernized, and although hardly the lap of luxury—none has a bathtub—they are light, clean, cheap, and have gleaming wooden floors. Room 8 is the largest, accommodating four people. The old-fashioned dining room has a cozy, slightly faded charm, and some of the fixed-price menus showcase regional cuisine. ✉ *2 Porte de Laon, 02380,* ☎ *03–23–52–69–70,* FAX *03–23–52–69–79. 7 rooms. Restaurant, no air-conditioning, minibars. MC, V. Closed Christmas week.*

Soissons

35 *19 km (12 mi) south of Coucy via D1.*

Although much damaged in World War I, Soissons commands attention for its two huge churches, one intact, one in ruins. The Gothic **Cathédrale Notre-Dame** was appreciated by Rodin, who famously declared that "there are no hours in this cathedral, but rather eternity." The interior, with its pure lines and restrained ornamentation, creates a more harmonious impression than the asymmetrical, one-towered facade. The most remarkable feature, however, is the rounded two-story transept, an element more frequently found in the German Rhineland than in France. Rubens's freshly restored *Adoration of the Shepherds* hangs on the other side of the transept. ✉ *Pl. Fernand-Marquigny.* ⏲ *Daily 9:30–noon and 2:30–5:30.*

The twin-spire facade, arcaded cloister, and airy refectory, constructed from the 14th to the 16th centuries, are all that is left of the hilltop abbey church of **St-Jean-des-Vignes,** which was largely destroyed just after the Revolution. Its fallen stones were used to restore the cathedral and neighboring homes. But the church remains the most impressive sight in Soissons, its hollow rose window peering out over the town like the eye of some giant Cyclops. ✉ *Cours St-Jean-des-Vignes.* 🎫 *Free.* ⏲ *Mon.–Sat. 9–12:30 and 1:30–6, Sun. 10–12:30 and 1:30–7.*

Partly housed in the medieval church of St-Léger, the **Musée de Soissons,** the town museum, has a varied collection of local archaeological finds and paintings, with fine 19th-century works by Gustave Courbet and Eugène Boudin. ✉ *2 rue de la Congrégation,* ☎ *03–23–59–15–90.* 🎫 *Free.* ⏲ *Wed.–Mon. 10–noon and 2–5.*

Dining and Lodging

$$$$ ★ **Château de Courcelles.** East of Soissons, along the Vesle River on the Champagne border, is this luxurious and refined château run by easy-going Frédéric Nouhaud. Its pure, classical Louis XIV facade harmonizes oddly with the sweeping brass main staircase attributed to Jean Cocteau. Rooms vary in size and grandeur; the former outbuildings have been converted into large family-size suites. Wind down in the cozy bar next to a roaring fire while anticipating excellent fare, including seasonal game, prepared by chef Eric Samson and served up in the stately dining room. A formal garden and pool are the gateway to 40 acres of parkland and a tree-shaded canal. ✉ *8 rue du Château, 02220 Courcelles-sur-Vesle (20 km/12 mi east of Soissons via N31),* ☎ *03–23–74–13–53,* FAX *03–23–74–06–41,* WEB *www.chateau-de-courcelles.com. 11 rooms, 7 suites. Restaurant, bar, no air-conditioning, cable TV, minibars, tennis court, pool, sauna, some pets allowed (€45 fee). AE, DC, MC, V.*

$–$$ **Abbaye.** The shambling village of Longpont, on the northeast fringe of the Forest of Retz, boasts a ruined Cistercian abbey, a turreted 14th-century gateway, and this ivy-clad, foursquare hotel. The cavernous dining room welcomes all with massive wooden tables, a crackling fireplace, and generous portions of family cooking, much of it prepared over a charcoal grill, with mushrooms, game, and duck with cherries among the favorites. To work it all off, you can rent a bike from the hotel to explore the forest. Rooms are calm and look out over either the forest or the abbey ruins. ✉ *8 rue des Tourelles, 02600 Longpont (14 km/9 mi southwest of Soissons via N2/D17),* ☎ *03–23–96–10–60,* FAX *03–23–96–10–60. 11 rooms, 1 with bath, 10 with showers. Restaurant, bar, no TV in some rooms. MC, V.*

Blérancourt

36 *23 km (14 mi) northwest of Soissons via D6.*

The village of Blérancourt is address to the **Musée National de la Coopération Franco-Américaine** (Museum of French-American Cooperation). Two style-setting pavilions and monumental archways are all that remain of the original château, built in 1612–19 by the great architect Salomon de Brosse but largely demolished during the French Revolution. American Anne Morgan founded the museum in 1924. The airy, modern museum contains art and documents charting Franco-American relations, with a section on American involvement in World War I. A beguiling female portrait by Missouri Postimpressionist Richard Miller stands out: an American Mona Lisa. The trim gardens include a bronze casting of the statue of George Washington by Jean-Antoine Houdon and an arboretum. ✉ *Off D939,* ☎ *03–23–39–60–16.* *€2.45.* ⏲ *Tues.–Sun. 10–12:30 and 2–6:30.*

Noyon

37 *14 km (9 mi) northwest of Blérancourt, 37 km (23 mi) northwest of Soissons.*

Noyon is an often overlooked cathedral town that owed its medieval importance to the cult of 7th-century St. Eloi, patron of blacksmiths and a former town bishop. Its second famous son, the Protestant theologian John Calvin, was born here in 1509. The old streets around the cathedral are at their liveliest during the Saturday morning market.

Constructed between 1140 and 1290, the **Cathédrale St-Eloi** was one of the earliest attempts at building a full-fledged Gothic cathedral. This feat is evident in the four-story nave; the intermittent use of rounded as well as pointed arches; and the thin, pointed lancet (as opposed to rose) windows in the austere facade. Pause for a wry smile at the "piazza" in front of the cathedral, with its elegant town houses arranged in a semicircle in bashful imitation of St. Peter's in Rome; then head down the cobbled lane to the left of the facade to admire the timber-front 16th-century library behind the cathedral. ✉ *Pl. du Parvis.* ⏲ *Daily 8–noon and 2–6.*

Dining and Lodging

$–$$ **St-Eloi.** Between the train station and the cathedral, this hotel charms with its provincial elegance. The redbrick and timber Victorian exterior, marble-lined reception area, and airy dining room are all staunchly French bourgeois. The spacious, pastel rooms have high ceilings; several have views of the interior courtyard. Avoid, however, the chain hotel–like annex. Affordable prix-fixe menus are available in the restaurant, which does not serve Sunday dinner. ✉ *81 bd. Carnot, 60400,* ☎ *03–44–44–01–49,* FAX *03–44–09–20–90,* WEB *www.hotelsainteloi.fr. 22 rooms. Restaurant, bar, cable TV, Internet, some pets allowed (€6 fee). AE, DC, MC, V. Closed mid-July–mid-Aug.*

Compiègne

38 *24 km (15 mi) southwest of Noyon via N32.*

Compiègne, a bustling town of some 40,000 people, is at the northern limit of the Forêt de Compiègne, on the edge of the misty plains of Picardy; this being prime hunting country, you can be sure there's a former royal hunting lodge in the vicinity. The one here enjoyed its heyday in the mid-19th century under upstart emperor Napoléon III. But the town's history stretches farther back—to Joan of Arc, who was captured in battle and held prisoner here, and to its 15th-century Hôtel de Ville (Town Hall), with its exceptional Flamboyant Gothic facade; and farther forward—to the World War I armistice, signed in Compiègne Forest on November 11, 1918.

★ The 18th-century **Palais de Compiègne** was restored by Napoléon I and favored for wild weekends by his nephew Napoléon III. The first Napoléon's legacy is more keenly felt: his state apartments have been refurbished using the original designs for hangings and upholstery, and bright silks and damasks adorn every room. Much of the mahogany furniture gleams with ormolu, and the chairs sparkle with gold leaf. Napoléon III's furniture looks ponderous in comparison, but fans of the Second Empire style love its lavish opulence. Behind the palace is a gently rising 4-km (2½-mi) vista, inspired by the park at Schönbrunn, in Vienna, where Napoléon I's second wife, Empress Marie-Louise, grew up. Also here is the **Musée du Second Empire,** a collection of Napoléon III–era decorative arts, including works by the caricaturist Honoré Daumier. Make time, too, for the **Musée de la Voiture** and its display of carriages, coaches, and old cars, including the *Jamais Contente* (*Never Satisfied*), the first car to reach 100 kph (62 mph). ✉ *Pl. du Général-de-Gaulle,* ☎ *03–44–38–47–00.* *€5.45.* ⏲ *Wed.–Mon. 10–6.*

A collection of 85,000 miniature soldiers—fashioned of lead, cardboard, and other materials—that depicts military uniforms through the ages is found in the **Musée de la Figurine Historique** (Toy Soldier Museum). ✉ *28 pl. de l'Hôtel-de-Ville,* ☎ *03–44–40–72–55.* *€1.85.* ⏲ *Mar.–Oct., Tues.–Sat. 9–noon and 2–6, Sun. 2–6; Nov.–Feb., Tues.–Sat. 9–noon and 2–5, Sun. 2–5.*

Some 7 km (4 mi) east of Compiègne via N31 and D546, off the road to Rethondes, is the **Wagon de l'Armistice** (Armistice Railcar), a replica of the one in which the World War I armistice was signed in 1918. In 1940 the Nazis turned the tables and made the French sign their own surrender in the same place—accompanied by Hitler's infamous jig for joy—then tugged the original car off to Germany, where it was later destroyed. The replicated car is part of a small museum in a leafy clearing. ✉ *Clairière de l'Armistice,* ☎ *03–44–40–09–27.* 🎫 *€1.55.* ⏲ *Apr.–Oct., Wed.–Mon. 9–noon and 2–6:30; Nov.–Mar., Wed.–Mon. 9:30–11:45 and 2–5:30.*

Dining and Lodging

$$ ✕🏨 **France.** A former 17th-century coaching inn, the hotel is central, cheap, and the epitome of French Provincial. Rooms have matching fruit-and-flower wallpaper and bedspreads and range in size from nook-and-cranny to family sleeper. The main restaurant with its brass lights, plush curtains, and waiters in black tie, tries valiantly to be upper crust while the brasserie serves a lighter more casual fare. ✉ *17 rue Eugène-Floquet, 60200,* ☎ *03–44–40–02–74,* FAX *03–44–40–48–37,* WEB *www.logisdefrance.fr. 20 rooms. Restaurant, brasserie, bar, no air-conditioning, some pets allowed (€7 fee). MC, V.*

Pierrefonds

★ 39 *14 km (9 mi) southeast of Compiègne via D973.*

★ Dominating the attractive lakeside village of Pierrefonds is its huge ersatz medieval castle. Built on a mound in the 15th century, the **Château de Pierrefonds** was comprehensively restored and re-created in the 1860s to imagined former glory at the behest of upstart emperor Napoléon III, then seeking to cash in on the fashion for neo-Gothic and the 19th-century craze for the Middle Ages. Architect Viollet-le-Duc left a crenellated fortress with a fairy-tale silhouette, although, like the fortified town of Carcassonne, which he also restored, Pierrefonds is more a construct of what Viollet-le-Duc thought it should have looked like than what it really was. A visit takes in the chapel, barracks, and the majestic keep holding the lord's bedchamber and reception hall, which is bordered by a spiral staircase whose lower and upper sections reveal clearly what is ancient and modern in this former fortress. Don't miss the plaster casts of tomb sculptures from all over France in the cellars, and the **Collection Monduit**—industrially produced, larger-than-life lead decorations made by the 19th-century firm that brought the Statue of Liberty to life. ☎ *03–44–42–72–72.* 🎫 *€5.55.* ⏲ *Mon.–Sat. 10–12:30 and 2–5, Sun. 10–5:30.*

OFF THE BEATEN PATH

MORIENVAL – This village, 6 km (4 mi) south of Pierrefonds via D335, is known for its modest 11th-century Romanesque church, one of the key buildings in architectural history. It was here, in the 1120s, that masons first hit on the idea of using stone vaults supported on "ribs" springing diagonally from column to column, an architectural breakthrough that formed the structural basis of the Gothic style. The trend was soon picked up at the great basilica of St-Denis near Paris and swept through northern France during the years that followed.

Dining and Lodging

$–$$ ✕🏨 **Relais Brunehaut.** Just down the valley from Pierrefonds, in the hamlet of Chelles, is this quaint hotel-restaurant with a view of the abbey church next door. It's made up of a tiny ensemble of stucco buildings, bordered by several acres of pleasant park and a small duck-populated river. An old wooden water mill in the dining room and the good, simple seasonal fare make eating here a pleasure. The dining room is closed Monday and Tuesday. ✉ *3 rue de l'Église, 60350 Chelles (5 km/3 mi east of Pierrefonds on D85),* ☎ *03–44–42–85–05,* FAX *03–44–42–83–30. 7 rooms. Restaurant. MC, V.*

CHAMPAGNE AND THE ARDENNES

Champagne, a place name that has become a universal synonym for joy and festivity, is a word of humble origin. Like *campagna,* its Italian counterpart, it is derived from the Latin *campus,* which means "open field." In French campus became *champ,* with the old language extending this to *champaign,* for "battlefield," and *champaine,* for "district of plains." *Battlefield* and *plains* both accurately describe the province, as Champagne is crisscrossed by Roman roads along which defenders and invaders have clashed for two millennia.

Today, of course, the province is best known for its champagne vineyards, which start just beyond Château-Thierry, 96 km (60 mi) northeast of Paris, and continue along the towering Marne Valley to Epernay. Cheerful villages line the Route du Vin (Wine Road), which twines north to Reims, the capital of bubbly. As you head farther northeast, rolling chalk hills give way to the rugged Ardennes Forest, close to the Belgian border and Lorraine.

Château-Thierry

40 *94 km (59 mi) northeast of Paris via A4, 51 km (32 mi) southeast of Pierrefonds.*

Built along the Marne River beneath the ruins of a hilltop castle that dates from the time of Joan of Arc, and within sight of the American **Belleau Wood** War Cemetery, Château-Thierry is best known as the birthplace of the French fabulist Jean de La Fontaine (1621–95). The 16th-century mansion where de La Fontaine was born is now a museum, the **Musée Jean de La Fontaine,** furnished in the style of the 17th century. It contains de La Fontaine's bust, portrait, and baptism certificate, plus editions of his fables magnificently illustrated by Jean-Baptiste Oudry (1755) and Gustave Doré (1868). ✉ *12 rue Jean-de-La-Fontaine,* ☎ *03–23–69–05–60.* 🎫 *€3.* ⏲ *Wed.–Mon. 10–noon and 2–5.*

Épernay

41 *50 km (31 mi) east of Château-Thierry via N3 or D3 and D1.*

Unlike Reims with its numerous treasures, the town of Épernay, on the south bank of the Marne, appears to live only for champagne. Unfortunately, no relation exists between the fabulous wealth of Épernay's illustrious wine houses and the drab, dreary appearance of the town as a whole. Most champagne firms are spaced out along the long, straight avenue de Champagne, and although their names may provoke sighs of wonder, their facades are either merely functional or overdressy. The attractions are all underground.

Of the various champagne houses open to the public, **Mercier** offers the best deal; its sculpted, labyrinthine cellars contain one of the world's largest wooden barrels (with a capacity of more than 215,000 bottles). A tour of the cellars takes 45 minutes in the relative comfort of a small train. A glass of champagne is your post-visit reward. ✉ *75 av. de Champagne,* ☎ *03–26–51–22–22,* FAX *03–26–51–22–23.* 🎫 *€4.60.* ⏲ *Weekdays 9:30–11:30 and 2–4:30. Closed Tues., Wed. in Jan.–Mar.*

To understand how the region's still wine became sparkling champagne, head across the Marne to **Hautvillers.** Here the monk Dom Pérignon (1638–1715)—upon whom, legend has it, blindness conferred the gifts of exceptional taste buds and sense of smell—invented champagne as everyone knows it by using corks for stoppers and blending wines from different vineyards. Dom Pérignon's simple tomb, in a damp, dreary Benedictine abbey church (now owned by Moët et Chandon), is a forlorn memorial to the hero of one of the world's most lucrative drink industries.

Dining and Lodging

$$$–$$$$ ✕🏨 **Briqueterie.** Épernay is short on good hotels, so it's worth driving south to Vinay to find this luxurious manor. The spacious rooms are modern; ask for one overlooking the extensive gardens. The chef has the Mediterranean on his mind, hence the lobster and prawns in citrus sauce. For more regional fare try the Champagne snails with herbed butter and, for dessert, the *crêpe soufflée au marc de champagne* (a crepe filled with pastry cream and flavored with brandy). ✉ *4 rte. de Sézanne, 51530 Vinay (6 km/4 mi south of Épernay),* ☎ *03–26–59–99–99,* FAX *03–26–59–92–10. 40 rooms, 2 suites. Restaurant, bar, cable TV, minibars, Internet, pool, gym, sauna, some pets allowed (€8 fee). AE, MC, V. Closed late Dec.*

Nightlife and the Arts

The leading wine festival in the Champagne region is the **Fête St-Vincent** (named for the patron saint of vine growers), held on either January 22 or the following Saturday in Ambonnay, 24 km (15 mi) east of Épernay.

Châlons-en-Champagne

42 *34 km (21 mi) east of Épernay via N3.*

Strangely enough, the official administrative center of the champagne industry is not Reims or Épernay but Châlons-en-Champagne. Yet this large town is mainly of interest for its vast cathedral and smaller, early Gothic church.

★ With its twin spires, Romanesque nave, and early Gothic choir and vaults, the church of **Notre-Dame-en-Vaux** bears eloquent testimony to Châlons's medieval importance. The small **museum** beside the excavated cloister contains outstanding medieval statuary. ✉ *Rue Nicolas-Durand,* ☎ *03–26–64–03–87.* 🎫 *€4.* ⏲ *Apr.–Sept., Wed.–Mon. 10–noon and 2–6; Oct.–Mar., Wed.–Fri. 10–noon and 2–5, weekends 10–noon and 2–6.*

The 13th-century **Cathédrale St-Étienne** (✉ Rue de la Marne) is a harmonious structure with large nave windows and tidy flying buttresses; the exterior effect is marred only by the bulky 17th-century Baroque west front.

Dining and Lodging

$$–$$$ ✕🏨 **Angleterre.** Rooms at this stylish spot in central Châlons have elaborate decor and marble bathrooms; those in the back are quietest. Particularly outstanding is the restaurant (closed Sunday; no lunch Saturday): chef Jacky Michel's creations include *sandre* (perch-pike) cooked in champagne and seasoned roast duck, as well as the seasonal dessert *tout-pommes,* featuring five variations on the humble apple. Breakfast is a superb buffet. ✉ *19 pl. Monseigneur-Tissier, 51000,* ☎ *03–26–68–21–51,* FAX *03–26–70–51–67,* WEB *www.hotel-dangleterre.com. 25 rooms. Restaurant, bar, minibars, Internet, some pets allowed (€8 fee). AE, DC, MC, V. Closed mid-July–early Aug. and late Dec.–early Jan.*

En Route The grapes of Champagne flourish on the steep slopes of the Montagne de Reims—more of a forest-topped plateau than a mountain—northwest of Châlons. Take D1 northwest, then turn right on D37 to Ambonnay to join the Route des Vins (Wine Road). This winds around the vine-entangled eastern slopes of the Montagne through such pretty wine villages as the aptly named **Bouzy** (known for its fashionable if overpriced red), **Verzy, Mailly-Champagne, Chigny-les-Roses,** and **Rilly-la-Montagne.**

L'Épine

43 *7 km (4 mi) east of Châlons.*

The tiny village of L'Épine is dominated by its church, the twin-towered Flamboyant Gothic **Basilique de Notre-Dame de l'Épine.** The church's facade is a magnificent creation of intricate patterns, spires, and an interior that exudes elegance and restraint.

Dining and Lodging

$$$ ★ ✕ 🏨 **Aux Armes de Champagne.** The highlight of this cozy former coaching inn (just opposite the town church, so ask for a table with a view) is the restaurant, with its renowned champagne list and imaginative, often spectacular cuisine by chef Gilles Blandin. Among his specialties are artichokes with local goat cheese, and red mullet prepared with juice from roast veal. (The restaurant is closed Monday in winter; no dinner is served Sunday.) Rooms are furnished with solid, traditional reproductions, wall hangings, and thick carpets. No. 21, with wood beams, is especially nice. ✉ *31 av. du Luxembourg, 51460,* ☎ *03–26–69–30–30,* FAX *03–26–66–92–31,* WEB *www.auxarmesdechampagne.com. 37 rooms. Restaurant, bar, no air-conditioning, cable TV, minibars, cable TV, Internet, tennis court. AE, DC, MC, V. Closed Jan. 1–Feb. 8*

Reims

11 km (7 mi) north of Rilly-la-Montagne, 44 km (27 mi) northwest of Châlons via N44, 144 km (90 mi) northeast of Paris.

Although most of its historic buildings were flattened in World War I and replaced by drab, modern architecture, those that do remain are of royal magnitude. Top of the list goes to the city's magnificent cathedral, in which the kings of France were crowned until 1825, while the Musée des Beaux-Arts has a stellar collection, including the famed Jacques-Louis David painting of Marat in his bath. Reims sparkles with some of the biggest names in champagne production, and the thriving industry has conferred wealth and sometimes an arrogant reserve on the region's inhabitants. Nevertheless, the maze of champagne cellars constitutes another fascinating sight of the city. Several champagne producers organize visits to their cellars, combining video presentations with guided tours of their cavernous, hewn-chalk underground warehouses. For a complete list of champagne cellars, head to the **tourist office** (✉ 2 rue Guillaume-de-Machault, ☎ 03–26–77–45–25), next to the cathedral.

★ 44 The tour of the **Taittinger** cellars is the most spectacular of the champagne producer visits. It includes a champagne *dégustation* (tasting) afterward. ✉ *9 pl. St-Nicaise,* ☎ *03–26–85–84–33.* 🎫 *€5.50.* ⌚ *Mar.–Nov., daily 9:30–noon and 2–4:30; Dec.–Feb., weekdays 9:30–noon and 2–4:30.*

45 The 11th-century **Basilique St-Rémi** honors the 5th-century saint who gave his name to the city. Its interior seems to stretch into the endless distance, an impression created by its relative murk and lowness. The airy four-story Gothic choir contains some fine original 12th-century stained glass. Like its sister cathedral, the basilica puts on indoor **son-et-lumière** shows every Saturday evening at 9:30 from late June to early October. They are preceded by a tour of the building and are free. ✉ *53 rue St-Rémi,* ☎ *03–26–85–31–20.* ⌚ *Daily 8–6.*

Basilique St-Rémi 45
Cathédrale Notre-Dame . .48
Crypto-portique 49
Mumm 52
Musée des Beaux-Arts . .47
Palais du Tau 46
Porte Mars . .50
Salle de Reddition . . .51
Taittinger . . .44

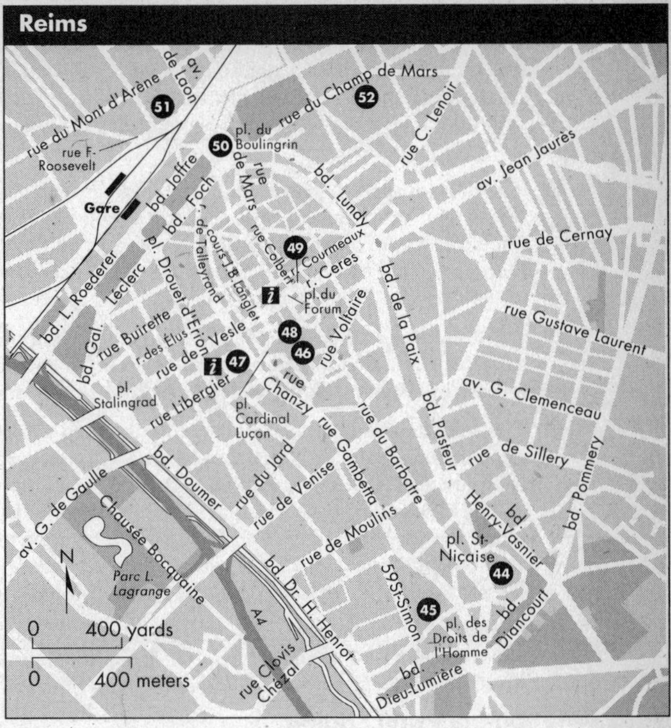

(46) The **Palais du Tau** (formerly the Archbishop's Palace), alongside the cathedral, houses an impressive display of tapestries and coronation robes, as well as several statues rescued from the cathedral facade before they fell off. The second-floor views of Notre-Dame are terrific. ✉ *2 pl. du Cardinal Luçon,* ☎ *03–26–47–81–79.* *€5.55.* *July–Aug., daily 9:30–6:30; mid-Mar.–June and Sept.–mid-Nov., daily 9:30–12:30 and 2–6; mid-Nov.–mid-Mar., weekdays 10–noon and 2–5, weekends 10–noon and 2–6.*

(47) The **Musée des Beaux-Arts** (Museum of Fine Arts), two blocks southwest of the cathedral, has an outstanding collection of paintings: no fewer than 27 Corots are here, as well as Jacques-Louis David's celebrated and unforgettable portrait of the revolutionary polemicist Jean-Paul Marat, stabbed in his bath by Charlotte Corday. ✉ *8 rue Chanzy,* ☎ *03–26–47–28–44.* *€3.* *Wed.–Mon. 10–noon and 2–6.*

★ (48) The **Cathédrale Notre-Dame** was the age-old setting for the coronations of the French kings. Clovis, king of the Franks in the 6th century, was baptized in an early structure on this site; Joan of Arc led her recalcitrant Dauphin here to be crowned King Charles VII; Charles X's coronation, in 1825, was the last. The high, solemn nave is at its best in summer, when the light shows up the plain lower walls. The east-end windows have stained glass by Marc Chagall. Admire the vista toward the west end, with an interplay of narrow pointed arches. The glory of Reims's cathedral is its facade: it's so skillfully proportioned that initially you have little idea of its monumental size. Above the north (left) door hovers the *Laughing Angel,* a delightful statue whose famous smile threatens to melt into an acid-rain scowl. Pollution has succeeded war as the ravager of the building's fabric. Restoration is an ongoing process. With the exception of the 15th-century towers, most of the original building went up in the 100 years after 1211. A stroll around the outside reinforces the impression of harmony, discipline, and decorative richness. The east end presents an idyllic sight across well-tended lawns. Spectacular **son-et-lumière** shows are performed both inside (small charge) and outside (free) the cathedral on Friday and Saturday evenings from July to mid-September. ✉ *Pl. du Cardinal-Luçon.* ⊙ *Daily 7:30–7:30.*

49 The Gallo-Roman **Cryptoportique,** an underground gallery and crypt, now a semi-subterranean passageway, was constructed around AD 200 under the forum of what was Reim's predecessor, the Roman town of Durocortorum. ✉ *Pl. du Forum,* ☎ *03–26–85–23–36.* ⊙ *Mid-June–mid-Sept., Tues.–Sun. 2–6.*

50 The **Porte Mars** (✉ Rue de Mars), an unlikely but impressive 3rd-century Roman arch adorned by worn bas-reliefs depicting Jupiter, Romulus, and Remus, looms up across from the train station.

51 The **Salle de Reddition** (Surrender Room), near the train station, also known as the Salle du 8 mai 1945, is a well-preserved map-covered room used by General Eisenhower as Allied headquarters at the end of World War II. It was here that General Alfred Jodl signed the German surrender at 2:41 AM on May 7, 1945. Fighting officially ceased at midnight the next day. ✉ *12 rue Franklin-Roosevelt,* ☎ *03–26–47–84–19.* 🎫 *€1.55.* ⊙ *Wed.–Mon. 10–noon and 2–6.*

52 **Mumm** is one of the few champagne houses to give out free samples after a tour. ✉ *34 rue du Champ-de-Mars,* ☎ *03–26–49–59–70.* 🎫 *€5.* ⊙ *Mar.–Oct., daily 9–11 and 2–5; Nov.–Feb., daily 2–5.*

Dining and Lodging

$$ ✕ **Vigneron.** This little brasserie in a 17th-century mansion is cozy and cheerful, with two tiny dining rooms displaying a jumble of champagne-related paraphernalia. The food is delightful as well: relatively cheap, distinctly hearty, and prepared with finesse. Try the pigs' feet or andouillettes slathered with delicious mustard made with champagne. ✉ *1 pl. Paul-Jamot,* ☎ *03–26–79–86–86. MC, V. Closed weekends, late Dec.–early Jan., and most of Aug.*

$$$$ ★ ✕🏨 **Boyer.** The top attraction at this hotel—a late-19th-century château surrounded by a hilly park and with a gilt-trimmed interior—is Gérard Boyer, one of the country's most highly rated chefs, whose delectable dishes range from wild mushrooms in cream to scallops with endive confit. The extensive wine list pays homage to Reims's champagne heritage. The restaurant is closed Monday, and no luncheon is offered Tuesday; reservations and jacket and tie are all essential. ✉ *Les Crayères, 64 bd. Henri-Vasnier, 51100,* ☎ *03–26–82–80–80,* FAX *03–26–82–65–52,* WEB *www.gerardboyer.com. 19 rooms. Restaurant, bar, cable TV, minibars, Internet, some pets allowed (€20 fee). AE, DC, MC, V. Closed late Dec.–mid-Jan.*

$$–$$$ ✕🏨 **Cheval Blanc.** This hotel, owned for five generations by the hospitable Robert family, is in the small village of Sept-Saulx, southeast of Reims. Guest rooms overlook a parklike glade on the small Vesle River—some are quite small, but the newer suites are larger and have modern furnishings. Restaurant specialties include St-Pierre fish seasoned with Chinese pepper and pigeon with dried raisins. ✉ *Rue du Moulin, 51400 Sept-Saulx (24 km/15 mi southeast of Reims via D8),* ☎ *03–26–03–90–27,* FAX *03–26–03–97–09. 25 rooms. Restaurant, no air-conditioning, cable TV, minibars, Internet, tennis court, fishing. AE, DC, MC, V. Closed late Jan.–mid-Feb.*

$$ ✕🏨 **La Paix.** A modern eight-story hotel, 10 minutes' walk from the cathedral, La Paix has stylish rooms with 18th- and 19th-century reproductions, a pretty garden, and a rather incongruous chapel. Its

brasserie-style restaurant serves good, though not inexpensive, cuisine (mainly grilled meats and seafood). ✉ *9 rue Buirette, 51100,* ☎ *03–26–40–04–08,* FAX *03–26–47–75–04,* WEB *www.bw-hotel-de-la-paix.com. 91 rooms, 21 suites. Restaurant, pool, bar, cable TV, minibars, some pets allowed (€8 fee). AE, DC, MC, V.*

THE NORTH AND CHAMPAGNE A TO Z

To research prices, get advice from other travelers, and book travel arrangements, visit www.fodors.com.

AIRPORTS

If you are coming from the U.S. and most other destinations, count on arriving at Paris's Charles de Gaulle or Orly airports. Charles de Gaulle offers easy access to the northbound A1 and the TGV line for Lille. If coming from London, consider the occasional direct flights from Heathrow to Lille-Lesquin and from Gatwick to Beauvais.

BOAT AND FERRY TRAVEL

Ferry and hovercraft companies travel between northern France and the United Kingdom. Companies traveling between Calais and Dover include Hoverspeed, P&O Stena, and Seafrance. The sole operator of the route between Boulogne and Folkestone is Hoverspeed. For more information, *see* Boat and Ferry Travel *in* Smart Travel Tips A to Z.

BUS TRAVEL

In the Picardy region, the main bus operator is **Courriers Automobiles Picards**; their main hub is Gare Routière in Amiens (✉ Rue de la Vallée, Amiens, ☎ 03–22–92–27–03). In the Champagne region, services are run by STDM Trans-Champagne; the main hub is Reims, where buses depart from the train station. Some sample bus links include Reims to Troyes (via STDM Trans-Champagne); Reims to Laon (one a day via RTA); Amiens to Arras (via Courriers Automobiles Picards); Boulogne to Calais (via Cariane Littoral); and Arras to Lille (via Colvert). There are many other links, so always check in with the regional tourist office or information window at a big gateway rail or bus station to get printed bus schedules.

➤ BUS INFORMATION: **Cariane Littoral** (☎ 03–21–34–74–40). **Colvert** (☎ 03–21–22–62–62). **Courriers Automobiles Picards** (BP 59, 80136 Rivery, ☎ 03–22–70–70–70, FAX 03–22–70–70–71). **RTA** (☎ 03–23–50–68–50). **STDM Trans-Champagne** (86 rue des Fagnières, 51000 Châlons-en-Champagne, ☎ 03–26–65–17–07).

CAR RENTAL

Be aware that the Avis offices at the Calais car ferry and Hoverport terminals may not always be staffed. Look for instructions on how to use the red phones provided in these offices to reach the central office in the town of Calais, which will handle your rental.

➤ LOCAL AGENCIES: **Avis** (✉ 36 pl. d'Armes, Calais, ☎ 03–21–34–66–50; ✉ Calais car ferry terminal, ☎ 03–21–96–47–65; ✉ Calais Hoverport, ☎ 03–21–96–66–52; ✉ Cour de la Gare, Reims, ☎ 03–26–47–10–08). **Europcar** (✉ Gare Lille-Europe, av. Le Corbusier, Lille, ☎ 03–20–06–01–46; ✉ Gare Lille-Flandre, rue de Tournai, ☎ 03–20–06–10–04). **Hertz** (✉ 5 bd. d'Alsace-Lorraine, Amiens, ☎ 03–22–91–26–24; ✉ 10 bd. Daunou, Boulogne-sur-Mer, ☎ 03–21–31–53–14).

CAR TRAVEL

Two highways head north from Paris. Busy A1 passes close to Compiègne and Arras (where A26 branches off to Calais) before reaching Lille. Journey time is about 1 hour and 40 minutes to Arras and 2½ hours to Lille. The new, much quieter A16 leads from L'Isle-Adam, north of Paris, up to Beauvais and Amiens, before veering northwest to Abbeville and around the coast to Boulogne, Calais, and Dunkerque. Journey time is about 90 minutes to Amiens and 2½ hours to Boulogne. If you're arriving by car via the Channel Tunnel, you'll disembark at Coquelles, near Calais, and join A16 not far from its junction with A26, which heads to Arras (75 minutes) and Reims (2½ hours). A4 heads east from Paris to Reims; allow 90 minutes to two hours, depending on traffic.

A26 heads inland from Calais and St-Omer to Arras (where it intersects with A1), Laon, and Reims, the latter directly linked to Paris by A4. A16 follows the railroad around the coast from Belgium and Dunkerque past Calais, Boulogne, Le Touquet, Abbeville, Amiens, and Beauvais to Paris.

EMERGENCIES

➤ CONTACTS: **Ambulance** (☎ 15). **Regional hospitals** (✉ 1 pl. Victor-Pauchet, Amiens, ☎ 03–22–66–80–00; ✉ 8 av. Henri-Adnot, Compiègne, ☎ 03–44–23–60–00; ✉ 51 bd. de Belfort, Lille, ☎ 03–20–87–48–48; ✉ American Hospital, 47 rue Cognac-Jay, Reims, ☎ 03–26–78–78–78).

TOURS

Service des Visites Guidées in Boulogne's Château-Musée arranges trips to Boulogne's old town and port for groups of up to 30 people; the cost for two hours totals €60 for two or more.

➤ FEES AND SCHEDULES: **Service des Visites Guidées** (✉ Rue Bernet, Boulogne-sur-Mer, ☎ 03–21–80–56–78).

BUS TOURS

The Lille Tourist Office is a mine of information about companies that operate bus tours through northern France. Loisirs-Accueil Nord organizes bus trips to Boulogne and Flanders and can arrange fishing, walking, and beer-tasting tours.

➤ FEES AND SCHEDULES: **Lille Tourist Office** (✉ 42 pl. Rihour, ☎ 03–20–21–94–21, WEB www.lilletourism.com). **Loisirs-Accueil Nord** (✉ 6 rue Gauthier-de-Châtillon, Lille, ☎ 03–20–57–59–59).

TRAIN TRAVEL

TGV (*Trains à Grande Vitesse*) trains speed from Paris (Gare du Nord) to Lille (255 km/165 mi) in just one hour. A separate TGV service links Paris (Gare du Nord) to Arras (50 minutes) and Dunkerque (two hours). The Paris–Boulogne–Calais train chugs unhurriedly around the coast, taking nearly three hours to cover 300 km (185 mi) via Amiens. There is also frequent daily service from Paris (Gare du Nord) to Compiègne and Noyon, as well as to Laon (taking up to two leisurely hours to cover 140 km/87 mi). Regular trains cover the 170 km (105 mi) from Paris (Gare de l'Est) to Reims in 1½ hours. Eurostar trains, via the Channel Tunnel, link London to Lille in two hours; some stop at Fréthun, just outside Calais.

It's easy to get around this region by train. Most sites can be reached by regular train service, except for the war cemeteries and the château in Pierrefonds. The Lille–Calais regional line (TER) stops at St-Omer. From Calais it follows the coast to Boulogne, Montreuil, Étaples (with a bus link to Le Touquet 6½ km/4 mi away), Abbeville, and Amiens, where a change is needed to reach Beauvais or Reims (via Laon). Trains leave Reims for Épernay and Châlons.

➤ TRAIN INFORMATION: **SNCF** (☎ 08–36–35–35–35, WEB www.sncf.com).

TRAVEL AGENCIES

➤ LOCAL AGENT REFERRALS: **Carlson Wagons-lit** (✉ 1 rue Paul-Bert, Calais, ☎ 03–21–34–79–25; ✉ 9 rue Faidherbe, Lille, ☎ 03–20–55–05–76).

VISITOR INFORMATION

The principal regional tourist offices in Amiens, Lille, and Reims are good sources of information about the region. Other, smaller towns also have their own tourist offices, listed below by town.

➤ TOURIST INFORMATION: **Abbeville** (✉ 1 pl. de l'Amiral-Courbet, ☎ 03–22–24–27–92). **Amiens** (✉ 6 bis rue Dusevel, ☎ 03–22–71–60–50, WEB www.amiens.com-tourisme). **Arras** (✉ Hôtel de Ville, pl. des Héros, ☎ 03–21–51–26–95). **Beauvais** (✉ 1 rue Beauregard, ☎ 03–44–45–08–18). **Boulogne-sur-Mer** (✉ Forum Jean-Noël, quai de la Poste, ☎ 03–21–31–68–38). **Calais** (✉ 12 bd. Clemenceau, ☎ 03–21–96–62–40). **Compiègne** (✉ Pl. de l'Hôtel-de-Ville, ☎ 03–44–40–01–00). **Eu** (✉ 41 rue Paul-Bignon, ☎ 02–35–86–04–68). **Laon** (✉ Pl. du Parvis, ☎ 03–23–20–28–62). **Le Touquet** (✉ Palais de l'Europe, pl. de l'Hermitage, ☎ 03–21–06–72–00). **Lille** (✉ 42 pl. Rihour, ☎ 03–20–21–94–21, WEB www.lilletourism.com). **Montreuil-sur-Mer** (✉ 21 rue Carnot, ☎ 03–21–06–04–27). **Noyon** (✉ Pl. de l'Hôtel-de-Ville, ☎ 03–44–44–21–88). **Pierrefonds** (✉ Rue Louis-d'Orléans, ☎ 03–44–42–81–44). **Reims** (✉ 2 rue Guillaume-de-Machault, ☎ 03–26–77–45–25, WEB www.tourism.fr-reims). **St-Omer** (✉ 4 rue du Lion-d'Or, ☎ 03–21–98–08–51).

8 ALSACE, LORRAINE, AND FRANCHE-COMTÉ

Only the Rhine River separates Germany from Alsace-Lorraine, a region that often looks and even sounds German. But its heart—after all, its natives were the first to sing the "Marseillaise"—is passionately French. In Alsace, wind along the Route du Vin through vineyards and storybook villages, then explore Strasbourg, which for all its medieval charms rivals Paris in history and haute cuisine. In mellow Lorraine, trace Joan of Arc's childhood, then discover the elegant 18th-century town of Nancy. Great art treasures—the Grünewald altarpiece at Colmar is one—also entice, as do hikes in the forested wilds of Franche-Comté.

Updated by
Nicola Keegan

Introduction by
Nancy Coons

WHO PUT THE HYPHEN IN ALSACE-LORRAINE? The two regions, long at odds physically and culturally, were bonded when Kaiser Wilhelm sliced off the Moselle chunk of Lorraine and sutured it, à la Dr. Frankenstein, to Alsace, claiming the unfortunate graft as German turf. Though their names to this day are often hyphenated, Alsace and Lorraine have always been two separate territories, with distinctly individual characters. It is only their recent German past that ties them together—it wasn't until 1879, as a concession after France's surrender in 1871, that the newly hyphenated "Alsace-Lorraine" became part of the enemy's spoils. At that point the region was systematically Teutonized—architecturally, linguistically, culinarily (" . . . ve haff our own vays of cookink sauerkraut!")—and the next two generations grew up culturally torn. Until 1918, that is, when France undid its defeat and reclaimed its turf. Until 1940, when Hitler snatched it back and reinstated German textbooks in the primary schools. Until 1945, when France once again triumphantly raised the *bleu-blanc-rouge* over Strasbourg.

But no matter how forcefully the French tout its hard-won Frenchness, Alsace's German roots go deeper than the late 19th century, as one look at its storybook medieval architecture will attest. In fact, this strip of vine-covered hills squeezed between the Rhine and the Vosges mountains was called Prima Germania by the Romans, and belonged to the fiercely Germanic Holy Roman Empire for more than 700 years. Yet west of the Vosges, Lorraine served under French and Burgundian lords as well as the Holy Roman Empire, coming into its own under the powerful and influential dukes of Lorraine in the Middle Ages and Renaissance. Stanislas, the duke of Lorraine who transformed Nancy into a cosmopolitan Paris of the East, was Louis XV's father-in-law. Thus Lorraine's culture evolved as decidedly less German than its neighbor to the southeast.

But that's why these days most travelers find Alsace more exotic than Lorraine: its gabled, half-timber houses, ornate wells and fountains, oriels (upstairs bay windows), storks' nests, and carved-wood balustrades would serve well as a stage set for the tale of William Tell and satisfy a visitor's deepest craving for well-preserved Old World atmosphere. Strasbourg, perhaps France's most fascinating city outside Paris, offers all this ambience, and urban sophistication as well. And throughout Alsace, hotels are well scrubbed, with tile bathrooms, good mattresses, and geraniums spilling from every windowsill. Although the cuisine leans toward wursts and sauerkraut, sophisticated spins on traditional fare have earned it a reputation—perhaps ironic, in some quarters—as one of the gastronomic centers of France. In fact, it has been crudely but vividly put that Alsace combines the best of both worlds: one dines in France but washes up, as it were, in Germany.

Lorraine, on the other hand, has suffered in recent years, and a decline in its northern industry and the miseries of its small farmers have left much of it tarnished and neglected—or, as others might say, kept it unspoiled. Yet Lorraine's rich caches of verdure, its rolling countryside dotted with *mirabelle* (plum) orchards and crumbling-stucco villages, abbeys, fortresses, and historic cities (majestic Nancy, war-ravaged Verdun) offer a truly French view of life in the north. Its borders flank Belgium, Luxembourg, and Germany's mellow Mosel (also spelled Moselle). Home of Baccarat and St-Louis crystal (thanks to limitless supplies of firewood from the Vosges Forest), the origin of the Gregorian chant, birthplace of Art Nouveau and Joan of Arc, Lorraine-the-underdog has long had something of its own to contribute. Although it may lack the Teutonic comforts of Alsace—it subscribes to the more laissez-faire school of innkeeping (concave mattresses, dusty bolsters, creaky floors)—it serves its regional delicacies with flair: *tourte Lorraine* (a pork-and-beef pie), madeleines (shell-shape butter cakes), mirabelle plum tarts, and the famous local quiche.

There's even more novelty to be found south of Alsace and Lorraine: folkloric Franche-Comté. With its forested pre-Alpine mountains, weathered-wood and stone chalets, green-velvet pastures, and cheese cooperatives, it reminds nearly everyone of a certain cuckoo-clock country just over the border. In the misty Jura mountain range, sturdy shoes and topographical maps are de rigueur, with a decidedly un-Swiss reward at the end of a hiker's day: superb and eccentric Jura wines, a panoply of subtly smoked sausages, and the discreet hospitality that makes this the *bouche à l'oreille* (word of mouth) retreat of ski-weary Parisians.

Pleasures and Pastimes

Dining

If Alsace cooking tends to be heavy—*choucroute* (sauerkraut served with ham and sausages) and *baeckoffe* (a hearty meat-and-potato casserole) are two mainstays—there is sophistication, too: foie gras accompanied by a glass of *vendange tardive* (late-harvested) Gewürztraminer, and trout and chicken cooked in Riesling, the classic wine of Alsace. Snails and seasonal game are other favorites, as are Muenster cheese, salty *bretzel* loaves, and briochelike *kouglof* bread. Carp fried in bread crumbs is a specialty of southern Alsace. Lorraine, renowned for quiches, is also famous for its madeleines, *dragées* (almond candies), macaroons, and the lovely little *mirabelle,* a small yellow plum juicy with heady, perfumed nectar. Lorraine shares the Alsatian love of pastry and fruit tarts, served as often at 4 in the afternoon, with coffee, as an after-dinner dessert. Restaurant prices tend to be lower in Lorraine than in Alsace, but only in German-influenced Alsace will you find *winstubs* (pronounced *veen*-shtoob), cozy, paneled inns serving hearty regional specialties or, between meals, wine and snacks. Mountain-smoked hams and sausages, mushrooms, and freshwater fish are menu mainstays in the Jura. Hard, flavorsome Comté and Beaufort are the choice local Gruyère-style cheeses, along with blue-stripe Morbier, satiny Vacherin (often served melted in its box), and Cancaillotte, its flavor milder than its reek. *Tartiflettes* (diced potatoes in bacony cheese sauce) is a rib-sticking mainstay.

CATEGORY	COST*
$$$$	over €30
$$$	€20–€30
$$	€12–€20
$	under €12

**per person for a main course only, including tax (19.6%) and service; note that if a restaurant offers only prix-fixe (set-price) meals, it has been given the price category that reflects the full prix-fixe price.*

Lodging

Accommodations are easier to find in Lorraine and the Jura than in Alsace, where advance reservations are essential in summer. Alsace is rich in *gîtes,* country houses that can be rented. Throughout Alsace, hotels are models of good housekeeping. Lorraine tends to lack the Teutonic comforts of Alsace but is coming around as renovations get under way.

Assume all hotel rooms have air-conditioning, telephones, TV, and private bath unless otherwise noted. Internet, when listed in facilities, means in-room data-ports and/or public-area computers provide on-line access.

CATEGORY	COST*
$$$$	over €180
$$$	€120–€180
$$	€60–€120
$	under €60

**All prices are for a standard double room in high season, including tax (19.6%) and service charge.*

Outdoor Activities and Sports

The region is ideal for outdoor activities: bicycling along the banks of rivers in Lorraine, horseback riding through forests, fishing in the angler's paradise of Franche-Comté, or hiking in the Vosges and Jura mountains.

Exploring Alsace, Lorraine, and Franche-Comté

Most itineraries begin by exploring this region to the west—nearest Paris—where the battlegrounds of Verdun provide a poignant introduction to Lorraine. Linger in the artistic city of Nancy and then head east to Strasbourg (145 km/90 mi), a city of such historic and cultural importance that it is worth exploring in depth. From here tour the rest of Alsace, following the photogenic Route du Vin (Wine Road) to Mulhouse. Finally, head south to Besançon and the spectacular scenery of Franche-Comté and the Jura.

Great Itineraries

You can cover most of Alsace-Lorraine and Franche-Comté in about nine days. With six days you can see the northern part of Lorraine, from Verdun to Nancy, and most of Alsace. Three days will give you just enough time to explore Alsace, including the cosmopolitan city of Strasbourg.

Numbers in the text correspond to numbers in the margin and on the Lorraine, Alsace, Franche-Comté, Nancy, and Strasbourg maps.

IF YOU HAVE 3 DAYS

Explore Alsace, beginning with a day and night in the delightful city of **Strasbourg** 27–40. The next day start out early, cruising south along the Route du Vin to pretty **Obernai** 41; the charming villages of **Barr** 43, **Andlau** 44, and **Dambach-la-Ville** 45; and the dramatic castle in **Haut-Koenigsbourg** 47. Spend the night in the wine town of **Ribeauvillé** 48 or medieval **Riquewihr** 49. On day three soak up the art and atmosphere in **Colmar** 50—whose museum headlines the world-famous Grünewald altarpiece—or tour industrial museums in **Mulhouse** 52.

IF YOU HAVE 6 DAYS

Coming from Paris, start at the moving **Verdun** 19 battlefields; then head east to the cathedral city of **Metz** 20. On day two concentrate on **Nancy** 1–18, where you'll find some of the most elegant 18th-century architecture in France on tap. Spend your third evening in **Strasbourg** 27–40 and your fourth in or around **Obernai** 41, visiting **Barr** 43 and environs en route. Take in bustling **Sélestat** 46, with its fine churches, on day five, along with **Haut-Koenigsbourg** 47 and **Ribeauvillé** 48, ending up in **Riquewihr** 49. On day six head to **Colmar** 50 or **Mulhouse** 52.

Lorraine

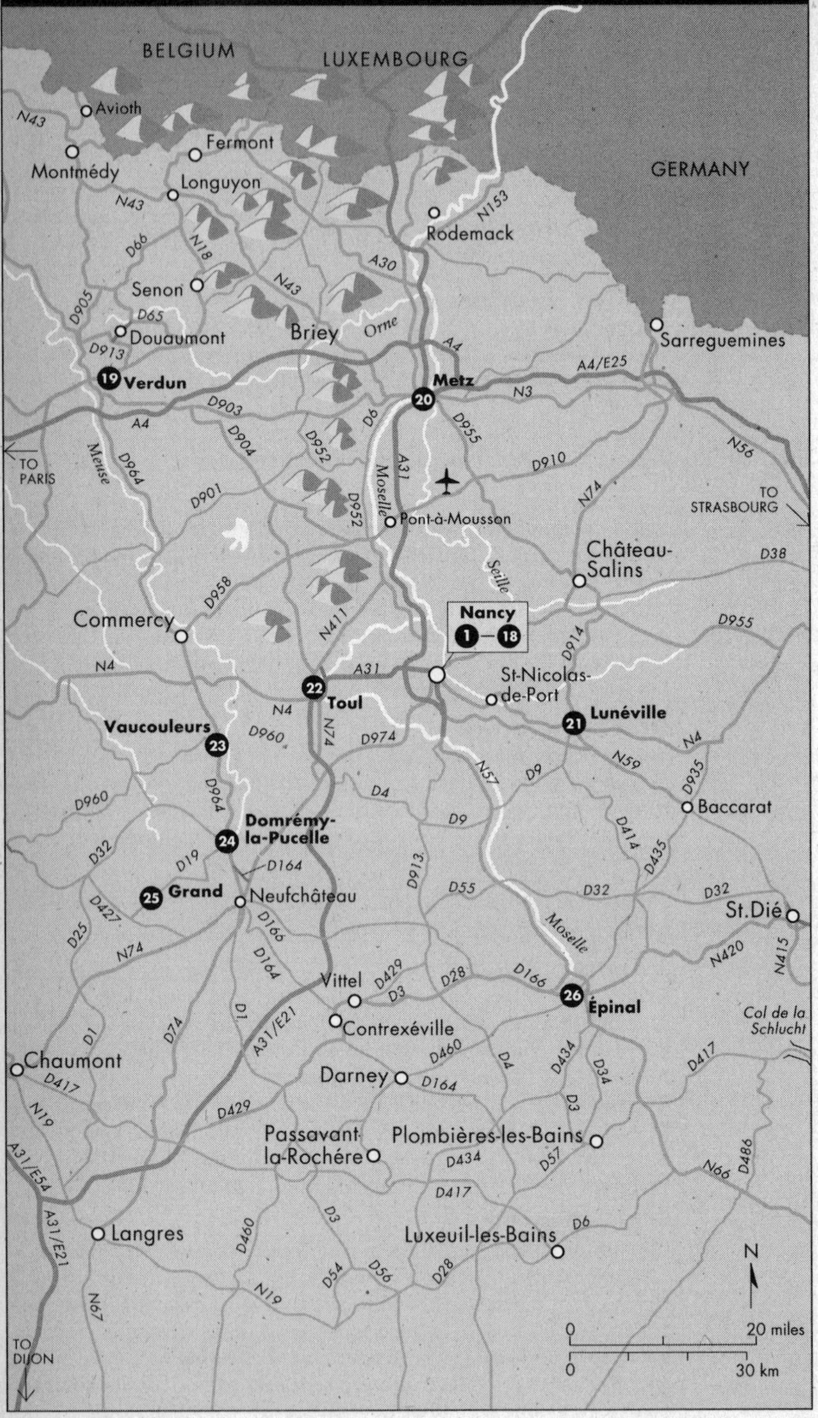

BELGIUM
LUXEMBOURG
GERMANY
Avioth
Montmédy
Fermont
Longuyon
Rodemack
Senon
Douaumont
Briey
Orne
Sarreguemines
Verdun
Metz
TO PARIS
Meuse
Moselle
Pont-à-Mousson
TO STRASBOURG
Château-Salins
Seille
Nancy
1–18
Commercy
Toul
St-Nicolas-de-Port
Lunéville
Vaucouleurs
Baccarat
Domrémy-la-Pucelle
Grand
Neufchâteau
St.Dié
Vittel
Contrexéville
Épinal
Col de la Schlucht
Chaumont
Darney
Passavant-la-Rochère
Plombières-les-Bains
Langres
Luxeuil-les-Bains
TO DIJON
N
0
20 miles
0
30 km

Alsace

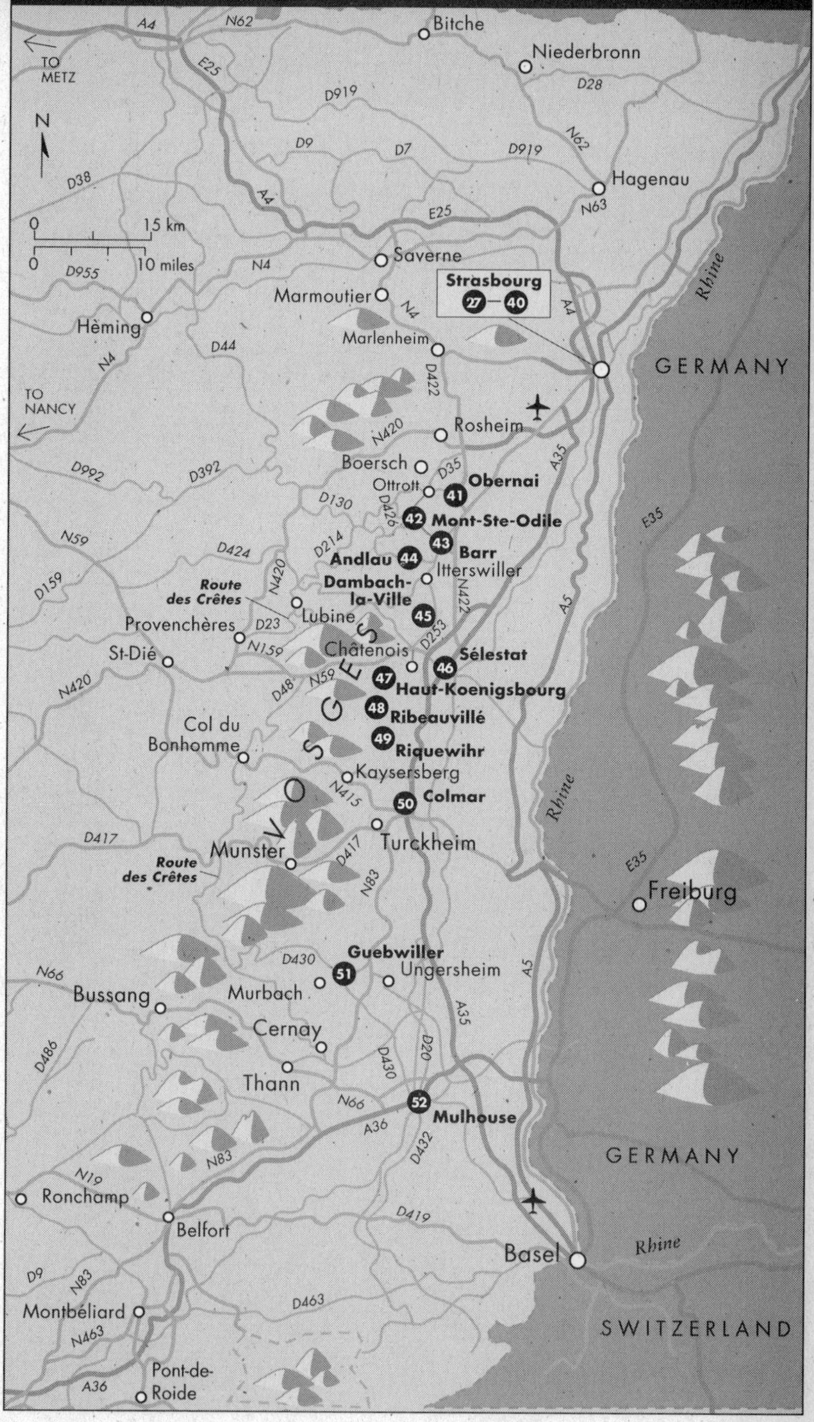

Bitche
Niederbronn
TO METZ
A4
N62
E25
D919
D28
N62
D9
D7
D919
Hagenau
N63
N
D38
A4
E25
0
15 km
0
10 miles
D955
N4
Saverne
Marmoutier
Strasbourg
27
40
Rhine
Hèming
N4
A4
Marlenheim
D44
N4
D422
GERMANY
TO NANCY
N420
Rosheim
A35
D992
D392
Boersch
D35
Ottrott
41
Obernai
D130
D426
42
Mont-Ste-Odile
E35
N59
D214
43
Barr
D424
Andlau
44
Itterswiller
N420
D159
Route des Crêtes
Dambach-la-Ville
N422
A5
Lubine
45
Provenchères
D23
D253
N159
Châtenois
46
Sélestat
St-Dié
D48
N59
47
Haut-Koenigsbourg
N420
VOSGES
48
Ribeauvillé
Col du Bonhomme
49
Riquewihr
Kaysersberg
N415
50
Colmar
Rhine
Turckheim
D417
Munster
D417
Route des Crêtes
N83
E35
Freiburg
Guebwiller
D430
51
Ungersheim
N66
A5
Bussang
Murbach
A35
Cernay
D486
D430
D20
Thann
N66
52
Mulhouse
A36
D432
GERMANY
N83
N19
Ronchamp
Belfort
D419
Basel
Rhine
D9
N83
D463
Montbéliard
N463
SWITZERLAND
Pont-de-Roide
A36

Franche-Comté

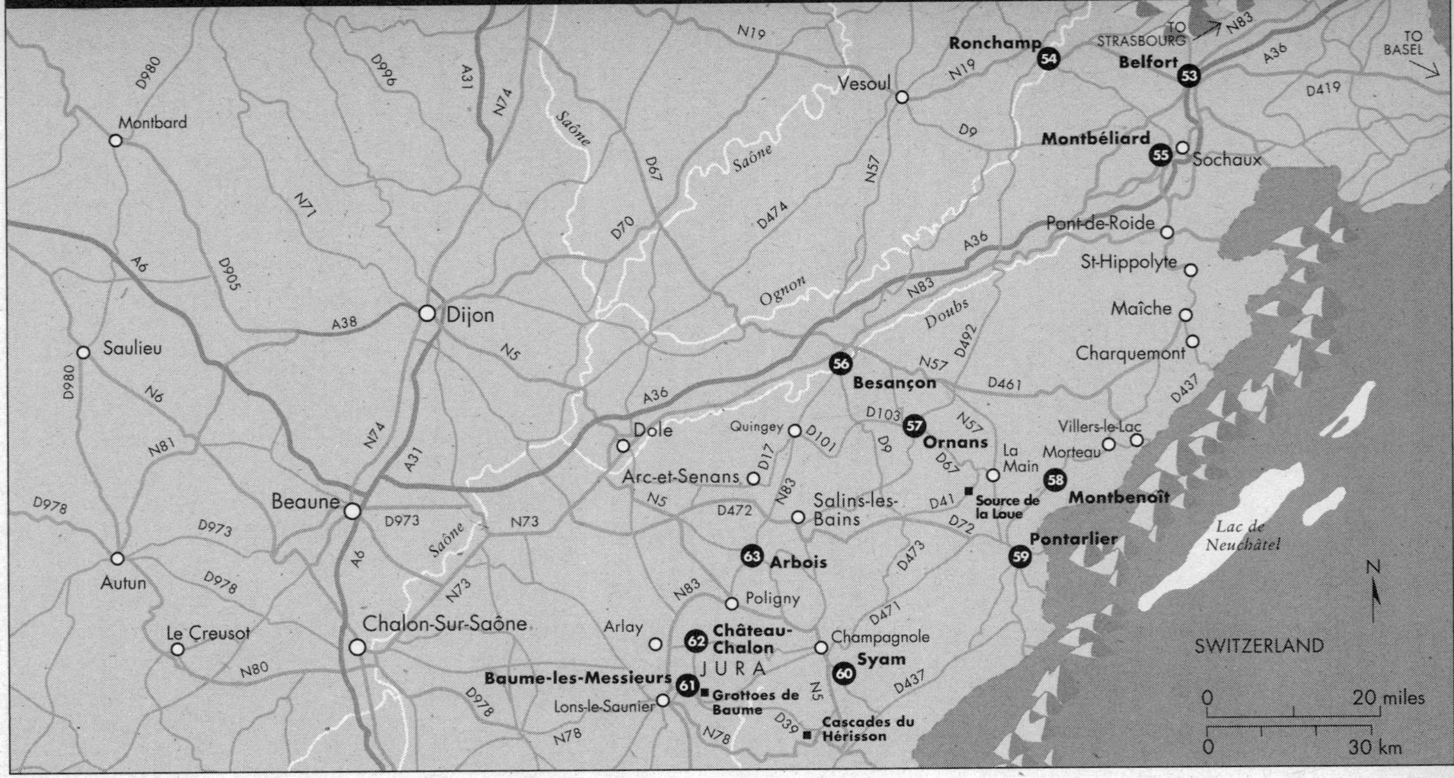

IF YOU HAVE 9 DAYS

Begin in **Verdun** ⑲ and **Metz** ⑳; then head south through Lorraine to the crumbling cathedral town of **Toul** ㉒ and to Joan of Arc's birthplace in **Domrémy-la-Pucelle** ㉔. Spend day three in **Nancy** ①–⑱. On day four make **Strasbourg** ㉗–㊵ your goal. The next day follow the Route du Vin to **Obernai** ㊶, **Mont-Ste-Odile** ㊷, and **Barr** ㊸. Continue south to **Sélestat** ㊻, **Haut-Koenigsbourg** ㊼, **Ribeauvillé** ㊽, and **Riquewihr** ㊾. On day seven head to one of the following cities: **Colmar** ㊿, to see its splendid Unterlinden Museum; **Mulhouse** (52), if you're interested in visiting museums of industry and technology; or **Belfort** (53), for its monuments. Spend the night in Colmar or Belfort, or head that night to **Besançon** (56). Explore this historic Franche-Comté town on the morning of day eight; then head to scenic riverside **Ornans** (57) before wheeling west to the wine town of **Arbois** (63). Use Arbois as a base to explore the grandiose Jura scenery at the Reculée des Planches, the Cirque du Fer-à-Cheval, **Baume-les-Messieurs** (61), and the hilltop village of **Château-Chalon** (62).

When to Tour Alsace-Lorraine and Franche-Comté

Outside tourist-packed high summer, June and September are the warmest and sunniest months. Many of the region's towns and villages, especially the wine villages of Alsace, stage summer festivals, including the spectacular pagan-inspired burning of the three pine trees in Thann (late June), the Flower Carnival in Sélestat (mid-August), and the wine fair in Colmar (first half of August). Some of the region's top sights, however—notably Haut-Koenigsbourg—can be besieged by tourists in July and August, so if you're there then, try to visit early in the morning. Although Lorraine is a lusterless place in winter, the Vosges and Jura mountains make attempts at being ski venues—plentiful snow cannot always be guaranteed—while Strasbourg pays tribute to the Germanic tradition with a Christmas fair.

NANCY

For architectural variety, few French cities match Nancy, which is in the heart of Lorraine, 146 km (91 mi) east of Paris. Medieval ornamentation, 18th-century grandeur, and Belle Epoque fluidity rub shoulders in the town center, where the bustle of commerce mingles with stately elegance. Its majesty derives from a long history as domain to the powerful dukes of Lorraine, whose double-barred crosses figure prominently on local statues and buildings. Never having fallen under the rule of the Holy Roman Empire, or, more recently, the Germans, this Lorraine city retains an eminently Gallic charm.

The city is at its most sublimely French in its harmoniously constructed squares and buildings, which, as vestiges of the 18th century, have the quiet refinement associated with the best in French architecture. Curiously enough, it was a Pole, and not a Frenchman, who was responsible for much of what is beautiful in Nancy. Stanislas Leszczynski, ex-king of Poland and father of Marie Leczinska (who married Louis XV of France) was given the kingdom of Lorraine-Habsburg by his royal son-in-law on the understanding that on his death it would revert to France. Stanislas installed himself in Nancy and devoted himself to the glorious embellishment of the city. Today place Stanislas remains one of the loveliest and most perfectly proportioned squares in the world, with place de la Carrière—reached through Stanislas's Arc de Triomphe—with its elegant, homogeneous 18th-century houses, its close rival for this honor.

The Historic Center

Concentrated northeast of the train station, this neighborhood—rich in architectural treasures as well as museums—includes classical place Stanislas and the shuttered, medieval *vieille ville* (Old Town).

A Good Walk

Begin your walk at the symbolic heart of Nancy, **place Stanislas** ①. On the western corner is the **Musée des Beaux-Arts** ②, the Fine Arts Museum. Cross place Stanislas diagonally and head south down rue Maurice Barrès to the Baroque **Cathédrale** ③. On leaving, turn left on rue St-Georges and right up rue des Dominicains, stopping to admire the elegant stonework on No. 57, the Maison des Adams, named for the sculptors who lived in (and decorated) the edifice in the 18th century.

Recross place Stanislas and go through the monumental Arc de Triomphe, entering into peaceful **place de la Carrière** ④. At the colonnaded Palais du Gouvernement, former home of the governors of Lorraine, turn right into the vast, formal city park known as **La Pépinière** ⑤. From the park's entrance at the foot of place de la Carrière, head straight under the arches and into the Vieille Ville (Old Town). Dominating the square is the basilica of **St-Epvre** ⑥, clearly constructed to make up for the absence of a Gothic cathedral in Nancy.

Head immediately right up picturesque Grande-Rue, with its antiques shops, bookstores, and artisanal bakeries behind brightly painted facades. On your right is the **Palais Ducal** ⑦. Here is the main branch of the Musée Historique Lorraine, a marvelous complex that covers art as well as regional lore. The neighboring **Musée des Arts et Traditions Populaires** ⑧ occupies the Couvent des Cordeliers, combining a folk-arts museum and a Gothic chapel. At the end of Grande-Rue is the **Porte de la Craffe** ⑨, the last of Nancy's medieval fortifications.

TIMING

Depending on how much time you spend in the museums, this walk could take an hour or a whole day. Note that all the museums are closed on Tuesday.

Sights to See

❸ **Cathédrale.** This vast, frigid edifice was built in the 1740s in a ponderous Baroque style, eased in part by the florid ironwork of Jean Lamour. Its most notable interior feature is a murky 19th-century fresco in the dome. The **Trésor** (Treasury) contains minute 10th-century splendors carved of ivory and gold. ✉ *Rue St-Georges, Ville Neuve.*

★ ❽ Just up the street from the Palais Ducal, the quirky, appealing **Musée des Arts et Traditions Populaires** (Museum of Folk Arts and Traditions) is housed in the **Couvent des Cordeliers** (Convent of the Franciscans, who were known as Cordeliers until the Revolution). It re-creates how local people lived in pre-industrial times, using a series of evocative rural interiors. Craftsmen's tools, colorful crockery, somber stone fireplaces, and dark waxed-oak furniture accent the tableaulike settings. Also within the religious complex, the dukes of Lorraine are buried in the crypt of the adjoining **Église des Cordeliers,** a Flamboyant Gothic church; the *gisant* (reclining statue) of Philippa de Gueldra, second wife of René II, executed in limestone in flowing detail, is a moving example of Renaissance portraiture. The octagonal Ducal Chapel was begun in 1607 in the Renaissance style, modeled on the Medici Chapel in Florence. ✉ *66 Grande-Rue, Vieille Ville,* ☎ *03–83–32–18–74.* 🎫 *€3.30 (€4.60 joint ticket with Musée Historique).* ⏲ *May–Sept., Wed.–Mon. 10–6; Oct.–Apr., Wed.–Sat. and Mon. 10–noon and 2–5, Sun. 10–noon and 2–6.*

Avenue Foch . 12
Brasserie l'Excelsior . . . 13
Cathédrale . . . 3
Musée des Arts 8
Musée des Beaux-Arts . . . 2
Musée de l'École de Nancy 10
No. 1 rue Louis-Majorelle . . . 11
No. 2 rue Bénit 16
No. 9 rue Chanzy 15
No. 40 rue Henri-Poincaré 14
Nos. 42-44 rue St-Dizier 18
Palais Ducal/ Musée Historique Lorrain 7
La Pépinière . . 5
Place de la Carrière 4
Place Stanislas . 1
Porte de la Craffe 9
Rue Raugraff . 17
St-Epvre 6

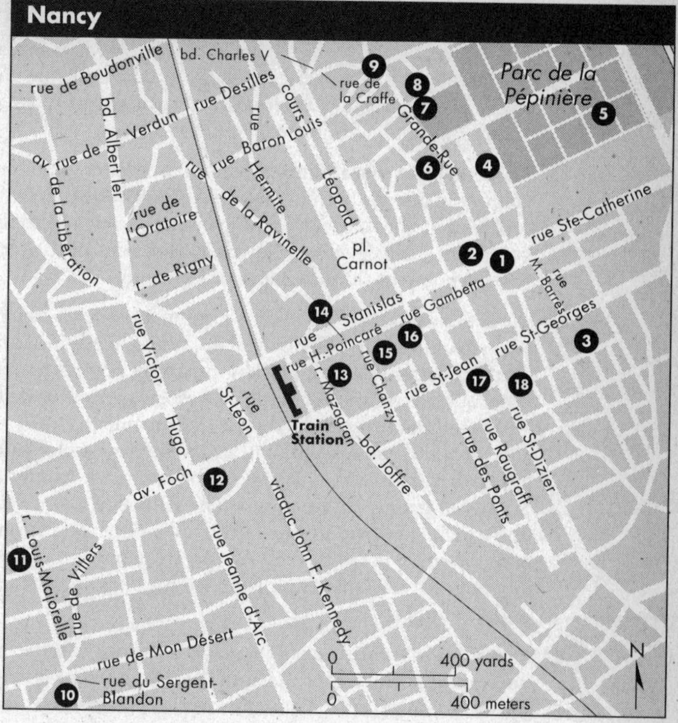

★ ❷ **Musée des Beaux-Arts** (Fine Arts Museum). In a splendid building that now spills over into a spectacular new wing, a broad and varied collection of art treasures lives up to the noble white Héré facade. Most striking are the freeze-the-moment realist tableaux painted by native son Emile Friant at the turn of the 20th century. A sizable collection of Lipschitz sculptures includes portrait busts of Gertrude Stein, Jean Cocteau, and Coco Chanel. You'll also find 19th- and 20th-century paintings by Monet, Manet, Utrillo, and Modigliani; a Caravaggio *Annunciation* and a wealth of old masters from the Italian, Dutch, Flemish, and French schools; and impressive glassworks by Nancy native Antonin Daum. The showpiece is Rubens's massive *Transfiguration.* Good commentary cards in English are available in every hall. ✉ *Pl. Stanislas, Ville Royale,* ☎ *03–83–85–30–72.* 💶 *€5.35.* ⏲ *Wed.–Mon. 10:30–6.*

❼ **Palais Ducal** (Ducal Palace). This palace was built in the 13th century and completely restored at the end of the 15th century and again after a fire at the end of the 19th century. The main entrance to the palace, and the **Musée Historique Lorrain** (Lorraine History Museum), which it now houses, is 80 yards down the street from the spectacularly flamboyant Renaissance portal. A spiral stone staircase leads up to the palace's most impressive room, the **Galerie des Cerfs** (Stags Gallery). Exhibits here (including pictures, armor, and books) recapture the Renaissance mood of the 16th century—one of elegance and merrymaking, with an undercurrent of stern morality: an elaborate series of huge tapestries, *La Condemnation du Banquet* (Condemnation of the Banquet), expounds on the evils of drunkenness and gluttony. Exhibits showcase Stanislas and his court, including "his" oft-portrayed dwarf; a section on Nancy in the revolutionary era; and works of Lorraine native sons, including a collection of Jacques Callot engravings and a handful of Georges de La Tour works. ✉ *64 Grande-Rue, Vieille Ville,* ☎ *03–*

83–32–18–74. *€3.10 (€4.60 joint ticket with Musée des Arte et Traditions).* *Wed.–Mon. 10–12:30, 2–6.*

5 **La Pépinière.** This lovely, landscaped city park has labeled ancient trees, a rose garden, playgrounds, a carousel, and a small zoo. ✉ *Entrance off pl. de la Carrière, Vieille Ville.*

4 **Place de la Carrière.** Lined with pollarded trees and handsome 18th-century mansions (another successful collaboration between Stanislas and Héré), this elegant rectangle leads from place Stanislas to the colonnaded facade of the **Palais du Gouvernement** (Government Palace), former home of the governors of Lorraine.

★ 1 **Place Stanislas.** With its severe, gleaming-white Classical facades given a touch of Rococo jollity by fanciful wrought gilt-iron railings, this perfectly proportioned square will probably remind many of Versailles. The square is named for Stanislas Leszczynski, twice dethroned as king of Poland but offered the throne of Lorraine by Louis XV (his son-in-law) in 1736. Stanislas left a legacy of spectacular buildings, undertaken between 1751 and 1760 by architect Emmanuel Héré and ironwork genius Jean Lamour. The sculpture of Stanislas dominating the square went up in the 1830s, when the square was named after him. Framing the exit is the **Arc de Triomphe,** erected in the 1750s to honor Louis XV. The facade trumpets the gods of war and peace; Louis's portrait is here.

9 **Porte de la Craffe.** The only remains of Nancy's medieval fortifications loom at one end of the Grande-Rue. Built in the 14th and 15th centuries, this arch served as a prison through the Revolution. The thistle and cross are symbols of Lorraine.

6 **St-Epvre.** A 275-ft spire towers over this splendid neo-Gothic church rebuilt in the 1860s. Most of the 2,800 square yards of stained glass were created by the Geyling workshop in Vienna; the chandeliers were made in Liège, Belgium; many carvings are the work of Margraff of Munich; the heaviest of the eight bells was cast in Budapest; and the organ, though manufactured by Merklin of Paris, was inaugurated in 1869 by Austrian composer Anton Bruckner. ✉ *Pl. de la Carrière, Vieille Ville.*

Art Nouveau Nancy

Nancy was a principal source of the revolution in decorative arts that produced Art Nouveau and Jugendstil (the German version of Art Nouveau). Inspired and coordinated by the glass master Émile Gallé, the local movement, formalized in 1901 as L'École de Nancy, nurtured the floral *pâte de verre* (literally, glass dough) works of Antonin Daum and Gallé; the Tiffany-esque stained-glass windows of Jacques Gruber; the fluidity of Louis Majorelle's furniture designs; and the sinuous architecture of Lucien Weissenburger, Émile André, and Eugène Vallin. Thanks to these artists, Nancy's downtown architecture gives the impression of a living garden suspended above the sidewalks.

A Good Walk

The **Musée de l'École de Nancy** ⑩ is the best place to immerse yourself in the fanciful style that crept into interiors and exteriors throughout Nancy. To get to the museum from the busy shopping street rue St-Jean (just up rue des Dominicains from place Stanislas), take Bus 5 or 25 uphill and get off at place Pain-Levée. From the museum turn left down rue du Sergent Blandan and walk about four blocks to **No. 1 rue Louis-Majorelle** ⑪. Cut east to place de la Commanderie and head up **avenue Foch** ⑫ to admire the colorful structures at Nos. 71, 69, and

41. Hike over the Viaduct Kennedy and the *gare* (train station), turn left past the department store Printemps, and follow rue Mazagran to the **Brasserie l'Excelsior** ⑬. Turn right toward **No. 40 rue Henri-Poincaré** ⑭. Turn right and walk past **No. 9 rue Chanzy** ⑮ (now the Banque Nationale de Paris). Head left to find **No. 2 rue Bénit** ⑯, with its ornate metal structure. Head south to rue St-Jean; at the corner of **rue Raugraff** ⑰ are two bay windows, remnants of stores that were once here. Continue down rue St-Jean and turn right to find **Nos. 42–44 rue St-Dizier** ⑱. Many more Art Nouveau addresses are scattered throughout the city; you can get a detailed map at the tourist office.

TIMING

Allow a full morning to linger in the Musée de l'École de Nancy and then, during the course of about an hour and a half, wander back circuitously toward the Vieille Ville, stopping to admire Art Nouveau masterworks along the way.

Sights to See

⓬ **Avenue Foch.** This busy boulevard lined with mansions was built for Nancy's affluent 19th-century middle class. At No. 69, the occasional pinnacle suggests Gothic influence on a house built in 1902 by Émile André, who designed the neighboring No. 71 two years later. No. 41, built by Paul Charbonnier in 1905, bears ironwork by Majorelle.

⓭ **Brasserie l'Excelsior.** This bustling brasserie has a severely rhythmic facade that is invitingly illuminated at night. The popular restaurant continues to evoke the turn of the 20th century, both in its historic decor and its fin-de-siècle perfume. ✉ *5 rue Mazagran, Art Nouveau.*

★ ❿ **Musée de l'École de Nancy** (School of Nancy Museum). The only museum in France devoted to Art Nouveau is housed in an airy turn-of-the-last-century garden–town house. It was built by Eugène Corbin, an early patron of the School of Nancy. There isn't a straight line in the house; pianos ooze, bedsteads undulate; the wood itself, hard and burnished as it is, seems to have melted and re-formed. ✉ *36 rue du Sergent-Blandan, Art Nouveau,* ☎ *03–83–40–14–86.* *€4.60 (€6.15 for joint ticket with Musée des Beaux-Arts).* ⏲ *Mon. 2–6, Wed.–Sun. 10–6.*

⓫ **No. 1 rue Louis-Majorelle.** This villa was built in 1902 by Paris architect Henri Sauvage for Majorelle himself. Sinuous metal supports seem to sneak up on the unsuspecting balcony like swaying cobras, and there are two grand windows by Gruber: one lighting the staircase (visible from the street) and the other set in the dining room on the south side of the villa (peek around from the garden side). ✉ *Art Nouveau.*

⓰ **No. 2 rue Bénit.** This elaborately worked metal exoskeleton, the first in Nancy (1901), is as functional as it is beautiful. The fluid decoration reminds you of the building's past as a seed supply store. Windows were worked by Gruber; the builders were Henry-Barthélemy Gutton (architect) and Henri Gutton (engineer); Victor Schertzer conceived the metal frame. ✉ *Art Nouveau.*

⓯ **No. 9 rue Chanzy.** Designed by architect Émile André, this lovely structure—now a bank—can be visited during business hours. You can still see the cabinetry of Majorelle, the decor of Paul Charbonnier, and the stained-glass windows of Gruber. ✉ *Art Nouveau.*

⓮ **No. 40 rue Henri-Poincaré.** The Lorraine thistle and brasserie hops weave through this undulating exterior, designed by architects Émile Toussaint and Louis Marchal. Victor Schertzer conceived this metal structure in 1908, after the success of No. 2 rue Bénit. Gruber's windows are enhanced by the curving metalwork of Majorelle. ✉ *Art Nouveau.*

18 **Nos. 42–44 rue St-Dizier.** Eugène Vallin and Georges Biet left their mark on this graceful 1903 bank structure, open weekdays 8:30–5:30. ✉ *Art Nouveau.*

17 **Rue Raugraff.** Once there were two stores here, both built in 1901. The bay windows are the last vestiges of the work of Charles Vallin, Émile André, and Eugène Vallin. ✉ *At corner of rue St-Jean, Art Nouveau.*

Dining and Lodging

$$–$$$ ✕ **Capucin Gourmand.** With a chic decor making the most of Nancy's Art Nouveau pâte de verre, including a giant chandelier and glowing mushroom lamps on the tables, this landmark puts its best foot forward under chef Hervé Fourrière. Soigné specialties include a light lobster lasagna with mushrooms, beef marrow served in the bone with truffles and white beans, and a trio of fresh mango desserts. The choice of Toul wines is extensive. ✉ *31 rue Gambetta, Ville Royale,* ☎ *03–83–35–26–98. Reservations essential. AE, MC, V. Closed Mon., Aug., and end Feb.–early March. No dinner Sun.*

$$ ✕ **Gastrolâtre.** Under the inspired direction of chef Patrick Tanesy, this stylish checked-cloth bistro off place Stanislas serves sophisticated regional cooking. Combinations include baeckoffe with foie gras, mullet with pigs' feet, and authentic *bouchée à la reine* (pastry shell with creamed meat) complete with cock's comb, sweetbreads, and morel mushrooms. Reserve ahead for summer terrace dining. ✉ *1 pl. de Vaudemont, Vieille Ville,* ☎ *03–83–35–51–94. MC, V. Closed Sun. No lunch Mon.*

$ ★ ✕ **Au P'tit Cuny.** If you were inspired by the rustic exhibits of the Musée des Arts et Traditions Populaires, cross the street and sink your teeth into authentic Lorraine cuisine in the form of choucroute, *tête de veau* (veal head), or tangy veal *tourte* (pie). ✉ *99 Grande-Rue, Vieille Ville,* ☎ *03–83–32–85–94. MC, V. Closed Sun.–Mon.*

$$$–$$$$ ★ ✕🏨 **Grand Hôtel de la Reine.** This hotel is every bit as grand as place Stanislas, on which it stands; the magnificent 18th-century building is officially classified as a historic monument. Rooms are in a suitably flamboyant Louis XV style; the most luxurious look out onto the square. The restaurant, Le Stanislas, is run by ambitious Eric Cizeron, whose sophisticated touch bodes well for diners: beef carpaccio with truffles, *dorade* crisped in sesame seeds, and poached plums stuffed with Roquefort. ✉ *2 pl. Stanislas, Ville Royale 54000,* ☎ *03–83–35–03–01,* FAX *03–83–32–86–04,* WEB *www.concorde.hotels.com. 42 rooms. Restaurant, bar, minibars, cable TV, some pets allowed (fee). AE, DC, MC, V.*

$ 🏨 **Carnot.** This somewhat generic downtown hotel, with 1950s-style comforts and mostly tiny rooms, is handy to cours Léopold parking and backs up on the Old Town. Corner rooms are sizable, rooms in the rear quiet. ✉ *4 cours Léopold, Vieille Ville 54000,* ☎ *03–83–36–59–58,* FAX *03–83–37–00–19. 33 rooms. Bar, no air-conditioning, no TV in some rooms, some pets allowed (fee). MC, V.*

$ 🏨 **Hôtel de Guise.** Deep in the shuttered Old Town, this hotel is in a formerly noble mansion with a magnificent stone-floor entry. Three and a half years of renovation were completed in early 2002 and rooms are now furnished with period pieces. Breakfast on the once-grand main floor and an excellent location make this a good choice if you're a bargain-hunting romantic. ✉ *18 rue de Guise, Vieille Ville 54000,* ☎ *03–83–32–24–68,* FAX *03–83–35–75–63. 42 rooms, 6 junior suites. MC, V.*

Nightlife and the Arts

On summer evenings (June–September) at 10 PM, place Stanislas comes alive with a **sound-and-light show,** and the doors of the magnificent

Hôtel de Ville are opened to the public (€2.30). Nancy's **Orchestre Symphonique et Lyrique** (✉ 1 rue Ste-Catherine, Ville Royale, ☎ 03–83–85–30–65) is a highly rated classical orchestra.

Le Chat Noir (✉ 63 rue Jeanne-d'Arc, Ville Neuve, ☎ 03–83–28–49–29) draws a thirtysomething crowd to retro-theme dance parties. **Métro** (✉ 1 ter rue du Général-Hoche, Ville Neuve, ☎ 03–83–40–25–13) is a popular dance club. **La Place** (✉ 9 pl. Stanislas, Ville Royale, ☎ 03–83–35–24–14) attracts a young upscale crowd that comes to dance.

Shopping

Daum (✉ 17 rue des Cristalleries, Vieille VIlle, ☎ 03–83–30–80–20) sells deluxe crystal and examples of the city's traditional Art Nouveau pâte de verre. **Librairie Lorraine** (✉ 93 Grande-Rue, Vieille Ville, ☎ 03–83–36–79–52), across from the Musée des Arts et Traditions, is an excellent bookstore devoted entirely to Lorraine history and culture.

LORRAINE

In long-neglected Lorraine there are hidden treasures worth digging up. You can study the evolution of Gregorian chant in the municipal museum in Metz, where it was first codified. You can observe the luster of Baccarat crystal at its ancient factory, and the consummate artistry of Daum glassware in Nancy, where it sprang from the roots of Art Nouveau. You can hear the church bells in which Joan of Arc discerned voices challenging her to save Orléans, and stand on the wounded earth of Verdun. And throughout Lorraine you'll find the statue of the region's patron saint, St. Nicholas—old St. Nick himself—with three children in a *saloir* (salting tub). Every December 6 Lorraine schoolchildren reenact the legend: a greedy butcher slaughters and salts down three children as hams, but when St. Nicholas drops by his place for a meal, he discovers the dastardly deed and brings them back to life.

Verdun

⓳ *66 km (41 mi) west of Metz, 93 km (58 mi) northwest of Nancy, 262 km (164 mi) east of Paris.*

A key strategic site along the Meuse Valley, Verdun is known, above all, for the 10-month battle between the French and the Germans in World War I that left more than 350,000 dead and nine villages wiped off the map. Both sides fought with suicidal fury, yet no significant ground was gained or lost. The French declared victory once they regained the 10 km (6 mi) the Germans had taken, but bloody scrapping continued until the Armistice, leaving a total of more than 700,000 dead. To this day, the scenes of battle are scarred by bomb craters, stunted vegetation, and thousands of unexploded mines and shells, rendering the area permanently uninhabitable.

The most shocking memorial of the carnage is the **Ossuaire de Douaumont,** 10 km (6 mi) north of the city. The bizarre, evocative structure—a little like a cross, a lot like a bomb—rears up over an endless sea of graves, its ground-level windows revealing undignified heaps of human bones harvested from the killing fields. Climb to the top of the tower (€1) for a view of the cemetery. In the basement a film is shown that dwells on the agony of the senseless butchery. ☎ *03–29–84–54–81,* WEB *www.verdun-douaumont.com.* 🎫 *Slide show €3.* ⏲ *Mar. and Oct., daily 9–noon and 2–5:30; Apr., daily 9–6; May–Aug., daily 9–6:30; Sept., daily 9–noon and 2–6; Nov., daily 9–noon and 2–5.*

The square, modern **Mémorial de Verdun** (Verdun Memorial), in the town of Fleury-devant-Douaumont, is a World War I museum with emotionally charged texts and video commentary, as well as uniforms, weapons, and the artwork of soldiers (Art Nouveau vases hammered from artillery shells). ☎ *03–29–84–35–34.* €4.60. *Mid-Apr.–Dec., daily 9–6; Feb.–Mar., daily 9–noon and 2–6.*

Dining and Lodging

$$–$$$ **Coq Hardi.** This large, steep-roof, half-timber hotel, built in 1827 on the bank of the Meuse, is a Lorraine landmark, with comfy, unpretentious rooms and a familial welcome. Now young chef Frédèric Engel brings a breath of fresh air to the place. His training at Buerehiesel and Crocodile in Strasbourg shows, blending fashionable Mediterranean touches with Lorraine tradition: frothy pea-soup "cappuccino" with Spanish ham, pig's foot stuffed with foie gras, and raspberry-lemon gratin. ✉ *8 av. de la Victoire, 55100,* ☎ *03–29–86–36–36,* FAX *03–29–86–09–21,* WEB *www.coq-hardi.com. 36 rooms. Restaurant, bar, no air-conditioning, minibars, cable TV, some pets allowed (fee). AE, DC, MC, V.*

Metz

★ 20 *66 km (41 mi) east of Verdun, 53 km (33 mi) north of Nancy, 160 km (100 mi) northwest of Strasbourg.*

Despite its industrial background, Metz, the capital of the Moselle region, is one of France's greenest cities: parks, gardens, and leafy squares frame an imposing mix of military and classical architecture, all carved out of the region's yellow sandstone. At the Old Town's heart is one of the finest Gothic cathedrals in France.

The **Musée d'Art et d'Histoire** (Museum of Art and History), two blocks up from the cathedral in a 17th-century former convent, has a wide-ranging collection of French and German paintings from the 18th century on; military arms and uniforms; and religious works of art stored in the **Grenier de Chèvremont,** a granary built in 1457. Best by far are the stelae, statuary, jewelry, and arms evoking the city's Gallo-Roman and Merovingian past. Not to be missed: the ethereal reconstruction of the ancient chapel of St-Pierre-aux-Nonnains. Unfortunately, the museum's labyrinth of stairways excludes wheelchairs, strollers, and poor navigators. ✉ *2 rue du Haut-Poirier,* ☎ *03–87–68–25–00.* €4.60. *Daily 10–5.*

★ At 137 ft from floor to roof, the **Cathédrale St-Étienne** (✉ Pl. des Armes) is one of France's tallest; and thanks to nearly 1½ acres of window space, one of the brightest. The narrow 13th- to 14th-century nave channels the eye toward the dramatically raised 16th-century choir, whose walls have given way to richly colored, gemlike glass created by masters old and modern, including artist Marc Chagall. The oldest windows—on the right rear wall of the transept above the modern organ—date from the 12th century; their dark, mosaiclike simplicity are in stark contrast to the ethereality of the new stained glass. A pair of symmetrical 290-ft towers flank the nave, marking the division between the two churches that were merged to form the cathedral. The **Grand Portal,** beneath the large rose window, was reconstructed by the Germans at the turn of the 20th century; the statues of the prophets include, on the right, *Daniel,* sculpted to resemble Kaiser Wilhelm II (his unmistakable upturned mustache was shaved off in 1940).

The lively **Marché Couvert** (Market Hall; ✉ Pl. de la Cathédrale) was built as a bishop's palace at the end of the 18th century, but the Revolution nipped this decadence in the bud, and it was converted to its current, more practical use. The right flank offers artisanal farm-cured cheeses and still-flopping seafood. At the bottom of the hill that slopes down rue d'Estrées from the market, veer left and cut right over the rushing river for picturesque views of bridges and balconies laden with flowers.

Take in the broad perspective of grand Classical symmetry on the **place de la Comédie,** with its turn-of-the-last-century Protestant temple. The curving sandstone buildings date from the 18th century and include the opera, theater, and département seat.

The small, heavily restored church of **St-Pierre-aux-Nonnains** (✉ Rue Poncelet) has round stones and rows of red bricks thought to date from the 4th century, predating Attila the Hun's sacking of Metz; thus, Metz claims the oldest church in France.

But you may want to skip the church itself: the best of the rare Merovingian ornaments salvaged from the 6th-century version of the chapel are displayed in a full reproduction in the Museum of Art and History, demonstrating as chronologies never can how early Christian times mixed the cultures and tastes of Celts, Romans, and Gauls.

Dining and Lodging

$$–$$$ ✕ **La Dinanderie.** Chef Claude Piergiorgi serves inventive cuisine—scallops with delicate bacon threads, farm pigeon in salt crust, and pear gratin with gingerbread ice cream—with dependable flair. The intimate restaurant is across the Moselle, a 10-minute hike from the cathedral. *✉ 2 rue de Paris, ☎ 03–87–30–14–40. AE, MC, V. Closed Sun.–Mon.*

$ ✕ **La Baraka.** Below the cathedral, this classic French-Moroccan couscous spot offers a fiery but delicious and digestible break from French cooking. *✉ 25 pl. de Chambre, ☎ 03–87–36–33–92. MC, V. Closed Wed. and mid-July–mid-Aug.*

$ ✕ **Le Dauphiné.** Come to this unpretentious barrel-vaulted lunch spot for *tourte Lorraine* (meat pie), a plat du jour with delicious gratin potatoes, and a generous slice of fruit tart. Locals claim permanent lunch stations, but there's room upstairs, too. It's between the cathedral and the museum. *✉ 8 rue du Chanoine-Collin, ☎ 03–87–36–03–04. MC, V. Closed Sun. No dinner Mon.–Thurs.*

$ ✕ **Le Grand Café.** Catercorner from the cathedral entrance, this stylish Belle Epoque–style brasserie has tables spilling onto place d'Armes. Lorraine specialties include *cochon de lait* (suckling pig), local lamb and rabbit, and succulent lard-roasted potatoes. *✉ 14 pl. d'Armes, ☎ 03–87–75–35–09. MC, V.*

$ ✕ **Pont St-Marcel.** Murals, dirndl skirts, and rib-sticking old-style cuisine make this a culinary plunge into Lorraine culture. There's quiche, of course, but also stewed rabbit, *potée* (boiled pork and cabbage), and carp. The list of Lorraine wines (from Toul) is encyclopedic, with the oak-cured red from Laroppe worth the splurge. In summer, reserve a spot on the tiny terrace on the river. *✉ 1 rue du Pont St-Marcel, ☎ 03–87–30–12–29. AE, DC, MC, V.*

$$–$$$ 🏨 **Royal Bleu Marine.** This fully modernized hotel, taken over and buffed up by the Campanile chain, occupies a sumptuous Belle Epoque building not far from the train station. Rooms come in a choice of styles (old-fashioned luxury versus simpler modernity); all are soundproof. *✉ 23 av. Foch, 57011, ☎ 03–87–66–81–11, FAX 03–87–56–13–16, WEB www.bleumarine.fr. 62 rooms. Restaurant, bar, minibars, cable TV, Internet, gym, sauna. AE, DC, MC, V.*

$$ ★ 🏨 **Cathédrale.** From its waxed plank floors, ironwork banister, beamed ceilings, and French windows to its views of the cathedral, this gem of a hotel is reason enough to spend the night in Metz. The country-chic bedspreads, linen drapes, and hand-painted furniture are the work of

the friendly owner; she collected all the antiques, too. Breakfast is served in the Baraka, downstairs. ✉ *25 pl. de Chambre, 57000,* ☎ *03–87–75–00–02,* FAX *03–87–75–40–75.* WEB *www.hotelcathedrale-metz.fr. 20 rooms. Restaurant, bar, cable TV, Internet. AE, DC, MC, V.*

Lunéville

21 *30 km (19 mi) southeast of Nancy.*

Lunéville rose to prominence at the start of the 18th century when Duke Léopold of Lorraine had the château built by Mansart's pupil Germain Boffrand, who also designed the Baroque town church of St-Jacques (of note for its carved pulpit and choir stalls). The château's chief glory days, however, came under King Stanislas, who held court here from 1735 to 1760, treating Lunéville as his own (scaled-down) version of Versailles. After Stanislas died, Lorraine reverted to the French crown, and Lunéville lost its luster. Although you can wander at leisure in the regimented château gardens, which have been painstakingly restored, much of the château itself is off-limits to the public.

The **Musée** (Town Museum), in one wing of the château, has an eclectic spectrum of local pottery, archeological finds, and French paintings, including one work by Lunéville's most famous son—the 17th-century master of flickering candlelight, Georges de La Tour, whose career is evoked here by a short film. ✉ *Pl. du Château-Stanislas,* ☎ *03–83–76–23–57.* 🎫 *€2.30.* ⏲ *Wed.–Mon. 10–noon and 2–5.*

The small industrial town of St-Nicolas-de-Port, 18 km (11 mi) northwest of Lunéville, is saved from mediocrity by its colossal basilica. Legend has it that a finger of St. Nicholas was brought to the town during the 11th-century Crusades. Sheltering such a priceless relic, the **Basilique de St-Nicolas-de-Port** (1495–1555) was rapidly besieged by pilgrims (including Joan of Arc, who came to ask St. Nicholas's blessing on her famous journey to Orléans). The simplified column capitals and elaborate rib vaulting are shining examples of Flamboyant Gothic enjoying a final fling before the gathering impetus of the Renaissance, as are the 280-ft onion-dome towers, almost symmetrical but, as was the Gothic wont, not quite. Inside, the slender, freestanding 90-ft pillars in the transept are the highest in France.

Dining and Lodging

$$$–$$$$ ✕🏨 **Château d'Adoménil.** This steep-roofed, pink-walled, ivy-covered 18th-century château makes a stylish base for visiting Nancy, Baccarat, and St-Nicolas-de-Port. Flamboyant owner Michel Million is a skilled chef, and his elegant dining room showcases his specialties, which range from roast pike-perch with wild mushrooms to grilled foie gras and frogs'-legs omelet, perfect with a bottle of Côtes de Toul, the tangy local wine. Rooms in the château have weighty regional furniture; those in the annex—the converted stable—offer a mix of modern and Neoclassical designs. ✉ *54300 Rehainviller (4 km/2½ mi southwest of Lunéville),* ☎ *03–83–74–04–81,* FAX *03–83–74–21–78. 12 rooms. Restaurant, pool. AE, DC, MC, V. Closed Jan.–mid-Feb. and Sun.–Mon. in Nov.–Apr. No dinner Sun., no lunch Tues.*

Toul

22 *23 km (14 mi) west of Nancy.*

The old town of Toul, nestled behind mossy, star-shape ramparts, has been a bishopric since AD 365 and merited visits from the Frankish king Clovis to study the Christian faith; from Charlemagne in passing; and from a young, premilitary Joan of Arc, who was sued in the Toul court for breach of promise when she threw over a beau for the voice of God. In 1700, under Louis XIV, the military engineer Vauban built the thrusting ramparts around the town.

The ramshackle streets of central Toul haven't changed much for centuries—not since the embroidered twin-tower facade, a Flamboyant Gothic masterpiece, was woven onto the **Cathédrale St-Étienne** in the second half of the 15th century. The cathedral's interior, begun in 1204, is long (321 ft), airy (105 ft high), and more restrained than its exuberant facade. On one side of the cathedral are the 14th-century **cloisters**, and on the other is a pleasant **garden** behind the **Hôtel de Ville** (Town Hall), built in 1740 as the Bishop's Palace. ✉ *Pl. d'Armes.* ⏲ *Summer, daily 9–6; winter, daily 9–dark.*

The **Musée Municipal** (Town Museum), in a former medieval hospital, has a well-preserved *Salle des Malades* (Patients' Ward) dating from the 13th century. Archaeological finds, ceramics, tapestries, and medieval sculpture are on display. ✉ *25 rue Gouvion-St-Cyr,* ☎ *03–83–64–13–38.* 🎫 *€2.60.* ⏲ *Apr.–Oct., Wed.–Mon. 9:30–noon and 2–6; Nov.–Mar., Wed.–Mon. 2–6.*

Dining

$$–$$$ ✕ **Le Dauphin.** In a bleak industrial neighborhood and with a dated decor, this grand restaurant seems out of place in humble Toul. But the modern and imaginative cooking of Christophe Vohmann draws kudos for its exotic touches and balance of flavor—opt for the langoustines with ginger and radishes or the local foie gras with artichokes. ✉ *65 allée Gaumiron,* ☎ *03–83–43–13–46. AE, DC, MC, V. Closed Mon. and mid-July–mid-Aug. No dinner Sun.*

Vaucouleurs

23 *24 km (15 mi) southwest of Toul on D960.*

Below the medieval walls and ruins of Robert de Baudricourt's ancient château in the modest market town of Vaucouleurs, you can see the **Porte de France,** through which Joan of Arc led her armed soldiers to Orléans. The barefoot Maid of Orléans spent a year within these walls, first wheedling an audience with Baudricourt and then, having convinced him of the necessity of her mission, learning to ride and to sword-fight.

Dining and Lodging

$ ✕🏨 **Relais de la Poste.** On the main street, this simple hotel has quiet rooms and a pleasant, intimate restaurant. The good regional menu is served noon and night. A friendly family cooks, serves the meals, and checks you in. ✉ *12 av. André-Maginot, 55140,* ☎ *03–29–89–40–01,* FAX *03–29–89–40–93. 9 rooms. Restaurant, bar, Internet. AE, MC, V. Closed Fri.–Sun. in Nov.–May; last 2 wks Dec.*

Domrémy-la-Pucelle

24 *40 km (25 mi) southwest of Toul, 19 km (12 mi) south of Vaucouleurs.*

Joan of Arc was born in Domrémy-la-Pucelle in a stone hut in either 1411 or 1412. You can see it as well as the church where she was baptized, the actual statue of St. Marguerite before which she prayed, and the hillside where she tended sheep and first heard voices telling her to take up arms and save France from the English.

The humble stone-and-stucco **Maison Natale Jeanne d'Arc** (Joan of Arc Birthplace)—an irregular, slope-roof former cowshed—has been preserved with some reverence. The museum, the **Centre Johannique,** shows a film (French only) while mannequins in period costume present

Joan of Arc's amazing story. After she heard mystical voices, Joan walked 19 km (12 mi) to Vaucouleurs. Dressed and mounted like a man, she led her forces to lift the siege of Orléans, defeated the English, and escorted the unseated Charles VII to Reims, to be crowned king of France. Military missions after Orléans failed—including an attempt to retake Paris—and she was captured at Compiègne. The English turned her over to the Church, which sent her to be tried by the Inquisition for witchcraft and heresy. She was convicted, excommunicated, and burned at the stake in Rouen—but was she? There are some far-fetched theories that she was never actually burned; that she was allegedly a distant relative of the royal family and not quite the "peasant" she was made out to be. ✉ *2 rue de la Basilique,* ☎ *03–29–06–95–86.* *€3.* *Apr.–Sept., daily 9–noon and 2–6:30; Oct.–Mar., Wed.–Mon. 9:30–noon and 2–5.*

The ornate late-19th-century **Basilique du Bois-Chenu** (Aged-Forest Basilica), a pleasant walk up a country road from Joan of Arc's birthplace, has enormous painted panels telling her story in glowing Pre-Raphaelite tones. Here you can see Joan's budding role as symbol of French nationalist pride, passionately illustrated in the shadow of Prussian defeat.

Lodging

$ **Jeanne d'Arc.** Stay next door to Joan of Arc's childhood church and wake to the bells that accompanied her voices. Accommodations are considerably less evocative, in jazzy '60s tile and paneling, but bathrooms are spotless and breakfasts (in-room only) generous. ✉ *1 rue Principale, 88630,* ☎ *03–29–06–96–06. 12 rooms. No credit cards. Closed mid-Nov.–Mar.*

Grand

25 *15 km (9 mi) southwest of Domrémy-la-Pucelle: From Domrémy follow signs down country roads west toward Grand.*

In the tiny, enigmatic hamlet of Grand, a natural spring developed into a center for the worship of the Gallo-Roman sun god Apollo-Grannus. It was important enough to draw the Roman emperors Caracalla and Constantine. Thus, Grand today is a treasure trove of classical ruins.

At the entry to the village the remains of a large **amphitheater** that once seated 20,000 are being reconstructed as an outdoor theater; displays illustrate its history. In a tiny museum in the upper village there is a marvelously expressive floor **mosaic** with realistic animal details. Surrounding the mosaic are scraps of exotic stone and relics transported from across two continents, bearing witness to this isolated village's opulent past. ☎ *03–29–06–63–43.* *Amphitheater and mosaic €3.* *Apr.–Sept., daily 9–noon and 2–7; Oct.–mid-Dec. and mid-Jan.–Mar., Wed.–Mon. 10–noon and 2–5.*

Épinal

26 *84 km (53 mi) southeast of Domrémy, 69 km (43 mi) south of Nancy, 97 km (61 mi) north of Belfort.*

On the Moselle River at the feet of the Vosges, Épinal, a printing center since 1735, is famous throughout France for boldly colored prints, popular illustrations, and hand-colored stencils. **L'Imagerie Pellerin,** the artisanal workshop, has a slide show tracing the history of local printing. ✉ *42 bis quai de Dogneville,* ☎ *03–29–31–28–88.* *Free; guided tour with slide show €4.75.* *Tours at 9:30, 11, 3, and 4:30 for 1 hour. Gallery-salesroom open between tours Sept.–June, Mon.–Sat. 9–noon and 2–6:30, Sun. 2–6:30; July–Aug., Mon.–Sat. 9–7, Sun. 2–7.*

On an island in the Moselle in the center of Épinal, the spectacular **Musée Départemental d'Art Ancien et Contemporain** (Museum of Antiquities and Contemporary Art) is in a renovated 17th-century hospital, whose Classical traces are still visible under a dramatic barrel-vaulted skylight. It contains France's fourth-largest collection of contemporary art, as well as Gallo-Roman artifacts; rural tools and local faïence; and Old Masters, including some fine drawings and watercolors by Fragonard and Boucher. ✉ *1 pl. Lagarde,* ☎ *03–29–82–20–33.* €4.60. ⏲ *Wed.–Mon. 10–6.*

The small but bustling Old Town is anchored by the lovely old **Basilique St-Maurice,** a low gray-stone basilica blending Romanesque and Gothic styles. Its deep 15th-century entry porch prepares you for passing into dark, sacred space. ✉ *Pl. St-Goëry,* ☎ *03–29–82–58–36.*

STRASBOURG

Though centered in the heart of Alsace 490 km (304 mi) east of Paris, and drawing appealingly on Alsatian Gemütlichkeit (friendliness), the city of Strasbourg is a cosmopolitan French cultural center and, in many ways, the unofficial capital of Europe. Against an irresistible backdrop of old half-timber houses, waterways, and the colossal single spire of its red-sandstone cathedral, which seems to insist imperiously that you pay homage to its majestic beauty, Strasbourg is an incongruously sophisticated mix of museums, elite schools (including that notorious hothouse for blooming politicos, the École Nationale d'Administration, or National Administration School), international think tanks, and the European Parliament.

The Romans knew Strasbourg as Argentoratum before it came to be known as Strateburgum, or City of (Cross) Roads. After centuries as part of the Germanic Holy Roman Empire, the city was united with France in 1681, but retained independence regarding legislation, education, and religion under the honorific title Free Royal City. Since World War II Strasbourg has become a symbolic city, embodying Franco-German reconciliation and the wider idea of a united Europe. The city center is effectively an island within two arms of the River Ill; most major sites are found here, but the northern districts also contain some fine buildings erected over the last 100 years, culminating in the Palais de l'Europe.

Note to drivers: the new configuration of downtown streets makes it difficult to approach the center via the autoroute exit marked STRASBOURG CENTRE. Instead, hold out for the exit marked PLACE DE L'ÉTOILE and follow signs to CATHÉDRALE/CENTRE VILLE. At place du Corbeau, veer left across the Ill, and go straight to the place Gutenberg parking garage, a block from the cathedral.

The Historic Heart

This central area, from the cathedral to picturesque Petite France, concentrates the best of Old Strasbourg, with its twisting backstreets, flower-lined courts, tempting shops, and inviting winstubs (wine taverns).

A Good Walk

Begin at place Gutenberg and head up rue des Hallebardes. To see a bit of Strasbourg's appealing combination of cozy winstubs, medieval alleys, and chic shops, turn left up rue des Orfevres (marked RUE PITTORESQUE); then circle right down rue Chaudron and again down rue du Sanglier. Head back right down rue des Hallebardes and onto place de la Cathédrale, passing the landmark Maison Kammerzells.

Emerging from this close-packed warren of dark-timber buildings and narrow streets, you'll confront the magnificent **Cathédrale Notre-Dame** ㉗. Continue across the square to the **Musée de l'Oeuvre Notre-Dame** ㉘, with its collection of statuary. Leaving the museum, turn right and approach the vast neighboring palace, the **Palais Rohan** ㉙. Once the headquarters of the powerful prince-bishops, the Rohans, it now houses the art and archaeology museums.

Once out of the château's entry court, double back left and turn left again, following rue des Rohan to the river. From here you can take a boat tour of the Old Town. Veer right away from the water and cross place du Marché aux Cochons de Lait (Suckling Pig Market Square) and place de la Grande Boucherie (Grand Slaughterhouse Square) to reach the **Musée Historique** ㉚, with its collection of paintings, weapons, and furniture from Strasbourg (reopening 2005 after renovations). Across the street is the modern glass entrance to the **Ancienne Douane** ㉛, the former customs house, now a vast venue for temporary exhibitions. Over the Ill, cross Pont du Corbeau and veer right to the **Musée Alsacien** ㉜, where you can get a glimpse of how Alsatian families used to live.

Now cross back over the river on the Pont St-Nicolas and follow the riverside promenade west to the picturesque quarter of **Petite France** ㉝. At Pont St-Martin, take rue des Dentelles to rue du Bain aux Plantes. Explore the alleys, courtyards, cafés, and shop windows as you work your way west. Eventually you'll reach the four monumental **Ponts Couverts** ㉞. Just beyond the bridges lies the grass-roof dam, the **Barrage Vauban** ㉟. Climb to the top; from here you'll see a gleaming glass-frame building, the **Musée d'Art Moderne et Contemporain** ㊱.

TIMING

Allow at least a full day to see Strasbourg—perhaps visiting the Old Town and cathedral in the morning, ending at 12:30 with the astronomical clock, and then lunch on a nearby backstreet. The afternoon might allow a museum stop and time to wander through Petite France. Two days would allow more museum time; a third day would allow you to take in the monumental sights on place de la République and the Palais de l'Europe.

Sights to See

㉛ **Ancienne Douane** (Old Customs House). In 2000, a terrible fire ravaged this old customs house set on the Ill River; extensive repairs are expected to continue until 2004. When operational, the airport-hangar scale and flexible walls here lend themselves to enormous expositions of Old Master paintings as well as archaeology and history. ✉ *1 rue de Vieux-Marché-aux-Poissons,* ☎ *03–88–52–50–00.* *Unavailable at press time.*

㉟ **Barrage Vauban** (Vauban Dam). Just beyond the Ponts Couverts is the grass-roof Vauban Dam, built by its namesake in 1682. Climb to the top for wide-angle views of the Ponts Couverts and, on the other side, the Museum of Modern Art. Then stroll through its echoing galleries, where magnificent cathedral statuary lies scattered among pigeon droppings. ✉ *Ponts Couverts.* *Free.* ⏲ *Mid-Oct.–mid-Mar., daily 9–7; mid-Mar.–mid-Oct., daily 9–8.*

★ ㉗ **Cathédrale Notre-Dame.** Rosy, ornately carved Vosges sandstone masonry covers the facade of this most novel and Germanic of French cathedrals, a triumph of Gothic art begun in 1176. Not content with the outlines of the walls themselves, medieval builders encased them in a

Strasbourg

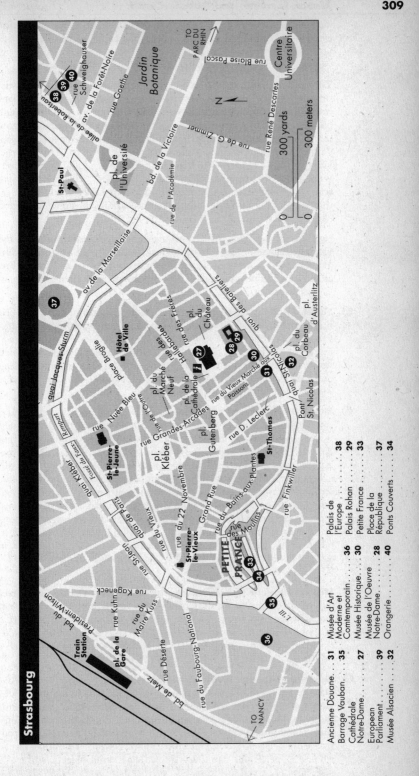

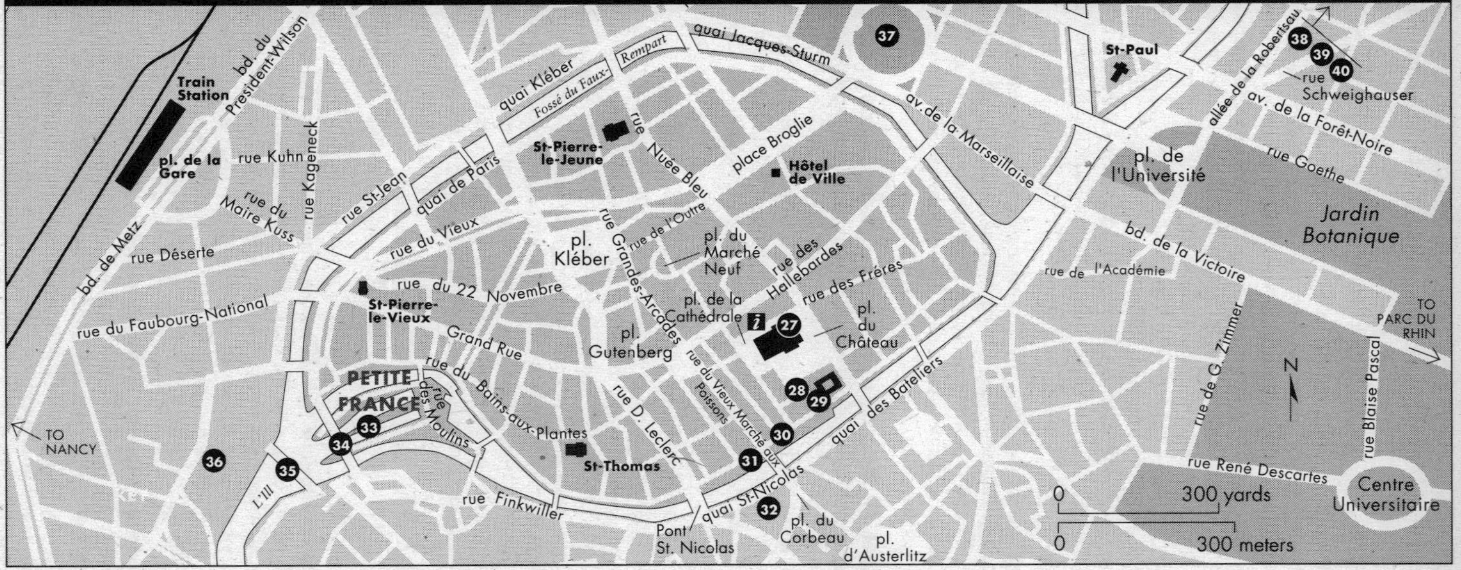

Ancienne Douane. . . **31**
Barrage Vauban. . . . **35**
Cathédrale Notre-Dame. **27**
European Parliament. **39**
Musée Alsacien **32**
Musée d'Art Moderne et Comtemporain **36**
Musée Historique. . . . **30**
Musée de l'Oeuvre Notre-Dame. **28**
Orangerie **40**
Palais de l'Europe **38**
Palais Rohan **29**
Petite France **33**
Place de la République **37**
Ponts Couverts **34**

lacy exoskeleton of slender shafts of stone. The off-center **spire,** finished in 1439, looks absurdly fragile as it tapers skyward some 466 ft; you can nonetheless climb its 330 steps to the top to take in sweeping views of the city, the Vosges Mountains, and the Black Forest.

The interior presents a stark contrast to the facade: it is older (mostly finished by 1275), and the nave's broad windows emphasize the horizontal rather than the vertical. Note Hans Hammer's ornately sculpted pulpit (1484–86) and the richly painted 14th- to 15th-century organ loft that rises from pillar to ceiling. The left side of the nave is flanked with richly colored Gothic windows honoring the early leaders of the Holy Roman Empire—Otto I and II, and Heinrich I and II. The **choir** is not ablaze with stained glass but framed by chunky Romanesque masonry. The elaborate 16th-century **Chapelle St-Laurent,** to the left of the choir, merits a visit; turn to the right to admire the **Pilier des Anges** (Angels' Pillar), an intricate column dating from 1230.

Just beyond the pillar, the Renaissance machinery of the 16th-century **Horloge Astronomique** (Astronomical Clock) whirs into action daily at 12:30 PM (but the line starts at the south door at 11:45 AM): macabre clockwork figures enact the story of Christ's Passion. ✉ *Pl. de la Cathédrale.* 🎫 *Clock €.7; spire €3.*

㉜ **Musée Alsacien** (Alsatian Museum). In this labyrinthine half-timber home, with layers of carved balconies sagging over a cobbled inner courtyard, local interiors have been faithfully reconstituted. The diverse activities of blacksmiths, clog makers, saddlers, and makers of artificial flowers are explained with the help of old-time artisans' tools and equipment. ✉ *23 quai St-Nicolas,* ☎ *03–88–52–50–00.* 🎫 *€3.* ⏲ *Wed.–Mon. 10–6.*

㊱ **Musée d'Art Moderne et Contemporain** (Modern and Contemporary Art Museum). A magnificent sculpture of a building that sometimes dwarfs its contents, this spectacular museum frames a relatively thin collection of new, esoteric, and unsung 20th-century art. Downstairs, a permanent collection of Impressionists and modernists up to 1950 is heavily padded with local heroes but happily fleshed out with some striking furniture; all are juxtaposed for contrasting and comparing, with little to no chronological flow. Upstairs, harsh, spare new works must work hard to live up to their setting; few contemporary masters are featured. Drawings, aquarelles, and paintings by Gustave Doré, a native of Alsace, are enshrined in a separate room. ✉ *1 pl. Hans-Jean Arp,* ☎ *03–88–23–31–31.* 🎫 *€4.05.* ⏲ *Tues.–Wed. and Fri.–Sun. 11–7, Thurs. noon–10.*

㉚ **Musée Historique** (Local History Museum). This museum, in a step-gabled slaughterhouse dating from 1588, was temporarily closed for extensive renovations at press time; it is expected to reopen by late 2005. It contains a collection of maps, armor, arms, bells, uniforms, traditional dress, printing paraphernalia, and two huge relief models of Strasbourg. ✉ *2 rue du Vieux-Marché-aux-Poissons.*

★ ㉘ **Musée de l'Oeuvre Notre-Dame** (Museum of Works from Notre-Dame). There is more to this museum than the usual assembly of dilapidated statues rescued from the local cathedral before they fell off the walls (*those* you'll find rotting in the Barrage Vauban). Sacred sculptures stand in churchlike settings, and secular exhibits are enhanced by the building's fine old architecture. Subjects include a wealth of Flemish and Upper Rhine paintings, stained glass, gold objects, and massive, heavily carved furniture. ✉ *3 pl. du Château,* ☎ *03–88–32–88–17.* 🎫 *€3.* ⏲ *Tues.–Sun. 10–6.*

29 **Palais Rohan** (Rohan Palace). The exterior of Robert de Cotte's massive Neoclassical palace (1732–42) is starkly austere. But the glamour is inside, in Robert le Lorrain's magnificent ground-floor rooms, led by the great **Salon d'Assemblée** (Assembly Room) and the book- and tapestry-lined **Bibliothèque des Cardinaux** (Cardinals' Library). The library leads to a series of less august rooms that house the **Musée des Arts Décoratifs** (Decorative Arts Museum) and its elaborate display of ceramics. This is a comprehensive presentation of works by Hannong, a porcelain manufacturer active in Strasbourg from 1721 to 1782; dinner services by other local kilns reveal the influence of Chinese porcelain. The **Musée des Beaux-Arts** (Fine Arts Museum), also in the château, includes masterworks of European painting from Giotto and Memling to El Greco, Rubens, and Goya. Downstairs, the **Musée Archéologique** (Archaeology Museum) displays regional archaeological finds, including gorgeous Merovingian treasures. ✉ *2 pl. du Château,* ☎ *03–88–52–50–00.* 🎫 *€7.50 all museums; €4.50 each museum.* ⏲ *Wed.–Mon. 10–6.*

★ 33 **Petite France.** With its gingerbread half-timber houses that seem to lean precariously over the canals of the Ill, its shops, and inviting little restaurants, this is the most magical neighborhood in Strasbourg. Wander up and down the tiny streets that connect rue du Bain aux Plantes and rue des Dentelles to Grand' Rue, and stroll the waterfront promenade.

34 **Ponts Couverts** (Covered Bridges). These three bridges, distinguished by their four stone towers, were once covered with wooden shelters. Part of the 14th-century ramparts that framed Old Strasbourg, they span the Ill as it branches into four fingerlike canals.

Beyond the Ill

If you've seen the center and have time to strike out in new directions, head across the Ill to view two architectural landmarks unrelated to Strasbourg's famous medieval past: place de la République and the Palais de l'Europe.

A Good Walk

North of the cathedral, walk up rue des Hallebardes and turn left on rue du Dôme. Take a right onto place Broglie and continue up this main thoroughfare across the river to the striking circle of red-sandstone buildings on **place de la République** (37). Back at the river, head for a bus stop on avenue de la Marseillaise and take Bus 23 to the **Palais de l'Europe** (38) for a guided tour (by appointment, arranged in advance). You may also want to visit the sleek new digs of the **European Parliament** (39), just across the river. From here plunge into the greenery of the **Orangerie** (40). Indulge in a three-hour lunch at the stellar Buerehiesel or have a picnic on a bench.

TIMING

Basing your schedule on your tour appointment at the Palais de l'Europe, allow about a half day for this walk; if need be, you can while away the wait in the Orangerie.

Sights to See

39 **European Parliament.** This sleek building testifies to the growing importance of the governing body of the European Union, which used to make do with rental offices in the Palais de l'Europe. Eurocrats continue to commute between Brussels, Luxembourg, and Strasbourg, hauling their staff and files with them. One week per month, visitors can slip into the hemicycle and witness the tribune in debate, complete with simultaneous translation. ✉ *Behind the Palais de l'Europe, 03–88–17–52–85.* 🎫 *Free.* ⏲ *Call ahead to see if Parliament is in session.*

40 **Orangerie.** Like a private backyard for the Eurocrats in the Palais de l'Europe, this delightful park is laden with flowers and punctuated by noble copper beeches. It contains a lake and, close by, a small reserve of rare birds, including flamingos and noisy local storks. ✉ *Av. de l'Europe.*

38 **Palais de l'Europe.** Designed by Paris architect Henri Bernard in 1977, this Continental landmark is headquarters to the Council of Europe, founded in 1949 and independent of the European Union. A guided tour introduces you to the intricacies of its workings and may allow you to eavesdrop on a session. Arrange your tour by telephone in advance; appointments are fixed according to language demands and usually take place in the afternoon. Note: You must provide a *pièce d'identité* (ID) before entering. ✉ *Av. de l'Europe,* ☎ *03–90–21–49–40 for appointments.* *Free.* *Guided tours by appointment weekdays.*

37 **Place de la République.** The spacious layout and ponderous architecture of this monumental *cirque* (circle) have nothing in common with the Old Town except for the local red sandstone. A different hand was at work here—that of occupying Germans, who erected the former Ministry (1902); the Academy of Music (1882–92); and the Palais du Rhin (1883–88). The handsome neo-Gothic church of **St-Paul** and the pseudo-Renaissance **Palais de l'Université** (University Palace), constructed between 1875 and 1885, also bear the German stamp. Heavy turn-of-the-century houses, some reflecting the whimsical curves of the Art Nouveau style, frame **allée de la Robertsau,** a tree-lined boulevard that would not look out of place in Berlin.

Dining and Lodging

$$$$ ★ ✕ **Buerehiesel.** This lovely Alsatian farmhouse, reconstructed in the Orangerie, warrants a pilgrimage if you are willing to pay for the finest cooking in Alsace. Antoine Westermann stands in the upper echelon of chefs while remaining true to the ingredients and specialties of his native Alsace: *schniederspaetzle* (onion-perfumed ravioli) with frogs' legs, duck braised and caramelized in Asian spices, and plum tart Tatin with vanilla ice cream. European *parlementaires* come on foot; others might come on their knees. ✉ *4 parc de l'Orangerie,* ☎ *03–88–45–56–65. Reservations essential. AE, DC, MC, V. Closed Tues.–Wed., 3 wks Jan., and 3 wks in Aug.*

$$$–$$$$ ★ ✕ **Crocodile.** Chef Émile Jung is celebrated throughout the region for his Alsatian dishes prepared with urbane finesse: truffle turnover, warmed goose liver with rhubarb, and bitter-chocolate cherry cake. The restaurant's opulent decor makes a sophisticated backdrop for a sensual meal. It's more central than the Buerehiesel and nearly as revered. ✉ *10 rue de l'Outre,* ☎ *03–88–32–13–02. Reservations essential. Jacket and tie. AE, DC, MC, V. Closed Sun.–Mon. and 3 wks in July.*

$$ ✕ **Maison Kammerzell.** This restaurant glories in its richly carved, half-timber 16th-century building—probably the most familiar house in Strasbourg. Fight your way through the tourist hordes on the terrace and ground floor to one of the atmospheric rooms above, with their gleaming wooden furniture and stained-glass windows. Foie gras and choucroute are best bets, though you may want to try the chef's pet discovery, choucroute with freshwater fish. ✉ *16 pl. de la Cathédrale,* ☎ *03–88–32–42–14. AE, DC, MC, V.*

$–$$ ★ ✕ **Chez Yvonne.** Behind red-checked curtains you'll find artists, tourists, lovers, and heads of state sitting elbow-to-elbow in this classic winstub. All come to savor steaming platters of local specialties: watch for duck confit on choucroute, and *tête de veau* (veal head) in white wine. Warm Alsatian fabrics dress tables and lamps, the china is regional, the photos historic, and the ambience chic—and no kitsch. ✉ *10 rue* *du Sanglier,* ☎ *03–88–32–84–15. AE, DC, MC, V. Closed Sun. and mid-July–mid-Aug. No lunch Mon.*

$ ✕ **St-Sépulcre.** Shared plank tables, a jovial red-vested patron (with a nose to match), and a wisecracking waitstaff enhance the convivial welcome at this no-frills, down-home winstub. A massive ham sits casually on the counter, and slabs of it find their way onto every platter—even the salads. A crock of crunchy pickles, chewy bread, and a cereal bowl heaped with fresh horseradish accompany every order except dessert. ✉ *15 rue des Orfèvres,* ☎ *03–88–32–39–97. MC, V. Closed Sun.*

$ ★ ✕ **Suzel.** This cozy little tearoom in Petite France mixes rustic-chic blandishments (blue gingham, artfully arranged bric-a-brac, rows of potted boxwood) with excellent and unpretentious regional food. There's rabbit stew with dumplings, fresh trout, baeckoffe, fruit tarts, and good wines. It's also marvelous for an atmospheric afternoon tea break. Too bad it's closed nights. ✉ *2 rue des Moulins at rue Bain-aux-Plantes,* ☎ *03–88–23–10–46. MC, V. Closed Mon. No dinner.*

$$$$ **Régent-Contades.** This sleek, modern hotel is in a revamped mansion in a residential turn-of-the-20th-century district close to the Ill (ask for a room with a view of St-Paul's). It's intimate, quiet, and homey in an aristocratic way. First-class amenities add to the appeal of the spacious rooms. ✉ *8 av. de la Liberté, 67000,* ☎ *03–88–15–05–05,* FAX *03–88–15–05–15,* WEB *www.regent-hotels.com. 45 rooms. Bar, minibars, cable TV, Internet, some pets allowed (fee), sauna. AE, DC, MC, V.*

$$$$ **Régent-Petite France.** Opposite the Ponts Couverts and surrounded by rushing canals, this boldly modern luxury hotel occupies a former ice factory in the heart of Strasbourg's quaintest quarter. A spacious marble vestibule, vivid graffiti art, and sculptural room furnishings contrast sharply with the half-timber houses and roaring river viewed from nearly every room. The restaurant, Le Pont Tournant, offers summer tables over the torrent. ✉ *5 rue des Moulins, 67000,* ☎ *03–88–76–43–43,* FAX *03–88–76–43–76,* WEB *www.regent-hotels.com. 72 rooms. Restaurant, bar, minibars, cable TV, Internet. AE, DC, MC, V.*

$$–$$$ **Cathédrale.** Expansion and renovation have brought this superbly positioned hotel more than up to par, with a sleek marble lobby, with lounges, bar, and breakfast room rich with ancient beams and sandstone. Rooms feature dark timbers, and most have windows framing a view of the Maison Kammerzell or the cathedral. For summer drinks and breakfast, there's a garden courtyard cloistered from the outside world. ✉ *12 pl. de la Cathédrale, 67000,* ☎ *03–88–22–12–12,* FAX *03–88–23–28–00,* WEB *www.hotel-cathedrale.fr. 47 rooms. Bar, minibars, cable TV, some Internet, parking (fee). AE, DC, MC, V.*

$$–$$$ **Rohan.** Across from the cathedral on a picturesque pedestrian street, this modest little hotel has a welcoming air and a marvelous sense of French style, from the Louis XV furniture to the gilt mirrors. Though swagged in rich fabrics, rooms are fully modern, with impeccable all-tile baths. ✉ *17 rue Maroquin, 67000,* ☎ *03–88–32–85–11,* FAX *03–88–75–65–37,* WEB *www.hotel-rohan.com. 36 rooms. Minibars, cable TV, Internet, parking (fee), some pets allowed (fee). AE, DC, MC, V.*

$$ **Gutenberg.** In a 200-year-old mansion just off place Gutenberg, this sturdy urban hotel has rooms with fresh, old-fashioned wallpaper and built-in wood cabinetry. Charming little fifth-floor lofts reveal roof timbers. ✉ *31 rue des Serruriers, 67000,* ☎ *03–88–32–17–15,* FAX *03–88–75–76–67. 42 rooms. No air-conditioning in some rooms, Internet. MC, V. Closed 1st 2 wks in Jan.*

Nightlife and the Arts

The annual **Festival de Musique** (Music Festival) is held from June to early July at the Palais des Congrès and at the cathedral; contact the

Amis de la Musique (✉ 1 av. de la Marseillaise, ☎ 03–88–39–64–10) for information. The **Opéra du Rhin** (✉ 19 pl. Broglie, ☎ 03–88–75–48–23) has a sizable repertoire. Classical concerts are staged by the **Orchestre Philharmonique** (✉ Palais des Congrès, ☎ 03–88–15–09–09).

The Old Town neighborhood east of the cathedral, along rue des Frères, is the nightlife hangout for university students and twentysomethings; among its handful of heavily frequented bars is **Le Velvet** (✉ 6 rue Tonnelet Rouge, ☎ 03–88–37–95–84). **Le Chalet** (✉ 376 rte. de La Wantzenau, ☎ 03–88–31–18–31) is the biggest and most popular disco, but it is some 10 km (6 mi) northeast of the city center.

Outdoor Activities

The **Port Autonome de Strasbourg** (☎ 03–88–84–13–13) organizes 75-minute boat tours along the Ill four times a day in winter and up to every half hour from 9:30 to 9, April–October. Boats leave from behind the Palais Rohan; the cost is €6.30.

Shopping

The lively city center is full of boutiques, including chocolate shops and delicatessens selling locally made foie gras. Look for warm paisley linens and rustic homespun fabrics, Alsatian pottery, and local wines. Forming the city's commercial heart are **rue des Hallebardes,** next to the cathedral; **rue des Grandes Arcades,** with its shopping mall; and **place Kléber.** An **antiques market** takes place behind the cathedral on rue du Vieil-Hôpital, rue des Bouchers, and place de la Grande Boucherie every Wednesday and Saturday morning.

ALSACE

The Rhine River forms the eastern boundary of both Alsace and France. But the best of Alsace is not found along the Rhine's industrial waterfront. Instead it's nestled in the Ill Valley at the base of the Vosges, southwest of cosmopolitan Strasbourg. Northwest is Saverne and the beginning of the Route du Vin, the great Alsace Wine Road, which winds its way south through the Vosges foothills, fruitful vineyards, and medieval villages that would serve well as stage-sets for Rossini's *William Tell.* Signs for the road help you keep your bearings on the twisty way south, and you'll find limitless opportunities to stop at wineries and sample the local wares. At the industrial town of Mulhouse, you leave behind the charms of Alsace and head into the historic wilds of Franche-Comté.

Obernai

41 *35 km (22 mi) south of Saverne, 27 km (17 mi) southwest of Strasbourg.*

Obernai is a thriving, colorful Renaissance market town with a medieval belfry, a Renaissance well, and a late-19th-century church. Place du Marché, in the heart of town, is dominated by the stout, square 13th-century **Kapelturm Beffroi** (Chapel Tower Belfry), topped by a pointed steeple flanked at each corner by frilly openwork turrets added in 1597. An elaborate Renaissance well near the belfry, the **Puits à Six-Seaux** (Well of Six Buckets), was constructed in 1579; its name recalls the six buckets suspended from its metal chains. The twin spires of the parish church of **St-Pierre–St-Paul** compete with the belfry for skyline preeminence. They date, like the rest of the church, from the 1860s, although the 1504 Holy Sepulchre altarpiece in the north transept is a survivor from the previous church.

Dining and Lodging

$$ ★ ✕🏨 **L'Ami Fritz.** This welcoming inn combines style, rustic warmth, and three generations of family tradition. Patrick Fritz's sophisticated twists on regional specialties include feather-light blood sausage in flaky pastry, a delicate choucroute of grated turnips, and freshwater fish. Don't miss the fruity red wine, an Ottrott exclusive. Pretty, impeccable rooms decked in toile de Jouy and homespun checks are available in the historic house; avoid the less appealing residence across the village. ✉ *8 rue des Châteaux, 67530 Ottrott (3 km/2 mi from Obernai),* ☎ *03–88–95–80–81,* FAX *03–88–95–84–85,* WEB *www.amifritz.com. 39 rooms. Restaurant, no air-conditioning in some rooms, minibars, Internet, pool, some pets allowed (fee). AE, DC, MC, V.*

$ ✕🏨 **La Cloche.** Leaded glass, dark oak, and Hansi-like murals set the tone in this sturdy half-timber 14th-century landmark on Obernai's market square. Standard local dishes and blackboard specials draw locals on market days. Rooms are well equipped and country-pretty; two double-decker duplex rooms accommodate four. ✉ *90 rue Général-Gouraud, 67210,* ☎ *03–88–95–52–89,* FAX *03–88–95–07–63,* WEB *www.la-cloche.com. 20 rooms. Restaurant, bar, Internet. AE, DC, MC, V. Closed 1st 2 wks in Jan.*

Shopping

Dietrich (✉ 58 and 74 rue du Général-Gouraud, ☎ 03–88–95–57–58) has a varied selection of Beauvillé linens, locally hand-blown Alsatian wine glasses, and Obernai-patterned china.

Mont-Ste-Odile

★ 42 *12 km (8 mi) southwest of Obernai, 42 km (26 mi) southwest of Strasbourg.*

Mont-Ste-Odile, a 2,500-ft hill, has been an important religious and military site for 3,000 years. The eerie 9½-km-long (6-mi-long) **Mur Païen** (Pagan Wall), up to 12 ft high and, in parts, several feet thick, rings the summit; its mysterious origins and purpose still baffle archaeologists. The Romans established a settlement here and, at the start of the 8th century Odile, daughter of Duke Etichon of Obernai, who had been born blind, founded a convent on the same spot after recovering her sight while being baptized. The relatively modern convent is now a workaday hostelry for modern pilgrims on group retreats. Odile—the patron saint of Alsace—died here in AD 720; her sarcophagus rests in the 12th-century **Chapelle Ste-Odile.** The spare, Romanesque **Chapelle de la Croix** adjoins St-Odile.

Barr

43 *11 km (7 mi) southeast of Mont-Ste-Odile, 8 km (5 mi) south of Obernai, 33 km (20 mi) southwest of Strasbourg.*

Barr is a thriving, semi-industrial town surrounded by vines, with some charming narrow streets (notably rue des Cigognes, rue Neuve, and the tiny rue de l'Essieu), a cheerful Hôtel de Ville, and a decorative arts museum. Most buildings date from after a catastrophic fire in 1678; the only medieval survivor is the Romanesque tower of St-Martin, the Protestant church.

Admire original furniture, local porcelain, earthenware, and pewter at the **Musée de la Folie Marco,** in a mansion built by local magistrate Félix Marco in 1763. One section of the museum explains the traditional process of *schlittage*: sleds, bearing bundles of freshly sawn tree trunks, once slid down the forest slopes over a "corduroy road" made of logs. ✉ *30 rue du Dr-Sultzer,* ☎ *03–88–08–94–72; 03–88–08–66–*

65 winter. €3. *End of June–Sept., Wed.–Mon. 10–noon and 2–6; early June, Oct., and Dec., weekends 10–noon and 2–6.*

Andlau

44 *3 km (2 mi) southwest of Barr, 37 km (23 mi) southwest of Strasbourg.*

Andlau has long been known for its magnificent abbey. Built in the 12th century, the **Abbaye d'Andlau** has the richest ensemble of Romanesque sculpture in Alsace. Sculpted vines wind their way around the doorway as a reminder of wine's time-honored importance to the local economy. A statue of a female bear, the abbey mascot—bears used to roam local forests and were bred at the abbey until the 16th century—can be seen in the north transept. Legend has it that Queen Richarde, spurned by her husband, Charles the Fat, founded the abbey in AD 887 when an angel enjoined her to construct a church on a site to be shown to her by a female bear.

Dining and Lodging

$$–$$$ **Hotel Arnold.** This yellow-wall, half-timber hillside hotel overlooks the cute wine village of Itterswiller; most rooms have views across the vines. The cheapest rooms, on the top floor, have a shower and no balcony; the priciest have a bath and a balcony facing south. The wood-beamed lobby with its wrought-iron staircase has the same quaint charm as the hotel restaurant across the street, with its old winepress and local Alsace wines served by the jug; homemade foie gras and venison in cranberry sauce top the menu, along with sauerkraut and baeckoffe. *98 route des Vins, 67140 Itterswiller (3 km/2 mi south of Andlau on D253),* ☎ *03–88–85–50–58,* FAX *03–88–85–55–54,* WEB *www.hotel-arnold.com. 29 rooms. Restaurant, no air-conditioning, minibars, cable TV, Internet, some pets allowed (fee). AE, MC, V. Closed 1st ½ of Feb. No dinner Sun., Mon. May–Nov.*

Dambach-la-Ville

45 *5 km (3 mi) southeast of Andlau, 42 km (26 mi) southwest of Strasbourg. From Andlau take D253 to the junction with D603; keep right; about 1 km (½ mi) later, turn right, then left through Itterswiller before turning right toward Dambach-la-Ville.*

One of the prettiest village along the Alsace Wine Road, Dambach-la-Ville is a fortified medieval town protected by ramparts and three powerful 13th-century gateways. It is particularly rich in half-timber, high-roof houses from the 17th and 18th centuries, clustered mainly around **place du Marché** (Market Square). Also on the square is the 16th-century Hôtel de Ville (Town Hall).

En Route Just south of Dambach is the imposing **Château d'Ortenburg,** constructed in 1000 by Wernher d'Ortenburg and restored in 1258 by Rodolphe de Habsbourg, one of the founders of the great Habsburg empire.

Dining and Lodging

$ **Au Raisin d'Or.** Set around the corner from the village church and halfway up the street that climbs straight into the vineyards, this unpretentious hotel is where you'll get a down-to-earth welcome and a hearty meal in a typical Alsace dining room with heavy wooden tables and checked tablecloths. Hearty fare like sauerkraut, sausage meat, and potatoes are staple offerings. Rooms are on the small side, with functional dark-wood furnishings, but the best have balconies overlooking the street. *28 bis rue Clemenceau, 67650,* ☎ *03–88–92–48–66,* FAX *03–88–92–61–42,* WEB *www.au-raisin-dor.com. 8 rooms. Restaurant,* *bar, no air-conditioning, minibars. DC, MC, V. Closed 1st ½ of Jan. and Mon. No lunch Tues.*

Sélestat

46 *9 km (5 mi) southeast of Dambach, 19 km (12 mi) south of Barr, 47 km (29 mi) southwest of Strasbourg.*

Sélestat, midway between Strasbourg and Colmar, is a lively, historic town with a Romanesque church and a library of medieval manuscripts. Head directly to the Vieille Ville and explore the quarter on foot. The church of **St-Foy** (✉ Pl. du Marché-Vert) dates from between 1155 and 1190; its Romanesque facade remains largely intact (the spires were added in the 19th century), as does the 140-ft octagonal tower over the crossing. Sadly, the interior was mangled during the centuries, chiefly by the Jesuits; their most inspired legacy is the Baroque pulpit of 1733 depicting the life of St. Francis Xavier. Note the Romanesque bas-relief next to the baptistery, originally the lid of a sarcophagus.

Among the precious medieval and Renaissance manuscripts on display at the **Bibliothèque Humaniste** (Humanist Library), a major library founded in 1452 and installed in the former Halle aux Blés, are a 7th-century lectionary and a 12th-century Book of Miracles. ✉ *1 rue de la Bibliothèque,* ☎ *03–88–58–07–20.* *€3.50.* ⏲ *Sept.–June, Mon. and Wed.–Fri. 9–noon and 2–6, Sat. 9–noon; July–Aug., Mon. and Wed.–Fri. 9–noon and 2–6, weekends 9–noon and 2–5.*

Dining

$$$$ ★ ✕ **L'Auberge de l'Ill.** With its windows opening over the swans on the Ill river and an entire family carrying on a grand tradition, this is the ultimate Alsatian inn. England's Queen Mother, Marlene Dietrich, and Montserrat Caballé are just a few of the famous who have feasted here, but, oddly, this place has never been as famous as it should be, the long trek from Paris to Alsace perhaps the reason. With both feet firmly fixed in *la grande cuisine française,* master chef Paul Haeberlin creates his famous salmon soufflé, lamb chops in dainty strudel, and showstoppers like *le homard Prince Wladimir,* or lobster with shallots braised in champagne and crème fraîche. Germanic-Alsatian flair is apparent in such dishes as the truffled *baeckoffa* (baker's oven), a casserole-terrine of lamb and pork with leeks. The kitchen's touch is incredibly light (though not nouvelle, thank you) so you can even enjoy such master desserts as white peaches in vanilla syrup served in a chocolate "butterfly" with champagne sabayon sauce. ✉ *2 rue de Collonges, Illhaeusern (12 km/7 mi south of Sélestat),* ☎ *03–89–71–89–00,* FAX *03–89–71–82–83. AE, DC, MC, V. Reservations essential several weeks in advance. Closed Mon.–Tues. and Feb.*

Nightlife and the Arts

The colorful **Corso Fleuri** (Flower Carnival) takes place on the second Sunday in August, when the town decks itself—and the floats in its vivid parade—with a magnificent display of dahlias.

Haut-Koenigsbourg

47 *12 km (8 mi) west of Sélestat, 59 km (36½ mi) southwest of Strasbourg.*

One of the most popular spots in Alsace is the romantic, crag-top castle of Haut-Koenigsbourg, originally built as a fortress in the 12th century. ★ The ruins of the **Château du Haut-Koenigsbourg** were presented by the town of Sélestat to German emperor Wilhelm II in 1901. The château looked just as a kaiser thought one should, and he restored it with some diligence and no lack of imagination—squaring the main tower's original circle, for instance. The site, panorama, drawbridge, and amply furnished imperial chambers may lack authenticity, but they are undeniably dramatic. ☎ *03–88–92–11–46.* *Château €6.15.* *Jan.–Feb. and Nov.–Dec., daily 9:30–noon and 1–4:30; Mar.–Apr. and Oct., daily 9–noon and 1–5:30; May–June and Sept., daily 9–6; July–Aug., daily 9–6:30.*

Ribeauvillé

48 *14 km (9 mi) southwest of Sélestat, 63 km (39 mi) southwest of Strasbourg.*

The beautiful half-timber town of Ribeauvillé, surrounded by rolling vineyards and three imposing châteaux, produces some of the best Riesling in Alsace. (The Trimbach family has made Riesling and superb Gewürztraminer here since 1626.) The town's narrow main street, crowded with winstubs, pottery shops, bakeries, and wine sellers, is bisected by the 13th-century **Tour des Bouchers,** a clock-belfry completed (gargoyles and all) in the 15th century. Storks' nests crown several towers in the village.

Dining and Lodging

$–$$ ✕ **Zum Pfifferhüss.** This is a true-blood winstub, with yellowed murals, glowing lighting, and great local wines available by the glass. The cooking is pure Alsace, with German-scale portions of choucroute, ham hock, and fruit tarts. ✉ *14 Grand-Rue,* ☎ *03–89–73–62–28. MC, V. Closed Wed.–Thurs., 3 wks in Feb., 2 wks in July*

$$$ **Hostellerie des Seigneurs de Ribeaupierre.** On the edge of Ribeauvillé's old quarter, this gracious half-timber inn offers a warm regional welcome with a touch of flair. It has exposed timbers in pastel tones, sumptuous fabrics, and slick bathrooms upstairs, as well as a fire crackling downstairs on your way to the generous breakfast. ✉ *11 rue du Château, 68150,* ☎ *03–89–73–70–31,* FAX *03–89–73–71–21. 10 rooms. Bar, no room TVs, no air-conditioning. AE, MC, V. Closed Jan.–Feb.*

$$ **Hôtel de la Tour.** In the center of Ribeauvillé and across from the Tour des Bouchers, this hotel, with an ornate Renaissance fountain outside its front door, is a good choice for experiencing the atmospheric town by night. Rooms and amenities are modern; those on the top floor have exposed timbers and wonderful views of ramshackle rooftops. ✉ *1 rue de la Mairie, 68150,* ☎ *03–89–73–72–73,* FAX *03–89–73–38–74,* WEB *www.visit-alsace.com/hotel-la-tour. 34 rooms. Bar, no air-conditioning, some Internet, hot tub, sauna. AE, DC, MC, V.*

Shopping

Find rich paisley Alsatian tablecloths discounted at the factory outlet for **Beauvillé** (✉ 19 rte. de Ste-Marie-aux-Mines, ☎ 03–89–73–74–74), at the foot of forested hills just past the town center.

Riquewihr

★ 49 *5 km (3 mi) south of Ribeauvillé, 68 km (42 mi) south of Strasbourg.*

Riquewihr is a living museum of the quaint architecture and storybook allure of old Alsace. Its steep main street, ramparts, and winding back alleys have scarcely changed since the 16th century, and could easily serve as a film set. Merchants cater to the sizable influx of tourists with a plethora of kitschy souvenir shops; bypass them to peep into courtyards with massive wine presses, to study the woodwork and ornately decorated houses, to stand in the narrow old courtyard that was once the Jewish quarter, or to climb up a narrow wooden stair to the ramparts. You would also do well to settle into a winstub to sample some of Riquewihr's famous wines.

Dining and Lodging

$$ ✕🏨 **Sarment d'Or.** This cozy little hotel stands apart for its irreproachable modern comforts tactfully dovetailed with stone, dark timbers, and thick walls. The restaurant downstairs offers firelight romance and delicious cuisine—foie gras, frogs' legs in garlic cream, and breast of duck in pinot noir; it is closed Monday and does not serve dinner Sunday or lunch Tuesday. ✉ *4 rue du Cerf, 68340,* ☎ *03–89–86–02–86,* FAX *03–89–47–99–23. 9 rooms. Restaurant. MC, V. Closed Jan.*

Colmar

50 *16 km (10 mi) southeast of Riquewihr, 71 km (44 mi) southwest of Strasbourg.*

Much of Colmar's architecture is modern because of the destruction wrought by World Wars I and II. But the heart of this proud merchant town—an atmospheric maze of narrow streets lined with Renaissance houses restored to the last detail—outcharms Strasbourg. Old Town streets fan out from the beefy towered church of **St-Martin.** Each shop-lined backstreet winds its way to the 15th-century customs house, the **Ancienne Douane,** and the square and canals that surround it. The **Maison Pfister** (Pfister House; ✉ 11 rue Mercière), built in 1537, is the most striking of Colmar's many old dwellings. Note its decorative frescoes and medallions, carved balcony, and ground-floor arcades. Up the street from the Ancienne Douane on the Grand'Rue, the **Maison aux Arcades** (Arcades House) was built in 1609 in High Renaissance style with a series of arched porches (arcades) anchored by two octagonal towers

Calm canals wind through **La Petite Venise** (Little Venice), an area of bright Alsatián houses with colorful shutters and window boxes that's south of the center of town.

★ The **Musée d'Unterlinden,** once a medieval Dominican convent and hotbed of Rhenish mysticism, is now an important museum. The star attraction is one of the greatest art works of the 16th century, the ***Isenheim Altarpiece*** (1512–16), by Matthias Grünewald, majestically displayed in the convent's Gothic chapel. Originally painted for the Antoine convent at Isenheim, 32 km (20 mi) south of Colmar, the multipaneled altarpiece is framed with two-sided wings, which unfold to show the Crucifixion and Incarnation, with side panels illustrating the Annunciation and the Resurrection. Other panels depict the life of St. Anthony, notably the Temptation. Grünewald's altarpiece, replete with its raw realism (note the chamber pots, boil-covered bellies, and dirty linen), was believed to have miraculous healing powers over ergotism, a widespread disease in the Middle Ages. Produced by the ingestion of fungus-ridden grains, the malady caused its victims to experience delusional fantasies. Hallucinogenic, indeed, is the word to describe the proto-Expressionist power of Grünewald's tortured faces and poses, whose emotional power made a direct appeal to the pain-racked victims living out their last days at the convent. Arms and armor, stone sculpture, ancient wine presses and barrels, and antique toys cluster around the enchanting 13th-century cloister. Upstairs are fine regional furnishings and a collection of Rhine Valley paintings from the Renaissance, including Martin Schongauer's opulent 1470 altarpiece painted for Jean d'Orlier. ✉ *1 rue Unterlinden,* ☎ *03–89–20–15–50.* 🎫 *€5.50.* ⏲ *Apr.–Oct., daily 9–6; Nov.–Mar., Wed.–Mon. 9–12 and 2–5.*

★ The **Église des Dominicains** (Dominican Church) houses the Flemish-influenced *Madonna of the Rosebush* (1473), by Martin Schongauer (1445–91), the most celebrated painting by the noted 15th-century German artist. This work, stolen from St-Martin's in 1972 and later recovered and hung here, has almost certainly been reduced in size from its original state but retains enormous impact. The grace and intensity of the Virgin match that of the Christ child; yet her slender fingers dent the child's soft flesh (and his fingers entwine her curls) with immediate intimacy. Schongauer's text for her crown is: ME CARPES GENITO TUO O SANTISSIMA VIRGO ("Choose me also for your child, o holiest Virgin"). ✉ *Pl. des Dominicains,* ☎ *03–89–24–46–57.* 🎫 *€1.30.* ⏲ *Apr.–Dec., daily 10–1 and 3–6.*

The **Musée Bartholdi** (Bartholdi Museum) is the birthplace of Frédéric-Auguste Bartholdi (1834–1904), the local sculptor who designed the Statue of Liberty. Exhibits of Bartholdi's works claim the ground floor; a reconstruction of the artist's Paris apartments and furniture are upstairs; and, in adjoining rooms, the creation of Lady Liberty is explored. ✉ *30 rue des Marchands,* ☎ *03–89–41–90–60.* 🎫 *€4.* ⏲ *Mar.–Dec., Wed.–Mon. 10–noon and 2–6.*

Dining and Lodging

$$ ✕ **Chez Hansi.** Named for the Rockwell-like illustrator whose beclogged folk children adorn most of the souvenirs of Alsace, this hypertraditional beamed tavern in the Old Town serves excellent down-home classics such as choucroute and pot-au-feu, prepared and served with a sophisticated touch despite the waitresses' dirndls. ✉ *23 rue des Marchands,* ☎ *03–89–41–37–84. MC, V. Closed Wed.–Thurs. and Jan.*

$–$$ ✕ **Au Koïfhus.** Not to be confused with the shabby little Koïfhus on rue des Marchands, this popular landmark serves huge portions of regional standards, plus changing specialties: roast quail and foie gras on salad, game stews with spaetzle (dumplings), and freshwater fish. Choose between the big, open dining room, glowing with wood and warm fabric, and a shaded table on the broad, lovely square. ✉ *2 pl. de l'Ancienne-Douane,* ☎ *03–89–23–04–90. DC, MC, V. Closed Thurs. and Jan.*

$$$–$$$$ ★ 🏨 **Le Maréchal.** A maze of narrow, creaky corridors connects the series of Renaissance houses that make up this romantic riverside inn. Rooms are small but lavished with extravagant detail, from glossy rafters to rich fabrics to fourposter beds. A vivid color scheme—scarlet, sapphire, candy pink—adds to the Vermeer atmosphere. This is not a high-tech luxury hotel: it's an endearing, quirky, lovely old place hanging over a Petite Venise canal. The gastronomic restaurant, A l'Echevin, offers such dishes as terrine of rouget, leeks, truffles, and pigeon breast and foie gras crisped in pastry. ✉ *4 pl. des Six-Montagnes-Noires, 68000,* ☎ *03–89–41–60–32,* FAX *03–89–24–59–40,* WEB *www.hotel-le-marechal.com. 30 rooms. Restaurant, minibars, cable TV, some Internet, some pets allowed (fee). AE, DC, MC, V.*

$$ 🏨 **Rapp.** In the old town, just off the Champ de Mars, this solid, modern hotel has business-class comforts, a professional and welcoming staff, and a good German-scale breakfast. There's even an extensive indoor-pool complex, including sauna, steam bath, and workout equipment—all included in the low price. ✉ *1 rue Weinemer, 68000,* ☎ *03–89–41–62–10,* FAX *03–89–24–13–58,* WEB *www.rapp-hotel.com. 42 rooms. Restaurant, bar, no air-conditioning, cable TV, pool, gym. AE, DC, MC, V.*

The Arts

During the first half of August, Colmar celebrates with its annual **Foire Régionale des Vins d'Alsace,** an Alsatian wine fair in the Parc des Expositions. Events include folk music and theater performances and, above all, the tasting and selling of wine.

Guebwiller

51 *26 km (16 mi) southwest of Colmar, 25 km (16 mi) north of Mulhouse, 94 km (58 mi) south of Strasbourg.*

Despite its admirable churches, fine old buildings, and pleasantly authentic feeling, Guebwiller is often overlooked.

The **Église St-Léger** (✉ Pl. St-Léger), built in 1180–1280, is one of the most harmonious Romanesque churches in Alsace, though its original choir was replaced by the current Gothic one in 1336. The bare, solemn interior is of less interest than the three-tower exterior. The towers match—almost: the one on the left has small turrets at the base of its steeple, while the one on the right is ringed by triangular gables. The octagonal tower over the crossing looms above them both, topped by a seldom-visited stork's nest. The surrounding square has a lively weekly market.

The **Église Dominicaine** (✉ Rue de l'Hôpital) has an unmistakable silhouette thanks to the thin, lacy lantern that sticks out of its roof like an effeminate chimney. Its large 14th-century nave is adorned with frescoes and contains a fine rood screen.

Guebwiller's third and largest church, **Notre-Dame** (✉ Rue de la République), has a Baroque grandeur that would not be out of keeping in Paris—a reflection of the wealth of the Benedictine abbey in nearby Murbach, whose worldly friars, fed up with country life, opted for the comparatively brighter lights of Guebwiller in the mid-18th century. The monks—who needed a noble pedigree of four generations to qualify for the cloth—outmaneuvered church authorities by pretending to take temporary exile in Guebwiller while "modernizing" Murbach Abbey, thus circumventing the need for papal permission before abbeys could move. As a token gesture, the crafty clerics smashed the nave of Murbach Abbey, then failed to replace it and refused to budge from their "temporary" home. Instead, they commissioned Louis Beuque to design this new church in Guebwiller (1762–85). The interior is majestic without being overbearing. The gold-and-marble high altar fits in better, perhaps, than does the trick 3-D–effect stucco Assumption (1783), an example of Baroque craftsmanship at its most outlandish.

The **Musée du Florival** is in one of the 18th-century canons' houses alongside Notre-Dame. It has a fine collection of ceramics designed by Théodore Deck (1823–91), a native of Guebwiller who was director of the renowned Sèvres porcelain factory near Paris. It also contains archaeological treasures, artifacts from everyday life, and religious sculpture. ✉ *1 rue du 4-Février,* ☎ *03–89–74–22–89.* €2.30. ⏲ *Mon. and Wed.–Fri. 2–6, weekends 10–noon and 2–6.*

OFF THE BEATEN PATH

ECOMUSÉE DE HAUTE-ALSACE – Great for kids, this open-air museum near Ungersheim, southeast of Guebwiller (via D430), is really a small village created from scratch in 1980, including 70 historic peasant houses and buildings typical of the region. The village is crisscrossed by donkey carts and wagons, and behind every door lie entertaining demonstrations of the old ways. An off-season visit is a study in local architecture; in high season the place comes alive. Small restaurants, snack bars, a playground, and a few amusement rides are scattered about for breaks. Inexpensive lodging is available on-site. ☎ *03–89–74–44–74.* €*13.* ⏲ *July–Aug., daily 9–7; Apr.–June and Sept., daily 9:30–6; Mar. and Oct., daily 10–5; Nov.–Feb., daily 10:30–5.*

Mulhouse

52 *23 km (14 mi) southeast of Guebwiller, 35 km (22 mi) south of Colmar.*

An unremarkable industrial town, Mulhouse (pronounced moo-*looze*) nonetheless rates a visit for its superb car and train museums, as well as for its art and fabric museums.

Some 500 vintage and modern cars, dating from the steam-powered Jacquot of 1878 and spanning 100 different makes, are housed at the **Musée National de l'Automobile** (National Car Museum). ✉ *192 av. de Colmar,* ☎ *03–89–33–23–23.* *€10.* *Daily 10–6.*

A reconstructed Stephenson locomotive of 1846 sets the wheels rolling at the **Musée Français du Chemin de Fer** (National Train Museum). Stock is spread over 12 tracks, including a panoply of steam trains and the BB 9004 electric train. ✉ *2 rue Alfred-de-Glehn,* ☎ *03–89–42–83–33.* *€7.40.* *Apr.–Sept., daily 9–6; Oct.–Mar., daily 9–5.*

Dutch and Flemish masters of the 17th to 18th centuries—including Brueghel, Teniers, and Ruisdael—top the bill at the **Musée des Beaux-Arts** (Fine Arts Museum), complemented by French painters such as Boudin, Courbet, and Bouguereau. ✉ *4 pl. Guillaume-Tell,* ☎ *03–89–45–43–19.* *Free.* *Wed.–Mon., 10–noon and 2–6.*

The **Musée de l'Impression sur Étoffes** (Museum of Fabric Printing) traces the history and development of industrial cloth printing in Alsace. Like the more famous Provençal cottons, these fine floral and geometric prints were first imported from India; feast your eyes on ancient samples and presses. ✉ *14 rue Jean-Jacques Henner,* ☎ *03–89–46–83–00.* *€5.55.* *Daily 10–6.*

Lodging

$–$$ **Salvator.** Mulhouse is an industrial city of limited beauty, but you may wish to overnight here if you're keen to do justice to some or all of the excellent local museums. The functional, postwar Salvator Hotel wins few plaudits for character, but with its large glass windows (nicely double-paned against the noise) it feels lighter and airier than most and is pleasantly situated near a grid of pedestrian streets. ✉ *7 rue Louis-Pasteur, 68100,* ☎ *03–89–45–28–32,* FAX *03–89–56–49–59,* WEB *www.hotelsalvator.fr. 50 rooms. Bar, no air-conditioning in some rooms, cable TV. MC, V.*

FRANCHE-COMTÉ

The name of the Jura Mountains—that huge natural barrier some 240 km (150 mi) long that throws its curved length between France and Switzerland—was known to Julius Caesar, who referred to them in his *Commentaries* as the Mons Jura. Jura is derived from *juria,* which means "forest," and no more fitting phrase could be found to describe this region than that of "the forested mountains." It is the name by which the region of the Franche-Comté—the "free country"—is best known among foreign visitors. The Franche-Comté extends from Belfort to Besançon, then clockwise through the Jura's great expanses of quiet, untouched land with rivers, waterfalls, and its challenging range of mountains, where you can climb, ski, and enjoy the solitude. From this region it is an easy trip to Burgundy and the Rhône Valley.

Belfort

53 *40 km (25 mi) southwest of Mulhouse, 146 km (90½ mi) southwest of Strasbourg.*

A beefy citadel and colossal stone lion bear witness to the distinguished military history of the stubborn warrior-town of Belfort. In the heart of town is a 36-ft-high **Lion,** sculpted in red sandstone by Frédéric-Auguste Bartholdi, best known as the creator of the Statue of Liberty in New York Harbor. The lion was commissioned to celebrate Belfort's heroic resistance during the Franco-Prussian War (1870–71), when the town, under the leadership of General Denfert-Rochereau, withstood a 103-day siege, surrendering only after the rest of France had capitulated. The Prussian leader Otto von Bismarck was so impressed by Belfort's plucky resistance that he granted the town independent status. Although Alsace was returned to France in 1918, Belfort maintained its special status—meaning that the Territoire de Belfort (Belfort Territory) remains by far the smallest *département* (province) in France. ✉ *Pl. des Bourgeois.* *To climb up to see statue of lion €1.*

Belfort's Lion sits proudly at the foot of Vauban's impregnable hilltop château, the **Musée d'Art et d'Histoire** (Museum of Art and History), which contains Vauban's 1687 scale model of the town plus a detailed section on military history. There's also a collection of paintings and sculpture from the 16th through 19th centuries. From the ramparts you can look out over the Old Town toward the Vosges Mountains to the north and the Jura to the south. ☎ *03–84–54–25–52.* *Château free, museum €2.75 (free Wed.).* *May–Sept., daily 10–7; Oct.–Apr., Wed.–Mon. 10–noon and 2–5.*

Dining and Lodging

$$ ✕ **Pot-au-Feu.** This rustic bistro, tucked in a 16th-century *cave* (cellar) at the foot of the citadel, serves good regional specialties, such as Jura sausages and *coq au vin jaune* (chicken in Jura wine) and features—of course—a savory, long-simmered pot-au-feu. ✉ *27 bis Grande-Rue,* ☎ *03–84–28–57–84. AE, MC, V. No lunch Sat., Sun., Mon., no dinner Sun. Closed 2 wks in Aug.*

$$–$$$ ✕ **Château Servin.** Set in a garden and built in 1885, this hotel maintains that era's stuffy grandeur, although a frayed Gothic air has entered the picture. Dark polished woodwork, heavy floral carpets, fringe, gilt, and lace close you in, whether in the velour-beswagged rooms or the stately restaurant (closed Friday; no dinner Sunday). Chef Dominique Mathy creates classic dishes—sole soufflé in lobster sauce, fresh foie gras with poppy seeds, and hot cherry soufflé. ✉ *9 rue du Général-Négrier, 90000,* ☎ *03–84–21–41–85,* FAX *03–84–57–05–57. 8 rooms. Restaurant, no air-conditioning. AE, DC, MC, V.*

Ronchamp

54 *21 km (13 mi) west of Belfort via N19.*

The little town of Ronchamp, in the windswept Haute-Saône département, was once renowned for having France's deepest coal-mine shaft (3,300 ft). The mine's huge chimney still towers above the valley, but Ronchamp is now the site of one of Europe's most famous ★ postwar buildings. The hilltop chapel of **Notre-Dame-du-Haut** was designed by Swiss-born French architect Le Corbusier in 1951 to replace a church destroyed during World War II. The chapel's curved, sloping white walls, small, irregularly placed windows, and unadorned, slug-shape gray-concrete roof are unique. Many consider it Le Corbusier's masterpiece. ☎ *03–84–20–65–13.* *€1.50.* *Mid-Mar.–Oct., Wed.–Mon. 9:30–6:30; Nov.–mid-Mar., Wed.–Mon. 10–4.*

Montbéliard

55 *16 km (10 mi) south of Belfort.*

Montbéliard is an industrial town that is home base for the giant Peugeot automobile company and presided over by a stately castle. Only two round towers of the **Château** remain from the heyday of the princes of Württemberg, who once ruled this Renaissance principality; its more classical portions, dating from the 18th century, contain a museum devoted to insects, geological and archaeological finds, and local clocks and music boxes. ✉ *Rue du Château,* ☎ *03–81–99–22–61.* *May–Sept. €4.60, Oct.–Apr. €1.50.* *Wed.–Mon. 2–6.*

Across the rail line in the neighboring suburb of Sochaux, Peugeot's production methods and colorful history can be explored at the **Musée de l'Aventure Peugeot** (Peugeot Adventure Museum). You can also tour the factory (children under 14 are not allowed). ✉ *Carrefour de l'Europe,* ☎ *03–81–94–48–21; 03–81–33–27–46 to arrange factory tours.* *Museum €4.60, factory tour free.* *Museum daily 10–6; factory tours 8:30 AM weekdays (English-speaking guides available).*

Besançon

56 *80 km (50 mi) southwest of Montbéliard, 238 km (147 mi) southwest of Strasbourg.*

The former capital of the Franche-Comté, Besançon is a graceful, old gray-stone city nestled in a vast bend of the River Doubs. Its defensive potential was quickly realized by Vauban, whose imposing citadel remains the town's architectural focal point. The town has long been a clock-making center and, more recently, was the birthplace of the rayon industry. Famous offspring include Auguste and Louis Lumière, the inventors of a motion-picture camera, and the poet Victor Hugo, born in 1802 while his father was garrisoned here.

A 75-minute **boat trip** along the Doubs River provides a good introduction to Besançon. Boats leave from Pont de la République and take in a lock and the 400-yard tunnel under the citadel. ☎ *03–81–68–13–25.* *€8.* *July–early Sept., weekdays 10, 2:30, 4:30, weekends 10, 2:30, 4:30, and 6; May–June, weekends 2:30 and 4:30.*

Wander around the quayside to the **Musée des Beaux-Arts et d'Archéologie** (Museum of Fine Arts and Archaeology) to see its collection of tapestries, ceramics, and paintings by Bonnard, Renoir, and Courbet. ✉ *1 pl. de la Révolution,* ☎ *03–81–87–80–49.* *€3.25.* *June–Oct., Wed.–Mon. 9:30–6; Nov.–May, Wed.–Mon. 9:30–noon and 2–6.*

Besançon was once a great watch- and clock-making center, and the **Musée du Temps** (Museum of Time) houses an extensive collection of fine old timepieces. Even if you're not interested in watches, you can still enjoy touring the lovely Renaissance **Palais Granvelle** (1540), which will be the museum's new home once renovations are complete, scheduled at press time for the end of June 2002. ✉ *Palais Granvelle, Grande-Rue,* ☎ *03–81–87–81–61.* *€3.* *Oct.–Apr., Wed.–Sat. 1–5:30, Sun. 1–6; May–Sept., Wed.–Sun. 1–7.*

Besançon's oldest street, **Grande-Rue,** leads from the river toward the citadel, past fountains, wrought-iron railings, and stately 16th- to 18th-century mansions. Victor Hugo was born at No. 140, the Lumière brothers just opposite.

The **Horloge Astronomique,** at the foot of the citadel, is a stupendous 19th-century astronomical clock with 62 dials and automatons that spring into action just before the hours are sounded. ✉ *2 rue du Chapitre,* ☎ *03–81–81–12–76.* 🎫 *€2.30.* ⏲ *Apr.–Sept., tours hourly Wed.–Mon. 9:50–11:50 and 2:50–5:50; Oct.–Mar., tours hourly Thurs.–Mon. 9:50–11:50 and 2:50–5:50.*

The **Citadelle,** perched on a rocky spur 350 ft above the town, has a triple ring of ramparts now laid out as promenades and studded with Vauban's original watchtowers. Inside are museums devoted to natural history, regional folklore, agricultural tools, and the French Resistance during World War II. There also are shops and restaurants. ☎ *03–81–65–07–54.* 🎫 *Joint ticket with citadel and museums €6.15.* ⏲ *Late Mar.–June and Sept.–Oct., daily 9–6; July–Aug., daily 9–7; Nov.–Mar., daily 10–5.*

Dining and Lodging

$$$ ✕ **Mungo Park.** This former warehouse on the bank of the Doubs is now a bright glassed-in restaurant. Chefs Jocelyne Choquart and Benoît Rotschi bring local ingredients forward into this century—Jura snails in horseradish cream, chicken breast with morel mushrooms and vin jaune, and a sweet, hot dessert soup of walnuts, vin jaune, and nutmeg. ✉ *11 rue Jean-Petit,* ☎ *03–81–81–28–01. Reservations essential. AE, MC, V. Closed Sun., Mon., 1 wk in Feb., and 2 wks in Aug.*

$$ ★ ✕ **Poker d'As.** Carved-wood tables and cowbells counterbalanced by swagged tulle and porcelain capture the ethnic-chic of this landmark restaurant's cuisine. Earning kudos for his *cuisine du terroir* (regional cooking), chef Raymond Ferreux animates his upscale experiments with splashes of local color: Jura *morteau* (sausage) sautéed with artichokes and cèpes, and pressed partridge with wild mushrooms. ✉ *14 Clos St-Amour,* ☎ *03–81–81–42–49. AE, DC, MC, V. Closed Mon. and late July–early Aug. No dinner Sun.*

$ ✕ **Bistrot du Jura.** In an intimate, downscale setting of checkered tiles and bentwood, sample home-cooked regional specialties such as herring with steamed potatoes and andouillette in Jura wine—a fine selection of which is served by the glass. The owner keeps proud standards but irregular hours; call in advance. ✉ *35 rue Charles-Nodier,* ☎ *03–81–82–03–48. MC, V. Closed weekends.*

$$$ ★ 🏨 **Castan.** Just below the citadel, in a courtyard behind a tangle of ancient trees and crumbling Roman pillars, this noble 17th- and 18th-century mansion has become a chic *relais* (inn). Rooms are atmospheric and exquisitely decorated: Regency moldings, period fabrics, luxurious baths, and a private collection of regional bibelots set the tone. ✉ *6 sq. Castan, 25000,* ☎ *03–81–65–02–00,* FAX *03–81–83–01–02,* WEB *www.hotelcastan.fr. 10 rooms. Bar, no air-conditioning, Internet, some pets allowed (fee), parking (fee). AE, MC, V.*

$$ 🏨 **Paris.** Extensive renovations have given this standby a sleek new look, with a mahogany-lined lobby and freshly decorated rooms. These overlook the quiet, tree-lined courtyard, which provides a note of serenity although you're deep in the heart of commercial Besançon. It's well run and unpretentious. ✉ *33 rue des Granges, 25000,* ☎ *03–81–81–36–56,* FAX *03–81–61–94–90. 48 rooms. Bar, no air-conditioning. AE, DC, MC, V.*

$ 🏨 **Granvelle.** Convenient to the citadel and set back from Old Town streets, this modest, straightforward lodging has freshly decorated rooms, including some with shared bathrooms that are bargains. ✉ *13 rue du Général-Lecourbe, 25000,* ☎ *03–81–81–33–92,* FAX *03–81–81–31–77,* WEB *www. hotel-granvelle.fr. 30 rooms, 26 with bath. Bar, no air-conditioning, some minibars, some pets allowed (fee). DC, MC, V.*

Ornans

57 *26 km (16 mi) south of Besançon.*

In the pretty village of Ornans you can enjoy the views of the steep-roof old houses lining the Loue River and see the birthplace of the great French painter Courbet. Gustave Courbet (1819–77), the pioneering French realist painter who influenced Édouard Manet, was an assertive, full-bearded radical who spent his last years in Swiss exile after toppling Napoléon's column on place Vendôme during the Paris Commune in 1871. The **Musée de la Maison Natale de Courbet** (Courbet Birthplace Museum)—a rambling 18th-century mansion—hardly goes with his tempestuous image and provides a sedate setting for souvenirs, documents, drawings, sculptures, and paintings. Courbet is best known for his magisterial *Burial at Ornans* (now in the Musée d'Orsay in Paris), which, with its procession of somber peasants, became the defining landmark of French realist painting. ✉ *Pl. Robert-Fernier,* ☎ *03–81–62–23–30.* 🎫 *€3.* ⏲ *July–Aug., daily 10–6; Apr.–June and Sept.–Oct., daily 10–noon and 2–6; Nov.–Mar., Wed.–Mon. 10–noon and 2–6.*

Montbenoît

58 *40 km (25 mi) southeast of Ornans.*

The tiny village of Montbenoît is dominated by its **Ancienne Abbaye,** which dates from the 11th century. The vast cloisters, conservative for their Flamboyant times, were added in the 15th century. Take time to study the superbly carved wood **choir stalls** (1525–27), which offer a Renaissance interpretation of biblical tales: Samson, for instance, wears natty hose and a lace ruff collar as Delilah takes to his flowing locks with a pair of oversize scissors. ☎ *03–81–38–10–32.* 🎫 *€1.50.* ⏲ *July–Aug., Mon.–Sat. 10–noon and 2–6, Sun. 11:15–noon and 2–6; Sept.–June, check at tourist office. Guided tours of kitchen and refectory July–Aug. by request.*

Dining and Lodging

$$ ✕🏨 **France.** Flocks of Swiss gourmands cross the border (just two minutes away) to this spot in Villers-le-Lac, to savor chef Hugues Droz's exotic but earthy cuisine: lobster in vanilla and escargots in Pernod (the restaurant is closed Monday and does not serve dinner Sunday or lunch Tuesday). The spare, modern rooms are somewhat noisy. Breakfast, however, is bountiful. ✉ *8 pl. Maxime-Cupillard, 25130 Villers-le-Lac (24 km/15 mi northeast of Montbenoît),* ☎ *03–81–68–00–06,* FAX *03–81–68–09–22. 14 rooms. Restaurant. AE, DC, MC, V. Closed Jan.*

Pontarlier

59 *38 km (22 mi) southwest of Ornans.*

Pontarlier, with its old streets, churches, and gateways, was once France's main center for the production of absinthe—a notorious anise-based aperitif, the forerunner of Ricard and Pernod. It was banned in 1915 for inducing alcoholism and even madness. The **Musée Municipal** has a section on the history of the *fée verte* (green fairy), as absinthe was called. Porcelain and local paintings are also on display. ✉ *2 pl. d'Arçon,* ☎ *03–81–38–82–14.* 🎫 *€2.30.* ⏲ *Wed.–Mon. 10–noon and 2–6, Sat. 2–6, Sun. 3–7.*

OFF THE BEATEN PATH

CHÂTEAU DE JOUX – Just south of Pontarlier via N57, this fortress perched on a steep hill glowers across the Jura landscape toward the Swiss border. Founded in the 11th century, it retains its round medieval towers, drawbridges, and 17th-century ramparts. The dungeon holds a sturdy collection of old guns and weapons (guided tours only; allow one hour). ☎ *03–81–69–47–95.* ✉ *€5.* ⏲ *July–Aug., daily 9–6; Feb.–June and Sept., daily 10–11:30 and 2–4:30; Oct.–Jan., daily tours at 10, 11:15, 2, and 3:30.*

Dining and Lodging

$–$$ **Raison d'Or.** You can't miss this colorful, turn-of-the-20th-century mansion on the main village street in Malbuisson. Its cheerful green-and-yellow walls reflect the relaxed mood at this large, old-fashioned family-run hotel. The garden backs onto the Lac de St-Point, and some rooms overlook the lake; a handful also have private balconies. Lobster and freshly caught fish are on offer most days in the light, elegant restaurant. There's also a smaller dining room that concentrates on cheese dishes, and a tearoom. ✉ *65 Grande-Rue, 25160 Malbuisson (16 km/10 mi south of Pontarlier via D437),* ☎ *03–81–69–34–80,* FAX *03–81–69–35–44. 54 rooms. Restaurant, bar, tea shop, no air-conditioning, some pets allowed (fee). DC, MC, V. Closed mid-Nov.–mid-Dec.*

Syam

60 *48 km (30 mi) southwest of Pontarlier: take D72 and D471 to Champagnole, then N5 south (toward Geneva) before bearing left on D127.*

Syam, nestled in the lush Ain Valley, forged into the limelight in the second decade of the 19th century as an ironworks center. The **Forges de Syam** (Syam Ironworks) was built in 1813; iron was hauled in by train, then dragged down to the riverside by oxen. Simple lodgings were built on-site, now occupied by the nearly 50 people who still work here, making nails, locks, tools, and machinery. "Hot-rolling" and "hard-drawing" techniques are explained at the museum (with video presentation). ☎ *03–84–51–61–00.* ✉ *€1.85.* ⏲ *July–Aug., Wed.–Mon. 10–6; May–June and Sept., weekends 10–6.*

The founder of the forge, Alphonse Jobez, was clearly flushed with pride when he built the **Château de Syam,** a sturdy, square, yellow-front neo-Palladian villa. Finished in 1818, this grandiose self-homage has outsize Ionic pilasters at each corner and, inside, a theatrical colonnaded rotunda ringed with balconies and Pompeiian grotesques. Guided tours take you through restored rooms. ☎ *03–84–51–61–25.* ✉ *€3.80.* ⏲ *July–Sept., Fri.–Mon. 2–6.*

Baume-les-Messieurs

61 *33 km (21 mi) west of Syam.*

A rambling little stone village in a breathtaking landscape of cliffs and forests, Baume-les-Messieurs has a venerable medieval abbey and an underground network of caves. Its Romanesque stonework resonant with history, the 12th-century **Abbaye** has time-worn courtyards and a tenderly painted 16th-century Flemish altarpiece donated by the Belgian town of Ghent. ☎ *03–81–84–27–98.* ✉ *Free.* ⏲ *Daily 9–8.*

The **Grottes de Baume,** 2 km (1 mi) outside town, consists of 650 yards of skillfully lighted galleries 400 ft underground, containing a river, a lake, and weird-shape stalactites and stalagmites (the temperature is chilly, so bring along a sweater). The largest cave is more than 200 ft high, and classical music blasts out to heighten the dramatic effect. The ceilings are clustered with hundreds of tiny mink-brown bats. ✉ *Chalet de Guide,* ☎ *03–84–44–61–58.* ✉ *€3.80.* ⏲ *Apr.–Sept., daily 9:30–noon and 2–6.*

Five kilometers (3 miles) outside Baume-les-Messieurs (south on D4 and then west on D71) is the **Belvedère des Roches de Baume** (Baume Rocks Overlook); watch for signs. The plummeting view of the ring of chalky cliffs hemming the village is spectacular. You can also hike the rim of the cirque, following the Grand Randonée (national hiking trail, GR59).

Dining and Lodging

$ ★ **Chambre d'Hôte/Étape Gourmande.** This bed-and-breakfast and casual restaurant is nestled in the abbey itself, featuring groin-vaulted stonework, a vast Gothic fireplace, and a weathered refectory table in the breakfast room. Enjoy salads, Charolais beef with morels, and regional cheese dishes placed to melt in the fireplace. If you're lucky, you can even stay in one of the three vast, beamed rooms furnished casually with mismatched collectibles and woodstoves. The romantic views of surrounding forests and cliffs defy description. ✉ *Abbaye de Baume-les-Messieurs, 39210,* ☎ *03–84–44–64–47. 3 rooms. Restaurant, no air-conditioning, some pets allowed (fee). MC, V.*

Château-Chalon

★ 62 *13 km (8 mi) north of Baume-les-Messieurs.*

The medieval village of Château-Chalon, on a rocky promontory vertiginously high above local vineyards, is renowned for its legendary vin jaune, said to keep for 200 years without losing its vigor. Though there's very little to "do" here, you could easily lose yourself for a day in its atmosphere: the restored stonework, restrained shop fronts, and archaic street signs help to keep out the 20th century. You can sample the nutty, sherrylike flavor of vin jaune at the **Fruitière Vinicole,** opposite the 10th-century St-Pierre church. Walk off any aftereffects with a stroll through the narrow, twisting streets.

OFF THE BEATEN PATH

CHÂTEAU D'ARLAY – This 18th-century château, 8 km (5 mi) west of Château-Chalon, contains sumptuously carved regional furniture dating from the same period. The outstanding wine produced here can be sampled (and purchased) in the château's cellar, open Monday–Saturday 8–noon and 2–6. Combine your visit with a walk around the magnificent park, with its grotto, medieval ruins, and alley of ancient *tilleuls* (lime trees). Stop at the Volerie des Rapaces, where (at 4 and 5 PM) trained eagles and other birds of prey perform wide-winged acrobatics overhead. The Jardin des Jeux (Garden of Games) is a manicured vegetable garden designed on a parlor-game theme and is great fun for kids. ✉ *Rue Haute-du-Bourg,* ☎ *03–84–85–04–22. Château and volerie: €8.30. Mid-June–mid-Sept., Mon.–Sun. 2–6. Volerie also open Apr.–Oct., weekends 2–6.*

Arbois

63 *24 km (15 mi) north of Château-Chalon.*

The pretty wine-market town of Arbois is worth a stop for its fine restaurant, Jean-Paul Jeûnet. It also has a museum dedicated to the vine and to Louis Pasteur (1822–95), the famous bacteriologist and father of pasteurization, who grew up in Arbois.

The **Maison de Pasteur,** Louis Pasteur's family home, is fully furnished in authentic style, containing many of his possessions. ✉ *83 rue de Courcelles,* ☎ *03–84–66–11–72. €5. Guided tours on the ½ hr June–Sept., daily 9:45–11:45 and 2:15–5:15; Apr.–May and early Oct. afternoons only.*

The Arbois vineyard is one of the finest in eastern France; to learn more about it, visit the **Musée de la Vigne et du Vin** (Vineyard and Wine Museum) and peruse its collection of tools and documents. ✉ *Château Pécauld,* ☎ *03–84–66–40–45.* *€3.25.* *Mar.–Oct., Wed.–Mon. 10–noon and 2–6; Nov.–Feb., Wed.–Mon. 2–6.*

A short excursion south along D469 takes you into the magnificent **Reculée des Planches,** a dramatic rocky valley created by glacial erosion and peppered with caves and waterfalls. ☎ *03–84–66–07–96 cave access information.* *Caves €5.10.* *Apr.–June and Sept., daily 10–noon and 2–5; July–Aug., daily 9:30–6.*

Continue along D469 from the Reculée des Planches to the beautiful, rocky **Cirque du Fer à Cheval** (Horseshoe Circle), with its panoramic view of U-shape cliffs (10 minutes' walk from parking.) Watch for signs.

Dining and Lodging

$$$ ★ ✕ **Jean-Paul Jeûnet.** One of the most lauded eateries in the Jura occupies an ancient stone convent, its massive beams enhanced with subtle lighting and contemporary art (closed Tuesday, September to June, with no lunch Wednesday). Chef Jeûnet's devotion to local flora and fauna has evolved into a bold, earthy, flavorful cuisine: crayfish sausage, prawns with heather flowers, and even sheep's-milk sorbet. The chef's father, a prize-winning sommelier, has established a worthy cellar. Guest rooms are pleasant and modern with pretty pine furniture. ✉ *9 rue de l'Hôtel-de-Ville, 39600,* ☎ *03–84–66–05–67,* FAX *03–84–66–24–20,* WEB *www.recptionfrance.com. 17 rooms. Restaurant, some pets allowed (fee). DC, MC, V. Closed Dec.–Jan.*

$–$$ **Hôtel des Messageries.** This dignified, vine-covered inn on Arbois's main street has moderate rooms with flossy baroque touches and a warm public ambience enhanced by grand spaces full of old wood and stone. ✉ *2 rue des Courcelles, 39600,* ☎ *03–84–66–15–45,* FAX *03–84–37–41–09. 26 rooms. Bar, no air-conditioning. MC, V. Closed Dec.–Jan.*

ALSACE, LORRAINE, AND FRANCHE-COMTÉ A TO Z

To research prices, get advice from other travelers, and book travel arrangements, visit www.fodors.com.

AIRPORTS

Most international flights to Alsace land at Mulhouse-Basel Airport, on the Franco-Swiss border; some others at Entzheim, near Strasbourg. Metz-Nancy and Mirecourt (Vittel/Épinal) also have tiny airports for charter- and private-plane landings.

BUS TRAVEL

The two main bus companies are Les Rapides de Lorraine, based in Nancy, and Compagnie des Transports Strasbourgeois, based in Strasbourg. Various regional bus lines can connect you with towns and villages such as Mont-St-Odile, and those departing from Colmar for the towns along the Route du Vin, such as Riquewihr and Ribeauvillé; getting there when you want is another problem entirely. Bus routes run to Metz and Verdun from Nancy; Nancy, Strasbourg, and Colmar all have city buses. Bus routes to Franche-Comté villages are run by Monte-Jura Buses. There are many other routes throughout Alsace, Lorraine, and Franche-Comté, so always check in with the regional tourist office or information window at a gateway rail or bus station to get printed bus schedules.

➤ BUS INFORMATION: **Les Rapides de Lorraine** (✉ 52 blvd. d'Austrasie, 54000 Nancy, ☎ 03–83–32–34–20). **Compagnie des Transports Strasbourgeois** (✉ 14 rue de la Gare-aux-Marchandises, 67200 Strasbourg, ☎ 03–88–77–70–70). **Monts-Jura Buses** (✉ 4 rue Berthelot, Besançon, ☎ 03–81–63–44–44).

CAR RENTAL

➤ LOCAL AGENCIES: **Avis** (✉ 7 pl. Flore, Besançon, ☎ 03–81–80–91–08; ✉ Pl. de la Gare, Strasbourg, ☎ 03–88–32–30–44). **Europcar** (✉ 18 rue de Serre, Nancy, ☎ 03–83–37–57–24). **Hertz** (✉ 7 pl. Thiers, Nancy, ☎ 03–83–32–13–14; ✉ Pl. Flore, Besançon, ☎ 03–81–47–43–23).

CAR TRAVEL

A4 heads east from Paris to Strasbourg, via Verdun, Metz, and Saverne. It is met by A26, descending from the English Channel, at Reims. A31 links Metz to Nancy, continuing south to Burgundy and Lyon. The quickest route from Paris to Besançon and the Jura is on A6 (to Beaune) and then A36; A5 from Paris to Besançon is swift and direct.

N83/A35 connects Strasbourg, Colmar, and Mulhouse. A36 continues to Belfort and Besançon. A4, linking Paris to Strasbourg, passes through Lorraine via Metz, linking Lorraine and Alsace. Picturesque secondary roads lead from Nancy and Toul through Joan of Arc country and on to Épinal. Several scenic roads climb switchbacks over forested mountain passes through the Vosges, connecting Lorraine to Alsace and Alsace to Belfort. And Alsace's Route du Vin, winding from Marlenheim, in the north, all the way south to Thann, is the ultimate touring experience.

EMERGENCIES

➤ CONTACTS: **Ambulance** (☎ 15). **Hôpital Central** (✉ 29 av. du Mal-de-Lattre-de-Tassigny, 54000 Nancy, ☎ 03–83–85–85–85). **Hôpital Civil** (✉ 1 place de l'Hôpital, 67000 Strasbourg, ☎ 03–88–11–67–68).

LODGING

APARTMENT AND VILLA RENTALS

Contact Gîtes de France for its brochure on "Gîtes de France" in the Jura. The list includes both bed-and-breakfasts and houses for rent.

➤ LOCAL AGENTS: **Gîtes de France** (✉ 8 rue Louis Rousseau, 39016 Lons-le-Saunier, ☎ 03–84–87–08–88, WEB www.gitesdefrance.com).

OUTDOORS AND SPORTS

A guide to bicycling in the Lorraine is available from the Comité Départemental de Cyclisme. The Comité Régional de Tourisme provides full details on hiking and biking in Franche-Comté. The Fédération Jurassienne de Randonnée Pédestre publishes a brochure on trails in the Jura. For a list of signposted trails in the Vosges foothills, contact the Sélestat Tourist Office (☞ Visitor Information, *below*). A brochure on fishing is available by writing to Agence de Développement Économique du Doubs. For information on horseback riding in the area, contact the Délégation Départementale de Tourisme Équestre.

➤ BICYCLING: **Comité Départemental de Cyclisme** (✉ 33 rue de la République, 54950 Laronxe).

➤ FISHING: **Agence de Développement Économique du Doubs** (✉ Av. de la Gare d'Eau, 25031 Besançon).

➤ HIKING: **Comité Régional de Tourisme** (✉ 9 rue de Pontarlier, 25000 Besançon). **Fédération Jurassienne de Randonnée Pédestre** (✉ Hôtel du Département, B.P. 652, 39021 Lons-le-Saunier).

➤ HORSEBACK RIDING: **Délégation Départementale de Tourisme Équestre** (✉ 4 rue des Violettes, 67201 Eckbolsheim, ☎ 03–88–77–39–64).

TOURS

Walking tours of Strasbourg's Old Town are given by a tourist office guide at 2:30 every Saturday afternoon in low season, daily at 10:30 in July and August (€6.15). For information contact the tourist office. Minitrain tours of the Old Town with commentary leave from place du Château from April through October (€4.61). In Besançon you can take a minitrain tour from the center up to the citadel, including recorded commentary and access to the various museums at the top.

➤ FEES AND SCHEDULES: **Besançon minitrain tours** (☎ 03–81–65–07–50). **Strasbourg minitrain tours** (☎ 03–88–77–70–03). **Strasbourg tourist office** (✉ Pl. de la Cathédrale, ☎ 03–88–52–28–28, WEB www.strasbourg.com).

TRAIN TRAVEL

Mainline trains leave Paris (Gare de l'Est) every couple of hours for the four-hour, 500-km (315-mi) journey to Strasbourg. Some stop in Toul, and all stop in Nancy, where there are connections for Épinal and Gérardmer. Trains run three times daily from Paris to Verdun and more often to Metz (around three hours to each). Mainline trains stop in Mulhouse (four to five hours) en route to Basel. Three high-speed TGV (*Trains à Grande Vitesse*) leave Paris (Gare de Lyon) daily for Besançon (2½ to 3 hours).

Several local trains a day run between Strasbourg and Mulhouse, stopping in Sélestat and Colmar. Several continue to Belfort and Besançon. Local trains link Besançon to Lons-le-Saunier, occasionally stopping in Arbois. Other towns, such as Obernai, Montbenoît, and Pontarlier, are accessible, with planning, by train. But without any bus connection you'll need a car to visit smaller villages and the region's spectacular natural sights.

➤ TRAIN INFORMATION: **SNCF** (☎ 08–36–35–35–35, WEB www.sncf.com).

TRAVEL AGENCIES

➤ LOCAL AGENT REFERRALS: **Havas Voyages** (✉ 23 rue de la Haute-Montée, Strasbourg, ☎ 03–88–32–99–77). **Carlson Wagons-Lit** (✉ 30 pl. Kléber, Strasbourg, ☎ 03–88–32–16–34; ✉ 2 rue Raymond-Poincaré, Nancy, ☎ 03–83–35–06–97).

VISITOR INFORMATION

The principal regional tourist offices are in Besançon, Nancy, and Strasbourg. Other tourist offices are listed by town below the principal offices.

➤ TOURIST INFORMATION: **Besançon** (✉ 2 pl. de la 1e–Armée Française, ☎ 03–81–82–80–77, WEB www.besancon.com). **Nancy** (✉ 14 pl. Stanislas, ☎ 03–83–35–22–41, WEB www.ot-nancy.fr). **Strasbourg** (✉ 17 pl. de la Cathédrale, ☎ 03–88–52–28–28, WEB www.strasbourg.com; ✉ Pl. de la Gare, ☎ 03–88–32–51–49; there is also a city tourist office at the train station). **Belfort** (✉ 2 bis bd. Clemenceau, ☎ 03–84–55–90–90). **Colmar** (✉ 4 rue Unterlinden, ☎ 03–89–20–68–95). **Guebwiller** (✉ 73 rue de la République, ☎ 03–89–76–10–63). **Lons-le-Saunier** (✉ 1 rue Louis-Pasteur, ☎ 03–84–24–65–01). **Metz** (✉ Pl. d'Armes, ☎ 03–87–55–53–76, WEB www.tourisme.mairie.metz.fr). **Mulhouse** (✉ 9 av. du Maréchal-Foch, ☎ 03–89–35–48–48, WEB www.tourism-mulhouse.com). **Obernai** (✉ 59 rue du Général-Gouraud, ☎ 03–88–95–64–13, WEB www.oberni.fr). **Saverne** (✉ 37 Grand'Rue, ☎ 03–88–91–80–47). **Sélestat** (✉ 10 bd. Leclerc, ☎ 03–88–58–87–20). **Toul** (✉ Parvis de la Cathédrale, ☎ 03–83–64–11–69). **Verdun** (✉ Pl. de la Nation, ☎ 03–29–86–14–18, WEB www.verdun.tourisme.com).

9 BURGUNDY

Having done its duty by producing a blissful wealth of what many pronounce the world's greatest wines and harboring a knee-weakening concentration of magnificent Romanesque abbeys, Burgundy hardly needs to be beautiful as well—but it is. Its green-hedgerowed countryside and densely forested Morvan, its manor houses and scattered villages, and its numerous lovely (and stellar) vineyards deserve to be rolled on the palate and savored. Like glasses filled with Clos de Vougeot, the sights here—from the stately hub of Dijon to the medieval sanctuaries of Cluny and Clairvaux—invite the wanderer to tarry and partake of their mellow splendor.

Updated by Christopher Mooney

Introduction by Nancy Coons

DRAIN TO THE DREGS BURGUNDY'S FULL-BODIED VISTAS: rolling hillsides carpeted in emerald green, each pasture cross-hatched with hedgerows, peppered with cows, quilted with vineyards. Behind a massive quarried-stone wall, a château looms, seemingly untouched by time, the only hints of habitation the featherbeds airing from casement windows and a flock of sheep mowing the grounds. Tightly clustered villages, slate roofs surviving from the days when they protected against brigands, encircle one central church spire, a lightning rod for the local faithful. On a hilltop high over the patchwork of green rises a pale, patrician edifice of white rock, a Romanesque church of such austerity and architectural purity that it harks back to the early Roman temples on which it was modeled. And deep inside a musty *cave* or perhaps a wine cellar redolent of cork and soured grapes, a row of glasses gleams like a treasured necklace, their garnet contents waiting to be swirled, sniffed, and savored.

You may often fall under the influence of extraordinary wine during a sojourn in Burgundy, but the beauty surrounding you will not be a boozy illusion. Passed over by revolutions, both republican and industrial, unscarred by world wars, and relatively inaccessible thanks to necessarily circuitous country roads, the region still reflects the pastoral prosperity it enjoyed under the Capetian dukes and kings.

Those were the glory days—the era of a Burgundy self-sufficient enough to hold its own against the emerging spread of France and the fading of the Holy Roman Empire—a period characterized by the expansive influence of the dukes of Bourgogne. Consider the Capetians, history-book celebrities all: there was Philippe the Bold, with his power-brokered marriage to Marguèrite of Flanders. There was Jean sans Peur, who murdered Louis d'Orléans in a cloak-and-dagger affair in 1407 and was himself murdered in 1419 on a dark bridge while negotiating a secret treaty with the future Charles VII. There was Philippe le Bon, who threw in with the English against Joan of Arc, and of course Charles the Bold, whose temerity stretched the boundaries of Bourgogne—already bulging with Flanders, Luxembourg, and Picardie—to include most of Holland, Lorraine, Alsace, and even French Switzerland. He met his match in 1477 at the battle of Nancy, where he and his boldness were permanently parted. Nonetheless, you can still see Burgundian candy-tile roofs in Fribourg, Switzerland, his easternmost conquest.

Yet the Capetians in their acquisitions couldn't hold a candle to the Light of the World: the great Abbaye de Cluny, founded in 910, grew to such overweening ecclesiastic power that it dominated the European Church on a papal scale for some four centuries. It was Urban II himself who dubbed it "*la Lumière du Monde.*" And like the Italian popes, Cluny, too, indulged a weakness for worldly luxury and knowledge, both sacred and profane. In nearby Clairvaux, St-Bernard himself spoke up in outrage, chiding the monks who, although sworn to chastity and poverty, kept mistresses, teams of horses, and a library of unfathomable depth that codified classical and Eastern lore for all posterity—that is, until it was burned in the War of Religions and its wisdom lost for all time. The abbey itself followed after, destroyed for its wealth of quarry stone after the French Revolution.

Neighboring abbeys, perhaps less glorious than Cluny but with more humility than hubris, fared better. The stark geometry of the Cistercian abbeys—Clairvaux, Cîteaux—stand in silent rebuke to Cluny's excess. The basilicas at Autun, Vézelay, and Paray le Monial remain today in all their noble simplicity, yet manifest some of the finest Romanesque sculpture ever created; the tympanum at Autun rejects all time frames in its visionary daring. And anchored between Autun and Vézelay the broad massif of the Morvan rises up, its dewy green flanks densely wooded in oak and beech. Hidden streams, rocky escarpments, dark forests, and meadows alive with falcons and hoopoes—a hiker's dream—are protected today by the Parc Naturel Régional du Morvan.

It's almost unfair to the rest of France that all this history, all this art, all this natural beauty comes with delicious refreshments. As if to live up to the extraordinary quality of its Chablis, its Chassagne-Montrachet, its Nuits-St-Georges, its Gevrey-Chambertin, Burgundy flaunts some of the best good, plain food in the world. Two poached eggs in savory wine sauce, a slab of ham in aspic, a platter of beef stew, a half-dozen earthy snails—no frills needed—just the pleasure of discovering that such homely material could resonate on the tongue, and harmonize so brilliantly with the local wine. This is simplicity raised to Gallic heights, embellished by the poetry of one perfect glass of pinot noir paired with a licensed and diploma'd *poulet de Bresse* (Bresse chicken), sputtering in unvarnished perfection on your white-china plate.

Thus you may find that food and drink entries take up as much space in your travel diary as the sights you see. And that's as it should be in such well-rounded, full-bodied terrain.

Pleasures and Pastimes

Abbeys

From the sober beauty of splendid and well-preserved Fontenay to the majestic ruins of Cluny and the isolated remains of Pontigny and Clairvaux, the abbeys of Burgundy are an evocative part of the region's storied past. Reminders of medieval religious luminaries—notably Thomas à Becket and Bernard of Clairvaux—are everywhere, and they inject a sense of living history into a visit to the region.

Dining

Dijon ranks with Lyon as one of the unofficial gastronomic capitals of France, and Burgundy's hearty traditions help explain why. Parisian gourmands think nothing of driving three hours to sample the cuisine of Beaune's Jean Crotet or Vézelay's Marc Meneau. Game, freshwater trout, garlicky *jambon persillé* (ham flavored with parsley), coq au vin, snails, and, of course, beef Bourguignon number among the region's specialties. Sadly, mustard production is no longer the mainstay of Dijon (it has been displaced by the more profitable colza plant, from which cooking oil is made), but one or two people continue to make it by hand (importing the seed from Canada). *Pain d'épices*, a dense spice cake, is the delectable dessert staple of the region.

Like every other part of France, Burgundy has its own cheeses. The Abbaye de Cîteaux, birthplace of Cistercian monasticism in Burgundy, has produced a mild cheese for centuries. Chaource and the hearty, melt-in-your-mouth Époisses are also treats—as are Bleu de Bresse and Meursault. Meat and poultry—including Charolais beef from the regional breed of cattle and poulet de Bresse, the only regionally certified breed of chicken in France—are often served in rich, wine-based sauces.

CATEGORY	COST*
$$$$	over €30
$$$	€20–€30
$$	€12–€20
$	under €12

**per person for a main course only, including tax (19.6%) and service; note that if a restaurant offers only prix-fixe (set-price) meals, it has been given the price category that reflects the full prix-fixe price.*

Hiking and Horseback Riding

The Parc Naturel Régional du Morvan, with its rocky escarpments, hidden valleys, rushing streams, thick forests, and wooded hills, is marvelous for hiking and horseback riding, especially in spring and fall.

Lodging

Burgundy is seldom deluged by tourists, so finding accommodations is not usually a problem. But it is still wise to make advance reservations, especially in the wine country (from Dijon to Beaune). If you intend to visit Beaune for the Trois Glorieuses wine festival in November, make your hotel reservation several months in advance. Note that nearly all country hotels have restaurants, and you are usually expected to eat at them. Some towns have a large number of inexpensive hotels. In Dijon you can find them around place Émile Zola; in Beaune look around place Madeleine; in Auxerre they're tucked away in the streets heading down from Cathédrale St-Étienne; in Tournus and Avallon check out the Old Town sections. Assume all hotel rooms have air-conditioning, TV, telephones, and private bath except when noted. Internet, when listed in facilities, means in-room data-ports and/or public-area computers provide on-line access.

CATEGORY	COST*
$$$$	over €180
$$$	€120–€180
$$	€60–€120
$	under €60

**All prices are for a standard double room in high season, including tax (19.6%) and service charge.*

Wine

Geography and centuries of tradition have given the wines of Burgundy a worldwide fame, each region producing a wine of distinctive quality: Chablis (dry white wine), Côte de Nuits (rich and full-flavored red wine), Côte de Beaune (delicately flavored red and white wines), Côte Chalonnaise (full-flavored red, white, and sparkling wines), Mâcon (earthy flavored white wines), or Beaujolais (fresh and fruity wine). The famous vineyards south of Dijon—the Côte de Nuits and Côte de Beaune—are among the world's most distinguished and picturesque. You can sample a selection at the Marché aux Vins in Beaune, an old town clustered around the patterned-tile roofs of its medieval hôtel-Dieu (hospital). Or go directly to the vineyards (of course, the hope is that you'll purchase a case). Don't expect to unearth many bargains, however. Less expensive Burgundies can be found between Chalon and Mâcon.

Exploring Burgundy

The best way to enter Burgundy is southeast from Paris by car. First, explore the northwest part of the region, from Sens to Autun, with a rewarding detour to the town of Troyes, in Champagne, and the Loire Valley, equally renowned for its wines, in the west, around the Parc du Morvan. Go next to Burgundy's wine country, which begins at Dijon and stretches south down the Saône Valley through charming Beaune to Mâcon.

Great Itineraries

You could easily spend two weeks in Burgundy—visiting the sights, tasting the wine, and filling up on the hearty food. If, however, you have only three days, you can take in two of Burgundy's most interesting cities—Dijon and Beaune. With five days you can explore the northeast part of the region, from Sens to Beaune. Eight days will give you time to get to the Parc du Morvan and the Côte d'Or, which is studded with Burgundy's finest vineyards.

Numbers in the text correspond to numbers in the margin and on the Burgundy, Troyes, and Dijon maps.

IF YOU HAVE 3 DAYS

Start with Burgundy's two most interesting cities: first, the age-old capital of Burgundy, **Dijon** ㉞–㊺—former haunt of the dukes of Burgundy, who were among the richest people in the late Middle Ages and bequeathed to the city a dazzling legacy of art, goldsmithing, and tapestry; and second, on to medieval **Beaune** ㊽ to view its majestic Hospice, founded by Chancellor Rolin, the great patron of Jan van Eyck and Rogier van der Weyden, whose *Last Judgement* altarpiece takes pride of place here. Between touring the two towns, visit the famous Burgundy vineyards around **Clos de Vougeot** ㊻—if you're lucky, you'll catch one of the *vendanges* (grape harvests).

IF YOU HAVE 5 DAYS

Make your first stop out of Paris the small town of **Sens** ①, with its vast cathedral and its 13th-century Palais Synodal. Then head for the serene abbey in **Pontigny** ⑯ and the Ancien Hôpital in **Tonnerre** ⑲. End the day tasting the famous white wine in **Chablis** ⑱ and spend the night there. Begin day two with a visit to **Auxerre** ⑰ and its cathedral before going on to ancient **Clamecy** ㉚ and the world-famous basilica in **Vézelay** ㉛. Stay overnight in dramatic **Avallon** ㉜, with its medieval church of St-Lazarus. Get to **Dijon** ㉞–㊺ by day three and stay two nights. On day five take a short run down the wine-producing Côte d'Or to **Beaune** ㊽.

IF YOU HAVE 9 DAYS

Make **Troyes** ②–⑭, with its medieval pedestrian streets, your first stop. On day two head south to see **Tonnerre** ⑲, the Renaissance châteaux of **Tanlay** ⑳, **Ancy-le-Franc** ㉑, and the Cistercian **Abbaye de Fontenay** ㉒. End the day in **Dijon** ㉞–㊺. Give yourself two days and nights in Dijon and then go to **Beaune** ㊽ for another night. While you're in the vicinity, drive south down the Saône River to medieval **Tournus** ㊿ and the abbey of St-Philibert, as well as the ruined abbey of **Cluny** (51). The next day drive north to see the cathedral and Roman remains in **Autun** ㉖, the **Château de Sully** ㉕, the hilltop town of **Châteauneuf-en-Auxois** ㉔, and the basilica in **Saulieu** ㉓; end up in **Avallon** ㉜. On day six drive through the **Parc Naturel Régional du Morvan** ㉝ and visit the village of **Château-Chinon** ㉗, the imposing cathedral in **Nevers** ㉘, and the abbey church in **La Charité-sur-Loire** ㉙, before returning to Avallon. Spend the next two days and nights around **Auxerre** ⑰, **Chablis** ⑱, or **Sens** ①. These make good bases for exploring unspoiled **Clamecy** ㉚, the vineyards around Chablis, the abbey in **Pontigny** ⑯, and the basilica in **Vézelay** ㉛.

When to Tour Burgundy

May in Burgundy is especially nice, as are September and October, when the sun is still warm on the shimmering golden trees and the grapes, now ready for harvesting, are scenting the air with anticipation. Many festivals also take place around this time.

NORTHWEST BURGUNDY

In the Middle Ages, Sens, Auxerre, and Troyes, which are in the neighboring Champagne region (but included here), came under the sway of the Paris-based Capetian kings, who erected mighty Gothic cathedrals in those towns. Outside these major centers of northwest Bur-

Burgundy

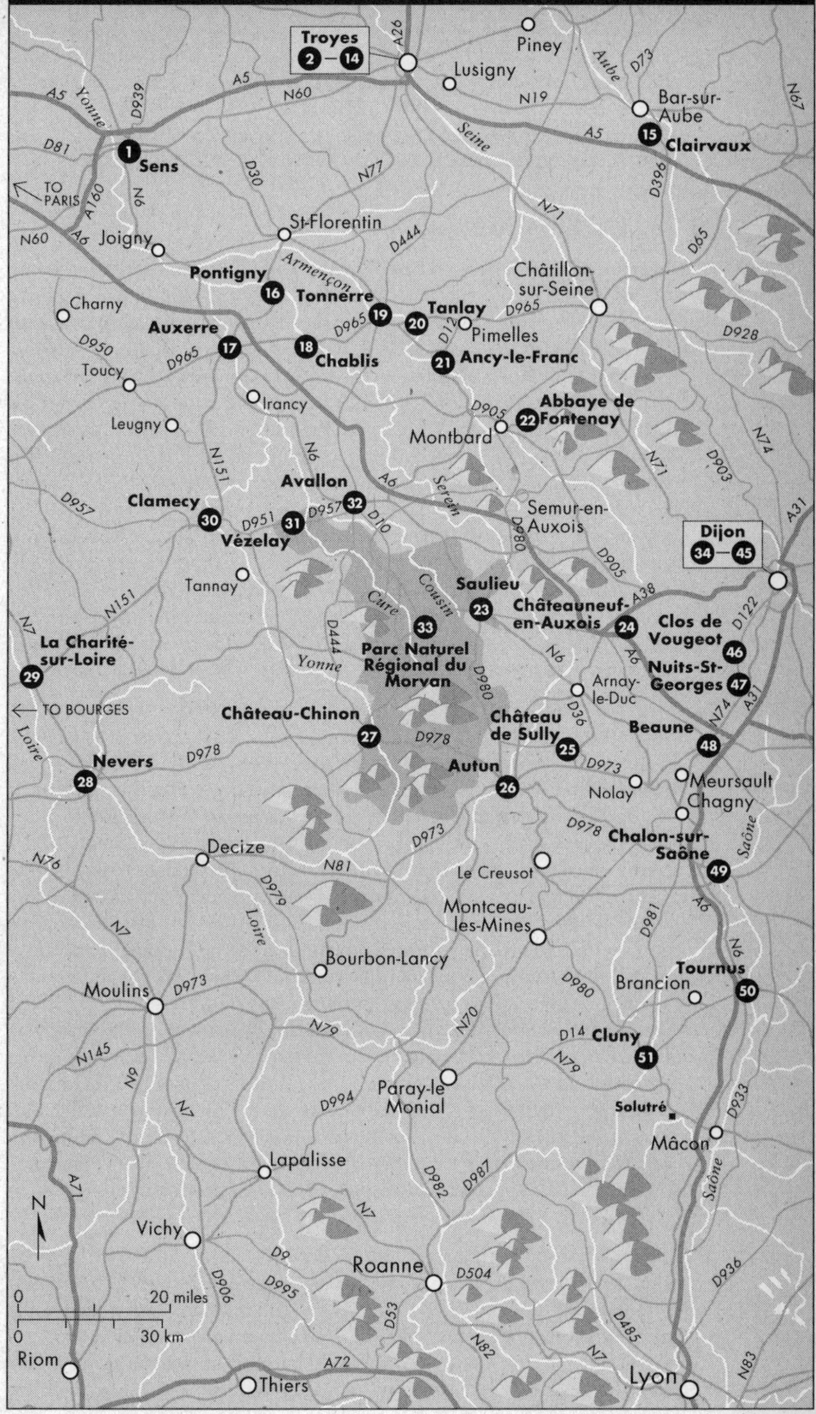

Troyes 2–14
Piney
Lusigny
Bar-sur-Aube
15 Clairvaux
1 Sens
TO PARIS
Joigny
St-Florentin
Pontigny 16
Tonnerre 19
Tanlay 20
Pimelles
Châtillon-sur-Seine
Charny
Auxerre 17
18 Chablis
21 Ancy-le-Franc
Toucy
Irancy
Leugny
Abbaye de Fontenay 22
Montbard
Avallon 32
Clamecy 30
31 Vézelay
Semur-en-Auxois
Dijon 34–45
Tannay
Saulieu 23
Châteauneuf-en-Auxois 24
Clos de Vougeot 46
Nuits-St-Georges 47
La Charité-sur-Loire 29
TO BOURGES
33 Parc Naturel Régional du Morvan
Arnay-le-Duc
Château-Chinon 27
Château de Sully 25
Beaune 48
Nevers 28
Autun 26
Nolay
Meursault
Chagny
Chalon-sur-Saône 49
Decize
Le Creusot
Montceau-les-Mines
Tournus 50
Bourbon-Lancy
Brancion
Moulins
Cluny 51
Paray-le-Monial
Solutré
Mâcon
Lapalisse
Vichy
Roanne
Riom
Thiers
Lyon
Yonne
Armençon
Seine
Aube
Serein
Cousin
Cure
Loire
Saône
A5
A6
A26
A31
A38
A71
A72
A160
N6
N7
N9
N19
N60
N67
N70
N71
N74
N76
N77
N79
N81
N82
N83
N145
N151
D9
D10
D12
D14
D30
D36
D53
D65
D73
D81
D122
D396
D444
D485
D504
D903
D905
D906
D928
D933
D936
D939
D950
D951
D957
D965
D973
D978
D979
D980
D981
D982
D987
D994
D995
N
0 20 miles
0 30 km

gundy, countryside villages are largely preserved and the surprisingly rural landscape seems to have remained the same for centuries. Here "life in the fast lane" is considered a reference to the Paris-bound A6 expressway. Arriving from Paris, most travelers drive southeast into Burgundy on A6 (or, as an alternative, on A5 direct to Troyes, first sneaking into Champagne), before making a clockwise loop around the Parc du Morvan, visiting the small cities and ancient abbeys in the area.

Sens

❶ *112 km (70 mi) southeast of Paris on N6.*

It makes sense for Sens to be your first stop in Burgundy since it's only 60 minutes by car from Paris on N6, a fast road that hugs the pretty Yonne Valley south of Fontainebleau. Historically linked more with Paris than with Burgundy, Sens was for centuries the ecclesiastical center of France and is still dominated by its **Cathédrale St-Étienne,** once the French sanctuary for Thomas à Becket and a model for England's Canterbury Cathedral. You can see the cathedral's 240-ft south tower from far away; the highway forges straight past it. The pompous 19th-century buildings lining the narrow main street—notably the meringue-y Hôtel de Ville—can give you a false impression if you're in a hurry: the streets leading off it near the cathedral (notably rue Abelard and rue Jean-Cousin) are full of half-timber medieval houses. On Monday the cathedral square is crowded with stalls, and the beautiful late-19th century Baltard-style market—a distant cousin of Baltard's iron-and-glass Halles Centrales once extant in Paris—throbs with people buying meat and produce. A smaller market is held on Friday morning.

Begun around 1140, the cathedral once had two towers; one was topped in 1532 by an elegant though somewhat incongruous Renaissance campanile that contains two monster bells; the other collapsed in the 19th century. Note the trifoil arches decorating the exterior of the remaining tower. The gallery, with statues of former archbishops of Sens, is a 19th-century addition, but the statue of St. Stephen, between the doors of the central portal, is thought to date from the late 12th century. The vast, harmonious interior is justly renowned for its stained-glass windows; the oldest (circa 1200) are in the north transept and include the stories of the Samaritans and the Prodigal Son; those in the south transept were manufactured in 1500 in Troyes and include a much-admired *Tree of Jesse.* Stained-glass windows in the north of the chancel retrace the story of Thomas à Becket: Becket fled to Sens from England to escape the wrath of Henry II before returning to his cathedral in Canterbury, where he was murdered in 1170. Below the window (which shows him embarking on his journey in a boat, and also at the moment of his death) is a medieval statue of an archbishop said to have come from the site of Becket's home in Sens. Years of restoration work have permitted the display of his *aube* (vestment) in the annex to the Palais Synodal. ✉ *Pl. de la République,* ☎ *03–86–64–15–27.*

The roof of the 13th-century **Palais Synodal** (Synodal Palace), alongside Sens's cathedral, is notable for its Burgundian yellow, green, and red diamond-tile motif—incongruously (and misleadingly) added in the mid-19th century by medieval monument restorer Viollet-le-Duc. Its six grand windows and vaulted Synodal Hall are outstanding architectural features, but the building now functions as an exhibition space. Annexed to the Palais Synodal is an ensemble of Renaissance buildings from whose courtyard there is a fine view of the cathedral's Flamboyant Gothic south transept, constructed by master stonemason Martin Chambiges at the start of the 16th century (rose windows were his specialty, as you can appreciate here). Inside is a museum with archaeological finds from the Gallo-Roman period, including the *trésor de Villethierry,* a cache of bronze popular jewelry unearthed during the construction of A5, exceptional stelae depicting various trades, and the remains of Roman baths discovered in situ 20 years ago. The cathedral treasury, now on the museum's second floor, is one of the richest in France, comparable to that of Conques. It contains a collection of miters, ivories, the shrouds of St. Sivard and St. Loup, and sumptuous reliquaries. But the star of the collection is Thomas à Becket's restored brown- and silver-edged linen robe. His chasuble, stole, and sandals, too fragile to display, await similar help. ☎ *03–86–64–46–27.* €3. *June–Sept., daily 10–noon and 2–6; Oct.–May, Wed. and weekends 10–noon and 2–6, Mon. and Thurs.–Fri. 2–6.*

Dining and Lodging

$$–$$$ ★ ✕ **Le Clos des Jacobins.** With its pale orange walls and exceptional fish specialties, this restaurant in the center of town strikes a happy balance between elegant and casual. Try the €15 lunch *menu du marché,* which may include *matelotte d'oeufs pochés à l'Irancy* (poached eggs in Irancy wine sauce), and *blanc de turbot au Noilly-Prat* (turbot with Noilly-Prat vermouth). ✉ *49 Grande-Rue,* ☎ *03–86–95–29–70. AE, MC, V.*

$$$ ★ ✕ **La Lucarne aux Chouettes.** There's nothing Hollywoodesque about actress Leslie Caron's charmingly rustic riverside hotel and restaurant, the "Owl's Nest," set in four 17th-century buildings. The lovely white-washed-brick dining room, with its ingenious twisted rope chandeliers, has a homey-meets-elegant feel, as do the rooms: "The Loft" is an enormous wood-beamed aerie atop the house (the bathroom is in the room itself—just as it was in the rip-roaring days of the 1680s), while "The Suite" glows with a portrait of Sarah Bernhardt. The legendary hostess (the beloved Lili-Gigi-Fanny of everyone's memories) is often on hand to greet all and sundry. In summer enjoy the terrace over the Yonne. The town itself, a *bastide* (fortified town, built on a grid pattern), is entered and exited via sturdy, angular 13th- and 14th-century gateways. ✉ *Quai Bretoche, 89500 Villeneuve-sur-Yonne (12 km/7 mi south of Sens on N6),* ☎ *03–86–87–18–26,* FAX *03–86–87–22–63. 4 rooms. Restaurant, no air-conditioning, cable TV. AE, MC, V.*

$$–$$$ ★ ✕ **Hôtel de Paris et de la Poste.** Owned for the last several decades by the Godart family, the modernized Paris & Poste, which began life as a post house in the 1700s, is a convenient and pleasant stopping point. Rooms are clean, spacious and well equipped; most open onto a patio (No. 42, is especially nice). But it's the traditional red-and-gold restaurant (with great home-smoked salmon), padded, green leather armchairs in the lounge, and little curved wooden bar that give this place its comfy charm. ✉ *97 rue de la République, 89100,* ☎ *03–86–65–17–43,* FAX *03–86–64–48–45. 21 rooms. Restaurant, some air-conditioning, cable TV, free parking. AE, DC, MC, V.*

$$$–$$$$ ★ **Château de Prunoy.** Though it's a little out of the way, this château and park—built by one of Louix XVI's finance ministers—is spectacular enough to be worth the trip. Grand public rooms are a stylish blend of Louis Seize gilt-trimmed antiques and grandmother's knick-knackery although many of the guest rooms seem to be the suave result of an elegant decorator (but do avoid the one designed as a Japanese teahouse). Quirky flea-market finds help make it all very *chez soi,* right down to the presence of the owner's friendly Labradors. Dinner is not especially grand but the dining salon itself is country-adorable. ✉ *89120 Charny (40 km/25 mi southwest of Sens, 40 km/25 mi northwest of Auxerre on N6 to D943 to D18),* ☎ *03–86–63–66–91,* FAX *03–86–63–77–79,* WEB *www.chateaudeprunoy.com. 19 rooms, 4 suites. Restaurant, no air-conditioning, pool, gym, sauna, tennis court. AE, DC, MC, V.*

Nightlife and the Arts

Sens is known throughout France for **Les Synodales**, an annual dance festival held in late June and July, which headlines distinguished dancers and other artists from around the world. Events are held in front of the cathedral and in surrounding streets; contact the tourist office for information.

Troyes

★ *64 km (40 mi) northeast of Sens, 150 km (95 mi) east of Paris.*

The inhabitants of Troyes would be insulted if you mistook them for Burgundians. Troyes is the historic capital of the counts of Champagne; as if to prove the point, its historic town center is shaped like a champagne cork, the part corresponding to the rounded top enclosed by a loop of the Seine. It was also the home of the late-12th-century writer Chrétien (or Chrestien) de Troyes, who, in seeking to please his patrons Count Henry the Liberal and Marie de Champagne, penned the first Arthurian legends. Few, if any, other French town centers contain so much to see and do. A web of enchanting pedestrian streets with timber-frame houses, magnificent churches, fine museums, and a wide choice of restaurants make Troyes appealing. Keep in mind, however, that you're looking at a model of historical preservation. Despite its being one of the first French towns to be classed a *secteur sauvegardé* (protected zone) by then–Minister of Culture André Malraux, modern development and several major fires have removed large chunks of Troyes (brace yourself for the '70s concrete of the Quartier du 14 Juillet, intersected by the boulevard of the same name).

The center of Troyes is divided by the boulevard Dampierre, a broad, busy thoroughfare. On one side is the quiet cathedral quarter, on the other the more upbeat commercial part. Keep your eyes peeled for the delightful architectural accents that make Troyes unique: *essentes*, geometric chestnut tiles that keep out humidity and are fire resistant; and sculpted *poteaux* (in Troyes they are called *montjoies*), carvings at the joint of corner structural beams. There's a lovely one of Adam and Eve next door to the hotel Les Comtes de Champagne. Along with its neighbors Provins and Bar-sur-Aube, Troyes was one of Champagne's major fair towns in the Middle Ages. The wool trade gave way to the cotton textile trade in the 18th century, and today Troyes draws busloads of shoppers from all over Europe to its outlet clothing stores.

The **tourist office** (✉ 16 bd. Carnot, ☎ 03–25–82–62–70, WEB www.ot-troyes.fr) has information and sells museum passes that admit you to the four major museums for €9.50—a 50% saving.

❷ Although Troyes is on the Seine, it is the capital of the Aube *département* (province) and is run from the elegant **Préfecture.** The building looks out from behind its gleaming gilt-iron railings across both the Bassin de la Préfecture, an arm of the Seine, and the place de la Libération.

❸ Across the Bassin is the **Hôtel-Dieu** (hospital), fronted by superb wrought-iron gates (from the 18th century) and topped with the blue-and-gold fleurs-de-lis emblems of the French monarchy. Around the corner is the entrance to the **Apothicairie de l'Hôtel-Dieu Le Comte,** the former medical laboratory, the only part of the Hôtel-Dieu open to visitors. Inside, time has been suspended: floral-painted boxes and ceramic jars containing medicinal plants line the antique shelves. ✉ *Quai des Comtes-de-Champagne,* ☎ *03–25–80–98–97.* 🎫 *€3.* ⏲ *July–Aug., Wed.–Mon. 10–6; Sept.–June, Wed. and weekends 2–6.*

❹ The **Musée d'Art Moderne** (Modern Art Museum) is housed in the 16th- to 17th-century former bishop's palace. Its magnificent interior, with

Basilique St-Urbain 8
Cathédrale St-Pierre-St-Paul 5
Hôtel de Vauluisant . . . 14
Hôtel de Ville 9
Hôtel-Dieu . . . 3
Hôtel du Petit Louvre 7
Maison de l'Outil 12
Musée d'Art Moderne 4
Musée St-Loup 6
Préfecture 2
St-Jean 10
St-Pantaléon . . . 13
Ste-Madeleine . . 11

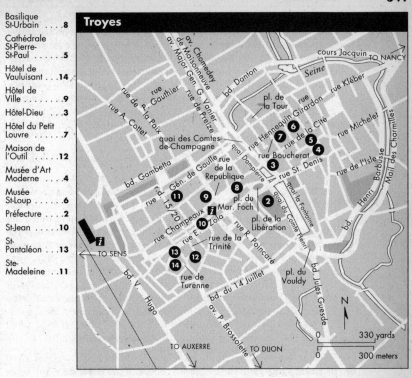

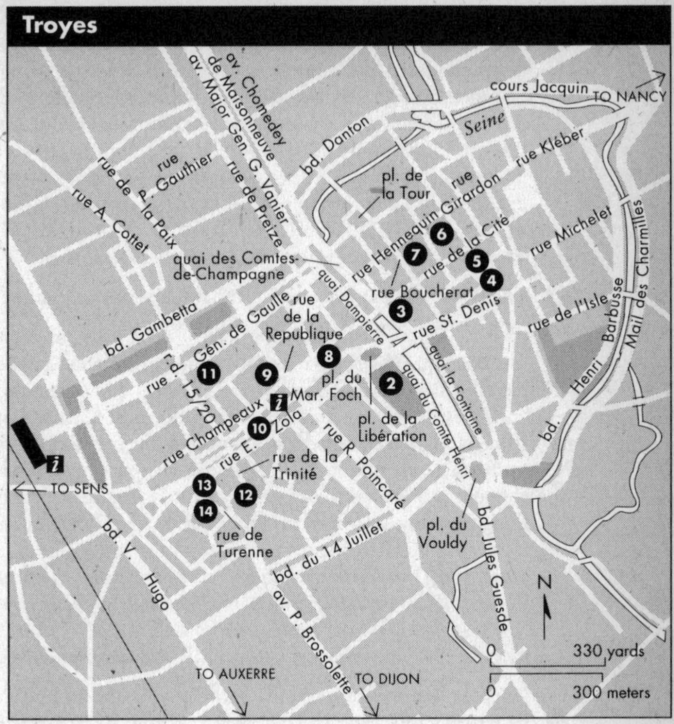

a wreath-and-cornucopia carved oak fireplace, ceilings with carved wood beams, and a Renaissance staircase, now contains the Lévy Collection of modern art—including an important group of works by Claude Derain. In the back are formal gardens. ✉ *Palais Épiscopal, pl. St-Pierre,* ☎ *03–25–76–26–80.* 🎫 *€5.* ⏲ *Tues.–Sun. 11–6.*

❺ The Flamboyant Gothic **Cathédrale St-Pierre–St-Paul** dominates with its 200-ft towers (undergoing restoration at press time); note the incomplete single-tower west front, the small Renaissance campaniles on top of the tower, and the artistry of Martin Chambiges, who worked on Troyes's facade (with its characteristic large rose window) around the same time as he did the transept of Sens. At night the floodlit features burst into dramatic relief. The cathedral's vast five-aisle interior, refreshingly light thanks to large windows and the near-whiteness of the local stone, dates mainly from the 13th century. It has fine examples of 13th-century stained-glass in the choir, such as the *Tree of Jesse* (a popular regional theme), and richly colored 16th-century glass in the nave and west front rose window. The choir stalls and organ were requisitioned from Clairvaux Abbey. One of the chapels contains black-basalt tombstones marking the remains of Count Henry I of Champagne, carved in 1792 after the count's palace was destroyed, and the cathedral treasury displays such curiosities as a piece of St. Bernard of Clairvaux's skull. The arcaded triforium above the pillars of the choir was one of the first in France to be glazed rather than filled with stone. Across the street from the cathedral, behind an iron fence, is an unusual, lopsided, late-medieval **grange aux dîmes** (tithe barn) with a peaked roof. It is used as a warehouse by the wine maker next door. ✉ *Pl. St-Pierre,* ☎ *03–25–76–98–18.* 🎫 *Free.* ⏲ *July–mid-Sept., daily 9–1 and 2–7; mid-Sept.–Feb., daily 10–noon and 2–4; Mar.–June, daily 10–noon and 2–5.*

6 Facing the cathedral square, the buildings of the former Abbaye St-Loup now house the **Musée St-Loup,** an arts and archaeology museum. Exhibits are devoted to natural history, with impressive collections of birds and meteorites; local archaeological finds, especially gold-mounted 5th-century jewelry and a Gallo-Roman bronze statue of Apollo; medieval statuary and gargoyles; and paintings from the 15th to 19th centuries, including works by Rubens, Anthony Van Dyck, Antoine Watteau, François Boucher, and Jacques-Louis David. ✉ *1 rue Chrestien-de-Troyes,* ☎ *03–25–76–21–60.* 🎫 *€5.* 🕒 *Sept.–June, Wed.–Mon. 10–noon and 2–6; July–Aug., Wed.–Mon. 10–noon and 2–7.*

7 The **Hôtel du Petit Louvre** (✉ Rue Boucherat) is a handsome, 16th-century former *relais de diligence* (coaching inn).

8 The **Basilique St-Urbain** was built between 1262 and 1286 by Pope Urban IV, who was born in Troyes. St-Urbain is one of the most remarkable churches in France, a perfect culmination of Gothic's quest to replace stone walls with stained glass. Its magnificently long and narrow porch frames a 13th-century *Last Judgment* tympanum, whose highly worked elements include a frieze of the dead rising out of their coffins (note the grimacing skeleton) and an enormous crayfish, a testament to the local river culture. Inside, a chapel on the south side houses the *Vièrge au Raisin* (*Virgin with Grapes*), clutching Jesus with one hand and a bunch of Champagne grapes in the other. ✉ *Pl. Vernier,* ☎ *03–25–73–37–13.* 🎫 *Free.* 🕒 *July–Aug., daily 10:30–7; 1st 2 wks in Sept., daily 10:30–5; mid-Sept.–June, daily 10–noon and 2–4.*

9 Place du Maréchal-Foch, the main square of central Troyes, is flanked by cafés, shops, and the delightful facade of the **Hôtel de Ville** (Town Hall). In summer the square is filled with people from morning to night.

10 The clock tower of the church of **St-Jean** is an unmistakable landmark. England's warrior king Henry V married Catherine of France here in 1420. The church's tall 16th-century choir contrasts with the low nave, constructed earlier. ✉ *Pl. du Marché au Pain.* ☎ *03–25–73–06–96.* 🎫 *Free.* 🕒 *July–Aug., daily 10:30–7; 1st 2 wks in Sept., daily 10:30–5; mid-Sept.–June, daily 10–noon and 2–4.*

11 **Ste-Madeleine,** the oldest church in Troyes, is best known for its elaborate triple-arched stone rood screen separating the nave and the choir. Only six other such screens still remain in France—most were dismantled during the French Revolution. This filigreed Flamboyant Gothic beauty was carved with panache by Jean Gailde between 1508 and 1517. ✉ *Rue de la Madeleine.* ☎ *03–25–73–82–90.* 🎫 *Free.* 🕒 *July–Aug., daily 10:30–7; 1st 2 wks in Sept., daily 10:30–5; mid-Sept.–June, daily 10–noon and 2–4.*

12 There's a practical reason why the windows of the **Maison de l'Outil** (Tool and Craft Museum) are filled with bizarre and beautiful outsize models—like a winding staircase and a globe on a swivel. It's the display venue for the "final projects" created by apprentice Compagnons de Devoir, members of the national craftsmen's guild whose school is in Troyes. The museum, in the 16th-century Hôtel de Mauroy, also contains a collection of paintings, models, and tools relevant to such traditional wood-related trades as carpentry, clog making, and barrel making—including a medieval anvil, called a *bigorne.* ✉ *7 rue de la Trinité,* ☎ *03–25–73–28–26.* 🎫 *€5.* 🕒 *Weekdays 9–1 and 2–6:30, weekends 10–1 and 2–6.*

13 The 16th- to 18th-century church of **St-Pantaléon** primarily serves the local Polish community. A number of fine canopied stone statues, many of them the work of the Troyen Dominique le Florentin, deco-

rator to François I, are clustered around its pillars. ✉ *Rue de Turenne,* ☎ *03–25–73–06–99.* 🎟 *Free.* ⏲ *July–Aug., daily 10:30–12:30 and 2:30–6:30; 1st 2 wks in Sept., daily 10:30–12:30 and 2:30–5:30; mid-Sept.–June, daily 10–noon and 2–4.*

14 The 16th- to 17th-century **Hôtel de Vauluisant** houses two museums: the **Musée de Vauluisant** (History Museum) and the **Musée de la Bonneterie** (Textile Museum). The former traces the development of Troyes and southern Champagne, with a section devoted to religious art; the latter outlines the history and manufacturing process of the town's 18th- to 19th-century textile industry. ✉ *4 rue Vauluisant,* ☎ *03–25–76–21–60.* 🎟 *Joint ticket for both museums €5.* ⏲ *Sept.–June, Wed.–Sun. 10–noon and 2–6; July–Aug., Wed.–Mon. 10–6.*

Dining and Lodging

The pleasure of Troyes is its Old Town, Vieux Troyes. This is where you want your hotel to be or—at least within walking distance of it. If you want to dine informally, it's also the area to find a restaurant, especially along rue Champeaux.

$$$–$$$$ ★ ✕ **Le Clos Juillet.** The best restaurant in Troyes, Le Clos Juillet also spotlights one of the largest wine cellars in Champagne. Chef Philippe Collin concentrates his considerable skills on local produce and traditions but also throws in some exotic curveballs—oysters poached in cider, sea bream and caramelized leek tart, lobster couscous and fruit-filled Vietnamese rolls served with balsamic vinegar syrup. ✉ *22 bd. du 14-Juillet,* ☎ *03–25–73–31–32. AE, MC, V. Closed Sun.–Mon., Feb., and last 2 wks of Aug.*

$$$–$$$$ ✕ **Valentino.** Across the back courtyard from the Relais St-Jean is this comfortable, sea green–painted restaurant with a glassed-in terrace (tables are set outside in summer). Oysters are served as a complement to the menu's fish specialties—try them *en gelée d'eau de mer* (sea water aspic), chilled and served on a bed of *crème fraîche* with rock salt on the side. ✉ *11 cour de la Rencontre,* ☎ *03–25–73–14–14. AE, MC, V. Closed Mon., last wk of Aug., 1st 3 wks of Jan., Sun. nights in winter. No lunch Sat.*

$–$$ ✕ **La Taverne de l'Ours.** This popular, convivial brasserie has faux Art Nouveau and neo-Gothic furbelows, brass globe lamps, and plushy seating alcoves. It also has delicious, hearty cuisine, such as roast *cochon de lait* (suckling pig) straight off the spit. The €11 lunch menu is a real bargain, and even tastier when accompanied by the grapey, dark pink rosé *des Riceys* from the Champagne–Burgundy border. Happily, this place is open year-round. ✉ *2 rue Champeaux,* ☎ *03–25–73–22–18. AE, MC, V.*

$$$ ★ 🏨 **Le Champ des Oiseaux.** Idyllically situated in Troyes' oldest quarter, this is the finest hotel in town—an ensemble of three pink-and-yellow 15th- and 16th-century houses (their bright colors part of a town campaign to "medievalize" half-timber facades). Inside are stylish floral prints and 15th-century scrollwork panels. The biggest room, the Suite Médiévale, is under the oak-beamed eaves. Downstairs is a lovely breakfast room with a stone fireplace, as well as a vine-clad inner courtyard for summer mornings. ✉ *20 rue Linard Gonthier, 10000,* ☎ *03–25–80–58–50,* FAX *03–25–80–98–34. 12 rooms. No air-conditioning, cable TV, Internet. AE, MC, V.*

$$–$$$ 🏨 **Relais St-Jean.** This calm half-timber hotel, in the pedestrian zone near St-Jean, has fully equipped, good-size rooms—some connected by a path running through the second floor's tree-filled atrium. Black-leather chairs and mirrored walls in the bar contrast rudely with the wicker and plants of an adjoining room. But have a drink here, and good-natured owner Monsieur Rinaldi will gladly stop to chat. The hotel has no restaurant, but next door is the friendly **Valentino** (✉ 11 cour de la Rencontre, ☎ 03–25–73–14–14), which has dining in its courtyard. ✉ *49 rue Paillot-de-Montabert, 10000,* ☎ *03–25–73–89–90,* FAX *03–25–73–88–60. 25 rooms. Bar, minibars, Internet. AE, DC, MC, V. Closed mid-Dec.–early Jan.*

$$ **Royal.** This modern hotel benefits by being less than a five-minute walk from Vieux Troyes and from the train and bus station (with windows open, you can hear the passing TGV and the busy boulevard below—close them and it's dead quiet). Rooms are standard for a refurbished hotel: smallish, with either double or single beds, a desk, and a couple of chairs. The comfy bar, with its black-leather chairs, is a good evening hangout. ✉ *22 bd. Carnot, 10000,* ☎ *03–25–73–19–99,* FAX *03–25–73–47–85. 37 rooms. Restaurant, bar, some air-conditioning, minibars, Internet. AE, DC, MC, V.*

$ **Les Comtes de Champagne.** In Vieux Troyes's former mint is this bargain hotel. The topsy-turvy building, with its solid, squat staircase and faded floral wallpaper, has a nice inner courtyard with large vines and a philodendron. The two couples who co-manage, the Gribourets and the Picards, are friendly folk. ✉ *56 rue de la Monnaie, 10000,* ☎ *03–25–73–11–70,* FAX *03–25–73–06–02. 35 rooms, 5 with bath. MC, V.*

Shopping

If there's an ideal place for a shopping spree, it's Troyes. Many clothing manufacturers are just outside town, clustered together in two large suburban malls: **Marques Avenue,** in St-Julien-les-Villas (take N71 toward Dijon); and **Marques City** and the American outlet store **McArthur Glen,** in Pont-Ste-Marie (take N77 toward Chalons-sur-Marne). Ralph Lauren and Calvin Klein at McArthur Glen face off with Laura Ashley at Marques Avenue and Doc Martens at Marques City, to name a few of the shops. The malls are open Monday 2–7, Tuesday–Friday 10–7, and Saturday 9:30–7.

Clairvaux

15 *55 km (34 mi) east of Troyes via N19.*

Although much of it has been replaced by a sprawling 19th-century prison, the **Abbaye de Clairvaux,** once the Cistercian mother abbey of Champagne and northern Burgundy, is well worth the detour from Troyes. St. Bernard, a native of Fontaine-les-Dijon, founded Clairvaux (meaning "bright valley") only two years after his entry into Cîteaux, in 1115, and three years before establishing the community of Fontenay, in 1118. Subsequently known as Bernard of Clairvaux, he went on to condemn the behavior of Peter Abelard, preach the Second Crusade in Vézelay, and decry the lavish pomp of Cluny. The 12th-century vaulted halls of the lay brothers' dormitory remain, as do parts of the once-flourishing 18th-century abbey. ✉ *Off N19 (watch for signs),* ☎ *03–25–27–88–17.* ⏲ *May–Oct., Sat. only. Guided tours at 2, 3, 4, and 5. Bring ID.*

Pontigny

16 *60 km (37 mi) south of Troyes, 56 km (35 mi) southeast of Sens.*

Pontigny can easily be mistaken for another drowsy, dusty village, but the once proud **Abbaye de Pontigny** is as large as many cathedrals. In the 12th and 13th centuries it sheltered three archbishops of Canterbury, including St. Thomas à Becket (from 1164 to 1166). His path to refuge from the king of England was followed by his successor, Stephen Langton (here from 1207 to 1215), and, lastly, Edmund of Abingdon—whose body, naturally mummified in the years following his death in

1240, has been venerated (as St. Edmund) by centuries of English pilgrims to Pontigny). His Baroque tomb, whose occupant is supposedly very much intact, can be seen at the rear of the church, although peeking through one of the openings is now strictly forbidden. The abbey was founded in 1114, but the current church was finished around 1150. By Burgundian standards the church and lay brothers' quarters (all that remain) were precociously Gothic—the first buildings in the region to have rib vaults. Inside, it is surprisingly Baroque—particularly beautiful are the late-17th-century wooden choir stalls, carved with garlands and angels. On the grassy lawn next to the church is a large, plate-shape 12th-century **fountain** with 31 spigots and sculpted Gothic feet—one of the few functioning medieval abbey fountains remaining in Europe. ☎ *03–86–47–54–99.* *Free, €3 for a guided tour.* *June–Oct., daily 9–7; Nov.–May, daily 10–5, except during services.*

Auxerre

⓱ *21 km (13 mi) southwest of Pontigny, 58 km (36 mi) southeast of Sens.*

Auxerre is the jewel of Burgundy's Yonne region—a beautifully laid-out town with three imposing and elegant churches climbing the large hill on which the town perches over the Yonne River. Its steep, undulating streets are full of massively photogenic, half-timber houses in every imaginable style and shape. Although, as late-medieval towns go, it is much more harmonious and architecturally interesting than flat, half-destroyed Troyes, Auxerre is underappreciated—perhaps because of its location, midway between Paris and Dijon.

The town's dominant feature is the ascending line of three magnificent churches—St-Pierre, St-Étienne, and St-Germain—and the **Cathédrale St-Étienne,** in the middle, rising majestically above the squat houses around it. The 13th-century choir, the oldest part of the edifice, contains its original stained glass, dominated by brilliant reds and blues. Beneath the choir, the frescoed 11th-century Romanesque crypt keeps company with the treasury, which has a panoply of medieval enamels, manuscripts, and miniatures. A 75-minute son-et-lumière show focusing on Roman Gaul is presented every evening from June to September. ✉ *Pl. St-Étienne,* ☎ *03–86–52–31–68.* *Crypt and treasury €2 each; €3.84 Passport ticket allows entry to crypt and treasury plus St-Germain.* *Easter–Nov., Mon.–Sat. 9–noon and 2–6, Sun. 2–6.*

Fanning out from Auxerre's main square, **place des Cordeliers** (just up from the cathedral), are a number of venerable, crooked, steep streets lined with half-timber and stone houses, each one a gem. The best way to see them is to start from the riverside on the quai de la République, where you find the tourist office (and can pick up a handy local map), and continue along the quai de la Marine. The medieval arcaded gallery of the **Ancien Evêché** (Old Bishop's Palace), now an administrative building, is just visible on the hillside beside the tourist office. At **9 rue de la Marine** (which leads off one of several riverside squares) are the two oldest houses in Auxerre, dating from the end of the 14th century. Continue up the hill to rue de l'Yonne, which leads into the **rue Cochois.** Here, at No. 23, is the appropriately topsy-turvy home and shop of *maître verrier* (lead-glass maker) P. Defert. Closer to the center of town, the most beautiful of Auxerre's many *poteaux* (the carved tops of wooden corner posts) can be seen at **8 rue Joubert**: the building dates from the late 15th century and its Gothic tracery windows, acorns, and oak leaves are an open-air masterpiece.

North of place des Cordeliers is the former **Abbaye de St-Germain,** which stands parallel to the cathedral some 300 yards away. The church's earliest aboveground section is the 12th-century Romanesque bell tower, but the extensive underground crypt was inaugurated by Charles the Bald in 859 and contains its original Carolingian frescoes and Ionic capitals. It's the only monument of its kind in Europe—a labyrinth retaining the plan of the long-gone church built above it—and was a place of pilgrimage until Huguenots burned the remains of its namesake, a Gallo-Roman governor and bishop of Auxerre, in the 16th century. Several hundred years of veneration had already seen the burial of 33 bishops of Auxerre as close to the central tomb of St-Germain as they could physically get. The frescoes are a testimony to the brief artistic sophistication of the Carolingian Renaissance: Witness St. Stephen running from a stone-hurling crowd towards the disembodied hand of God, a date-bearing palm tree, and the reversed images of a young bishop and an old one teaching each other. ✉ *Pl. St-Germain,* ☎ *03–86–51–09–74.* 🎫 *€4.* ⏲ *Guided tours of crypt Oct.–Apr., daily 10, 11, and 2–5; May–Sept., daily every ½ hr between 10 and 5:30.*

Dining and Lodging

$$–$$$ ✕ **La Chamaille.** This restaurant is remarkably low-key for its culinary aspirations. The mood is set by a babbling brook running through the garden and the exposed brick walls in the dining room. Try the rabbit in a rich brown sauce and pastry. You'll be hard-pressed to find room for the apple flan, but you must—it's delectable. Prices are reasonable, especially for the four-course menu, which includes a half bottle of regional wine, for €32. ✉ *4 rte. de Boiloup, Chevannes (10 km/6 km south of Auxerre),* ☎ *03–86–41–24–80. Reservations essential. AE, MC, V. Closed Mon.–Tues.*

$$–$$$ ✕ **Jardin Gourmand.** As its name implies, this restaurant in a former manor house has a pretty garden (*jardin*) where you can eat in summer. The interior is accented by sea-green and yellow panels and is equally congenial and elegant. Terrine of pheasant breast is a specialty, and hope that the superb snails with barley and chanterelles is available. The staff is discreet and friendly. ✉ *56 bd. Vauban,* ☎ *03–86–51–53–52. AE, MC, V. Closed Mon.*

$–$$ ★ 🏨 **Château de Ribourdin.** Retired farmer Claude Brodard began building his *chambres d'hôtes* (bed-and-breakfast) in an old stable six years ago, and the result is cozy, comfortable, and reasonably priced. Château de la Borde, named for another small manor (and former family-run establishment) nearby, is the smallest, sunniest, and most intimate room; all overlook Monsieur Brodard's fields. Homemade preserves—cassis, quince, and carrot—are served at breakfast. ✉ *89240 Chevannes (8 km/5 mi southwest of Auxerre on D1),* ☎ *03–86–41–23–16,* FAX *03–86–41–23–16. 5 rooms. No air-conditioning, no room phones, no room TVs, pool. No credit cards.*

$ 🏨 **Normandie.** Set in a rather grand 19th-century mansion, the vine-covered Normandie is in the center of Auxerre, just a short walk from the cathedral. Rooms are unpretentious and clean. There's a billiard room, and the terrace is a nice place to relax after a long day of sightseeing. ✉ *41 bd. Vauban, 89000,* ☎ *03–86–52–57–80,* FAX *03–86–51–54–33. 47 rooms. Bar, no air-conditioning, no room phones, no room TVs, gym, sauna. AE, DC, MC, V.*

Chablis

18 *16 km (10 mi) east of Auxerre, 70 km (44 mi) south of Troyes, 183 km (114 mi) southeast of Paris.*

The pretty little village of Chablis, famous for its white wine, nestles on the banks of the River Serein and is protected, perhaps from an ill wind, by the massive, round, turreted towers of the Porte Noël gateway. Although in America Chablis has become a generic name for cheap white wine, it's not so in France: there it's a sharp, slightly acacia-tasting wine of tremendous character, with the Premier Cru and Grand Cru wines standing head to head with the best French whites. Prices in the local shops tend to be inflated, so your best bet is to buy directly from a vineyard; keep in mind that most are closed Sunday.

Dining and Lodging

$$–$$$ ★ ✕ 🏨 **Hostellerie des Clos.** The moderately priced, simple yet comfortable rooms at this inn have floral curtains and wicker tables with chairs. But most of all, come here for chef Michel Vignaud's cooking, some of the best in the region. ✉ *18 rue Jules-Rathier, 89800,* ☎ *03–86–42–10–63,* FAX *03–86–42–17–11. 26 rooms. Restaurant, cable TV, minibars, Internet. AE, MC, V. Closed late Dec.–mid-Jan., Wed.*

$ 🏨 **Domaine de Montpierreux.** This private manor on a truffle farm south of Chablis has five immaculate rooms on its top floor. All are delightful, with paisley fabrics and at least one piece of antique furniture. The friendly owners help to make this a very comfortable base for exploring the area. Breakfast is served. ✉ *89290 Venoy (10 km/4 mi south of Chablis, 10 km/6 mi north of Auxerre on D965),* ☎ *03–86–40–20–91,* FAX *03–86–40–28–00. 5 rooms. No credit cards.*

Tonnerre

⑲ *16 km (10 mi) northeast of Chablis, 60 km (37 mi) south of Troyes.*

The small town of Tonnerre was mostly rebuilt after a devastating fire in 1556. A good spot from which to survey the 16th-century reconstruction and the Armançon Valley is the terrace of the church of **St-Pierre.**

The town's chief attraction, the high-roofed **Ancien Hôpital,** or hôtel-Dieu (hospital), was built in 1293 and has survived the passing centuries—flames and all—largely intact. The main room, the **Grande Salle,** is 280 ft long and retains its oak ceiling; it was conceived as the hospital ward and after 1650 served as the parish church. The original hospital church leads off from the Grande Salle; in the adjoining **Chapelle du Revestière,** a dramatic 15th-century stone group represents the *Entombment of Christ.* Look for good finds at the **Salon des Antiquaires** (antiques fair), held here on All Saints' weekend (the second weekend in November). ✉ *Rue du Prieuré,* ☎ *03–86–54–33–00.* 🎫 *€4.* ⏲ *June–Sept., Wed.–Mon. 10–noon and 1:30–6:30; Apr.–May and Oct.–Nov., weekends 1:30–6:30.*

Tanlay

⑳ *10 km (6 mi) east of Tonnerre, 45 km (28 mi) northeast of Auxerre.*

Tanlay is best known for its **Château de Tanlay.** Built around 1550, it is an example of the influence of the classical on Renaissance design. The vestibule, framed by wrought-iron railings, leads to a wood-paneled salon and dining room filled with period furniture. A graceful staircase climbs to the second floor, which has a frescoed gallery and ornate fireplaces. A small room in the tower above was used as a secret meeting-place by Huguenot Protestants during the 1562–98 Wars of Religion; note the cupola with its fresco of scantily clad 16th-century religious personalities. ☎ *03–86–75–70–61.* 🎫 *Guided tours, €6; grounds only, €4.* ⏲ *Apr.–Nov. 15, Wed.–Mon. 9:30–11:30 and 2:15–5:15.*

Lodging

$ 🏨 **Chez Batreau.** Set in the lovely little farming village of Cruzy-le-Chatel, on a hillside close to Tanlay, this inn comes with its own walled garden. Rooms are large and filled with family furnishings; beds sag a little. Nonetheless, the rooms are good value for the money, especially the one at the end of the hall, whose exposed timbers and cross beams form a sort of loft. ✉ *89740 Cruzy-le-Chatel (12 km/7 mi from Tanlay),* ☎ *03–86–75–22–76. 4 rooms, 2 with bath. No credit cards.*

Ancy-le-Franc

21 *14 km (9 mi) southeast of Tanlay, 63 km (40 mi) northeast of Auxerre, 51 km (32 mi) north of Avallon.*

Ancy-le-Franc is famous for its Renaissance château. Built from Sebastiano Serlio's designs, with interior blandishments by Primaticcio, both of whom worked at the court of François I (1515–47), the **Château d'Ancy-le-Franc** has an Italian flavor. The plain, majestic exterior contrasts with the sumptuous rooms and apartments, many—particularly the magnificent Chambre des Arts (Art Gallery)—with carved or painted walls and ceilings and original furnishings. Such grandeur won the approval of the Sun King, Louis XIV, no less, who once stayed in the Salon Bleu (Blue Room). Adjoining the château is a small **Musée de l'Automobile.** ✉ *Pl. Clermont-Tonnerre,* ☎ *03–86–75–14–63.* *Château and museum, €7; museum only, €3.* ⏲ *Early Apr.–mid-Nov., guided château tours at 10, 11, 2, 3, 4, 5, and 6 (last one at 5 mid-Sept.–mid-Nov.).*

Abbaye de Fontenay

★ 22 *46 km (29 mi) southeast of Tonnerre, 104 km (75 mi) southeast of Auxerre.*

Just east of Montbard is the best-preserved of the Cistercian abbeys, the Abbaye de Fontenay, founded in 1118 by St. Bernard. The same Cistercian criteria applied to Fontenay as to Pontigny: no-frills architecture and an isolated site—the spot was especially remote, for it had been decreed that these monasteries could not be established anywhere near "cities, feudal manors, or villages." The monks were required to live a completely self-sufficient existence, with no contact whatsoever with the outside world. By the end of the 12th century the buildings were finished, and the abbey's community grew to some 300 monks. Under the protection of Pope Gregory IX and Hughes IV, duke of Burgundy, the monastery soon controlled huge land holdings, vineyards, and timberlands. It prospered until the 16th century, when religious wars and administrative mayhem hastened its decline. Dissolved during the French Revolution, the abbey was used as a paper factory until 1906. Fortunately, the historic buildings emerged unscathed. The abbey is surrounded by extensive gardens dotted with the fountains that gave it its name. The church's solemn interior is lightened by windows in the façade and by a double row of three narrow windows, representing the Trinity, in the choir. A staircase in the south transept leads to the wood-roofed dormitory (spare a thought for the bleary-eyed monks, obliged to stagger down for services in the dead of night). The chapter house, flanked by a majestic arcade, and the scriptorium, where monks worked on their manuscripts, lead off from the adjoining cloisters. Fontenay retains one of the oldest forges in Europe, dating from the 13th century (including the massive fireplace) and once powered by the river. ✉ *Marmagne,* ☎ *03–80–92–15–00.* *€8.* ⏲ *Mid-Mar.–mid-Nov., daily 9–noon and 2–6; mid-Nov–mid-Mar., daily 2–5.*

Saulieu

23 *46 km (29 mi) south of Fontenay, 62 km (37 mi) northwest of Beaune, 77 km (49 mi) west of Dijon.*

Saulieu's reputation belies its size: it is renowned for good food (Rabelais, that roly-poly 16th-century man of letters, extolled its gargantuan hospitality) and Christmas trees (a staggering million are packed and sent off from the area each year). The town's **Basilique de St-Andoche** (✉ Pl. du Docteur Roclore) is almost as old as that of Vézelay, though less imposing and much restored. Note the Romanesque capitals. The **Musée François Pompon,** adjoining the basilica, is a museum devoted, in part, to the work of animal-bronze sculptor Pompon (1855–1933), whose smooth, stylized creations seem contemporary but predate World War II. The museum also contains Gallo-Roman funeral stones, sacred art, and a room devoted to local gastronomic lore. ✉ *Rue Sallier,* ☎ *03–80–64–19–51.* *€3.5.* *Apr.–Sept., Wed.–Mon. 10–12:30 and 2–6; Oct.–Mar., Wed.–Mon. 10–12:30 and 2–5:30.*

Dining and Lodging

$$$$ ★ **La Côte d'Or.** Originally a historic coaching auberge, this is now one of the region's finest hotels and restaurants, celebrated as the home base for chef Bernard Loiseau, one of France's culinary superstars. He made his mark by offering up a feather-light nouvelle version of rich Burgundian fare, as is shown by his foie gras and fowl in a pureed truffle sauce. Almost more delicious is the setting: a chapel-like wood-beam dining room with a lush flower garden radiating around it. Guest rooms combine exposed beams and glass panels with cheerful traditional furnishings; a newer annex has the most comfortable (and air-conditioned) rooms, while the more stylish accommodations (styles range from Louis XVI to Empire) are in the main house. Some are tiny (one is complete with porthole window), some are luxurious (one has a comfy balcony overlooking the countryside)—no matter which you book, try to get a room facing the garden courtyard. ✉ *2 rue d'Argentine (off N6), 21210 Saulieu,* ☎ *03–80–90–53–53,* FAX *03–80–64–08–92. 33 rooms. Restaurant, some air-conditioning, cable TV, health club, Internet, meeting room. AE, DC, MC, V.*

$$ **Chez Camille.** Small, quiet, and friendly sum up this hotel in a 16th-century house with an exterior so ordinary you might easily pass it by. But within, rooms have period furniture and original wooden beams; ask for No. 22 or No. 23, the most dramatic, with a beamed ceiling that looks like spokes in a wheel. Traditional Burgundian fare—duck and boar are specialties—makes up the menu in the glass-roof restaurant. ✉ *1 pl. Édouard-Herriot, 21230 Arnay-le-Duc (on N6 between Saulieu and Beaune),* ☎ *03–80–90–01–38,* FAX *03–80–90–04–64. 11 rooms. Restaurant, cable TV, Internet. AE, DC, MC, V.*

Châteauneuf-en-Auxois

24 *41 km (25 mi) east of Saulieu, 35 km (22 mi) northwest of Beaune.*

The tiny hilltop town of Châteauneuf-en-Auxois catches your eye from A6. Turn off at Pouilly-en-Auxois and take any one of the three narrow, winding roads up, and you'll suddenly feel you've entered the Middle Ages. The town's modest 15th-century church ministered to as as many as 500 souls when the village was at its zenith. In the last few years tourists have discovered the charm of this village, so try to avoid it on weekends.

The **château,** built in the 12th and 15th centuries (with some later modifications), commands a broad view over rolling farmland as far as the eye can see. ☎ *03–80–49–21–89.* *€3.5.* *Apr.–May and Sept., Thurs.–Mon. 9:30–12:30 and 2–6; June–Aug., Thurs.–Mon. 9:30–12:30 and 2–7; Oct.–Mar., Thurs.–Mon. 10–noon and 2–4.*

Clustered behind the château are houses for ordinary folk, at least a score of them notable for their 14th- and 15th-century charm, where today only about 80 people live. One of these, the charming **Monsieur Simon** (☎ 03–80–49–21–59), is so proud of his village that he gladly takes small groups on tours of the sights.

Dining and Lodging

$$$$ ✕🏨 **Château la Chassagne.** Feel like a king or a queen for a night at this former estate where you can even arrive by private plane or helicopter and be picked up in a Rolls-Royce. Rooms have high ceilings and are spacious; the modern iron-and-cane furnishings are obviously expensive, but of somewhat questionable taste. The grounds include a golf range, tennis court, and swimming pool. Nouvelle cuisine is served in the restaurant, but the chef seems to focus more on artistic presentation than creative flavoring; still, it's enjoyable. ✉ *21410 Pont-de-Pany (12 km/7 mi from Châteauneuf-en-Auxois off A38, shortly after the junction with A6),* ☎ *03–80–49–76–00,* FAX *03–80–49–76–19. 11 rooms. Restaurant, cable TV, driving range, 2 tennis courts, pool. AE, DC, MC, V. Closed Nov.–Mar.*

$$ ✕🏨 **Hostellerie du Château.** This hotel is in an ancient timbered building in the shadow of the town castle. The restaurant serves classical Bourgogne fare—roasted Époisses (local cow's-milk cheese) on a salad bed with walnuts, noisettes of lamb with thyme, and coq au vin; it is closed Tuesday and doesn't serve dinner Monday, except in July and August. Rooms vary considerably—from small to commodious; the best have a view of the castle. ✉ *Châteauneuf-en-Auxois, 21320 Pouilly,* ☎ *03–80–49–22–00,* FAX *03–80–49–21–27. 17 rooms. Restaurant, no air-conditioning, no room telephones, no room TV. AE, DC, MC, V. Closed late Nov.–early Feb.*

Château de Sully

㉕ *37 km (28 mi) south of Châteauneuf-en-Auxois, 43 km (27 mi) southeast of Saulieu.*

"The Fontainbleau of Burgundy" was how Madame de Sévigné described this turreted Renaissance château, continuing on to proclaim the inner court, whose Italianate design was inspired by Serlio, as the latest in chic. The building is magnificent, landmarked by four lantern-topped corner towers, which loom over a romantic moat filled with the waters of the River Drée. Originally constructed by the de Rabutin family and once owned by Gaspard de Saulx-Tavannes—an instigator of the St. Bartholomew's Day Massacre, August 24, 1572, he reputedly ran through Paris's streets yelling, "Blood, blood! The doctors say that bleeding is as good for the health in August as in May!"—the château was partly reconstructed in elegant Règence style in the 18th century. Marshal MacMahon, president of France from 1873 to 1879, was born here, in 1808. ☎ *03–85–82–10–27.* 🎫 *Guided tours €5.5; grounds €2.5.* ⊙ *Château 45-min guided tours June–Sept. (call for times). Grounds daily 10–noon and 2–6.*

Autun

㉖ *20 km (12 mi) southwest of Sully, 41 km (25 mi) south of Saulieu, 49 km (30 mi) west of Beaune.*

One of the most richly endowed *villes d'art* in Burgundy, Autun is a great draw for fans of both Gallo-Roman and Romanesque art. The name derives from Augustodonum—city of Augustus—and it was Augustus Caesar who called it "the sister and rival of Rome itself." You may still see traces of the Roman occupation—dating from when

Autun was much larger and more important than it is today—in its well-preserved archways, Porte St-André and Porte d'Arroux, and the Théâtre Romain, once the largest arena in Gaul. Parts of the Roman walls surrounding the town also remain and give a fair indication of its size in those days. The curious Pierre de Couhard, a pyramidlike Roman construction, has so far baffled archaeologists, who are undecided as to its significance. Perhaps not unsurprisingly, this Roman outpost became a center for the new 12th-century style based on Roman precedent, the Romanesque, and its greatest sculptor, Gislebertus, left his precocious mark on the town cathedral. Several centuries later, Napoléon and his brother Joseph studied here at the military academy.

★ Autun's principal monument is the **Cathédrale St-Lazarus,** a Gothic cathedral in Classical clothing. It was built between 1120 and 1146 to house the relics of St. Lazarus; the main tower, spire, and upper reaches of the chancel were added in the late 15th century. Lazarus's tricolor tomb was dismantled in 1766 by canons: vestiges of exquisite workmanship can be seen in the neighboring Musée Rolin. The same canons also did their best to transform the Romanesque-Gothic cathedral into a Classical temple, adding pilasters and other ornaments willy-nilly. Fortunately, the lacy Flamboyant Gothic organ tribune and some of the best Romanesque stonework, including the inspired nave capitals and the tympanum above the main door, emerged unscathed. Jean-Auguste-Dominique Ingres's painting *The Martyrdom of St. Symphorien* has been relegated to a dingy chapel in the north aisle of the nave. The *Last Judgment,* above the main door, was plastered over in the 18th century, which preserved not only the stylized Christ and elongated apostles but also the inscription GISLEBERTUS HOC FECIT (Gislebertus did this). Christ's head, which had disappeared, was found by a local canon shortly after World War II. Make sure to visit the cathedral's **Salle Capitulaire,** which houses Gislebertus's original capitals, distinguished by their relief carvings. The cathedral provides a stunning setting for **Musique en Morvan,** a festival of classical music held in July. ✉ *Pl. St-Louis.*

The **Musée Rolin,** across from the cathedral, was built by Chancellor Nicholas Rolin, an important Burgundian administrator and art patron (he's immortalized in one of the Louvre's greatest paintings, Jan van Eyck's *Madonna and the Chancellor Rolin*). The museum is noteworthy for its early Netherlandish paintings and sculpture, including the magisterial *Nativity* painted by the Maître de Moulins in the 15th century. But the collection's star is a Gislebertus masterpiece, the *Temptation of Eve,* which originally topped one of the side doors of the cathedral. Try to imagine the missing elements of the scene: Adam on the left and the devil on the right. ✉ *3 rue des Bancs,* ☎ *03–85–52–09–76.* 🎫 *€3.* ⏲ *Oct.–Mar., Wed.–Sat. 10–noon and 2–4, Sun. 10–noon and 2:30–5; Apr.–Sept., Wed.–Mon. 9:30–noon and 1:30–6.*

The **Théâtre Romain,** at the edge of town on the road to Chalon-sur-Saône, is a historic spot for lunch. Pick up the makings for a picnic in town and eat it on the stepped seats, where as many as 15,000 Gallo-Roman spectators perched during performances two millennia ago. In August a Gallo-Roman performance—the only one of its kind—is put on by locals wearing period costume. The peak of a Gallo-Roman pyramid can be seen in the foreground.

The **Temple of Janus,** in a field at the edge of town as you leave for Château-Chinon, is a Celtic temple built in the Roman style by the local Eduan tribe. It may have honored the horse goddess Eponna, a maternal figure, or Cernunnos, a war god.

Dining and Lodging

$$–$$$$ ✕🏨 **Hôtel St-Louis et de la Poste.** Autun's best hotel, in a former post house, is noteworthy more for its history than its pretensions to elegance. It has Mexican wrought-iron furnishings and a remarkable family-size suite—it was while making a speech from this room's balcony in 1815 on his way back to Paris that Napoléon was rebuffed by crowds; George Sand also stayed here. The staff is friendly and helpful, and the restaurant, La Rotonde, is one of Autun's best. ✉ *6 rue de l'Arbalète, 71400,* ☎ *03–85–52–01–01,* FAX *03–85–86–32–54. 39 rooms. Restaurant, no air-conditioning, no-smoking rooms, minibars, cable TV, Internet. AE, DC, MC, V.*

$$–$$$$ ✕🏨 **Hôtel des Ursalines.** Placed above the Roman ramparts of the old city, this converted 17th-century convent offers spacious, well-kept rooms overlooking a simple, geometric *style Française* garden. The restaurant, adorned with red-velvet flocking and run by Paul Bocuse protégée Bruno Schlewitz, is worth a trip in itself, especially for the escargots with dried tomatoes and garlic *confit*. Some guest rooms have fine views of the surrounding Morvan mountains, and breakfast is served in the historic chapel area. ✉ *14 rue Rivault,* ☎ *03–85–86–58–58,* FAX *03–85–86–23–07. 40 rooms, 3 apartments. No air-conditioning, cable TV, minibars, Internet, no-smoking rooms. AE, DC, MC, V.*

Château-Chinon

27 *37 km (23 mi) west of Autun, 62 km (38 mi) south of Avallon.*

The late president François Mitterrand was a former mayor of the small town of Château-Chinon, the capital of the Morvan. One of his legacies is the brash, colorful, and controversial **Fontaine de Niki de St-Phalle,** in front of the Hôtel de Ville. At the **Musée du Septennat** (Septennate Museum)—the name refers to the seven-year French presidency—is an astonishing variety of gifts Mitterrand received while president. ✉ *6 rue du Château,* ☎ *03–86–60–67–62.* 🎫 *€4.* ⏲ *Early Feb.–Apr. and Oct.–Dec., Wed.–Mon. 10–1 and 2–7; May–June and Sept., daily 10–1 and 2–6; July–Aug., daily 10–1 and 2–7.*

The 👍 **Musée du Costume** (Clothing Museum) exhibits French clothing from the 18th century. ✉ *4 rue du Château,* ☎ *03–86–85–18–55.* 🎫 *€4.* ⏲ *Oct.–Apr., Wed.–Mon. 10–1 and 2–6; May–June and Sept., Wed.–Mon. 10–1 and 2–6; July–Aug., daily 10–1 and 2–7.*

$$ ✕🏨 **Le Vieux Morvan.** This family-run, clean, and simple—emphasis on simple—pension was Monsieur le Présidènt François Mitterrand's unofficial headquarters during his 14-year reign, and it still attracts its share of presidential pilgrims. The guest rooms are standard-issue, but the excellent 130-seat restaurant offers a panoramic view of the Morvan. Try the very copious *tête de veau* (calf's head)—which just happens to be the favorite dish of Mitterrand's successor, Jacques Chirac. ✉ *8 pl. Gudin,* ☎ *03–86–85–05–01,* FAX *03–86–85–05–01. 24 rooms. MC, V. Closed Jan.*

Nevers

28 *64 km (40 mi) west of Château-Chinon, 119 km (74 mi) south of Auxerre, 239 km (149 mi) southeast of Paris.*

Burgundy's western outpost, Nevers, on the banks of the Loire, has been producing earthenware since the late 16th century. Promoted initially by Italian craftsmen, the industry suffered during the French Revolution, but five or six traditional manufacturers remain. An extensive selection of Nevers earthenware, retracing its stylistic development, can be admired at the **Musée Municipal** (Town Museum). ✉ *Promenade* *des Remparts, ☎ 03–86–71–67–90. €2.30. ⏲ May–Sept., daily 10–6:30; Oct.–Apr., Wed.–Sat. 1–5:30, Sun. 10–noon and 2–5:30.*

Part of Nevers's medieval walls extend behind the Town Museum, culminating in the intimidating gateway known as the **Porte du Croux** (built in 1393), which, thanks to its turrets and huge, sloping roof, resembles a small castle.

The **Cathédrale** (✉ Rue du Cloître-St-Cyr) has a 170-ft square tower, two apses, and two choirs—one Romanesque, one Gothic—in place of a narthex. The **Palais Ducal** (✉ Pl. de la République), beyond the cathedral, has a sumptuous, large-windowed Renaissance facade but, unfortunately, is closed to the public.

Across the park that can be entered from place Carnot is the **Couvent St-Gildard,** the convent where St. Bernadette of Lourdes (1844–79) spent the last 13 years of her life. A small museum contains mementos and outlines her life story (she claimed to have seen the Virgin several times in 1858 and was canonized in 1933). ✉ *Rue St-Gildard,* ☎ *03–86–71–99–50. Free. ⏲ Apr.–Oct., daily 7 AM–7:30 PM; Nov.–Mar., daily 7:30–noon and 2–7.*

Dining and Lodging

$$–$$$ ✕ **La Cour St-Étienne.** The food is delicious, exquisitely presented, and an excellent value, and the ambience is serene. Enjoy lunch on the terrace overlooking the courtyard or in one of the cozy dining rooms. Farm-raised veal medallions with morels are just one of the specialties. ✉ *Rue St-Etienne,* ☎ *03–86–36–74–57. Reservations essential. MC, V. Closed Sun.–Mon., Aug. and 1st 2 wks of Jan. Sun.–Mon.*

$$–$$$ ✕🏨 **La Renaissance.** Sole braised in grapefruit and port, Charolais beef served with a cream and morel sauce, oven-roasted crayfish—this is the kind of enlightened Morvanese cuisine that comes out of Jean-Claude Dray's kitchen. Tipple some of the wonderful Burgundies from the extensive wine cellar, finish off the meal with something sweet from the dessert wagon, then stumble upstairs to one of La Renaissance's comfortable modern rooms. There's no dinner Sunday, and the restaurant is closed Monday. ✉ *2 rue de Paris, 58470 Magny-Cours (12 km/7½ mi south of Nevers on the RN7),* ☎ *03–86–58–10–40,* FAX *03–86–21–22–60. 9 rooms. Parking (fee). AE, DC, MC, V. Closed Feb. and 1st 2 wks Aug.*

The Arts

Jazz à Nevers is just that—a jazz festival that takes place in Nevers in the spring (☎ 03–86–57–88–51 for more information).

La Charité-sur-Loire

29 *24 km (15 mi) northwest of Nevers, 94 km (58 mi) south of Auxerre.*

La Charité-sur-Loire is best known for its medieval church. Unlike those of Pontigny and Fontenay, the abbey church of **Ste-Croix-Notre-Dame** was dependent on Cluny; when it was consecrated by Pope Pascal II in 1107, it was the country's second-largest church. Fire and neglect have taken their toll on the massive original edifice, and these days the church is cut in two by pretty place Ste-Croix (where the nave used to be), with the single-tower facade separated from the imposing choir and transept. A fine view of the church's exterior can be seen from Square des Bénédictins, just off Grande-Rue.

Clamecy

30 *51 km (32 mi) northeast of La Charité-sur-Loire, 44 km (27 mi) south of Auxerre.*

Slow-moving Clamecy is not on many tourist itineraries, but its tumbling alleyways and untouched ancient houses epitomize *la France profonde* (the French heartland). The multishape roofs, dominated by the majestic square tower of the church of **St-Martin,** an ensemble that hasn't changed in centuries, are best viewed from the banks of the Yonne River. The river played a crucial role in Clamecy's development; trees from the nearby Morvan Forest were chopped down and floated to Paris in huge convoys. The history of this form of transport (*flottage*), which lasted until 1923, is detailed in the Musée Municipal (Town Museum), also known as the **Musée d'Art et d'Histoire Romain Rolland** (Romain Rolland Museum of Art and History). Native son Rolland, Nobel Laureate for literature in 1915, spent his final years in a small literary community in nearby Vézelay. Faïence and paintings from the 17th–19th centuries are also on display. ✉ *Av. de la République,* ☎ *03–86–60–67–61.* 🎫 *€2.30.* ⏲ *Easter–Oct., Wed.–Mon. 10–noon and 2–6; Nov.–Easter, Mon. and Wed.–Sat. 10–noon and 3–6.*

In homage to the logs that were once floated downriver, *bûchette* (a log-shape sugared-almond candy) has long been a favorite of Clamecyçois. Sample it at **Avignon** (✉ 22 rue de la Monnaie, near steps leading to St-Martin), a pastry shop and tearoom.

Lodging

$ **Hostellerie de la Poste.** This family-run hotel, in an old coaching stop in the heart of Clamecy, has a welcoming feel. The old-fashioned rooms are small and worn but tidy and clean. It's a popular place for lunching locals, who all seem to be warmly greeted by name at the desk. Regional fare is served; menus start at €16. ✉ *4 pl. Émile Zola, 58500,* ☎ *03–86–27–01–55,* FAX *03–86–27–05–99. 16 rooms. Restaurant, bar. AE, MC, V.*

Vézelay

31 *24 km (15 mi) east of Clamecy, 51 km (32 mi) south of Auxerre, 13 km (8 mi) southwest of Avallon.*

In the 11th and 12th centuries one of the most important places of pilgrimage in the Christian world, Vézelay today is a somewhat isolated, picturesque village set on a peak. Its one main street, rue St-Étienne, climbs steeply to the summit and its medieval basilica, world-famous for its Romanesque sculpture. In summer you have to leave your car at the bottom and walk up. Off-season you can drive up and look for a spot to park in the square.

It's easy to ignore this tiny village, but don't: hidden under its narrow *ruelles* (small streets) are Romanesque cellars that once sheltered pilgrims and are now opened to visitors by homeowners in summer. Sections of several houses have arches and columns dating from the 12th and 13th centuries: don't miss the hostelry across from the tourist office and, next to it, the house where Louis VII, Eleanor of Aquitaine, and the king's adviser Suger stayed when they came to hear St. Bernard preach the Second Crusade in 1146.

★ In the 11th and 12th centuries the celebrated **Basilique Ste-Madeleine** was one of the focal points of Christendom. Pilgrims poured in to see the relics of St. Mary Magdalene (in the crypt) before setting off on the great trek to the shrine of St. James at Santiago de Compostela, in northwest Spain. Several pivotal church declarations of the Middle Ages were made from here, including St. Bernard's preaching of the Second Crusade (which attracted a huge French following) and Thomas à Becket's excommunication of English king Henry II. By the mid-13th century the authenticity of St. Mary's relics was in doubt; others had been discovered in Provence. The basilica's decline continued until the French Revolution, when the basilica and adjoining monastery buildings were sold by the state. Only the basilica, cloister, and dormitory escaped demolition, and were falling into ruin when ace restorer Viollet-le-Duc, sent by his mentor Prosper Merimée, rode to the rescue in 1840 (he also restored the cathedrals of Laon and Amiens and Paris's Notre-Dame).

Today the basilica, under the patrimony of UNESCO, has recaptured some of its glory and is considered to be one of France's most prestigious Romanesque showcases. The exterior tympanum was redone by Viollet-le-Duc (have a look at the eroded original as you exit the cloister), but the narthex (circa 1150) is a Romanesque masterpiece. Note the interwoven zodiac signs and depictions of seasonal crafts along its rim, similar to those at both Troyes and Autun. The pilgrims' route around the building is indicated by the majestic flowers over the left-hand entrance, which metamorphose into full-blown blooms on the right; an annual procession is still held on July 22. Among the most beautiful scenes on the nave capitals is one of Moses grinding grain (symbolizing the Old Testament) into flour (the New Testament), which St. Paul collects in a sack.

The basilica's exterior is best seen from the leafy terrace to the right of the facade. Opposite, a vast, verdant panorama encompasses lush valleys and rolling hills and hedgerows. In the foreground is the Flamboyant Gothic spire of St-Père-sous-Vézelay, a tiny village 3 km (2 mi) away that is the site of Marc Meneau's famed restaurant. ✉ *Pl. de la Basilique,* ☎ *03–86–33–39–50.* 🎫 *Free; donation of €3 for guided visit.* ⏲ *Daily 8–8, except during offices Mon.–Sat. 12:30–1:15 and 6–7, Sun. 11–12:15.*

Just 10 km (6 mi) out of Vézelay in the small town of Bazoches-du-Morvan is the **Château de Bazoches,** the former home of Maréchal de Vauban. Built in the 12th century in the form of a trapezium with four towers and a keep, the building was bought by Vauban in 1675 with the money Louis XIV awarded him for devising the parallel trenches successfully used in the siege of Maastricht. Vauban transformed the building into a fortress and created many of his military engineering designs here. These and furnishings of his day are on display. ✉ *Bazoches-du-Morvan,* ☎ *03–86–22–10–22.* 🎫 *Free.* ⏲ *Late Mar.–early Nov., daily 9:30–noon and 2:15–6.*

Dining and Lodging

$ ✕ **Le Bougainville.** One of the few affordable restaurants in this well-heeled town is in an old house with a fireplace in the dining room and the requisite Burgundian color scheme of brown, yellow, and ocher. Philippe Guillemard presides in the kitchen, turning out regional favorites such as hare stew, crayfish, escargot ragout in Chardonnay sauce, and venison with chestnuts. He has also devised a vegetarian menu—a rarity in Burgundy—with deeply satisfying dishes like terrine of Époisses cheese and artichokes. ✉ *26 rue St-Etienne,* ☎ *03–86–33–27–57. MC, V. Closed Wed. and Dec.–Jan. No dinner Tues.*

$$$$ ✕🏨 **L'Espérance.** Noted chef Marc Meneau is justly renowned for his original creations, such as roast veal in a bitter caramel-based sauce and turbot in a salt-crust *croûte.* The setting—by a stream and a large, statue-filled garden with Vézelay in the background—is exquisite. Accommodations, which vary in price, come in a trinity of delights: charming rooms overlooking the garden, full suites in a renovated mill by the trout stream, and rooms in the annex, the Pré des Marguerites, where rooms are done up in a cozy *style Anglaise.* ✉ *89450 St-Père-sous-Vézelay,* ☎ *03–86–33–39–10,* FAX *03–86–33–26–15. Reserva-*

tions essential. 44 rooms. Restaurant, some air-conditioning, cable TV, minibars, Internet, pool. AE, DC, MC, V. Closed Feb., Tue., lunch Wed.

$$ ✕🏨 **Poste et du Lion d'Or.** On a small square in the lower part of town is this old-fashioned, rambling hotel. A terrace out front welcomes you; the good-size rooms have traditional chintzes. The comfortable restaurant is a popular spot with locals, who come for the regional fare, such as roast partridge in black currant sauce and rabbit casserole. ✉ *Pl. du Champ de Foire, 89450,* ☎ *03–86–33–21–23,* FAX *03–86–32–30–92. 39 rooms. Restaurant, bar, no air-conditioning. AE, MC, V. Closed mid-Nov.–mid-Mar.*

$$$ 🏨 **Résidence Hôtel Le Pontot.** With Vézelay's limited lodging you would do well to book ahead, especially for this historic fortified house with sumptuous little rooms and a lovely garden. Another advantage is the hotel's location in the center of the village halfway up the hill. ✉ *Pl. du Pontot, 89450,* ☎ *03–86–33–24–40,* FAX *03–86–33–30–05. 10 rooms. No air-conditioning, no room TV. DC, MC, V. Closed mid-Nov.–mid-Apr.*

Avallon

32 *13 km (8 mi) east of Vézelay, 105 km (65 mi) northeast of Nevers, 52 km (42 mi) southeast of Auxerre.*

Avallon is on a spectacular promontory jutting over the Vallée du Cousin. Its old streets and ramparts are pleasant places to stroll, and its medieval market-town ambience is appealing. It has enough cafés, bars, and shops to make it interesting, yet it's small enough that you can quickly become familiar with it and turn it into your base for exploring the rest of the region. The main sight to see in town is the work of Romanesque stone carvers whose imaginations ran riot on the portals and 15th-century belfry of the venerable church of **St-Lazarus.**

Dining and Lodging

$$–$$$ ✕🏨 **Moulin des Ruats.** Once an old flour mill, the Moulin des Ruats became a family hotel in 1924 and is now a comfortable country inn run by Monsieur Rossi. Guest rooms are pretty country-French in style; some have balconies overlooking the Cousin River. Ask for one that has been renovated; No. 11, for instance, with its exposed beams and a cozy alcove. The restaurant, fronting the river, serves traditional Bourgogne fare with a strong Provençal accent. Be forewarned that dishes can be uneven: you're better off choosing simple rather than complex preparations, although you can't go wrong with the distinctive foie gras salad. ✉ *89200 Vallée du Cousin (4 km/2½ mi southwest of Avallon),* ☎ *03–86–34–97–00,* FAX *03–86–31–65–47. 25 rooms. Restaurant. AE, DC, MC, V. Closed Dec., Jan.*

$–$$$ ★ ✕🏨 **Les Capucins.** On a peaceful square 10 minutes from the town center, this intimate hotel has rooms in a range of prices. It's better known for its lovely restaurant, however, whose mirrored walls set off the hosts' collection of painted-glass cookie jars, *seaux à biscuits,* dating from the early part of the century. The prix-fixe menus are dominated by regional fare—pike perch, snails and the *oeufs en meurette* (eggs poached in broth and red wine). A garden makes a pleasant spot for breakfast and aperitifs, and there are small, cozy rooms for a postprandial drink. ✉ *6 av. Paul-Doumer (also known as av. de la Gare), 89200,* ☎ *03–86–34–06–52,* FAX *03–86–34–58–47. 8 rooms, 7 with bath. Restaurant. AE, MC, V. Closed Dec.–Jan.*

Parc Naturel Régional du Morvan

33 *Take D944 out of Avallon and then turn left on D10 to Quarré-les-Tombes.*

The vast Parc du Morvan encompasses a 3,500-square-km (1,351-square-mi) chunk of Burgundy. A network of roads and ***Grandes Randonnées*** (GRs, or Long Trails) winds around the park's lush forests, granite outcroppings, photogenic lakes, idyllic farms, and tiny villages. Hiking in the Morvan is not strenuous, but it is enchanting: every turn down a trail provides a new idyllic scene. Numerous itineraries through the park are mapped and marked (maps for specific trails are available from local tourist offices). About fifty 5- to 15-km (3- to 9-mi) routes are good for day hikes; another 10 or so trails of around 110 km (68 mi) each are good for much longer walks.

Quarré-les-Tombes, one of the best little villages peppering the park, is so named because of the empty prehistoric stone tombs discovered eerily arrayed in a ring around its church. Eight kilometers (5 miles) south of Quarré-les-Tombes is the **Rocher de la Pérouse,** a mighty rocky outcrop worth scrambling up for a view of the park and the Cure and Cousin valleys.

Some 25 **gîtes d'étapes** (simple bed-and-breakfasts, also known as *chambres d'hôte*) en route provide for overnight stays (to make reservations, call ☎ 03–86–78–74–93). Twenty-one gîtes have facilities for you and your horse to stay overnight. For the pamphlet "Le Morvan à Cheval," which lists stables and gîtes for overnight accommodations, contact the **Parc Natural Régional du Morvan** (✉ Maison du Parc, St-Brisson, ☎ 03–86–78–79–00, FAX 03–86–78–74–22). Horses can be rented from several stables: **La Ferme des Ruats** (✉ off N6, between St-Émilion and Bussières, ☎ 03–86–33–16–57), **Le Triangle** (✉ Usy, ☎ 03–86–33–32–78), and **La Vieille Diligence** (✉ Rive Droite, Lac des Settons, 58230 Montsauche, ☎ 03–86–84–55–22).

DIJON

314 km (195 mi) southeast of Paris, 100 km (62 mi) east of Avallon.

The wine-mustard center of the world, site of an important university, and studded with medieval art treasures, Dijon—linked to Paris by expressway (A6/A38) and the high-speed TGV (Train à Grande Vitesse)—is the age-old capital of Burgundy. Throughout the Middle Ages, Burgundy was a duchy that led a separate existence from the rest of France, culminating in the rule of the four "Grand Dukes of the West" between 1364 and 1477—Philippe le Hardi (the Bold), Jean Sans Peur (the Fearless), Philippe le Bon (the Good), and the unfortunate Charles le Téméraire (the Foolhardy, whose defeat by French king Louis XI at Nancy spelled the end of Burgundian independence). A number of monuments date from this period, including the Palais des Ducs (Ducal Palace), now largely converted into an art museum. The city has magnificent half-timber houses and *hôtels particuliers,* some rivaling those in Paris. But the most striking ensemble of buildings is its three central churches, built one following the other for three distinct parishes—St-Bénigne, its facade distinguished by Gothic galleries; St-Philibert, Dijon's only Romanesque church (with Merovingian vestiges); and St-Jean, an asymmetrical building now used as a theater.

Dijon's fame and fortune outlasted its dukes, and the city continued to flourish under French rule from the 17th century on. It has remained the major city of Burgundy—it is the only one with more than 150,000 inhabitants. Its site, on the major European north–south trade route and within striking distance of the Swiss and German borders, has helped maintain its economic importance. It's also a cultural center—just a portion of its museums are mentioned below. And many of the gastronomic specialties that originated here are known worldwide, although unfortunately the Dijon traditions have largely passed into legend. They include snails (now, shockingly, mainly imported from the Czech Republic), mustard (the handmade variety is a lost art), and cassis (a blackcurrant liqueur often mixed with white wine—preferably Burgundy Aligoté—to make *kir*, the popular aperitif).

The Historic Center

A Good Walk

Begin at the **Palais des Ducs** ㉞, Dijon's leading testimony to bygone splendor; these days it contains an art museum. Cross to the left side of place de la Libération and take rue des Bons-Enfants, where you'll find the **Musée Magnin** ㉟, with exhibits of furniture and paintings. Continue on to rue Philippe Pot to see the elegant **Chambre des Métiers** ㊱. Just south of here is the **Palais de Justice** ㊲, with its elaborate Baroque facade. Turn onto rue Jean-Baptiste-Liégeard, where the imposing pink-and-yellow limestone Hôtel Legouz de Gerland watches over the street from its distinctive *échauguettes* (faceted towers). Return to rue de la Liberté to get to the church of **St-Michel** ㊳. West of here, behind the palace, is **Notre-Dame** ㊴, one of the city's oldest churches. The rue Verrerie, behind Notre-Dame and the Palais des Ducs, is lined with half-timber houses. Facing the church on rue de la Chouette is the elegant **Hôtel de Vogüé** ㊵. Walk from here to the somewhat plain **Cathédrale St-Bénigne** ㊶. In the former abbey of St-Bénigne is the **Musée Archéologique** ㊷. The former Cistercian convent houses two museums, the **Musée d'Art Sacré** and **Musée de la Vie Bourguignonne** ㊸. Behind the train station is the **Musée d'Histoire Naturelle** ㊹, in the lovely Jardin de l'Arquebuse, the botanical garden. More links with Dijon's medieval past can be found west of the town center, beyond the train station, just off avenue Albert-1er, including the gateway to the celebrated **Chartreuse de Champmol** ㊺, where the spotlight is held by the Claus Sluter masterpiece the *Puits de Moïse* (*Well of Moses*).

Sights to See

㊶ **Cathédrale St-Bénigne.** The chief glory of this comparatively austere cathedral is its atmospheric 11th-century crypt—a forest of pillars surmounted by a rotunda. ✉ *Pl. St-Bénigne.*

㊱ **Chambre des Métiers.** This stately mansion with Gallo-Roman *stelae* incorporated into the walls (a quirky touch) was built in the 19th century. ✉ *Rue Philippe Pot.*

★ ㊺ **Chartreuse de Champmol.** All that remains of this former charterhouse—a half-hour walk from Dijon's center and now surrounded by a psychiatric hospital—are the exuberant 15th-century gateway and the *Puits de Moïse* (*Well of Moses*), one of the greatest—perhaps the greatest—examples of late-Netherlandish sculpture. The well was designed by Flemish master Claus Sluter, who also created several other masterpieces during the late 14th and early 15th centuries, including the tombs of the dukes of Burgundy. If you closely study Sluter's six large sculptures, you will discover the Middle Ages becoming the Renaissance right before your eyes. Representing Moses and five other prophets, they are set on a hexagonal base in the center of a basin and remain the most compellingly realistic figures ever crafted by a medieval sculptor.

Dijon

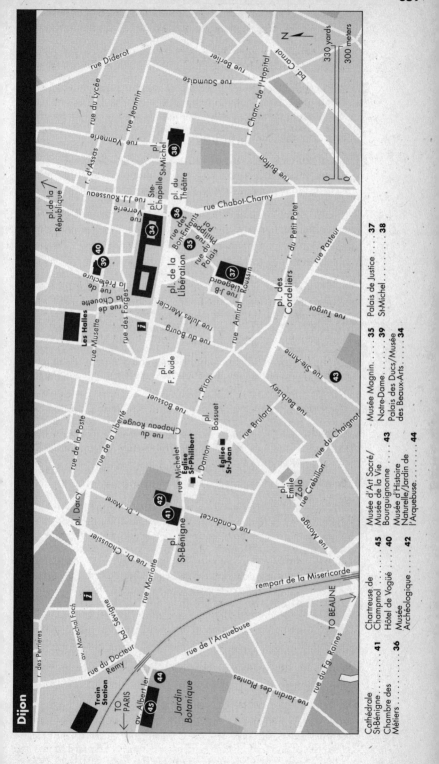

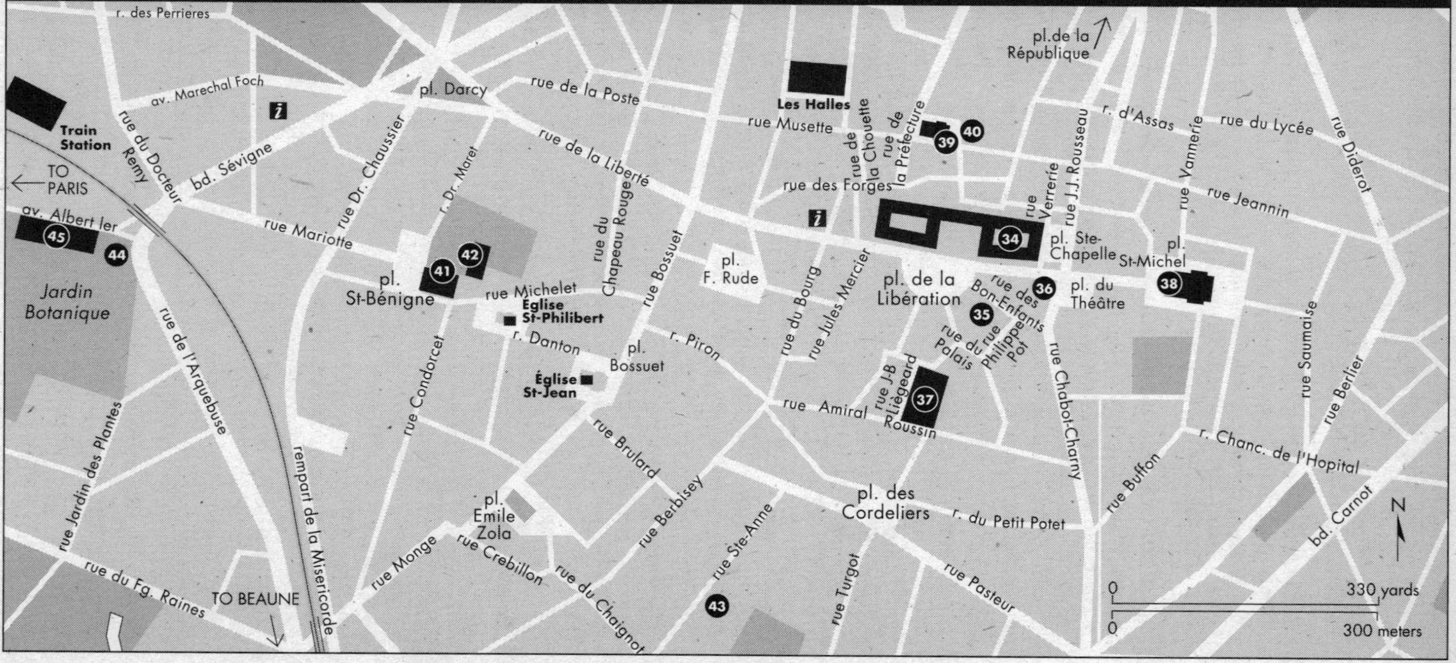

Cathédrale St-Bénigne **41**
Chambre des Métiers **36**
Chartreuse de Champmol **45**
Hôtel de Vogüé **40**
Musée Archéologique **42**
Musée d'Art Sacré/ Musée de la Vie Bourguignonne **43**
Musée d'Histoire Naturelle/Jardin de l'Arquebuse. **44**
Musée Magnin. **35**
Notre-Dame. **39**
Palais des Ducs/Musée des Beaux-Arts **34**
Palais de Justice **37**
St-Michel. **38**

40 **Hôtel de Vogüé.** This stately 17th-century mansion has a characteristic red, yellow, and green Burgundian tile roof—a tradition whose disputed origins lie either with the Crusades and the adoption of Arabic tiles or with Philip the Bold's wife, Marguerite of Flanders. ✉ *Rue de la Chouette.*

42 **Musée Archéologique** (Archaeological Museum). This museum, in the former abbey buildings of the church of St-Bénigne, traces the history of the region through archaeological finds. ✉ *5 rue du Dr-Maret,* ☎ *03–80–30–88–54.* 🎫 *€1.50.* ⏲ *June–Sept., Wed.–Mon. 9:30–6; Oct.–May, Wed.–Mon. 9–noon and 2–6.*

43 **Musée d'Art Sacré and Musée de la Vie Bourguignonne** (Museum of Religious Art and Museum of Burgundian Traditions). In the former Cistercian convent, one museum contains religious art and sculpture; the other has crafts and artifacts from Burgundy, including old storefronts saved from the streets of Dijon that have been reconstituted, Hollywood moviemaking style, to form an imaginary street. ✉ *17 rue Ste-Anne,* ☎ *03–80–30–65–91.* 🎫 *€1.* ⏲ *Wed.–Mon. 9–noon and 2–6.*

44 **Musée d'Histoire Naturelle** (Natural History Museum). The museum is in the impressive botanical garden, the **Jardin de l'Arquebuse,** a pleasant place to stroll amid the wide variety of trees and tropical flowers. ✉ *1 av. Albert-1er,* ☎ *03–80–76–82–76 for museum; 03–80–76–82–84 for garden.* 🎫 *Museum €1.50, garden free.* ⏲ *Museum Wed.–Mon. 9–noon and 2–6; garden daily 7:30–6 (until 8 PM in summer).*

35 **Musée Magnin.** In a 17th-century mansion, this museum showcases a private collection of original furnishings and paintings from the 16th to the 19th centuries. ✉ *4 rue des Bons-Enfants,* ☎ *03–80–67–11–10.* 🎫 *€2.20.* ⏲ *Tues.–Sun. 10–noon and 2–6.*

39 **Notre-Dame.** One of the city's oldest churches, Notre-Dame stands out with its spindlelike towers, delicate arches gracing its facade, and 13th-century stained glass. Note the windows in the north transept tracing the lives of five saints, as well as the 11th-century Byzantine cedar Black Virgin. ✉ *Rue de la Préfecture.*

★ 34 **Palais des Ducs.** The elegant, classical exterior of the former palace can best be admired from the half-moon place de la Libération and the Cour d'Honneur. The **kitchens** (circa 1450), with their six huge fireplaces and (for its time) state-of-the-art aeration funnel in the ceiling, and the 14th-century **chapter house** catch the eye, as does the 15th-century **Salle des Gardes** (Guard Room), with its richly carved and colored tombs and late-14th-century altarpieces. The palace now houses one of France's major art museums, the **Musée des Beaux-Arts** (Fine Arts Museum). Here are displayed the magnificent tombs sculpted by celebrated artist Claus Sluter for dukes Philip the Bold and his son John the Fearless—note their dramatically moving mourners, hidden in shrouds. These are just two of the highlights of a rich collection of medieval objects and Renaissance furniture gathered here as testimony to Marguerite of Flanders, wife of Philip the Bold, who brought to Burgundy not only her dowry, which was the country of Flanders itself, but also a host of distinguished artists—including Rogier van der Weyden, Jan van Eyck, and Claus Sluter. Their artistic legacy can be seen in this collection, as well as at several of Burgundy's other museums and monuments. Among the paintings are works by Italian Old Masters and French 19th-century artists, such as Théodore Géricault and Gustave Courbet, and their realist and Impressionist successors, notably Édouard Manet and Claude Monet. ✉ *Cour de Bar du Palais des États,* ☎ *03–80–74–52–70.* 🎫 *€3.50.* ⏲ *Wed.–Mon. 10–6.*

37 **Palais de Justice.** The meeting place for the old regional Parliament of Burgundy serves as a reminder that Louis XI incorporated the province into France in the late 15th century. ✉ *Rue du Palais.*

38 **St-Michel.** This church, with its chunky Renaissance facade, takes you forward 300 years from when Notre-Dame was built. ✉ *Pl. St-Michel.*

Dining and Lodging

As one of the longtime culinary capitals of France, Dijon has many superb restaurants, with three areas popular for casual dining. One is around place Darcy, a square catering to all tastes and budgets: choose from the bustling Concorde brasserie, the quiet bar of the Hôtel de la Cloche, the underground Caveau de la Porte Guillaume wine-and-snack bar, or—for your sweet tooth—the Pâtisserie Darcy. For a really inexpensive meal, try the cafeteria Le Flunch on boulevard de Brosses (near place Darcy). Two other areas for casual dining in the evening are place Émile Zola and the old market (Les Halles), along rue Bannelier.

$$$$ ✕ **Central Grill Rôtisserie.** This grill room, attached to the Central Ibis Hotel, is a good alternative to the gastronomic sophistication of Dijon and offers a taste of Burgundian food the way it used to be. There are carpaccio and smoked salmon in addition to heavier *abats* (organ meats) dishes. ✉ *3 pl. Grangier,* ☎ *03–80–30–44–00. AE, DC, MC, V. Closed Sun.*

$$$–$$$$ ✕ **Billoux.** A local celebrity, Jean-Pierre Billoux made his name as chef for other establishments, but for the past five years he's owned this bright and beautiful Napoléon III–style restaurant. Billoux's touch can take the lowest farmyard chicken and turn it into an absurdly divine dish. Most house specialties are inventive, the welcome is always convivial, and the wine list reads like a who's who of the region's best—but not necessarily best-known—wine makers. The lunch menu, at €30 (including wine), is a terrific introduction to modern Burgundian cuisine. ✉ *13 pl. de la Libération,* ☎ *03–80–38–05–05. Reservations essential. AE, DC, MC, V. Closed Mon. No dinner Sun.*

$$$–$$$$ ★ ✕ **La Dame d'Aquitaine.** In a happy marriage between two of France's greatest gastronomic regions, chef Monique Saléra, from Pau, and her Dijonnais husband create a wonderful blend of regional cuisines. The foie gras and duck, in confit or with cèpes, come from Saléra's native region; the coq au vin, snails, and *lapin à la moutarde* (rabbit with mustard) from her husband's Burgundy; the *magret de canard aux baies de cassis* (duck breast with cassis berries) is a hybrid. The moderate prix-fixe menus are extremely good value. ✉ *23 pl. Bossuet,* ☎ *03–80–30–45–65. Reservations essential. AE, DC, MC, V. Closed Sun. No lunch Mon.*

$$$–$$$$ ★ ✕ **Toison d'Or.** A collection of superbly restored 16th-century buildings belonging to the Burgundian Company of Wine Tasters forms the backdrop to this pleasant restaurant. It is lavishly furnished but also quaint (candlelight in the evening). The food is good, especially the langoustines with ginger and the nougat-and-honey dessert. After dinner you can visit the small wine museum in the cellar. ✉ *18 rue Ste-Anne,* ☎ *03–80–30–73–52. Reservations essential. Jacket required. AE, DC, MC, V. No dinner Sun.*

$$–$$$ ✕ **Bistrot des Halles.** Of the many restaurants in the area, this one is the best value. Well-prepared dishes range from escargots to boeuf bourguignonne with braised endive. Dine either at the sidewalk tables or inside, where traditional French decor—mirrors and polished wood—predominates. ✉ *8 rue Bannelier,* ☎ *03–80–49–94–15. MC, V. No dinner Sun.*

$$–$$$ ✕ **Thibert.** From starters like oysters in green-apple puree to entrées like perch with blood pudding to desserts such as rice pudding topped with caramelized spices, a dinner here takes two-fisted Burgundian fare and makes it into an elegantly refined affair. The menu changes often at this Art Deco restaurant, while the prices are gentler than you might expect. ✉ *10 pl. Wilson,* ☎ *03–80–67–74–64. Reservations essential. Jacket and tie. MC, V. Closed Sun., early Jan., and Aug. No lunch Mon.*

$ ✕ **Les Moules Zola.** If you love mussels, this is the place. Mussels and only mussels—prepared a half-dozen ways, from traditional *moules marinières* (mussels cooked with white wine) to mussels with Dijon mustard—are served. Large picture windows look over the square, and the ambience is jovial—conversation hums to the music of empty shells clattering into bowls. ✉ *3 pl. Émile-Zola,* ☎ *03–80–58–93–26. Reservations essential. MC, V.*

$$$–$$$$ ✕🏨 **Chapeau Rouge.** A player piano in the bar and an elegant staircase give this hotel a degree of charm that the rooms, though clean and well appointed, lack. The restaurant, renowned as a haven of classic regional cuisine, serves snails cooked in basil and stuffed pigeon. The staff and owner Patrick Lagrange are attentive. ✉ *5 rue Michelet, 21000,* ☎ *03–80–30–28–10,* FAX *03–80–30–33–89. 30 rooms. Restaurant, bar, Internet. AE, DC, MC, V.*

$$$–$$$$ 🏨 **Hôtel Sofitel Dijon–La Cloche.** In use since the 19th century, La Cloche is a successful cross between a luxury chain and a grand hotel. The entry hall is imposing, and the gleaming bar has stylish leather-covered chairs. Rooms are large and plush; try to get one overlooking the tiny, tranquil back garden with its reflecting pool. The garden is also the backdrop for La Rotonde restaurant, but opt for the more relaxed Les Caves de la Cloche, in the cellar, which offers French singalongs with dinner and a choice of Burgundies. ✉ *14 pl. Darcy, 21000,* ☎ *03–80–30–12–32,* FAX *03–80–30–04–15. 53 rooms, 15 suites. 2 restaurants, bar, no-smoking floor, Internet, cable TV, minibars, gym, sauna. AE, DC, MC, V.*

$$ 🏨 **Hôtel Wilson.** This hotel in a 17th-century post house is connected by a walkway to the Thibert restaurant. Rooms are modern and comfortable. ✉ *Pl. Wilson, 21000,* ☎ *03–80–66–82–50,* FAX *03–80–36–41–54. 27 rooms. No air-conditioning, Internet, parking (fee). AE, MC, V.*

$–$$ 🏨 **Central Ibis.** This central old hotel, now part of a national chain, offers comfort in excess of price. Rooms are clean if ordinary. ✉ *3 pl. Grangier, 21000,* ☎ *03–80–30–44–00,* FAX *03–80–30–77–12. 90 rooms. Restaurant, air-conditioning, cable TV, minibars, no-smoking floor, Internet. AE, DC, MC, V.*

$ 🏨 **Le Jacquemart.** In old Dijon, in a neighborhood known for its antiques shops, Le Jacquemart is housed in an 18th-century building with high-ceilinged rooms and warm, rustic furniture. It's a quiet, restful spot and thus very popular, so make sure you book well in advance. ✉ *32 Rue Verrerie, 21000,* ☎ *03–80–60–09–60,* FAX *03–80–60–09–69. 30 rooms, 2 suites. No air-conditioning, Internet, parking (fee). MC, V.*

Nightlife and the Arts

Dijon stages **L'Été Musical** (the Musical Summer), a predominantly classical music festival in June; the tourist office can supply the details. For three days in June the city hosts **Arts in the Streets** (☎ 03–80–65–91–00 for information), an event at which dozens of painters exhibit their works. During the **Bell-Ringing Festival,** in mid-August, St-Bénigne's bells chime and chime. In September Dijon puts on the **Festival International de Folklore.** November in Dijon is the time for the **International Gastronomy Fair.**

L'An Fer (✉ 8 rue Pierre-Marceau, ☎ 03–80–70–03–69) caters to a slightly youngish clientele. **Bahia Brazil** (✉ 39 rue des Godrans, ☎ 03–80–30–90–19), a piano bar, is pleasant for a romantic drink. **L'Endroit** (✉ Centre Dauphine, ☎ 03–80–30–60–63) is a popular Dijon disco. The bar **Le Messire** (✉ 3 rue Jules-Mercier, ☎ 03–80–30–16–40) attracts an older crowd.

Shopping

The auction houses in Dijon are good places to prospect for antiques and works of art. Tempting food items—mustard, snails, and candy (including snail-shape chocolates—escargots de Bourgogne) can easily be found in the pedestrian streets in the heart of Dijon.

En Route A31 connects Dijon to Beaune, 40 km (25 mi) south. But if you prefer a leisurely route through the vineyards, chug along D122, the **route des Grands Crus,** past venerable properties such as Gevrey-Chambertin, Chambolle-Musigny, and Morey-St-Denis, to Clos de Vougeot.

THE WINE COUNTRY

Burgundy—Bourgogne to the French—has given its name to one of the world's great wines. Although many people will allow a preference for Bordeaux, Alsatian, Loire, or Rhône Valley wines, the great French gourmands often confess that the precious red nectars of Burgundy have no rivals, and they treat them with reverence. So for some travelers a trip to Burgundy's Wine Country takes on the feel of a spiritual pilgrimage. East of the Parc du Morvan the low hills and woodland gradually open up, and vineyards, clothing the contour of the land in orderly beauty, even in winter, appear on all sides. The vineyards' steeply banked hills stand in contrast to the region's characteristic gentle slopes. Burgundy's most famous vineyards run south from Dijon through Beaune to Mâcon along what has become known as the Côte d'Or (*or* doesn't mean gold here, but is an abbreviation of *orient,* or east). Here you can go from vineyard to vineyard tasting the various samples (both the powerfully tannic aged reds and the less tannic younger ones). Purists will remind you that you're not supposed to drink them but simply taste them, then spit them into the little buckets discreetly provided. But who wants to be a purist?

Clos de Vougeot

46 *17 km (11 mi) south of Dijon.*

The reason to come to Vougeot is to see its *grange viticole* (wine-making barn) surrounded by its famous vineyard—a symbolic spot for all Burgundy viticulturists. The **Château du Clos de Vougeot** was constructed in the 12th century by Cistercian monks from neighboring Cîteaux—who were in need of wine for mass and also wanted to make a diplomatic offering—and completed during the Renaissance. It's best known as the seat of Burgundy's elite company of wine lovers, the Confrérie des Chevaliers du Tastevin, who gather here in November at the start of an annual three-day festival, Les Trois Glorieuses. Josephine Baker sampled wine here once. You can admire the château's cellars, where ceremonies are held, and ogle the huge 13th-century grape presses, true marvels of medieval engineering. ☎ *03–80–62–86–09.* €*3.* ⏲ *Apr.–Sept., daily 9–6:30; Oct.–Mar., weekdays and Sun. 9–11:30 and 2–5:30, Sat. 9–5.*

Near Clos de Vougeot is the **Abbaye de Cîteaux,** where the austere Cistercian order was founded in 1098 by Robert of Molesmes. The abbey has housed monks for more than 900 years. ✉ *Off D996 (signs point* *the way along a short country road that breaks off from the entry road to Château de Gilly),* ☎ *03–80–62–15–00.* ✉ *€7.* ⏲ *May–Oct., Mon. and Wed.–Sat. 9:15–noon and 1:45–4:45; Sun. after 10:30 mass. Guided tours available.*

Dining and Lodging

$$$–$$$$ ✕🏨 **Château de Gilly.** Considered by some an obligatory stop on their tour of Burgundy's vineyards, this château has almost become too popular for its own good (a conference center on-site doesn't help things). Formerly an abbey and a government-run avant-garde theater, the château does have vestiges worthy of its Relais & Châteaux parentage: painted ceilings, a vaulted crypt-cellar (now the dining room), suits of armor. Guest rooms have magnificent beamed ceilings and lovely views, but standard-issue fabrics, reproduction furniture, and ordinary bathrooms will greatly benefit from planned renovations. The restaurant's menu includes pastries made with Cîteaux's famous handmade cheese and pike perch with a *pain d'épices* (spice bread) crust. "An elegant form of dress" at dinner is requested. There's no need to swim in the moat—a pool was added in 1998. ✉ *Gilly-les-Cîteaux, 21640,* ☎ *03–80–62–89–98,* FAX *03–80–62–82–34. 38 rooms. Restaurant, no air-conditioning, cable TV, Internet, tennis court, pool, meeting room. AE, DC, MC, V. Closed in Feb.*

Nuits-St-Georges

47 *27 km (17 mi) south of Dijon, 20 km (12 mi) north of Beaune, 5 km (3 mi) south of Clos de Vougeot.*

Wine has been made in Nuits-St-Georges since Roman times; its "dry, tonic, and generous qualities" were recommended to Louis XIV for medicinal use. There isn't much to see or do here—it mostly serves as a good stop while visiting the surrounding area.

Dining and Lodging

$–$$ ✕ **Toute Petite Auberge.** Vosne-Romanée, the greatest vine village on the Côte, also entices with one of the most charming restaurants in Burgundy. No surprises on the menu (jambon persillé, coq au vin, crème brûlée, etc.), but everything is excellent and prices are more than reasonable. As you would expect, the wine list is top-notch. ✉ *No. 5, rte. nationale 74 (2 km/1.2 mi north of Nuits-St-George),* ☎ *03–80–61–02–03. Reservations essential. MC, V. Closed Aug. No lunch Mon.*

$ ✕ **Au Bois de Charmois.** Three kilometers (2 miles) out of Nuits-St-Georges, on the way toward Meuilley, is this marvelous little inn serving local fare at great prices—a three-course lunch (sample the huge plate of garlicky frogs' legs) is only €10. An even less-expensive menu is available at lunch on weekdays. It's especially pleasant to sit in the courtyard under the ancient trees, though even on chilly, gray days the small dining room is full of good cheer. ✉ *Rte. de la Serrée,* ☎ *03–80–61–04–79. MC, V. Closed Mon.*

$$$ 🏨 **Domaine Comtesse Michel de Loisy.** Comtesse Christine de Loisy is an institution unto herself in the Nuits-St-Georges area: an internationally traveled, erudite *dame d'un certain âge,* who is also a well-known oenologist and local historian. Rooms in her eclectic *hôtel particulier* are furnished with fine antiques, tapestries, chintz-covered walls, and Oriental carpets, and memorably temper grandeur with old-fashioned charm. Four of the five have a view of the flower-filled courtyard or the magnificent winter garden. The hotel offers an optional two-day program of wine tastings, Burgundy-focused meals, and vineyard excursions. ✉ *B.P. 1, 28 rue Général de Gaulle, 21701,* ☎ *03–80–61–02–72,* FAX *03–80–61–36–14. 5 rooms. No air-conditioning, no room TVs, no minibars. AE, MC, V. Closed mid-Nov.–mid-Mar.*

$ **Albizzia.** The Dufouleur family, Burgundian wine growers since the sixteenth century, run this charming *chambre d'hôte* in the small village of Quincey, just outside Nuits-St-George. Facing the night-lit church in the village square, the B&B is in an old stone farmhouse, entirely renovated, with two very cozy double rooms. Breakfast in summer is served in the beautiful garden, and wine tastings (with local cheeses) are held year-round in the Dufouleur cellar. For those of more sanguine interests, the landlords organize wild boar and deer hunts. ✉ *Place de l'Eglise, 21701 Quincey (4 km/2.5 miles south of Nuits-St-George),* ☎ *03–80– 61–13–23,* FAX *03–80–61–13–23. 2 rooms. No air-conditioning, no room TVs, no minibars. AE, MC, V.*

Beaune

48 *26 km (16 mi) south of Clos de Vougeot, 40 km (25 mi) south of Dijon, 315 km (197 mi) southeast of Paris.*

Beaune is sometimes considered the wine capital of Burgundy because it is at the heart of the region's vineyards, with the Côte de Nuits to the north and the Côte de Beaune to the south. In late November the famous wine auction at the Hospices de Beaune pulls in connoisseurs and the curious from France and abroad. Despite the hordes, Beaune remains one of France's most attractive provincial towns.

★ Some of the region's finest vineyards are owned by the **Hospices de Beaune** (better known to some as the **Hôtel-Dieu**), founded in 1443 as a hospital to provide free care for men who had fought in the Hundred Years' War. A visit to the Hospices (across from the city's tourist office) is one of the highlights of a stay in Beaune; its tiled roofs and Flemish architecture have become icons of Burgundy, and in fact the same glowing colors and intricate patterns are seen throughout the region. Misleadingly appearing to be medieval, the interior was repainted by 19th-century Gothic restorer Viollet-le-Duc. Of special note are the **Grand' Salle,** more than 165 ft long, with the original furniture, a great wooden roof, and the picture-postcard **Cour d'Honneur.** The Hospices carried on its medical activities until 1971—its nurses still wearing their habitlike uniforms—and the hospital's history is retraced in the museum, whose wide-ranging collections contain some weird and wonderful medical instruments from the 15th century. You can also see a collection of tapestries that belonged to the repentant founder of the Hospices, ducal chancellor Nicolas Rolin, who hoped charity would relieve him of his sins—one of which was collecting wives. Outstanding are both the tapestry he had made for Madame Rolin III, with its repeated motif of "my only star," and one relating the legend of St. Eloi and his miraculous restoration of a horse's leg. But the star of the collection is Rogier Van der Weyden's stirringly composed 15th-century Flemish masterpiece *The Last Judgment,* ordered for the hospital by Rolin. A son-et-lumière show is presented every evening from April to mid-November. ✉ *Rue de l'Hôtel-Dieu,* ☎ *03–80–24–45–00.* *€5.* ⏲ *Late Mar.–mid-Nov., daily 9–6:30; mid-Nov.–Mar., daily 9–11:30 and 2–5:30.*

A series of tapestries relating the life of the Virgin hangs in Beaune's main church, the 12th-century **Collégiale Notre-Dame.** ✉ *Just off av. de la République.*

In the candlelighted cellars of the **Marché aux Vins** (Wine Market) you can taste several regional wines. (You can also visit most of the Burgundian vineyards themselves and get free tastings of their wines, which may be more interesting than those available at the Marché aux Vins; of course, they hope that you'll buy a case or two.) Perhaps the best reason to visit the Marché aux Vins is to see the building's Burgundian Romanesque architecture mixed with Gothic additions. Even Viollet-le-Duc left his mark by adding the galleries to the right of the portal. ✉ *Rue Nicolas Rolin,* ☎ *03–80–25–08–20.* *Entry and tasting €8.* ⏲ *Daily 9:30–noon and 2–6.*

For a break and a snack of handmade pain d'épices in all shapes and incarnations, stop by **Mulot and Petitjean** (✉ Pl. Carnot).

Dining and Lodging

$$$–$$$$ ✕ **L'Écusson.** Don't be put off by its unprepossessing exterior: this is a comfortable, friendly, thick-carpeted restaurant with good-value prix-fixe menus. Showcased is chef Jean-Pierre Senelet's sure-footed culinary mastery with dishes like boar terrine with dried apricot and juniper berries, and roast crayfish with curried semolina and ratatouille. ✉ *Pl. Malmédy,* ☎ *03–80–24–03–82. Reservations essential. AE, DC, MC, V. Closed Sun. No lunch Mon.*

$–$$ ✕ **Le Gourmandin.** In the center of Beaune, chef Alain Billard and Isabelle Crotet (daughter of Jean) serve regional fare at their intimate bistro. It's simple, in the style of a 1930s café, with black-and-white tabletops and art posters on the walls. Pork shank and shoulder stewed with beans and cabbage—*potée Bourguignonne*—is a delicious staple, accompanied by a fine list of wines from small vineyards. Le Gourmandin also has rooms from €54 to €69. ✉ *8 pl. Carnot,* ☎ *03–80–24–07–88. MC, V.*

$–$$ ✕ **La Grilladine.** Chef Jean-Marc Jacquel's cuisine, though not elaborate, is good, hearty Burgundy fare: boeuf Bourguignon and oeufs en meurette. The prix-fixe menus are extremely reasonable. Warm and cheerful, the room allures with rose-pink tablecloths, exposed stone walls, and an ancient beam supporting the ceiling. ✉ *17 rue Maufoux,* ☎ *03–80–22–22–36. Reservations essential. MC, V. Closed Mon. and end Nov.–mid-Dec.*

$–$$ ✕ **Ma Cuisine.** Fabienne Parra-Escoffier, the owner of this great little restaurant, was a sommelier before she went into the restaurant business, which explains the restaurant's marvelous wine list; her husband runs a wineshop next door. The menu, chalked up on a board, changes daily depending on what Escoffier finds in the market, but there are always her delicious parsleyed ham, fricasseed chicken, and tuna tartare. Ask for a table in the courtyard for warm-weather dining. ✉ *Passage Ste-Hélène,* ☎ *03–80–22–30–22. Reservations essential. MC, V. Closed weekends and Aug. No lunch Wed.*

$$$$ ★ ✕🏨 **Hostellerie de Levernois.** The Crotets' hotel-restaurant, a Relais & Châteaux property, gleams with light from its large picture windows. The cuisine is still of the highest standard but the stylishly decorated lodgings are looking a just a tad shopworn; those in the modern building in the landscaped garden are more up to date. In the kitchen Jean works with his sons, Christophe and Guillaume, who have a more nouvelle approach. Meals are occasions to be savored, but they are also expensive; menus begin at €53 (€30 at lunch) and may spotlight pigeon with foie gras and truffles or smoked salmon with vine shoots. ✉ *Rte. de Verdun-sur-le-Doubs, 21200 Levernois (3 km/2 mi east of Beaune),* ☎ *03–80–24–73–58,* FAX *03–80–22–78–00. 15 rooms, 1 suite. Restaurant, cable TV, minibars, Internet. AE, DC, MC, V.*

$$$–$$$$ ✕🏨 **Lameloise.** This small, unpretentious hotel on the outskirts of Chagny, south of Beaune, may be the only Relais & Châteaux property to stock crayons for kids. But don't be misled: the clientele is well heeled. Rooms are deluxe, with token rustic touches. Confident and consistent, chef-owner Jacques Lameloise cooks luxurious but not stuffy dishes, such as roast pigeon with minced truffles and snails in garlic-flavored bouillon. ✉ *36 pl. d'Armes, 71150 Chagny (14 km/9 mi south* *of Beaune), ☎ 03–85–87–65–85, FAX 03–85–87–03–57. 16 rooms. Restaurant, cable TV, minibars, Internet. Reservations essential. AE, MC, V. Closed late Dec.–late Jan., Wed., Thurs. lunch in winter.*

$$ ✕ **Central.** A well-run establishment with several modernized rooms, the Central lives up to its name. The stone-walled restaurant is cozy—some might say cramped—and the consistently good cuisine is popular with locals, who come to enjoy oeufs en meurette and coq au vin. Service is efficient, if a little hurried. A rate that includes dinner is obligatory for tour groups in July and August. ✉ *2 rue Victor-Millot, 21200, ☎ 03–80–24–77–24, FAX 03–80–22–30–40. 20 rooms. Restaurant, no air-conditioning in some rooms, cable TV, minibars, parking. MC, V. Closed late Nov.–mid-Dec.*

$$–$$$ **Château de Chorey-les-Beaune.** To really soak up the flavor of the vineyards, stay at the Germain family's winery and B&B north of Beaune. Guest rooms are up a circular stone staircase; furnishings are from the attic. Though it's a bit rustic and casual, it's the kind of place where you can open the windows and let the country air, perfumed by grapes, waft in. A good breakfast is served but no dinner; you may have a chance to try their wine before going out to eat in Beaune. ✉ *21200 Chorey-les-Beaune (1½ km/1 mi north of Beaune), ☎ 03–80–22–06–05, FAX 03–80–24–03–93. 7 rooms. Minibars (each floor), parking (fee) MC, V. Closed Dec.–Apr.*

$$ **Hôtel de la Cloche.** In a 15th-century residence in the heart of town, this hotel has rooms furnished with care by owners Monsieur and Madame Lamy, both of whom are always on hand to assist. The best rooms, those with a full bath, are more expensive; the smaller yet delightful attic rooms, each with a shower and separate toilet, are less. Breakfast is served on the garden terrace in summer. ✉ *40–42 rue Faubourg-Madeleine, 21200, ☎ 03–80–24–66–33, FAX 03–80–24–04–24. 22 rooms. Restaurant, cable TV, minibars, Internet, parking (fee). AE, MC, V. Closed late Dec.–mid-Jan.*

The Arts

In July Beaune celebrates its annual **International Festival of Baroque Music,** which draws big stars of the music world. On the third Sunday in November at the Hospices is Beaune's famous wine festival, **Les Trois Glorieuses.** For both festivals, contact Beaune's Office de Tourisme (✉ 1 rue de l'Hôtel-Dieu, ☎ 03–80–26–21–35, FAX 03–80–25–04–81).

Chalon-sur-Saône

49 *29 km (18 mi) south of Beaune, 127 km (79 mi) north of Lyon.*

Chalon-sur-Saône's medieval heart is close to the bank of the Saône River, around the former Cathédrale St-Vincent (now a parish church), which displays a jumble of styles. This area was reconstructed to have an Old World charm, but the rest of Chalon is a modern, commercial, cosmopolitan city—the cultural and shopping center of southern Burgundy. Chalon is the birthplace of Nicéphore Niepce (1765–1833), whose early experiments, developed further by Jacques Daguerre, qualify him as the father of photography.

The **Musée Nicéphore Niepce,** occupying an 18th-century house overlooking the Saône, retraces the early history of photography and motion pictures with the help of some pioneering equipment. It also includes a selection of contemporary photographic work and a lunar camera used during the U.S. Apollo program. But the star of the museum is the primitive camera used to take the first photographs in 1816. ✉ *28 quai des Messageries, ☎ 03–85–48–41–98. €2, free Wed. Sept.–June, Wed.–Mon. 9:30–11:30 and 2:30–5:30; July–Aug., Wed.–Mon. 10–6.*

Dining and Lodging

$$$–$$$$ ✕ **Moulin de Martorey.** A beautiful restaurant set on the bank of the Orbize River in a converted water mill. The cogs and wheels inside make for a charming note, but when the sun is out you'll want a table on the terrace next to the water. The chef, Jean-Pierre Gillot, excels at elaborate dishes like frogs' legs fricasseed with garlic and nettles, and escargots served three ways: in a red wine sauce, with olives and sun-dried tomatoes, and with wild celery. ✉ *St-Rémy (3 km/2 mi south of Chalon on the N6),* ☎ *03–85–48–12–98. MC, V. Closed Aug. and Mon.–Tues. No dinner Sun.*

$$–$$$ ★ ✕🏨 **Moulin d'Hautrive.** Once a mill built by Cistercian monks in the 12th century, it's now a comfortable hotel in the country. Every room has blackened ancient beams, antiques, and bric-a-brac. The restaurant's four-course, €36 menu may include frogs' legs in cream with basil, and pigeon with semolina and spices. The restaurant is closed Monday and does not serve dinner Sunday. ✉ *Hameau de Chaublanc, 71350 St-Gervais-en-Vallière (24 km/15 mi north of Chalon, 12 km/7 mi south of Beaune),* ☎ *03–85–91–55–56,* FAX *03–85–91–89–65. 22 rooms. Restaurant, cable TV, health club, hot tub, tennis court, pool, sauna. AE, MC, V.*

$$ ✕🏨 **St-Georges.** Close to the train station and town center, this friendly, white-walled hotel is tastefully modernized and has many spacious rooms. Its cozy restaurant is known locally for its efficient service and menus of outstanding value, with such specialties as veal kidney with mustard; it is closed in early August and does not serve lunch Saturday. ✉ *32 av. Jean-Jaurès, 71100,* ☎ *03–85–90–80–50,* FAX *03–85–90–80–55. 48 rooms. Restaurant, cable TV, minibars, cable TV, Internet. AE, DC, MC, V.*

The Arts

For two weeks in July all of Chalon becomes a stage as street theater groups from around the world come to perform in the annual **Chalon in the Streets Festival.**

Tournus

50 *27 km (17 mi) south of Chalon-sur-Saône, 30 km (18 mi) north of Mâcon.*

Tournus, which retains much of the charm of the Middle Ages and the Renaissance and has one of Burgundy's most spectacular and best-preserved Romanesque buildings, has long been overshadowed as a tourist attraction by other medieval Burgundian towns. But it's worth a stop, and it's also a great spot for a picnic, especially along the left bank (*rive gauche*) of the Saône River. The **tourist office** (✉ 2 pl. Carnot, ☎ 03–85–51–13–10) has a map of the town's many *traboules*—its hidden covered walkways—which are fun to explore.

The 17th-century **Hôtel-Dieu** (hospital) reopened in mid-1999 after extensive renovation. Particularly noteworthy is its pharmacy. In one wing is the Musée de Greuze, displaying the work of painter Jean-Baptiste Greuze (1725–1805), a native of Tournus, as well as pieces by other painters past and present, sculpture, and archaeological finds. ✉ *Rue de l'Hôpital,* ☎ *03–85–51–23–50.* 🎫 *€4.* ⏲ *Apr.–Oct., Wed.–Mon. 11–6.*

The abbey church of **St-Philibert,** despite its massiveness—unadorned cylindrical pillars more than 4 ft thick support the nave—is spacious and light. No effort was made to decorate or embellish the interior, whose sole hint of frivolity is the alternating red and white stones in the nave arches. The crypt—with its chapels containing 12th-century frescoes of *Christ in Majesty* and the *Virgin with Child*—and former abbey buildings, including the cloister and magnificent 12th-century refectory, can also be visited. ✉ *Pl. de l'Abbaye.*

Dining and Lodging

$$–$$$$ ★ ✕🏨 **Aux Terrasses.** For an enjoyable meal of the region's products at reasonable prices—such as chef Michel Carrette's fricassee of rabbit with pepper—this is the place. (The restaurant is closed Sunday dinner and Monday.) Many French, German, and Dutch travelers stop here for dinner and a night's rest. Rooms are reasonably large and comfortable, with standard floral decor. ✉ *18 av. du 23-Janvier, 71700,* ☎ *03–85–51–01–74,* FAX *03–85–51–09–99. 18 rooms. Restaurant. MC, V. Closed early Jan.–early Feb.*

$$ ✕🏨 **Le Rempart.** This hotel, originally a 15th-century guardhouse built on the town ramparts, has an elegant foyer and dining room incorporating Romanesque pillars. Rooms are modern, functional, and kept up. Double-glazed windows keep out traffic noise. At the restaurant, prix-fixe dinners begin at €27; the cooking, though competently prepared by chef Daniel Rogie, doesn't live up to its reputation; you may wish to dine elsewhere. ✉ *2–4 av. Gambetta, 71700,* ☎ *03–85–51–10–56,* FAX *03–85–40–77–22. 31 rooms, 6 suites. Restaurant, bar, minibars. AE, DC, MC, V.*

$ ✕🏨 **Le Coq d'Or.** For inexpensive prix-fixe menus, this cheerful hotel-restaurant is the spot, with main courses ranging in price from €9 to €14. The traditional fare is reliable, from onion soup and steak to poulet de Bresse and fruit tarts, and many dishes are cooked on an open-hearth grill. The exposed beams, peach-tone tablecloths, and friendly service add up to coziness. Guest rooms are bare-bones but clean. The best one, No. 8, is at the quiet rear of the building. ✉ *1 rue Pasteur, 71700,* ☎ *03–85–51–35–91. 6 rooms. Restaurant, no air-conditioning, no room TV, no minibars. MC, V.*

En Route The best way to reach Cluny from Tournus is to use picturesque D14. Along the way you pass the fortified hilltop town of **Brancion,** with its old castle and soaring keep, before turning left at Cormatin.

Cluny

51 *36 km (22 mi) southwest of Tournus, 50 km (31 mi) south of Chalon-sur-Saône, 24 km (15 mi) northwest of Mâcon.*

The village of Cluny is legendary for its medieval abbey, once the center of a vast Christian empire and today one of the most towering of medieval ruins. Unfortunately, only one transept of this mammoth church remains standing, thanks to the mobs of the French Revolution—one reason art historians have written themselves into knots tracing the fundamental influence of its architecture in the development of early Gothic style. Founded in the 10th century, the **Ancienne Abbaye** was the largest church in Europe until the 16th century, when Michelangelo built St. Peter's in Rome. Cluny's medieval abbots were as powerful as popes; in 1098 Pope Urban II (himself a Cluniac) assured the head of his old abbey that Cluny was the "light of the world." That assertion, of dubious religious validity, has not stood the test of time—after the Revolution the abbey was sold as national property and much of it used as a stone quarry. Today Cluny stands in ruins, a reminder of the limits of human grandeur. The ruins, however, suggest the size and glory of the abbey at its zenith, and piecing it back together in your mind is part of the attraction.

In order to get a clear sense of what you are looking at, start at the **Porte d'Honneur,** the entrance to the abbey from the village, whose classical architecture is reflected in the pilasters and Corinthian columns of the **Clocher de l'Eau-Bénite** (a majestic bell tower), crowning the only remaining part of the abbey church, the south transept. Between the two are the reconstructed monumental staircase, which led to the portal of the abbey church, and the excavated column bases of the vast narthex. The entire nave is gone. On one side of the transept is a national horse-breeding center (*haras*) founded in 1806 by Napoléon and constructed with materials from the destroyed abbey; on the other is an elegant pavilion built as new monks' lodgings in the 18th century. The gardens in front of it once contained an ancient lime tree (destroyed by a 1982 storm) named after Abélard, the controversial philosopher who sought shelter at the abbey in 1142. Off to the right is the 13th-century *farinier* (flour mill), with its fine oak-and-chestnut roof and collection of exquisite Romanesque capitals from the disappeared choir. The **Musée Ochier,** in the abbatial palace, contains Europe's foremost Romanesque lapidary museum. Vestiges of both the abbey and the village constructed around it are conserved here, as well as part of the Bibliothèque des Moines (Monks' Library). ☎ *03–85–59–12–79,* WEB *http://perso.wanadoo.fr/otcluny.* 🎫 *Abbey and museum, €5; museum only, €2.5.* ⏲ *Abbey and museum Nov.–mid-Feb., daily 10–noon and 2–4; mid-Feb.–Mar., daily 10–noon and 2–5; Apr.–June, daily 9:30–noon and 2–6; July–Aug., daily 9–7; Sept., daily 9–6; Oct., daily 9:30–noon and 2–5.*

The village of Cluny was built to serve the abbey's more practical needs, and several fine Romanesque houses around the rue d'Avril and the rue de la République, including the so-called **Hôtel de la Monnaie** (Abbey Mint; ✉ 6 rue d'Avril, ☎ 03–85–59–25–66) are prime examples of the period's different architectural styles. Parts of the town ramparts, the much-restored 11th-century defensive **Tour des Fromages** (✉ 6 rue Mercière, ☎ 03–85–59–05–34), now home to the tourist office, and several noteworthy medieval churches also remain.

Dining and Lodging

$$–$$$ ✕🏨 **Bourgogne.** Get into Cluny's medieval mood at this old-fashioned hotel dating from 1817, where parts of the abbey used to be. It has a small garden and an atmospheric restaurant with sober pink palette and comfort cuisine, such as *volaille de Bresse au Noilly et morilles* (Bresse chicken with Noilly Prat and morels. The evening meal is mandatory in July and August, and lunch is not served on Tuesday or Wednesday. ✉ *Pl. de l'Abbaye, 71250,* ☎ *03–85–59–00–58,* FAX *03–85–59–03–73. 15 rooms. Restaurant, bar, some air-conditioning. AE, DC, MC, V. Closed mid-Nov.–early Mar.*

$–$$$ ✕🏨 **Hôtel de l'Abbaye.** This modest hotel is a five-minute walk from the center. The three rooms to the right of the dining room are the best value. The restaurant serves rich, hearty local fare that's less elaborate than at the Bourgogne but better; if you're feeling adventurous, try the *pâté en croûte de grenouilles au Bleu de Bresse* (frog and Bresse blue-cheese pie). The prix-fixe menus are very reasonable, and the restaurant is closed Monday and doesn't serve dinner Sunday. ✉ *Av. Charles-de-Gaulle, 71250,* ☎ *03–85–59–11–14,* FAX *03–85–59–09–76. 12 rooms. Restaurant. AE, MC, V. Closed mid-Jan.–mid-Feb.*

The Arts

The ruined abbey of Cluny forms the backdrop of the **Grandes Heures de Cluny** (☎ 03–85–59–05–34 for details), a classical music festival held in August.

BURGUNDY A TO Z

To research prices, get advice from other travelers, and book travel arrangements, visit www.fodors.com.

AIRPORTS

The Dijon Airport serves domestic flights between Paris and Lyon.

➤ AIRPORT INFORMATION: **Dijon Airport** (☎ 03–80–67–67–67).

BIKE & MOPED TRAVEL

Details about recommended bike routes and where to rent bicycles (train stations are a good bet) can be found at most tourist offices. La Peurtantaine arranges bicycle tours of Burgundy.

➤ BIKE TOURS: **La Peurtantaine** (✉ Accueil Morvan Environment, École du Bourg, 71550 Anost, ☎ 03–85–82–77–74).

BUS TRAVEL

Local bus services are extensive; where the biggest private companies, Les Rapides de Bourgogne and TRANSCO, do not venture, the national SNCF routes often do. TRANSCO's No. 44 bus travels through the Côte d'Or wine region, connecting Dijon, Beaune, Vougeot, Nuits St-Georges, and other towns. Les Rapides des Bourgogne connects many towns: Auxerre to Chablis, Avallon to Vézelay, Autun to Beaune and Dijon, and to Chalon-sur-Saône's train station where you can bus over to Cluny. A SNCF route connects Saulieu, Montbard (near Fontenay), Autun, and Avallon. Cars Taboreau have lines that enter the Parc du Morvan. Always inquire at the local tourist office for timetables and ask your hotel concierge for information.

➤ BUS INFORMATION: **Les Rapides des Bourgogne** (✉ 3 rue des Fontenottes, Auxerre, ☎ 03–86–94–95–00). **TRANSCO** (✉ Rue des Perrières, Dijon, ☎ 03–80–42–11–00). For SNCF, see Train Information, *below*.

CAR RENTAL

➤ LOCAL AGENCIES: **Avis** (✉ 5 av. du Maréchal-Foch, Dijon, ☎ 03–80–43–60–76). **Europcar** (✉ 47 rue Guillaume-Tell, Dijon, ☎ 03–80–43–28–44). **Hertz** (✉ 18 bis av. Foch, Dijon, ☎ 03–80–43–55–22).

CAR TRAVEL

Although bus lines do service smaller towns and scenic byways, traveling through Burgundy by car allows you to explore its meandering country roads at leisure. A6 is the main route through the region; A6 heads southeast from Paris through Burgundy, passing Sens, Auxerre, Chablis, Avallon, Saulieu, Beaune, and Mâcon before continuing on to Lyon and the south. A38 provides a quick link between A6 and Dijon; A31 heads down from Dijon to Beaune, a distance of 45 km (27 mi). A38 leads from A6 to Dijon, 290 km (180 mi) southeast of Paris; the trip takes 2½–3½ hours, depending on traffic. If you have more time, take N6 to Sens, just 110 km (68 mi) southeast of Paris; then continue southeast. N6 is a slower, prettier option. Troyes and Dijon are linked via A5 and A31. Other smaller roads lead off the main routes to the little villages.

OUTDOORS & SPORTS

From April to November Air Escargot arranges hot-air balloon rides over the countryside.

➤ HOT-AIR BALLOONING: **Air Escargot** (✉ 71150 Remigny, ☎ 03–85–87–12–30).

TOURS

For general information on tours in Burgundy, contact the regional tourist office, the Comité Régional du Tourisme. Tours of Beaune with a guide and a wine tasting can be arranged in advance through the Beaune tourist office. Gastronomic weekends, including wine tastings, are organized by Bourgogne Tour.

➤ CONTACTS: **Beaune tourist office** (✉ Rue de l'Hôtel-Dieu, ☎ 03–80–26–21–30). **Bourgogne Tour** (✉ 11 rue de la Liberté, 21000 Dijon, ☎ 03–80–30–49–49). **Comité Régional du Tourisme** (✉ B.P. 1602, 21035 Dijon Cedex, ☎ 03–80–50–90–00).

TRAIN TRAVEL

The TGV zips out of Paris (Gare de Lyon) to Dijon (75 minutes), Mâcon (100 minutes), and on to Lyon (two hours). Trains run frequently, though the fastest Paris–Lyon trains do not stop at Dijon or go anywhere near it. Some TGVs stop at Le Creusot, between Chalon and Autun, 90 minutes from Paris. There is also TGV service directly from Roissy Airport to Dijon (1 hour, 50 minutes). Sens is on a mainline route from Paris (45 minutes). The region has two local train routes: one linking Sens, Joigny, Montbard, Dijon, Beaune, Chalon, Tournus, and Mâcon and the other connecting Auxerre, Avallon, Clamecy, Autun, and Nevers. If you want to get to smaller towns or to vineyards, use bus routes or opt for the convenience of renting a car.

➤ TRAIN INFORMATION: **SNCF** (☎ 08–36–35–35–35, WEB www.sncf.com).

TRAVEL AGENCIES

➤ LOCAL AGENT REFERRALS: **Air France** (✉ 29 pl. Darcy, Dijon, ☎ 03–80–42–89–90). **Wagons-Lits** (✉ 8 av. du Maréchal-Foch, Dijon, ☎ 03–80–45–26–26).

VISITOR INFORMATION

Following are principal regional tourist offices, listed by town, as well as addresses of other tourist offices in towns mentioned in this chapter.

➤ TOURIST INFORMATION: **Autun** (✉ 2 av. Charles-de-Gaulle, ☎ 03–85–86–80–38, WEB www.autun.com). **Auxerre** (Principal regional tourist office, ✉ 1 quai de la République, ☎ 03–86–52–06–19, WEB www.burgundy-tourism.com/patrimoine/auxerre.htm). **Avallon** (✉ 4 rue Bocquillot, ☎ 03–86–34–14–19). **Beaune** (✉ Rue de l'Hôtel-Dieu, ☎ 03–80–26–21–30, WEB www.beaune-burgundy.com). **Clamecy** (✉ Rue du Grand-Marché, ☎ 03–86–27–02–51). **Cluny** (✉ 6 rue Mercière, ☎ 03–85–59–05–34, WEB www.perso.wanadoo.fr/otcluny). **Dijon** (principal regional tourist office, ✉ 29 pl. Darcy, close to cathedral, ☎ 03–80–44–11–44, WEB www.ot-dijon.fr). **Mâcon** (Principal regional tourist office, ✉ 1 pl. St-Pierre, ☎ 03–85–21–07–07). **Sens** (✉ Pl. Jean-Jaurès, ☎ 03–86–65–19–49). **Tournus** (✉ 2 pl. Carnot, ☎ 03–85–51–13–10). **Troyes** (✉ 16 bd. Carnot, ☎ 03–25–82–62–70, WEB www.ot-troyes.fr; ✉ Rue Mignard, ☎ 03–25–73–36–88). **Vézelay** (✉ Rue St-Pierre, ☎ 03–86–33–23–69).

10 LYON AND THE ALPS

In this diverse region—where the local chefs rival their cosmopolitan Parisian counterparts—the art of fine dining and other earthly pleasures have been perfected. You can ski in the shadow of Mont Blanc, hike the trails over Alpine slopes, sail across stunningly idyllic Lake Annecy, and enjoy a broad palette of Lyon's cultural offerings. You can visit the Roman sites and medieval towns—reminders of other eras—or take a heady trip along the Beaujolais Wine Road to discover the region's refreshingly unaffected vintages.

Updated by George Semler

Introduction by Nancy Coons

AS THE NOBLE RHÔNE COURSES ITS WAY DOWN from Switzerland, flowing out of Lake Geneva and being nudged west and south by the flanking Jura Mountains and the Alps, it meanders through France at its wholesome best. Here you'll find the pretty towns and fruity purple wines of Beaujolais, the brawny, broad-shouldered cuisine of Lyon, the extraordinary beauty of the Alps, and the friendly wine villages that loom high on the steep hills bordering the Rhône as it wends its long, low roll to the Mediterranean. Deep gorges carve the Ardèche to its west, cutting grooves through a no-man's-land of ragged stone and pine. There is history to be found here, but the kind that treads lightly: the ruins at Vienne mark the region's Gallo-Roman roots with more grace than pomp, while Lyon's gigantic amphitheater and intimate Odéon confirm Roman Lugdunum's 2000 years of bright cultural history.

So relax and dig into the *terroir,* or earth. Strike up a flirtation with saucy Beaujolais, the region's pink-cheeked country lass, blushing voluptuously next to Burgundy, its noble neighbor. The very names of Beaujolais's robust wines conjure up a wildflower bouquet: Fleurie, Chiroubles, Juliénas, St-Amour. Glinting purple against red-checked linens in a Lyonnais *bouchon,* they flatter every delight on the blackboard menu: a salty chew of sausage, a crunch of bacon, a spurt of boudin noir bursting from its casing, a tangle of country greens in a tangy mustard vinaigrette, or a taste of crackling roast chicken.

If you are what you eat, then Lyon itself is real and hearty, as straightforward and unabashedly simple as a *poulet de Bresse.* Yet the refinements of world-class opera, theater, and classical music thrive happily in Lyon's gently patinaed urban milieu, one strangely reminiscent of 1930s Paris—lace curtains in overpainted storefronts, elegant bourgeois town houses, deep-shaded parks, and low-slung bridges lacing back and forth over the broad, lazy Saône and Rhône rivers. Far from the madding immensity of Paris, here you can immerse yourself in what feels, tastes, and smells like the antique France of yore.

When you've had your fill of this, then pack a picnic of victuals to tide yourself over and take to the hills. If you head west, the Gorges de l'Ardèche swallow you up in a craggy world of chasms and stone villages; if you head northeast, you'll ease slowly into the Alps, a world of green-velvet slopes and cold, icy mist, ranging from the modern urban hub of Grenoble to the ethereal crystal lake of Annecy, to the state-of-the-art ski resorts of Chamonix and Megève. The grand finale: awe-inspiring Mont-Blanc, at 15,700 ft Western Europe's tallest peak. End your day's exertions on the piste or the trail with a bottle of gentian-perfumed Suze, repair to your fir-enclosed chalet, and dress down for a hearty mountain-peasant supper of raclette, fondue, or cheesy *ravioles,* all by a crackling fire.

Grouped together in this book solely for geographic convenience, Lyon and the Alps are as alike as chocolate and broccoli. Lyon is fast, congested, and saturated with culture (and smog). Lyon may be the gateway to the Alps, but otherwise the two halves of the region could be on different continents. While in the bustling city, it's hard to believe the pristine Alps are only an hour away from this rich metropolis by train. Likewise, while in a small Alpine village you could almost forget that France has any big, noisy cities at all—much less one of the biggest and noisiest just on the other side of the mountains. Leaving Lyon, few travelers can resist paying a call on the Alps. Everything you imagine when you hear their name—soaring snowcaps, jagged ridges, crystalline lakes—is true. Their major outpost—Grenoble—buzzes with Alpine talk, propelling visitors away from city life and into the great Alpine high.

Pleasures and Pastimes

Dining

Throw out the dieter's notebook and roll up your sleeves—it is time to *eat!* Food lovers celebrate Lyon's cuisine and rank it among the most complete and diverse in the world. At its extreme, this is not dining for the fainthearted. The flavors are strong and cholesterol-heavy, the portions are trenchermen-huge (oddly enough, many of these time-honored dishes were first created by women, one reason so many Lyon dining establishments are nicknamed La Mère). Typical dishes are *sabodet,* a sausage made of pig's head; *gâteau de foie de volaille* (chicken liver pudding); *museau vinaigrette* (pickled beef muzzle); and the daunting *tête de veau* (calf's head). There are also exquisitely light delicacies like *quenelles* (poached fish dumplings, often in sauce Nantua), which appear on tables in restaurants from the most elegant on down. Lyon is most famous for its traditional *bouchons* (taverns), with homey wooden benches, zinc counters, and paper tablecloths, which serve salads, pork products like garlicky *rosette* sausage, and sturdy main courses such as tripe, veal stew, and *andouillette* (chitterling sausage). Also the word for cork, *bouchon* in this case, refers to the handfuls of straw used by grooms to *bouchonner* (rub down) horses after a day's ride. Taverns supplied piles of straw at the door and sold simple fare to horsemen. Unfortunately, the bouchon tradition has led to a host of modern-day fakes, so look for the little plaque at the door showing Gnafron, a Grand Guignol character, raising a glass of the grape, a seal of approval from the town's historical association.

If you're not enthralled by traditional Lyonnais fare (there's only so much pork tripe and pike dumpling you can consume in a day), turn to the full rainbow of Lyon's vast modern and postmodern culinary wealth: butter and creams from the north, Charolais beef to the west, olive oil, and seafood from the Rhône estuary and the Mediterranean to the south, and game and highland delicacies from the Alps to the east. The Dombes is rich in game and fowl; the chicken is famous, especially *poulet de Bresse,* usually cooked with cream. Thrush, partridge, and hare star along the Rhône. Local cheeses include St-Marcellin, Roquefort, Beaufort, Tomme, and goat's-milk Cabecou. Privas has its *marrons glacés* (candied chestnuts), Montélimar its nougats. Alpine rivers and lakes supply abundant pike and trout. In the Alps try a raclette, melted cheese over potatoes. Mountain herbs yield liqueurs and aperitifs such as tangy, dark Suédois; sweet, green Chartreuse; and bittersweet Suze (made from gentian).

CATEGORY	COST*
$$$$	over €38
$$$	€31–€38
$$	€15–€30
$	under €15

**per person for a main course only, including tax (19.6%) and service; note that if a restaurant offers only prix-fixe (set-price) meals, it has been given the price category that reflects the full prix-fixe price.*

Lodging

Hotels, inns, bed-and-breakfasts, *gites d'étapes* (hikers' way stations), and *tables d'hôte* run the gamut from grande luxe to spartanly rustic in this ample region. Many places expect you to have your evening meal there, especially in summer. In winter Alpine travelers are generally free

Lyon and the Alps

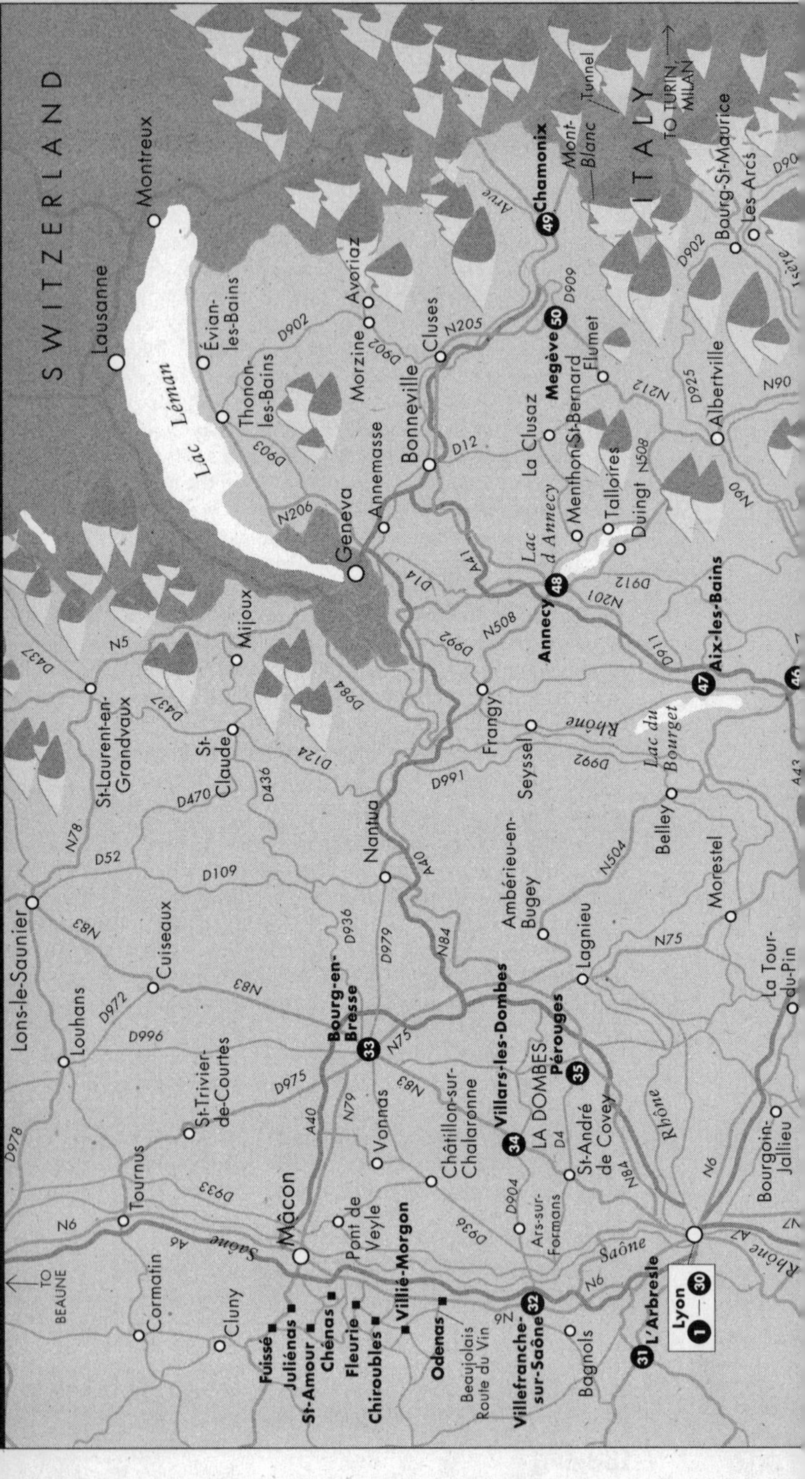

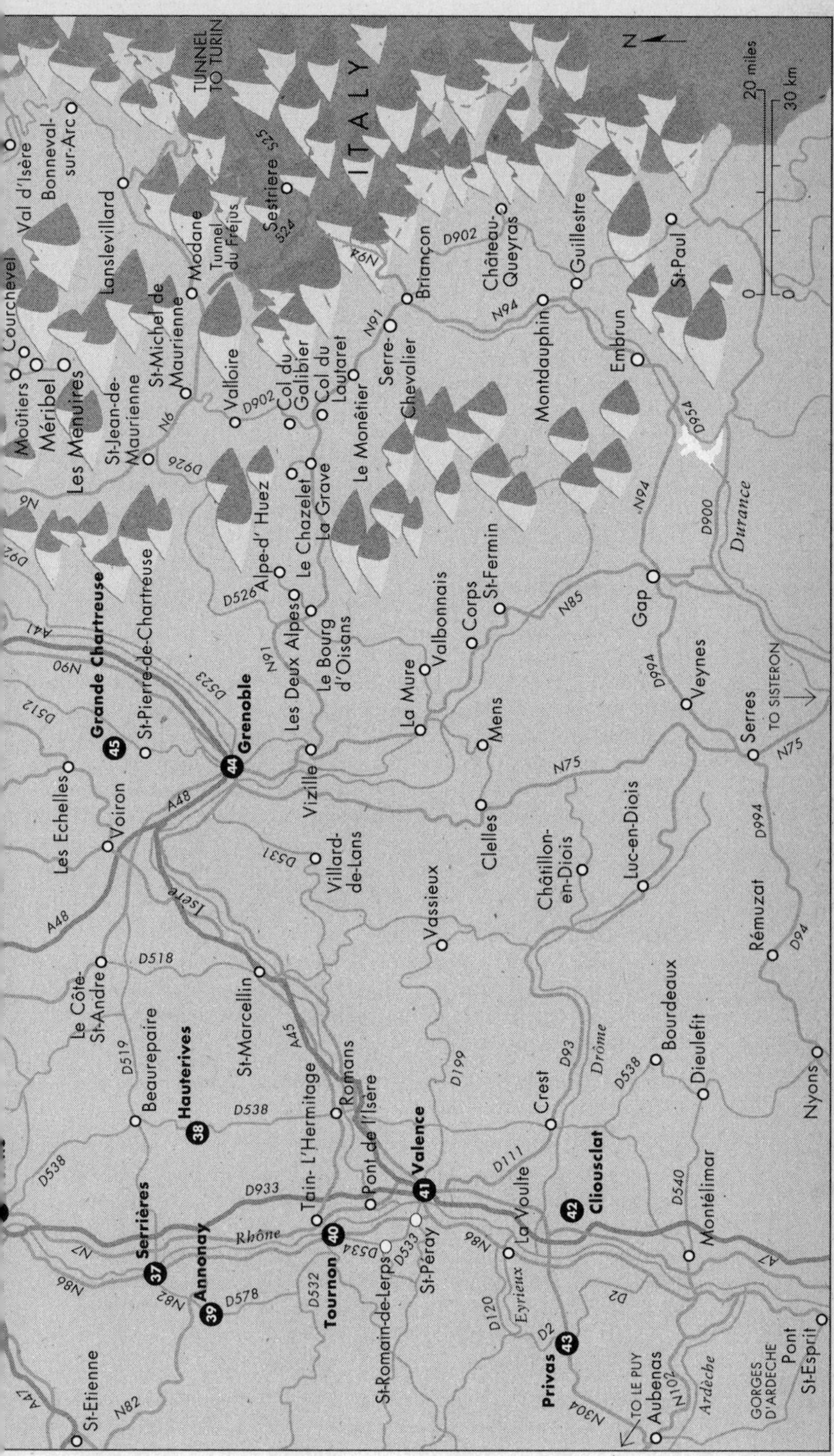

ITALY
TUNNEL TO TURIN
N
0 20 miles
0 30 km
Val d'Isère
Bonneval-sur-Arc
Courchevel
Moûtiers
Méribel
Les Menuires
Lanslevillard
Modane
Tunnel du Fréjus
Sestriere
S25
S24
St-Michel de Maurienne
St-Jean-de-Maurienne
Valloire
Col du Galibier
Col du Lautaret
Le Monêtier
Serre-Chevalier
Briançon
N94
D902
Château-Queyras
Montdauphin
Guillestre
St-Paul
Embrun
D954
N91
N6
D926
Alpe-d' Huez
Le Chazelet
La Grave
D526
Les Deux Alpes
Le Bourg d'Oisans
Valbonnais
Corps
St-Fermin
N85
Gap
D900
Durance
Grande Chartreuse
St-Pierre-de-Chartreuse
A41
N90
D512
D523
Grenoble
Vizille
La Mure
Mens
D994
Veynes
TO SISTERON
Serres
N75
Les Echelles
Voiron
A48
D531
Villard-de-Lans
Clelles
Châtillon-en-Diois
Luc-en-Diois
Vassieux
Isère
Le Côte-St-André
D518
St-Marcellin
Rémuzat
D94
Beaurepaire
D519
Hauterives
D538
A45
Romans
D199
Bourdeaux
Dieulefit
Nyons
Drôme
D93
Crest
Tain-L'Hermitage
Pont de l'Isère
Valence
D933
D111
Cliousclat
D540
Montélimar
Serrières
Annonay
N7
Rhône
Tournon
D534
D533
St-Romain-de-Lerps
St-Péray
La Voulte
N86
D578
N82
D532
D120
Eyrieux
D2
Privas
A7
St-Etienne
A47
N304
TO LE PUY
Aubenas
N102
Ardèche
GORGES D'ARDECHE
Pont St-Esprit
37
38
39
40
41
42
43
44
45

to choose breakfast only, *demi-pension*, with breakfast and dinner, or *pension complète*, with three meals a day. Check on meal plans when booking your reservations. Assume all hotel rooms have air-conditioning, TV, telephones, and private bath unless otherwise noted. Internet, when listed in facilities, means in-room data-ports and/or public-area computers provide on-line access.

CATEGORY	COST*
$$$$	over €123
$$$	€84–€123
$$	€46–€83
$	under €46

All prices are for a standard double room in high season, including tax (19.6%) and service charge.

Skiing

The area's most famous ski venue is Chamonix. Chic, expensive Megève, Courchevel, and fashionable Méribel are also world-class spots. Val d'Isère is one of Europe's poshest. Nearby Tignes and novice-friendly Morzine are also good bets. L'Alpe d'Huez is near Grenoble. The ski season lasts from December through April.

Exploring Lyon and the Alps

East-central France can be divided into two areas: the Alps and "not the Alps." The second area includes Lyon—a magnet for the surrounding region, including the vineyards of Beaujolais—and the area south of Lyon, dominated by the mighty Rhône as it flows toward the Mediterranean. This chapter is divided into four chunks: Lyon, France's "second city"; Beaujolais and La Dombes—where hundreds of wine *caves* alternate with glacier-created lakes and golden towns built of *pierres dorées*, soft, golden-color stones that come from the local hillsides; the Rhône Valley, studded with quaint villages and hilltop castles; and Grenoble and the Alps, where you'll often find down-home friendliness on tap at sky-high ski resorts.

Great Itineraries

As you plan your trip, remember that although you can make good time along the highways, you'll have to slow down on lesser roads and in the Alps. In more rural and mountainous regions avoid making your daily itineraries too ambitious.

Numbers in the text correspond to numbers in the margin and on Lyon and the Alps and Lyon maps.

IF YOU HAVE 3 DAYS

To enjoy some of France's best cooking, best museums, and best theater, concentrate on ☒ **Lyon** ①–㉚, but take a day to head down the Rhône to see the Roman ruins in **Vienne** ㊱. If you're hungry for mountains and the wide open spaces, spend your second two days around the lake in ☒ **Annecy** ㊽ or in the dramatic Alps, using ☒ **Megève** ㊿— where the amusements tend to outpace the skiing—as your base.

IF YOU HAVE 7 DAYS

Stay in ☒ **Lyon** ①–㉚ for at least two days. If you love wine, travel up the Saône Valley, through the villages along the **Beaujolais Wine Road,** and then head to ☒ **Bourg-en-Bresse** ㉝ or medieval ☒ **Pérouges** ㉟ for the third night. On day four make ☒ **Annecy** ㊽, with its medieval Old Town, your destination; be sure to drive around the lake to lovely Talloires; stay in either one. The next day travel along the narrow roads connecting small villages via mountain passes in the Alps. Stop in the fashionable mountain resort town of **Megève** ㊿ before you drive to elegant **Chambéry** ⑯. On day six visit the abbey of **Grande Chartreuse** ⑮; then either go to **Grenoble** ⑭ to see the Grenoble Museum's fabulous collection or zip via the autoroute to **Valence** ⑪ to view its Old Town's cathedral and art museum. On the final day, drive through the spectacular Ardèche Gorge if you are heading for Provence, making a stop in **Privas** ⑬. Or you can return to Lyon via **Vienne** ㊱ to see the Roman sites.

When to Tour Lyon and the Alps

Midsummer can be hot and sticky. The best time of year in Lyon and the Rhône Valley is autumn, when the lakes are still warm, grape harvesting is under way, and many festivals are taking place. Note, however, that many of Lyon's hotels book early for September and October, when delegates attend conventions there. Winter tends to be dreary, though the crystal mist hovering over the Rhône can be beautiful. In the Alps summer is the time to hike, explore isolated villages, and admire the vistas; in winter the focus is snow and skiing. In early spring and late autumn many hotels in the Alps are closed.

LYON

Lyon and Marseille both claim to be France's "second city." In terms of size and industrial importance, Marseille probably grabs that title. But for tourist appeal, Lyon, 462 km (287 mi) southeast of Paris, is the clear winner. Easily accessible by car or by train, Lyon's speed and scale are human in ways that Paris may have lost forever. Lyon has its share of historic buildings and quaint *traboules* (from the Latin *transambulare,* or walk-through), which are the passageways under and through town houses dating from the Renaissance (in Vieux Lyon) and the 19th century (in La Croix Rousse). Originally designed as dry, high-speed shortcuts for silkweavers delivering their wares, these passageways were used by the French Resistance during World War II to elude German street patrols. The city's setting at the confluence of the Saône and the Rhône is a spectacular riverine landscape overlooked from the heights to the west by the imposing Notre-Dame de Fourvière church and from the north by the hilltop neighborhood of La Croix Rousse. And when it comes to dining, you will be spoiled for choice—Lyon has more good restaurants per square mile than any other European city except Paris.

Lyon's development owes much to its riverside site halfway between Paris and the Mediterranean and within striking distance of Switzerland, Italy, and the Alps. Lyonnais are proud that their city has been important for more than 2,000 years: Romans made their Lugdunum (the name means "hill of the crow"), the second largest Roman city after Rome itself, capital of Gaul around 43 BC. The remains of the Roman theater and the Odéon, the Gallo-Roman music hall, are among the most spectacular Roman ruins in the world. In the middle of the city is the Presqu'île, a fingerlike peninsula between the rivers, only half a dozen blocks wide and about 10 km (6 mi) long, where modern Lyon throbs with shops, restaurants, museums, theaters, and a postmodern, Jean Nouvel–designed opera house. West of the Saône is Vieux Lyon (Old Lyon), with its peaceful Renaissance charm and lovely traboules and patios; above it is the old Roman district of Fourvière. To the north is the hilltop Croix Rousse District, where Lyon's silkweavers once operated their looms in lofts designed as workshop dwellings, while across the Rhône to the east is a mix of older residential areas, the famous Halles de Lyon market, and the ultramodern Part-Dieu business and office district with its landmark *gratte-ciel* (skyscraper) beyond.

Basilique de Notre-Dame-de-Fourvière .11
Basilique de Saint-Martin d'Ainay 25
Cathédrale St-Jean 8
Centre d'Histoire de la Resistance et de la Déportation .27
Hôtel Bullioud . .14
Hôtel Paterin .13
Hôtel de Ville . .20
Institut Lumière .28
Jardin Archéologique . .7
Jardin des Chartreux . . .16
Jardin des Plantes 17
Loge du Change .3
Maison des Canuts 18
Maison du Crible 6
Musée des Arts Décoratifs . . .23
Musée des Beaux-Arts . .21
Musée de la Civilisation Gallo-Romaine .10
Musée Historique de Lyon/ Musée de la Marionnette . .4
Musée Historique des Tissus . . .24
Musée Urbain Tony Garnier . .30
Opéra de Lyon 22
Parc de la Tête d'Or . . .29
Place Bellecour .1
Place Carnot .26
Place des Terreaux 19
Rue du Boeuf .5
Rue St-Jean . . .2
St-Paul 15
Théâtres Romains 9
Tour Métallique . .12

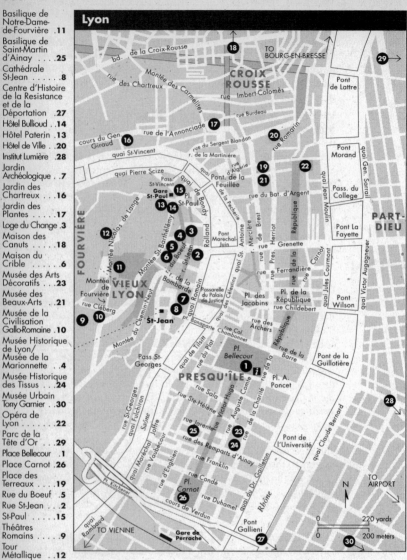

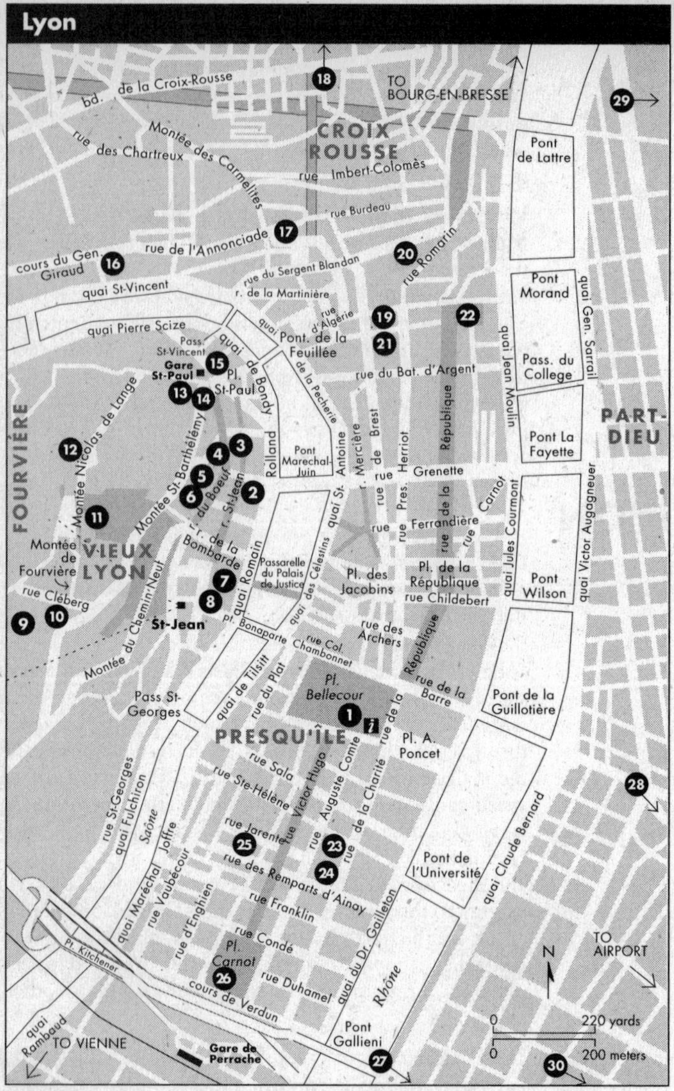

All in all, Lyon is a city of ups and downs: from the Presqu'île to the top of the Croix Rousse or from Vieux Lyon to the top of the Roman Fourvière, from a simple bouchon with checked tablecloths to a stunningly haute-cuisine establishment such as Paul Bocuse (this is where the superstar chef became world famous) or Leon de Lyon. Consider taking advantage of the *Clés de Lyon* (Keys to Lyon), a three-day museum pass costing €14.

Vieux Lyon and Fourvière

Vieux Lyon—one of the richest groups of urban Renaissance dwellings in Europe—has narrow cobblestone streets, 15th- and 16th-century mansions, lovely *traboules* (passageways) and patios, small museums, and the cathedral. When Lyon became an important silkweaving town in the 15th century, Italian merchants and bankers built dozens of Renaissance town houses. Officially catalogued national monuments, the courtyards and passageways are open to the public during the morning. The excellent Renaissance Quarter map of the traboules and courtyards of Vieux Lyon, available at the tourist office and in most hotel lobbies, offers the city's most gratifying exploring (use the silver buttons at the top of entryway door-buzzer panels to give you access). Above Vieux Lyon, in hilly Fourvière, are the remains of two Roman theaters and the Basilique de Notre-Dame, visible from all over the city.

A Good Walk

Start your walk armed with free maps from the Lyon tourist office on Presqu'île's **place Bellecour** ①. Cross the square and head north along lively rue du Président-Herriot; turn left onto place des Jacobins and explore rue Mercière and the small streets off it. Cross the Saône on the Passerelle du Palais de Justice (Palace of Justice Footbridge); now you are in Vieux Lyon. Facing you is the old Palais de Justice. Turn right and then walk 200 yards along quai Romain Rolland to No. 17, where there is a traboule that leads to No. 9 rue des Trois Maries. Take a right to get to small **place de la Baleine.** Exit the square on the left (north) side and go right on historic **rue St-Jean** ②. All along rue St-Jean are traboules and patios leading into lovely courtyards with spiral staircases and mullioned windows. Head up to cobblestoned place du Change; on your left is the **Loge du Change** ③ church. Take rue Soufflot and turn left onto rue de Gadagne. The Hôtel de Gadagne now houses two museums: the **Musée Historique de Lyon** ④, with medieval sculpture and local artifacts, and the Musée de la Marionnette, a puppet museum.

Walk south along **rue du Boeuf** ⑤, parallel to rue St-Jean, with its many traboules, courtyards, and spiral staircases. Just off tiny place du Petit-Collège, at No. 16, is the **Maison du Crible** ⑥, with its pink tower. Cut through the traboule at 31 rue du Boeuf into rue de la Bombarde and go left to get to the **Jardin Archéologique** ⑦, a small garden with two excavated churches. Alongside the gardens is the solid **Cathédrale St-Jean** ⑧, itself an architectural history lesson. The *ficelle* (funicular railway) runs from the cathedral to the top of Colline de Fourvière (Fourvière Hill). Take the Montée de Fourvière to the **Théâtres Romains** ⑨, the well-preserved remnants of two Roman theaters. Overlooking the theaters is the semi-subterranean **Musée de la Civilisation Gallo-Romaine** ⑩, a repository for Roman finds. Continue up the hill and take the first right to the mock-Byzantine **Basilique de Notre-Dame-de-Fourvière** ⑪.

Return to Vieux Lyon via the Montée Nicolas-de-Lange, which are stone stairs at the foot of the metal tower, the **Tour Métallique** ⑫. You will emerge alongside the St-Paul train station. Venture onto rue Juiverie, off place St-Paul, to see two splendid Renaissance mansions, the **Hôtel Paterin** ⑬, at No. 4, and the **Hôtel Bullioud** ⑭, at No. 8. On the northeast side of place St-Paul is the church of **St-Paul** ⑮. Behind the church, cross the river on the Passarelle St-Vincent and take a left on quai St-Vincent; 200 yards along on the right is the **Jardin des Chartreux** ⑯, a small park. Cut through the park up to cours du Général Giraud and then turn right to place Rouville. Rue de l'Annonciade leads from the square to the **Jardin des Plantes** ⑰, the botanical gardens.

TIMING

Spend the morning ambling around Vieux Lyon's traboules and patios. After a trip to the top of the Fourvière hill for a look at the basilica and the Roman ruins, have lunch in one of Vieux Lyon's many bouchons. (There is also a spectacular restaurant overlooking all of Lyon next to the basilica.) In the afternoon explore the Croix Rousse District and its traboules and museums. Note that most museums are closed Monday.

Sights to See

11 **Basilique de Notre-Dame-de-Fourvière.** The pompous late-19th-century basilica, at the top of the ficelle, is—for better or worse—the symbol of Lyon. Its mock-Byzantine architecture and hilltop site make it a close relative of Paris's Sacré-Coeur. Both were built to underline the might of the Roman Catholic Church after the Prussian defeat of France in 1870 gave rise to the birth of the anticlerical Third Republic. The excessive gilt, marble, and mosaics in the interior underscore the Church's wealth, although they masked its lack of political clout at that time. One of the few places in Lyon where you can't see the basilica is the adjacent terrace, whose panorama reveals the city—with the cathedral of St-Jean in the foreground and the glass towers of the reconstructed Part-Dieu business complex glistening behind. For a yet more sweeping view, climb the 287 steps to the basilica observatory. ✉ *Pl. de Fourvière, Fourvière.* 🎫 *Observatory €1.53.* ⏲ *Observatory Easter–Oct., daily 10–noon and 2–6; Nov.–Easter, weekends 2–6. Basilica daily 8–noon and 2–6.*

8 **Cathédrale St-Jean.** Solid and determined—it withstood the sieges of time, revolution, and war—the cathedral's stumpy facade is stuck almost bashfully onto the nave. Although the mishmash inside has its moments—the fabulous 13th-century stained-glass windows in the choir and the varied window tracery and vaulting in the side chapels—the interior lacks drama and harmony. Still, it is an architectural history lesson. The cathedral dates from the 12th century, and the chancel is Romanesque, but construction continued over three centuries. The 14th-century astronomical clock, in the north transept, is a marvel of technology very much worth seeing. It chimes a hymn to St. John on the hour at noon, 2, 3, and 4 as a screeching rooster and other automatons enact the Annunciation. History majors will want to know that in 1600 Henri IV came to Lyon to meet his Italian fiancée, Marie de' Medici, who was on her way from Marseille; he took one look at her, gave her the okay, and they were married immediately in this cathedral. To the right of the Cathédrale St-Jean stands the 12th-century **Manécanterie** (choir school). ✉ *70 rue St-Jean, Vieux Lyon,* ☎ *04–78–92–82–29.*

14 **Hôtel Bullioud.** This Renaissance mansion, close to the Hôtel Paterin, is noted for its courtyard, with an ingenious gallery (1536) built by Philibert Delorme, one of France's earliest and most accomplished exponents of Classical architecture. He also worked on a pair of spectacular châteaux in central France, Fontainebleau and Chenonceau. ✉ *8 rue Juiverie, off pl. St-Paul, Vieux Lyon.*

13 **Hôtel Paterin.** This is a particularly fine example of the type of splendid Renaissance mansion found in the area. ✉ *4 rue Juiverie, off pl. St-Paul, Vieux Lyon.*

7 **Jardin Archéologique** (Archaeological Garden). This garden contains the excavated ruins of two churches that succeeded one another on this spot. The foundations of the churches were unearthed during a time when apartment buildings—constructed here after churches had been destroyed during the Revolution—were being demolished. One arch still remains and forms part of the ornamentation in the garden. ✉ *Entrance on rue de la Bombarde, Vieux Lyon.*

16 **Jardin des Chartreux.** This garden is just one of several small, leafy parks in Lyon. It's a peaceful place to take a break while admiring the splendid view of the river and Fourvière Hill. ✉ *Entrance on quai St-Vincent, Presqu'île.*

⓱ **Jardin des Plantes** (Botanical Garden). In the peaceful, luxurious Botanical Garden are remnants of the once-huge **Amphithéâtre des Trois Gauls** (Three Gauls Amphitheater), built in AD 19. ✉ *Entrance on rue de la Tourette, Vieux Lyon.* ⏲ *Dawn to dusk.*

❸ **Loge du Change.** Originally a center for the moneychanging activities that took place here in the late 15th and 16th centuries, the building was constructed by Simon Gourdet in the mid-16th century and completely redesigned in 1747 by Jean-Baptiste Roche, using plans supplied by his famous colleague Jacques-Germain Soufflot, architect of Paris's Panthéon. After serving as an inn during the French Revolution, the Loge became a Protestant church in 1803, and is now one of Vieux Lyon's prime concert venues. ✉ *Pl. du Change, Vieux Lyon.*

❻ **Maison du Crible.** This 17th-century mansion is one of Lyon's oldest. In the courtyard you can glimpse a charming garden and the original Tour Rose—an elegant pink tower. The higher the tower in those days, the greater the prestige—this one was owned by the tax collector—and it's not so different today. ✉ *16 rue du Boeuf (off pl. du Petit-Collège), Vieux Lyon.* 🎫 *Free.* ⏲ *Daily 10–noon and 2–6.*

❿ **Musée de la Civilisation Gallo-Romaine** (Gallo-Roman Civilization Museum). Since 1933, systematic excavations have unearthed vestiges of Lyon's opulent Roman precursor. The statues, mosaics, vases, coins, and tombstones are excellently displayed in this semisubterranean museum next to the Roman theaters. The large, bronze Table Claudienne is inscribed with part of Emperor Claudius's speech to the Roman Senate in AD 48, conferring senatorial rights on the Roman citizens of Gaul. ✉ *17 rue Clébert, Fourvière,* ☏ *04–72–38–81–90.* 🎫 *€3.* ⏲ *Wed.–Sun. 9:30–noon and 2–6.*

❹ **Musée Historique de Lyon** (Lyon Historical Museum). This museum is housed in the city's largest ensemble of Renaissance buildings, the Hôtel de Gadagne, built between the 14th and 16th centuries. Medieval sculpture, furniture, pottery, paintings, and engravings are on display. Also housed here is the **Musée de la Marionnette** (Puppet Museum), tracing the history of marionettes, beginning with Guignol and Madelon (Lyon's Punch and Judy, created by Laurent Mourguet in 1795). ✉ *1 pl. du Petit-Collège, Vieux Lyon,* ☏ *04–78–42–03–61.* 🎫 *€3.84.* ⏲ *Wed.–Mon. 10:45–6.*

❶ **Place Bellecour.** Shady, imposing place Bellecour is one of the largest squares in France and is Lyon's fashionable center, midway between the Saône and the Rhône. Classical facades erected along its narrower sides in 1800 lend architectural interest. The large, bronze equestrian statue of Louis XIV, installed in 1828, is the work of local sculptor Jean Lemot. On the south side of the square is the **tourist office** (☏ 04–72–77–69–69). ✉ *Presqu'île.*

❺ **Rue du Boeuf.** Like the parallel rue St-Jean, rue du Boeuf has lovely traboules, courtyards, spiral staircases, towers, or facades, all lovely to see. The traboule at No. 31 rue du Boeuf hooks through and out on to rue de la Bombarde. No. 36 has a notable courtyard, although at No. 19 is the standout Maison de l'Outarde d'Or, so named for the Great Bustard, a goose-like gamebird, in the coat of arms over the door. The late-15th-century house and courtyard inside have spiral staircases in the towers, which were built as symbols of wealth and power. The Hotel Tour Rose at No. 22 has, indeed, a beautiful *tour rose* (pink tower) in the inner courtyard. At the corner of place Neuve St-Jean and rue du Boeuf is the famous sign portraying the bull for which rue du Boeuf is named, the work of the Renaissance Italy–trained French sculptor Jean de Bologne. No. 18 contains Antic Wine, the emporium of

English-speaking Georges Dos Santos, "the flying sommelier," who is a wealth of information (throw away this book and just ask Georges). No. 20 conceals one of the rare open-shaft spiral staircases allowing you to see all the way up the core. At No. 16 is the Maison du Crible, and No. 14 has another splendid patio. ✉ *Vieux Lyon.*

❷ **Rue St-Jean.** Once Vieux Lyon's major thoroughfare, this street leads north from place St-Jean to place du Change, where moneychangers operated during medieval trade fairs. Many area streets were named for their shops, still heralded by intricate iron signs. The elegant houses along the street were built for illustrious Lyonnais bankers and Italian silk merchants during the French Renaissance. The traboule at No. 54 leads all the way through to rue du Boeuf No. 27. Beautiful Renaissance courtyards can be visited at No. 50, No. 52, and No. 42. At No. 27 rue St-Jean an especially lovely traboule winds through to No. 6 rue des 3 Maries. No. 28 has a pretty courtyard; No. 24, the Maison Laurencin, has another; Maison Le Viste at No. 21 has a splendid facade. The courtyard at No. 18 merits a close look. The houses at No. 5 place du Gouvernment and No. 7 and No. 1 Rue St-Jean also have facades you won't want to miss. ✉ *Vieux Lyon.*

⓯ **St-Paul.** The 12th-century church of St-Paul is noted for its octagonal lantern, its frieze of animal heads in the chancel, and its Flamboyant Gothic chapel. ✉ *Pl. St-Paul, Vieux Lyon.*

❾ **Théâtres Romains** (Roman Theaters). Two ruined, semicircular Roman-built theaters are tucked into the hillside, just down from the summit of Fourvière. The **Grand Théâtre,** the oldest Roman theater in France, was built in 15 BC to seat 10,000. The smaller **Odéon,** with its geometric flooring, was designed for music and poetry performances. Lyon International Arts Festival performances are held here each September. ✉ *Colline Fourvière, Fourvière.* 🎫 *Free.* ⏲ *Daily 9–dusk.*

⓬ **Tour Métallique** (Metal Tower). Beyond Fourvière Basilica is this skeletal metal tower built in 1893 and now a television transmitter. The stone staircase, the **Montée Nicolas-de-Lange,** at the foot of the tower, is a direct but steep route from the basilica to the St-Paul train station. ✉ *Colline Fourvière, Fourvière.*

Presqu'île and the Croix Rousse District

Presqu'île, the peninsula flanked by the Saône and the Rhône, is Lyon's modern center, with fashionable shops, a trove of restaurants and museums, and squares with fountains and 19th-century buildings. This is the core of Lyon, where you'll be tempted to wander the streets from one riverbank to the other and to explore the entire stretch from the Gare de Perrache railroad station to the place Bellecour and up to place des Terreaux.

The hillside and hilltop district north of place des Terreaux, the Croix Rousse District, is flanked by the Jardins des Plantes on the west and the Rhône on the east. It once resounded to the clanking of looms churning out the silks and other cloth that made Lyon famous. By the 19th century more than 30,000 *canuts* (weavers) worked on looms on the upper floors of the houses. So tightly packed were the buildings that the only way to transport fabrics was through the traboules, which had the additional advantage of protecting the fine cloth in bad weather.

A Good Walk

Armed with a detailed map available from the Lyon Tourist Office, you could spend hours "trabouling" on the Croix Rousse hillside, which is still busy with textile merchants despite the demise of the old-style cottage industry of silk weaving. In the very northern part of the Croix Rousse District you can see old-time looms at the **Maison des Canuts** ⑱. For an impromptu tour of the area, walk along rue Imbert-Colomès. At No. 20, turn right through the traboule that leads to rue des Tables Claudiennes and right again across place Chardonnet. Take the Passage Mermet alongside the church of St-Polycarpe; then turn left onto rue Leynaud. A traboule at No. 32 leads to the Montée St-Sébastien. Here is a transfixing trompe l'oeil on the Mur des Canuts, a large wall painted with depictions of local citizens sitting and walking up a passageway of steps. Exit the Croix Rousse District by taking rue Romarin down to **place des Terreaux** ⑲.

The sizable place des Terreaux has two notable buildings: on the north side is the **Hôtel de Ville** ⑳, the Town Hall; on the south side is the elegant **Musée des Beaux-Arts** ㉑, the art museum. To reach the barrel-vaulted **Opéra de Lyon** ㉒, walk east across place des Terreaux and through the ground floor of the Hôtel de Ville (go around if it's closed). For a culinary delight, detour to the east over the Rhône by walking south along the boulevard de la Republique; at place Regaud turn left and head over the Pont Lafayette for a 2 km (1½ mi) walk to **Les Halles de Lyon,** the city's main produce market—in a city where food is worshipped, this is one of its many temples. Backtrack over the river and check out Lyon's fashionable shops by walking down the pedestrian-only rue de la République and cross place Bellecour. Continue 300 yards farther (now rue de la Charité) to the **Musée des Arts Décoratifs** ㉓, a decorative arts museum. Next door is the **Musée Historique des Tissus** ㉔, a textile museum.

Now cut west across rue des Remparts d'Ainay to the **Basilique de Saint-Martin d'Ainay** ㉕, the abbey church of one of the oldest monasteries in the Lyon region. The lovely, archaic **Voûte d'Ainay** just past the church was the former gateway to the abbey. Just outside to the left is the much filmed and photographed restaurant Comptoir Abel Bar, also known as À La Voûte d'Ainay. Continue south to **place Carnot** ㉖ and the Gare de Perrache railway and subway station.

After crossing the Rhône on Pont Galliéni and going up avenue Berthelot, visit the **Centre d'Histoire de la Résistance et de la Déportation** ㉗, which focuses on Lyon's Resistance movement during World War II. If you're a film buff, head to the **Institut Lumière** ㉘. From the center walk east along avenue Berthelot to avenue Jean-Jaurès; take a right and then a left on grande rue de Guillotière, then another right on rue Premier-Film. To return to Presqu'île, walk west to Pont de la Guillotière.

If you've seen all of Lyon's main cultural sights and want to indulge your children, take the métro from Perrache train station to Masséna and the **Parc de la Tête d'Or** ㉙, which has a small zoo and pony rides. If you're an architecture buff, take the métro from place Bellecour to Monplaisir-Lumière (it's a bit of a long trip) and walk 10 minutes south along rue Antoine to the **Musée Urbain Tony Garnier** ㉚, usually referred to as the Cité de la Création.

TIMING

It will take you at least three hours to explore Presqu'île and the Croix Rousse District. A full day would be even better. The Musée des Beaux-Arts deserves at least two hours, the Musée des Arts Décoratifs and the Musée Historique des Tissus another 45 minutes each. The explorations east of the Rhône might entail another half day. Note that most museums are closed Monday; the Musée des Beaux-Arts is open Monday but closed Tuesday.

Sights to See

25 **Basilique de Saint-Martin d'Ainay.** The abbey church of one Lyon's most ancient monasteries, this fortified church dates back to a 10th-century Benedictine abbey and a 9th-century sanctuary before that. The millenary energy field is palpable around this hulking structure, especially near the back side of the apse where the stained-glass windows glow richly in the twilight. One of the earliest buildings in France to be classified as a national monument, in 1844, it contains murals and frescoes in the interior, disappointingly severe compared to the quirky, rough exterior. ✉ *Place de l'Abbaye d'Ainay, Presqu'île,* ☎ *04–78–72–10–03.* 🎫 *Free.* ⏲ *Daily 9–1, 4-7.*

27 **Centre d'Histoire de la Résistance et de la Déportation** (Museum of the History of the Resistance and the Deportation). During World War II, especially after 1942, Lyon played an important role in the Resistance movement against the German occupation of France. Displays include equipment, such as radios and printing presses, photographs, and exhibits recreating the clandestine lives and heroic efforts of Resistance fighters. ✉ *14 av. Berthelot, Part-Dieu,* ☎ *04–78–72–23–11.* 🎫 *€4.* ⏲ *Wed.–Sun. 9–5:30.*

20 **Hôtel de Ville** (Town Hall). Architects Jules Hardouin-Mansart and Robert de Cotte redesigned the very impressive facade of the Town Hall after a 1674 fire. The rest of the building dates from the early 17th century. ✉ *Pl. des Terreaux, Presqu'île.*

OFF THE BEATEN PATH

LES HALLES DE LYON – For a sensorial feast you won't soon forget, walk over west of the Rhône to Les Halles de Lyon, the city's main produce market, especially on Saturday, Sunday, or a holiday morning when the place crackles with excitement. On the left bank of the Rhône on Part-Dieu's Cours Lafayette, the market offers everything from pristine lettuce to wild mushrooms to poulet de Bresse to caviar, from 150 kinds of cheese at the Alain Martinet stand to the "*Rolls de l'huitre*" (Rolls-Royce of oysters) at Chez Georges. The *salons de dégustation* (tasting rooms) are in fact raging restaurants with a joie de vivre hard to surpass in Lyon or anywhere else. Maison Monestir, le Jardin des Halles, Chez Léon, Au Patio are all good, but Maison Rousseau, with its raised platforms amid the produce for serving oysters and snails with marvelous bread, St-Marcellin cheese, and a white Côtes du Rhône is the best.

28 **Institut Lumière.** On the site where the Lumière brothers invented the first cinematographic apparatus, this museum has daily showings of early films and contemporary movies as well as a permanent exhibit about the Lumières. Researchers can have access to the archives, which contain numerous films, books, periodicals, director and actor information, photo files, posters, and more. ✉ *25 rue Premier-Film, Part-Dieu,* ☎ *04–78–78–18–95.* 🎫 *€4.* ⏲ *Tues.-Fri. 9–12:30 and 2–6, weekends 2–6.*

18 **Maison des Canuts** (Silk Weavers' Museum). Despite the industrialization of silk and textile production, old-time Jacquard looms are still in action at this historical house in the Croix Rousse. The weavers are happy to show children how to operate a miniature loom. ✉ *12 rue d'Ivry, La Croix Rousse,* ☎ *04–78–28–62–04.* 🎫 *€3.* ⏲ *Sept.–July, weekdays 8:30–noon and 2–6:30, Sat. 9–noon and 2–6; Aug., Tues.–Fri. 8:30–noon and 2–6:30, Sat. 9–noon and 2–6.*

★ 23 **Musée des Arts Décoratifs** (Decorative Arts Museum). Housed in an 18th-century mansion, this museum has fine collections of silverware, furniture, objets d'art, porcelain, and tapestries. ✉ *34 rue de la Char-*

ité, Presqu'île, ☎ *04–78–38–42–00.* 🎫 *€6 (joint ticket with the nearby Musée Historique des Tissus).* ⏲ *Tues.–Sun. 10–5:30.*

❷❶ **Musée des Beaux-Arts** (Fine Arts Museum). In the elegant 17th-century Palais St-Pierre, once a Benedictine abbey, this museum has one of France's largest collections of art after that of the Louvre, including Rodin's *Walker,* Byzantine ivories, Etruscan statues, and Egyptian artifacts. Amid Old Master, Impressionist, and modern paintings are works by the tight-knit Lyon School, characterized by exquisitely rendered flowers and overbearing religious sentimentality. Note Louis Janmot's *Poem of the Soul,* immaculately painted visions that are by turns heavenly, hellish, and downright spooky. ✉ *Palais St-Pierre, 20 pl. des Terreaux, Presqu'île,* ☎ *04–72–10–17–40.* 🎫 *€4.* ⏲ *Wed.–Sun. 10:30–6.*

NEED A BREAK? For an adorable perch over the Rhône and a perfect sunset observation point, **Pieds Humides** (✉ 15 Quai Victor Augagneur, Part-Dieu)—literally, "wet feet"—is a nonpareil little kiosk for a coffee, a *pot de vin,* or a passable *plat du jour.*

❷❹ **Musée Historique des Tissus** (Textile History Museum). On display is a fascinating exhibit of intricate carpets, tapestries, and silks, including Asian tapestries from as early as the 4th century, Turkish and Persian carpets from the 16th to the 18th centuries, and 18th-century Lyon silks, so lovingly depicted in many portraits of the time and still the star of many costume exhibits mounted throughout the world today. ✉ *34 rue de la Charité, Presqu'île,* ☎ *04–78–38–42–00.* 🎫 *€6 (joint ticket with Musée des Arts Décoratifs).* ⏲ *Tues.–Sun. 10–5:30.*

❸⓪ **Musée Urbain Tony Garnier** (Tony Garnier Urban Museum). Also known as the Cité de la Création (City of Creation), this project was France's first attempt at low-income housing. Over the years, tenants have tried to bring some art and cheerfulness to their environment: twenty-two giant murals depicting the work of Tony Garnier, the turn-of-the-20th-century Lyon architect, were painted on the walls of these huge housing projects built in 1920 and 1933. Artists from around the world, with the support of UNESCO, have added their vision to the creation of the ideal housing project. To get there, take the métro from place Bellecour to Monplaisir-Lumière and walk 10 minutes south along rue Antoine. ✉ *4, rue Serpollières, Part-Dieu,* ☎ *04–78–75–16–75.* 🎫 *€4.* ⏲ *Daily 2–6.*

❷❷ **Opéra de Lyon.** The barrel-vaulted Lyon Opera, a reincarnation of a moribund 1831 building, was designed by star French architect Jean Nouvel and built in the early '90s. It incorporates a columned exterior, soaring glass vaulting, Neoclassical public spaces, an all-black interior down to and including the bathrooms and toilets, and the latest backstage magic. High above, looking out between the heroic statues lined up along the parapet, is a small restaurant, Les Muses. ✉ *Pl. de la Comédie, Presqu'île,* ☎ *04–72–00–45–00; 04–72–00–45–45 for tickets.*

❷❾ **Parc de la Tête d'Or** (Golden Head Park). On the bank of the Rhône, this 300-acre park has a lake, pony rides, and a small zoo. It's ideal for an afternoon's outing with children. Take the métro from Perrache train station to Masséna. ✉ *Pl. du Général-Leclerc, quai Charles-de-Gaulle, Cité Internationale.* 🎫 *Free.* ⏲ *Dawn–dusk.*

❷❻ **Place Carnot.** Spread out in front of the Perrache train station built in 1857, this bustling square holds an excellent Christmas market from early December through New Year's. The two main monuments represent La République and (the seated figure) the City of Lyon. The

Brasserie Georges, dating from 1836, has hosted legendary personalities from Mistinguet to Jacques Brel and Johnny Halliday. ✉ *Presqu'île.*

19 **Place des Terreaux.** The four majestic horses rearing up from a monumental 19th-century fountain in the middle of this large square are by Frédéric-Auguste Bartholdi, who also sculpted New York Harbor's Statue of Liberty. The 69 fountains embedded in the wide expanse of the square are illuminated by fiber optics at night. The notable buildings on either side are the Hôtel de Ville and the Musée des Beaux-Arts. ✉ *Presqu'île.*

Dining and Lodging

$$$$ ★ ✕ **Léon de Lyon.** Chef Jean-Paul Lacombe's innovative uses of the region's butter, cream, and foie gras put this restaurant at the forefront of the city's gastronomic scene. Dishes such as fillet of veal with celery and leg of lamb with fava beans are memorable; suckling pig comes with foie gras, onions, and a truffle salad. Alcoves and wood paneling in this 19th-century house add charm to the mix. Prix-fixe menus are €91 and €115. ✉ *1 rue Pléney, Presqu'île,* ☎ *04–72–10–11–12. Reservations essential. Jacket required. AE, MC, V. Closed Sun.–Mon. and 1st 3 wks Aug.*

$$$$ ★ ✕ **Les Loges.** With dazzlers like roast wild boar with rosemary raisins and poached red pears or cinnamon chicken with Swiss chard on his bill of fare, it's little wonder their creator, Nicolas Le Bec, was named Gault-Millau Chef of the Year 2002. Vegetables triumph here, so much so that this young Breton chef lists them first on the menu for each entrée. To top it all off, mahogany chairs, modern art, and a giant medieval hearth make for a stunning setting. ✉ *6 rue du Boeuf, Vieux Lyon,* ☎ *04–72–77–44–44. AE, DC, MC, V. Sun., Mon., and Aug 4–26.*

$$$$ ★ ✕ **Paul Bocuse.** Parisians actually jump on the express TGV to dine at this culinary shrine north of Lyon in Collonges-au-Mont-d'Or, then snooze through the return trip to the capital. Whether Bocuse—who kickstarted the "new" French cooking back in the 1970s and became a superstar chef in the process—himself is here or not, the legendary black-truffle soup in pastry crust Bocuse created to honor President Giscard d'Estaing will be. So will the frogs'-leg soup with watercress, the green-bean and artichoke salad with foie gras, or the Bresse chicken cooked *en vessie* (in a bladder). Like the desserts, the grand dining room is done in traditional style. Call ahead if you want to find out whether Bocuse or one of his chefs will be cooking, and book far in advance. ✉ *50 quai de la Plage, Collonges-au-Mont-d'Or, Pont de Collonges Nord,* ☎ *04–72–42–90–90. Reservations essential. Jacket required. AE, DC, MC, V.*

$$–$$$$ ✕ **Pierre Orsi.** Pierre Orsi's lavish restaurant, a pink-stucco wonder, is alongside a tiny tree-lined square. Marble floors, brocade draperies, bronze nudes, and gilt-frame paintings make it glamorously festive. The foie gras ravioli with truffles and the mesclun with goat cheese are hard acts to follow, though the dessert of sliced figs with pistachio ice cream holds its own. ✉ *3 pl. Kléber, Presqu'île,* ☎ *04–78–89–57–68. Reservations essential. Jacket required. AE, MC, V. Closed Sun. except holidays.*

$$–$$$ ✕ **L'Alexandrin.** Chef Alex Alexanian's take on nouvelle cuisine is everything to every mouth. If succulent game is your weakness, this is the place, especially during hunting season. If you're tired of oversaturated Lyonnaise cuisine, try the special *"fruits et légumes"* menu, a creative feast of fresh goodies selected each morning from Les Halles market, around the corner. Whether a dish centers on veal, rabbit, or sole, Alexanian's touch is always light on calories and heavy on fla-

vor. ✉ *83 rue Moncey, Part-Dieu,* ☎ *04–72–61–15–69. MC, V. Closed Sun.–Mon. and July 29–Aug. 20.*

$$ ✕ **Café des Fédérations.** For 80 years this sawdust-strewn café with homey red-checked tablecloths has reigned as one of the city's leading *bouchons* (historic taverns). It may have overextended its stay, however, and is trading on past glory. Readers report a desultory hand in the kitchen, and native Lyonnais seem to head elsewhere. Still, Raymond Fulchiron not only serves deftly prepared local classics like *boudin blanc* (white-meat sausage) but also stops by to chat with you, making you feel at home. ✉ *8 rue du Major-Martin, Presqu'île,* ☎ *04–78–28–26–00. DC, MC, V. Closed weekends and Aug.*

$$ ★ ✕ **L'Etage.** Hidden over Place des Terreaux, this semi-secret upstairs dining room prepares some of Lyon's finest new cuisine. A place at the window (admittedly hard to come by), overlooking the facade of the Beaux Arts academy across the square, is a moment to remember, especially if it's during the December 8th Festival of Lights. ✉ *4 place des Terreaux, Presqu'île,* ☎ *04–78–28–19–59. AE, DC, MC, V. Closed Feb., July 22–Aug. 22, Sun., Mon.*

$$ ✕ **Maison Villemanzy.** A former cook from Léon de Lyon owns this delightful restaurant on the Croix Rousse hills, from which there are outstanding views. The cuisine is a modern, lighter version of Lyonnais fare, though you can still expect veal and chicken cooked in butter and cream to be on the menu. The prix-fixe dinner is a bargain at €18. ✉ *5 Montée St-Sébastien, La Croix Rousse,* ☎ *04–78–39–37–00. MC, V. Closed Sun. and 1st 2 wks in Jan. No lunch Mon.*

$$ ★ ✕ **Les Muses.** High up under the glass vault of the Opéra de Lyon is this small restaurant run by Philippe Chavent. Look out the glass front between statues of the Muses to the Hôtel de Ville. The quality of the nouvelle cuisine makes it hard to choose between the choices offered, but don't pass up the salmon in butter sauce with watercress mousse. ✉ *Opéra de Lyon, Presqu'île,* ☎ *04–72–00–45–58. Reservations essential. AE, MC, V. Closed Sun.*

$$ ✕ **Le Nord.** Should you want to keep some change in your pocket and still sample cooking by Paul Bocuse–trained chefs, lunch at his bistro in downtown Lyon. The specialties here are dishes from the *rotissoire.* Be sure to order the *frîtes* (fries)—they are some of the country's best. The night menu is €18. Incidentally, Bocuse now has another spot that showcases Provençal cooking: **Le Sud,** at 11 place Antonin-Poncet, Presqu'île (☎ 04–72–77–80–00). ✉ *18 rue Neuve, Presqu'île,* ☎ *04–72–10–69–69. AE, DC, MC, V.*

$–$$ ✕ **Anticipation.** Light, creative dishes using the region's famed specialties (such as poulet de Bresse) are carefully prepared here by John Rosiak, a former cook at Georges Blanc. The homey feel makes it a place where you can settle in for an evening of good fare and fun. ✉ *8 rue Chavanne, Presqu'île,* ☎ *04–78–30–91–92. AE, MC, V. Closed Mon. No dinner Sun.*

$–$$ ✕ **Brunet.** Tables are crammed together in this tiny bouchon-tavern where the decor is limited to past menus inscribed on mirrors and a few photographs. The food is good, traditional Lyonnais fare; besides the mandatory andouillette sausage and tripe, there is usually excellent roast pork on the menu. On a busy night expect it to be crowded—but it's all part of the fun. ✉ *23 rue Claudia, Presqu'île,* ☎ *04–78–37–44–31. MC, V. Closed Sun.–Mon. and Aug.*

$–$$ ✕ **Chez Hugon.** This typical bouchon-tavern with red-checked tablecloths is behind the Musée des Beaux-Arts and is one of the city's top-rated insider spots. Practically a club, it's crowded with regulars, who keep busy trading quips with the owner while Madame prepares the best *tablier de sapeur* (tripe marinated in wine and fried in breadcrumbs) in town. Whether you order the hunks of homemade pâté, the stewed chicken in wine vinegar sauce, or the plate of *ris de veau* (sweetbreads), your dinner will add up to good, inexpensive food and plenty of it. ✉ *12 rue Pizay, Presqu'île,* ☎ *04–78–28–10–94. MC, V. Closed weekends and Aug.*

$–$$ ★ ✕ **Comptoir Abel.** This absolutely charming 400-year-old house is one of Lyon's most famous, and most frequently filmed and photographed taverns. Simple wooden tables in wood-paneled dining rooms, quirky art on every wall, heavy-bottomed *pot lyonnais* wine bottles: every detail is lovingly pampered and produced. The *salade Lyonnaise* (green salad with homemade croutons and sautéed bacon, topped with a poached egg) or the *rognons madère* (kidneys in a madeira sauce) are standouts. ✉ *25 rue Guynemer, Presqu'île,* ☎ *04–78–37–46–18. AE, DC, MC, V. Closed Sat., Sun., and Dec. 22–Jan. 2.*

$–$$ ✕ **Le Vivarais.** Robert Duffaud's simple, tidy restaurant is an outstanding culinary value. Don't expect napkins folded into flower shapes—the excitement is on your plate, with dishes like *lièvre royale* (hare rolled and stuffed with foie gras and a hint of truffles). ✉ *1 pl. du Dr-Gailleton, Presqu'île,* ☎ *04–78–37–85–15. Reservations essential. AE, MC, V. Closed Sun. and 1st 2 wks Aug.*

$ ✕ **Brasserie Georges.** This inexpensive brasserie at the south end of rue de la Charité next to the Perrache train station is one of the city's largest and oldest, founded in 1836 but now in a palatial Art Deco building. Meals range from hearty veal stew or sauerkraut and sausage to more refined fare. The kitchen could be better—stick with the great standards, such as *saucisson brioché* (sausage in brioche stuffed with truffled foie gras)—but the ambience is as delicious as it comes. ✉ *30 cours Verdun, Perrache,* ☎ *04–72–56–54–54. AE, DC, MC, V.*

$ ★ ✕ **Café 203/Café 100 Tabac.** These two clever sister bistros near the opera are young, hot, and happening. One is named for the Peugeot 203 (an antique model of which is parked outside), and the other is a play on "100/sans" (100 percent–without) tobacco—yes, you read it here: a smoke-free restaurant in Europe. The Italianate cuisine is fresh and original, fast, inexpensive, and delicious. For a quick pre- or post-opera meal, this is the spot. ✉ *9 rue du Garet and 23 rue de l'Arbre Sec, Presqu'île,* ☎ *04–78–42–24–62. AE, DC, MC, V. Closed Sun., lunch except Sat. from Sept. to Easter.*

$ ✕ **Jura.** The rows of tables, the 1934 mosaic tile floor, and the absence of anything pretty gives this place the feel of a men's club. The mustachioed owner, looking as if he stepped out of the turn-of-the-20th-century prints on the walls, acts gruffly but with a smile, as his wife rushes around. The game and steak dishes are robust, as is the *cassoulet des escargots* (stew of beans, mutton, and snails). For dessert, stick with the fine cheese selection. ✉ *25 rue Tupin, Presqu'île,* ☎ *04–78–42–20–57. MC, V. Closed weekends in summer and Aug. No lunch Sun.–Mon.*

$ ✕ **Les Lyonnais.** This popular brasserie, decorated with photographs of local celebrities, is particularly animated. The simple food—chicken simmered for hours in wine, meat stews, and grilled fish—is served on bare wood tables. A blackboard announces plats du jour, which are less expensive than items on the printed menu. Try the *caille aux petits legumes* (quail with vegetables), for a change from heavier bouchon fare such as *la quenelle* (pike dumpling) or *l'andouillette* (sausage). ✉ *1 rue Tramassac, Vieux Lyon,* ☎ *04–78–37–64–82. MC, V. Closed Aug. and the 1st wk Jan.*

$ ★ ✕ **Mâchonnerie.** The word *mâchon* comes from the morning snack of the silkweaver or *canut,* and has come to mean the typical food of the Lyon region. This is one of Lyon's most respected popular bistros under the *ficelle,* the funicular up to the Fourvière hill. Try the *andouillettes* (sausage). ✉ *36 rue Tramassac, Vieux Lyon,* ☎ *04–78–42–*

24–62. AE, DC, MC, V. Closed Sun. and lunch except Sat. from Sept. to Easter.

$$$$ ★ ✕ 🏨 **La Tour Rose.** Philippe Chavent's silk-swathed Vieux Lyon hotel occupies a Renaissance-period convent set around a gorgeous Florentine-style courtyard under a rose-washed tower. The glass-roofed restaurant occupies a former chapel and offers a fetching view of the hanging garden overhead. Each guest room is named for a famous silk-weaving concern and decorated in its goods; taffetas, plissés, and velvets cover walls, windows, and beds in daring, even startling styles. The signature specials here—smoked-duck soup, skate in oyster coulis, hibiscus sorbet—are well worth all the extra *louis d'or.* ✉ *22 rue du Boeuf, Vieux Lyon, 69005,* ☎ *04–78–37–25–90,* FAX *04–78–42–26–02,* WEB *www.slh.com. 12 rooms. Restaurant, bar, cable TV, minibars, meeting rooms, parking (fee). AE, DC, MC, V.*

$$$$ ★ 🏨 **La Cour des Loges.** Carl XVI Gustaf of Sweden and Juan Carlos of Spain, Celine Dion, and the Rolling Stones have all graced this most eye-popping of Lyon hotels. Spectacularly renovated around a glassed-in Renaissance courtyard, this former Jesuit convent is now an extravaganza of glowing fireplaces, Florentine crystal chandeliers, Baroque credenzas, high beamed ceilings, mullioned windows, guest rooms swathed in Venetian red and antique Lyon silks, suites that are like artist ateliers, and Phillipe Starck bathrooms. The restaurant, **Les Loges,** is one Lyon's most talked-about, since it is run by Nicolas Le Bec, a young Breton who was named Gault-Millau Chef of the Year 2002. In addition, there is a cellar-level wine bar and a tapas bar with a lovely vaulted-ceiling. ✉ *6 rue du Boeuf, Vieux Lyon, 69005,* ☎ *04–72–77–44–44,* FAX *04–72–40–93–61,* WEB *www.courdesloges.com. 52 rooms. Restaurant, bar, tapas bar, cable TV, minibars, pool, health club, sauna, meeting rooms, parking (fee). AE, DC, MC, V.*

$$$$ ★ 🏨 **Villa Florentine.** High above the Old Town, near the Roman theaters and the basilica, this pristine hotel was once a 17th-century convent—and everyone knows the sisters always enjoyed the best real estate in town. It has beamed and vaulted ceilings, terraces, and particularly marvelous views, which are seen to best advantage from the pool and the excellent restaurant, Les Terrasses de Lyon. In time-warp fashion, 17th-century Italianate architectural details are contrasted with the latest in bright postmodern Italian furnishings. ✉ *25–27 Montée St-Barthélémy, Fourvière, 69005,* ☎ *04–72–56–56–56,* FAX *04–72–40–90–56,* WEB *www.villaflorentine.com. 11 rooms, 8 suites. Restaurant, bar, outdoor café, cable TV, minibars, Internet, meeting rooms, pool, parking (fee). AE, DC, MC, V.*

$$$–$$$$ 🏨 **Grand Hôtel Concorde.** This Belle Epoque hotel off place de la République has a courteous and efficient staff. Rooms have high ceilings, mostly modern furnishings, and one special piece such as an armoire or writing desk. Erté prints try hard to set a stylish tone in the guest rooms, the Rhône is just across the street, and tour group bookings are kept happy and contented. ✉ *11 rue Grôlée, Presqu'île, 69002,* ☎ *04–72–40–45–45,* FAX *04–78–37–52–55,* WEB *www.grand-hotel-concorde.com. 140 rooms. Restaurant, bar, cable TV, meeting rooms, no smoking areas, parking (fee). AE, DC, MC, V.*

$$$–$$$$ 🏨 **Grand Hôtel Mercure Saxe-Lafayette.** There are times when a good chain hotel is needed: this one, part of the Mercure line, has super king-size beds, large bathrooms and towels, reassuring uniformity, and an English-speaking staff. It's in Part-Dieu, the business section of town, not far from the train station (a shuttle is available), though this makes it a little less convenient for shopping or hanging out in Vieux Lyon. There are any number of facilities here, but this place may have seen one too many tired businessmen for its own good. ✉ *29 rue de Bon-*

nel, Part-Dieu, 69003, ☎ *04–72–61–90–90,* FAX *04–72–61–17–54,* WEB *www.mercure.com. 156 rooms. Restaurant, bar, cable TV, minibars, Internet, health club, parking (fee). AE, DC, MC, V.*

$$–$$$ **Globe et Cecil.** This impeccably bright and clean hotel tucked in just one block north of Place Bellecour is in the very heart of Lyon. The rooms are as cheery and fresh as the lobby; the staff is effervescent and pleasant, and the cost-value ratio is a definite boon to the soul (and wallet/purse). What this place may lack in time-varnished charm it compensates for with crisp, polite efficiency and comfort. ✉ *21 rue Gasparin, Presqu'île, 69002,* ☎ *04–78–42–58–95,* FAX *04–72–41–99–06,* WEB *www.globeetcecilhotel.com. 60 rooms. Bar, cable TV, parking (fee). AE, DC, MC, V.*

$$–$$$ **Grand Hôtel des Beaux-Arts.** Half the rooms at this hotel are termed "inspired worlds," where an artist has developed a decorating theme through his paintings, some of which are on display in the room. In Room 309, for instance, the paintings of Carmelo Zagari are used to lead you into the world of the theater. Should you want a more conventional sleeping environment, other rooms are traditionally furnished. A buffet breakfast is served. ✉ *Rue du Président Édouard-Herriot, pl. des Jacobins, Presqu'île, 69002,* ☎ *04–78–38–09–50,* FAX *04–78–42–19–19,* WEB *www.grandhotelbeauxarts.com. 75 rooms. Bar, cable TV, minibars, parking (fee). AE, DC, MC, V.*

$$ **Hôtel des Artistes.** This intimate hotel on an elegant square opposite the Théâtre des Célestins has long been popular among stage and screen artists; black-and-white photographs of actors and actresses adorn lobby walls. Rooms are smallish but modern and comfortable, and the friendly reception and great location appeal to all comers. ✉ *8 rue Gaspard-André, Presqu'île, 69002,* ☎ *04–78–42–04–88,* FAX *04–78–42–93–76. 45 rooms. No air-conditioning, minibars. AE, DC, MC, V.*

$ **Hôtel Bayard.** Rooms at this hotel in the heart of town each have a distinctive look. One favorite, No. 2, overlooks the large square and has a canopy bed. For a group, opt for No. 15, which sleeps four. Only breakfast is served, but there are dozens of restaurants nearby. ✉ *23 pl. Bellecour, Presqu'île, 69002,* ☎ *04–78–37–39–64,* FAX *04–72–40–95–51,* WEB *www.hotelbayard.com. 22 rooms. Bar, no air-conditioning, cable TV, parking (fee). MC, V.*

$ **Hôtel du Théâtre.** The friendly and enthusiastic owner is sufficient enough reason to recommend this small hotel. But its location and reasonable prices make it even more commendable. Rooms are simple but clean; those overlooking place des Célestins not only have a theatrical view but also a bathroom with a tub. Those facing the side have a shower only. Breakfast is included. ✉ *10 rue de Savoie, Presqu'île, 69002,* ☎ *04–78–42–33–32,* FAX *04–72–40–00–61. 21 rooms. Bar, no air-conditioning, parking (fee). MC, V.*

Nightlife and the Arts

Lyon is the region's liveliest arts center; check the weekly *Lyon-Poche*, published on Wednesday and sold at newsstands, for cultural events and goings-on at the dozens of discos, bars, and clubs.

For darts and pints and jazz on weekends, head to the **Albion Public House** (✉ 12 rue Ste-Catherine, Presqu'île, ☎ 04–78–28–33–00), where they even accept British pounds. The low-key, chic **L'Alibi** (✉ 13 quai Romain-Roland, Vieux Lyon, ☎ 04–78–42–04–66) has a laser show along with the music. **Bar Live** (✉ 13 pl. Jules Ferry, Vieux Lyon, ☎ 04–72–74–04–41) is in the old Brotteaux train station and is the current drinking haunt. Romantics rendezvous at the **Bar de la Tour Rose** (✉ 22 rue du Boeuf, Vieux Lyon, ☎ 04–78–37–25–90).

Bouchon aux Vin (✉ 64 rue Mercière, Presqu'île, ☎ 04–78–42–88–90) is a wine bar with 30-plus vintages. Computer jocks head into cyberspace at **Le Chantier** (✉ 18–20 rue Ste-Catherine, Presqu'île, ☎ 04–78–39–05–56), while their friends listen to jazz and nibble on tapas. Caribbean and African music pulses at **Le Club des Iles** (✉ 1 Grande-Rue des Feuillants, Presqu'île, ☎ 04–78–39–16–35). Live jazz is played in the stone-vaulted basement of **Hot Club** (✉ 26 rue Lanterne, Presqu'île, ☎ 04–78–39–54–74). A gay crowd is found among the 1930s blandishments at **La Ruche** (✉ 22 rue Gentil, Presqu'île, ☎ 04–78–39–03–82). **Villa Florentine** (✉ 25 Montée St-Barthélémy, Fourvière, ☎ 04–72–56–56–56) is a quiet spot for sipping a drink to the strains of a harpist, who plays on Friday and Saturday. **La Cave des Voyageurs** (✉ 7 pl. St-Paul–St-Barthélémy, Vieux Lyon, ☎ 04–78–28–92–28) just below the St-Paul train station is a cozy place to try some top wines.

Café-Théâtre de L'Accessoire (✉ 26 rue de l'Annonciade, Presqu'île, ☎ 04–78–27–84–84) is a leading café-theater where you can eat and drink while watching a review. **Le Complexe du Rire** (✉ 7 rue des Capucins, Presqu'île, ☎ 04–78–27–23–59) is a lively satirical and comic review above Place des Terreaux. The café-theater **Espace Gerson** (✉ 1 pl. Gerson, Vieux Lyon, ☎ 04–78–27–96–99) presents revues in conjunction with dinner. The **Opéra de Lyon** (✉ 1 pl. de la Comédie, Presqu'île, ☎ 04–72–00–45–45) presents plays, concerts, ballets, and opera from October to June. Lyon's Société de Musique de Chambre performs at **Salle Molière** (✉ 18 quai Bondy, Vieux Lyon, ☎ 04–78–28–03–11).

Early fall sees the renowned **Biennale de la Danse** (Dance Biennial), which occurs in even years. September is the time for the **Foire aux Tupiniers** (☎ 04–78–37–00–68), a pottery fair. October brings the **Festival Bach** (☎ 04–78–72–75–31). The **Biennale d'Art Contemporain** (Contemporary Art Biennial; ☎ 04–78–30–50–66) is held in odd years in October. The **Festival du Vieux Lyon** (☎ 04–78–42–39–04) is a music festival in November and December. On December 8, the Fête de La Immaculée Conception (Feast of the Immaculate Conception), startling lighting creations transform the city into a fantasy for the marvelous **Fête de Lumière,** Lyon's Festival of Lights.

Shopping

Lyon has the region's best shopping; it is still the nation's silk-and-textile capital, and all big-name designers have shops here. For chic clothing try the stores on rue du Président Édouard-Herriot and rue de la République in the center of town. Lyon's biggest shopping mall is the **Part-Dieu Shopping Center** (✉ Rue du Dr-Bouchut, Part-Dieu, ☎ 04–72–60–60–62), where there are 14 movie theaters and 250 shops. France's major department stores are well represented in Lyon. **Galeries Lafayette** (✉ in Part-Dieu Shopping Center, Part-Dieu, ☎ 04–72–61–44–44; ✉ 6 pl. des Cordeliers, Presqu'île, ☎ 04–72–40–48–00; ✉ 200 bd. Pinel, Villeurbanne, ☎ 04–78–77–82–12) has always brought Parisian flair to its outlying branches. **Printemps** (✉ 42 rue de la République, Presqu'île, ☎ 04–72–41–29–29) is the Lyon outpost of the big Paris store.

Captiva (✉ 10 rue de la Charité, Perrache, ☎ 04–78–37–96–15) is the boutique of a young designer who works mainly in silk. **Les Gones** (✉ 33 rue Leynaud, Croix Rousse, ☎ 04–78–28–40–78), in the Croix Rousse, is a boutique carrying the work of several young designers. The workshop of **Monsieur Georges Mattelon** (✉ Rue d'Ivry, Presqu'île, ☎ 04–78–28–62–04) is one of the oldest silk-weaving shops in Lyon. Lyonnais designer **Clémentine** (✉ 18 rue Émile-Zola, Presqu'île) is good for well-cut, tailored clothing. **Étincelle** (✉ 34 rue St-Jean, Vieux Lyon) has trendy outfits for youngsters.

For antiques, wander down **rue Auguste-Comte** (from place Bellecour to Perrache). **Image en Cours** (✉ 26 rue du Boeuf, Vieux Lyon) sells superb engravings. **La Maison des Canuts** (✉ 10–12 rue d'Ivry, Croix Rousse) carries local textiles. Fabrics can be also found at the **Boutique des Soyeux Lyonnais** (✉ 3 rue du Boeuf, Vieux Lyon).

For arts and crafts there are several places where you can find irresistible objects. Look for Lyonnais puppets on **place du Change**—or try the **Marché des Artistes** (Artists' Market; ✉ Quai Romain-Rolland, 5e, Vieux Lyon), every Sunday morning from 7 to 1. Also held on Sunday morning is the **Marché des Artisans** (Crafts Market; ✉ Quai Fulchiron, 5e, Vieux Lyon). A **Marché des Puces** (Flea Market; ✉ 1 rue du Canal in Villeurbanne; take Bus 37, Villeurbanne) takes place on Thursday and Saturday mornings 8–noon and on Sunday 6–1. For **secondhand books** try the market along quai de la Pêcherie (2e) near place Bellecour, held every Saturday and Sunday 10–6.

Food markets are held from Tuesday through Sunday on boulevard de la Croix-Rousse (4^{e}), at Les Halles on cours Lafayette (3^{e}), on quai Victor Augagneur (3^{e}), and on quai St-Antoine (2^{e}). For up-to-the-minute information on food, restaurants, and great wines, don't miss the (English speaking) "flying sommelier," Georges Dos Santos at **Antic Wine** (✉ 18 rue du Boeuf, Vieux Lyon, ☎ 04–78–37–08–96). A wine shop with an excellent selection is **À Ma Vigne** (✉ 18 rue Vaubecour, Presqu'île, ☎ 04–78–37–05–29). **La Compagnie Beaujolaise 3è Fleuve** (✉ 7 rue Colonel Chambonnet, Presqu'île, ☎ 04–78–42–70–96) offers excellent *3ème fleuve* (Lyon's third river: Beaujolais) products, from wines to pots lyonnais to olive oils. **Cave de la Côte** (✉ 5 rue Pleney, Presqu'île, ☎ 04–78–42–93–20) also has good wines. For chocolates head to **Bernachon** (✉ 42 cours Franklin-Roosevelt, Les Brotteaux); some say it is the best *chocolaterie* in France. **La Boîte à Dessert** (✉ 1 rue de l'Ancienne-Préfecture, Presqu'île) makes luscious peach turnovers. For culinary variety, shop **Les Halles** (✉ 102 cours Lafayette, Part-Dieu). **Pignol** (✉ 17 rue Émile-Zola, Presqu'île) is good for meats and sandwich-makings. **Reynon** (✉ 13 rue des Archers, Presqu'île) is the place for charcuterie. For fragrances, photos, furniture, philosophy, and comprehensive Oriental tea culture, **Cha Yuan** (✉ 7–9 rue des Remparts d'Ainay, Presqu'île) is the best boutique in Lyon.

BEAUJOLAIS AND LA DOMBES

North of Lyon along the Saône are the vineyards of Beaujolais, a thrill for any oenophile. In the area around Villefranche, small villages—perhaps comprising a church, a bar, and a boulangerie—pop up here and there out of the rolling vine-covered hillsides. Lyon's tourist office has a decent map of the Beaujolais region; even better is the "Vignobles de Beaujolais" map, available in Villefranche's tourist office. Beaujolais wine is made exclusively from the *gamay noir à jus blanc* grape. The region's best wines are all labeled "Grand Cru," a more complex version of the otherwise light, fruity Beaujolais. For the price of one bottle, you can spend an afternoon getting a wealth of knowledge (and a little buzz) by visiting one of the village *caves* (cellars where wine is made, stored, and sold), from big-time tourist operators to mom-and-pop stops. Make sure the ones you pick have DÉGUSTATION signs out front. Signs that say VENTE EN DIRECT (sold directly from the property) and VENTE AU DÉTAIL (sold by the bottle) are also good indicators.

East of the Saône is the fertile land of La Dombes, where ornithologists flock to see migratory bird life. North of La Dombes and east of the Beaujolais wine villages is Bourg-en-Bresse, famous for its marvelous church and a breed of poultry that delights gourmands; it makes a good base after Lyon. South toward the Rhône, the great river of southern France, is the well-preserved medieval village of Pérouges.

L'Arbresle

31 *16 km (10 mi) northwest of Lyon.*

If you love modern architecture, don't miss Éveux, outside L'Arbresle. Here the stark, blocky Dominican convent of **Ste-Marie de la Tourette** protrudes over the hillside, resting on slender pillars that look like stilts and revealing the minimalist sensibilities of architect Le Corbusier, who designed it in 1957–59. ☎ *04–74–01–01–03.* €5. *July–Aug., daily 9–noon and 2–6; Sept.–June, weekends 2–6.*

Villefranche-sur-Saône

32 *6 km (4 mi) east of Ars-sur-Formans, 31 km (19 mi) north of Lyon.*

The lively industrial town of Villefranche-sur-Saône is the capital of the Beaujolais region and is known for its *vin nouveau* (new wine). Thanks to marketing hype, this youthful, fruity red wine is eagerly gulped down around the world every year on the third Thursday of November.

Dining and Lodging

$$ ✕ **Juliénas.** This simple little restaurant delivers what other, pricier restaurants in town don't, won't, or can't: bistro fare that does honor to traditional Beaujolais cookery. All the all-stars are here: andouillette, hot sausage, pork with tarragon, and, for dessert, a luscious île flottante. The €17 prix-fixe menu, served lunch and dinner, is one of the best deals in the region. ✉ *236 rue d'Anse,* ☎ *04–74–09–16–55. AE, MC, V. Closed Mon. No dinner Sun.*

$$$$ ★ ✕ **Château de Bagnols.** This intimate and exquisite 13th-century castle southwest of Villefranche is filled with period glassware, fabrics, and porcelain to go with the antique furniture. The 17th- and 18th-century murals were inspired by Lyon's textile industry. Rooms are huge, as are the baronial bathrooms. Those in the main château evoke the 18th century, while the ones in La Résidence, converted stables, and carriage houses, are rustic-contemporary. Wine tastings are held in the beautiful stone *cuvage* (wine-pressing room). ✉ *69620 Bagnols (15 km/9 mi southwest of Villefranche on D38 to Tarare),* ☎ *04–74–71–40–00,* FAX *04–74–71–40–49,* WEB *www.bagnols.com. 12 rooms, 4 apartments. Restaurant, bar, cable TV, minibars, pool, library, parking. AE, DC, MC, V.*

Beaujolais Route du Vin

16 km (10 mi) north of Villefranche-sur-Saône, 49 km (30 mi) north of Lyon.

Not all Beaujolais wine is promoted as vin nouveau—that's just a marketing gimmick celebrated in full force on the third Thursday of November annually, both here in this region and around the world. Wine classed as "Beaujolais Villages" is higher in alcohol and produced from a clearly defined region northwest of Villefranche. Beaujolais is made from one single variety of grape, the *gamay noir à jus blanc.* However, there are 12 different appellations: Beaujolais, Beaujolais Villages, Brouilly, Chénas, Chiroubles, Côte de Brouilly, Fleurie, Juliénas, Morgon, Moulin à Vent, Régnié, and St-Amour. The Beaujolais Route du

Vin (Wine Road), a narrow strip just 23 km (14 mi) long, is home to nine of these deluxe Beaujolais wines, also known as *grands crus.* Most villages have a *cave* (communal cellar) or *coopérative* where you can taste and buy. The **École Beaujolaise des Vins** (Beaujolais School of Wine; ✉ Villefranche, ☎ 04–74–02–22–81) organizes lessons in wine tasting and on creating your own cellar.

In the southernmost and largest *vignoble* (vineyard) of the Beaujolais crus is **Odenas,** producing Brouilly, a soft, fruity wine best consumed young. In the vineyard's center is towering Mont Brouilly, a hill whose vines produce a tougher, firmer wine classified as Côte de Brouilly. From Odenas take D68 via St-Lager to **Villié-Morgon,** in the heart of the Morgon vineyard; robust wines that age well are produced here. At Monternot, east of Villié-Morgon, you will find the 15th-century **Château de Corcelles,** noted for its Renaissance galleries, canopied courtyard well, and medieval carvings in its chapel. The guardroom is now an atmospheric tasting cellar. ✉ *Off D9 from Villié-Morgon,* ☎ *04–74–66–72–42.* ⏲ *Mon.–Sat. 10–noon and 2:30–6:30.*

From Villié-Morgon D68 wiggles north through several more wine villages, including **Chiroubles,** where a rare, light wine best drunk young is produced. The wines from **Fleurie** are elegant and flowery. Well-known **Chénas** is favored for its two crus: the robust, velvety, and expensive Moulin à Vent, and the fruity and underestimated Chénas. The wines of **Juliénas** are sturdy and a deep color; sample them in the cellar of the town church (closed Tuesday and lunchtime), amid bacchanalian decor. **St-Amour,** west of Juliénas, produces light but firm reds and a limited quantity of whites. The famous white Pouilly-Fuissé comes from the area around **Fuissé.**

Bourg-en-Bresse

33 *43 km (27 mi) east of St-Amour on N79, 65 km (40 mi) northeast of Lyon.*

Cheerful Bourg-en-Bresse is esteemed among gastronomes for its fowl—striking-looking chickens with plump white bodies and bright blue feet, the *poulet de Bresse.* The town's southeasternmost district, Brou, is its most interesting and the site of a singular church. This is a good place to stay before or after a trip along the Beaujolais Wine Road.

The **Église de Brou,** a marvel of the Flamboyant Gothic style, is no longer in religious use. The church was built between 1506 and 1532 by Margaret of Austria in memory of her husband, Philibert le Beau, Duke of Savoy, and their finely sculpted tombs highlight the rich interior. **Son-et-lumière** shows—on Easter and Pentecost Sunday and Monday, and on Thursday, Saturday, and Sunday from May through September—are magical. A massive restoration of the roof has brought it back to its 16th-century state with the same gorgeous, multicolor, intricate patterns found throughout Burgundy. The museum in the nearby **cloister** stands out for its paintings: 16th- and 17th-century Flemish and Dutch artists keep company with 17th- and 18th-century French and Italian masters, 19th-century artists of the Lyon School, Gustave Doré, and contemporary local painters. ✉ *63 bd. de Brou,* ☎ *04–74–22–83–83.* 🎫 *€5.* ⏲ *Apr.–Sept., daily 9–12:30 and 2–6:30; Oct.–Mar., daily 9–noon and 2–5.*

Dining and Lodging

$$–$$$ ★ ✕ **L'Auberge Bressane.** Overlooking the Brou church, the modern, polished dining room and chef Jean-Pierre Vullin's cuisine are a good combination. Frogs' legs and Bresse chicken with wild morel cream sauce are specialties; also try the *quenelles de brochet* (poached fish dumplings).

Jean-Pierre wanders through the dining room ready for a chat while his staff provides excellent service. Don't miss the house aperitif, a champagne cocktail with fresh strawberry puree. The wine list has 300 vintages. ✉ *166 bd. de Brou,* ☎ *04–74–22–22–68. Reservations essential. AE, DC, MC, V.*

$$ ✕ **La Petite Auberge.** This cozy flower-decked inn is in the countryside on the outskirts of town. Madame Bertrand provides games for children. Chef Philippe Garnier has a subtle way with mullet (he grills it in saffron butter) and Bresse chicken (browned in tangy cider vinegar). ✉ *St-Just, rte. de Ceyzeriat,* ☎ *04–74–22–30–04. MC, V. Closed Jan. and Tues. No dinner Mon.*

$$$$ ✕🏨 **Georges Blanc.** This simple 19th-century inn full of antique country furniture makes a fine setting for poulet de Bresse, truffles, and lobster, all featured on this legendary menu. The restaurant is closed Wednesday and Thursday (except for dinner June to mid-September). The 30 guest rooms range from (relatively) simple to luxurious. It's worth the trip from Bourg-en-Bresse, but be sure you have enough money to burn. ✉ *Pl. du Marché, 01540 Vonnas (19 km/12 mi from Bourg-en-Bresse),* ☎ *04–74–50–90–90,* FAX *04–74–50–08–80,* WEB *www.georgesblanc.com. 48 rooms. Restaurant, minibars, cable TV, tennis court, pool, meeting rooms, helipad, parking. AE, DC, MC, V. Reservations essential. Closed Jan.–mid-Feb.*

Villars-les-Dombes

34 *29 km (18 mi) south of Bourg-en-Bresse, 37 km (23 mi) north of Lyon.*

Villars-les-Dombes is the unofficial capital of La Dombes, an area once covered by a glacier. When the ice retreated, it left a network of lakes and ponds that draws anglers and bird-watchers today. The 56-acre **Parc des Oiseaux,** one of Europe's finest bird sanctuaries, is home-sweet-home to 400 species of birds (some 2,000 individuals from five continents); 435 aviaries house species from waders to birds of prey; and tropical birds in vivid hues fill the indoor birdhouse. Allow two hours. ✉ *Off N83,* ☎ *04–74–98–05–54.* €6. ⏲ *Easter–Sept., daily 9–7; Oct.–Easter, daily 9–dusk.*

En Route N83 skirts the Dombes region's largest lake, the **Grand Étang de Birieux,** en route from Villars-les-Dombes to St-André de Covey.

Pérouges

★ 35 *21 km (13 mi) southeast of Villars-les-Dombes, 36 km (22 mi) northeast of Lyon.*

Wonderfully preserved (though a little too precious), hilltop Pérouges, with its medieval houses and narrow cobbled streets surrounded by ramparts, is just 200 yards across. Hand weavers first brought it prosperity; the industrial revolution meant their downfall, and by the late 19th century the population had dwindled from 1,500 to 12. Now the government has restored the most interesting houses, and a potter, bookbinder, cabinetmaker, and weaver have given the town a new lease on life. A number of restaurants make Pérouges a good lunch stop.

Encircling the town is **rue des Rondes**; from this road you can get fine views of the countryside and, on clear days, the Alps. Park your car by the main gateway, **Porte d'En-Haut,** alongside the 15th-century fortress-church. Rue du Prince, the town's main street, leads to the **Maison des Princes de Savoie** (Palace of the Princes of Savoie), formerly the home of the influential Savoie family that once controlled the eastern part of France. Note the fine watchtower. **Place de la Halle,** a pretty square with great charm, around the corner from the Maison des

Princes de Savoie, is the site of a lime tree planted in 1792. The **Musée de Vieux Pérouges** (Old Pérouges Museum), to one side of the place de la Halle, contains local artifacts and a reconstructed weaver's workshop. The medieval **garden** is noted for its array of rare medicinal plants. ✉ *Pl. du Tilleul,* ☎ *04–74–61–00–88.* *€3.* ⏲ *May–Sept., daily 10–noon and 2–6.*

Dining and Lodging

$$$–$$$$ ★ ✕🏨 **Ostellerie du Vieux Pérouges.** Extraordinary even by French standards, this historic inn has antiques, gigantic stone hearths, and glossy wood floors and tables. Rooms in the geranium-decked 15th-century Au St.-Georges et Manoir manor are more spacious—but also nearly twice the cost—than those in L'Annexe and have marble bathrooms and period furniture (one or two rooms even have their own garden). In the restaurant, fine cuisine is served on pewter plates by waitresses in folk costumes. ✉ *Pl. du Tilleul, 01800 Pérouges,* ☎ *04–74–61–00–88,* FAX *04–74–34–77–90,* WEB *www.hostellerie.com. 28 rooms. Restaurant, bar, no air-conditioning, cable TV, minibars, meeting rooms. AE, DC, MC, V.*

THE RHÔNE VALLEY

At Lyon, the Rhône, joined by the Saône, truly comes into its own, plummeting south in search of the Mediterranean. The river's progress is often spectacular, as steep vineyards conjure up vistas that are more readily associated with the river's Germanic cousin, the Rhine. All along the way, small-town vintners invite you to sample their wines. Early Roman towns like Vienne and Valence reflect the Rhône's importance as a trading route. To the west is the rugged, rustic Ardèche *département* (province), where time seems to have slowed to a standstill.

Vienne

36 *27 km (17 mi) south of Lyon via A7.*

One of Roman Gaul's most important towns, Vienne became a religious and cultural center under its count-archbishops in the Middle Ages and retains considerable historic charm despite being a major road and train junction. The tourist office anchors cours Brillier in the leafy shadow of the Jardin Public (Public Garden). The €5 Passport admits you to most local monuments and museums; it's available at the tourist office or at the first site that you visit.

On quai Jean-Jaurès, beside the Rhône, is the church of **St-Pierre.** Note the rectangular 12th-century Romanesque bell tower with its arcaded tiers. The lower church walls date from the 6th century. Although religious wars deprived the cathedral of **St-Maurice** of many of its statues, much original decoration is intact; the portals on the 15th-century facade are carved with Old Testament scenes. The cathedral was built between the 12th and 16th centuries, with later additions, such as the splendid 18th-century mausoleum to the right of the altar. A frieze of the zodiac adorns the entrance to the vaulted passage that once led to the cloisters but now opens onto place St-Paul.

Place du Palais is the site of the remains of the **Temple d'Auguste et de Livie** (Temple of Augustus and Livia), accessible via place St-Paul and rue Clémentine; they probably date in part from Vienne's earliest Roman settlements (1st century BC). The Corinthian columns were walled in during the 11th century, when the temple was used as a church; in 1833 Prosper Mérimée intervened to have the temple restored. The last vestige of the city's sizable Roman baths is a **Roman gateway** (✉ Rue Chantelouve) decorated with delicate friezes.

The **Théâtre Romain** (Roman Theater), on rue de la Charité, is one of the largest in Gaul (143 yards across). It held 13,000 spectators and is only slightly smaller than Rome's Theater of Marcellus. Rubble buried Vienne's theater until 1922; excavation has uncovered 46 rows of seats, some marble flooring, and the frieze on the stage. Concerts take place here in summer. ✉ *7 rue du Cirque,* ☎ *04–74–85–39–23.* 🎫 *€3.* ⏲ *Apr.–Aug., daily 9–12:30 and 2–6; Sept.–mid-Oct., Tues.–Sun. 9–12:30 and 2–6; mid-Oct.–Mar., Tues.–Sat. 9:30–12:30 and 2–5, Sun. 1:30–5:30.*

Rue des Orfèvres (off rue de la Charité) is lined with Renaissance facades and distinguished by the church of **St-André-le-Bas,** once part of a powerful abbey. If possible, venture past the restoration now in progress to see the finely sculpted 12th-century capitals (made of Roman stone) and the 17th-century wood statue of St. Andrew. It's best to see the cloisters during the music festival held here and at the cathedral from June to August. ✉ *Cour St-André,* ☎ *04–74–85–18–49.* 🎫 *€3.* ⏲ *Apr.–mid-Oct., Tues.–Sun. 9:30–1 and 2–6; mid-Oct.–Mar., Tues.–Sat. 9:30–12:30 and 2–5, Sun. 2–6.*

Across the Rhône from the town center is the excavated **Cité Gallo-Romaine** (Gallo-Roman City), covering several acres. Here you can find villas, houses, workshops, public baths, and roads, all built by the Romans. 🎫 *€5.* ⏲ *Daily 9–6.*

Dining

$$ ✕ **Le Bec Fin.** With its understatedly elegant dining room and an inexpensive weekday menu, this unpretentious eatery opposite the cathedral is a good choice for lunch and dinner. Red meat, seafood, and freshwater fish are well prepared here. Try the turbot cooked with saffron. ✉ *7 pl. St-Maurice,* ☎ *04–74–85–76–72. Reservations essential. AE, DC, MC, V. Closed Mon. No dinner Sun.*

Serrières

37 *32 km (20 mi) south of Vienne, 59 km (37 mi) south of Lyon.*

Riverboats traditionally stop at little Serrières, on the Rhône's west bank. Life on the water is depicted at the **Musée des Mariniers du Rhône** (Boatmen's Museum), in the wooden-roof Gothic chapel of St-Sornin. ☎ *04–75–34–01–26.* 🎫 *€3.* ⏲ *Apr.–Oct., weekends 3–6.*

Dining and Lodging

$$–$$$ ✕🏨 **Schaeffer.** Guest rooms here are decorated in contemporary style, but the real draw is the dining room, where chef Bernard Mathé invents variations on traditional French dishes: smoked duck cutlet in lentil stew or lamb with eggplant in anchovy butter. The number of desserts is overwhelming, but pistachio cake with bitter chocolate is the clear winner. Reservations are essential for the restaurant. Menus run from €40 to €60. ✉ *Quai Jules Roche, 07340,* ☎ *04–75–34–00–07,* FAX *04–75–34–08–79. 11 rooms. Restaurant, bar, cable TV, minibars, meeting rooms. AE, DC, MC, V. Closed Mon., dinner Sun., 1st 3 wks Jan.*

Hauterives

38 *28 km (17 mi) east of Serrières, 40 km (25 mi) south of Vienne.*

Hauterives would be just another quaint village on the eastern side of the Rhône if not for the **Palais Idéal,** one of Western Europe's weirdest constructions. A fantasy constructed entirely of stones (called *galets*) from the nearby Galaure River, it was the life's work of a local postman, Ferdinand Cheval (1836–1924), who was haunted by visions of faraway mosques and temples. One of many wall inscriptions reads "1879–1912: 10,000 days, 93,000 hours, 33 years of toil." ☎ *04–75–68–81–19,* FAX *04–75–68–88–15.* 🎫 *€5.* 🕘 *Mid-Apr.–mid-Sept., daily 9–7; mid-Sept.–mid-Apr., daily 9:30–5:30.*

Dining and Lodging

$$ ✕🏨 **Le Relais.** A stone's throw from the Palais Idéal, this rustic inn is a good place for a meal—and a night's stay, if desirable. Rooms are small and could use refurbishing in the not-too-distant future. Owner Roland Graillat is better as a chef—roast partridge and delicately seasoned frogs' legs are good bets. From September to June the restaurant is closed Monday and does not serve dinner Sunday. ✉ *Pl. de l'Église, 26390,* ☎ *04–75–68–81–12,* FAX *04–75–68–92–42. 13 rooms. Restaurant, bar, no air-conditioning, cable TV, minibars, terrace café. AE, DC, MC, V. Closed Jan.–Feb.*

Annonay

39 *44 km (27 mi) south of Vienne, 43 km (27 mi) southeast of St-Étienne.*

The narrow streets and passageways of central Annonay are full of character. The town, which grew up around the leather industry, is best known as the home of Joseph and Étienne Montgolfier, who, in 1783, invented the hot-air balloon (known in French as a *montgolfière*). The first flight was on June 4, 1783, from place des Cordeliers (although a commemorating obelisk is on avenue Marc-Seguin); the flight lasted a half hour and reached 6,500 ft.

Local history and folklore are evoked at the **Musée Vivarais César Filhol,** between the Mairie (Town Hall) and the church of Notre-Dame. ✉ *15 rue Béchetoille,* ☎ *04–75–33–24–51.* 🎫 *€3.* 🕘 *July–Aug., Tues.–Fri. 3–6, weekends 3–6; Sept.–June, Wed. and weekends 3–6.*

Tournon

40 *37 km (23 mi) southeast of Annonay, 59 km (37 mi) south of Vienne.*

Tournon is on the Rhône at the foot of granite hills. Its hefty **Château,** dating from the 15th and 16th centuries, is the chief attraction. The castle's twin terraces have wonderful views of the Old Town, the river, and—towering above Tain-l'Hermitage across the Rhône—the steep vineyards that produce Hermitage wine, one of the region's most refined—and costly—reds. In the château is a museum of local history, the **Musée Rhodanien** (or du Rhône). ✉ *Pl. Auguste-Faure,* ☎ *04–75–08–10–23.* 🎫 *€4.* 🕘 *June–Aug., Wed.–Mon. 10–noon and 2–6; Apr.–May and Sept.–Oct., Wed.–Mon. 2–6.*

👶 A ride on one of France's last steam trains, the **Chemin de Fer du Vivarais,** makes an adventurous two-hour trip 33 km (21 mi) along the narrow, rocky Doux Valley to Lamastre and back to Tournon. ✉ *Departs from Tournon station,* ☎ *04–78–28–83–34.* 🎫 *Round-trip €18.* 🕘 *June–Aug., daily 10 AM; May and Sept., weekends 10 AM.*

Dining and Lodging

$$$ ✕🏨 **Michel Chabran.** This modern interpretation of Drôme-style stone and wood design has floral displays, airy picture windows over the garden, and guest rooms with a touch of contemporary Danish influence. Next to the main road, sleeping with the windows open can make for a noisy night (though the air-conditioning largely solves that). The restaurant serves a truffle menu from December to March and imaginative and light fare such as mille-feuille de foie gras with artichokes and lamb from Rémuzat. ✉ *29 av. du 45e Parallèle, 26600 Pont de l'Isère (on left [east] bank of the Rhône, 10 km/6 mi south of Tournon via N7 and 7 km/4 mi north of Valence),* ☎ *04–75–84–60–09,* FAX *04–75–84–59–65. 12 rooms. Restaurant, terrace café, cable TV, minibars, pool, meeting room, parking (fee). AE, DC, MC, V. Closed Mon. Nov.–Mar. No dinner Sun.*

$–$$ ✕🏨 **Reynaud.** Tain-l'Hermitage, across the Rhône from Tournon, entices with this fine inn and restaurant. The dining room is comfortable and traditional, the river magnificent. Rooms are on the small side but cozy and tastefully furnished. The classic cuisine is excellent, with specialties from poached egg with foie gras to pigeon fillet in black-currant sauce. ✉ *82 av. du Président-Roosevelt, Tain-l'Hermitage, 07300,* ☎ *04–75–07–22–10,* FAX *04–75–08–03–53. 13 rooms. Restaurant, bar, cable TV, minibars, parking (fee). AE, DC, MC, V. Closed Mon., Jan., and 1 wk in Aug. No dinner Sun.*

En Route From Tournon's place Jean-Jaurès, slightly inland from the château, follow signs to the narrow, twisting **Route Panoramique**; the views en route to the old village of **St-Romain-de-Lerps** are breathtaking. In good weather the panorama at St-Romain includes 13 départements, Mont Blanc to the east, and arid Mont Ventoux to the south. D287 winds down to St-Péray and Valence; topping the **Montagne de Crussol,** 650 ft above the plain, is the ruined 12th-century **Château de Crussol.**

Valence

41 *17 km (11 mi) south of Tournon, 92 km (57 mi) west of Grenoble, 127 km (79 mi) north of Avignon.*

Largish Valence, the Drôme département capital, is the region's market center. Steep-curbed alleyways called *côtes* extend into the old town from the Rhône. At the center of the Old Town is the cathedral of **St-Apollinaire.** Although begun in the 12th century in the Romanesque style, it is not as old as it looks: parts of it were rebuilt in the 17th century, with the belfry rebuilt in the 19th. The **Musée des Beaux-Arts** (Fine Arts Museum), next to the cathedral of St-Apollinaire, in the former 18th-century bishops' palace, displays archaeological finds as well as sculpture and furniture and drawings by landscapist Hubert Robert (1733–1808). ✉ *Pl. des Ormeaux,* ☎ *04–75–79–20–80.* 🎫 *€3.* ⏲ *Mon.–Tues. and Thurs.–Fri. 2–6, Wed. and weekends 9–noon and 2–6.*

Dining and Lodging

$$$$ ★ ✕🏨 **Pic.** Kubla Khan would have decamped Xanadu in a minute for this Drôme pleasure palace. The Maison Pic has been a culinary landmark for decades, although its (too?) glossy Relais & Château makeover into a full-scale hotel has nearly obliterated any traces of its time-stained past. Not that you will complain—much of the decor is to die for: vaulted white salons, red-velvet sofas, 18th-century billiard tables, gigantic Provençal (that's where the Pic family started) armoires, lovely gardens, and an eye-popping pool make this a destination in itself. The famous restaurant is going stronger than ever—try the truffle-flavored *galettes* (pancakes) with asparagus or bass with caviar (served either "avec modération" or "passionnément") to see how Anne-Sophie, great-granddaughter of the founding matriarch, is continuing the family legacy. Dine in the cardinal-red dining room seated on Louis Seize–style bergères or, in summer, on the shaded terrace, then repair upstairs to the guest rooms, done in a mix of rustic antiques and high-style fabrics. A café, the Auberge du Pin, entices with much lower prices. ✉ *285 av. Victor-Hugo, 26000,* ☎ *04–75–44–15–32,* FAX *04–75–40–*

96–03, WEB *www.pic-valence.com. 12 rooms, 3 apartments. Restaurant, bar, terrace café, cable TV, minibars, meeting rooms, pool, parking (fee). AE, DC, MC, V. Closed Mon. No dinner Sun.*

Shopping

In the small town of Romans, 15 minutes northeast of Valence via D532, is a score of retail outlets for designer shoes. Romans, with its tradition of leather making, has become the major factory center for the production of high-quality shoes. Many of the top European designers are represented, and their products may be had at bargain prices from any number of stores. **Charles Jourdan** (✉ Galerie Fan Halles, ☎ 04–75–02–32–36) is perhaps the highest-quality brand name represented in Romans. **Chaussures Tchlin** (✉ Quai Chopin, ☎ 04–75–72–51–41) is a longtime mainstay for French shoes. **Stephane Kelian** (✉ 11 pl. Charles-de-Gaulle, ☎ 04–75–05–23–26) is a name that speaks hip and high style.

En Route The prettiest route between Valence and Privas is N86, on the right bank of the Rhône; after 16 km (10 mi) and just before La Voulte, turn onto the scenic D120, which follows the Eyrieux Valley as far as Les Ollières-sur-Eyrieux; then turn south along D2, under the thick canopy of horse-chestnut trees.

Cliousclat

42 *21 km (13 mi) south of Valence, 27 km (17 mi) north of Montélimar.*

Less than 10 km (6 mi) off A7 and N7, the roads running south from Valence to Montélimar and on to Provence, is the delightful, tiny village of Cliousclat. It's built on a hillside, with room for just one narrow street running through it. There's not much to do or see, but its charming atmosphere and its gorgeous views make it very appealing. While you're here, however, drop in at the small **Histoires de Poteries** (Pottery History Museum) to see the work of local potters. You might want to buy some of the lovely wares, too. ☎ *04–75–63–15–60.* *€3.* *Apr.–June, Tues.–Sun. 2–7; July–Aug., daily 10–1 and 2–8; Sept., Tues.–Sun. 10–noon and 2–7; Oct., Tues.–Sun. 2–6.*

Dining and Lodging

$$ ★ **La Treille Muscate.** Between Lyon and Avignon there is no better place to spend a night than at this gem of a hotel. Lovingly collected antiques and clay-tile floors with throw rugs make each room different. Room No. 11 has a huge terrace overlooking fields to the Rhône. The restaurant serves top-quality products such as Sisteron lamb, Mediterranean fish, and homemade foie gras. The friendly owner, Madame de Laître, speaks English fluently but politely refrains from doing so until you have exhausted your French. ✉ *26270 Cliousclat,* ☎ *04–75–63–13–10,* FAX *04–75–63–10–79. 12 rooms. Restaurant, terrace café, cable TV, minibars. AE, DC, MC, V. Closed Wed. and mid-Dec.–Feb.*

Privas

43 *41 km (25 mi) southwest of Valence.*

The capital of the spectacular Ardèche département, renowned for its caves and rocky gorges, Privas makes a good base for exploring the region. The tourist office, just off place Charles-de-Gaulle, can provide details. A Protestant stronghold during the 16th-century Wars of Religion, Privas was razed by Louis XIII in 1629, following a 16-day siege. The Pont Louis XIII (Louis XIII Bridge), over the River Ouvèze, commemorates the town's return to royal good graces. It eventually became a peaceful administrative town, best known for the production of that French delicacy known as *marrons glacés* (candied chestnuts).

Dining

$ ✕ **Lous Esclos.** This strikingly modern restaurant has more windows than walls—all overlooking the wild Ardèche landscape. The chef's masterpieces include goose and snail in flaky pastry—at prices that are too good to be true. ✉ *Alissas (5 km/3 mi southeast of Privas on D2),* ☎ *04–75–65–12–73. MC, V. Closed late-Dec.–mid-Jan.*

The Ardèche Valley

Aubenas is 30 km (18 mi) south of Privas on N104, 74 km (46 mi) northeast of Alés; Pont-St-Esprit is 43 km (27 mi) south of Montélimar, 45 km (28 mi) north of Avignon.

For the 120 km (75 mi) that the Ardèche River flows from its source to the Rhône, there is a spectacular panoply of nature—basins of orchards, vertical cliffs, and spectacular gorges—plus medieval villages guarded by castles perched high up on rocky promontories. A good base is in or near the small town of **Aubenas,** which has a thriving silk industry and a 12th-century castle (with later additions) that is now the town hall. The Ardèche River's source can be traced at the **Col de la Chavade** (4,154 ft); take N102 west from Aubenas toward Mayres, 38 km (24 mi) upstream.

East of Aubenas via D104 and D579 is a 40-km (25-mi) stretch known as **La Valée Moyenne** (Middle Valley), where you'll find a number of small villages and a dramatic gorge. Pass through Rochecolombe and Balazuc to get to the small medieval village of **Voqüssmé.** Just before Ruoms, make a detour right on D245 for 3½ km (2 mi) en route to the tiny village of **Labesume.** The houses here are all built out of natural stone and would appear to be unnoticeable, as if camouflaged, except for their balconies. Labesume is at the southern end of the **Gorges de la Beaume,** a 40-km (25-mi) gorge cut through by the Beaume River as it tumbles down from the Tanarque Massif to join the Ardèche River at Ruoms.

The last 58 km (35 mi) of the valley, from Vallon-Pont-d'Arc to Pont-St-Esprit, are particularly magnificent. Here you'll find another dramatic gorge, the 41-km-long (26-mi-long) **Gorges de l'Ardèche.** Route D290 runs from Vallon-Pont-d'Arc along the edge of the gorge on the side of the Gras Plâteau; stop periodically to look down. Your first stop should be at the **Pont d'Arc,** where the river flows under a natural arch 112 ft high and 194 ft wide. From here on, the river makes some spectacular bends and varies from tumbling through rapids to a gentle meander. The most dramatic view of the gorge is from **Serre de Toure Belvédère,** about 11 km (7 mi) from Vallon, where you can peer down 750 ft to the river. Another 11 km (7 mi) along, the **Gournier Belvédère** gives you a view of the river tumbling its way through the Gournier Toupine Rocks. All along the gorge are caverns and grottoes. The best is **Marzal Aven,** with its large calcite formations. To reach it, turn left onto D590 just after the Gournier Belvédère and drive about 5 km (3 mi); the entrance to the main cave is down 743 steps to the Salle du Tombeau (Tomb Cave), where translucent sheets of stalactites seem like shielding drapes to bear and deer bones. Spend a fascinating hour underground being guided through the fantastic caves, but be sure to take a sweater, as it can be chilly. 🎫 *€5.* ⏲ *Mid-Apr.–Sept., daily 9–6; mid-Mar.–mid-Apr. and Oct.–Nov., weekends 11, 3, and 5.*

Take one last look at the gorge at the **Ranc-Pointu Belvédère,** where the Le Louby River joins the Ardèche. This viewpoint overlooks the river's last enclosed bend, so don't pass up a stop here. The gorge then ends, and the countryside opens up to a fertile valley. Cross over the suspension bridge at **Pont-St-Esprit** and turn left on D941 to reach the Rhône and the north–south route A7 heading toward Montélimar.

Dining and Lodging

$$$ ✕🏨 **La Bastide du Soleil.** Nestled in a 17th-century castle in the heart of the medieval village of Vinezac, the rooms here are modern and charming, while the excellent restaurant specializes in an ever-changing seasonal menu based on fresh local produce. Menus range from economical prix-fixe menus to an elaborate taster's menu. ✉ *07110 Vinezac (off Rte. D104 10 km/6 mi southwest of Aubenas),* ☎ *04–75–36–91–66,* FAX *04–75–36–91–59. 6 rooms. Restaurant, cable TV, minibars. AE, DC, MC, V. Closed Jan. 1–Feb. 29.*

$$ ✕🏨 **Les Cedres.** A friendly husband-and-wife team (she speaks English) efficiently manages this moderately priced hotel. Rooms are small but cozy; ask for one overlooking the garden (smaller and more expensive, but better) instead of the parking lot. Half have small terraces; those without terraces are air-conditioned. The restaurant serves simple fare of sautéed fish, regional stews, and meats with Provençal sauces. ✉ *07260 Joyeuse (20 km/12 mi southwest of Aubenas),* ☎ *04–75–39–40–60,* FAX *04–75–39–90–16. 40 rooms. Restaurant, bar, cable TV, minibars, pool, fishing. AE, DC, MC, V. Closed mid-Oct.–mid-Apr.*

Outdoor Activities and Sports

If you're interested in kayaking or canoeing through the Gorges de l'Ardèche, contact **Alpha Bateaux** (✉ 07150 Vallon Pont d'Arc, ☎ 04–75–88–08–29). A two-person canoe costs about €55 per day, and a one-person kayak is about €35.

GRENOBLE AND THE ALPS

This is double-treat vacationland: in winter some of the world's best skiing is found in the Alps; in summer chic spas, shimmering lakes, and hilltop trails offer additional delights. The Savoie and Haute-Savoie départements occupy the most impressive territory; Grenoble, in the Dauphiné, is the Alps' gateway and the area's only city. It's all at the nexus of highways from Marseille, Valence, Lyon, Geneva, and Turin.

The skiing season for most French resorts runs from December 15 to April 15. By late December resorts above 3,000 ft usually have sufficient snow. January is apt to be the coldest—and therefore the least popular—month; in Chamonix and Megève, this is the time to find hotel bargains. At the high-altitude resorts the skiing season lasts until May. In summer the lake resorts, as well as the regions favored by hikers and climbers, come into their own. Let's not forget that this is the region where Stendhal was born, and where the great 18th-century philosopher Jean-Jacques Rousseau lived out his old age. Worldly pleasures also await: incredibly charming Annecy, set with arcaded lanes and quiet canals in the old quarter around the lovely 16th-century Palais de l'Isle; the Old Master treasures on view at Grenoble's Musée; and the fashionable lakeside promenades of spa towns like Aix-les-Bains are just some of the civilized enjoyments to be discovered here.

Grenoble

44 *104 km (65 mi) southeast of Lyon, 138 km (86 mi) northeast of Montélimar.*

Capital of the Dauphiné (Lower Alps) region, Grenoble sits at the confluence of the Isère and Drac rivers and lies nestled within three *massifs* (mountain ranges): La Chartreuse, Le Vercors, and Belledonne. This cosmopolitan city's skyscrapers seem intimidating by homey French standards. But along with the city's nuclear research plant, they bear witness to the fierce local desire to move ahead with the times, and it's not surprising to find one of France's most noted universities here. Grenoble's main claim to fame is as the birthplace of the great French novelist Henri Beyle (1783–1842), better known as Stendhal, author of *The Red and the Black* and *The Charterhouse of Parma.* The heart of the city forms a crescent around a bend of the Isère, with the train station at the western end and the university all the way at the eastern tip. As it fans out from the river toward the south, the crescent seems to develop a more modern flavor. The hub of the city is **place Victor Hugo,** with its flowers, fountains, and cafés, though most sights and nightlife are near the Isère in place St-André, place de Gordes, and place Notre-Dame; avenue Alsace-Lorraine, a major pedestrian street lined with modern shops, cuts right through it. The layout of the city is very tricky, so it is best to stop into the city tourist office for detailed maps and directions.

Near the center curve of the River Isère is a **Téléphérique** (cable car), starting at quai St-Stéphane-Jay, which whisks you over the River Isère and up to the hilltop and its **Fort de la Bastille,** where there are splendid views. Walk back down via the footpath through the Jardin Dauphinoise. €7 *round-trip.* *Apr.–Oct., daily 9 AM–midnight; Nov.–Dec. and Feb.–Mar., daily 10–6.*

On the north side of the River Isère is rue Maurice-Gignoux, lined with gardens, cafés, mansions, and a 17th-century convent that contains the **Musée Dauphinois,** featuring the history of mountaineering and skiing. The *Premiers Alpins* section explores the evolution of the Alps and its inhabitants. ✉ *30 rue Maurice-Gignoux,* ☎ *04–76–85–19–01.* *€4.* *Nov.–Apr., Wed.–Mon. 10–6; May–Oct., Wed.–Mon. 10–7.*

The church of **St-Laurent,** near the Musée Dauphinois, has a hauntingly ancient 6th-century crypt—one of the country's oldest Christian monuments—supported by a row of formidable marble pillars. ✉ *2 pl. St-Laurent,* ☎ *04–76–44–78–68.* *€3.* *Wed.–Mon. 8–noon and 2–6.*

On the south side of the River Isère and nearly opposite the cable-car stop is the Jardin de Ville—an open space filled with immense plane trees—where a handsome conical tower with slate roof marks the **Palais Lesdiguières.** This was built by the right hand of King Henri IV, the Duc de Lesdiguières (1543–1626), and possibly the prototype for Stendhal's voraciously egoistic protagonists (as Constable of France, the duke had a reign of terror, marrying his young lover Marie Vignon–31 years his junior—after having her husband assassinated). A master urbanist, Lesdiguières did much to establish the Grenoble you see today, so it may only be apt his palace is now the **Musée Stendhal,** where family portraits trace the life of Grenoble's greatest writer amidst elegant wooden furniture turned out by the Hache family dynasty of famous woodworkers.

Although some of the city's residents will be surprised that non-natives know who Stendhal (much less Henri Beyle) is, there is no denying that this great author remains Grenoble's most famous native son. Copies of original manuscripts and major memorabilia will please fans, who will wish to then pay a call to the **Maison Stendhal,** at 20 Grande Rue, Stendhal's grandfather's house and the place where the author spent the "happiest days of his life"; you can also take a stroll back over to the **Jardin de Ville**, where the author met his first "love" (basically unrequited), the actress Virginie Kubly. The city tourist office distributes a **"Stendhal itinerary"** that also includes the author's birthplace, at 14 rue Hébert, now a repository for memorabilia on the Resistance and deportations of World War II. ✉ *1 rue Hector-Berlioz,* ☎ *04–76–42–02–62.* 🎫 *Free.* ⏲ *Oct.–June, Tues.–Sun. 2–6; July–Sept., Tues.–Sun. 9–12 and 2–6.*

Several blocks east of the Musée Stendhal is place de Lavalette, on the south side of the river where most of Grenoble is concentrated, and site of the **Musée de Grenoble,** formerly the Musée de Peinture et de Sculpture (Painting and Sculpture Museum). Founded in 1796 and since enlarged, it is one of France's oldest museums and the first to concentrate on modern art (Picasso donated his *Femme Lisant* in 1921); a modern addition incorporates the medieval Tour de l'Isle (Island Tower), a Grenoble landmark. The collection includes 4,000 paintings and 5,500 drawings, among them works from the Italian Renaissance, Rubens, Flemish still lifes, Zurbaran, and Canaletto; Impressionists such as Renoir and Monet; and 20th-century works by Matisse (*Intérieur aux Aubergines*), Signac, Derain, Vlaminck, Magritte, Ernst, Miró, and Dubuffet. Modern art lovers should also check out the **Centre National d'Art Contemporain** (✉ 155 cours Berriat, ☎ 04–76–21–95–84). Behind the train station in an out-of-the-way district, it is noted for its distinctive warehouse museum and cutting-edge collection. ✉ *5 pl. de Lavalette,* ☎ *04–76–63–44–44.* 🎫 *€4.* ⏲ *Wed. 11–10, Thurs.–Mon. 11–7.*

Place St-André is a medieval square, now filled with umbrella-shaded tables and graced with the **Palais de Justice** on one side and the **Église St-André** on the other. For a tour of Grenoble's oldest and most beautiful streets, head to the area around **La Halle Sainte-Claire,** the splendid glass-and-steel-covered market in place Sainte-Claire, several blocks southeast of the Jardin de Ville. Facing the market's spouting fish fountain on the facade, to your right at the end of the street you will see the Baroque entryway to the Lyçee et College Stendhal.

Dining and Lodging

$$$ ✕ **Auberge Napoléon.** This alpine gourmand haven is where elfin chef Agnès Chotin puts together the best table in Grenoble with *terroir* creations ranging from *daube de sanglier en aumonière croustillante* (wild boar stewed in port wine with lemon crust) or *crème de potiron* (cream of squash soup). ✉ *7 rue Montorge,* ☎ *04–76–87–80–67. AE, DC, MC, V. Closed July 30–Aug. 20, Mon.–Wed. lunch, and Sun.*

$ ✕ **Café de la Table Ronde.** The second oldest café in France, junior only to the Procope in Paris, this was a favorite haunt of Henri Beyle as well as the spot where Choderlos de Laclos sought inspiration for his 1784 *Liaisons Dangereuses.* Known for gatherings of "*les mordus*" (literally the "bitten," or passionate ones), the café still hosts poetry readings and concerts. ✉ *7 pl. St-André,* ☎ *04–76–44–51–41. AE, DC, MC, V.*

$$$$ ★ ✕🏨 **Park Hôtel Grenoble.** Grenoble's finest hotel, with spacious corner rooms over the leafy Parc Paul Mistral, is more than comfortable. This smoothly run establishment attends to your every need with skill and good cheer, from recommendations around town to dinner in front of a roaring fire in Le Parc, the excellent restaurant. Try the sumptuous *foie gras de canard poelé aux figues* (duck liver sautéed with figs) and the *tournedos de charolais aux morilles* (Charolais beef with morels) with a Château Fombrauge, Saint Emilion '95 grand cru. ✉

10 place Paul Mistral, 38000, ☎ 04–76–85–81–23, FAX 04–76–46–49–88, WEB www.park-affaires.com. 40 rooms, 12 apartments. Restaurant, bar, cable TV, minibars, hot tubs, meeting rooms, parking (fee). AE, DC, MC, V.

$$$ ★ ✕🏨 **Chavant.** Dining under the watchful eye of the charming Danièle Chavant is a pleasure at this ivy-covered mansion. The lobster smothered in truffles is wonderfully wicked and wholly delicious, while the *civet de biche en robe d'automne* (venison with apples, potatoes, and turnips in a daube sauce) is unforgettable. Rooms are elegant and spacious, overlooking meadows and forests beyond the lush garden and pool. ✉ *Rue Bresson, 38320 Bressons (8 km/5 mi south of Grenoble),* ☎ *04–76–25–25–38,* FAX *04–76–25–15–14,* WEB *www.chavant.fr. 7 rooms. Restaurant, cable TV, minibars, pool, meeting rooms, parking. AE, DC, MC, V. Closed Dec. 25–31. Restaurant closed Sat. lunch, Sun. dinner, Mon.*

$$–$$$ ★ ✕🏨 **Château de la Commanderie.** This 13th-century castle has been owned by the same family for 200 years, as the ancestral portraits peering down over grandfather clocks suggest. Each room in the new 20th-century annex differs in design, but all share the same light color scheme and fresh feeling. Hot oysters coated with chopped watercress and venison fillet are representative of chef Denis Coutarel's flair and creativity. ✉ *17 av. D'Echirolles, 38320 Eybens (5 km/3 mi south of Grenoble),* ☎ *04–76–25–34–58,* FAX *04–76–24–07–31,* WEB *www.commanderie.fr. 25 rooms. Restaurant, cable TV, minibars, pool, meeting rooms. AE, DC, MC, V. Closed Dec. 23–Jan. 8. Restaurant closed Sun. dinner, Mon. lunch.*

$–$$ 🏨 **Europe.** This modest hotel at the edge of old Grenoble on a corner of Place Grenette is handy for its central location. As it is an easy walk from the river, the Jardin de Ville, and the city museums, once you're ensconced here, you're set to explore the town. Rooms are adequate and the staff is helpful. ✉ *22 place Grenette,* ☎ FAX *04–76–46–16–94. 45 rooms. Breakfast room, cable TV, minibars, health club, meeting rooms, parking (fee). AE, DC, MC, V.*

Nightlife and the Arts

Look for the monthly *Grenoble-Spectacles* for a list of events around town. **La Soupe aux Choux** (✉ 7 rte. de Lyon) is the spot for jazz.

Cinq Jours de Jazz is just that—five days of jazz—in February or March. In summer, classical music characterizes the **Session Internationale de Grenoble-Isère.**

Outdoor Activities and Sports

The **Maison de la Randonnée** (✉ 7 rue Voltaire, ☎ 04–76–51–76–00) can provide you with information on places to hike around Grenoble.

En Route If you have time only for a brief glimpse of the Alps, take N91 out of Grenoble toward Briançon, past the spectacular mountain scenery of **L'Alpe d'Huez, Les Deux Alpes,** and the **Col du Galibier.** Or take D512 north from Grenoble for 17 km (11 mi), fork left, and follow small D57-D as far as you can (only a few miles) before leaving your car for the 30-minute climb to the top of the 6,000-ft **Charmant Som peak.** Your reward will be a stunning view of the Grande Chartreuse Monastery to the north. If you're heading to Provence and using Grenoble as your gateway through the Alps, be sure to take N76, which cuts through the mountains and presents some majestic scenery. From spring through fall the valleys are lush with greenery; in winter they are snow-covered bowls attracting skiers. Along the way you'll pass many small villages tucked inside mountain ridges, which guard them from winter winds.

Grande Chartreuse

45 *23 km (14 mi) north of Grenoble; head north on D512 and fork left 8 km (5 mi) on D520-B just before St-Pierre-de-Chartreuse.*

St. Bruno founded this 12-acre monastery in 1084; it later spawned 24 other charterhouses in Europe. Burned and rebuilt several times, it was stripped of possessions during the French Revolution, when the monks were expelled. On their return they resumed making their sweet liqueur, Chartreuse, the 132-plant–based formula which is today known to only a few monks. Sold worldwide, Chartreuse is a main source of income for the monastery. Enclosed by wooded heights and limestone crags, the monastery is austere and serene. Although it is not open to visitors, you can see the road that goes to it.

The **Musée de la Correrie,** near the road to the monastery, has exhibits on monastic life and sells the monks' distillation. ☎ *04–76–88–60–45.* 🎫 *€4.* ⏲ *Easter–Oct., daily 10–noon and 2–6.*

Chartreuse is also sold in **Voiron,** 26 km (16 mi) west of St-Pierre-de-Chartreuse and 27 km (17 mi) northwest of Grenoble; free tastings are offered. ✉ *10 bd. Edgar-Kofler,* ☎ *04–76–05–81–77.* ⏲ *Spring–fall, daily 8:30–11:30 and 2–5:30; winter, weekdays 8:30–11:30 and 2–5:30.*

Chambéry

46 *44 km (27 mi) northeast of Voiron, 40 km (25 mi) north of St-Pierre-de-Chartreuse, 55 km (34 mi) north of Grenoble.*

Elegant old Chambéry is the region's shopping hub. Townspeople congregate for coffee and people-watching on pedestrians-only **place St-Léger.** The town's highlight is the 14th-century **Château des Ducs de Savoie.** Its Gothic Ste-Chapelle has good stained glass and houses a replica of the Turin Shroud. ✉ *Rue Basse du Château,* ☎ *no phone.* 🎫 *€4.* ⏲ *Guided tours May–June and Sept., daily at 10:30 and 2:30; July–Aug., daily at 10:30, 2:30, 3:30, 4:30, and 5:30; Mar.–Apr. and Oct.–Nov., Sat. at 2:15, Sun. at 3:30.*

Dining and Lodging

$$$$ ★ ✕🏨 **Château de Candie.** This rambling manor on a hill east of Chambéry makes a delightful base. Owner Lhostis Didier, an avid antiques collector, spent four years renovating. Linger over a lavish breakfast in your large room—No. 106, a corner room with a view, has honey-gold beams, a grandfather clock, and a carved armoire. For dinner the chef's dishes include rabbit terrine with shallot compote and an *escalope de fruits de mer,* where the copious seafood is arranged in the shape of a lobster. ✉ *Rue du Bois de Candie, 73000 Chambéry-le-Vieux (6 mi/4 mi east of Chambéry),* ☎ *04–79–96–63–00,* FAX *04–79–96–63–10. 17 rooms, 3 apartments. Restaurant, bar, no air-conditioning, cable TV, minibars, pool, park, meeting rooms. AE, MC, V.*

Outdoor Activities and Sports

Go horseback riding in the foothills of the Alps with a horse from the **Centre Équestre** (✉ Chenin des Bigornes, Voglans, ☎ 04–79–54–47–52).

Aix-les-Bains

47 *14 km (9 mi) north of Chambéry, 106 km (65 mi) east of Lyon.*

The family resort and spa town of Aix-les-Bains takes advantage of its position on the eastern side of **Lac du Bourget,** the largest natural freshwater lake in France, with a fashionable lakeshore esplanade. Although the lake is icy cold, you can sail, fish, play golf and tennis, or picnic on the 25 acres of parkland at the water's edge. (Try to avoid it on weekends, when it gets really crowded.) The main town of Aix is 3 km (2 mi) inland from the lake itself. Its sole reason for being is its thermal waters. Many small hotels line the streets, and streams of the weary take to the baths each day; in the evening, for a change of pace, they play the slot machines at the casino or attend tea dances.

The Roman Temple of Diana (2nd to 3rd centuries AD) now houses the **Musée Archéologique** (Archaeology Museum); enter via the tourist office on place Mollard. The ruins of the original Roman baths are underneath the present **Thermes Nationaux** (National Thermal Baths), built in 1934. ⏲ *Guided tours only Apr.–Oct., Mon.–Sat. at 3; Nov.–Mar., Wed. at 3.*

OFF THE BEATEN PATH **ABBAYE DE HAUTECOMBE** – Mass is celebrated with Gregorian chants at this picturesque spot, a half-hour boatride from Aix-les-Bains. ☎ *04–79–54–26–12.* 🎫 *€10.* ⏲ *Departures from Grand Pont, Mar.–June and Sept.–Oct.,,daily at 2:30; July–Aug., daily at 9:30, 2, 2:30, 3, 3:30, and 4:30.*

Outdoor Activities and Sports

Some brave souls pursue water sports on the lake, but most swim in the local ***piscine*** (pool; ✉ Av. Daniel-Rops). There's also an attractive 18-hole **golf course** (✉ Av. du Golf).

En Route Fast A41 links Aix-les-Bains and Annecy. For a prettier if longer route, go 24 km (15 mi) on D911; turn left onto D912 at La Charniaz to snake the 24 km (15 mi) north to Annecy along the Montagne du Semnoz.

Annecy

★ 48 *33 km (20 mi) north of Aix-les-Bains, 137 km (85 mi) east of Lyon, 43 km (27 mi) southwest of Geneva.*

Jewel-like Annecy is on crystal-clear **Lac d'Annecy** (Annecy Lake), surrounded by snow-tipped peaks. Though the canals, flower-decked bridges, and cobbled pedestrian streets are filled on market days—Tuesday and Friday—with shoppers and tourists, the town is still tranquil. Does it seem to you that the River Thiou flows backward, that is, out of the lake? You're right: it drains the lake, feeding the town's canals. Most of the Old Town is now a pedestrian zone lined with half-timber houses. Here is where the best restaurants are, so you'll probably be back in the evening.

Meander through the Old Town, starting on the small island in the River Thiou, at the 12th-century **Palais de l'Isle** (Island Palace), once site of courts of law and a prison, now a landmark and one of France's most photographed sites. It houses the Musée d'Histoire d'Annecy (Museum of Annecy History) and is where tours of the old prisons and cultural exhibitions begin. ☎ *04–50–33–87–30.* 🎫 *€5.* ⏲ *June–Sept., daily 10–6; Oct.–May, Wed.–Mon. 10–noon and 2–6.*

From the towers of the medieval **Château d'Annecy,** high on a hill opposite the Palais, there are good views of the lake. This mighty castle of four towers (the oldest is from the 12th century) has a stout defensive outer wall and an inner courtyard whose several dwellings reflect different eras of Annecy history (covered in a small permanent exhibit on-site). ☎ *04–50–33–87–31.* 🎫 *€5.* ⏲ *June–Sept., daily 10–6; Oct.–May, Wed.–Mon. 10–noon and 2–6.*

A drive around Lake Annecy—or at least along its eastern shore, which is the most attractive—is a must; set aside a half day for the 40-km (25-mi) trip. Picturesque **Talloires,** on the eastern side, has many hotels and restaurants. Just after Veyrier-du-Lac, keep your eyes open for the privately owned medieval **Château de Duingt.** Continue around the ★ eastern shore to get to the magnificently picturesque **Château de Menthon-St-Bernard.** The exterior is the stuff of fairy tales; the interior is even better. The castle's medieval rooms—many adorned with tapestries, Romanesque frescoes, Netherlandish sideboards, and heraldic motifs—have been lovingly restored by the owner, who can actually trace his ancestry directly back to St. Bernard. All in all, this is one of the loveliest dips into the Middle Ages you can make in eastern France. You can get a good view of the castle by turning onto the Thones road out of Veyrier. ☎ *04–50–60–12–05.* *€5.* ⏲ *July–Aug., daily 2–4:30; May–June and Sept., Tues., Thurs., and weekends 2–4:30; Oct.–Apr., Thurs. and weekends 2–4:30.*

Dining and Lodging

$ ✕ **L'Estamille.** The decor is always changing at this restaurant, as it sells its furnishings and decorations in addition to the food. So it's no surprise that it feels like an antiques store—albeit one serving modern, inexpensive cuisine such as grilled river perch and raclette (a round of cheese baked with potatoes). ✉ *4 quai E. Chappuis,* ☎ *04–50–45–21–16. MC, V.*

$ ✕ **L'Étage.** This small second-floor restaurant serves inexpensive local fare—from cheese and beef fondue to grilled freshwater fish from Lake Annecy, and raclette made from the local Reblochon cheese. Minimal furnishings and plain wooden tables give it a rather austere look, but the often lively crowd makes up for it by creating true bonhomie. ✉ *13 rue Paquier,* ☎ *04–50–51–03–28. AE, DC, MC, V.*

$$$$ ★ ✕ **Auberge de l'Éridan.** Every room in this elegant Third-Empire mansion offers a spectacular view of Lake Annecy, but most everyone will be too knocked out by what's going on in the dining room to even notice. Marc Veyrat, the only six-starred Michelin chef on the planet—three here and three for his restaurant in Megève (☞ *below* for a perspective on his house style)—performs miracles with local Alpine produce, most of which the self-taught shepherd handpicks himself during daily treks through the idyllic mountain pastures that surround the hotel. The hikes are part of the Veyrat myth, as is the signature black hat he wears 24 hours a day. The reality is that this is home to one of the savviest self-promoters in the business, who also just so happens to be an extraordinarily gifted chef. The menu changes according to the seasons, the chef's whims, and what the mountain hikes bring in. Upstairs, luxe guest rooms and suites await those who just want to repair and digest the great feast. ✉ *13 vieille route des Pensières, Veyrier-du-Lac (5½ km/3½ mi from Annecy on D909),* ☎ *04–50–60–24–00,* FAX *04–50–60–23–00,* WEB *www.marcveyrat.com. 9 rooms, 3 suites. Restaurant, bar, cable TV, minibars, park, parking (fee). AE, DC, MC, V. Closed Dec.–Mar. 20, and Mon. (except July and Aug.) and Tues. No lunch Wed.*

$$$$ ✕ **L'Impérial Palace.** Though the Palace, across the lake from the town center, is Annecy's leading hotel, it lacks depth of character. In contrast to its Belle Epoque exterior, the spacious, high-ceiling guest rooms are done in the subdued colors so loved by contemporary designers. The better rooms face the public gardens on the lake; waking up to breakfast on the terrace is a great way to start the day. Service is professional, but you pay for it. Fine cuisine is served in the stylish La Voile; the food in Le Jackpot Café, in the casino, is acceptable and less costly. ✉ *32 av. Albigny, 74000,* ☎ *04–50–09–30–00,* FAX *04–50–09–33–33,* WEB *www.lac-annecy.com. 91 rooms, 7 suites. 2 restaurants, bar, cable TV, minibars, health club, meeting rooms, casino, parking (fee). AE, DC, MC, V.*

$$ ★ **Hôtel du Palais de l'Isle.** Steps away from the lake, in the heart of Old Annecy, is this delightful small hotel. Without destroying the building's ancient feel, rooms have a cheery, contemporary look and Philippe Starck furnishings; some have a view of the Palais de l'Isle. Rates reflect the size of the room. Breakfast is served. Though the area is pedestrian-only, you can drive up to unload luggage. ✉ *13 rue Perrière, 74000,* ☎ *04–50–45–86–87,* FAX *04–50–51–87–15. 26 rooms. No air-conditioning, cable TV. AE, MC, V.*

Outdoor Activities and Sports

Bikes can be rented at the **train station** (✉ Pl. de la Gare). Mountain bikes are available from **Loca Sports** (✉ 37 av. de Loverchy, ☎ 04–50–45–44–33). **Sports Passion** (✉ 3 av. du Parmelan, ☎ 04–50–51–46–28) is a convenient source for bikers. From April through October you can take an hour-long cruise around Lake Annecy on the ***M.S. Libellule*** (✉ Compagnie des Bateaux du Lac d'Annecy, 2 pl. aux Bois, ☎ 04–50–51–08–40) for €9.

Chamonix

49 *94 km (58 mi) east of Annecy, 83 km (51 mi) southeast of Geneva.*

Chamonix is the oldest and biggest of the French winter-sports resort towns. It was the site of the first Winter Olympics, held in 1924. As a ski resort, however, it has its limitations: The ski areas are spread out, none is very large, and the lower slopes often suffer from poor snow conditions. On the other hand, some runs are extremely memorable, such as the 20-km (12-mi) run through the **Vallée Blanche** or the off-trail area of **Les Grands Montets.** And the situation is getting better: many lifts have been added, improving access to the slopes as well as lessening lift lines. In summer it's a great place for hiking, climbing, and enjoying outstanding views. If you're heading to Italy via the Mont Blanc Tunnel, Chamonix will be your gateway.

The world's highest **cable car** soars 12,000 ft up the Aiguille du Midi, providing positively staggering views of 15,700-ft **Mont Blanc,** Europe's loftiest peak. Be prepared for a lengthy wait, both going up and coming down—and wear warm clothing. *€45 round-trip.* ⏲ *May–Sept., daily 8–4:45; Oct.–Apr., daily 8–3:45.*

Dining and Lodging

$$$$ ✕ **Hameau Albert 1er.** At Chamonix's most desirable hotel, rooms are furnished with elegant reproductions, and most have balconies. Many, such as No. 33, have unsurpassed views of Mont Blanc. Choose between rooms in the original building or Alpine lodge–style accommodations—with touches of contemporary rustic elegance—in the complex known as Le Hameau. The dining room also has stupendous Mont Blanc views. Pierre Carrier's cuisine is best characterized as perfectly prepared and presented, though sometimes not so interesting or original. ✉ *119 impasse du Montenvers, 74400,* ☎ *04–50–53–05–09,* FAX *04–50–55–95–48,* WEB *www.hameaualbert.fr. 17 rooms, 12 suites, 3 chalets, 12 rooms in farmhouse. 2 restaurants, bar, cable TV, minibars, pool, hot tub, health club, meeting rooms, parking (fee). AE, DC, MC, V. Closed 2 wks in May, 3 wks in Nov.*

$$$–$$$$ ✕ **Mont-Blanc.** In the center of town, this Belle Epoque hotel has catered to the rich and famous since 1878. Family owned, it is permeated by a sense of well-being; the staff is warm and efficient. High ceilings give guest rooms a majestic feel, accentuated by warm, pale colors, and period pieces. Most rooms look onto Mont Blanc or Mont Brevant. Dining on chef Morand's creations in the restaurant, Le Matafan, is a refined pleasure. Besides classic French dishes (try the

succulent crayfish with shallots and chanterelle mushrooms), many foods available only locally are served, such as a delicious lake fish known as *fera.* ✉ *62 allée Majestic, 74400,* ☎ *04–50–53–05–64,* FAX *04–50–55–89–44,* WEB *www.chamonixhotels.com. 34 rooms, 8 suites. Restaurant, bar, cable TV, minibars, 2 tennis courts, pool, parking (fee). AE, DC, MC, V. Closed Nov.*

$–$$ ✕ **Auberge Croix-Blanche.** In the heart of Chamonix, this small inn has modest and tidy rooms, each with a good-sized bathroom—from one you can even lie in the tub and look out the window at Mont Blanc. Make sure you ask for one of the newly renovated rooms. The hotel has no restaurant, but right next door is the Brasserie de L'M, where reasonably priced Savoie specialties are served. The hotel shuttle bus can take you to the slopes. ✉ *87 rue Vallot, 74404,* ☎ *04–50–53–00–11,* FAX *04–50–53–48–83. 35 rooms. Restaurant, bar, no air-conditioning, cable TV, minibars. AE, DC, MC, V. Closed 2 May–29 June.*

Nightlife

Chamonix is a lively place at night with its discos and late-night bars. A popular place to start or end the evening is at the **Casino** (✉ Pl. de Saussure, ☎ 04–50–53–07–65), which has a bar, a restaurant, roulette, and blackjack. Entrance to the casino is €12, though entry is free to the slot machine rooms.

Outdoor Activities and Sports

Contact the **Chamonix Tourist Office** for information on skiing in the area. Want to try bobsledding? Two approximately 3,000-ft-long runs are open winter and summer at **Parc de Loisirs des Planards** (☎ 04–50–53–08–07). Chamonix's indoor **skating rink** (☎ 04–50–53–12–36) is open year-round, Thursday–Tuesday 3–6 and Wednesday 3–11. Admission is €4, and skates are €3.

The **Sports Centre Olympide** (☎ 04–50–53–09–07) has an indoor-outdoor Olympic-size pool. Hang gliding and paragliding can be arranged through **Chamonix Parapente** (☎ 04–50–55–99–22). **Espace Sensations** (☎ 04–50–55–99–49) also organizes hang gliding and paragliding at a cost of €76. Mont Blanc provides the backdrop to golf at the course in **Les Praz de Chamonix** (✉ Rte. de Tignes, ☎ 04–50–53–06–28); it's open daily May–November; greens fees are €55. Horseback rides are organized by the **Club Hippique La Guérinière** (☎ 04–50–53–42–84); an hour's trek is €15.

Megève

50 *35 km (22 mi) west of Chamonix, 69 km (43 mi) southeast of Geneva.*

The smartest of the Mont Blanc stations, idyllic Alpine Megève is not only a major ski resort but also a chic winter watering hole that draws royalty, celebrities, and fat wallets from all over the world (many will fondly recall Cary Grant bumping into Audrey Hepburn here in the opening scenes of the 1963 thriller *Charade*). The aprés-ski amusements tend to submerge the skiing here because the slopes are comparatively easy, and beginners and skiers of only modest ability will find Megève more to their liking than Chamonix. This may account for Megève's having one of France's largest ski schools. Ski passes purchased here cover the slopes not only around Megève but also in Chamonix. In summer the town is a popular spot for golfing and hiking. From Megève the drive along N212 to Albertville goes along one of the prettiest little gorges in the Alps.

Dining and Lodging

$$$$ ✕🏨 **Chalet du Mont d'Arbois.** This rustic but sophisticated mountain resort—part of a vast, upscale development next to the ski lifts, 3 km (2 mi) up from Megève on Mont d'Arbois—is run by Nadine de Rothschild. Most come here for a few days or more to ski or hike. Rooms have fine views, antiques, and down comforters. The restaurant is the most prestigious in the area and serves delicious spit-roasted meats and fish (try salmon in red-wine sauce) as well as many wines from—*bien sûr*—the baroness's Bordeaux vineyards. ✉ *447 chemin Rocaille, 74120,* ☎ *04–50–21–25–03,* FAX *04–50–21–24–79,* WEB *www.chalet-montarbois.com. 19 rooms, 4 suites. Restaurant, bar, no air-conditioning, cable TV, minibars, golf course, tennis court, pool, health club, hot tub. AE, DC, MC, V. Closed May–mid-June and Oct.–mid-Dec.*

$$$$ ★ ✕🏨 **La Ferme de Mon Père.** This amazing Savoyard inn is the newest culinary shrine in Europe, now packed with critics and millionaires fighting to pay astronomic prices in order to taste the creations of the newest superstar of the food world, Marc Veyrat. Past and future fittingly collide in the eye-dazzling surroundings—a farmhouse that looks like it was put together by a Ralph Lauren on acid. Farm implements, drying hams, old pots, and even moss growing out of the rough-hewn floorboards all conjure up Farmhouse Chic with a vengeance. Amusing is the bread cart—an antique crib. Not amusing, however, are the stables that Veyrat has concocted for resident cows, goats, sheep, and chickens—they can be seen through glass panels in the floor, allowing the animals and humans to eye each other as one devours the other. In this world of foot-and-mouth and mad cow disease, this borders on the grotesque. Foodies insist that Veyrat's creations—bass cooked on a rock, eggs infused with lichen and nutmeg, coquilles St-Jacques served up with a purée of dates in an essence of pink grapefruit, lobster with lovage and licorice root—hurtle the lessons of Escoffier far into the 21st century. There are those, however, who will carp that the concept of Alpine haute cuisine is at best an oxymoron. ✉ *367 route du Crêt,* ☎ *04–50–21–01–01,* WEB *www.marcveyrat.com. AE, DC, MC, V. Closed Mon., Tues.–Thurs. lunch, and Dec. 15–Mar. 31.*

$$$ ✕🏨 **Les Fermes de Marie.** By reassembling four Alpine chalets brought down from the mountains and decorating rooms with old Savoie furniture (shepherds' tables, sculptured chests, credenzas), Jocelyne and Jean-Louis Sibuet have created a luxury hotel with a delightfully rustic feel. Both a summer and winter resort, it has shuttle-bus service to ski lifts in season and a spa providing a wide range of services in this most tranquil of settings. In the kitchen, chef Christophe Cote creates fine cuisine based on local products. ✉ *Chemin de Riante Colline, 74120,* ☎ *04–50–93–03–10,* FAX *04–50–93–09–84,* WEB *www.c-h-m.com. 69 rooms. 3 restaurants, bar, no air-conditioning, cable TV, minibars, pool, gym, spa, parking. AE, DC, MC, V. Closed Apr.–May and Oct.–Nov.*

$$ ✕🏨 **Les Cîmes.** Friendly owners Monsieur and Madame Bourdin put their hearts into running this tiny, reasonably priced hotel with small, neat rooms and a pleasant little restaurant. Simple food is served, such as roast lamb or grilled fish. Breakfast is included in room rates. The hotel's only drawback is its location on a main street entering Megève, which can be a little noisy. ✉ *341 av. Charles Feige, 74120,* ☎ *04–50–21–01–71,* FAX *04–50–58–70–95. 8 rooms. Restaurant, no air-conditioning, cable TV, minibars, parking (fee). V.*

$$$–$$$$ 🏨 **Hôtel Mont-Blanc.** Each guest room at this hotel in the heart of Megeve's pedestrian-only zone has a different theme, from Austrian to English to Haute Savoie; half have a small balcony overlooking the courtyard—an ideal spot for summer breakfasts and evening cocktails. Wood predominates, as does artwork collected from all over Europe. Public areas are comfortable, from the lounge with huge easy chairs to the leather-bound library that doubles as a tearoom and bar. ✉ *Pl. de l'Eglise, 74120,* ☎ *04–50–21–20–02,* FAX *04–50–21–45–28. 40 rooms. Bar, no air-conditioning, minibars, pool, library. AE, DC, MC, V. Closed May 1–June 10.*

Outdoor Activities and Sports

For information about skiing in the area, contact the **Megève Tourist Office.** In summer you can play at the 18-hole **Megève Golf Course** (✉ Golf du Mont d'Arbois, ☎ 04–50–21–29–79); it costs about €5 per round.

LYON AND THE ALPS A TO Z

To research prices, get advice from other travelers, and book travel arrangements, visit www.fodors.com.

AIR TRAVEL

CARRIERS

Air France, British Airways, and many other major carriers have connecting services from Paris into Aéroport-Lyon-Saint-Exupéry in Satolas. Only domestic airlines, such as Air France, fly into Grenoble Airport.

AIRPORTS

The region's international gateway airport is Aéroport-Lyon-Saint-Exupéry, 26 km (16 mi) east of Lyon, in Satolas. There are domestic airports at Grenoble, Valence, Annecy, Chambéry, and Aix-les-Bains.

To get between the Aéroport-Lyon-Saint-Exupéry and downtown Lyon take the Satobus, a shuttle bus that goes to the city center between 5 AM and 9 PM and to the train station between 6 AM and 11 PM; journey time is 35–45 minutes, and the fare is €6.92. There's also a bus from Satolas to Grenoble; journey time is just over an hour, and the fare is €18. A taxi into Lyon costs about €30. Taking a taxi from the small Grenoble airport to downtown Grenoble is expensive, but it may be your only option.

➤ AIRPORT INFORMATION: **Aéroport-Lyon-Saint-Exupéry** (☎ 04–72–22–72–21 for information). **Satobus** (☎ 04–72–22–71–28).

BUS TRAVEL

Where there is no train service, SNCF often provides bus transport. Buses cover the entire region, but Lyon and Grenoble are the two main bus hubs for long-distance (national and international) routes. From these towns, buses go to the smaller towns. Many ski centers, such as Chamonix, have shuttle buses connecting them with surrounding villages. Tourist destinations, such as Annecy, have convenient bus links with Grenoble. There are many other routes, so always check in with the regional tourist office or information window at a gateway rail or bus station to get printed bus schedules.

➤ BUS INFORMATION: **SNCF** (☎ 02–38–53–94–75, WEB www.sncf.com).

CAR RENTAL

➤ LOCAL AGENCIES: **Avis** (✉ 1 av. du Dr-Desfrançois, Chambéry, ☎ 04–79–33–58–54, FAX 04–79–15–13–63; ✉ in Aéroport Lyon-Saint-Exupéry). **Hertz** (✉ 16 rue Émile-Gueymard, Grenoble, ☎ 04–76–43–12–92, FAX 04–76–47–97–26; ✉ 11 rue Pasteur, Valence, ☎ 04–75–44–39–45, FAX 04–75–44–76–88).

CAR TRAVEL

A6 speeds south from Paris to Lyon (463 km/287 mi). The Tunnel de Fourvière, which cuts through Lyon, is a classic hazard, and at peak times you may sit idling for hours. Lyon is 313 km (194 mi) north of Marseille on A7. To get to Grenoble (568 km/352 mi from Paris) from Lyon, take A43. Coming from the south, take A7 to Valence and then swing east on A49 to Grenoble. Access to the Alps is easy from Geneva or Italy (via the Tunnel du Mont Blanc at Chamonix or the Tunnel du Fréjus from Turin). Another popular route into the Alps, especially coming north from Provence, is from Sisteron via N85.

ROAD CONDITIONS

Regional roads are fast and well maintained, though smaller mountainous routes can be difficult to navigate and high passes may be closed in winter.

EMERGENCIES

In case of an emergency, call the fire department or the police. Samu, in Lyon, provides emergency medical aid and ambulance service. Lyon has several all-night pharmacies. One of the largest, with an equivalence chart of foreign medicines, is Pharmacie Blanchet. In Grenoble contact Europ'ambulance.

➤ CONTACTS: **Police** (☎ 17). **Fire department** (☎ 18). **Europ'ambulance,** Grenoble (☎ 04–76–33–10–03). **Pharmacie Blanchet,** Lyon (✉ 5 pl. des Cordeliers, ☎ 04–78–37–81–31). **Samu,** Lyon (☎ 04–72–33–15–15).

TOURS

BOAT TOURS

Navig-Inter arranges daily boat trips from Lyon along the Saône and Rhône rivers.

➤ FEES AND SCHEDULES: **Navig-Inter** (✉ 13 bis quai Rambaud, 69002 Lyon, ☎ 04–78–42–96–81).

BUS TOURS

Philibert runs bus tours of the region from April to October starting in Lyon.

➤ FEES AND SCHEDULES: **Philibert** (✉ 24 av. Barthélémy-Thimonier, B.P. 16, 69300 Caluire, ☎ 04–72–23–10–56, FAX 04–72–27–00–97).

WALKING TOURS

The Lyon tourist office organizes walking tours of the city in English, as well as minibus tours.

➤ FEES AND SCHEDULES: **Lyon Tourist Office** (✉ Pl. Bellecour, ☎ 04–72–77–69–69).

TRAIN TRAVEL

The high-speed TGV (*Train à Grande Vitesse*) to Lyon leaves Paris (from Gare de Lyon) hourly and arrives in just two hours. There are also six TGVs daily between Paris's Charles de Gaulle Airport and Lyon. The TGV also has less frequent service to Grenoble, where you can connect to local SNCF trains headed for villages in the Alps. South of Lyon the TGV goes to Avignon and then splits and goes either to Marseille or Montpellier. The trips from Lyon to Marseille and Lyon to Montpellier take about 1½ hours. Major rail junctions include Grenoble, Annecy, Valence, Chambéry, and Lyon, with frequent train service to other points.

➤ TRAIN INFORMATION: **SNCF** (☎ 08–36–35–35–35, WEB www.sncf.com).

TRANSPORTATION AROUND LYON

Lyon's good subway system serves both of the city's train stations. A single ticket costs €1.23, and a 10-ticket book is €10.46. A day pass for bus and métro is €3.69 (available from bus drivers and the automated machines in the métro). Lyon Espace Affaires runs a fleet of well-kept taxi-vans in the city.

➤ CONTACTS: **Lyon Espace Affaires** (☎ 04–78–39–26–11).

TRAVEL AGENCIES

➤ LOCAL AGENT REFERRALS: **American Express** (✉ 6 rue Childebert, 69002 Lyon, ☎ 04–72–77–74–50). **Carlson Wagons-lit** (✉ 2 bd. des Alpes, 38240 Melan, ☎ 04–76–04–24–00, FAX 04–76–04–24–02).

VISITOR INFORMATION

Contact the Comité Régional du Tourisme Rhône-Alpes for information on Lyon and the Alps. The Maison du Tourisme deals with the Isère département and the area around Grenoble. Local tourist offices for towns mentioned in this chapter are listed by town below.

➤ TOURIST INFORMATION: **Comité Régional du Tourisme Rhône-Alpes** (✉ 78 rte. de Paris, 69260 Charbonnières-les-Bains, ☎ 04–72–59–21–59, FAX 04–72–59–21–60, WEB www.rhonealpes-tourisme.com). **Maison du Tourisme** (✉ 14 rue de la République, B.P. 227, 38019 Grenoble, ☎ 04–76–42–41–41, FAX 04–76–00–18–98, WEB www.grenoble-isere-tourisme.com). **Annecy** (✉ Centre Bonlieu, 1 rue Jean-Jaurès, ☎ 04–50–45–00–33, WEB www.lac-annecy.com/). **Aubenas** (✉ Centre Ville, ☎ 04–75–89–02–03). **Bourg-en-Bresse** (✉ 6 av. d'Alsace-Lorraine, ☎ 04–74–22–49–40). **Chambéry** (✉ 24 bd. de la Colonne, ☎ 04–79–33–42–47). **Chamonix** (✉ 85 pl. du Triangle de l'Amitié, ☎ 04–50–53–00–24, WEB www.chamonix.com/). **Courchevel** (✉ La Croisette, ☎ 04–79–08–00–29, WEB www.courchevel.com/). **Évian-les-Bains** (✉ Pl. d'Allinges, ☎ 04–50–75–04–26, WEB www.evian.fr/). **Grenoble** (✉ 14 rue de la République, ☎ 04–76–42–41–41, WEB www.ville-grenoble.fr/; ✉ Train station, ☎ 04–76–54–34–36). **Lyon** (✉ Pl. Bellecour, ☎ 04–72–77–69–69, WEB www.lyon-france.com/; ✉ Av. Adolphe Max near cathedral, ☎ 04–72–77–69–69; ✉ Perrache train station). **Megève** (✉ Rue Monseigneur Conseil, ☎ 04–50–21–27–28, WEB www.megeve.com/). **Montélimar** (✉ Allées Provençales, ☎ 04–75–01–00–20). **Privas** (✉ 3 rue Elie-Reynier, ☎ 04–75–64–33–35). **Tournon** (✉ Mairie de Tournon, ☎ 04–75–08–10–23, WEB www.ville-tournon.com/). **Valence** (✉ Parvis de la Gare, ☎ 04–75–44–90–40). **Vienne** (✉ Cours Brillier, ☎ 04–74–53–80–30).

11 THE MASSIF CENTRAL

Continental France's wildest region, the Massif Central, offers a top-ten medley of land, lots of land, including windswept plains, snowcapped mountains, volcanic plateaus, and romantic forests. This is a country of early-to-bed and early-to-rise, the better to take delight in the great outdoors, where unblemished landscapes and spectacular panoramas seem to appear around nearly every turn. As the most untamed part of a very civilized country, the Massif Central is a refreshing contrast to cosmopolitan France.

Updated by Chris Mooney

Introduction by Nancy Coons

IT IS NOT FOR NOTHING THAT THEY CALL this region *massif*. Stretching over a vast landscape that manages to border both Beaune and Avignon as well as both Toulouse and Tours, it covers a truly massive portion of the nation. But what's here? The answer to that question is: very little you've ever heard of. If the points of France's topographic star are its outthrust limbs—Alsace, Provence, the Basque Country, Bretagne—then this is the country's underbelly: raw, unprotected, and unrevealed. Its biggest city? Clermont-Ferrand, best known as the home of the Michelin Tire Man. Its most (in)famous city? Vichy, whose dubious distinction it is to bear the name of the Nazi puppet government Pétain established there.

It's a pity that the Massif Central doesn't automatically bring to mind French culture or civilization, as it is also the setting for Bourges, which is graced with a fabulous Gothic cathedral and the medieval mansion of Jacques Coeur, and for Roanne, site of that culinary shrine La Maison Troisgros. Yet this region is home to another side of France—usually the last one you might choose to explore. For aside from the occasional bicycle-with-baguette ride, few outsiders know natural France, the nation of rugged country carved deep with torrential rivers and sculpted with barren and beautiful landscapes begging to be hiked, climbed, or surveyed on horseback. Windswept plains are punctuated with tiny villages cut into time-ravaged stone. The silhouettes of volcanic cones pierce the horizon and speak of a landscape still forming, even as the rivers gouge out canyons of dizzying depth. The Gorges du Tarn is one of France's most famous natural landmarks, and the volcano-top village of Puy-de-Dôme one of its most admired phenomena.

Battles have raged across this rugged land since the dawn of history: Romans versus Arvernes (the original Celtic settlers), Gauls versus Visigoths, Charlemagne versus Saracens, the dukes of Bourbon versus Francis I, and Huguenots versus Catholics in the Wars of Religion. Small wonder, then, that the Auvergnois kept to themselves during the Revolution, thereby managing to escape much of its mayhem. Collaborating with Hitler under Pétain's Vichy-based government spared the region from bombing in World War II. Thus little was lost—though, some might add, little was there in the first place.

This is truly *la France profonde,* or deepest France, sought by lovers of natural beauty, scorned for the most part by seekers of art museums and grand châteaux. But before you turn the page in search of a more tourist-intensive region, take note of a simple truth: the more rural the region, the better the cheese. And any area that proffers crusty yellow Cantal, redolent of volcanic ash; nutty-smooth St-Nectaire; mild and tangy Bleu d'Auvergne; and the world-famous Roquefort, salty-sharp and sheepy . . . well, perhaps the landscape hasn't gone to waste after all. As the lucky travelers who venture to discover the Massif Central realize, there are few greater pleasures than a day's hard hiking in France's deepest backcountry, then sitting down at night to a local roadhouse feast. After all, the way to France's heart is almost always through its stomach, and the Massif Central is indeed the nation's heartland.

Pleasures and Pastimes

Dining

Food in the Massif Central is fuel for the body; fine dining it is not. But there are a few regional specialties: *aligot* (puree of potatoes with Tomme de Cantal cheese and garlic), *cousinat* (chestnut soup), *sanflorin* (fried pork and herbs in pastry), and *salmis de colvert Cévenole* (wild duck sautéed in red wine and onions). Several well-known cheeses are also made here: Roquefort, creamy Bleu d'Auvergne, Gaperon with garlic, and the delightfully nutty St-Nectaire. In summer, bakers turn *myrtilles* (blueberries) into tangy pies and tarts.

CATEGORY	COST*
$$$$	over €30
$$$	€20–€30
$$	€12–€20
$	under €12

**per person for a main course only, including tax (19.6%) and service; note that if a restaurant offers only prix-fixe (set-price) meals, it has been given the price category that reflects the full prix-fixe price.*

Lodging

Because the region was difficult to get to for so long, you won't find a broad selection of accommodations. The larger towns generally have modest hotels, the villages have small inns, and a few châteaux dot the countryside. In July and August rates are higher and rooms are at a premium, so be sure to make reservations in advance. Many hotels are closed from November to March. Assume all rooms have air-conditioning, TV, telephones, and private bath unless otherwise noted. Internet, when listed in facilities, means in-room data-ports and/or public-area computers provide on-line access.

CATEGORY	COST*
$$$$	over €180
$$$	€120–€180
$$	€60–€120
$	under €60

**All prices are for a standard double room for two, including tax (19.6%) and service charge.*

Outdoor Activities and Sports

With its volcanic peaks and impressive gorges, the Massif Central is a great alternative to the Alps for outdoor adventures. Bicycling and mountain biking (mountain bikes are known as *vélos touts terrains*, or VTT) over the hills and along country roads is a good way to see the region; bikes can be rented at train stations in most towns. For serious hiking, strike out along the extensive network of trails that crisscrosses the large Parc National des Volcans and follow the Gorges du Tarn. Kayaking down the Gorges du Tarn is also popular. For gentler walking from village to village and valley to valley, follow the Monts du Cantal. During winter there is limited skiing around Le Mont-Dore and Mt. Aigoual in the Causses, a high limestone plateau.

Exploring the Massif Central

The Massif Central is roughly demarcated by Burgundy, the Rhône River, Languedoc-Roussillon, and the Dordogne River valley. France's central highlands offer dramatic untouched terrain, quiet medieval villages, imposing castles, and few large towns: Clermont-Ferrand (population 150,000), in the center of the region, is the major metropolis; elegant, infamous Vichy and industrial St-Étienne are two other cities. At the center of the region is the Auvergne, where the expansive Parc National des Volcans, the grand Gorges du Tarn, and the magnificent Cévennes Mountains, cut by canyons, are favorite destinations of nature lovers.

The Massif Central

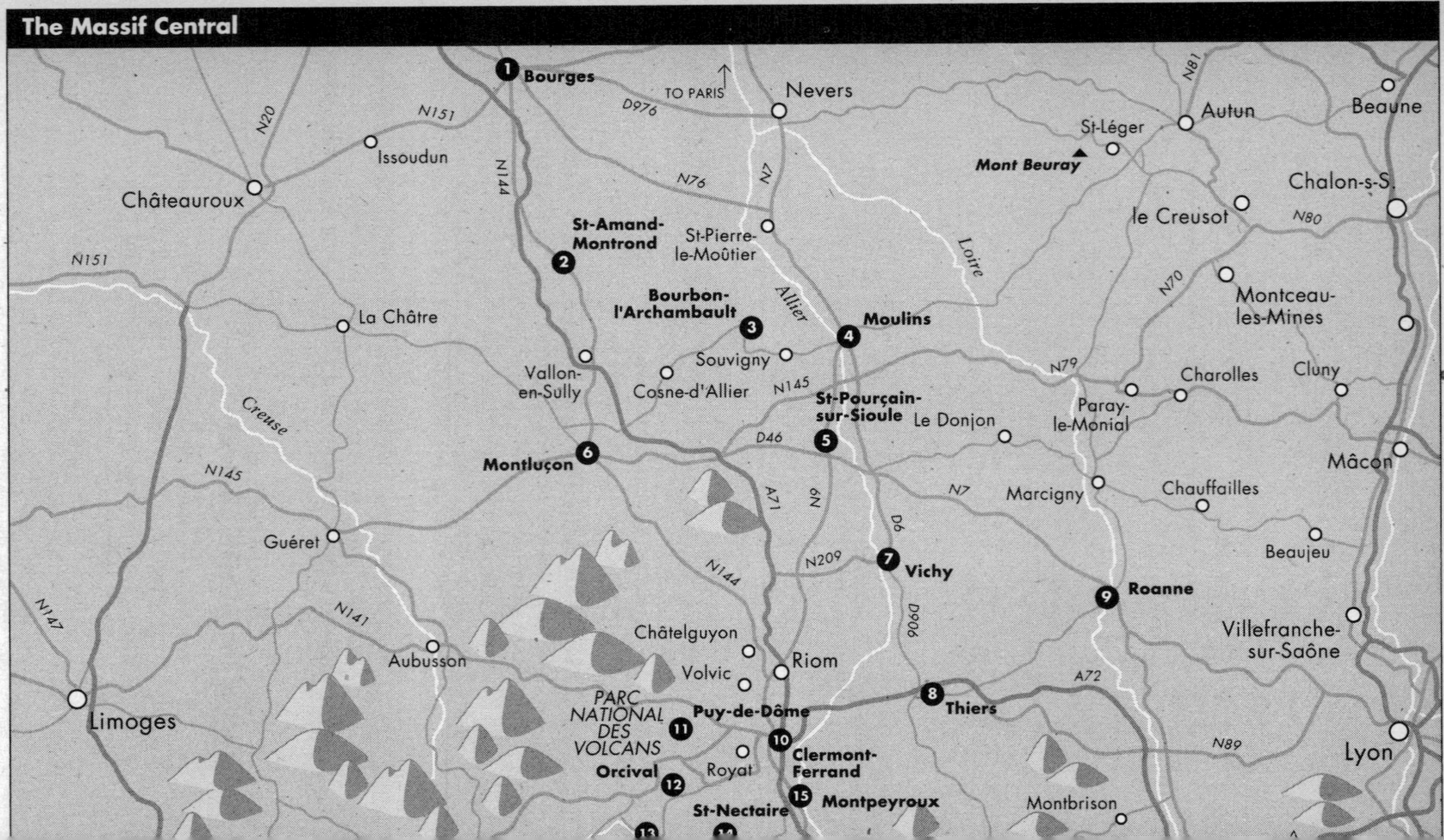

Rhône
A7
N82
Tournon
St-Etienne
Yssingeaux
Privas
Aubenas
N86
Pont-St-Esprit
Avignon
Vallon-Pont-d'Arc
N106
Nîmes
St-Laurent-les-Bains
Loire
La Chaise-Dieu
16
Le Puy-en-Velay
Langogne
Le Bleymard
Villefort
Alès
Anduze
N110
St-Jean-du-Gard
N106
Meyrueis
CORNICHES DES CÉVENNES
N102
Brioude
Allier
Monistrol-d'Allier
N88
Mende
Ispagnac
Florac
26
N106
Ste-Énimie
25
Gorges du Tarn
Gorges de la Jonte
27
Le Vigan
Nant
Couvertoirade
Cirque de Navacelles
D590
N108
Les Vignes
Le Rozier
La Couvertoirade
Besse
A75
St-Flour
17
N9
Laguiole
20
Canyon de la Dourbie
N9
24
Millau
Séverac-le-Château
Lac Pavin
Condat
N122
D926
Murat
Le Lioran
Espalion
D92
N88
Roquefort-sur-Soulzon
Riom-ès-Montagne
Pas de Peyrol
Monts du Cantal
Plaisance
Conques
23
Rodez
Tarn
Bort-les-Orgues
Salers
18
19
D920
22
Dordogne
Mauriac
Aurillac
Lot
N140
N122
Figeac
21
Albi
Aveyron
N89
N120
Sousceyrac
N140
Tulle
Gramat
N20
20 miles
30 km
Brive-la-Gaillarde
N

Great Itineraries

Because the Massif Central is so big, it's almost impossible to see everything in a short trip. But with 3–10 days you can get a fair sense of the region.

Numbers in the text correspond to numbers in the margin and on the Massif Central map.

IF YOU HAVE 3 DAYS

Begin your first day in the former, short-lived capital of France, **Bourges** ①, a medieval city adorned with one of the tallest Gothic cathedrals in the country, and certainly one of its most beautiful medieval palaces; spend the night there or in nearby **St-Amand-Montrond** ② at the Château de la Commanderie. On day two explore Bourbonnais country, with stops in **Bourbon-l'Archambault** ③ for its weathered mansions. Head to medieval **Moulins** ④ to gape at its Flamboyant Gothic cathedral and overnight at one of the lovely hotels here. On day three drive through the Parc National des Volcans to see a natural wonder, the stone formation of **Puy-de-Dôme** ⑪; then visit the Romanesque church in **Orcival** ⑫.

IF YOU HAVE 9 DAYS

You can cover much of the region by car if you don't mind a lot of driving. Begin with lunch in **Bourges** ① and then head to the Château de la Commanderie, near **St-Amand-Montrond** ②, to stay the night. The second day explore **Bourbon-l'Archambault** ③ and **Moulins** ④, home of the Bourbons and another good place to spend a night. On day three pass through **Vichy** ⑦ on your way to **Thiers** ⑧ to ponder its House of the Seven Deadly Sins; stop in **Roanne** ⑨ for the night and try to dine at the superb Troisgros restaurant. On the fourth day drive south to **Le Puy-en-Velay** ⑯ and then on to overnight near the **Gorges du Tarn** ㉕. On day five explore the gorge, then head for the **Gorges de la Jonte** ㉗ on your way back westward toward Millau. On day six head over to **Rodez** ㉓ to see its pink-sandstone cathedral en route to the basilica in **Conques** ㉒. By nightfall get to **Aurillac** ⑲ or **Salers** ⑱. Spend day seven exploring the *cols* (passes) and valleys in this area and the sparse lands around **Laguiole** ⑳ and **St-Flour** ⑰. On day eight travel through the **Parc National des Volcans** around the **Puy-de-Dôme** ⑪, perhaps spending the night in **St-Nectaire** ⑭ or **Montpeyroux** ⑮. On your last day make your way to **Clermont-Ferrand** ⑩ and then on to home.

When to Tour the Massif Central

Autumn, when the sun is still warming the shimmering, golden trees, and early spring, May particularly, when the wildflowers are in bloom, are the best times to visit central France. In summer the *canicule* (literally, dog days) can be oppressive, and the sky is often cloudy; in winter it's cold, and a snowstorm can make a catastrophic intrusion, unless getting snowed in by a cozy fire somewhere in France's central highlands is just what you're looking for.

THE BOURBONNAIS

The northern part of the Massif Central, from Bourges south to Montluçon and east to Vichy, is known as the Bourbonnais, for the dynasty of kings that it spawned.

Bourges

❶ *243 km (151 mi) south of Paris, 70 km (42 mi) west of Nevers, 153 km (92 mi) east of Tours.*

Find your way to Bourges, and you'll find yourself at the center of France. Or rather, medieval France—modern times have largely passed by this neck of the woods, and the result is a preserved market town with an immensely high cathedral and streets lined with timber-frame houses right out of the Middle Ages. Pedestrians-only rue Mirabeau and rue Coursarlon are particularly appealing places to stroll and shop. In the early 15th century the town was home-base for France's most flamboyant art patron and fashion plate, Jean, Duc de Berry, whose enormous expenditure on castles, jewels, and art helped create the French devotion to the *plasir de vie*. Later in the 15th century, it served as temporary capital for Charles VII, who had been forced to flee invading British forces. The town hero at that time was Jacques Coeur, the son of a local fur trader, who amassed a fortune as the king's finance minister. His lavish early-Renaissance palace still stands as one of central France's foremost sights.

★ Approaching the town, you'll see the soaring towers of the 13th-century **Cathédrale St-Étienne.** For connoisseurs of Gothic architecture, this cathedral is one of the skyscrapers of the Middle Ages. The architects who completed the nave in 1280 really pushed the envelope, as shown by the side aisles flanking the nave, which rise to an astonishing 65 ft—high enough to allow windows to be placed above the level of the second side aisles. The nave of the cathedral of Senlis is shorter than the aisles here. The central portal is a masterpiece of sculpture: cherubim, angels, saints, and prophets cluster mightily in the archway. The interior is sleek, elegant, and entirely given over to heaven-seeking vertical forces, particularly as there are no transepts, crossings, or lanterns here. Study the stained-glass windows in the aisles, which are relatively close to the ground. Note several pillars still painted in royal blue and gold—they serve as testimony to the great wealth and power this church once enjoyed, also seen in the massive crypt, one of the last to be built in France. ✉ *Off rue Porte Jaune.*

★ Once showplace for the staggeringly wealthy Jacques Coeur, the **Palais Jacques-Coeur** is one of the most important late-Gothic dwellings in France. Notice its vaulted chapel, the wooden ceilings covered with original paintings, and the dining room with its tapestries and massive fireplace—all set-pieces of International Gothic, the last gasp of the medieval style throughout Europe. There are few furnishings to be seen, but the storybook Gothic building itself is beautiful, from the carving- and fresco-decorated walls to the sculpture-covered facade (spot the celebrated stone carvings of courtiers staring out of "windows"). As well as being Charles VII's finance minister, Coeur was a great art patron (along with Jean, Duc de Berry, he sponsored some of the finest illuminated 15th-century books of hours) and helped spread a taste for Italy's new Renaissance style. ✉ *Rue Jacques-Coeur,* ☎ *02–48–24–06–87.* 🎫 *€5.50.* ⏲ *Apr.–June and Sept.–Oct., daily 9–noon and 2–6; Nov.–Mar., daily 9–noon and 2–5; July–Aug., daily 9–noon and 2–7; 45-min guided tours only, begin 15 mins after the hr.*

Dining and Lodging

$$–$$$ ✕🏨 **Hotel de Bourbon.** Set on beautiful grounds close to Bourges's medieval quarter, this former 17th-century abbey combines the grandeur of vaulted ceilings with the modern comforts of contemporary furnishings, a conference center, and an Internet connection in every room. Adjacent to the hotel is its restaurant, L'Abbaye Saint-Ambroix. Chef Pascale Auger has a light, innovative touch with fish and does playful desserts such as strawberries with rosemary. The restaurant also has an extensive wine cellar for intrepid tipplers. ✉ *Bd. de la République, 18000 Bourges,* ☎ *02–48–70–80–00,* FAX *02–48–70–*

21–22. 57 rooms. Restaurant, bar, cable TV, minibars, Internet, no-smoking rooms, meeting room, parking (fee). AE, DC, MC, V.

$$ ✕🏨 **Auberge du Moulin de Chaméron.** Out in the country with only the owls to keep you awake at night, this hotel is a peaceful place to stay. Though rooms in this modern, almost motel-like building are small, with standard hotel furnishings that make them seem even smaller, most open out onto the lovely garden. At the other end of the garden is the restaurant, in a former mill. Dining outside on the terrace in the twilight or in either of the cozy, beamed dining rooms is a fine way to end the day. The cooking is not fancy, but the produce is fresh, and the beef is prime Charolais. ✉ *18210 Bannegon (40 km/25 mi from Bourges),* ☎ *02–48–61–83–80 for hotel; 02–48–61–84–48 for restaurant,* FAX *02–48–61–84–92. 12 rooms, 1 apartment. Restaurant, cable TV, minibars, Internet, pool. AE, DC, MC, V. Closed mid-Nov.–Mar.*

$$–$$$ 🏨 **Hôtel d' Angleterre.** This efficient hotel in the center of town near the palace is popular with business travelers. It was recently acquired by the Best Western chain, and its rooms make up for their lack of character with soothing modern conveniences. The restaurant, decorated in Louis XVI style, has prix-fixe menus starting at €15. ✉ *1 pl. des Quatre-Piliers, 18000 Bourges,* ☎ *02–48–24–68–51,* FAX *02–48–65–21–41,* WEB *www.bw-fa-champlain.com/eng/index.html. 31 rooms. Restaurant, bar, cable TV, minibars. AE, DC, MC, V.*

St-Amand-Montrond

❷ *44 km (27 mi) south of Bourges, 54 km (33 mi) north of Montluçon.*

The small market town of St-Amand-Montrond is a convenient stopping point when you're heading south into the heart of the Massif Central. If time permits, visit the **town museum,** a former hôtel particulier dating from the 16th century, for an account of the region's history all the way from the Stone Age to the present. ✉ *Off pl. du Marché,* ☎ *02–48–96–55–20.* 🎫 *€2.5.* ⏲ *Mon. and Wed.–Sat. 10–noon and 2–6, Sun. 2–6.*

Also worth exploring is the **Montrond Fortress,** once a residence of Louis II. Though it's in ruins, you can wander around and imagine its former grandeur.

OFF THE BEATEN PATH

ABBAYE DE NOIRLAC – Twenty kilometers (12 miles) northwest of St-Amand is this abbey constructed in 1150, still one of the finest examples of medieval monastic architecture in France. The abbey church is intact, with 13th- and 14th-century arcades flanking the south cloister; also standing are the monastery, the chapter house, and the monks' hall. ✉ *18200 Bruère-Allichamps,* ☎ *02–48–62–01–01.* 🎫 *€5.5.* ⏲ *Feb.–Sept., daily 9:45–noon and 1:45–5; Oct.–Jan., Wed.–Mon. 9:45–noon and 1:45–5.*

Dining and Lodging

$$$$ ★ ✕🏨 **Château de la Commanderie.** You won't regret going out of your way to reach this impressive 11th-century château-inn, where you'll stay in style in large, elegant rooms. The main building, of gleaming white stone, is adorned with mansard roof, turrets, and towers and looks suitably storybooklike. Dinner can be arranged with the hosts, the Comte and Comtesse de Jouffrey-Gonsans (jacket and tie, *s'il vous plâit*) in the paneled dining room. Expect well-prepared family fare, often including perfectly aged Charolais beef. ✉ *D144 at Farges-Allichamps, 18200 Farges-Allichamps (44 km/27 mi south of Bourges on N144 and 12 km/7 mi northwest of St-Amand-Montrond),* ☎ *02–48–61–04–19,* FAX *02–48–61–01–84,* WEB *ila-chateau.com/command. 7 rooms. No air-conditioning, no room phones, no room TVs. AE, MC, V.*

$-$$ ✕🏨 **La Poste–Le Relais.** The main draw is the restaurant—where reasonably priced, delicious food is prepared with loving care and fresh ingredients from imaginative recipes (note that it's closed Sunday and doesn't serve dinner Monday). Rooms are small and plainly furnished, but perfectly adequate. ✉ *9 rue du Docteur Vallet, 18200,* ☎ *02–48–96–27–14,* FAX *02–48–96–97–74. 18 rooms. Restaurant, no air-conditioning. AE, MC, V. Closed Nov.–Mar.*

Bourbon-l'Archambault

❸ *48 km (58 mi) northeast of Montluçon.*

During the 17th–19th centuries Bourbon-l'Archambault functioned as a ritzy thermal spa; illustrious figures such as Talleyrand, France's powerful foreign minister, took the waters here. But the fancy for fashionable spas, which proved fleeting, left the town a little less noble. Nevertheless, the weathered buildings and the ruined 14th-century **château**—once quarters for tourists of nobility—still have an appealing, faded glory. ✉ *Rue du Château,* ☎ *no phone.* ⏲ *Mid-Apr.–mid-Oct., daily 2–6.*

Dining and Lodging

$$-$$$ ✕🏨 **Grand Hotel Montespan-Talleyrand.** Napoléon's foreign minister, Charles Maurice de Talleyrand, used to come here for the thermal baths, as did Madame de Sevigny—just two members of an A-list 19th-century clientele. The hotel is actually a converted trio of houses with a sumptuous (tapestries and antiques) reading room, covered passageway to the bathhouse, and a swimming pool amid formal French gardens. The rooms are big, but for true grandeur spring for one of the apartment-size suites. The service is very accommodating, one reason many guests here are habitués. The restaurant's food is heavy, but consistently good. ✉ *2–4 pl. des Thermes, 18200,* ☎ *04–70–67–00–24,* FAX *04–70–67–12–00. 48 rooms, 4 suites. Restaurant, no air-conditioning, pool. AE, MC, V. Closed Nov.–Apr.*

$ 🏨 **Les Trois Puits.** Like any good French inn, Les Trois Puits (*puits* is regional jargon for "welcome") offers no-frills lodgings and warm, friendly service. The just-renovated rooms are comfortable, the bathrooms are unusually spacious, and the restaurant serves honest and hearty fare. ✉ *Rue des Trois-Puits, 18200,* ☎ *04–70–67–08–35. 10 rooms. Restaurant, no air-conditioning. AE, MC, V.*

Moulins

❹ *12 km (7 mi) east of Souvigny, 291 km (182 mi) south of Paris, 98 km (61 mi) southeast of Bourges, 54 km (32 mi) southeast of Nevers.*

Once the capital of the dukes of Bourbon, Moulins has a compact medieval center dominated by its cathedral. The oldest part (1474–1507) of the **Cathédrale Notre-Dame** (✉ Rue de Paris), in Flamboyant Gothic style, is known for its stained-glass windows. In the 15th century such windows served as picture books for illiterate peasants, enabling them to follow the story of the crusades of Louis IX. The cathedral's other medieval treasure is the triptych by the Maître de Moulins—one of the greatest, although still sadly anonymous, artists of early Renaissance France—painted toward the end of the 15th century. The painter mixed classicizing style with realistic details—notice the Virgin is not as richly clothed as the duke and duchess of Bourbon, who commissioned the painting. The town's belfry, known as the **Jacquemart** (✉ Pl. de l'Hôtel), was built in 1232 and rebuilt in 1946 after it ignited during a fireworks display. **The Musée du Folklore** (Folklore Museum), in a 15th-century mansion next door to the Jacquemart, is filled with costumes, farming implements, and other reminders of Moulins's past.

✉ 4 pl. de l'Ancien Palais, ☎ 04–70–44–39–03. ✉ €4. ⊙ Daily 10–noon and 2–6, 45-min guided tours.

Dining and Lodging

$$ ✕ **Cours.** Easily the best in town, this chic brasserie-style restaurant in a lovely vine-covered building serves classic dishes with creative twists, perfectly turned out. Service is impeccable, and the wine list is balanced and sanely priced. The €15 menu fixe is outstanding. *✉ 36–38 cours Jean-Jaurès, ☎ 04–70–44–25–66. MC, V. Closed Wed., 1st 2 wks July.*

$$$ ★ ✕🏨 **Paris-Jacquemart.** This family-owned hotel, just a block from the town's medieval quarter, is a genuine delight—traditional France at its very best. Service is efficient and welcoming. Rooms are suitably large, with high ceilings and 19th-century antiques. The menus range from a weekday special at €23 to a €69 deal for a three-course combination meal, usually including a hearty portion of Charolais beef. *✉ 21 rue de Paris, 03000 Moulins, ☎ 04–70–44–00–58, FAX 04–70–34–05–39. 22 rooms, 5 suites. Restaurant, minibars, cable TV, pool, parking (fee). AE, DC, MC, V. Closed 1st 3 wks Jan., last 2 wks June.*

$$–$$$ 🏨 **Chalet.** In the quiet Bourbonnaise countryside, in its own park next to a lovely fish pond, this *Relais de silence* hotel is the perfect place to hole up for a few days and forget about the outside world. Most of the bright, spacious rooms are done up with vintage wallpaper and elegant period furniture (others are more modern). The restaurant is very good, in the same league as the Paris-Jacquemart, which means you can stay holed up and not feel you're missing out on something. *✉ Target, 03140 Coulandon (7 km/4½ mi from Moulins), ☎ 04–70–46–00–66, FAX 04–70–44–07–09. 28 rooms. Restaurant, no air-conditioning, no room phones, no room TVs. AE, MC, V. Closed mid-Dec.–mid-Jan.*

St-Pourçain-sur-Sioule

5 *31 km (19 mi) south of Moulins, 59 km (37 mi) east of Montluçon, 27 km (18 mi) northwest of Vichy.*

Most of the region's wine comes from the attractive little village of St-Pourçain-sur-Sioule—one of the oldest viticulture centers in France. The wine, which varies considerably in quality and price, is generally not found in other parts of France and is often a good value.

Dining and Lodging

$–$$ ✕🏨 **Le Chêne Vert.** This traditional hotel is, as the French say, "correct," meaning, clean, comfortable, and well-serviced. Rooms are large and nicely decorated; many have been recently renovated. Tasty, uncomplicated fare is served in the two dining rooms—veal kidneys in mustard, superb Charolais beef, rabbit in aspic—all to be washed down with excellent St-Pourcain. *✉ 35 Bd. Ledru Rollin, 03500, ☎ 04–70–45–40–65, FAX 04–70–45–68–50. 29 rooms. Restaurant. AE, MC, V. Closed 2 wks. Jan., Sun. in winter*

$$$$ 🏨 **Château de Boussac.** Although the turrets and moat suggest its defensive role in the past, this château-inn is fully modernized. Despite being a working Charolais cattle ranch, it is very quiet. Lovely breakfasts are served in guest rooms, which are furnished with antiques. In the evening you can enjoy an aperitif with the Marquis and Marquise de Longueil before the table d'hôte dinner (advance arrangements required) is served. *✉ Target, 03140 Chantelle (10 km/6 mi from St-Pourçain on D987), ☎ 04–70–40–63–20, FAX 04–70–40–60–03. 3 rooms. Restaurant, no air-conditioning, no room TVs. AE, MC, V. Closed Dec.–Mar.*

Montluçon

❻ *94 km (58 mi) south of Bourges, 54 km (34 mi) south of St-Amand-Montrond, 59 km (37 mi) west of St-Pourçain.*

Montluçon is best known for its Bourbon castle and its Old Quarter, where small 16th- and 17th-century houses line the streets. Built during the Hundred Years' War, the **Château de Montluçon** is remarkably well preserved. It houses the **Musée des Musiques Populaires** (Museum of Folk Music), with a collection of local artifacts from the 18th and 19th centuries, including a historical account of the hurdy-gurdy, a traditional stringed instrument. ☎ *04–70–02–56–56.* €4. *Easter–Oct., Tues.–Sun. 2–7.*

Dining and Lodging

$$ **Le Grenier à Sel.** On the ground floor of a private villa in the center of town, this restaurant is the meeting place for the town's bigwigs. They come for chef Morlon's classic French cuisine and the excellent service. Choose from such dishes as foie gras *chaud* (warm foie gras) or *sandre* (pike perch) poached in wine with a light beurre blanc sauce. Menus start at €19. Should you choose to spend the night, the five rooms upstairs are small but pretty. ✉ *Pl. des Toiles, 8 rue St-Anne,* ☎ *04–70–05–53–79,* FAX *04–70–05–87–91. 5 rooms. AE, DC, MC, V. Closed Mon. Sept.–June. No dinner Sun.*

$$ **Château de Fragne.** The Comtesse de Montaignac has opened five rooms as guest accommodations in her 18th-century château, set on sizable grounds just 15 minutes from town. A random assortment of furniture, some from the turn of the last century, gives rooms a haphazard feel, but all are quite comfortable. In the morning enjoy an excellent breakfast (€8), and if you make advance arrangements, a table d'hôte dinner in the evening. ✉ *03190 Verneix (northeast of Montluçon on D302 or Exit 10 of A71),* ☎ *04–70–07–88–10,* FAX *04–70–07–83–73. 4 rooms, 1 suite. No air-conditioning, minibars. AE, DC, MC, V. Closed Nov.–Apr.*

En Route Between Montluçon and Bourbon-l'Archambault is the delightful rural town of **Cosne-d'Allier** (Exit 10 off A71 to D94 east), where locals come to market. Look for the small, top-value market restaurant **Globe,** at 61 rue de la République, for bosky specialties such as hare with wild mushrooms in season.

Vichy

❼ *91 km (56 mi) southeast of Montluçon, 30 km (19 mi) south of St-Pourçain, 54 km (33 mi) north of Clermont-Ferrand, 349 km (216 mi) south of Paris.*

Vichy, one of the few large towns in the region, does not have the depth of character you'd expect from a place whose mineral waters attracted the Romans and, later, Paris haute society. Nobles such as France's greatest woman of letters, the Marquise de Sévigné—who once famously wrote, "The countryside here alone would cure me"—and her friend the Duchess of Angoulême started the trend in the 17th century; Napoléon III entered the scene in the mid-19th century, and the arrival of the railroad in the early 20th century attracted the middle classes.

When France fell to the Germans in 1940 and the country was divided under direct and indirect German control, the Pétain government moved to Vichy, using its hotels as embassies and ministries. After the war the puppet government left a stain of infamy on the city. Today Vichy is trying to overcome its past, as well as the perception that it's only a place for retirement. A stretch of the River Allier is being transformed into a lake, and large conference facilities and thermal baths have been built. Although there are no old, famous buildings to admire, the city has a **thermal spa** (✉ Rue Callou, ☎ 04–70–97–39–59) that looks like a mosque. Nighttime sights include the **Grand Casino,** which contains an opera house, in the Parc des Sources. Around the park is a shopping area; the **tourist office** (✉ 19 rue du Parc, ☎ 04–70–98–71–94) is on the western side.

Dining and Lodging

$ ✕ **L'Alambic.** A master with local produce, chef-owner Jean-Jacques Barbot creates such dishes as fish, caught fresh from nearby streams, grilled with endives, and lentil salad using the famous tiny *lentilles de Puy.* Menus start at €25. ✉ *8 rue Nicolas-Larbaud,* ☎ *04–70–59–12–71. MC, V. Closed late Feb.–early Mar., late Aug.–early Sept., and Mon. No lunch Tues.*

$ ✕ **Le Piquenchagne.** Classic cooking to perfection is chef Vincent's motto—and he lives up to it. Try the *lapin* (rabbit) roasted with coriander and cumin or the sautéed fresh bream. Service is smoothly orchestrated by Madame Vincent. ✉ *69 rue de Paris,* ☎ *04–70–98–63–45. AE, MC, V. Closed Wed., during Feb. school holidays. No dinner Tues.*

$$ 🏨 **Hôtel Arverna.** This hotel in an 18th-century building in the center of town provides excellent value for the money. The owner, who has traveled the world extensively, provides a friendly welcome. Rooms are modest but functional (Nos. 101 and 102 are the best); bathrooms are clean. ✉ *12 rue Debrest, 03200,* ☎ *04–70–31–31–19,* FAX *04–70–97–86–43,* WEB *www.groupcitotel.com/web/citoan.html. 22 rooms, 4 suites. No air-conditioning, cable TV, parking (fee). AE, DC, MC, V. Closed Dec. 15–Jan. 5.*

AUVERGNE

Auvergne, the real heart of central France, is home to the Parc National des Volcans, which is characterized by *puys,* craggy lava peaks. Medieval villages perch on the hilltops, and outdoor markets make the narrow streets come alive. Many of these country villages are now being transformed into skiing and hiking resorts. Industry is also a focus in such towns as Thiers, Roanne, St-Étienne, and Clermont-Ferrand—though good restaurants, museums, and churches are to be found in these areas as well. Everywhere there is a harmony between religious architecture and the terrain from which it rises, be it a mountain crest, as at St-Nectaire, or the hollow of a green valley nestling its church, as at Orcival.

Thiers

❽ *34 km (21 mi) south of Vichy, 47 km (29 mi) northeast of Clermont-Ferrand.*

Built on a steep hill, Thiers is a slightly grimy but nonetheless fascinating 18th- and 19th-century town famous for its cutlery. It supplies 70% of France's carving and cutting needs, producing everything from table knives to daggers. In the old days, while the River Durolle turned the massive grindstones, craftsmen would lie on planks over the icy water to hone their blades on the stone. Today's factories use less exotic methods, but the tourist office gives demonstrations of the old way (as well as maps and information). Be prepared for stiff walking—the streets run only up and down! Follow rue Conchette, then rue Bourg to appealing place du Pirou, where there is a wonderful example of ancient half-timber architecture, the 15th-century **Maison du Pirou**

(Pirou House). At 11 rue de Pirou is the **Maison des Sept Péchés Capitaux** (House of the Seven Deadly Sins)—look at the carvings on the ends of the beams, and you'll know why it is so named).

On rue de la Coutellerie are old knife-making workshops and the 15th-century **Maison des Coutelliers** (Cutlery House), a small museum and workshop with demonstrations covering five centuries of knife making. ✉ *58 rue de la Coutellerie,* ☎ *04–73–80–58–86.* *€4.* ⏲ *Oct.–May, Tues.–Sun. 10–noon and 2–6; June and Sept., daily 10–noon and 2–6:30; July–Aug., daily 10–6:30.*

Dining

$ ✕ **Le Coutelier.** Housed in a former *coutelier*'s (cutler's) shop, this restaurant is filled with old Thiers cutlery. The fare is traditional Auvergne style—dishes such as lentils with bacon and sausage, chicken cooked in wine, and, most traditional of all, *truffade* (a potato dish with ham, cheese, and green salad). ✉ *4 pl. du Palais,* ☎ *04–73–80–79–59. MC, V. Closed June. No dinner Mon.–Thurs. in winter, no dinner Mon. in summer.*

Roanne

9 *59 km (37 mi) east of Thiers, 87 km (54 mi) west of Lyon, 98 km (61 mi) southeast of Moulins, 389 km (243 mi) south of Paris.*

The industrial city of Roanne is probably on your itinerary for only one reason—the world-famous Troisgros restaurant.

Dining and Lodging

$$$$ ★ ✕🏨 **Troisgros.** For more than four decades one of the most revered restaurants in France, Troisgros is an obligatory pilgrimage stop for foodies (book weekends two months in advance) interested in the mainstays of haute cuisine. Happily, you'll find the old magic is still here—quite a feat for a place that first set up shop in Roanne's station hotel in 1930. The third generation is now at the helm, and they have learned their lessons well, if the Menu dans la Tradition (€83) is any proof: lightly sautéed foie gras with grilled groundnuts, frogs'-leg lasagna, regional cheeses, and the most celebrated dessert trolley in France are just a few highlights. Service is often incomparable, not surprising with a waiter-to-diner ratio of three to one. You don't have to deprive your heirs to dine here, however: you can also enjoy the Troisgros's buffet breakfast—a dazzling spread—and the Grand Dessert, a high tea served in mid-afternoon. The restaurant is closed Tuesday and Wednesday, and reservations are essential. This is now officially La Maison Troisgros, for the family now owns the adjacent hotel as well. As in the restaurant, decor here is modern, so if you're out for charm, escape to the hotel's lovely garden-courtyard. ✉ *Pl. Jean Troisgros (across from train station), 42300,* ☎ *04–77–71–66–97,* FAX *04–77–70–39–77. 9 rooms, 4 apartments, 1 suite. Restaurant, cable TV, minibars. AE, DC, MC, V. Closed 3 wks during school holidays in Feb. and 1st 2 wks Aug.*

Clermont-Ferrand

10 *40 km (24 mi) west of Thiers, 400 km (248 mi) south of Paris, 178 km (110 mi) west of Lyon.*

Known to historians as the hometown of Vercingétorix, who rallied the Arvernes to defeat Julius Caesar in 52 BC (and who is immortalized in Astérix comic books), Clermont-Ferrand is the only large city in Auvergne. A bustling, modern commercial center that is home to the Michelin tire company's headquarters, Clermont-Ferrand probably won't draw you for more than a few hours. But the city serves as an ideal transfer point to the rest of Auvergne. It has some good museums and a small Old Quarter dominated by its cathedral.

The monolithic **Cathédrale Notre-Dame-de-l'Assomption** (✉ Pl. de la Victoire) was constructed of an especially durable black volcanic stone that enabled the pillars to be thinner and the interior to soar to greater heights than ever before. Originally it was built in Romanesque style in the 13th century, but a subsequent renovation gave it a much more Gothic appearance. In 1884 the two spires were added in accordance with plans drawn up by Viollet le Duc, to imitate the style of the 13th and 15th centuries.

The older **Notre-Dame-du-Port** (✉ Rue du Port) was built of sandstone and has an entirely different feel from the cathedral. Though founded in the 6th century, renovations in the 11th and 12th centuries gave it a Romanesque look. Note the choir loft with carved capitals that illustrate such tales as the struggle between Virtue and Vice and the fall of Adam and Eve.

Housed in a former Ursuline convent, the **Musée des Beaux-Arts** (Fine Arts Museum) has a beautifully designed exhibit on the history of painting and sculpture. ✉ *Pl. Louis-Deteix,* ☎ *04–73–16–11–30.* 🎫 *€4.* ⏲ *Tues.–Sun. 10–6.*

The **Musée du Ranquet** houses an assortment of artifacts, from ancient musical instruments to the world's first calculating machine, invented in the 17th century by native son Blaise Pascal. ✉ *34 rue des Gras,* ☎ *04–73–37–38–63.* 🎫 *€2.5.* ⏲ *Tues.–Sun. 10–noon and 1–6.*

Dining and Lodging

$$$–$$$$ ★ ✕ **Bernard Andrieux.** Chef Bernard Andrieux cooks deceptively simple dishes such as salmon with truffle sauce and *escalope de foie chaud de canard* (hot scalloped duck liver). The restaurant's elegance—cream-color walls, white linens, and well-spaced tables—reflects the prices (the least expensive prix-fixe menu is €28) but not the suburban location. ✉ *Rte. de la Baraque (3 km/2 mi northwest of Clermont-Ferrand on D141A),* ☎ *04–73–19–25–00,* FAX *04–73–19–25–04. AE, DC, MC, V. Closed Sun. mid-Aug.–mid-July, 1st wk in May, school holidays in Feb., and Mon.*

$$ 🏨 **Hôtel de Lyon.** With its exposed timbers, this centrally located hotel stands out in contrast to the surrounding buildings made of volcanic stone and concrete, but don't expect much more than clean rooms and perfunctorily efficient service. ✉ *16 pl. de Jaude, 63000,* ☎ *04–73–93–32–55,* FAX *04–73–93–54–33. 32 rooms. Restaurant, no air-conditioning. AE, DC, MC, V.*

Parc National des Volcans and Puy-de-Dôme

★ ⓫ *18 km (11 mi) west of Royat on D68, 24 km (15 mi) west of Clermont-Ferrand.*

Stretching 150 km (90 mi) from north to south, the **Parc National des Volcans** (National Park of Volcanoes) contains 80 or so dormant volcanoes, with all kinds of craters, dikes, domes, prismatic lava flows, caldera cones, and basaltic plateaus dotting the grounds. The volcanoes are (relatively) young; the most recent is only 6,000 to 8,000 years old, which explains why their shapes are so well preserved.

The most famous *puy* (peak) of all is also the most convenient, ideal for the day-trip crowd based at Clermont-Ferrand, 12 km (7 mi) to the north. As the highest volcano in the Mont-Dôme range, the Puy-de-Dôme, at 4,800 ft, is one heck of a climb—just ask the Tour de France riders, who consider it one of the most challenging stages of the bike race. The Romans built a temple to Mercury here; its ruins were uncovered in 1872. The number of tourists, especially in July and August, is tremendous—Puy-de-Dôme is one of the most visited sights in France. Count on spending most of the day here, and bring your walking shoes so that you can follow the trails up to magnificent panoramas. If you're set on a bird's-eye view, parasailing, hot-air ballooning, and hang gliding can be arranged.

To reach the summit, take Bus 14 from the train station or place de Jaude in Clermont-Ferrand to Royat. From here walk 6 km (4 mi) along the road toward Col de Ceyssat until you come to the *sentier des muletiers* (path of the mule-keepers), a wide, rocky switchback trail leading to the top. If you're not up for the hike, take an excursion bus from Clermont-Ferrand (such as those run by Voyages Maisonneuve). The road to the peak is mostly paved, so if you want hardcore nature, you're out of luck. Luckily, once you are at the top there are trails in every direction—one two-hour hike takes you to a cone-shape crater. The *salle d'exposition* (exhibition hall) in Royat has good hiking maps. *€4.5 per car except July and Aug. (when access by shuttle bus only, €3). Mar. and Nov., daily 8–6; Apr. and Oct., daily 8–8; May–Sept., daily 7 AM–10 PM; Dec., weekends 7–5:30.*

Orcival

12 *13 km (8 mi) southwest of Puy-de-Dôme, 22 km (14 mi) southwest of Clermont-Ferrand.*

Mont-Dôme was a major hurdle for pilgrims making the long walk to Santiago de Compostela in Spain. To house them, five major sanctuaries—St-Austremoine d'Issoire, Notre-Dame-du-Port, Notre-Dame d'Orcival, St-Nectaire, and St-Saturnin—were erected in the 12th century. Of these vaulted Romanesque hospices, **Notre-Dame d'Orcival** (1146–78) was the most famous. Step inside to inspect a most unusual statue of the Virgin carrying an adult-looking Child.

En Route From Orcival take D27, which joins D983, for a beautiful ride over the **Col de Guery** pass, at 4,160 ft.

Le Mont-Dore

13 *19 km (12 mi) south of Orcival.*

On the Dordogne River at the head of the sheltered Chaudefour Valley, Le Mont-Dore was once a Roman spa town. Today it still has hot springs, though the town now derives much of its income as a convenient, although not particularly attractive, summer and winter resort. Ski trails (mostly intermediate level) radiate from the town center and a *téléphérique* (cable car) climbs the peaks.

Dining and Lodging

$ ✕ **Le Boeuf dans l'Assiette.** This restaurant provides simple fare for ravenous skiers and hikers. With a three-course menu and a bottle of St-Pourçain wine, two people can replenish their energy for less than €27. *9 av. Michel-Bertrand, ☎ 04–73–65–01–23. MC, V. Closed Mon.*

$$ ★ **Château de Bassignac.** A fortified 16th-century manor decorated with family antiques, Bassignac is a working farm, but the owners leave that aspect of the business to their children. Monsieur Besson is an artist who conducts painting classes; Madame Besson acts like everyone's mother. In the evening you can sit before the fire mellowing with a glass of Armagnac after a day of fly-fishing on the nearby River Sumène. In

winter the château is open only by advance arrangement. ✉ *Brousse, 15240 Bassignac (on edge of village, 14 km/9 mi southwest of Bort-les-Orgues on D922; 55 km/34 mi from Le Mont-Dore),* ☎ FAX *04–71–40–82–82. 4 rooms. No air-conditioning, no room TVs, fishing. No credit cards.*

St-Nectaire

⓮ *16 km (10 mi) east of Le Mont-Dore, 44 km (27 mi) southwest of Clermont-Ferrand.*

In the upper part of the village of St-Nectaire is a Romanesque hospice—you may want to give thanks here after surviving the challenge of driving over the passes. But your true reward is St-Nectaire's superb, soft, nutty-tasting cheese, made here since the 3rd century.

Lodging

$$ **Relais Mercure.** On the site of the former Roman baths, in a dignified 19th-century building, is this attractive, modern hotel. Soaring ceilings in the palatial public areas and picture windows in the restaurant and bar give the place a light, airy feel. Part of the reliable Mercure chain, the hotel has all the amenities, from cable TV to direct-dial phones and in-room modem lines. The grounds in back, rising protectively from the hotel, include a tranquil arboretum. ✉ *63710 St-Nectaire,* ☎ *04–73–88–57–00,* FAX *04–73–88–57–02. 71 rooms. Restaurant, bar, cable TV, minibars, Internet, pool, health club, hot tub. AE, DC, MC, V.*

Montpeyroux

⓯ *20 km (12 mi) east of St-Nectaire, 23 km (13 mi) south of Clermont-Ferrand.*

This medieval village, perched on a knoll just 8 km (5 mi) off A75 Exit 7, has made a comeback. By the early 19th century, 445 inhabitants lived within its granite walls, going out each day to tend the vineyards. Then came the phylloxera, in the later part of the century, which destroyed the vines. The village's population dwindled to 125 people, and its once proud homes fell into disrepair. In the 1970s, however, came recognition in France that its many medieval relics needed to be preserved and Montpeyroux's rebirth began. Now the village has 360 residents, restored houses, and an annual festival of flowers the third week in May. There isn't actually that much to see here, except for the 13th-century round donjon and a restaurant or two. Nonetheless, the views from the village of the sprawling landscape and the distant volcanic mountains, combined with a prevailing sense of serenity, make it quite appealing.

Lodging

$–$$ **Chez Astruc.** Owner M. Astruc's enthusiasm for the village—he is its mayor—and his knowledge of the area make staying at this charming four-story inn a pleasure. The Astrucs live on the top floor; guest rooms—not large but pleasant if a bit fussy—are on the lower three floors. Ask to stay on the second floor, where two rooms have balconies and views of the countryside. ✉ *63720 Montpeyroux,* ☎ *04–73–96–69–42. 5 rooms. No air-conditioning. No credit cards.*

En Route The route south from Besse is splendid if you take D978 through the **Monts du Cantal, Monts du Condat,** and **Riom-les-Montagnes.** The route becomes even more dramatic when, at Riom, D62 leads west from Besse, and D680 heads through the **Cirque de Falgoux,** whose tricky twists and turns will require all your attention.

Le Puy-en-Velay

16 *130 km (81 mi) southeast of Clermont-Ferrand, 76 km (47 mi) southwest of St-Étienne.*

Le Puy-en-Velay is a stunning sight, built up on the *puys* that rise from the fertile valley like pyramids. These solidified-lava peaks are crowned with man-made monuments: on the lowest, a statue of St. Joseph and the Infant Jesus; on the highest, the 11th-century chapel of St-Michel; on another, a huge statue of the Virgin. Most spectacular of the monuments is the Romanesque cathedral of **Notre-Dame-du-Puy,** built of polychrome lava and balanced atop the fourth narrow pinnacle, reachable only by a long flight of steps.

Dining and Lodging

✕ **Régina.** In the town center (ask for a room at the rear), the hotel's building dates from the late 19th century, but recent renovations, including updates like Internet connections and Jacuzzis, have kept clientele equipped with all the modern essentials. A big selling point of the hotel is the restaurant, with its cozy interior and veranda, which makes it one of the prettiest addresses in town year-round—and one of the most delicious: desserts are to die for, and the bread is *fait maison* (homemade). ✉ *34 bd. du Mal-Fayolle, 18200,* ☎ *04–71–09–14–71,* FAX *04–71–09–18–57. 27 rooms. Restaurant, cable TV, minibars, Internet, some in-room hot tubs. AE, MC, V.*

St-Flour

17 *110 km (69 mi) east of Le Puy-en-Velay, 74 km (46 mi) west of Aurillac.*

St-Flour is a medieval enclave perched on the edge of an escarpment with cliffs dropping down on three sides. The age of the town becomes even more apparent as you drive from the newer *ville basse* (lower town) up to the ancient *ville haute* (upper town). Narrow cobblestone streets meander between 16th- and 17th-century buildings.

The **Musée de la Haute-Auvergne** (Auvergne Museum), in the former bishop's palace, presents some local archaeological finds but is mostly filled with artifacts and furnishings used by residents over the last 300 years. ✉ *1 pl. d'Armes,* ☎ *04–71–60–61–34.* *€3.8.* *Mid-Oct.–mid-Apr., Mon.–Sat. 10–noon and 2–6; mid-Apr.–July and Sept.–mid-Oct., daily 10–noon and 2–6; July–Aug., daily 10–noon and 2–7.*

Across the square from the Musée de la Haute-Auvergne is the **Musée Alfred Douët.** The 13th-century building, renovated in the 16th century, has on display tapestries and furnishings from the 16th, 17th, and 18th centuries. The objects are laid out just as they might have been when the building was occupied by the consul-general. ✉ *Pl. d'Armes,* ☎ *04–71–60–44–99.* *€4.* *Mid-Apr.–mid-Oct., daily 9–noon and 2–6; mid-Oct.–mid-Apr., Mon.–Sat. 9–noon and 2–6.*

Lodging

$$ **Grand Hôtel de l'Europe.** The choice of hotels in St-Flour's ville haute is limited; the family-run Europe is the best. A long, horizontal building on the edge of town, it overlooks the valley below and the hills beyond—this view being a large part of the hotel's appeal. Ask for a room—and in the restaurant, a table—with a view of the valley. Rooms, though not large, are old-fashioned, homey, and comfortable. ✉ *12–13 cours Spy des Ternes, 15100,* ☎ *04–71–60–03–64,* FAX *04–71–60–03–45. 44 rooms. Restaurant, bar, no air-conditioning, cable TV. AE, DC, MC, V.*

En Route At nearly 5,249 ft, the **Pas de Peyrol** is Auvergne's highest pass. Leave your car in the parking lot and take the 30-minute walk to the summit of ★ **Puy Mary.** The views from here are tremendous: 13 valleys radiate from the mountain, funneling their streams into some of France's major rivers.

Salers

★ 18 *11 km (7 mi) west of the Pas de Peyrol, 20 km (12 mi) south of Mauriac, 43 km (25 mi) north of Aurillac.*

Medieval Salers, perched on a bluff above the Maronne Valley, is filled with tourists—little wonder, since this town cannot fail to seduce most visitors. In the 15th century the people of Salers, feeling isolated in the country, began building protective ramparts and the town subsequently won the right to govern itself. Many 15th- and 16th-century houses of black lava stone remain, now filled with boutiques and small restaurants. Although this was once an important cattle-market town, farming today plays a smaller role than tourism—though you still may be awakened by the sound of cowbells. On market days **Grande-Place,** in the heart of the village, is very busy.

About 15 km (9 mi) south of Salers, the valley ridges are so beautiful that you could spend a day or two exploring the region's tiny, winding roads. The *cols* (mountain passes) are high enough (plus or minus 3,000 ft) to have snow in the winter, but they are really quite gentle, and they provide a good view of the comely valleys below. Find your way to the small *hameau* (hamlet) of **Fontanges,** with its tiny chapel hollowed out of a limestone bluff on which stands a white Madonna. The sweet hillside village of Tournemire and its **Château Anjony** are also worth a visit. *Château: ☎ 04–71–47–64–11. €5. Mar.–mid-Nov., Mon.–Sat. 2–5:30.*

Lodging

$$–$$$ ★ **Château de la Vigne.** Monsieur and Madame du Fayet de la Tour's château-inn retains elements of its past roles as an 8th-century Merovingian castle and medieval fortress, though it was rebuilt in the 15th century. Family coats of arms and stained-glass windows decorate the best guest room, where Jean-Jacques Rousseau is said to have stayed in 1767. Elsewhere furnishings are sparse and bathrooms makeshift. A table d'hôte dinner of regional dishes is served in the splendid dining room. *✉ 15700 Ally (16 km/10 mi from Salers), ☎ FAX 04–71–69–00–20. 4 rooms. No air-conditioning, no room TVs. No credit cards. Closed mid-Oct.–late Mar.*

$$ **Hôtel des Remparts.** From its position atop the ramparts, this hotel has spectacular panoramic views. Rooms are simple and functional. The management likes to quote half-pension rates, which you should resist if you are staying for more than one night. *✉ Esplanade de Barrouze, 15410 Salers, ☎ 04–71–40–70–33, FAX 04–71–40–75–32. 18 rooms. Restaurant, no air-conditioning. MC, V. Closed late Oct.–late Dec.*

Aurillac

19 *42 km (26 mi) south of Salers, 157 km (97 mi) southwest of Clermont-Ferrand.*

The prefecture and market town of Aurillac, at the edge of the Monts du Cantal, bustles by day and becomes a sleepy country village at night. The oldest part of town—a small area—has an old cheese market, ancient houses, and narrow streets that twist along the banks of the River Jordanne. Locals and tourists spend their days at the cafés on place du Palais-de-Justice, the main square. Stop by the tourist office here for a free walking-tour map—well worth following.

At the **Musée d'Art et d'Archéologie** (Art and Archaeology Museum), remains of a Gallo-Roman temple and various religious objects are on display. A unique collection of umbrellas from the past three centuries—about half of all French umbrellas are made in Aurillac—is also housed here. ✉ *Centre Pierre Mendès-France, 37 rue des Carmes,* ☏ *04–71–45–46–10.* 🎫 *€3.* 🕒 *Apr.–Oct., Tues.–Sat. 10–noon and 2–6; July–Aug., Tues.–Sat. 10–noon and 2–6, Sun. 2–6.*

Dining and Lodging

$–$$ ✕ **Poivre et Sel.** This intimate, friendly bistro serves a refined version of Auvergne fare. It is a good place to try Salers beef, as well as other regional dishes such as *salmis de colvert Cévenole* (ragout of game). Two menus are offered, for €10 and €26. ✉ *4 rue du 14-Juillet,* ☏ *04–71–64–20–20. MC, V. Closed Sun.–Mon.*

$$ 🏨 **Grand Hôtel de Bordeaux.** There are advantages to this Best Western hotel—its central location, its private garage, and its professional staff. Otherwise, rooms are what you'd expect from this chain—compact but clean, functional, and adequate, though some have views of the gardens of the Palais de Justice. ✉ *2 av. de la République, 15000,* ☏ *04–71–48–01–84,* FAX *04–71–48–49–93,* WEB *www.bestwestern.fr. 30 rooms, 3 suites. Bar, some air-conditioning, cable TV, Internet. AE, DC, MC, V. Closed end Dec.–early Jan.*

GORGE COUNTRY

Breathtaking gorges carved into the limestone plateaus of the Causses mark the landscape here. Millennia ago, pressure caused fractures and cleavages that trapped torrential rains. Through thousands of years the swirling waters ate into the mass of stone, gouging out the canyons and caves and the underground rivers and lakes that are today such wonders to the tourist, boatman, and geologist. The most famous of these are the Gorges du Tarn, a wilderness filled with sudden views of dramatic silhouettes of red and yellow cliffs. The lovely, old, rural towns make perfect bases for exploring the area, which also headlines some great medieval churches.

Laguiole

20 *85 km (53 mi) southeast of Aurillac, 56 km (35 mi) north of Rodez.*

On the high basalt plateau, Laguiole is more than 3,000 ft above sea level. In winter the wind roars across the land, piling up snow on ski trails; in summer the sun scorches it; in spring and fall the angled sunlight dances on the granite outcroppings. The town is known for its hardy breed of Aubrac cattle; for its distinctive cheese made from unpasteurized cows' milk, flavored by the varied local flora; and for its spring-hinged pocket knife. You can visit the factory, the **Societé Forge de Laguiole** (☏ 05–65–48–43–34), where they make these knives, which have a slightly curved handle and a long blade; buy one here or in town.

Dining and Lodging

$$$$ ★ ✕🏨 **Michel Bras.** Despite the flowery prose used by the Brases to describe their contemporary hotel-restaurant, it does not really "mold itself perfectly to the countryside," but stands on a promontory like a spaceship about to be launched. To be fair, the rooms are bright and comfortable and the views of the granite outcrops are haunting. But the main draw is Michel Bras's unique creations—foie gras with apri-

cots and honey vinegar and asparagus with truffle vinaigrette—as well as his more classic Aubrac beef and wild boar dishes. The €42 lunch menu is worth a visit for itself. ✉ *Rte. de l'Aubrac, 12210,* ☎ *05–65–51–18–20,* FAX *05–65–48–47–02,* WEB *www.relaischateaux.fr. 15 rooms. Restaurant, cable TV, minibars, Internet. AE, DC, MC, V. Closed Mon. No lunch Tues., except July–Aug. and Nov.–Easter.*

$$ ✕🏨 **Grand Hôtel Auguy.** A good alternative to the high-priced Michel Bras, the Auguy has basic, standard-issue rooms. Ask for one of the quieter ones away from the street. Owner Isabelle Auguy is a creative cook who uses her grandparents' rustic recipes but gives them a lighter touch. The foie gras salad is a delight, as are the Aubrac beef and the fresh trout. The restaurant is closed Monday and does not serve dinner Sunday. ✉ *2 allée de l'Amicale, 12210,* ☎ *05–65–44–31–11,* FAX *05–65–51–50–81. 20 rooms. Restaurant, bar, no air-conditioning, cable TV, minibars, Internet. AE, DC, MC, V. Closed Dec.–Jan.*

Figeac

21 *66 km (44 mi) southwest of Aurillac, 38 km (24 mi) west of Conques, 43 km (27 mi) northwest of St-Cirq-Lapopie.*

The old town of Figeac, which has a lively Saturday-morning market, was once a major stopping point for pilgrims heading toward Santiago de Compostela in Spain. Many of the 13th-, 14th-, and 15th-century houses in the old part of town have been carefully restored; note their octagonal chimneys and *soleilhos* (open attics used for drying flowers and wood). The elegant 13th-century **Hôtel de la Monnaie,** a block from the Célé River, is a characteristic old Figeac house. Probably used as a money-changing office in the Middle Ages, today it houses the **tourist office** and a museum of relics. ✉ *Pl. Vival,* ☎ *05–65–34–06–25.* 🎫 *€2.5.* ⏲ *July–Aug., daily 10–1 and 2–7; Sept.–June, Mon.–Sat. 11–noon and 2:30–5:30.*

Jean-François Champollion (1790–1830), one of the first men to decipher Egyptian hieroglyphics, was born in Figeac. The **Musée Champollion** (leave place Vival on rue 11-Novembre, take the first left, and follow it as it veers right) contains a casting of the Rosetta stone (whose original was discovered in the Nile River delta), which Champollion used to decode Pharaonic writing. A varied collection of Egyptian antiquities is also on display. ✉ *5 impasse Champollion,* ☎ *05–65–50–31–08.* 🎫 *€3.* ⏲ *Mar.–June and Sept.–Oct., Tues.–Sun. 10–noon and 2:30–6:30; Nov.–Feb., Tues.–Sun. 2–6; July–Aug., daily 10–noon and 2:30–6:30.*

Dining and Lodging

$$$$ ✕🏨 **Château du Viguier du Roy.** Everything—the tower, the cloister, the gardens, the wood beams, the tapestries, and the canopy beds—in this medieval palace, once the residence of the king's *viguier* (representative), has been painstakingly restored. Rooms throughout are regal. The restaurant, La Dinée du Viguier, serves excellent prix-fixe meals. ✉ *rue Droite, 46100,* ☎ *05–65–50–05–05,* FAX *05–65–50–06–06. 18 rooms, 3 suites. Restaurant,no-smoking rooms, cable TV, minibars, Internet, pool. AE, DC, MC, V. Closed early–mid-Dec. and early Jan.–Mar.*

$$–$$$ 🏨 **Ferme Auberge Domaine des Villedieu.** This lovely farmhouse-inn, partly dating from the 16th century, is lovingly run by the Villedieu family. Not only are there cozy rooms in ancient (restored) outbuildings such as the former bakery, but you can also look forward to a fireside dinner of cassoulet in a bubbling earthenware casserole accompanied by homemade foie gras and a local Cahors wine. ✉ *Rte. D13, Vallée du Célé, 46100 Boussac (10 km/6 mi from Figeac),* ☎ *05–65–40–06–*

63, FAX *05–65–40–09–22. 5 rooms. Dining room, no air-conditioning, pool. DC, MC, V.*

En Route Leave Figeac on the road to Rodez and take D52, a small road on your left: it leads through the beautiful Lot Valley to D901, which goes to Conques.

Conques

22 *44 km (27 mi) east of Figeac, 39 km (24 mi) northwest of Rodez, 56 km (35 mi) south of Aurillac.*

The pretty red-ochre houses of Conques harmonize perfectly with the surrounding rocky gorge. The village was put on the map by its Benedictine abbey, whose outstanding Romanesque church was one of the principal stopping points on the pilgrimage route between Le Puy-de-Dôme and Santiago de Compostela.

★ Begun in the early 11th century, the abbey church of **Ste-Foy** had its heyday in the 12th and 13th centuries, after which the flood of pilgrims, and their revenue, dried up. The two centuries of success were due to the purloined relics of Ste-Foy (St. Faith), a 13-year-old Christian girl who was martyred in 303 in Agen, where her remains were jealously guarded. A monk from Conques venerated them so highly that he traveled to Agen, joined the community of St. Faith, and won their trust. After 10 years they put him in charge of guarding the saint's relics, whereupon he stole them and brought them back to Conques. Devastated by Huguenot hordes, the church languished until the 19th century, when the writer Prosper Mérimée raised the money to salvage it. Ste-Foy clings to a hill so steep that even driving and walking—let alone building—are still precarious activities. The church's interior is high and dignified; the ambulatory was given a lot of wear by medieval pilgrims, who admired the church's most precious relic, a 10th-century wooden statue of Ste-Foy encrusted with gold and precious stones. You can see this statue in the treasury, off the recently restored cloister.

The **Musée Docteur Joseph-Fau** (Trésor II), opposite the pilgrims' fountain near Ste-Foy, houses a collection of 17th-century furniture, neo-Gothic reliquaries, and tapestries from Ste-Foy Abbey. €4. *Sept.–June, Mon.–Sat. 9–noon and 2–6, Sun. 2–6; July–Aug., Mon.–Sat. 9–noon and 2–7, Sun. 2–7.*

Rodez

23 *39 km (24 mi) southeast of Conques, 46 km (29 mi) southeast of Rocamadour.*

Rodez, capital of the Aveyron, stands on a windswept hill. At its center is the pink-sandstone **Cathédrale Notre-Dame** (13th–15th centuries). Its sober bulk is lightened by decorative upper stories, completed in the 17th century, and by the magnificent 285-ft bell tower. The renovated **Cité Quartier,** once ruled by medieval bishops, lies behind the cathedral. On tiny place de l'Olmet, just off place du Bourg, is the 16th-century **Maison d'Armagnac,** a fine Renaissance mansion with a courtyard and an ornate facade covered with medallion emblems of the counts of Rodez. The extensively modernized **Musée Denys Puech,** an art museum, is just east of the wide boulevard that circles the old town. ✉ *Pl. Clemenceau,* ☎ *05–65–42–70–64.* €3. *Mon. 2–7, Wed.–Sat. 10–noon and 2–6, Sun. 2–6.*

Dining and Lodging

$$–$$$$ ✕ **Goûts et Couleurs.** In an intimate, pastel-color atmosphere, enjoy the à la carte selections or the prix-fixe seasonal menus (€22 and

€52), which have such selections as pan-fried calf's liver stuffed with cabbage, or rabbit with fresh herbs. In summer lunch and dinner are served on the beautiful terrace. ✉ *38 rue de Bonald,* ☎ *05–65–42–75–10. MC, V. Closed Sun.–Mon. and mid-Jan.–mid-Feb.*

$–$$ ★ ✕🏨 **La Diligence.** Talented chef Joël Delmas makes succulent mille-feuilles of lamb kidneys and a superb banana coconut tart, among other fine dishes. Equally impressive are the prices: prix-fixe lunches start at €14. The restaurant is closed Tuesday September–June and doesn't serve dinner Monday September–June. Rooms, furnished in modern style, are not luxurious, but they are adequate and modestly priced. ✉ *12330 Vallady (10 km/6 mi northwest of Rodez on Rte. N140 near village of Nuces),* ☎ *05–65–72–60–20. 6 rooms. Restaurant, no air-conditioning. MC, V. Closed 1st 2 wks Jan.*

En Route If you are traveling from Rodez to the east in the direction of Millau, skip N88 and treat yourself to the shorter and prettier route D28, off N88.

Millau

24 *66 km (41 mi) southeast of Rodez, 248 km (154 mi) south of Clermont-Ferrand.*

Millau is primarily a jumping-off point for exploring the magnificent gorges that cut through the limestone *causses* (plateaus). Give yourself time to wander through the Old Quarter, especially around place du Maréchal-Foch, with its 800-year-old arcades. Browse through the shops on place des Mandarous and place de la Tine for leather goods, by-products of all those sheep producing the milk for Roquefort cheese.

In Roman times Millau produced pottery and sent its vases as far afield as Scotland. Some of these artifacts, collected from the nearby archaeological site, are in the **Musée de Millau.** ✉ *Hôtel de Pégayrolles, Pl. Foch,* ☎ *05–65–59–01–08.* 🎫 *€4.* ⏲ *Apr.–Sept., daily 10–noon and 2–6; Oct.–Mar., Mon.–Sat. 10–noon and 2–6.*

Lodging

$$ 🏨 **Château de Creissels.** This hotel, in an ancient 12th-century fort, has rooms furnished in simple country style with modern accents. A few have a terrace overlooking the small village of Creissels. Dinner is served in the medieval allure of the vaulted cellar. ✉ *Rte. de Ste-Afrique, 12100 Millau (3 km/2 mi outside town on D992),* ☎ *05–65–60–31–79,* FAX *05–65–61–24–63. 30 rooms. Restaurant, no air-conditioning. MC, V. Closed mid-Dec.–mid-Feb.*

Outdoor Activities and Sports

Mountain bikes, a good way to explore the gorges, can be rented from **William Orts** (✉ 21 bd. de l'Ayrolle, ☎ 05–65–61–14–29).

Gorges du Tarn

★ 25 *Extends from Le Rozier (16 km/10 mi northeast of Millau) to Florac, 75 km (47 mi) to the northeast.*

Though not quite as awesome as the Grand Canyon, the Gorges du Tarn (Tarn Gorge) is very beautiful and dramatic. Route D907 leads into its mouth and runs along it, 1,968 ft below the clifftop. Beginning at **Le Rozier,** the Tarn River, flowing out of the gorge, is joined by the Jonte, coming from the Gorges de la Jonte. Follow D907B to **Les Vignes,** where the gorge opens into a little valley. Take D995 to the top, along some challenging switchbacks, and follow signs for **Point Sublime,** where you'll find the views that justify the name. After Les Vignes the gorge becomes even more dramatic, with sheer cliffs and rock faces dappled with grays, whites, and blues. In summer you can take a boat through this stretch; a bus takes you to the embarkation point.

At the **Cirque des Baumes,** just before the village of La Malène, the cliffs form a natural amphitheater. Continue on to **Les Détroits** (the straits), the gorge's narrowest section, where the tumbling waters barely squeeze through. After passing **La Malène,** note the 15th-century **Château de la Caze,** with its imposing parade of turrets. Beyond the castle, just before the village of St-Chély-du-Tarn, is the **Cirque de Pournadoires,** and catercorner to it is another, larger natural amphitheater. On summer nights it is the site of a son-et-lumière show. But don't make a point of seeing it: the gorge looks far more beautiful under natural light.

Ste-Énimie, the gorge's major town, is mired under a flood of tourists in summer. In its little church ceramic tiles tell the 7th-century legend of Ste-Énimie, the beautiful sister of the Frankish king. When she was about to marry, she fell ill with leprosy and was scorned by her suitor. On the advice of an angel she was cured at the fountain of Burle, where she then founded a convent. Its ruins can still be seen, as can the fountain. From Ste-Énimie, the road winds through the valley, opening out just before the small market town of **Florac.**

Dining and Lodging

$–$$ ✕🏨 **Le Vallon.** Locals are drawn year-round by the simple yet good fare at this restaurant-inn in the touristy town of Ispagnac, along the gorge. Prix-fixe menus range from €10 to €25; €15 buys you a very respectable four-course repast, which might include an omelet, a salad, a casserole, and some cheese. Rooms are simple, clean, and inexpensive. ✉ *Rte. D907B, 48320 Ispagnac,* ☎ *04–66–44–21–24,* FAX *04–66–44–26–05,* WEB *www.hotelvallon.com. 24 rooms. Restaurant, bar, no air-conditioning. AE, MC, V. Closed late Dec.–Jan.*

Outdoor Activities and Sports

For kayaking down through the Gorges du Tarn, try **Canyon Location** (✉ Rte. de Millau, Ste-Énimie, ☎ 04–66–48–50–52). Trips can be as short as 9 km (5½ mi) and as long as 72 km (50 mi). **FREMYC** (✉ Meyrueis, ☎ 04–66–45–61–54) is another outfit for kayaking the Gorges du Tarn, which also organizes horseback riding, rents mountain bikes, and sends you riding the winds in a hang glider (*parapente*).

En Route Between Florac and St-Jean-du-Gard, the **Corniches des Cévennes** road winds its way through spectacular scenery. Follow D907 from Florac; then take a left on D983 toward St-Laurent-de-Trèves. From here the road ascends the **Col du Rey,** high above the valley.

Meyrueis

❷❻ *35 km (22 mi) southwest of Florac, 43 km (27 mi) east of Millau.*

The Jonte and Betuzon rivers join at the village of Meyrueis (2,300 ft/690 m), whose warm days and cool nights make it a perfect base for exploring the gorgeous Gorges du Tarn, Gorges de la Jonte, and other nearby caves, causses, and cirques. Meyrueis itself has a medieval round tower, part of ancient fortifications, which houses the tourist office, as well as a ruined château high above. The narrow streets of the oldest part of town, once within the walls, conceal a minuscule Jewish quarter and a noble house you can stay in. A self-guided walking tour will introduce you to everyone once worth knowing in Meyrueis, as well as show you where they lived, prayed, and administered justice.

Dining and Lodging

$$$ ★ ✕ 🏨 **Château d'Ayres.** A Benedictine monastery before the Wars of Religion, this aristocratic manor house has been transformed into a marvelous country retreat. A serene pool reflects the vine-covered building, and spacious grounds include a tennis court and pool. Inside are comfortable public spaces and two dining rooms where delightful Auvergne meals are served: Aubrac beef and Mt. Aigoual mushrooms are just some of the regional riches. Up the broad stone staircase are spacious, high-ceilinged guest rooms. ✉ *Rte. d'Ayres, 48150 (1½ km/1 mi east of Meyrueis by D57),* ☎ *04–66–45–60–10,* FAX *04–66–45–62–26,* WEB *www.karenbrown.com/franceinns/chateaudayres.html. 20 rooms, 7 suites. Restaurant, no air-conditioning, cable TV, minibars, tennis court, pool, horseback riding. AE, DC, MC, V. Closed mid-Nov.–late Mar.*

$ 🏨 **La Renaissance.** Just off shady place d'Orléans is this small 16th-century mansion owned by the Bourguet family since it was built. Over the centuries they have furnished it with antiques, beautiful linen-fold paneling, and family portraits. Don't expect to find telephones in rooms (although there are TVs) or an elevator. A nice breakfast room overlooks the garden, but other meals are served at the neighboring Hôtel du St-Sauveur (also owned by the Bourguets), whose restaurant and wine list are of gastronomic note. ✉ *Rue de la Ville, 48150,* ☎ *04–66–45–60–19,* FAX *04–66–45–68–81. 20 rooms. No air-conditioning, cable TV. AE, DC, MC, V. Closed Nov.–Mar.*

Gorges de la Jonte

27 *Extends from Meyrueis (35 km/22 mi southwest of Florac) 21 km (13 mi) west to Le Rozier (16 km/11 mi northeast of Millau).*

The splendid Gorges de la Jonte (Jonte Gorge) is narrower than the Gorges du Tarn. At its depths flows the Jonte River. Start from the village of **Meyrueis,** where the gorge is at its broadest. Within a short distance the gorge narrows, and the eroded limestone cliffs form strange pinnacle shapes. A good spot to stop for a snack is **Les Douzes.** From here proceed to the deepest part of the gorge, along the cliffside. Past **Truel,** a cluster of houses clinging to the cliff face, is a lookout where for a moment the view opens to reveal two levels of cliffs—**Les Terrasses de Truel**—then closes again before Le Rozier. Four kilometers (2½ miles) from Rozier a sign to the right directs you up to the **Belvédère des Vautours,** a natural reserve for birds of prey. Over the past two decades these birds have been reestablished on the causse, offering you a rare chance to see them in their proper habitat—as well as marvel at the cliff-hanging views. ☎ *04–66–45–60–33 for information about bird reserve.* 🎫 *€5.5.* ⏲ *Apr.–Nov., daily 10–7.*

THE MASSIF CENTRAL A TO Z

To research prices, get advice from other travelers, and book travel arrangements, visit www.fodors.com.

AIR TRAVEL

The major airport for the region, at Clermont-Ferrand, has regularly scheduled flights to Paris (Orly), Bordeaux, Dijon, Lyon, Marseille, Nantes, Nice, and Toulouse on Air France, and direct international flights to Geneva, Milan, and London on Air France, British Airways, and Swissair. TAT (Transport Aérien Transrégional) flies from Paris's Orly Airport to Rodez.

➤ Airlines and Contacts: **TAT** (☎ 01–42–79–05–05 for reservations in Paris; 05–65–42–20–30 in Rodez).

AIRPORTS

Clermont-Ferrand has the major regional airport; there is also a small airport in Rodez.

➤ AIRPORT INFORMATION: **Clermont-Ferrand** (☎ 04–73–62–71–00).

BUS TRAVEL

Where there is no train service, the SNCF will often provide bus transports. Contact local tourist offices for schedules and advice for this national service plus the two main regional outfits, T2C Transports Urbains and Voyages Coudert.

➤ BUS INFORMATION: **SNCF** (☎ 08–36–35–35–35, WEB www.sncf.com). **T2C Transports Urbains** (17 bd. R. Schumann, 63000 Clermont Ferrand, ☎ 04–73–28–56–56). **Voyages Coudert** (7 pl. Renoux, 63013 Clermont Ferrand, ☎ 04–73–92–00–40).

CAR RENTAL

➤ LOCAL AGENCIES: **Avis** (✉ 22 bd. Etienne-Clémentel, Clermont-Ferrand, ☎ 04–73–25–72–06, FAX 04–73–25–86–34; ✉ Clermont-Ferrand Airport, ☎ 04–73–91–18–08, FAX 04–73–61–06–93; ✉ Clermont-Ferrand train station, ☎ 04–73–91–72–94, FAX 04–73–90–74–11). **Europcar** (✉ Rue Émile-Loubet, ☎ 04–73–92–70–26, FAX 04–73–90–28–10; ✉ Clermont-Ferrand Airport, ☎ 04–73–92–70–26). **Hertz** (✉ 71 av. de l'Union Soviétique, Clermont-Ferrand, ☎ 04–73–92–36–10, FAX 04–73–90–46–47; ✉ Clermont-Ferrand Airport, ☎ 04–73–62–71–93, FAX 04–73–62–71–96).

CAR TRAVEL

There is only one way to *really* explore the region, and that is by car. Although national highways will get you from one place to another fairly expediently, the region's beauty is best discovered on the small roads that twist through the mountains and along the gorges. Take A10 from Paris to Orléans, then A71 into the center of France. From Paris, Bourges is 229 km (137 mi), and Clermont-Ferrand is 378 km (243 mi). Coming from Lyon it takes less than 90 minutes to drive the 179 km (111 mi) on A72 to Clermont-Ferrand. Entry into Auvergne from the south is mostly on small curving national roads, though the new A75 will eventually link Montpellier with Clermont-Ferrand through Millau; portions of the autoroute are already completed and open to vehicles.

OUTDOORS AND SPORTS

Rafting trips of the Gorges du Tarn can be arranged through Service Loisirs or the Association Le Merlet. From April to November, float through the skies above the volcanoes in a balloon; contact Objectif.

➤ CANOEING, KAYAKING, AND RAFTING: **Association Le Merlet** (✉ Rte. de Nîmes, St-Jean du Gard, ☎ 04–66–85–18–19). **Service Loisirs** (✉ Haute-Loire, ☎ 05–61–09–20–80).

➤ HOT-AIR BALLOONING: **Objectif** (✉ 44 av. des États-Unis, 63057 Clermont-Ferrand, ☎ 04–73–29–49–49, FAX 04–73–34–11–11).

TRAIN TRAVEL

The fastest way from Paris (Gare de Lyon) to Clermont-Ferrand, the capital of Auvergne, is on the high-speed TGV (*Trains à Grande Vitesse*) via Lyon, where you change for the regular train to Clermont-Ferrand. Regular SNCF trains also go from Paris to Bourges and Clermont-Ferrand and from Nantes, Limoges, Toulouse, Brive, Bordeaux, and Nîmes to Clermont-Ferrand.

➤ TRAIN INFORMATION: **SNCF** (☎ 08–36–35–35–35, WEB www.sncf.com).

TRAVEL AGENCIES

➤ LOCAL AGENT REFERRALS: **Centre Auvergne Tourisme** (✉ 9 rue Ballainvilliers, 63000 Clermont-Ferrand, ☎ 04–73–90–10–20). **Voyagers Maisonneuve** (✉ 24 rue Georges-Clemenceau, 63000 Clermont-Ferrand, ☎ 04–73–93–16–72).

VISITOR INFORMATION

The main tourist office for the region is the Comité Régional du Tourisme D'Auvergne. Other departmental and regional tourist offices are listed below by town.

➤ DEPARTMENTAL TOURIST OFFICES: **Comité Régional du Tourisme D'Auvergne** (✉ 43 av. Julien, 63011 Clermont-Ferrand, ☎ 04–73–29–49–49, FAX 04–73–34–11–11, WEB www.crt-auvergne.fr/uk.htm). **Allier** (✉ 11 rue François-Péron, 03000 Moulins, ☎ 04–70–44–14–14). **Aveyron** (✉ Pl. Maréchal-Foch, 12000 Rodez, ☎ 05–65–68–02–27). **Cantal** (✉ Pl. du Square, 15000 Aurillac, ☎ 04–71–48–46–58). **Cher** (✉ 5 rue de Séaucourt, 18000 Bourges, ☎ 02–48–67–00–18). **Haute-Loire** (✉ Pl. du Breuil, 43000 Le Puy-en-Velay, ☎ 04–71–09–38–41). **Lot** (✉ Pl. François-Mitterrand, 46000 Cahors, ☎ 05–65–53–20–65, WEB www.tourisme-lot.com). **Lozère** (✉ 14 bd. Henri-Bourrillon, 48000 Mende, ☎ 04–66–65–60–00). **Puy-de-Dôme** (✉ 26 rue St-Esprit, 63000 Clermont-Ferrand, ☎ 04–73–42–21–21).

➤ LOCAL TOURIST OFFICES: **Bourbon-l'Archambault** (✉ 1 pl. de Thermes, 03160, ☎ 04–70–67–09–79, WEB www.bourbon-archambault.auvergne.net). **Montluçon** (✉ 5 pl. Piquand, 03100, ☎ 04–70–05–11–44, WEB www.montlucon.auvergne.net). **Montpeyroux** (✉ Les Pradets-Lebourg, 63114, ☎ 04–73–96–68–80). **Moulins** (✉ 11 rue François Péron, 03006, ☎ 04–70–44–14–14, WEB www.moulins.auvergne.net). **Orcival** (✉ Le Bourg, 63210, ☎ 04–73–65–92–25). **St-Amand-Montrond** (✉ Pl. de la République, 78200, ☎ 02–48–96–16–86). **St-Nectaire** (✉ Les Grands Thérmes, 63710, ☎ 04–73–88–50–86). **St-Pourçain-sur-Sioule** (✉ 13 pl. Maréchal Foch, 03500, ☎ 04–70–45–32–73). **Thiers** (✉ Pl. du Pirou, 63300, ☎ 04–73–80–10–74).

12 PROVENCE

Provence means dazzling light and an arid, rocky countryside striped with vineyards, fields of lavender, and silvery olive groves. The early Romans staked a claim here and left epic monuments behind to prove it. Later, van Gogh and Cézanne abstracted it into geometric daubs of vivid paint; then, in the late 20th century, essayist Peter Mayle bought a house and spread the word—bringing the rest of the world running. From the marshlands of the Camargue to the honey-gold hill towns of the Luberon, this alluring land has a way of touching something ancient in all of us.

Updated by Christopher Mooney

Introduction by Nancy Coons

AS YOU APPROACH PROVENCE there is a magical moment when you finally leave the north behind: cypresses and red-tile roofs appear; you hear the screech of the cicadas and catch the scent of wild thyme and lavender. Along the highway, oleanders bloom on the center strip against a backdrop of austere, sun-filled landscapes, the very same that inspired the Postimpressionists.

Then you notice a hill town whose red roofs skew downhill at Cubist angles, sun-bleached and mottled with age. Your eye catches the rhythm of Romanesque tiles overlapping in sensual, snaking rows, as alike and yet as varied as the reeds in a pan pipe, their broad horizontal flow forming a foil for the dark, thrusting verticals of the cypresses, and the ephemeral, willowy puffs of the silvery olive. Overhead, the sky is an azure prism thanks to the famous mistral—a fierce, cold wind that razors through the Rhône Valley—which often scrubs the torpid sky to crystal blue. Sheep bells *tonk* behind dry rock walls, while your ear picks up from the distance the pulsing roar of the sea. The Phoenicians, the Greeks, and the Romans recognized a new Fertile Crescent and founded vital civilizations here, leaving traces untouched by millennia of clean, dry air. Nowhere else in France, and rarely in the Western world, can you touch antiquity with this intimacy—its exoticism, its purity, eternal and alive. This is Provence the primordial.

But there's another Provence in evidence today, a disarming culture of *pastis* (an anise-based aperitif), *pétanque* (lawn bowling), and shady plane trees, where dawdling is a way of life, where you may take root in a sidewalk café and listen to the trickling fountain, putter aimlessly down narrow cobbled alleyways, heft melons in the morning marketplace and, after a three-hour lunch, take a postprandial snooze in the cool blue shadow cast by a 500-year-old olive tree.

Until the cell phone rings, that is. Because ever since Peter Mayle abandoned the London fog and described with sensual relish a life of unbuttoned collars and espadrilles in his best-selling *A Year in Provence*, the world has beaten a path here. Now Parisians are heard in the local marketplaces passing the word on the best free-range rabbit, the purest olive oil, the lowest price on a five-bedroom *mas* (farmhouse) with vineyard and pool. And a chic *bon-chic-bon-genre* city crowd languishes stylishly at the latest country inn and makes an appearance at the most fashionable restaurant. Ask them, and they'll agree: ever since Princess Caroline of Monaco moved to St-Rémy, Provence has become the new Côte d'Azur.

But chic Provence hasn't eclipsed idyllic Provence, and it's still possible to melt into a Monday-morning market crowd, where blue-aproned *paysannes* scoop gnarled fistfuls of mesclun into a willow basket, matron-connoisseurs paw through bins containing the first Cavaillon asparagus, a knot of *pépés* in workers' blues takes a pétanque break . . . welcoming all into the game.

Relax and join them—and plan to stay around a while. Yes, there are plenty of sights to see: some of the finest Roman ruins in Europe, from the Pont du Gard to the arenas at Arles and Nîmes; the pristine Romanesque abbeys of Senanque and de Montmajour; bijoux chapels and weathered mas; the feudal châteaux at Tarascon and Beaucaire; the monolithic Papal Palace in old Avignon; and everywhere vineyards, pleasure ports, and sophisticated city museums. But allow yourself time to feel the rhythm of modern Provençal life, to listen to the pulsing *breet* of the cicadas, to breath deep the perfume of wild herbs and old stone, and feel the velvety air of a summer night on your skin. . . .

Pleasures and Pastimes

Architecture and Antiquities

Churches, châteaux, and abbeys are sprinkled throughout the countryside of Provence, a surprising concentration of them pure Romanesque—that is, built in the solid progression of arches and barrel vaults that marked Roman engineering and was mimicked by architects up through the 12th and 13th centuries. Although you'll find Roman traces throughout Provence (in fact, its name comes from the Roman's *provincia,* or "the province"), the most beautifully preserved are concentrated around the Rhône, their main shipping artery. There are two arenas (in Arles and Nîmes), the ancient Hellenistic settlement outside St-Rémy (Glanum), the miraculously preserved temple in Nîmes (Maison Carrée), a theater in Orange, and two villages in Vaison-la-Romaine.

Dining

Now universally emulated for its winning combination of simplicity, healthy ingredients, and vivid sun-kissed flavors, Provençal cooking glories in olive oil, garlic, tomatoes, olives, and the ubiquitous wild herbs that crunch underfoot. France's greatest chefs scour lively markets for melons still warm from the morning sun, and buy glistening olives by the pailful. You can't lose when you start with an icy pastis, that pale yellow, anise-based aperitif; smear your toast with *tapenade,* a delicious paste of olives, capers, and anchovies; heap aioli, a garlicky mayonnaise, on your fresh fish; and rub thyme and garlic on your lamb. No meal is complete without a round of goat cheese, sun-ripened fruit, and a chilled bottle of rosé from the surrounding hills.

CATEGORY	COST*
$$$$	over €30
$$$	€20–€30
$$	€12–€20
$	under €12

**per person for a main course only, including tax (19.6%) and service; note that if a restaurant offers only prix-fixe (set-price) meals, it has been given the price category that reflects the full prix-fixe price.*

Lodging

Accommodations in this oft-visited part of France range from luxurious villas to elegantly converted *mas* (farmhouses) to modest city-center hotels. Reservations are essential for much of the year, and many hotels are closed in winter. Assume all hotel rooms have air-conditioning, TV, telephones, and private bath unless otherwise noted. Internet, when listed in facilities, means in-room data-ports and/or public-area computers provide on-line access.

CATEGORY	COST*
$$$$	over €180
$$$	€120–€180
$$	€60–€120
$	under €60

**All prices are for a standard double room in high season, including tax (19.6%) and service charge.*

Markets

At Provençal markets, seafood, poultry, olives, melons, and asparagus cry out to be gathered in a basket, arranged lovingly in pottery bowls, and cooked in their purest form. For picnics, stock up on tubs of tapenade and *anchoïade* (anchovy spread), dried game sausage, tangy marinated seafood, and tiny pucks of withered goat cheese. In fact, you can usually also pick up any silverware, linens, pottery, and articles of clothing you may need from hawkers in nearby stalls. And antiques and *brocantes* (collectibles) are never far away, sometimes providing the most authentic local souvenirs.

Exploring Provence

Bordered to the west by the Languedoc and melting to the south and east into the blue waters of the Mediterranean, Provence falls easily into four areas. The Camargue is at the heart of the first, flanked by Nîmes and picturesque Arles to the east. Northeast of Arles, the rude and rocky Alpilles jut upward, their hillsides green with orchards and olive groves; here you'll find feudal Les Baux and the Greco-Roman enclave of St-Rémy, now fashionable with the Summer People. The third area, which falls within the boundaries of the Vaucluse, begins at Avignon and extends north to Orange and Vaison-la-Romaine, then east to the forested slopes of the Luberon. The fourth area encompasses Cézanne country, east of the Rhône, starting in Aix-en-Provence, then winding southward to Marseille and east along the Mediterranean coast to the idyllic Iles d'Hyères.

Great Itineraries

Peter Mayle's book *A Year in Provence* prescribes just that, but even a year might not be long enough to soak up all the charm of this captivating region. In three days you can see three representative (and very different) towns: Arles, Avignon, and St-Rémy; with seven days you can easily add the Camargue, the Luberon, and Aix-en-Provence; with 10 days you can add Vaison-la-Romaine and Marseille. The following are suggested itineraries for touring the area; another option is to base yourself in one place and take day trips from there.

To make the most of your time in the region, plan to divide your days between big-city culture, backcountry tours, and waterfront leisure. You can "do" Provence at an if-this-is-Tuesday breakneck pace, but its rural roads and tiny villages reward a more leisurely approach. Provence is as much a way of life as a region charged with tourist must-sees, so you should allow time to enjoy its old-fashioned pace. Hot afternoons tend to mean siestas, with signs of life discernible only as the shadows under the *platanes* (plane trees) start to lengthen and locals saunter out to play *boules* (the French version of boccie, or lawn bowling) and sip long drinks of cooling pastis.

Numbers in the text correspond to numbers in the margin and on the Provence, Nîmes, Arles, Avignon, and Marseille maps.

IF YOU HAVE 3 DAYS

The best gateway to the region is **Avignon** ㉘–㉟, where tiny, narrow streets cluster around the 14th-century Palais des Papes, as if still seeking the protection afforded them when this massive structure represented the supreme Christian authority of the world back in the 14th century. Then make an afternoon outing west to the **Pont du Gard** ① aqueduct, a majestic relic from the ancient Romans that strikes all as more a work of art than a practical construction. On day two stop briefly in **Nîmes** ②–⑩ to see the antiquities of the Arènes and the Maison Carrée—a striking contrast to this busy commercial center—then head into atmospheric old **Arles** ⑭–㉓, inspiration to van Gogh, who captured the beauty of the Arlésienne, with her delicate pointed features, in some of his finest portraits. On day three drive through the countryside, stopping at the **Abbaye de Montmajour** ㉔—whose cloisters are a particularly charming spot when the oleander trees are in bloom—and the medieval hill town of **Les Baux-de-Provence** ㉕; stay overnight in **St-Rémy-de-Provence** ㉖, with its Roman ruins and recognizable van Gogh landmarks.

IF YOU HAVE 7 DAYS

Visit **Orange** (37) on your first day before stopping to see the **Pont du Gard** (1)—both the ancient Roman theater in Orange and the famous aqueduct will allow you to travel back two millennia in time. Spend two nights in **Avignon** (28)–(35) and don't forget to visit the Bridge of St-Bénézet (made famous in the old song "Sur le pont d'Avignon"). In the morning stop briefly in **Nîmes** (2)–(10) on your way to the fortified town of **Aigues-Mortes** (11) and make a slight detour through the Camargue to **Arles** (14)–(23). The next morning explore Arles's Roman remains. Try to get to the rocky perch of **Les Baux-de-Provence** (25) by lunchtime and then continue to **St-Rémy-de-Provence** (26) to see where van Gogh set up his easel. On day five wend your way through **L'Isle-sur-la-Sorgue** (41) to **Gordes** (43), in the Luberon Mountains, one of Provence's most famous *villages perchés* (perched villages). Spend the night in the hilltop village of **Bonnieux** (47) and drive over the windswept spine of the Luberon on your way south to **Aix-en-Provence** (48)–(54); spend two days there visiting the marvelous 18th-century mansions, the museums, and its Cours Mirabeau, which is to Aix what the Champs-Élysées is to Paris.

IF YOU HAVE 10 DAYS

To the seven-day itinerary, add a day visiting ruins in the Rhône-side Roman market town of **Vaison-la-Romaine** (38) and drive the winding back roads of the neighboring Mont Ventoux region, where fruited plains give way to forested heights. Or make a broader sweep through the Camargue to include the eccentric seaside town of **Stes-Maries-de-la-Mer** (13), its gloomy Romanesque church (full of Gypsy tributes to the two St. Marys and their servant girl Sarah). Then take the time to experience the urban vitality of **Marseille** (56)–(67), or cool your heels at the gently gentrified seaside retreat of **Cassis** (69).

When to Tour Provence

Spring and fall are the best months to experience the dazzling light, rugged rocky countryside, and fruitful vineyards of Provence. Though the lavender fields show peak color in mid-July, summertime here is beastly hot; worse, it's always crowded on the beaches and connecting roads. Winter has some nice days, when genuine locals are able to enjoy their cafés and their town squares tourist-free, but it often rains, and the razor-sharp mistral can cut to the bone.

NÎMES, ARLES, AND THE CAMARGUE

Though Roman remains are found throughout Provence, their presence is strongest where the rivers meander their way to the sea on the region's western flank: the beautiful Pont du Gard aqueduct and the arenas in Nîmes and Arles. Just west and south of these landmarks, the Camargue is a vast watery plain formed by the sprawling Rhône delta and extending over 800 square km (300 square mi).

Pont du Gard

★ ❶ *22 km (13 mi) southwest of Avignon, 37 km (23 mi) southwest of Orange, 48 km (30 mi) north of Arles.*

No other architectural sight in Provence rivals the Pont du Gard, a mighty, three-tiered aqueduct midway between Nîmes and Avignon. Erected some 2,000 years ago as part of a 48-km (30-mi) canal supplying water to Roman Nîmes, it is astonishingly well preserved. In the early morning the site offers an amazing blend of natural and classical beauty—the rhythmic repetition of arches resonates with strength, bearing testimony to an engineering concept relatively new in the 1st century AD, when it was built under Emperor Claudius. Later in the day crowds become a problem, even off-season. You can approach the aqueduct from either side of the Gardon River. If you choose the north side (Rive Gauche), you'll be charged €3.5 to park (stay as close to the booth as possible because unfortunately break-ins are a problem). The walk to the *pont* (bridge) is shorter and the views arguably better from here. It costs less (€2.75) to park on the south side (Rive Droite), and there's a tourist office with information and postcards—but this is also the side the tour buses prefer. Access to the spectacular walkway along the top is indefinitely blocked due to ongoing restoration work.

Nîmes

20 km (13 mi) southwest of the Pont du Gard, 43 km (26 mi) south of Avignon, 121 km (74 mi) west of Marseille, 711 km (427 mi) south of Paris.

If you've come to the south seeking Roman treasures, you need look no further than Nîmes (pronounced *neem*): The Arènes and Maison Carrée are among continental Europe's best-preserved antiquities. But if you've come seeking a more modern mythology—of lazy, graceful Provence—give Nîmes a wide berth. It's a feisty, run-down rat race of a town, with jalopies and Vespas roaring irreverently around the ancient temple. Its medieval Old Town has none of the gentrified grace of those in Arles or St-Rémy. Yet its rumpled and rebellious ways trace directly back to its Roman incarnation, when its population swelled with newly victorious soldiers, arrogant after their conquest of Egypt in 31 BC.

Already anchoring a fiefdom of pre-Roman *oppida* (elevated fortresses) before ceding to the empire in the 1st century BC, this ancient city grew to formidable proportions under the Pax Romana. Its next golden age bloomed under the Protestants, who established an anti-Catholic stronghold here and wreaked havoc on iconic architectural treasures—not to mention the papist minority. Their massacre of some 200 Catholic citizens is remembered as the Michelade; many of those murdered were priests sheltered in the *évêché* (bishop's house), now the Museum of Old Nîmes.

A locally produced lightweight serge (a densely woven fabric) brought fame to Nîmes more than once. Legend has it that Christopher Columbus admired its durability and used it for sails; its reputation spread, and it was exported worldwide from the ports of Genoa (Gênes in French). Levi Strauss found its sturdy texture strong enough for gold miners' pants and Americanized its name from *bleu de Gênes* to blue jeans. The now-ubiquitous fabric's name traces back to its origins: *de Nîmes,* or denim.

★ ❷ The **Arènes** (Arena) is considered the best-preserved Roman amphitheater in the world. A miniature of the Colosseum in Rome, it stands more than 520 ft long and 330 ft wide, with a seating capacity of 24,000. Bloody gladiator battles and theatrical wild-boar chases drew crowds to its bleachers. Nowadays its most colorful use is the ***corrida,*** the bullfight that transforms the arena (and all of Nîmes) into a sangria-flushed homage to Spain. ✉ *Bd. Victor-Hugo,* ☎ *04–66–76–72–77.* 🎫 *€5; joint ticket to Arènes and Tour Magne €5.25.* ⏲ *May–Sept., daily 9–6:30; Oct.–Apr., daily 9–noon and 2–5.*

❸ The **Musée des Beaux-Arts** (Fine Arts Museum) contains a vast Roman mosaic; the marriage ceremony depicted provides intriguing insights into the Roman aristocratic lifestyle. Paintings (by Nicolas Poussin, Pieter Brueghel, Peter Paul Rubens) and sculpture (by Auguste Rodin) form

Provence

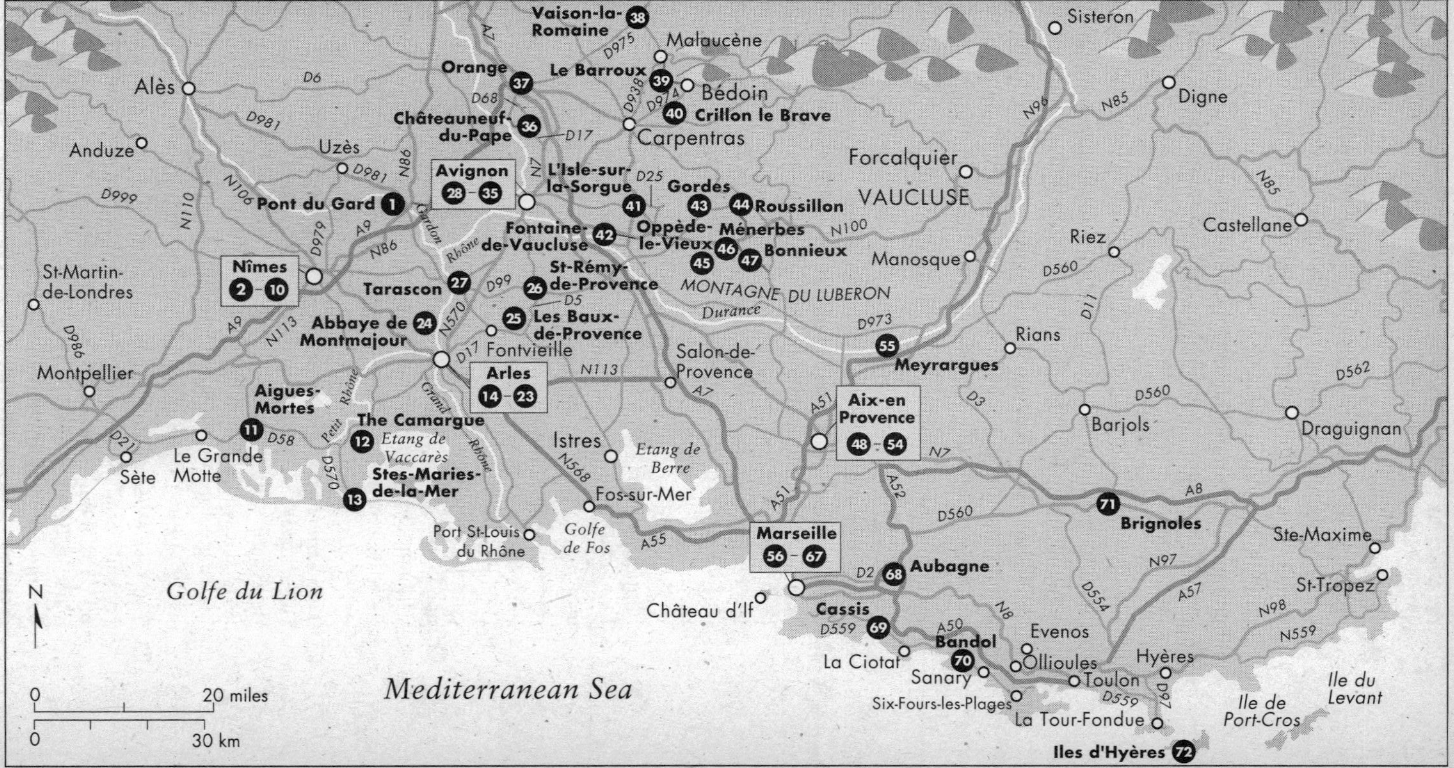
Vaison-la-Romaine 38
Malaucène
Orange 37
Le Barroux 39
Bédoin
Crillon le Brave 40
Carpentras
Châteauneuf-du-Pape 36
Alès
Anduze
Uzès
Avignon 28–35
L'Isle-sur-la-Sorgue 41
Gordes 43
Roussillon 44
Pont du Gard 1
Fontaine-de-Vaucluse 42
Oppède-le-Vieux 45 46
Ménerbes
Bonnieux 47
Nîmes 2–10
St-Martin-de-Londres
Tarascon 27
St-Rémy-de-Provence 26
MONTAGNE DU LUBERON
Durance
Abbaye de Montmajour 24
Les Baux-de-Provence 25
Fontvieille
Montpellier
Arles 14–23
Salon-de-Provence
Aigues-Mortes 11
The Camargue 12
Etang de Vaccarès
Istres
Etang de Berre
Sète
Le Grande Motte
Stes-Maries-de-la-Mer 13
Fos-sur-Mer
Port St-Louis du Rhône
Golfe de Fos
Golfe du Lion
Mediterranean Sea
Sisteron
Digne
Forcalquier
VAUCLUSE
Castellane
Riez
Manosque
Rians
Meyrargues 55
Aix-en Provence 48–54
Barjols
Draguignan
Brignoles 71
Marseille 56–67
Château d'If
Aubagne 68
Cassis 69
La Ciotat
Bandol 70
Sanary
Six-Fours-les-Plages
Evenos
Ollioules
Toulon
Hyères
La Tour-Fondue
Ste-Maxime
St-Tropez
Ile de Port-Cros
Ile du Levant
Iles d'Hyères 72
Gardon
Rhône
Petit Rhône
Grand Rhône
A7
A8
A9
A51
A52
A55
A57
A50
N7
N8
N85
N86
N96
N97
N98
N100
N106
N110
N113
N559
N568
N570
D2
D3
D5
D6
D11
D17
D21
D25
D58
D68
D97
D99
D554
D559
D560
D562
D570
D938
D973
D974
D975
D979
D981
D986
D999
N
0
20 miles
0
30 km

the mainstay of the collection. ✉ *Rue de la Cité-Foulc,* ☎ *04–66–67–38–21.* 🎫 *€4.* ⏲ *Tues.–Sun. 11–6.*

4 The **Musée Archéologique et d'Histoire Naturelle** (Museum of Archaeology and Natural History) is rich in local archaeological finds, mainly statues, busts, friezes, tools, coins, and pottery. ✉ *Bd. de l'Amiral-Courbet,* ☎ *04–66–67–25–57.* 🎫 *€4.50.* ⏲ *Tues.–Sun. 11–6.*

Destroyed and rebuilt in several stages, with particular damage by rampaging Protestants who slaughtered eight priests from the neighbor-
5 ing *évêché* (bishop's house), the **Cathédrale Notre-Dame et St-Castor** (✉ Pl. aux Herbes) still shows traces of its original construction in 1096. A remarkably preserved Romanesque frieze portrays Adam and Eve cowering in shame, the gory slaughter of Abel, and a flood-wearied Noah. Inside, look for the 4th-century sarcophagus (third chapel on the right) and a magnificent 17th-century chapel (in the apse).

6 The **Musée du Vieux Nîmes** (Museum of Old Nîmes), in the 17th-century bishop's palace opposite the cathedral, has embroidered garments in exotic and vibrant displays. Look for the 14th-century jacket made of blue-serge de Nîmes, the famous fabric from which Levi-Strauss first fashioned blue jeans. ✉ *Pl. aux Herbes,* ☎ *04–66–36–00–64.* 🎫 *€4.50.* ⏲ *Tues.–Sun. 11–6.*

Lovely and forlorn in the middle of a busy downtown square, the
★ 7 exquisitely preserved **Maison Carrée** (Square House) strikes a timeless balance between symmetry and whimsy, purity of line and richness of decor. Built around 5 BC and dedicated to Caius Caesar and his grandson Lucius, it has survived subsequent use as a medieval meeting hall, an Augustine church, a storehouse for Revolutionary archives, and a horse shed. It was modeled on the Temple to Apollo in Rome. Alas, its interior now serves as a slapdash display space for temporary exhibitions. ✉ *Bd. Victor-Hugo,* ☎ *04–66–36–26–76.* 🎫 *Free.* ⏲ *May–Oct., daily 9–7; Nov.–Apr., daily 9–noon and 2–6.*

The glass-fronted Carré d'Art (it's directly opposite the Maison Carrée) was designed by British architect Sir Norman Foster as its neighbor's stark contemporary mirror: it literally reflects the Maison Carrée's creamy symmetry and figuratively answers it with a featherlight deconstructed colonnade. Homages aside, it looks like an airport termi-
8 nal. It now houses the **Musée d'Art Contemporain** (Contemporary Art Museum), featuring art dating from 1960 onward and temporary exhibits of new works. ✉ *Pl. de la Maison Carrée,* ☎ *04–66–76–35–70.* 🎫 *€4.50.* ⏲ *Tues.–Sun. 10–6.*

9 The shattered Roman ruin known as the **Temple de Diane** (Temple of Diana) dates from the 2nd century BC. The temple's function is unknown, though it is thought to have been part of a larger Roman complex that is still unexcavated. In the Middle Ages Benedictine nuns occupied the building before it was converted into a church. Destruction came during the Wars of Religion.

10 The **Tour Magne** (Magne Tower), at the far end of the Jardin de la Fontaine, is all that remains of a tower the emperor Augustus had built on Gallic foundations; it was probably used as a lookout post. Despite a loss of 30 ft over the course of time, it still provides fine views of Nîmes for anyone energetic enough to climb the 140 steps. ✉ *Quai de la Fontaine,* ☎ *04–66–67–29–11.* 🎫 *Tour Magne €2.50, joint ticket with Arènes €5.25.* ⏲ *May–Oct., daily 9–7; Nov.–Apr., daily 9–5.*

Dining and Lodging

$$ ✕ **Le Jardin d'Hadrien.** This enclave, with its quarried white stone, ancient plank-and-beam ceiling, and open fireplace, would be a culinary

Arènes 2
Cathédrale Notre-Dame et St-Castor 5
Maison Carrée 7
Musée Archéologique et d'Histoire Naturelle 4
Musée d'Art Contemporain 8
Musée des Beaux-Arts . . . 3
Musée du Vieux Nîmes 6
Temple de Diane 9
Tour Magne 10

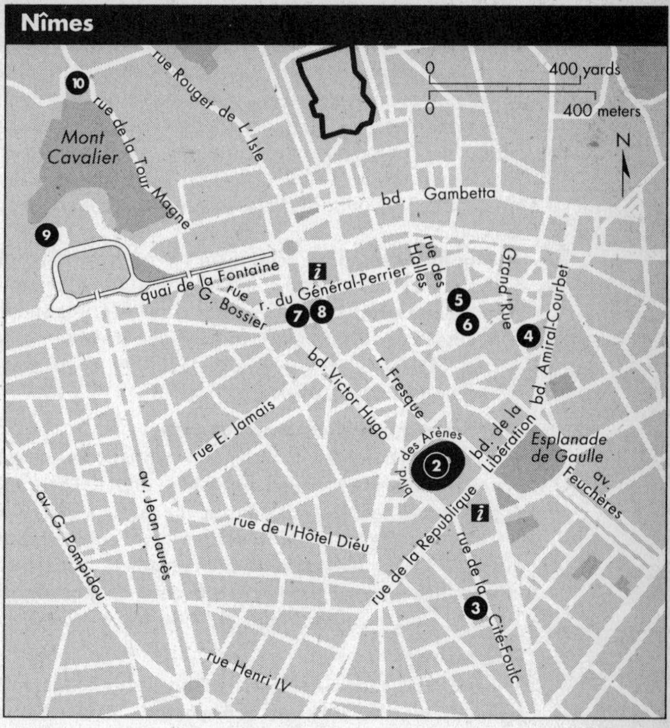

haven even without its lovely hidden garden, a shady retreat for summer meals. Fresh cod crisped in salt and olive oil, zucchini flowers filled with *brandade* (the creamy, light paste of salt cod and olive oil), and a frozen parfait perfumed with licorice all show chef Alain Vinouze's subtle skills. Prix-fixe menus are €15 and €25. ✉ *11 rue Enclos Rey,* ☎ *04–66–21–86–65. AE, MC, V.*

$ ★ ✕ **Chez Jacotte.** Duck into an Old Town back alley and into this cross-vaulted grotto that embodies Nîmes's Spanish-bohemian flair. Candlelight flickering on rich tones of oxblood, ocher, and cobalt enhances the warm welcome of red-haired owner Jacotte Friand. Mouthwatering goat-cheese-and-fig gratin, mullet crisped in olive oil and basil, herb-crusted lamb, and seasonal fruit crumbles show off chef Christophe Ciantar's flair with local ingredients. ✉ *15 rue Fresque (impasse),* ☎ *04–66–21–64–59. MC, V. Closed Sun.–Mon. No lunch Sat.*

$ ✕ **Vintage Café.** This popular Old Town wine bar draws a loyal crowd of oenophiles for serious tastings and simple, compatible regional specialties—for example, hot lentil salad with smoked haddock, and goat cheese terrine. Ocher, bright ceramics, and warm-color lamplight enhance the artful Mediterranean decor. Summer nights on the terrace are idyllic. ✉ *7 rue de Bernis,* ☎ *04–66–21–04–45. MC, V. Closed Sun.–Mon. No lunch Sat.*

$$ **La Baume.** In the heart of scruffy Old Nîmes, this noble 17th-century *hôtel particulier* (mansion) has been reincarnated as a stylish hotel with an architect's eye for mixing ancient detail with modern design. The balustraded stone staircase is a protected historic monument, and stenciled beamed ceilings, cross vaults, and archways counterbalance hot ocher tones, swags of raw cotton, leather, and halogen lighting. ✉ *21 rue Nationale, 30000,* ☎ *04–66–76–28–42,* FAX *04–66–76–28–45,* WEB *www.new-hotel.com. 34 rooms. Cable TV, Internet. AE, DC, MC, V.*

$$ ★ **Royal Hôtel.** Jazz, art-deco ironwork, and caged birds set the Latin tone at this bohemian, shabby-chic urban hotel, where whitewash and scrubbed concrete set off 1930s details and trendy flea-market finds. Bathrooms are newly tiled and amenities reasonably up to date. Its Spanish restaurant serves tapas on the pedestrian place d'Assas, but the lobby bar is where you'd expect to run across Picasso slumming over absinthe. ✉ *3 bd. Alphonse Daudet, 30000,* ☎ *04–66–58–28–27,* FAX *04–66–58–28–28. 27 rooms. Restaurant, bar, no air-conditioning, parking (fee). AE, MC, V.*

$ **Amphithéâtre.** Just behind the arena, this big, solid old private home has fortunately fallen into the hands of a loving owner, who has stripped and refinished 18th-century double doors and fitted out rooms with restored-wood details and antique bedroom sets. ✉ *4 rue des Arènes, 30420,* ☎ *04–66–67–28–51,* FAX *04–66–67–07–79. 17 rooms. No air-conditioning, cable TV. AE, MC, V.*

Outdoor Activities and Sports

The **corrida** (bullfight) is the quintessential Nîmes experience, taking place as it does in the ancient Roman arena. There are usually three opportunities a year, always during the carnival-like citywide *férias* (festivals): in early spring (mid-February), at Pentecost (end of May), and during the wine harvest (end of September). For tickets and advance information contact the Arena's ***bureau de location*** (ticket office; ✉ 1 rue A. Ducros, 30900 Nîmes, ☎ 04–66–67–28–02).

Shopping

The only authentic commercial maker of brandade, Nîmes's signature salt cod-and-olive oil paste, is **Raymond** (✉ 24 rue Nationale, ☎ 04–66–67–20–47). It's paddled fresh into a plastic carton or sold in sealed jars so you can take it home.

Aigues-Mortes

⓫ *13 km (8 mi) east of La Grande Motte, 41 km (25 mi) south of Nîmes, 48 km (30 mi) southwest of Arles.*

Like a tiny illumination in a medieval manuscript, Aigues-Mortes is a precise and perfect miniature fortress-town contained within symmetrical crenellated walls, its streets laid out in geometric grids. Now awash in a flat wasteland of sand, salt, and monotonous marsh, it was once a major port town from which no less than St-Louis himself (Louis IX) set sail to conquer Jerusalem in the 13th century. In 1248 some 35,000 zealous men launched 1,500 ships toward Cyprus, engaging the infidel on his own turf and suffering swift defeat; Louis himself was briefly taken prisoner. A second launching in 1270 led to more crushing loss, and Louis succumbed to the plague.

Louis's state-of-the-art **fortress-port** remains astonishingly well preserved. Its stout walls now contain a small Provençal village milling with tourists, but the visit is more than justified by the impressive scale of the original structure. ✉ *Porte de la Gardette,* ☎ *04–66–53–61–55.* *€5.* ⏲ *Easter–late May, daily 10–6; late May–mid-Sept., daily 9:30–8; mid-Sept.–Easter, daily 10–5.*

It's not surprising that the town within the rampart walls has become tourist oriented, with the usual plethora of gift shops and postcard stands. But **place St-Louis,** where a 19th-century statue of the father of the fleur-de-lis reigns under shady pollards, has a mellow village feel. The pretty, bare-bones **Église Notre-Dame des Sablons,** on one corner of the square, has a timeless air (the church dates from the 13th century, but the stained glass is ultramodern).

Dining and Lodging

$$–$$$ ★ ✕🏨 **Les Arcades.** Long a success as an upscale seafood restaurant, this beautifully preserved 16th-century house now has big, airy rooms, some with tall windows overlooking a green courtyard. Pristine white-stone walls, color-stained woodwork, and rubbed-ocher walls frame antiques and lush fabrics. Classic cooking includes lotte (monkfish) in saffron and poached turbot in hollandaise. ✉ *23 bd. Gambetta, 30220,* ☎ *04–66–53–81–13,* FAX *04–66–53–75–46. 9 rooms. Restaurant, minibars, cable TV, Internet, pool. AE, DC, MC, V. Closed early March and late Nov.*

$$ 🏨 **Les Templiers.** In a 17th-century residence within the ramparts, this delightful hotel sets the stage with stone, stucco, and terra-cotta floors. Furnishings are classically simple and softened with antiques. On the ground floor are two small, cozy sitting areas; breakfast, weather permitting, is served in the small courtyard. ✉ *23 rue de la République, 30220,* ☎ *04–66–53–66–56,* FAX *04–66–53–69–61. 11 rooms. No air-conditioning, cable TV, minibars, Internet, parking (fee). MC, V. Closed Nov.–Feb.*

The Camargue

⓬ *19 km (12 mi) east of Aigues-Mortes, 15 km (9 mi) south of Arles.*

For about 800 square km (309 square mi), the vast alluvial delta of the Rhône known as the Camargue stretches to the horizon, an austere, unrelievedly flat marshland, scoured by the mistral and swarmed over by mosquitoes. Between the endless flow of sediment from the Rhône and the erosive force of the sea, its shape is constantly changing. Even the Provençal poet Frederic Mistral described it in bleak terms: *"Ni arbre, ni ombre, ni âme"* ("Neither tree, nor shade, nor a soul").

Yet its harsh landscape harbors a concentration of exotic wildlife unique in Europe, and its isolation has given birth to an ascetic and ancient way of life that transcends national stereotype. It's a strange region, one worth discovering slowly, either on foot or on horseback—especially as its wildest reaches are inaccessible by car. People find the Camargue intriguing, but birds find it irresistible. Its protected marshes lure some 400 species, including more than 160 in migration. As you drive the scarce roads that barely crisscross the Camargue, you'll usually be within the boundaries of the **Parc Regional de Camargue.** Unlike state and national parks in the United States, this area is privately owned and utilized following regulations imposed by the French government. The principal owners are the *manadiers* (the Camargue equivalent of a small-scale rancher) and their *gardians* (a kind of open-range cowboy), who keep it for grazing their wide-horn bulls and their dappled-white horses. When it's not participating in a bloodless bullfight (mounted players try to hook a red ribbon from its horns), a bull may well end up in the wine-rich regional stew called *gardianne de taureau.* Riding through the marshlands in leather pants and wide-rimmed black hats and wielding long prongs to prod their cattle, the gardians themselves are as fascinating as the wildlife. Their homes—tiny and whitewashed—dot the countryside.

The easiest place to view bird life is in a private reserve just outside the regional park called the **Parc Ornithologique du Pont de Gau** (Pont du Gau Ornithological Park). On some 150 acres of marsh and salt lands, birds are welcomed and protected (but in no way confined); injured birds are treated and kept in large pens, to be released if and when able to survive. A series of boardwalks (including a short, child-friendly inner loop) snakes over the wetlands, the longest leading to a blind, where a half hour of silence, binoculars in hand, can reveal unsuspected satisfactions. ☎ *04–90–97–82–62.* 🎟 *€5.* ⏲ *Oct.–Mar., daily 10–sunset; Apr.–Sept., daily 9–sunset.*

If you're an even more committed nature lover, venture into the inner sanctum of the Camargue, the **Réserve Nationale de Camargue.** This intensely protected area contains the central pond called **Le Vaccarès,** mostly used for approved scientific research. Pick up maps and information at the **Centre d'Information** (☎ 04–90–97–86–32, FAX 04–90–97–70–82), open April–September, daily 9–6, and October–March, Saturday–Thursday 9:30–5; it's just up D570 from the Parc Ornithologique. To explore this area, you'll have to strike out on foot, bicycle, or horseback (the **Association Camarguaise de Tourisme Equestre** publishes a list of stables where you can rent horses; copies are available at the information center or the Stes-Maries tourist office). Note that you are not permitted to diverge from marked trails.

Stes-Maries-de-la-Mer

13 *32 km (20 mi) southeast of Aigues-Mortes, 129 km (80 mi) west of Marseille, 39 km (24 mi) south of Arles.*

The principal town within the confines of the Parc Régional de Camargue, Stes-Maries is a beach resort with a fascinating history. Provençal legend has it that around AD 45 a band of the very first Christians were rounded up and set adrift at sea without provisions in a boat without a sail. Their stellar ranks included Mary Magdalene, Martha, and Mary Salome, mother of apostles James and John; Mary Jacoby, sister of the Virgin; and Lazarus, not necessarily the one risen from the dead. Joining them in their fate was a dark-skinned servant girl named Sarah. Miraculously, their boat washed ashore at this ancient site, and the grateful Marys built a chapel in thanks. The pilgrims attracted to Stes-Maries aren't all lighting candles to the two St. Marys: Sarah has been adopted as an honorary saint by the Gypsies of the world. Two extraordinary festivals celebrating the Marys take place every year in Stes-Maries, one on May 24–25 and the other on the Sunday nearest to October 22.

What is most striking to a visitor entering the damp, dark, and forbidding fortress-church, ★ **Église des Stes-Maries,** is its novel character. Almost devoid of windows, its tall, barren single nave is cluttered with florid and sentimental ex-votos (tokens of blessings, prayers, and thanks) and primitive and sentimental artworks depicting the famous trio. Another oddity brings you back to the 20th century: a sign on the door forbids visitors from entering *torso nu* (topless). For outside its otherworldly role Stes-Maries is first and foremost a beach resort: dead flat, whitewashed, and more than a little tacky. Unless you've made a pilgrimage here for the sun and sand, don't spend much time in the town center; if you've chosen Stes-Maries as a base for viewing the Camargue, stay in one of the discreet *mas* (country inns) outside its city limits.

Lodging

$$ ★ **Mas de Cacharel.** On 170 acres of private marshland bordering the Réserve Départemental de Camargue, this low-slung, low-key haven is set well back from D85 just north of Stes-Maries. A simple retreat, it has a lodgelike central breakfast hall complete with Provençal furniture and a pleasantly smoky grand fireplace. Spartan rooms (no TV) are arranged motor-court style, so most have windows that overlook the eternal stretch of reeds and birds. ✉ *13460 Stes-Maries-de-la-Mer (4 km/2 mi north of town on D85),* ☎ *04–90–97–95–44,* FAX *04–90–97–87–97. 16 rooms. Bar, no air-conditioning, pool, horseback riding. MC, V.*

Arles

38 km (24 mi) north of Stes-Maries-de-la-Mer, 92 km (57 mi) northwest of Marseille, 36 km (22 mi) south of Avignon, 31 km (19 mi) east of Nîmes.

If you were obliged to choose just one city to visit in Provence, lovely little Arles would give Avignon and Aix a run for their money. It's too chic to become museumlike yet has a wealth of classical antiquities and Romanesque stonework, quarried-stone edifices and shuttered town houses, and graceful, shady Old Town streets and squares. Throughout the year there are pageantry, festivals, and cutting-edge arts events. Its panoply of atmospheric restaurants and picturesque small hotels makes it the ideal headquarters for forays into the Alpilles and the Camargue.

A Greek colony since the 6th century BC, little Arles took a giant step forward when Julius Caesar defeated Marseille in the 1st century BC. The emperor-to-be designated Arles a Roman colony and lavished funds and engineering know-how on it. It became an international crossroads by sea and land and a market to the world, with goods from Africa, Arabia, and the Far East. The emperor Constantine himself moved to Arles and brought with him Christianity.

The remains of this golden age are reason enough to visit Arles today, yet its character nowadays is as gracious and low-key as it once was cutting-edge. Seated in the shade of the plane trees on place du Forum or strolling the rampart walkway along the sparkling Rhône, you'll see what enchanted Gauguin and drove van Gogh frantic with inspiration.

Note: If you plan to visit many of the monuments and museums in Arles, buy a *visite generale* ticket for €9. This covers the entry fee to the Musée de l'Arles Antique and any and all of the other museums and monuments (except the independent Museon Arlaten), which normally charges €2 each per visit. It's good for the length of your stay.

★ 14 Though it's a hike from the center, a good place to set the tone and context for your exploration of Arles is at the state-of-the-art **Musée de l'Arles Antique** (Museum of Ancient Arles). The bold, modern triangular structure was built in 1995 on the site of an enormous Roman *cirque* (chariot-racing stadium). You'll learn about all Arles in its heyday, from the development of its monuments to details of daily life in Roman times. Ask for the English-language guidebook. ✉ *Presqu'île du Cirque Romain,* ☎ *04–90–18–88–88.* 🎫 *€5.5.* ⏲ *Apr.–mid-Oct., daily 9–7; mid-Sept.–Mar., daily 10–5.*

15 A good way to plunge into post-Roman Arles is through the quirky old **Museon Arlaten** (Museum of Arles). Created by the father of the Provençal revival, turn-of-the-century poet Frédéric Mistral, it enshrines a seemingly bottomless collection of regional treasures. Following Mistral's wishes, women in full Arlésienne costume oversee the labyrinth of lovely 16th-century halls. ✉ *29 rue de la République,* ☎ *04–90–93–58–11.* 🎫 *€4.* ⏲ *Apr.–Sept, daily 9:30–12:30 and 2–6; Oct.–Mar., Tues.–Sun. 10–12:30 and 2–5:30.*

16 At the entrance to a 17th-century Jesuit college you can access the ancient underground galleries called the **Cryptoportiques.** Dating from 30 BC to 20 BC, this horseshoe of vaults and pillars buttressed the ancient forum from below ground. Yet openings let in natural daylight, and artworks of considerable merit and worth were unearthed here, adding to the mystery of these passages' true function. ✉ *Rue Balze,* ☎ *04–90–49–36–74.* 🎫 *€2.5.* ⏲ *Apr.–Sept. daily 9–7; Oct.–Mar., daily 10–4:30.*

Arènes 20
Cloître St-Trophime . . .18
Crypto-portiques . . .16
Église St-Trophime . . .17
Espace Van Gogh . .23
Musée de l'Arles Antique 14
Musée Réattu 21
Museon Arlaten 15
Place Lamartine . . .22
Théâtre Antique 19

Arles

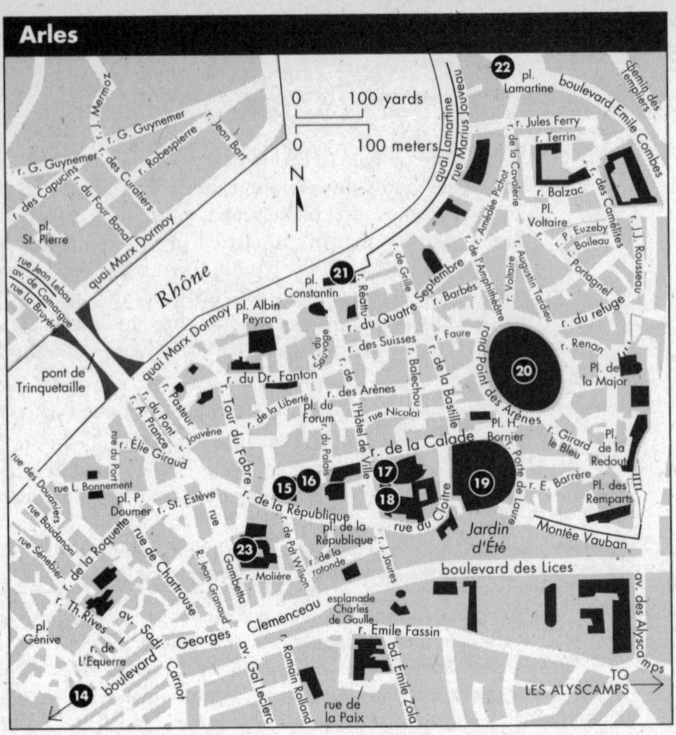

Classed as a world treasure by UNESCO, the extraordinary Romanesque **Église St-Trophime** (✉ Pl. de la République) alone would justify a visit to Arles, though it's continually upstaged by the antiquities around it. Its transepts date from the 11th century and its nave from the 12th; the church's austere symmetry and ancient artworks (including a stunning Roman-style 4th-century sarcophagus) are fascinating in themselves. But it is the church's superbly preserved Romanesque sculpture on the 12th-century **portal**—its entry facade—that earns it international respect.

★ 17

18 Tucked discreetly behind St-Trophime is a peaceful haven, the **Cloître St-Trophime** (St-Trophime Cloister). A Romanesque treasure worthy of the church, it's one of the loveliest cloisters in Provence. ☎ *04–90–49–36–74.* 🎫 *€2.5.* ⏲ *Apr.–Sept., daily 9–7; Oct.–Mar., daily 10–4:30.*

19 Directly up rue de la Calade from place de la République are the picturesque ruins of the **Théâtre Antique** (Ancient Theater), built by the Romans under Augustus in the 1st century BC. Now overgrown and a pleasant, parklike retreat, it once served as an entertainment venue to some 20,000 spectators. Today it serves as a concert stage for the Festival d'Arles (in July and August) and site of the Recontres Internationales de la Photographie (Photography Festival). ✉ *Rue de la Calade,* ☎ *04–90–49–36–74.* 🎫 *€2.5.* ⏲ *Apr.–Sept., daily 9–7; Oct.–Mar., daily 10–4:30.*

20 Rivaled only by the even better-preserved version in Nîmes, the **Arènes** (Arena) dominates old Arles: Its four medieval towers are testimony to its transformation from classical sports arena to feudal fortification in the middle ages. Younger than Arles's theater, it dates from the 1st century AD, and unlike the theater, seats 20,000 to this day. Its primary function is as a venue for the traditional spectacle of the corridas, or bullfights, which take place annually during the *feria pascale,* or Easter

Close-Up

VAN GOGH IN ARLES AND ST-RÉMY—"WHAT A LOVELY COUNTRY, AND WHAT LOVELY BLUE AND WHAT A SUN!"

It was the light that drew Vincent van Gogh to Arles. For a man raised under the iron-gray skies of the Netherlands and the gaslight pall of Paris, Provence's clean, clear sun was a revelation. In his last years he turned his frenzied efforts toward capturing the resonance of " . . .golden tones of every hue: green gold, yellow gold, pink gold, bronze or copper colored gold, and even from the yellow of lemons to the matte, lusterless yellow of threshed grain."

Arles, however, was not drawn to van Gogh. Though it makes every effort today to make up for its misjudgment, Arles treated the artist very badly during the time he passed here near the end of his life—a time when his creativity, productivity, and madness all reached a climax. It was in 1888 that he settled in to work in Arles with an intensity and tempestuousness that first drew, then drove away his companion Paul Gauguin, with whom he had dreamed of founding an artists' colony. Astonishingly productive—he applied a pigment-loaded palette knife to some 200 canvases in that year alone—he nonetheless lived within intense isolation, counting his sous, and writing his visions in lengthy letters to his long-suffering, infinitely patient brother Theo. Often heavy-drinking, occasionally whoring, Vincent alienated his neighbors, driving them to distraction and ultimately goading them to action.

In 1889 the people of Arles circulated a petition to have him evicted, a shock that left him more and more at a loss to cope with life and led to his eventual self-commitment to an asylum in nearby St-Rémy. The houses he lived in are no longer standing, though many of his subjects remain as he saw them (or are restored to a similar condition). The paintings he daubed and splashed with such passion have been auctioned elsewhere. Thus you have to go to Amsterdam or Moscow to view van Gogh's work. But with a little imagination you can glean something of van Gogh's Arles from a tour of the modern town. In fact, the city has provided helpful markers and a numbered itinerary to guide you between landmarks. You can stand on the place Lamartine, where his famous Maison Jaune stood until it was destroyed by World War II bombs.. *Starry Night* may have been painted from the quai du Rhône just off place Lamartine, though another was completed at St-Rémy. The Café La Nuit on place Forum is an exact match for the terrace platform, scattered with tables and bathed in gaslight under the stars, from the painting *Terrace de café le Soir*; Gauguin and van Gogh used to drink here. (Current owners have determinedly maintained the fauve color scheme to keep the atmosphere.) Both the Arènes and Les Alyscamps were featured in paintings, and the hospital where he broke down and cut off his ear lobe is now a kind of shrine, its garden reconstructed exactly as it figured in *Le Jardin de l'Hôtel-Dieu*. The drawbridge in *Le pont de Langlois aux Lavandières* has been reconstructed outside of town, at Port-de-Bouc, 3 km (2 mi) south on D35.

About 25 km (15½ mi) away is St-Rémy-de-Provence, where van Gogh retreated to the asylum St-Paul-de-Mausolée. Here he spent hours in silence, painting the cloisters. On his ventures into town he painted the dappled lime trees at the intersection of boulevard Mirabeau and boulevard Gambetta.

And on the route between the towns and, in fact, in traveling anywhere nearby, you'll see the orchards whose spring blooms ignite joyous explosions of yellow and cream, olive groves twisting like dancers in silver and green, ocher houses and red roofs, star-spangled crystalline skies—the stuff of inspiration.

festival. ✉ *Rond Point des Arènes,* ☎ *04–90–49–36–74.* 🎫 €2.5. ⏲ *Apr.–Sept., daily 9–7; Oct.–Mar., daily 10–4:30.*

Though it makes every effort today to make up for its misjudgment, Arles treated Vincent van Gogh very badly during the time he passed here near the end of his life. It was 1888 when he settled in to work in Arles with an intensity and tempestuousness that drove away his colleague and companion Paul Gauguin and alienated his neighbors. In 1889 the people of Arles circulated a petition to have him evicted, a shock that left him more and more at a loss to cope with life and led to his voluntary commitment to an insane asylum in nearby St-Rémy. Thus Arles can't boast a single van Gogh painting—even so, did they have to name their art museum after Jacques Réattu, a local painter
21 of confirmed mediocrity? The **Musée Réattu** lavishes three rooms on his turn-of-the-19th-century ephemera but redeems itself with a decent collection of 20th-century works. The best thing about the Réattu may be the building, a Knights of Malta priory dating from the 15th century. ✉ *Rue Grand Prieuré,* ☎ *04–90–49–36–74.* 🎫 €2.5. ⏲ *Apr.–Sept., daily 9–7; Oct.–Mar., daily 10–4:30.*

You'll have to go to Amsterdam to view van Goghs. But the city has provided helpful markers and a numbered itinerary to guide you from one landmark to another—many of them recognizable from beloved
22 canvases. You can stand on **Place Lamartine** (between the rail station and the ramparts), where he lived in the famous Maison Jaune (Yellow House); it was destroyed by bombs in 1944. *Starry Night* may have been painted from the quai du Rhône, just off place Lamartine. The most strikingly resonant site, impeccably restored and landscaped to match one of van Gogh's paintings, is the courtyard garden of what
23 is now the **Espace van Gogh** (✉ Pl. Dr. Félix Rey), featured in *Le Jardin de l'Hôtel-Dieu.* This was the hospital to which the tortured artist repaired after cutting off his earlobe—contrary to myth, he didn't cut off his entire ear and, in fact, made the desperate gesture in homage to Gauguin, whom he had come to idolize, following the fashion in Provençal bullrings for a matador to present his lady love with an ear from a dispatched bull—and its cloistered grounds have become something of a shrine for visitors. For more information about Van Gogh, see the Close-Up Box, "Van Gogh in Arles and St-Rémy," *below.*

OFF THE BEATEN PATH

LES ALYSCAMPS – Though this romantically melancholy Roman cemetery lies away from the Old Town, it's worth the hike—certainly, van Gogh thought so, as several of his famous canvases prove. This long necropolis amassed the remains of the dead from antiquity to the Middle Ages. Greek, Roman, and Christian tombs line the long shady road that was once the entry to Arles—the Aurelian Way. ☎ *04–90–49–36–74.* 🎫 €2.5. ⏲ *Apr.–Sept., daily 9–7; Oct.–Mar., daily 10–4:30.*

Dining and Lodging

$–$$ ✕ **L'Affenage.** A vast smorgasbord of Provençal hors d'oeuvres draws loyal locals to this former fire-horse shed. They come here for heaping plates of fried eggplant, tapenade, chickpeas in cumin, and a slab of ham carved off the bone. In summer you can opt for just the first-course buffet and go back for thirds; reserve a terrace table out front. ✉ *4 rue Molière,* ☎ *04–90–96–07–67. AE, MC, V. Closed Sun. and 3 wks in Aug.*

$–$$ ★ ✕ **Brasserie Nord-Pinus.** With its tile-and-ironwork interior straight out of a design magazine and its place du Forum terrace packed with all the right people, this cozy-chic retro brasserie showcases the superb but unpretentious cooking of Jean-André Charial, trained at the hallowed L'Oustau de la Baumanière. The cuisine is light, simple, and purely

Provençal. ✉ *Pl. du Forum,* ☎ *04–90–93–44–44. Reservations essential. AE, DC, MC, V. Closed Feb. and Wed. Nov.–Mar.*

$–$$ ✕ **La Gueule du Loup.** Serving as hosts, waiters, and chefs, the ambitious couple who own this restaurant tackle serious cooking—monkfish and squid in saffron, lamb in pastry lined with tapenade, and crème brûlée perfumed with orange blossoms. Jazz music and vintage magic-act posters bring the old Arles stone-and-beam rooms up to date. ✉ *39 rue des Arènes,* ☎ *04–90–96–96–69. MC, V. Closed Sun.–Mon. Oct.–Mar.; closed Sun. Apr.–Sept. No lunch Mon.*

$$$$ ✕ **Le Mas de Peint.** This may be the ultimate mas experience, set as it is in a 17th-century farmhouse on some 1,250 acres of Camargue ranch land. Provençal fabrics and antiques complement the old stone floors, and rooms are lavished with brass beds, monogrammed linens, and even canopied bathtubs. At dinnertime you (and some non-resident visitors) gather in the kitchen for sophisticated specialties using home-grown products. ✉ *Le Sambuc, 13200 Arles (20 km/12 mi south of town),* ☎ *04–90–97–20–62,* FAX *04–90–97–22–20,* WEB *www.ila-chateau.com/manade/. 8 rooms, 3 apartments. Restaurant, cable TV, pool, horseback riding. AE, DC, MC, V. Closed mid-Jan.–mid-Mar.*

$$$–$$$$ **Jules César.** This pleasant landmark, once a Carmelite convent but styled like a Roman palace, anchors the lively (often noisy) boulevard des Lices. Low-slung, with rooms on the small side, it's not a grand luxury palace; rather, it's an intimate, traditional hotel, conservatively decorated with richly printed fabrics and burnished woodwork. Some windows look over the pool and some over the pretty cloister, where breakfast is served under a vaulted stone arcade—a nice break from all the hubbub outside the door. ✉ *Bd. des Lices, 13200,* ☎ *04–90–93–43–20,* FAX *04–90–93–33–47. 50 rooms, 5 suites. 2 restaurants, cable TV, minibars, Internet, pool, parking (fee). AE, DC, MC, V. Closed mid-Nov.–late Dec.*

$$$–$$$$ ★ **Nord-Pinus.** The adventurer and mail-order genius J. Peterman would feel right at home in this quintessentially Mediterranean hotel on place du Forum; Hemingway certainly did. Travel relics, kilims, oil jars, angular wrought iron, and colorful ceramics create a richly atmospheric stage-set. Its scruffy art-director chic is not for everyone: traditionalists should head for the mainstream luxuries of the Jules César. ✉ *Pl. du Forum, 13200,* ☎ *04–90–93–44–44,* FAX *04–90–93–34–00,* WEB *www.nord-pinus.com. 25 rooms. Cable TV, minibars, parking (fee). AE, DC, MC, V.*

$$ **Arlatan.** Built by the counts of Arlatan, this noble 15th-century stone house stands on the site of a 4th-century basilica. Rows of rooms horseshoe around a fountain courtyard, each decorated with a lovely, light hand. Recent renovations have added seven modern rooms and pretty breakfast salons, and a pool is in the works. ✉ *26 rue du Sauvage, 13200,* ☎ *04–90–93–56–66,* FAX *04–90–49–68–45. 41 rooms, 7 suites. Dining room, bar, cable TV, minibars, Internet, pool. AE, DC, MC, V.*

$ **Le Cloître.** Built as a private home, this grand old medieval building has luckily fallen into the hands of a couple devoted to making the most of its historic details—with their own bare hands. They've chipped away plaster from pristine quarry-stone walls, cleaned massive beams, restored tile stairs, and mixed natural chalk and ocher to plaster the walls. ✉ *16 rue du Cloître, 13200,* ☎ *04–90–96–29–50,* FAX *04–90–96–02–88. 30 rooms. AE, MC, V.*

$ ★ **Muette.** With 12th-century exposed stone walls, a 15th-century spiral stair, weathered wood, and an Old Town setting, a hotelier wouldn't have to try very hard to please. But the couple who own this place do: hand-stripped doors, antiques, sparkling blue-and-white-tile baths, hair dryers, good mattresses, Provençal prints, and fresh sunflowers in every room show they care. ✉ *15 rue des Suisses, 13200,* ☎ *04–90–96–15–39,* FAX *04–90–49–73–16,* WEB *perso.wanadoo.fr/hotel-muette. 18 rooms. No air-conditioning, cable TV. AE, MC, V.*

Nightlife and the Arts

To find out what's happening in and around Arles (even as far away as Nîmes and Avignon), the free weekly **Le César** lists films, plays, cabarets, and jazz and rock events. It's distributed at the tourist office and in bars, clubs, and cinemas. In high season the cafés stay lively 'til the wee hours; in winter the streets empty out by 11. **Le Cargo de Nuit** (✉ 7 av. Sadi-Carnot, ☎ 04–90–49–55–99) is the main venue for live jazz, reggae, and rock, with a dance floor next to the stage. Though Arles seems to be one big sidewalk café in warm weather, the place to tipple is the hip bar **Le Cintra,** in the Hôtel Nord-Pinus.

THE ALPILLES AND THE RHÔNE FORTRESSES

The low mountain range called the Alpilles (pronounced ahl-*pee*-yuh) forms a rough-hewn, rocky landscape that rises into nearly barren limestone hills, the flanking fields silvered with ranks of twisted olive trees and alleys of gnarled *amandiers* (almond trees). There are superb antiquities in St-Rémy and feudal ruins in Les Baux. West of the Alpilles, the fortresses of Tarascon and Beaucaire guard the Rhône between Avignon and the sea.

Abbaye de Montmajour

24 *5 km (3 mi) northeast of Arles, 17 km (10½ mi) south of Tarascon.*

An extraordinary structure looming over the marshlands north of Arles, this magnificent Romanesque abbey stands in partial ruin. Begun in the 12th century by a handful of Benedictine monks, it grew according to an ambitious plan of church, crypt, and cloister. Under the management of corrupt lay monks in the 17th century, it grew more sumptuous; when those lay monks were ejected by the church, they sacked the place. After the Revolution it was sold to a junkman, and he tried to pay the mortgage by stripping off and selling its goods. A 19th-century medieval revival spurred its partial restoration, but its 18th-century portions remain in ruins. Ironically, because of this mercenary history, what remains is a spare and beautiful piece of Romanesque architecture. The **cloister** rivals that of St-Trophime in Arles for its balance, elegance, and air of mystical peace: van Gogh was drawn to its womblike isolation and came often to the abbey to paint and reflect. ☎ *04–90–54–64–17.* 🎫 *€5.* ⏲ *Apr.–Sept., daily 9–7; Oct.–Mar., Wed.–Mon. 10–1 and 2–5.*

Les Baux-de-Provence

★ 25 *18 km (11 mi) northeast of Arles, 29 km (18 mi) south of Avignon.*

When you first search the craggy hilltops for signs of Les Baux-de-Provence (pronounced lay-*bo*), you may not quite be able to distinguish between bedrock and building, so naturally do the ragged skyline of towers and crenellation blend into the sawtooth jags of stone. This tiny château-village ranks as one of the most visited tourist sites in France, a tour-de-force blend of natural scenery and medieval ambience of astonishing beauty.

From this intimidating vantage point, the lords of Les Baux ruled throughout the 11th and 12th centuries over one of the largest fiefdoms in the south. Only in the 19th century did Les Baux find new purpose: the mineral bauxite, valued as an alloy in aluminum production, was discovered in its hills and named for its source. A profitable industry sprang up that lasted into the 20th century before fading into history.

Today Les Baux offers two faces to the world: its beautifully preserved medieval village and the ghostly ruins of its fortress, once referred to as the *ville morte* (dead town). In the village, lovely 12th-century stone houses, even their window frames still intact, shelter the shops, cafés, and galleries that line the steep cobbled streets.

The 17-acre clifftop sprawl of ruins is contained under the umbrella name the **Château des Baux.** At the entry, the Tour du Brau contains the **Musée d'Histoire des Baux,** a small collection of relics and models. Its exit gives access to the wide and varied grounds, where Romanesque chapels and towers mingle with skeletal ruins. The tiny **Chapelle St-Blaise** shelters a permanent music-and-slide show called *Van Gogh, Gauguin, Cézanne au Pays de l'Olivier,* of artworks depicting olive orchards in their infinite variety. ☎ *04–90–54–55–56.* *€5.5.* *Mar.–June and Sept.–Oct., daily 9–7; July–Aug., daily 9 AM–9:30 PM; Nov. and Feb., daily 9–6; Dec.–Jan., daily 9–5.*

Dining and Lodging

$$–$$$$ ★ **L'Oustau de la Baumanière.** Sheltered by rocky cliffs below the village of Les Baux, this long-famous hotel, with its formal landscaped terrace and broad swimming pool, has a guest list studded with names like Winston Churchill, Elizabeth Taylor, and Picasso. The interior is luxe-Provençal, thanks to tile floors, arched stone ceilings, and brocaded settees done up in Canovas and Halard fabrics. Guest rooms—breezy, private, and beautifully furnished with antiques—were renovated in 1999, but the basic style remains archetypal Baux. These rooms are set in three buildings on broad landscaped grounds, the best of which are in the enchanting Le Manoir. As for the famed Baumanière restaurant, chef Jean-André Charial's hallowed reputation continues to attract culinary pilgrims (too many, it would appear from the noisy crowds that drive up the nearby road to the hotel). You can't blame them: the Oustau tradition is a veritable museum of Provençal tradition, but one that has been given a nouvelle face-lift—lobster cooked in Châteauneuf-du-Pape and set on a bed of polenta is a typical dazzler. If you're only dining here, be sure to make reservations. Note that from November to December and in March the restaurant is closed Wednesday and does not serve lunch Thursday; during January and February both the hotel and restaurant are closed. If you want the Oustau experience at just half the price, why not opt for a room a kilometer (half mile) away at **La Cabro d'Or** (☎ 04–90–54–33–21, FAX 04–90–54–45–98)—although run by the same owners, it is cheaper, more rustic, more private, and don't be surprised to see a resident billy-goat wander by your guest-room window. ✉ *Val d'Enfer, 13520,* ☎ *04–90–54–33–07,* FAX *04–90–54–40–46,* WEB *www.oustaudebaumaniere.com. 22 rooms; 8 rooms in La Cabro. Restaurant, cable TV, minibars, 2 tennis courts, pool, horseback riding. AE, DC, MC, V. Closed Jan.–Feb.*

$ **La Reine Jeanne.** At this modest but majestically placed inn right at the entrance to the village, you can stand on balconies and look over rugged views worthy of the châteaux up the street. Rooms are small, simple, and—despite the white vinyl-padded furniture—lovingly decorated. Reserve in advance for one of the two rooms with a balcony, though even one of the tiny interior rooms gives you the right to spend an evening in Les Baux after the tourists have drained away. Good home-style cooking is served in the restaurant, which has views both from inside and outside on the pretty terrace. ✉ *13520,* ☏ *04–90–54–32–06,* FAX *04–90–54–32–33. 10 rooms. Restaurant, no air-conditioning, cable TV. MC, V. Closed Jan.*

$$$ **Mas de L'Oulivié.** Built to look ancient, with recycled roof tiles and hand-waxed chalk walls, this mas is clarity itself, with a cool, clean look and a low-key aura. There's no upscale restaurant—just easy and unpretentious lunches by the pool (grilled meats, salads, and goat cheese). Eight rooms on the upper floor of the main house are pretty enough, with floral-print curtains and rich carpets, but ask for one with doors opening onto the lavender gardens and olive groves. ✉ *Below Les Baux, D27 direction Fontvieille, Les Arcoules, 13520,* ☏ *04–90–54–35–78,* FAX *04–90–54–44–31,* WEB *www.masdeloulivie.com. 23 rooms. Restaurant, cable TV, minibars, Internet, tennis court, pool. AE, DC, MC, V. Closed Dec.–Feb.*

St-Rémy-de-Provence

★ 26 *8 km (5 mi) north of Les Baux, 24 km (15 mi) east of Arles, 19 km (12 mi) south of Avignon.*

Something felicitous has happened in this market town in the heart of the Alpilles—a steady infusion of style, of art, of imagination—all brought by people with a respect for local traditions and a love of Provençal ways. Here more than anywhere you can meditate quietly on antiquity, browse redolent markets with basket in hand, and enjoy urbane galleries, cosmopolitan shops, and specialty food boutiques. An abundance of choices in restaurants, mas, and even châteaux awaits you; the almond and olive groves conceal dozens of stone-and-terra-cotta gîtes, many with pools.

First established by an indigenous Celtic-Ligurian people who worshiped the god Glan, the village Glanum was adopted and gentrified by the Greeks of Marseille in the 2nd and 3rd centuries before Christ. Rome moved in to help ward off Hannibal, and by the 1st century BC Caesar had taken full control. The Via Domitia, linking Italy to Spain, passed by its doors, and the main trans-Alpine pass emptied into its entrance gate. Under the Pax Romana there developed a veritable city, complete with temples and forum, luxurious villas and baths.

The Romans eventually fell, but a town grew up next to their ruins, taking its name from their protectorate Abbey St-Remi, in Reims. It grew to be an important market town, and wealthy families built fine mansions in its center—among them the family de Sade (whose black-sheep relation held forth in the Lubéron at Lacoste). Another famous native son was the eccentric doctor, scholar, and astrologist Michel Nostradamus (1503–66), who is credited by some as having predicted much of the modern age.

Perhaps the best known of St-Rémy's residents was the ill-fated Vincent van Gogh. Shipped unceremoniously out of Arles at the height of his madness (and creativity), he committed himself to the asylum St-Paul-de-Mausolé.

To approach Glanum, you must park in a dusty roadside lot on D5 south of town (toward Les Baux). But before crossing, you'll be confronted with two of the most miraculously preserved classical monuments in France, simply called **Les Antiques.** Dating from 30 BC, the **Mausolée** (mausoleum), a wedding-cake stack of arches and columns, lacks nothing but its finial on top, yet it is dedicated to a Julian (as in Julius Caesar), probably Caesar Augustus. A few yards away stands another marvel: the **Arc Triomphal,** dating from AD 20.

Across the street from Les Antiques and set back from D5, a slick visitor center prepares you for entry into the ancient village of **Glanum** with scale models of the site in its various heydays. A good map and an English brochure guide you stone by stone through the maze of foundations, walls, towers, and columns that spreads across a broad field; helpfully, Greek sites are noted by numbers, Roman ones by letters. ✉ *Off D5, direction Les Baux, info phone at Hôtel de Sade,* ☎ *04–90–92–64–04.* 🎫 *€5 (€6 includes entry to Hôtel de Sade).* ⏲ *Apr.–Sept., daily 9–7; Oct.–Mar., daily 9–noon and 2–5.*

You can cut across the fields from Glanum to **St-Paul-de-Mausolée,** the lovely, isolated asylum where van Gogh spent the last year of his life (1889–90). But enter it quietly: it shelters psychiatric patients to this day—all of them women. You're free to walk up the beautifully manicured garden path to the church and its jewel-box Romanesque **cloister,** where the artist found womblike peace. ✉ *Next to Glanum, off D5, direction Les Baux,* ☎ *04–90–92–77–00.* 🎫 *€2.5.* ⏲ *May–Sept., daily 8–7; Oct.–Apr., daily 8–5.*

Within St-Rémy's fast-moving traffic loop, a labyrinth of narrow streets leads you away from the action and into the slow-moving inner sanctum of the **Vieille Ville** (Old Town). Here trendy, high-end shops mingle pleasantly with local life, and the buildings, if gentrified, blend in unobtrusively.

Make your way to the **Hôtel de Sade,** a 15th- and 16th-century private manor now housing the treasures unearthed with the ruins of Glanum. The de Sade family built the house around remains of 4th-century baths and a 5th-century baptistery, now nestled in its courtyard. ✉ *Rue du Parage,* ☎ *04–90–92–64–04.* 🎫 *€2.5 (€6 includes Glanum entry).* ⏲ *Feb.–Mar. and Oct., Tues.–Sun. 10–noon and 2–5; Apr.–Sept., Tues.–Sun. 10–noon and 2–6; Nov.–Dec., Wed. and weekends 10–noon and 2–5.*

Dining and Lodging

$$–$$$ ✕ **Maison Jaune.** This modern retreat in the Old Town draws crowds of summer people to its pretty roof terrace, with accents of sober stone and lively contemporary furniture both indoors and out. The look reflects the cuisine: with vivid flavors and a cool, contained touch, chef François Perraud prepares grilled sardines with crunchy fennel and lemon confit, and veal lightly flavored with olives, capers, and celery. The prix-fixe menus are good values at €28 and €47. ✉ *15 rue Carnot,* ☎ *04–90–92–56–14. Reservations essential. MC, V. Closed Mon. No lunch Tues.*

$–$$ ★ ✕ **L'Assiette de Marie.** Marie Ricco is a collector, and she's turned her tiny restaurant into a bower of attic treasures. Seated at an old school desk, you choose from the day's specials, all made with Marie's Corsican-Italian touch—marinated vegetables with tapenade, a cast-iron casserole of superb pasta, satiny *panetone* (flan). ✉ *1 rue Jaume Roux,* ☎ *04–90–92–32–14. Reservations essential. MC, V. Closed Mon. Nov.–Easter. No lunch Tues.*

$ ✕ **La Gousse d'Ail.** Another intimate, indoor Old Town hideaway, this family-run bistro lives up to its name (the Garlic Clove), serving robust, highly flavored southern dishes in hearty portions. Aim for Thursday night, when there's Gypsy music and jazz. ✉ *25 rue Carnot,* ☎ *04–90–92–16–87. AE, MC, V. Closed Jan.–Feb. except occasional weekends.*

$$$–$$$$ ★ ✕🏨 **Domaine de Valmouriane.** In this genteel mas-cum-resort, beautifully isolated within a broad park, overstuffed English-country decor mixes cozily with cool Provençal stone and timber. The restaurant is masterminded by chef Pierre Walter, who is determined to please with

fresh game, seafood, local oils, and truffles; his desserts have won him national standing. But it's the personal welcome from English owner Judith McHugo that makes you feel like a weekend guest. The pool is most inviting, surrounded by a slate walk and delightful gardens. ✉ *Petite rte. des Baux (D27), 13210,* ☎ *04–90–92–44–62,* FAX *04–90–92–37–32,* WEB *www.valmouriane.com. 14 rooms. Restaurant, cable TV, minibars, tennis court, pool, hot tub, steam room, billiards. AE, DC, MC, V.*

$$$ ★ ✕🏨 **Bistrot d'Eygalières.** Belgian chef Wout Bru's understated restaurant in nearby Eygalières is quickly gaining a reputation (and stars) for its elegant, light, and subtly balanced cuisine, like sole with goat cheese, lobster salad with candied tomatoes, and foie gras carpaccio with summer truffles. The wine list is both eclectic and thorough, though prices are a bit on the high side. Guest rooms are very chic, very comfortable; Wout's wife, Suzy, has a wonderful eye and a welcoming disposition. ✉ *Rue de la République, 13810 Eygalières, 10 km/6 mi southeast of Saint-Rémy-de-Provence on the D99 and then the D24,* ☎ *04–90–90–60–34,* FAX *04–90–90–60–37. Reservations essential. 4 rooms. Restaurant, minibars. AE, DC, MC, V.*

$$$–$$$$ 🏨 **Château des Alpilles.** At the end of an alley of grand old plane trees, this early 19th-century manor house reigns over a vast park off D31. If its public spaces are cool and spare to the point of sparseness, guest rooms are warm and fussy, with lush Provençal prints and polished antiques (plus some jarring 1970s touches). Outer buildings offer jazzy-modern apartments with kitchenettes, and the poolside grill gives you a noble perspective over the park. ✉ *Ancienne rte. du Grès, 13210,* ☎ *04–90–92–03–33,* FAX *04–90–92–45–17. 16 rooms, 4 suites. Cable TV, minibars, cable TV, 2 tennis courts, pool, sauna. AE, DC, MC, V. Closed mid-Nov.–mid-Dec. and Jan.–mid-Feb.*

$$$–$$$$ 🏨 **Mas de Cornud.** An American stewards the wine cellar and an Egyptian runs the kitchen, but the attitude is pure Provence: David and Nito Carpita's house and rooms have turned their farmhouse, just outside St-Rémy, into a bed-and-breakfast filled with French country furniture and objects from around the world. The welcome is so sincere you'll feel like one of the family in no time. Table d'hôte dinners, cooking classes, and tours can be arranged. Breakfast is included. ✉ *Rte. de Mas-Blanc, 13210,* ☎ *04–90–92–39–32,* FAX *04–90–92–55–99,* WEB *www.masdecornud.com. 5 rooms, 1 suite. Dining room, no air-conditioning, pool. No credit cards. Closed Jan.–Feb.*

$$ 🏨 **Château de Roussan.** In a majestic park shaded by ancient plane trees, this 18th-century château is a helter-skelter of brocantes and bric-a-brac, and the bathrooms have an afterthought air about them. Cats outnumber the staff. Yet if you're the right sort for this place—backpackers, romantic couples on a budget, lovers of atmosphere over luxury—you'll blossom in this three-dimensional costume-drama scene. ✉ *Rte. de Tarascon, 13210,* ☎ *04–90–92–11–63,* FAX *04–90–92–50–59,* WEB *www.alpilles.com/ang1ax.htm. 22 rooms. Restaurant, cable TV. MC, V.*

Shopping

Every Wednesday morning St-Rémy hosts one of the most popular and picturesque **markets** in Provence, during which place de la République and narrow Old Town streets overflow with fresh produce, herbs, and olive oil by the vat, as well as fabrics and brocantes (antiques).

Tarascon

27 *16 km (10 mi) west of St-Rémy, 17 km (11 mi) north of Arles, 25 km (15 mi) east of Nîmes.*

Tarascon's claim to fame is as the haunt the mythical Tarasque, a monster that was said to emerge from the Rhône to gobble up children and cattle. Luckily, St. Marthe, who washed up at Stes-Maries-de-la-Mer, tamed the beast with a sprinkle of holy water, after which the inhabitants slashed it to pieces. This dramatic event is celebrated on the last weekend in June with a parade, and was immortalized by Alphonse Daudet, who lived in nearby Fontvieille, in his tales of a folk hero known to all French schoolchildren as *Tartarin de Tarascon*. Unfortunately, a saint has not yet been born who can vanquish the fumes that emanate from Tarascon's enormous paper mill, and the hotel industry is suffering for it.

★ Nonetheless, with the walls of its formidable **Château** plunging straight into the roaring Rhône, this ancient city on the river presents a daunting challenge to Beaucaire, its traditional enemy across the water. Begun in the 13th century by the noble Anjou family on the site of a Roman *castellum,* it grew through the generations into a splendid structure, crowned with both round and square towers and elegantly furnished. Complete with a moat, a drawbridge, and a lovely faceted spiral staircase, it retains its beautiful decorative stonework and original window frames. ☎ *04–90–91–01–93.* ▭ *€5.* ⏲ *Apr.–Sept., daily 9–7; Oct.–Mar., Wed.–Mon. 9–noon and 2–5.*

AVIGNON AND THE VAUCLUSE

Anchored by the magnificent papal stronghold of Avignon, the Vaucluse spreads luxuriantly east of the Rhône. Its famous vineyards—Châteauneuf-du-Pape, Gigondas, Vacqueyras, Beaumes-de-Venise—seduce connoisseurs, and its Roman ruins in Orange and Vaison-la-Romaine draw scholars and arts lovers. Arid lowlands dotted with orchards of olives, apricots, and almonds give way to a rich and wild mountain terrain around the formidable Mont Ventoux and flow into the primeval Luberon, made a household name by Peter Mayle. The hill villages around the Luberon—Gordes, Roussillon, Oppède, Bonnieux—are as lovely as any you'll find in the south of France.

Avignon

24 km (15 mi) northeast of Tarascon, 82 km (51 mi) northwest of Aix-en-Provence, 95 km (59 mi) northwest of Marseille, 224 km (140 mi) south of Lyon.

From its famous Palais des Papes (Papal Palace), where seven exiled popes camped between 1309 and 1377 after fleeing from the corruption and civil strife of Rome, to the long, low bridge of childhood song fame stretching over the river, you can beam yourself briefly into 14th-century Avignon, so complete is the context, so evocative the setting. Yet the town is anything but a museum; it surges with modern ideas and energy and thrives within its ramparts as it did in the heyday of the popes—and, like those radical church lords, is sensual, cultivated, and cosmopolitan, with a taste for laic pleasures. Avignon remained papal property until 1791, and elegant mansions bear witness to the town's 18th-century prosperity.

★ 28 The colossal **Palais des Papes** creates a disconcertingly fortresslike impression, underlined by the austerity of its interior. Most of the original furnishings were returned to Rome with the papacy, others were lost during the French Revolution. Some imagination is required to picture its earlier medieval splendor, awash with color and with worldly clerics enjoying what the 14th-century Italian poet Petrarch called "licentious banquets." On close inspection, two different styles of building emerge at

Avignon

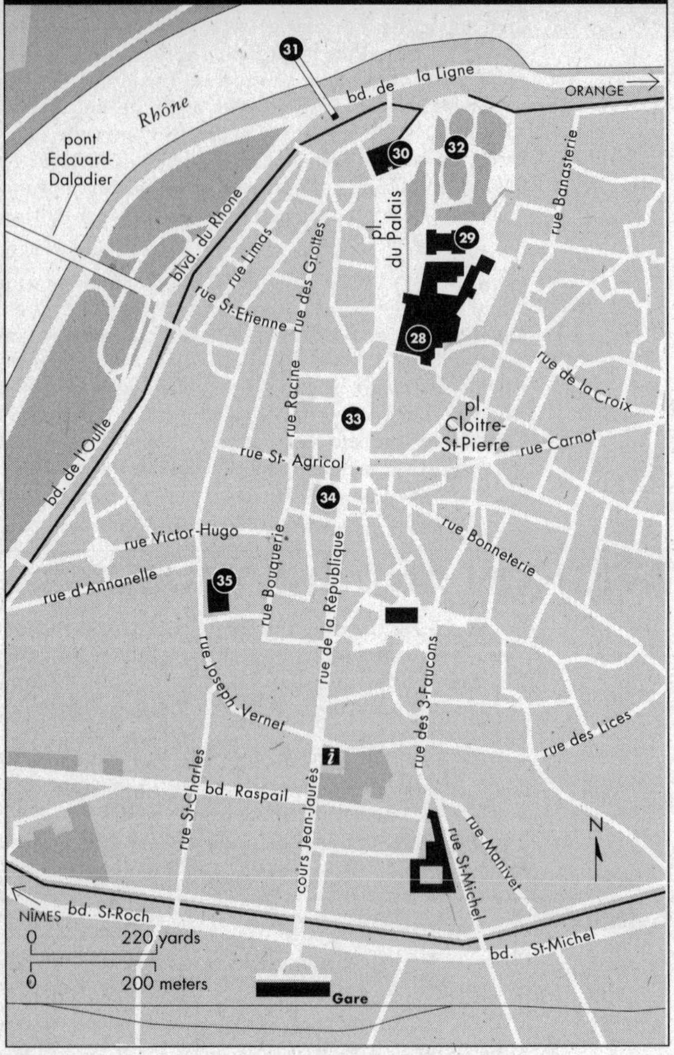

the palace: the severe **Palais Vieux** (Old Palace), built between 1334 and 1342 by Pope Benedict XII, a member of the Cistercian order, which frowned on frivolity, and the more decorative **Palais Nouveau** (New Palace), built in the following decade by the artsy, lavish-living Pope Clement VI. The Great Court, entryway to the complex, links the two.

The main rooms of the Palais Vieux are the **Consistory** (Council Hall), decorated with some excellent 14th-century frescoes by Simone Martini; the **Chapelle St-Jean** (original frescoes by Matteo Giovanetti); the **Grand Tinel,** or Salle des Festins (Feast Hall), with a majestic vaulted roof and a series of 18th-century Gobelin tapestries; the **Chapelle St-Martial** (more Giovanetti frescoes); and the **Chambre du Cerf,** with a richly decorated ceiling, murals featuring a stag hunt, and a delightful view of Avignon. The principal attractions of the Palais Nouveau are the **Grande Audience,** a magnificent two-nave hall on the ground floor, and, upstairs, the **Chapelle Clémentine,** where the college of cardinals once gathered to elect the new pope. ✉ *Pl. du Palais,* ☎ *04–90–27–*

50–00. 🎟 *€7 entry includes choice of guided tour or individual audio guide; €8.5 includes audio guided tour to pont St-Bénézet.* ⏲ *Nov.–Mar., daily 9:30–5:45; Apr.–June and Oct., daily 9–7; July (during theater festival), daily 9–9; Aug.–Sept., daily 9–8.*

29 The **Cathédrale Notre-Dame-des-Doms,** first built in a pure Provençal Romanesque style in the 12th century, was quickly dwarfed by the extravagant palace that rose beside it. It rallied in the 14th century with the addition of a cupola—which promptly collapsed. As rebuilt in 1425, it's a marvel of stacked arches with a strong Byzantine flavor and is topped nowadays with a gargantuan Virgin Mary lantern—a 19th-century afterthought—whose glow can be seen for miles around. ✉ *Pl. du Palais,* ☎ *04–90–86–81–01.* ⏲ *Mon.–Sat. 7–7, Sun. 9–7.*

30 The **Petit Palais,** the former residence of bishops and cardinals, houses a large collection of Old Master paintings. The majority are Italian works from the Early Renaissance schools of Siena, Florence, and Venice—styles with which the Avignon popes would have been familiar. Later key works to seek out include Sandro Botticelli's *Virgin and Child* and Venetian paintings by Carpaccio and Giovanni Bellini. ✉ *Pl. du Palais,* ☎ *04–90–86–44–58.* 🎟 *€4.7.* ⏲ *Oct.–May, Wed.–Mon. 9:30–1 and 2–5:30; June–Sept., Wed.–Mon. 10–1 and 2–6.*

★ 31 The **Pont St-Bénézet** (St. Bénézet Bridge) is the subject of the famous children's song: "*Sur le pont d'Avignon on y danse, on y danse . . .*" ("On the bridge of Avignon one dances, one dances . . ."). Unlike London Bridge, this one still stretches its arches across the river, but only partway: half was washed away in the 17th century. Its first stones allegedly laid with the miraculous strength granted St-Bénézet in the 12th century, it once reached all the way to Villeneuve. ✉ *Port du Rochre.*

32 The hilltop garden known as **Rocher des Doms** (Rock of the Domes), with statuary and swans under grand Mediterranean pines, offers extraordinary views of the palace, the rooftops of Old Avignon, the Pont St-Bénézet, and formidable Villeneuve across the Rhône. On the horizon loom Mont Ventoux, the Luberon, and Les Alpilles. ✉ *Montée du Moulin off pl. du Palais.*

33 The **Place de l'Horloge** (Clock Square) is the social nerve center of Avignon, where the concentration of bistros, brasseries, and restaurants draws swarms of locals to the shade of its plane trees.

Housed in a pretty little Jesuit chapel on the main shopping street, the 34 **Musée Lapidaire** gathers a collection of classical sculpture and stonework from Gallo-Roman times (1st and 2nd centuries), as well as pieces from the Musée Calvet's collection of Greek and Etruscan works. They are haphazardly labeled and insouciantly scattered throughout the noble chapel, itself slightly crumbling but awash with light. ✉ *27 rue de la République,* ☎ *04–90–85–75–38.* 🎟 *€1.5.* ⏲ *Wed.–Mon. 10–1 and 2–6.*

Worth a visit for the beauty and balance of its architecture alone, the 35 fine old **Musée Calvet** contains a rich collection of antiquities and classically inspired works. Recent acquisitions are Neoclassical and Romantic and almost entirely French, including works by Manet, Daumier, and David. The main building itself is a Palladian-style jewel in pale Gard stone dating from the 1740s; and the garden is so lovely that it may distract you from the paintings. ✉ *65 rue Joseph-Vernet,* ☎ *04–90–86–33–84.* 🎟 *€5.* ⏲ *Wed.–Mon. 10–1 and 2–6.*

Dining and Lodging

$$ ✕ **Brunel.** Stylishly redecorated in a hip, contemporary retro-bistro style in urbane shades of gray, this Avignon favorite entices with the passionate Provençal cooking of Avignon-born and -bred chef Roger

Brunel. This is down-home bistro cooking based on a sophisticated larder: parchment-wrapped mullet with eggplant and tomatoes, chicken roasted with garlic confit (preserves), and caramelized apples in tender pastry. The prix-fixe menus run €26 and €51. ✉ *46 rue de la Balance,* ☎ *04–90–85–24–83. Reservations essential. MC, V.*

$$ ★ ✕ **La Cuisine de Reine.** Glassed into the white-stone cloister of the trendy art gallery called Les Cloître des Arts, this chic bistro has theatrical dell'arte decor and a young, laid-back waitstaff. The blackboard lists eclectic dishes: duck in rosemary honey and salmon tartare with eggplant caviar and citrus vinaigrette. Or join the cashmere-and-loafer set for the €18 Saturday brunch buffet. ✉ *83 rue Joseph-Vernet,* ☎ *04–90–85–99–04. AE, DC, MC, V. Closed Sun.*

$ ★ ✕ **Le Grand Café.** Behind the Papal Palace, in a massive former factory—note the carefully preserved industrial decay—this hip entertainment complex combines an international cinema, a bar, and this popular bistro. Gigantic 18th-century mirrors and dance-festival posters hang on crumbling plaster and brick, and votive candles half-light the raw metal framework—an inspiring environment for intense film talk and a late supper of foie gras, goat cheese, or marinated artichokes. The prix-fixe menu is €25. ✉ *La Manutention, 4 rue des Escaliers Ste-Anne,* ☎ *04–90–86–86–77. MC, V. Closed Mon. Aug.–June.*

$ ✕ **Maison Nani.** Crowded inside and out with trendy young professionals, this pretty lunch spot serves stylish home cooking in generous portions without the fuss of multiple courses. Choose from heaping salads sizzling with fresh meat, enormous kebabs, and a creative quiche du jour. It's just off rue de la République. ✉ *29 rue Théodore Aubanel,* ☎ *04–90–82–60–90. No credit cards. Closed Sun. No dinner Mon.–Thurs.*

$$$$ ★ ✕🏨 **Hôtel de la Mirande.** This *petit palais* is a designer's dream of a hotel, set just below the Papal Palace. Inside you step into 18th-century Avignon, thanks to antique parquet floors, painted coffered ceilings, sumptuous antiques, and other superb grand siècle touches (those rough sisal mats on the floors were the height of chic back in the Baroque era). The central lounge is a skylighted and jazz-warmed haven. Upstairs, guest rooms are both gorgeous and comfy, with extraordinary baths and even more extraordinary handmade wall coverings. The costume-drama dining room provides an idyllic setting for the restaurant's sophisticated cuisine. Look for friendly Friday-night cooking classes in the massive downstairs "country" kitchen. ✉ *Pl. de la Mirande, 84000,* ☎ *04–90–85–93–93,* FAX *04–90–86–26–85. 19 rooms, 1 suite. Restaurant, bar, cable TV, minibars, Internet, meeting room, parking (fee). AE, DC, MC, V.*

$$$–$$$$ ✕🏨 **Hôtel d'Europe.** Once host to guests like Napoléon and Emperor Maximilian, this vine-covered 16th-century home is regally discreet and classic. Set in a walled court shaded by trees, the splendor continues inside with Aubusson tapestries, porcelains, and Provençal antiques. Guest rooms are mostly emperor-size, with two suites overlooking the Papal Palace. The restaurant, La Vieille Fontaine, is one of Avignon's finest; during the festival period, tables in the courtyard are highly coveted and are top places to preen while enjoying such delights as hot duck fois gras with peaches. ✉ *12 pl. Crillon, 84000,* ☎ *04–90–14–76–76,* FAX *04–90–14–76–71,* WEB *www.hotel-d-europe.fr. 44 rooms. Restaurant, cable TV, minibars, Internet, meeting room, parking (fee). AE, DC, MC, V.*

$$ 🏨 **Du Palais des Papes.** Despite its mere two-star rating, this is a remarkably solid, comfortable hotel, ideally situated just off the place de Palais. Recently updated with chic ironwork furniture and rich fabrics, the exposed-stone-and-beam decor fulfills fantasies of a medieval city—but one with good tile baths (top rooms include Nos. 10, 11, 12,

20, and 21). ✉ *1 rue Gérard-Philippe, 84000,* ☎ *04–90–86–04–13,* FAX *04–90–27–91–17,* WEB *www.avignon-et-provence.com/hotel-le-lutrin-palais-des-papes. 23 rooms. Bar, cable TV, minibars, Internet, no-smoking rooms. AE, DC, MC, V.*

$$ ★ **Hôtel du Blauvac.** Just off rue de la République and place de l'Horloge, this 17th-century nobleman's home has been divided into 16 guest rooms. Many have pristine exposed stonework, aged-oak details, and lovely tall windows that look, alas, onto backstreet walls. Pretty fabrics and a warm, familial welcome more than compensate, however. ✉ *11 rue de la Bancasse, 84000,* ☎ *04–90–86–34–11,* FAX *04–90–86–27–41. 16 rooms. No air-conditioning, cable TV, Internet, free parking. AE, DC, MC, V.*

$ **Hôtel de Mons.** Tatty and almost intolerably eccentric, this is a neo-Gothic budget flophouse after Edward Gorey's own heart, first built as a 13th-century chapel. Transformation took some maneuvering, but guest rooms with baths (with '70s-style decor) have been fitted into crooked nooks and crannies, while retaining some period detail (slanting spiral stairs, quarried stone). Breakfast is served in a groin-vaulted crypt. Location is everything: it's two steps off place de l'Horloge. And it's dirt cheap. ✉ *5 rue de Mons, 84000,* ☎ *04–90–82–57–16,* FAX *04–90–85–19–15. 11 rooms, 10 with bath. No air-conditioning, cable TV. AE, MC, V.*

Nightlife and the Arts

Held annually in July, the Avignon festival, known officially as the **Festival Annuel d'Art Dramatique** (Annual Festival of Dramatic Art), has brought the best of world theater to this ancient city since 1947. Some 300 productions take place every year; the main performances are at the Palais des Papes (for tickets and information contact ☎ 04–90–27–66–50).

Within its fusty old medieval walls, Avignon teems with modern nightlife well into the wee hours. At **AJMI** (Association Pour le Jazz et la Musique Improvisée, ✉ 4 rue Escaliers Ste-Anne, ☎ 04–90–86–08–61), in La Manutention, you can hear live jazz acts of some renown. At the cabaret **Dolphin Blues** (✉ Chemin de L'île Piot, ☎ 04–90–82–46–96), a hip mix of comedy and music dominates the repertoire, and there's children's theater as well. **Le Rouge Gorge** (✉ 10 bis rue Peyrollerie, behind palace, ☎ 04–90–14–02–54) presents a dinner show and after-dinner dancing every Friday and Saturday night.

Shopping

Avignon has a cosmopolitan mix of French chains, youthful clothing shops (it's a college town), and a few plummy shops. **Rue des Marchands** off place Carnot is one shopping stretch, but **rue de la République** is the main artery.

Châteauneuf-du-Pape

36 *18 km (11 mi) north of Avignon, 23 km (14 mi) west of Carpentras.*

The countryside around this very famous wine center is a patchwork of rolling vineyards. Imposing gates and grand houses punctuate the scene, as symmetrical and finely detailed as the etching on a wine label, and signs beckon you to follow the omnipresent smell of fermenting grapes to its source.

Once the table wine of the Avignon popes, who kept a fortified summer house here (hence the name of the town, which means "new castle of the pope"), the vineyards of Châteauneuf-du-Pape had the good fortune to be wiped out by phylloxera in the 19th century—good in that its revival as a muscular and resilient mix of up to 13 varietals has moved it to the forefront of French wines. To learn more, stop in at the **Musée des Outils de Vignerons Père Anselme,** a private collection of tools and equipment displayed in the *caveau* (wine cellar) of the Brotte family. ✉ *Rte. d'Avignon,* ☎ *04–90–83-70–07.* *Free.* *Daily 9–noon and 2–6.*

If you're disinclined to spend your holiday sniffing and sipping in a dark basement, climb the hill to the ruins of the **Château.** Though it was destroyed in the Wars of Religion and its remaining donjon blasted by the Germans in World War II, it still commands magnificent views.

Dining and Lodging

$–$$ ✕ **Le Pistou.** This friendly little inn serves sophisticated cooking by a chef in love with things Provençal, from marketing to cooking all-day daubes and marking his whims on a blackboard. The welcome is warm, and the fixed-price menus start at the low end. ✉ *15 rue Joseph-Ducos,* ☎ *04–90–83–71–75. MC, V. Closed Mon. No dinner Sun.*

$$ ✕ **La Garbure.** With four rooms decked out in soft pastel ruffles upstairs and a new, low-price *menu terroir* (prix-fixe menu of regional specialties), this pretty inn aims to please. Look for potted quail in Carpentras truffles and stuffed rabbit with subtle thyme sauce (the restaurant is closed Sunday, October through June, and does not serve Sunday lunch in season, July–September). ✉ *3 rue Joseph-Ducos 84230,* ☎ *04–90–83–75–08,* FAX *04–90–83–52–34. 4 rooms. Restaurant, cable TV, minibars. MC, V.*

Orange

37 *10 km (6 mi) north of Châteauneuf-du-Pape, 31 km (19 mi) north of Avignon, 193 km (121 mi) south of Lyon.*

Even less touristy than Nîmes and just as eccentric, the city of Orange (pronounced oh-*rawnzh*) nonetheless draws thousands every year to ★ its spectacular **Théâtre Antique,** a colossal Roman theater built in the time of Caesar Augustus. Its vast stone stage wall, bouncing sound off the facing hillside, climbs four stories high, and the niche at center stage contains the original statue of Augustus, just as it reigned over centuries of productions of classical plays. Today this theater provides a backdrop for world-class theater and opera. ✉ *Pl. des Frères-Mounet,* ☎ *04–90–34–70–88.* *€4.75, joint ticket with Musée Municipal.* *Apr.–Oct., daily 9–6:30; Nov.–Mar., daily 9–noon and 1:30–5.*

The small **Musée Municipal** (Town Museum) displays antiquities unearthed around Orange, including three detailed marble *cadastres* (land survey maps) dating from the 1st century. Upstairs are Provençal fabrics manufactured in local mills in the 18th century and a collection of faïence pharmacy jars. ✉ *Pl. des Frères-Mounet,* ☎ *04–90–34–70–88.* *€4.75, joint ticket with theater.* *Apr.–Sept., daily 9–6:30; Oct.–Mar., daily 9–noon and 1:30–5.*

North of the city center is the **Arc de Triomphe,** which once straddled the Via Agrippa between Lyon and Arles. Three arches support a heavy double attic (horizontal top) floridly decorated with battle scenes and marine symbols, references to Augustus's victories at Actium. The arch, which dates from about 20 BC, is superbly preserved, particularly the north side, but to view it on foot, you'll have to cross a roundabout seething with traffic. ✉ *North of center on av. de l'Arc, in direction of Gap.*

Dining and Lodging

$$–$$$ ✕ **La Yaka.** At this intimate, unpretentious bistro, you are greeted by the beaming owner, who is also your host and waiter, then pampered with specialties that are emphatically *style grandmère* (like Grandma used to make: rabbit stew, *caillette,* or pork-liver meat loaf, and even canned peas with bacon). It's all served up in charming stone-and-beam rooms. ✉ *24 pl. Sylvain,* ☎ *04–90–34–70–03. MC, V. Closed Wed. and Nov. No dinner Tues.*

$$ 🏨 **Arène.** On a quiet square in the Old Town center, this comfortable old hotel has attentive owners and a labyrinth of rooms done in rich colors and heavy fabrics. The nicest ones look out over the square. As it's built of several fine old houses strung together, there's no elevator, but a multitude of stairways compensates. ✉ *Pl. de Langues, 84100,* ☎ *04–90–11–40–40,* FAX *04–90–11–40–45. 30 rooms. Cable TV, minibars, Internet, parking (fee). AE, DC, MC, V.*

The Arts

Every July **Les Chorégies d'Orange** echo tradition and present operatic and classical music spectacles under the summer stars (☎ 04–90–34–24–24, FAX 04–90–11–04–04; or write to ✉ Chorégies, B.P. 205, 84107 Orange Cedex well in advance).

Vaison-la-Romaine

38 *27 km (17 mi) northeast of Orange, 30 km (19 mi) northeast of Avignon.*

This ancient town thrives as a modern market center yet retains an irresistible Provençal charm, with medieval backstreets, lively squares lined with cafés, and, as its name implies, the remains of its Roman past. Vaison's well-established Celtic colony joined forces with Rome in the 2nd century BC and grew to powerful status in the empire's glory days. No gargantuan monuments were raised, yet the luxurious villas surpassed even those of Pompeii.

There are two broad fields of **Roman ruins,** both in the center of town: before you pay entry at either of the ticket booths, pick up a map (with ★ English explanations) at the **Maison du Tourisme et des Vins** (☎ 04–90–36–02–11), which sits between them; it's open July–August, daily 9–12:30 and 2–6:45; September–June, Monday–Saturday 9–noon and 2–5:45. Like a tiny Roman forum, the **Maison des Messii** spreads over the field and hillside in the heart of town. Its skeletal ruins of villas, landscaped gardens, and museum lie below the ancient theater, all of which are accessed next to the booth across from the tourist office. Closest to the entrance, the foundations of the **Maison des Messii** (Messii House) retain the outlines of its sumptuous design. A formal garden echoes a similar landscape of the time; wander under its cypresses and flowering shrubs to the **Musée Archéologique Théo-Desplans** (Théo-Desplans Archaeology Museum). In this streamlined venue the accoutrements of Roman life have been amassed and displayed by theme: pottery, weapons, representations of gods and goddesses, jewelry, and sculpture. Cross the park behind the museum to climb into the bleachers of the 1st-century **theater,** which is smaller than Orange's but is still used today for concerts and plays. Across the parking lot is the **Quartier de la Villasse,** where the remains of a lively market town evoke images of main-street shops, public gardens, and grand private homes, complete with floor mosaics. The most evocative image of all is in the area of the *thermes* (baths): a neat row of marble-seat toilets. ✉ *Av. Général-de-Gaulle at pl. du 11 Novembre,* ☎ *04–90–36–02–11.* 🎫 *Ruins, museum, and cloister €6.50.* ⏲ *Museum Mar.–May and Oct., daily 10–12:30 and 2:30–6;*

June–Sept., daily 9:30–6; Nov.–Feb., daily 10–11:30 and 2–4. Villasse June–Sept., daily 9:30–noon and 2–6; Mar.–May and Oct., daily 10–12:30 and 2–6; Nov.–Feb., daily 10–noon and 2–4:30.

Take the time to climb up into the **Haute Ville,** a medieval neighborhood perched high above the river valley. Its 13th- and 14th-century houses owe some of their beauty to stone pillaged from the Roman ruins below, but their charm is from the Middle Ages.

If you're in a medieval mood, stop into the sober Romanesque **Cathédrale Notre-Dame-de-Nazareth,** based on recycled fragments and foundations of a Gallo-Roman basilica. Its richly sculpted **cloister** is the key attraction. ✉ *Av. Jules-Ferry.* ⊙ *June–Sept., daily 9:30–noon and 2–5:30; Mar.–May and Oct., daily 10–noon and 2–5:30; Nov.–Feb., daily 10–noon and 2–4.*

One last highlight: the remarkable single-arch **Pont Romain** (Roman Bridge), built in the 1st century, stands firm across the Ouvèze River.

Dining and Lodging

$$ ★ ✕🏨 **Le Beffroi.** On a clifftop in the Old Town, this elegant grouping of 16th-century homes makes a fine little hotel. The extravagant salon decked out in period style leads to the sizable rooms with beams and antiques; the big corner rooms have breathtaking views. From April through October dine on local specialties under the fig tree in the intimate enclosed garden court. By day you can enjoy a simple salad on the garden terrace or take a dip in the rooftop pool. ✉ *Rue de l'Évêché, 84110,* ☎ *04–90–36–04–71,* FAX *04–90–36–24–78. 22 rooms. Restaurant, no air-conditioning, cable TV, pool. AE, DC, MC, V. Closed Feb.–mid-Mar.*

$$ ✕🏨 **Château de la Baude.** Just 6 km (4 mi) outside Vaison, this fortified medieval farm has been converted into a bed-and-breakfast retreat, complete with swimming, tennis, Ping-Pong, pétanque, and 9 acres of grounds. There are table d'hôte dinners and sleek beamed rooms, and breakfast is served under the grape trellis. ✉ *La Baude, 84110 Villedieu,* ☎ *04–90–28–95–18,* FAX *04–90–28–91–05,* WEB *www.eurobandb.com/gites/labaud_e.htm. 4 rooms, 2 suites. Restaurant, no air-conditioning, cable TV, minibars, tennis court, pool, health center. AE, DC, MC, V.*

$$ 🏨 **Évêché.** In the medieval part of town, this turreted 16th-century former bishop's palace has just four small rooms. The warm welcome and rustic charm—delicate fabrics, exposed beams, wooden bedsteads—have garnered a loyal following among travelers who prefer B&B character to modern luxury. ✉ *Rue de l'Évêché, 84110,* ☎ *04–90–36–13–46,* FAX *04–90–36–32–43. 4 rooms, 1 suite. No credit cards.*

Le Barroux

39 *16 km (10 mi) south of Vaison-la-Romaine, 34 km (21 mi) northeast of Avignon.*

Of all the marvelous hilltop villages stretching across the south of France, this tiny ziggurat of a town may be unique: it is 100% boutique-and-gallery-free and has only one tiny old *épicerie* (small grocery) selling canned goods, yellowed postcards, and today's *Le Provençal.* You are forced, therefore, to look around you and listen to the trickle of the ancient fountains at every labyrinthine turn.

The **château** is its main draw, though its perfect condition reflects a complete restoration after a World War II fire. Grand vaulted rooms and a chapel date from the 12th century, and other halls serve as venues for contemporary art exhibits. ☎ *04–90–62–35–21.* 🎫 *€3.* ⊙ *Apr.–May, weekends 10–7; June, weekdays 2–7, weekends 10–7; July–Sept., daily 10–7; Oct., daily 2:30–7.*

Dining and Lodging

$–$$ **Les Géraniums.** Though it has simple, pretty rooms, many with views sweeping down to the valley, this family-run auberge emphasizes its restaurant. A broad garden terrace stretches along the cliffside, where you can sample herb-roasted rabbit, a truffle omelet, and local cheeses. Half-pension is strongly encouraged. New rooms in the annex across the street take in panoramic views. *Pl. de la Croix, 84330, 04–90–62–41–08, FAX 04–90–62–56–48. 22 rooms. Restaurant, bar, no air-conditioning. AE, DC, MC, V. Closed Jan.–Feb.*

Crillon le Brave

40 *12 km (7 mi) south of Malaucène (via Caromb), 21 km (13 mi) southeast of Vaison-la-Romaine.*

The main reason to come to this tiny village, named after France's most notable soldier-hero of the 16th century, is to stay or dine at its hotel, the Hostellerie de Crillon le Brave. But it's also pleasant—perched on a knoll in a valley shielded by Mont Ventoux, with the craggy hills of the Dentelles in one direction and the hills of the Luberon in another. Today the village still doesn't have even a *boulangerie* (bakery), let alone a souvenir boutique.

Dining and Lodging

$$$–$$$$ **Hostellerie de Crillon le Brave.** The views from the interconnected hilltop houses of this Relais & Châteaux property are as elevated as its prices, but for this you get a rarefied stage-set of medieval luxury. A cozy-chic southern touch informs book-filled salons and brocante-trimmed guest rooms, some with terraces looking out onto infinity. In the stone-vaulted dining room, stylish French cuisine is served. Wine tastings and regional discovery packages encourage longer stays. *Pl. de l'Église, 84410, 04–90–65–61–61, FAX 04–90–65–62–86, WEB www.crillonlebrave.com. 23 rooms. Restaurant, no air-conditioning in some rooms, cable TV, Internet, baby-sitting, massage, pool. AE, DC, MC, V. Closed Jan.–mid-Mar.*

L'Isle-sur-la-Sorgue

41 *18 km (11 mi) south of Malaucène, 41 km (25 mi) southeast of Orange, 26 km (16 mi) east of Avignon.*

Crisscrossed with lazy canals and alive with moss-covered waterwheels that once drove its silk, wool, and paper mills, this old valley town retains a gentle appeal—except, that is, on Sunday, when it transforms itself into a Marrakech of marketeers, its streets crammed with antiques and brocantes, its cafés swelling with crowds of bargain seekers making a day of it. There are also street musicians, food stands groaning under mounds of rustic breads, vats of tapenade, and cloth-lined baskets of spices, and miles of café tables offering ringside seats to the spectacle. On a nonmarket day life returns to its mellow pace, with plenty of antiques dealers open year-round, as well as fabric and interior design shops, bookstores, and food stores for you to explore.

The token sight to see is L'Isle's 17th-century church, the **Collégiale Notre-Dame-des-Anges,** extravagantly decorated with gilt, faux marble, and sentimental frescoes. Its double-colonnaded facade commands the center of the Old Town.

Dining and Lodging

$$$–$$$$ **La Prévôté.** With all the money you saved bargaining on that chipped Quimper vase, splurge on lunch at this discreet, pristine spot hidden off a backstreet courtyard. The cuisine has won top awards for chef

Roland Mercier—try his cannelloni stuffed with salmon and goat cheese, or tender duckling with lavender honey. The prix-fixe menus start at €22 and top out at €54. ✉ *4 rue Jean-Jacques-Rousseau,* ☎ *04–90–38–57–29. Reservations essential. MC, V. Closed Mon. (Dec.–June), Nov., and 2 wks in Feb. No dinner Sun.*

$ ✕ **Lou Nego Chin.** In winter you sit shoulder to shoulder in the cramped but atmospheric dining room (chinoiserie linens, brightly hued tiles), but in summer tables are strewn across the quiet street, on a wooden deck along the river. Ask for a spot at the edge so you can watch the ducks play, then order the inexpensive house wine and the menu du jour, often a goat-cheese salad and a good, garlicky stew. ✉ *12 quai Jean Jaurès,* ☎ *04–90–20–88–03. MC, V. Closed Mon. No dinner Sun.*

$–$$ ★ ✕ **Le Mas de Cure-Bourse.** This graceful old 18th-century post-coach stop is well outside the fray, snugly hedge-bound in the countryside amid 6 acres of fruit trees and fields. Rooms are freshly decked out in Provençal prints and painted country furniture. You'll be served sophisticated home cooking with a local touch. The restaurant is closed Monday, and lunch is not served Tuesday. ✉ *Rte. de Caumont, 84800,* ☎ *04–90–38–16–58,* FAX *04–90–38–52–31. 13 rooms. Restaurant, no air-conditioning, cable TV, pool. MC, V. Closed 3 wks in Nov., first 2 wks in Jan.*

$ ✕ **La Gueulardière.** After a Sunday glut of antiquing along the canals, you can dine and sleep just up the street in a hotel full of collectible finds, from the school posters in the restaurant to the oak armoires and brass beds that furnish the simple lodgings. Each room has French windows that open onto the enclosed garden courtyard, where you can enjoy a private breakfast in the shade. ✉ *1 rue d'Apt, 84800,* ☎ *04–90–38–10–52,* FAX *04–90–20–83–70. 5 rooms. Restaurant, no air-conditioning. AE, DC, MC, V.*

Shopping

Of the dozens of antiques shops in L'Isle, one conglomerate concentrates some 40 dealers under the same roof: **L'Isle aux Brocantes** (✉ 7 av. des Quatre Otages, ☎ 04–90–20–69–93); it's open Saturday–Monday. Higher-end antiques are concentrated next door at the twin shops of **Xavier Nicod et Gérard Nicod** (✉ 9 av. des Quatre Otages, ☎ 04–90–38–35–50 or 04–90–38–07–20). **Maria Giancatarina** (✉ 4 av. Julien Guigue [across from train station], ☎ 04–90–38–58–02) showcases beautifully restored linens, including *boutis* (Provençal quilts).

Fontaine-de-Vaucluse

42 *8 km (5 mi) east of L'Isle-sur-la-Sorgue, 33 km (20 mi) east of Avignon.*

★ The **Fontaine de Vaucluse,** for which the town is named, is a strange and beautiful natural phenomenon that has been turned into a charming, albeit slightly tacky, tourist center—like a tiny Niagara Falls—and should not be missed if you're either a connoisseur of rushing water or a fan of foreign kitsch. There's no exaggerating the magnificence of the *fontaine* itself, a mysterious spring that gushes from a deep underground source that has been explored to a depth of 1,010 ft . . . so far. Framed by towering cliffs, a broad, pure pool wells up and spews dramatically over massive rocks down a gorge to the village, where its roar soothes and cools the tourists who crowd the riverfront cafés.

You must pay to park and then run a gauntlet of souvenir shops and tourist traps on your way to the top. But even if you plan to make a beeline past the kitsch, do stop in at the legitimate and informative **Moulin Vallis-Clausa.** A working paper mill, it demonstrates a reconstructed 15th-century waterwheel that drives timber crankshafts to mix rag pulp, while artisans roll and dry thick paper *à l'ancienne* (in the old manner). Watching the process is fascinating and free of charge, though it's almost impossible to resist buying note cards, posters, even lampshades fashioned from the pretty stuff. Fontaine was once a great industrial mill center, but its seven factories were closed by strikes in 1968 and never recovered. ☏ *04–90–20–34–14.* ⏲ *Sept.–June, daily 9–noon and 2–6; July–Aug., daily 9–7.*

Fontaine has its own ruined **Château,** perched romantically on a forested hilltop over the town and illuminated at night. First built around the year 1000 and embellished in the 13th century by the bishops of Cavaillon, it was destroyed in the 15th century and now forms little more than a saw-tooth silhouette against the sky.

The Renaissance poet Petrarch, driven mad with unrequited love for a beautiful married woman named Laura, retreated to this valley to nurse his passion in a cabin with "one dog and only two servants." Sixteen years in this wild isolation didn't ease the pain, but the serene landscape inspired him to poetry. The small **Musée-Bibliothèque Pétrarch,** built on the site of his stay, displays prints and engravings of the virtuous lovers. ☏ *04–90–20–37–20.* 🎟 *€3.* ⏲ *Apr.–May., Wed.–Mon. 10–noon and 2–6; June–Sept., Wed.–Mon. 10–12:30 and 1:30–6; Oct., weekends 10–noon and 2–5.*

Dining and Lodging

$ ✕🏨 **Le Parc.** In a spectacular riverside locale in the shadow of the ruined château, this solid old hotel has basic, comfortable rooms (whitewashed stucco, all-weather carpet) with clean bathrooms and no creaks; five of them offer river views. The restaurant (closed Wednesday) spreads along the river in a pretty park, with tables shaded by trellises heavy with grapes and trumpet vine. Moderately priced daily menus include river-fresh salmon. ✉ *Rue de Bourgades, 84800,* ☏ *04–90–20–31–57,* FAX *04–90–20–27–03. 12 rooms. Restaurant, no air-conditioning. AE, DC, MC, V. Closed Jan.–mid-Feb.*

En Route Gordes is only a short distance from Fontaine de Vaucluse, but you need to wind your way south, east, and then north on D100A, D100, D2, and D15 to skirt the impassable hillside. It's a lovely drive through dry, rocky country covered with wild lavender and scrub oak and may tempt you to a picnic or a walk.

Gordes

★ 43 *16 km (10 mi) southeast of Fontaine-de-Vaucluse, 35 km (22 mi) east of Avignon.*

Gordes was once merely an unspoiled hilltop village; it is now a famous unspoiled hilltop village surrounded by luxury vacation homes, modern hotels, restaurants, and B&Bs. No matter: the ancient stone village still rises above the valley in painterly hues of honey gold, and its mosaiclike cobbled streets—lined with boutiques, galleries, and real-estate offices—still wind steep and narrow to its Renaissance château—making this certainly one of the most beautiful and picturesque towns in Provence. The only way to see the interior of the **château** is to view its ghastly collection of photo paintings by pop artist Pol Mara, who lived in Gordes. It's worth the price of admission to look at the fabulously decorated stone fireplace, created in 1541. ☏ *04–90–72–02–75.* 🎟 *€4.* ⏲ *Wed.–Mon. 10–noon and 2–6.*

★ Just outside Gordes, on a lane heading north from D2, follow signs to the **Village des Bories.** Found throughout this region of Provence, the bizarre and fascinating little stone hovels called *bories* are concentrated some 20 strong in an ancient community. Their origins are provocatively vague: built as shepherds' shelters with tight-fitting, mortarless stone in a hivelike form, they may date to the Celts, the Ligurians, even the Iron Age—and were inhabited or used for sheep through the 18th century. ☎ *04–90–72–03–48.* €5.5. *Daily 9–sunset or 8, whichever comes 1st.*

If you've dreamed of Provence's famed lavender fields, head to a wild valley some 4 km (2 mi) north of Gordes (via D177) to find the beautiful 12th-century Romanesque **Abbaye de Sénanque,** which floats above a redolent sea of lavender (in full bloom in July and August). Begun in 1150 and completed at the dawn of the 13th century, the **church** and adjoining **cloister** are without decoration but still touch the soul with their chaste beauty. In this orbit, the graystone buildings seem to have special resonance—ancient, organic, with a bit of the borie about it. Next door, the enormous vaulted **dormitory** contains an exhibition on the abbey's construction, and the **refectory** shelters a display on the history of Cistercian abbeys. ☎ *04–90–72–05–72.* €4.75. *Mar.–Oct., Mon.–Sat. 10–noon and 2–6, Sun. 2–6; Nov.–Feb., weekdays 2–5, weekends 2–6.*

Dining and Lodging

$$ ✕ **Comptoir du Victuailler.** Across from the château, this tiny but deluxe bistro entices with daily *aioli,* a smorgasbord of fresh cod and lightly steamed vegetables crowned with the garlic mayonnaise. Evenings are reserved for intimate, formal indoor meals à la carte—roast Luberon lamb, beef with truffle sauce. The '30s-style bistro tables and architectural lines are a relief from Gordes's ubiquitous rustic-chic. ✉ *Pl. du Château,* ☎ *04–90–72–01–31. Reservations essential. MC, V. Closed Wed. Sept.–May. No dinner Tues. mid-Nov.–Easter.*

$$–$$$ **Domaine de l'Enclos.** This cluster of private stone cottages has newly laid antique tiles and fresh faux-patinas that keep it looking fashionably old. There are panoramic views and a pool, baby-sitting services and swing sets, and an aura that is surprisingly warm and familial for an inn of this sophistication. ✉ *Rte. de Sénanque, 84220,* ☎ *04–90–72–71–00,* FAX *04–90–72–03–03,* WEB *www.guideweb.com/provence/hotel/enclos. 12 rooms, 5 apartments. Restaurant, no air-conditioning, pool. AE, MC, V.*

$$–$$$ ✕ **Ferme de la Huppe.** This 17th-century stone farmhouse with a well in the courtyard, a swimming pool in the garden, and rooms with pretty prints and secondhand finds is in the countryside outside Gordes. Dine poolside on three styles of roast lamb, prepared by the proprietors' son, Gerald Konings, but reserve ahead: the restaurant (closed Thursday) is as popular as the hotel. ✉ *84220 Les Pourquiers (3 km/2 mi east of Gordes, R156),* ☎ *04–90–72–12–25,* FAX *04–90–72–01–83. 9 rooms. Restaurant, no air-conditioning, pool. MC, V. Closed end Dec.–Mar.*

$$–$$$ **Les Romarins.** At this small hilltop inn on the outskirts of Gordes you can gaze at the town across the valley while having breakfast on a sheltered terrace in the morning sun. Rooms are clean, well lighted, and feel spacious—ask for either No. 1, in the main building, from whose white-curtained windows you can see forever, or the room with a terrace in the atelier. Oriental rugs, antique furniture, and a pool add to your contentment. ✉ *Rte. de Sénanque, 84220,* ☎ *04–90–72–12–13,* FAX *04–90–72–13–13. 10 rooms. No air-conditioning, cable TV, pool. AE, MC, V.*

Roussillon

★ 44 *10 km (6 mi) east of Gordes, 45 km (28 mi) east of Avignon.*

In shades of deep rose and russet, this quintessential hilltop cluster of houses blends into the red-ocher cliffs from which its stone was quarried. The ensemble of buildings and jagged, hand-cut slopes are equally dramatic, and views from the top look out over a landscape of artfully eroded bluffs that Georgia O'Keefe would have loved.

This famous vein of natural ocher, which spreads some 25 km (15 mi) along the foot of the Vaucluse plateau, has been mined for centuries, beginning with the ancient Romans, who used it for their pottery. You can visit the old **Usine Mathieu de Roussillon** (Roussillon's Mathieu Ochre Works) to learn more about ocher's extraction and its modern uses. There are explanatory exhibits, ocher powders for sale, and guided tours in English on advance request. ✉ *On D104 southeast of town,* ☎ *04–90–05–66–69.* ⏲ *Mar.–Nov., daily 10–7.*

$$–$$$ ★ ✕🏨 **Mas de Garrigon.** An exquisite hotel, tastefully decorated in classic Provençal style, the Garrigon has spacious rooms, a cozy library, and views of the surrounding ocher cliffs. It also showcases the best restaurant (by far) in Roussillon—which is a good thing, as the management takes it very personally if you pass on their demi-pension offer. So don't: the food is superb—monkfish in salt crust, straw-baked lamb with rosemary jus, inventive vegetable courses, plus wonderful desserts—and the family welcome is warm and genuine. ✉ *Rte. de St-Saturnin-d'Apt (3 km/2 mi north on the D2), 84220,* ☎ *04–90–05–63–92,* FAX *04–90–05–70–01. 9 rooms. No air-conditioning, cable TV, pool, parking (fee). AE, DC, MC, V.*

$$ 🏨 **Ma Maison.** In the valley 4 km (2½ mi) below Roussillon, this isolated 1850 mas has been infused with a laid-back, cosmopolitan style by its artist-owners. It includes a big saltwater pool, an idyllic garden, a massive country kitchen, and views toward Bonnieux and the Luberon. ✉ *Quartier Les Devens, 84220,* ☎ *04–90–05–74–17,* FAX *04–90–05–74–63,* WEB *www.mamaison-provence.com. 4 rooms, 2 suites. No air-conditioning, pool. MC, V. Closed Nov.–Apr.*

Oppède-le-Vieux

45 *25 km (15½ mi) southeast of Avignon, 15 km (9 mi) southwest of Gordes.*

Follow signs toward Oppède; you'll occasionally be required to follow signs for Oppède-le-Village, but your goal will be marked with the symbol of *monuments historiques*: Oppède-le-Vieux. A Byronesque tumble of ruins arranged against an overgrown rocky hillside, Oppède's charm—or part of it—lies in its preservation. Taken over by writers and artists who have chosen to live here and restore but not develop it, the village has a café or two but little else. Bring a lunch, wander, and contemplate.

Cross the village square, pass through the old city gate, and climb up steep trails past restored houses to the church known as **Notre-Dame-d'Alydon.** First built in the 13th century, its blunt buttresses were framed into side chapels in the 16th century; you can still see the points of stoned-in Gothic windows above. The marvelous hexagonal bell tower sprouts a lean, mean gargoyle from each angle. It once served as part of the village's fortifications.

Head left past the cliff-edge wall, plunge into the rock tunnel, and clamber up to the ruins of the **château,** built in the 13th century and then transformed in the 15th century. From the left side of its great square tower, look down into the dense fir forests of the Luberon's north face.

En Route As you drive along D188 between Oppède and Ménerbes, the rolling rows of grapevines are punctuated by stone farmhouses. But something is different: these farmhouses have electric gates, tall arborvitae hedges, and swimming pools. Peter Mayle isn't the only outsider who came to vacation here and contrived to stay.

Ménerbes

46 *5 km (3 mi) east of Oppède-le-Vieux, 30 km (19 mi) southeast of Avignon.*

The town of Ménerbes clings to a long, thin hilltop over this sought-after valley, looming over the surrounding forests like a great stone ship. At its prow juts the **Castellet,** a 15th-century fortress. At its stern looms the 13th-century **Citadelle.** These redoubtable fortifications served the Protestants well during the War of Religions—until the Catholics wore them down with a 15-month siege.

A campanile tops the Hôtel de Ville (Town Hall), on pretty **place de l'Horloge** (Clock Square), where you can admire the delicate stonework on the arched portal and mullioned windows of a Renaissance house. Just past the tower on the right is an overlook taking in views toward Gordes, Roussillon, and Mont Ventoux.

But what you really came to see is **Peter Mayle's house,** right? Do its current owners a favor and give it a wide berth: after years of tour buses spilling the curious into the private driveway to crane their necks and snap pictures, the heirs to the stone picnic table, the pool, and Faustin's grapevines wish the books had never been written. And besides, Peter Mayle has moved to Lourmarin now, on the other side of the mountain. Do leave these folk in peace.

Seven kilometers (4 miles) east of Ménerbes is the eagle's-nest village of Lacoste, presided over by the once magnificent Château de Sade, erstwhile retreat to the notorious Marquis de Sade (1740–1814) when he wasn't on the run from authorities. For some years, the wealthy Paris couturier Pierre Cardin has been restoring the castle and in 2001 premiered the first **Festival Lacoste.**

Lodging

$$$ **Hostellerie Le Roy Soleil.** In the imposing shadow of the Luberon, this luxurious country inn has pulled out all stops on comfort and decor: marble and granite bathrooms, wrought-iron beds, and coordinated fabrics. But the integrity of its 17th-century building, with thick stone walls and groin vaults and beams, redeems it just short of pretentiousness and makes it a lovely place to escape to. ✉ *Rte. des Beaumettes, 84560,* ☎ *04–90–72–25–61,* FAX *04–90–72–36–55,* WEB *www.roy-soleil.com. 19 rooms. Restaurant, bar, no air-conditioning, cable TV, minibars, tennis court, pool. AE, MC, V. Closed Nov.–mid-Mar.*

Bonnieux

★ 47 *11 km (7 mi) south of Roussillon, 45 km (28 mi) north of Aix-en-Provence.*

The most impressive of the Luberon's hilltop villages, Bonnieux rises out of the arid hills in a jumble of honey-color cubes that change color subtly as the day progresses. The village is wrapped in crumbling ramparts and dug into bedrock and cliff. Most of its sharply raked streets take in wide-angle valley views, though you'll get the best view from the pine-shaded grounds of the 12th-century church, reached by stone steps that wind past tiny niche houses.

Dining and Lodging

$–$$ ★ ✕ **Auberge de la Loube.** The chef's inclusion in a Peter Mayle book hasn't gone to his toque: for simple, unpretentious Provençal food perfectly prepared, nothing beats this idyllic little restaurant in the neighboring hamlet of Buoux. Meals are served on a covered terrace out back.

The gargantuan starters are famous and fabulous, as are house specialties like scrambled eggs with truffles and roasted leg of lamb. Sunday lunch is a feast worthy of Pagnol. ✉ *Quartier la Loube/Buoux,* ☎ *04–90–74–19–58,* FAX *04–90–74–19–58. MC, V.*

$–$$ ✕ **Le Fournil.** In a natural grotto deep in stone, lighted by candles and arty torchères, this restaurant would be memorable even without its trendy look and stylishly presented Provençal cuisine. Try the adventurous dishes such as the crisped pigs'-feet *galette* (patty) and check out the informed wine list. ✉ *5 pl. Carnot,* ☎ *04–90–75–83–62,* FAX *04–90–75–96–19. MC, V.*

$$–$$$ ★ **Hostellerie du Prieuré.** Not every hotel has its own private chapel, but this gracious inn occupies an 18th-century abbey, right in the village center. From the firelit salon to the dining room burnished with Roussillon ocher, it casts a pleasantly warm glow. Summer meals and breakfasts are served in the enclosed garden oasis. Rooms have plush carpets and antiques. The Coutaz family has been in the hotel business since Napoléon III, and it shows. ✉ *In center of village, 84480,* ☎ *04–90–75–80–78,* FAX *04–90–75–96–00,* WEB *www.esprit-de-france.com. 10 rooms. Restaurant, no air-conditioning, tennis court. MC, V. Closed Nov.–Feb.*

$$ ★ **Le Clos du Buis.** At this B&B, whitewash and quarry tiles, lovely tiled baths, and carefully juxtaposed antiques create a regional look in the guest rooms. Public spaces, with scrubbed floorboards, a fireplace, and exposed stone, are free for your use around the clock. It even has a pool and a pretty garden, and it's all overlooking the valley from the village center. ✉ *Rue Victor Hugo, 84480,* ☎ *04–90–75–88–48,* FAX *04–90–75–88–57,* WEB *www.luberon-news.com/le-clos-du-buis. 6 rooms. No air-conditioning, pool. MC, V.*

AIX-EN-PROVENCE AND THE MEDITERRANEAN COAST

The southeastern part of this area of Provence, on the edge of the Côte d'Azur, is dominated by two major towns: Aix-en-Provence, considered the main hub of Provence and the most cultural town in the region; and Marseille, a vibrant port town that combines seediness with fashion and metropolitan feistiness with classical grace. For a breathtaking experience of the dramatic contrast between the azure Mediterranean sea and the rocky, olive tree–filled hills, take a trip along the coast east of Marseille and make an excursion to the Iles d'Hyères.

Aix-en-Provence

★ *48 km (29 mi) southeast of Bonnieux, 82 km (51 mi) southeast of Avignon, 176 km (109 mi) west of Nice, 759 km (474 mi) south of Paris.*

Gracious, cultivated, and made all the more cosmopolitan by the presence of some 30,000 international university students, the lovely old town of Aix (pronounced *ex*) was once the capital of Provence. The vestiges of that influence and power—fine art, noble architecture, and graceful urban design—remain beautifully preserved today. That and its thriving market, vibrant café life, and world-class music festival make Aix vie with Arles and Avignon as one of the towns in Provence that shouldn't be missed.

The Romans were first drawn here by mild thermal baths, naming the town Aquae Sextiae (Waters of Sextius) in honor of the consul who founded a camp near the source in 123 BC. Just 20 years later some 200,000 Germanic invaders besieged Aix, but the great Roman general Marius flanked them and pinned them against the mountain known ever since as Ste-Victoire. Marius remains a popular local first name to this day.

Under the wise and generous guidance of Roi René (King René) in the 15th century, Aix became a center of Renaissance arts and letters. At the height of its political, judicial, and ecclesiastic power in the 17th and 18th centuries, Aix profited from a surge of private building, each grand *hôtel particulier* (mansion) vying to outdo its neighbor. Its signature *cours* (courtyards) and *places* (squares), punctuated by grand fountains and intriguing passageways, date from this time.

It was into this exalting elegance that artist Paul Cézanne (1839–1906) was born, though he drew much of his inspiration from the raw countryside around the city and often painted Ste-Victoire. A schoolmate of Cézanne's made equal inroads: the journalist and novelist Émile Zola (1840–1902) attended the Collège Bourbon with Cézanne and described their friendship as well as Aix itself in several of his works. You can still sense something of the ambience that nurtured these two geniuses in the streets of modern Aix.

Under the deep shade of tall plane trees whose branches interlace over
48 the street, **Cours Mirabeau** prevails as the city's social nerve center. One side of the street is lined with dignified 18th-century hôtels particuliers; you can view them from a comfortable seat in one of the dozen or so cafés and restaurants that spill onto the sidewalk on the other side.

49 In the **Musée du Vieil Aix** (Museum of Old Aix), an eclectic assortment of local treasures resides in a 17th-century mansion, from faïence to *santons* (terra-cotta figurines) to ornately painted furniture. The building itself is lovely, too. ✉ *17 rue Gaston-de-Saporta,* ☎ *04–42–21–43–55.* *€2.5.* *Apr.–Oct., Tues.–Sun. 10–noon and 2:30–6; Nov.–Mar., Tues.–Sun. 10–noon and 2–5.*

50 The **Musée des Tapisseries** (Tapestry Museum), housed in the 17th-century **Palais de l'Archevêché** (Archbishop's Palace), displays a sumptuous collection of tapestries that once decorated the walls of the bishop's quarters. Its broad courtyard is used for the main opera productions of the Festival International d'Art Lyrique. ✉ *Pl. de l'Ancien-Archevêché,* ☎ *04–42–23–09–91.* *€1.5.* *Wed.–Mon., 10–noon and 2–5:45.*

★ 51 The **Cathédrale St-Sauveur** (✉ Rue Gaston de Saporta) juxtaposes so many eras of architectural history, all clearly delineated and preserved, it's like a survey course in itself. It has a double nave, Romanesque and Gothic side by side, and a Merovingian (5th-century) **baptistery,** its colonnade mostly recovered from Roman temples built to honor pagan deities. Shutters hide the ornate 16th-century carvings on the **portals,** opened by a guide on request. The guide can also lead you into the tranquil Romanesque **cloisters** next door, so that you can admire its carved pillars and slender columns. As if these treasures weren't enough, the cathedral also houses an extraordinary 15th-century triptych painted by Nicolas Froment in the heat of inspiration following his travels in Italy and Flanders. Called the ***Triptyque du Buisson Ardent*** (*Burning Bush Triptych*), it depicts the generous art patrons King René and Queen Jeanne kneeling on either side of the Virgin, who is poised above a burning bush. These days, to avoid light damage, it's only opened for viewing on Tuesday from 3 to 4.

52 The 12th-century **Église St-Jean-de-Malte** (✉ intersection of rue Cardinale and rue d'Italie) served as a chapel of the Knights of Malta, a medieval order of friars devoted to hospital care. It was Aix's first attempt at the Gothic style. It was here that the counts of Provence were

Atelier Cézanne . . . **54**
Cathédrale St-Sauveur . . **51**
Cours Mirabeau . . . **48**
Église St-Jean-de-Malte **52**
Musée Granet **53**
Musée des Tapisseries/ Palais de l'Archevêché . **50**
Musée du Vieil Aix **49**

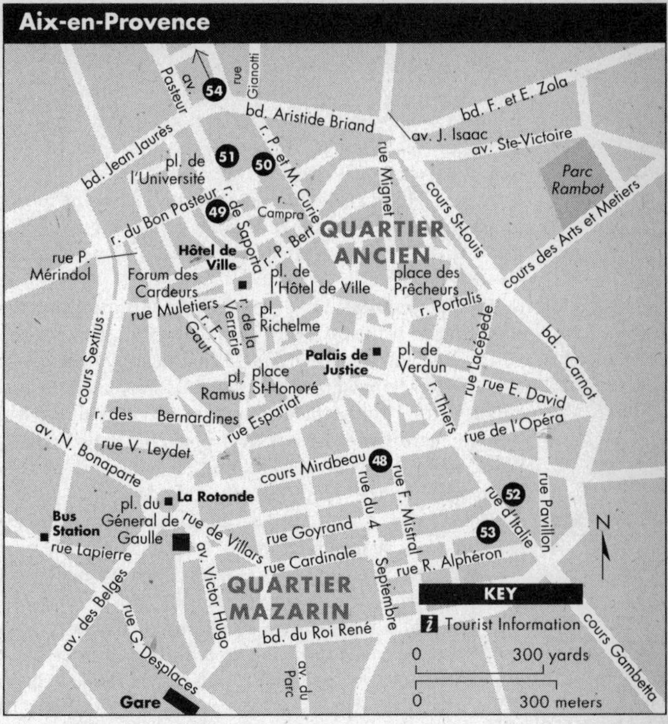

buried throughout the 18th century; their tombs (in the upper left) were attacked during the Revolution and have been only partially repaired.

In the graceful Quartier Mazarin, below the cours Mirabeau, the
53 **Musée Granet** was once the Ecole de Dessin (Art School) that granted Cézanne a second prize in 1856. Cézanne drawings and watercolors have been moved here from his studio, and there are eight of his paintings as well. You'll also find Rubens, David, Ingres, and a group of sentimental works by the museum's namesake, François Granet (1775–1849). In the archaeology section are statues and busts recovered from the early Roman settlement. ✉ *Pl. St-Jean-de-Malte,* ☎ *04–42–38–14–70.* 🎫 €2. ⏲ *Wed.–Mon., 10–noon and 2–6.*

54 Just north of the Old Town loop is the **Atelier Cézanne** (Cézanne Studio). After the death of his mother forced the sale of the painter's beloved country retreat, known as Jas de Bouffan, he had this studio built just above the town center. In the upstairs work space Cézanne created some of his finest paintings, including *Les Grandes Baigneuses* (*The Large Bathers*). But what is most striking is its collection of simple objects that once featured prominently in the portraits and still lifes he created—redingote, bowler hat, ginger jar, and all. ✉ *9 av. Paul-Cézanne,* ☎ *04–42–21–06–53.* 🎫 €4. ⏲ *Apr.–Sept., daily 10–noon and 2:30–6; Oct.–Mar., daily 10–noon and 2–5. Guided tours Wed. and Sat. at 10 and 3 (English on request).*

Dining and Lodging

$$$–$$$$ ★ ✕ **Le Clos de la Violette.** Whether you dine under the chestnut trees or in the airy, pastel dining room, you'll get to experience the cuisine of one of the south's top chefs, Jean-Marc Banzo. Banzo spins tradition into gold, from pressed crab on a humble chickpea salad to langoustine tails on shortbread with coral ravioli. The restaurant isn't far from the Atelier Cézanne, outside the Old Town ring. Reservations essential. ✉ *10 av. de la Violette,* ☎ *04–42–23–30–71. Jacket required. AE, MC, V. No lunch Mon.*

$$–$$$ ✕ **Brasserie Les Deux Garcons.** The food is rather ordinary—stick to the *coquillages* (oysters and clams) or the smoked-duck salad—but eating isn't what you come here for. It's the linen-decked sidewalk tables facing onto the cours Mirabeau, the white-swathed waiters, and the blackboard menu—making this one of the most picture-perfect cafés in France. Dining inside is less glamorous, but the murals and gilt-ivory grace notes date from the restaurant's founding, in 1792. Cézanne, Zola, and Cocteau were devoted regulars. ✉ *53 cours Mirabeau,* ☎ *04–42–26–00–51. MC, V.*

$$ ✕ **Les Bacchanales.** Despite a slightly self-important air and a position on a tourist-trap street off cours Mirabeau, this is a pleasant, intimate restaurant with inviting daub-filled beams, yellow-ocher stucco, and Louis XIII chairs. Fixed-price menus may include a delicate octopus salad, stuffed guinea hen, *rouget* (mullet) perfumed with sage and fennel, and caramelized pears over pistachio ice cream. As the name implies, wine figures large here, and the list is extensive. ✉ *10 rue de la Couronne,* ☎ *04–42–27–21–06. AE, MC, V.*

$$$$ ★ **Villa Gallici.** A Provençal dream, shaded by ancient cypress and plane trees and landscaped with jars of laurel and topiary boxwood, this luxurious hilltop garden retreat stands serenely apart from the city center on the outskirts of town (offering great views), but the shops of Cours Mirabeau are only a 15-minute walk away. Have breakfast on the spectacular shaded terrace, tea by the pool, then retreat to your adorable room swagged with rich florals or red-checked plaids (No. 2 is a stunner)—two top decorators own this place, now one of the most coveted reservations in Provence. Meals are served up in candlelit salons but the fine Le Clos de Violette restaurant is just next door if you want a break from all this beauty. ✉ *Av. de la Violette, 13100,* ☎ *04–42–23–29–23,* FAX *04–42–96–30–45. 18 rooms, 4 suites. Restaurant, cable TV, Internet, pool. AE, DC, MC, V.*

$$$–$$$$ **Augustins.** The best aspect of this Old Town hotel, just a half block back from cours Mirabeau, is its reception area: the groin-vaulted stone, stained glass, and ironwork banister date from the 15th century, when the house was an Augustinian convent. The rooms are perfectly nice but a bit of a letdown, with heavy carpeting and fabric-covered walls. Bathrooms are all-white tile and marble. ✉ *3 rue de la Masse, 13100,* ☎ *04–42–27–28–59,* FAX *04–42–26–74–87. 29 rooms. Cable TV. AE, DC, MC, V.*

$$–$$$ **Nègre-Coste.** Its prominent cours Mirabeau position and its lavish public areas make this 18th-century town house a popular hotel. Provençal decor and newly tiled bathrooms live up to the lovely ground-floor salons. It's worth the price to open your shutters in the morning and lean out over the cours Mirabeau with a cup of café crème in hand. ✉ *33 cours Mirabeau, 13100,* ☎ *04–42–27–74–22,* FAX *04–42–26–80–93. 37 rooms. Minibars. AE, DC, MC, V.*

$$ **St-Christophe.** With so few midprice *hôtels de charme* in Aix and a distinct shortage of regional style, you might as well opt for this glossy art deco–style hotel, where the comfort and services are remarkable for the price. Rooms are slickly done in deep jewel tones, and the top-floor rooms have artisanal tiles in the bathrooms. ✉ *2 av. Victor-Hugo, 13100,* ☎ *04–42–26–01–24,* FAX *04–42–38–53–17,* WEB *www.francemarket.com/stchristophe. 58 rooms, 7 suites. Restaurant, cable TV, parking (fee). AE, MC, V.*

$–$$ ★ **Quatre Dauphins.** In the quiet Mazarin quarter, this modest but impeccable lodging inhabits a noble hôtel particulier. Its pretty, comfortable little rooms have been spruced up with *boutis* (Provençal quilts), Les Olivades fabrics, quarry tiles, jute carpets, and hand-painted furniture.

The house-proud but unassuming owner-host bends over backward to please. ✉ *55 rue Roux Alphéran, 13100,* ☎ *04–42–38–16–39,* FAX *04–42–38–60–19. 12 rooms. No air-conditioning. MC, V.*

Nightlife and the Arts

To find out what's going on in town, pick up a copy of the events calendar *Le Mois à Aix* or the bilingual city guide *Aix la Vivante* at the tourist office. **Le Scat Club** (✉ 11 rue de la Verrerie, ☎ 04–42–23–00–23) is the place for live soul, funk, reggae, rock, blues, and jazz. For a night of playing roulette and the slot machines, head for the **Casino Municipal** (✉ 2 bis av. N.-Bonaparte, ☎ 04–42–26–30–33).

Every July during the **Festival International d'Art Lyrique** (International Opera Festival; ☎ 04–42–17–34–00 for information), you can see world-class opera productions in the courtyard of the Palais de l'Archevêché.

Shopping

Aix is a market town, and a sophisticated **food and produce market** sets up every morning on place Richelme; just up the street, on place Verdun, is a good high-end ***brocante*** (collectibles market) Tuesday, Thursday, and Saturday mornings. A famous Aixois delicacy is *calissons,* a blend of almond paste and glazed melon in almond shapes. The most picturesque shop specializing in calissons is **Bechard** (✉ 12 cours Mirabeau). **Leonard Parli** (✉ 35 av. Victor-Hugo), near the train station, also offers a lovely selection of calissons.

In addition to its old-style markets and jewel-box candy shops, Aix is a modern shopping town—perhaps the best in Provence. The winding streets of the Vieille Ville above cours Mirabeau—centered around **rue Clemenceau, rue Marius Reinaud, rue Espariat, rue Aude,** and **rue Maréchal Foch**—have a head-turning parade of goods.

Meyrargues

55 *12 km (19 mi) northwest of Aix-en-Provence on the N96.*

A picturesque village dominated by a feudal fortress, Meyrargues has been a pilgrimage stop for more than nine centuries. The fortress, transformed into a chateau in the 17th century and into a four-star hotel in 1952, remains the chief attraction, but the little town nestled beneath the chateau's monumental flight of steps is perfectly charming in itself. The clay santons, or terra-cotta figurines, from the village factory are much coveted, the surrounding woods are great for horseback riding, and Monsieur Sallier's wines (Château de Vauclaire, Coteaux d'Aix) are among the most *buvable* in the region. There are two ancient chapels in the village, and three arches of a Roman aqueduct that once fed Aix-en-Provence still stand in a valley just behind the chateau's cemetery.

Dining and Lodging

$$$–$$$$ ★ ✕🏨 **Château de Meyrargues.** A Celtic outpost in 600 BC, a military fortress in AD 900: few places, even in France, have as much history as the Château de Meyrargues. Fewer still take paying guests. Constructed over six centuries, the imposing chateau, with its massive stones walls and staircase, is a truly formidable sight, perched high above the Durance Valley, lording over the medieval village from the top of a rocky outcrop, surrounded by hills of pine. The views are breathtaking, as are the spacious, Provençal-decorated rooms and luxurious baths. If you can't stay the night, at least try to fit in lunch or dinner in the excellent restaurant. ✉ *13650 Meyrargues,* ☎ *04–42–63–49–90,* FAX *04–42–63–49–92. 8 rooms, 3 suites. Restaurant, pool, 2 tennis courts. AE, DC, MC, V.*

Marseille

31 km (19 mi) south of Aix-en-Provence, 188 km (117 mi) west of Nice, 772 km (483 mi) south of Paris.

Much maligned, Marseille is often given a wide berth by travelers in search of a Provençal idyll. It's their loss, for they miss its Cubist jumbles of white stone rising up over a picture-book seaport, bathed in light of blinding clarity and crowned by larger-than-life neo-Byzantine churches. Its neighborhoods teem with multiethnic life, its souklike African markets reek deliciously of spices and coffees, its labyrinthine Old Town is painted in broad strokes of saffron, cinnamon, and robin's-egg blue. Feisty and fond of broad gestures, Marseille is a dynamic city, as cosmopolitan now as when the Phoenicians first founded it, and with all the exoticism of the international shipping port it has been for 2,600 years. Vital to the Crusades in the Middle Ages and crucial to Louis XIV as a military port, Marseille flourished as France's market to the world—and still does today.

The heart of Marseille is clustered around the Vieux Port—immortalized in all its briny charm in the 1961 Leslie Caron film version of *Fanny.* The hills to the south of the port are crowned with mega-monuments, such as Notre-Dame de la Garde and Fort St-Jean. To the north lies the ramshackle hilltop Old Town known as Le Panier. East of the port you'll find the North African neighborhood and, to its left, the famous thoroughfare called La Canebière. South of the city, the clifftop waterfront highway leads to obscure and colorful ports and coves.

One of many museums devoted to Marseille's history as a shipping port,
56 the **Musée de la Marine** (Marine Museum) concentrates on the 17th century to today. It's all about boats: there are steamboats and sailboats and schooners in miniature, as well as a collection of paintings and prints of the port in action. ✉ *Palais de la Bourse, 7 La Canebière, La Canebière,* ☎ *04–91–39–33–33.* 🎫 €2. ⏲ *Daily 10–6.*

★ 57 The modern, open-spaced **Musée d'Histoire de Marseille** (Marseille History Museum) illuminates Massalia's history by mounting its treasure of archaeological finds in didactic displays. There's a real Greek-era wooden boat in a hermetically sealed display case. ✉ *Centre Bourse, entrance on rue de Bir-Hakeim, Vieux Port,* ☎ *04–91–90–42–22.* 🎫 €2. ⏲ *Mon.–Sat. noon–7.*

58 The **Jardin des Vestiges** (Garden of Remains), just behind the Marseille History Museum, stands on the site of Marseille's classical waterfront and includes remains of the Greek fortifications and loading docks. It was discovered in 1967 when roadwork was being done next to the Bourse (Stock Exchange). ✉ *Centre Bourse, Vieux Port,* ☎ *04–91–90–42–22.* 🎫 *€2 includes entry to Museum of History.* ⏲ *Mon.–Sat. noon–7.*

★ 59 **Le Panier** is the old heart of Marseille, a maze of high shuttered houses looming over narrow cobbled streets, *montées* (stone stairways), and tiny squares. Long decayed and neglected, it is the principal focus of the city's efforts at urban renewal. Wander this atmospheric neighborhood at will, making sure to stroll along rue du Panier, the montée des Accoules, rue du Petit-Puits, and rue des Muettes.

★ 60 At the top of the Panier district, the **Centre de la Vieille Charité** (Center of the Old Charity) is a superb ensemble of 17th- and 18th-century architecture designed as a hospice for the homeless by Marseillais artist-architects Pierre and Jean Puget. Even if you don't enter the museums, walk around the inner court, studying the retreating perspective of triple arcades and admiring the Baroque chapel with its novel

Abbaye St-Victor **65**
Cathédrale de la Nouvelle Major **61**
Centre de la Vielle Charité **60**
Ferry Boat **64**
Fort St-Nicolas/ Fort St-Jean **66**
Jardin des Vestiges **58**
Musée des Docks Romains **63**
Musée d'Histoire de Marseille . . . **57**
Musée de la Marine **56**
Musée du Vieux Marseille . . . **62**
Notre-Dame-de-la-Garde **67**
Le Panier . . . **59**

Marseille

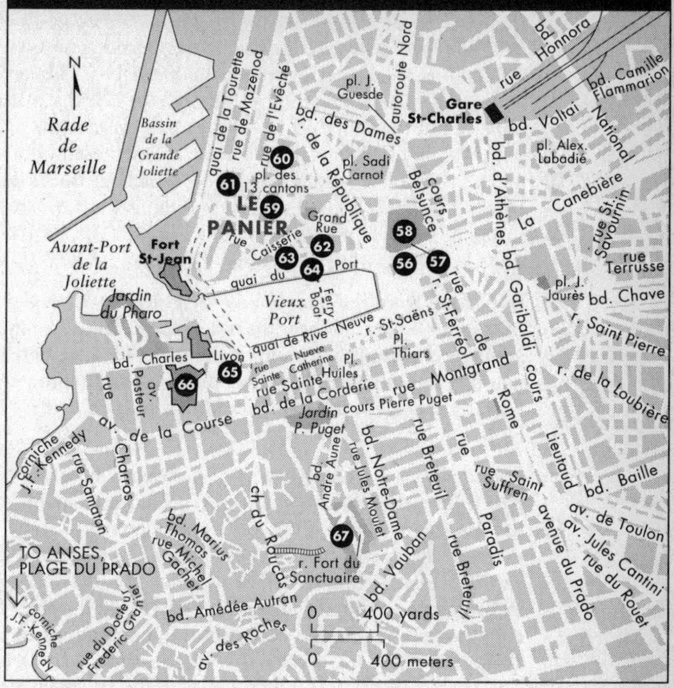

egg-peaked dome. Of the complex's two museums, the larger is the **Musée d'Archéologie Méditerranéenne** (Museum of Mediterranean Archaeology), with a sizable collection of pottery and statuary from classical Mediterranean civilization, elementally labeled (for example, "pot"). There's also a display on the mysterious Celt-like Ligurians who first peopled the coast, cryptically presented with emphasis on the digs instead of the finds themselves. The best of the lot is the evocatively mounted Egyptian collection, the second largest in France after the Louvre's. There are mummies, hieroglyphs, and gorgeous sarcophagi in a tomblike setting. Upstairs, the **Musée d'Arts Africains, Océaniens, et Amérindiens** (Museum of African, Oceanic, and American Indian Art) creates a theatrical foil for the works' intrinsic drama: the spectacular masks and sculptures are mounted along a pure black wall, lighted indirectly, with labels across the aisle. ✉ *2 rue de la Charité, Panier,* ☎ *04–91–14–58–80.* 🎫 *€2 per museum.* 🕓 *May–Sept., Tues.–Sun. 11–6; Oct.–Apr., Tues.–Sun. 10–5.*

61 A gargantuan, neo-Byzantine 19th-century fantasy, the **Cathédrale de la Nouvelle Major** (✉ Pl. de la Major, Vieux Port) was built under Napoléon III—but not before he'd ordered the partial destruction of the lovely 11th-century original, once a perfect example of the Provençal Romanesque style. You can view the flashy decor—marble and rich red porphyry inlay—in the newer of the two churches; the medieval one is being restored.

62 The **Musée du Vieux Marseille** (Museum of Old Marseille)—in the 16th-century **Maison Diamantée** (one of the few buildings in this quarter that would be spared by Hitler), so called because of its beveled-stone diamondlike facade—concentrates on Marseille's Provençal personality. Reopened in 2002 after sizeable renovations, the collection includes beautifully carved wooden furniture, crèches, and santons, and 19th-

century costume. ✉ *Rue de la Prison, Vieux Port,* ☎ *04–91–13–89–00 for information.*

In 1943 Hitler destroyed the neighborhood along the quai du Port—some 2,000 houses—displacing some 20,000 citizens. This act of brutal urban renewal, ironically, laid the ground open for new discoveries. When Marseille began to rebuild in 1947, they dug up remains of a Roman shipping warehouse full of the terra-cotta jars and amphorae that once lay
63 in the bellies of low-slung ships. The **Musée des Docks Romains** (Roman Docks Museum) created around it demonstrates the scale of Massalia's shipping prowess. ✉ *Pl. de Vivaux, Vieux Port,* ☎ *04–91–91–24–62.* *€2. Oct.–May, Tues.–Sun. 10–5; June–Sept., Tues.–Sun. 11–6.*

64 Departing from the quai below the Hôtel de Ville, the **Ferry Boat** is a Marseille treasure. To hear the natives pronounce "fer-ry bo-at" (they've adopted the English) is one of the joys of a visit here. For a pittance you can file onto this little wooden barge and chug across the Vieux Port. ✉ *Travels between pl. des Huiles on quai de Rive Neuve side and Hôtel de Ville on quai du Port, Vieux Port.* *€1.*

Founded in the 4th century by St-Cassien, who sailed into Marseille's port full of fresh ideas on monasticism acquired in Palestine and Egypt,
★ 65 the **Abbaye St-Victor** grew to formidable proportions. With its severe exterior of crenellated stone and the spare geometry of its Romanesque church, the structure would be as much at home in the Middle East as its founder had been. The Saracens destroyed the first structure, so the abbey was rebuilt in the 11th century and fortified against further onslaught in the 14th. By far the best reason to come is the **crypt,** St-Cassien's original, which lay buried under the medieval church's new structure. In evocative nooks and crannies you'll find the 5th-century sarcophagus that allegedly holds the martyr's remains. Upstairs look for the reliquary containing what's left of St. Victor himself, who was ground to death between millstones, probably by Romans. *Crypt entry €2. Daily 8:30–6:30.*

66 The twin structures of **Fort St-Nicolas and Fort St-Jean** flank the entrance to the Vieux Port. In order to keep the feisty, rebellious Marseillais under his thumb, Louis XIV had the fortresses built with the guns pointing *inward.* To view them, climb up to the Jardin du Pharo.

Towering above the city and visible for miles around, the preposter-
67 ously overscaled neo-Byzantine monument called **Notre-Dame-de-la-Garde** was erected in 1853 by the ever-tasteful Napoléon III. Its interior is a Technicolor bonanza of red-and-beige stripes and glittering mosaics. The gargantuan *Madonna and Child,* on the steeple (almost 30 ft high), is covered in real gold leaf. The boggling panoply of naive ex-votos, mostly thanking the Virgin for death-bed interventions and shipwreck survivals, makes the pilgrimage worth it. ✉ *On foot, climb up cours Pierre Puget, cross jardin Pierre Puget, cross bridge to rue Vauvenargues, and hike up to pl. Edon. Or catch Bus 60 from cours Jean-Ballard, Garde Hill.* ☎ *04–91–13–40–80.* *May–Sept., daily 7 AM–8 PM; Oct.–Apr., daily 7–7.*

OFF THE BEATEN PATH ★

CHÂTEAU D'IF – François I, in the 16th century, recognized the strategic advantage of an island fortress surveying the mouth of Marseille's vast harbor, so he had one built. Its effect as deterrent was so successful that it never saw combat, and was eventually converted into a prison. It was here that Alexandre Dumas locked up his most famous character, the Count of Monte Cristo. Though he was fictional, the hole Dumas had him escape through is real enough, and is visible in the cells today. Video monitors playing relevant scenes from dozens of Monte Cristo films bring each tower and cell to life. On the other hand, the real-life Man in the Iron Mask, whose cell is still being shown, was not actually imprisoned here. The boat ride (from the quai des Belges, €8) and the views from the broad terrace alone are worth the trip. ☎ 04–91–59–02–30, WEB www.monuments-france.fr. ☒ Château €4. ☉ Apr.–Sept., daily 9–7; Oct.–Mar., Tues.–Sun. 9–5:30.

Dining and Lodging

$$$–$$$$ ✕ **Chez Fonfon.** Tucked into a storybook film set of a fishing port east
★ of the center, this landmark draws the Marseillais for plain, fresh seafood and classic bouillabaisse. Alexandre Pinna, the owner's son, has taken over from the late, great chef Fonfon, but the restaurant's cachet survives. ☒ 140 rue du Vallon des Auffes, Vieux Port, ☎ 04–91–52–14–38. Reservations essential. AE, DC, MC, V. Closed 2 wks in Jan. No dinner Sun.

$$$ ✕ **Mets de Provence.** Climb the sleazy wharf-side stairs and enter a cosseted Provençal world. With boats bobbing out the window and a landlubbing country decor, this romantic restaurant makes the most of Marseille's split personality. Classic Provençal hors d'oeuvres—tapenade, brandade, aioli—lead into seafood (dorade roasted with fennel and licorice) and meats (rack of lamb in herb pastry). The four-course lunch (€30, including wine) is marvelous. ☒ 18 quai de Rive-Neuve, Vieux Port, ☎ 04–91–33–33–38. AE, MC, V. Closed Sun. No lunch Mon.

$$–$$$ ✕ **Baie des Singes.** On a tiny rock-ringed lagoon as isolated from the nearby city as if it were a desert island, this cinematic corner of paradise was once a customs house under Napoléon III. You can rent a mattress and lounge chair, dive into the turquoise water, and shower off for the only kind of food worthy of such a locale: fresh fish. It's all served at terrace tables overlooking the water. ☒ Anse des Croisettes, Les Goudes, Les Goudes, ☎ 04–91–73–68–87. AE, DC, MC, V. Closed Oct.–Mar.

$$ ✕ **Les Arcenaulx.** At this book-lined, red-walled haven in the stylish book-and-boutique complex of this renovated arsenal, you can have a sophisticated regional lunch—and read while you're waiting. Look for mussels in saffron with buckwheat crepes, carpaccio of cod with crushed olives, or rabbit with garlic confit. The terrace (on the Italian-scaled cours d'Estienne d'Orves) is as pleasant as the interior. ☒ 25 cours d'Estienne d'Orves, Vieux Port, ☎ 04–91–59–80–30. AE, DC, MC, V. Closed Sun.

$ ✕ **Etienne.** This historic Le Panier hole-in-the-wall has more than just
★ good fresh-anchovy pizza from a wood-burning oven. There are also fried squid, eggplant gratin, a slab of rare-grilled beef big enough for two, and the quintessential pieds et paquets, Marseille's earthy classic of sheep's feet and stuffed tripe. ☒ 43 rue de la Lorette, Vieux Port, ☎ no phone. No credit cards.

$$$$ ✕▣ **Le Petit Nice.** On a rocky promontory overlooking the sea, this
★ fantasy villa was bought from a countess in 1917 and converted to a hotel/restaurant. The Passédat family has been getting it right ever since, with father and son manning the exceptional kitchen (one of the coast's best), creating truffled brandade, sea anemone beignets, fresh fish roasted whole, and licorice soufflé (the restaurant is closed Sunday; prix-fixe menus are €110 and €139). Most rooms are sleek and minimalist, with some art deco–cum–postmodern touches, while outside the fetching pool is illuminated at night by antique gaslight fixtures. ☒ Anse de Maldormé, corniche J.-F.-Kennedy, Vieux Port 13007, ☎ 04–91–59–25–92, FAX 04–91–59–28–08, WEB www.petitnice-passedat.com. 15 rooms. Restaurant, cable TV, minibars, Internet, pool, free parking. AE, DC, MC, V.

$$$ ★ **Mercure Beauvau Vieux Port.** The antiques are real, the woodwork burnished with age; add a little marble, a touch of brass, and deep carpet underfoot, and you have an idea of this intimate urban hotel's genuine Old World charm. George Sand kept a suite here—knowing that makes the plush retro appearance of all the rooms, with paisleys and moiré, seem all the more appropriate. Port-view rooms more than justify the splurge. ✉ *4 rue Beauvau, Vieux Port 13001,* ☎ *04–91–54–91–00; 800/637–2873 for U.S. reservations,* FAX *04–91–54–15–76. 71 rooms. Bar, no-smoking rooms, cable TV, minibars, Internet. AE, DC, MC, V.*

$–$$ **Alizé.** On the Vieux Port, its front rooms taking in postcard views, this straightforward lodging has been modernized to include tight double windows, slick modular baths, and a laminate-and-all-weather carpeted look. Public spaces have exposed stone and preserved details, and a glass elevator whisks you to your floor. It's an excellent value and location for the price. ✉ *35 quai des Belges, Vieux Port 13001,* ☎ *04–91–33–66–97,* FAX *04–91–54–80–06. 37 rooms. Cable TV. AE, DC, MC, V.*

$ **Hermès.** Just around the corner from the Quai du Port, this modest city hotel has been smartly renovated. Rooms are snug and modular, with all-new baths. Ask for one of the fifth-floor rooms with tiny balconies overlooking the port—or the crow's-nest *nuptiale* double with a private rooftop terrace. ✉ *2 rue Bonneterie, Vieux Port 13002,* ☎ *04–96–11–63–63,* FAX *04–96–11–63–64. 29 rooms. Cable TV, minibars, Internet. AE, DC, MC, V.*

Nightlife and the Arts

With a population of more than 800,000, Marseille is a big city by French standards, with all the nightlife that entails. Arm yourself with *Marseille Poche,* a glossy monthly events minimagazine; the monthly *In Situ,* a free guide to music, theater and galleries; *Sortir,* a weekly about film, art, and concerts in southern Provence; or *TakTik,* a hip weekly on theater and art. They're all in French. Rock, jazz, and reggae concerts are held at the **Espace Julien** (✉ 39 cours Julien, Préfecture, ☎ 04–91–24–34–10). **Le Trolleybus** (✉ 24 quai de Rive Neuve, Bompard, ☎ 04–91–54–30–45) is the most popular disco in town, with a young, *branché* (hip) crowd. Classical music concerts are given in the **Abbaye St-Victor** (☎ 04–91–05–84–48 for information). Operas and orchestral concerts are held at the **Opéra Municipal** (✉ 2 rue Molière, Vieux Port, ☎ 04–91–55–21–24).

Outdoor Activities and Sports

Marseille's waterfront position makes it easy to swim and sunbathe within the city sprawl. From the Vieux Port, Bus 83 or Bus 19 will take you to the vast green spread of reclaimed land called the **Parc Balnéaire du Prado.** Its waterfront is divided into beaches, all of them public and well equipped. The beach surface varies between sand and gravel.

Marseille is a major center for diving (*plongée*), with several organizations offering *baptêmes* (baptisms, or first dives) to beginners. The coast is lined with rocky inlets, grottos, and ancient shipwrecks, not to mention thronging with aquatic life. For general information contact the **Centre de Loisirs des Goudes** (✉ 2 bd. Alexandre Dumas, Saint-Giniez 13008, ☎ FAX 04–91–25–13–16).

Shopping

The locally famous bakery **Four des Navettes** (✉ 136 rue Sainte, Garde Hill, ☎ 04–91–33–32–12), up the street from Notre-Dame-de-la-Garde, makes orange-spice, shuttle-shape *navettes.* These cookies are modeled on the little boat in which Mary Magdalene and Lazarus washed up onto Europe's shores. **Savon de Marseille** (Marseille soap) is a household standard in France, often sold as a satisfyingly crude and hefty block in odorless olive-oil green. But its chichi offspring are dainty pastel guest soaps in almond, lemon, vanilla, and other scents.

Aubagne

68 *16 km (10 mi) east of Marseille, 36 km (22 mi) south of Aix-en-Provence.*

This easygoing, plane tree–shaded market town is an ideal spot to spend the morning browsing through the Old Town or basking on the broad tree-lined squares. Aubagne claims the title of *santon*-making capital of Provence. The craft, originally from Marseille, was focused here at the turn of the 20th century, when artisans moved inland to make the most of local clay. The more than a dozen studios in town are set up for you to observe the production process. Make sure you visit Aubagne on a market day, when the sleepy center is transformed into a tableau of Provençal life. The Tuesday market is the biggest.

The town is proud of its native son, the dramatist, filmmaker, and chronicler of all things Provençal, Marcel Pagnol, best known as the author of *Jean de Florette* and *Manon des Sources* (*Manon of the Springs*) and the stories that comprise the Fanny trilogy. You can study miniature dioramas of scenes from Pagnol stories at **Le Petit Monde de Marcel Pagnol** (The Small World of Marcel Pagnol). ✉ *Esplanade de Gaulle.* *Free.* ⏲ *Daily 9–noon and 2–6.*

Even if you haven't read Pagnol's works or seen his films, you can enjoy the **Circuit Pagnol,** a hike in the rough-hewn, arid *garrigues* (scrublands) behind Marseille and Aubagne. Here Pagnol spent his idyllic summers, described in his *Souvenirs d'un Enfance* (*Memories of a Childhood*). When he grew up to be a famous playwright and filmmaker, he shot some of his best work in these hills. After Pagnol's death, Claude Berri came back to find a location for his remake of *Manon des Sources* but found it so altered by brush fires and power cables that he chose to shoot in the Luberon instead. Although the trail may no longer shelter the pine-shaded olive orchards of its past, it still gives you the chance to walk through primeval Provençal countryside and rewards you with spectacular views of Marseille and the sea. ✉ *To access marked trail by yourself, drive to La Treille, northeast of Aubagne, and follow signs. For an accompanied tour with literary commentary, contact the tourist office:* ☎ *04–42–03–49–98.*

Another claim to fame for Aubagne: it is the headquarters for the French Foreign Legion. The legion was created in 1831, and accepts recruits from all nations, no questions asked. The **Musée de la Légion Étrangère,** named after the distinctive white caps of the *légionnaires,* does its best to polish the image by way of medals, uniforms, weapons, and photographs. ✉ *Caserne Viénot (to get there, take a left off D2 onto D44A just before Aubagne),* ☎ *04–42–18–82–41.* *Free.* ⏲ *June–Sept., Tues.–Thurs. and weekends 10–noon and 3–7, Fri. 10–noon; Oct.–May, Wed. and weekends 10–noon and 2–6.*

Dining

$–$$ ✕ **La Farandole.** Cosseted here by rustic Provençal lemon-print cloths, lace curtains, and the region's typical bow-legged chairs, you can enjoy good home cooking with local regulars who claim the same table every day. The inexpensive daily menu highlights panfried chicken livers on a green salad, *rascasse* (a local fish) with sorrel, or garlicky steak and *frites* (fries); wine is included. ✉ *6 rue Martino (just off cours Maréchal, on a narrow street leading into the Old Town),* ☎ *04–42–03–26–36. MC, V. Closed Sun. No dinner Mon.*

Cassis

69 *11 km (7 mi) south of Aubagne, 30 km (19 mi) east of Marseille, 42 km (26 mi) west of Toulon.*

Surrounded by vineyards, flanked by monumental cliffs, guarded by the ruins of a medieval castle, and nestled around a picture-perfect fishing port, Cassis is the prettiest coastal town in Provence. Stylish without being too recherché, it provides shelter to numerous pleasure-boaters, who restock their galleys at its market, replenish their nautical duds in its boutiques, and relax with a bottle of Cassis and a platter of sea urchins in one of its numerous waterfront cafés. Pastel houses set at Cubist angles frame the port, and the mild rash of parking-garage architecture that scars its outer neighborhoods doesn't spoil the general effect, one of pure and unadulterated charm.

The **Château de Cassis** has loomed over the harbor since the invasions of the Saracens in the 7th century, evolving over the centuries into a walled enclosure crowned with stout watchtowers. It's private property today and best viewed from a port-side café.

You can't visit Cassis without touring the **Calanques,** the fjordlike finger bays that probe the rocky coastline. Either take a sightseeing cruise or hike across the clifftops, clambering down the steep sides to these barely accessible retreats. Or you can combine the two, going in by boat and hiking back; make arrangements at the port. The Calanque closest to Cassis is the least attractive: **Port Miou** was a stone quarry until 1982, when the Calanques became protected sites. Now this calanque is an active leisure and fishing port. **Calanque Port Pin** is prettier, with wind-twisted pines growing at angles from the white-rock ★ cliffs. But it's the third calanque that's the showstopper: the **Calanque En Vau** is a castaway's dream, with a tiny beach at its root and jagged cliffs looming overhead. The series of massive cliffs and calanques stretches all the way to Marseille.

Dining and Lodging

$$$–$$$$ ✕ **Chez Nino.** This is the best of the many restaurants lining the harbor, with top-notch Provençal food and wine and a spectacular terrace view. The owners, Claudie and Bruno, are extremely hospitable as long as you stick to the menu—don't ask for sauce on the side—and you are as passionate about fish and seafood as they are. The sardines in *escabeche* are textbook perfect, as are the grilled fish and the bouillabaisse. ✉ *Quai Barthélémy,* ☎ *04–42–01–74–32. AE, DC, MC, V. Closed mid-Dec.–mid-Feb. and Mon. off-season. No dinner Sun. off-season.*

$$–$$$ ✕ **Monsieur Brun.** One of the most authentic meals you can have in Cassis is a platter of raw shellfish. At this terrace brasserie on the west side of the port, a multitier tower of shellfish on a bed of kelp is served with nothing but bread, butter, and a finger towelette. Have the nutty little *bleues,* the local oyster, but *oursins* (sea urchins) are a Cassis specialty, and these are brought in daily by the chef's fisherman friend. Omelets and salads are alternatives. ✉ *2 quai Calendal,* ☎ *04–42–01–82–66. No credit cards. Closed mid-Dec.–mid-Jan.*

$$ ★ ✕🏨 **Jardin d'Émile.** Tucked back from the waterfront under quarried cliffs and massive parasol pines, this stylish, cozy inn takes in views of the cape. Rooms are intimate, with rubbed-chalk walls, scrubbed pine, and weathered stone. The restaurant is atmospheric, on a sheltered terrace surrounded by greenery and, by night, the illuminated cliffs. Regional specialties with a cosmopolitan twist—such as snapper filled with goat cheese and wrapped in eggplant—are served on locally made pottery. ✉ *Plage du Bestouan, 13260,* ☎ *04–42–01–80–55,* FAX *04–42–01–80–70,* WEB *www.lejardindemile.fr. 7 rooms. Cable TV. AE, DC, MC, V.*

$$$ **Les Roches Blanches.** First built as a private home in 1887, this cliff-side villa takes in smashing views of the port and the Cap Canaille, both from the best rooms and from the panoramic dining hall. The beautifully landscaped terrace is shaded by massive pines, and the horizon pool appears to spill into the sea. Yet the aura is far from snooty or deluxe; it's friendly, low-key, and pleasantly mainstream. ✉ *Rte. des Calanques, 13260,* ☏ *04–42–01–09–30,* FAX *04–42–01–94–23,* WEB *www.roches-blanches-cassis.com. 19 rooms, 5 suites. 2 restaurants, no air-conditioning, pool. AE, MC, V.*

Outdoor Activities and Sports

To go on a **boat ride** to Les Calanques, get to the port around 10 AM or 2 PM and look for a boat that's loading passengers. Round-trips should include visits to at least three Calanques and average €10. To **hike** the Calanques, gauge your skills: the GR98 (marked with red-and-white bands) is the most scenic, but requires scrambling to get down the sheer walls of En Vau. The alternative is to follow the green markers and approach En Vau from behind. If you're ambitious, you can hike the length of the GR98 between Marseille and Cassis, following the coastline.

En Route From Cassis head east out of town and cut sharply right up the **route des Crêtes.** This road takes you along a magnificent crest over the water and up to the very top of **Cap Canaille.** Venture out on the vertiginous trails to the edge, where the whole coast stretches below.

Bandol

70 *25 km (15½ mi) southeast of Cassis, 15 km (9 mi) west of Toulon.*

Although its name means wine to most of the world, Bandol is also a popular and highly developed seaside resort town. It has seafood snack shacks, generic brasseries, a harbor packed with yachts, and a waterfront promenade. Yet the east end of town conceals lovely old villas framed in mimosas, bougainvillea, and pine. And a port-side stroll up the palm-lined allée Jean-Moulin feels downright Côte d'Azur. But be warned: the sheer concentration of high-summer crowds can not be exaggerated. If you're not a beach lover, pick up an itinerary from the tourist office and visit a few Bandol vineyards just outside town.

Dining

$$$–$$$$ ✕ **Auberge du Port.** This is a fish-first-and-foremost establishment, with a terrace packed night and day—and not because of the splendid view it offers of Ile Bandor. Going off menu for a daily catch special can be costly, but worth it if a memorable fish-dish experience has so far eluded you on the trip. Otherwise, try the excellent *friture* of small fish fried with lemon or the classic fish stew *bourride.* Get here early for something especially fresh and savory. And book ahead. ✉ *9 allée Jean-Moulin,* ☏ *04–94–29–42–63. Reservations essential. MC, V.*

Brignoles

71 *86 km (47 mi) northwest of Bandol, 70 km (39 mi) north of Toulon.*

This rambling backcountry hill town, crowned with a medieval chateau, is the market center for the wines of the Var and the crossroads of this green, ungentrified region—until now, that is. With a Ducasse restaurant now in the region, real estate has rocketed, and le tout Paris whispers that this little corner of nowheresville is The next Luberon. The main point of interest in the region is the **Abbaye de La Celle,** a 12th-century Benedictine abbey that served as a convent until the 17th century, when it was closed because its young nuns had began to run wild and were known less for their chastity than "the color of their petticoats and the name of their lover." There's a refectory and a ruined cloister; the simple Romanesque chapel still serves as the parish church.

Dining and Lodging

$$$–$$$$ ★ ✕ 🏨 **Hostellerie de l'Abbaye de La Celle.** Superchef Alain Ducasse's country inn is buried in the unspoiled backcountry north of Toulon, just southwest of Brignoles. Up the road from the town's royal abbey, this beautifully restored 18th-century *bastide* (country house)—a dream in ocher-yellow walls, Arles green shutters, and white stone trim—was once part of the convent where future queens of Provence were raised. Guest rooms mix Louis XVI and regional accents; half are split-level with their own gardens, some with views of vineyards, others of a park thick with chestnut and mulberry trees. Beds are enormous—none more so than those of the Charles de Gaulle Suite (where the prime minister once stayed). Fish arrives daily from Marseilles, goat cheese is made in nearby Banon, and delights such as wild mushrooms sautéed with crayfish, and rabbit with olives and polenta top chef Benoît Witz's menu, whose creations glorify the rustic. Why not enjoy his crisp French toast with strawberries in the rose arbor? ✉ *Pl. du Général-de-Gaulle, 83170 La Celle,* ☎ *04–98–05–14–14,* FAX *04–98–05–14–15,* WEB *www.abbaye-celle.com. 10 rooms. Restaurant, no air-conditioning, cable TV, minibars, Internet, pool, meeting room. AE, DC, MC, V.*

Iles d'Hyères

72 *32 km (20 mi) off the coast south of Hyères. To get to the islands, follow the narrow Giens Peninsula to La Tour-Fondue, at its tip. Boats (leaving every half hour in summer, every 60 or 90 minutes the rest of the year, for €12 round-trip) make a 20-minute beeline to Porquerolles. For Port-Cros and Levant, you'll depart from Port d'Hyères at Hyères-Plages.*

Off the southeastern point of France's star and spanning some 32 km (20 mi), this archipelago of islands could be a set for a pirate movie; in fact, it has featured in several, thanks to a soothing microclimate and a wild and rocky coastline dotted with palms. And not only film pirates made their appearance: in the 16th century the islands were seeded with convicts to work the land. They soon ran amok and used their adopted base to ambush ships heading into Toulon.

A more wholesome population claims the islands today. They are made up of three main areas. **Port-Cros** is a national park, with both its surface and underwater environs protected. **Levant** has been taken ★ over, for the most part, by nudists. **Porquerolles** is the largest and best of the lot—and a popular escape from the modern world. Off-season, it's a castaway delight of pine forests, sandy beaches, and vertiginous cliffs above rocky coastline. Inland, its preserved pine forests and orchards of olives and figs are crisscrossed with dirt roads to be explored on foot or on bikes; except for the occasional jeep or work truck, the island is car-free. In high season (April to October), day-trippers pour off the ferries and surge to the beaches.

Dining and Lodging

$$$ ★ ✕ 🏨 **Mas du Langoustier.** Amid lush terrain at the westernmost point of the Ile de Porquerolles, 3 km (2 mi) from the harbor, this luxurious hideout is a popular getaway. Owner Madame Richard will pick you up at the port in her Dodge; her grandmother was given the island as a wedding gift. Choose between big California-modern rooms and charming old-style rooms in the original section. Chef Joël Guillet creates inspired southern French cuisine, to be accompanied by the rare island rosé. ✉ *Pointe du Langoustier, 83400 Ile de Porquerolles,* ☎

04–94–58–30–09, FAX *04–94–58–36–02,* WEB *www.langoustier.com. 49 rooms. Restaurant, cable TV, minibars, Internet, tennis court, beach, billiards. AE, DC, MC, V. Closed Nov.–Apr.*

$$–$$$ ✕☒ **Les Glycines.** In soft shades of yellow-ocher and sky-blue, this sleekly modernized little bastide has an idyllic enclosed courtyard. Back rooms look over a jungle of mimosa and eucalyptus. Public salons have Provençal chairs and fabrics. The restaurant, where food is served on the terrace or in the garden, proffers port-fresh tuna and sardines. The inn is just back from the port in the village center. ✉ *Pl. d'Armes, 83400 Ile de Porquerolles,* ☎ *04–94–58–30–36,* FAX *04–94–58–35–22. 11 rooms. Restaurant, bar, no air-conditioning, cable TV, minibars, Internet. AE, MC, V.*

Outdoor Activities and Sports

You can rent a mountain bike (*velo tout-terrain,* or VTT) for a day to pedal the paths and clifftop trails of Porquerolles at **Cycle Porquerol** (✉ Rue de la Ferme, ☎ 04–94–58–30–32). **L'Indien** (✉ Pl. d'Armes, ☎ 04–94–58–30–39) offers a wide variety of bikes. **Locamarine 75** (✉ On port, ☎ 04–94–58–35–84) rents motorboats to amateurs with or without license.

PROVENCE A TO Z

To research prices, get advice from other travelers, and book travel arrangements, visit www.fodors.com.

AIR TRAVEL

Marseille is served by frequent flights from Paris and London, and daily flights from Paris arrive at the smaller airport at Nîmes, which serves Arles and the Camargue (the trip takes about an hour). There are direct flights in summer from the United States to Nice, 160 km (100 mi) from Aix-en-Provence.

BIKE AND MOPED TRAVEL

Bikes can be rented from the train stations in Aix-en-Provence, Arles, Avignon, Marseille, Nîmes, and Orange at a cost of about €6 per day. Contact the Comité Départemental de Cyclotourisme for a list of scenic bike routes in Provence.

➤ BIKE MAPS: **Comité Départemental de Cyclotourisme** (✉ Les Passadoires, 84420 Piolenc).

BUS TRAVEL

A moderately good network of bus services—run by a perplexing number of independent bus companies (for best advice on schedules, consult the town tourist office or your hotel concierge)—links places not served, or poorly served, by train. If you plan to explore Provence by bus, Avignon, Marseille, Aix-en-Provence, and Arles are good bases. Avignon is also the starting point for excursion-bus tours and boat trips down the Rhône. In most cases, you can buy bus tickets on the bus itself.

Aix-en-Provence: One block west of La Rotonde, the station (rue Lapierre) is crowded with many bus companies, which offer numerous regional connections, the farthest links being Orange, Nice, Marseille, Avignon, and Arles. **Arles:** The gare routière (av. Paulin Talabot) is adjacent to the train station. Five buses leave daily for Aix-en-Provence and Marseille (only two run on weekends); others travel daily to Avignon and Nîmes. **Avignon:** The bus station is right by the rail station on boulevard St-Roch; lines connect to nearby towns such as Châteauneuf-du-Pape and Fontaine-de-Vaucluse. **Les Baux:** Buses here head for Avignon or Arles. **Nîmes:** The bus station (rue Ste-Félicité) connects with Montpellier, Pont du Gard, and many other places.

Marseille: The station (3 pl. Victor Hugo) is next to the train station and offers myriad connections to cities and small towns. St-Remy-de-Provence is 40 minutes from Avignon by bus. **Orange:** The station is on cours Pourtoules, on the eastern edge of city city, and offers links to Avignon, Vaison-la-Romaine, and Marseille. **Pont du Gard:** This is a 40-minute ride from Nîmes; you are dropped off 1 km (½ mi) from the bridge at the Auberge Blanche. **Stes-Maries-de-la-Mer:** As the gateway to the Camargue region (in which there is little or no public transportion), buses head here from Arles, Nîmes, and Aigues-Mortes.

➤ BUS INFORMATION: **Les Cars Lieutaud** (☎ 04–90–36–05–22, WEB www.cars-lieutaud.fr). **Ceyte Tourisme Méditerranée** (☎ 04–90–93–74–90). For a complete list of bus web sites for the region, log on to WEB www.provence-jouques.com/fr/venir/venir15.html.

CAR RENTAL

➤ LOCAL AGENCIES: **Avis** (✉ 11 bd. Gambetta, Aix, ☎ 04–42–21–64–16; ✉ at train station, Avignon, ☎ 04–90–27–96–10; ✉ at train station, Marseille, ☎ 04–91–64–71–00; ✉ 19 av. Charles de Gaulle, Orange, ☎ 04–90–34–11–00).

Budget (✉ Bd. St-Roch, Avignon, ☎ 04–90–27–94–95; ✉ 42 bd. Edouard Daladier, Orange, ☎ 04–90–34–00–34).

Hertz (✉ 43 av. Victor Hugo, Aix, ☎ 04–42–27–91–32; ✉ 2A av. Monclar, Avignon, ☎ 04–90–14–26–90; ✉ train station, Marseille, ☎ 04–91–90–14–03).

CAR TRAVEL

A6/A7 (a toll road) from Paris, known as the Autoroute du Soleil—the Highway of the Sun—takes you straight to Provence, when it divides at Orange, 659 km (412 mi) from Paris; the trip can be done in a fast five or so hours.

After route A7 divides at Orange, A9 heads west to Nîmes (723 km /448 mi from Paris) and continues into the Pyrénées and across the Spanish border. Route A7 continues southeast from Orange to Marseille, on the coast (1,100 km/680 mi from Paris), while A8 goes to Aix-en-Provence (with a spur to Toulon) and then to the Côte d'Azur and Italy.

LODGING

APARTMENT AND VILLA RENTALS

Properties for rent in Provence are listed by the national house-rental agency, Gîtes de France. Regional offices are in Bouches-du-Rhône, Gard, Var, and Vaucluse. In addition, each of the tourist offices in towns in the region usually publishes lists of independent rentals (*locations meublés*), many of them inspected and classified by the tourist office itself.

➤ LOCAL AGENTS: **Bouches-du-Rhône** (✉ Domaine du Vergon, B.P. 26, 13370 Mallemort, ☎ 04–90–59–49–40, FAX 04–90–59–16–75). **Gard** (✉ 3 pl. des Arènes, B.P. 59, 30007 Nîmes Cedex 4, ☎ 04–66–27–94–94, FAX 04–66–27–94–95). **Var** (✉ 1 bd. Maréchal Foch, Draguignan, ☎ 04–94–50–93–93, FAX 04–94–50–93–90). **Vaucluse** (✉ Pl. Campana, B.P. 164, 84008 Avignon Cedex 1, ☎ 04–90–85–45–00).

B&BS

Gîtes de France, the French national network of vacation lodging, rates participating B&Bs for comfort and lists them in a catalog. For chambres d'hotes regulated by this national network, contact the local branches, divided by *départements* (administrative regions).

TOURS

PRIVATE GUIDES

Bus tours through the Camargue, either 5-hour or 9-hour, are offered, departing from Arles, by Cars de Camargue. For €46, Taxis T.R.A.N. can take you round-trip from Nîmes to the Pont du Gard (ask the taxi to wait while you explore for 30 minutes).

➤ CONTACTS: **Cars de Camargue** (24 bd. G. Clemenceau, Arles, ☎ 04–90–96–94–78). **Taxis T.R.A.N.** (☎ 04–66–29–40–11).

WALKING TOURS

The tourist offices in Arles, Nîmes, Avignon, Aix-en-Provence, and Marseille all organize a full calendar of walking tours (some in summer only).

TRAIN TRAVEL

The new high-speed TGV *Méditerranée* line ushers in a new era in *Trains à Grande Vitesse* travel in France; the route (lengthened last year from the old terminus, Valence, in Haute Provence) means that you can travel from Paris's Gare de Lyon to Avignon in two hours and 40 minutes, with a mere three hour trip to Nîmes, Aix-en-Provence, and Marseille. Not only is the idea of Provence as a day-trip now possible (though, of course, not advisable), you can even whisk yourself there directly upon arrival at Paris's Charles de Gaulle airport.

After the main line of the TGV divides at Avignon, the westbound link heads to Nîmes and points west; heading east, the line connects with Orange. The southeast-bound link takes in Marseille, Toulon, and the Côte d'Azur. Montpellier is the stop after Nîmes, with other links at Béziers and Narbonne. There is also frequent service by daily local trains to other towns in the region from these main TGV stops. With high-speed service now connecting Nîmes, Avignon, and Marseille, travelers without cars will find a Provence itinerary much easier to pull off. For full information on the TGV *Méditerranée,* log onto the TGV web-site; you can purchase tickets on this web site or through RailEurope, and you should always buy your TGV tickets in advance.

Aix-en-Provence: The station (pl. Victor Hugo) is a 5-minute walk from place du Général-de-Gaulle and offers many connections, with hourly departures to Marseille. **Arles:** The train station (av. Paulin Talabot) has frequent trains to Avignon, Nîmes, Marseille, and other stops. **Avignon:** The Gare d'Avignon (bd. St-Roch) is across from the entrance to the walled city—easy connections here include Arles, Nîmes, Marseille, and Aix-en-Provence. **Marseille:** The station (esplanade St-Charles) serves all regions of France and is at northern end of center city, a 20-minute walk from the Old Town. Trains run almost hourly to Arles, Aix-en-Provence, Avignon, and Nice. **Nîmes:** Frequent trains connect with Arles, Avignon, Montpellier, and Marseille; to reach the Old Town from the station, walk north on av. Fauchères. **Orange:** The center city is a 15-minute walk from the train station—walk from av. Frédéric Mistral to rue de la République, then follow signs.

➤ TRAIN INFORMATION: **SNCF** (☎ 08–36–35–35–35, WEB www.sncf.com). **TGV** (WEB www.tgv.com).

TRAVEL AGENCIES

➤ LOCAL AGENT REFERRALS: **Havas** (✉ 4 bd. des Lices, Arles, ☎ 04–90–18–31–31; ✉ 35 rue de la République, Avignon, ☎ 04–90–80–66–80; ✉ 44 bd. Victor Hugo, Nîmes, ☎ 04–66–36–99–99; ✉ 34 rue de la République, Orange, ☎ 04–90–11–44–44). **Nouvelle Frontières** (✉ 14 rue Carnot, Avignon, ☎ 04–90–82–31–32). **Provence-Camargue Tours** (✉ 1 rue Émile Fassin, Arles, ☎ 04–90–49–85–58).

VISITOR INFORMATION

Regional tourist offices prefer written queries only. The mother lode of general information is the Comité Regional du Tourisme de Provence-Alpes-Côte d'Azur. For information specific to one département, contact the following: Comité Départemental du Tourisme des Bouches-du-Rhône, Comité Départemental du Tourisme du Var, Comité Départemental du Tourisme de Vaucluse. Local tourist offices for major towns covered in this chapter can be phoned, faxed, or addressed by mail.

➤ REGIONAL TOURSIT OFFICES: **Comité Regional du Tourisme de Provence-Alpes-Côte d'Azur** (✉ 12 pl. Joliette, 13002 Marseille, ☏ 04–91–56–47–00, FAX 04–91–56–47–01, WEB www.crt-paca.fr/fre/accueil flash.jsp). **Comité Départemental du Tourisme des Bouches-du-Rhône** (✉ 13 rue Roux de Brignole, 13006 Marseille, ☏ 04–91–13–84–13, FAX 04–91–33–01–82, WEB www.visitprovence.com). **Comité Départemental du Tourisme du Var** (✉ 1 bd. Maréchal Foch, 83300 Draguignan, ☏ 04–94–50–55–50, FAX 04–94–50–55–51, WEB www.tourismevar.com). **Comité Départemental du Tourisme de Vaucluse** (✉ B.P. 147, 84008 Avignon Cedex 1, ☏ 04–90–80–47–00, FAX 04–90–86–86–08).

➤ LOCAL TOURIST OFFICES: **Aix** (✉ 2 pl. du Général-de-Gaulle, B.P. 160, 13605 Cedex 1, ☏ 04–42–16–11–61, FAX 04–42–16–11–62, WEB www.aixenprovencetourism.com). **Arles** (✉ 35 pl. de la République, 13200, ☏ 04–90–18–41–21, FAX 04–90–93–17–17, WEB www.ville-arles.fr). **Avignon** (✉ 41 cours Jean-Jaurès, 84000, ☏ 04–90–82–65–11, FAX 04–90–82–95–03, WEB www.ot-avignon.fr). **Marseille** (✉ 4 La Canebière, 13001, ☏ 04–91–13–89–00, FAX 03–91–13–89–20, WEB www.marseille-tourisme.com). **Nîmes** (✉ 6 rue Auguste, 3000, ☏ 04–66–67–29–11, FAX 04–66–21–81–04, WEB www.ot-nimes.fr). **Orange** (✉ 5 cours A. Briand, 84100, ☏ 04–90–34–70–88, FAX 04–90–34–99–62, WEB www.provence-orange.com). **St-Rémy** (✉ Pl. Jean-Jaurès, 13210, ☏ 04–90–92–05–22, FAX 04–90–92–38–52, WEB www.saintremy-de-provence.com).

13 THE CÔTE D'AZUR

This is the Riviera of Hollywood lore, a land of sunglasses, convertibles, and palm trees lording it over indigo surf. From glamorous St-Tropez and Cannes through picturesque Antibes to sophisticated Nice, this sprawl of pebble beaches and ocher villas has captivated sun lovers and socialites since the days of the Grand Tour. Artists, too: Renoir, Matisse, Picasso, and Cocteau all reveled in its light and left an impressive legacy of modern art behind them. If you weary of the coast, it's three quick heel-clicks into another world: just behind the shore lie the golden hill towns of Old Provence: St-Paul, Vence, and Grasse.

Revised and updated by Chris Mooney

Introduction by Nancy Coons

WITH THE ALPS AND PRE-ALPS PLAYING bodyguard against inland winds and the sultry Mediterranean warming the breezes, the Côte d'Azur is pampered by a nearly tropical climate. This is where the dreamland of azure waters and indigo sky begins, with balustraded white villas edging the blue horizon, evening air perfumed with jasmine and mimosa, and parasol pines silhouetted against sunsets of ripe apricot and gold. As emblematic as the sheet-music cover for a Jazz Age tune, the Côte d'Azur seems to epitomize happiness, a state of being the world pursues with a vengeance.

But the Jazz Age dream confronts modern reality: on the hills that undulate along the blue water, every cliff, cranny, gully, and plain bristles with cubes of hot-pink cement and iron balconies, each skewed to catch a glimpse of the sea and the sun. Like a rosy rash, these crawl and spread, outnumbering the trees and blocking each other's views. Their owners and renters, who arrive on every vacation and at every holiday—Easter, Christmas, Carnival, All Saints' Day—choke the tiered highways with bumper-to-bumper cars, and on a hot day in high summer the traffic to the beach—slow-flowing at any time—coagulates and blisters in the sun.

There has always been a rush to the Côte d'Azur, starting with the ancient Greeks, who were drawn eastward from Marseille to market their goods to the natives. From the 18th-century English aristocrats who claimed it as one vast spa to the 19th-century Russian nobles who transformed Nice into a tropical St. Petersburg to the 20th-century American tycoons who cast themselves as romantic sheiks, the beckoning coast became a blank slate for their whims. Like the modern vacationers who followed, they all left their mark—villas, shrines, Moroccan-fantasy castles-in-the-air—temples all to the sensual pleasures of the sun and sultry sea breezes. Artists, too, made the Côte d'Azur their own, as museum goers who have studied the sunny legacy of Picasso, Renoir, Matisse, and Chagall will attest. Today's admirers can take this all in, along with the Riviera's textbook points of interest: animated St-Tropez; the Belle Epoque aura of Cannes; the towns made famous by Picasso—Antibes, Vallauris, Mougins; the urban charms of Nice; and several spots where the per-capita population of billionaires must be among the highest on the planet: Cap d'Antibes, Villefranche-sur-Mer, and Monaco. The latter, once a Belle Epoque fairyland, has for some time been known as the Hong Kong of the Riviera, a bustling community where the sounds of drills tearing up the ground for new construction has mostly replaced the clip-clop of the horse-drawn fiacres. The ghosts of Grace Kelly and Cary Grant must have long since gone elsewhere.

Veterans know that the beauty of the Côte d'Azur coastline is only skin deep, a thin veneer of coddled glamour that hugs the water and hides a much more ascetic region up in the hills. These low-lying mountains and deep gorges are known as the *arriére-pays* (backcountry) for good cause: they are as aloof and isolated as the waterfront resorts are in the swim. Medieval stone villages cap rocky hills and play out scenes of Provençal life—the game of boules, the slowly savored *pastis* (the anise-and-licorice-flavored spirit mixed slowly with water), the farmers' market—as if the ocean were a hundred miles away. Some of them—Èze, St-Paul, Vence—have become virtual Provençal theme parks, catering to busloads of tourists day-tripping from the coast. But just behind them, dozens of hill towns stand virtually untouched, and you can lose yourself in a cobblestone maze.

You could drive from St-Tropez to the border of Italy in three hours and take in the entire Riviera, so small is this renowned stretch of

Mediterranean coast. Along the way you'll undoubtedly encounter the downside: jammed beaches, insolent waiters serving frozen seafood, traffic gridlock. But once you dabble your feet off the docks in a picturesque port full of brightly painted boats, or drink a Lillet in a hilltop village high above the coast, or tip your face up to the sun from a boardwalk park bench and doze off to the rhythm of the waves, you—like the artists and nobles who paved the way before you—will very likely be seduced to linger.

Pleasures and Pastimes

Art

Because the Côte d'Azur has long nurtured a relationship among artists, art lovers, and wealthy patrons, this region is blessed with superb art museums. Renoir, Picasso, Matisse, Chagall, Cocteau, Léger, and Dufy all left their mark here; museums devoted to their work are scattered along the coast. Formidable collections of modern masters and contemporary works can be seen in the museums of Nice and at the Fondation Maeght above St-Paul. St-Tropez has a good collection of Impressionist paintings of its port at the Musée de l'Annonciade.

Beaches

With their worldwide fame as the earth's most glamorous beaches, the real thing often comes as a shock to first-timers: much of the Côte d'Azur is lined with rock and pebble, and the beaches are narrow swaths backed by city streets or roaring highways. Only St-Tropez and isolated bits around Fréjus and Antibes have sandy waterfronts, hence, their legendary popularity. Many beaches are privately operated, renting parasols and mattresses to anyone who pays; if you're a guest at one of the local hotels, you'll get a discount, but beach access is not included in the price of your stay. Fees for private beaches average €6–€10 for a dressing room and mattress, between €2 and €4 for a parasol, and between €4 and €5 for a cabana to call your own. Private beaches alternate with open stretches of public frontage served by free toilets and open showers.

Dining

Typical throughout Provence, but especially at home with a slab of fresh coastal fish, the garlicky mayonnaise called aioli is a staple condiment. Even more pungent is the powerful paste called *anchoiade,* made of strong, salty anchovies. The Provençal version of pesto, basil-y *pistou* flavors a hearty vegetable soup called *soupe au pistou.* Fresh Mediterranean fish, such as *rouget* (mullet) and *loup* (sea bass), are often served grilled with a crunch of fennel. Your plate may be garnished with ratatouille, or with zucchini flowers stuffed and fried in batter. Niçois specialties include the *pissaladière,* the father of modern pizza, topped with a heap of caramelized onions. It's a good picnic takeout, as is a hefty *pan bagnat,* a pitalike bun with tuna, hard-boiled eggs, tomatoes, and olives. Try *socca,* a paste of ground chickpeas smeared on a griddle and scraped up like a gritty pancake; *petits farcis,* a selection of red peppers, zucchini, and eggplant stuffed with spicy sausage paste and roasted; and sardine beignets, fresh, whole sardines fried in a thick puff of spicy batter.

CATEGORY	COST*
$$$$	over €30
$$$	€20–€30
$$	€12–€20
$	under €12

**per person for a main course only, including tax (19.6%) and service; note that if a restaurant offers only prix-fixe (set-price) meals, it has been placed in the price category that reflects the full prix-fixe price.*

Lodging

If you've come from other regions in France—even western Provence—you'll notice a sharp hike in hotel prices, costly by any measure, but actually vertiginous in summer. In Cannes and Nice the grand hotels are big on prestige and weak on swimming pools, which are usually just big enough to dip in; their private beaches are on the opposite side of the busy street, and you pay for access, just as nonguests do. It is up in the hills above the coast that you'll find the charm you expect from France, both in sophisticated hotels with gastronomic restaurants and in friendly mom-and-pop auberges (inns); the farther north you drive, the lower the prices.

Assume all hotel rooms have air-conditioning, TV, telephones, and private bath unless otherwise noted.

CATEGORY	COST*
$$$$	over €180
$$$	€120–€180
$$	€60–€120
$	under €60

**All prices are for a standard double room for two, including tax (19.6%) and service charge.*

Exploring the Côte d'Azur

You can visit any spot between St-Tropez and Menton in a day trip; the hilltop villages and towns on the coastal plateau are just as accessible. Thanks to the efficient raceway, A8, you can whisk at high speeds to the exit nearest your destination up or down the coast; thus, even if you like leisurely exploration, you can zoom back to your home base at day's end. Above the autoroute, things slow down considerably, but you'll find exploring the winding roads and overlooks between villages an experience in itself.

Great Itineraries

Numbers in the text correspond to numbers in the margin and on The Côte d'Azur: St-Tropez to Cannes; The Côte d'Azur: Cannes to Menton; Nice; and Monaco maps.

IF YOU HAVE 3 DAYS

Base yourself in **Antibes** ⑩, exploring the **Cap d'Antibes** ⑫—one of the few places in the region where the legend lingers; rich and residential, this 2-mi-long peninsula is studded with private delights (great villas) and public wonders (the Jardin Thuret). Make a day-trip westward to **Cannes** ⑧, a town that maintains its grand-tour grace and glamour even after the film stars head home from its famous film festival; then stop in Picasso country at **Vallauris** ⑭; or head inland for **St-Paul-de-Vence** ⑲ and **Vence** ⑱, two gorgeous hill towns famous for their art treasures (Matisse's *Chapelle du Rosaire* and the *Fondation Maeght* among them). On day three explore the museums and Old Town of **Nice** ㉒–㊴, where buildings are sumptuously adorned with wedding-cake half-domes and cupolas.

IF YOU HAVE 5 DAYS

Spend your first day and night in **St-Tropez** ①, whose fishing-village cachet translates into port-front cafés thick with young gentry affecting nonchalance but peeping furtively over their sunglasses in hope of sighting a film star, then make an excursion up to the hill villages of **Ramatuelle** ② and **Gassin** ③—the latter has a fetching medieval ambience. The next day cruise (or, in high summer, crawl along) the coastal highway N98, stopping to visit **Fréjus** ⑤, home to Roman ruins and a fine cathedral.

The Côte d'Azur: St-Tropez to Cannes

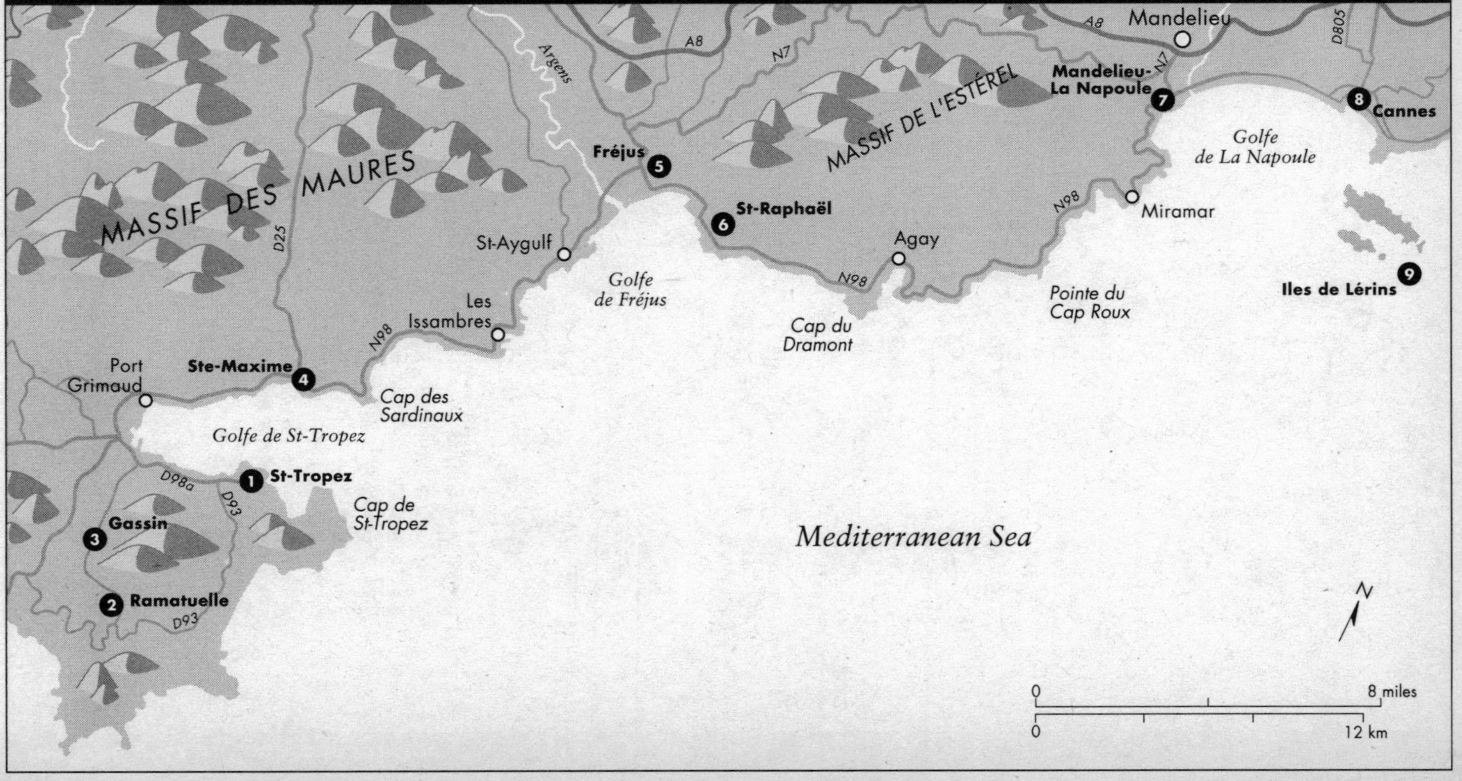

The Côte d'Azur: Cannes to Menton

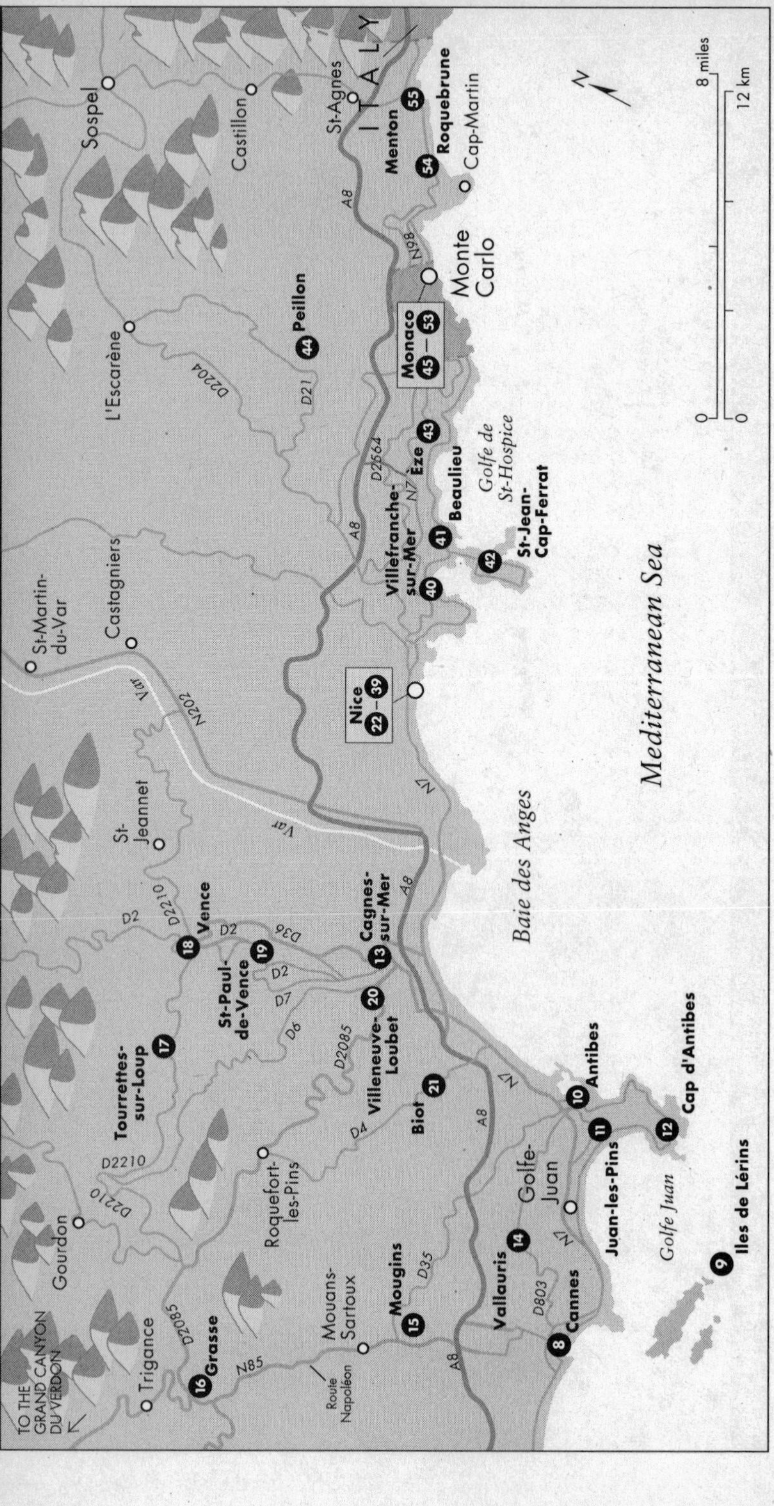

Still on N98, wind around the dramatic Corniche de l'Estérel and make a triumphant entry into **Cannes** ⑧, straight down La Croisette. Spend your third morning in **Antibes** ⑩—be sure to visit the famous Chateau Grimaldi and Picasso museum—then head inland for an afternoon in **St-Paul-de-Vence** ⑲ or **Vence** ⑱, both good stopovers (and where hotel dining rooms are often hung with Braque sketches). Day four could be spent in **Nice** ㉒–㊴, full of big-city textures, scents, and history, rich with museums, and colored with its own cuisine and patois. Then escape for a quiet night in **St-Jean-Cap-Ferrat** ㊷, a lush peninsula that shelters the lovely gardens of the Musee Ephrussi de Rothschild. On your last day bet your return ticket on the baccarat tables in **Monaco** ㊺–㊿.

IF YOU HAVE 10 DAYS

Expand the five-day itinerary with a second night in Cannes so you can make a boat trip to one of the idyllic **Iles de Lérins** ⑨. Spend two nights in Nice so you can take in the Matisse and Chagall museums and see the Baroque churches in the Old Town. Then spend two nights in **Menton** 55—some say this is the most romantic townscape on the Riviera—so you can visit the market and make an excursion to **Roquebrune** 54 to see its château and walk the length of the cape.

When to Tour

Unless you enjoy jacked-up prices, traffic jams, and sardine-style beach crowds, avoid the coast like the plague in July and August. Many of the better restaurants simply shut down to avoid the coconut-oil crowd, and the Estérel is closed to hikers during this flash-fire season. Cannes books up early for the film festival in May, so aim for another month (April, June, September, or October). Between Cannes and Menton, the Côte d'Azur's gentle microclimate usually provides moderate winters; it is protected by the Estérel from the mistral wind that razors through Fréjus and St-Raphaël.

ST-TROPEZ TO ANTIBES

Flanked at each end by subtropical capes and crowned by the red-rock Estérel, this stretch of the coast has a variety of waterfront landmarks. St-Tropez first blazed into fame when it was discovered by painters like Paul Signac and writers like Colette. Since then it has never looked back, and remains one of the most animated little stretches of territory on the Côte d'Azur, flooded at high season with people who like to roost at waterfront cafés and watch the passing parade. St-Tropez vies with Cannes for name recognition and glamour, but the more modest resorts—Ste-Maxime, Fréjus, and St-Raphaël—offer a more affordable Riviera experience. Historic Antibes and jazzy Juan-les-Pins straddle the subtropical peninsula of Cap d'Antibes.

St-Tropez

❶ *35 km (22 mi) southwest of Fréjus, 66 km (41 mi) northeast of Toulon.*

At first glance, it really doesn't look all that lovely: there's a moderately pretty port full of bobbing boats, a picturesque Old Town in candied-almond hues, sandy beaches, and old-fashioned squares with plane trees and *pétanque* (lawn bowling) players. So what made St-Tropez a household word? In two words: Brigitte Bardot. When this *pulpeuse* (voluptuous) teenager showed up in St-Tropez on the arm of the late Roger Vadim in 1956 to film *And God Created Woman,* the heads of the world snapped to attention. Neither the gentle descriptions of writer Guy de Maupassant (1850–93) nor the watercolor tones of Impressionist Paul Signac (1863–1935) nor the stream of painters who followed him (including Matisse and Bonnard) could focus the world's attention on this seaside hamlet as could this one luscious female, in head scarf, Ray-Bans, and capri pants. With the film world following in her steps, St-Tropez became the hot spot it to some extent remains. What makes it worthwhile is if you get up early (before the 11 o'clock breakfast rush at Le Gorille Café and other port-side spots lining quai Suffern and quai Jean-Jaurès) and wander the medieval backstreets and waterfront by yourself. You'll experience what the artists first found to love and what remains of the village's real charms: its soft light, warm pastels, and the scent of the sea wafting in from the waterfront.

Anything associated with the distant past almost seems absurd in St-Tropez. Still, the place has a history that predates the invention of the string bikini, and people have been finding reasons to come here since AD 68, when a Roman soldier from Pisa named Torpes was beheaded for professing his Christian faith in front of Emperor Nero, transforming this spot into a place of pilgrimage. Since then people have come for the sun, the sea, and, much more recently, the celebrities. The latter stay hidden in villas, so the people you'll see are mere mortals, lots of them, many intent on displaying the best (or at least the most) of their youth, beauty, and wealth. Still, if you take an early morning stroll along the harbor or down the narrow medieval streets—the rest of the town will still be sleeping off the Night Before—you'll see just how charming St-Tropez is, with its tiny squares and rich pastel-color houses. There's a weekend's worth of boutiques to explore and many cute cafés where you can sit under colored awnings and watch the spectacle that is St-Trop (*trop* in French means too much) saunter by.

The legacy of the artists who loved St-Tropez has been preserved in ★ the extraordinary **Musée de l'Annonciade** (Annunciation Museum), a 14th-century chapel converted to an art museum that alone merits a visit to St-Tropez. Works by Signac, Matisse, Signard, Braque, Dufy, Vuillard, and Rouault, many of them painted in (and about) St-Tropez, trace the evolution of painting from Impressionism to Expressionism. ✉ *Quai de l'Épi/pl. Georges Grammont,* ☎ *04–94–97–04–01.* 🎫 *€5.5.* ⏲ *June–Sept., Wed.–Mon. 10–noon and 3–7; Oct.–May, Wed.–Mon. 10–noon and 2–6.*

From the quai, head up rue Laugier and rue de la Citadelle to the 16th-century **Citadelle,** which stands in a lovely hilltop park. Inside its donjon the **Musée Naval** (Naval Museum) displays ship models, cannons, and pictures of St-Tropez from its days as a naval port. ✉ *Rue de la Citadelle,* ☎ *04–94–97–59–43.* 🎫 *€4.* ⏲ *Dec.–Easter, Wed.–Mon. 10–noon and 1–5; Easter–Oct., daily 10–6.*

From the citadel head back down and lose yourself in the **Quartier de la Ponche,** the Old Town maze of backstreets and old ramparts daubed in shades of gold, pink, ocher, and sky-blue. Trellised jasmine and wrought-iron birdcages hang from shuttered windows, and many of the tiny streets dead-end at the sea. Wander back across rue Citadelle to the medieval rue Miséricorde, which leads to the 17th-century Chapelle de la Miséricorde, and on to rue Gambetta.

Dining and Lodging

$$$$ ✕ **Les Mouscardins.** Breton-born chef Laurent Tarridec has left the Bistrot des Lices for a spectacular seaside locale offering 180-degree sea views, just on the edge of St-Tropez's Old Town. His cooking, however, maintains the sophisticated tradition of upscale Provençal cuisine: opt for a frothy mullet soup, an earthy *galette* of chestnuts and morel mushrooms, the house bourride, or the tender, long-simmered veal. Fixed-price menus are €43 and €56. ✉ *Tour du Portalet,* ☎ *04–94–97–29–00. AE, DC, MC, V. Closed mid-Nov.–mid-Dec. and mid-Jan.–mid-Feb.*

$$ ✕ **Lou Revelen.** Strike a pose on the throw-pillow-y couch by the fireplace or people-watch from the terrace: this smart, stagy restaurant caters to the glamorous and their wanna-bes. There's also, not incidentally, good Provençal cooking: try duck carpaccio, garlicky-sweet eggplant terrine, or basil-perfumed lamb; the fennel-grilled fish of the day is a mainstay. ✉ *4 rue des Remparts,* ☎ *04–94–97–06–34. MC, V.*

$–$$ ✕ **Le Girelier.** Like his father before him, chef Yves Rouet makes an effort to prepare Mediterranean-only fish for his buffed and bronzed clientele, who enjoy the casual sea-shanty decor and the highly visible Vieux Port terrace tables. Grilling is the order of the day, with most fish sold by weight, but this is also a stronghold of bouillabaisse. ✉ *Quai Jean-Jaurès,* ☎ *04–94–97–03–87. AE, DC, MC, V. Closed Oct.–Mar. (with the occasional exception).*

$$$$ ✕🏨 **Le Byblos.** Arranged like a toy Provençal village, fronted with stunning red, rust, and yellow facades, and complete with ocher-stucco cottagelike suites grouped around courtyards landscaped with palms, olive trees, and lavender, this landmark stresses fitness and beauty treatment. Guest rooms are *à la Provencal* but modern in comfort. Chef Georges Pelissier creates artful classics with a Mediterranean touch: sea bass roasted with salsify and garlic chips or rib-sticking beef tournedos with foie gras. Or opt for more nouvelle Med fireworks on offer at the new **Spoon Byblos** (✉ entrance on Ave. du Maréchal-Foch, ☎ ☎ 04–94–56–68–20), the latest outpost of superstar chef Alain Ducasse. At evening, all head to the hotel's Caves du Roy—a gigantic disco extravaganza. ✉ *Av. Paul-Signac, 83990,* ☎ *04–94–56–68–00,* FAX *04–94–56–68–01,* WEB *www.byblos.com. 80 rooms, 11 suites. 2 restaurants, cable TV, minibars, Internet, health center, meeting room, pool, gym, spa, nightclub. AE, DC, MC, V. Closed mid-Oct.–Easter.*

$$$$ ✕🏨 **La Résidence de la Pinède.** Perhaps the most opulent of St. Tropez's luxe hangouts, this balustraded white villa and its broad annex sprawl elegantly along a private waterfront, wrapped around an isolated courtyard and a pool shaded by parasol pines. Louis XVI bérgères, a beam here and there, gilt frames, indirect spots, and oh-so-comfy beds make for a cosetting if overly homogenized interior. Pay extra for a seaside room, where you can lean over the balcony and take in broad views of the coast and the large seafront restaurant; the chef has a celebrated reputation, and you'll understand why after one taste of his truffled ravioli. ✉ *Plage de la Bouillabaisse, 83991,* ☎ *04–94–55–91–00,* FAX *04–94–97–73–64,* WEB *www.residencepinede.com. 39 rooms, 4 suites. Restaurant, cable TV, minibars, Internet, pool, meeting room. AE, DC, MC, V. Closed mid-Oct.–Mar.*

$$–$$$ 🏨 **Ermitage.** Surrounded by mimosas and lemon trees, this big, old-fashioned, tangerine-hued hotel is on a hill above town and, from its back rooms and garden, commands striking sea views. The fireplace and colonial rattan in the bar; the solid, light-bathed rooms in soft pastels; and owner Annie Bolloreis's friendly welcome make this a real charmer. ✉ *Av. Paul-Signac, 83990,* ☎ *04–94–97–52–33,* FAX *04–94–97–10–43. 26 rooms. Bar, no air-conditioning. MC, V.*

$$ ★ 🏨 **Lou Cagnard.** Inside an enclosed garden courtyard, this pretty little hotel is owned by an enthusiastic young couple who are fixing it up room by room. Five ground-floor rooms open onto the lovely manicured garden, where breakfast is served in the shade of a fig tree. Freshly decorated rooms have regional tiles and Provençal fabrics. ✉ *18 av. Paul Roussel, 83900,* ☎ *04–94–97–04–24,* FAX *04–94–97–09–44. 19 rooms. No air-conditioning. MC, V. Closed Nov.–late Dec.*

Nightlife and the Arts

The most elite and sought-after nightspot in St-Tropez is the evergreen **Les Caves du Roy,** in the Byblos Hotel (✉ Av. Paul-Signac, ☎ 04–94–

97–16–02). **Le Papagayo** (✉ Résidence du Port, ☎ 04–94–54–88–18), a vast disco, caters to a crowd of young teens and twentysomethings. The **VIP Room** (✉ Residence du Port, ☎ 04–94–97–14–70) draws a chic mix of young professionals and baby boomers. Every July and August, **classical music concerts** are given in the gardens of the Château de la Moutte (✉ Rte. des Salins). For ticket information inquire at the tourist office (☎ 04–94–97–45–21).

Outdoor Activities and Sports

The best ***plages*** (beaches) are scattered along a 5-km (3-mi) stretch reached by the Route des Plages (Beach Road); the most fashionable are **Moorea, Tahiti,** and **Club 55.** Those beaches close to town—**Plage des Greniers** and the **Bouillabaisse**—are accessible on foot, but many prefer the 10-km (6-mi) sandy crescent at **Les Salins** and the long sandy stretch of the **Plage de Pampelonne,** 4 km (3 mi) from town. Bicycles are an ideal way to get to the beach; try **Espace 93** (✉ 2 av. Général-Leclerc, ☎ 04–94–55–80–00) or **Holiday Bikes** (✉ 14 av. Général-Leclerc, ☎ 04–94–97–09–39).

Shopping

Rue Sibilli, behind the quai Suffren, is lined with all kinds of trendy boutiques. The **place des Lices** overflows with produce, regional foods, clothing, and *brocantes* (collectibles) on Tuesday and Saturday mornings. The picturesque little fish market fills up **place aux Herbes** every morning.

Ramatuelle

❷ *12 km (7 mi) southwest of St-Tropez.*

A typical hilltop whorl of red-clay roofs and dense inner streets topped with arches and lined with arcades, this ancient market town was destroyed in the Wars of Religion and rebuilt as a harmonious whole in 1620, complete with venerable archways and vaulted passages. Now its souvenir shops and galleries attract day-trippers out of St-Tropez, who enjoy the pretty drive through the vineyards as much as the village itself. The town cemetery is the final resting place of Gérard Phillipe, an aristocratic heartthrob who died in 1959 after making his mark in such films as *Le Diable au Corps.*

En Route From Ramatuelle the lovely ride to the hilltop village of Gassin takes you through vineyards and woods full of twisted cork oaks over the highest point of the peninsula (1,070 ft).

Dining and Lodging

$$$–$$$$ ✕🏨 **Les Moulins.** A satellite of planet St-Tropez, this new outpost of showbiz chef Christophe Leroy lures off-duty celebrities and the swank to its lovely perch near Pampelonne beach. Ceiling fans, rattan chairs, and blonde-wood accents heighten the pleasure of the scrumptious dishes served here—don't miss out on the vichyssoise with truffles. Upstairs are five cozy, rustic guest rooms. ✉ *Route des Plages, 83350,* ☎ *04–94–97–17–22,* FAX *04–94–79–72–70. 5 rooms. Restaurant, cable TV. AE, MC, V. Closed Nov.–Mar.*

$$ ✕🏨 **Ferme Ladouceur.** Not far from the talcum-powder beach of Pampelonne and surrounded by vineyards is this *naif* farmhouse, domain of Constance Ladouceur, whose paintings adorn the hallways and whose restaurant is a draw for budget-minded locals. Quirky, simple, affordable—little wonder you need to book here far in advance. ✉ *Quartier La Rouillère, 83350,* ☎ *04–94–79–24–22,* FAX *04–94–79–12–14. 7 rooms. Restaurant, no air-conditioning, no room phones, no room TVs. AE, MC, V. Closed Nov.–Mar.*

Gassin

❸ *7 km (4 mi) north of Ramatuelle.*

Though not as picturesque as Ramatuelle, this hilltop village gives you spectacular views over the surrounding vineyards and St-Tropez's bay. In winter, before the summer haze drifts in and after the mistral has given the sky a good scrub, you may be able to make out a brilliant white chain of Alps looming on the horizon. There's less commerce here to keep you distracted; for shops, head to Ramatuelle.

Dining and Lodging

$$$$ ★ **Villa Belrose.** This spanking-new Hollywood palace, perched on the highest point of the peninsula, has unrivaled views of the Gulf of St-Tropez and the kind of decadently rich élan that would make Scott and Zelda feel right at home. Rooms are spacious yet cozy, with marble bathrooms and romantic balconies. Besides the 180-degree views, the restaurant, run by Alain Ducasse disciple Thierry Thiercelin, supplies first-rate Mediterranean cuisine, pleasant service, and a top-drawer wine list. ✉ *Bd. Crète, 83580,* ☏ *04–94–55–97–97,* FAX *04–94–55–97–98. 36 rooms, 2 suites. Restaurant, bar, minibars, Internet, pool, spa. AE, DC, MC, V. Closed Nov.–Feb.*

Ste-Maxime

❹ *8 km (5 mi) east of Port-Grimaud, 33 km (20 mi) east of St-Tropez.*

You may be put off by the heavily built-up waterfront bristling with parking-garage-style apartments and hotels, and its position directly on the waterfront highway, but Ste-Maxime is an affordable family resort with fine sandy beaches. It even has a sliver of car-free Old Town and a stand of majestic plane trees sheltering central place Victor-Hugo. The main beach, north of town, is the wide and sandy La Nartelle.

Fréjus

❺ *19 km (12 mi) northeast of Ste-Maxime, 37 km (23 mi) northeast of St-Tropez.*

After a stroll on the sandy curve along the tacky, overcommercial Fréjus-Plage (Fréjus Beach), turn your back on modern times and head uphill to Fréjus-Centre. Here you'll enter a maze of narrow streets lined with small shops barely touched by the cult of the lavender sachet. The farmers' market (Monday, Wednesday, and Saturday mornings) is as real and lively as any in Provence, and the cafés encircling the fountains and squares nourish an easygoing social scene.

Yet Fréjus has the honor of owning some of the most important historic monuments on the coast. Founded in 49 BC by Julius Caesar himself and named Forum Julii, this quiet town was once a thriving Roman city of 40,000 citizens. Today you can see the remains: just outside the Old Town is the Roman **Théâtre Antique**; its remaining rows of arches are mostly intact, and much of its stage works is still visible at its center. The **Arènes** (often called the Amphithéâtre) is still used today for concerts and bullfights. Back down on the coast, a big French naval base occupies the spot where ancient Roman galleys once set out to defeat Cleopatra and Mark Anthony at the Battle of Actium.

★ Fréjus is also graced with one of the most impressive religious monuments in Provence: called the **Groupe Épiscopal,** it's made up of an early Gothic **cathedral,** a 5th-century Roman-style **baptistery,** and an early Gothic **cloister,** its gallery painted in sepia and earth tones with a phantasmagoric assortment of animals and biblical characters. Off the entrance and gift shop is a small museum of finds from Roman Fréjus, including a complete mosaic and a sculpture of a two-headed Hermès. ✉ *58 rue de Fleury,* ☎ *04–94–51–26–30.* *Cathedral free; cloister, museum, and baptistery €4.* ⏲ *Cathedral daily 8:30–noon and 2–6. Cloister, museum, and baptistery Apr.–Sept., daily 9–7; Oct.–Mar., Tues.–Sun. 9–noon and 2–5.*

St-Raphaël

❻ *1 km (½ mi) southeast of Fréjus, 41 km (25½ mi) southwest of Cannes.*

Right next door to Fréjus, with almost no division between, is St-Raphaël, a sprawling resort town with a busy downtown anchored by a casino. It's also a major sailing center, has five golf courses nearby, and draws the weary and indulgent to its seawater-based thalassotherapy. It serves as a major rail crossroads, the closest stop to St-Tropez. The port has a rich history: Napoléon landed at St-Raphaël on his triumphant return from Egypt in 1799; it was also from here in 1814 that he cast off for Elba in disgrace. And it was here, too, that the Allied forces landed in their August 1944 offensive against the Germans.

Dining and Lodging

$$$ ✕ **La Bouillabaisse.** Enter through the beaded curtain covering the open doorway to a wood-paneled room decked out with starfish and the mounted head of a swordfish: this classic hole-in-the-wall has a brief, straightforward menu inspired by the fish markets. You might have the half lobster with spicy *rouille* (peppers and garlic whipped with olive oil), the seafood-stuffed paella, or the generous house bouillabaisse. ✉ *50 pl. Victor-Hugo,* ☎ *04–94–95–03–57. AE, MC, V. Closed Mon.*

$$–$$$ **Excelsior.** This urban hotel has been under the careful management of one family for three generations. Its combination of straightforward comforts and a waterfront position in the center of town attracts a regular clientele. Rooms are plush and pastel, bathrooms up to date. ✉ *Promenade du Pdt-René Coty, 83700,* ☎ *04–94–95–02–42,* FAX *04–94–95–33–82,* WEB *www.excelsior-hotel.com. 36 rooms. Restaurant, café, cable TV, minibars. AE, DC, MC, V.*

$ ★ **Le Thimothée.** The new owners of this bargain lodging are throwing themselves wholeheartedly into improving an already attractive 19th-century villa. They've also restored the garden, with its grand palms and pines shading the walk to the pretty little swimming pool. Though it's tucked away in a neighborhood far from the waterfront, top-floor rooms have poster-perfect sea views. ✉ *375 bd. Christian-Lafon, 83700,* ☎ *04–94–40–49–49,* FAX *04–94–19–41–92,* WEB *www.provenceweb.fr/83/thimothee. 12 rooms. No air-conditioning in some rooms, cable TV, minibars, pool. AE, MC, V.*

En Route The rugged **Massif de l'Estérel,** between St-Raphaël and Cannes, is a hiker's dream. Made up of rust-red volcanic rocks (porphyry) carved by the sea into dreamlike shapes, the harsh landscape (now made even harsher due to the ravages of forest fires set by greedy developers) is softened by patches of lavender, scrub pine, and gorse. Take N7, the mountain route to the north, to lose yourself in the desert landscape far from the sea. Or stay on N98, the **Corniche de l'Estérel** (the coastal road along the dramatic corniche), past tiny calanques and sheer rock faces plunging down to the waves.

Mandelieu–La Napoule

❼ *32 km (20 mi) northeast of St-Raphaël, 8 km (5 mi) southwest of Cannes.*

La Napoule is the small, old-fashioned port village devoured by the big-fish resort town of Mandelieu. You can visit Mandelieu for a golf-and-sailing retreat—the town is replete with many sporting facilties and hosts a bevy of sporting events, including sailing regattas, windsurfing contests, golf championships (there are two major golf courses in Mandelieu right in the center of town by the sea), and, every August, the Kelly Challenge, a rowing regatta named after Grace Kelly's father, who was a keen oarsman—and La Napoule for a port-side stroll, a meal, or a tour of its peculiar castle.

Set on Pointe des Pendus (Hanged Man's Point), the **Château de la Napoule,** looming over the sea and the port, is a bizarre hybrid of Romanesque, Gothic, Moroccan, and Hollywood cooked up by the eccentric American sculptor Henry Clews. Working with his architect wife, he transformed the 14th-century bastion into something that suited his own expectations and then filled the place with his fantastical sculptures. Today, the château's foundation hosts visiting writers and artists, who set to work surrounded by Clews's gargoyle-ish sculptures. ✉ *Av. Henry Clews,* ☎ *04–93–49–95–05.* 🎫 *€4.* ⏲ *Guided visits Mar.–June and Sept.–Nov., Wed.–Mon. at 3 and 4; July–Aug., Wed.–Mon. at 3, 4, and 5.*

Dining and Lodging

$$$–$$$$ ✕ **L'Oasis.** This gothic villa by the sea is home to Stéphane Raimbault, a master of Provençal cuisine and a great connoisseur of Asian techniques and flavorings. The combination creates unexpected delights—Jabugo ham with anise, lobster, and ginger, or Thai-spiced crayfish with squid-ink ravioli—and, sometimes, as is inevitable with all artists, the odd disaster, like foie gras served on a bed of Swiss chard and drowned in vinegar. More often than not, however, Raimbault delivers on his promise. ✉ *Rue J. H. Carle,* ☎ *04–93–49–95–52. AE, DC, MC, V.*

$$–$$$ ★ ✕ **Le Boucanier.** The drab, low-ceiling dining room is upstaged by wraparound plate-glass views of the marina and château at this waterfront favorite. Locals gather here for mountains of oysters and whole fish, simply grilled and served with a drizzle of fruity olive oil, a pinch of rock salt, or a brief flambé in pastis. ✉ *Port La Napoule,* ☎ *04–93–49–80–51. AE, DC, MC, V.*

$$$–$$$$ 🏨 **Le Domaine d'Olival.** Set back from the coast on its own vast landscaped grounds along the Siagne River, this inn has a Provençal feel that belies its waterfront-resort situation. Bright rooms with country-fresh fabrics have built-in furniture and small kitchenettes. Balconies, ideal for breakfast, overlook the semitropical garden. ✉ *778 av. de la Mer, 06210,* ☎ *04–93–49–31–00,* FAX *04–92–97–69–28,* WEB *www.hotels-tradition.com/olival. 7 rooms, 11 suites. Cable TV, minibars, Internet, tennis court, pool. AE, DC, MC, V. Closed Nov.–mid-Jan.*

Outdoor Activities and Sports

The **Golf Club de Cannes-Mandelieu** (✉ Rte. du Golf, ☎ 04–92–97–32–00) is one of the most beautiful in the south of France; It is bliss to play on English turf, under Mediterranean pines with mimosa blooming here and there in the spring. The club has two courses—one with 18 holes (par 71) and one with nine (par 33).

Cannes

8 *73 km (45 mi) northeast of St-Tropez, 33 km (20 mi) southwest of Nice, 908 km (563 mi) southeast of Paris.*

A tasteful and expensive breeding ground for the upscale (and those who are already "up"), Cannes is a sybaritic heaven for those who believe that life is short and sin has something to do with the absence of a tan. Backed by gentle hills and flanked to the south by the Estérel, warmed by dependable sun but kept bearable in summer by the cool Mediterranean breeze, Cannes is pampered with the luxurious climate that has made it one of the most popular and glamorous resorts in Europe. For 150 years the cynosure of sun worshipers, it has been further glamorized by the success of its film festival.

Its bay served as nothing more than a fishing port until 1834, when an English aristocrat, Lord Brougham, made an emergency stopover with his sick daughter and fell in love with the site. He had a home built here and returned every winter for a sun cure—a ritual quickly picked up by his peers. With the democratization of modern travel, Cannes has become a tourist and convention town; there are now 20 compact Twingos for every Rolls-Royce. But glamour—and the perception of glamour—is self-perpetuating, and as long as Cannes enjoys its ravishing climate and setting, it will maintain its incomparable panache. If you're a culture-lover into art of the noncelluloid type, however, you should look elsewhere—there is only one museum here, and that one is devoted to history. Still, as his lordship understood, this is a great place to pass the winter.

Pick up a map at the tourist office in the **Palais des Festivals,** the scene of the famous Festival International du Film, known as the Cannes Film Festival. As you leave the information center, follow the Palais to your right to see the red-carpeted stairs where the stars ascend every year. Set into the surrounding pavement, the **Allée des Etoiles** (Stars' Walk) enshrines some 300 autographed imprints of film stars' hands—of Dépardieu, Streep, and Stallone, among others.

The most delightful thing to do is to head to the famous mile-long waterfront promenade, **La Croisette,** which starts at the western end by the Palais des Festivals, and let the *esprit de Cannes* take control. This is precisely the sort of place for which the verb *flâner* (to dawdle, saunter) was invented, so stroll through the palm trees and flowers and crowds of strolling poseurs (furs coats in tropical weather, cell phones on Rollerblades, and sunglasses at night). Head east past the broad expanse of private beaches, glamorous shops, and luxurious hotels (such as the wedding-cake Carlton, famed for its see-and-be-seen terrace-level brasserie). The beaches along here are almost all private, though open for a fee—each beach is marked with between one and four little lifebuoys, rating their quality and expense.Two blocks behind La Croisette lies **rue d'Antibes,** Cannes's main high-end shopping street. At its western end is **rue Meynadier,** packed tight with trendy clothing boutiques and fine food shops. Just beyond, the covered **Marché Forville** is the scene of the animated morning food market.

Climb up rue St-Antoine into the picturesque Old Town neighborhood known as **Le Suquet,** on the site of the original Roman *castrum*. Shops proffer Provençal goods, and the atmospheric theme restaurants give you a chance to catch your breath; the pretty pastel shutters, Gothic stonework, and narrow passageways are lovely distractions. The hill is crowned by the 11th-century château, housing the **Musée de la Castre,** and the imposing four-sided **Tour du Suquet** (Suquet Tower), built in 1385 as a lookout against Saracen-led invasions. ✉ *Pl. de la Castre, Le Suquet,* ☎ *04–93–38–55–26.* 🎫 *€1.5.* ⏲ *Apr.–June, Wed.–Mon. 10–noon and 2–6; July–Sept., Wed.–Mon. 10–noon and 3–7; Oct.–Dec. and Feb.–Mar., Wed.–Mon. 10–noon and 2–5.*

Dining and Lodging

$–$$ ✕ **La Mère Besson.** This long-standing favorite continues to please a largely foreign clientele with its regional specialties such as sweet-and-sour sardines *à l'escabèche* (marinated), monkfish Provençal (with tomatoes, fennel, and onion), and roast lamb with garlic puree. The formality of the damask linens and still-life paintings is moderated by clatter from the open kitchen. The lunch menu is €15; dinners are €22 and €26. ✉ *13 rue des Frères-Pradignac, La Croisette,* ☎ *04–93–39–59–24. AE, DC, MC, V. Closed Sun. Sept.–June. No lunch Sat. and Mon., except during festivals.*

$–$$ ★ ✕ **Montagard.** This extraordinary newcomer serves elegant, imaginative vegetarian cuisine—rare in France—in a chic, low-key setting. A turnover stuffed with pumpkin and chestnuts may be trimmed with deep-fried pumpkin rings and ruby beet chips, or you may select from a choice of three fish. Strains of Keith Jarrett waft through the artful mise-en-scène, with its high-design chairs and warm shades of ocher. Fixed-menu prices start at €18. ✉ *6 rue Maréchal Joffre, La Croisette,* ☎ *04–93–39–98–38. MC, V. Closed Sun.–Mon.*

$ ✕ **Bouchon d'Objectif.** Popular and unpretentious, this tiny bistro serves inexpensive Provençal menus prepared with a sophisticated twist. Watch for terrine of hare with sultanas and Armagnac, stuffed sardines, or a trio of fresh fish with aioli. An ever-changing gallery display of photography adds a hip touch to the simple ocher-and-aqua room. ✉ *10 rue Constantine, La Croisette,* ☎ *04–93–99–21–76. AE, MC, V. Closed Mon.*

$$$$ ★ **Carlton Inter-Continental.** As one of the turn-of-the-19th-century pioneers of this resort town, this deliciously pompous neoclassical landmark quickly staked out the best position: La Croisette seems to radiate symmetrically from its figurehead waterfront site. Seafront rooms have a retro Laura Ashley look; those on the back compensate with cheery Provençal prints. The restaurant is luxe, the brasserie swank, and the Bar des Célébrités lives up to its name during the film festival. ✉ *58 bd. de la Croisette, La Croisette 06414,* ☎ *04–93–06–40–06,* FAX *04–93–06–40–25,* WEB *www.interconti.com. 295 rooms, 18 suites. 3 restaurants, bar, no-smoking rooms, cable TV, minibars, Internet, health club, beach, casino, meeting room, parking (fee). AE, DC, MC, V.*

$$$$ **Majestic.** Classical statuary and tapestries set the aristocratic tone at this other La Croisette "palace"; it is grand but gracious, with a quieter feel than most of its neighbors. Its romantic poolside terrace and Egyptian/Art Deco bar give a nod to cinematic glamour. Ask for one of the rooms newly redone in retro style. ✉ *14 bd. de la Croisette, La Croisette 06400,* ☎ *04–92–98–77–00,* FAX *04–93–38–97–90,* WEB *www.lucienbarriere.com. 305 rooms, 23 suites. Restaurant, bar, cable TV, minibars, Internet, pool, sauna, health club, meeting room, parking (fee). AE, DC, MC, V. Closed mid-Nov.–Dec.*

$$–$$$ **Splendid.** If you covet a waterfront position but can't afford the grand hotels on La Croisette, consider this traditional 1873 palace overlooking La Pantiéro and the old port. Rooms are a bit creaky but sleekly decorated, and though the bathrooms have '60s tiling, they're well maintained. There are flowers and fruit in rooms, robes and kitchenettes in those with sea views, and pretty Provençal furniture in the breakfast room. ✉ *Allées de la Liberté, entrance at 4–6 rue Félix-Faure, La Croisette 06407,* ☎ *04–93–99–53–11,* FAX *04–93–99–55–02. 64 rooms. Cable TV, minibars, kitchenettes. AE, DC, MC, V.*

$$ ★ **Molière.** Plush, intimate, and low-key, this hotel, a short stroll from the Croisette, has pretty tile baths and small rooms in cool shades of peach, indigo, and white-waxed oak. Nearly all overlook the vast, enclosed front garden, where palms and cypresses shade terrace tables, and breakfast is served most of the year. ✉ *5 rue Molière, La Croisette 06400,* ☎ *04–93–38–16–16,* FAX *04–93–68–29–57. 42 rooms. Cable TV, minibars. AE, MC, V. Closed mid-Nov.–end Dec.*

$ **Albert Ier.** In a quiet residential area above the Forville market—a 10-minute walk uphill from La Croisette and the beach—this neo-Deco mansion has pretty rooms in pastels, as well as tidy tile baths and an enclosed garden. You can have breakfast on the flowered, shady terrace or in the family-style salon. The hotel has had the same owner since 1980, and it shows. ✉ *68 av. de Grasse, Le Suquet 06400,* ☎ *04–93–39–24–04,* FAX *04–93–38–83–75. 11 rooms. No air-conditioning, cable TV, minibars, free parking. MC, V.*

Nightlife and the Arts

The Riviera's cultural calendar is splashy and star-studded, and never more so than during the **International Film Festival** in May. The film screenings are not open to the public, so unless you have a pass, your star-studded glimpses will be on the streets or in restaurants (though if you hang around in a tux, a stray ticket might come your way).

As befits a glamorous seaside resort, Cannes has two casinos. The famous **Casino Croisette** (✉ in Palais des Festivals, La Croisette, ☎ 04–92–98–78–00) draws more crowds to its slot machines than any other casino in France. The **Carlton Casino Club** (✉ 58 bd. de la Croisette, La Croisette, ☎ 04–92–99–51–00) retains an exclusive atmosphere in its posh seventh-floor hideaway.

To make the correct entrance at the popular **Le Cat Corner** (✉ 22 rue Macé, La Croisette, ☎ 04–93–39–31–31), have yourself whisked by limo from the steak house Le Farfalla. **Jimmy'z** (✉ Palais des Festivals, La Croisette, ☎ 04–93–68–00–07) cabaret shows are legendary. After many metamorphoses, **César Palace** (✉ 48 bd. de la République, La Croisette, ☎ 04–93–68–23–23) remains one of the main disco draws.

Outdoor Activities and Sports

Most of the **beaches** along La Croisette are owned by hotels and/or restaurants, though this doesn't necessarily mean the hotels or restaurants front the beach. It does mean they own a patch of beachfront bearing their name, where they rent out chaises longues, mats, and umbrellas to the public and hotel guests (who also have to pay). Public beaches are between the color-coordinated private beach umbrellas and offer simple open showers and basic toilets.

Sailboats can be rented from **Camper & Nicholson's** (✉ Port Canto, La Croisette) and the **Yacht Club de Cannes** (✉ Palm Beach Port, La Croisette). Windsurfing equipment is available from **Le Club Nautique La Croisette** (✉ Plage Pointe Palm-Beach, La Croisette) and the **Centre Nautique Municipal** (✉ 9 rue Esprit-Violet, La Croisette). The **Majestic Ski Club** (Ponton du Majestic; ✉ At Majestic's private beach, La Croisette, ☎ 04–92–98–77–47) can take you waterskiing or pull you on a ski-board, an inflatable chair, or take you up over the water on a parachute.

Iles de Lérins

❾ *15–20 minutes by ferry off the coast of Cannes.*

When you're glutted on glamour, you may want to make a day trip to the peaceful Iles de Lérins (Lérins Islands); boats depart from Cannes's Vieux Port. Allow at least a half day to enjoy either of the islands; you can see both only if you get an early start. You have two options: **Horizon/Caribes Company** (✉ Jetée Edouard, ☎ 04–92–98–71–36) or the less comfortable **Estérel Chanteclair** (✉ Promenade La Pantiéro, ☎ 04–93–39–11–82).

It's a 15-minute, €9 round-trip to **Ile Ste-Marguerite.** Its Fort Royal, built by Richelieu and improved by Vauban, offers views over the ramparts to the rocky island coast and the open sea.

Behind the prison buildings is the **Musée de la Mer** (Marine Museum), with its Roman boat dating from the 1st century BC and its collection of amphorae and pottery recovered from ancient shipwrecks. ☎ *04–93–43–18–17.* ✉ *€1.5.* ⏲ *Oct.–Dec. and Feb.–Mar., Wed.–Mon. 10:30–12:15 and 2:15–4:30; Apr.–June and Sept., Wed.–Mon. 10:30–12:15 and 2:15–5:30; July–Aug., Wed.–Mon. 10:30–12:15 and 2:15–6:30.*

Ile St-Honorat can be reached in 20 minutes (€9 round-trip) from the Vieux Port. Smaller and wilder than Ste-Marguerite, it is home to an active monastery and the ruins of its 11th-century predecessor.

Antibes

❿ *11 km (7 mi) northeast of Cannes, 15 km (9 mi) southeast of Nice.*

With its broad stone ramparts scalloping in and out over the waves and backed by blunt medieval towers and a skew of tile roofs, Antibes is one of the most romantic old towns on the Mediterranean coast. As gateway to the Cap d'Antibes, Antibes's Port Vauban Harbor has some of the largest yachts in the world tied up at its berths—their millionaire owners won't find a more dramatic spot to anchor, with the tableau of the snowy Alps looming behind and the formidable medieval block towers of the Fort Carré guarding entry to the port. Stroll Promenade Amiral-de-Grasse along the crest of Vauban's sea walls, and you'll understand why Picasso was inspired here to paint on a panoramic scale. Yet a few steps inland you'll enter a souklike maze of atmospheric old streets.

To visit Old Antibes, pass through the **Porte Marine,** an arched gateway in the rampart wall. Follow rue Aubernon to **cours Masséna,** where the little sheltered market sells lemons, olives, and hand-stuffed sausages, and the vendors take breaks in the shoebox cafés flanking one side. From cours Masséna head up to the **Église de l'Immaculée-Conception** (✉ Pl. de la Cathédrale), which served as the region's cathedral until the bishopric was transferred to Grasse in 1244. Its stout medieval watchtower was built in the 11th century with stones "mined" from Roman structures. Inside is a Baroque altarpiece painted by the Niçois artist Louis Bréa in 1515.

★ Next door to the cathedral, the medieval **Château Grimaldi** rises high over the water on a Roman foundation. The Grimaldi family—which still rules Monaco today in the person of Prince Rainier—lived here until the Revolution, but this fine old castle was little more than a monument until in 1946 its curator offered use of its vast chambers to Picasso, and at a time when that extraordinary genius was enjoying a period of intense creative energy. The result is now housed in the **Musée Picasso,** a bounty of exhilarating paintings, ceramics, and lithographs inspired by the sea and by Greek mythology—all very Mediterranean. Even those who are not great Picasso fans should enjoy his vast paintings on wood, canvas, paper, and walls, alive with nymphs, fauns, and centaurs. The museum houses more than 300 works by the artist, as well as pieces by Miró, Calder, and Léger. ✉ *Pl. du Château,* ☎ *04–92–90–54–20.* ✉ *€5.* ⏲ *June–Sept., Tues–Sun. 10–6; Oct.–May, Tues.–Sun. 10–noon and 2–6.*

The Bastion St-André, a squat Vauban fortress, now contains the **Musée Archéologique** (Archaeology Museum). Its collection focuses on Antibes's classical history, displaying amphorae and sculptures found in local digs as well as in shipwrecks from the harbor. ✉ *Av. Général-Maizières,* ☎ *04–92–90–54–35.* ✉ *€3.* ⏲ *Tues.–Sun. 10–noon and 2–6.*

Dining and Lodging

$$$$ ✕ **La Jarre.** You can dine under the beams or the ancient fig tree at this lovely little garden hideaway, just off the ramparts and behind the cathedral. Open only for dinner, it has an ambitious menu (€55) of Provençal specialties filtered through an international lens: tabbouleh topped with mullet and sharp black tapenade, sweet-and-sour duck breast, shrimp grilled in ginger, and apricot nougat. ✉ *14 rue St-Esprit,* ☎ *04–93–34–50–12. MC, V. Closed mid-Oct.–Easter. No lunch.*

$$$–$$$$ ✕ **La Bonne Auberge.** In a graceful inn set back from the overbuilt sprawl along N7, Chef Philippe Rostang cooks up classic, conservative specialties such as lamb slow-simmered in herbs, lobster salad with tiny ravioli, and airy fish soufflés. The dining room is a pastel haven of exposed beams, fresh flowers, and soft lighting. The dinner menu is €32. ✉ *Quartier de la Brague (4 km/2 mi east of Antibes),* ☎ *04–93–33–36–65. AE, MC, V. Closed Mon., except July–Aug. Closed mid-Nov.–mid-Dec. No dinner Sun., except July–Aug.*

$–$$ ★ ✕ **Le Brûlot.** One street back from the market, this bistro remains one of the busiest in Antibes. Burly Chef Christian Blancheri hoists anything from pigs to apple pies in and out of his roaring wood oven, and it's all delicious. Watch for the sardines *à l'escabèche* (in a tangy sweet-sour marinade), sizzling lamb chops, or grilled fresh fish. ✉ *3 rue Frédéric Isnard,* ☎ *04–93–34–17–76. MC, V. Closed Sun., last 2 wks of Aug., and last wk of Dec.–1st wk Jan. No lunch Mon.*

$$ 🏨 **Auberge Provençale.** The six rooms in this onetime abbey come complete with exposed beams, canopy beds, and lovely antique furniture. The dining room and the arbored garden are informed with the same impeccable taste; the menu allures with fresh seafood inventions such as rascasse (rock fish) sausage with mint, as well as bouillabaisse and duck grilled over wood coals. The restaurant is closed Monday and at lunch Tuesday. ✉ *61 pl. Nationale, 06600,* ☎ *04–93–34–13–24,* FAX *04–93–34–89–88. 6 rooms. Restaurant, cable TV, minibars, free parking. AE, DC, MC, V. Closed Jan.*

$$ 🏨 **Le Mas Djoliba.** Tucked into a residential neighborhood on the crest between Antibes and Juan, this converted Provençal farmhouse is surrounded by greenery and well protected from traffic noise. Rooms, decked out in bright colors and floral prints, have views of the garden or the sea. Note that in summer the restaurant serves half board only. ✉ *29 av. de Provence, 06600,* ☎ *04–93–34–02–48,* FAX *04–93–34–05–81,* WEB *www.hotel-pcastel-djoliba.com. 13 rooms. Restaurant, cable TV, minibars, Internet, pool. AE, DC, MC, V. Closed Nov.–Jan.*

Nightlife and the Arts

La Siesta (✉ Rte. du Bord de Mer, Antibes, ☎ 04–93–33–31–31) is an enormous summer entertainment center with seven dance floors (some on the beach), bars, slot machines, and roulette.

Outdoor Activities and Sports

Antibes and Juan together claim 25 km (15½ mi) of coastline and 48 **beaches** (including Cap d'Antibes). In Antibes you can choose between small sandy inlets—such as **La Gravette,** below the port; the central **place de Ponteil;** and **Plage de la Salis,** toward the Cap—rocky escarpments around the Old Town; or the vast stretch of sand above the Fort Carré.

Juan-les-Pins

⓫ *5 km (3 mi) southwest of Antibes.*

If Antibes is the elderly, historic parent, then Juan-les-Pins is the jazzy younger-sister resort town that, with Antibes, bracelets the wrist of the Cap d'Antibes. The scene along Juan's waterfront is something to behold, with thousands of international sunseekers flowing up and down the promenade or lying flank to flank on its endless stretch of sand. Along with two of the Riviera's most beloved hotels, Juan is famous for the quality—some pundits say quantity—of its nightlife. There are numerous nightclubs where you can do everything but sleep, ranging from casinos to discos to strip clubs (rather a bore—after all, the beach here was one of the first in France to offer topless bathing). If all this sounds like too much hard work, wait for July's jazz festival—one of Europe's most prestigious—or simply repair to the Juana or Les Belles Rives (☞ *below*); if you're lucky enough to be a guest at either hotel, you'll understand why F. Scott Fitzgerald set his *Tender in the Night* in Juantibes, as both places retain the golden glamour of the Riviera of yore.

Dining and Lodging

$$$$ ★ ✕ **La Terrasse.** The renowned restaurant of the historic Hotel Juana, this was where superstar chef Alain Ducasse first earned his toque. When he left, all Juan-les-Pins heaved a high-octane sigh of relief when he was replaced by the equally superlative Christian Morisset, who maintains top honors with such dishes as sea bass steamed with Menton lemon, lamb roasted in Vallauris clay, and Tour d'Argent-style roasted duck. Menus run from €95 to €140. The decor is potted palms, plate glass, and a bit too glossy for its own good. ✉ *Av. Georges-Gallice,* ☎ *04–93–61–08–70. AE, MC, V. Closed Nov.–Mar.*

$$$$ ★ ✕🏨 **Belles Rives.** If "living well is the best revenge," then vacationers at this landmark hotel should know. Not far from the one-time villa of Gerald and Sara Murphy—those Roaring Twenties millionaires who devoted their life to proving this maxim—the Belles Rives became the home-away-from-home for F. Scott Fitzgerald and his wife Zelda (chums of the Murphys). Lovingly restored, the public salons' Neoclassical Moderne chic proves that what's old is new again: France's stylish young set now make this endearingly historic place one of their favorites. The restaurant's classic cuisine is impeccably served; for the most magical effect, dine on the terrace on a fine summer night, with the sea lapping below and stars twinkling in the velvety Mediterranean sky. No pool, but that's no loss—the beach is nearby. ✉ *Bd. Baudoin, 06160,* ☎ *04–93–61–02–79,* FAX *03–93–67–43–51,* WEB *www.bellesrives.com. 42 rooms. Restaurant, bar, cable TV, minibars, Internet, beach. AE, MC, V. Closed late-Oct.–mid-Apr.*

$$$$ ★ ✕🏨 **Juana.** The luxuriously renovated Juana is one of the defining monuments of 1930s Côte d'Azur architectural style. Run by the Barrache family since it opened in 1931, the hotel retains a wonderful Gatsby feel, with striped awnings and white balustrades. Pine trees tower over the grounds and the white-marble pool, balconies offer sunset views of the Esterel red-cliff mountains, while rooms are cool and plain-pastel, with marble and acajou accents. Though two blocks from the waterfront, the Juana has its own private sand beach. The excellent restaurant is La Terrasse. ✉ *Av. Georges-Gallice, 06160 Juan-les-Pins,* ☎ *04–93–61–08–70,* FAX *04–93–61–76–60,* WEB *www.hotel-juana.com. 45 rooms, 5 suites. Restaurant, bar, cable TV, minibars, Internet, pool, meeting room, parking (fee). AE, MC, V. Closed Nov.–Mar.*

$$ 🏨 **Le Mimosa.** The fabulous setting, in an enclosed hilltop garden studded with tall palms, mimosas, and tropical greenery, makes up for the hike down to the beach. Rooms are small and modestly decorated in Victorian florals, but ask for one with a balcony: many look over the garden and sizable pool. ✉ *Rue Pauline 06160, Antibes,* ☎ *04–93–61–04–16,* FAX *04–92–93–06–46. 34 rooms. No air-conditioning, cable TV, pool, free parking. MC, V. Closed Oct.–Apr.*

Nightlife and the Arts

The glassed-in complex of the **Eden Casino** (✉ Bd. Baudoin, Juan-les-Pins, ☎ 04–92–93–71–71) houses restaurants, bars, dance clubs, and a casino. Every July the **Festival de Jazz d'Antibes-Juan-les-Pins** (☎ 04–92–90–50–00 for information) challenges Montreux for its stellar lineup and romantic venue under ancient pines. This place hosted the European debut performances of such stars as Meels Dah-*vees* (Miles Davis) and Ray Charles. It can only be hoped that by now they've changed the tacky stage decor—a gigantic "rendition" of a Picasso dove.

Cap d'Antibes

⓬ *2 km (1 mi) south of Antibes.*

This extravagantly beautiful peninsula, protected from the concrete plague infecting the mainland coast, has been carved up into luxurious estates shaded by thick, tall pines. Since the 19th century its wild greenery and isolation have drawn a glittering guest list of aristocrats, artists, literati, and the merely fabulously wealthy: Guy de Maupassant, Anatole France, Claude Monet, the Duke and Duchess of Windsor, the Greek shipping tycoon Stavros Niarchos, and the cream of the Lost Generation, including Ernest Hemingway, Gertrude Stein, and Scottie and Zelda Fitzgerald. Now the most publicized focal point is the Hotel Eden Roc, rendezvous and weekend getaway of film stars.

You can sample a little of what draws famous people to the site by walking up the chemin de Calvaire from the Plage de la Salis in Antibes (about 1 km/¾ mi) and taking in the extraordinary views from the hill that supports the old lighthouse, the **Phare de la Garoupe** (Garoupe Lighthouse). Next to the lighthouse, the 16th-century double chapel of **Notre-Dame-de-la-Garoupe** contains ex-votos and statues of the Virgin, all in memory of and for the protection of sailors. ☎ *04–93–67–36–01.* ⏲ *Easter–Sept., daily 9:30–noon and 2:30–7; Oct.–Easter, daily 10–noon and 2:30–5.*

Another lovely walk (about 1½ km/1 mi), along the **Sentier Tirepoil,** begins at the cape's pretty Plage de la Garoupe and winds along dramatic rocky shores, magnificent at sunset. The final destination of the ★ Sentier Tirepoil is the **Villa Eilenroc,** designed by Charles Garnier, who created the Paris Opera—which should give you some idea of its style. It commands the tip of the peninsula from a grand and glamorous garden. You may swan around the grounds freely, but the house remains closed (unless the owners, on a good day, choose to open the first floor to visitors). ✉ *At peninsula's tip,* ☎ *04–93–67–74–33.* 🎫 *Free.* ⏲ *Mid-Sept.–June, Tues.–Wed. 9–5.*

To fully experience the Riviera's heady hothouse exoticism, visit the ★ glorious **Jardin Thuret** (Thuret Garden), established by botanist Gustave Thuret in 1856 as a testing ground for subtropical plants and trees. Thuret was responsible for the introduction of the palm tree, forever changing the profile of the Côte d'Azur. On his death the property was left to the Ministry of Agriculture, which continues to dabble in the introduction of exotic species. ✉ *Bd. du Cap,* ☎ *04–93–67–88–00.* 🎫 *Free.* ⏲ *Weekdays 8:30–5:30.*

At the southwest tip of the peninsula, an ancient battery contains the **Musée Naval et Napoléonien** (Naval and Napoleonic Museum), where you can peruse a collection of watercolors of Antibes, platoons of lead soldiers, and scale models of military ships. ✉ *Batterie du Grillon, av. Kennedy,* ☎ *04–93–61–45–32.* 🎫 *€3.* ⏲ *Weekdays 9:30–noon and 2:15–6, Sat. 9:30–noon.*

Dining and Lodging

$$$$ ★ ✕ **Restaurant de Bacon.** Since 1948, under the careful watch of the Sordello brothers, this has been *the* spot for seafood on the Côte d'Azur. The catch of the day may be minced in lemon ceviche, floating in a top-of-the-line bouillabaisse, or simply grilled with fennel, crisped with hillside herbs. The warm welcome, discreet service, sunny dining room, and dreamy terrace over the Baie des Anges justify extravagance. Fixed menu prices are €45 and €70. ✉ *Bd. de Bacon,* ☎ *04–93–61–50–02. Reservations essential. AE, DC, MC, V. Closed Mon. and Nov.–Jan.*

$$$$ ★ ✕🏨 **Imperial Garoupe.** The newest Provençal palace in the Cap is a terra-cotta oasis of Mediterranean comfort and glitz. It offers all the perks of a luxury hotel—superequipped bathrooms, floor-to-ceiling chintz, thick towels, and daily deliveries of fresh fruit—at about half the cost of its neighbors. All rooms open onto the patio and swimming pool, but the beşt is No. 35, which has its own terrace. ✉ *770 chemin Garoupe, 06160,* ☎ *04–92–93–31–61,* FAX *04–92–93–31–62. 30 rooms, 4 suites. Restaurant, cable TV, minibars, pool. AE, DC, MC, V. Closed Nov.–mid-Apr.*

$$$ ★ 🏨 **La Baie Dorée.** Clinging to the waterfront and skewed toward the open sea, this elegant little inn provides private sea-view terraces off every room. Guest rooms are plush and subdued, yet even the small standard doubles feel deluxe when you look out the window. The public grounds and terraces fall in tiers down to the water, from the shaded restaurant to the private beach on the Baie de la Garoupe. ✉ *579 bd. de la Garoupe, 06160,* ☎ *04–93–67–30–67,* FAX *04–92–93–76–39. 17 rooms. Restaurant, cable TV, minibars, beach. MC, V. Closed Nov.–mid-Dec.*

Cagnes-sur-Mer

⓭ *21 km (13 mi) northeast of Cannes, 10 km (6 mi) north of Antibes, 14 km (9 mi) southwest of Nice.*

Although from N7 you may be tempted to give wide berth to the congested sprawl of Cagnes-sur-Mer, follow the signs inland and up into **Haut-de-Cagnes.** Its steep-cobbled Old Town is crowned by the fat, crenellated **Château de Cagne,** built in 1310 by the Grimaldis and reinforced over the centuries. Within are vaulted medieval chambers, a vast Renaissance fireplace, a splendid 17th-century trompe-l'oeil fresco of the fall of Phaëthon from his sun-chariot, and three small specialized collections dealing with the history of the olive; memorabilia of the cabaret star Suzy Solidor; and a collection of modern Mediterranean artists, including Cocteau and Dufy. ✉ *Pl. Grimaldi,* ☎ *04–93–20–87–29.* 🎫 *€3.* ⏲ *Oct. and Dec.–Easter, Wed.–Mon. 10–noon and 2–5; Easter–Sept., Wed.–Sun. 10–noon and 2–6.*

After staying up and down the coast, August Renoir (1841–1919) settled in a house in Les Collettes, just east of the Old Town, now the **Musée Renoir.** Here he passed the last 12 years of his life, painting the landscape around him, working in bronze, and rolling his wheelchair through the luxuriant garden, tiered with roses, citrus groves, and some of the most spectacular olive trees along the coast. You can view his home as it has been preserved by his children, as well as 11 of his last paintings. ✉ *Av. des Collettes,* ☎ *04–93–20–61–07.* 🎫 *€3.* ⏲ *June–Oct., Wed.–Mon. 10–noon and 2–6; Nov.–May, Wed.–Mon. 10–noon and 2–5. Guided tours in English, Thurs. July–Aug.*

THE HILL TOWNS: ON THE TRAIL OF PICASSO AND MATISSE

The hills that back the Côte d'Azur are often called the *arrière-pays,* or backcountry. This particular wedge of backcountry—behind the coast between Cannes and Antibes—has a character all its own: deeply, unself-consciously Provençal, with undulating fields of lavender watched over by villages perched in golden stone. Many of these villages look as if they do not belong to the last century—but they do, since they played the muse to some of modern art's most famous exemplars, notably Pablo Picasso and Henri Matisse. A highlight here is the Maeght Foundation, in St-Paul de Vence, one of France's leading museums of modern art. Its neighbor, Vence, has the Chapelle du Rosaire, entirely designed and decorated by Matisse. It's possible to get a small taste of this backcountry on a day trip out of Fréjus, Cannes, or Antibes; even if you're vacationing on the coast, you may want to settle in for a night or two.

Of course, you'll soon discover the stooped, stone row houses that are now galleries and boutiques offering everything from neo-Van Gogh sofa art to assembly-line lavender sachets, and everywhere you'll hear the gentle *breet-breet* of mechanical souvenir *cigales* (cicadas). So if you're at all allergic to souvenir shops and middlebrow art galleries, aim to visit off-season or after hours, when the stone-paved alleys empty of tourists and the scent of strawberry potpourri is washed away by the natural perfume of bougainvillea and jasmine wafting from terra-cotta jars.

Vallauris

14 *6 km (4 mi) northeast of Cannes, 6 km (4 mi) west of Antibes.*

In the low hills over the coast, dominated by a blocky Renaissance château, this ancient village was ravaged by waves of the plague in the 14th century, then rebuilt in the 16th century by 70 Genoese families imported to repopulate the abandoned site. They brought with them a taste for Roman planning—hence the grid format in the Old Town—but, more important in the long run, a knack for pottery making. Their skills and the fine clay of Vallauris proved to be a marriage made in heaven, and the village thrived as a pottery center for hundreds of years.

In the 1940s Picasso found inspiration in the malleable soil and settled here in a simple stone house, creating pottery art with a single-minded passion. But he returned to painting in 1952 to create one of his masterworks in the château's Romanesque chapel, the vast multipanel oil-on-wood composition called *La Guerre et la Paix* (*War and* ★ *Peace*). The chapel is part of the **Musée National Picasso** today, where several of Picasso's ceramic pieces are displayed. There's also a group of paintings by a contemporary of Picasso's, Italian artist Alberto Magnelli. ✉ *Pl. de la Libération,* ☎ *04–93–64–16–05.* €2.75. *June–Sept., Wed.–Mon. 10–6:30; Oct.–May, Wed.–Mon. 10–noon and 2–6.*

Mougins

15 *8 km (5 mi) north of Cannes, 11 km (7 mi) northwest of Antibes, 32 km (20 mi) southwest of Nice.*

Passing through Mougins, a popular summer-house community convenient to Cannes and Nice, you may perceive little more than suburban sprawl. But in 1961 Picasso found much to admire and settled into a *mas* (farmhouse) that verily became a pilgrimage spot for artists and art lovers; he died there in 1973.

You can find Picasso's final home and see why, of all spots in the world, he chose this one, by following D35 to the ancient ecclesiastical site of **Notre-Dame-de-Vie.** This was the hermitage, or monastic retreat, of the Abbey of Lérins, and its 13th-century bell tower and arcaded chapel form a pretty ensemble. Approached through an allée of ancient cypresses, the house Picasso shared with his wife, Jacqueline, overlooks the broad bowl of the countryside (unfortunately now blighted with modern construction).

Dining and Lodging

$$$$ ★ ✕🏨 **Moulin de Mougins.** A temple of taste housed in a 16th-century olive mill on a hill above the coastal fray, this legendary and sophisticated inn houses one of the best restaurants in the region. It used to be a de rigueur lunch trip out of Cannes, especially back when it hosted the annual Elizabeth Taylor AIDS benefit during the film fest; since celebrity chef Roger Vergé relocated to the Roger Vergé Ecole de Cuisine at Mougins's Restaurant L'Amandier and set Serge Chollet at the helm, however, the loyal clientele has begun to sigh for the good old days. Still, the sun-drenched Mediterranean cuisine is excellent and redolent of the market, with the freshest fish and whitest asparagus. Inside are intimate, beamed dining rooms; in summer dine outside under the awnings. Guest rooms are elegantly rustic; the apartments are small but deluxe. ✉ *Notre-Dame-de-Vie, 06250,* ☎ *04–93–75–78–24,* FAX *04–93–90–18–55,* WEB *www.relaischateaux.fr/mougins. 3 rooms, 4 apartments. Restaurant, cable TV, minibars. Reservations essential. AE, DC, MC, V. Closed Feb; rest. closed Mon.*

Grasse

16 *10 km (6 mi) northwest of Mougins, 17 km (10½ mi) northwest of Cannes, 22 km (14 mi) northwest of Antibes, 42 km (26 mi) southwest of Nice.*

High on a plateau over the coast, this busy, modern town is usually given a wide berth by anyone who isn't interested in its prime tourist industry, the making of perfume. But its unusual art museum featuring works of the 18th-century artist Fragonard and the picturesque backstreets of its very Mediterranean Old Town round out a pleasant day trip from the coast.

It's the Côte d'Azur's hothouse climate, nurturing nearly year-round shows of tropical-hue flowers, that fosters Grasse's perfume industry. It takes 10,000 flowers to produce 2.2 pounds of jasmine petals, and nearly 1 ton of petals to distill 1½ quarts of essence; this helps justify the sky-high cost of perfumes, priced by the proportion of essence in the final blend.

You can't visit the laboratories where the great blends of Chanel, Dior, and Guerlain are produced. But to accommodate the crowds of tourists who come here wanting to know more, Grasse has three functioning perfume factories that create simple blends and demonstrate production techniques for free.

Fragonard (✉ Rte. de Cannes Les 4-Chemins, ☎ 04–93–77–94–30) operates in a factory built in 1782. **Galimard** (✉ 73 rte. de Cannes) traces its pedigree back to 1747. **Molinard** (✉ 60 bd. Victor-Hugo, ☎ 04–93–36–01–62) was established in 1849.

The **Musée International de la Parfumerie** (International Museum of Perfume), not to be confused with the museum in the Fragonard factory, traces the 3,000-year history of perfume-making. The museum has a room equipped with potbellied copper stills and old machines, and labels guide you through the steps of production during different eras. ✉ *8 pl. du Cours,* ☎ *04–93–36–80–20.* €3. ⏲ *June–Sept., daily 10–7; Oct.–May., Wed.–Sun. 10–12:30 and 2–5:30.*

The **Musée Fragonard** headlines the work of Grasse's most famous son, Jean-Honoré Fragonard (1732–1806), one of the great French artists of the period. The lovely villa contains a collection of drawings, engravings, and paintings by the artist. Other rooms in the mansion display works by Fragonard's son Alexandre-Evariste and his grandson Théophile. ✉ *23 bd. Fragonard,* ☎ *04–93–36–02–71.* €3. ⏲ *June–Sept., daily 10–7; Oct.–May, Wed.–Sun. 10–12:30 and 2–5:30.*

The **Musée d'Art et d'Histoire de Provence** (Museum of the Art and History of Provence), just down from the Fragonard perfumery, has a large collection of faïence from the region, including works from Moustiers, Biot, and Vallauris. Also on display in this noble 18th-century mansion are *santons* (terra-cotta figurines), furniture, local paintings, and folk costumes. ✉ *2 rue Mirabeau,* ☎ *04–93–36–01–61.* €3. ⏲ *June–Sept., daily 10–7; Oct.–May., Wed.–Sun. 10–12:30 and 2–5:30.*

Continue down rue Mirabeau and lose yourself in the dense labyrinth of the **Vieille Ville** (Old Town), its steep, narrow streets thrown into shadow by shuttered houses five and six stories tall. On a clifftop overlook at the Old Town's edge, the Romanesque **Cathédrale Ste-Marie** (✉ Pl. de la Cathédrale) contains three paintings by Rubens, a triptych by the Provençal painter Louis Bréa, and *Lavement des Pieds* (*Washing of the Feet*), by the young Fragonard.

Dining and Lodging

$ ✕ **Arnaud.** Just off place aux Aires, this easygoing corner bistro serves up inventive home cooking under a vaulted ceiling decorated with stenciled grapevines. Choose from an ambitious and sophisticated menu of à la carte specialties—three kinds of fish in garlic sauce, *pieds et paquets* (pigs' feet and tripe), or a hearty *confit de canard* (preserved duck). ✉ *10 pl. de la Foux,* ☎ *04–93–36–44–88. MC, V.*

$$$$ ★ ✕ **La Bastide Saint-Antoine.** The cicadas live better than most humans at this picture-perfect 18th-century estate overlooking the Estéval and once home of an industrialist who hosted Kennedys and Rolling Stones. Now the domain of celebrated chef Jacques Chibois, it welcomes you with old stone walls, shaded walkways, enormous pool, and a mouthwatering ocher-hued and blue-shuttered mansion draped with red trumpet-flowered bignonia and purple bougainvillea. The guest rooms glossily mix Louis Seize–style chairs, Provençal embroidered bedspreads, and high-tech delights (massaging showers). While the restaurant is exceedingly excellent and expensive (L'Elegance de Lobster in a Rainbow of Petals and Herbs will run you €51), lunch is a bargain €45. Prices are in top category, but some rooms hover close to $$$ level. ✉ *48 av. Henri-Dunant, 06130,* ☎ *04–93–70–94–94,* FAX *04–93–70–94–95,* WEB *www.jacques-chibois.com. 8 rooms, 3 suites. Restaurant, no air-conditioning, cable TV, minibars, pool, shop. AE, DC, MC, V.*

Route Napoléon

Extends 176 km (109 mi) from Grasse to Sisteron.

One of the most famous and panoramic roads in France is the Route Napoléon, taken by Napoléon Bonaparte in 1815 after his escape from imprisonment on the Mediterranean island of Elba. Napoléon landed at Golfe-Juan, near Cannes, on March 1 and forged northwest to Grasse, then through dramatic, hilly countryside to Castellane, Digne, and Sisteron. Commemorative plaques bearing the imperial eagle stud the route, inspired by Napoléon's remark, "The eagle will fly from steeple to steeple until it reaches the towers of Notre-Dame." Nowadays there are some lavender-honey stands and souvenir shacks, but they are few and far between. It's the panoramic views as the road winds its way up into the Alps that make this a route worth taking. If you like scenic drives, follow the Route Napoléon to Trigance and on to the spectacular gorge called the **Grand Canyon du Verdon.** You can then continue on to the heart of the Var and Moustiers-Ste-Marie (covered below), where famed chef Alain Ducasse has set up shop.

Tourrettes-sur-Loup

17 *5 km (3 mi) west of Vence, 24 km (15 mi) west of Nice.*

In this steep-sloped old hill town the wind blows colder, the surrounding forest is dense and arid, and the coast seems hours—and ages—away (though it's less than an hour's drive from Nice). From the town square that doubles as a parking lot with an ongoing pétanque game on one side, to the sharp-raked, tortuous streets snaking down the slopes of the Old Town, this is Old Provence without the stage makeup. Yes, there are dozens of galleries and arts-and-crafts shops, but they are owned and run by real artists and artisans who have made a life for themselves in this intimate community.

Vence

18 *4 km (2 mi) north of St-Paul, 22 km (14 mi) north of Nice.*

Encased behind stone walls inside a thriving modern market town is **la Vieille Ville,** the historic part of Vence, which dates from the 15th century. Though crowded with boutiques and souvenir shops, it's slightly more conscious of its history than St-Paul—plaques guide you through its historic squares and *portes* (gates). Wander past the pretty Place du Peyra, with its fountains, to place Clemenceau, with its ocher-color Hôtel de Ville (town hall), to Place du Frêne, with its ancient ash tree planted in the 16th century.

In the Old Town center, the **Cathédrale de la Nativité de la Vierge** (Cathedral of the Birth of the Virgin, on place Godeau) was built on the Romans' military drilling field and traces bits and pieces to Carolingian and even Roman times. It's a hybrid of Romanesque and Baroque styles, expanded and altered over the centuries. In the baptistery is a ceramic mosaic of Moses in the bulrushes by Chagall.

★ On the outskirts of "new" Vence, toward St-Jeannet, the **Chapelle du Rosaire** (Chapel of the Rosary) was decorated with beguiling simplicity and clarity by Matisse between 1947 and 1951—the chapel was the artist's gift to nuns who had nursed him through illness. It reflects the reductivist style of the era: walls, floor, and ceiling are gleaming white, and the small stained-glass windows are cool greens and blues. "Despite its imperfections I think it is my masterpiece . . . the result of a lifetime devoted to the search for truth," wrote Matisse, who designed and dedicated the chapel when he was in his eighties and nearly blind. ✉ *Av. Henri-Matisse,* ☎ *04–93–58–03–26.* €2.5. ⏲ *Tues. and Thurs. 10–11:30 and 2–5:30; Mon., Wed., and Sat. 2–5:30.*

Dining and Lodging

$$$ ★ ✕ **Jacques Maximin.** This temperamental superchef has found peace of mind in a gray-stone farmhouse covered with wisteria—his home and his own country restaurant. Here he devotes himself to creative country cooking superbly prepared and unpretentiously priced—white beans in rich squid ink, Mediterranean fish grilled in rock salt and olive

oil, and candied-eggplant sorbet. The yellow dining room is airy and uncluttered; the garden is a palm-shaded delight. ✉ *689 chemin de la Gaude,* ☎ *04–93–58–90–75. AE, MC, V. Closed Mon. and mid-Nov.–mid-Dec. No dinner Sun. Sept.–June.*

$$–$$$ ✕ **La Farigoule.** A long, beamed dining room that opens onto a shady terrace casts an easygoing spell and serves as an hors d'oeuvre for some sophisticated Provençal cooking. Watch for tangy pissaladieres with sardines marinated in ginger and lemon, salt-cod ravioli, lamb with olive polenta, and a crunchy parfait of honey and hazelnuts. Fixed-menu dinners are €21 and €34. ✉ *15 rue Henri-Isnard,* ☎ *04–93–58–01–27. MC, V. Closed Wed., 1st 2 wks Nov., end Dec.–early Jan., 2 wks Feb. No lunch Tues. Oct.–Apr. and Thurs. May–Sept.*

$$ ★ **Villa Roseraie.** This quiet little inn outside the center is a pet project of the enthusiastic young owners, Monsieur and Mme. Ganier, who have scoured antiques shops for regional details and invested in fine local tiles and fabrics. You can enjoy a generous breakfast on the terrace and lounge by the pool much of the year, and it's a quick walk down to Old Vence. ✉ *51 av. Henri-Giraud, 06140,* ☎ *04–93–58–02–20,* FAX *04–93–58–99–31. 14 rooms. No air-conditioning, minibars, pool. AE, MC, V.*

St-Paul-de-Vence

⑲ *18 km (11 mi) north of Nice, 4 km (2 mi) south of Vence.*

The medieval village of St-Paul-de-Vence can be seen from afar, standing out like its companion, Vence, against the skyline. In the Middle Ages St-Paul was basically a city-state, and it controlled its own political destiny for centuries. But by the early 20th century St-Paul had faded to oblivion, overshadowed by the growth of Vence and Cagnes—until it was rediscovered in the 1920s when a few penniless artists began paying for their drinks at the local auberge with paintings. Those artists turned out to be Signac, Modigliani, and Bonnard, who met at the Auberge de la Colombe d'Or, now a sumptuous inn, where the walls are still covered with their ink sketches and daubs. Nowadays art of a sort still dominates in the myriad tourist traps that take your eyes off the beauty of St-Paul's old stone houses and its rampart views. The most commercially developed of Provence's hilltop villages, St-Paul is nonetheless a magical place when the tourist crowds thin. Artists are still drawn to its light, its pure air, its wraparound views, and its honey-color stone walls, soothingly cool on a hot Provençal afternoon. Film stars continue to love its lazy yet genteel ways, lingering on the garden-bower terrace of the Colombe d'Or and challenging the locals to a game of pétanque under the shade of the plane trees.

★ Many people come to St-Paul just to visit the **Fondation Maeght,** founded in 1964 by art dealer Aimé Maeght and set on a wooded clifftop high above the medieval town. It's not just a small modern art museum but an extraordinary marriage of the arc-and-plane architecture of José Sert; the looming sculptures of Miró, Moore, and Giacometti; and a humbling hilltop perch of pines, vines, and flowing planes of water. On display is an intriguing and ever-varying parade of the work of modern masters, including the wise and funny late-life masterwork *La Vie* (*Life*), by Chagall. ☎ *04–93–32–81–63.* *€8.* *July–Sept., daily 10–7; Oct.–June, daily 10–12:30 and 2:30–6.*

Dining and Lodging

$$$$ ★ ✕ **La Colombe d'Or.** The art display here may cause a double take—are those really Mirós, Bonnards, Picassos, Légers, and Braques hanging on the rustic walls? Yes, they were indeed given in payment by the artists in hungrier days. This idyllic old auberge was the heart and soul of St-Paul's artistic revival, and the cream of 20th-century France lounged together under its fig trees—Picasso and Chagall, Maeterlinck and Kipling, Yves Montand and Simone Signoret (who met and married here). Today, the inn's *pastorale* history is the lure, not the food, which is unambitious bordering on fine, but high-priced nonetheless. Give in to the green-shaded loveliness of the terrace and the creamy manners of the waitstaff. A dinner table here is lorded over by a ceramic Léger mural, while the pool is an idyllic garden bower, complete with a Calder, and there's even a Braque by the fireplace in the bar. Rooms are spartan and don't live up to the luxury-level prices. This is a guarded star—there are minuses here but where else can you enjoy your Campari sitting under a Braque? Reserve well in advance for guest rooms. ✉ *Pl. Général-de-Gaulle, 06570,* ☎ *04–93–32–80–02.* FAX *04–93–32–77–78. 16 rooms, 10 suites. Restaurant, bar, some air-conditioning, cable TV, minibars, Internet, pool. AE, DC, MC, V. Closed Nov.–late Dec.*

$$$$ ★ ✕🏨 **Le Saint-Paul.** Right in the center of the labyrinth of stone alleys, with views over the ancient ramparts, this luxurious inn (a Relais & Châteaux property) fills a noble 15th-century house with comfort and charm. Provençal furniture, golden quarried stone, and lush reproduction fabrics warm the salons and restaurant; rooms are decked in sleek pastels and sprig prints, and a few have balconies over the valley. The restaurant, serving sophisticated regional specialties such as eggplant terrine with *pistou* (Provençal pesto), and sole with bacon and pumpkin puree, is a cut above as well. And a candlelit meal on the terrace, where flowers spill from every niche, is a romantic's dream. (Off-season, the restaurant is closed Wednesday, and lunch is not served Tuesday.) ✉ *86 rue Grande, 06570,* ☎ *04–93–32–65–25,* FAX *04–93–32–52–94,* WEB *www.relaischateaux.fr/stpaul/. 15 rooms, 3 suites. Restaurant, bar, cable TV, minibars, Internet. AE, DC, MC, V. Closed early Jan.–mid-Feb.*

$$ 🏨 **Le Hameau.** Less than 1½ km (1 mi) outside St-Paul, with views of the valley and the village, this lovely little inn is a jumble of terraces, trellises, archways, and honeysuckle vines. The main hotel, built in 1920, has good-sized rooms and old Provençal furniture; or you can opt for the 18th-century farmhouse, with smaller, more modern rooms but wonderful views. The friendly new owners have built a sizable new pool. ✉ *528 rte. de La Colle, 06570,* ☎ *04–93–32–80–24,* FAX *04–93–32–55–75. 17 rooms. Cable TV, minibars, Internet, pool. MC, V. Closed mid-Nov.–mid-Feb. (except Christmas–New Year's).*

Villeneuve-Loubet

20 *10 km (6 mi) north of Antibes, 17 km (10½ mi) southwest of Nice, 20 km (12 mi) northeast of Cannes.*

This tiny village, its medieval château heavily restored in the 19th century, is best known for its lower sprawl of overbuilt beachfront, heavily charged with concrete high-rises with all the architectural charm of a parking ramp. If you're a foodie, you may want to make a pilgrimage uphill to the eccentric **Musée de l'Art Culinaire** (Museum of Culinary Arts), a shrine to the career of the great chef Auguste Escoffier (1846–1935), the founding father of the modern school of haute cuisine. In his birthplace are illustrations of his creations and a collection of fantastical menus. ✉ *3 rue Escoffier,* ☎ *04–93–20–80–51.* 🎫 *€4.* ⏲ *Sept.–June, Tues.–Sun. 2–6; July–Aug., Tues.–Sun. 2–7.*

Biot

21 *6 km (4 mi) northeast of Antibes, 15 km (9 mi) northeast of Cannes, 18 km (11 mi) southwest of Nice.*

Rising above an ugly commercial-industrial quarter up the coast from Antibes, Biot (pronounced bee-*otte*) sits neatly on a hilltop, welcoming day-trippers into its self-consciously quaint center. For centuries the center for a pottery industry known for its fine yellow clay that stretched into massive, solid oil jars, it has in recent generations made a name for itself as a glass-art town. Nowadays its cobbled streets are lined with glass boutiques and galleries. Yet despite the commercialism, traces of the feel of Old Provence remain, especially in the evening after the busloads of shoppers leave and the deep-shaded *placettes* (small squares) under the plane trees fall quiet.

Long a regular on the Côte d'Azur, Fernand Léger fell under Biot's spell and bought a mas (farmhouse) here in 1955 to house an unwieldy collection of his sculptures. The modernized structure of the **Musée National Fernand-Léger** is striking, its facade itself a vast mosaic in his signature style of heavily outlined color fields. Within you can trace the evolution of Léger's technique, from his fascination with the industrial to freewheeling abstractions. ✉ *Chemin du Val de Pomme,* ☎ *04–92–91–50–30.* 🎫 *€6.* ⏲ *July–Sept., Wed.–Mon. 11–6; Oct.–June, Wed.–Mon. 10–12:30 and 2–5:30.*

On the edge of town follow the pink signs to **La Verrerie de Biot** (Biot Glassworks), founded in the 1950s. Here you can watch glassblowers at work, visit the extensive galleries of museum-quality art glass, and start a collection of bubble-glass goblets, cruets, or pitchers. ✉ *5 chemin des Combes,* ☎ *04–93–65–03–00.* ⏲ *May–Sept., daily 10–7; Oct.–Apr., Mon.–Sat. 10:30–1 and 2:30–6:30.*

Dining and Lodging

$–$$ ✕ **Chez Odile.** Biot's more expensive addresses are hard put topping the excellent fare on offer at this family-run bistro. Courses are simple—Provençal vegetable platters, hot sausage, stuffed rabbit, fresh-fruit tarts—but extremely tasty and copious. On hot summer evenings a table on the pretty terrace is a must. The €15 lunch menu is a great bargain. ✉ *Chemin des Bachettes,* ☎ *04–93–65–15–63. AE, DC, MC, V.*

$ ★ ✕🏨 **Galerie des Arcades.** Tucked away behind the quiet palm-lined place des Arcades in the Old Town, this combination hotel/restaurant/art gallery draws a loyal clientele. They come for unpretentious, authentic Provençal food: rabbit sautéed in fresh herbs, stuffed sardines, or a Friday aioli (fish and crudités served with garlic mayonnaise). Ask for one of the three *grandes chambres* (large rooms) and revel in antiquity: four-poster beds, beams, and a tapestry-rich color scheme. ✉ *14 pl. des Arcades, 06410,* ☎ *04–93–65–01–04,* FAX *04–93–65–01–05. 12 rooms. Restaurant, no air-conditioning, no room phones, no room TVs. AE, DC, MC, V.*

NICE

As the fifth-largest city in France, this distended urban tangle is often avoided, but that decision is one to be rued: Nice's waterfront, paralleled by the famous Promenade des Anglais and lined by grand hotels, is one of the noblest in France. It is capped by a dramatic hilltop château, below which the slopes plunge almost into the sea and at whose base a bewitching warren of ancient Mediterranean streets unfold.

It was in this old quarter, now Vieux Nice, that the Greeks established a market-port in the 4th century BC and named it Nikaia. After falling to the Saracen invasions, Nice regained power and developed into an important port in the early Middle Ages. In 1388, under Louis d'Anjou, Nice, along with the hill towns behind, effectively seceded from the

Nice

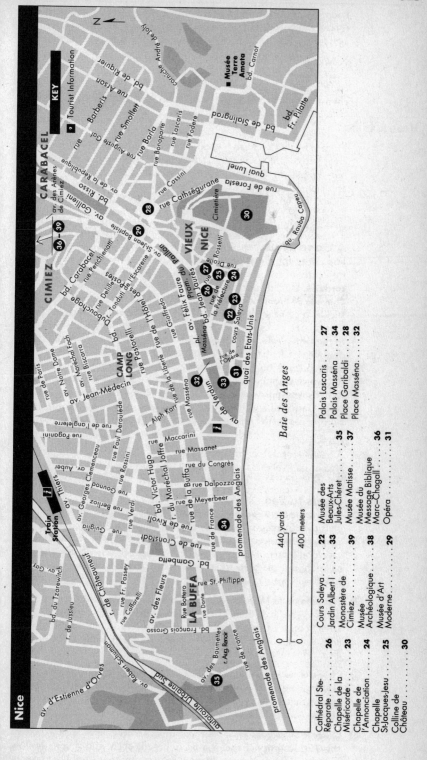

Cathédral Ste-Réparate	26
Chapelle de la Miséricorde	23
Chapelle de l'Annonciation	24
Chapelle St-Jacques-Jesu	25
Colline de Château	30
Cours Saleya	22
Jardin Albert I	33
Monastère de Cimiez	39
Musée Archéologique	38
Musée d'Art Moderne	29
Musée des Beaux-Arts Jules-Chéret	35
Musée Matisse	37
Musée du Message Biblique Marc–Chagall	36
Opéra	31
Palais Lascaris	27
Palais Masséna	34
Place Garibaldi	28
Place Masséna	32

county of Provence and allied itself with Savoie as the Comté de Nice (Nice County). It was a relationship that lasted some 500 years and added rich Italian flavor to the city's culture, architecture, and dialect.

Nowadays Nice strikes an engaging balance between historic Provençal grace, port-town exotica, urban energy, whimsy, and high culture. You could easily spend your vacation here, attuned to Nice's quirks, its rhythms, its very multi-culti population, and its Mediterranean tides.

Vieux Nice

Framed by the "château"—really a rocky promontory—and cours Saleya, Nice's Old Town is its strongest drawing point and, should you only be passing through, the best place to capture the city's historic atmosphere. Its grid of narrow streets, darkened by houses five and six stories high with bright splashes of laundry fluttering overhead and jewel-box Baroque churches on every other corner, creates a magic that seems utterly removed from the Côte d'Azur fast lane.

A Good Walk

First, head for the morning flower market on the **cours Saleya** ㉒. At the center of cours Saleya is the florid, Baroque **Chapelle de la Miséricorde** ㉓. Thread your way into the Old Town maze to the extravagant **Chapelle de l'Annonciation** ㉔. Continue up Poissonerie to rue de la Place Vieille, then head right to rue Droite; the **Chapelle St-Jacques-Jesu** ㉕ looms large and spare. Turn left on rue Rossetti and cross the square to the **Cathédrale Ste-Réparate** ㉖. Now take a break from the sacred, doubling back up rue Rossetti and continuing left up narrow rue Droite to the magnificent **Palais Lascaris** ㉗. Head next to boulevard Jean-Jaurès, which empties onto the grand, arcaded **place Garibaldi** ㉘; one of its five street spokes points straight to the **Musée d'Art Moderne** ㉙. From place Garibaldi and boulevard Jean-Jaurès, wind your way up to the ruins of the castle, now a park called the **Colline de Château** ㉚.

TIMING

Aim for morning on this walk, so you'll see the market on cours Saleya at its liveliest. If you include a visit to the Palais Lascaris and a visit to the Musée Terra Amata, this would make a full day's outing.

Sights to See

㉖ **Cathédrale Ste-Réparate.** An ensemble of columns, cupolas, and symmetrical ornaments dominates the Old Town, flanked by its own 18th-century bell tower and capped by its glossy ceramic-tile dome. The cathedral's interior, restored to a bright palette of ocher, golds, and rusts, has elaborate plasterwork and decorative frescoes on every surface. ✉ *Rue Ste-Réparate, Vieux-Nice.*

㉓ **Chapelle de la Miséricorde.** A superbly balanced *pièce-montée* (wedding cake) of half-domes and cupolas, this chapel is decorated within an inch of its life with frescoes, faux marble, gilt, and crystal chandeliers. A magnificent Bréa altarpiece crowns the ensemble. ✉ *Cours Saleya., Vieux-Nice.*

㉔ **Chapelle de l'Annonciation.** This 17th-century Carmelite chapel is a classic example of pure Niçoise Baroque, from its sculpted door to its extravagant marble work and the florid symmetry of its arches and cupolas. ✉ *Rue de la Poissonerie, Vieux-Nice.*

㉕ **Chapelle St-Jacques-Jesu.** If the Old Town's other chapels are jewel boxes, this 17th-century chapel is a barn: broad, open, and ringing hollow, this church seems austere by comparison, but that's only because the theatrical decoration is spread over a more expansive surface. ✉ *Corner of rue Droite and rue Gesu, Vieux-Nice.*

30 **Colline de Château** (Château Hill). Though nothing remains of the once-massive medieval stronghold but a few ruins left after its 1706 dismantling, this park still bears its name. From here take in extraordinary views of the Baie des Anges, the length of the Promenade des Anglais, and the red-ocher roofs of the Old Town. ⏲ *Daily 7–7.*

22 **Cours Saleya.** This street is framed with 18th-century houses and shaded by plane trees. The tall yellow-stone building at the far-east end was home to Henri Matisse from 1921 to 1938.

29 **Musée d'Art Moderne.** The assertive contemporary architecture of the Modern Art Museum makes a bold and emphatic statement regarding Nice's presence in the modern world. The art collection inside focuses intently and thoroughly on contemporary art from the late 1950s onward. ✉ *Promenade des Arts, Vieux-Nice,* ☎ *04–93–62–61–62.* 🎟 *€4.* ⏲ *Mon., Wed.–Thurs., and weekends 11–6; Fri. 11–10.*

27 **Palais Lascaris.** The aristocratic Lascaris Palace was built in 1648 for Jean-Baptiste Lascaris-Vintimille, *marechal* to the duke of Savoy. The magnificent vaulted staircase, with its massive stone balustrade and niches filled with classical gods, is surpassed in grandeur only by the Flemish tapestries (after Rubens) and the extraordinary trompe-l'oeil fresco depicting the fall of Phaëthon. ✉ *15 rue Droite, Vieux-Nice,* ☎ *04–93–62–05–54.* 🎟 *€4.* ⏲ *Tues.–Sun. 10–noon and 2–6.*

28 **Place Garibaldi.** Encircled by grand vaulted arcades stuccoed in rich yellow, the broad pentagon of this square could have been airlifted out of Turin. In the center, the shrinelike fountain sculpture of Garibaldi seems to be surveying you as you stroll under the arcades and lounge in its cafés.

Along the Promenade des Anglais

Nice takes on a completely different character west of cours Saleya, with broad city blocks, vast Neoclassical hotels and apartment houses, and a series of inviting parks dense with palm trees, greenery, and splashing fountains. From the Jardin Albert Ier, once the delta of the Paillon River, the famous promenade des Anglais stretches the length of the city's waterfront. The original promenade was the brainchild of Lewis Way, an English minister in the then-growing community of British refugees drawn to Nice's climate. Nowadays it's a wide multilane boulevard thick with traffic—in fact, it's the last gasp of the N98 coastal highway. Beside it runs its charming parallel, a wide, sun-washed pedestrian walkway with intermittent steps leading down to the smooth-rock beach. A daily parade of *promeneurs,* rollerbladers, joggers, and sun baskers strolls its broad pavement, looking out over the hypnotic blue expanse of the sea. Only in the wee hours is it possible to enjoy the waterfront stroll as the cream of Nice's international society once did, when there was nothing more than hoofbeats to compete with the roar of the waves.

A Good Walk

From the west end of cours Saleya, walk down rue St-François-de-Paule past the Belle Epoque **Opéra** ㉛. Continue up the street, then head right up rue de l'Opéra to **Place Masséna** ㉜, framed in broad arcades and opening onto the vast, green **Jardin Albert I** ㉝. Three long blocks past the Casino Ruhl, you'll reach the gates and park of the imposing **Palais Masséna** ㉞. Walk along the waterfront for a few blocks, past busy boulevard Gambetta, then head inland up tiny rue Sauvan. Cross boulevard Grosso and head diagonally up the hill on avenue des Baumettes. In this quiet, once luxurious neighborhood is the **Musée des Beaux-Arts Jules-Chéret** ㉟, built in extravagant Italianate style.

TIMING

This walk covers a long stretch of waterfront, so it may take up to an hour to stroll the length of it. Allow a half day if you intend to explore the Palais Massena or the Musée des Beaux Arts.

Sights to See

33 **Jardin Albert I** (Albert I Garden). Along the Promenade des Anglais, this luxurious garden stands over the delta of the River Paillon, underground since 1882. Every kind of flower and palm tree grows here, thrown into exotic relief by night illumination.

35 **Musée des Beaux-Arts Jules-Chéret** (Jules-Chéret Fine Arts Museum). In a 19th-century Italianate mansion, the museum has a fine collection of paintings by Nice artists of the era, including works by the museum's namesake. It also has a small collection of Impressionist works, two pieces by Rodin, and some ceramic pieces by Picasso. ✉ *33 av. des Baumettes, Centre-Ville,* ☏ *04–92–15–28–28.* 🎫 €4. ⏲ *Oct.–Apr., Tues.–Sun. 10–noon and 2–5; May–Sept., Tues.–Sun. 10–noon and 2–6.*

31 **Opéra.** A half block west of the cours Saleya stands a flamboyant Italian-style theater designed by Charles Garnier, architect of the Paris Opéra. It's home today to the Opéra de Nice, with a permanent chorus, orchestra, and ballet corps. ✉ *4 rue St-François-de-Paule, Vieux-Nice/Port,* ☏ *04–92–17–40–40.*

34 **Palais Masséna** (Masséna Palace). This handsome Belle Epoque building, housing the **Musée d'Art et d'Histoire** (Museum of Art and History), is undergoing a complete renovation and is scheduled to reopen sometime in 2002. ✉ *Entrance at 65 rue de France, Centre-Ville,* ☏ *04–93–88–11–34.*

32 **Place Masséna.** As cours Saleya is the heart of the Old Town, so this broad square is the heart of the city as a whole. It's framed by an ensemble of Italian-style arcaded buildings first built in 1815, their facades stuccoed in rich red ocher.

Cimiez

Once the site of the powerful Roman settlement Cemenelum, the hilltop neighborhood of Cimiez—4 km (2 mi) north of cours Saleya—is Nice's most luxurious quarter (use Bus 15 from place Massena or avenue Jean-Médecin to visit its sights).

A Good Walk

Begin at the **Musée du Message Biblique Marc-Chagall** (36), which houses one of the finest collections of Chagall's works based on biblical themes. Then make the pilgrimage to the center of Cimiez and the **Musée Matisse** (37), where an important collection of Matisse's life work is amassed in an Italianate villa. Just behind, the **Musée Archéologique** (38) displays a wealth of Roman treasures. Slightly east of the museum is the thriving **Monastère de Cimiez** (39), a Franciscan monastery.

TIMING

Between bus connections and long walks from sight to sight, this walk is a half-day commitment at minimum. Or if you plan to really spend time in the Matisse Museum and the Chagall Museum, it could easily become a day's outing.

Sights to See

39 **Monastère de Cimiez.** This fully functioning monastery is worth the pilgrimage. You'll find a lovely **garden**, replanted along the lines of the original 16th-century layout; the **Musée Franciscain**, a didactic museum tracing the history of the Franciscan order; and a 15th-century **church**

containing three works of remarkable power and elegance by Bréa. ✉ *Pl. du Monastère, Cimiez,* ☎ *04–93–81–00–04.* 🎫 *Free.* ⏲ *Mon.–Sat. 10–noon and 3–6.*

38 **Musée Archéologique** (Archaeology Museum). This museum, next to the Matisse Museum, has a dense and intriguing collection of objects extracted from the digs around the Roman city of Cemenelum, which flourished from the 1st to 5th centuries. ✉ *160 av. des Arènes-de-Cimiez, Cimiez,* ☎ *04–93–81–59–57.* 🎫 *€4.* ⏲ *Apr.–Sept., Tues.–Sun. 10–noon and 2–6; Oct.–Mar., Tues.–Sun. 10–1 and 2–5.*

★ 37 **Musée Matisse.** In the '60s the city of Nice bought this lovely, light-bathed 17th-century villa, surrounded by the ruins of Roman civilization, and restored it to house a large collection of Henri Matisse's works. Matisse settled in Nice in 1917, seeking a sun cure after a bout with pneumonia, and remained here until his death in 1954. During his years on the Côte d'Azur, Matisse maintained intense friendships and artistic liaisons with Renoir, who lived in Cagnes, and with Picasso, who lived in Mougins and Antibes. Settling first along the waterfront, he eventually moved up to the rarified isolation of Cimiez and took an apartment in the Hôtel Regina (now an apartment building), where he lived out the rest of his life. Matisse walked often in the parklands around the Roman remains and was buried in an olive grove outside the Cimiez cemetery. The collection of artworks includes several pieces the artist donated to the city before his death; the rest were donated by his family. In every medium and context—paintings, gouache cutouts, engravings, and book illustrations—it represents the evolution of his art, from Cézanne-like still lifes to exuberant dancing paper dolls. Even the furniture and accessories speak of Matisse, from the Chinese vases to the bold-printed fabrics with which he surrounded himself. A series of black-and-white photographs captures the artist at work, surrounded by personal—and telling—details. ✉ *164 av. des Arènes-de-Cimiez, Cimiez,* ☎ *04–93–81–08–08.* 🎫 *€4.* ⏲ *Apr.–Sept., Wed.–Mon. 10–6; Oct.–Mar., Wed.–Mon. 10–5.*

★ 36 **Musée du Message Biblique Marc-Chagall** (Marc Chagall Museum of Biblical Themes). This museum has one of the finest permanent collections of Chagall's (1887–1985) late works. Superbly displayed, 17 vast canvases depict biblical themes, each in emphatic, joyous colors. ✉ *Av. du Dr-Ménard (head up av. Thiers, then take a left onto av. Malausséna, cross railway tracks, and take first right up av. de l'Olivetto), Cimiez,* ☎ *04–93–53–87–20.* 🎫 *€5, in summer €6.* ⏲ *July–Sept., Wed.–Mon. 10–6; Oct.–June, Wed.–Mon. 10–5.*

Dining and Lodging

$$–$$$ ✕ **Grand Café de Turin.** Whether you squeeze onto a banquette in the dark, low-ceiling bar or win a coveted table under the arcaded porticoes on place Garibaldi, this is *the* place to go for shellfish in Nice: sea snails, clams, plump *fines de claires*, and salty *bleues* oysters, and urchins by the dozen. It's packed noon and night. ✉ *5 pl. Garibaldi, Vieux-Nice,* ☎ *04–93–62–29–52. AE, DC, MC, V. Closed June.*

$$–$$$ ✕ **L'Olivier.** In this hole-in-the-wall bistro on place Garibaldi, two brothers have gone back to their roots, and all of Nice has followed. Frank Musso, trained at the Tour d'Argent in Paris, concentrates his sophisticated gifts on simple dishes: tripe simmered in tomatoes, daubes and pork confits, and crepes with homemade bitter-orange marmalade. His brother Christian provides the cheery welcome. Dinner menus are €19 to €28. ✉ *2 pl. Garibaldi, Vieux-Nice,* ☎ *04–93–26–89–09. Reservations essential. AE, MC, V. Closed Sun. and Aug. No dinner Wed.*

$$ ★ ✕ **La Mérenda.** The back-to-bistro boom climaxed here when Dominique Le Stanc retired his crown at the Negresco to take over this tiny, unpretentious landmark of Provençal cuisine. Now he and his wife work in the miniature open kitchen, creating the ultimate versions of stuffed sardines, pistou, and slow-simmered *daubes* (beef stews). To reserve entry to the inner sanctum, you must stop by in person (there is no telephone). The dinner menu is €25. ✉ *4 rue de la Terrasse, Vieux-Nice,* ☎ *no phone. No credit cards. Closed weekends, last wk July, 1st 2 wks Aug., and school holidays.*

$ ✕ **Chez René/Socca.** This back-alley landmark is the most popular dive in town for socca, the chickpea-pancake snack food unique to Nice. Rustic olive-wood tables line the street, and curt waiters splash down your drink order. For the food, you get in line at the Socca, choose your €3 plate (or plates), and carry it steaming to the table yourself. It's off place Garibaldi on the edge of the old town, across from the *gare routière* (bus station). ✉ *2 rue Miralheti, Vieux-Nice,* ☎ *04–93–92–05–73. No credit cards.*

$ ✕ **Lou Pilha Leva.** Not as well known as Chez René but much more serious about the socca it serves, this street stand just south of place St-François offers good, fresh-cooked versions of petits farcis, chickpea socca, quichelike *tourta de blea,* and pissaladières as well as full meals of homemade pasta, pizza, stockfish (stewed salt cod), and polenta, all made on the premises. Order food at the window, drinks at the table. ✉ *10 rue du Collet, on pl. Centrale, Vieux-Nice,* ☎ *04–93–13–99–08. MC, V.*

$$$$ ★ ✕🏨 **La Perouse.** Just past the Old Town, at the foot of the château, this hotel is a secret treasure cut into the cliff (an elevator takes you up to reception). Some of the best rooms (including Raoul Dufy's favorite) not only have views of the azure sea but also look down into an intimate garden with lemon trees and a cliffside pool. The restaurant serves meals in the candlelit garden May–September. ✉ *11 quai Rauba-Capeau, Le Château 06300,* ☎ *04–93–62–34–63,* FAX *04–93–62–59–41,* WEB *www.hroy.com/la-perouse. 64 rooms. Restaurant, cable TV, minibars, Internet, health club, meeting room, pool, sauna. AE, DC, MC, V.*

$$$–$$$$ ✕🏨 **Beau Rivage.** Occupying an imposing late-19th-century town house near cours Saleya, this hotel (guests included Chekhov, Matisse, and Nietzsche) is just a few steps from the best parts of Old Nice and the beach, though other buildings have long since blocked its sea views. The rooms are standard and a bit stuffy, done in a color scheme of pinks and teals. The restaurant, however, is fabulous. ✉ *24 rue St-François-de-Paule, Vieux-Nice 06000,* ☎ *04–93–80–80–70,* FAX *04–93–80–55–77. 118 rooms. Restaurant, no-smoking rooms, cable TV, minibars, beach. AE, DC, MC, V.*

$$ 🏨 **La Fontaine.** Downtown and a block from the waterfront, this immaculate, simply designed hotel offers a friendly welcome from its house-proud owners. Rooms are small and comfortable, in cheery blues and yellows and with bathrooms freshly tiled. It even has a pretty little courtyard where breakfast is served. ✉ *49 rue de France, Vieux-Nice 06000,* ☎ *04–93–88–30–38,* FAX *04–93–88–98–11. 28 rooms. Cable TV, minibars, Internet. AE, DC, MC, V.*

$$ ★ 🏨 **Windsor.** This is a memorably eccentric hotel with a vision: most of its white-on-white rooms either have frescoes of mythic themes or are works of artists' whimsy. But the real draw of this otherworldly place is its astonishing city-center garden—a tropical oasis of lemon, magnolia, and palm trees. You can breakfast or dine here by candlelight (guests only) and dip into the small, shrubbery-screened pool. ✉ *11 rue Dalpozzo, Vieux-Nice 06000,* ☎ *04–93–88–59–35,* FAX *04–93–*

88–94–57, WEB *www.webstore.fr/windsor. 57 rooms. Restaurant, bar, no air-conditioning in some rooms, cable TV, minibars, pool. AE, DC, MC, V.*

$ **Felix.** On popular, pedestrian rue Masséna and a block from the beach, this tiny hotel is owned by a hard-working couple (both fluent in English) who make you feel welcome. Rooms are compact but neat and bright, so they don't feel as small, and four have tiny balconies providing a ringside seat over the pedestrian thoroughfare. ✉ *41 rue Masséna, Vieux-Nice 06000,* ☎ *04–93–88–67–73,* FAX *04–93–16–15–78. 14 rooms. Cable TV, minibars, Internet. AE, DC, MC, V.*

Nightlife and the Arts

The **Casino Ruhl** (✉ 1 Promenade des Anglais, Vieux-Nice, ☎ 04–93–87–95–87), gleaming neon-bright and modern, is a sophisticated Riviera landmark. If you're all dressed up and have just won big, invest in a drink in the intimate walnut-and-velour **Bar Anglais** (✉ 37 Promenade des Anglais, Vieux-Nice, ☎ 04–93–88–39–51), in the landmark Hôtel Negresco.

In July the **Nice Jazz Festival** (☎ 04–92–17–77–77 for information) draws international performers from around the world. Classical music and ballet performances take place at Nice's convention center, the **Acropolis** (✉ Palais des Congrès, Esplanade John F. Kennedy, Centre-Ville, ☎ 04–93–92–83–00). The season at the **Opéra de Nice** (✉ 4 rue St-François-de-Paul, Vieux-Nice, ☎ 04–92–17–40–40) runs from September to June.

Outdoor Activities and Sports

Nice's **beaches** extend all along the Baie des Anges, backed full-length by the Promenade des Anglais. Public stretches alternate with posh private beaches that have restaurants—and bar service, mattresses and parasols, waterskiing, parasailing, windsurfing, and jet-skiing. Some of the handiest private beaches are the **Beau Rivage** (☎ 04–92–47–82–83), across from the cours Saleya, and the **Ruhl** (☎ 04–93–87–09–70), across from the casino.

Shopping

Olive oil by the gallon in cans with colorful, old-fashioned labels is sold at tiny **Alziari** (✉ 14 rue St-François-de-Paule, Vieux-Nice). A good source for crystallized fruit, a Nice specialty, is the **Confiserie du Vieux Nice** (✉ 14 quai Papacino, Vieux-Nice), on the west side of the port. The venerable **Henri Auer** (✉ 7 rue St-François-de-Paule, Vieux-Nice) has sold crystallized fruit since 1820. For fragrances, linens, and pickled-wood furniture, head to **Boutique 3** (✉ 3 rue Longchamp, Vieux-Nice), run by three Niçoise women of rare talent and taste.

Seafood of all kinds is sold at the **fish market** (✉ Pl. St-François, Vieux-Nice) every morning except Monday. At the daily **flower market** (✉ Cours Saleya, Vieux-Nice) you can find all kinds of plants and fruits and vegetables. The **antiques and brocante market** (✉ Pl. Robilante, Vieux-Nice), by the old port, is held from Tuesday through Saturday.

En Route The lay of the land east of Nice is nearly vertical, as the coastline is one great cliff, a corniche terraced by three parallel highways—the **Basse Corniche,** the **Moyenne Corniche,** and the **Grande Corniche**—that snake along its graduated crests. The lowest (*basse*) is the slowest, following the coast and crawling through the main streets of resorts—including downtown Monte Carlo. The highest (*grande*) is the fastest, but its panoramic views are blocked by villas, and there are few safe overlooks. The middle (*moyenne*) offers views down over the shoreline and villages and passes through a few picturesque towns.

THE EASTERN CÔTE D'AZUR

You may build castles in Spain or picture yourself on a South Sea island, but when it comes to serious speculation about how to spend that first $10 million and slip easily into the life of the idle rich, most people head for France and the stretch of coast that covers the eastern Côte d'Azur. Here, backed by the mistral-proof Alps and coddled by mild Mediterranean breezes, waterfront resorts—Villefranche and Menton—draw energy from the thriving city of Nice, while jutting tropical peninsulas—Cap Ferrat, Cap Martin—frame the tiny principality of Monaco. Here the corniche highways snake above sparkling waters, their pink-and-white villas turning faces toward the sun. Cliffs bristle with palm trees and parasol pines, and a riot of mimosa, bougainvillea, jasmine, and even cactus blooms in the hothouse climate. Crowded with sunseekers, the Riviera still reveals quiet corners with heart-stopping views of sea, sun, and mountains—all within one memorable frame.

Villefranche-sur-Mer

★ 40 *10 km (6 mi) east of Nice.*

Nestled discreetly along the deep scoop of harbor between Nice and Cap Ferrat, this pretty watercolor of a fishing port seems surreal, flanked as it is by the big city of Nice and the assertive wealth of Monaco. The town is a stage-set of brightly colored houses—the sort of place where *Fanny* could have been filmed. Genuine fishermen actually skim up to the docks here in weathered-blue *barques,* and the streets of the Old Town flow directly to the waterfront, much as they did in the 13th century. The deep harbor, in the caldera of a volcano, was once preferred by the likes of Onassis and Niarchos and royals on their yachts (today, unfortunately, these are usually replaced by warships as a result of the presence of a nearby naval base). The character of Villefranche was subtly shaped by the artists and authors who gathered at the Hôtel Welcome—Diaghilev and Stravinsky, taking a break from the Ballet Russe in Monaco; Somerset Maugham and Evelyn Waugh; and, above all, Jean Cocteau, who came here to recover from the excesses of Paris life. Behind towering gates and secluded groves are the private vacation villas of some of the wealthiest people on earth. The most celebrated is La Leopolda, built in the early 20th century by King Leopold of Belgium for his mistress; the villa is private but has a famous garden staircase, gloriously immortalized in the film *The Red Shoes,* whose endless stairs may be glimpsed through gates on the road below the villa.

So enamored was Jean Cocteau of this painterly fishing port that he decorated the 14th-century **Chapelle St-Pierre** with images from the life of St. Peter and dedicated it to the village's fishermen. ✉ *Pl. Pollanais,* ☎ *04–93–76–90–70.* 🎫 *€2.* ⏲ *Mid-June–mid-Sept., Tues.–Sun. 10–noon and 4–8:30; mid-Sept.–mid-Nov., Tues.–Sun. 9:30–noon and 2–6; end Dec.–Mar., Tues.–Sun. 9:30–noon and 2–5:30; Apr.–mid-June, Tues.–Sun. 9:30–noon and 3–7.*

Running parallel to the waterfront, the extraordinary 13th-century **rue Obscure** (literally, Dark Street) is entirely covered by vaulted arcades; it sheltered the people of Villefranche when the Germans fired their parting shots—an artillery bombardment—near the end of World War II. The stalwart 16th-century **Citadelle St-Elme,** restored to perfect condition, anchors the harbor with its broad, sloping stone walls. Beyond its drawbridge lie the city's administrative offices and a group of minor gallery-museums, with a scattering of works by Picasso and Miró. Whether or not you stop into these private collections of local art (all free of charge), you are welcome to stroll around the inner grounds and to circle the imposing exterior.

Lodging

$$–$$$ ★ **Hôtel Welcome.** When Villefranche harbored a community of artists and writers, this waterfront landmark was their adopted headquarters. Somerset Maugham holed up in one of the tiny crow's-nest rooms at the top, and Jean Cocteau moved into one of the corners. Evelyn Waugh and Richard Burton used to tie one on in the bar. It's comfortable and modern, with the best rooms brightened with vivid colors and stenciled quotes from Cocteau. The views are spectacular. ✉ *Quai Courbet, 06230,* ☎ *04–93–76–27–62,* FAX *04–93–76–27–66. 32 rooms. 2 restaurants, bar, some air-conditioning, cable TV, minibars, Internet, health club. AE, DC, MC, V. Closed mid-Nov.–mid-Dec.*

Beaulieu

41 *4 km (2 mi) east of Villefranche, 14 km (9 mi) east of Nice.*

With its back pressed hard against the cliffs of the corniche and sheltered between the peninsulas of Cap Ferrat and Cap Roux, this once-grand resort basks in a tropical microclimate that earned its central neighborhood the name *Petite Afrique*. The town was the pet of 19th-century society, and its grand hotels welcomed Empress Eugénie, the Prince of Wales, and Russian nobility.

★ One manifestation of Beaulieu's Belle Epoque excess is the eye-knocking **Villa Kerylos,** a mansion built in 1902 in the style of classical Greece. It was the dream house of the amateur archaeologist Théodore Reinach, who commissioned an Italian architect to surround him with Grecian delights: cool Carrara marble, rare fruitwoods, and a dining salon where guests reclined to eat *à la Greque*. Don't miss this—it's one of the most unusual houses in the south of France. ✉ *Rue Gustave-Eiffel,* ☎ *04–93–01–01–44.* €7. ⏲ *Mid-Feb.–mid-Nov., daily 10:30–6; mid-Dec.–mid-Feb., weekdays 2–6, weekends 10:30–6; July–Aug., daily 10:30–7.*

Dining and Lodging

$$$$ ★ **Métropole.** Affluent beachcombers have been coming to this palace for more than 100 years, attracted by the saltwater pool and beautiful seaside terrace. The Restoration-style furniture and subdued beige and blue-gray tones in the guest rooms offer a welcome change from the Provençal patterns that tyrannize the region. New chef Christian Métral has enlivened the Mediterranean-based cuisine with tempura starters, oyster and squid cassoulet, and citrus-caramelized endives. ✉ *Bd. Mar. Leclerc, 06160,* ☎ *04–93–01–00–08,* FAX *04–93–01–18–51. 35 rooms, 5 suites. Restaurant, cable TV, minibars, pool, beach. AE, DC, MC, V. Closed mid-Oct.–mid-Dec.*

St-Jean-Cap-Ferrat

★ 42 *2 km (1 mi) south of Beaulieu on D25.*

This luxuriously sited pleasure port moors the peninsula of Cap Ferrat; from its port-side walkways and crescent of beach you can look over the sparkling blue harbor to the graceful green bulk of the corniches. Yachts purr in and out of port, and their passengers scuttle into cafés for take-out drinks to enjoy on their private decks.

★ Between the port and the mainland, the gaudily beautiful **Villa Ephrussi de Rothschild** stands as witness to the wealth and worldly flair of the baroness who had it built. Constructed in 1905 in neo-Venetian style (its flamingo-pink facade was thought not to be in the best of taste by the local gentry), the house was baptised "Ile-de-France" in hommage to the Baroness Bétrice de Rothschild's favorite ocean liner (her staff used to wear sailing costumes and her ship travel-kit is on view in her bedroom). Precious artworks, tapestries, and furniture adorn the salons. The grounds are landscaped with no fewer than seven theme gardens; be sure to allow yourself time to wander here, as this is one of the few places on the coast where you'll be allowed to experience the lavish pleasures characteristic of the Belle Epoque Côte d'Azur. Tea and light lunches are served in a glassed-in porch overlooking the grounds and spectacular views of the coastline. ✉ *Av. Ephrussi,* ☎ *04–93–01–33–09.* 🎟 *Access to ground floor and gardens €8; guided tour upstairs €2 extra.* ⏲ *Feb.–June and Sept.–Nov., daily 10–6; July–Aug., daily 10–7; Nov.–Jan., weekdays 2–6, weekends 10–6.*

The residents of Cap Ferrat fiercely protect it from curious tourists; its grand old villas are hidden for the most part in the depths of tropical gardens. You can nonetheless walk its entire **coastline promenade** if you strike out from the port; from the restaurant Capitaine Cook, cut right up avenue des Fossés, turn right on avenue Vignon, and follow the chemin de la Carrière. The 11-km (7-mi) walk passes through rich tropical flora and, on the west side, over white cliffs buffeted by waves. When you've traced the full outline of the peninsula, veer up the chemin du Roy past the fabulous gardens of the **Villa des Cèdres,** once owned by King Leopold II of Belgium at the turn of the last century; you'll reach the **Plage de Passable,** from which you cut back across the peninsula's wrist. A shorter loop takes you from town out to the **Pointe de St-Hospice,** much of the walk shaded by wind-twisted pines. From the port climb avenue Jean Mermoz to place Paloma and follow the path closest to the waterfront. At the point are an 18th-century prison tower, a 19th-century chapel, and unobstructed views of Cap Martin.

Dining and Lodging

$$$ ✕ **Le Sloop.** This sleek port-side restaurant caters to the yachting crowd and sailors who cruise into dock for lunch. The focus is fish, of course: *soupe de poisson* (fish soup), *St-Pierre* (John Dory) steamed with asparagus, roasted whole sea bass. Its outdoor tables surround a tiny "garden" of potted palms. The menu is €25. ✉ *Port de Plaisance,* ☎ *04–93–01–48–63. AE, MC, V. Closed Wed. mid-Sept.–mid-Apr. No lunch Wed.–Thurs. mid-Apr.–mid-Sept.*

$$–$$$ ★ 🏨 **Brise Marine.** With a glowing Provençal-yellow facade, bright blue shutters, and balustraded sea terrace, this lovely vision fulfills most desires for that perfect, picturesque Cap Ferrat hotel. Pretty pastel guest rooms feel like bedrooms in a private home—many offer window views of the gorgeous peninsula stunningly framed by statuesque palms. ✉ *58 av. Jean Mermoz, 06230,* ☎ *04–93–76–04–36,* FAX *04–93–76–11–49,* WEB *www.hotel-brisemarine.com. 16 rooms. Bar, cable TV, minibars. AE, DC, MC, V. Closed Nov.–Jan.*

Èze

43 *2 km (1 mi) east of Beaulieu, 12 km (7 mi) east of Nice, 7 km (4 mi) west of Monte Carlo.*

Towering like an eagle's nest above the coast and crowned with ramparts and the ruins of a medieval château, Èze (pronounced *ehz*) is unfortunately the most accessible of all the perched villages. Consequently, it's by far the most commercialized, surpassing St-Paul-de-Vence for the tackiness of its souvenir shops and the indifference of its waiters. It is, nonetheless, spectacularly sited; if you can manage to shake the crowds and duck off to a quiet overlook, the village commands splendid views up and down the coast, one of the draws that once lured fabled visitors—lots of crowned heads, Georges Sand, Friedrich Nietzsche—and residents: Consuelo Vanderbilt, when she was tired of being duchess of Marlborough, traded in Blenheim Palace for a custom-built house here.

From the crest-top **Jardin Exotique** (Tropical Garden), full of rare succulents, you can pan your videocam all the way around the hills and waterfront. But if you want a prayer of a chance of enjoying the magnificence of this lovely stone village, come at dawn or after sunset—or (if you have the means) spend the night—and the day elsewhere. The church of **Notre-Dame,** consecrated in 1772, glitters inside with Baroque retables and altarpieces. Èze's tourist office, on place du Gal-de-Gaulle, can direct you to the numerous footpaths that thread Èze with the coast's three corniche highways.

Dining and Lodging

$$ ✕ **Troubadour.** Amid the clutter and clatter, this is a wonderful find: comfortably relaxed, this old family house proffers pleasant service and excellent dishes, like roasted scallops with chicken broth and squab with citrus zest and beef broth. Full-course menus range from €27 to €38. ✉ *4 rue du Brec,* ☎ *04–93–41–19–03. AE, MC, V. Closed Mon., Fri. lunch, 1st wk July and early Dec.*

$ ✕ **Loumiri.** Classic Provençal and regional seafood dishes are tastily prepared and married with decent, inexpensive wines at this cute little bistro near the entrance to the Old Village. The best bet is to order *à l'ardoise*—that is, from the blackboard listing of daily specials. The lunch menu prix-fixe (€15) is the best deal in town. Dinner menus start at €20 and top out at €27. ✉ *Av. Jardin Exotique,* ☎ *04–93–41–16–42. AE, MC, V. Closed Mon., Wed. dinner, Feb.*

$$$$ ★ ✕ **Château de la Chèvre d'Or.** Though on the main tourist thoroughfare, these weathered-stone houses allow you to turn your back on the world and drink in unsurpassed sea views. More than half the creamy white rooms look over the water, and the others compensate with exposed stone, beams, and burnished antiques. The three restaurants all take in the views, too, as does the Louis XIII–style bar. It is the luxurious if occasionally precious main restaurant that draws kudos for its delicate stuffed pastas and near-crunchy risotto, its buttery mullet fillets, and its gingerbread soufflés. The swimming pool alone, clinging like a swallow's nest to the hillside, may justify the investment, as do the liveried footmen who greet you at the village entrance to wave you VIP style past the cattle-drive of tourists. ✉ *Rue du Barri, 06360,* ☎ *04–92–10–66–66,* FAX *04–93–41–06–72,* WEB *www.relaischateaux.com. 23 rooms, 9 suites. 3 restaurants, cable TV, minibars, Internet, tennis court, pool. AE, DC, MC, V. Closed Dec.–Feb.*

$$$$ ★ ✕ **Château Eza.** Vertiginously perched on the edge of a cliff 3,000 feet above the crouching tiger of St Jean-Cap Ferrat, this former residence of Prince William of Sweden is one of the most dramatic, romantic, and expensive joints on the entire Mediterranean coast. Rooms are spread among a cluster of 13th century buildings on cobblestoned streets too narrow for cars. Most have private entrances and all are luxed out to the max: canopy beds, costly objets d'art and antiques, exquisite carpets and tapestries, wood-burning fireplaces and unbelievable views. If you're not staying the night, the views from the panoramic restaurant and outdoor terrace are just as good. The wine list is one of the best on the Côte, though the food has slipped a notch and service can be haughty. Still, for fairy-tale experiences, the surroundings are hard to beat. ✉ *06360,* ☎ *04–93–41–12–24,* FAX *04–93–41–16–64,* WEB *www.slh.fr. 7 rooms, 3 suites. Restaurant, minibars. AE, DC, MC, V. Closed Apr.–Oct.*

Peillon

★ 44 *15 km (9 mi) northeast of Nice via D2204 and D21.*

Perhaps because it's difficult to reach and not on the way to or from anything else, this idyllic village has maintained the magical ambience of its medieval origins. You can hear the bell toll here, walk in silence along its weathered cobblestones, and smell the thyme crunching underfoot if you step past its minuscule boundaries onto the unspoiled hillsides. And its streets are utterly and completely commerce-free; the citizens have voted to vaccinate themselves against the plague of boutiques, galleries, and cafés that have afflicted its peers along the coast.

Dining and Lodging

$$–$$$ ★ ✕🏨 **Auberge de la Madone.** With its shaded garden terrace and its impeccable, bright-colored rooms, this inn is a charming oasis. A lunch of sea bass, pigeon, and goat cheese on the flowery veranda is everything the south of France should be. The inn has a tennis court on the slope above it and, in the village annex Lou Pourtail, six little rooms offering shelter at bargain rates. ✉ *06440 Peillon Village,* ☎ *04–93–79–91–17,* FAX *04–93–79–99–36. 20 rooms. Restaurant, no air-conditioning, no-smoking rooms, minibars, Internet, tennis court. MC, V. Closed late Oct.–late Dec. and Jan.*

Monaco

7 km (4 mi) east of Èze, 21 km (13 mi) east of Nice.

It's positively feudal, the idea that an ancient dynasty of aristocrats could still hold fast to its patch of coastline, the last scrap of a once-vast domain. But that's just what the Grimaldi family did, clinging to a few acres of glory and maintaining their own license plates, their own telephone area code (377—don't forget to dial this when calling Monaco from France or other countries), and their own highly forgiving tax system. Yet the Principality of Monaco covers just 473 acres and would fit comfortably inside New York's Central Park or a family farm in Iowa. And its 5,000 pampered citizens would fill only a small fraction of the seats in Yankee Stadium.

The present ruler, Prince Rainier III, traces his ancestry to Otto Canella, who was born in 1070. The Grimaldi dynasty began with Otto's great-great-great-grandson, Francesco Grimaldi, also known as Frank the Rogue. Expelled from Genoa, Frank and his cronies disguised themselves as monks and in 1297 seized the fortified medieval town known today as Le Rocher (the Rock). Except for a short break under Napoléon, the Grimaldis have been here ever since, which makes them the oldest reigning family in Europe (they also seem to be the tackiest, considering all the lurid tabloid coverage of princesses Caroline and Stephanie).

In the 1850s a Grimaldi named Charles III made a decision that turned the Rock into a giant blue chip. Needing revenues but not wanting to impose additional taxes on his subjects, he contracted with a company to open a gambling facility. The first spin of the roulette wheel was on December 14, 1856. Almost overnight, a threadbare principality became an elegant watering hole for European society. Profits were so great that Charles eventually abolished all direct taxes.

But it's the tax system, not the gambling, that has made Monaco one of the most sought-after addresses in the world. It bristles with gleaming glass-and-concrete corncob-towers 20 and 30 stories high and with vast apartment complexes, their terraces, landscaped like miniature gardens, jutting over the sea. You now have to look hard to find

Casino 45
Cathédrale de l'Immaculée–Conception . .51
Jardin Exotique 53
Musée Napoléon . . .50
Musée National . . .48
Musée Océano-graphique . .52
Opéra 46
Palais Princier 49
Sun Casino 47

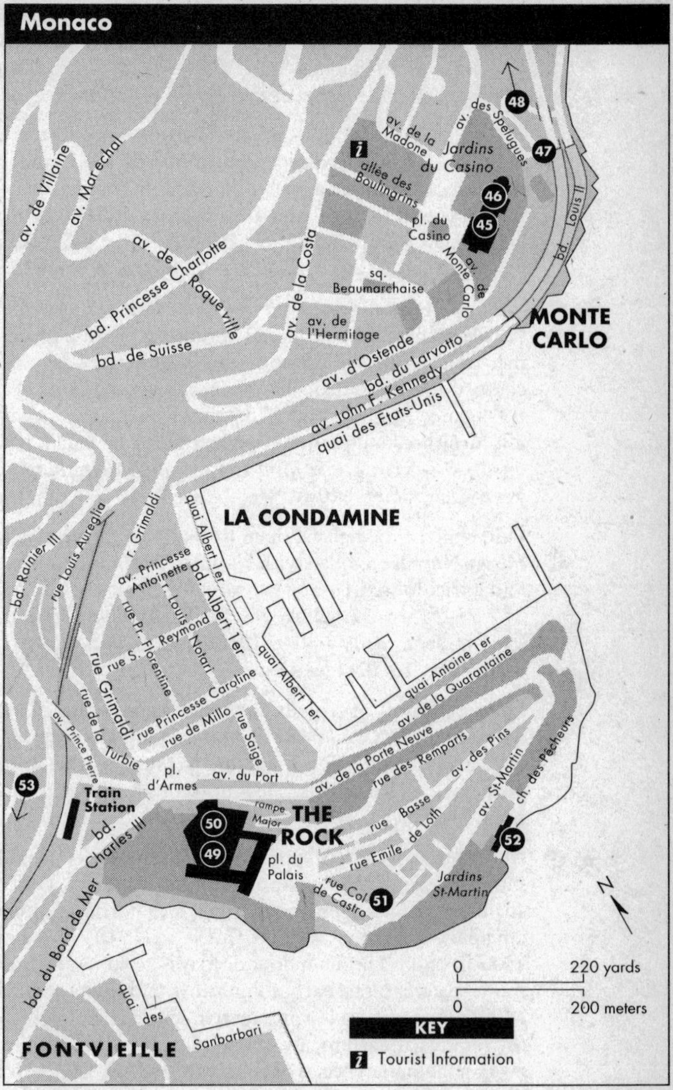

the Belle Epoque grace of yesteryear—but if you spend some time at the Casino, the Opéra, or the Louis XV restaurant, you may be able to conjure up Monaco's elegant past and the much-missed spirit of Princess Grace.

★ 45 Place du Casino is the center of Monte Carlo, and the **Casino** is a must-see, even if you don't bet a sou. Into the gold-leaf splendor of the Casino, the hopeful traipse from tour buses to tempt fate beneath the gilt-edged Rococo ceiling. Jacket and tie are required in the back rooms, which open at 3 PM. Bring your passport (under-21s not admitted). ✉ *Pl. du Casino*, ☎ *377/92–16–20–00*, WEB *www.sbm.mc.* ⊙ *Daily, noon–4* AM.

46 In the true spirit of the town, it seems that the **Opéra de Monte-Carlo** (✉ Pl. du Casino, ☎ 377/92–16–22–99), with its 18-ton gilt-bronze chandelier and extravagant frescoes, is part of the Casino complex. The grand theater was designed by Charles Garnier, who also built the Paris Opéra; Its main auditorium, the Salle Garnier, was inaugurated by Sarah Bernhardt in 1879.

47 Some say the most serious gamblers play at **Sun Casino,** in the Monte Carlo Grand Hotel, by the vast convention center that juts over the water. ✉ *12 av. des Spélugues,* ☎ *377/92–16–21–23.* ⏲ *Tables open weekdays at 5 PM and weekends at 4 PM; slot machines open daily at 11 AM.*

48 From Place des Moulins an elevator descends to the Larvotto Beach complex, artfully created with imported sand, and the **Musée National,** housed in a Garnier villa within a rose garden. It has a beguiling collection of 18th- and 19th-century dolls and automatons. ✉ *17 av. Princesse Grace,* ☎ *377/93–30–91–26.* 🎟 *€5.* ⏲ *Easter–Aug., daily 10–6:30; Sept.–Easter, daily 10–12:15 and 2:30–6:30.*

49 West of Monte Carlo stands the famous Rock, crowned by the **Palais Princier,** where the royal family resides. A 40-minute guided tour (summer only) of this sumptuous chunk of history, first built in the 13th century and expanded and enhanced over the centuries, reveals an extravagance of 16th- and 17th-century frescoes, as well as tapestries, gilt furniture, and paintings on a grand scale. ✉ *Pl. du Palais,* ☎ *377/93–25–18–31.* 🎟 *€5; joint ticket with Musée Napoléon, €6.50.* ⏲ *June–Oct., daily 9:30–5.*

50 One wing of the palace, open throughout the year, is taken up by the **Musée Napoléon,** filled with Napoléonic souvenirs—including that hat and a tricolor scarf—and genealogical charts. ✉ *In Palais Princier,* ☎ *377/93–25–18–31.* 🎟 *€3; joint ticket with palace apartments, €6.50.* ⏲ *June–Sept., daily 9:30–6:30; Oct.–mid-Nov., daily 10–5; Dec.–May, Tues.–Sun. 10:30–12:30 and 2–5.*

51 Follow the flow of crowds down the last remaining streets of medieval Monaco to the **Cathédrale de l'Immaculée-Conception** (✉ Av. St-Martin), an uninspired 19th-century version of the Romanesque style. Nonetheless, it harbors a magnificent altarpiece, painted in 1500 by Bréa, and the tomb of Princess Grace.

★ 52 At the prow of the Rock, the grand **Musée Océanographique** (Oceanography Museum) perches dramatically on a cliff. It's a splendid Edwardian structure, built under Prince Albert I to house specimens collected on amateur explorations. Jacques Cousteau (1910–97) led its missions from 1957 to 1988. The main floor displays skeletons and taxidermy of enormous sea creatures; early submarines and diving gear dating from the Middle Ages; and a few interactive science displays. The main draw is the famous **aquarium,** a vast complex of backlighted tanks containing every imaginable species of fish, crab, and eel. ✉ *Av. St-Martin,* ☎ *377/93–15–36–00.* 🎟 *€9.50.* ⏲ *July–Aug., daily 9–8; Sept. and Apr.–June, daily 9–7; Oct. and Mar., daily 9:30–7; Nov.–Feb., daily 10–6.*

★ 53 Carved out of the rock face and one of Monte Carlo's most stunning escape hatches, the **Jardin Exotique de Monaco** (Monaco Exotic Garden) is studded with thousands of succulents and cactii, all set along promenades, belvederes over the sea, and even framing faux boulders (actually hollow sculptures). There are rare plants from Mexico and Africa, and the hillside plot, threaded with bridges and grottoes, can't be beat for coastal splendor. ✉ *Blvd. du Jardin Exotique,* ☎ *377/93–30–33–65.* 🎟 *€6.40.* ⏲ *May–Aug. 9–7; Sept.–Apr. 9–5.*

Dining and Lodging

$$$$ ★ ✕ **Le Louis XV.** This sumptuous neo-Baroque restaurant, in the Hôtel de Paris, stuns with royal pomp that is nonetheless upstaged by its product: the superb cuisine of Alain Ducasse, one of Europe's most celebrated chefs. Ducasse often refers to his deceptively simple style as "country cooking," where caviar and truffles slum happily with stockfish (stewed salt cod) and tripe. In short, it's a panoply of Mediterranean

delights. If your wallet is a fat one, this is a must. Menus run from €132 to €151. ✉ *Hôtel de Paris, pl. du Casino,* ☎ *377/92–16–30–01. AE, DC, MC, V. Closed Wed. Sept.–mid-June, Tues., 2 wks in Feb.–early Mar., 2 wks in late Nov.–late Dec. No lunch Wed. mid-June–Aug.*

$$$–$$$$ ✕ **Café de Paris.** This landmark Belle Epoque brasserie, across from the Casino, offers the usual classics (shellfish, steak tartare, matchstick frites, and fish boned table-side). Supercilious, super-pro waiters fawn gracefully over titled preeners, gentlemen, jet-setters, and tourists alike. Happily, there's good hot food until 2 AM. Menus run from €31 to €62. ✉ *Pl. du Casino,* ☎ *377/92–16–20–20. AE, DC, MC, V.*

$$ ✕ **Castelroc.** With its tempting pine-shaded terrace just across from the entrance to the palace, this popular local lunch spot serves up specialties of cuisine Monegasque, ranging from anchoiade to stockfish. There are only fixed-price menus at €37. ✉ *Pl. du Palais,* ☎ *377/93–30–36–68. AE, MC, V. Closed Sat. and Dec.–Jan.*

$$$$ **Hermitage.** A riot of frescoes and plaster flourishes embellished with gleaming brass, this landmark 1900 hotel, set back a block from the Casino scene, nonetheless maintains a relatively low profile. Even if you're not staying, come to see the glass-dome Art Nouveau vestibule, designed by Gustav Eiffel. The best rooms face the sea or angle toward the port. ✉ *Sq. Beaumarchais, 98005,* ☎ *377/92–16–40–00,* FAX *92–16–38–52,* WEB *www.montecarloresort.com. 195 rooms, 14 junior suites, 18 suites. Restaurant, bar, cable TV, minibars, Internet, health club, pool, parking (fee). AE, DC, MC, V.*

$$$$ **Hôtel de Paris.** Built in 1864 on an extravagant scale, this vestige of the Belle Epoque has one of the most prestigious addresses in Europe. The cavernous lobby is a veritable crossroads of the buffed and befurred Euro-gentry, and rooms—fresh, pretty, and not in the least grandiose—overlook the casino, the gardens, and those on higher floors, the sea. ✉ *Pl. du Casino, 98000,* ☎ *377/92–16–30–00,* FAX *92–16–38–50,* WEB *www.sbm.mc. 141 rooms, 40 suites, 19 junior suites. 4 restaurants, no-smoking rooms, cable TV, minibars, Internet, health club, pool, spa, parking (fee). AE, DC, MC, V.*

$$$$ **Monte Carlo Grand Hotel.** Sprawling long and low along the waterfront at Monte Carlo's base, this ultramodern airport-scale complex is so vast it commands a full-time staff of upholsterers. Bright rooms decked in vivid hues angle onto the open sea. The bars, casino, boutiques, and mall-size lobby easily contain megaconventions, but vacationers will feel at home, too. ✉ *12 av. des Spélugues, 98000,* ☎ *377/93–50–65–00,* FAX *93–30–01–57,* WEB *www.monaco.mc/granotel/. 619 rooms, 69 apartments. 3 restaurants, bar, cable TV, minibars, Internet, cabaret, health club, meeting room, pool, health club, hot tub, casino, parking (fee). AE, DC, MC, V.*

$$$ **Alexandra.** The friendly proprietress, Madame Larouquie, makes you feel right at home at this central, comfortable spot just north of the Casino. Though the color schemes clash and the bedrooms are spare, bathrooms are spacious and up to date, and insulated windows keep traffic noise out. ✉ *35 bd. Princesse-Charlotte, 98000,* ☎ *377/93–50–63–13,* FAX *92–16–06–48. 56 rooms. Cable TV, minibars. AE, DC, MC, V.*

Nightlife and the Arts

There's no need to go to bed before dawn in Monte Carlo when you can go to the **casinos.** Monte Carlo's spring arts festival, **Printemps des Arts,** takes place from early April to mid-May and includes the world's top ballet, operatic, symphonic, and chamber-music performers. Year-round, opera, ballet, and classical music can be enjoyed at the magnificently sumptuous Salle Garnier auditorium of the **Opéra de Monte-Carlo** (✉ Pl. du Casino, ☎ 337/92–16–22–99, WEB www.opera.mc), the main venue of the Opéra de Monte-Carlo and the Orchestre

Philharmonique de Monte-Carlo, both worthy of the magnificent hall.

Outdoor Activities and Sports

The **Monte Carlo Tennis Tournament** is held during the spring arts festival. When the tennis stops, the auto racing begins: the **Grand Prix de Monaco** (☎ 377/93–15–26–00 for information) takes place in mid-May.

Roquebrune–Cap-Martin

54 *5 km (3 mi) east of Monaco.*

In the midst of the frenzy of overbuilding that defines this last gasp of the coast before Italy, two twinned havens have survived, each in its own way: the perched old town of Roquebrune, which gives its name to the greater area, and Cap-Martin—luxurious, isolated, and exclusive. With its tumble of raked tile roofs and twisting streets, fountains, archways, and quiet squares, Roquebrune retains many of the charms of a hilltop village, although it has become heavily gentrified and commercialized. W. Somerset Maugham—who once memorably described these environs as a "sunny place for shady people"—resided in the town's grandest villa for many years.

Roquebrune's main attraction is its **Château Féodal** (Feudal Castle): Around the remains of a 10th-century tower, the Grimaldis erected an impregnable fortress that was state-of-the-art in the 16th century, with crenellation, watchtowers, and a broad moat. *€3. ⏲ Oct.–Jan., daily 10–12:30 and 2–5; Feb.–May, daily 10–12:30 and 2–6; June–Sept., daily 10–12:30 and 3–7:30.*

In the **cemetery,** Swiss-French architect Le Corbusier lies buried with his wife in a tomb of his own design. He kept a humble *cabanot* (beach bungalow) on the rocky shore of the Cap-Martin, where he drowned while swimming in 1965.

★ You can see the glorious flora of the cape by walking the **Promenade Le Corbusier.** It leads over chalk cliffs and through dense Mediterranean flora to the famed modernist architect's "Cabanon" bungalow (plans are in the works to open this as a museum—check with local tourist office)—a tiny retreat, as much outdoors as in and designed along the rigorous lines he preferred. Park at the base of the cape on avenue Winston-Churchill and follow the signs.

Menton

55 *1 km (¾ mi) east of Roquebrune, 9 km (5½ mi) east of Monaco.*

Menton, the most Mediterranean of the French resort towns, rubs shoulders with the Italian border and owes its balmy climate to the protective curve of the Ligurian shore. Its picturesque harbor skyline seems to beg artists to immortalize it, while its Cubist skew of terra-cotta roofs and yellow-ocher houses, Baroque arabesques capping the church facades, and ceramic tiles glistening on their steeples all evoke the villages of the Italian coast. Menton is the least pretentious of the Côte d'Azur resorts and all the more alluring for its modesty.

The **Basilique St-Michel** (✉ Parvis St-Michel), a majestic Baroque church, dominates the skyline of Menton with its bell tower. Beyond the beautifully proportioned facade—a 19th-century addition—the richly frescoed nave and chapels contain several works by Genovese artists and a splendid 17th-century organ.

Just above the main church, the smaller **Chapelle de l'Immaculée-Conception** answers St-Michel's grand gesture with its own pure Baroque beauty, dating from 1687. Between 3 and 5 you can slip in to see the graceful trompe l'oeil over the altar and the ornate gilt lanterns early penitents carried in processions.

Two blocks below the square, **rue St-Michel** serves as the main commercial artery of the Vieille Ville, lined with shops, cafés, and orange trees. Between the lively pedestrian rue St-Michel and the waterfront, the marvelous **Marché Couvert** (Covered Market) sums up Menton style with its Belle Epoque facade decorated in jewel-tone ceramics. Inside, it's just as appealing, with merchants selling chewy bread, mountain cheeses, oils, fruit, and Italian delicacies in Caravaggio-esque disarray.

On the waterfront opposite the market, a squat medieval bastion crowned with four tiny watchtowers houses the **Musée Jean-Cocteau.** Built in 1636 to defend the port, it was spotted by the artist-poet-filmmaker Jean Cocteau (1889–1963) as the perfect site for a group of his works. There are bright, cartoonish pastels of fishermen and wenches in love, and a fantastical assortment of ceramic animals in the wrought-iron windows he designed. ✉ *Vieux Port,* ☎ *04–93–57–72–30.* 🎫 *€3.* ⏲ *Wed.–Mon. 10–noon and 2–6.*

The 19th-century Italianate **Hôtel de Ville** conceals another Cocteau treasure: it was he who decorated the **Salle des Mariages** (Marriage Room), the room in which civil marriages take place, with vibrant allegorical scenes. ✉ *17 av. de la République.* 🎫 *€2.* ⏲ *Weekdays 8:30–12:30 and 1:30–5.*

At the far west end of town stands the 18th-century **Palais Carnolès** (Carnolès Palace) in vast gardens luxuriant with orange, lemon, and grapefruit trees. It was once the summer retreat of the princes of Monaco; nowadays it contains a sizable collection of European paintings from the Renaissance to the present day. Green-thumbers should also head to the **Val Rahmeh Botanical Garden** (✉ Av. St-Jacques), planted by Maybud Campbell in the 1910s, much prized by connoisseurs, bursting with rare ornamentals and subtropical plants, and adorned with water-lily pools and fountains. ✉ *3 av. de la Madone,* ☎ *04–93–35–49–71.* 🎫 *Free.* ⏲ *Wed.–Mon. 10–noon and 2–6.*

Dining and Lodging

$$–$$$ ★ ✕🏨 **Aiglon.** Sweep down the curving stone stair to the terrazzo mosaic lobby of this lovely 1880 garden villa and wander out for a drink or a meal by the pool. Or settle onto your little balcony overlooking the grounds and a tiny wedge of sea. The poolside restaurant, Le Riaumont, serves classic seafood by candlelight; breakfast is served in a shady garden shelter. From here it's a three-minute walk to the beach. ✉ *7 av. de la Madone, 06502,* ☎ *04–93–57–55–55,* FAX *04–93–35–92–39,* WEB *http://perso.wanadoo.fr/aiglon. 28 rooms, 2 apartments. Restaurant, bar, no room TV, Internet, pool. AE, MC, V.*

Nightlife and the Arts

In August the **Festival de Musique de Chambre** (Chamber Music Festival) takes place on the stone-paved plaza outside the church of St-Michel. The **Fête du Citron** (Lemon Festival), at the end of February, celebrates the lemon with floats and sculptures like those of the Rose Bowl Parade, all made of real fruit.

THE CÔTE D'AZUR A TO Z

To research prices, get advice from other travelers, and book travel arrangements, visit www.fodors.com.

AIR TRAVEL

There are frequent flights between Paris and Nice on Air Liberté, AOM, and Air France, as well as direct flights on Delta Airlines from New York. The flight time between Paris and Nice is about one hour.

AIRPORTS

The Nice–Côte d'Azur Airport sits on a peninsula between Antibes and Nice.

➤ AIRPORT INFORMATION: **Nice–Côte d'Azur Airport** (✉ 7 km/4 mi from Nice, ☎ 04–93–21–30–30).

BUS TRAVEL

Buses allow you to penetrate deeper into villages and backcountry spots not on the rail line; Pick up a schedule for local and commercial excursion buses at the train station, at tourist offices, and at the local *gare routière* (bus station). Phocéens Santa Azur (Voyages) is the best bus service covering the Côte d'Azur region, with buses departing from Nice, Antibes, Cannes, Menton, and Mandelieu and regular minibus service between Nice, Marseilles, Touilon, and some towns inland of Nice. Alpes-Maritimes Bus Services—RCA Transport (Rapides Côte d'Azur) covers the coastal area, from Menton to Villeneuve Loubet, and inland, to Peille and Aspremont; Routes run between Nice and Cannes, with stops at Cagnes-sur-Mer and Juan-les-Pins and they also service Menton, Villefranche, St-Jean-Cap-Ferrat, Èze, and Monaco (plus a "rapid" airport service from Menton and/or Monaco to Nice International). SAP offers buses serving Vence, St-Paul, La Colle-sur-Loup, St-Laurent-du-Var, and Nice. Compagnie des Autobus de Monaco covers that principality. Rapides Côte d'Azur traffics the routes in and around Cannes, while SODETRAV buses head to and from St-Tropez and St-Raphael. In addition, the national SNCF service covers more distant locales.

➤ BUS INFORMATION: ✉ **Agence Intercars** (✉ 5 bd. Jean Jaures, Nice, ☎ 04–93–80–08–70, WEB www.intercars.fr). **Alpes-Maritimes Bus Services—RCA Transport (Rapides Cote d'Azur)** (✉ 5 bd. Jean Jaures, Nice, ☎ 04–93–85–64–44, WEB www.rca.tm.fr/2index.htm). **Phocéens Santa Azur (Voyages)** (✉ 4 Place Massena, Nice, ☎ 04–93–13–18–20; ✉ 5 square Merimee, Cannes, ☎ 04–93–39–79–40; ✉ 8 pl. de Gaul, Antibes, ☎ 04–93–34–15–98). **SAP (Société Automobile de Provence)** (✉ ☎ 04–93–58–37–60).

CAR RENTAL

Most likely you'll want to rent your car at one of the main rail stops, either St-Raphäel, Nice, Monaco, or Menton, or at the airport in Nice, where all major companies are represented.

➤ LOCAL AGENCIES: **Avis** (✉ 2 av. des Phocéens, Nice, ☎ 04–93–80–63–52; ✉ Nice airport, ☎ 04–93–21–42–80; ✉ 190 pl. Pierre Coullet, St-Raphaël, ☎ 04–94–95–60–42). **Budget** (✉ 23 rue de Belgique, Nice, ☎ 04–93–16–24–16; ✉ Nice Airport, ☎ 04–93–21–36–50; ✉ 40 rue Waldeck–Rousseau, St-Raphaël, ☎ 04–94–82–24–44). **Europcar** (✉ 3 av. Gustave V, Nice, ☎ 04–92–14–44–50; ✉ Nice Airport, ☎ 04–93–21–43–54; ✉ 47 av. de Grande-Bretagne, Monaco, ☎ 377–93–50–74–95; ✉ 54 pl. Pierre Coullet, St-Raphaël, ☎ 04–94–95–56–87). **Hertz** (✉ 1 prom. Anglais, Nice, ☎ 04–93–87–11–87; ✉ Nice airport, ☎ 04–93–21–36–72; ✉ 32 rue Waldeck–Rousseau, St-Raphaël, ☎ 04–94–95–48–68; ✉ 27 bd. Albert I, Monaco, ☎ 377–93–50–79–60).

CAR TRAVEL

The best way to explore the secondary sights in this region, especially the backcountry hill towns, is by car. It also allows you the freedom to zip along A8 between the coastal resorts and to enjoy the tremendous views from the three corniches that trace the coast from Nice to the Italian border. N98, which connects you to coastal resorts in between, can be extremely slow, though scenic. A8 parallels the coast from above St-Tropez to Nice to the resorts on the Grand Corniche; N98 follows the coast more closely. From Paris the main southbound artery is A6/A7, known as the Autoroute du Soleil; it passes through Provence and joins the eastbound A8 at Aix-en-Provence.

LODGING

APARTMENT AND VILLA RENTALS

The tourist offices of individual towns often publish lists of *locations meublés* (furnished rentals), sometimes vouched for by the tourist office and rated for comfort. Gîtes de France is a nationwide organization that rents *gîtes ruraux* (rural vacation lodgings) by the week, usually outstanding examples of a region's character. The headquarters for the regions covered in this chapter are listed below. Write or call for a catalog, then make a selection and reservation.

➤ LOCAL AGENTS: **Gîtes de France Var** (✉ Rond-Point du 4 Décembre 1974, B.P. 215, 83006 Draguignan Cedex, ☎ 04–94–50–93–93, FAX 04–94–50–93–90). **Gîtes de France des Alpes-Maritimes** (✉ 55 Promenade des Anglais, B.P. 1602, 06011 Nice Cedex 01, ☎ 04–92–15–21–30, FAX 04–93–86–01–06, WEB www.crt-riviera.fr/gites06).

OUTDOORS AND SPORTS

This is golf country, and you can pick up the brochure and map *Les Golfs du Soleil* (*Golf Courses of the Sun*) and *Destination Golf* at local tourist offices to get a complete listing of golf courses and facilities from St-Tropez to Monaco.

TOURS

BUS TOURS

Santa Azur organizes all-day or half-day bus excursions to sights near Nice, including Monaco, Cannes, and nearby hill towns, either leaving from its offices or from several stops along the Promenade des Anglais, mainly in front of the big hotels. In Antibes, Phocéens Voyages organizes similar bus explorations of the region.

➤ FEES AND SCHEDULES: **Phocéens Voyages** (✉ 8 pl. de Gaulle, Antibes, ☎ 04–93–34–15–98). **Santa Azur** (✉ 11 av. Jean-Médecin, Nice, ☎ 04–93–85–46–81).

PRIVATE GUIDES

The city of Nice arranges individual guided tours on an à la carte basis according to your needs. For information contact the Bureau d'Accueil and specify your dates and language preferences.

➤ CONTACTS: **Bureau d'Accueil** (☎ 04–93–14–48–00).

TRAIN TOURS

A small tourist train goes along the Nice waterfront from in front of the Casino Ruhl, along cours Saleya, and up to the Château.

➤ FEES AND SCHEDULES: **Tourist train** (☎ 04–93–92–45–59).

TRAIN TRAVEL

Nice is the major rail crossroads for trains arriving from Paris and other northern cities, as well as from Italy. This coastal line, working eastward from Marseille and west from Ventimiglia, stops at Fréjus, Antibes, Monaco, and Menton. There is no rail access to St-Tropez; St-Raphaël is the nearest stop. To get from Paris to Nice, you can take the TGV, though it only maintains high speeds to Valence before returning to conventional rails and rates.

You can easily move along the coast by train on the Côte d'Azur line, a dramatic and highly tourist-pleasing route that offers panoramic views as it rolls from one famous resort to the next. But train travelers will have difficulty getting up to St-Paul, Vence, Peillon, and other back-country villages; that you must accomplish by bus or car.

➤ TRAIN INFORMATION: **SNCF** (☎ 08–36–35–35–35, WEB www.sncf.com).

TRAVEL AGENCIES

➤ LOCAL AGENT REFERRALS: **American Express Voyages** (✉ 11 Promenade des Anglais, Nice, ☎ 04–93–16–53–51; ✉ 35 bd. Princess Charlotte, Monte Carlo, ☎ 377/93–25–74–45; ✉ 8 rue des Belges, Cannes, ☎ 04–93–38–15–87). **Havas Voyages** (✉ 12 av. Félix Faure, Nice ☎ 04–93–62–76–30; ✉ 64 av. Commandant Guilbaud, St-Raphael, ☎ 04–94–19–82–20; ✉ 17 bd. Louis Blanc, St-Tropez, ☎ 04–94–56–64–64).

VISITOR INFORMATION

For information on travel within the department of Var (St-Tropez to La Napoule), write to the Comité Départmental du Tourisme du Var. The Comité Régional du Tourisme Riviera Côte d'Azur provides information on tourism throughout the department of Alpes-Maritimes, from Cannes to the Italian border. Local tourist offices in major towns discussed in this chapter are listed below by town.

➤ TOURIST INFORMATION: **Antibes/Juan-les-Pins** (✉ 11 pl. de Gaulle, 06600 Antibes, ☎ 04–92–90–53–00, FAX 04–92–90–53–01). **Cannes** (✉ Palais des Festivals, Esplanade G. Pompidou, B.P. 272, ☎ 04–93–39–24–53, FAX 04–92–99–84–23, WEB www.cannes-on-line.com). **Comité Départmental du Tourisme du Var** (✉ 1 bd. Maréchal Foch, 83300 Draguignan, ☎ 03–94–50–55–50, FAX 04–94–50–55–51). **Comité Régional du Tourisme Riviera Côte d'Azur** (✉ 55 Promenade des Anglais, B.P. 1602, 06011 Nice Cedex 1, ☎ 04–93–37–78–78, WEB www.crt-riviera.fr). **Fréjus** (✉ 325 rue Jean-Jaurès, B.P. 8, 83601, ☎ 04–94–51–83–83, FAX 04–94–51–00–26). **Grasse** (✉ Palais des Congrés, 22 Cours Honoré Cresp, ☎ 04–93–36–66–66, FAX 04–93–36–86–36, WEB www.ville-frejus.fr). **Menton** (✉ Palais de l'Europe, av. Boyer, 06500, ☎ 04–92–41–76–76, FAX 04–92–41–76–78). **Monaco** (✉ 2a bd. des Moulins, 98000 Monte Carlo, ☎ 377/92–16–61–66, FAX 377–92–16–60–00, WEB www.monaco-tourism.com). **Nice** (✉ 5 Promenade des Anglais, 06000, ☎ 04–92–14–48–00, FAX 04–92–14–48–03, WEB www.nicetourism.com; or in person at the train station or airport). **St-Paul-de-Vence** (✉ 2 rue Grande, 06570, ☎ 04–93–32–86–95, FAX 04–93–32–60–27). **St-Raphaël** (✉ Rue Waldeck-Rousseau, 83700, ☎ 04–94–19–52–52, FAX 04–94–83–85–40, WEB www.saint-raphael.com). **St-Tropez** (✉ Quai Jean-Jaurès, B.P. 183, 83992, ☎ 04–94–97–45–21, FAX 04–94–97–82–66, WEB www.ot-saint-tropez.com). **Vence** (✉ Pl. du Grand Jardin, 06140, ☎ 04–93–58–06–38, FAX 04–93–58–91–81).

14 CORSICA

"The best way of knowing Corsica," Napoléon said, "is to be born there." Not everyone has had his luck, so chances are you'll be arriving on the overnight ferry from Marseille. Famed as a Mediterranean-bound "mountain in the sea," Corsica is known for its unspoiled, spectacular scenery, its medieval villages, and for its capital at Ajaccio. But don't overlook the highland capital of Corsican independence at Corte, the graceful port of Bastia, the Castagniccia chestnut forest, or the beaches at Calvi—all important acts in the rich drama that is Corsica.

Updated by George Semler

Introduction by George Semler

FORMING A VERTICAL GRANITE WORLD of its own in the Mediterranean between Provence and Tuscany, Corsica is France's own Wild West: a powerful natural setting and, literally, a breath of fresh air. Corsica is where you go to clear your head, to get away from it all and find your magnetic north, a microcosm of mountains, beaches, fishing ports, wilderness, and the purest strain of proto-Mediterranean culture. Mountain people born and bred, Corsicans have historically distrusted the sea and the cosmopolitan coastal landing points, open to invading forces. The true Corsican is a highland spirit, at home in the dense undergrowth of the *maquis*—the all-sustaining chestnut forest—or the Laricio pines that climb the upper reaches of what Guy de Maupassant christened his "mountain in the sea."

Corsica's gifts of artistic and archaeological treasures, crystalline waters, granite peaks, and pine forests add up to one of France's wildest and most unspoiled sanctuaries—a logical crucible for the emergence of a force such as Napoléon Bonaparte. Its strategic location 168 km (105 mi) south of Monaco and 81 km (50 mi) west of Italy has made Corsica a prize hotly contested by a succession of Mediterranean powers, notably Genoa, Pisa, and France. Their vestiges remain: the city-state of Genoa ruled Corsica for more than 200 years, leaving impressive citadels, churches, bridges, and nearly 100 medieval watchtowers around the island's coastline. The Italian influence is also apparent in village architecture and in the Corsican language, a combination of Italian, Tuscan dialect, and Latin.

Corsica seems immense, far larger than its 215 km (133 mi) length and 81 km (50 mi) width, partly because its rugged, mountainous terrain makes for slow traveling and partly because the landscape and the culture vary greatly from one microregion to another. Much of the part of Corsica that is not wooded or cultivated is covered with a dense thicket of undergrowth, called the maquis, a variety of wild and aromatic plants including lavender, myrtle, and heather that gave Corsica one of its sobriquets, "the perfumed isle." The maquis, famous for harboring fugitives, became the term used for the French Resistance movement during World War II. In Corsica "going underground" meant taking to the maquis.

Along with the word *maquis,* the term *vendetta* is one of Corsica's contributions to world lexicography. The rough-and-ready legend associated with the island comes from a long tradition of apparent lawlessness and deeply entrenched clannishness. As justice from "the Continent," whether France or Italy, was usually slow and often unsatisfying, Corsican clans frequently fought each other in blood feuds of honor and revenge.

Famous as the birthplace of Napoléon Bonaparte (who never returned to the island after beginning his military career), Corsica's real national hero is Pasquale Paoli, who framed the world's first republican constitution for his independent Corsican nation in 1755. Paoli's ideas significantly influenced the French Revolution, as well as the founding fathers of the United States. Inspiration for generations of literati from Homer to Mérimée, Boswell, Dumas, and Balzac, Corsica has always been, in Greek, *Kallisté,* "the most beautiful," a sylvan land and repository for romantic characters from Mérimée's Robin Hood–like *bandit d'honneur* Colomba to comic-book Asterix's pal Aucatarinabellachichix. In the end you'll find Corsica composed of equal parts vendetta, witchcraft, dream hunters, shepherds improvising the rough and haunting Corsican polyphony, megalithic menhirs, chestnuts, free-range livestock, powerful cheeses, and—always—the bittersweet, lemon-pepper fragrance of the maquis, an aroma like no other, described by Dorothy Carrington in her *Granite Island* as "akin to incense," and the only fitting perfume for Balzac's "back of beyond."

Pleasures and Pastimes

Dining

Authentic Corsican fare based on free-range livestock, game (especially wild boar), herbs, and wild mushrooms is best found October–June in the tiny villages of the mountainous interior. *Civets* (delicious meaty stews) headline many menus, as do many versions of the prototypical, hearty Corsican soup (alternately known as *soupe paysanne, soupe corse,* and *soupe de montagne*) made from herbs and vegetables simmered for hours with a ham bone. Seafood dishes are available on the coast: particularly good is *aziminu,* a rich bouillabaisse. Everywhere you'll find all kinds of *charcuterie* (pork products): *lonzu* (shoulder), *coppa* (fillet), and *figatelli* (liver sausage) are standard cuts, along with *prisuttu* (cured ham). Among Corsican cheeses, the most emblematic is really not a cheese at all: *brocciu* (pronounced broach) is similar to ricotta and is used in omelets, *fiadone* (cheesecake), *fritelli* (chestnut-flour doughnuts), and as stuffing for trout or rabbit. Cheeses from Corsica's microregions include *bastelicaccia,* a soft, creamy sheep cheese, and the harder and sharper *sartenais.* Many of the most powerful cheeses are simply designated as *brebis* (sheep) or *chèvre* (goat). Chestnuts and chestnut flour also play an important part in Corsican gastronomy: in *castagna* (Corsican for chestnut), a cake; *panetta,* a kind of bread; *canistrelli,* dry cookies; beignets (fried dough), often made of chestnut flour; *pulenta,* a doughy chestnut-flour bread; and *Pietra,* chestnut beer. Be sure, too, to try some of Corsica's best wines: Arenas, Orenga de Gaffory, or Gentile, from the Patrimonio vineyards; Domaine Peraldi, Clos de Capitoro, or Clos Alzeto, from Ajaccio; Fiumicicoli, from Sartène; or Domaine de Torracia, from Porto-Vecchio.

CATEGORY	COST*
$$$$	over €23
$$$	€15–€23
$$	€8–€14
$	under €8

**per person for a main course only, including tax (19.6%); note that if a restaurant offers only prix-fixe (set-price) meals, it is given a price category that reflects prix-fixe price.*

Lodging

The quantity of construction around Porto-Vecchio in the 1950s was so horrifying to Corsicans that, with some extra unwanted encouragement from separatist bombers, they resolved to avoid excessive tourist-driven development. Instead, *fermes-auberges* (farmhouse-inns) are being restored at a rapid clip, and tastefully designed hotels are being built. During the peak season (from July to mid-September) prices are higher, and some hotels insist that breakfast and dinner be included as part of the price. The best seaside hotels are priced only marginally lower than on the Riviera, but lodgings in the interior villages remain substantially cheaper. Off-season, good prices can be found all over. Assume all rooms have air-conditioning, TV, telephones, and private bath unless otherwise noted.

CATEGORY	COST*
$$$$	over €115
$$$	€61–€115
$$	€38–€60
$	under €38

**All prices are for a standard double room for two, including tax (19.6%) and service charge.*

Outdoor Activities

From the wild, undeveloped strands of the northern Cap Corse (Cape Corsica) to the Riviera-like tourist beaches near Calvi and Propriano, the island's coastline is astonishingly varied. In summer, during the *canicule* (literally, dog days), Corsicans take to the rivers, always cooler than the Mediterranean. Others take on the rugged GR 20 (Grande Randonnée 20); considered one of Europe's greatest hiking trails, it requires from 70 to 100 hours to complete. Planned in stages from one mountain refuge to another, the well-marked GR 20 is the ultimate way to see Corsica. If you are traveling by car, short probes along the GR 20 are easily feasible. In addition to the GR 20 there are shorter cross-island, coast to coast ("*Tra mare a mare*") hikes with villages and refuges at convenient intervals. Horseback excursions and round-the-island sailing cruises are also good ways to connect with the great-outdoors aspect of Corsica. Golf options begin with the Robert Trent Jones course at Sperone, near Bonifacio. Downhill, cross-country, and mountain skiing are an option above 1,400 meters from December to March. Check with tourist offices or bookstores for hiking guides, maps, ski conditions, charts, and sailing contacts.

Exploring Corsica

Leaving Marseille (on the excellent SNCM *Ferryterranée,* which also departs from Toulon and Nice) at sunset and arriving in Ajaccio at sunrise are among the finest moments of any trip to Corsica. Inasmuch as Napoléon claimed he could identify the fragrance of the Corsican maquis from many miles out at sea, approaching the island by some means other than a boat seems like heresy. The northern half of the island (Haute Corse) is generally wilder than the southern half (Corse du Sud), which is hotter and more barren. On the other hand, southern Corsica's archaeological sites at Filitosa and Pianu de Levie, the Col de Bavella and its majestic Laricio pine forest, and the towns of Sartène and Bonifacio all rank indisputably among the island's finest treasures. The least interesting part of the island is the coast road between Porto-Vecchio and Bastia, although one of the prettiest drives is the tour around the northward-pointing finger of Cap Corse. Don't hesitate to drive into the interior highlands, the true Corsica; if you spend too much time at sea level you'll be missing the remote villages and dramatic heights for which the island is famous.

Great Itineraries

Three days is barely sufficient time to visit Corsica's three main cities and some of the island's prettiest sites. In five days you can cover most of Haute Corse, and in 10 days it is possible, though not necessarily advisable, to see the whole island. The danger is spending too much time car-bound. One approach is to settle in Corte, near the island's center, setting out each day on a quest to see different attractions.

Numbers in the text correspond to numbers in the margin and on the Corsica and Ajaccio maps.

IF YOU HAVE 3 DAYS

Ajaccio ①–⑧ is a good place to start. After a walk through the market and the Musée Fesch, a two-hour drive over the Vizzavona Pass to **Corte** ⑱ will place you at the island's historical heart for the night. Explore the town and the nearby Restonica gorges the next day. On day three drive through the chestnut forest, the Castagniccia region, visiting small villages along the way. Find your way out of La Castagniccia via Folelli, stopping for lunch (call ahead for reservations) in **Murato** ㉝. Save the afternoon and evening for exploring **Bastia** ㊵ before shipping out for the mainland.

Corsica

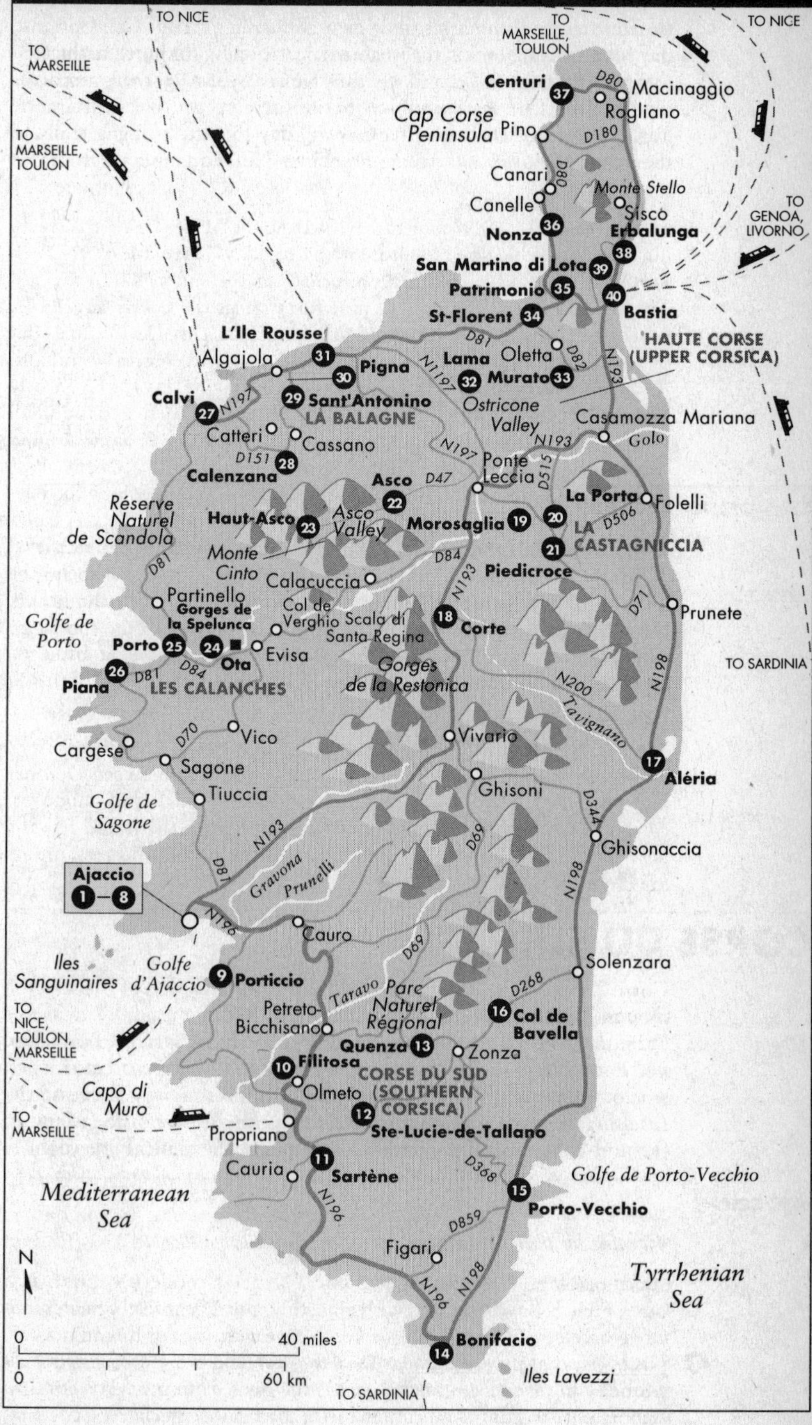

TO NICE
TO MARSEILLE
TO MARSEILLE, TOULON
TO MARSEILLE, TOULON
TO NICE
TO GENOA, LIVORNO
Centuri 37
Macinaggio
Rogliano
D80
Cap Corse Peninsula
Pino
D180
Canari
D80
Monte Stello
Canelle
Sisco
Nonza 36
Erbalunga 38
San Martino di Lota 39
Patrimonio 35
40 Bastia
St-Florent 34
L'Ile Rousse
D81
Oletta
D82
HAUTE CORSE (UPPER CORSICA)
Algajola 31
Pigna 30
N1197
Lama 32
Murato 33
N193
Calvi 27
N197
29 Sant'Antonino
LA BALAGNE
Ostricone Valley
Casamozza Mariana
Catteri
Cassano
N193
Golo
D151 28
Calenzana
N197
Ponte Leccia
D515
Asco 22
D47
La Porta
Folelli
Réserve Naturel de Scandola
Haut-Asco 23
Asco Valley
Morosaglia 19
20
LA CASTAGNICCIA
D506
21
D81
Monte Cinto
D84
Piedicroce
Calacuccia
N193
Partinello
Gorges de la Spelunca
Col de Verghio
Scala di Santa Regina
18 Corte
D71
Prunete
Golfe de Porto
Porto 25
24 Ota
Evisa
TO SARDINIA
26 Piana
D81
D84
LES CALANCHES
Gorges de la Restonica
N200
N198
Tavignano
Vico
D70
Vivario
Cargèse
Sagone
17 Aléria
Ghisoni
Tiuccia
Golfe de Sagone
D344
N193
D69
Ghisonaccia
Ajaccio 1–8
D81
Gravona
Prunelli
N198
N196
Cauro
D69
Iles Sanguinaires
Golfe d'Ajaccio
9 Porticcio
Solenzara
Taravo
Parc Naturel Régional
D268
TO NICE, TOULON, MARSEILLE
Petreto-Bicchisano
16 Col de Bavella
Quenza 13
Zonza
10 Filitosa
CORSE DU SUD (SOUTHERN CORSICA)
Olmeto
Capo di Muro
12 Ste-Lucie-de-Tallano
TO MARSEILLE
Propriano
11 Sartène
D368
Cauria
Golfe de Porto-Vecchio
Mediterranean Sea
N196
15 Porto-Vecchio
D859
Figari
N198
N196
Tyrrhenian Sea
N
0 40 miles
0 60 km
14 Bonifacio
Iles Lavezzi
TO SARDINIA

IF YOU HAVE 5 DAYS

Follow the three-day itinerary in a more leisurely fashion and spend the fourth and fifth nights in or near **Bastia** ㊵. Tour Cap Corse on day four, starting out on the eastern side, stopping for lunch in the fishing port of **Centuri** ㊲, and visiting **Nonza** ㊱, **St-Florent** ㉞, and the vineyards of the **Patrimonio** ㉟ before driving up over the Col de Teghime (at sunset, if possible). Spend day five exploring Bastia and then continue overnight to the French or Italian mainland.

IF YOU HAVE 10 DAYS

Start in **Ajaccio** ①–⑧, visiting the market and the Musée Fesch and reaching the megalithic site at **Filitosa** ⑩ by midday. Have a look through **Sartène** ⑪ and drive into **Bonifacio** ⑭ as the sun sets into the sea. The next day get to the Laricio pine forest, near the **Col de Bavella** ⑯, to see or even walk to the famous granite peaks. Tiny D268 comes out on the east coast at N198, which will take you up to **Aléria** ⑰ and into **Corte** ⑱ on N200. Make Corte your base: devote day three to Corte and the Restonica Gorge, day four to the **Asco** ㉒, day five to the small villages in **La Castagniccia.** On day six take the **Scala di Santa Regina** drive through the Aitone Forest. Spend the night in **Ota** ㉔. Pass through the Scandola Natural Reserve on day seven, reaching the Riviera-like **Calvi** ㉗ by evening. Dally at the beach in Calvi on day eight. In the evening drive through La Balagne to **L'Ile Rousse** ㉛ and medieval **Lama** ㉜. On the ninth day drive around Cap Corse and spend the night in **Erbalunga** ㊳, **San Martino di Lota** ㊴, or **Bastia** ㊵. On the morning of day 10 hike up to the Bocca di Santo Lunardo or go to the beach at Erbalunga; in the afternoon explore Bastia and then head back to the mainland.

When to Tour Corsica

The best time to visit Corsica is fall or spring, when the weather is cool. Most Corsican culinary specialties are at their best between October and June. Try to avoid July and August, when French and Italian vacationers fill hotels and push up prices. In winter the island has the best weather in France, but a majority of the hotels and restaurants are closed.

CORSE DU SUD

Corse du Sud includes the French administrative capital of Ajaccio, the mountainous zones of the Cinarca and Alta Rocca, megalithic treasures at Filitosa and Levie, and the fortresslike towns of Sartène, Bonifacio, and Porto-Vecchio. Perhaps because southern Corsica is on the French side of the island, it seems more Continentalized. Forest fires and the resulting flooding scarred much of the southern part of the island in the mid-'90s, though the irrepressible maquis has quickly regrown.

Ajaccio

40 mins by plane, 5–10 hrs by ferry from Marseille, Nice, or Toulon.

Ajaccio, Napoléon's birthplace and Corsica's modern capital, is a busy, French-flavored town with a bustling port, beautiful beaches, ancient streets, and, in the Musée Fesch, five centuries of Italian masterpieces.
❶ Start at the spectacular **food market** held every morning except Monday in place Campinchi, across the quai from the ferry port, an opportunity to admire an enticing parade of Corsican cheeses, pastries, sausages, and everything from traditional chestnut-flour beignets to prehistoric *rascasse* (red scorpion fish). The latter are found at the fish market tucked in under the Hôtel de Ville, across from the southeast corner of the square.

Cathédrale . . . 6
Chapelle Impérial 7
Food market 1
Hôtel de Ville 3
Maison Bonaparte . . . 4
Musée Fesch 8
Place Maréchal–Foch 2
St-Jean Baptiste 5

Ajaccio

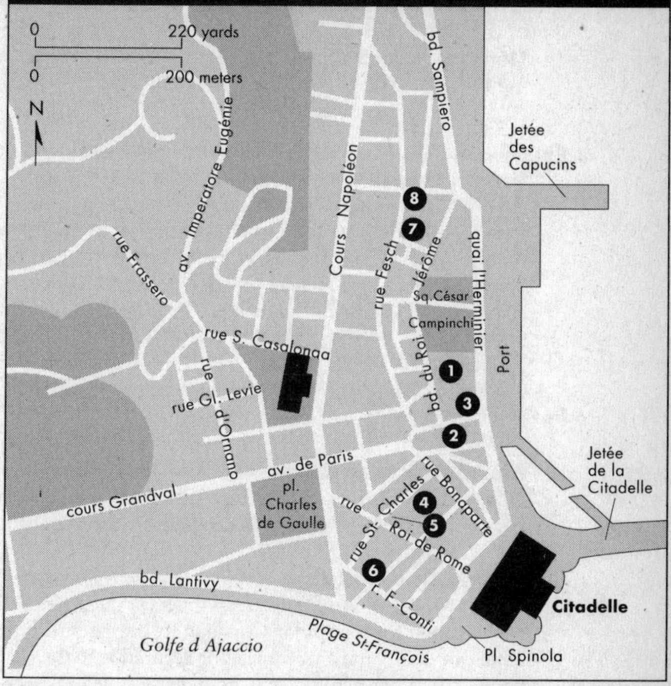

Rows of stately palm trees lead up to a marble statue of Napoléon on
2 3 **Place Maréchal-Foch,** the city's main square. The **Hôtel de Ville** (town hall) has an Empire-style grand salon hung with portraits of a long line of Bonapartes. You'll find a fine bust of Letizia, Napoléon's formidable mother; a bronze death mask of the emperor himself; and a frescoed ceiling that depicts Napoléon's meteoric rise. ✉ *Pl. Maréchal-Foch,* ☎ *04–95–21–90–15.* 🎫 *€2.* ⏲ *Apr.–Oct., weekdays 9–noon and 2:30–5:30; Nov.–Mar., weekdays 9–noon and 2–5.*

Two short blocks left of the statue of Napoléon on place Maréchal-
4 Foch, is the **Maison Bonaparte** (Bonaparte House). Here Napoléon was born on August 15, 1769. Today this large (once middle-class) house contains a museum with portraits and cameos of the entire Bonaparte clan. Search out the two genealogical documents that are family trees woven out of actual human hair. ✉ *Rue St-Charles,* ☎ *04–95–21–43–89.* 🎫 *€4.* ⏲ *Mon. 2–5, Tues.–Sat. 10–noon and 2–5, Sun. 10–noon and 2–5.*

At the corner of rue St-Charles and rue Roi-de-Rome are the city's old-
5 est houses, opposite the tiny church of **St-Jean Baptiste.** They were built shortly after the town was founded in 1492. For a look at the Citadelle, walk east down rue Roi-de-Rome to boulevard Danielle Casanova. At the corner, the **Musée du Capitellu** is a fascinating private museum tracing the history of Ajaccio through the career of a single family. ✉ *18 bd. Danielle Casanova,* ☎ *04–95–21–50–57.* 🎫 *€4.* ⏲ *Mon.–Sat. 10–12 and 2–6, Sun. 10–12.*

6 The 16th-century Baroque **Cathédrale** where Napoléon was baptized is at the end of rue St-Charles. The interior is covered with trompe-l'oeil frescoes, and the high altar, from an old church in Lucca, Italy, was donated by Napoléon's sister Eliza after he made her princess of Tuscany. Above the altar, look for Eugène Delacroix's famous painting *Virgin of Sacré Coeur.* ✉ *Rue F.-Conti.*

❼ The Renaissance-style **Chapelle Impérial** (Imperial Chapel) was built in 1857 by Napoléon's nephew, Napoléon III, to accommodate the tombs of the Bonaparte family (Napoléon Bonaparte himself is buried in the Hôtel des Invalides in Paris). A Coptic crucifix taken from Egypt during the general's 1798 campaign hangs over the chapel's main altar. ⊠ *50 rue Fesch.* ⊡ *€3.* ⊙ *Tues.–Sat. 10–12:30 and 3–7.*

★ ❽ Adjacent to the Chapelle Impérial, the **Musée Fesch** houses a fine collection of Italian masters, ranging from Botticelli and Canaletto to De Tura—part of a massive collection of 30,000 paintings bought at bargain prices following the French Revolution by Napoléon's uncle, Cardinal Fesch, the archbishop of Lyon. Thanks to his nephew's military conquests, the cardinal was able to amass (steal, some would say) many celebrated Old Master paintings, the most famous of which are now in the Louvre. ⊠ *50 rue Fesch,* ☎ *04–95–21–48–17.* ⊡ *€5.38.* ⊙ *Apr.– June and Sept.–Oct., Wed.–Mon. 9:30–noon and 3–6:30; Jul.–Aug., Tues.–Sat. 9–midnight, Sun.–Mon. 9:30–noon and 3–6:30; Nov.–Mar., Wed.–Mon. 9:30–noon and 2:30–6.*

NEED A BREAK?	After visiting the Old Quarter, walk down to the Plage St-François to the **Café Fesch** to enjoy a cup of coffee while you contemplate the sparkling expanse of the Golfe d'Ajaccio. **Le Cohiba,** next door, is another good choice.

Dining and Lodging

$$–$$$ ✗ **A La Funtana.** A fountain greets diners at the door of this noted restaurant, named for a popular Corsican folk song. Fresh flowers and Oriental carpets are the only touches of decoration in the simple white dining room. The house specialty is homemade foie gras; other items worth sampling include *morilles* (morels) in foie gras and homemade sorbets. ⊠ *7 rue Notre-Dame,* ☎ *04–95–21–78–04. AE, DC, MC, V. Closed mid-June–mid-July and Mon.*

$$–$$$ ✗ **Auberge de Prunelli.** This cheerful riverside inn overlooking the
★ Prunelli River has a good-value, three-course prix-fixe menu for €17. You can also choose from such regional specialties as sea-urchin beignets with brocciu, brocciu omelets, trout, roast *cabrit* (kid), or figatelli sausage from the excellent à la carte menu. ⊠ *Pisciatellu (11 km/7 mi south of Ajaccio just off N196; look for the turnoff onto D55B just before crossing the river),* ☎ *04–95–20–02–75. Reservations essential. MC, V. Closed Tues.*

$$–$$$ ✗ **Le Floride.** This port restaurant overlooking the docks serves simple but sound combinations of maritime and upland products. Fresh fish and shellfish are the specialty, with spaghetti *au langouste* (with lobster) one of the stars in chef Nicolas Baubé's firmament of seafood creations. ⊠ *Rue Charles Ornano s/n, Port,* ☎ *04–95–22–67–48. AE, DC, MC, V. Closed Mon.*

$–$$ ✗ **20123.** This well-loved Ajaccio favorite is known for its traditional cuisine, fresh fish from the nearby market, and, in season, game specials such as *civet de sanglier* (wild boar stew) with *trompettes de la mort* (wild mushrooms) served in a bubbling earthenware casserole. ⊠ *2 rue Roi-de-Rome,* ☎ *04–95–21–50–05. MC, V. Closed Mon., Tues. and Jan. 15–Feb. 15. No lunch June 15–Sept. 15.*

$$$$ ✗⊡ **Eden Roc.** The modern Eden Roc overlooks the gulf in Ajaccio's most exclusive suburb. Gardens surround the swimming pool, and a tiny beach lies across the road. Rooms are large and luxurious, each with a terrace and sea view. The restaurant is a favorite outing for Ajaccio gourmands. ⊠ *Rte. des Iles Sanguinaires, 20000 (8 km/5 mi from center of town),* ☎ *04–95–51–56–00,* 𝖥𝖠𝖷 *04–95–52–05–03,* 𝖶𝖤𝖡 *www.edenroc-corsica. fr. 45 rooms. Restaurant, piano bar, cable TV, minibars, pool, health club, meeting rooms, beach, parking (fee). AE, DC, MC, V.*

$$$–$$$$ ✕🏨 **La Dolce Vita.** Spread out over flower-filled terraces at the edge of the Golfe d'Ajaccio, this hotel-restaurant is lavishly Italianate. The spectacular swimming pool overlooks the sea, and the restaurant ranks as one of the island's best for stylish interpretations of traditional Corsican dishes. ✉ *Rte. des Iles Sanguinaires, 20000 (8 km/5 mi from center of town),* ☎ *04–95–52–42–42,* FAX *04–95–52–07–15. 32 rooms. Restaurant, bar, cable TV, minibars, pool, beach, free parking. AE, DC, MC, V. Closed Nov. 1–Mar. 31.*

$$$ ★ 🏨 **Hôtel San Carlu.** On the edge of the Old Town, this friendly hotel overlooking the ramparts and the sea is an ideal base for exploring Ajaccio. Rooms are clean and comfortable; those on the Golfe d'Ajaccio side (east) on the third floor get an abundance of morning sunshine streaming across the beds and into the bathtubs, not a bad way to greet a new day on the Isle de la Beauté. ✉ *8 bd. Danielle Casanova, 20000,* ☎ *04–95–21–13–84,* FAX *04–95–21–09–99. 40 rooms. No air-conditioning, minibars. AE, DC, MC, V.*

Nightlife and the Arts

Many of Ajaccio's top nightspots are 4 km (2½ mi) north of town, in the Santa-Lina District along route des Iles Sanguinaires. **La Cinquième Avenue** (✉ Rte. des Iles Sanguinaires) is a leading dance-until-dawn venue for all ages, the younger the better. **Le Sun** (✉ Rte. des Iles Sanguinaires) draws the usual suspects and the party-hardened. For in-town action, **Le Pigalle** (✉ Pl. Charles de Gaulle) is a spot to check. **L'Entreacte** (✉ Bd. Lantivy, next to casino) is a popular stop on the night circuit. A continuing success in Ajaccio's night scene is **Le Privilège** (✉ Rue Macchini, pl. Charles-de-Gaulle). **Le Cohiba** (✉ Bd. Lantivy, 1 Résidence Diamant) is a vibrant music bar. **La Place** (✉ Bd. Lantivy) is another well-known boîte and piano bar. On the road to the airport, **Le Duplex** (✉ Av. Campo dell'Oro) is a brash young addition to the disco scene in the Corsican capital.

The **Fête de la Miséricorde** (Feast of Our Lady of Mercy), on March 18, spotlights the Procession de la Madunnuccia (Procession of the Madonna), Ajaccio's patron saint. In May all Ajaccio celebrates during its festive **Carnival.** In July you can attend the **Rencontres Internationales de Musique,** a gathering of classical music and opera performers. A major festival, the **Fêtes Napoléoniennes,** is held on August 15, Napoléon's birthday.

Outdoor Activities and Sports

NAVE VA (✉ 2 rue J. B. Marcaggi, ☎ 04–95–21–83–98) operates boating excursions to the Iles Sanguinaires, Reserve Naturelle de Scandola, Girolata, Calanches de Piana, and the chalk cliffs of Bonifacio. **BMS** (✉ Quai de la Citadelle, ☎ 04–95–21–33–75) rents bicycles year-round. **Locacorse** (✉ 10 av. Bévérini-Vico, ☎ 04–95–20–71–20) has bike rentals from April through September. The **Centre de Randonnées Équestres de St-Georges** (✉ Domaine de Campicciolі, rte. de Vigna Piana, ☎ 04–95–25–34–83) rents horses and organizes outings along the former mule paths. The **Poney-Club d'Ajaccio** (✉ Campo dell' Oro, ☎ 04–95–23–03–10) is a popular option for horse rentals. For fishing, swimming, underwater diving, kayaking, or windsurfing, head to **Club des Calanques** (✉ Hôtel des Calanques, rte. des Sanguinaires, ☎ 04–95–21–39–65). **Les Dauphins** (✉ Rte. des Sanguinaires, Plage de Barbicaja, ☎ 04–95–52–07–78) has water-sports gear among other offerings. For information about sailing, contact the **Ligue Corse de Voile** (✉ Port de la Citadelle, ☎ 04–95–21–07–79). A popular spot to rent a sailboat is at the **Tahiti Nautic Club d'Ajaccio** (✉ Plage du Ricanto, ☎ 04–95–20–05–95).

Shopping

Much more than just a bookstore specializing in books about Corsica, **Librairie la Marge** (✉ 7 rue Emmanuelle-Arène) is a hub of Corsican culture, where you can also buy music and attend poetry readings. **Paese Nostru** (✉ Passage Guinguetta) sells Corsican crafts of all kinds. **U Tilaghju** (✉ Rue Forcioli Conti), one of several artisanal shops near the cathedral, has an impressive collection of ceramics.

Porticcio

❾ *17 km (10½ mi) south of Ajaccio on N196.*

Across the Prunelli River south of Ajaccio, Porticcio is the capital's fancy suburb and luxurious beach resort town. It's primarily notable for its seawater cures at the **Institut de Thalassothérapie** (Institute of Thalassotherapy), on the Punta di Porticcio, and the *grand luxe* Le Maquis hotel.

Dining and Lodging

$$$$ ★ ✕ 🏨 **Le Maquis.** The Maquis ranks as one of the island's (even France's) finest *hôtels de charme.* The quaint, ivy-covered building reaches down to a private beach. Rooms have views of the sea or the hills. At the candlelight restaurant L'Arbousier, with its ancient beams taken from what was once the Ajaccio prison, a blend of traditional and nouvelle cuisine is served: fish tartare, scrambled eggs with truffles, and fresh tagliatelle. ✉ *D55, 20166 Porticcio,* ☎ *04–95–25–05–55,* FAX *04–95–25–11–70,* WEB *www.slh.com/lemaquis. 19 rooms. Restaurant, bar, cable TV, minibars, tennis court, indoor and outdoor pool, beach, park, meeting rooms, no pets. AE, DC, MC, V.*

Outdoor Activities and Sports

Bikes are a great way to explore the beach; **Avis** (✉ Hôtel Marina Viva) rents them. Kids love **Aqua Cyrné Gliss** (✉ follow signs in Porticcio, ☎ 04–95–25–17–48), a water park with water slides and swimming pools. Admission is €11.53, and it's open mid-June–mid-September, daily 10:30–7, plus two nights a week (usually Tuesday and Friday).

Filitosa

★ ❿ *71 km (43 mi) southeast of Ajaccio off N196.*

Filitosa is the site of Corsica's largest grouping of megalithic menhir statues. Bizarre, life-size stone figures of ancient warriors rise up mysteriously from the undulating terrain, many with human faces that have been flattened over time by erosion. A small museum on the site houses archaeological finds, including the menhir known as *Scalsa Murta,* whose delicately carved spine and rib cage make it difficult to believe the statue dates from some 5,000 years ago. Be sure to buy the excellent guidebook in English (€5) by experts Cesari and Acquaviva. You can study it over a snack at the pleasant museum café. *Contact Centre Préhistorique Filitosa,* ☎ *04–95–74–00–91 for information.* 🎫 *Guided tours in English €6.* ⏲ *June–Aug., daily 8–7.*

Sartène

⓫ *27 km (16 mi) southeast of Filitosa on N196.*

The hillside town of Sartène was called the "most Corsican of all Corsican towns" by French novelist Prosper Mérimée. Dorothy Carrington, author of *Granite Island,* the definitive work in English (and probably in any language) on Corsica, described it as one of the least changed places on Corsica. Founded in the 16th century, Sartène has survived pirate raids and bloody feuding among the town's families.

The word "vendetta" is believed to have originated here as the result of a 19th-century family feud so serious that French troops were brought in as a peacekeeping buffer force. Centuries of fighting have left the town with a somewhat eerie and menacing atmosphere. Perhaps adding to this is the annual Good Friday *catenacciu* (enchaining) procession in which an anonymous penitent, dragging ankle chains, lugs a heavy cross through the village streets.

The most interesting part of town is **Vieux Sartène** (Old Sartène), surrounded by ancient ramparts. Start at place de la Libération, the main square. To one side is the **Hôtel de Ville** (town hall), in the former Genoese governor's palace. For a taste of the Middle Ages, slip through the tunnel in the Town Hall to place du Maggiu and the old quarter of **Santa Anna,** a warren of narrow, cobbled streets lined with granite houses. Scarcely 100 yards from the Hôtel de Ville, down a steep and winding street, a 12th-century ***tour de guet*** (watchtower) stands out in sharp contrast to the modern apartment buildings behind.

Sartène is the center for research into Corsica's prehistory, thanks to its proximity to Pianu de Levie and numerous dolmens and megalithic statues. For a look at some of the island's best prehistoric relics, head to the **Musée Départemental de Préhistoire Corse** (Regional Museum of Corsican Prehistory), in the town's former prison. ✉ *Rue Croce,* ☎ *04–95–77–01–09.* 🎫 *€4.* ⏲ *Apr.–Oct., Mon.–Sat. 10–noon and 2–6; Nov.–Mar., weekdays 10–noon and 2–5.*

Dining

$$ ✕ **Auberge de Santa Barbara.** This excellent restaurant is just 1 km (½ mi) north of Sartène. Known as one of the top specialists in authentic Corsican cuisine, chef Giselle Lovighi also serves innovative seafood specialties such as shrimp soufflé and crayfish salad. ✉ *Rte. de Propriano, Alzone, Sartène,* ☎ *04–95–77–09–06. MC, V. Closed Mon. lunch and Oct. 15–Mar. 15.*

Outdoor Activities and Sports

Horses can be rented from the **Ferme Équestre de Baracci** (✉ Propriano, ☎ 04–95–76–08–02), just north of Sartène; 5- to 15-day seaside and mountain outings are also arranged. Another way to see the area is to hike along the **Tra Mare a Mare** (Sea-to-Sea Trail) from Propriano to Porto-Vecchio. Roadside information points suggest itineraries.

Ste-Lucie-de-Tallano

⑫ *15 km (9 mi) northeast of Sartène, 12 km (7 mi) southeast of Levie on D268.*

The pretty little village of Ste-Lucie-de-Tallano is in the heart of Mérimée country, the setting for *Colomba,* the tale of a beautiful young Corsican woman caught in an Andromaque-like web of love, honor, vendetta, and death. Driving up the Rizzanese Valley, the Spin' a Cavallu (Horse's Back) Bridge, one of the oldest and loveliest Genoese bridges on the island, is the first important sight. The St-François convent and the church of Ste-Lucie are the main religious buildings in town.

Dining

$$–$$$ ✕ **Vecchiu Mulinu.** This restored mill serves simple but delicious *cuisine du terroir* (regional country cooking). The local Fiumicicoli red is the perfect match. ✉ *Bains de Caldanes,* ☎ *04–95–77–00–54. Reservations essential. MC, V. Closed Mon. Oct.–Easter.*

En Route Five kilometers (3 miles) east of Ste-Lucie-de-Tallano on the Zonza road (D268), the 3½-km (2-mi) walk up to the **Pianu de Levie** (Levie Plateau) offers a look at one of Corsica's best archaeological sites. The **Castellu de Cucurruzzu** is a Torréen fortress, 3,500 years old. A 20-minute additional walk from Cucurruzzu is another Torréen fortress, the **Castellu de Capula.** In Levie the **Musée Archéologique** (Archaeology Museum) (☎ 04–95–78–46–34; €4) displays prehistoric discoveries; it is open July–September, daily 9:30–6, and October–June, weekdays 10–noon and 2–4.

Quenza

13 *8 km (5½ mi) west of Zonza on D420.*

Quenza is known for its 10th-century chapel of **Santa Maria.** It is also the headquarters of **I Muntagnoli Corsi** (☎ 04–95–78–64–05), which organizes guided hikes into the Coscione Forest.

Dining and Lodging

$$$–$$$$ **Auberge Sole e Monti.** One of southern Corsica's best options for authentic Corsican cooking and a standout as a hotel as well, this place is worth a detour. Rooms are modern and well kept, and the staff is friendly. Try the local version of *soupe corse* (Corsican soup) and, in summer, trout with wild mint and brocciu. Be sure to reserve in advance. ✉ *20122 Quenza (1 km/½ mi east of town on the Zonza rd.),* ☎ *04–95–78–62–53,* FAX *04–95–78–63–88. 20 rooms. Restaurant, bar, no air-conditioning, park, parking, no pets. AE, DC, MC, V. Closed Dec.–Mar.*

Bonifacio

14 *52 km (31 mi) southeast of Sartène via N196.*

The ancient fortress town of Bonifacio occupies a spectacular clifftop aerie above a harbor carved from limestone cliffs. It is just 13 km (8 mi) from Sardinia, and the local speech is heavily influenced by the accent and idiom of that nearby Italian island. Established in the 12th century as Genoa's first Corsican stronghold, Bonifacio remained Genoese through centuries of battles and sieges. As you wander the narrow streets of the **Haute Ville** (Upper Village), inside the walls of the citadel, think of Homer's *Odyssey.* It is here, in the harbor, that scholars have placed the catastrophic encounter (Chapter X) between Ulysses's fleet and the Laestrygonians, who hurled lethal boulders down from the cliffs.

From place d'Armes at the city gate, enter the **Bastion de l'Étendard** (Bastion of the Standard); you can still see the system of weights and levers used to pull up the drawbridge. The former garrison now houses life-size dioramas of Bonifacio's history. €4. *Mid-June–mid-Sept., daily 9–7.*

In the center of the maze of cobbled streets that makes up the citadel is the 12th-century church of **Ste-Marie-Majeure,** with buttresses attaching it to surrounding houses. Inside the church, note the Renaissance baptismal font, carved in bas-relief, and the 3rd-century white-marble Roman sarcophagus. Walk around the back to see the loggia, which is built above a huge cistern that stored water for use in times of siege, as did the circular silos seen throughout the town.

From Bonifacio you can take a **boat trip** to the Dragon Grottoes and Venus's Bath (the trip takes one hour on boats that set out every 15 minutes during July and August) or the Lavezzi Islands. (✉ Boats leave from outside Hôtel La Caravelle; ☎ 04–95–75–05–93 for information).

Dining and Lodging

$$$ ✕ **La Rascasse.** In prime position to haul the freshest seafood from the boat to your table, this portside spot is an old favorite in Bonifacio. Try the fish for which the restaurant is named, the prehistorically spiny (and light) *rascasse* (red sea–scorpion fish). ✉ *Quai Comparetti,* ☎ *04–95–73–01–26. AE, DC, MC, V. Closed Nov.–Easter.*

$$–$$$ ★ ✕ **Le Voilier.** This popular year-round restaurant in the port serves carefully selected and prepared fish and seafood, along with fine Corsican sausage and traditional cuisine from *soupe Corse* to *fiadone* (cheesecake). ✉ *Quai Comparetti,* ☎ *04–95–73–07–06. AE, DC, MC, V. Closed Jan. 1–Mar. 20 and Mon. Oct.–Dec. No dinner Sun.*

$$ ✕ **Les 4 Vents.** This friendly restaurant near the Sardinia boat terminal is popular with the yachting crowd and family groups. In winter the kitchen serves up Alsatian specialties like sauerkraut and sausages. In summer the focus is on barbecued fish and meats, as well as typical Corsican dishes. ✉ *29 quai Bando di Ferro,* ☎ *04–95–73–07–50. MC, V. Closed mid–late Nov. and Tues. Nov.–June.*

$$$$ 🏨 **Hôtel le Genovese.** This small, intimate hotel is built into the ramparts of the upper town's citadel. Peach fabric wallcoverings set the rooms aglow. Upstairs rooms have superb views over the cliffs and out to Sardinia. ✉ *Quartier de Citadelle, Haute Ville, 20169,* ☎ *04–95–73–12–34,* FAX *04–95–73–09–03,* WEB *www.woda.fr-aa-genovese. 15 rooms. Bar, minibars, cable TV, pool, parking, no pets. AE, DC, MC, V.*

Nightlife and the Arts

Party early at the *avant-boîte* ("before club," until 2) at **B-52** (✉ Quai Comparetti, ☎ 04–95–73–57–52), in the port. Raging until sunrise is the happening **Lollapalooza** (✉ Quai Comparetti, ☎ 04–95–73–04–54), open around the clock in summer.

The **Fête Millénaire de Bonifacio,** Bonifacio's celebration of the 1,000th anniversary of its founding, is held in early June and has become a well-attended annual event, with concerts, processions, and street dances.

Outdoor Activities and Sports

The area around Bonifacio is ideal for water sports. Contact **Club Atoll** (✉ Rte. de Porto-Vecchio, ☎ 04–95–73–02–83). The best golf course on Corsica (and one of the best in the Mediterranean), a 20,106-ft par-72 gem designed by Robert Trent Jones, is at **Sperone** (✉ Domaine de Sperone, ☎ 04–95–73–17–13), just east of Bonifacio.

Shopping

Pierres de Cade (✉ Haute Ville) has a good selection of beautiful objects carved out of wood from Corsica's rich forests of chestnut and juniper.

Porto-Vecchio

⑮ *27 km (16 mi) north of Bonifacio via N198.*

The old walled town of Porto-Vecchio has become synonymous with mass tourism dominated by tour operators from Italy, so you might want to consider skipping it. The town's network of medieval streets has now been largely given over to bistros, boutiques, and cafés. Nonetheless, the Gulf of Porto-Vecchio is lined with beautiful beaches.

Dining and Lodging

$$$$ ✕🏨 **Belvédère.** This intimate little hotel is nearly surrounded by water and sandy beaches. Rooms decorated in blue and white make you feel like part of the seascape. The restaurant *gastronomique* is deservedly famous throughout Corsica and beyond, while the grill, *Mari i Terra* serves simpler fare cooked over coals. ✉ *Baie de Santa Giulia, 20137*

(5 km/3 mi south of town), ☎ *04–95–70–54–13,* FAX *04–95–70–42–63. 16 rooms. Restaurant, bar, minibars, cable TV, pool, park, beach, parking, no pets. AE, DC, MC, V. Closed Nov.–Apr.*

$$$$ ✕🏨 **Grand Hôtel de Cala Rossa.** This famous hotel and restaurant built over the water merits a look, even though the luxurious surroundings and overdeveloped Porto-Vecchio tourist scene are probably not the Corsica you had in mind. Nouvelle Mediterranean cuisine with a Corsican flair is featured in the restaurant, long considered one of the island's premier dining spots. ✉ *Rte. de Cala Rossa, 20137 (8 km/5 mi north of Porto-Vecchio),* ☎ *04–95–71–61–51,* FAX *04–95–71–60–11,* WEB *www.hotel-calarossa.com. 55 rooms. Restaurant, bar, minibars, cable TV, 2 tennis courts, beach, park, parking, no pets. AE, DC, MC, V. Closed Nov.–Apr.*

En Route Porto-Vecchio backs onto Corsica's largest cork-oak forest, **L'Ospédale.** An excursion across the forest on D368, climbing 49 km (30 mi) to the mountain pass of **Col de Bavella,** is one of the island's most magical tours, and should not be missed. Opt in favor of the alternative—a flat, straight road up the east coast—only if you have a boat leaving Bastia in two hours.

Col de Bavella

★ ⓰ *50 km (31 mi) northeast of Porto-Vecchio on D368 and D268.*

The granite peaks known as the **Aiguilles de Bavella** (Needles of Bavella) tower some 6,562 ft overhead as you reach the Col de Bavella (Bavella Pass). Hiking trails are well marked. The narrow but mostly well-paved roadway over the pass will take you back to the coast along the Solenzara River. If you stop and peer carefully into its depths, you may be able to see wild Corsican trout dining on their usual fare of aquatic insects.

Dining and Lodging

$ ★ ✕🏨 **Le Refuge.** Near the top of the spectacular drive from Porto-Vecchio to the Col de Bavella, follow signs for Le Refuge, an inexpensive little *gîte d'étape* (hikers' inn). Here, by a roaring fire, you can enjoy a hearty lunch or dinner of Corsican mountain fare or spend a night in simple but adequate accommodations under immense laricio pines. Demi-pension is often required here; inquire when booking. ✉ *Cartalavonu (2 km/1½ mi off D368 to the left),* ☎ *04–95–70–00–39. 4 double rooms, 30 single dormitory bunks without bath. MC, V.*

Aléria

⓱ *32 km (20 mi) north of Solenzara on N198, 70 km (63 mi) north of Porto-Vecchio, 48 km (29 mi) southeast of Corte.*

Just before the village of Aléria are the ruins of the Roman city of the same name. On a pine-studded plateau is the carefully restored 16th-century **Fort de Matra,** which houses the **Musée Jérôme Carcopino.** On display are pottery and tools found on the site, as well as Etruscan, Greek, and Roman artifacts dating from as far back as 500 BC. 🎫 €4. ⏲ *Apr.–Oct., daily 8–noon and 2–7; Nov.–Mar., Mon.–Sat. 8–noon and 2–5.*

Dining

$$ ✕ **Chez Mathieu.** This beachside restaurant, open year-round, specializes in very fresh *loup* (sea bass) and *dorade* (sea bream). In summer if you have dinner on the beach at sunset (before driving back up into the mountains at Corte), you can get—aside from the best fresh fish—a sense of Corsica's unique geographical diversity. ✉ *Plage Padulone,* ☎ *04–95–57–12–03. MC, V.*

Outdoor Activities and Sports

At Aléria's **beach** you can go surf casting, swimming, or sailing. The beach stretches north from the mouth of the Tavignano River and gets wilder the farther north you go. **Camping-Bungalows Marina d'Aléria** (✉ at intersection of N200 and the beach, ☎ 04–95–57–01–42) rents all kinds of nautical equipment.

HAUTE CORSE

Haute Corse (Upper Corsica) encompasses the northeastern end of the island and is, indeed, higher in mean altitude than Corse du Sud, topped by the 8,876-ft Monte Cinto. Most Corsica enthusiasts agree that Haute Corse is richer than other parts of this "mountain in the sea" in the attributes that are typically Corsican: highland forests, remote villages, hidden cultural gems, and alpine lakes and streams. In the center of Haute Corse is the city of Corte, Corsica's historic heart. To the east is the forested region of La Castagniccia, named for the abundance of *châtaigniers* (chestnut trees). This is one of Corsica's treasures, especially in the fall, when fallen leaves and chestnuts blanket the ground. The forest's tiny roadways go through villages with stunning Baroque churches and houses still roofed in traditional blue-gray slate. To the north is Cap Corse: the 105-km (65-mi) drive along the coastal route D80, from the town of Patrimonio to the city of Bastia, takes about three hours (four with lunch in Centuri and five with a run up the Col de Ste-Lucie). Bastia is Corsica's most Italianate city and projects a dramatic contrast to the tidier and more "Continental" Ajaccio.

Corte

★ 18 *48 km (30 mi) northwest of Aléria on N200, 83 km (51 mi) northeast of Ajaccio, 70 km (43 mi) southwest of Bastia.*

Set amid spectacular cliffs and gorges at the confluence of the Tavignano, Restonica, and Orta rivers, Corte is the spiritual heart and soul of Corsica. Capital of Pasquale Paoli's government from 1755 to 1769, it was also where Paoli established the Corsican University in 1765. Closed by the victorious French in 1769, the university, always a symbol of Corsican identity, was reopened in 1981.

To reach the upper town and the 15th-century château overlooking the rivers, walk up the cobblestone ramp from place Pasquale-Paoli. Stop in lovely **place Gaffori** at one of the cafés or restaurants. Note the bullet-pocked house where the Corsican hero Gian Pietro Gaffori and his wife, Faustina, held off the Genoese in 1750.

★ The **Citadelle,** a Vauban-style fortress (1769–78), is built around the original 15th-century fortification at the highest point of the cliff, with the river below. It contains the **Musée de la Corse** (Corsica Museum), dedicated to the island's history and ethnography. ☎ *04–95–45–25–45.* 🎫 *€6.* ⊙ *Nov.–Apr., Tues.–Sat. 10–5; May–Oct., daily 10–8.*

The **Palais National** (National Palace), just outside the citadel and above place Gaffori, is the ancient residence of Genoa's representatives in Corsica and was the seat of the Corsican parliament from 1755 to 1769. The building is now part of the Corsican University. ✉ *Pl. du Poilu.* ⊙ *Weekdays 2–6.*

For an unforgettable view of the river junction and the Genoese bridge below, the citadel's tiny watchtower above and the mountains behind, walk left along the citadel wall to the **Belvédère.**

Leave the Haute Ville and go through the tiny alleys of the **Quartier de Chiostra.** Follow the cobblestone path (as you look down) to the right from the Belvédère, bearing right and across at the **Chapelle St-Théophile.** Coming into the tiny square on your left, don't miss the open stone staircase on the opposite wall, or the prehistoric fertility goddess carved into the wall to the left next to the pottery artisans' shop. After leaving this little space, continue downhill, and you will rejoin the ramp leading into place Pasquale-Paoli.

The **Gorges de la Restonica** (Restonica Gorge) make a spectacular day hike. At the top of the Restonica Valley, leave your car in the parking area at the end of the road. A two-hour climb will take you to **Lac de Mélo,** a trout-filled mountain lake 6,528 ft above sea level. Surrounded by a circle of craggy granite peaks, the lake is the site of a classical concert in early August. Another hour up is the usually snow-bordered **Lac de Capitello.** Information on trails is available from the tourist office or the Parc Naturel Régional. At the Restonica Gorge, light meals are served in the stone shepherds' huts at the **Bergeries de Grotelle.**

Dining and Lodging

$$$ ★ ✕ 🏨 **Auberge de la Restonica.** Above the crystalline Restonica River, this cozy inn—known for its hearty Corsican fare—has seven charming rooms (one of which is a duplex apartment) in a hunting lodge-like building over rushing water. The cuisine is well known in and around Corte. ✉ *Vallée de la Restonica, 20250,* ☎ *04–95–45–25–25,* FAX *04–95–61–15–79. 7 rooms. Restaurant, pool. AE, DC, MC, V. Closed Nov. 4–Feb. 28.*

$$$ 🏨 **Hôtel Dominique Colonna.** Originally the modern annex across the parking lot from the Auberge de la Restonica, this comfortable spot has sliding glass and screen doors leading directly out to breakfast nooks next to the stream. Owner Dominique "Dumé" Colonna, one of France's (and certainly Corsica's) greatest soccer stars, drops by from time to time. ✉ *Vallée de la Restonica, 20250,* ☎ *04–95–45–25–65,* FAX *04–95–61–03–91. 28 rooms. Restaurant, no air-conditioning, minibars, pool, park, parking. AE, DC, MC, V. Closed Nov. 11–Mar. 14*

Morosaglia

19 *14 km (9 mi) southeast of Ponte Leccia, 9 km (5 mi) east of La Porta.*

The town of Morosaglia is the birthplace of Pasquale Paoli, Corsica's most celebrated national hero and author of the first republican constitution, drafted for Corsica in 1755 (with reverberations extending to the founding fathers of the United States). Letters, portraits, and memorabilia from Paoli's life are on display at the **Maison de Pasquale Paoli** (Pasquale Paoli House). ☎ *04–95–61–04–97.* 🎫 *€4.* ⏲ *Spring–fall, daily 9–noon and 2:30–7:30; winter, daily 1–5.*

La Porta

20 *9 km (5 mi) west of Morosaglia, 14½ km (9 mi) north of Piedicroce on D515.*

As the name of the village suggests, La Porta (the Door) is an entranceway to La Castagniccia. The **St-Jean-Baptiste** church here is widely accepted as the crowning glory of Corsican Baroque art. The bright ocher facade and the five-story bell tower are feasts for the eyes, as are the paintings inside. Look for the *Martyrdom of St. Eulalie of Barcelona* (1848), by Louis Destouches (1819–81), just inside on the left.

Dining

$$–$$$ ✕ **U Fragnu.** After you've exited La Castagniccia near La Porta, head north to this restaurant for some exquisite local country cooking. Madame Garelli is a specialist in *soupe de berger* (shepherd's soup)—made from a restored original recipe recovered after painstaking research. ✉ *Rte. de Vescovato, Venzolasca (7 km/4 mi north of Folelli on N198, then 2 km/1 mi up D37),* ☎ *04–95–36–62–33. Reservations essential. No credit cards. No lunch Thurs.–Sat. Nov.–Mar.*

$$ ✕ **L'Ampugnani–Chez Elisabeth.** This excellent restaurant is known throughout Corsica as a treasury of fine local cooking. Specializing in *cuisine du terroir* (local country cooking), it offers such dishes as a superb leg of lamb with herbs and *figatellu* (liver sausage). ✉ *La Porta,* ☎ *04–95–39–22–00. Reservations essential. MC, V. Closed Mon. Oct.–Easter.*

Piedicroce

★ 21 *14 km (9 mi) south of La Porta on D515, 66 km (40 mi) south of Bastia.*

Piedicroce's panoramic view of La Castagniccia is superb. Be sure to stop in to visit the vividly painted Baroque church of **St-Pierre-et-St-Paul,** one of the finest of its type in the area. The nearby mineral springs of **Orezza** are reputed to have miraculous powers. The **Fium Alto,** running along the road that goes northeast to Folelli, is one of Corsica's best trout streams. To exit La Castagniccia, follow signs for **Folelli** (37 km/22 mi north) or Bastia (66 km/40 mi north).

Dining and Lodging

$$ ★ ✕ **Le Refuge.** A handy midway point in the labyrinthine La Castagniccia, this hotel-restaurant is a good place for a delicious meal based on the Rafalli family's home-processed charcuterie and a night's sleep in the small but cozy quarters overlooking the Castagniccia and the valley of the Fium Alto. ✉ *20229 Piedicroce,* ☎ *04–95–35–82–65,* FAX *04–95–35–84–42. 20 rooms. Restaurant, bar, no air-conditioning. MC, V. Closed Nov.*

Asco

22 *22 km (13 mi) west of Ponte Leccia: 2 km (1 mi) north of Ponte Leccia, D147 turns off N197 toward the village of Asco, 16 km (10 mi) away.*

The Asco Valley is studded with beehives, and honey and cheese abound in Asco's shops. Don't miss the Genoese bridge below Asco or, even better, a swim in the river. Above Asco the granite gorge becomes a cool pine forest, perfect for hiking. Follow the road for another 12 km (7 mi) past the village, ending at the top against a wall of mountains. The Asco Valley runs west to an awe-inspiring barrier of mountains crowned by **Monte Cinto,** rising to 8,795 ft, the highest point in Corsica. As you travel up the valley, the maquis-covered slopes give way to a sheer granite gorge hung with sweet-smelling juniper. This is certainly a drive well worth making in daylight, although if you must make the trip up at night, you can ogle the scenery on your way down the next day.

Haut-Asco

23 *13 km (8 mi) west of Asco.*

Haut-Asco is the starting point for the eight- to nine-hour (round-trip) walk up **Monte Cinto.** From the top, on a clear day, you can see the entire island and even the Apennines on the Italian mainland. Clouds and mist gather after about 10 AM, however, particularly in summer. For this reason a 4 AM start is recommended. Questions can be answered at Le Chalet.

Dining and Lodging

$–$$ ✕🏨 **Le Chalet.** This tidy hideaway at the very top of the island has a simple, no-frills restaurant serving Corsican cuisine. Walls are covered with photographs of famous mountaineers. Along with the 22 private rooms there are also a hikers' dormitory, a bar, and a store selling supplies to trekkers, who use the chalet as a way station from the GR 20. *✉ 20276 Haut-Asco, ☎ FAX 04–95–47–81–08. 22 rooms, plus dormitory without bath. Restaurant, bar, no air-conditioning. MC, V. Closed early Nov.–early May.*

Outdoor Activities and Sports

From at least December to April, Corsica's upper reaches are snowed in, creating options for both alpine and cross-country skiing; consult the **Club Alpin Français** (☎ 04–95–22–73–81) in Ajaccio. For information about hiking up Monte Cinto, in Bastia contact the **Office National des Forêts** (☎ 04–95–32–81–90).

La Scala di Santa Regina

★ *9 km (5 mi) south of Ponte Leccia, D84 leaves N193, starts up the Golo River, and turns into La Scala di Santa Regina.*

This road, known as La Scala di Santa Regina (Stairway of the Holy Queen), is one of the most spectacular on the island. It's also one of the most difficult to navigate, especially in winter. The route follows the twisty path of the Golo River, which has carved its way through layers of red granite, forming dramatic gorges and waterfalls. Be prepared to stop for herds of animals crossing the road. Follow the road to the **Col de Verghio** (Verghio Pass) for superb views of Tafunatu, the legendary perforated mountain, and Monte Cinto. On the way up you'll pass through the **Valdo Niello Forest,** Corsica's most important woodlands, filled with pines and beeches. The col is considered the border between Haute Corse and Corse du Sud. As you descend from the Verghio Pass through the **Forêt d'Aitone** (Aitone Forest), note how well manicured it is—the pigs, goats, and sheep running rampant through the tall Laricio pines keep it this way. As you pass the village of Evisa, with its orange roofs, look across the impressive **Gorges de Spelunca** (Spelunca Gorge) to see the hill village of Ota. A small road on the right will take you across the gorge, where there's an ancient Genoese-built bridge.

Ota

24 *16 km (10 mi) northwest of Evisa on La Scala di Santa Regina.*

The tiny village of Ota, overlooking the **Gorges de Spelunca,** has traditional stone houses that seem to be suspended on the mountainside, an amazing view of the surrounding mountains, and a number of trailheads. It's an excellent base for hiking in the area.

Dining and Lodging

$–$$ ✕🏨 **Chez Félix.** This homey place serves as dining room, taxi stand, and town hall. Cheerful owner Marinette Ceccaldi cooks up heaping portions of Corsican specialties ranging from wild boar to chestnut-flour beignets. Suites are decorated with curios and antiques, each with a balcony overlooking the gorge. Rooms are comfortable and rustic; some have private bathrooms, others share. The hotel has a van that will transport you out to hiking routes. ✉ *Pl. de la Fontaine, 20150,* ☎ FAX *04–95–26–12–92. 4 2-bedroom apartments, 36 beds in 4- and 6-bed rooms with shared bath. Restaurant, bar, no air-conditioning. AE, DC, MC, V.*

Porto and Les Calanches

25 *5 km (3 mi) west of Ota, 30 km (19 mi) south of Calvi.*

The flashy resort town of Porto doesn't have much character, but its setting on the crystalline **Golfe de Porto** (Gulf of Porto), surrounded by massive pink-granite mountains, is superb. Activity focuses on the small port, where there is a boardwalk with restaurants and hotels. A short hike from the boardwalk will bring you to a 16th-century Genoese tower that overlooks the bay. Boat excursions leave daily for the **Réserve Naturel de Scandola.** Detour south of Porto on D81 to get to **Les Calanches,** jagged outcroppings of red rock considered among the most extraordinary natural sites in France. Look for arches and stelae, standing rock formations shaped like animals and phantasmagoric human faces.

Piana

26 *11 km (7 mi) south of Porto, 71 km (44 mi) north of Ajaccio.*

Piana overlooks Les Calanches and the Golfe de Porto. Explore the crooked streets of the Old Town and climb up to the old fortress at the top of **Capo Rosso** to admire the craggy rocks that jut out from the water.

Dining and Lodging

$$–$$$ ✕🏨 **Les Roches Rouges.** On the hillside just below the Capo Rosso, this rambling old mansion has a distinctive British flavor. The vast Empire-style restaurant is classified as a historic monument. Try the fish soup or grilled lobster. ✉ *Rte. de Porto, 20115,* ☎ *04–95–27–81–81,* FAX *04–95–27–81–76. 20 rooms. Restaurant, bar, pool, no pets. AE, DC, MC, V. Closed Nov.–Mar.*

$$$ 🏨 **Capo Rosso.** The Capo Rosso sits high in the hills overlooking the gulf, just yards from Les Calanches. The views—whether enjoyed from your room, the outdoor pool, or the restaurant's terrace—are dramatic. Rooms are modern and functional more than charming, but all the comforts are in place. ✉ *20115 Piana,* ☎ *04–95–27–82–40,* FAX *04–95–27–80–00. 57 rooms. Restaurant, bar, no air-conditioning, pool, no pets. AE, DC, MC, V. Closed mid-Oct.–Easter.*

Calvi

27 *92 km (58 mi) north of Piana, 159 km (100 mi) north of Ajaccio.*

Calvi, Corsica's slice of the Riviera, has been described by author Dorothy Carrington as "an oasis of pleasure on an otherwise austere island." Calvi grew rich by supplying products to Genoa; its citizens remained loyal supporters of Genoa long after the rest of the island declared independence. Calvi also claims to be the birthplace of Christopher Columbus. During the 18th century the town endured assaults from Corsican nationalists, including celebrated patriot Pasquale Paoli. Today Calvi sees a summertime invasion of tourists, drawn to the 6-km (4-mi) stretch of sandy white beach, the citadel, and the buzzing nightlife.

The Genoese **Citadelle,** perched on a rocky promontory at the tip of the bay, competes with the beach as a major attraction. An inscription above the drawbridge—CIVITAS CALVI SEMPER FIDELIS (The citizens of Calvi always faithful)—reflects the town's unswerving allegiance to Genoa. At the welcome center, just inside the gates, you can see a video on the city's history and arrange to take a guided tour given in English (three times a day) or a self-guided walking tour. ✉ *Up the hill off av. de l'Uruguay,* ☎ *04–95–65–36–74.* *Guided tour and video show €7.69.* ⏲ *Tours Easter–early Oct., daily at 10, 4:30, and 6:30.*

Stop in at the 13th-century church of **St-Jean-Baptiste** (✉ Pl. d'Armes); it contains an interesting Renaissance baptismal font. Look up to see the rows of pews screened by grillwork: the chaste young women of Calvi's upper classes sat here.

Dining and Lodging

$$$ ★ ✕ **Chez Tao.** At Chez Tao, a mandatory stop on almost everyone's itinerary, you can rub elbows with the town's glitterati on the ocher-color 16th-century terraces that look out over the bay. Seafood is what everyone eats, but food plays second fiddle to the atmosphere, which includes Corsican folk singing and a tinkling piano until the wee hours. ✉ *Pl. de la Citadelle,* ☎ *04–95–65–00–73. AE, DC, MC, V. Closed mid-Sept.–Easter.*

$$$ ✕ **Emile's.** With panoramic views of the port, this is a lucky place to find a table in summer. Classic French cuisine with *terroir* (local Corsican) touches is available, but fish and seafood hold center stage. ✉ *Quai Landry,* ☎ *04–95–65–09–60. AE, DC, MC, V. Closed Dec. 1–Jan. 15, Mon. in winter, and Tues. year-round.*

$$$ ✕ **L'Ile de Beauté.** One of Calvi's most celebrated restaurants has been pulling in crowds since 1929. Metal suns adorn the walls of the dining room, where the menu has many delights of seafood and upland dishes ranging from lobster fricassee to wild boar stew. ✉ *Quai Landry,* ☎ *04–95–65–00–46. AE, DC, MC, V. Closed Oct.–Apr. No lunch Wed.*

$$$$ ★ ✕🏨 **La Villa.** On a hill with marvelous views of the town and the citadel, this Relais & Châteaux hotel feels like a Mediterranean-modern villa. The gorgeous architecture leans heavily toward arched loggias and wrought iron, and fountains, paintings, and sculpture abound. Rooms are large and have terra-cotta floors and balconies. The canopied dining area overlooks the pool, surrounded by a fragrant garden. ✉ *Chemin de Notre Dame de la Serra, 20260,* ☎ *04–95–65–10–10,* FAX *04–95–65–10–50,* WEB *www.relaischateaux.fr. 26 rooms. Restaurant, bar, minibars, pool, hair salon, Turkish bath, tennis, health club. AE, DC, MC, V. Closed Jan.–Mar.*

$$$ ★ ✕🏨 **Le Signoria.** This 17th-century country manor (and annex) has homey bedrooms and large bathrooms. From the pool and patio there are panoramic views of the mountains and the bay. The renowned restaurant serves imaginative regional cuisine (it's closed for lunch, except on weekends from July through August). ✉ *Rte. de la Forêt de Bonifato, 20260 (5 km/3 mi from Calvi),* ☎ *04–95–65–93–00,* FAX *04–95–65–38–77. 18 rooms. Restaurant, bar, pool, Turkish baths, free parking, no pets. AE, MC, V. Closed Nov.–Easter.*

$$–$$$ ✕🏨 **Le Magnolia.** Rooms in this cozy 19th-century former mansion situated between the church and the marketplace are named after French literary figures: the Verlaine overlooks rooftops to the port. Cupids and cherubs perch over beds. The restaurant is in the garden under a giant magnolia tree—thus the name of the hotel. ✉ *Pl. du Marché, 20260,* ☎ *04–95–65–19–16,* FAX *04–95–65–34–52. 11 rooms. Restaurant, bar, minibars, no pets. DC, MC, V. Closed Jan. 15–Mar. 15.*

Nightlife and the Arts

The cabaret-restaurant **Chez Tao** (✉ Pl. de la Citadelle, ☎ 04–95–65–00–73) is the "in" spot in town. **L'Eden Port** (✉ Quai Landry, ☎ 04–

95–62–10–32) is one of Calvi's hot piano bars, on Quai Landry next to the port Captaincy. **La Camargue,** on the outskirts of town (✉ on N167) is the town's biggest dance club. **L'Acapulco** (✉ on N167) draws a friendly crowd. Note that a free *navette* (shuttle bus) cruises downtown Calvi until dawn collecting and returning club goers.

The **Calvi Jazz Festival** is held the last week of June. **Rencontres Polyphoniques,** an international choral festival, is held in mid-September. **Les Rencontres d'Art Contemporain de Calvi** shows contemporary painting and sculpture under the arcades of the Citadelle from mid-June to the end of August. **Festiventu,** a celebration of wind-powered sports, musical instruments, and scientific artifacts, happens in late October.

Outdoor Activities and Sports

The **GR 20** begins near Calvi and follows the watershed line on the crests of the mountains northwest–southeast to Ste-Lucie de Porto-Vecchio. Contact the tourist office for information. For water-sports, diving, and boating information and equipment rental, contact **Calvi Nautique Club** (✉ Port de Plaisance, ☎ 04–95–65–10–65). The **Centre Équestre de Calvi** (✉ Rte. de Pietramaggiore, ☎ 04–95–65–22–22) arranges tours on horseback.

Shopping

The major shopping streets are rue Clemenceau and boulevard Wilson. Look for pottery, for which the region is known. Corsican knives are another specialty item, as are regional charcuterie, cheeses, and jams.

Calenzana

㉘ *13 km (8 mi) from Calvi: head east on N197 for 5 km (3 mi), then south on D151.*

Leaving Calvi via the rose-color hill towns of La Balagne—"the garden of Corsica"—will take you through some memorable towns and villages. Calenzana is the jumping-off point for the GR 20, Corsica's challenging 20-day hike over the crest of its mountainous interior. It is also the home of the spectacular wine cellar of the Orsini vineyards, the **Cave du Domaine Orsini** (✉ Clos Rochebelle, tours scheduled by appointment; ☎ 04–95–62–81–01).

The 11th-century church of **Ste-Restitute,** about 1 km (½ mi) beyond town, has an altar backed by medieval frescoes depicting the life of St. Restitute. Legend has it that the saint was martyred here in the 3rd century, and when the people of the town began building a church on a separate site, the stone blocks were moved here each night by two huge white bulls. Apparently, so the story goes, this happened several times before the townsfolk finally got the divine message and changed building sites.

Sant'Antonino

㉙ *7 km (4 mi) north of Cateri on D13 and across the gorge.*

The medieval, stone hilltop village of Sant'Antonino, believed to date from the 9th century, is one of the oldest still-inhabited places on the island. The view over La Balagne from here is just spectacular.

Pigna

★ ㉚ *7 km (4 mi) northeast of Sant'Antonino on D151.*

The unusual village of Pigna is dedicated to bringing back traditional Corsican music and crafts. Here you can listen to folk songs in cafés, visit workshops, and buy handmade musical instruments. The Casa

Musicale, a concert hall, auberge, and restaurant, is at the center of it all. During the first half of July, the Casa Musicale hosts a Festivoce (song festival) of vocalists and a capella groups.

Dining and Lodging

$–$$ ✕🏨 **Casa Musicale.** This magnetic spot has traditional local cuisine, music of all kinds—often authentic Corsican polyphonic singing—and a lovely view over La Balagne down to Calvi. Rooms are simple but elegant, with whitewashed walls and rustic furniture; they sleep two, three, or four. ✉ *20220 Pigna,* ☎ *04–95–61–77–31,* FAX *04–95–61–74–28. 7 rooms. Restaurant, bar, no air-conditioning, minibars. MC, V. Closed Jan. 5–Mar. 5. No dinner Sun.–Mon. except July 14–Aug. 30.*

Shopping

The **Casa di l'Artigiani** (☎ 04–95–61–77–29) sells a panoply of local crafts, from jam and honey to musical instruments and hand-knit sweaters.

L'Ile Rousse

31 *10 km (6 mi) northeast of Algajola, 37 km (22 mi) southwest of St-Florent.*

L'Ile Rousse, named for the mass of reddish rock now connected to the town by a causeway, is a favorite spot of French vacationers who come to bask in its Riviera-like mise-en-scène. A small two-car train runs from here along the coast to Calvi, delivering sun-worshipers to beaches not accessible by road.

Dining and Lodging

$$ ✕🏨 **A Pasturella.** This picturesque hotel in Monticello, 5 km (3 mi) southeast of L'Ile Rousse, has simple rooms with modern furnishings and geranium-filled window boxes overlooking the mountains. The widely admired restaurant specializes in seafood and Corsican dishes. ✉ *20220 Monticello (5 km/3 mi outside L'Ile Rousse),* ☎ *04–95–60–05–65,* FAX *04–95–60–21–78. 14 rooms. Restaurant, bar. AE, MC, V. Closed mid-Nov.–mid-Dec.*

$$$ 🏨 **La Pietra.** This modern building is one of those places where it is more pleasurable to be on the inside looking out: the views from its windows are stunning. Built into the red-granite rocks across from the port of L'Ile Rousse, this comfortable spot combines contemporary taste, friendly service, and unbeatable seascapes. ✉ *Chemin du Phare, 20217,* ☎ *04–95–63–02–30,* FAX *04–95–60–15–92. 40 rooms. Restaurant, bar, no pets. AE, MC, V. Closed Oct. 30–Mar. 31.*

Outdoor Activities and Sports

Two of the best **beaches** in the area are the **Plage d'Ostriconi,** at the mouth of the Ostriconi River (20 km/13 mi north of town), and the wilder and much-frequented-by-nudists **Plage Saleccia,** used in the 1960s filming of *The Longest Day.*

Shopping

Baked goods, local wines, and herbs from the maquis can be bought at the famous L'Ile Rousse **market** (✉ Pl. Paoli), classified as a national monument, open every morning.

Lama

32 *15 km (9 mi) southeast of L'Ile Rousse, 57 km (24 mi) north of Corte.*

The charmingly restored medieval village of Lama is only 10 minutes up the Ostriconi Valley and is a handy place to spend a night on your way to Cap Corse. Everyone from the mayor to local children works to accommodate visitors; people say hello in the streets and seem to know where you are staying. Once a prosperous olive-growing town, the village was nearly deserted after a 1971 fire destroyed 35,000 olive trees in a single afternoon. Carefully cultivated tourism has put Lama back on the map.

Dining and Lodging

$$ ✕ **U Campu Latinu.** Skillfully built into an ancient *bergerie,* using old stones and drywall construction, this flower-festooned restaurant overlooks Lama, the sea, and the mountains. Try an omelet or lasagna prepared with mint and brocciu, or lamb grilled over coals with maquis herbs. ✉ *At top of Village de Lama; walk or drive up from main square,* ☎ *04–95–48–23–83. DC, MC, V. Closed Sept.–June.*

$$–$$$ ✕ **Auberge de Lama.** Pierre-Jean and Françoise Costa make you part of their life, whether on horseback, on a wild boar hunt, or by showing you Lama's hidden corners and secret spots. Lodgings are scattered throughout the village in small stone cottages that sleep from two to eight. The lively restaurant, open year-round, is the town's informal nerve center. Excellent Corsican specialties are served, such as a mint-and-brocciu omelet or roast kid. ✉ *20218 Lama,* ☎ *04–95–48–22–99,* FAX *04–95–48–23–77. 50 cottages. Restaurant, bar, no air-conditioning, kitchenettes, no pets. DC, MC, V.*

Outdoor Activities and Sports

Riding along the old mule trails on horseback is an excellent way to see the countryside; for this and nearly any other outdoor activity you can imagine, from hang-gliding to canyoning to a wild boar hunt, contact Pierre-Jean Costa at **Corse Escapades** (✉ Village de Lama, 20218 Lama, ☎ 04–95–48–22–99, FAX 04–95–48–23–77).

Murato

33 *15 km (9 mi) west of Lama, 12 km (7 mi) south of Bastia: take N193 to D82 to D305 at Rutalli.*

The village of Murato has two excellent restaurants (Le Monastère and Le Ferme Campo di Monte) as well as a remarkable 12th-century Pisan church, one of Corsica's finest and foremost architectural treasures.

The polychrome, green-marble, and white-limestone **Église Mosaïque de San Michele de Murato** (Mosaic Church of San Michele of Murato) suggests many interpretations. Look for the relief depicting Eve tempted by a serpent, covering her nakedness with an oversized hand. The site overlooks the Golfe de St-Florent. When the *libecciu* (a powerful and persistent west wind) is blowing full force, even the Continent (the mainland) is sometimes visible.

Dining

$$–$$$ ★ ✕ **Le Ferme Campo di Monte.** The Julliard sisters prepare what is widely regarded as Corsica's most authentic cuisine at this lovely 350-year-old stone farmhouse. Especially good are the *storzapreti* (brocciu croquettes). ✉ *D305 Rutali-Murato,* ☎ *04–95–37–64–39. Reservations essential. AE, DC, MC, V. Closed for lunch except Sun., closed Mon.–Wed. Sept.–June.*

$$ ★ ✕ **Le Monastère.** This handsome stone structure in the middle of town, within walking distance of the church, serves excellent roast kid and lamb cooked in herbs. If the Campo di Monte is booked, this is a great alternative. ✉ *D305 Rutali-Murato,* ☎ *04–95–37–64–18. Reservations essential. AE, DC, MC, V. Open only for specific reservations Oct.–June.*

St-Florent

34 *28 km (17 mi) northeast of the exit for Lama on D81, 46 km (28½ mi) northeast of L'Ile Rousse.*

St-Florent is a postcard-perfect village nestled into the crook of the Golfe de St-Florent between the rich Nebbio Valley and the desert of Agriates. The town has a crumbling citadel and a yacht basin ringed by shops and restaurants.

Be sure to seek out the interesting Romanesque **Santa Maria Assunta** (✉ Rue Agostino Giustiniani), just outside the village. Standing in isolated splendor among the vineyards, this 12th-century white-limestone church is one of only two Pisan churches remaining on the island. The facade and interior columns support a menagerie of sculpted human faces, snakes, snails, and mythical animals.

Dining and Lodging

$$ ✕ **La Rascasse.** This fine restaurant overlooking the port is known for its excellent fish stews and fresh seafood dishes. Try to get an upstairs table for a better view of the gulf. The *civet de lotte* (stewed monkfish) and the warm scallop salad are especially good. ✉ *Esplanade du Port,* ☎ *04–95–37–06–69. AE, DC, MC, V. Closed Mon. Apr.–June and Sept.*

$$$ **Hôtel de l'Europe.** This centrally located, venerable, and elegant spot is open nearly all winter and has spectacular views over the sea. Rooms are spacious and well decorated, and the café downstairs doubles as the town nerve center. ✉ *Pl. du Village, 20217,* ☎ *04–95–37–00–03,* FAX *04–95–37–17–36. 22 rooms. Restaurant, bar, no air-conditioning, minibars, no pets. AE, MC, V. Closed Jan.–Feb.*

Patrimonio

35 *5 km (3 mi) northeast of St-Florent, 18 km (11 mi) west of Bastia.*

Patrimonio lies at the base of the Cap Corse Peninsula, among vineyards that produce most of Corsica's best wines. The most prestigious of the Patrimonio vineyards is the **Orenga de Gaffory** (☎ 04–95–30–11–38) operation, a hard-to-beat combination of wine brewery and art gallery. Tours of the vineyards and of the Orenga de Gaffory gallery can be arranged; open weekdays 9–noon and 3–6. **Antoine Arena** (☎ 04–95–37–08–27) is one of the leading young vintners. **Dominique Gentile** (☎ 04–95–37–01–54) is a leading Patrimonio wine maker who combines old techniques and modern technology.

Nightlife and the Arts

The **Nuits de la Guitare** music festival during the third week of July is one of Corsica's top musical events, featuring blues, jazz, and flamenco guitarists from all over the world.

Outdoor Activities and Sports

One of the most spectacular mountain **hiking** routes in Corsica follows the crest of Cap Corse over the 4,287-ft Monte Stello, from which you can see the hills of Tuscany and Provence. Contact the Parc Naturel Régional de la Corse for details.

Nonza

36 *14 km (9 mi) north of Patrimonio, 8 km (5 mi) south of Canelle.*

On your way along Cap Corse, be sure to stop in Nonza. This vertiginous crag seems impossibly high over its famous black beach, the legacy of a former asbestos mine down the coast at Canari. The beach is accessible only by trudging down the 600 steps from Nonza, and no doubt this is the reason why it's usually deserted. The chapel is dedicated to the martyred St. Julie, whose severed breasts, it is said, became the double fountain known as the *Fontaine aux Mamelles* (Fountain of Mammaries) on the way down to the beach. The spectacular gravity-defying tower was constructed by Pasquale Paoli in 1760. Its squared corners made it easier to defend, as famed Captain Casella proved in 1768 when he stood off 1,200 French troops.

Dining and Lodging

$$ ✕🏨 **Auberge Patrizi.** On a shady terrace in the center of town, this place serves excellent Corsican cuisine in a lively setting. It also has rooms—small and a little too close to the road—with spectacular views. ✉ *Pl. du Village, 20217,* ☎ *04–95–37–82–16,* FAX *04–95–37–86–40. 13 rooms. Restaurant, bar, no air-conditioning, no pets. AE, MC, V. Closed Nov.–Mar.*

Centuri

37 *55 km (34 mi) north of Patrimonio, 41 km (25 mi) north of Nonza.*

Centuri (pronounced *chen*-toori), Cap Corse's top fishing port, is a good place for lunch on your way around the cape. The late afternoon arrival and unloading of the fishing boats is also an event for which it is worth staying around.

Dining and Lodging

$$–$$$ ✕🏨 **Le Vieux Moulin.** Old World charm and authentic Corsican flavor characterize this place. The main house was built in 1870 as a private residence; the eight-room annex is less antique but no less inviting, with bougainvillea cascading from its balconies. Boat rides, diving, and fishing trips can be arranged, and tennis courts are nearby. The restaurant specializes in Centuri's famous seafood. ✉ *Rte. de Cap Corse, 20238 Centuri Port,* ☎ *04–95–35–60–15,* FAX *04–95–35–60–24. 14 rooms. Restaurant, bar, no air-conditioning, pool, 2 tennis courts, no pets. AE, DC, MC, V. Closed Nov.–Mar.*

En Route From Centuri continue along the D80 coastal road to the **belvedere** near the Moulin Mattei Windmill at Col de Serra on the tip of the peninsula. As you round the tip, you can see some of Corsica's 90 **Genoese watchtowers,** as well as Giraglia Island, with its lighthouse. Take D253 north to reach the fishing village of **Barcaggio.** A long, sandy beach extends east from the village, ending in a path leading to the 16th-century Tour D'Agnello. The **Finocchiarola Islands,** a protected aviary reserve that can be visited by boat from Macinaggio, are visible off the northeast corner of the peninsula. As you head down the east coast of Cap Corse on D80, you might want to make a detour on D180 through the **Col de Ste-Lucie** to the **Tour de Sénèque,** home of the Roman philosopher and writer Seneca after he was exiled for seducing the niece of Emperor Claudius. Farther south on D80, a drive up D32 to the town of **Sisco** will take you to within a 2-km (1-mi) walk of the Romanesque church of San Michele, built in 1030.

Erbalunga

38 *40 km (25 mi) southeast of Centuri, 10 km (6 mi) north of Bastia.*

Erbalunga is one of the most charming villages on Cap Corse's east coast, with stone houses sloping gently down to a Genoese tower built into a rock ledge. Probably because Erbalunga was so attractive, though possibly because it was French poet Paul Valéry's ancestral home, a colony of artists settled here in the 1920s.

Lodging

$$$–$$$$ ★ **Castel' Brando.** This 19th-century mansion has dark-green shutters and terra-cotta tiles. The spacious rooms are furnished with country-style antiques and dried flowers. The large pool and the terrace, where breakfast is served, are in the garden. ✉ *Off D80 (mailing address: B.P. 20), 20222 Erbalunga,* ☎ *04–95–30–10–30,* FAX *04–95–33–98–18,* WEB *www.castelbrando.corsica-net.com. 27 rooms. Kitchenettes, cable TV, heated pool, cable TV, no pets. AE, MC, V. Closed Nov. 1–Mar. 15.*

San Martino di Lota

39 *12 km (7 mi) north of Bastia.*

Just 20 minutes from downtown Bastia, the turnoff to the perched village of San Martino di Lota winds through thick vegetation as the flat blue expanse of the Tyrrhenian Sea spreads out below. A hike up to the mountain pass, **Bocca di Santo Lunardo,** above the village, is a perfect way to develop a ravenous appetite: the trek takes between six and eight hours round-trip and provides fantastic views of Cap Corse, the Tyrrhenian Sea, and the Tuscan hills.

Dining and Lodging

$$ ✕ **La Corniche.** The Anziani family runs this excellent hotel-restaurant serving innovative Corsican fare such as *cabri aux herbes du maquis* (roast kid in maquis herbs) and wild boar terrine. The menu changes four times a year, as the seasons bring different ingredients into the kitchen. (October–April the restaurant is closed Monday and does not serve dinner Sunday.) The rooms are simply furnished in light pastels and have panoramic views of the sea. ✉ *20200 San Martino di Lota,* ☎ *04–95–31–40–98,* FAX *04–95–32–37–69. 18 rooms. Restaurant, bar, no air-conditioning, minibars, pool, no pets. AE, DC, MC, V. Closed Dec.–Jan.*

Bastia

40 *13 km (7 mi) south of San Martino di Lota, 10 km (6 mi) south of Erbalunga, 23 km (14 mi) east of St-Florent, 93 km (58 mi) northeast of Calvi, 170 km (105 mi) north of Bonifacio, 153 km (95 mi) northeast of Ajaccio.*

Bastia, its name derived from the word bastion, was named for the fortress the Genoese built here in the 14th century as a stronghold against rebellious islanders and potential invaders. Today the city is Corsica's business center and largest town. Despite sprawling suburbs, the center of Bastia retains the timeless, salty flavor of an ancient Mediterranean port. The **Terra Vecchia** (Old Town) is best explored on foot. Start at the wide, palm-filled **place St-Nicolas,** bordered on one side by docked ships looming large in the port and on the other by two blocks of popular cafés along boulevard Général-de-Gaulle.

From place St-Nicolas head south on boulevard Général-de-Gaulle, which becomes rue Napoléon, for two blocks to the **Église de la Conception** (Church of the Conception; ✉ Rue Napoléon), occupying a pebble-studded square. Step inside to admire the church's ornate 18th-century interior, although the lighting is poor, requiring a bright day to see much detail. The walls are covered with a riot of wood carvings, gold, and marble, and the ceiling is painted with vibrant frescoes. **Place du Marché,** the market square, behind the church, buzzes with activity every morning except Monday. The warren of tiny streets that make up the old fishermen's quarter begins at the far side of the square.

To the south is the picturesque **Vieux Port** (Old Port), along quai des Martyrs de la Libération, dominated by the hilltop citadel. The harbor, lined with excellent seafood restaurants, is berthed by several million-dollar yachts, but you can still find many bright red-and-blue fishing boats and tangles of old nets and lines. A walk around the port takes you to **Terra Nova** (New Town), a maze of not-so-new streets and houses at the base of the 15th-century fortress. Climb the Escalier Romieu steps beside the leafy Jardins Romieu for a sweeping view of the Italian islands of Capraia, Elba, and Montecristo.

The **Palais des Nobles Douzes** (also known as the Palais des Gouverneurs Genois, or Genoese Governors' Palace), whose vaulted, colonnaded galleries once held the **Musée d'Ethnographie Corse** (Corsican Ethnographic Museum) is presently closed. If visits are allowed, don't miss the *Casablanca,* a French submarine used by the Resistance with swastikas on the turret representing downed Nazi aircraft. ✉ *Pl. du Donjon,* ☎ *04–95–31–09–12.*

A network of cobbled alleyways rambles across the citadel to the 15th-century **Cathédrale Ste-Marie** (✉ Rue Notre-Dame). Inside, classic Baroque abounds in an explosion of gilt decoration. The 18th-century silver statue of the Assumption is paraded at the head of a religious procession every August 15. The sumptuous Baroque style of the **Chapelle Ste-Croix** (Chapel of the Holy Cross), behind the cathedral, makes it look more like a theater than a church. The chapel owes its name to a blackened oak crucifix, dubbed "Christ of the Miracles," discovered by fishermen at sea in 1428 and venerated to this day by Bastia's fishing community.

Dining and Lodging

$$–$$$ ✕ **La Citadelle.** This rustic and intimate spot, arranged around an ancient oil press, is near the Governor's Palace on the heights of the Terra Nova. Dishes are carefully and elegantly prepared and presented; especially tasty is the rockfish soup, a delicious dark and thick potage. ✉ *5 rue du Dragon,* ☎ *04–95–31–44–70. AE, MC, V. Closed Sun.*

$$ ★ ✕ **A Scaletta.** Enjoy the view of the Old Port as you choose from a host of fish and seafood specials at this popular spot. (Lavezzi, next door, has the same view, fine cuisine, and higher prices.) The cuisine in this rollicking little bistro is traditional Corsican with maritime leanings. ✉ *4 rue St-Jean,* ☎ *04–95–32–28–70. AE, DC, MC, V. Closed Sun.*

$$$–$$$$ 🏨 **Pietracap.** Perched on a hillside five minutes north of Bastia, Pietracap is a strikingly modern hotel nestled in a fragrant garden. The large rooms have stark, white, modern furnishings and balconies. The lobby and hallways are decorated with bold canvases painted by the amiable owner's brother. ✉ *20 rte. de San Martino di Lota, 20200 Pietranera-Bastia,* ☎ *04–95–31–64–63,* FAX *04–95–31–39–00. 39 rooms. Restaurant, bar, cable TV minibars, pool, bicycles, park, no pets. AE, DC, MC, V. Closed mid-Dec.–early Mar.*

$$ 🏨 **Posta Vecchia.** The top selling point of this hotel in an old building not far from place St-Nicolas is its quai-side location. The unpretentious rooms have floral wallpaper and wood-beam ceilings; some are quite small. Ask for one in the main house facing the port. ✉ *Quai des Martyrs-de-la-Libération, 20200,* ☎ *04–95–32–32–38,* FAX *04–95–32–14–05. 49 rooms. No air-conditioning, no pets. AE, DC, MC, V.*

Nightlife and the Arts

L'Alba (✉ 22 quai des Martyrs-de-la-Libération, ☎ 04–95–31–13–25) is a piano bar with occasional cabaret and floor shows. **L'Apo Beach** (✉ in La Marana, 10 km/6 mi south of Bastia, ☎ 04–95–33–36–83) is *the* place to go dancing. A younger set gathers at **Mayflower** (✉ Port de Plaisance, ☎ 04–95–32–33–14) to hear loud rock and roll. Musicians fill the lively patio of the **Pub Chez Assunta** (✉ Pl. Fontaine Nueve 4, ☎ 04–95–34–11–40) on most summer nights. For a night of traditional Corsican music, head to **U-Fanale** (✉ Vieux Port, ☎ 04–95–32–68–38).

One of Corsica's major carnivals, the **Fête du Christ Noir** (Feast of the Black Christ), dedicated to Bastia's most important religious icon, is on May 3. The **Fête de St-Jean,** on Midsummer's Eve (June 23), means concerts in all of Bastia's Baroque spaces. A **Film Festival of Mediterranean Cultures** is held every November. An **International Music Festival** is in early December.

Outdoor Activities and Sports

Golf at the nine-hole **Bastia Golf Club** (✉ Castellarèse, rte. de l'Aéroport, Borgo, 12 km/7 mi south of Bastia, ☎ 04–95–38–33–99). **Corsica Loisirs** (✉ 31 av. Émile-Sari, ☎ 04–95–32–54–34) organizes fishing outings and rents equipment. Bikes can be rented from **Objectif Nature** (✉ 3 rue Notre-Dame-de-Lourdes, ☎ 04–95–32–54–34). Horses are available at the **Société Hippique Urbaine de Bastia La Marana** (☎ 04–95–33–53–08 or 04–95–30–37–62) for galloping jaunts along the coast.

Shopping

Casa di l'Artigiani (✉ 5 rue des Terrasses) has a wide selection of local crafts. The **Mattei Cap Corse** store (✉ Pl. St-Nicolas) sells the Mattei family's special Cap Corse liqueur (made from grapes). At the **market** (✉ Pl. du Marché, behind St-Jean-Baptiste), everything from local cheeses to charcuterie to myrtle liqueur is sold on weekday mornings.

CORSICA A TO Z

To research prices, get advice from other travelers, and book travel arrangements, visit www.fodors.com.

AIR TRAVEL

CARRIERS

Air France has daily service connecting Paris and Lyon with Ajaccio, Bastia, and Calvi. Compagnie Corse Méditérranée connects Ajaccio and Bastia to Nice and Marseille, with several flights a day. Delta connects with Air France for flights from the United States to Corsica from May to October. TAT (Transport Aérien Transrégional) flies to Figari from Paris. Air Balagne, ATM (Air Transport Méditérranée), and Kyrnair are airlines with intra-island flights.

➤ AIRLINES AND CONTACTS: **Air Balagne** (☎ 04–95–65–02–97). **Air France** (☎ 04–95–29–45–45 Ajaccio; 01–45–46–90–00 Paris). **ATM** (☎ 04–95–76–04–99). **Compagnie Corse Méditérranée** (☎ 04–95–29–05–00 Ajaccio). **Delta** (☎ 800/241–4141). **Kyrnair** (☎ 04–95–20–52–29). **TAT** (☎ 04–95–71–01–20).

AIRPORTS

Corsica has four major airports: Ajaccio, Bastia, Calvi, and Figari. The airports at Ajaccio and Bastia run regular shuttle-bus services to and from town. At Figari a bus meets all incoming flights and will take passengers as far as Bonifacio and Porto-Vecchio for about €15.38. From Calvi the best way to get into town is to take a taxi for about €15.38.

➤ AIRPORT INFORMATION: **Bastia–Poretta** (☎ 04–95–55–96–96). **Figari–Sud Corse** (☎ 04–95–71–10–10). **Ajaccio–Campo dell'Oro** (☎ 04–95–23–56–56). **Calvi–Ste Catherine** (☎ 04–95–65–88–88).

BOAT AND FERRY TRAVEL

Regular car ferries run from Marseille, Nice, and Toulon to Ajaccio, Bastia, Calvi, L'Ile Rousse, and Propriano. These crossings take from 5 to 10 hours, with sleeping cabins available. The high-speed ferry from Nice to either Calvi or Bastia takes about three hours. Package deals, which include making the crossing with a car, an onboard cabin, and a hotel in Corsica, are available from SNCM, the Société Nationale Maritime Corse-Méditérranée. Connections from the Italian mainland are run by Corsica Ferries. Moby Lines also runs Italian mainland connections. Sardinia can be reached by ferry from Bastia or Bonifacio on Navarma Lines. Saremar also runs ferries to Sardinia.

➤ BOAT AND FERRY INFORMATION: **CMN** (✉ Compagnie Méridionale de Navigation, Ajaccio, ☎ 04–95–21–20–34; ✉ Bastia, ☎ 04–95–31–63–38). **Corsica Ferries** (✉ Bastia, ☎ 04–95–32–95–95; ✉ Genoa, Italy, ☎ 010–59–33–01). **Moby Lines** (✉ Bastia, ☎ 04–95–31–46–29; ✉ Bonifacio, ☎ 04–95–73–00–29; ✉ Genoa, Italy, ☎ 010–20–56–51). **Navarma Lines** (✉ 4 rue Luce-de-Casablanca, Bastia, ☎ 04–95–31–46–29). **Saremar** (✉ Gare Maritime, Bonifacio, ☎ 04–95–73–06–75). **SNCM** (✉ Paris, ☎ 01–49–24–24–24; ✉ Marseille, ☎ 04–91–56–30–30; ✉ Nice, ☎ 04–93–13–66–99; ✉ Toulon, ☎ 04–94–16–66–66; ✉ Ajaccio, ☎ 04–95–29–66–99; ✉ Bastia, ☎ 04–95–54–66–88; ✉ Calvi, ☎ 04–95–65–01–38; ✉ L'Ile Rousse, ☎ 04–95–60–09–56).

BUS TRAVEL

The local bus network is geared to residents who take it to school and work. At least two buses a day connect all the southern towns with Ajaccio, while northern towns are connected by bus to Bastia.

➤ BUS INFORMATION: **Autocars Eurocorse** (☎ 04–95–31–03–79). **Autocars "Les Beaux Voyages"** (☎ 04–95–65–11–35). **Autocars Les Rapides Bleus** (☎ 04–95–31–03–79). **Autocars Santini** (☎ 04–95–37–02–98).

CAR RENTAL

Hertz serves the entire island; its 18 offices are at all airports and harbors and in the major towns. Be sure to reserve at least two weeks in advance in July and August.

➤ LOCAL AGENCIES: **Avis Ollandini** (✉ Ajaccio Airport, ☎ 04–95–23–25–14). **Europcar** (✉ 1 rue du Nouveau Port, Bastia, ☎ 04–95–31–59–29). **Hertz** (✉ Ajaccio Airport, ☎ 04–95–22–14–84; ✉ 8 cours Grandval, Ajaccio, ☎ 04–95–21–70–94; ✉ Sq. St-Victor, Bastia, ☎ 04–95–31–14–24; ✉ Quai du Commerce, Bonifacio, ☎ 04–95–73–02–47; ✉ 2 rue Maréchal-Joffre, Calvi, ☎ 04–95–65–06–64).

CAR TRAVEL

Though driving is undoubtedly the best way to explore the island's scenic stretches, note that winding, mountainous roads and uneven surfaces can actually double or triple your expected travel time. The Michelin 1/200,000 map No. 90 is essential. Be prepared for spelling anomalies, many of which are Corsican, not French. Drive defensively: you'll find that others on the road tend to move at terrifying speeds.

OUTDOORS AND SPORTS

Canoeing, kayaking, and rafting are popular pastimes on the mountain rivers; for details write the Association Municipale de Ponte-Leccia.

➤ CANOEING, KAYAKING, AND RAFTING: **Association Municipale de Ponte-Leccia** (✉ 20218 Ponte Leccia).

TOURS

AIRPLANE TOURS

ATM and Kyrnair arrange sightseeing tours by plane.

➤ FEES AND SCHEDULES: **ATM** (☎ 04–95–76–04–99). **Kyrnair** (☎ 04–95–20–52–29).

BOAT TOURS

Most of Corsica's spectacular scenery is best viewed from the water. Colombo Line and Promenades en Mer, in Calvi, organize whole-day glass-bottom boat tours of Girolata, the Scandola Nature Reserve, and the Golfe de Porto. The Promenades en Mer, in Ajaccio, organizes daily trips (at 9 and 2) to the Iles Sanguinaires. Vedettes Christina and Vedettes Méditérranée arrange outings from Bonifacio to the Iles Lavezzi, Les Calanches, and Les Grottes.

➤ FEES AND SCHEDULES: **Colombo Line** (✉ Quai Landry, Calvi, ☎ 04–95–65–32–10). **Promenades en Mer** (✉ Port de l'Amirauté, 20000 Ajaccio, ☎ 04–95–23–23–38; ✉ Porto Marine, Calvi, ☎ 04–95–26–15–16). **Vedettes Christina** (☎ 04–95–73–14–69). **Vedettes Méditérranée** (☎ 04–95–73–07–71).

BUS TOURS

Ollandini arranges whole- and half-day bus tours of the island, leaving from Ajaccio.

➤ FEES & SCHEDULES: **Ollandini** (✉ 1 rte. d'Alata, Ajaccio, ☎ 04–95–21–10–12).

WALKING TOURS

Two- and three-day guided hikes through the mountains and lake region are organized by the Associu di Muntagnoli Corsi.

➤ FEES AND SCHEDULES: **Associu di Muntagnoli Corsi** (✉ Quartier Pentaniedda, 20122 Quenza, ☎ 04–95–78–64–05).

TRAIN TRAVEL

The main line of Corsica's simple rail network runs from Ajaccio, in the west, to Corte, in the central valley, then divides at Ponte Leccia. From here one line continues to L'Ile Rousse and Calvi, in the north, and the other to Bastia, in the northeast. Another service runs four times daily between Ajaccio and Bastia. In summer a small train connects Calvi and L'Ile Rousse, stopping at numerous beaches and resorts. Telephone numbers for local train stations are listed below by town.

➤ TRAIN INFORMATION: **SNCF Ajaccio** (☎ 04–95–23–11–03). **SNCF Bastia** (☎ 04–95–32–60–06). **SNCF Calvi** (☎ 04–95–65–00–61). **SNCF Ponte Leccia** (☎ 04–95–47–61–29).

TRAVEL AGENCIES

➤ LOCAL AGENT REFERRALS: **Corse Itineraries** (✉ 32 cours Napoléon, Ajaccio, ☎ 04–95–51–01–10, FAX 04–45–21–52–30). **Corse Voyages** (✉ Immeuble Les Remparts, bd. Wilson, Calvi, ☎ 04–95–65–26–71). **Cyrnea Tourisme** (✉ 9 av. Xavier-Luciani, Corte, ☎ 04–95–46–24–62, FAX 04–95–46–11–22). **Kallistour** (✉ 6 av. Maréchal-Sebastiani, Bastia, ☎ 04–95–31–71–49, FAX 04–95–32–35–73).

VISITOR INFORMATION

The Agence du Tourisme de la Corse can provide information about the whole island. The Parc Naturel Régional de la Corse, Corsica's wildlife and natural-resource management authority, controlling well over a third of the island, can provide trail maps, booklets, and a wide variety of information. Local tourist offices are listed below by town.

➤ TOURIST INFORMATION: **Agence du Tourisme de la Corse** (✉ 17 bd. Roi-Jérôme, 20000 Ajaccio, ☎ 04–95–51–77–77, FAX 04–95–51–14–40). **Ajaccio** (✉ Hôtel de Ville, pl. Foch, ☎ 04–95–51–53–03). **Bas-**

tia (✉ Pl. St-Nicolas, ☎ 04–95–54–20–40). **Bonifacio** (✉ Rue des Deux Moulins, ☎ 04–95–73–11–88). **Calvi** (✉ Port de Plaisance, ☎ 04–95–65–16–67). **Corte** (✉ La Citadelle, ☎ 04–95–46–26–70). **L'Ile Rousse** (✉ Pl. Paoli, ☎ 04–95–60–04–35). **Levie–Alta Rocca** (✉ Rue Sorba, ☎ 04–95–78–41–95). **Parc Naturel Régional de la Corse** (✉ Rue du Général-Fiorella, ☎ 04–95–21–56–54; ✉ Mailing address: B.P. 417, 20100 Ajaccio). **Piana** (✉ Hôtel de Ville, ☎ 04–95–27–84–42). **Piedicroce–Castagniccia** (✉ Piedicroce, ☎ 04–95–35–82–54). **Porticcio** (✉ 428 bd. Rive Sud, ☎ 04–95–25–01–00). **Porto Vecchio** (✉ Rue du Député de Rocca Serra, ☎ 04–95–70–09–58). **Propriano** (✉ Port de Plaisance, ☎ 04–95–76–01–49). **Sartène** (✉ Rue Borgo, ☎ 04–95–77–15–40). **Sollacaro-Filitosa** (✉ Filitosa, ☎ 04–95–74–07–64). **St-Florent** (☎ 04–95–37–06–04).

15 THE MIDI-PYRÉNÉES AND THE LANGUEDOC-ROUSSILLON

The Midi-Pyrénées and the Languedoc-Roussillon form the main body of France's traditional southwestern region. Sports- and nature-lovers flock here to enjoy the natural beauty of the area, of which Toulouse—a university town of rosy pink brick—is the cultural star. Here, too, are Albi and its wonderful Toulouse-Lautrec Museum; Moissac and its famous Romanesque cloister; the once-upon-a-timeliness of Carcassonne; the spa towns that enliven the Pyrénées; and the relatively undiscovered city of Montpellier. And when you see picturesque Collioure's stunning Mediterranean setting, you'll understand why Fauvists Matisse and Derain went color-berserk while there.

Revised and updated by George Semler

Introduction by George Semler

LIKE THE MOST CELEBRATED DISH OF THIS AREA, cassoulet, the southwestern region of France itself is a diverse and multifaceted feast. Just as it would be a gross oversimplification to call cassoulet baked beans, southwestern France is more than just Toulouse, the peaks of the Pyrénées, and the fairy-tale ramparts of Carcassonne. Rolling, sunbaked plains and stone- and shrub-covered hills dotted with ruins of ancient civilizations parallel the burning coastline; the fortifications and cathedrals of once-great cities like Béziers and Narbonne stand miragelike in the Mediterranean haze; and Collioure and the famed Côte Vermeille immortalized by Picasso and Matisse nestle colorfully just north of the border with Spain. Nevertheless, just as cassoulet *toulousain* (made with goose) is the variety you are most apt to find all over France, so the city of Toulouse tops the tourist "bill of fare" here. Serving as gateway to the region, alive with music, sculpture, and architectural gems, and vibrant with students, Toulouse is all that more famous regional capitals would like to have remained, or become. Sinuously spread along the romantic banks of the Garonne as it meanders north and west from the Catalan Pyrénées on its way to the Atlantic, *la ville en rose*—so-called for its redbrick buildings—has a Spanish sensuality unique in all Gaul, a feast for eyes and ears alike. Toulouse was the ancient capital of the province called Languedoc, so christened when it became royal property in 1270, meaning the country where *oc*—instead of the *oil* or *oui* of northeastern France—meant yes.

Outside Toulouse, the countrysides of the Midi-Pyrénées and Languedoc-Roussillon are studded with highlights, like so many raisins sweetening up a spicy stew. Albi, with its Toulouse-Lautrec legacy, is a star attraction, while each outlying town—from Montauban to Moissac to Auch, Mirepoix, or Cordes-sur-Ciel—has artistic and architectural secrets waiting to be uncovered. Besides Albi's Toulouse-Lautrec Museum, other art museums not to miss here are Montauban's Musée Ingres, devoted to France's most accomplished Neoclassical painter, and Ceret's Musée d'Art Moderne, which is packed with Picassos, Braques, and Chagalls.

There is also an "open-air museum" prized by artists and poets: the Côte Vermeille, or Vermilion Coast, centered around the fishing village of Collioure, where Matisse, Derain, and the Fauvists committed chromatic mayhem in the early years of the 20th century. The view of the Côte Vermeille from the Alberes mountain range reveals a bright-yellow strand of beach curving north and east toward the Camargue wetlands. From the vineyards above Banyuls-sur-Mer to the hills Hannibal traversed with his regiment of elephants, this storied coast has been irresistible to everyone from Pompey to Louis XIV. The Mediterranean smooth and opalescent at dawn; villagers dancing sardanas to the music of the raucous and ancient woodwind *flavioles* and *tenores*; the flood of golden light so peculiar to the Mediterranean . . . everything about it seems to be asking to be immortalized in oil paint on canvas. The heart of the region is Collioure, with its narrow, cobbled streets and pink-and-mauve houses. A town of espadrille merchants, anchovy packers, and lateen-rigged fishing boats in the shadow of its 13th-century Château Royal, Collioure, home of the late novelist Patrick O'Brian, is now as much a magnet for tourists as it ever was a lure for artists.

The abundant mountains, lakes, rivers, wide green valleys, and arid limestone plateaus make many of the areas in this chapter ideal for outdoor activities. The Ariège Valley and the Pyrénées Orientales provide a dramatic route through Cathar country and the Cerdagne Valley on the way to the Mediterranean. For the *sportif,* options run from kayaking and windsurfing to climbing up to high Pyrenean lakes and peaks, exploring mountain monasteries such as St-Martin de Canigou, fly-fishing the upper Aude and Ariège rivers, or walking up to the Spanish border at the Gorges de Carança above Thuès-entre-Valls or the Col de Nuria above Eyne. To finish off on a cultural high note, take in the famous Romanesque cloister of St-Guilhem-le-Désert and the nearby student mecca of Montpellier, home to a fine university, museum, and the Ricardo Bofill–designed Quartier Antigone, the old city's nod to the future.

Pleasures and Pastimes

Dining

Languedoc is known for powerful and strongly seasoned cooking. Garlic and goose fat are generously used in traditional recipes, though modern chefs have come skilled at preserving traditional tastes in lighter formats. Be sure to try some of the renowned foie gras (goose liver) and *confit de canard* (preserved duck). The most famous regional dish is cassoulet, a succulent white-bean stew with *confit d'oie* (preserved goose) or *confit de canard,* spicy sausage, pork, and sometimes lamb. Other specialties might include *farci du lauragais,* a kind of pork pancake, or *gigot de sept heures,* a leg of lamb cooked for seven hours. In the Gers *département* (province) finish your meal with a glass of Armagnac, the local brandy distilled throughout the province. In the Pyrénées look for rich, dark *civet d'isard* (stewed mountain goat) or *trinchat,* a Cerdagne Valley specialty of mashed half-frozen cabbage, potato, and bacon. In the Roussillon and along the Mediterranean coast from Collioure up through Perpignan to Narbonne, the prevalent Catalan cuisine features olive oil–based cooking and sauces such as the classic aioli (crushed and emulsified garlic and olive oil).

CATEGORY	COST*
$$$$	over €23
$$$	€15–€23
$$	€8–€14
$	under €8

**per person for a main course only, including tax (19.6%); note that if a restaurant offers only prix-fixe (set-price) meals, it has been given the price category that reflects the full prix-fixe price.*

Lodging

Hotels range from Mediterranean modern to medieval baronial to Pyrenean chalet; most are small and cozy rather than luxurious. Toulouse has the usual range of big-city hotels; make reservations well in advance if you plan to visit in spring or fall. Look for *gîtes d'étape* (hikers' waystations) and table d'hôtes (bed-and-breakfasts), which offer excellent value and a chance to meet local and international travelers and sample life on the farm, as well as the delights of *cuisine du terroir* (country cooking). Assume all hotel rooms have air-conditioning, TV, telephones, and private bath unless otherwise noted. Internet, when listed in facilities, means in-room data-ports and/or public-area computers provide on-line access.

CATEGORY	COST*
$$$$	over €123
$$$	€84–€123
$$	€46–€83
$	under €46

**All prices are for a standard double room, including tax (19.6%) and service charge.*

Outdoor Activities and Sports

The Pyrénées Orientales (Eastern Pyrénées) between Prades and Foix offer great and relatively easy walking, though sturdy legs and sensible shoes come in handy. The rough waters of the Tarn and Aveyron gorges are perfect for canoeing and kayaking; the peaceful Quercy River is better for a gentler trip. Skiing—downhill or cross-country—is excellent in the Pyrénées, with more than two dozen ski resorts along the central and eastern part of the range. There are also equestrian tours, fishing opportunities, and several superb golf courses.

Exploring the Midi-Pyrénées and the Languedoc-Roussillon

France's largest region, Midi-Pyrénées spreads from the Dordogne in the north to the Spanish border along the Pyrénées. Radiating out from Toulouse to the surrounding towns of Albi, Carcassonne, Montauban, and Auch, and up through the Ariège Valley into the Pyrénées Orientales, the central and southern parts of the Midi-Pyrénées are rich in history, natural resources, art, and architecture. Languedoc-Roussillon fits in along the Mediterranean from Collioure north through Perpignan, Narbonne, Beziers, and Montpellier, all once part of Catalonia and the crown of Aragon's medieval Mediterranean empire. Montpellier is at the dead center of the Mediterranean coastline, a five-hour train ride from Paris, Nice, and Barcelona.

This chapter divides the region into three sections. The first covers the lively city of Toulouse. The second encompasses the area to the north and west of Toulouse, including the Gers *département*, Albi, the Lot Valley, Montauban, and verdant Gascony. The third extends southeast into the Languedoc-Roussillon and up the Mediterranean coast to the now-inland crossroads of Narbonne.

Great Itineraries

Getting to know this vast region would take several weeks, or even years. But it is possible to sample its finest offerings in three to seven days, if that's all you have.

Numbers in the text correspond to numbers in the margin and on the Midi-Pyrénées and the Languedoc-Roussillon and Toulouse maps.

IF YOU HAVE 3 DAYS

Bask in the rich rose color of **Toulouse** ①–㉔ for a day and then head to **Cordes** ㉖, a fortified medieval village. Make Toulouse-Lautrec's home town, **Albi** ㉕, your home for the night. On day three explore the medieval citadel at **Carcassonne** ㉜.

IF YOU HAVE 7 TO 10 DAYS

Spend the first day and a half in **Toulouse** ①–㉔; then drive west to **Auch** ㉛, the capital of the Gers département. Next, head north to the old Roman town of **Lectoure** ㉚. Next up is a true high point of the trip: the famous Romanesque sculptures of the abbey church at **Moissac** ㉘. On day three study up on the university town of **Montauban** ㉗ before visiting the medieval age in **Cordes** ㉖. Spend the night in **Albi** ㉕. On the fourth day go south to **Carcassonne** ㉜ for more medieval history, before heading to **Mirepoix** ㉝, near the castle town of **Foix** ㉞ for the night. The next day drive into the Pyrénées, passing through **Tarascon-sur-Ariège** ㉟ to see the Grotte de Niaux, the mountain resorts of **Ax-les-Thermes** ㊱, and **Font-Romeu** ㊲. Spend the night in nearby **Eyne** ㊳ before continuing east out of the Pyrénées toward the Mediterranean. Stop in the fortified town of **Villefranche-de-Conflent** ㊴ and the Abbaye de St-Martin-de-Canigou. Pass through the spa town of **Vernet-les-Bains** ㊵ on your way to **Prades** ㊶ and the

The Midi-Pyrénées and the Languedoc-Roussillon

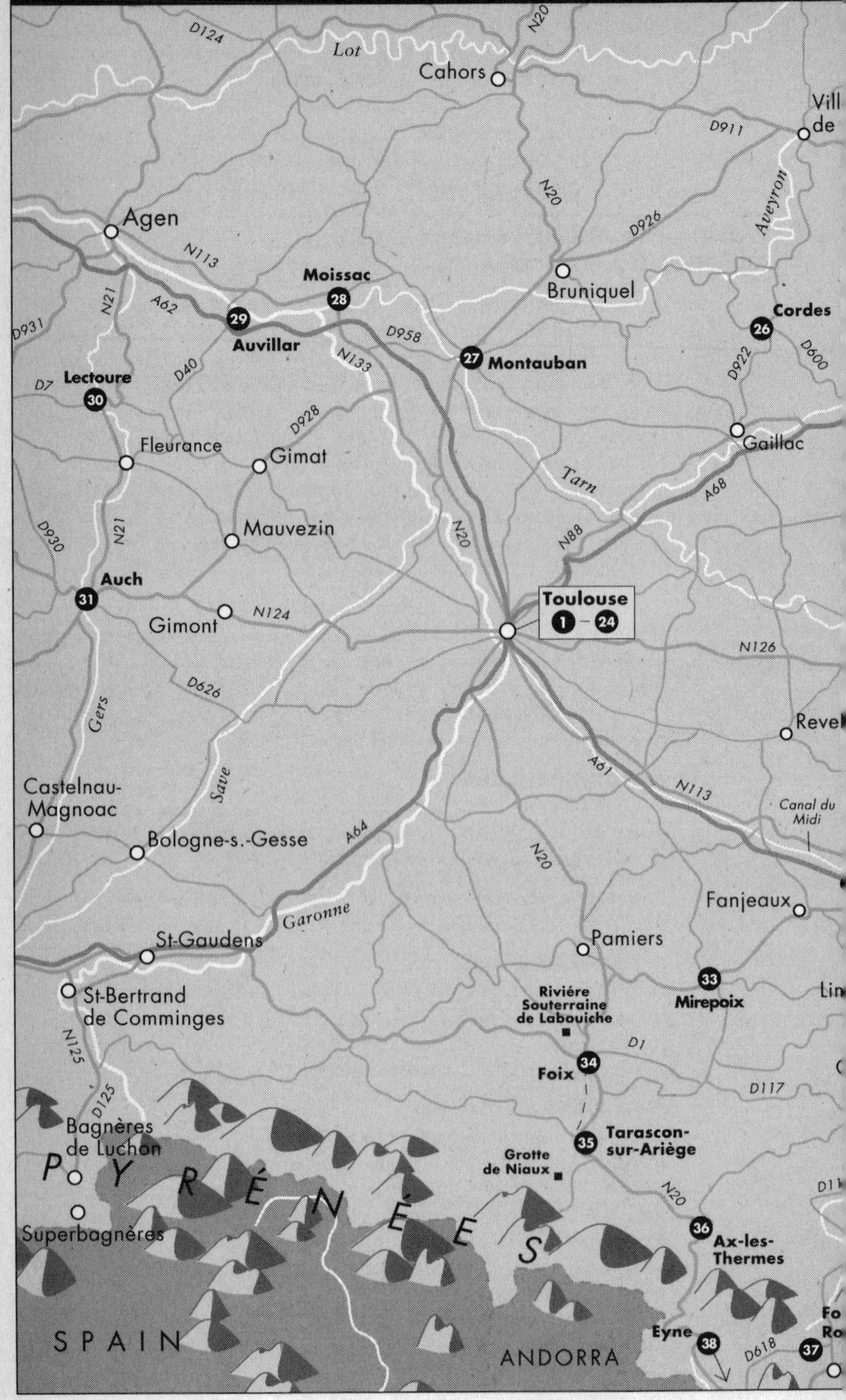

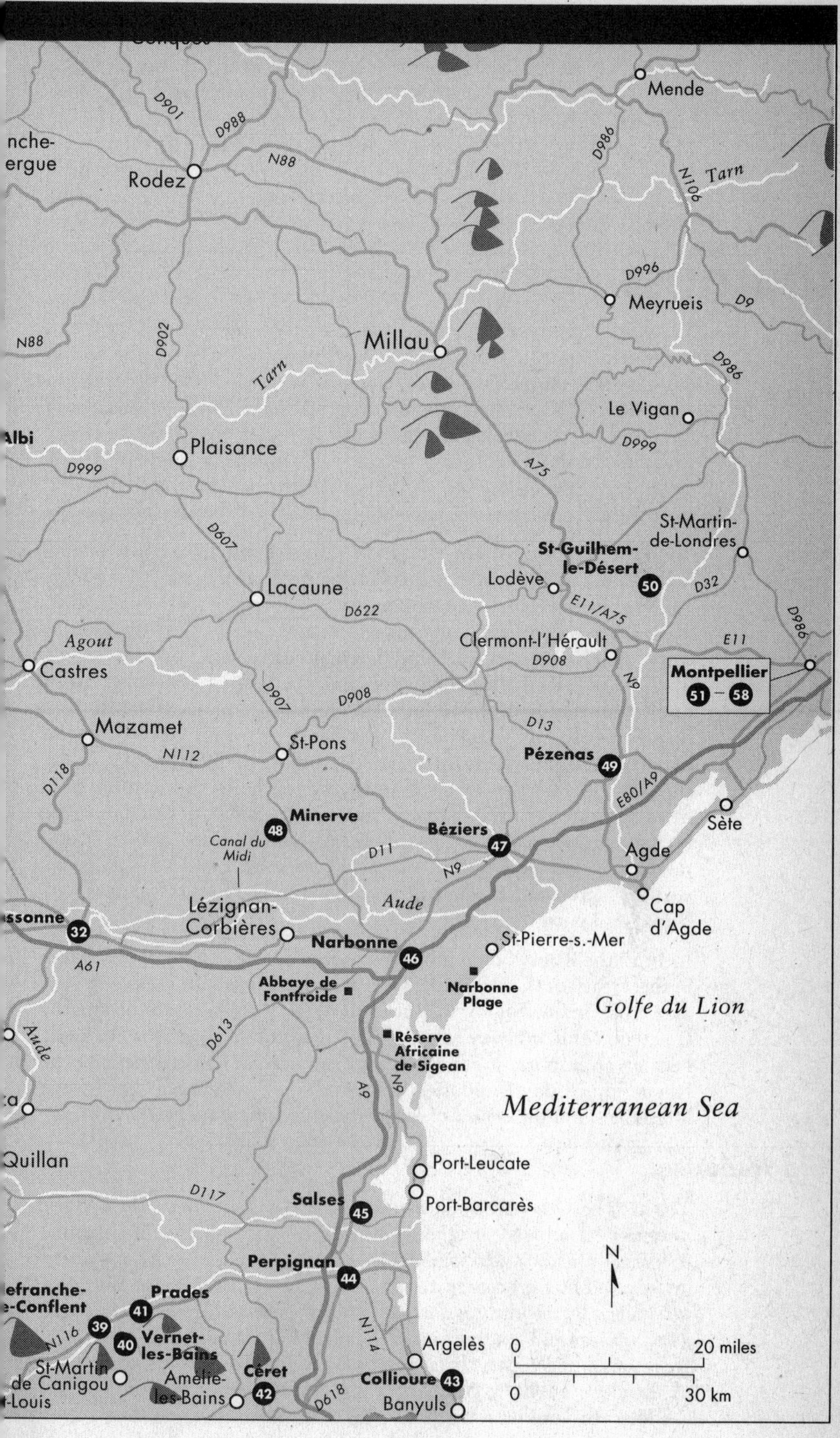

Mende
Rodez
Tarn
Meyrueis
Millau
Le Vigan
Albi
Plaisance
St-Martin-de-Londres
St-Guilhem-le-Désert
50
Lodève
Lacaune
Clermont-l'Hérault
Agout
Castres
Montpellier
51 – 58
Mazamet
St-Pons
Pézenas
49
Sète
Minerve
48
Canal du Midi
Béziers
47
Agde
Cap d'Agde
Aude
Lézignan-Corbières
32
Narbonne
46
St-Pierre-s.-Mer
Abbaye de Fontfroide
Narbonne Plage
Golfe du Lion
Réserve Africaine de Sigean
Mediterranean Sea
Quillan
Port-Leucate
Port-Barcarès
Salses
45
Perpignan
44
Prades
41
39
Vernet-les-Bains
40
St-Martin de Canigou
Amélie-les-Bains
Céret
42
Argelès
Collioure
43
Banyuls
N
0
20 miles
0
30 km
D901
D988
N88
D986
N106
D996
D9
D902
D999
A75
D607
D622
D32
E11/A75
E11
D908
D907
N9
D13
N112
D118
E80/A9
D11
A61
D613
A9
D117
N116
N114
D618

Abbaye de St-Michel-de-Cuxa, and to **Céret** ㊷. Spend the sixth night in Roussillon's historic capital, **Perpignan** ㊹, or in the fishing village of **Collioure** ㊸. On the seventh day drive north to **Salses** ㊺, which Hannibal once passed through, before leaving this region at **Narbonne** ㊻. For your eighth day head north to the Languedoc frontier. Make a detour to the cloisters at **St-Guilhem-le-Désert** ㊿, then spend your last night in **Montpellier** (51)–(58); on your last day tour this city's fascinating *vielle ville* (old town), steeped in culture, history, and young blood (a famous university is based here).

TOULOUSE

The ebullient city of Toulouse is the capital of the Midi-Pyrénées and the fourth-largest city in France. Just 96 km (60 mi) from the border with Spain, Toulouse's flavor is in many ways closer to southern European Spanish than to northern European French. Weathered redbrick buildings line sidewalks, giving the city its nickname, "La Ville Rose" (the Pink City). Downtown, the sidewalks and restaurants pulse late into the night with tourists, workers, college students, and technicians from the giant Airbus aviation complex headquartered outside the city.

Toulouse was founded in the 4th century BC and quickly became an important part of Roman Gaul. In turn, it was made into a Visigothic and Carolingian capital before becoming a separate county in 843. Ruling from this Pyrenean hub that was one of the great artistic and literary capitals of medieval Europe, the counts of Toulouse held sovereignty over nearly all of the Languedoc and maintained a brilliant court known for its fine troubadours and literature. In the early 13th century Toulouse was attacked and plundered by troops representing an alliance between the northern French nobility and the papacy, ostensibly to wipe out the Albigensian heresy (Catharism), but more realistically as an expansionist move against the power of Occitania, the French southwest. The counts toppled, but Toulouse experienced a cultural and economic rebirth thanks to the *woad* (dye) trade; consequently, wealthy merchants' homes constitute a major portion of Toulouse's architectural patrimony.

In 1659 the Roussillon region was officially ceded to France by Spain in the Treaty of the Pyrénées, 17 years after Louis XIII conquered the area from Spain. Toulouse, at the intersection of the Garonne and the Canal du Midi, midway between the Massif Central and the Pyrénées, became an important nexus between Aquitania, Languedoc, and the Roussillon. Today Toulouse is France's second-largest university town after Paris and the center of France's aeronautical industry.

Old Toulouse

The area between the boulevards and the Garonne forms the historic nucleus of Toulouse. Originally part of Roman Gaul and later capital for Visigoths and Carolingians, by AD 1000 Toulouse was one of the artistic and literary centers of medieval Europe. Despite the 13th-century defeat by the lords of northern France, Toulouse quickly reemerged as a cultural and commercial power and has remained so ever since. Religious and civil structures bear witness to this illustrious past, even as the city's booming student life mirrors a dynamic present. This is the heart of Toulouse, with place du Capitole at its center.

The huge garage beneath place du Capitole is a good place to park, and offers easy walking distance to all the major sites. If you leave your car in another garage, you can take the subway that runs east–west to central Toulouse; it costs €1 for one zone, €1.50 for two.

A Good Walk

Start on **place du Capitole** ①, stopping at the donjon (dungeon or tower) next to the **Capitole/Hôtel de Ville** ②, where there is a tourist office with maps. Rue du Taur, off the square, leads to **Notre-Dame du Taur** ③. Continue along rue du Taur to the **Ancien Collège de Périgord** ④ to see the oldest part of the medieval university. Toulouse's most emblematic church, **St-Sernin** ⑤, is at the end of rue du Taur on place St-Sernin. Next door is the **Musée St-Raymond** ⑥, the city's archaeological museum.

Leave place St-Sernin and cut out along rue Bellegarde to the boulevard de Strasbourg, site of the vegetable and produce market. Take the boulevard to rue Victor-Hugo and the **Marché Victor Hugo** ⑦, the large market hall. Find your way back to place du Capitole, cross the square, and take rue Gambetta past the colorfully restored Art Nouveau facade on the left to rue Lakanal. To the right is the **Église des Jacobins** ⑧ with its famous palm vault, one of the city's most important architectural sites.

Back on rue Gambetta is the opulent **Hôtel de Bernuy** ⑨. Cut through rue Jean Suau to **place de la Daurade** ⑩. **Notre-Dame de la Daurade** ⑪ is the nonsteepled and domeless church on your left; the Café des Artistes is to the right. After a pause here, continue up quai de La Daurade past the sculpted goddesses on the facade of the École des Beaux-Arts to the **Pont Neuf** ⑫. Here you can cross the Garonne to the **Château d'Eau** ⑬, the water tower once used to store and pressurize the city's water system, now an excellent photographic gallery-museum. Or you can turn left on rue de Metz to the **Hôtel d'Assézat** ⑭, home of the Fondation Bemberg and its excellent collection of paintings. The nearby **Musée des Augustins** ⑮ has one of the world's best collections of Romanesque sculpture and is a de rigueur visit, especially on a rainy day.

Take a left on rue des Changes, once part of the Roman road that sliced through Toulouse from north to south; now it's a chic pedestrian-only shopping area. Stop to admire the **Hôtel d'Astorg** ⑯, the **Hôtel d'Arnault Brucelles** ⑰, and the **Hôtel Delpech** ⑱. Continue along rue des Changes to the intersection with rue de Temponières. Note the handsome wood-beam and brick building on the far right corner and the faux granite one at the near left, complete with painted lines between the "stones" and trompe-l'oeil windows (one of the clever ways the good citizens struggled to avoid paying the legendary window tax). The next street to the left, rue Tripière, loops through place du May onto rue du May, which leads to the **Musée du Vieux Toulouse** ⑲, housed in the Hôtel Dumay.

TIMING

This walk covers some 3 km (2 mi) and should take 3–4 hours, depending on how long you spend at each site. Most sites close punctually at noon, so it is essential that you get an early start. Or better yet, take a long lunch at some lovely spot and continue on again after 1 or 2, when places reopen.

Sights to See

❹ **Ancien Collège de Périgord** (Old Périgord College). The wooden gallery-like structure on the street side of the courtyard is the oldest remnant of the 14th-century residential college. ✉ *56–58 rue du Taur.*

❷ **Capitole/Hôtel de Ville** (Capitol/Town Hall). The 18th-century Capitole is home to the Hôtel de Ville and the city's highly regarded opera company. The reception rooms are open when not in use for official functions or weddings. Halfway up the **Grand Escalier** (Grand Stair-

Ancien Collège de Périgord 4
Capitole/Hôtel de Ville 2
Cathédrale St-Étienne . . .20
Château d'Eau 13
Église des Jacobins 8
Hôtel d'Arnault Brucelles 17
Hôtel d'Assézat . . .14
Hôtel d'Astorg 16
Hôtel de Bernuy 9
Hôtel de Clary 23
Hôtel Delpech 18
Hôtel du Vieux Raisin 22
Marché Victor Hugo 7
Musée des Augustins . . .15
Musée Paul Dupuy 21
Musée St-Raymond 6
Musée du Vieux Toulouse 19
Notre-Dame de la Dalbade . .24
Notre-Dame de la Daurade 11
Notre-Dame du Taur 3
Place du Capitole 1
Place de la Daurade 10
Pont Neuf . . .12
St-Sernin 5

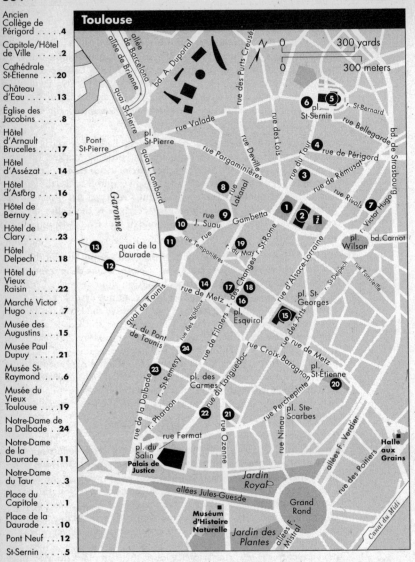

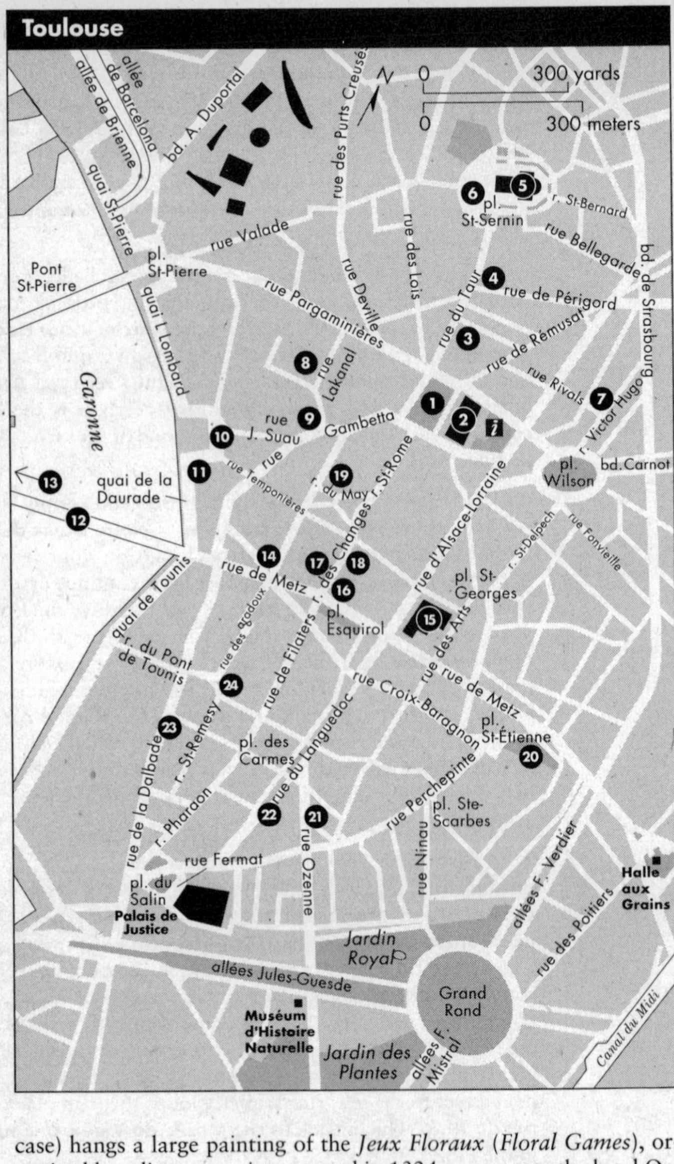

case) hangs a large painting of the *Jeux Floraux* (*Floral Games*), organized by a literary society created in 1324 to promote the local Occitanian language, Langue d'Oc. The festival continues to this day: poets give public readings here each May, and the best are awarded silver- and gold-plated violets, one of the emblems of Toulouse. At the top of the stairs is the **Salle Gervaise,** a hall used for weddings, over which hangs a series of paintings inspired by the themes of love and marriage. The mural at the far end of the room portrays the Isle of Cythères, where Venus received her lovers, alluding to a French euphemism for getting married: *embarquer pour Cythères* (to embark for Cythères). More giant paintings in the **Salle Henri-Martin,** named for the artist (1860–1943), show the passing seasons set against the eternal Garonne. Look for Jean Jaurès (1859–1914), one of France's greatest socialist martyrs, in *Les Rêveurs* (*The Dreamers*); he's wearing a boater and a beige coat. At the far left end of the elegant **Salle des Illustres** (Hall of the Illustrious) is a large painting of a fortress under siege, portraying the women of Toulouse slaying Simon de Montfort, leader of the Albigensian crusade against the Cathars, during the siege of Toulouse in 1218. ✉ *Pl. du Capitole,* ☎ *05–61–11–34–12.* 🎫 *Free.* ⏲ *Weekdays 8:30–5, weekends 10–6.*

⓭ **Château d'Eau.** This 19th-century water tower at the far end of the Pont Neuf, once used to store water and build water pressure, is now used for photography exhibits (it was built in 1823, the same year Nicéphore Nièpce created the first permanent photographic images). ✉ *1 pl. Laganne,* ☎ *05–61–77–09–40.* 🎫 *€3.* ⏲ *Wed.–Mon. 1:30–6.*

❽ **Église des Jacobins.** An extraordinary structure built in the 1230s for the Dominicans (renamed Jacobins in 1217 for their Parisian base in rue St-Jacques), this church has two rows of columns running the length of the nave—a standard feature of Dominican churches. The column on the right farthest from the entrance shoots up to reveal one of the world's two or three finest examples of palm-tree vaulting, the much-celebrated *Palmier des Jacobins,* a major masterpiece of Gothic art. The original refectory is used for temporary art exhibitions. The cloister is one of the city's esthetic and acoustical gems and in summer hosts piano and early music concerts. ✉ *Rue Lakanal s/n,* ☎ *05–61–22–21–92.* 🎫 *€2.20.* ⏲ *Daily 10-7.*

⓱ **Hôtel d'Arnault Brucelles.** One of the tallest and best of Toulouse's 49 towers can be found at this 16th-century mansion. ✉ *19 rue des Changes.*

⓮ **Hôtel d'Assézat.** Built in 1555 by Toulouse's top Renaissance architect, Nicolas Bachelier, this mansion, considered the city's most elegant, has arcades and ornately carved doorways. It is now home to the **Fondation Bemberg,** an exceptional collection of paintings ranging from Tiepolo to Toulouse-Lautrec, Manet, Monet, and Bonnard. Climb to the top of the tower for splendid views over the city's rooftops. ✉ *Rue de Metz.* 🎫 *€4.* ⏲ *Daily 10–noon and 2–6.*

⓰ **Hôtel d'Astorg.** This 16th-century mansion is notable for its lovely wooden stairways and galleries and for its top-floor *mirande,* a wooden balcony. ✉ *16 rue des Changes.*

❾ **Hôtel de Bernuy.** Now part of a school, this mansion, around the corner from the Église des Jacobins, was built for Jean de Bernuy in the 16th century, when Toulouse was at its most prosperous. De Bernuy made his fortune exporting woad, the dark-blue dye that brought unprecedented wealth to 18th-century Toulouse. De Bernuy's success is reflected in the use of stone, a costly material in this region of brick, and by the octagonal stair tower, the highest in the city. You may wander freely around the courtyard. ✉ *Rue Gambetta.*

⓲ **Hôtel Delpech.** Look for the biblical inscriptions carved in Latin in the stone under the windows. ✉ *20 rue des Changes.*

❼ **Marché Victor Hugo** (Victor Hugo Market). This hangarlike indoor market is always a refreshing stop. Consider eating lunch at one of the seven upstairs restaurants. **Chez Attila,** just to the left at the top of the stairs, is the best of them. ✉ *Pl. Victor-Hugo.*

⓯ **Musée des Augustins** (Augustinian Museum). In a former medieval Augustinian convent, the museum uses the sacristy, chapter house, and cloisters for displaying an outstanding array of Romanesque sculpture and religious paintings. ✉ *Rue de Metz,* ☎ *05–61–22–21–82.* 🎫 *Museum €2, exhibit €3, museum and exhibit €4; free Sun.* ⏲ *Wed. 10–9, Thurs.–Mon. 10–6.*

❻ **Musée St-Raymond.** The city's archaeological museum, next to the basilica of St-Sernin, has an extensive collection of imperial Roman busts, as well as ancient coins, vases, and jewelry. ✉ *Pl. St-Sernin,* ☎ *05–61–22–21–85.* 🎟 *€2.* ⏲ *Mon. and Wed.–Sat. 8–noon and 2–6, Sun. noon–6.*

⓳ **Musée du Vieux Toulouse** (Museum of Old Toulouse). This museum is worthwhile for the building itself as much as for its collection of Toulouse memorabilia, paintings, sculptures, and documents. Be sure to note the ground-floor fireplace and wooden ceiling. ✉ *7 rue du May,* ☎ *05–61–13–97–24.* 🎟 *€3.* ⏲ *June–Sept., Mon.–Sat. 3–6.*

⓫ **Notre-Dame de la Daurade.** Overlooking the Garonne is this 18th-century church. The name *Daurade* comes from *doré* (gilt), referring to the golden reflection given off by the mosaics decorating the 5th-century temple to the Virgin Mary that once stood on this site. ✉ *Pl. de la Daurade.*

❸ **Notre-Dame du Taur.** Built on the spot where St. Saturnin (or Sernin), the martyred bishop of Toulouse, was dragged to his death in AD 257 by a rampaging bull, this church is famous for its *cloche-mur,* or wall tower. The wall looks like an extension of the facade and has inspired many similar versions throughout the region. ✉ *Rue du Taur.*

❶ **Place du Capitole.** This vast, open square in the city center, lined with shops and cafés, is a good spot for getting your bearings or for soaking up some spring or winter sun. A very convenient parking lot is underneath.

❿ **Place de la Daurade.** On the Garonne, this is one of Toulouse's nicest squares. A stop at the Café des Artistes is almost obligatory. The corner of the quai offers a romantic view of the Garonne, the Hôtel Dieu across the river, and the Pont Neuf.

⓬ **Pont Neuf** (New Bridge). Despite its name, the graceful span of the Pont Neuf opened to traffic in 1632. The remains of the old bridge—one arch and the lighter-color outline on the brick wall of the **Hôtel-Dieu** (hospital)—are visible across the river. The 16th-century hospital was used for pilgrims on their way to Santiago de Compostela. Just over the bridge, on a clear day in winter, the snowcapped peaks of the Pyrénées are often visible in the distance, said to be a sign of imminent rain.

★ ❺ **St-Sernin.** Toulouse's most famous landmark and the world's largest Romanesque church once belonged to a Benedictine abbey, built in the 11th century to house pilgrims on their way to Santiago de Compostela in Spain. When illuminated at night, St-Sernin's five-tier octagonal tower glows red against the sky. Not all the tiers are the same: The first three, with their rounded windows, are Romanesque; the upper two, with pointed Gothic windows, were added around 1300. ✉ *Rue du Taur,* ☎ *05–61–21–70–18.* 🎟 *Crypt €3.* ⏲ *Daily 10–11:30 and 2:30–5:30.*

South of Rue de Metz

South of rue de Metz you'll discover the cathedral of St-Étienne, the antiques district along rue Perchepinte, and town houses and palaces along the way on rue Ninau, rue Ozenne, and rue de la Dalbade—all among the top sights in Toulouse.

A Good Walk

From the **Cathédrale St-Étienne** ⑳ walk down rue Fermat to place Stes-Scarbes and the 17th-century Hôtel du Bourg, at 6 rue Perchepinte, where you'll find the old antiques district, lined with noble 16th- to 18th-century houses all the way down to place du Salin. Take a left on rue Ninau; at No. 15 is the 16th-century Hôtel d'Ulmo, with its graceful tower, front stairs, courtyard, and interior garden; at No. 19 is the 18th-century Hôtel Castagnier. Place Montoulieu opens into rue Vélane, passing brick and timber-frame houses and the narrow 14th-century rue Neuve. At 16 rue Velane is the 17th-century Hôtel Penautier, with an elegant courtyard, stairway, and garden through the entryway next to the Laure Bandet antiques shop. Rue Vélane emerges back out on rue Perchepinte. Take a left on Perchepinte and a quick right onto rue de la Pléau to get to the **Musée Paul Dupuy** ㉑, a museum of medieval arts. Head right on rue Ozenne to No. 9, the 15th-century Hôtel de Dahus. Go left on rue du Languedoc; at No. 36 is the 15th- and 16th-century mansion **Hôtel du Vieux Raisin** ㉒, crowned by an unusual octagonal tower. Continue back down rue du Languedoc to place du Salin, where farmers sell homemade foie gras on market mornings. Rue de la Dalbade, parallel to the Garonne, leads past one stately facade after another. The finest is No. 25, the **Hôtel de Clary** ㉓, also known as the Hôtel de Pierre (not for Peter but for the stone [*pierre*] used in its construction). Continue up the street to the church of **Notre-Dame de la Dalbade** ㉔. From here cut through rue Pont de Tounis, go past the doorway on the left with the sculpted Gambrinus—legendary Flemish inventor of beer—then over the bridge (which used to span a branch of the Garonne) and out to quai de Tounis. The Pont Neuf is just up to the right.

TIMING

This walk will take you about three hours.

Sights to See

⓴ **Cathédrale St-Étienne.** The cathedral was erected in stages between the 13th and 17th centuries, though the nave and choir languished unfinished because of a lack of funds. A fine collection of 16th- and 17th-century tapestries traces the life of St. Stephen. In front of the cathedral is the city's oldest fountain, dating from the 16th century. ✉ *Pl. St-Étienne.*

㉓ **Hôtel de Clary.** This mansion, known as the Hôtel de Pierre because of its unusually solid *pierre* (stone) construction—at the time considered a sign of great wealth—is one of the finest 17th- and 18th-century mansions on the street. The ornately sculpted stone facade was built in 1608 by parliamentary president François de Clary. ✉ *25 rue de la Daurade.*

㉒ **Hôtel du Vieux Raisin.** Officially the Hôtel Maynier, named for the original owner, the house became the Vieux Raisin (Old Grape) after the early name of the street and even earlier inn. Built in 1550, the mansion has an octagonal tower, male and female figures on the facade, and allegorical sculptures of the three stages of life—infancy, maturity, and old age—over the windows to the left. ✉ *36 rue de Languedoc.*

㉑ **Musée Paul Dupuy.** This museum, dedicated to medieval applied arts, is housed in the Hôtel Pierre Besson, a 16th-century mansion. ✉ *13 rue de la Pleau,* ☎ *05–61–14–65–50.* 🎫 *€2.30.* ⏲ *Wed. 10–9, Thurs.–Mon. 10–5.*

㉔ **Notre-Dame de la Dalbade.** Originally Sancta Maria de Ecclesia Alba, in Langue d'Oc (Ste-Marie de l'Église Blanche, in French, or St. Mary of the White Church—*alba* meaning "white" as in "albino"), the name of the church evolved into "de Albata" and later "Dalbade." Ironically, one of its outstanding features today is the colorful 19th-century ceramic tympanum over the Renaissance door. ✉ *Pl. de la Dalbade.*

Dining and Lodging

$$$–$$$$ ★ ✕ **Michel Sarran.** This clean-lined post-nouvelle haven for what is arguably Toulouse's finest dining departs radically from traditional stick-to-your-ribs southwest France cuisine in favor of Mediterranean formulas suited to the rhythms and reasons of modern living. Foie gras soup with belon oysters, and *loup cuit et cru au chorizo* (sea-bass, cooked and raw, with chorizo sausage) are two examples of Michel Sarran's light but flavorful cuisine. ✉ *21 bd. A. Duportal,* ☎ *05–61–12–32–32. AE, DC, MC, V. Closed weekends; also July 27–Aug. 28 and Jan. 22–30.*

$$$–$$$$ ✕ **Toulousy–Jardins de l'Opéra.** Dominique Toulousy's elegant restaurant in the Grand Hôtel de l'Opéra is a perennial favorite. Intimate rooms and a covered terrace around a little pond make for undeniable charm, though some will find the grand flourishes—glass ceilings, *echt* statuary, and mammoth chandeliers—a little too, well, operatic, and might prefer the adjacent brasserie, Grand Café de l'Opéra. The food is an innovative departure from local fare, with Gascon and seductive nouvelle touches such as the ravioli stuffed with foie gras and truffle sauce. ✉ *1 pl. du Capitole,* ☎ *05–61–23–07–76. Reservations essential. AE, DC, MC, V.*

$$$ ✕ **Au Pois Gourmand.** A 40-minute walk (down the right bank of the river to the Pont des Catalanes, cross to the left bank, and continue along the gravel walkway to the fourth bridge downstream), or a 15-minute cab ride from the Pont Neuf, brings you to a lovely wooden house overlooking the Garonne and one of the best restaurants in Toulouse. Good-natured chef Jean-Claude Plazzotta, a specialist in wild mushrooms, herbs, and spices, takes you on a gastronomical tour of foie gras, lamb, *magret de canard* (duck breast), and squab. In summer dine in the garden or on the balcony with views over the river. ✉ *3 rue Heybrard,* ☎ *05–61–31–95–95. AE, DC, MC, V. Closed Sun. No lunch Sat. and Mon.*

$$$ ✕ **Brasserie des Beaux-Arts.** Overlooking the Pont Neuf, this elegant brasserie is the place to be at sunset. Watch the colors change over the Garonne from a quayside window or a sidewalk table while enjoying delicious seafood, including a dozen varieties of oysters. The house white wine, a local St-Lannes from the nearby Gers region, is fresh and fruity yet dry, and the service is impeccable. ✉ *1 quai de la Daurade,* ☎ *05–61–21–12–12. AE, DC, MC, V.*

$$–$$$ ★ ✕ **La Corde.** This little hideaway is worth taking the time to find. Built into a lovely 15th-century corner tower hidden in the courtyard of the 16th-century Hôtel Bolé, La Corde claims the distinction of being the oldest restaurant in Toulouse. Try the *effiloché de canard aux pêches* (shredded duck with caramelized peach). ✉ *4 rue Jules-Chalande,* ☎ *05–61–29–09–43. AE, DC, MC, V. Closed Sun. No lunch Mon.*

$$ ✕ **Au Bon Vivre.** This intimate bistro lined with tables with red-check tablecloths fills up at lunch and dinner every day. Quick, unpretentious, and always good, the house specialties include such dishes as roast monkfish in garlic, venison, and cassoulet. ✉ *15 pl. Wilson,* ☎ *05–61–23–07–17. AE, DC, MC, V.*

$$ ✕ **Chez Emile.** Downstairs you'll find a seafood menu that changes daily; if it's available, have the turbot in ginger. Upstairs is a cozy hideaway for a more traditional taste of Toulouse with classic specialties such as cassoulet and magret de canard. ✉ *13 pl. St-Georges,* ☎ *05–61–21–05–56. Reservations essential. AE, DC, MC, V. Closed last wk in Aug. and Sun.–Mon.*

$$$$ ★ 🏨 **Grand Hôtel de l'Opéra.** In a former 17th-century convent, this downtown doyen has an Old World feel with 21st-century amenities. Grandeur is the keynote in the lobby, complete with marble columns and Second Empire bergeres and sofas of tasseled velvet. Guest rooms are plush, with

rich fabrics and painted headboards in many, while three restaurants range from provincial bistro to international gourmet (☞ Jardins de l'Opera, *above*). Even though you are on busy place du Capitole, this hotel is a tranquil oasis of luxury. ✉ *1 pl. du Capitole, 31000,* ☎ *05–61–21–82–66,* FAX *05–61–23–41–04,* WEB *www.grand-hotel-opera.com. 49 rooms. 2 restaurants, café, cable TV, minibars, pool, health club, meeting rooms, parking (fee). AE, DC, MC, V.*

$$$ ★ **Hôtel des Beaux-Arts.** In the thick of the most Toulousain part of town, over the Pont Neuf and next to the Hôtel d'Assézat, this cozy place has small but tasteful rooms; the best have tiny terraces overlooking the Garonne. The staff is cheery and helpful. ✉ *1 pl. du Pont-Neuf, 31000,* ☎ *05–34–45–42–42,* FAX *05–34–45–42–43,* WEB *www.hotelsdecharmetoulouse.com. 19 rooms. Cable TV, minibars, parking (fee). AE, DC, MC, V.*

$$ **Grand Hôtel d'Orléans.** This picturesque former stagecoach relay station was built in 1867 and still retains a certain 19th-century charm. Four floors of wooden balustrades overhung with plants look down over a central patio. Guest rooms are small but cozy. ✉ *72 rue Bayard, 31000 (near Matabiau railroad station),* ☎ *05–61–62–98–47,* FAX *05–61–62–78–24. 56 rooms. Restaurant, cable TV, parking (fee). AE, DC, MC, V.*

$–$$ **Hôtel Albert I.** The building may seem undistinguished and the reception hall is no Versailles, but the rooms are cheerful and spacious (especially the older ones with giant fireplaces and mirrors). The extremely warm and personable owner, Madame Hilaire, is on hand to give suggestions of all kinds. A Continental breakfast is served, and nearby parking can be arranged by the hotel. ✉ *8 rue Rivals, 31000,* ☎ *05–61–21–17–91,* FAX *05–61–21–09–64. 50 rooms. Cable TV, parking (fee). AE, DC, MC, V.*

Nightlife and the Arts

For a schedule of events, contact the city tourist office. If you want to stay up late—and they do in Toulouse—a complete list of clubs and discos can be found in the weekly *Toulouse Pratique,* available at any newsstand. As for cultural highlights, so many opera singers perform at the **Théâtre du Capitole** and the **Halle aux Grains** that the city is known as the *capitale du bel canto*. The opera season lasts from October until late May, with occasional summer presentations as well. A wide variety of dance companies perform in Toulouse: the **Ballet du Capitole** stages classical ballets; **Ballet-Théâtre Joseph Russilo** and **Compagnie Jean-Marc Matos** put on modern-dance concerts. The **Centre National Chorégraphique de Toulouse** welcomes international companies each year in the St-Cyprien quarter.

The most exciting music venue in Toulouse is the auditorium-in-the-round **Halle Aux Grains** (✉ Pl. Dupuy, ☎ 05–61–63–18–65). **Théâtre du Capitole** (✉ Pl. du Capitole, ☎ 05–61–23–21–35) is the orchestra, opera, and ballet specialist. **Théâtre Daniel Sorano** (✉ 35 allée Jules-Guesde, ☎ 05–61–25–66–87) stages dramatic productions and concerts. **Théâtre de la Digue** (✉ 3 rue de la Digue, ☎ 05–61–42–97–79) is a theater and dance venue. **Théâtre du Taur** (✉ 69 rue du Taur, ☎ 05–61–21–77–13) puts on theatrical productions of every stripe and spot.

For general carousing and carrying on, the **Bagamoyo** (✉ 27 rue des Couteliers, ☎ 05–62–26–11–36) is a lively spot for nocturnal snacks of simple but delicious African fare. **Bar Basque** (✉ 7 pl. St-Pierre, ☎ 05–61–21–55–64) is one of the many good watering holes around place St-Pierre. **Le Bistro à Vins** (✉ 5 rue Riguepels, ☎ 05–61–25–20–41), near the Cathedral of St-Étienne, is a hot spot for the third-Thursday-in-November Beaujolais Nouveau blowout. Brazilian guitarists perform at **La Bonita** (✉ 112 Grand-Rue St-Michel, ☎ 05–62–26–36–45). For jazz, try **Le Café des Allées** (✉ 64 allée Charles-de-Fitte, ☎ 05–62–27–14–46), a hothouse for local musicians. **Café Le Griot** (✉ 34 rue des Blanchers, ☎ 05–62–36–41–56) features a number of American duos and trios.

At **El Mexicano** (✉ 37 rue de l'Industrie, ☎ 05–61–63–17–36) a crush of people inhales tequila and 3-inch-thick steaks. **La Péniche** (✉ Canal de Brienne, 90 allée de Barcelone, ☎ 05–61–21–13–40) is a local gay bar. Begin your night on the town at **Père Louis** (✉ 45 rue des Tourneurs, ☎ 05–61–21–33–45), an old-fashioned winery (and restaurant), with barrels used as tables plus vintage photographs. **Puerto Habana** (✉ 12 port St-Étienne, ☎ 05–61–54–45–61) is the place for salsa music. If you're looking for onion soup and other treats in the wee hours, head for **St-André** (✉ 39 rue St-Rome, ☎ 05–61–22–56–37), open from 7 PM to dawn (closed Sunday). Local glitterati and theater stars go to **L'Ubu** (✉ 16 rue St-Rome, ☎ 05–61–23–97–80), the city's top nightspot for 20 years.

Outdoor Activities and Sports

Toulouse is just 100 km (60 mi) from the nearest peaks. For information about hiking, skiing, mountain refuges, and just about anything having to do with the Pyrénées, check with the **Pyrénées Club** (✉ 29 rue du Taur, ☎ 05–61–21–11–44). A top-ranked 18-hole golf course near Toulouse is the **Golf Club de Toulouse** (✉ Vieille Toulouse, ☎ 05–61–73–45–48). On the outskirts of Toulouse is the popular 18-hole **Golf Club de Toulouse Palmola** (✉ Rte. d'Albi, ☎ 05–61–84–20–50). If you want to go horseback riding, try **Pony City** (✉ St-Paul, 40 km/25 mi east of Toulouse, ☎ 05–63–42–06–45).

Shopping

Toulouse is a chic design outlet for clothing and artifacts of all kinds. **Rue St-Rome, rue Croix Baragnon, rue des Changes,** and **rue d'Alsace-Lorraine** are all good shopping streets.

ALBI AND THE GERS

Along the banks of the Tarn to the northeast of Toulouse is Albi, Toulouse's rival in rose colors. West from Albi, along the river, the land opens up to the rural Gers *département,* home of the heady brandy Armagnac and heart of the former dukedom of Gascony. Studded with châteaux—from simple medieval fortresses to ambitious classical residences—and with tiny, isolated villages, the Gers is an easy place to fall in love with, or in.

Albi

★ ㉕ *75 km (47 mi) northeast of Toulouse.*

Toulouse-Lautrec's native Albi is a well preserved and busy provincial market town. In its heyday, Albi was a major center for the Cathars, members of a dualistic and ascetic religious movement critical of the hierarchical and worldly ways of the Catholic Church. Pick up a copy of the excellent visitor booklet (in English) from the **tourist office** (✉ Pl. Ste-Cécile, ☎ 05–63–49–48–80), and follow the walking tours—of the Old City, the old ramparts, and the banks of the River Tarn.

The huge **Cathédrale Ste-Cécile,** with its intimidating clifflike walls, resembles a cross between a castle and an ocean liner. It was constructed as a symbol of the Church's return to power after the 13th-century crusade that wiped out the Cathars. The interior is an astonishingly ornate contrast to the massive austerity of the outer walls. Maestro Donnelli and a team of 16th-century Italian artists covered every possible surface with religious scenes and brightly colored patterns. The most striking fresco is a 15th-century depiction of the Last Judgment, on the west wall. ✉ *Pl. Ste-Cécile.*

★ The **Musée Toulouse-Lautrec** occupies the **Palais de la Berbie** (Berbie Palace), set between the cathedral and the Pont Vieux (Old Bridge) in a garden designed by the famed André Le Nôtre (creator of the famous "green geometries" at Versailles). Built in 1265, the fortress was transformed in 1905 into a museum to honor Albi's most famous son, Belle Epoque painter Henri de Toulouse-Lautrec (1864–1901). Toulouse-Lautrec left Albi for Paris in 1882, and soon became famous for his colorful and tumultuous evocations of the lifestyle of bohemian glamour found in and around Montmartre. Son of a wealthy and aristocratic family (Lautrec is a town not far from Toulouse), the young Henri suffered from a genetic bone deficiency and broke both legs as a child, which stunted his growth. The artist's fascination with the decadent side of life led to an early grave at the age of 37 and Hollywood immortalization in the 1954 John Huston film *Moulin Rouge.* With more than 1,000 of the artist's works, the Albi exhibit is the country's largest Toulouse-Lautrec collection. ✉ *Just off pl. Ste-Cécile,* ☎ *05–63–49–48–70.* 🎫 *€4, gardens free.* ⏲ *May–Sept., daily 10–noon and 2–6; Oct.–Apr., Wed.–Mon. 10–noon and 2–5.*

From the central square and parking area in front of the Palais de la Berbie, walk to the 11th- to 15th-century college and **Cloître de St-Salvy** (cloister; ✉ Rue Ste-Cécile). Next, visit Albi's finest restored traditional house, the **Maison du Vieil Albi** (Old Albi House; ✉ Corner of rue de la Croix-Blanche and Puech-Bérenguer). If you're a real fan of Toulouse-Lautrec, you might view his birthplace, the **Maison Natale de Toulouse-Lautrec** (✉ 14 rue Henri de Toulouse-Lautrec), although there are no visits as the house, the Hôtel Bosc, remains a private residence. Rue de l'Hôtel de Ville, two streets west of the Maison Natale, leads past the Mairie (City Hall), with its hanging globes of flowers, to Albi's main square, **place du Vigan.** Take a break in one of the two main cafés, Le Pontie or Le Vigan.

Dining and Lodging

$$$ ✕ **Le Moulin de la Mothe.** Set at the foot of Albi Cathedral, this onetime mill on the bank of the Tarn is neatly tucked into the river, surrounded by lush vegetation. Chef-owner Michel Pellaprat specializes in inventive cooking *à l'albeigeoise*—his hare sausage in beetroot vinaigrette is sublime—based on high-quality products of the Tarn region. ✉ *Rue de la Mothe,* ☎ *05–63–60–38–15. AE, MC, V. Closed at All Saints (Nov. 1), Feb.; Sun. dinner except July–Aug.; Tues. dinner Sept. 15–Apr. 30.*

$$ ✕ **Le Jardin des Quatre Saisons.** A good-value menu and superb fish dishes are the reasons for this restaurant's excellent reputation. Chef-owner Georges Bermond's house specialties include mussels baked with leeks and *suprême de sandre* (a freshwater fish cooked in wine), and change with *les saisons.* ✉ *19 bd. de Strasbourg,* ☎ *05–63–60–77–76. AE, MC, V. Closed Mon. No dinner Sun.*

$$$–$$$$ ✕🏨 **Hostellerie St-Antoine.** Founded in 1734, this hotel in the center of town is one of the oldest in France. Run by the same family for five generations, this lineage is attested to by the presence of some Toulouse-

Lautrec sketches given to the owner's great-grandfather, a friend of the painter. Modern renovations have made it eminently comfortable. Room 30 has a pleasing view of the garden; pristine white furnishings give it a spacious feel. The superb restaurant serves classic Gallic cuisine, such as *foie gras de canard* (duck liver) and saddle of hare with a foie gras–based sauce. ✉ *15 rue St-Antoine, 81000,* ☎ *05–63–54–04–04,* FAX *05–63–47–10–47,* WEB *www.saint-antoine-albi.com. 43 rooms. Restaurant, cable TV, minibars, meeting rooms, parking (fee). AE, DC, MC, V.*

$$ ✕🏨 **Hôtel Chiffre.** In a centrally located town house, this hotel has impeccable rooms overlooking a cozy garden. The restaurant, the Bateau Ivre, is one of Albi's finest. ✉ *50 rue Séré-de-Rivières, 81000,* ☎ *05–63–48–58–48,* FAX *05–63–47–20–61,* WEB *www.hotelchiffre.com. 36 rooms. Restaurant, cable TV, minibars, meeting rooms, parking (fee). AE, DC, MC, V.*

$$ ✕🏨 **Mercure Albi Bastides.** This converted 18th-century *vermicellerie* (noodle mill), across the river from the old center of Albi, has rooms that are functional and modern, if somewhat cramped. The views of the Tarn and the Pont Vieux are spectacular, however. In the stylish restaurant (which does not serve lunch weekends), try chef Gérard Belbèze's regional specialties or his "Toulouse-Lautrec menu." ✉ *41 rue Porta, 81000,* ☎ *05–63–47–66–66; 800/637–2873 U.S. reservations; 0181/741–3100 U.K. reservations,* FAX *05–63–46–18–40,* WEB *www.accor-hotels.com. 56 rooms. Restaurant, minibars, parking (fee). AE, DC, MC, V.*

$$ 🏨 **La Pérouse.** This intimate and tasteful enclave is centrally located and supremely quiet. Rooms are comfortable, and the garden is a lush and shady spot to rest between sorties in and around Albi. There's also a secluded swimming pool. ✉ *21 pl. Lapérouse, 81000,* ☎ *05–63–54–69–22,* FAX *05–63–38–03–69. 26 rooms. Pool, parking (fee). AE, DC, MC, V.*

$ 🏨 **Le George V.** This little in-town B&B is near the cathedral and the train station. Each room is unique, and the garden makes for a pleasant retreat in summer. ✉ *29 av. Maréchal-Joffre, 81000,* ☎ *05–63–54–24–16,* FAX *05–63–49–90–78. 9 rooms. No air-conditioning, terrace café, garden, parking (fee). AE, DC, MC, V.*

Outdoor Activities and Sports

A leading 18-hole golf course facility is **Golf d'Albi** (✉ Château de Lasbordes, ☎ 05–63–54–98–07). **Golf de Florentin-Gaillac** (✉ Le Bosc, Florentin, 29 km/17 mi from Albi, ☎ 05–63–55–20–50) attracts serious golfers.

Shopping

Around **place Ste-Cécile** are numerous clothing, book, music, and antiques shops. The finest foie gras in town is found at **Albi Foie Gras** (✉ 29 rue Mariès, ☎ 05–63–38–21–23). **L'Artisan Chocolatier** (✉ 4 rue Dr-Camboulives, on pl. du Vigan, ☎ 05–63–38–95–33) is famous for its chocolate.

Albi has many **produce markets**: one takes place Tuesday through Sunday in the market halls near the cathedral; another is held on Sunday morning on place Ste-Cécile. A Saturday-morning **flea and antiques market** is held in the Halle du Castelviel (✉ Pl. du Castelviel).

Cordes

★ 26 *25 km (15 mi) northwest of Albi, 80 km (50 mi) northeast of Toulouse.*

The picture-book hilltop village of Cordes, built in 1222 by Count Raymond VII of Toulouse, is one of the most impressively preserved *bastides* (fortified medieval towns built along a strict grid plan) in France. When mists steal up from the Cérou Valley and enshroud the hillside, Cordes appears to hover in midair, hence its nickname, Cordes-sur-Ciel (Cordes-on-Sky/Heaven). Many of the restored medieval houses are occupied by artisans and craftspeople; the best crafts shops are found along the main street, Grande-Rue. The village's venerable covered market, supported by 24 octagonal stone pillars, is also noteworthy, as is the nearby well, which is more than 300 ft deep.

Dining and Lodging

$$$–$$$$ ★ ✕🏨 **Le Grand Écuyer.** The dramatic hilltop setting of this hotel suits it well—it's a perfectly preserved Gothic mansion. Rooms have period furnishings; the best, Planol, Horizon, and Ciel, have grand views of the rolling countryside. Yves Thuriès is one of the region's best chefs and chocolatiers; sample his salmon and sole twist in vanilla or the guinea fowl supreme in pastry. Menus begin around €30 and culminate in a seven-course gourmet extravaganza that costs more than €77. ✉ *Rue Voltaire, 81170,* ☎ *05–63–53–79–50,* FAX *05–63–53–79–51,* WEB *www.thuries.fr. 13 rooms. Restaurant, bar, cable TV, minibars, parking (fee). AE, DC, MC, V. Closed mid-Oct.–early Apr.*

$$ ✕🏨 **L'Hostellerie du Vieux Cordes.** This magnificent 13th-century house is built around a lovely courtyard dotted with tiny white tables and shaded by a 200-year-old wisteria. Guest rooms are richly decorated but not nearly as opulent as the vast crimson dining rooms (the restaurant is closed Monday from November to Easter and also the month of January). ✉ *Rue St-Michel, 81170,* ☎ *05–63–53–79–20,* FAX *05–63–56–02–47,* WEB *www.thuries.fr. 21 rooms. Restaurant, no air-conditioning, cable TV, minibars. AE, DC, MC, V. Closed Jan. 1–mid-Feb.*

Montauban

27 *59 km (37 mi) west of Cordes, 55 km (33 mi) north of Toulouse.*

Montauban, built in 1144, was one of the first bastides in France. The town is best known as the birthplace of the great painter Jean-Auguste-Dominique Ingres (1780–1867), and is home to a superb collection of ★ his works. The **Musée Ingres,** overlooking the Tarn River, is housed in what was originally the château of Edward the Black Prince (1330–76), who was briefly ruler of the English principality of Aquitaine. The château was later converted into a bishop's palace in the 17th century. Ingres has the second floor to himself; note the contrast between his love of myth (*Ossian's Dream*) and his deadpan, uncompromising portraiture (*Madame Gonse*). Ingres was the last of the great French Classicists, who favored line over color and used classical antiquity as a source for subject matter. However, Ingres fell out of favor with the strict Neoclassicists of his day as a result of his unusual combination of superb draftsmanship and sensuality. Later, artists such as Degas, Renoir, and Picasso acknowledged their debt to Ingres. Most paintings here are from Ingres's excellent private collection, ranging from his followers (Théodore Chassériau) and precursors (Jacques-Louis David) to Old Masters. Across from the museum adorning place Bourdelle is *The Death of the Last Centaur,* an allegorical bronze by sculptor Antoine Émile Bourdelle (1861–1929), which symbolically depicts the struggles of the man/artist, lyre in hand, overcome by the obstacles of life but still triumphant. ✉ *19 rue de l'Hôtel de Ville,* ☎ *05–63–22–12–92.* 🎫 *€3.* ⏲ *July–Aug., Mon.–Sat. 9:30–noon and 1:30–6, Sun. 1:30–6; Sept.–June, Tues.–Sat. 10–noon and 2–6.*

Beyond the Musé Ingres, there are several other notable sights in town. The 14th-century **Pont Vieux** (Old Bridge), with its seven pointed arches, is another of Montauban's attractions. A chapel dedicated to St. Catherine, protector of mariners (Montauban had some 3,000 river men during the 18th century), used to stand on the fourth piling until it was washed away by a flood in the 18th century. In the 12th-century arcaded and brick-vaulted **place National,** in the center of Montauban, look for the simple wooden cross marking the medieval execution and pillory site (it's in front of the Brasserie des Arts, a good spot for lunch or coffee). Note the sundial on the north side of the square with its carpe diem inscription UNA TIBI ("one for you"—meaning, your hour will come). Markets are held on the square almost every day; Wednesday markets are held across the river on place Lalaque. The **Hôtel Lefranc-de-Pompignon** is a classic 17th- to 18th-century *portail monumentale* (monumental entryway) just north of the Église St-Jacques. One of Montauban's architectural gems, this redbrick portico with its wrought-iron grill announced the residence of M. Lefranc-de-Pompignon (whose unsuccessful tenure at Paris's Royal Academy was once mocked by Voltaire). ✉ *Rue Armand Cambon s/n.*

The mid-13th-century **Église St-Jacques** (✉ Pl. Victor Hugo), with its Toulouse-style steeple, is a dark, single-nave church of austere dignity. The 17th- to 18th-century **Notre-Dame Cathedral** (✉ Pl. Franklin Roosevelt) was built of white stone to contrast with the city's predominant redbrick architecture and to proclaim Catholicism's triumph over Protestantism. On display here is a poorly illuminated Ingres masterpiece, *The Vow of Louis XIII.*

Dining and Lodging

$$$–$$$$ ✕ **Les Saveurs d'Ingres.** Cyril Paysserand's *cuisine d'auteur* is some of the best experimental fare in the area, served in a graceful vaulted dining room in midtown Montauban, just a few doors up from the Ingres Museum. Not unlike Ingres himself, Paysserand sticks with the classical canons prepared in sensual yet always novel ways. If you've maxed out on cassoulet and web-footed fare in general, try the frogs' legs here or the *bécasse* (woodcock) in season for a welcome change of pace. ✉ *13 rue de l'Hôtel de Ville,* ☎ *05–63–91–26–42. AE, DC, MC, V. Closed Sun.–Mon.*

$$ 🏨 **Hôtel du Midi–Mercure.** Refurbished in 1999 by the Mercure chain, the Hôtel du Midi combines Old World elegance with modern comforts. A plaque on the hotel's facade attests that Manuel Azaña, last president of the Spanish Republic, died here in exile in 1940. ✉ *12 rue Notre-Dame, 82000,* ☎ *05–63–63–17–23,* FAX *05–63–66–43–66,* WEB *www.accor.hotel.fr. 40 rooms. Restaurant, bar, cable TV, minibars, parking (fee). AE, DC, MC, V.*

Moissac

★ 28 *29 km (18 mi) west of Montauban, 72 km (45 mi) northwest of Toulouse.*

Moissac has both the region's largest (and most beautiful) Romanesque cloisters and one of its most remarkable abbey churches. The port—at the confluence of the Tarn, Aveyron, and Garonne rivers, and the lateral canal—is a surprising sight so far from the sea. For a spectacular view over this Mississippi-like riverine expanse, France's widest, head to the lookout point at Boudou, 2 km (1 mi) west of Moissac off route N113.

★ Little is left of the original 7th-century **Abbaye St-Pierre,** and subsequent religious wars laid waste to its 11th-century replacement. Today's abbey, dating mostly from the 15th century, narrowly escaped demolition early in the 20th century when the Bordeaux-Sète railroad was rerouted within feet of the cloisters. Each of the 76 capitals has a unique pattern of animals, geometric motifs, and religious or historical scenes. Look for the Cain and Abel story on the 19th column to the right of the entry point. The 63rd column (fourth back from the northeast corner) shows St-Sernin being dragged to his death by a bull. The highlight of the abbey church is the 12th-century south portal, topped with carvings illustrating the Apocalypse. Especially noteworthy is the representation of a sweetly mournful Jeremiah, author of the Old Testament Book of Lamentations, on the lower part of the door. The **Musée des Arts et Traditions Populaires** (Folk Art Museum), in the abbey, contains regional treasures and a room of local costumes. ✉ *6 bis rue de l'Abbaye,* ☎ *05–63–04–05–73.* 🎫 *Cloisters and museum €3.84.* ⏲ *Oct.–Mar., Tues.–Sun. 9–noon and 2–5; Apr.–June and Sept., Tues.–Sun 9–noon and 2–6; July–Aug., Tues.–Sun. 9–noon and 2–7.*

Dining and Lodging

$$$–$$$$ ★ ✕🏨 **Le Pont Napoléon.** One of France's rising culinary stars, Michel Dussau, who trained with Alain Ducasse (and others), is a master of refined simplicity and innovative combinations of regional products. Try such dishes as scallops with chestnut-flour pasta or foie gras *pôelé* (sautéed goose liver), and anything made with Moissac's *chasselas* grape (the restaurant is closed Wednesday). Guest rooms are furnished with elegant, authentic antiques; some have lovely views of the Tarn and the bridge. ✉ *2 allée Montbello, 82200,* ☎ *05–63–04–01–55,* FAX *05–63–04–34–44,* WEB *www.canalalaune.fr. 12 rooms. Restaurant, bar, cable TV. AE, DC, MC, V. Closed Wed. and Jan. 5–20.*

$$ 🏨 **Chapon Fin.** For a more protected, in-town hotel just a minute from Moissac's cloister and St-Pierre church, this sturdily traditional 150-year-old French town house offers economy, comfort, and intimacy in Moissac's quiet (yet, at times, bustling) central square. The hotel's gourmet restaurant serves typical southwestern French specialties. Just outside the door, the Saturday and Sunday morning markets are a potpourri of *produits du terroir* (farm produce) featuring, of course, duck-related items. ✉ *82200, Place des Récollets,* ☎ *05–63–04–04–22,* FAX *05–63–04–58–44. 27 rooms. Restaurant, bar. AE, DC, MC, V.*

Auvillar

29 *23 km (14 mi) west of Moissac.*

Officially classified as one of France's most beautiful villages, Auvillar is centered on its gorgeous, covered **Halle aux Grains** (Grain Market), a circular structure built in 1825. Most other buildings in the town are equally lovely, including the stone-and-brick **Tour de l'Horloge** (Clock Tower), now connected to the town's only hotel, the 18th-century brick-and-beam **Maison des Consuls** (Consuls' House), once the local magistrate's home.

Dining and Lodging

$–$$ ✕🏨 **L'Horloge.** This cozy spot next to (and named for) Auvillar's trademark clock tower is the town's de facto hub and nerve center. The restaurant is a combination brasserie, *bouchon,* and full-scale dining establishment all in one, with menus and *formules* for all tastes and tendencies. The rooms are modest and intimate, and Madame Martigue and her staff are warm and welcoming. ✉ *Place de l'Horloge, 82340,* ☎ *05–63–39–89–82,* FAX *05–63–39–75–20. 10 rooms. Restaurant, café, bar, no air-conditioning, garden. Closed Dec. 16–Jan. 19. Restaurant closed Fri. and Sat. lunch mid-Oct.–mid-Apr. AE, DC, MC, V.*

Lectoure

30 *57 km (35 mi) southwest of Moissac, 94 km (58 mi) northwest of Toulouse.*

Once a Roman city and a fortified Gallic town, Lectoure stands on a promontory above the Gers Valley in the heart of the former dukedom of Gascony. Lectoure was ravaged in 1473 when Louis XI attacked its fortress and established direct royal rule by killing the last count of Armagnac, but there's still plenty to see in its old arched streets. The 13th-century **Fontaine Diane** (Diana Fountain; ✉ Rue Fontélie) is the town's most interesting monument, as well as a visual feast. The 15th- to 16th-century **Cathédrale St-Gervais et St-Protais** (✉ Pl. de la Cathédrale) is an enormous structure for a town of this size and is an immense trove of art and architectural treats.

The **Musée Municipal** (Town Museum), near the cathedral, is in the vaulted cellars of the former **Palais Épiscopal** (Bishop's Palace), now the Town Hall. It contains an array of 2,000-year-old Gallo-Roman artifacts ranging from tweezers and hairbrushes to Latin-engraved pre-Christian altars and heads of sacrificial bulls. Ask about the sculpture of Priapus, god of fertility, and what happened to his allegedly heroic virility. ✉ *Pl. de la Cathédrale, in the Hôtel de Ville,* ☎ *05–62–68–70–22.* 🎫 *€4.* ⏲ *Daily 9–noon and 2–6.*

Dining and Lodging

$$–$$$ ★ ✕🏨 **Hôtel de Bastard.** This elegant hotel and restaurant on an 18th-century estate is the creation of chef Jean-Luc Arnaud and his wife, Anne (who speaks excellent English). The rooms, while not spacious, are modern and comfortable and have fine views over the fields. The innovative cuisine is prepared with fresh local produce; try the *il était trois foies,* foie gras prepared three ways—raw, steamed, and grilled—all with herbs and vegetables. ✉ *Rue Lagrange, 32700,* ☎ *05–62–68–82–44,* FAX *05–62–68–76–81,* WEB *www.hotel-de-bastard.com. 29 rooms. Restaurant, bar, no air-conditioning, cable TV, garden, pool. AE, DC, MC, V. Closed Dec. 18–Feb. 1.*

Auch

31 *24 km (14 mi) south of Fleurance, 77 km (46 mi) west of Toulouse, 73 km (44 mi) northeast of Tarbes.*

Auch, the capital of the Gers département, is best known for its stunning Gothic **Cathédrale de Ste-Marie.** Most of the stained-glass windows in the choir were done by Arnaud de Moles; vividly colorful, they portray biblical figures and handsome pre-Christian sibyls, or prophetesses. The oak choir stalls are intricately carved with more than 1,500 biblical and mythological figures that took 50 years and three generations of artisans to complete. In June, classical music concerts are held here. ✉ *Pl. Salinis.* 🎫 *€2.50.* ⏲ *Daily 8–noon and 2–6.*

On the first floor of the 15th-century brick and wood-beam Maison Fedel, on the other side of the cathedral, is the **tourist office** (✉ 1 rue Dessoles), where you can obtain maps and information.

Across place Salinis is a terrace overlooking the Gers River. A monumental flight of 370 steps leads down to the riverbank. Halfway down is the **Statue of D'Artagnan,** the musketeer immortalized by Alexandre Dumas. Although Dumas set the action of his historical novel *The Three Musketeers* in the 1620s, the true D'Artagnan—Charles de Batz—was born in 1620, probably in Castlemore, near Lupiac, and did not become a musketeer until 1645.

Off place Salinis, in a wood-beam and brick house known as the **Maison d'Henri IV** (✉ 32 rue d'Espagne), the French and Navarran monarch is said to have cavorted with several of his 57 mistresses. A left at the end of rue d'Espagne will take you through one of the *pousterles,* steep and narrow alleys leading up from the river.

The **Musée des Jacobins,** behind the former Archbishop's Palace (now the Préfecture), has a fine collection of Latin-American art, pre-Columbian pottery, and Gallo-Roman relics. Look for the white-marble epitaph dedicated by a grief-stricken Roman mistress to her dog Myia, for whose "*douces morcures*" ("sweet love bites") she mourned. ✉ *Rue Daumesnil,* ☎ *05–62–05–74–79.* *€4.* *May–Oct., Tues.–Sun. 10–noon and 2–6; Nov.–Apr., Tues.–Sat. 10–noon and 2–5.*

Dining and Lodging

$$ ★ ✕ **Café Gascon.** This ramshackle and romantic little spot is right over the Halles aux Herbes. The fare is typical country Gascon with innovative personal touches such as the *salade folle* (duck prepared three different ways) with apples, tomatoes, and raspberries on lettuce). Chef, poet, and painter Georges Nosella is likely to come out to your table and serve your *café gascon* (coffee, whipped cream, and flaming Armagnac) with grace and humor. ✉ *5 rue Lamartine,* ☎ *05–62–61–88–08. AE, DC, MC, V. Closed Sun. Sept.–June and Mon.*

$$$–$$$$ ★ ✕ **Hôtel de France.** Roland Garreau's gourmet restaurant, Le Jardin des Saveurs, is an institution at this classic central Auch hotel; his specialty is the reduction or lighter interpretation of traditional country cooking. The duplex suite behind the circular dormer window on the facade facing the square is worth a look, if not occupied, even if you resist the temptation to spend the $350 it costs to sleep there. Other rooms are cozy, if a little small and overly fabric-filled. ✉ *Pl. de la Libération, 32000,* ☎ *05–62–61–71–71,* FAX *05–62–61–71–81,* WEB *www.auchgarreau.com. 29 rooms. Restaurant, bar, cable TV, shop, parking (fee). AE, DC, MC, V. Closed Jan. 2–14*

Shopping

Caves de l'Hôtel de France (✉ Rue d'Étigny) sells a wide selection of Armagnac.

LANGUEDOC-ROUSSILLON

Draw a line between Toulouse and Narbonne, on the Mediterranean: the area to the south down to the Pyrénées, long dominated by the House of Aragón, the ruling family of adjacent Catalonia, is known as the Roussillon. Rolling plains sweep along its northern border; the Pyrénées line the southern end; and craggy hills, divided by gorges, lie in between. On the eastern side are the Mediterranean and the Côte Vermeille (Vermilion Coast)—home to the villages once so beloved by Matisse, Picasso, and other great artists of the early 20th century; on the western side is the Ariège Valley. The Languedoc begins south of Narbonne at Salses and extends to the region's hub, the elegant city of Montpellier.

Carcassonne

★ 32 *88 km (55 mi) southeast of Toulouse, 105 km (65 mi) south of Albi.*

Set atop a hill overlooking lush green countryside and the Aude River, Carcassonne is a medieval town that looks lifted from the pages of a storybook—literally, perhaps, as its circle of towers and battlements (comprising the longest city walls in Europe) is said to be the setting for Charles Perrault's classic tale *Puss in Boots*. The oldest sections of the walls, built by the Romans in the 1st century AD, were later enlarged, in the 5th century, by the Visigoths. Charlemagne once set siege to the settlement in the 9th century, only to be outdone by one Dame Carcas, a clever woman who boldly fed the last of the city's wheat to a pig in full view of the conqueror; Charlemagne, thinking this indicated endless food supplies, promptly decamped, and the exuberant townsfolk named their city after her. During the 13th century, Louis IX (St. Louis) and his son Philip the Bold strengthened Carcassonne's fortifications—so much so that the town became considered inviolable by marauding armies and was duly nicknamed "the virgin of Languedoc." A town that can never be taken in battle is often abandoned, however, and for centuries thereafter Carcassonne remained under a Sleeping Beauty spell. It was only awakened during the mid-19th-century craze for chivalry and the Gothic style, when, in 1835, the historic-monument inspector (and poet) Prosper Mérimée arrived. He was so appalled by the dilapidated state of the walls he commissioned the painter and historian Viollet-le-Duc (who found his greatest fame restoring Paris's Notre-Dame) to restore the town. Today the 1844 renovation is considered almost as much a work of art as the medieval town itself. No matter if the town is more Viollet than authentic medieval, it still remains one of the most romantic sights in France.

The town is divided by the river into two parts—La Cité, the fortified upper town, and the lower, newer city (the *ville basse*), known simply as Carcassonne. Unless you are staying at a hotel in the upper town, you are not allowed to enter it with your car; you must park in the lot (€2) across the road from the drawbridge. Be aware that the train station is in the lower town, which means either a cab ride, a 45-minute walk up to La Cité, or a ride on the *navette* shuttle bus. Plan on spending at least a couple of hours exploring the walls and peering over the battlements across sun-drenched plains toward the distant Pyrénées. Once inside the walls of the upper town, a florid carousel announces that 21st-century tourism is about to take over. The streets are lined with souvenir shops, crafts boutiques, restaurants, and tiny "museums" (i.e., a Cathars Museum, a Hat Museum), all out to make a buck and rarely worth that. Staying overnight within the ancient walls lets you savor the timeless atmosphere after the daytime hordes are gone.

The 12th-century **Château Comtal** is the last inner bastion of Carcassonne. It has a drawbridge and a museum, the **Musée Lapidaire,** where stone sculptures found in the area are on display. ☏ *04–68–11–70–77.* ✉ €*5.* ⏲ *June–Sept., daily 9–6; Oct.–May, daily 9–noon and 2–5.*

The best part about the the ville basse, built between the Aude and the Canal du Midi, is the **Musée des Beaux-Arts** (Fine Arts Museum). It houses a nice collection of porcelain, 17th- and 18th-century Flemish paintings, and works by local artists—including some stirring battle scenes by Jacques Gamelin (1738–1803). ✉ *Rue Verdun,* ☏ *04–68–77–73–70.* ✉ *Free.* ⏲ *Mon.–Sat. 10–noon and 2–5.*

Dining and Lodging

$$$ ✕ **Le Languedoc.** This restaurant in the ville basse serves up light versions of the region's specialties, from confit to game. In summer the flowery patio is a perfect spot for a long evening dinner. Be sure to try the quail with foie gras, if available. ✉ *32 allée d'Iéna,* ☏ *04–68–25–22–17. MC, V. Closed mid-Dec.–mid-Jan. and Mon. No dinner Sun. July–Oct.*

$$$$ ✕🏨 **La Cité.** Set within the walled upper town, this is *the* spot for celebrities in Carcassonne. This ivy-covered former episcopal palace offers creature comforts the ascetic Cathars would have hated. Afternoon tea is in the library or rotunda lounge with its antique-tile floors, detailed woodwork, and leaded windows (with storybook views). Dining in the sumptuous La Barbacane restaurant—all double-vaulted ceiling, ogival windows, and agate-green walls—is an event. For more casual fare, try the brasserie Chez Saskia or, in summer, the bistro outside on a charmingly cobbled square. A pool, set like a sapphire in the garden, beckons on hot days. ✉ *Pl. de l'Église, 11000 La Cité de Carcassonne,* ☎ *04–68–71–98–71,* FAX *04–68–71–50–15.* WEB *www.hoteldelacite.orient-express.com. 66 rooms. 2 restaurants, pool, cable TV, minibars, garden, meeting rooms, parking (fee). AE, DC, MC, V. Closed early Jan.–mid-Feb.*

$$$–$$$$ ★ ✕🏨 **Domaine d'Auriac.** Former rugby star and present star-chef Bernard Rigaudis and his family maintain a countrified atmosphere in this elegant 19th-century manor house southwest of Carcassonne. Room prices vary according to size and view; the largest look out onto a magnificent park and vineyards. Next to a terrace planted with mulberry trees, the restaurant, famed as one of the best in the area, offers superlative Languedoc cuisine; enjoy the Provençal-style salon festooned with copper pots while savoring truffled pigeon, John Dory in blueberry wine, and game dishes, in season, accompanied by rare regional vintages. ✉ *Rte. de St-Hilaire, 11330 Auriac (4 km/2½ mi southwest of Carcassonne),* ☎ *04–68–25–72–22,* FAX *04–68–47–35–54.* WEB *www.relaischateaux.fr. 26 rooms. Restaurant, bar, golf course, tennis court, pool. AE, MC, V. Closed last 2 wks Feb., last 2 wks Nov., 1st wk Dec.*

$$$ 🏨 **Château de Garrevaques.** Equidistant (50 km/31 mi) from Toulouse, Carcassonne, and Albi, this château on 8 acres of parkland makes a convenient base camp for all three. Built in 1470 and restored in the early 19th century, it is owned by Madame Combes, who will happily show you the family heirlooms. Rooms are spacious, baronial, and furnished with antiques. Continental breakfast is included in room rates. The table d'hôte dinner is a good chance to sample the local country cooking (advance reservations are required). ✉ *81700 Garrevaques (5 km/3 mi northwest of Revel),* ☎ *05–63–75–04–54,* FAX *05–63–70–26–44.* WEB *www.garrevaques.com. 8 rooms, 1 suite. Restaurant, tennis court, pool, billiards. AE, DC, MC, V.*

$$ 🏨 **Hôtel Montségur.** With its ville basse location, this hotel is especially convenient. Rooms on the first two floors have Louis XV and Louis XVI furniture, some of it genuine; those above are more romantic, with gilt-iron bedsteads under sloping oak beams. ✉ *27 allée d'Iéna, 11000,* ☎ *04–68–25–31–41,* FAX *04–68–47–13–22. 21 rooms. Restaurant, bar, no air-conditioning, cable TV, parking (fee). AE, DC, MC, V. Closed mid-Dec.–mid-Jan.*

The Arts

Carcassonne hosts a major arts festival in July, with dance, theater, classical music, and jazz; for details, contact the **Théâtre Municipal** (✉ B.P. 236, rue Courtejaire, 11005, ☎ 04–68–25–33–13; 04–68–77–71–26 for reservations). The city usually goes medieval in mid-August with **Les Médiévales,** a festival of troubadour song, rich costumes, and jousting performances (some years the event isn't held; check with tourist office). The Bastille Day fireworks over La Cité are spectacular.

Mirepoix

33 *48 km (29 mi) southwest of Carcassonne, 88 km (53 mi) southeast of Toulouse, 35 km (22 mi) northeast of Foix.*

The 13th-century walled town of Mirepoix is in the heart of Cathar country. A good time to come here is during Mirepoix's Medieval Festival, always in July, when a historical procession is held on the third Sunday of the month. The town is built around the lovely, medieval main square, **place Général-Leclerc,** surrounded by 13th- to 15th-century houses with intricately carved timbers forming arcades or porticoes called *couverts*.

Dining and Lodging

$$–$$$ ✕ **La Porte d'Aval.** Next to one of Mirepoix's key monuments, a fortified entryway, this elegant spot serves quail, wild pigeon, fresh fish, and a sampling of *cuisine du terroir* (local country cooking). The terrace is the place to be in summer. ✉ *Cours Maréchal de Mirepoix,* ☎ *05–61–68–19–19. AE, DC, MC, V. Closed Mon. and Nov.*

$$ ✕ **La Brasserie Llobet.** Tucked under the wooden arches Mirepoix is known for, this simple *cuisine du terroir* (country cooking) specialist does cassoulets, confits, or fish with equal aplomb and with minimal wear and tear on the wallet. ✉ *3 pl. Philippe de Levis,* ☎ *05–61–69–44–34. AE, DC, MC, V. Closed Tues. dinner, Wed.*

$$$ ★ **La Maison des Consuls.** This extraordinary 14th-century townhouse hotel on the central square is a classified historic site. The 500-year-old carved timber gargoyles concentrated around the hotel facade make the exquisitely restored interior even more surprising. Each room is decorated in a different color, most with exposed beams. The Chambre de Dame Louise and the Chambre du Maréchal, both overlooking the square, are the best. ✉ *Pl. des Couverts, 09500 Mirepoix,* ☎ *05–61–68–81–81,* FAX *05–61–68–81–15,* WEB *www.pyrenevoyages.com. 7 rooms, 1 suite. No air-conditioning, parking (fee). AE, DC, MC, V.*

Foix

34 *16 km (10 mi) north of Tarascon-sur-Ariège, 84 km (52 mi) south of Toulouse, 35 km (22 mi) southwest of Mirepoix, 138 km (86 mi) west of Perpignan.*

Nestled in the Ariège Valley, Foix is the capital of the Ariège département. Notice the fancy 19th-century administrative buildings south of avenue Fauré, the town's major thoroughfare. Now that you're in the thick of the Midi-Pyrénées, try to do some hiking. East of Foix is one of the best routes, the **Sentier Cathare** (Path of the Cathars)—a tough, hundred-mile trail that takes you through a chain of cliff-side châteaux all the way to the Mediterranean. Pick up maps in Toulouse.

The **Château de Foix,** sitting impregnably on a promontory above the town and river, has three enormous towers reaching skyward like sentinels. The castle **museum** features regional history and archaeological finds. ✉ *Rue Mercadal,* ☎ *05–61–65–56–05.* €3.84. *Daily 10–noon and 2–5:30.*

A 5-km (3-mi) drive northwest from Foix along D1 leads to the **Rivière Souterraine de Labouiche** (Labouiche Subterranean River), a mysterious underground stream whose waters have tunneled a 5-km (3-mi) gallery through the limestone. The 75-minute boat trip covers a 1½-km (1-mi) stretch, past weirdly shaped, subtly lighted stalactites and stalagmites, ending at a subterranean waterfall. Dry land is 230 ft overhead. ☎ *05–61–65–04–11.* €7. *Apr.–mid-June and mid-Sept.–mid-Nov., daily 2–5; mid-June–mid-Sept., daily 10–noon and 2–5.*

Dining and Lodging

$$–$$$ ✕ **Le Phoebus.** The views across the Ariège and over the Château de Foix, which once belonged to the illustrious Gaston Phoebus himself, the most famous of the counts of Foix, are superb. The Phoebus is known for game specialties in season and cuisine du terroir, such as *foie de canard mi-cuit* (half-cooked duck liver) and *rable de lièvre au poivrade* (hare in pepper sauce). ✉ *3 cours Irénée Cros,* ☎ *05–61–65–10–42. AE, DC, MC, V. Closed Mon. and mid-July–mid-Aug. No lunch Sat.*

$$ ✕🅃 **Audoye-Lons.** This former post house in the town center has comfortable, modernized rooms that vary in size. The restaurant is reasonably priced and overlooks the Ariège; it is closed Saturday in winter. ✉ *4 pl. Georges-Duthil, 09000,* ☎ *05–61–65–52–44,* FAX *05–61–02–68–18. 39 rooms, 24 with bath or shower. Restaurant, parking (fee). AE, DC, MC, V. Closed Dec. 20–Jan. 20.*

Outdoor Activities and Sports

The rivers and mountain lakes here are excellent trout habitat. Beginner and advanced fishing courses are run by **Loisirs Accueil** (✉ Service Pêche, 14 rue Lazéma, 09000, ☎ 05–61–65–01–15).

Tarascon-sur-Ariège

35 *16 km (10 mi) south of Foix.*

Tarascon is best known for its superb, extensive grotto, whose collection of prehistoric art is second only to that of the Lascaux. As you enter Tarascon, veer left along D8 to the **Grotte de Niaux,** which contains scores of red-and-black Magdalenian rock paintings done in charcoal and iron oxide. Stylized horses, goats, deer, and bison, dating from about 20,000 BC, gallop around a naturally circular underground gallery (known as the Salon Noir, or Black Room) 1 km (½ mi) inside the entrance. Now that the famous caves at Lascaux in the Dordogne can be seen only in reproduction, this is the finest assembly of prehistoric art open to the public anywhere in France. ☎ *05–61–05–88–37 (guided tours only; call ahead for reservations and to check schedule).* €6.92. ⏲ *July–Sept., tours daily every 45 mins 8:30–11:30 and 1:30–5:15; Oct.–June, tours daily at 11, 3, and 4:30.*

Ax-les-Thermes

36 *26 km (15 mi) southeast of Tarascon-sur-Ariège, 104 km (64 mi) southwest of Carcassonne.*

A summer and winter resort town, Ax-les-Thermes has more than 80 mineral springs—at one, in the middle of town, you can often see local merchants on a coffee break or lunch hour reading the newspaper with trousers rolled to the knees and legs immersed. There are ski stations in Ax-Bonascre and Ascou-Pailhères, 5 km (3 mi) from town, and cross-country skiing is available at the Plateau de Beille and Domaine de Chioula, 10 km (6 mi) from town; For complete information, contact the **tourist office** (☎ 05–61–64–60–60). After a day of skiing, come back to Ax for a thermal hot bath—an unbeatable winter combination. Crisscrossing the surrounding heights are 400 km (248 mi) of hiking trails.

Font-Romeu

37 *75 km (45 mi) southeast of Ax-les-Thermes, 87 km (54 mi) southeast of Tarascon-sur-Ariège, 88 km (55 mi) southwest of Perpignan.*

In this high-altitude vacation spot, French Olympians trained for the Mexico City games of 1968. The views over the Cerdagne Valley from the balcony across from the tourist office should not be missed. Sports facilities include various ski lifts (one operates from the center of town), an ice rink, a riding school, a swimming pool, tennis courts, and a nine-hole golf course. Known for the sunniest slopes and best snow-making machines in the area, the skiing can get very crowded during peak Christmas and Easter vacation weekends. The **École de Ski Français** (☎ 04–68–30–03–74) is a local resource for sport fans.

Dining and Lodging

$$ ✕🏨 **Pyrénées.** This modern hotel perched above the Cerdagne Valley offers stunning views over the sunniest and widest highland space in the Pyrénées. A five-minute walk from the gondola ski lift up to the snow (or to hiking trails in summer), this handy spot is also next to Font Romeu's best restaurant, Le Chalet à Fondue. The rooms are small but command unforgettable panoramas, while the hotel pool seems all but suspended over the valley. ✉ *Pl. des Pyrénées, 66120,* ☎ *04–68–30–01–49,* FAX *04–68–30–35–98. 37 rooms. Restaurant, bar, no air-conditioning, no room TVs, pool, sauna. AE, DC, MC, V.*

Outdoor Activities and Sports

For general advice and ski equipment in Font-Romeu, look for the knowledgeable and English-speaking Roy van der Groen at **Sport 2000** (✉ 102 av. Emmanuel Brousse, ☎ 04–68–30–15–99, FAX 04–68–30–09–34).

Font-Romeu's 9-hole golf course, at **Golf de Font-Romeu** (✉ Espace Sportif Colette Besson, ☎ 04–68–30–38–09), is a rare high-altitude course offering excellent views and some challenging mountaineering as well. For fly-fishing, contact **Marc Ribot** (✉ 6 impasse des Lutins, ☎ 04–68–30–30–93, FAX 04–68–30–06–75), who can arrange for guides, equipment, and fly-fishing courses.

Eyne

38 *12 km (7 mi) southeast of Font-Romeu, 5 km (3 mi) southwest of Mont-Louis.*

Eyne Village, with a grand total of zero in-town commercial establishments—not even a café or a bakery—is one of the purest and best-preserved villages remaining in the broad Pyrenean valley of the Cerdagne. There are archaeological walks to megalithic menhirs and dolmens, a ski station uphill (2 km/1 mi away), and hiking trails to neighboring villages and thermal springs. Nestled below a nationally classified botanical park, the **Réserve Naturelle d'Eyne,** the town has been famous since the 17th century as the point where Atlantic and Mediterranean weather systems and vegetation converge. Information about the park can be obtained at the park headquarters and museum (☎ 04–68–04–08–05), in Eyne Village.

Dining and Lodging

$$–$$$ ★ ✕🏨 **Cal Pai.** In a lovely old farmhouse filled with heavy wooden beams and massive granite pillars, this *gîte d'étape* (way station for hikers and skiers) has a variety of accommodations (doubles, dormitory-style beds, with bathrooms and without) and table d'hôte (communal prix-fixe dinners) of uncommon quality—note that the room rate includes breakfast and dinner (confirm when booking, as rate schedule may change). Manager and chef Françoise Massot knows every wild mushroom and raspberry in the valley and puts them to delicious use in memorable breakfasts and dinners. ✉ *Eyne Village,* ☎ *04–68–04–06–96. 15 rooms without bath. Dining room, no air-conditioning. No credit cards.*

Villefranche-de-Conflent

39 *6 km (4 mi) west of Prades, 30 km (18 mi) east of Mont-Louis, 49 km (30 mi) southwest of Perpignan.*

Named for its location at the confluence of the Têt and Cady rivers, this village has remnants of an 11th-century fortress, with Vauban improvements from the 17th century. Cross the tiny St-Pierre Bridge over the Têt and use the pink-marble "stairway of a thousand steps" to climb up to Fort Liberia for views of the village, the Canigou, and the valleys east to Prades. A guided tour of the ramparts and the town can be arranged in advance by calling the **Villefranche tourist office** (☎ 04–68–96–22–96).

Le petit train jaune ("Little Yellow Train") is a fun way to see some of the most spectacular countryside in the Pyrénées. This life-size toy train makes the 63-km (40-mi) 3-hour trip from Villefranche to La Tour de Carol about five times a day. When the weather is nice, ride in one of the open-air cars. For information about hours and prices, contact the Villefranche tourist office.

Dining and Lodging

$$$ ✕ **Auberge Saint-Paul.** One of the best-known tables in the area, this warm stone-surrounded refuge is known for its fine Catalan and Roussillon cuisine, such as *truite à la llosa* (trout on slate slabs) and *civet d'isard* (stewed mountain goat). ✉ *7 pl. de l'Église,* ☎ *04–68–96–30–95. Reservations essential. MC, V. Closed Mon.*

$$ ✕🏨 **Auberge du Cèdre.** This comfortable little inn over the river commands fine views of the fortress. Rooms are small but cozy. Pyrenean and Catalan specialties are served on a little glassed-in porch suspended over the Têt. Reservations are essential at the restaurant; call before you go to make sure it's open. For guests at the inn, the room rate includes breakfast and dinner. ✉ *Domaine Ste-Eulalie, 66500,* ☎ *04–68–96–05–05,* FAX *04–68–96–09–50. 6 rooms. Restaurant, bar, no air-conditioning, no room TVs. AE, DC, MC, V.*

Vernet-les-Bains

40 *12 km (7 mi) southwest of Prades, 55 km (34 mi) west of Perpignan.*

English writer Rudyard Kipling came to take the waters in Vernet-les-Bains, a long-established spa town. The hilltop village church is dwarfed by imposing Mont Canigou; even higher up is the medieval abbey, which you can trek to by leaving your car first in Casteil, 2 km (1 mi) ★ farther on, and completing the journey to the **Abbaye St-Martin du Canigou** on foot. Brace yourself for the steep half-hour climb but the blisters will be worth it—this is one of the most photographed abbeys in Europe, thanks to its sky-kissing perch atop a triangular promontory at an altitude of nearly 3,600 ft. It was constructed in 1007 by Count Guifred of Cerdagne in expiation for murdering his son. Although the abbey was perhaps too diligently restored by the bishop of Perpignan early in the 20th century, part of the cloisters, along with the higher (and larger) of the two churches, dates from the 11th century. The lower church, dedicated to Notre-Dame-sous-Terre, is even older. Rising above is a stocky, fortified bell tower. Although the hours vary, masses are sung daily; call ahead to confirm. ☎ *04–68–05–50–03.* 🎫 *€3.* ⏲ *Mid-June–mid-Sept., visits daily at 10, noon, 2, 3, 4, and 5; mid-Sept.–mid-June, Mon.–Sat. at 10, 12:30, 2:30, 3:30, and 4:30, Sun. 11 and 12:30.*

Prades

41 *6 km (4 mi) east of Villefranche-de-Conflent, 43 km (27 mi) west of Perpignan.*

Once home to Catalan cellist Pablo Casals, the market town of Prades is famous for its annual summer music festival (from late July to mid-August), the **Festival Pablo Casals.** Founded by Casals in 1950, the music ★ festival is primarily held at the medieval **Abbaye de St-Michel de Cuxa,** (✉ Km 3/2 mi on D7 south of Prades and Codalet, ☎ 04–68–96–15–35, 🎫 €3; ⏲ Daily 9:30–11:30 and 2–5). One of the gems of the Pyrénées, the abbey's sturdy, crenellated four-story bell tower is visible from afar. If the remains of the cloisters here seem familiar, it may be because you have seen the missing pieces at New York City's Cloisters Museum. The 10th-century pre-Romanesque church is a superb aesthetic and acoustical venue for the summer cello concerts. The six-voice Gregorian vespers service held (somewhat sporadically—call to confirm) at 7 PM in the monastery next door is hauntingly simple, and medieval in tone and texture.

Céret

42 *68 km (41 mi) southeast of Prades, 35 km (21 mi) west of Collioure, 31 km (19 mi) southwest of Perpignan.*

The "Barbizon of Cubism," Céret achieved immortality when leading 20th-century artists found this small Pyrenean town irresistible at the beginning of this century. Here in this medieval enclave set on the banks of the Tech River, Picasso and Gris developed a vigorous new way of seeing that would result in the fragmented forms of Cubism, a thousand years removed from the Romanesque sculptures of the Roussillon chapels and cloisters. Adorned by cherry orchards, the town landscapes have been captured in paintings by Picasso, Gris, Dufy, Braque, Chagall, Kisling, and others. Some of these are on view in the ★ fine collection of the **Musée d'Art Moderne** (Modern Art Museum). ✉ *8 bis Maréchal-Joffre,* ☎ *04–68–87–27–76.* 💶 *€6 (free to age 16).* ⏲ *May–Sept., Wed.–Mon. 10–6.*

After visiting the Modern Art Museum, stroll through pretty **Vieux Céret** (Old Céret): find your way through **place des Neufs Jets** (Nine Fountains Square), around the church, and out to the lovely fortified **Porte de France** gateway. Then walk over the single-arched **Vieux Pont** (Old Bridge).

Dining and Lodging

$$$ ★ ✕🏨 **Les Feuillants.** One of the top restaurants in the area, this elegant place offers cuisine, wine, and traditional design, adding another element to Céret's surprising artistic heritage. The "Atlantique en Mediterranée" theme embraced by chef Robert Abraham, formerly of the Brittany coast's St-Malo, produces an original fusion of recipes from all over France, with a hint of Catalonian *cuisine d'auteur* thrown in. Flowers and herbs adorn the dishes of the *menu découverte* (discovery menu), a very personal version of a taster's menu. Guest rooms, though few, are gems (rates include breakfast and dinner). ✉ *1 bd. La Fayette,* ☎ *04–68–87–37–88,* FAX *04–68–87–49–44,* WEB *www.contactles-feuillants.com. 3 rooms, 3 apartments. Restaurant, cable TV, parking. AE, DC, MC, V. Closed Mon., 2 wks in Feb., and 2 wks in Nov. No dinner Sun.*

$$ 🏨 **Les Arcades.** This comfortable spot in mid-Céret looks, smells, and feels exactly the way an inn ensconced in the heart of a provincial French town should. That the world-class collection of paintings of the Musée d'Art Moderne and the top-rated Les Feuillants restaurant (☞ *above*) are both just across the street puts it over the top. ✉ *1 pl. Picasso, 66400 Céret,* ☎ *04–68–87–12–30,* FAX *04–68–87–49–44. 31 rooms. No air-conditioning, cable TV, parking (fee). AE, DC, MC, V.*

Collioure

43 *35 km (21 mi) east of Céret, 27 km (17 mi) southeast of Perpignan.*

The heart of Matisse Country, this pretty seaside fishing village with a sheltered natural harbor has become a summer magnet for tourists (beware the crowds in July and August). Painters such as Henri Matisse, André Derain, Henri Martin, and Georges Braque—who were dubbed Fauves for their "savage" (*fauve* means "wild animal") approach to color and form—were among the early discoverers of Collioure. The view they admired remains largely unchanged today: to the north, the rocky Ilot St-Vincent juts out into the sea, a modern lighthouse at its tip, while inland the Albères Range rises to connect the Pyrénées with the Mediterranean. Collioure continues to play the muse to the entire Côte Vermeille—after all, it gave rise to the name of the Vermilion Coast because Matisse daringly painted Collioure's yellow-sand beach using a bright red terra-cotta hue. Matisse set up shop in the summer of 1905 and was greatly inspired by the colors of the town's terra-cotta roofs. The town's information center, behind the Plage Boramar, has an excellent map that points out the main locales once favored by the Fauve painters.

Near the old Quartier du Mouré is the 17th-century church of **Notre-Dame-des-Anges** (✉ Pl. de l'Église). It has exuberantly carved altarpieces by celebrated Catalan master Josef Sunyer and a pink-dome bell tower that doubled as the original lighthouse.

A slender jetty divides the Boramar Beach, beneath the church, from the small landing area at the foot of the **Château Royal,** a 15th-century castle remodeled by Vauban 200 years later. ☎ *04–68–82–06–43.* 🎫 *€3.* ⏲ *Mar.–Oct., daily 10–noon and 2–5.*

Dining and Lodging

$$$$ ✕🏨 **Relais des Trois Mas.** Overlooking Collioure from the cliffs south of town, this hotel has small but interestingly furnished rooms—headboards, for example, are made from antique Spanish doors. Rooms are named for painters whose work appears on the bathroom tiles. The views are spectacular. Below is a pebbled beach, though you may prefer the small pool (hewn from rock) or the huge Jacuzzi. Dine at the restaurant, La Balette, on the terrace or in one of the two small dining rooms looking over the harbor. ✉ *Rte. de Port-Vendres, 66190,* ☎ *04–68–82–05–07,* FAX *04–68–82–38–08. 19 rooms, 4 suites. Restaurant, 2 dining rooms, cable TV, minibars, garden, pool, gym, hot tub, beach. AE, DC, MC, V. Closed mid-Nov.–mid-Dec.*

$$ ★ ✕🏨 **Les Templiers.** Universally considered the "soul" of Collioure, this place merits a visit on every itinerary. Owner Jojo Pous, son of the force behind Collioure's art colony, has more than 2,500 original works hanging from every nook and cranny. The bar itself is a work of art, curved like the hull of a skiff and ending with a wood sculpture of a mermaid suckling an infant sailor. Collioure is Catalan in all senses but cartographically, so the food here is mostly Catalan and usually excellent; be sure to try dishes that feature the town's fabled anchovies. The rooms overlooking the château are cozy. ✉ *Quai de l'Amirauté, 66190,* ☎ *04–68–98–31–10,* FAX *04–68–98–01–24. 43 rooms. Restaurant, bar, café, no air-conditioning, cable TV. AE, DC, MC, V. Closed early Jan.–early Feb.*

Perpignan

44 *27 km (17 mi) northwest of Collioure, 64 km (40 mi) south of Narbonne, 204 km (126 mi) southeast of Toulouse.*

In medieval times Perpignan was the second city of Catalonia (after Barcelona), before falling to Louis XIII's French army in 1642. The Spanish influence is evident in Perpignan's leading monument, the fortified **Palais des Rois de Majorque** (Kings of Majorca Palace), begun in the 14th century by James II of Majorca. Highlights here are the majestic **cour d'Honneur** (Courtyard of Honor), the two-tier Flamboyant Gothic chapel of **Ste-Croix,** and the **Grande Salle** (Great Hall) with its monumental fireplaces. ✉ *Rue des Archers,* ☎ *04–68–34–48–29.* 🎫 *€2.* ⏲ *Daily 9–5.*

Now a rather dispiriting city (and don't venture to any of the suburbs), Perpignan's centre ville is still alluring, landmarked by a medieval monument, the 14th-century **Le Castillet,** with its tall, crenellated twin towers. Originally this hulking brick building was the main gate to the city; later it was used as a prison. Now the **Casa Pairal,** a museum devoted to Catalan art and traditions, is housed here. ✉ *Pl. de Verdun,* ☎ *04–68–35–42–05.* *Free.* *Wed.–Mon. 9–noon and 2–6.*

The **Promenade des Plantanes,** across boulevard Wilson from Le Castillet, is a cheerful place to stroll among flowers, plane trees, and fountains. To see other interesting medieval buildings, walk along the streets—the **Petite Rue des Fabriques d'En Nabot** is the best—near Le Castillet and the adjacent place de la Loge, the town's nerve center. Note the frilly wrought-iron campanile and dramatic medieval crucifix on the **Cathédrale St-Jean** (✉ Pl. Gambetta).

The **Loge de Mer** (Maritime Exchange; ✉ Rue de la Loge), a graceful 14th-century building, was once the chamber of commerce for maritime trade.The 15th-century **Palais de la Députation** (✉ Rue de la Loge) was once the seat of the permanent deputy, or representative of the Catalan Corts (parliament). The massive arched entryway is typical of the Catalonian, or House of Aragon, civil design of that period.

Dining and Lodging

$$$–$$$$ ✕ **Chapon Fin.** An upscale crowd pours into this excellent restaurant in the Park hotel to sample the subtle, understated cuisine. Three prix-fixe menus showcase authentic Mediterranean food. Try the *civet de homard au vieux banyuls* (lobster stewed in aged Banyuls wine). ✉ *18 bd. Jean-Bourrat,* ☎ *04–68–35–14–14. AE, DC, MC, V. Closed Sun. No lunch Mon.*

$$ ★ ✕ **La Casa Sansa.** This very Catalan, very popular restaurant serves fine regional specialties in an atmosphere thick with tastefully designed local color. Paintings on Rousillon themes crowd the walls. ✉ *2 rue Fabrique d'en Nadal,* ☎ *04–68–34–21–84. Reservations essential. AE, DC, MC, V. Closed Sun. No lunch Mon.*

$$$ ★ ✕ **Park.** Don't be deceived by the undistinguished facade: this family-run hotel enjoys ironclad prestige in Perpignan. Although some of the guest rooms are small, most are luxurious, soundproof, and air-conditioned. The spectacular suite (300 square ft for €260) is the top room in the house, and the hotel restaurant is excellent. ✉ *18 bd. Jean-Bourrat, 66000,* ☎ *04–68–35–14–14,* FAX *04–68–35–48–18,* WEB *www.parkhotel-fr.com. 67 rooms, one suite. Restaurant, bar, cable TV, minibars, parking (fee). AE, DC, MC, V.*

$–$$ **Hôtel de la Poste et de la Perdrix.** If you're looking for an inexpensive place with Old French charm in the center of town next to Le Castillet, don't miss this little spot. Rooms, like the hotel, are simple and poetic, as opposed to pampered and prosaic. The cuisine is Catalan. ✉ *6 rue Fabriques Nabot, 66000,* ☎ *04–68–34–42–53,* FAX *04–68–34–58–20. 38 rooms. Restaurant, no air-conditioning, no room TVs, parking (fee). AE, DC, MC, V.*

Shopping

Rue des Marchands, near Le Castillet, is thick with chic shops. **Maison Quinta** (✉ Rue Louis Blanc) is a top design and architectural artifacts store. Excellent local ceramics can be found at the picturesque **Sant Vicens Crafts Center** (✉ Rue Sant Vicens, off D22 east of town center).

Salses

45 *16 km (10 mi) north of Perpignan, 48 km (30 mi) south of Narbonne.*

Salses has a history of sieges. History relates that Hannibal stormed through the town with his elephants on his way to the Alps in 218 BC, though no trace of his passage remains. The colossal and well-preserved

Fort de Salses, built by Ferdinand of Aragon in 1497 and equipped for 300 horses and 1,000 soldiers, fell to the French under Cardinal Richelieu in 1642 after a three-year siege. Bulky round towers ring the rectangular inner fort, and the five-story keep, with its narrow corridors and small-scale drawbridges, was designed to keep the fort's governor safe to the last. ☏ *04–68–38–60–13.* €4. *July–Aug., daily 9–6; Sept.–June, daily 9:30–11:30 and 2–5:30; Nov.–Easter, 9:30–11:30 and 2–4.*

Narbonne

46 *64 km (40 mi) north of Perpignan, 60 km (37 mi) east of Carcassonne, 94 km (58 mi) south of Montpellier.*

In Roman times, bustling, industrial Narbonne was the second-largest town in Gaul (after Lyon) and an important port, though today little remains of its Roman past. Until the sea receded during the Middle Ages, Narbonne prospered. The town's former wealth is evinced by the 14th-century **Cathédral St-Just** (✉ Rue Armand-Gauthier); its vaults rise 133 ft from the floor, making it the tallest cathedral in southern France. Only Beauvais and Amiens, in Picardy, are taller, and as at Beauvais, the nave at Narbonne was never built.

Richly sculpted cloisters link the cathedral to the former **Palais des Archevêques** (Archbishops' Palace), now home to **museums** of archaeology, art, and history. Note the enormous palace kitchen and the late-13th-century keep, the Donjon Gilles-Aycelin; climb the 180 steps to the top for a view of the region and the town. ✉ *Palais des Archevêques,* ☏ *04–68–90–30–30.* *€5 (includes all town museums). May–Sept., daily 9–noon and 2–6; Oct.–Apr., Tues.–Sun. 10–noon and 2–5:30.*

On the south side of the Canal de la Robine is the **Musée Lapidaire** (Sculpture Museum), in the handsome 13th-century former church of **Notre-Dame de la Mourguié.** Classical busts, ancient sarcophagi, lintels, and Gallo-Roman inscriptions await you. ✉ *Pl. Lamourguier,* ☏ *04–68–65–53–58.* *€5 (includes all town museums). May–Sept., daily 9–noon and 2–6; Oct.–Apr., Tues.–Sun. 10–noon and 2–5:30.*

For the nearest decent beach, follow pretty D168 as it winds its way over the Montagne de la Clape to **Narbonne-Plage,** 15 km (9 mi) away. Just up the coast in St-Pierre-sur-Mer is the curious **Gouffre de l'Oeil-Doux,** an inland lake fed by seawater.

Dining and Lodging

$$$ ✕ **Le Relais du Val d'Orbieu.** This pretty spot 14 km (8 mi) west of town is a viable solution to Narbonne's scarcity of good hotels. Owner Jean-Pierre Gonsalvez speaks English and is extremely helpful. Grouped around a courtyard, most rooms are reached through covered arcades. The better ones are pleasantly simple, with bare tile floors and large French windows leading onto terraces; the standard ones are slightly smaller and do not have terraces or views. The restaurant (no luncheon served November–March) lacks intimacy but is more than serviceable. ✉ *D24, 11200 Ornaisons (14 km/8 mi west of Narbonne),* ☏ *04–68–27–10–27,* FAX *04–68–27–52–44,* WEB *www.relaisvaldorbieu.com. 13 rooms, 7 apartments. Restaurant, no air-conditioning, cable TV, minibars, garden, tennis court, pool. AE, DC, MC, V.*

$$ ✕ **Languedoc.** In this old-fashioned, early 20th-century hotel downtown, the smallish rooms vary in style and comfort; a full bath is an extra €15. La Petite Cour restaurant (closed Monday, no dinner Sunday) serves inexpensive regional dishes, with menus starting at €14. ✉ *22 bd. Gambetta, 11100,* ☏ *04–68–65–14–74,* FAX *04–68–65–81–*

48. 38 rooms, 34 with bath or shower; 2 suites. Restaurant, piano bar, parking (fee). AE, DC, MC, V.

Béziers

47 *20 km (12 mi) northeast of Narbonne, 54 km (33 mi) southwest of Montpellier.*

The Languedoc's *capital du vin* (wine capital)—crowds head here for *dègustation* tastings during the October wine harvest festival—and centerpiece of the Canal du Midi, Béziers owes its reputation to the genius of native son and royal salt-tax collector Pierre-Paul Riquet (that's his statue presiding over the allées Paul Riquet). He was a visionary at a time when roads were in deplorable shape and grain was transported on the backs of mules, dying a pauper in 1680, a year before the canal's completion (it was begun by the ancient Romans) and the revolutionizing of commerce in the south of France. Few would have predicted much of a future for Béziers in July of 1209, after Simon de Montfort, leader of the crusade against the Cathars, scored his first major victory here, massacring 20,000. Today the Canal du Midi hosts mainly pleasure cruisers, and Béziers sits serenely on its perch overlooking the distant Mediterranean and the foothills of the Cévennes Mountains. Early August sees the four-day *féria*—a festival with roots in Spain and replete with gory bullfighting (you've been warned).

Just off allées Paul Riquet on place G. Péri is a statue that has come to represent Béziers's other local hero, the mythical figure **Pépézuc** (the statue is actually made up of the body of one Roman emperor, topped by the head of another). Legend has it that Pépézuc defended the town against the onslaught of the English led by the Black Prince. At one corner of place G. Péri, Béziers's only **12th-century house** (⊠ Rue du Chapeau Rouge), with arcaded windows and carved heads, survives as a testament to Languedoc prior to the 13th-century Albigensian Crusade.

The heavily restored **Église de la Madeleine** (⊠ off rue de la République), with its distinctive octagonal tower, was the site of the beginning of the massacre, which occurred in 1209. About 7,000 townspeople who had sought refuge from Simon de Montfort in the church were burned alive before he turned his attention to sacking the town; the event is known as "*le grand mazel*" ("the great bonfire"). Restoration work means that you may only be able to admire the crenellations, gargoyles, floral frieze, and crooked arches of the late 11th-century pentagonal apse.

Béziers's late-19th-century **Halles** (Market Hall) was done in the style of the architect Baltard, who built the original Les Halles in Paris. This is a particularly beautiful example, with large stone cabbages gracing the entrance like urns. ⊠ *Entrances on rue Paul Riquet, pl. Pierre Sémard.* ⏲ *Daily 6:30–12:30.*

The **Ancienne Cathédrale St-Nazaire** (⊠ Pl. des Albigeois) was rebuilt over several centuries after the sack of Béziers. Note the medieval wall along rue de Juiverie, which formed the limit between the cathedral precincts and the Jewish quarter of town. The western facade resembles a fortress for good reason: it served as a warning to would-be invaders. Look for the magnificent 17th-century walnut organ and the frescoes about the lives of St. Stephen and others. Adjoining the cathedral are a 14th-century cloister and the **Jardin des Evêques** (Bishops' Garden), conceived of as a terraced garden descending to the banks of the Orb. The views from here, which take in Béziers's five bridges, are magnificent. ⊠ *Pl. des Albigeois.* ⏲ *Oct.–Apr., daily 10–noon and 2–5:30; May–Sept., daily 10–7.*

Dining and Lodging

$$$–$$$$ ✕🏨 **Château de Lignan.** Set in its own park, this elegant estate northwest of Béziers has four slender roof-tiled towers, lending a vaguely Italianate feel to go with the austere stucco facade. Pity that rooms have little to distinguish them from standard chain hotels except their size and louvered windows, but the restaurant is exceptional. The octagonal sprawl of the skylit dining room is cheery and welcoming. Simple, streamlined fare such as strongly flavored *loup en papillote* (sea perch cooked in foil) makes a perfect prelude to the vanilla ice cream–filled baked pears. ✉ *Pl. de l'Église, 34490 Lignan-sur-Orb (6 km/4 mi northwest of Béziers),* ☎ *04–67–37–91–47,* FAX *04–67–37–99–25,* WEB *www.chateauxhotels.com. 50 rooms. Restaurant, cable TV, minibars, garden, pool, parking. AE, MC, V.*

Outdoor Activities

Daylong excursions on the Canal du Midi include passage over the canal bridge spanning the Orb and through the nine locks; one popular canal-boat operator is **Crosières Cathy** (✉ Regimont, 34310 Poilhes, ☎ 04–67–03–72–16). Some companies working the Canal de Midi have extensive routes, some as far as the Mediterranean resort town of Agde, 21 km (14 mi) away. **Les Bâteaux du Soleil** (✉ 6 rue Chassefière, 34300 Agde, ☎ 04–67–94–08–79, FAX 04–67–21–28–38) includes some wide-ranging excursions.

Minerve

48 *40 km (25 mi) west of Béziers, 30 km (19 mi) northwest of Narbonne.*

Surrounded by the meandering, juniper-covered limestone gorges of the Vallée de la Cesse, Minerve is the quintessential medieval hilltop village. The town sheltered a large number of heretics at the start of the Albigensian Crusade. But its defensive position was no match for Simon de Montfort's army in July 1210, when after a seven-week siege the dehydrated citizens capitulated and 180 Cathar *Perfecti* (elite Cathari) were burned. De Montfort's army had blocked the village well with the aid of a catapult called La Malvoisine (the Evil Neighbor), which has been reconstructed on its original strategic site. Stroll around the remaining fortifications and try to imagine the assault. Around Minerve are a number of geological and archaeological curiosities, including *ponts naturels* (natural bridges), enormous tunnels in the rock cut by the path of the Cesse River, prehistoric grottoes, and dolmens.

Maps and information are available from the somewhat hidden **Syndicat d'Initiative** (✉ Pl. du Monument aux Morts, ☎ 04–68–91–81–43), the tourist office in the center of the village. You can also get addresses of local winemakers who produce the classed wine Minervois (a rough, fruity red) from grapes grown in arid, pebbly soil.

The austere, Romanesque **Église St-Etienne** has one of the oldest altar tables in Europe, dating from AD 456. Next to the church is a carving of a dove, a monument to the village's resistance during the Crusades. The château was destroyed by Simon de Montfort. Only the curious, candlelike **Tour du Guet** (Watchtower) remains on a ledge at the far end of the village.

The **Musée Hurepel** re-creates the events of the Albigensian Crusade in a series of figurine-populated dioramas and does a good job of explaining how villagers would have interacted with the Cathars they sheltered. ✉ *5 rue des Martyrs,* ☎ *04–68–91–12–26.* 🎫 *€3.* ⏲ *Apr.–late Sept., daily 10:30–12:30 and 2–6:30; other times by appointment only.*

Dining and Lodging

$$ ✕ 🏨 **Relais Chantovent.** Overlooking the gorges of the Brian River, this oak-beamed, terra-cotta-tile restaurant and inn is decorated with exceptional paintings by local artists. Rooms are basic but quaint, with old lamps, framed prints, and wooden furniture. Owners Maïté and Loulou Evenou serve up elegantly garnished local fare, including strong, salty *jambon de la Montagne Noire* (Black Mountain ham) and trout in a cream and red-pepper sauce. The €15 menu is a bargain. The restaurant is closed Monday, and there is no dinner Sunday. ✉ *17 Grande-Rue, 34210 Minerve,* ☎ *04–68–91–14–18,* FAX *04–68–91–81–99. 10 rooms. Restaurant, no air-conditioning, no room TVs. MC, V. Mid-Dec.–late Mar.*

$$–$$$ ★ 🏨 **Les Aliberts.** Ensconced among the vine- and asphodel-covered hills outside Minerve, with stunning views of the Pyrénées and the Montagne Noire, this *gîte* (hiker's way-station) is in a restored and renovated set of 12th- to 17th-century farm buildings. Cosmopolitan owners Pascal and Monique Bourgogne treat guests like friends. The majestic main farmhouse has common rooms with an enormous fireplace, library, and piano. The five cozy houses (€475 to €975 per week), without phones, range in style from Scandinavian to Asian to French contemporary; all have full kitchens and fireplaces. Meals and breakfasts can be ordered in advance. ✉ *Les Aliberts, 34210 Minerve (off D10 south toward Olonzac),* ☎ *04–68–91–81–72,* FAX *04–68–91–22–95,* WEB *www.gite.com/aliberts. 5 houses, with 13 rooms total. No room TVs, Internet, library, pool, laundry facilities. No credit cards.*

Pézenas

49 *23 km (14 mi) northeast of Béziers, 52 km (32 mi) southwest of Montpellier.*

Pézenas retains the courtly appearance and feel it acquired in the 16th century, when the Estates General of the Languedoc, the regional administrative body, governed from here. The town made its fortune with 16th- to 18th-century textile fairs, at which denim was sold. Hence you have Pézenas's architectural richness: around every picturesque corner is another *hôtel particulier* (town-house mansion)—and because of architectural competition that once existed among the wealthy, they are all unique. Some notable streets are rue Triperie Vieille; rue de la Foire, where you'll find the Maison Carrion de Nizas and the Hôtel de Wicque; cour Jean-Jaurès, famous for its Maison Émile Mâzuc, at No. 10; place du 14 Juillet and its outstanding Hôtel des Barons de Lacoste; and rue Émile Zola, home to the Maison de Jacques Coeur. At the end of rue Émile Zola is a rounded archway leading into the rue Juiverie, also called La Carriera, which in the Occitan language denotes a Jewish ghetto.

The tourist office, which organizes a variety of tours of Pézenas, is in the **Maison du Barbier Gély** (✉ 1 pl. Gambetta), once home to Molière's barber and friend, Monsieur Gély. Pézenas's most impressive hôtel particulier is the **Hôtel d'Alfonce,** with its twisted Baroque columns, three-tiered balustraded loggia overlooking the garden, and vinelike corner staircase. This was the residence of the Prince de Conti, who sponsored visits by Molière and his acting troupe in 1650, 1653, and 1655. *Le Médecin Volant* (*The Flying Doctor*) may have premiered here shortly before Conti, mad from syphilis, purged his illustrious court. The owners, Monsieur Aubert and his daughter, give private tours of their family home. ✉ *Rue Conti,* 🎫 *€2.* ⏱ *June–Sept., Mon.–Sat. 10–noon and 2–6.*

Nightlife and the Arts

As part of **La Mirondela Del Arts** festival in July and August, Molière's spirit comes alive with performances by comedy troupes; there are also Occitan-language music and poetry events. In February the town's medieval mascot, **Le Poulain** (a giant horse made out of chestnut and cloth), gets toted around in honor of Carnival.

St-Guilhem-le-Désert

50 *44 km (28 mi) north of Pézenas, 40 km (25 mi) northwest of Montpellier.*

The name of this ancient abbey on the Santiago de Compostela pilgrimage route conjures up visions of windswept sands. Actually, it's nowhere near the desert—the term refers to its isolated, inhospitable location. Poised at the top of the Verdus Estuary in the Gellone Valley, among the heather-covered Hérault gorges, the abbey was founded in 804 by Guilhem d'Orange, count of Toulouse and cousin of Charlemagne. St. Guilhem was seeking to retire from war with the Saracens and to live a monastic life when his cousin presented him with a piece of the true cross. The remote site chose itself: Guilhem was a devout follower of Benoît d'Aniane, reformer of the Benedictine order and abbot in nearby Aniane.

A massive 140-year-old plane tree dominates place de la Liberté, on which sits all that remains of the Abbaye St-Guilhem-le-Désert, the **abbey church,** and some beautiful arcaded medieval houses; look for large, dried *cardabelle* flowers, native to the region, decorating people's homes. The nave of the somber church, with its austere tower, dates to the 11th century and the apse to the 12th, built over a Carolingian crypt: note the unusual tribunes in the transept. What's left of St-Guilhem's remains are in a reliquary in the wall, recovered from an 1817 flood. Another niche contains the fragment of the cross. But the **altar** in the chapel is the real attraction here: thought to be from the 12th century, it's made entirely of white marble, with a black marble base, and the tracings of Christ were once filled with colored glass.

Around a square pool filled with carp, the **cloître** is a place of reflection for the nine young Carmelite nuns who live here and cultivate the garden encircling the apse. The beautiful sculptures that once decorated the cloister, including ***Daniel in the Lion's Den,*** were bought in the early 20th century by art collector George Grey Barnard for New York's Cloisters. ✉ *In abbey church.* ⏲ *Sept.–Mar., daily 10:30–12:30 and 2–5; Apr.–Aug., daily 9:30–7.*

The abbeys of St-Guilhem and Aniane built the impressive **Pont du Diable** (Devil's Bridge) in the mid-11th century to straddle the Hérault at the entrance to its gorges. Legend has it that the devil, wanting to prevent St-Guilhem from building the bridge, threatened to damn the first man who crossed it. A dog was prudently sent instead. ✉ *Just south of St-Guilhem on D4, heading toward D27 and Aniane.*

Montpellier

40 km (25 mi) southeast of St-Guilhem-le-Désert, 42 km (26 mi) southwest of Nîmes.

Vibrant Montpellier (pronounced monh-pell-*yay*), capital of the Languedoc-Roussillon region, has been a center of commerce and learning since the Middle Ages, when it was crossroads for pilgrims on their way to Santiago de Compostela, in Spain, and an active shipping center trading in spices from the East. With its cargo of exotic luxuries, it also imported Renaissance learning, and its university—founded in the 14th century—has nurtured a steady influx of ideas through the centuries. Though the port silted up by the 16th century, Montpellier never became a backwater, and as a center of commerce and conferences it keeps its focus on the future. An imaginative urban planning program has streamlined the 17th-century Vieille Ville (Old Town), and monumental perspectives dwarf passersby on the 17th-century Promenade du Peyrou. An even more utopian venture in urban planning is the Antigone district: a vast, harmonious 100-acre complex designed in 1984 by Barcelona architect Ricardo Bofill. A student population of some 65,000 keeps things lively, especially on the place de la Comédie, the city's social nerve center. The Old Town is a pedestrian paradise; you can travel around the entire city on the excellent bus system (the gare routière station is by the train terminal on rue Jules Ferry).

★ 51 52 The **Promenade du Peyrou** is easy to find: its enormous **Arc de Triomphe,** designed by d'Aviler in 1689 and finished by Giral in 1776, looms majestically over the peripheral highway that loops around the city center. Both were dedicated to Louis XIV at the end of the 17th century. The noble scale of the harmonious stone constructions and the sweeping perspectives they frame make for an inspiring stroll through this posh stretch of town. At the end of the park is the **Château d'Eau,** a Corinthian temple and the terminal for **les Arceaux,** an 18th-century aqueduct; on a clear day the view from here is spectacular, taking in the Cévennes Mountains, the sea, and an ocean of red-tile roofs (it's worth it to come back here at night to see the entire promenade lit up).

Boulevard Henri IV runs north from the Promenade du Peyrou to
53 France's oldest botanical garden, the **Jardin des Plantes,** planted on order of Henri IV in 1593. An exceptional range of plants, flowers, and trees grows here. *Free.* *Gardens Mon.–Sat. 9–noon and 2–5. Greenhouses weekdays 9–noon and 2–5, Sat. 9–noon.*

After taking in the broad vistas of the Promenade de Peyrou, cross over into the Vieille Ville and wander its maze of narrow streets, full of pretty shops and intimate restaurants. At the northern edge of the
54 Old Town, visit the imposing **Cathédrale St-Pierre** (✉ Pl. St-Pierre), its fantastical and unique 14th-century entry porch alone worth the detour: two cone-topped towers—some five stories high—flank the main portal and support a groin-vaulted shelter. The interior, despite 18th-century reconstruction, maintains the formal simplicity of its 14th-century origins.

55 Next door to the cathedral, peek into the noble **Faculté de Médecine,** on rue de l'École de Médecine, one of France's most respected medical schools, founded in the 14th century and infused with generations of international learning—especially Arab and Jewish scholarship.

From the medical school follow rue Foch, which slices straight east. The number of bistros and brasseries increases as you leave the Old Town to cross place des Martyrs; veering right down rue de la Loge,
56 you spill out onto the festive gathering spot known as **Place de la Comédie.** Anchored by the Neoclassical 19th-century **Opéra-Comédie,** this broad square is a beehive of leisurely activity, a cross between Barcelona's Ramblas and a Roman *passagiata* (afternoon stroll, en masse). Brasseries, bistros, fast-food joints, and cinemas draw crowds, but the pleasure is getting there and seeing who came before, in which shoes, and with whom.

From place de la Comédie, boulevard Sarrail leads north past the shady
★ 57 esplanade Charles de Gaulle to the **Musée Fabre.** A mixed bag of ar-

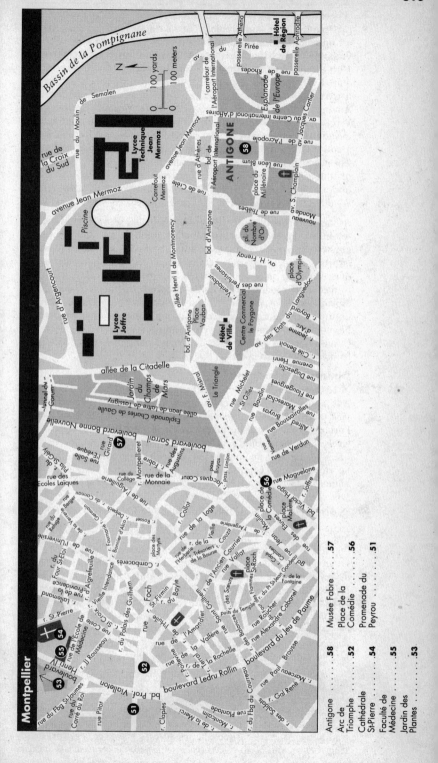

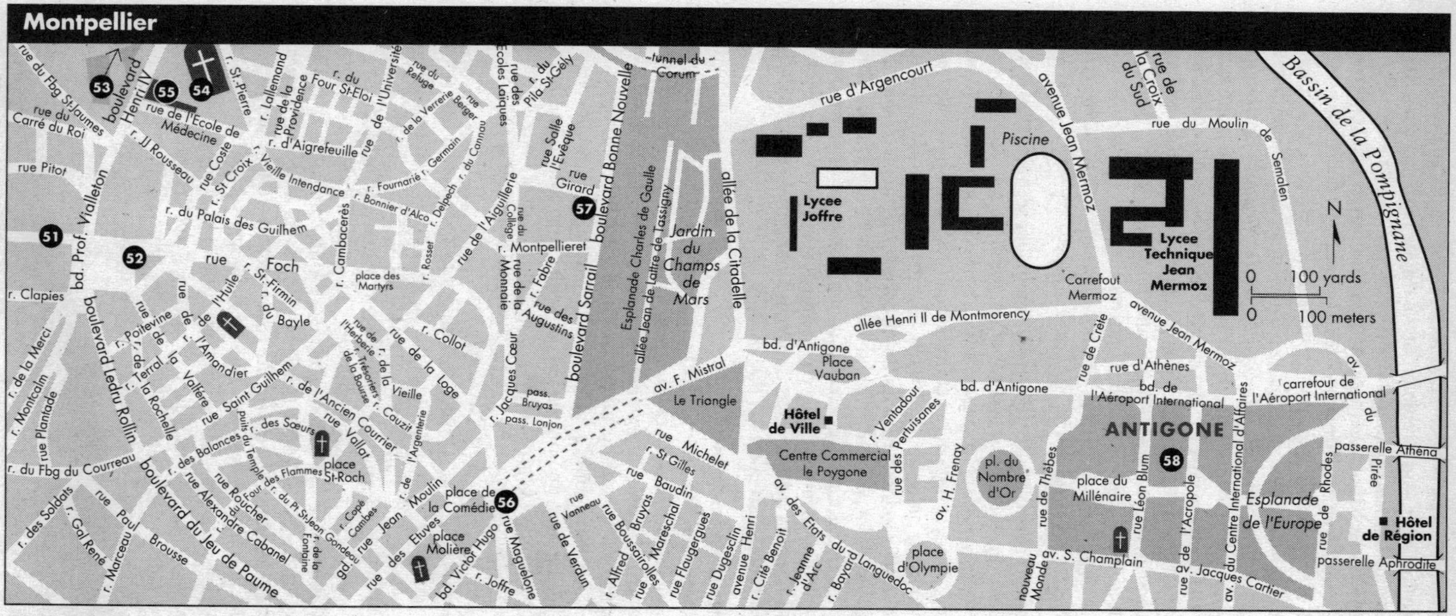

Antigone	58	Musée Fabre	57
Arc de Triomphe	52	Place de la Comédie	56
Cathédrale St-Pierre	54	Promenade du Peyrou	51
Faculté de Médecine	55		
Jardin des Plantes	53		

chitectural styles (a 17th-century *hôtel,* a vast Victorian wing with superb natural light, and a remnant of a Baroque Jesuit college), this rich art museum has a surprisingly big collection, thanks to its namesake. François-Xavier Fabre, a native of Montpellier, was a student of the great 18th-century French artist David, who established roots in Italy and acquired a formidable collection of masterworks—which he then donated to his hometown, supervising the development of this fine museum. Among his gifts were the *Mariage Mystique de Sainte Catherine,* by Veronese, and Poussin's coquettish *Venus et Adonis.* Later contributions include a superb group of 17th-century Flemish works (Rubens, Steen), a collection of 19th-century French canvases (Géricault, Delacroix, Corot, Millet) that inspired Gauguin and Van Gogh, and a growing group of 20th-century acquisitions that buttress a legacy of paintings by early Impressionist Frédéric Bazille. ✉ *3 bd. Bonne Nouvelle,* ☎ *04–67–14–83–00.* 🎫 *€3.* ⏲ *Tues.–Fri. 9–5:30, weekends 9:30–5.*

At the far-east end of the city loop, Montpellier seems to transform itself into a futuristic ideal city, all in one smooth, low-slung postmod-
58 ern style. This is the **Antigone** district, the result of city planners' efforts (and local industries' commitment) to pull Montpellier up out of its economic doldrums. It worked. This ideal neighborhood, designed by the Catalan architect Ricardo Bofill, covers 100-plus acres with plazas, esplanades, shops, restaurants, and low-income housing, all constructed out of stone-colored, pre-stressed concrete. Be sure to visit place du Nombre d'Or—symmetrically composed of curves—and the 1-km-long (½-mi-long) vista that stretches down a mall of cypress trees to the glass-fronted **Hôtel de Region** (✉ Av. du Pirée).

Dining and Lodging

$$$–$$$$ ✕ **Le Chandelier.** On the sixth and seventh floors of a building in the Antigone district, this restaurant has dramatic views, impeccable service, and bold blue-and-yellow Mediterranean decor. Chef Gilbert Furlan's inventive cuisine takes Provençal ingredients to sophisticated levels: sample his squid sautéed in fresh thyme, dried mullet eggs with brandade mousse, and pigeon roasted with cinnamon and nutmeg. The licorice-honey ice cream makes a fine dessert. There's a good range of Languedoc wines available. ✉ *Pl. Zeus 39,* ☎ *04–67–15–34–38. AE, DC, MC, V. Closed Sun. No lunch Mon.*

$$ ✕ **Alexandre.** If you're making a run out to the seaside, this is a good choice for lunch. Tons of nutty, salty oysters are cultivated in the nearby *étangs* (ponds); you can sample them in the elegant surroundings of Louis XV furnishings while gazing out over the Mediterranean. Other choices include a splendid array of seafood dishes. ✉ *Esplanade de la Capitainerie, La Grande-Motte (21 km/13 mi southeast of Montpellier),* ☎ *04–67–56–63–63. AE, MC, V. Closed Mon. No dinner Sun.*

$$ ★ ✕ **Le Petit Jardin.** On a quiet Old Town backstreet, this simple restaurant lives up to its name: you dine looking over (or seated in) a lovely, deep-shaded garden with views of the cathedral. A simple omelet with pepper sauce, spicy bourride, or hearty *osso buco* (veal shanks in saffron-tomato sauce) mirror the welcome, which is warm and unpretentious. ✉ *20 rue Jean-Jacques Rousseau,* ☎ *04–67–60–78–78. AE, DC, MC, V. Closed Mon.*

$$$$ ★ ✕🏨 **Le Jardin des Sens.** Blink and look again: twins Laurent and Jacques Pourcel, trained under separate masters, combine forces here to achieve a quiet, almost cerebral cuisine based on southern French traditions. At every turn are happy surprises: foie gras crisps, dried-fruit risotto, and lamb sweetbreads with *gambas* (prawns). A modest lunch menu (in the $$ category) lets you indulge on a budget. Decor is minimal stylish, with steel beams and tables on three tiers. With ultramodern Relais & Châteaux rooms on site, it doesn't matter that you're far from the historic center—or does it? Truth is, this is in a rather *delabré* working-class neighborhood and from the outside looks like an anonymous warehouse. ✉ *11 av. St-Lazare,* ☎ *04–99–58–38–38,* FAX *04–99–58–38–39,* WEB *www.jardindessens.com. 12 rooms, 2 apartments. Restaurant, bar, cable TV, minibars, pool, meeting rooms, park, parking (fee). AE, DC, MC, V. Both restaurant and hotel closed Sun. No lunch Mon.*

$$ ★ **Le Guilhem.** On the same quiet backstreet as the restaurant Le Petit Jardin, this jewel of a *hôtel de charme* beads together a chain of 16th-century houses. Rebuilt from ruins to include an elevator and state-of-the-art white-tile baths, it nonetheless retains original casement windows (many overlooking the extraordinary old garden), slanting floors, and views toward the cathedral. Soft yellows and powder blues add to its gentle, *temps passé* atmosphere. Tiny garret-style rooms at the top are great if you're traveling alone; if not, ask for the largest available. ✉ *18 rue Jean-Jacques-Rousseau, 34000,* ☎ *04–67–52–90–90,* FAX *04–67–60–67–67,* WEB *www.hotel-guilhem.fr. 33 rooms. No air-conditioning, cable TV, parking (fee). MC, V.*

Nightlife and the Arts

Concerts are performed in the 19th-century **Théâtre des Treize Vents** (✉ Allée Jules-Milhau, ☎ 04–67–58–08–13). The **Orchestre Philharmonique de Montpellier** (☎ 04–67–61–66–16) is a young and energetic group of some reputation, performing regularly in the Opéra Berlioz in the Corum conference complex. The resident **Opéra de Montpellier** (☎ 04–67–60–19–99) performs in the very imposing Opéra-Comédie on place de la Comédie. For rousing student hangouts, head to **place Jean-Jaurès.**

Outdoor Activities

Although Montpellier's medieval port may have been silted in, it's still a quick jaunt to the nearest **beach,** via the narrow causeway that straddles the ponds and open coastline to the city's south. You can abandon your car in the low dunes to clamber over to the water, or make a beeline for the architectural monstrosities—pyramidal residential pods—that have transformed **La Grande-Motte** and **La Grau-du-Roi** into extremely popular sandy-beach resorts.

THE MIDI-PYRÉNÉES AND THE LANGUEDOC-ROUSSILLON A TO Z

To research prices, get advice from other travelers, and book travel arrangements, visit www.fodors.com.

AIR TRAVEL

CARRIERS

Air France has regular flights between Paris and Toulouse; Montpellier is served by frequent flights from Paris and London. TAT (Transport Aérien Transrégional) has direct flights from Paris's Orly Airport to Rodez.

➤ AIRLINES & CONTACTS: **Air France** (☎ 08–02–80–28–02). **TAT** (reservations: ☎ 01–42–79–05–05 Paris; 05–65–42–20–30 Rodez).

AIRPORTS

All international flights arrive at Toulouse's Blagnac Airport, a 20-minute drive from the center of the city. Airport shuttles run regularly (every half hour between 8:15 AM and 8:45 PM) from the airport to the bus station in Toulouse (at the train station; fare €4) and also at 9:20 PM, 10 PM, and 10:45 PM. From the Toulouse bus station to the airport, buses leave every half hour 5:30 AM–8:30 PM.

➤ AIRPORT INFORMATION: **Blagnac Airport** (☎ 05–61–42–44–65). **Airport Montpellier-Méditerranée** (☎ 04–67–20–85–00).

BUS TRAVEL

As in most rural regions in France, there is an array of bus companies (in addition to SNCF buses, Intercars, Semvat, Courriers du Midi, Salt Autocars, among others) threading the Midi-Pyrénées countryside; be sure to stop in the bigger tourist offices on your route to inquire in advance for detailed bus schedules and advice on which bus routes to use for your sightseeing itinerary. Toulouse's bus links include Albi, Auch, Castres, Foix, and Montauban; Albi connects with Cordes (summer only) and Montauban; Montauban with Moissac and Auch; Montpellier with Béziers. For Courriers Catalans and Car Inter 66 buses to the Côte Vermeille, Collioure, Céret, and Prades, depart from Perpignan. Everyone says you should take the train to Carcassonne, although buses do head there.

➤ BUS INFORMATION: **Montpellier Gare Routière** (☎ 04–67–92–01–43). **Toulouse Gare Routière** (☎ 04–61–61–67–67).

CAR RENTAL

➤ LOCAL AGENCIES: **Avis** (✉ 13 bd. Conflent, Perpignan, ☎ 04–68–34–26–71; ✉ Blagnac Airport, Toulouse, ☎ 05–61–30–04–94). **Budget** (✉ Montpellier train station, ☎ 04–67–92–69–00). **Hertz** (✉ Pl. Lagarrasic, Auch, ☎ 05–62–05–26–26; ✉ 5 av. Chamier, Montauban, ☎ 05–63–20–29–00; ✉ 18 rue Jules Ferry, Montpellier, ☎ 04–67–58–65–18).

CAR TRAVEL

The fastest route from Paris to Toulouse (700 km/435 mi southwest) is via Bordeaux on A10, then A62; the journey time is about nine hours. If you choose to head south over the Pyrénées to Barcelona, the Tunnel du Puymorens saves half an hour of switchbacks between Hospitalet and Porta, but in good weather and with time to spare the drive over the Puymorens Pass is spectacular. Plan on taking three hours between Toulouse and Font-Romeu and another three to Barcelona. The fastest route from Toulouse to Barcelona is the four-hour, 421-km (253-mi) drive via Carcassonne and Perpignan on A61 and A9, which becomes A7 at Le Perthus.

A62/A61 slices through the region on its way through Carcassonne to the coast at Narbonne, where A9 heads south to Perpignan. At Toulouse, where A62 becomes A61, various highways fan out in all directions: N124 to Auch; N117/E80 to St-Gaudens, Tarbes, and Pau; A62/N20 to Montauban and Cahors; N20 south to Foix and the Ariège Valley; N88 to Albi and Rodez. A9 (La Languedocienne) is the main highway artery that connects Montpellier with Beziers to the south and Nîmes to the north.

MUSIC FESTIVALS

Fifty music festivals a year take place in the smaller towns throughout the region; the Comité Régional du Tourisme (CRT) and larger tourist offices can provide a list of dates and addresses. For complete musical information contact the Délégation Musicale Régionale.

➤ CONTACTS: **Délégation Musicale Régionale** (✉ 56 rue du Taur, 31080 Toulouse, ☎ 05–61–29–21–00).

OUTDOORS AND SPORTS

For information on canoeing or kayaking, contact the Ligue de Canoë-Kayak. For information on hiking or horseback riding, contact the Comité de Randonnées Midi-Pyrénées. Local tourist offices also have detailed maps of more than 3,220 km (2,000 mi) of marked trails. The

Comité Regional du Tourisme du Languedoc-Roussillon publishes a brochure on golf courses in the area and sells a pass honored at 14 courses.

➤ CANOEING, KAYAKING, AND RAFTING: **Ligue de Canoë-Kayak** (✉ 16 rue Guillemin-Tarayre, 31000 Toulouse, ☎ 05–61–62–65–05).

➤ GOLF: **Comité Regional du Tourisme du Languedoc-Roussillon** (✉ 20 rue de la République, 34000 Montpellier, ☎ 04–67–22–81–00, FAX 04–67–58–06–10, WEB www.cr-languedocroussillon.fr/tourisme/).

➤ HIKING: **Comité de Randonnées Midi-Pyrénées** (CORAMIP; ✉ 14 rue Bayard, 31000 Toulouse, ☎ 05–61–99–44–00).

TOURS

Contact the Toulouse tourist office for information about walking tours and bus tours in and around Toulouse. Ask for the encyclopedic, superbly entertaining, and English-speaking Gilbert Casagrande for a nonpareil tour of Toulouse. The Comité Régional du Tourisme has a brochure, "1,001 Escapes in the Midi-Pyrénées," with descriptions of weekends and short organized package vacations.

In addition to publishing map itineraries that you can follow yourself, the **Montpellier tourist office** (☎ 04–67–60–60–60) provides guided walking tours of the city's neighborhoods and monuments daily in summer and on Wednesday and Saturday during the school year (roughly, September–June). They leave from the place de la Comédie. There are also **horse-drawn carriage** tours between the square and the Esplanade Charles de Gaulle; you can go for 15 minutes up to an hour and a half (information ☎ 04–67–92–47–60). A small **tourist train** with broadcast commentary leaves from the Esplanade between 2 and 9, Monday through Saturday (information ☎ 04–67–60–60–60).

➤ CONTACTS: **Comité Régional du Tourisme** (CRT; ✉ 54 bd. de l'Embouchure, 31200 Toulouse, ☎ 05–61–13–55–55). **Montpellier** (✉ 30 allée Jean de Lattre de Tassigny, Esplanade Comédie, ☎ 04–67–60–60–60). **Toulouse tourist office** (✉ Donjon du Capitole, ☎ 05–61–11–02–22).

TRAIN TRAVEL

The regional French rail network in the southwest provides regular service to many towns, though not all. Béziers is linked by train to Carcassonne, Perpignan, Narbonne, and Montpellier, as well as Paris (but via slow trains that take hours not via TGVs). There's no train service to Pézenas, Minerve, and St-Guilhem. Most trains for the southwest leave from Paris's Gare d'Austerlitz. There are direct trains to Toulouse, Carcassonne, and Montauban. For Rodez, change in Brive, and for Auch, in Toulouse. Seven trains leave Paris (Gare de Lyon) daily for Narbonne and Perpignan; a change at Montpellier is often necessary. Most of these trips take between six or seven hours. Note that at least three high-speed TGV (*Trains à Grande Vitesse*) per day leave Paris (Gare Montparnasse) for Toulouse; the journey time is five hours. A TGV line also connects to TGV that serves Montpellier.

Within the Midi-Pyrénées region, Toulouse is the biggest hub, with a major line linking Carcassonne, Béziers, Narbonne (change here for Perpignan), and Montpellier; trains also link up with Albi and Montauban; the latter connects with Moissac. Montpellier connects with Carcassonne, Perpignan, Narbonne, Béziers, and other towns.

➤ TRAIN INFORMATION: **SNCF** (☎ 08–36–35–35–35, WEB www.sncf.com).

TRAVEL AGENCIES

➤ LOCAL AGENT REFERRALS: **Havas** (✉ 2 pl. de la Comédie, Montpellier, ☎ 04–67–91–31–70; ✉ 73 rue d'Alsace-Lorraine, Toulouse, ☎

05–61–23–16–35). **Wagons-Lits** (✉ Voyages Dépêche, 42 bis rue d'Alsace-Lorraine, Toulouse, ☎ 05–62–15–42–70).

VISITOR INFORMATION

The regional tourist office for the Midi-Pyrénées is the Comité Régional du Tourisme. For Pyrénées-Roussillon information, contact the Comité Départemental de Tourisme. For the Languedoc-Roussillon contact the Comité Régional du Tourisme du Languedoc-Roussillon. Local tourist offices are listed by town below.

➤ Tourist Information: **Comité Régional du Tourisme** (CRT; ✉ 54 bd. de l'Embouchure, 31200 Toulouse, ☎ 05–61–13–55–55). **Comité Départemental de Tourisme** (✉ Quai de Lattre de Tassigny, B.P. 540, 66005 Perpignan, ☎ 04–68–34–29–94). **Comité Régional du Tourisme du Languedoc-Roussillon** (✉ 20 rue de la République, 34000 Montpellier, ☎ 04–67–22–81–00, FAX 04–67–58–06–10, WEB www.cr-languedocroussillon.fr/tourisme/). **Albi** (✉ Pl. Ste-Cécile, ☎ 05–63–49–48–80, WEB www.mairie-albi.fr). **Auch** (✉ 1 rue Dessoles, ☎ 05–62–05–22–89). **Béziers** (✉ Palais des Congrès, 29 av. St-Saëns, ☎ 04–67–76–47–00). **Carcassonne** (✉ 15 bd. Camille-Pelletan, ☎ 04–68–25–07–04, WEB www.carcassonne.org). **Céret** (✉ 1 bd. Clemenceau, ☎ 04–68–87–00–53, WEB www.ot-ceret.fr). **Collioure** (✉ Pl. 18-juin, ☎ 04–68–82–15–47, WEB www.collioure.com). **Cordes** (✉ Maison Fonpeyrouse, ☎ 05–63–56–00–52). **Eyne** (✉ Eyne Station, ☎ 04–68–04–08–01). **Fleurance** (✉ Pl. de la République 2, ☎ 05–62–64–00–00). **Foix** (✉ 45 Cours G.-Fauré, ☎ 05–61–65–12–12). **Font-Romeu** (✉ Av. E. Brousse, ☎ 05–68–30–68–30). **Larressingle** (✉ Syndicat D'Initiative, ☎ 05–62–28–37–02). **Lectoure** (✉ Pl. de l'Église, ☎ 05–62–68–76–98). **Minerve** (✉ Pl. du Monument aux Morts, ☎ 04–68–91–81–43). **Mirepoix** (✉ Pl. Mar.-Leclerc, ☎ 05–61–68–83–76). **Montauban** (✉ Ancien College, B.P. 201, ☎ 05–63–63–60–60, WEB www.officetourisme.montauban.com). **Moissac** (✉ 6 pl. Durand de Bredon, ☎ 05–63–04–01–85). **Mont-Louis** (✉ Rue Vauban, ☎ 04–68–04–21–97). **Montpellier** (✉ 30 allée Jean de Lattre de Tassigny, Esplanade Comédie, ☎ 04–67–60–60–60, WEB www.ot-montpellier.fr). **Narbonne** (✉ Pl. Roger-Salengro, ☎ 04–68–65–15–60). **Perpignan** (✉ Quai de Lattre de Tassigny, ☎ 04–68–66–30–30). **Pézenas** (✉ 1 pl. Gambetta, ☎ 04–67–98–36–40, WEB www.perpignantourisme.com). **Prades** (✉ 4 rue Victor-Hugo, ☎ 04–68–05–41–02). **St-Guilhem-le-Désert** (✉ 2 rue de la Font du Portal, ☎ 04–67–57–44–33). **Toulouse** (✉ Donjon du Capitole, ☎ 05–61–11–02–22, WEB www.ot-toulouse.fr). **Villefranche-de-Conflent** (✉ Pl. de l'Eglise, ☎ 05–62–64–00–00).

16 THE BASQUE COUNTRY, THE BÉARN, AND THE HAUTES-PYRÉNÉES

Few other regions of mainland France can claim such dramatic extremes: from Atlantic beaches and the Basque Country's lush green hills to the Béarn's rolling meadows, lofty heights, and rushing salmon streams, to the granite walls of Gavarnie, the greatest natural marvel of the Hautes-Pyrénées. Whether you head for Bay of Biscay resorts like Biarritz, picturesque villages like St-Jean-de-Luz, or the towering peaks of the central Pyrenean cordillera, you'll discover some of France's most fascinating man-made and natural wonders here.

Revised and updated by George Semler

Introduction by George Semler

RECENTLY, A PELOTA-PLAYING MAYOR IN THE PROVINCE OF SOULE welcomed a group of travelers by blithely announcing that the Basque Country is the most beautiful in the world, that the Basque people were very probably directly descended from Adam and Eve via the lost city of Atlantis, that his own ancestors fought in the Crusades, and that Christopher Columbus was almost certainly a Basque. There, in short order, was a composite picture of the pride, dignity, and humor of the Basques. And if Columbus was not a Basque (a claim historians very much doubt), at least historians know that whalers of the regional village of St-Jean-de-Luz sailed as far as America in their three-masted ships and that Juan Sebastián Elkano, from the Spanish Basque village of Guetaria was one of those intrepid adventurers who did indeed complete Magellan's voyage around the world.

From berets and pelota matches to Basque cooking, the culture of this little "country" straddling the French and Spanish Pyrénées has cast its spell in the far corners of the earth. And continues to do so—just witness the best-seller status of Mark Kurlansky's 1999 *The Basque History of the World.* Today travelers bruised by the crowding and commerce of more frequented parts of France are increasingly heading to this southwest corner to enjoy the region's relatively undiscovered panoply of rich cultures and landscapes. In an easy stretch, a midsummer's day begun surfing in Biarritz could end glacier skiing at sunset at the Brèche de Roland above Gavarnie. The ocher sands along the Bay of Biscay and the bright reds and blues of the St-Jean-de-Luz fishing fleet are less than an hour from the emerald-green hills of St-Jean-Pied-de-Port in the Basque Pyrénées. Atlantic salmon and native Pyrenean trout still thrive in the River Nive, while puff-ball sheep tumble through moist highland pastures.

Center stage is held by the three French Basque provinces—Labourd, Soule, and Basse Navarre—which share a singularly distinct culture with their four cousin Basque provinces in Spain: jai alai, whaleboat regattas, stone lifting, world-famous cuisine, and a mysterious and ancient non-Indo-European language all its own. In fact, the origins of this culture remain obscure. The purported resemblance of the Basque evening (or war) call, the *irrinzina,* to that of the Upper Amazon Indians only adds to the mystery, as does the common use by both the Basques and the ancient Mayans of base 20 to reckon math. Some trace Basque origins back to the Berbers of North Africa, though the most tenable and logical theory is that they are descended from the aboriginal Iberian peoples who were most successful in defending their language and cultural identity from the influence of Roman and Moorish domination felt elsewhere on the Peninsula.

At the Basque Country's eastern edge, the ski and spelunking town of Pierre-St-Martin marks the start of the Béarn, with its splendid capital city of Pau and the pristine valleys of Aspe, Ossau, and Barétous descending from the Pyrénées. Sauveterre-de-Béarn's medieval drawbridge, Navarrenx and its *bastide* over the rushing Gave d'Oloron, and the Romanesque and Mudejar Ste-Croix church at Oloron-Ste-Marie provide stepping-stones into the limestone heights surrounding the 8,263-ft Pic d'Anie, the highest point in the Béarn.

East through the Aubisque Pass, at the Béarn's eastern limit, is the heart of the Hautes-Pyrénées, where France's highest Pyrenean peaks—Vignemale (10,820 ft) and Balaïtous (10,321 ft)—compete with some of the Pyrénées' most legendary natural treasures: the Cirque de Gavarnie, the world's most spectacular cirque (or natural amphitheater), is centered around a 1,400-ft waterfall. The nearby Brèche de Roland is a dramatic breach, or cleft, in the rock wall between France and Spain, while to the east, the Cirque de Troumouse is the largest of its kind in all the Pyrénées. When you get your fill of mountaintop vistas and Basque peaks, you can head to the regional spa towns and coastal cities refined enough to have once welcomed half the crowned heads of Europe. It was Empress Eugènie who gave Biarritz its coming-out party, changing it, in the era of Napoléon III, from a simple bourgeois town into an international favorite. Today you can still enjoy the Second Empire trimmings by winding down from sightseeing with a turn at the roulette table in the town's casino.

Pleasures and Pastimes

Basque Sports

Perhaps the best-known and most spectacular of Basque sports is the ancestral ball game of pelota, a descendant of the medieval *jeux de paume* (literally, palm games), a fundamental part of rural Basque culture. A Basque village without a fronton (backboard and pelota court) is as unimaginable as an American town without a baseball diamond. There are many versions and variations on this graceful and rapid sport, played with the bare hand, with wooden bats, or with curved basketlike gloves; a real wicker *chistera*—the wicker bat used in the game—is an interesting souvenir to buy (and makes a very pretty fruit basket, but let no Basque hear that bit of heresy). Other rural Basque sports include scything, wood-chopping and -sawing, sack hauling, stone lifting, long-distance racing, tug-of-war, whaleboat rowing competitions, and, for those who really want to take the weight of the world on their shoulders, *orga yoko*, or cart lifting—hefting and moving a 346-kilo (761-pound) hay wagon (you read it here).

Dining

Dining in this region is invariably a feast, whether it's on seafood or upland dishes ranging from beef to lamb to game birds such as the famous migratory *palombes* (wood pigeons). Dishes to keep in mind include *ttoro* (hake stew), *pipérade* (tomatoes and green peppers cooked in olive oil, and often scrambled eggs), *bakalao al pil-pil* (cod cooked in oil "*al pil-pil*"—at the precise temperature so that oil makes this bubbling noise as the fish creates its own sauce), *marmitako* (tuna and potato stew), and *zikiro* (roast lamb). Béarn is famous for its *garbure*, thick vegetable soup with *confit de canard* (preserved duck) and *fèves* (broad beans). *Civets* (stews) made with *isard* (wild goat) or wild boar are other specialties. La Bigorre and the Hautes-Pyrénées are equally dedicated to garbure, though they may call their version *soupe paysanne bigourdane* (Bigorran peasant soup) to distinguish it from that of their neighbors.

CATEGORY	COST*
$$$$	over €23
$$$	€15–€23
$$	€8–€14
$	under €8

**per person for a main course only, tax (19.6%) included; note that if a restaurant offers only prix-fixe (set-price) meals, it is given a price category that reflects prix-fixe price.*

Hiking

The Pyrénées are best explored on foot—and after a day of hiking along the gorges and into the mountains the hearty regional cuisine makes perfect sense. The lengthy GR (Grande Randonnée) 10, a trail marked by discreet red-and-white paint markings, runs all the way from the

Atlantic at Hendaye to Banyuls-sur-Mer on the Mediterranean, through villages and up and down mountains. Along the way are mountain refuges. The HRP (Haute Randonnée Pyrénéenne, or High Pyrenean Hike) stays closer to the border crest, following the terrain through both France and Spain, irrespective of national borders. Local trails are also well indicated, usually with blue or yellow markings. Some of the classic walks in the Basque Pyrénées include the Iparla Ridge walk between Bidarrai and St-Étienne-de-Baïgorry, the Santiago de Compostela Trail's dramatic St-Jean-Pied-de-Port to Roncesvalles walk over the Pyrénées, and the Holçarté Gorge walk between Larrau and Ste-Engrâce. Trail maps are available from local tourist offices.

Lodging

From palatial beachside splendor in Biarritz to simple mountain auberges in the Basque Country to Pyrenean refuges in the Hautes-Pyrénées, the gamut of lodging in southwest France is ample. For top value and camaraderie, look for *gîtes* or *tables d'hôtes* (rustic bed-and-breakfasts and way stations for hikers and skiers) where all guests dine together. Be sure to book summer lodging on the Basque coast well in advance, particularly for August. In the Hautes-Pyrénées only Gavarnie during its third-week-of-July music festival presents a potential booking problem. An even better approach is to make it up as you go along: the surprises are usually very pleasant. Assume all hotel rooms have air-conditioning, TV, telephones, and private bath unless otherwise noted.

CATEGORY	COST*
$$$$	over €123
$$$	€84–€123
$$	€46–€83
$	under €46

**All prices are for a standard double room, including tax (19.6%) and service charge.*

Exploring the Basque Country, Béarn, and Hautes-Pyrénées

Bayonne and Pau are the urban bookends for this southwest corner of France. But whether you approach from the Atlantic or the Mediterranean, you won't want to miss Gavarnie, Ste-Engrâce, St-Jean-Pied-de-Port, Sauveterre-de-Béarn, Ainhoa, or St-Jean-de-Luz. Trans-Pyrenean hikers (and drivers) generally prefer moving from west to east for a number of reasons, especially the excellent light of the late afternoon and evening during the prime months of May to October.

Great Itineraries

Consider Dax and Eugénie-les-Bains as excellent side trips to the basic itinerary outlined here. Begin in Bayonne, exploring the Basque coast, and then head east into the Atlantic Pyrénées. Explore the Béarn as carefully as time permits—Sauveterre-de-Béarn, Oloron-Ste-Marie, and Pau—before continuing on to La Bigorre, the Hautes-Pyrénées, and Gavarnie.

Numbers in the text correspond to numbers in the margin and on the Basque Country and the Hautes-Pyrénées maps.

IF YOU HAVE 3 DAYS

There is nothing leisurely about this three-day tour, nor is there time to do much walking, which is why it's recommended only if you have limited time and unlimited curiosity. Begin in **Bayonne** ①, spending a morning exploring the town. See the cathedral and the Bonnat Mu-

Basque Country and the Hautes-Pyrénées

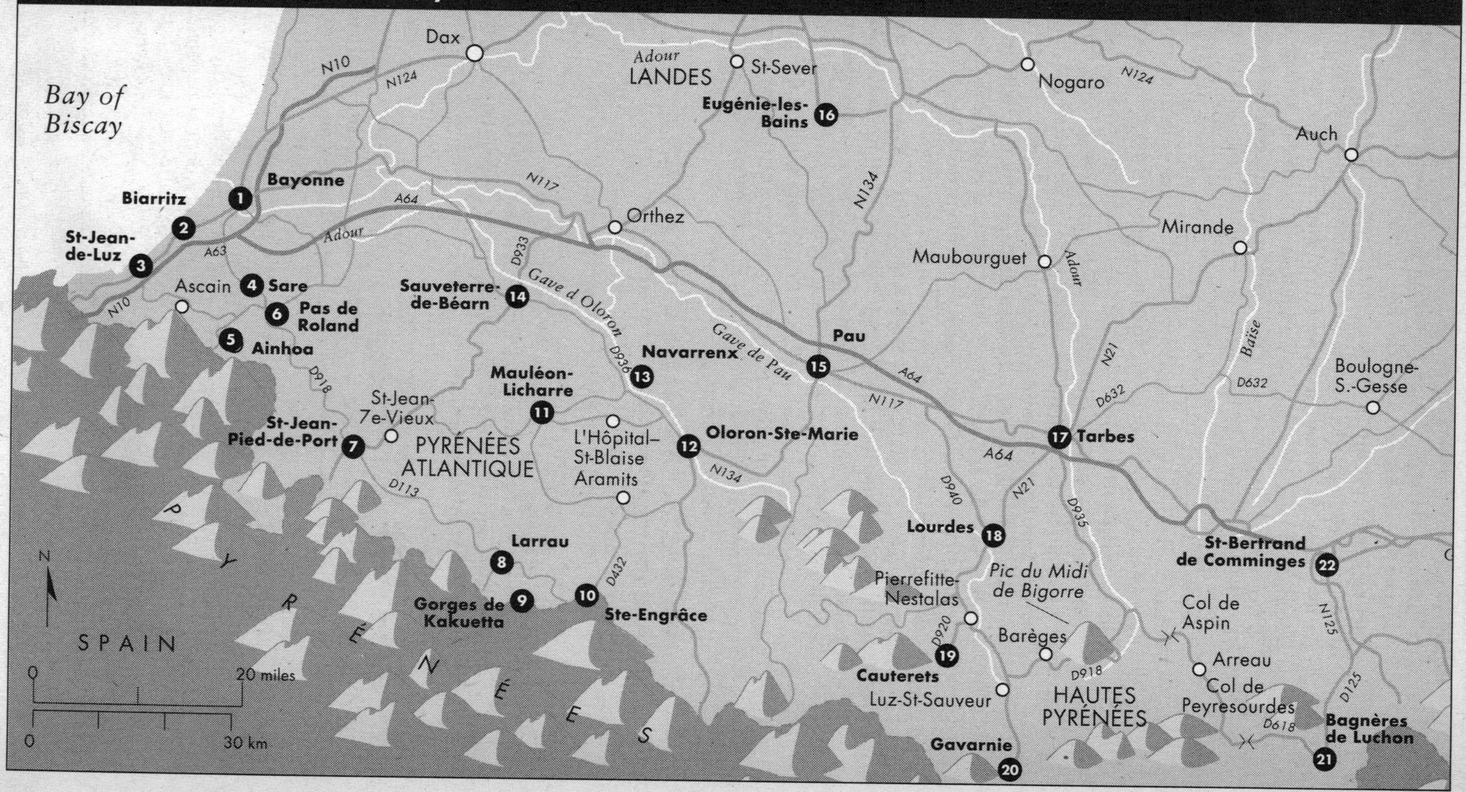

seum before hitting **Biarritz** ② in time for afternoon tea. Spend the night in **St-Jean-de-Luz** ③. On day two drive through **Sare** ④ and **Ainhoa** ⑤ and past **Pas de Roland** ⑥ on the way up the Nive River to **St-Jean-Pied-de-Port** ⑦ for lunch. Explore the Haute Soule during the afternoon: drive through the Irati Forest to **Larrau** ⑧ and **Ste-Engrâce** ⑩ on the way through **Oloron-Ste-Marie** ⑫ to **Pau** ⑮ for the night. On day three have a look around Pau, see **Lourdes** ⑱ at midday, and get up to **Gavarnie** ⑳ in time to see the sunset from the legendary Hôtel du Cirque et de la Cascade.

IF YOU HAVE 8 DAYS

Begin in **Bayonne** ①, spending a morning exploring the town. See the cathedral and the Bonnat Museum. The second day head back to the coast at **Biarritz** ② for some time at the beach. Spend the night in **St-Jean-de-Luz** ③. On day three climb La Rhune (or take the little train to the top) for a stunning view over the entire Basque coast. Drive through **Sare** ④ and **Ainhoa** ⑤ and past **Pas de Roland** ⑥ on the way up the Nive River to **St-Jean-Pied-de-Port** ⑦ for the night. Explore the town and the Haute Soule on your fourth morning: drive through the Irati Forest to **Larrau** ⑧ and do the Holçarté Gorges walk to **Ste-Engrâce** ⑩ if there is time; return to Larrau if not. On day five explore the lower Soule, **Oloron-Ste-Marie** ⑫, and **Pau** ⑮. On day six walk around Pau, tour the château, then head up to **Eugénie-les-Bains** ⑯ and the fabulous domains created by superstar restaurateur-hotelier Michel Guéard. After a day and night of blissful *luxe, calme, et volupté,* it will be time to check out your more spiritual side in **Lourdes** ⑱ on the seventh day. Then make the ascent to **Gavarnie** ⑳ in time to see the sun set from the Hôtel du Cirque et de la Cascade. On day eight explore the area around Gavarnie.

When to Tour the Basque Country, Béarn, and Hautes-Pyrénées

From early May through late October is the best time to explore this region. June and September are the height of the season. July is the only month you can be nearly 100% sure of being to able to, say, walk safely over the glacier to the Brèche de Roland. In winter, beach life is over and the Pyrénées are snowed in; many hotels and restaurants close. Only for skiing and the pleasure of the nearly total absence of tourists is the winter season recommended.

THE BASQUE COAST

The French Basque coast—a world of its own with its own language, sports, and folklore—occupies France's southwesternmost corner along the Spanish border. Inland, the area is laced with rivers: the Bidasoa River border with Spain marks the southern edge of the region, and the Adour River, on its northern edge, separates the Basque country from the neighboring Les Landes. The Nive River flows through the heart of the verdant Basque littoral to join the Adour at Bayonne, and the smaller Nivelle River flows into the Bay of Biscay at St-Jean-de-Luz. Bayonne, Biarritz, and St-Jean-de-Luz are the main towns along the coast, all less than 40 km (25 mi) from the first peak of the Pyrénées.

Bayonne

❶ *48 km (30 mi) southwest of Dax, 184 km (114 mi) south of Bordeaux, 295 km (183 mi) west of Toulouse.*

At the confluence of the Adour and Nive rivers, Bayonne, France's most Basque city, was in the 4th century a Roman fort, or *castrum,* and for 300 years (1151–1451) a British colony. Source of the name of the bayonet blade (from the French *baïonnette*), invented here in the 17th century, today's Bayonne is more famous for its ham (*jambon de Bayonne*) and for the annual Basque pelota world championships held in September. Even though the port is spread out along the Adour estuary some 5 km (3 mi) from the sea, the two rivers and five bridges lend this small gem of a city a definite maritime feel. The quai-front houses, the intimate place Pasteur, the Château-Vieux, the elegant 18th-century homes along rue des Prébendés, the 17th-century ramparts, and the cathedral are some of the town's not-to-be-missed sights. The **Cathédrale** (called both Ste-Marie and Notre-Dame) was built mainly in the 13th century, and is one of France's southernmost examples of Gothic architecture. Its 13th- to 14th-century cloisters are among its best features. The airy, modernized **Musée Bonnat,** in itself reason enough to visit Bayonne, has a notable treasury of 19th-century paintings collected by French portraitist and historical painter Léon Bonnat (1833–1922). ✉ *5 rue Jacques-Lafitte,* ☎ *05–59–59–08–52.* 🎫 *€3.* ⏲ *Wed.–Mon. 10–noon and 2:30–6:30.*

Dining and Lodging

$$$–$$$$ ★ ✕ **Auberge du Cheval Blanc.** This innovative Basque establishment in the Petit Bayonne quarter near the Bonnat Museum serves a combination of *cuisine du terroir* (home-style regional cooking) and original concoctions in contemporary surroundings. Jean-Claude Tellechea showcases fresh fish as well as upland specialties from the Basque hills, sometimes joining the two in ground-breaking dishes such as the *merlu rôti aux oignons et jus de volaille* (hake roasted in onions with essence of poultry). ✉ *68 rue Bourgneuf,* ☎ *05–59–59–01–33. MC, V. Closed Sun. dinner, Mon. except Aug., June 25–July 2, Feb. 10–Mar. 8.*

$$$ ✕🏨 **Le Grand Hôtel.** Just down the street from the Château-Vieux, this central spot has pleasant, comfortable rooms with an Old World feel. The restaurant, Les Carmes, built in a former Carmelite convent, is excellent. ✉ *21 rue Thiers, 64100,* ☎ *05–59–59–62–00,* FAX *05–59–59–62–01,* WEB *www.bw-legrandhotel.com. 54 rooms. Restaurant, bar, cable TV, minibars, parking (fee). AE, DC, MC, V.*

Biarritz

❷ *8 km (5 mi) south of Bayonne, 190 km (118 mi) southwest of Bordeaux, 50 km (31 mi) north of San Sebastián, 115 km (69 mi) west of Pau.*

Biarritz rose to prominence when rich and royal Carlist exiles from Spain set up shop here in 1838. Unable to visit San Sebastián on the Spanish coast, they sought a summer watering spot as close as possible to their old stamping ground. Among the exiles was Eugénie de Montijo, soon destined to become empress of France. Half the crowned heads of Europe slept in Eugénie's villa, now the Hótel du Palais. Whether you consider Napoléon III's bombastic architectural legacies an eyesore or part of the fun—they at least have the courage of their convictions. Biarritz no longer lays claim to the title "the resort of kings and the king of resorts"—but there is no shortage of deluxe hotel rooms or bow-tied gamblers ambling over to the casino. Yet the old, down-to-earth charm of the former fishing village still manages to counterbalance the Second Empire aura.

Although far from as drop-dead stylish as it once was, the town is making a comeback as a swank surfing capital with its new casino and convention center. The **beaches** attract crowds—particularly the fine, sandy beaches of **Grande Plage** and the neighboring **Plage Miramar,** both set amid craggy natural beauty. The narrow streets around the cozy 16th-century church of **St-Martin** are a delight to explore. The harbor of the **Port des Pêcheurs** (Fishing Port) provides a tantalizing glimpse of the Biarritz of old. A walk along the beach promenades gives a view of the foaming breakers that beat constantly upon the sands, giving the name *Côte d'Argent* (Silver Coast) to the length of this part of the French Basque coast.

Dining and Lodging

$$$–$$$$ ✕ **Les Platanes.** Chef-owner Arnaud Daguin specializes in adapting country recipes and giving them a personal touch. Be sure to try his foie gras, which he gets from Auch, his hometown in Gers. The decor of the restaurant, in an old Basque town house, is comfortably formal. ✉ *32 av. Beau-Soleil,* ☎ *05–59–23–13–68. AE, DC, MC, V. Closed Mon.–Tues. except July 14–Aug 21.*

$$$$ ★ ✕🏨 **Hôtel du Palais.** Set on the beach, this majestic redbrick hotel with an immense driveway, a colonnade, lawns, and a semicircular dining room, still exudes an opulent, aristocratic air, no doubt left by Empress Eugénie a century ago when she built it as her Biarritz palace. Napoléonic frippery is everywhere in the public areas, but don't go looking for it in the more standard guest rooms, none of which have sea views. Of the three restaurants—the Hippocampe (where lunch is served beside the curved pool above the Atlantic), the regal Grand Siècle, and the seaside La Rotonde—be sure to book at the latter for chef Jean-Marie Gautier's innovative wonders, such as lobster gazpacho. ✉ *1 av. de l'Impératrice, 64200,* ☎ *05–59–41–64–00,* FAX *05–59–41–67–99,* WEB *www.hotel-du-palais.com. 134 rooms, 22 suites. Restaurant, bar, cable TV, minibars, pool, parking (fee). AE, DC, MC, V. Closed 2 wks in winter, dates vary.*

$$$ ★ ✕🏨 **Café de Paris.** This hotel is known for its popular restaurants. One is an elegant (and expensive) spot featuring such dishes as *ris de veau* (veal sweetbreads) and fish served with an imaginative nouvelle touch. The other is a less formal brasserie (with the same chefs). The haute cuisine restaurant is closed for lunch, as well as for dinner on Sunday; the brasserie is always open. Rooms are luxurious and many have ocean views. ✉ *5 pl. Bellevue, 64200,* ☎ *05–59–24–19–53,* FAX *05–59–24–18–20,* WEB *www.cafedeparis-biarritz.com. 18 rooms. Restaurant, bar, cable TV, minibars, pool, parking. AE, DC, MC, V. Closed mid-Nov.–mid-Mar.*

$$–$$$ ✕🏨 **Windsor.** This hotel, built in the 1920s, is close to the casino and the beach. Rooms are modern and cozy; those with sea views cost about twice as much as the ones facing the inner courtyard and street. The restaurant serves up a fine terrine de foie gras with Armagnac, and ravioli stuffed with crab. ✉ *19 bd. du Général-de-Gaulle, 64200,* ☎ *05–59–24–08–52,* FAX *05–59–24–98–90. 49 rooms. Restaurant, bar, no air-conditioning, parking (fee). AE, MC, V. Closed Jan.–mid-Mar.*

$$ 🏨 **Romance.** This tiny, early 19th-century villa on a quiet alley near the Hippodrome des Fleurs race track is an intimate refuge just ten minutes from downtown Biarritz. Madame Subra takes patient care of everyone here, while the minuscule garden is a dappled oasis of peace in the midsummer Biarritz maelstrom. Quarters are tight but homey. ✉ *6 allée des Acacias, 64200,* ☎ *05–59–41–25–65,* FAX *05–59–41–25–65. 10 rooms. No air-conditioning. AE, MC, V. Closed mid-Jan.–Mar. 1.*

$ 🏨 **Hotel Palym.** This excellent budget choice is stationed over a restaurant with a terrace five minutes from the Plage du Port-Vieux. Rooms range from low end without bath to slightly more expensive with complete in-room bath facilities. The restaurant serves all-you-can-eat paellas in summer, as well as acceptable prix-fixe menus and à la carte selections. ✉ *7 rue du Port-Vieux, 64200,* ☎ *05–59–24–16–56,* FAX *05–59–24–96–12,* WEB *www.palmarium.com. 28 rooms. Restaurant, bar, no air-conditioning, cable TV. AE, MC, V. Closed Jan.–mid-Mar.*

Nightlife and the Arts

At the **Casino de Biarritz** (✉ 1 av. Edouard-VII, ☎ 05–59–22–77–77) you can play the slots or blackjack, or go dancing at the Flamingo. **Le Queen's Bar** (✉ 25 pl. Clemenceau, ☎ 05–59–24–70–65) is a comfortable hangout both day and night. To keep your connections in cyberspace, **Internet & Café** (✉ 5 rue Jauerry, ☎ 05–59–24–03–31), behind the post office, provides the link.

Outdoor Activities and Sports

Désertours Aventure (✉ 65 av. Maréchal-Juin, ☎ 05–59–41–22–02) organizes rafting trips on the Nive River and four-wheel-drive vehicle tours through the Atlantic Pyrénées. **Golf de Biarritz** (✉ 2 av. Edith-Cavell, ☎ 05–59–03–71–80) has an 18-hole, par-69 course. **Pelote Basque: Biarritz Athletic-club** (✉ Parc des Sports d'Aguilera, ☎ 05–59–23–91–09) offers instruction in every type of Basque pelota including *main nue* (barehanded), *pala* (paddle), *chistera* (with a basketlike racket), and *cesta punta* (another game played with the same curved basket). On Wednesday and Saturday at 9 PM in July, August, and September, you can watch pelota games at the **Parc des Sports d'Aguilera** (☎ 05–59–23–91–09).

St-Jean-de-Luz

★ ❸ *23 km (16 mi) southwest of Bayonne, 24 km (18 mi) northeast of San Sebastián, 54 km (32 mi) west of St-Jean-Pied-de-Port, 128 km (77 mi) west of Pau.*

Along the coast between Biarritz and the Spanish border, St-Jean-de-Luz is memorable for its colorful harbor (scenes of which grace the celebrated New York City restaurant La Côte Basque), old streets, a curious church, and an elegant beach. The tree-lined **place Louis-XIV,** alongside the Hôtel de Ville (Town Hall), with its narrow courtyard and dainty statue of Louis XIV on horseback, is the hub of the town. Take a tour of the twin-towered **Maison Louis-XIV.** ✉ *Place Louis XIV,* ☎ *05–59–26–01–56.* 🎫 *€6.* ⏲ *July–Aug., 10–10; Apr.–Oct., daily 10:30–noon and 2–6:30; Nov.–Mar., by appointment.*

The church of **St-Jean-Baptiste** (✉ Pl. des Corsaires) has unusual wooden galleries lining the walls, creating a theaterlike effect.

Of particular note is the **Maison de l'Infante** (Princess's House), between the harbor and the bay, where Maria Teresa of Spain stayed prior to her wedding to the Sun King. The foursquare mansion now houses the **Musée Grévin,** which contains wax figures and period costumes. ✉ *Quai de l'Infante,* ☎ *05–59–51–24–88.* 🎫 *€6.* ⏲ *July–Aug., daily 10–10; Apr.–Oct., daily 10:30–noon and 2–6:30; Nov.–Mar., by appointment.*

Dining and Lodging

$$ ✕ **Chez Dominique.** A walk around the picturesque fishing port to the Ciboure side of the harbor will let you see the local side of St-Jean-de-Luz. The simple, home-style menu here is based on what the fishing fleet caught that morning; try the *marmitako,* a hearty fisherman's tuna stew. The views over the port are the best available. ✉ *15 quai M. Ravel,* ☎ *05–59–47–29–16. No credit cards. Closed Feb., Sun. dinner, Mon. except mid-June–end of Aug.*

$$ ✕ **La Taverne Basque.** This well-known midtown standard is one of the old faithful local dining emporiums, specializing in Basque cuisine with a definite maritime emphasis. Try the *ttoro* (a rich fish, crustacean, potato, and vegetable soup). ✉ *5 rue République,* ☎ *05–59–26–01–26. AE, DC, MC, V. Closed Mon.–Tues. except July–Aug.; month of Mar.*

$$ ✕ **Txalupa.** The name is Basque for "skiff" or "small boat," and you'll feel like you're in one when you're this close to the bay—yachts and fishing vessels go about their business just a few yards away. This well-known haunt with a terrace over the port serves the famous *jambon de Bayonne* (Bayonne ham) in vinegar and garlic sauce, as well as fresh fish and natural produce such as wild mushrooms. ✉ *Pl. Louis-XIV,* ☎ *05–59–51–85–52. AE, DC, MC, V.*

$ ✕ **Chez Pablo.** The simple, home-style menu is based on what the fishing fleet brought in early in the day; try the *marmitako,* a hearty fisherman's tuna stew. Long tables covered with red-and-white tablecloths, benches, and plaster walls make for a casual meal. ✉ *Rue Mme. Etxeto,* ☎ *05–56–26–37–81. No credit cards. Closed Sun.*

$$$$ **Le Grand Hôtel.** Completely overhauled and refitted in 2001, the Grand Hôtel has resumed its longstanding place as St-Jean-de-Luz's top hotel. Don't miss a meal at Le Rosewood, its top-rated restaurant overlooking the beach. The rooms are decorated in colorful pastels, wood, and marble, while the unbeatable location at the northern end of the St-Jean-de-Luz beach will make you feel like the Sun King himself. ✉ *43 bd. Thiers, 64500,* ☎ *05–59–26–35–36,* FAX *05–59–51–99–84,* WEB *www.luzgrandhotel.fr. 48 rooms, 2 suites, 2 apartments. Restaurant, bar, cable TV, minibars, pool. AE, DC, MC, V. Closed Dec.–early Apr.*

THE ATLANTIC PYRÉNÉES

The Atlantic Pyrénées extend eastward from the Atlantic to the Col du Pourtalet, and encompass Béarn and the mountainous part of the Basque Country. Watching the Pyrénées grow from rolling green foothills in the west to jagged limestone peaks to glacier-studded granite massifs in the Hautes-Pyrénées is an exciting process. The Atlantic Pyrénées' first major height is at La Rhune (2,969 ft), known as the Balcon du Côte Basque (Balcony of the Basque Coast). The highest Basque peak is at Orhi (6,617 ft); the Béarn's highest is Pic d'Anie (8,510 ft). Not until Balaïtous (10,381 ft) and Vignemale (10,820 ft), in the Hautes-Pyrénées, does the altitude surpass the 10,000-ft mark. Starting east from St-Jean-de-Luz up the Nivelle River, a series of picturesque villages that includes Ascain, Sare, Ainhoa, and Bidarrai leads up to St-Jean-Pied-de-Port and the Pyrénées.

This journey ends in Pau, far from the Pays Basque and set in the Béarn, akin in temperament to the larger region of which it is an enclave, Gascony. Gascony is purse-poor but certainly rich in scenery and lore. Its proud and touchy temperament is typified in literature by the character d'Artagnan in Dumas's *Three Musketeers* and in history by the lords of the château of Pau. An inscription over its entrance, TOUCHEZ-Y, SI TU L'OSES—"Touch this if you dare"—was that of Gaston Phoebus, a golden-haired and volatile count of Foix. An arts lover, he also had a hasty temper, which led him to murder his own brother and his only son.

Sare

❹ *14 km (8 mi) southeast of St-Jean-de-Luz, 9 km (5½ mi) southwest of Ainhoa on D118: take the first left.*

The gemlike village of Sare is built around a large fronton, or backboard, where a permanent pelota game rages around the clock. Not surprisingly, the Hôtel de Ville (town hall) offers a permanent exhibition on Pelote Basque (open July–August, daily 9–1 and 2–6:30; September–June, daily 3–6). Sare was a busy smuggling hub throughout the 19th century. Its chief attractions are colorful wood-beam and whitewashed Basque architecture, the 16th-century late-Romanesque church with its lovely triple-decker interior, and the **Ospitale Zaharra** pilgrim's hospice behind the church. More than a dozen tiny chapels sprinkled around Sare were built as ex-votos by seamen who survived Atlantic storms. Up the Sare Valley are the panoramic Col de Lizarrieta and the **Grottes de Sare,** where you can study up on Basque culture and history at a **Musée Ethnographique** (Ethnographical Museum) and take a guided tour (in five languages) for 1 km (½ mi) underground and see a son-et-lumière show. ☎ *05–59–54–21–88.* €5. *Mid-Feb.–Dec., Tues.–Sun. 11–7.*

West of Sare on D4, at the Col de St-Ignace, take the **Petit Train de la Rhune,** a tiny wood-paneled cogwheel train that reaches the less-than-dizzying speed of 5 mph while climbing up La Rhune peak. The views of the Bay of Biscay, the Pyrénées, and the grassy hills of the Basque farmland are wonderful. ☎ *05–59–54–20–26.* €7. *Round-trip (1 hr): Easter vacation and May–June, daily 10 and 3; July–Sept., daily every 35 mins.*

Dining and Lodging

$$ **Baratxartea.** This little inn 1 km (½ mi) from the center of Sare in one of the town's prettiest and most ancient *quartiers* is a find. Monsieur Fagoaga's family-run hotel and restaurant occupy a 16th-century town house complete with *colombiers* (pigeon roosts), and are surrounded by some of the finest rural Basque architecture in Labourd. ✉ *Quartier Ihalar, 64310 Itxassou,* ☎ *05–59–54–20–48,* FAX *05–59–47–50–84. 15 rooms. Restaurant, no air-conditioning, cable TV, no pets. AE, DC, MC, V. Closed Jan.–mid-Mar.*

Ainhoa

5 *9 km (5½ mi) east of Sare, 23 km (14 mi) southeast of St-Jean-de-Luz, 31 km (19 mi) northwest of St-Jean-Pied-de-Port.*

The Basque village of Ainhoa is officially registered among the villages selected by the national tourist ministry as the prettiest in France. The streets are lined with one lovely 16th- to 18th-century house after another, complete with whitewashed walls, flower-filled balconies, brightly painted shutters, and carved master beams. The church of **Notre-Dame de l'Assomption** has a traditional Basque three-tier wooden interior with carved railings and ancient oak stairs.

Dining and Lodging

$$$ ★ **Ithurria.** This is a registered historic monument, once a staging post on the fabled medieval pilgrims' route to Santiago de Compostela. If you are doing a modern version of the pilgrims' journey or just need a stopover on the way deeper into the mountains, the Ithurria—set in a 17th-century building in the prevailing Basque style and surrounded by a garden—will give you a fine atmospheric night. The rustic dining room is the gemstone here, with fare to match, combining inland game and fresh seafood from the Basque coast in creative ways. Guest rooms are modern and all are comfortable and done with impeccable taste. ✉ *Rue Principale, 64250,* ☎ *05–59–29–92–11,* FAX *05–59–29–81–28,* WEB *www.ithuria.com. 27 rooms. Restaurant, bar, no air-conditioning, minibars, pool, gym. AE, DC, MC, V. Closed Nov.–Apr. 1, Wed. except July–Aug.*

$–$$ **Oppoca.** This 17th-century *relais* or stagecoach relay station on Ainhoa's main square and pelota court is one of the prettiest typical Basque houses in one of France's prettiest towns. Rooms are small but adequate and the owners are a jolly group, always ready to share their local knowledge. ✉ *Place du Fronton, s/n, 64250,* ☎ *05–59–29–90–*

72, FAX 05–59–29–81–03. 12 rooms. Restaurant, bar, no air-conditioning, minibars. AE, DC, MC, V. Closed Dec.–Jan.

Pas de Roland

6 *15 km (9 mi) east of Ainhoa, 30 km (18 mi) northwest of St-Jean-Pied-de-Port; follow signs for Itxassou and proceed past the town up to the pass.*

Legend has it that the Pas de Roland (Roland's Footprint) was where the legendary medieval French hero Roland enabled Charlemagne's troops to pass by cutting a passageway through an impeding boulder with his mystical sword, Durandal. In the process he purportedly left his footprint in the rock, where the "evidence" remains to this day. The drive along this bend in the Nive River is a scenic detour off the D918 road up to St-Jean-Pied-de-Port.

Dining and Lodging

$–$$ **Hôtel du Pas du Roland.** Just upstream from the Pas de Roland, this rustic little inn is a good place for a meal or a night. Native trout are available from the nearby Nive River if you're skillful enough to capture one; otherwise, try the *pipérade basquaise au jambon* (an egg dish with tomatoes, green peppers, onions, and ham). Rooms are simple but clean and cozy. *Laxîa, 64250 Itxassou, 05–59–29–75–23, FAX 05–59–29–85–86. 9 rooms with showers and sinks, toilet in hall. Restaurant, bar, no air-conditioning, cable TV, parking. AE, DC, MC, V. Closed Dec.–Mar.*

St-Jean-Pied-de-Port

7 *54 km (33 mi) east of Biarritz, 46 km (28 mi) west of Larrau.*

St-Jean-Pied-de-Port, a fortified town on the Nive River, got its name from its position at the foot (*pied*) of the *port* (mountain pass) of Roncevaux (Roncesvalles). The pass was the setting for *La Chanson de Roland* (*The Song of Roland*), the 11th-century epic poem considered the true beginning of French literature. The bustling town center, a major stop for pilgrims en route to Santiago de Compostela, seems, after a tour through the Soule, like a frenzied metropolitan center—even in winter. In summer, especially around the time of Pamplona's San Fermin blowout (the running of the bulls, July 7–14), the place is filled to the gills and is somewhere between exciting and unbearable.

Walk into the old section through the Porte de France, just behind and to the left of the tourist office, climb the steps on the left up to the walkway circling the ramparts, and walk around to the stone stairway down to the rue de l'Église. The church of **Notre-Dame-du-Bout-du-Pont** (Our Lady of the End of the Bridge), known for its magnificent doorway, is at the bottom of this cobbled street. The church is a characteristically Basque three-tier structure, designed for women to sit on the ground floor, men to be in the first balcony, and the choir in the loft above. From the **Pont Notre-Dame** (Notre-Dame Bridge) you can watch the wild trout in the Nive (also an Atlantic salmon stream) as they sip mayflies off the surface. Note that fishing is *défendu* (forbidden) in town. Upstream, along the left bank, is another wooden bridge. Cross it and then walk around and back through town, crossing back to the left bank on the main road.

The **Relais de la Nive** bar and café—hanging over the river at the north end of the bridge in the center of town—is the perfect spot to have a coffee while admiring the reflection of the pont de Notre-Dame upstream and watching the trout working in the current.

On **rue de la Citadelle** are a number of sights of interest: the **Maison Arcanzola** (Arcanzola House), at No. 32 (1510); the **Maison des Évêques** (Bishops' House), at No. 39; and the famous **Prison des Évêques** (Bishops' Prison), next door to it. Continue up along rue de la Citadelle to get to the **Citadelle,** a classic Vauban fortress, now occupied by a school. The views from the Citadelle, complete with maps identifying the surrounding heights and valleys, are panoramic.

Dining and Lodging

$$–$$$ ✕ **Chez Arbillaga.** Tucked inside the citadel ramparts, this lively bistro is a sound choice for lunch or dinner. The food represents what the Basques do best: simple cooking of excellent quality, such as *agneau de lait à la broche* (roast lamb), in winter, or *coquilles St-Jacques au lard fumé* (scallops with bacon), in summer. ✉ *8 rue de l'Église,* ☎ *05–59–37–06–44. MC, V. Closed 1st 2 wks of June and Oct. and Wed. Jan.–May.*

$$$–$$$$ ★ ✕🏨 **Les Pyrénées.** This inn has the best restaurant in town, specializing in nouvelle Basque cuisine such as ravioli and prawns with caviar sauce and hot wild-mushroom terrine. Rooms are modern and vary in size; four have balconies. ✉ *19 pl. Charles de Gaulle, 64220,* ☎ *05–59–37–01–01,* FAX *05–59–37–18–97,* WEB *www.relais-chateaux.com/pyrenees. 18 rooms, 2 apartments. Restaurant, bar, cable TV, minibars, pool. AE, DC, MC, V. Closed last 3 wks Jan. and late Nov.–late Dec.*

$$ ✕🏨 **Central Hôtel.** Get the best quality for price in town at this family-run hotel and restaurant over the Nive, where trout could be literally (though illegally) caught from certain rooms. The wonderfully musical 200-year-old oak staircase is another memorable detail. The owners speak Basque, Spanish, French, English, and some German, so communicating is rarely a problem. The cuisine is superb, especially the lamb and *magret de canard* (duck breast). ✉ *1 pl. Charles de Gaulle, 64220,* ☎ *05–59–37–00–22,* FAX *05–59–37–27–79. 14 rooms. Restaurant, no air-conditioning, cable TV, no pets. AE, DC, MC, V. Closed mid-Dec.–early Mar.*

Larrau

❽ *46 km (28 mi) east of St-Jean-Pied-de-Port, 20 km (12 mi) west of Ste-Engrâce, 42 km (26 mi) southwest of Oloron-Ste-Marie.*

Larrau is a cozy way station on the road over the pass into Spain. The town has several hotels of distinction and a number of extraordinarily ancient, rustic mountain houses. Once known for its 19th-century forges, Larrau is now a winter base camp for hunters and a summer center for hikers. It's a good departure point for the **Holçarté Gorges walk.** This classic trek is a 90-minute round-trip hike, including a spectacular bridge that hangs 561 ft above the rocky stream bed. The full tour looping back around to the Logibar is a four-hour walk, while the hike over to Ste-Engrâce is a seven-hour trip each way, a good two-day project over and back. The well-marked trail begins at the Logibar Inn, 3 km (2 mi) east of Larrau.

Dining and Lodging

$$–$$$ ★ ✕🏨 **Hôtel Etxemaïté.** This sophisticated country inn has spectacular views and is one of the area's top dining spots (closed Monday and no dinner Sunday from mid-November to mid-May). The dining room seems suspended over the garden and often fills up in summer. The inn is well furnished with Basque antiques, including several unusual *susulia* chair-and-table combinations. The Basque cooking is excellent: terrine *de poule au foie gras* (hen with duck liver) is just one good choice. Rooms are done in light woods and cheery colors. ✉ *Rte. D26, 64560 Larrau,* ☎ *05–59–28–61–45,* FAX *05–59–28–72–71. 16 rooms. Restaurant,*

bar, air-conditioning, cable TV, park. AE, DC, MC, V. Closed mid–late Jan., Sun. night, Mon. Sept. 15–June 15.

$ ✕🏨 **Logibar.** This simple inn with a *gîte d'étape* (way station) for hikers serves nonpareil garbure and an even better *omelette aux cèpes* (wild mushroom omelet). Rooms are tiny but cozy, and the Quihilliry family, in its fourth generation running this well-known spot, has a knack for making you feel at home. ✉ *Rte. D26, 64560 Larrau,* ☎ *05–59–28–61–14,* FAX *05–59–28–61–14. 12 rooms. Restaurant, bar, no air-conditioning. MC, V. Closed early Dec.–early Mar.*

Gorges de Kakuetta

❾ *13 km (8 mi) east of Larrau, 3 km (2 mi) west of Ste-Engrâce.*

A right turn onto D113 at the confluence of the Uhaitxa and Larrau rivers will take you toward Ste-Engrâce and past one of the area's great natural phenomena, the Gorges de Kakuetta (the Basque spelling). A famous canyon cut through the limestone cliffs by the Uhaitxa River, the gorge is at times as narrow as 12 ft across while reaching depths of more than 1,155 ft. Stairways are cut into the rock, and hanging bridges span the watercourse. A waterfall and a grotto mark the end of the climb, a two-hour walk round-trip. This hike is recommended only during low-water conditions, normally between June and October. Good hiking shoes are indispensable. ☎ *05–59–28–73–44.* 🎫 *€4.* ⏲ *Mid-Mar.–mid-Nov., daily 8 AM–dark.*

Ste-Engrâce

❿ *66 km (40 mi) east of St-Jean-Pied-de-Port, 37 km (23 mi) southwest of Oloron-Ste-Marie, 100 km (62 mi) southwest of Pau.*

Ste-Engrâce is at the eastern edge of the Basque Country in the Haute Soule (Upper Soule). Soule is the smallest of the three French Basque provinces. Nearly all the inhabitants speak Euskera (Basque), a non-Indo-European language of uncertain (though probably native Pyrenean and Iberian) origins.

Medieval pilgrims on the way to Santiago de Compostela in northwest Spain once flocked to the village's lovely 11th-century church of **Ste-Engrâce** to venerate the arm of Sancta Gracia, a young Portuguese noblewoman martyred around the year 300. When pillaging Calvinists removed the cherished relic in 1569, a ring finger was sent from the scene of her martyrdom in Zaragoza to replace the stolen arm. The church has an asymmetrical, slanting roof, typical of the *maison Basque* (Basque house) design. Its gray stone contrasts eerily with the green hills and fields behind. The ornate interior is a surprising contrast to the church's stark exterior. The town remains a key crossroads for pilgrims traveling to Santiago and trans-Pyrenean trekkers going east across the "dragon's back," as generations of Pyreneists have respectfully dubbed the mountain range's jagged profile.

Lodging

$ 🏨 **Auberge Elichalt.** This cozy *gîte d'étape* (hikers' way station) and table d'hôte (bed and breakfast) has 50 beds in varying situations. There are double rooms, dormitory beds, and an apartment for rent, all in the shadow of the church. Monsieur and Madame Burguburu (Euskera for "head of town") can recommend hikes into the mountains. ✉ *64560 Ste-Engrâce,* ☎ *05–59–28–61–63,* FAX *05–59–28–75–54. 5 double rooms, 1 apartment for 5, 40 dormitory beds without bath. MC, V.*

Outdoor Activities and Sports

The nearby ski station, 10 km (6 mi) away in **Pierre-St-Martin,** has Alpine and Nordic skiing. If you're interested in fly-fishing, the **Gave d'Oloron** (*gave* is the word for river in the language of the Béarn), flowing through Sauveterre-de-Béarn, is a trout and Atlantic salmon fishery. On D919 between Aramits and Oloron-Ste-Marie, look for the Vert River and the nearby town of **Féas.** The gently flowing Vert is well populated with trout.

En Route The **Basse Soule** (Lower Soule), also known as the Barétous region, is a transition zone between the Basque Country and Béarn characterized by rolling green hills and cornfields. To explore the Basse Soule, take D132 from Pierre-St-Martin down to Arette. Drive the loop beginning west toward the hometown of the legendary Aramis of The Three Musketeers at **Aramits,** continuing through **Lannes, Trois-Villes, and Gotein,** with its characteristic *clocher-calvaire,* a three-peaked bell tower designed as an evocation of Calvary. Just short of Mauléon-Licharre on D918 is the rustic 11th-century **Chapelle St-Jean-de-Berraute,** built by the Order of Malta for pilgrims heading to Santiago de Compostela.

Mauléon-Licharre

⓫ *16 km (10 mi) southwest of Navarrenx, 40 km (24 mi) northeast of St-Jean-Pied-de-Port.*

Mauléon-Licharre, capital of the Soule, is the upland Basque Country's only industrial city, manufacturing rope-soled espadrilles. Spread along the banks of the Saison River, the 16th-century **Hôtel de Maytie** (also known as the Château d'Andurain), the 17th-century **Hôtel de Montréal,** and the remains of the 12th-century **château fort** fortress are the main spots to seek out.

Dining and Lodging

$$ ✕🏨 **Bidegain.** This classic 18th-century Basque town house is filled with heavy oak beams and creaky wooden stairs and floorboards. Just off the trout-filled Gave du Saison, this onetime stagecoach and pony-express relay station serves excellent Basque country cooking in a four-course, prix-fixe *formule* with a choice of four desserts. The shady garden out back is a cool and quiet summer retreat. ✉ *13 rue de Navarre, 64560 Mauléon-Licharre,* ☎ *05–59–28–16–05,* FAX *05–59–19–10–26,* WEB *www.bidegainhotel.fr. 20 rooms. Restaurant, no air-conditioning, cable TV. AE, DC, MC, V. Closed mid–late Jan., Sun. night, Mon. mid-Sept.–mid-June.*

Dining and Lodging

En Route From L'Hôpital-St-Blaise, a right on D936 will take you into Oloron-Ste-Marie. A left on D936 will take you to **Navarrenx** and **Sauveterre-de-Beárn,** both of them spectacular towns in the Soule region.

Oloron-Ste-Marie

⓬ *33 km (20½ mi) southwest of Pau on N134.*

Oloron-Ste-Marie straddles the confluence of two rivers, the Gave d'Aspe and the Gave d'Ossau. Trout and even the occasional Atlantic salmon can (with luck) be spotted when the sun is out. Originally an Iberian and later a Roman military outpost, the town was made a stronghold by the viscounts of Béarn in the 11th century.

The **Quartier Ste-Croix** occupies the once fortified point between the two rivers and is the most interesting part of town. The fortresslike church of Ste-Croix, with its Moorish-influenced cupola inspired by the mosque at Cordoba; the two Renaissance buildings nearby; and the 14th-century **Tour Grède** (Grède Tower) are the main attractions. A walk around the **Promenade Bellevue** along the ramparts below the west side of the church will give you a view down the Aspe Valley and into the mountains behind.

The 12th- and 13th-century **Église Ste-Marie,** in the **bourg de Ste-Marie** across the river on the left bank of the Gave d'Aspe, is famous for its surprisingly well-preserved Romanesque doorway of Pyrenean marble.

Dining and Lodging

$–$$ ✕ **Le Biscondau.** Come here to sample some of the finest garbure, the hearty peasant vegetable soup, in Oloron. The view over the Gave d'Ossau is at its best from the terrace in summer. ✉ *7 rue de la Filature,* ☎ *05–59–39–06–15. DC, MC, V. Closed Mon.*

$$–$$$ ✕🏨 **Alysson.** This modern building in the middle of town is a safe and sound, if charmless, place to spend a night in Oloron-Ste-Marie. The rooms are small but newly furnished and equipped. The restaurant serves excellent *garbures* (mountain soup with beans, vegetables, and duck confit) and *piperades* (red peppers, tomatoes, and eggs sautéed in goose fat and served with fatback or bacon). ✉ *Bd. Pyrénées, 64400,* ☎ *05–59–39–70–70,* FAX *05–59–39–24–47. 34 rooms. Restaurant, no air-conditioning, cable TV, garden, pool. AE, DC, MC, V.*

$ 🏨 **Chambre d'Hôtes Paris.** This bed-and-breakfast in Féas, run by Christian and Marie-France Paris, is a great deal, especially if you like fly-fishing. Christian, a registered guide, knows every trout in the Barétous by name. ✉ *64570 Féas (7½ km/5 mi past Oloron-Ste-Marie),* ☎ *05–59–39–01–10,* WEB *www.bwo.fr/destination-mouche/cparis. 3 rooms. No air-conditioning. No credit cards. Closed late Dec.–early Jan.*

Navarrenx

⓭ *19 km (11 mi) northwest of Oloron-Ste-Marie.*

Perched over the Gave d'Oloron, Navarrenx was built in 1316 as a *bastide* (fortified town) at an important crossroads on the Santiago de Compostela pilgrimage route. Henri d'Albret, king of Navarre, constructed the present ramparts in 1540. The bastion of Porte St-Antoine, with its miniature turret, is one of the Soule's best-known sights. The town motto, *Si You Ti Baou* (Béarnais for "If I should see you"), refers to the cannon guarding the approach to the town across the bridge. The Gave d'Oloron is an excellent trout and salmon river. Salmon angling is an important part of Navarrenx tradition: Every year a salmon-fishing championship takes place, during which spectators line the banks of the legendary salmon pool about 300 yards upstream from the bridge.

Dining and Lodging

$$ ✕🏨 **Hôtel du Commerce.** As the best restaurant and most traditional lodging in Navarrenx, the Commerce is an easy choice. Rooms are old-fashioned and cozy and have renovated, spacious bathrooms. The exquisite menu spotlights such items as *pigeonneau au style bécasse* (woodcock-style squab served up in a fragrant Madeira sauce), or *foie gras frais au myrtille* (fresh duck liver in a berry sauce). ✉ *Pl. des Casernes, 64190,* ☎ *05–59–66–50–16,* FAX *05–59–66–52–67,* WEB *www.hotel-commmerce.fr. 28 rooms. Restaurant, bar, no air-conditioning, cable TV. AE, DC, MC, V.*

Sauveterre-de-Béarn

14 *19 km (11 mi) northwest of Navarrenx, 39 km (23 mi) northwest of Oloron-Ste-Marie, 39 km (23 mi) northeast of St-Jean-Pied-de-Port.*

Make your first stop the terrace next to the church: the view from here takes in the Gave d'Oloron, the fortified 12th-century drawbridge, the lovely Montréal Tower, and the Pyrénées rising in the distance, and is among the finest in the region. The bridge, known both as the **Vieux Pont** (Old Bridge) and the Pont de la Légende (Bridge of the Legend), was named after the legend of Sancie, widow of Gaston V de Béarn. Accused of murdering a child after her husband's death in 1170, Sancie was subjected to the "Judgment of God" and thrown, bound hand and foot, from the bridge by order of her brother, the king of Navarre. When the river carried her safely to the bank, she was deemed exonerated of all charges.

Dining and Lodging

$$–$$$ ✕🏨 **Hôtel du Vieux Pont.** Former British journalists Paul and Sandie Williams have beautifully restored this medieval manor house built into the town's fortified 12th-century drawbridge. The views over the river and up to the ramparts of Sauveterre are superb. Rooms range from cozy and comfortable to grand and baronial (ask for the one in the corner, which has two views of the river and an immense bathroom). ✉ *Rue du Pont de la Légende, 64390 Sauveterre-de-Béarn,* ☎ *05–59–38–95–11,* FAX *05–59–38–99–10,* WEB *www.123voyage.com. 7 rooms. Restaurant, bar, no air-conditioning. AE, DC, MC, V.*

Pau

15 *106 km (63 mi) east of Bayonne and Biarritz.*

The busy and elegant town of Pau is the historic capital of Béarn, a state annexed to France in 1620. Pau was "discovered" in 1815 by British officers returning from the Peninsular War in Spain, and it soon became a prominent winter resort town. Fifty years later English-speaking inhabitants made up one-third of Pau's population. They started the Pont-Long Steeplechase, still one of the most challenging in Europe, in 1841; created France's first golf course here in 1856; and introduced fox hunting to the region.

Pau's regal past is commemorated at its **château,** begun in the 14th century by Gaston Phoebus, the flamboyant count of Béarn. The building was transformed into a Renaissance palace in the 16th century by Marguerite d'Angoulême, sister of François I. A woman of diverse gifts, her pastorales were performed in the château's sumptuous gardens. Her bawdy *Heptameron*—written at age 60—furnishes as much sly merriment today as it did when read by her doting kingly brother. Marguerite's grandson, the future king of France Henri IV, was born in the château in 1553. Exhibits connected to Henri's life and times are displayed regularly, along with portraits of the most significant of his alleged 57 lovers and mistresses. His cradle, a giant turtle shell, is on exhibit in his bedroom, one of the sumptuous, tapestry-lined royal apartments. ✉ *Rue du Château,* ☎ *05–59–82–38–00.* 🎫 *€5, Sun. €3.* ⏲ *Apr.–Oct., daily 9:30–11:30 and 2–5:45; Nov.–Mar., daily 9:30–11:30 and 2–4:30.*

The **Musée Béarnais,** on the fourth floor of the château, gives an overview of the region, encompassing everything from fauna to furniture to festival costumes. ☎ *05–59–27–07–36.* 🎫 *€2.* ⏲ *Apr.–Oct., daily 9:30–12:30 and 2:30–6:30; Nov.–Mar., daily 9:30–12:30 and 2:30–5:30.*

Dining and Lodging

$$–$$$ ✕ **Gousse d'Ail.** In the Hédas district, the deep mid-city canyon in the oldest part of Pau, this lovely hideaway is tucked under the stairway at the end of the street. Traditional Béarn cooking and international cuisine are served; try the magret de canard cooked over coals. ✉ *12 rue du Hédas,* ☎ *05–59–27–31–55,* FAX *05–59–06–10–53. AE, DC, MC, V. Closed Sun. No lunch Sat.*

$$ 🏨 **Hôtel de Gramont.** Five minutes from the château, the Gramont is a cozy and convenient base for exploring Pau. Ask for one of the *chambres mansardées* (dormered bedrooms) under the eaves overlooking the Hédas. ✉ *3 pl. de Gramont, 64000,* ☎ *05–59–27–84–04,* FAX *05–59–27–62–23. 36 rooms. No air-conditioning, cable TV. AE, DC, MC, V.*

Nightlife and the Arts

During the music and arts **Festival de Pau,** theatrical and musical events take place almost every evening from mid-July to late-August, nearly all of them gratis. Nightlife in Pau revolves around the Hédas district, where bars and restaurants line the alleys heading down into this onetime river gorge. The streets around Pau's imposing château are sprinkled with cozy pubs and dining spots, although the **casino** (✉ Parc Beaumont, ☎ 05–59–27–06–92) offers racier entertainment.

Outdoor Activities and Sports

Pau Golf Club (✉ Rue du Golf, Billère, ☎ 05–59–32–02–33), France's first golf course, is a lush 18-hole beauty. The **Haras National** (✉ 1 rue Mal-Leclerq, Gélos, ☎ 05–59–06–60–57) displays a stunning community of Thoroughbreds. **Hippodrome du Pont-Long** (✉ 462 bd. Cami-Salié, ☎ 05–59–32–02–33) runs one of the best steeplechases in Europe, and has horse races from October to May.

Eugénie-les-Bains

⑯ *45 km (30 mi) north of Pau, 140 km (87 mi) south of Bordeaux.*

Empress Eugénie popularized Eugénie-les-Bains at the end of the 19th century, and in return the villagers renamed the town after her. Michel and Christine Guérard brought the village back to life in 1973 by putting together one of France's most fashionable thermal retreats, which became the birthplace of nouvelle cuisine, thanks to the great talents of chef Michel. Their little kingdom now includes two restaurants, two hotels, a cooking school, and a spa. The 13 therapeutic treatments address everything from weight loss to rheumatism. Two springs are certified by the French Ministry of Health: L'Impératrice and Christine-Marie, whose 39°C (102°F) waters come from nearly 1,300 ft below the surface.

Dining and Lodging

$$$$ ✕🏨 **La Ferme aux Grives.** With four superb rooms for the lucky first-comers, Michel Guérard's delightfully re-created old coaching inn, set at one end of their Prés des Eugénie fiefdom (☞ *below*), is meant to be a more rustic alternative to their main flagship restaurant. Nature's bounty is the theme: a banquet table is laid out with vegetables and breads, darkened beams cast romantic shadows, and hunting paintings cover the walls. Grandmother's food is given a nouvelle spin, and nearly everything is *authentique*: even the suckling pig turns on a spit in the fireplace. ✉ *Eugénie-les-Bains,* ☎ *05–58–05–05–06,* FAX *05–58–51–10–10. 4 rooms. Restaurant, bar, no air-conditioning, cable TV, minibars. AE, DC, MC, V. Closed Jan. 3–Feb. 6.*

$$$$ ★ ✕🏨 **Les Prés d'Eugénie.** Ever since Michel Guérard's eponymously named restaurant fired the first shots of the nouvelle revolution of the late 1970s, the excellence of this suave culinary landmark has been a given (so much so that the breakfast here outdoes dinner at most other places). Thanks to Guérard's signature flair, *cuisine minceur*—the slimmer's dream—collides with the lusty fare of the Landes region (langoustines garnished with foie gras and mesclun greens, lobster with confetti-ed calf's head). In the lovely Second Empire–style hotel, set in a fine garden, grandeur prevails and rooms are formal. However, those in the "annex"—the former 18th-century **Couvent des Herbes**—have an understated luxe and look out over the herb garden. To top it all off, the complex includes an excellent spa, dance studio, two pools, and a nine-hole golf course, and "theme" weeks are devoted to cooking, perfumes, wines, or gardening. ✉ *40320 Eugénie-les-Bains,* ☎ *05–58–05–06–07; 05–58–05–05–05 for restaurant reservations,* FAX *05–58–51–10–10,* WEB *www.michelguerard.com. 35 rooms. Restaurant, bar, no air-conditioning, cable TV, minibars, golf course, 2 tennis courts, indoor pool, outdoor pool, gym. AE, DC, MC, V.*

$$ ★ ✕🏨 **La Maison Rose.** A low-cost, low-calorie alternative to Les Prés d'Eugénie (☞ *above*), Michel and Christine Guérard's newest hotel beckons with a sybaritically simple spa approach. Set in a renovated, superstylish 18th-century farmhouse adorned with old paintings hung with ribbons, rustic antiques, and Pays Basque handicrafts, this is a retreat that would have delighted the sober Madame de Maintenon—if she had wanted to lose weight, that is. This is a serious spa, complete with slimming cures and the most stylish relaxation room in France (oh, those Provençal-style chaises longues). No room service—everyone eats in the main dining room, a two-story, beam-ceiling delight. The kitchen's touch remains an inventive benediction to local produce. ✉ *40320 Eugénie-les-Bains,* ☎ *05–58–05–05–05,* WEB *www.michelguerard.com. 32 rooms. Restaurant, no air-conditioning, cable TV, minibars, kitchenette, pool, tennis, gym, parking, no pets. AE, DC, MC, V.*

THE HAUTES-PYRÉNÉES

The Hautes-Pyrénées include the highest and most spectacular natural wonders in the cordillera. Although mountain peaks soar in this region, there are also centers of more civilized charms—notably, the towns of Cauterets and Bagnères-de-Luchon, set in a spa region that once attracted such formidable luminaries as Montaigne, Madame de Maintenon, Henri IV, and the composer Rossini. Traditionally known as La Bigorre, the border with the Béarn is at the Col d'Aubisque southeast of Oloron-Ste-Marie, and the eastern border with the Haute Garonne is at the Col de Peyresourde just west of Bagnères-de-Luchon. The legendary Cirque de Gavarnie (natural mountain amphitheater), the Vignemale peak (10,817 ft) and glacier, the Balaïtous peak (10,312 ft), the Brèche de Roland, and the Cirque de Troumouse are the star attractions in the Hautes-Pyrénées.

Tarbes

17 *40 km (24 mi) east of Pau, 152 km (94 mi) southwest of Toulouse, 214 km (133 mi) southeast of Bordeaux.*

Tarbes is the commercial and administrative center of the Bigorre region and the Hautes-Pyrénées Département. If Tarbes is your point of entry into the Hautes-Pyrénées, stop by the **tourist office** (✉ 3 cours Gambetta, ☎ 05–62–51–30–31) for information, brochures, and maps of the region. The **Halle Marcadieu** is the commercial center. The Thursday market offers a chance to check out widely acclaimed local products ranging from the *choux-fleurs* (cauliflower) of Arros to the carrots of Asté, from the onions of Trébons to the famed *haricot tarbais,* a delicate-skinned kidney bean essential in any authentic garbure.

Tarbes was the **birthplace of Maréchal Ferdinand Foch** (✉ 2 rue de la Victoire, ☎ 05–62–93–19–02), the general most responsible for the 1918 Allied victory. The town is also home to the **Haras National** (✉ 70 av. du Régiment-de-Bigorre, ☎ 05–62–34–44–59), a stud farm and dressage academy. A nice place for a walk on a warm day is the **Jardin Massey** (Massey Garden), a luxuriant park that is home to ducks and an abundance of flowers in summer.

Dining and Lodging

$ ✕🏨 **Henri IV.** This comfortable spot in midtown Tarbes, near the Massey Garden and three blocks from the train station, is a safe if unspectacular choice for a night in town. The staff will direct you to the gastronomical star of Tarbes, L'Ambroisie, just two blocks toward the cathedral. ✉ *7 av. B. Barère, 65000,* ☎ *05–62–34–01–68,* FAX *05–62–93–71–32. 25 rooms. No air-conditioning, cable TV. AE, DC, MC, V.*

Lourdes

⓲ *41 km (27 mi) southeast of Pau, 19 km (12 mi) southwest of Tarbes.*

Five million pilgrims flock to Lourdes annually, many in quest of a miraculous cure for sickness or disability. A religious pilgrimage is one thing, but a sightseeing expedition has other requirements. The famous churches and grotto and the area around them are woefully lacking in beauty. Off-season, acres of empty parking lots echo. Shops are shuttered, restaurants closed. In season a mob jostles to see the grotto behind a forest of votive candles. Some pundits might say that Lourdes ingeniously combines the worst of both worlds.

In February 1858 Bernadette Soubirous, a 14-year-old miller's daughter, saw the Virgin Mary in the **Grotte de Massabielle,** near the Gave de Pau (in all, she had 18 visions). Bernadette dug in the grotto, releasing a gush of water from a spot where no spring had flowed before. From then on, pilgrims thronged the Massabielle rock for the water's supposed healing powers, though church authorities reacted skeptically. It took four years for the miracle to be authenticated by Rome and a sanctuary erected over the grotto. In 1864 the first organized procession was held. Today there are six official annual pilgrimages between Easter and All Saints' Day, the most important on August 15.

Lourdes celebrated the centenary of Bernadette Soubirous's visions by building the world's largest underground church, the **Basilique Souterraine St-Pie X,** with space for 20,000 people—more than the town's permanent population. Above St-Pie X stands the unprepossessing neo-Byzantine **Basilique du Rosaire** (1889). The **Basilique Supérieure** (1871), tall and white, hulks nearby.

The **Pavillon Notre-Dame,** across from St-Pie X, houses the **Musée Bernadette,** with mementos of Bernadette's life and an illustrated history of the pilgrimages. In the basement is the **Musée d'Art Sacré du Gemmail** (Museum of Stained-Glass Mosaic Religious Art). ✉ *72 rue de la Grotte,* ☎ *05–62–94–13–15.* 🎫 *Free.* ⏲ *July–Nov., daily 9:30–11:45 and 2:30–6:15; Dec.–June, Wed.–Mon. 9:30–11:45 and 2:30–5:45.*

Across the river is the **Moulin de Boly** (Boly Mill), where Bernadette was born on January 7, 1844. ✉ *12 rue Bernadette-Soubirous.* 🎫 *Free.* ⏲ *Easter–mid-Oct., daily 9:30–11:45 and 2:30–5:45.*

The **cachot,** a tiny room where, in extreme poverty, Bernadette and her family took refuge in 1856, can also be visited. ✉ *15 rue des Petits-Fossés,* ☎ *05–62–94–51–30.* *Free.* ⏲ *Easter–mid-Oct., daily 9:30–11:45 and 2:30–5:30; mid-Oct.–Easter, daily 2:30–5:30.*

The **château** on the hill above town can be reached by escalator, by 131 steps, or by the ramp up from rue du Bourg (from which a small Basque cemetery with ancient discoidal stones can be seen). Once a prison, the castle now contains the **Musée Pyrénéen,** one of France's best provincial museums, devoted to the popular customs, arts, and history of the Pyrénées. ✉ *25 rue du Fort,* ☎ *05–62–94–02–04.* *€5.* ⏲ *Easter–mid-Oct., daily 9–noon and 2–7 (last admission at 6); mid-Oct.–Easter, Wed.–Mon. 9–noon and 2–7 (last admission at 6).*

Dining and Lodging

$$ ✕ **Hôtel Albert/La Taverne de Bigorre.** The Moreau family's popular establishment serves traditional French mountain cooking such as hearty garbure. Rooms are clean and comfortable, with a personal touch that is very welcome in Lourdes. ✉ *21 pl. du Champ Commun, 65100,* ☎ *05–62–94–75–00,* FAX *05–62–94–78–45. 27 rooms. Restaurant, bar, no air-conditioning, parking (fee). AE, DC, MC, V. Closed mid-Nov.–mid-Dec. and Jan.*

Cauterets

19 *30 km (19 mi) south of Lourdes, 49 km (30 mi) south of Tarbes.*

Cauterets (which derives from the word for hot springs in the local *bigourdan* dialect) is a spa and resort town (for long-term treatments) high in the Pyrénées. It has been revered since Roman times for thermal baths thought to cure maladies ranging from back pain to female sterility. Novelist Victor Hugo (1802–85) womanized here; Lady Aurore Dudevant—better known as the writer George Sand (1804–76)—is said to have discovered her feminism here. Other famous visitors include Gastón Fébus, Chateaubriand, Sarah Bernhardt, King Edward VII of England, and Spain's King Alfonso XIII.

En Route Two kilometers (1 mile) south of Cauterets is the parking lot for the thermal baths, where the red-and-white-marked GR10 ***Sentier des Cascades*** (Path of the Waterfalls) departs for Pont d'Espagne. This famous walk (three hours round-trip) features stunning views of the waterfalls and abundant *marmottes* (Pyrenean groundhogs). From **Pont d'Espagne,** to which you can also drive, continue on foot or by chairlift to the plateau and a view over the bright blue **Lac de Gaube,** fed by the river of the same name. Above is **Le Vignemale** (10,817 ft), France's highest Pyrenean peak. Return via Cauterets to Pierrefitte-Nestalas and turn right on D921 up Luz-St-Saveur and Gavarnie.

Gavarnie

20 *30 km (19 mi) south of Cauterets on D921, 50 km (31 mi) south of Lourdes.*

The village of Gavarnie is a good base for exploring the mountains in the region. For starters, it's at the foot of the **Cirque de Gavarnie,** one of the world's most remarkable examples of glacial erosion and a daunting challenge to mountaineers. Horses and donkeys, rented in the village, are the traditional way to reach the head of the valley (though walking is preferable), where the Hôtel du Cirque has hosted six generations of visitors. When the upper snows melt, numerous streams tumble down from the cliffs to form spectacular waterfalls; the greatest of them, Europe's largest, is the **Grande Cascade,** dropping nearly 1,400 ft.

Another dramatic sight is 12 km (7 mi) west of the village of Gavarnie. Take D921 up to the Col de Boucharo, where you can park and walk five hours up to the **Brèche de Roland** glacier (you cross it during the last two hours of the hike). For a taste of mountain life, have lunch high up at the Club Alpin Français's **Refuge de Sarradets ou de la Brèche.** This is a serious climb, only feasible from mid-June to mid-September, for which you need (at least) good hiking shoes and sound physical conditioning. Crampons and ice axes are available for rent in Gavarnie; check with the Gavarnie tourist office for weather reports and for information about guided tours.

Dining and Lodging

$$–$$$ ✕ **Hôtel du Cirque.** With its legendary views of the Cirque de Gavarnie, this spot is magical at sunset. Despite its name it's just a restaurant, but not just any old eating establishment: the garbure here is as delicious as the sunset is grand. Seventh-generation owner Pierre Vergez claims his recipe using water from the Cirque and *cocos de Tarbes,* or *haricots tarbais* (Tarbes broad beans) is unique. ✉ *1-hr walk above the village of Gavarnie,* ☎ *05–62–92–48–02. MC, V. Closed mid-Sept.–mid-June.*

$$ ✕🏨 **Hôtel Marboré.** This multigabled house over a rushing mountain brook offers all the history and tradition of Gavarnie along with delightful creature comforts. Rooms are bright and pleasant and look out onto lush hillside meadows. The kind and lively owner-manager Roselyne Fillastre attends to all with great warmth and vivacity. The restaurant, too, is excellent: look forward to fine cuisine prepared with the freshest ingredients. ✉ *Village de Gavarnie, 65120,* ☎ *05–62–92–40–40,* FAX *05–62–92–40–30. 13 rooms. Restaurant, bar, no air-conditioning, cable TV. MC, V.*

Nightlife and the Arts

Every July Gavarnie holds an outdoor ballet and music performance, **La Fête des Pyrénées,** using the Cirque de Gavarnie as a backdrop; show time is at sunset. For information contact the tourist office (☎ 05–62–92–49–10).

En Route The dramatic mountain scenery is impressive all along D921 between Gavarnie and **Luz-St-Sauveur.** Continuing east from Luz-St-Sauveur along D918 toward Arreau, the road passes through the lively little spa town of **Barèges** and under the brow of the mighty **Pic du Midi de Bigorre,** a mountain peak towering nearly 10,000 ft above the Col du Tourmalet pass. The finest views—and the sharpest curves—are found toward the Col d'Aspin pass. Another spectacular road is D618 from Arreau over the **Col de Peyresourde** to Bagnères de Luchon.

Bagnères de Luchon

21 *150 km (93 mi) east of Gavarnie.*

The largest and most fashionable Pyrenean spa is Bagnères de Luchon (generally known simply as Luchon), at the head of a lush valley. Dubbed the *Reine des Pyrénées* (Queen of the Pyrénées), Luchon was considered by the Romans to rank second as a spa only to Naples. Thermal waters here cater to the vocal cords: opera singers, lawyers, and politicians hoarse from spurious electoral promises all pile in to breathe the healing vapors. The **Parc des Quinconces** is a pretty stroll in summer. Look for the beautiful Couteillas sculpture *Le Baiser à la Source* (*The Kiss at the Spring*), hidden under a pine tree.

On display at the **Musée du Pays de Luchon** (✉ 18 allée d'Étigny, ☏ 05–61–79–21–21) are exhibits about Pyrenean history and lore and artifacts such as a curious sculpture portraying a woman and a serpent.

Dining and Lodging

$$$–$$$$ **Hôtel Corneille.** This elegant spot with a lovely terrace and park has all the comforts you could want and then some. Most of the furnishings are original Napoléon III. The staff is very helpful and pleasant. *✉ 5 av. A. Dumas, 65100, ☏ 05–61–79–36–22, FAX 05–61–79–81–11. 56 rooms. Restaurant, bar, no air-conditioning, park, meeting rooms. AE, DC, MC, V. Closed end Nov.–mid-Dec.*

St-Bertrand de Comminges

22 *32 km (20 mi) north of Bagnères de Luchon, 57 km (35 mi) southeast of Tarbes, 107 km (66 mi) southwest of Toulouse.*

A Roman road once led directly from Luchon to St-Bertrand de Comminges (then a huge town of 60,000). This delightful village, whose inhabitants today number just over 200, is dwarfed beneath the imposing (mostly) 12th-century **Cathédrale Ste-Marie** (✉ Rue des Gouverneurs); don't miss the cloisters and the intricately and playfully carved wood choir stalls. Described as a land-bound Mont-St-Michel, St-Bertrand numbers old houses, sloping alleyways, and crafts shops that add to its charm. The summer music festival held here and in neighboring villages in July and August is excellent.

BASQUE COUNTRY AND THE HAUTES-PYRÉNÉES A TO Z

To research prices, get advice from other travelers, and book travel arrangements, visit www.fodors.com.

AIR TRAVEL

CARRIERS

Air France flies to Pau, Bayonne, and Biarritz from Paris and from other major European destinations. Air Littoral flies between Biarritz, Pau, Toulouse, Nice, and Marseille.

➤ AIRLINES AND CONTACTS: **Air France** (☏ 05–59–33–34–35). **Air Littoral** (☏ 05–59–33–26–64).

AIRPORTS

Biarritz-Parme Airport serves Bayonne and Biarritz and has several daily flights to and from Paris and several weekly to London, Marseille, Geneva, Lyon, Nice, and Pau. Pau-Pyrénées International Airport has 10 flights daily to and from Paris as well as flights to Nantes, Lyon, Marseille, Nice, Biarritz, Madrid, Rome, Venice, Milan, and Geneva.

➤ AIRPORT INFORMATION: **Biarritz-Parme Airport** (☏ 05–59–43–83–20). **Pau-Pyrénées International Airport** (☏ 05–59–33–33–00).

BUS TRAVEL

Various private bus concerns—STAB (serving the Bayonne–Anglet–Biarritz metropolitan areas) and ATCRB (up and down the coast and inland to many Basque towns)—service the region. Where they don't, the trusty SNCF national bus lines can occasionally come to the rescue. Beware of peak-hour traffic on roads in the summer, which can mean both delays in transport time and few seats on buses. Check in with the local tourist office for handy schedules or ask your hotel concierge for the best advice.

➤ BUS INFORMATION: **STAB–Biarritz** (Rue Louis Barthou, Biarritz, ☏ 05–59–24–26–53). **ATCRB** (☏ 05–59–26–06–99).

CAR RENTAL

➤ Local Agencies: **Avis** (✉ Biarritz-Parme Airport, Biarritz, ☏ 05–59–23–67–92; ✉ 107 bd. Général-de-Gaulle, Hendaye, ☏ 05–59–20–79–04; ✉ Pau-Pyrénées International Airport, Pau, ☏ 05–59–33–27–13; ✉ Train station, St-Jean-de-Luz ☏ 05–59–26–76–66). **Budget** (✉ Biarritz-Parme Airport, Biarritz, ☏ 05–59–23–58–62; ✉ Pau-Pyrénées International Airport, Pau, ☏ 05–59–33–77–45). **Eurodollar** (✉ Biarritz-Parme Airport, Biarritz, ☏ 05–59–41–21–12). **Europcar** (✉ Train station, Bayonne, ☏ 05–59–55–38–20; ✉ Biarritz-Parme Airport, Biarritz, ☏ 05–59–23–90–68; ✉ Pau-Pyrénées International Airport, Pau, ☏ 05–59–33–24–31). **Hertz** (✉ Biarritz-Parme Airport, Biarritz, ☏ 05–59–43–92–92; ✉ Pau-Pyrénées International Airport, Pau, ☏ 05–59–33–16–38).

CAR TRAVEL

A64 connects Pau and Bayonne in under an hour, and A63 runs up and down the Atlantic coast. N117 connects Hendaye with Toulouse via Pau and Tarbes. N134 connects Bordeaux, Pau, Oloron-Ste-Marie, and Spain via the Col de Somport and Jaca. The D918 from Bayonne through Cambo and along the Nive river to St-Jean-Pied-de-Port is a pretty drive, continuing on (as D919 and D920) through the Béarn country to Oloron-Ste-Marie and Pau.

ROAD CONDITIONS

Roads are occasionally slow and tortuous in the more mountainous areas, but valley and riverside roads are generally quite smooth and fast. D132, which goes between Arette and Pierre-St-Martin, can be snowed in between mid-November and mid-May, as can N134 through the Valley d'Aspe and the Col de Somport into Spain.

TOURS

In Biarritz, Aitzin organizes tours of Bayonne, Biarritz, the Basque coast, and the Basque Pyrénées. The Association des Guides, in Pau, arranges tours with guides of the city, the Pyrénées, and Béarn and Basque Country. The Bayonne tourist office gives guided tours of the city. La Guild du Tourisme des Pyrénées-Atlantiques offers information on and organizes visits and tours of the Basque Country and the Pyrénées. Guides Culturels Pyrénéens, in Tarbes, arranges many tours, including explorations on such themes as cave painting, art and architecture, Basque sports, hiking, and horseback riding.

➤ Contacts: **Aitzin** (☏ 05–59–24–36–05). **Association des Guides** (☏ 05–59–30–44–01). **Bayonne tourist office** (☏ 05–59–46–01–46). **Guides Culturels Pyrénéens** (☏ 05–62–44–15–44). **La Guild du Tourisme des Pyrénées-Atlantiques** (☏ 05–59–46–37–05).

TRAIN TRAVEL

High-speed trains (TGVs, Trains à Grande Vitesse) cover the 800 km (500 mi) from Paris to Bayonne in 4½ hours. To get to Pau, take the TGV to Bordeaux (three hours) and connect to Pau (two hours). Bayonne and Toulouse are connected by local SNCF trains via Pau, Tarbes, Lourdes, Lannemezan, and St-Gaudens. A local train runs along the Nive from Bayonne to St-Jean-Pied-de-Port. Local trains go between Bayonne and Biarritz and from Bayonne into the Atlantic Pyrénées, a slow but picturesque trip. Hendaye is connected to Bayonne and to San Sebastián via the famous *topo* (mole) train, so-called for the number of tunnels it passes through.

➤ Train Information: **SNCF** (☏ 08–36–35–35–35, WEB www.sncf.com).

TRAVEL AGENCIES

Note that the American Express agencies receive mail but don't do any banking transactions.

➤ LOCAL AGENT REFERRALS: **Adour Voyages** (✉ 3 rue Gardères, Biarritz, ☎ 05–59–24–14–25). **Agence Garrouste** (✉ 10 rue Thiers, Bayonne, ☎ 05–59–59–02–35). **American Express** (✉ 14 Chausée du Bourg, Lourdes, ☎ 05–62–94–40–84). **Havas Voyages** (✉ 5 rue Lormand, Bayonne, ☎ 05–59–46–29–26). **L'Accueil Pyrénéen** (✉ 26 av. Maransin, Lourdes, ☎ 05–62–94–15–62). **Maison du Pélérin** (✉ 12 av. Maransin, Lourdes, ☎ 05–62–94–70–05). **Saga Tours** (✉ 4 av. du Maréchal-Foch, Biarritz, ☎ 05–59–24–39–39).

VISITOR INFORMATION

The addresses of tourist offices in towns mentioned in this chapter are as follows.

➤ TOURIST INFORMATION: **Ainhoa** (✉ Mairie, ☎ 05–59–29–92–60). **Bagnères-de-Luchon** (✉ 18 allée d'Etigny, ☎ 05–61–79–21–21). **Bayonne** (✉ Pl. des Basques, ☎ 05–59–46–01–46). **Biarritz** (✉ 1 sq. Ixelles, ☎ 05–59–22–37–10). **Cauterets** (✉ 15 Cauterets, ☎ 05–62–92–50–27). **Gavarnie** (✉ in center of village, ☎ 05–62–92–49–10). **Hendaye** (✉ 12 rue des Aubépines, ☎ 05–59–20–00–34). **Lourdes** (✉ Pl. Beyramalu, ☎ 05–62–42–77–40). **Navarrenx** (✉ Mairie, ☎ 05–59–66–10–22). **Oloron-Ste-Marie** (✉ Pl. de la Résistance, ☎ 05–59–39–98–00). **Pau** (✉ Pl. Royale, ☎ 05–59–27–27–08). **St-Bertrand-de-Comminges** (✉ Mairie, ☎ 05–61–88–33–12). **St-Jean-de-Luz** (✉ Pl. Foch, ☎ 05–59–26–03–16). **St-Jean-Pied-de-Port** (✉ 14 pl. Charles-de-Gaulle, ☎ 05–59–37–03–57). **Sare** (✉ Mairie, ☎ 05–59–54–20–14). **Sauveterre-de-Béarn** (✉ Mairie, ☎ 05–59–38–50–17).

17 BORDEAUX, DORDOGNE, AND POITOU-CHARENTES

From the grand châteaux of Bordeaux country to the stone-cottage pastorale of Dordogne, from the broad, sandy beaches of Royan to the watery bower of the Marais Poitevin, this region offers a wondrous mix of high culture and gentle nature. And in the land of foie gras and cognac you'll eat (and quaff) like the kings (and queens) who once disputed this coveted southwest corner, staking it out with châteaux-forts and blessing it with Romanesque churches.

Revised and updated by Simon Hewitt

Introduction by Nancy Coons

IF YOU'RE LOOKING FOR THE GOOD LIFE, your search may be over. No other region of France packs such a concentration of fine wine, extraordinary spirits, and superb culinary delights as well as rib-sticking country cooking. It's almost too much to demand that it be lovely, too—but it is. Viewed by generations of British as the quintessential French escape, Dordogne is a picture-postcard fantasy of green countryside, stone cottages, and cliff-top châteaux, crowned by the enchanting medieval wine town of St-Émilion. The Atlantic coast north of Bordeaux offers elite enclaves of white-sand beach. The vineyards of Médoc extend their lush green rows to the south. And in the fertile outreaches of Charente, the canal-laced Marais Poitevin—France's "Green Venice"—is a luxuriant, watery bower.

It's no wonder the English fought for it so hard throughout the Hundred Years' War. This coveted corner of France was home to Eleanor of Aquitaine, and when she left her first husband, France's Louis VII, to marry Henry II of England, it came under English rule. Henry Plantagenet was, after all, a great-grandson of William the Conqueror, and the Franco-English ambiguity of the age exploded in a war that defined much of modern France and changed its face forever. Southwestern France was the stage upon which much of the war was conducted. Hence the region's defensive châteaux-forts; hence no end of Romanesque churches dedicated to the noble families' cause; and hence the steady flow of Bordeaux wines to England, where it is still dubbed "claret," after *clairet,* a light red version from earlier days.

What they sought, the world still seeks. The wines of Bordeaux tower as a standard against which other wines are measured, especially the burgeoning worldwide parade of Cabernets. From the grandest *premiers grands crus*—the Lafite-Rothschilds, the Margaux—to the modest *supérieur* in your picnic basket, the rigorously controlled Bordeaux commands respect. Fans and oenophiles come from around the world to pay homage; to gaze at the noble symmetry of estate châteaux, whose rows of green-and-black vineyards radiate in every direction; to lower a nose deep into a well-swirled glass, sucking in heady vapors of oak and almond and leather; and, finally, to reverently pack a few bloodline labels into a trunk or a suitcase for home.

The rest you will drink on site, from the mouthful of golden Graves that washes down the oysters to the syrupy sip of Sauternes that slips down with the foie gras to the last glass of Médoc paired with the salt-marsh lamb that leads to pulling the cork on a Pauillac—because there is, after all, cheese to come . . .

But brace yourself: you've barely scratched the culinary surface. Take a deep breath and head inland, following the winding sprawl of the Dordogne River into Duck Country. This is the land of the *gavée* goose, force-fed extravagantly to plump its liver into one of the world's most renowned delicacies. Duck and goose fat glistens on potatoes, on salty confits, on *rillettes d'oie,* a spread of potted duck that melts on the tongue as no butter ever could. Wild mushrooms and truffles weave their musky perfume through dense game pâtés. The wines, such as Bergerac and Cahors, are coarser here, as if to stand up to such an onslaught of earthy textures and flavors. And a snifter of amber cognac is de rigueur for the digestion.

Dining thus, in a vine-covered stone *ferme auberge* deep in the green wilds of Dordogne, the day's parade of châteaux and chapel tours blurring pleasantly into a reverie of picturesque history, you'll see what the Plantagenets were fighting for.

Pleasures and Pastimes

Beaches

French families concentrate on the resort towns of Royan and Arcachon, but there are plenty of other huge beaches where you can escape the crowds: along the forest-girdled Côte Sauvage (Wild Coast) north of Royan; along the shores of the islands of Ré, Aix, and Oléron; and beneath the huge dunes south of Arcachon.

Boat Trips

Although the region's two main islands, Ile de Ré and Ile d'Oléron, are linked to the mainland by bridges, boats still ply the Atlantic waters south of La Rochelle, visiting Fort Boyard and docking at Ile d'Aix. Explore the oyster beds of the Baie de Seudre or make an excursion across the Gironde to the Cordouan Lighthouse, stranded on a sandbank in mid-estuary. Ferries ply the Gironde from Royan and Blaye; punts, steered with long poles, glide peacefully along the canals of the Marais Poitevin; and the Dordogne River is a favorite with canoers.

Dining

Truffles, foie gras, walnuts, plums, trout, eel, oysters, and myriad succulent species of mushrooms jostle for attention on restaurant menus. The hearty food of Dordogne, the rich dairy produce of Poitou-Charentes, and shoals of succulent seafood from the Atlantic make for diversified table fare. The versatile wines of Bordeaux make fine accompaniments to most regional dishes. Cognac is de rigueur at the end of a meal; sweet, tangy *pineau des Charentes*—made from cognac and unfermented grape juice—at the beginning.

CATEGORY	COST*
$$$$	over €30
$$$	€20–€30
$$	€12–€20
$	under €12

**per person for a main course only, including tax (19.6%) and service; note that if a restaurant offers only prix-fixe (set-price) meals, it has been given the price category that reflects the full prix-fixe price.*

Lodging

Vacationers flock to the coast and islands, and for miles around hotels are booked solid for months in advance. Farther inland—except for the Dordogne Valley—the situation eases up, but there aren't as many places to stay. Advance booking is particularly desirable in Bordeaux, at any time, and in Dordogne, where hotels fill up quickly in midsummer. Many country or small-town hotels expect you to have at least one dinner with them, and if you have two meals a day with your lodging and stay several nights, you will save money. Prices offseason (October–May) often drop as much as 20%. Assume all hotel rooms have air-conditioning, TV, telephones, and private bath unless otherwise noted. Internet, when listed in facilities, means in-room data-ports and/or public-area computers provide on-line access.

CATEGORY	COST*
$$$$	over €180
$$$	€120–€180
$$	€60–€120
$	under €60

**All prices are for a standard double room in high season, including tax (19.6%) and service charge.*

Wine

No other part of France has such a concentrated wealth of top-class vineyards. The versatile Bordeaux region yields sweet and dry whites and fruity or full-bodied reds from a huge domain extending on either side of the Gironde (Blaye and Bourg to the north, Médoc and Graves to the south) and inland along the Garonne (Sauternes) and Dordogne (St-Émilion, Fronsac, Pomerol) or in between these two rivers (Entre-Deux-Mers). Farther north, the verdant hills of Cognac produce the world's finest brandy. Less familiar appellations are also worth seeking out, including Bergerac, Pécharmant, and Monbazillac, along the Dordogne River, and the lighter whites and reds of the Fiefs Vendéens, north of La Rochelle.

Exploring Bordeaux, Dordogne, and Poitou-Charentes

For three centuries during the Middle Ages, this region was a battlefield in the wars between the French and the English. Of the castles and châteaux dotting the area, those at Biron, Hautefort, and Beynac are among the best. Robust Romanesque architecture is more characteristic of this area than the airy Gothic style found elsewhere in France: Poitiers showcases the best examples, notably Notre-Dame-la-Grande, with its richly worked facade. The Romanesque style can also be admired at the nearby abbey of St-Savin, in Angoulême and Périgueux, and in countless village churches.

If there is a formula for enjoying this region, it should include cultural highlights, relaxing by the sea, tasting wine, and treating yourself to oysters, truffles, and foie gras. Swaths of sandy beaches line the Atlantic coast: well-heeled resorts like Royan and Arcachon are lined with glistening bodies baking in the sun. The world-famous vineyards of Médoc, Sauternes, Graves, Entre-Deux-Mers, Pomerol, and St-Émilion surround the elegant 18th-century city of Bordeaux, set on the southwest edge of the region near the foot of the Gironde Estuary.

But if you prefer solitude, you won't have any trouble finding it in the vast, underpopulated stretches inland toward the east in the rolling countryside of Dordogne, also chockfull of riverside châteaux, medieval villages, and prehistoric sites. To the north, the rural region of Poitou-Charentes stretches from Angoulême through cognac country to the Atlantic coast, and back inland through the canals around Niort to Poitiers. Between La Rochelle and Poitiers lies the Marais Poitevin, a marshy area known as "Green Venice" for its network of crisscrossing waterways.

Great Itineraries

To see all of the region in one trip would be overambitious, so you need to be selective. If you love the beach and the outdoors, head to the Royan Peninsula or the islands of Ré and Oléron. If you're a gourmand, go straight to Dordogne; if wine is your passion, use Bordeaux as your base. For nature, seek out the Marais-Poitevin. Following are some suggested itineraries.

Numbers in the text correspond to numbers in the margin and on the Bordeaux, Dordogne, and Poitou-Charentes map.

IF YOU HAVE 3 DAYS

Have a morning tour and lunch in vibrant **Bordeaux** ①–⑨ before heading on to medieval **St-Émilion** ⑭ during the afternoon. On the second day head north to **Cognac** ㉜ for lunch, visit a *chai* (brandy warehouse), then continue along the Charente Valley to spend the night in stately **Saintes** ㉝. On day three head up to **Ile de Ré** ㉟; Explore this

Bordeaux, Dordogne, and Poitou-Charentes

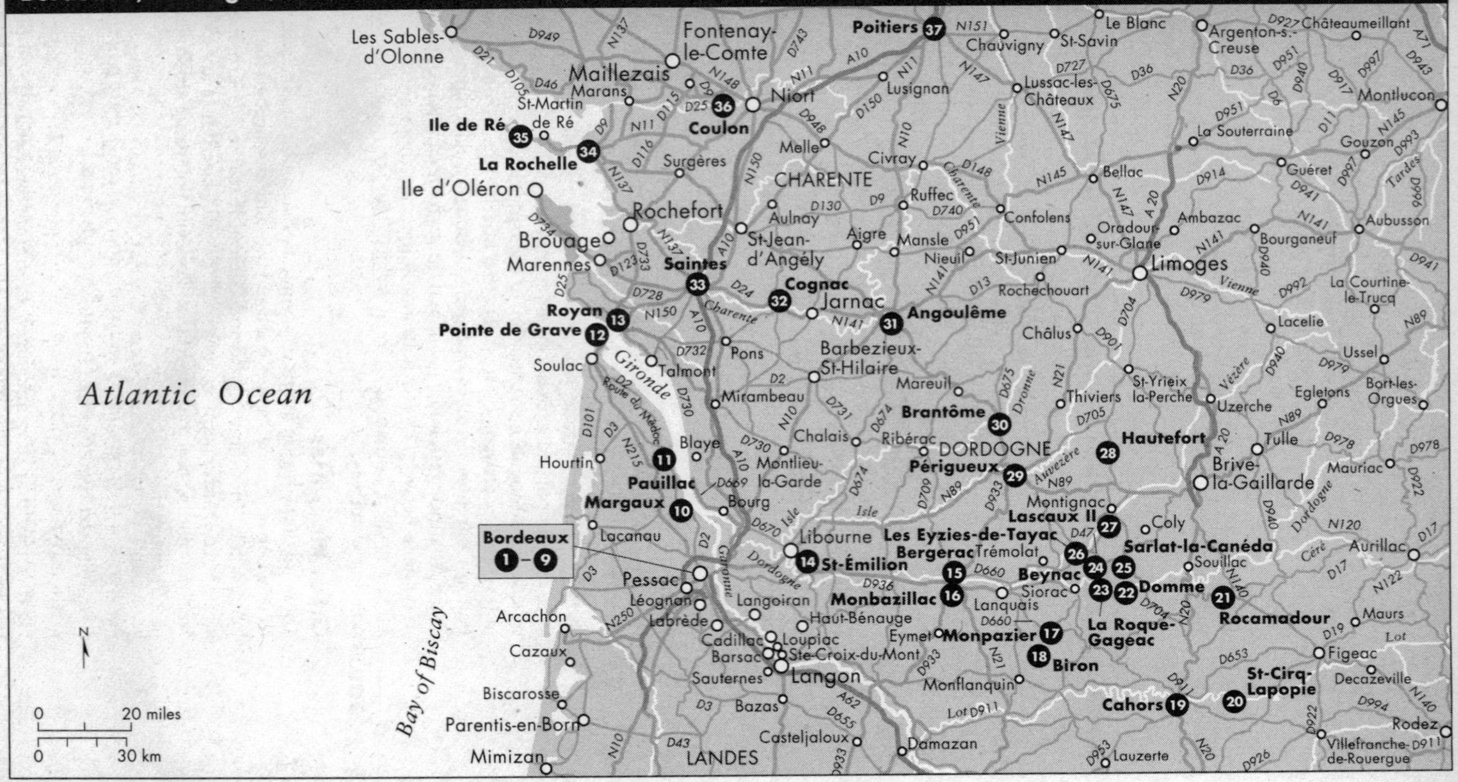

tranquil, verdant island before repairing to the old, bustling harbor town of **La Rochelle** ㉞.

IF YOU HAVE 7 DAYS

Finish off your morning tour with lunch in **Bordeaux** ①–⑨ before whizzing back to the Middle Ages in **St-Émilion** ⑭ during the afternoon. On the second day visit the fortified medieval village of **Monpazier** ⑰ and the mighty château in **Biron** ⑱, before veering north to overnight at **La Roque-Gageac** ㉓, huddled beneath a towering cliff. On day three head along the Dordogne River to the castle at **Beynac** ㉔, lunch on foie gras and truffles in the medieval market town of **Sarlat-la-Canéda** ㉕, then check out the cave paintings at the **Lascaux II** ㉗ or the archeological finds at the Musée Nationale de Préhistoire in **Les Eyzies-de-Tayac** ㉖. Rest up near **Hautefort** ㉘. On day four leave Dordogne via quaint **Brantôme** ㉚ en route to hilltop **Angoulême** ㉛. Try to get to **Cognac** ㉜ by afternoon to pay a call on a *chai* (brandy warehouse), then continue along the Charente Valley before spending the night in **Saintes** ㉝. On day five drive up to the lovely **Ile de Ré** ㉟. After an overnight, head to **La Rochelle** ㉞ where you can explore the old town and picturesque harbor, then enjoy your last overnight. On your final day head east to the Marais Poitevin, lunching in the pretty village of **Coulon** ㊱, and continuing to **Poitiers** ㊲ to end your tour.

When to Tour Bordeaux, Dordogne, and Poitou-Charentes

Spring and fall are the best times to visit—there aren't as many tourists around, and the weather is still pleasant. The *vendanges* (grape harvests) usually begin about mid-September in the Bordeaux region (though you can't visit the wineries at this time), and two weeks later in the Cognac region, to the north. A number of hotels close from the end of October through March.

THE BORDEAUX REGION

Bordeaux, the commercial and cultural center of southwest France, is ringed by renowned vineyards: Graves and pretty Sauternes, to the south; Pomerol and St-Émilion, to the east; and to the northwest, the dusty Médoc Peninsula, looking across the Gironde Estuary at the vineyards of Bourg and Blaye. Head southwest, and you'll find great swaths of pine forest, huge sand dunes, and the fancy resort of Arcachon.

Bordeaux

580 km (360 mi) southwest of Paris, 240 km (150 mi) northwest of Toulouse, 190 km (118 mi) northeast of Biarritz.

Bordeaux as a whole, rather than any particular points within it, is what you'll want to visit in order to understand why Victor Hugo described it as Versailles plus Antwerp, and why the great painter Goya chose it as his last home (he died here in 1828). The capital of southwest France and the region's largest city, Bordeaux remains synonymous with the wine trade: wine shippers have long maintained their headquarters along the banks of the Garonne, while buyers from around the world arrive for the huge biannual Vinexpo show. An aura of 18th-century elegance permeates downtown Bordeaux, where fine shops invite exploration. To the south of the city center are the old docklands, targeted for renewal—one train station has now been transformed into a big multiplex cinema—but still a bit shady. As a whole, Bordeaux is a less exuberant city than most others in France. That noted, lively and

Cathédrale St-André 7
Centre d'Art Plastique Contemporain .3
Grand Théâtre 6
Maison du Vin (CIVB) 5
Musée d'Aquitaine . .9
Musée des Beaux-Arts . . .8
Musée de Chartrons 4
Place de la Bourse 2
Pont de Pierre 1

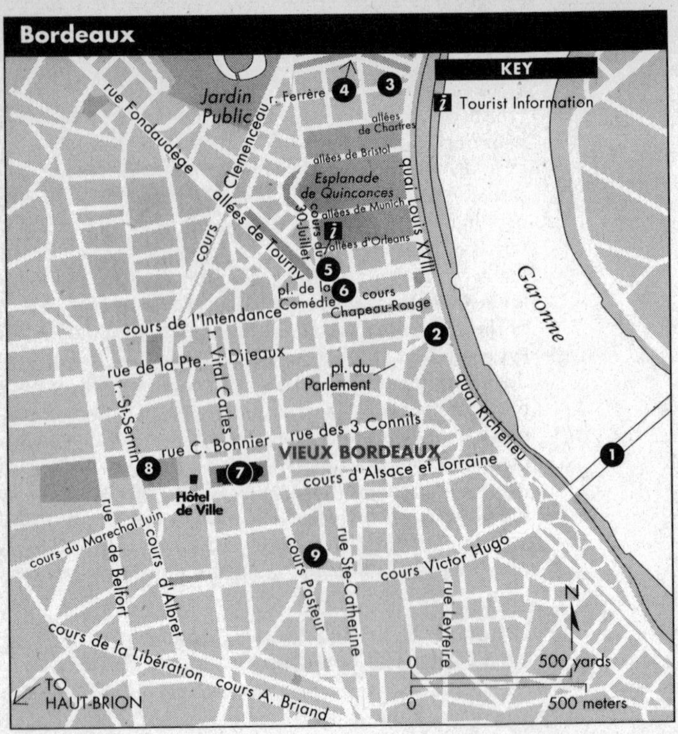

stylish elements are making a dent in the city's conservative veneer, and the cleaned-up riverfront is said by some to exude an elegance redolent of St. Petersburg. To get a feel for the historic port of Bordeaux, take the 90-minute boat trip that leaves quai Louis-XVIII every weekday afternoon, or take the regular passenger ferry that plies along the Garonne between Quai Richelieu and the Pont d'Aquitaine.

For a view of the picturesque quayside, stroll across the Garonne on
❶ the **Pont de Pierre** (Stone Bridge), the only bridge across the river until 1965; in calm weather you'll see a tethered balloon soaring 500 yards overhead, away to the left (€10). Return to the left bank and head north
❷ to **Place de la Bourse,** an open square (built 1730–55) ringed with large-windowed buildings designed by the era's most esteemed architect, Jacques-Ange Gabriel, who later worked for Marie-Antoinette at Versailles. Just north of the Esplanade des Quinconces, a sprawling square,
❸ is the two-story **Centre d'Art Plastique Contemporain** (Contemporary Arts Center), imaginatively housed in a converted 19th-century spice warehouse, the Entrepôt Lainé. Many shows here showcase cutting-edge artists who invariably festoon the huge expanse of the place with hanging ropes, ladders, and large video screens. There's a trendy restaurant on the roof next to the art library. ✉ *7 rue Ferrère,* ☎ *05–56–00–81–50.* 🎫 *€5.50.* ⏲ *Tues.–Sun. 11–6.*

❹ Close by along the quayside is the **Musée des Chartrons,** in an 18th-century vintner's house, retracing the history of the wine trade through a fine collection of old barrels and antique bottles. ✉ *41 rue Borie,* ☎ *05–57–87–50–60.* 🎫 *€3.05.* ⏲ *Weekdays 2–6.*

Turn back along the Garonne and cross Esplanade des Quinconces to
★ ❺ tree-lined cours du XXX-Juillet and the **Maison du Vin,** run by the CIVB (Conseil Interprofessionnel des Vins de Bordeaux), the headquarters of the Bordeaux wine trade. Before you go exploring the regional wine country, stop here to gain pointers from the staff (some English-speak-

ing) on the art of *dégustation* and pointers for where to go; their publication *Vineyards and Wine Cellars in the Bordeaux Area* is helpful. More importantly, tasting a red (like Pauillac or St-Émilion), a dry white (like an Entre-Deux-Mers or Côtes de Blaye), and a sweet white (like Sauternes or St-Macaire) will help you decide which of the seven wine regions to explore. Remember: Before visiting any country château vineyard, always call ahead to see if the tasting is free and whether you need an appointment—the staff here can help with these questions. You can also make purchases at the **Vinothèque** opposite this bureau. ✉ *1 cours du XXX-Juillet,* ☎ *05–56–00–22–66,* WEB *www.la-vinotheque.com.* 🎫 *Free.*

One block south is the city's leading 18th-century monument: the
6 **Grand Théâtre,** designed by Victor Louis and built between 1773 and 1780. The pride of the city, it is a building so magnificent that Charles Garnier did not hesitate to borrow major elements from its design when he built the Opéra in Paris. Its elegant exterior is ringed by graceful Corinthian columns, while the majestic foyer dazzles with a two-winged staircase and cupola. The theater hall has a frescoed ceiling with a shimmering chandelier composed of 14,000 Bohemian crystals. ✉ *Pl. de la Comédie,* ☎ *05–56–00–85–95.* 🎫 *€5. Contact tourist office for guided tours.*

Continue south on rue Ste-Catherine, then turn right on cours d'Al-
7 sace to reach the **Cathédrale St-André** (✉ Pl. Pey-Berland). This hefty edifice isn't one of France's finer Gothic cathedrals, but the intricate 14th-century chancel makes an interesting contrast with the earlier nave. Excellent stone carvings adorn the facade. You can climb the 15th-century, 160-ft **Tour Pey-Berland** for a view of the city; admission is €4, and it's open Tuesday–Sunday 10–noon and 2–5.

8 The nearby **Musée des Beaux-Arts,** across tidy gardens behind the ornate Hôtel de Ville (town hall), has a collection of works spanning the 15th–20th centuries, with important paintings by Paolo Veronese (*Apostle's Head*), Camille Corot (*Bath of Diana*), and Odilon Redon (*Chariot of Apollo*) and sculptures by Auguste Rodin. ✉ *20 cours d'Albret,* ☎ *05–56–10–20–56.* 🎫 *€4.* ⏲ *Wed.–Mon. 11–6.*

9 Two blocks south of the Cathédrale St-André is the **Musée d'Aquitaine,** an excellent museum that takes you on a trip through Bordeaux's history, with an emphasis on Roman, medieval, Renaissance, port-harbor, colonial, and 20th-century daily life. The detailed prehistoric section almost saves you a trip to Lascaux II, which is reproduced here in part. ✉ *20 cours Pasteur,* ☎ *05–56–01–51–00.* 🎫 *€4.* ⏲ *Mon.–Sat. 11–6.*

One of the region's most famous wine-producing châteaux is actually within the city limits: follow N250 southwest from central Bordeaux (in the direction of Arcachon) for 3 km (2 mi) to the district of Pessac, home to **Haut-Brion,** producer of the only non-Médoc wine to be ranked a *premier cru* (the most elite wine classification). The white château looks out over the celebrated pebbly soil. The wines produced at **La Mission–Haut Brion**, across the road, are almost as sought-after. ✉ *133 av. Jean-Jaurès, 33600 Pessac,* ☎ *05–56–00–29–31.* 🎫 *Free one-hour visits by appointment, Mon.–Fri. only, with tasting. Closed mid-July–mid-Aug.*

Dining and Lodging

Old Bordeaux has many small restaurants, particularly around the 18th-century place du Parlement, like bustling L'Ombrière (No. 14), with fairly priced steaks, and pricey Chez Philippe (No. 1), one of the city's top fish restaurants. What is lacking is charming hotels. You may want to consider staying outside Bordeaux, at the Château Lamothe in St-Sulpice et Cameyrac, 20 km (12 mi) east of the city, for instance.

$$$ ✕ **Estaquade.** *Le tout* Bordeaux now congregates at this fashionable spot, spectacularly set in a pierlike structure right on the Garonne River. Enormous bay windows allow you to drink in a beautiful panorama of the 18th-century place de la Bourse on the opposite bank. The cuisine is creative (prawn risotto, mullet with trout roe); the wine list has few selections to offer other than young Bordeaux, but that seems only fitting. ✉ *Quai des Queyries,* ☎ *05–57–54–02–50. AE, MC, V.*

$$ ✕ **Gravelier.** Anne-Marie, daughter of Pierre Troisgros of Roanne, married Yves Gravelier, and they combine their culinary talents here. In sparse decor, full of light and openness, imaginative cuisine is served: fillets of *rouget* (red mullet) with foie gras, and pigeon potpie with Chinese cabbage. The €20 lunch menu is a good deal. ✉ *114 cours de Verdun,* ☎ *05–56–48–17–15. AE, DC, MC, V. Closed Sun. and 1st 3 wks in Aug. No lunch Sat., no dinner Mon.*

$$ ★ ✕ **Vieux Bordeaux.** This lively, much-acclaimed nouvelle-cuisine haunt lies on the fringe of the old town. Chef Michel Bordage's menu is short but of high quality, complemented by three prix-fixe menus. His fish dishes are particularly tasty, such as the grilled *bar* (bass) on a peppery *galette* of crab. ✉ *27 rue Buhan,* ☎ *05–56–52–94–36. AE, DC, MC, V. Closed Sun., 1st ½ Feb., and Aug. No lunch Sat.*

$$$ ✕🏨 **Burdigala.** Of the three luxury hotels in Bordeaux, Burdigala (Latin for "Bordeaux") is the only one within walking distance of the center of town. The modern exterior is unappealing, the inside comfortable. The soundproof rooms are smart and neat; No. 416 is especially quiet and sunny. Deluxe rooms have marble bathrooms with whirlpool baths. The Jardin du Burdigala restaurant serves nouvelle cuisine. ✉ *115 rue Georges-Bonnac, 33000,* ☎ *05–56–90–16–16,* FAX *05–56–93–15–06,* WEB *www.burdigala.com. 68 rooms, 15 suites. Restaurant, cable TV, minibars, Internet, some pets allowed. AE, DC, MC, V.*

$$$ ✕🏨 **Sainte-Catherine.** This fully modernized hotel is in a 18th-century building in the old part of town. Service is limited, but the reception staff is helpful. The compact, pastel rooms are decorated with light floral fabrics. ✉ *27 rue du Parlement-Ste-Catherine, 33000,* ☎ *05–56–81–95–12,* FAX *05–56–44–50–51,* WEB *www.bordeaux-hotelquality.com. 84 rooms. Bar, cable TV, minibars, some pets allowed. AE, DC, MC, V.*

$$ 🏨 **Quatre Soeurs.** In an elegant 1840 town house near the Grand Théâtre, this hotel has sober, well-kept rooms of varying sizes, all renovated (with air-conditioning) in 1999–2000. It's changed a bit since Richard Wagner stayed here. ✉ *6 cours du XXX-juillet, 33000,* ☎ *05–57–81–19–20,* FAX *05–56–01–04–28,* WEB *www.4soeurs.free.fr. 34 rooms. Cable TV, Internet, some pets allowed. MC, V.*

Nightlife and the Arts

A respected and long-established Bordeaux hangout, **Les Argentiers** (✉ 33 rue des Argentiers) is the place for jazz. **L'Aztécal** (✉ 61 rue du Pas-St-Georges) is a comfortable spot for a drink. **Sénéchal** (✉ 57 bis quai de Paludate), near the station, is the place to dance the night away.

The **Grand Théâtre** (✉ Pl. de la Comédie, ☎ 05–56–00–85–95) puts on performances of French plays and occasionally operas. Bordeaux's four-day **Fête du Vin** (Wine Festival) at the end of June sees glass-clinking merriment along the banks of the Garonne.

Shopping

Between the cathedral and the Grand Théâtre are numerous pedestrian streets where stylish shops abound. For an exceptional selection of cheeses, go to **Jean d'Alos** (✉ 4 rue Montesquieu). The **Vinothèque** (✉ 8 cours du XXX-Juillet) sells top-ranked Bordeaux wines.

Route du Médoc

10 North of Bordeaux, the Route du Médoc wine road (D2) winds through the dusty Médoc Peninsula. Even the vines in Médoc look dusty, and so does the ugly town of **Margaux,** the area's unofficial capital, 27 km (17 mi) northwest of Bordeaux. Yet **Château Margaux,** housed in a coolly restrained Neoclassical building from 1802, is recognized as a producer of premiers crus, whose wine qualifies with Graves's Haut-Brion as one of Bordeaux's top five reds. The well-informed, English-speaking staff at the **Margaux Maison du Vin** (☎ 05–57–88–70–82, FAX 05–57–88–38–27) can direct you to such châteaux as **Lascombes** and **Palmer,** which have beautiful grounds, reasonably priced wines, and are open without reservations. In nearby Cussac, visit the winery and carriage museum at **Château Lanessan.**

★ 11 Some 90 km (56 mi) north of Bordeaux on highway D2 is **Pauillac,** home to three wineries—Lafite-Rothschild, Latour, and Mouton-Rothschild—that produce Médoc's other top reds. Renowned **Château Latour** (☎ 05–56–73–19–80) sometimes requires reservations a month in advance. If the posh prices of these fabled *grands crus* are not for you, rent a bike from the tourist office (La Verrerie, ☎ 05–56–59–03–08) and visit any of the less-expensive surrounding wineries. Of all the towns and villages in the Médoc, Pauillac is the prettiest; you may want to stroll along the riverfront and stop for refreshments at one of its restaurants.

Most of the great vineyards in this area are strictly private (the owners, however, are usually receptive to inquiries about visits from bona fide wine connoisseurs). One vineyard, however, has long boasted a ★ welcoming visitor center: **Mouton-Rothschild,** whose eponymous wine was brought to perfection in the 1930s by that flamboyant figure Baron Philippe de Rothschild, whose American-born wife, Pauline, was a great style-maker of the 1950s. The baron's daughter, Philippine, continues to lavish money and love on this growth, so wine lovers should flock here for either the one-hour visit, which includes a tour of the cellars, chais, and museum, or the slightly longer visit that tops off the tour with a tasting. ✉ *Le Pouyalet, 33250 Pauillac,* ☎ *05–56–73–21–29.* 🎫 *€5; with tasting, €12.50.* ⏲ *Apr.–Oct., daily 9:15–4.*

12 At the tip of the peninsula, near a memorial commemorating the landing of U.S. troops in 1917, is the **Pointe de Grave,** where you can take the *bac* (ferry) across the Gironde to Royan; it runs at least four times daily and costs €19.50 per car and €2.80 per passenger. During the half-hour crossing, keep an eye out for the **Phare de Cordouan** on your left, a lighthouse that looks as if it's emerging from the sea (it's actually built on a sandbank, exposed at low tide).

Dining and Lodging

$$$$ ★ ✕🏨 **Château Cordeillan-Bages.** This marble-faced, single-story 17th-century château just outside Pauillac is surrounded by the vines that produce its own *cru bourgeois*. Paris-trained chef Thierry Marx is the most highly rated in the region, and his fortes range from local salt-meadow lamb and spit-roasted kid with shallots to smoked eel with apple and crisp potato slices layered with oxtail and truffles (the restaurant is closed Monday and Tuesday and does not serve lunch Saturday). The guest rooms are cozy, comfortable, and Relais-&-Châteaux stylish. ✉ *61 rue des Vignerons, 33250 Pauillac (1½ km/1 mi south of town),* ☎

05–56–59–24–24, FAX *05–56–59–01–89,* WEB *www.relaischateaux.com/cordeillan. 25 rooms. Restaurant, bar, no air-conditioning in some rooms, cable TV, minibars, some pets allowed. AE, DC, MC, V. Closed mid-Dec.–end Jan.*

$$ **France & Angleterre.** A convenient choice for those who wish to explore Pauillac's lovely streets, this low-key spot offers some doubles overlooking the quaint waterfront. ✉ *3 quai Albert-Pichon, 33250 Pauillac,* ☎ *05–56–59–01–20,* FAX *05–56–59–02–31. 23 rooms. No air-conditioning, no room TVs, no pets. AE, DC, MC, V. Closed mid-Dec.–mid-Jan.*

Outdoor Activities and Sports

The **Médoc Marathon** (WEB www.marathondumedoc.com), on the first or second Saturday of September, is more than just a 42-km (26-mi) race through the vineyards: 50 groups of musicians turn out to serenade the runners, who can indulge in no fewer than 20 giant buffets en route, and drink free wine from two dozen estates along the way. Speed is not exactly of the essence for most competitors.

Royan

13 *104 km (65 mi) north of Bordeaux, 40 km (25 mi) south of Rochefort, 38 km (24 mi) southwest of Saintes.*

Royan is a commercialized resort town on the Atlantic whose vast seafront is packed to the gills in summer, although there are prettier beaches just north—in Pontaillac, St-Palais, and La Palymre (site of France's largest zoo, www.zoo-palmyre.fr). Boats leave Royan in summer for trips up the Gironde Estuary and across to the Phare de Cordouan lighthouse (☎ 05–46–06–42–36 for details).

Royan was tastefully rebuilt after being destroyed by German bombing in 1945. The imaginative domed, octagonal, concrete **Marché Central** (Central Market) merits a visit; it's open every morning, and ★ especially vibrant on Wednesday and Sunday. In the **Église Notre-Dame,** Guillaume Gillet's enormous 1950s concrete church with a breathtaking oval interior, the huge, unsupported sweep of the curved ceiling is a technical tour de force.

Lodging

$$–$$$ **Résidence de Rohan.** Royan is one of France's liveliest resorts during the summer, but its seafront is hardly the quietest place to spend the night. So take a short drive north of Royan, through Pontaillac to Vaux-sur-Mer, where the Résidence de Rohan is within skimming distance of the Plage de Nauzan. This old pink-and-white mansion is surrounded by trees. All rooms have a terrace or balcony, and most overlook the garden; the largest are in the annex. The reception areas have the plush-carpeted feel of a 1930s golf club, with velvet-lined armchairs in the lounge and mahogany seats in the bar. Snacks are served by the hotel's heated swimming pool. ✉ *Parc des Fées, 7 av. de Rohan, 17460 Vaux-sur-Mer (4 km/2½ mi northwest of Royan on D25),* ☎ *05–46–39–00–75,* FAX *05–46–38–29–99,* WEB *www.residence-rohan.com. 43 rooms. Bar, no air-conditioning, cable TV, Internet, tennis court, pool, some pets allowed. MC, V. Closed mid-Nov.–mid-Mar.*

En Route From Royan follow the Route Verte (Green Route) up the Gironde Estuary. Take D25 to the pleasant resort town of **St-Georges-de-Didonne** then continue south through pine forests and chalky cliffs to **Meschers** and Les Grottes de Matata, where you can sip tea or eat ice cream on a flower-bedecked terrace overlooking the estuary (from June through September). Farther south, **Talmont** is an unspoiled, car-free village renowned for its gently proportioned 12th-century pilgrim church jutting out over the water. Staying on D145, pause at the cheerful little harbor of **Mortagne-sur-Gironde**; then continue through pleasing hills, with beguiling views over the Gironde Estuary and vineyards, that produce cognac and then Bordeaux wines, as you progress south. **Blaye** has a vast Vauban citadel and a ferry that crosses to Lamarque, in the Médoc (four times a day for €14 per car and €4 per passenger). A scenic riverside road continues to **Bourg,** famed for its lightish red wines and Neoclassical château facing the river. From Bourg head southeast toward **Libourne,** skirting the town to the north to explore the vineyards of Fronsac, Pomerol, and Lalande-de-Pomerol, close to St-Émilion.

St-Émilion

★ ⓮ *128 km (80 mi) southeast of Royan, 35 km (23 mi) east of Bordeaux.*

Suddenly the sun-fired flatlands of Pomerol break into hills and send you tumbling into St-Émilion. This jewel of a town has old buildings of golden stone, ruined town walls, well-kept ramparts offering pleasing views, and a church hewn into a cliff. Sloping vineyards invade from all sides, and thousands of tourists invade down the middle, ravenous for the famous red wines and the scrumptious macaroons that bear the town's name. The medieval streets, delightfully cobblestoned, are filled with wine stores (St-Émilion reaches maturity earlier than other Bordeaux reds, and often offers a better value for the money than Médoc or Graves), crafts shops, and bakeries.

Tours of the pretty local vineyards—Château Pétrus and Cheval Blanc, among others—including wine tastings and train rides through the vineyards, are organized by the tourist office, the **Syndicat d'Initiative** (✉ Pl. des Créneaux, ☎ 05–57–55–28–28). The town's **Maison du Vin** (☎ 05–57–55–50–55, FAX 05–54–24–53–20) is helpful—ask where you can rent bikes to tour the wineries.

A stroll along the 13th-century ramparts takes you to the **Château du Roi** (King's Castle), built by occupying sovereign Henry III of England (1216–72). From the castle ramparts, steps lead down to **place du Marché,** a leafy square where cafés remain open late into the balmy summer night. Beware of the inflated prices charged at the café tables.

The **Église Monolithe** (Monolithic Church) is one of France's largest underground churches, hewn out of the rock face between the 9th and 12th centuries. Its spire-topped bell tower emerges from the bedrock, dominating the center of town. ✉ *Pl. du Marché.* 🎫 *€5.* ⏲ *Tours leave every 45 mins from tourist office, daily 10–11:30 and 2–5.*

Just south of the town walls is the **Château Ausone,** an estate that is ranked with Cheval Blanc as producing St-Émilion's finest wine.

Dining and Lodging

$–$$ ✕ **Chez Germaine.** Family cooking and regional dishes are the focus at this central St-Émilion eatery. The candlelit upstairs dining room and the terrace are both pleasant places to enjoy the reasonably priced set menus. Grilled meats and fish are house specialties; for dessert, go for the almond macaroons. ✉ *13 rue du Clocher,* ☎ *05–57–74–49–34. DC, V. Closed Sun.–Mon. and mid-Dec.–mid-Jan.*

$$$$ ✕🏨 **Grand Barrail.** This turn-of-the-20th-century luxury hotel just outside St-Émilion, flanked by a lake and vineyards, may seem a little stiff and heavy, but rooms are unusually large and smartly furnished; about half are in the former stables. Talented chef Fabrice Giraud serves pumpkin soup, and calamari and goat-cheese risotto, in the Belle Epoque dining room (no dinner Sunday; no lunch Tuesday, closed Monday out

Close-Up

BORDEAUX: A WINE-LOVER'S GAZETTEER

BARON PHILIPPE DE ROTHSCHILD, legendary owner of Bordeaux's famed Mouton-Rothschild vineyard, was famous for drinking *vin ordinaire* at most lunches and dinners. Indeed, any Frenchman knows you can't enjoy fine vintages at every meal. Still, if you're traveling to Bordeaux, you're going to want to enjoy some of the region's celebrated liquid *spécialités*. To find the best vineyards, just head in any direction from the city of Bordeaux. The city is at the hub of a patchwork of vineyards: the Médoc peninsula to the northwest; Bourg and Blaye across the estuary; St-Émilion inland to the east; then, as you wheel around clockwise, come Entre-Deux-Mers, Sauternes, and Graves.

The nearest vineyard to Bordeaux itself is, ironically, one of the best: Haut-Brion, on the western outskirts of the city, and one of the five châteaux to be officially recognized as a *premier cru* or first growth. There are only five premiers crus in all, and Haut-Brion is the only one not in the Médoc (Château Mouton-Rothschild, Château Margaux, Château Latour, and Château Lafite-Rothschild complete the list). The Médoc is subdivided into various appellations, wine-growing districts with their own specific characteristics and taste. Pauillac and Margaux host premiers crus; St-Julien and St-Estèphe possess many domaines of almost equal quality, followed by Listrac and Moulis; wines not quite so good are classed as Haut-Médoc or, as you move further north, Médoc pure and simple. Wines from the Médoc are made predominantly from the cabernet sauvignon grape, and can taste dry, even austere, when young. The better ones often need 15 to 25 years before "opening up" to reveal their complex spectrum of flavors.

When considering lighter reds for earlier consumption, serious connoisseurs will prefer to head southeast beyond Libourne to the stunning old town of St-Émilion. The surrounding vineyards see the fruity merlot grape in control, and wines here often have more immediate appeal than those of the Médoc. There are several small appellations apart from St-Émilion itself, the most famous being Pomerol, whose Château Pétrus is the world's most expensive wine.

South of St-Émilion is the region known as Entre-Deux-Mers ("between two seas"—actually the Dordogne and Garonne Rivers), whose dry white wine is particularly flavorsome if made from the vineyards near the ruined castle of Haut-Benauge. The picturesque villages of Loupiac and Sainte-Croix du Mont are sandwiched between the Garonne River and hillside vineyards producing sweet, not dry, white wine. But the best sweet wine produced hereabouts—some would say in the world—comes from across the Garonne and is made at Barsac and Sauternes. Nothing in the grubby village of Sauternes would suggest that mind-boggling wealth lurks amid the picturesque vine-laden slopes and hollows. The village has a wine shop where bottles gather dust on rickety shelves, next to handwritten price tags demanding small fortunes. Making Sauternes is a tricky business. Autumn mists steal up the valleys to promote *Botrytis cinerea*, a fungus known as *pourriture noble* or noble rot, which sucks moisture out of the grapes, leaving a high proportion of sugar. Up to seven successive harvests are undertaken at Château d'Yquem to assure the optimum selection. Heading back north toward Bordeaux you encounter the vineyards of the Graves region, so called because of its gravelly soil. The Graves is an extensive producer of white (mainly dry) wine as well as red, and some of the best is produced in the Pessac-Léognan appellation. As in Entre-Deux-Mers, the semillon and sauvignon grapes are to the fore. *Santé!*

of season). St-Émilions constitute at least 60% of the impressive wine list. ✉ *5 rue Marzelle, 33330 (4 km/2½ mi northwest of St-Émilion),* ☎ *05–57–55–37–00,* FAX *05–57–55–37–49,* WEB *www.grand-barrail.com. 28 rooms. Restaurant, cable TV, minibars, Internet, some pets allowed. AE, DC, MC, V. Closed 3 wks Feb., late Nov.–mid-Dec.*

$$$ ★ **Plaisance.** Across from the tourist office in the upper part of town is this sought-after hotel. Rooms are warm and appealing; the Descault Room has an excellent view of the vineyards. Dinner matches the St-Émilion wines; if you are not staying here, make this your number one choice for a leisurely meal, though you'll need to book ahead. Try the crab stuffed with cabbage, the pork with mango chutney, or the truffled bananas. ✉ *5 pl. du Clocher, 33330,* ☎ *05–57–55–07–55,* FAX *05–57–74–41–11,* WEB *www.hostellerie-plaisance.com. 19 rooms. Restaurant, cable TV, some minibars, some pets allowed. AE, DC, MC, V. Closed Jan.*

$$$$ **Château Lamothe.** St-Émilion's hotels are mostly in-and-out tourist stops, and those in Bordeaux lack charm; a nice alternative is this private manor house (advance reservations required) halfway between the two. The large guest rooms have big four-poster beds with soft cotton sheets; you may find them a little too frilly, but they are very comfortable. Owner Jacques Bastide speaks English and is extremely helpful with suggestions. ✉ *6 rte. du Stade, 33450 St-Sulpice et Cameyrac (25 km/16 mi west of St-Émilion, 20 km/12 mi northeast of Bordeaux),* ☎ *05–56–30–82–16,* FAX *05–56–30–88–33. 3 rooms. No air-conditioning, Internet, pool, fishing, no pets. MC, V.*

$$ **Commanderie.** Close to the ramparts, this 19th-century two-story hotel has a garden and a view of the vineyards. Rooms are small but clean and individually decorated with colorful prints; some have exposed stonework. ✉ *2 rue de la Porte-Brunet, 33300,* ☎ *05–57–24–70–19,* FAX *05–57–74–44–53. 17 rooms. Bar, no air-conditioning in some rooms, cable TV, Internet, no pets. MC, V. Closed late Dec.–Feb.*

DORDOGNE

Stretching along the Dordogne, Isle, Dronne, and Auvezère rivers, this region's wooded hills and valleys are full of romantic riverside châteaux, small medieval villages, and is one of the premier "prehistoric" destinations in Europe, as the region is dotted with noted sites, including the incomparable Lascaux cavern paintings (today, in reality, the not-so-incomparable Lascaux 2). You may want to spend a week exploring the small country roads and picnicking on riverbanks.

Bergerac

15 *87 km (54 mi) east of Bordeaux, 57 km (36 mi) east of St-Émilion.*

Cyrano never lived here, but no matter—the town still claims the long-nosed swashbuckler as a local son (his family had roots here but he was actually a Parisian playwright who lived 1619 to 1655). Bergerac is a lively town with ancient half-timber houses, narrow alleys, and colorful Wednesday and Saturday (the larger of the two) markets. Guided walking tours of the Old Town (1 hr, €4) leave from the **tourist office** (✉ 97 rue Neuve d'Argenson, ☎ 05–53–57–03–11). There are also hour-long cruises along the Dordogne (€6.30); check with the tourist office or the **cruise company** (☎ 05–53–24–58–80) for information.

The **Cloître des Récollets,** a former convent, is in the wine business. The convent's stone-and-brick buildings range in date from the 12th to the 17th centuries and include galleries, a large vaulted cellar, and a cloister, where the **Maison du Vin** (Wine Center) provides information on—and samples of—local vintages. ✉ *Quai Salvette,* ☎ *05–53–63–57–55.* 🎟 *Free.* ⏲ *Daily 10–12:30 and 1:30–6.*

You can learn about another local industry—tobacco growing—from its pre-Columbian origins to its spread worldwide, at the **Musée du Tabac** (Tobacco Museum). It's housed in the 17th-century Maison Peyrarède, near the quayside. ✉ *Pl. de Feu,* ☎ *05–53–63–04–13.* 🎟 *€3.* ⏲ *Tues.–Fri. 10–noon and 2–6, Sat. 10–noon and 2–5, Sun. 2:30–6:30.*

Dining and Lodging

$$ ✕🏨 **Bordeaux.** One of the better hotels in town, the family-owned Bordeaux has contemporary furnishings and neat rooms. Request one on the garden courtyard or No. 22, which is slightly more spacious. Though you're not obliged to eat at the restaurant, Le Terroir, it's difficult to refuse the marinated salmon in anisette and lime or the pan-fried *escalope de foie gras* (sautéed foie gras). The owner, Monsieur Maury, speaks fluent English. ✉ *38 pl. Gambetta, 24100,* ☎ *05–53–57–12–83,* FAX *05–53–57–72–14. 40 rooms. Restaurant, no air-conditioning, cable TV, pool, some pets allowed. AE, DC, MC, V. Closed mid-Dec.–end Jan.*

Monbazillac

⑯ *6 km (4 mi) south of Bergerac via D13.*

From the hilltop village of Monbazillac are spectacular views of the sweet wine–producing vineyards tumbling toward the Dordogne. The squat corner towers of the beautifully proportioned 16th-century gray-stone **Château de Monbazillac** pay tribute to the fortress tradition of the Middle Ages, but the large windows and sloping roofs reveal the Renaissance influence. Regional furniture and an ornate early 17th-century bedchamber enliven the interior. A wine tasting is included to tempt you into buying a case or two of the famous but expensive bottles. The restaurant on the grounds serves expensive meals. ☎ *05–53–61–52–52.* 🎟 *€5.65.* ⏲ *June–Sept., daily 10–12:30 and 2–7:30; mid-Feb.–May and Oct.–Dec., daily 10–noon and 2–5.*

Monpazier

⑰ *16 km (10 mi) southeast of Bergerac.*

Monpazier, on the tiny Drot River, is one of France's best-preserved bastide towns. It was built in ocher-color stone by English king Edward I in 1284 to protect the southern flank of his French possessions. The bastide has three stone gateways (of an original six), a large central square, and the church of **St-Dominique,** housing 35 carved-wood choir stalls and a would-be relic of the True Cross. Opposite the church is the finest medieval building in town, the **Maison du Chapître** (Chapter House), once used as a barn for storing grain. Its wood-beam roof is constructed of chestnut to repel insects.

Dining and Lodging

$ ✕🏨 **France.** Once an outbuilding on the estates of the Château de Biron, the Hôtel de France has never capitalized on its 13th-century heritage or its 15th-century staircase. Instead, it has remained a small, modest family-run hotel that caters less to tourists than to locals at its bar and restaurant, serving rich regional food. Rooms are a clutter of old furniture (with a plastic-cabinet shower and toilet squeezed into the corner); some are quite large. ✉ *21 rue St-Jacques, 24540,* ☎ *05–53–22–60–01,* FAX *05–53–22–07–27. 17 rooms. Restaurant, bar, no air-conditioning, no room TVs, no pets. MC, V.*

Biron

18 *8 km (5 mi) south of Monpazier via D53.*

Stop in Biron to see its massive hilltop castle, the **Château de Biron.** Highlights of the château, which with its keep, square tower, and chapel dates from the Middle Ages, include monumental staircases and the kitchen with its huge stone-slab floor. The classical buildings were completed in 1730. English Romantic poet Lord Byron (1788–1824) is claimed as a distant descendant of the Gontaut-Biron family, which lived here for 14 generations. ☎ *05–53–63–13–39.* €4.60. *Sept.–Nov. and Feb.–June, Wed.–Mon. 10–12:30 and 2–5:30; July–Aug., daily 10–7.*

Cahors

19 *60 km (38 mi) southeast of Monpazier via D660, 108 km (67 mi) northwest of Albi.*

Once an opulent Gallo-Roman town, Cahors, sitting snugly within a loop of the Lot River, is famous for its tannic red wine, known to the Romans as "black wine." Many of the small estates in the area offer tastings. The town's finest sight is the 14th-century **Pont Valentré,** a bridge with three elegant towers that constitutes a spellbinding feat of medieval engineering. Also look for the fortresslike **Cathédrale St-Étienne** (✉ off rue du Maréchal-Joffre), with its cupolas and cloisters connecting to the courtyard of the archdeaconry, which is awash with Renaissance decoration and thronged with townsfolk who come for art exhibits.

Dining and Lodging

$$$$ **Château de Mercuès.** The former home of the count-bishops of Cahors, on a rocky spur just outside town, has older rooms in baronial splendor (ask for one of these), as well as unappealing modern ones (which tend to attract midges). One of the best is "Tour," with a clever ceiling that slides back to expose the turret. Duck, lamb, and truffles reign in the restaurant, redecorated in 2001, but the high prices lead you to expect more creativity from chef Philippe Combet than is delivered. The restaurant is closed Monday, and there's no lunch Tuesday–Thursday. ✉ *46090 Mercuès (6 km/4 mi northwest of Cahors on road to Villeneuve-sur-Lot),* ☎ *05–65–20–00–01,* FAX *05–65–20–05–72,* WEB *www.relaischateaux.com/mercues. 24 rooms, 6 suites. Restaurant, no air-conditioning, cable TV, minibars, Internet, 2 tennis courts, pool, some pets allowed. AE, DC, MC, V. Closed Nov.–Easter.*

St-Cirq-Lapopie

20 *25 km (16 mi) east of Cahors via D653 and D662.*

The beautiful 13th-century village of St-Cirq (pronounced san-*sare*) is on a rocky spur 262 ft up, with nothing but a vertical drop to the Lot River below. Filled with artisans' workshops and not yet renovated à la Disney, the town has so many dramatic views you may end up spending several hours here. A mostly ruined château can be reached by a stiff walk along the path that starts near the Hôtel de Ville. Stop by the tourist office in the center of town for information.

Lodging

$$ **Pélissaria.** This intimate 16th-century hotel is small and simple but chock full of atmosphere. The best rooms look out across the village or the valley and river; some rooms in the garden have less grand views (Nos. 3 and 4 are very small). The lounge is a snug place to relax in front of the fire in the evening. ✉ *46330 St-Cirq-Lapopie,* ☎ *05–65–*

31–25–14, FAX 05–65–30–25–52. 10 rooms. Bar, no air-conditioning, pool, some pets allowed. MC, V. Closed Nov.–Mar.

Rocamadour

★ 21 *62 km (39 mi) north of St-Cirq, 46 km (29 mi) northwest of Figeac.*

Rocamadour is a medieval village that seems to defy the laws of gravity; it surges out of a cliff 1,500 ft above the Alzou River gorge—an awe-inspiring sight that makes this one of the most-visited tourist spots in France. The town got its name after the discovery in 1166 of the 1,000-year-old body of St. Amadour "quite whole." The body was moved to the cathedral, where it began to work miracles. Pilgrims flocked to the site, climbing the 216 steps to the church on their knees. Making the climb on foot is sufficient reminder of the medieval penchant for agonizing penance; today an elevator lifts weary souls. A very small number of people actually live in Rocamadour; what they think about the yearly influx of more than a million tourists and pilgrims can only be guessed at, and judging from the number of tacky souvenir shops in the village, not too poorly. Cars are not allowed; park in the lot below the town.

The staircase and elevator up to the **Cité Religieuse** start from place de la Carreta; if you walk, pause at the landing 141 steps up to admire the fort. Once up, you'll see tiny place St-Amadour and its seven sanctuaries: the basilica of **St-Sauveur** opposite the staircase; the **St-Amadour crypt** beneath the basilica; the chapel of **Notre-Dame** to the left; the chapels of **John the Baptist, St-Blaise,** and **Ste-Anne** to the right; and the Romanesque chapel of **St-Michel** built into an overhanging cliff. St-Michel's two 12th-century frescoes—depicting the Annunciation and the Visitation—have survived in superb condition. ✉ *Centre d'Accueil Notre-Dame.* *Tips at visitors' discretion.* ⏲ *Guided tours Mon.–Sat. 9–5; English-speaking guide available.*

The village of Rocamadour itself—the Cité Médiévale—though in parts grotesquely touristy, is full of beautifully restored structures, such as the 15th-century **Hôtel de Ville,** near the Porte Salmon, which houses the **tourist office** and an excellent collection of tapestries. Rue Piétonne is lined with creperies and tea salons. *Free.* ⏲ *Mon.–Sat. 10–noon and 3–8.*

Dining and Lodging

$$$–$$$$ ✕ **Château de la Treyne.** Part of the Relais & Châteaux group, this small hotel at Lacave, 6 mi (3½ km) northwest of Rocamadour, serenely guards the Dordogne as it has since the 14th century. Dinner is served in a paneled room with old portraits and a roaring fire. The spacious rooms are traditionally furnished with 19th-century paintings and country antiques. During high season you are expected to have dinner. ✉ *La Treyne, 46200 Lacave,* ☎ *05–65–32–60–60,* FAX *05–65–37–60–70. 15 rooms. Restaurant, minibars, Internet, tennis court, pool, sauna, some pets allowed. AE, DC, MC, V. Closed mid-Nov.–Feb.*

$$ ✕ **Beau Site.** This is the best of the few Old Town hotels. The charm of the ancient beams, exposed stone, and open hearth in the foyer ends, however, as you climb the stairs; rooms are modern and functional. The modern, large-windowed Jehan de Valon restaurant overlooks the canyon, serving foie gras, local lamb and walnut gateau. Best of all, you can park inside Rocamadour if you stay here. ✉ *Cité Médiévale, 46500,* ☎ *05–65–33–63–08,* FAX *05–65–33–65–23,* WEB *www.bw-beausite.com. 42 rooms. Restaurant, bar, no air-conditioning in some rooms, cable TV, Internet, some pets allowed. AE, DC, MC, V. Closed mid-Nov.–mid-Feb.*

$ 🏨 **Lion d'Or.** In the center of Rocamadour, this gently priced hotel conveniently has a restaurant on the premises. ✉ *Cité Médiévale, 46500,* ☎ *05–65–33–62–04,* FAX *05–65–33–72–54. 35 rooms. Restaurant, no air-conditioning, no room TVs, no pets. MC, V. Nov.–Feb.*

Domme

22 *50 km (31 mi) west of Rocadamour.*

The historic cliff-top village of Domme is famous for its **grottoes,** where prehistoric bison and rhinoceros bones have been discovered. You can visit the 500-yard-long illuminated galleries, which are lined with stalactites. ✉ *Entrance on pl. de la Halle.* 🎫 *€4.60.* ⏲ *Apr.–Sept., daily 9:30–noon and 2–6; Mar. and Oct., daily 2–6.*

Dining and Lodging

$$–$$$ ✕🏨 **Esplanade.** Make sure your room overlooks the Dordogne—the expansive view makes this hotel special. Rooms are small but modern, and the location on the edge of the square is perfect. Worthy chef René Gillard creates such specialties as foie de canard in pot-au-feu, and all kinds of truffle-filled dishes. The restaurant does not serve dinner on Monday February–April or lunch on Monday September–June. ✉ *Rue du Pont-Carrat, 24250 Domme,* ☎ *05–53–28–31–41,* FAX *05–53–28–49–92. 25 rooms. Restaurant, no air-conditioning, cable TV, some pets allowed. AE, DC, MC, V. Closed mid-Nov.–mid-Feb.*

La Roque-Gageac

23 *5 km (3 mi) northwest of Domme via D703.*

Across the Dordogne from Domme, in the direction of Beynac, huddled beneath a cliff, is La Roque-Gageac, one of the best-restored villages in the valley. Crafts shops line its narrow streets, dominated by the outlines of the 19th-century mock-medieval Château de Malartrie and the Manoir de Tarde, with its cylindrical turret.

Dining and Lodging

$$ ✕🏨 **Plume d'Oie.** This small inn overlooks the river and the limestone cliffs. Rooms, in light fabrics and wicker furniture, vary in size and price. La Plume d'Oie's major raison d'être, however, is the stone-walled restaurant, at which you are expected to have at least one meal. Chef-owner Marc-Pierre Walker prepares classic regional cuisine, such as fillet of beef cooked in red wine, and ragout of foie gras (the restaurant is closed Monday and does not serve lunch Tuesday). ✉ *24250 La Roque-Gageac,* ☎ *05–53–29–57–05,* FAX *05–53–31–04–81. 4 rooms. Restaurant, no air-conditioning, some pets allowed. MC, V. Closed late Nov.–mid-Dec. and early Mar.*

Beynac-et-Cazenac

24 *5 km (3 mi) west of La Roque-Gageac, 63 km (39 mi) east of Bergerac.*

The main reason to stop in Beynac is to see its medieval castle. Daringly perched atop a sheer cliff face beside an abrupt bend in the Dordogne, the muscular 13th-century **Château de Beynac** has unforgettable views from its battlements. ☎ *05–53–29–50–40.* 🎫 *€6.55.* ⏲ *Nov.–Feb., daily 11–5; Mar.–June and Sept.–Oct., daily 10–5:30; July–Aug., daily 10–7.*

The ruined castle of **Castlenaud,** containing a large collection of medieval arms, is just upstream from Beynac across the Dordogne; it's open May–October, daily 10–7, and admission is €6. Five kilometers

(3 miles) from Castlenaud is the turreted **Château des Milandes** (☎ 05–53–59–31–21), which is open mid-April–November, daily 10–noon and 2–5 (€7.50). It was once owned by the American-born cabaret star of Roaring '20s Paris, Josephine Baker, and there's a museum devoted to her memory. In summer there are falconry displays. From here D53 (via Belvès) leads southwest to Monpazier.

Sarlat-la-Canéda

★ 25 *10km (6 mi) northeast of Beynac, 74 km (46 mi) east of Bergerac.*

The small town of Sarlat (as it is usually known) is filled most days with tour groups, and is especially hectic on Saturday, market day: all the geese on sale are proof of the local addiction to foie gras. To do justice to the town's golden-stone splendor, wander through its medieval streets in the later afternoon or early evening, aided by the tourist office's walking map. The tourist office also organizes walking tours, which for €4 give you an in-depth look at the town's medieval buildings.

Of particular note is rue de la Liberté, which leads to **place du Peyrou,** anchored on one corner by the steep-gable Renaissance house where writer-orator Étienne de la Boétie (1530–63) was born. The elaborate turreted tower of the **Cathédrale St-Sacerdos** (✉ Pl. du Peyrou), begun in the 12th century, is the oldest part of the building and, along with the choir, all that remains of the original Romanesque structure. The sloping garden behind the cathedral, the **Cour de l'Évêché** (Bishop's Courtyard), contains a strange, conical tower known as the Lanterne des Morts (Lantern of the Dead), which was occasionally used as a funeral chapel. Rue d'Albusse, adjoining the garden behind the cathedral, and rue de la Salamandre are narrow, twisty streets that head to place de la Liberté and the 17th-century **Hôtel de Ville.** Opposite the town hall is the rickety former church of **Ste-Marie,** overlooking place des Oies. Ste-Marie points the way to Sarlat's most interesting street, **rue des Consuls.** Among its medieval buildings are the Hôtel Plamon, with broad windows that resemble those of a Gothic church, and, opposite, the 15th-century Hôtel de Vassal.

Dining and Lodging

$$ ★ ✕🏨 **St-Albert et Montaigne.** The Garrigou family has two hotels on this delightful square in the center of town. The Montaigne is in a manor; ask for lovely Room 33, with exposed beams. The St-Albert has simply furnished rooms of varying size. Hearty regional fare is served in the restaurant (closed Sunday dinner and Monday from November to Easter). Over dinner, discuss your next day's itinerary with Monsieur Garrigou: he not only knows the region well but is also the town's backroom politician. ✉ *10 pl. Pasteur, 24200,* ☎ *05–53–31–55–55,* FAX *05–53–59–19–99. 60 rooms. Restaurant, Internet, no pets. AE, MC, V.*

Les Eyzies-de-Tayac

26 *21 km (13 mi) northwest of Sarlat via D47.*

Many signs of prehistoric man have been discovered in the vicinity of Les Eyzies; a number of excavated caves and grottoes, some with wall paintings, are open for public viewing. At the **Grotte du Grand-Roc,** you can view weird-shape crystalline stalactites and stalagmites. ✉ *Rte. de la Gare,* ☎ *05–53–06–92–70.* 🎫 *€6.* ⏲ *Feb.–May and Sept.–Dec., daily 10–5; June–Aug., daily 9–7.*

The **Musée National de Préhistoire** (National Museum of Prehistory), in a Renaissance château, attracts large crowds to its renowned collection of prehistoric artifacts, including primitive sculpture, furniture, and tools. You can also get ideas at the museum about excavation sites to visit in the region. ✉ *Le Bourg,* ☎ *05–53–06–45–45.* 🎫 *€4.* ⏲ *Apr.–Oct., Wed.–Mon. 9:30–noon and 2–6; Nov.–Mar., Wed.–Mon. 9:30–noon and 2–5.*

Dining and Lodging

$$$–$$$$ ★ ✕🏨 **Vieux Logis.** This vine-clad manor house on the edge of Trémolat is one of the best hotels in Dordogne. The warm rooms vary in size; most face the well-tended garden and a rushing brook. One favorite, No. 22, has a terra-cotta tile floor, exposed beams, stone walls, and a suitelike bathroom. For dinner, the five-course Menu Vieux Logis (€45) might include the chef's forte, pigeon terrine (the restaurant is closed Tuesday from mid-January through May). ✉ *24510 Trémolat (24 km/15 mi west of Les Eyzies),* ☎ *05–53–22–80–06,* FAX *05–53–22–84–89. 19 rooms, 5 suites. Restaurant, no air-conditioning, cable TV, minibars, Internet, pool, some pets allowed. AE, DC, MC, V.*

$$$ ✕🏨 **Centenaire.** Though it's also a stylish, modern hotel, Le Centenaire is known foremost as a restaurant. Chef Roland Mazère adds flair to the preparation of local delights: risotto with truffles or snails with ravioli and gazpacho. The dining room's golden stone and wood beams retain local character (the restaurant does not serve lunch Tuesday or Wednesday; a jacket is required). Rooms, especially at the lower end of the price scale, are fairly small. ✉ *24620 Les Eyzies-de-Tayac,* ☎ *05–53–06–68–68,* FAX *05–53–06–92–41. 19 rooms. Restaurant, cable TV, minibars, pool, health club, sauna, no pets. AE, DC, MC, V. Closed Nov.–Mar.*

$$–$$$ 🏨 **Noyer.** This inn, in a steep-roofed 18th-century building west of Les Eyzies, is owned by Eric and Bettina Guilbert, who speak fluent English. The comfortable, provincial-style rooms are in the main building and in the former barn (avoid those on the ground floor: you can hear the upstairs plumbing). ✉ *Le Reclaud, 24260 Le Bugue (5 km/3 mi outside village; 11 km/7 mi west of Les Eyzies),* ☎ *05–53–07–11–73,* FAX *05–53–54–57–44,* WEB *www.perigord.com/aubergedunoyer. 10 rooms. No air-conditioning, no room TVs, pool, no pets. MC, V. Closed Nov.–Apr.*

Lascaux II

27 *27 km (17 mi) northeast of Les Eyzies via D706.*

The famous **Grotte de Lascaux** (Lascaux Caves), just outside Montignac, contain hundreds of prehistoric wall paintings—thought to be at least 20,000 years old. The undulating horses, cow, black bulls, and unicorn on this walls were discovered by chance in 1940. Although the caves have been sealed off to prevent damage, two of the galleries and many of the paintings have been reproduced in vivid detail in the Lascaux II exhibition center nearby. The copy is so good it is as awe-inspiring as the original. Unlike caves marked with authentic prehistoric art, Lascaux II is completely geared toward visitors, and you can watch a fancy presentation about cave art or take a tour in the language of your choice. Purchase tickets at the tourist office in Montignac before setting off. ✉ *Rte. de la Grotte,* ☎ *05–53–51–95–03.* 🎫 *€7.70.* ⏲ *Feb.–Dec., Tues.–Sun. 10–noon and 2–5.*

Hautefort

28 *28 km (18 mi) north of Lascaux.*

★ The reason to come to Hautefort is to see its castle, which presents a disarmingly arrogant face to the world. The silhouette of the **Château**

de Hautefort bristles with high roofs, domes, chimneys, and cupolas. The square-lined Renaissance left wing clashes with the muscular, round towers of the right wing, as the only surviving section of the original medieval castle—the gateway and drawbridge—plays referee in the middle. Adorning the inside are 17th-century furniture and tapestries. ✉ *Le Bourg,* ☎ *05–53–50–51–23.* *€6.50.* ⏲ *Easter–Nov., daily 2–6; Dec.–Easter, Sun. 2–6.*

Lodging

$$ **Enclos.** Out of a group of 250-year-old farm buildings on 4 acres of land, some 9 km (5 mi) west of Hautefort, Americans Robert and Dana Ornsteen have created a charming country base. They live in the main house, which also contains a living room and two small guest rooms. The *granges* (outbuildings) add five more guest rooms and a cottage. Exposed walls and beams and a restored bread-oven are among the features. Table d'hôte dinners are served once or twice a week. ✉ *Pragelier, 24390 Tourtoirac,* ☎ *05–53–51–11–40,* FAX *05–53–50–37–21. 7 rooms. No air-conditioning, pool, no pets. No credit cards.*

Périgueux

29 *40 km (24 mi) west of Hautefort via D5, 121 km (75 mi) northeast of Bordeaux, 85 km (53 mi) southeast of Angoulême.*

Périgueux is best known for its weird-looking cathedral. Finished in 1173 and restored in the 19th century, the **Cathédrale St-Front** looks like it might be on loan from Istanbul, given its shallow-scale domes and elongated conical cupolas sprouting from the roof like baby minarets. You may be struck by similarities with the Byzantine-style Sacré-Coeur in Paris; that's no coincidence—architect Paul Abadie (1812–84) had a hand in the design of both. ✉ *Pl. de la Clarté.*

Brantôme

30 *27 km (17 mi) northwest of Périgueux via D939, 59 km (37 mi) southeast of Angoulême.*

The beautiful old town of Brantôme, with its waterside abbey entirely ringed by the sparkling Dronne River, is often considered the gateway to (or from) the Dordogne region. It deserves a stop, even just for a walk along the river or through the old, narrow streets. At night the abbey is romantically floodlighted.

Lodging

$$ **Château de Laborie.** This country château is a step above your usual B&B. A long avenue of lime trees leads to the moat and handsome facade. Natty hostess Micheline "Dizzy" Duseau chats with all and offers advice on where to dine (one of these suggestions, the Terrace des Jardins, is below par). Rooms, furnished with hand-me-down antiques, are comfortable if a little stilted, though two rooms on the first floor are warmer and have fewer bourgeois pretensions. ✉ *La Borie, 24530 Champagnac-de-Belair (5 km/3 mi north of Brantôme),* ☎ *05–53–54–22–99,* FAX *05–53–08–53–78. 5 rooms. No air-conditioning, no room TVs, pool, no pets. No credit cards. Closed early Nov.–Easter.*

POITOU-CHARENTES

Poitou-Charentes occupies the northern part of the region covered in this chapter. Rural, rolling Poitou is named for the ancient town of Poitiers. Charentes refers to two départements linked by the Charente River: Charente-Maritime, with its islands and sandy Atlantic beaches, and inland Charente. Highlights of Poitou-Charentes include the

"Green Venice" of the Marais Poitevin and the town of Cognac, famed for its brandy.

Angoulême

31 *59 km (37 mi) northwest of Brantôme, 116 km (72 mi) south of Poitiers, 86 km (54 mi) northwest of Périgueux.*

Angoulême is divided, like many other French towns, between an old, picturesque section around a hilltop cathedral and a modern, industrial part sprawling along the valley and railroad below. The 19th-century novelist Honoré de Balzac is one of the town's adopted sons; he described Angoulême in his meaty novel *Lost Illusions*. The Ville Haute (Upper Town), known as *Le Plateau*, has a warren of quaint old streets around the Hôtel de Ville (Town Hall) and stunning views from the ramparts.

The 12th-century **Cathédrale St-Pierre** (✉ Pl. St-Pierre) bears little resemblance to the majority of its French counterparts because of the cupolas topping each of its three bays. The cathedral was partly destroyed by Calvinists in 1562, then restored in a heavy-handed manner in 1634 and 1866. Its main attraction is its magnificent Romanesque facade, whose layers of rounded arches bear 70 stone statues and bas-reliefs illustrating the Last Judgment.

Dining and Lodging

$–$$ ✕ **Tour des Valois.** Diagonally across from the market, this rustic 15th-century restaurant has a good choice of regional food. Sample one of André Gérard's veal dishes—the one using the local mustard from Jarnac is particularly good—and the locally made foie gras. ✉ *7 rue Massillon,* ☎ *05–45–95–23–64. AE, MC, V. Closed part of Feb., mid-Aug.–early Sept., and Mon. No dinner Sun.*

$$$$ ✕🏨 **Château de Nieuil.** An avenue of trees opening onto a circular lawn leads to this former hunting lodge—a huge Renaissance château with towers. Rooms vary: some have traditional furnishings and pastel blue fabric; others have a *petit salon* (small sitting area) or a garden view. If the reception area is small, the formidable dining room (no dinner Sunday; September to June closed Monday) has a large stone fireplace with sculpted family crests and a multifaceted chandelier. Enjoy superb lamb (a regional specialty) or scallop of milk-fed veal with grapes. ✉ *16270 Nieuil (40 km/24 mi east of Angoulême),* ☎ *05–45–71–36–38,* FAX *05–45–71–46–45. 11 rooms, 3 suites. Restaurant, bar, cable TV, minibars, Internet, tennis court, pool, baby-sitting service, some pets allowed. AE, DC, MC, V. Closed Nov.–Mar.*

$$ 🏨 **Mercure Hôtel de France.** On the edge of the Ville Haute, across from the covered market, this hotel has a traditional air. From the garden there are fine views of the city. Rooms lull in shades of pale blue with striped curtains and bedspreads. The staff is professional and accustomed to speaking English. In the restaurant (closed for lunch at weekends), solid regional cuisine is served. ✉ *1 pl. des Halles, 16000,* ☎ *05–45–95–47–95; 0181/741–3100 in U.K.; 800/637–2873 in U.S.;* FAX *05–45–92–02–70. 89 rooms. Restaurant, bar, Internet, some pets allowed. AE, DC, MC, V.*

Cognac

32 *42 km (28 mi) northwest of Angoulême.*

The black-walled town of Cognac seems an unlikely home for one of the world's most successful distilling trades. You may be disappointed initially by the town's unpretentious appearance but, like the distillate, it tends to grow on you. Cognac owed its early development to the transport of salt and wine along the Charente River. When 16th-century Dutch merchants discovered that the local wine was both tastier and easier to transport if distilled, the town became the heart of the brandy industry. Most cognac houses organize visits of their premises and chais. Wherever you decide to go, you will literally be inhaling the atmosphere of cognac—3% of the precious cask-bound liquid evaporates every year. This has two consequences: each chai smells delicious, and a small black fungus, which feeds on cognac's alcoholic fumes, forms on walls throughout the town.

The leading monument in Cognac is the former **Château François-Ier,** now the premises of Otard Cognac. Volatile Renaissance monarch François I was born here in 1494. The remaining buildings are something of a hodgepodge, though the chunky towers recall the site's fortified origins. The tour of Otard Cognac combines slick propaganda with historical comment on the drink itself. At the end you get to sample free cognac, and you can buy some at reduced prices. ✉ *127 bd. Denfert-Rochereau,* ☎ *05–45–35–72–68.* 🎫 *€3.* ⏲ *Guided tours on the hr, Apr.–Oct., daily 10–noon and 2–5.*

Hennessy, along the banks of the Charente and easily recognized by the company's mercenary emblem—an ax-wielding arm carved in stone—includes in its tour a cheerful jaunt across the Charente in old-fashioned boats. ✉ *Quai Richard-Hennessy,* ☎ *05–45–35–72–68,* WEB *www.hennessy-cognac.com.* 🎫 *€5.* ⏲ *June–Sept., Mon.–Sat. 9–6; Oct.–Dec. and Mar.–May, weekdays 10–5.*

Among the Cognac houses, **Martell** gives the most polished guided tour and its chais are perhaps more picturesque than Hennessy's. ✉ *7 pl. Édouard-Martell,* ☎ *05–45–36–33–33,* WEB *www.martell.com.* 🎫 *€4.* ⏲ *June–Sept., weekdays 9:30–5, weekends noon–5; Oct.–May, Mon.–Thurs. 9:30–11 and 2:30–5.*

Rue Saulnier, alongside the Hennessy premises, is the most atmospheric of the somber, sloping cobbled streets that compose the core of Cognac, dominated by the tower of **St-Léger** (✉ Pl. d'Armes), a church with a notably large Flamboyant Gothic rose window.

Busy boulevard Denfert-Rochereau twines around the old town, passing the town hall and the neighboring **Musée Municipal** (Town Museum) with its collection of cognac posters, glasses, and other marketing artifacts. ✉ *48 bd. Denfert-Rochereau,* ☎ *05–45–32–07–25,* WEB *www.ville-cognac.fr.* 🎫 *€2.20.* ⏲ *June–Sept., Wed.–Mon. 10–noon and 2–6; Oct.–May, Wed.–Mon. 2–5:30.*

Dining and Lodging

$$–$$$ ★ ✕🏨 **Pigeons Blancs.** "White Pigeons," a modernized coaching-inn on spacious grounds 1½ km (1 mi) from the center of Cognac, has been owned by the same family since the 17th century. Each room is different; one has a gabled ceiling supported by an ancient beam and a skylight. The major draw, though, is chef Jacques Tachet's cuisine: try his milk-fed lamb with *jus d'ail doux* (sweet garlic juice) or sea-bass in oyster sauce. The prix-fixe menus are good value at €19 and €29—arrange to have two meals per day with your room rate. ✉ *110 rue Jules-Brisson, 16100,* ☎ *05–45–82–16–36,* FAX *05–45–82–29–29. 7 rooms. Restaurant, bar, no air-conditioning, no pets. AE, DC, MC, V. Closed first half Jan.*

Nightlife and the Arts

La Maison Blanche (✉ 2 impasse de Moulins) is the place to party every night. Each September Cognac hosts a **crime film festival.**

Outdoor Activities and Sports

Hit the greens at the local 18-hole **golf course** (✉ in village of St-Brice, 5 km/3 mi east of Cognac, ☎ 05–45–32–18–17); fees range from €27 in peak season to €18 off-season.

Shopping

A bottle of old cognac makes a fine souvenir; try **La Cognathèque** (✉ 8 pl. Jean-Monnet), in Cognac itself, though you can sometimes find the same item infinitely cheaper at a local producer.

Saintes

33 *27 km (17 mi) northwest of Cognac via D24.*

On the banks of the Charente River, Saintes, littered with religious edifices and Roman ruins dating from the 1st century, exudes stately serenity. The town owes its development to the salt marshes that first attracted the Romans to the area some 2,000 years ago.

The Romans left their mark with the impressive **Arènes** (Amphitheater). There are several better-preserved examples in France, but few as old—it dates from AD 40 and could hold 15,000. You'll find it to the west of the town center, close to the church of St-Eutrope with its mighty spire (✉ Rue Lacurie, 🎫 Free, ⏲ Apr.–Oct., daily 9–7; Nov.–Mar., Tues.–Sun. 10–12:30 and 2–4:30). On the bank of the Charente stands a grand Roman triumphal arch, the **Arc de Germanicus,** dedicated to Emperor Tiberius and built in AD 19 as the entry to Saintes on the old Roman road from Lyon (the arch was moved to its present site in the 19th century). Boats leave alongside for river trips in summer (☎ 05–46–74–23–82 for details).

Climbing above the red roofs of the old town is the **Cathédrale St-Pierre** (✉ Pl. du Synode), which seems to stagger beneath the weight of its stocky tower. Engineering caution foiled plans for the traditional pointed spire, so the tower was given a shallow dome—incongruous, perhaps, but distinctive. The austere 16th-century interior is lined with circular pillars of formidable circumference. The narrow pedestrian-only streets clustered around the cathedral contrast with the broad boulevards that sweep through the town and over the river.

Saintes's ecclesiastical pride and joy is the **Abbaye aux Dames** (Ladies' Abbey), consecrated in 1047. The abbey church is fronted by an exquisite, intricately carved, arcaded facade. Although the Romanesque choir remains largely in its original form, the rest of the interior is less harmonious, as the abbey fell on hard times after the death of the last abbess—the 30th—in 1792. It became a prison, then a barracks, and it is now a cultural center for expositions. The brasserie opposite the abbey portals has inexpensive lunch menus (€10–€15). ✉ *7 pl. de l'Abbaye,* ☎ *05–46–97–48–48.* 🎫 *€3.* ⏲ *Apr.–Sept., daily 10–12:30 and 2–7; Oct.–Mar., Wed. and Sat. 10–12:30 and 2–7, Sun.–Tues. and Thurs.–Fri. 2–6.*

Dining and Lodging

$$$ ★ ✕🏨 **Relais du Bois St-Georges.** There are two buildings at this hotel: the smart Parc St-Georges, and the de luxe Pavillon du Lac. Rooms vary accordingly; some have contemporary furnishings, others traditional; some are miniduplexes with loft beds, others small with fold-down beds (one is named "Count de Monte Cristo's Prison Cell"); many have separate sitting areas. In the restaurant overlooking 15 acres of gardens and a lake, seafood and specialties from the Charente region become eye-catching creations in the hands of chef Christophe Gouard. ✉ *Le Pinier, cours Genêt, 17100,* ☎ *05–46–93–50–99,* FAX *05–46–93–*

34–93, WEB *www.relaisdubois.com. 27 rooms, 3 suites. Restaurant, bar, no air-conditioning in some rooms, cable TV, minibars, Internet, pool, some pets allowed. AE, MC, V.*

La Rochelle

★ 34 *65 km (42 mi) northwest of Saintes.*

La Rochelle is a vibrant, appealing town, with ancient streets and a picture-postcard harbor, the Vieux Port. Standing sentinel on either side of the harbor are two fortresslike 14th-century **towers,** the **Tour St-Nicolas** (to the left) and the **Tour de la Chaîne** (right); a third tower, the 15th-century **Tour de la Lanterne,** emerges a little farther along the quayside. You can climb to the top of any of them for a view of the bay toward Ile d'Aix. *Each tower €3.90; €7 all 3. Apr.–Sept., daily 10–7; Oct.–Mar., daily 10–12:30 and 2–5:30.*

Porte de la Grosse Horloge (Gate of the Giant Clock) is a massive stone gate marking the entrance to the narrow, bustling streets of the old town. From Porte de la Grosse Horloge head down rue du Palais and onto rue Gargoulleau: halfway down on the left is the 18th-century Bishop's Palace, now the **Musée des Beaux-Arts** (Museum of Fine Arts). ✉ *28 rue Gargoulleau,* ☎ *05–46–41–64–65. €3.50, joint ticket for all town museums €6.55. Mon. and Wed.–Sat. 10:30–12:30 and 1:30–6, Sun. 3–6.*

At the **Musée du Nouveau-Monde** (New World Museum), in an 18th-century building, old maps, engravings, watercolors, and even wall-paper evoke the commercial links between La Rochelle and the New World. ✉ *10 rue Fleuriau,* ☎ *05–46–41–46–50. €3.50, joint ticket for all town museums €6.55. Wed.–Mon. 10:30–12:30 and 1:30–6, Sun. 3–6.*

In summer, boats operated by **Inter-Iles** leave La Rochelle harbor daily for cruises to **Ile d'Aix,** and **Fort Boyard.** ✉ *Vieux Port,* ☎ *05–46–50–51–88. Round-trip: Ile d'Aix €15, Fort Boyard €12. Departure times vary; it's best to call ahead.*

Dining and Lodging

$$$ ★ ✕ **Richard Coutanceau.** Widely acknowledged as the region's premier chef, Richard Coutanceau deals imaginatively with fish and seafood in this sober, modern restaurant overlooking the bay and old port. Lobster, eel, bass with basil, and spider crab with asparagus number among his specialties. ✉ *Plage de la Concurrence,* ☎ *05–46–41–48–19,* WEB *www.relaischateaux.fr.coutanceau. AE, DC, MC, V. Closed Sun.*

$–$$ ✕ **André.** The salty decor is a bit excessive—fishing nets and posters of ocean liners. But the food and service have such gusto that you'll be caught up in the mood, especially if you order the monumental seafood platter and wash it down with white Charente wine. The three prix-fixe menus are priced from €20 to €30.50. ✉ *7 rue St-Jean-du-Pérot,* ☎ *05–46–41–28–24,* WEB *www.bar-andre.com. AE, DC, MC, V.*

$$–$$$ **Monnaie.** This 17th-century house by the Vieux Port has a wonderful lobby and cobblestone courtyard. Rooms are less inspiring; the quietest overlook the courtyard. Free parking is available adjacent to the hotel, a definite plus as it's only a few minutes' walk from the harbor and town. ✉ *3 rue de la Monnaie, 17000,* ☎ *05–46–50–65–65,* FAX *05–46–50–63–19,* WEB *www.hotel-monnaie.com. 31 rooms, 4 suites. No air-conditioning, cable TV, Internet, some pets allowed, free parking. AE, DC, MC, V.*

$$ ★ **Canne à Sucre.** Rooms in this 18th-century mansion are large and colorfully furnished. The owners speak good English, and breakfast is served in the courtyard in summer. ✉ *33 rue Thiers, 17000,* ☎ *05–*

46–41–62–23, FAX 05–46–41–10–76. 8 rooms. No air-conditioning, no pets. MC, V.

En Route If you're not going to head to the sea and the resort island of Ile de Ré, head inland from La Rochelle along D9 and D20 northeast toward Marans, once a thriving seaport but now linked to the sea only by canal. The landscape is flat, barren, almost eerie: this is the **Marais Desséché** (Dry Marsh), and your first encounter with the Marais Poitevin. The verdant, tree-lined waterways that form the more scenic **Marais Mouillé** (Wet Marsh) gradually take over as you continue east. Take D114 from Marans, then a left on D116 just before Courçon and head north to Maillezais and its ruined abbey. Return south on D15 and turn left to Damvix, continuing along the pretty, canal-like Sèvre Niortaise to Arçais and Coulon.

Ile de Ré

35 *44 km (28 mi) northwest of Rochefort via N137 and the Pont-Viaduc.*

L'Ile de Ré used to be a hush-hush, keep-it-quiet alternative to the Riviera. The few in the know enjoyed more than 50 km (31 mi) of beaches with fine white sands, an ornithological reserve, a citadel, a lighthouse, and great seafood, all baked by a sun that seems brighter here than anywhere else in France. But the secret is out and today the whole place smells more and more like burning money, with huge yachts in the old ports towns, intellectuals splitting hairs in cafés, and Rolex watches jingling on the dance floors. A toll bridge curves across just north of La Rochelle to this cheerful island just 26 km (16 mi) long and never more than 6 km (4 mi) wide. Vineyards sweep over the eastern part of the island; oyster beds straddle the shallow waters to the west.

The first village on the north coast reached from the mainland is **La Flotte.** The rectangular harbor hiding tiny fishing boats is surrounded by sturdy houses ready to stand against Atlantic gales. Ten km (6 mi) farther on is the largest village on the island, **St-Martin de Ré** (population 3,000). It has a lively harbor and a citadel built by ace military architect Sébastien de Vauban in 1681. Many of its streets also date from the 17th century, and the villagers' low, white houses are typical of that period. **Ars,** a smaller village 10 km (6 mi) farther west, has a black-and-white church spire, fine street market, and cute harbor.

If you go all the way to the northwestern end of Ile de Ré, be sure to climb up the **Phare de la Baleine** (Whale Lighthouse) for sweeping views of the Atlantic. At its foot is the Café de la Phare, which has a surprising Art Deco setting full of artsy '30s lamps and serves a good *poutargue,* a local specialty made from smoked cod roe accompanied by shallots and sour cream.

Dining and Lodging

$$$ ✕🏨 **Le Richelieu.** Eat chef Dominique Bourgeois's seafood as you gaze at the ocean. Let lobster and smoked oysters spark your taste buds for the excellent grilled turbot in beurre blanc and superb wine. Guest rooms are innocuously furnished but have all the amenities, from bathrobes to balconies. A separate building houses masseurs, beauticians, and thalassotherapy equipment. A beach fronts the hotel, but it's better for strolling than lounging. ✉ *44 av. de la Plage, 17630 La Flotte-en-Ré,* ☎ *05–46–09–60–70,* FAX *05–46–09–50–59. 39 rooms, 3 suites. Restaurant, no air-conditioning, cable TV, pool, beauty salon, massage, spa, 2 tennis courts, beach, no pets. AE, DC, MC, V. Closed early Jan.–mid-Feb.*

Coulon

36 *72 km (40 mi) southeast of La Rochelle.*

The photogenic village of Coulon is the best base for exploring the Marais Poitevin. The ideal way to explore the Marais is by rowboat—or, more typically, on a *pigouille* (a flat, narrow boat maneuvered with a long pole), which you can find in Coulon. They cost about €15 per hour per boat, maximum six persons, or you can hire a boat with a guide (for 45 minutes at €20). If your familiarity with French is decent, you'll get an earful of local lore as well. The town also has a lovely medieval church and a privately run folk museum, the **Musée Maraichin** (✉ Rue de l'Église). There are no regular hours: just show up and see if it's open; donations are accepted.

Dining and Lodging

$–$$ ✕ **Central.** Just opposite the church on the town square, this restaurant is a favorite haunt of the local bourgeoisie, who enjoy an obsequious welcome from the blue blazer–garbed owner. The fine choice of regional fare includes succulent lamb, eel fricassee, and warm oysters cooked with nettle leaves. Rooms are small and functional—good for an overnight stop, perhaps, but no longer. ✉ *4 rue d'Autremont, 79510,* ☎ *05–49–35–90–20. 5 rooms. Restaurant, no air-conditioning, no room TVs, no pets. MC, V. Closed part of Oct., part of Feb., and Mon. No dinner Sun.*

Outdoor Activities and Sports

One of the best ways to explore the area is by bicycle (a detailed map is advisable), rented from **La Libellule** (✉ 94 quai Louis-Tardy, ☎ 05–49–35–83–42).

Poitiers

★ 37 *76 km (48 mi) northeast of Coulon, 120 km (75 mi) northwest of Limoges, 340 km (212 mi) southwest of Paris.*

Thanks to its majestic hilltop perch above the Clain River and its position halfway along the Bordeaux–Paris trade route, Poitiers became an important commercial, religious, and university town in the Middle Ages. Life quieted down after the 17th century, but tranquillity has resulted in excellent architectural preservation.

The church of **Notre-Dame-la-Grande** (✉ Pl. Charles-de-Gaulle), in the town center, is an impressive example of the Romanesque architecture so common in western France. Its 12th-century facade, framed by rounded arches and decorated with a multitude of bas-reliefs and sculptures, was meticulously restored in 1994; a 15-minute light show highlights the details in color every evening from mid-June through September.

The **Cathédrale St-Pierre** (✉ Pl. de la Cathédrale), a few hundred yards beyond Notre-Dame-la-Grande, was built between the 12th and the 14th centuries. With a huge portal showing plump gargoyles without and tremendous open space and luminosity within, the largest church in Poitiers has a distinctive facade marked by two asymmetrical towers. The imposing interior is noted for its late 18th-century organ, stained glass, and 13th-century wooden choir stalls, claimed as the oldest in France.

The **Musée Ste-Croix** houses archaeological discoveries, traditional regional crafts, and European paintings from the 15th to the 19th centuries. The museum is part of a triad of museums. The Musée de Chièvres (✉ 9 rue Victor-Hugo, ☎ 05–49–41–42–21) displays Renaissance furniture, ceramics, and Old Master paintings. The **Hypogée Martyrium** (✉ 44 rue du Père-de-la-Croix, ☎ 05–49–01–68–85), a subterranean chapel with ancient sarcophagi and sculptures, has been closed for restoration for several years. ✉ *61 rue St-Simplicien,* ☎ *05–49–41–07–53.* *€2.50 (joint ticket for all museums); free Tues.* *Museums: Tues.–Fri. 10–noon and 1–5, weekends 10–noon and 2–6.*

★ **Planète Futuroscope,** just north of Poitiers, is a smorgasbord of cinema thrills that has attracted over 20 million visitors since it opened in 1987, making it western France's leading tourist attraction. Choose between half-dome screens (L'Omnimax); high-resolution screens (Cinéma Haute Résolution); theaters with mechanical seat effects (Cinémas Dynamiques); the Cinéma 360°, where you stand in mid-theater as nine images, shot in a circle, re-create a surf-pounding trimaran ocean race; the Magic Carpet, where a huge front screen is synchronized with another below your feet; Destination Cosmos, featuring the giant Hubble telescope; or Solido, where a pair of stereoscopic shades send you on a virtual swim. ✉ *Jaunay-Clan (Exit 28 off A10),* ☎ *05–49–49–59–84,* WEB *www.planete-futuroscope.com.* *€21–€30, depending on season.* *Apr.–Sept., daily 9 AM–10 PM; Oct.–Mar., daily 9–6.*

Dining and Lodging

$$–$$$ ✕ **Maxime.** Reasonable prix-fixe menus and chef Christian Rougier's cooking have made Maxime a crowd pleaser. Enjoy foie gras and duck salad in the pastel dining room lined with '30s-style frescoes. ✉ *4 rue St-Nicolas,* ☎ *05–49–41–27–37. Reservations essential. AE, DC, MC, V. Closed weekends and mid-July to mid-Aug.*

$$ **Europe.** An early 19th-century building with a modern extension houses this unpretentious hotel in the middle of town. Because it's off the main street and has a forecourt, rooms are quiet. It also has a pleasant garden in the back for an afternoon tea or an evening aperitif. ✉ *39 rue Carnot, 86000,* ☎ *05–49–88–12–00,* FAX *05–49–88–97–30. 85 rooms. No air-conditioning, cable TV, Internet, some pets allowed. AE, DC, MC, V.*

BORDEAUX, DORDOGNE, AND POITOU-CHARENTES A TO Z

To research prices, get advice from other travelers, and book travel arrangements, visit www.fodors.com.

AIR TRAVEL

➤ AIRLINES & CONTACTS: **Air France** (☎ 08–02–80–28–02).

AIRPORTS

Frequent daily flights on Air France link Bordeaux and the domestic airport at Limoges with Paris.

➤ AIRPORT INFORMATION: **Aéroport de Bordeaux-Mérignac** (☎ 05–56–34–50-50, WEB www.bordeaux.aeroport).

BUS TRAVEL

The regional bus operator is CITRAM; the main Gare Routière (bus terminal) is on Allées de Chartres (by Esplanade des Quinconces), near the Garonne river in Bordeaux. CITRAM buses cover towns in the wine country and beach areas not well served by rail (for instance, one or two buses run daily to St-Émilion and Pauillac). The Dordogne region is serviced by Trans-Périgord and CFTA; the region around La Rochelle by Océcars. Sarlat is a main bus hub, with connections to Les Eyzies, Périgueux, Bordeaux, and Souillac. The Sarlat-Périgueux line has a stop at Montignac for the Lascaux II caves. CITRAM buses from Cognac end up in Angoulême. Coulon in the Marais Poitevin is serviced by Casa Buses. Bus service in and around Poitiers is offered by Société des Transports Poitevins.

➤ BUS INFORMATION: **Casa** (13 chemin Fief-Binard, 79000, Niort, ☎ 05–49–24–93–47). **CFTA** (Gare Routière, pl. Francheville, 24000 Périgueux, ☎ 05–53–08–43–3). **CITRAM** (8 rue de Corneille, 33000 Bordeaux, ☎ 05–56–43–68–43). **Océcars** (31 rue des Rameaux, 17000, La Rochelle, ☎ 05–46–00–95–15). **Société des Transports Poitevins** (9 rue de Northampton, 86000 Poitiers, ☎ 05–49–44–77–00). **Trans-Périgord** (Cabant, 24250, Veyrines-de-Domme, ☎ 05–53–28–52–20).

CAR RENTAL

➤ LOCAL AGENCIES: **Avis** (✉ Gare St-Jean, Bordeaux, ☎ 05–56–91–65–50; ✉ 133 bd. du Grand-Cerf, Poitiers, ☎ 05–49–58–13–00; ✉ 166 bd. Joffre, La Rochelle, ☎ 05–46–41–13–55). **Hertz** (✉ Pl. de la Gare, Bergerac, ☎ 05–53–57–19–27; ✉ 105 bd. du Grand-Cerf, Poitiers, ☎ 05–49–58–24–24).

CAR TRAVEL

As the capital of southwest France, Bordeaux has superb transport links with Paris, Spain, and even the Mediterranean (A62 expressway via Toulouse). The A10, the Paris–Bordeaux expressway, passes close to Poitiers, Niort (Exit 33 for La Rochelle), and Saintes before continuing toward Spain as A63. Fast N137 connects La Rochelle with Saintes via Rochefort; Angoulême is linked to Bordeaux and Poitiers by N10 and to Limoges by N141; and D936 runs along the Dordogne Valley to Bergerac. N89 links Bordeaux to Périgueux, continuing to Limoges as N21.

EMERGENCIES

➤ CONTACTS: **Ambulance** (☎ 15). **Hôpital St-André** (✉ 1 rue Jean-Burguet, 33800 Bordeaux, ☎ 05–56–79–56–79).

TOURS

The Office de Tourisme in Bordeaux organizes four-hour coach tours of the surrounding vineyards every Wednesday and Saturday afternoon. The office has information on other wine tours and tastings, and on local and regional sights; a round-the-clock phone service in English is available.

➤ FEES & SCHEDULES: **Bordeaux Office de Tourisme** (✉ 12 cours du XXX-Juillet, 33080 Bordeaux cedex, ☎ 05–56–00–66–00).

TRAIN TRAVEL

Superfast TGV (*Trains à Grande Vitesse*) Atlantique service links Paris (Gare Montparnasse) to Bordeaux—585 km (365 mi) in three hours—with stops at Poitiers and Angoulême (change for Jarnac, Cognac, and Saintes); and to La Rochelle—465 km (290 mi) in three hours—with a stop in Niort. Trains link Bordeaux to Lyon (8–9 hours) and Nice (eight hours) via Toulouse. Six trains daily make the 3½-hour, 400-km (250-mi) trip from Paris to Limoges.

Bordeaux is the region's major train hub. Trains run regularly from Bordeaux to Bergerac (80 minutes), with occasional stops at St-Émilion, and three times daily to Sarlat (nearly three hours). At least six trains daily make the 90-minute journey from Bordeaux to Périgueux, and four continue to Limoges (2 hours, 20 minutes). Poitiers is the connecting point for Niort, La Rochelle, and Rochefort; Angoulême is the connecting point for Jarnac, Cognac, and Saintes.

➤ TRAIN INFORMATION: **SNCF** (☎ 08–36–35–35–35, www.ter–sncf.com/uk/poitou–charentes and WEB www.ter–sncf.com/uk/aquitaine).

TRAVEL AGENCIES

➤ LOCAL AGENT REFERRALS: **American Express** (✉ 14 cours de l'Intendance, Bordeaux, ☎ 05–56–00–63–33). **Carlson-Wagonlits** (✉ 43 rue de la Porte-Dijeaux, Bordeaux, ☎ 05–56–52–92–70).

VISITOR INFORMATION

The addresses of tourist offices in towns mentioned in this chapter are listed below.

➤ TOURIST INFORMATION: **Angoulême** (✉ 7 bis rue du Chat, ☎ 05–45–95–16–84, WEB www.tourisme.fr/angouleme). **Bergerac** (✉ 97 rue Neuve d'Argenson, ☎ 05–53–57–03–11). **Bordeaux** (✉ 12 cours du XXX-Juillet, ☎ 05–56–00–66–00, WEB www.bordeaux-tourisme.com). **Cognac** (✉ 16 rue du XIV-Juillet, ☎ 05–45–82–10–71, WEB www.tourism-cognac.com). **La Rochelle** (✉ Pl. de la Petite-Sirène, ☎ 05–46–41–14–68). **Limoges** (✉ 12 bd. Fleurus, ☎ 05–55–34–46–87). **Niort** (✉ Rue Ernest-Pérochon, ☎ 05–49–24–18–79). **Pauillac** (✉ La Verrerie, ☎ 05–56–59–03–08, WEB www.pauillac-Medoc.com). **Périgueux** (✉ 25 rue du Président-Wilson, ☎ 05–53–35–50–24). **Poitiers** (✉ 8 rue des Grandes-Écoles, ☎ 05–49–41–21–24). **Rochefort** (✉ Av. Sadi-Carnot, ☎ 05–46–99–08–60, WEB www.tourisme.fr/rochefort). **Royan** (✉ Rond-Point de la Poste, ☎ 05–46–05–04–71, WEB www.royan-tourisme.com). **St-Émilion** (✉ 15 rue du Clocher, ☎ 05–57–55–28–28). **Saintes** (✉ 62 cours National, ☎ 05–46–74–23–82, WEB www.ville-saintes.fr). **Sarlat** (✉ Pl. de la Liberté, ☎ 05–53–31–45–45).

18 BACKGROUND AND ESSENTIALS

BON APPÉTIT!: THE ART OF FRENCH COOKING

Born British, naturalized American, I am an unabashed chauvinist about French food. To wander through a French open market, the vegetables overflowing from their crates, the fruits cascading in casual heaps on the counter, is a sensual pleasure. To linger outside a bakery in the early morning, watching the fresh breads and croissants being lined up in regimental rows, must awaken the most fickle appetite. Just to read the menu posted outside a modest café alerts the imagination to pleasures to come.

Best of all, the French are happy to share their enthusiasm for good food with others. There are more good restaurants and eating places in France than in any other European country; the streets are lined with delicatessens, butchers, cheese shops, bakeries, and pastry shops. And I have yet to find a Frenchman, cantankerous though he may be, who does not warm to anyone who shows an interest in his national passion for wines and fine cuisine.

Fine cuisine does not necessarily mean fancy cuisine. Masters though French chefs are of the soufflé and the butter sauce, the salmon in aspic, and the strawberry *feuilleté* (puff pastry), such delicacies are reserved for celebration. Everyday fare is much more likely to be roast chicken, steak and *frîtes* (fries), an omelet, or a pork chop. Bread, eaten without butter, is mandatory at main meals, while the bottle of mineral water is almost as common as wine.

Where the French do score is in the variety and quality of their ingredients. Part of the credit must go to climate and geography—just look at the length of the French coastline and the part seafood plays in the cooking of Normandy, Brittany, and Provence. Count the number of rivers with fertile valleys for cattle and crops. Olives and fruit flourish in the Mediterranean sun, while the region from southwest of Paris running up north to the Belgian border is one of the great breadbaskets of Europe.

No one but the French identifies three basic styles of cuisine—classical, nouvelle, and regional. No other European nation pays so much attention to menus and recipes.

Most sophisticated are the sauces and soufflés, the mousselines and *macédoines* of classical cuisine. Starting in the 17th century, successive generations of chefs have lovingly documented their dishes, developing an intellectual discipline from what is an essentially practical art. As a style, classical cuisine is now outmoded, but its techniques form the basis of rigorous professional training in French cooking. In some measure, all other styles of cooking are based on its principles.

Nouvelle cuisine, for instance, is directly descended from the classics. Launched with great fanfare more than 20 years ago, it takes a fresh, lighter approach, with simpler sauces and a colorful view of presentation. First-course salads, often with hot additions of shellfish, chicken liver, or bacon, have become routine. For a while cooks experimented with such way-out combinations as vanilla with lobster and chicken with raspberries, but now new-style cooking has its own classics. Typical are *magrets de canard* (boned duck breasts) sautéed like steak and served with a brown sauce of wine or green peppercorns and pot-au-feu made of fish rather than the usual beef.

Many cooks have made a refreshing return toward country-style cooking. Indeed, many cooks never left it, for classical and nouvelle cuisines are almost exclusively the concern of professionals. However, regional dishes are cooked by everyone—at restaurants, at home, and in the café on the corner.

The city of Lyon exemplifies the best of regional cuisine. It features such local specialties as poached eggs in *meurette* (red-wine sauce), *quenelles* (fish dumplings) in crayfish sauce, sausage with pistachios, and chocolate gâteau (cake). The Lyonnais hotly dispute Paris's title as gastronomic capital of France, pointing to the number of prestigious restaurants in their city. What is more, some of the world's finest wines are produced only 150 km (90 mi) north, in Burgundy.

Lyon may represent the best of French regional cooking, but there's plenty to look for elsewhere. Compare the sole of Normandy, cooked with mussels in cream sauce, with the sea bass of Provence, flamed with dried fennel or baked with tomatoes and thyme. Contrast the butter cakes of Brittany with the yeast breads of Alsace, the braised endive of Picardy with the gratin of cardoons (a type of artichoke) found in the south.

Authentic regional specialties are based on local products. They have a character that may depend on climate (cream cakes survive in Normandy but not in Provence) or geography (each mountain area has its own dried sausages and hams). History brought spice bread to Dijon, a legacy of the days when the dukes of Burgundy controlled Flanders and the spice trade. Ethnic heritage explains ravioli around Nice, near the Italian border, waffles in the north near Belgium, and dumplings close to Germany. Modern ethnic influences show up in cities, with many an Arab pastry shop started by Algerian immigrants and many a restaurant run by Vietnamese.

Fundamental to French existence is the baker, the *boulanger.* From medieval times legislation has governed the weight and content of loaves of bread, with stringent penalties for such crimes as adulteration with sand or sawdust. Today the government pegs the price of white bread, and you'll find the famous long loaves a bargain compared with the price of brioche, croissants, or loaves of whole wheat (*pain complet*), rye (*pain de seigle*), and bran (*pain de son*). White bread can be bought as thin *flûtes* to slice for soup, as baguettes, or as the common, thicker loaves known simply as *pains*.

Since French bread stays fresh for only a few hours, it is baked in the morning for midday and baked again in the afternoon. A baker's day starts at 4 AM to give the dough time to rise. Sadly, there is a lack of recruits, so more and more French bread is being produced industrially, without the right nutty flavor and chew to the crisp crust. The clue to bread baked on the spot is the heady smell of fermenting yeast, so sniff out a neighborhood bakery before you buy.

If bread is the staff of French life, pastry is the sugar icing. The window of a city pastry shop (in the country, bakery and pastry shop are often combined) is a wonderland of éclairs and meringues, madeleines, puff pastry, spun sugar, and caramel. You'll find pies laden with seasonal fruit, nut cakes, and chocolate cakes, plus the baker's specialty, for he is certain to have one. Survey them with a sharp eye; they should be small (good ingredients are expensive) and impeccably alike in color and size (the sign of an expert craftsman). Last, the window should not be overflowing; because of the high cost, the temptation to cram the shelves with leftovers from the day before is strong.

The charcuterie is almost as French an institution as the bakery. *Chair cuite* means "cooked meat," and a charcuterie is a kind of delicatessen, specializing in pâtés, terrines, ham, and sausages. A charcuterie also sells long-lasting salads, such as cucumber, tomato, or grated carrot vinaigrette and root celery (celeriac) *rémoulade* (with mustard mayonnaise). Cooked "dishes of the day" may include coq au vin and *choucroute alsacienne* (sauerkraut with smoked pork hock). Often you'll also find such condiments as pickles, plus a modest selection of wines, cheeses, and desserts—rice pudding or baked apple, for example. Only bread is needed to complete the meal, and you're set for the world's best picnic!

French cheese deserves, and gets, close attention. Choosing a cheese is as delicate a matter as deciding on the right wine. In a good cheese shop you will be welcome to sample any of the cut cheeses, and assistants will gladly offer advice. One cardinal rule is to look for *fromage fermier* (farmhouse cheese), a rough equivalent of château-bottled wine. If the label says *lait cru* (raw milk)—even better; only when milk is unpasteurized does the flavor of some cheeses, Camembert, for example, develop properly. Try to keep a cheese cool without refrigeration and eat it as soon as you can. Delicate soft cheeses like Brie can become overripe within a matter of hours, one reason it is rare to find a wide-ranging selection of cheeses in a restaurant.

Many other kinds of specialty stores exist, often for local products. In Dijon, for instance, you'll find shops selling mustards in ornamental pots; in Gascony (near Bordeaux), it's foie gras and canned confit (preserved duck or goose). But the most famous concentration of food shops in the world must be clustered around place de la Madeleine in Paris. On one corner stands Fauchon, the dean of luxury food emporiums. Just across the square stands Hédiard, specializing in spices, rare fruits, and preserves.

If you're an early riser, there's a long wait until lunch, for snacks are not a French habit. The structure of a meal, its timing, and its content are taken seriously. The "grazing" phenomenon—minimeals snatched here and there throughout the day—is almost unheard of, and snacks are regarded as spoiling the appetite, not to mention being nutritionally unsound.

Still, the French light breakfast can come as no surprise; its unbeatable wake-up combination of croissant, brioche, or crusty roll with coffee has swept much of the world. Traditionally, the coffee comes as café au lait, milky and steaming in a wide two-handled bowl for dipping the bread.

At noon you'll be rewarded by what, for most French people, remains the main meal of the day. In much of the country, it is still true that everything stops for two hours; children return from school, and museums and businesses lock their doors. The pattern is much the same in provincial cities: restaurants, bistros, and cafés are crammed with diners, most of whom eat at least two and often three or more courses. Unfortunately, however, quick lunches are becoming more and more the norm in larger cities like Paris.

A big lunch keeps French adults going until evening, but you may want to follow the example of schoolchildren, who are allowed a treat on the way home. Often it is a *pain au chocolat* (chocolate croissant). By 8 you'll be ready for dinner and one of the greatest pleasures France has to offer.

The choice of restaurants in France is a feast in itself. At least once during your trip you may want to indulge in an outstanding occasion. But restaurants are just the beginning. You can also eat out in cafés, bistros, brasseries, fast-food outlets (they, too, have reached France), or auberges, which range from staid country inns to sybaritic hideaways.

Simplest is the café (where the espresso machine is king), offering drinks and such snacks as *croque monsieur* (toasted ham and cheese sandwich), *oeufs sur le plat* (fried eggs), *le hot dog,* and foot-long sandwiches of French bread. Larger-city cafés serve hot meals, such dishes as onion soup and braised beef with vegetables, consumed on marble-top tables to a background of cheerful banter. Like English pubs, French cafés are a way of life, a focal point for gossip and dominoes in practically every village.

The bistro, once interchangeable with the café, has taken a fashionable turn. In cities, instead of sawdust on the floor and a zinc-topped counter, you may find that a bistro is designer-decorated, serving new-style or fusion cuisine to a trendy, chattering crowd. If you're lucky, the food will be as witty and colorful as the clientele.

With few exceptions, brasseries remain unchanged—great bustling places with white-aproned waiters and hearty food. Go to them for oysters on the half shell and other fine seafood, garlic snails, *boudin* (black pudding), sauerkraut, and vast ice-cream desserts. Originally a brasserie brewed beer, and since many brewers came from Alsace on the borders of Germany, the cooking reflects their origins.

The importance placed on food in France is echoed by the number of gastronomic societies, from the Chevaliers du Tastevin to the Chaîne des Rôtisseurs and the Confrérie des Cordons Bleus, to mention only three. The French believe that good eating, at whatever level, is an art that merits considerable time and attention. They have done the hard work, and as a traveler you can reap the benefits.

— Anne Willan

Anne Willan is president and founder of the École de Cuisine La Varenne in Paris. She has a series on PBS, *Look and Cook with Anne Willan,* and has written numerous books, including *Cook It Right* and *La France Gastronomique.*

FURTHER READING

Books on Paris alone can fill several libraries. Two titles that have recently hit the best-seller lists are *Paris to the Moon,* by Adam Gopnik—the distinguished Paris-based correspondent of the *New Yorker*—and *The Flâneur,* by Edmund White, the brilliant belle-lettrist. For a look at American expatriates in Paris between the wars, read *Sylvia Beach and the Lost Generation* by Noel R. Fitch or *A Moveable Feast* by Ernest Hemingway. George Orwell's *Down and Out in Paris and London* gives an account of life on a shoestring in these two European capitals. More essays about Paris are excerpted in *A Place in the World Called Paris.* Yet another anthology of essays on Paris is the *Travelers' Tales Guides: Paris.* For a visual feast, delight in John Russell's *Paris*—a compendium of city scenes painted by great masters accompanied by an illuminating text.

Jules Verne's *Paris in the Twentieth Century* provides a view from the past of Paris in the future. A history of Paris from the Revolution to the Belle Epoque is found in Johannes Willms's *Paris: Capital of Europe. A Traveller's History of Paris* by Robert Cole is a good overview. Tyler Stovall's *Paris Noir: African-Americans in the City of Light* is a history of African-Americans in Paris. *Inside Paris* is a photography book of Paris interiors. Two unconventional guides to Paris are Karen Elizabeth Gordon's witty and surreal *Paris Out of Hand* and Lawrence Osborne's *Paris Dreambook.*

Three memoirs by Americans who have lived in Paris are Art Buchwald's *I'll Always Have Paris,* Edmund White's *The Flâneur,* and Stanley Karnow's *Paris in the Fifties. Paris Notebooks* by Mavis Gallant is her observations of Paris life. *Between Meals* by A. J. Liebling looks at the art of eating in Paris. *A Corner in the Marais: Memoir of a Paris Neighborhood* is Alex Karmel's history of the neighborhood. Edmund White and Hubert Sorin have also weighed in with *Our Paris: Sketches with Memory.*

The best introduction to modern France is John Ardagh's *France Today.* A witty but less complete survey of the country and its people is Theodore Zeldin's *The French.* Another entry on the list is Richard Bernstein's *Fragile Glory.* An immensely popular, if slightly satiric, introduction to French country life is provided by Peter Mayle's two autobiographical books on Provence, *A Year in Provence* and *Toujours Provence,* as well as his novel *Chasing Cézanne.*

Nancy Mitford's readable *The Sun King* covers the regal grandeur of the 17th century, while Alfred Cobban's workmanlike *History of Modern France* describes trends and events from the death of Louis XIV up to 1962. Another readable and fascinating book about French history is Barbara Tuchman's *A Distant Mirror.* Dorothy Carrington's classic work on Corsica, *Granite Island: A Portrait of Corsica,* is available at the library. For modern French history, particularly the Vichy era, a good bet is Robert Paxton's *Vichy France and the Jews.* For a scholarly study of Romanesque and Gothic architecture, read Henri Focillon's thoughtfully illustrated *The Art of the West,* available at the library.

Charles Dickens's *A Tale of Two Cities,* Flaubert's *Sentimental Education,* Henry James's *The Ambassadors,* Colette's *The Complete Claudine,* F. Scott Fitzgerald's *Tender Is the Night,* Hemingway's *The Sun Also Rises,* and Émile Zola's *La Curée, L'Assommoir, Nana,* and *La Débâcle* are just a handful of the classic novels set in France.

As for books about French wine and cuisine, Patricia Wells's *The Food Lover's Guide to Paris* and *The Food Lover's Guide to France* provide a good beginning. Waverly Root's *The Food of France* is a great accompaniment to any trip. Alexis Lichine's *Guide to Wines and Vineyards of France* is still the classic wine guide, though it's now only available from the library. For more books about French wine, try Robert M. Parker's *Bordeaux: A Comprehensive Guide to the Wines Produced from 1961–1990* and *Wines of the Rhône Valley.* A. J. Liebling's *Between Meals* provides a more literary and entertaining look at the fine art of eating in France.

FRANCE AT A GLANCE: A CHRONOLOGY

Here's a minihistory of France—an *aide mémoire* to monarchs and moments.

58–51 BC Julius Caesar conquers Gaul; writes up the war in *De Bello Gallico*.

52 BC Lutetia, later to become Paris, is built by the Gallo-Romans.

46 BC Roman amphitheater built at Arles.

14 BC Pont du Gard aqueduct at Nîmes is erected.

AD 406 Invasion by the Vandals (Germanic tribes).

451 Attila invades and is defeated at Châlons.

The Merovingian Dynasty

486–511 Clovis, king of the Franks (481–511), defeats the Roman governor of Gaul and founds the Merovingian dynasty. Great monasteries, such as those at Tours, Limoges, and Chartres, become centers of culture.

497 Franks convert to Christianity.

567 Frankish kingdom is divided into three parts—the eastern countries (Austrasia), later to become Belgium and Germany; the western countries (Neustria), later to become France; and Burgundy.

The Carolingian Dynasty

768–78 Charlemagne (768–814) becomes king of the Franks (768), conquers northern Italy (774), and is defeated by the Moors at Roncesvalles, Spain, after which he consolidates the Pyrénées border (778).

800 The pope crowns Charlemagne Holy Roman Emperor in Rome. Charlemagne expands the French kingdom far beyond its present borders and establishes a center for learning at his capital, Aix-la-Chapelle (Aachen, in present-day Germany).

814–987 After the death of Charlemagne the Carolingian line continues through a dozen or so monarchs, leading to a batch called Charles (the Bald, the Fat, the Simple) and a sprinkling of Louises over the centuries. Under the Treaty of Verdun (843), the empire is divided in two—the eastern half becoming Germany, the western half, France.

The Capetian Dynasty

987 Hugh Capet (987–996) is made king of France and establishes the principle of hereditary rule for his descendants. Settled conditions and the increased power of the Church see the flowering of Romanesque architecture in the cathedrals of Autun and Angoulême.

1066 Norman conquest of England by William the Conqueror (1028–87).

1067 Work begins on the Romanesque Bayeux Tapestry, celebrating the Norman Conquest.

ca. 1100 First universities in Europe include one in Paris. Development of European vernacular verse: *Chanson de Roland*.

1140 The Gothic style of architecture first appears at St-Denis and later becomes fully developed at the cathedrals of Chartres, Reims, Amiens, and Paris's Notre-Dame.

ca. 1150 Struggle between the Anglo-Norman kings (Angevin empire) and the French; when Eleanor of Aquitaine switches husbands (from Louis VII of France to Henry II of England), her extensive lands pass to English rule.

1257 Sorbonne University is founded in Paris.

The Valois Dynasty

1337–1453 Hundred Years' War between France and England: fighting for control of those areas of France gained by the English crown following the marriage of Eleanor of Aquitaine and Henry II.

1348–50 Black Death (plague) rages in France.

1428–31 Joan of Arc (1412–31), the Maid of Orléans, sparks the revival of French fortunes in the Hundred Years' War but is captured by the English and burned at the stake at Rouen.

1434 Johannes Gutenberg invents the printing press in Strasbourg, Alsace.

1453 France finally defeats England, terminating the Hundred Years' War and English claims to the French throne.

1475 Burgundy is at the height of its power under Charles the Bald.

1494 Italian wars: beginning of Franco-Hapsburg struggle for hegemony in Europe.

1515–47 Reign of François I, who imports Italian artists, including Leonardo da Vinci (1452–1519), and brings the Renaissance to France. The château of Fontainebleau is begun (1528).

1558 France captures Calais, England's last territory on French soil.

1562–98 Wars of Religion: Catholics versus Huguenots (French Protestants).

The Bourbon Dynasty

1589 The first Bourbon king, Henri IV (1589–1610), is a Protestant who converts to Catholicism and achieves peace in France. He signs the Edict of Nantes, giving limited freedom of worship to Protestants. The development of Renaissance Paris begins.

ca. 1610 Scientific revolution in Europe begins, marked by the discoveries of mathematician and philosopher René Descartes (1596–1650).

1643–1715 Reign of Louis XIV, the Sun King, a monarch who builds the Baroque power base of Versailles and presents Europe with a glorious view of France. With his first minister, Colbert, Louis makes France, by force of arms, the most powerful nation-state in Europe. He persecutes the Huguenots, who emigrate in great numbers, nearly ruining the French economy.

1660 Classical period of French culture: dramatists Pierre Corneille (1606–84), Molière (1622–73), and Jean Racine (1639–99), and painter Nicolas Poussin (1594–1665).

ca. 1715 Rococo art and decoration develop in Parisian boudoirs and salons, typified by the painter Antoine Watteau (1684–1721) and, later, François Boucher (1703–70) and Jean-Honoré Fragonard (1732–1806).

1700–onward Writer and pedagogue Voltaire (1694–1778) is a central figure in the French Enlightenment, along with Jean-Jacques Rousseau (1712–78) and Denis Diderot (1713–84), who in 1751 compiles the first modern encyclopedia. The ideals of the Enlightenment—for reason and scientific method and against social and political injustices—pave the way for the French Revolution. In the arts painter Jacques-Louis David (1748–1825) reinforces revolutionary creeds in his Neoclassical works.

1756–63 The Seven Years' War results in the loss by France of most of its overseas possessions and in the ascension of England as a world power.

1776 The French assist the Americans in the Revolutionary War. Ideals of liberty cross the Atlantic with the returning troops to reinforce new social concepts.

The French Revolution

1789–1804 The Bastille is stormed on July 14, 1789. Following upon early Republican ideals comes the Reign of Terror and the administration of the Directory under Robespierre. There are widespread political executions—Louis XVI and Marie-Antoinette are guillotined in 1793. Reaction sets in, and the instigators of the Terror are themselves executed (1794). Napoléon Bonaparte enters as Champion of the Directory (1795–99) and is installed as First Consul during the Consulate (1799–1804).

The First Empire

1804 Napoléon crowns himself emperor of France at Notre-Dame in the presence of the pope.

1805–12 Napoléon conquers most of Europe. The Napoleonic Age is marked by a Neoclassical artistic style called Empire as well as by the rise of Romanticism—characterized by such writers as François-Auguste-René de Chateaubriand (1768–1848) and Marie-Henri Stendhal (1783–1842) and the painters Eugène Delacroix (1798–1863) and Théodore Géricault (1791–1824)—which is to dominate the arts of the 19th century.

1812–14 Winter cold and Russian determination defeat Napoléon outside Moscow. The emperor abdicates and is transported to Elba.

Restoration of the Bourbons

1814–15 Louis XVIII, brother of the executed Louis XVI, regains the throne after the Congress of Vienna settles peace terms.

1815 The Hundred Days: Napoléon returns from Elba and musters an army on his march to the capital but lacks national support. He is defeated at Waterloo (June 18) and exiled to the island of St-Helena, in the south Atlantic.

1821 Napoléon dies in exile.

1830 Bourbon king Charles X, locked into a pre-Revolutionary state of mind, abdicates. A brief upheaval (called Three Glorious Days) brings Louis-Philippe, the Citizen King, to the throne.

1840 Napoléon's remains are brought back to Paris.

1846–48 Severe industrial and farming depression contributes to Louis-Philippe's abdication (1848).

Second Republic and Second Empire

1848–52 Louis-Napoléon (nephew and step-grandson of Napoléon I) is elected president of the short-lived Second Republic. He makes a successful attempt to assume supreme power and is declared emperor of France, taking the title Napoléon III.

ca. 1850 The ensuing period is characterized in the arts by the emergence of realist painters, such as Jean-François Millet (1814–75), Honoré Daumier (1808–79), and Gustave Courbet (1819–77), and late-Romantic writers, among them Victor Hugo (1802–85), Honoré de Balzac (1799–1850), and Charles Baudelaire (1821–87).

1863 Napoléon III inaugurates the Salon des Refusés in response to critical opinion. It includes work by Édouard Manet (1832–83), Claude Monet (1840–1926), and Paul Cézanne (1839–1906), and is commonly regarded as the birthplace of Impressionism and of modern art in general.

The Third Republic

1870–71 The Franco-Prussian War sees Paris besieged by and then fall to the Germans. Napoléon III takes refuge in England. France loses Alsace and Lorraine to Prussia before the peace treaty is signed.

1871–1914 Before World War I, France expands its industries and builds vast colonial empires in North Africa and Southeast Asia. Sculptor Auguste Rodin (1840–1917), composers Maurice Ravel (1875–1937) and Claude Debussy (1862–1918), and poets such as Stéphane Mallarmé (1842–98) and Paul Verlaine (1844–96) set the stage for modernism.

1870s Emergence of the Impressionist school of painting: Claude Monet, Auguste Renoir (1841–1919), Camille Pissarro (1830–1903), and Edgar Degas (1834–1917).

1889 The Eiffel Tower is built for the Paris World Exhibition. Centennial of the French Revolution.

1918–39 Between the wars Paris attracts artists and writers, including Americans Ernest Hemingway (1899–1961) and Gertrude Stein (1874–1946). France nourishes major artistic and philosophical movements: Constructivism, Dadaism, Surrealism, and Existentialism.

1939–45 At the beginning of World War II, France sides with the Allies until invaded and defeated by Germany in 1940. The French government, under Marshal Philippe Pétain (1856–1951), moves to Vichy and cooperates with the Nazis. French overseas colonies split between allegiance to the legal government of Vichy and declaration for the Free French Resistance, led (from London) by General Charles de Gaulle (1890–1970).

1944 D-Day, June 6: The Allies land on the beaches of Normandy and successfully invade France. Additional Allied forces land in Provence. Paris is liberated in August 1944, and France declares full allegiance to the Allies.

1944–46 A provisional government takes power under General de Gaulle; American aid assists French recovery.

The Fourth Republic

1946 France adopts a new constitution; French women gain the right to vote.

1954–62 The Algerian War leads to Algeria's independence from France. Other French African colonies gain independence.

1957 The Treaty of Rome establishes the European Economic Community (now known as the European Union—EU), with France as one of its members.

The Fifth Republic

1958–69 De Gaulle is the first president under a new constitution; he resigns in 1969, a year after widespread disturbances begun by student riots in Paris.

1981 François Mitterrand (1916–1996) is elected the first Socialist president of France since World War II.

1994 The Channel Tunnel (or Chunnel) opens; trains link London to Paris in three hours.

1995 Jacques Chirac, mayor of Paris, is elected president.

1997 The world's largest library, the Bibliothèque Nationale François-Mitterrand, is inaugurated in Paris. President Jacques Chirac calls early elections, a Socialist coalition wins a majority, and Lionel Jospin is appointed prime minister.

1999 The launch of the euro—the single European currency—sees prices in shops and restaurants commonly posted in both francs and euros.

2002 Throughout France, the widespread introduction of euro bills and coins goes off without a hitch.

FRENCH VOCABULARY

One of the trickiest French sounds to pronounce is the nasal final *n* sound (whether or not the *n* is actually the last letter of the word). You should try to pronounce it as a sort of nasal grunt—as in "huh." The vowel that precedes the *n* will govern the vowel sound of the word, and in this list we precede the final *n* with an *h* to remind you to be nasal.

Another problem sound is the ubiquitous but untransliterable *eu,* as in *bleu* (blue) or *deux* (two), and the very similar sound in *je* (I), *ce* (this), and *de* (of). The closest equivalent might be the vowel sound in "put," but rounded.

Words and Phrases

Basics

English	French	Pronunciation
Yes/no	Oui/non	wee/nohn
Please	S'il vous plaît	seel voo **play**
Thank you	Merci	mair-**see**
You're welcome	De rien	deh ree-**ehn**
That's all right	Il n'y a pas de quoi	eel nee ah pah de **kwah**
Excuse me, sorry	Pardon	pahr-**dohn**
Sorry!	Désolé(e)	day-zoh-**lay**
Good morning/ afternoon	Bonjour	bohn-**zhoor**
Good evening	Bonsoir	bohn-**swahr**
Goodbye	Au revoir	o ruh-**vwahr**
Mr. (Sir)	Monsieur	muh-**syuh**
Mrs. (Ma'am)	Madame	ma-**dam**
Miss	Mademoiselle	mad-mwa-**zel**
Pleased to meet you	Enchanté(e)	ohn-shahn-**tay**
How are you?	Comment ça va?	kuh-mahn-sa-**va**
Very well, thanks	Très bien, merci	tray bee-ehn, mair-**see**
And you?	Et vous?	ay **voo**?

Numbers

one	un	uhn
two	deux	deuh
three	trois	twah
four	quatre	**kaht**-ruh
five	cinq	sank
six	six	seess
seven	sept	set
eight	huit	wheat
nine	neuf	nuff
ten	dix	deess
eleven	onze	ohnz
twelve	douze	dooz

thirteen	treize	trehz
fourteen	quatorze	kah-**torz**
fifteen	quinze	kanz
sixteen	seize	sez
seventeen	dix-sept	deez-**set**
eighteen	dix-huit	deez-**wheat**
nineteen	dix-neuf	deez-**nuff**
twenty	vingt	vehn
twenty-one	vingt-et-un	vehnt-ay-**uhn**
thirty	trente	trahnt
forty	quarante	ka-**rahnt**
fifty	cinquante	sang-**kahnt**
sixty	soixante	swa-**sahnt**
seventy	soixante-dix	swa-sahnt-**deess**
eighty	quatre-vingts	kaht-ruh-**vehn**
ninety	quatre-vingt-dix	kaht-ruh-vehn-**deess**
one-hundred	cent	sahn
one-thousand	mille	meel

Colors

black	noir	nwahr
blue	bleu	bleuh
brown	brun/marron	bruhn/mar-**rohn**
green	vert	vair
orange	orange	o-**rahnj**
pink	rose	rose
red	rouge	rooje
violet	violette	vee-o-**let**
white	blanc	blahnk
yellow	jaune	zhone

Days of the Week

Sunday	dimanche	**dee**-mahnsh
Monday	lundi	**luhn**-dee
Tuesday	mardi	**mahr**-dee
Wednesday	mercredi	**mair**-kruh-dee
Thursday	jeudi	**zhuh**-dee
Friday	vendredi	**vawn**-druh-dee
Saturday	samedi	**sahm**-dee

Months

January	janvier	**zhahn**-vee-ay
February	février	**feh**-vree-ay
March	mars	marce
April	avril	a-**vreel**
May	mai	meh
June	juin	zhwehn
July	juillet	**zhwee**-ay
August	août	oot
September	septembre	sep-**tahm**-bruh
October	octobre	awk-**to**-bruh
November	novembre	no-**vahm**-bruh
December	décembre	day-**sahm**-bruh

Useful Phrases

Do you speak . . . English?	Parlez-vous . . . anglais?	par-lay **voo** **ahn-**glay
I don't speak . . . French	Je ne parle pas . . . français	zhuh nuh parl **pah** frahn-**say**
I don't understand	Je ne comprends pas	zhuh nuh kohm-prahn **pah**
I understand	Je comprends	zhuh kohm-**prahn**
I don't know	Je ne sais pas	zhuh nuh say **pah**
I'm American/ British	Je suis américain/ anglais	zhuh sweez a-may-ree-**kehn**/ahn-**glay**
What's your name?	Comment vous appelez-vous?	ko-mahn voo za-pell-ay-**voo**
My name is . . .	Je m'appelle . . .	zhuh ma-**pell** . . .
What time is it?	Quelle heure est-il?	kel air eh-**teel**
How?	Comment?	ko-**mahn**
When?	Quand?	kahn
Yesterday	Hier	yair
Today	Aujourd'hui	o-zhoor-**dwee**
Tomorrow	Demain	duh-**mehn**
This morning/ afternoon	Ce matin/cet après-midi	suh ma-**tehn**/set ah-pray-mee-**dee**
Tonight	Ce soir	suh **swahr**
What?	Quoi?	kwah
What is it?	Qu'est-ce que c'est?	kess-kuh-**say**
Why?	Pourquoi?	**poor**-kwa
Who?	Qui?	kee
Where is . . .	Où se trouve . . .	oo suh **troov**
the train station?	la gare?	la gar
the subway? station?	la station de? métro?	la sta-**syon** duh may-**tro**
the bus stop?	l'arrêt de bus?	la-**ray** duh **booss**
the airport?	l'aérogare?	lay-ro-**gar**
the post office?	la poste?	la post
the bank?	la banque?	la bahnk
the hotel?	l'hôtel?	lo-**tel**
the store?	le magasin?	luh ma-ga-**zehn**
the cashier?	la caisse?	la **kess**
the museum?	le musée?	luh mew-**zay**
the hospital?	l'hôpital?	lo-pee-**tahl**
the elevator?	l'ascenseur?	la-sahn-**seuhr**
the telephone?	le téléphone?	luh tay-lay-**phone**
Where are the rest rooms?	Où sont les toilettes?	oo sohn lay twah-**let**
Here/there	Ici/là	ee-**see**/la
Left/right	A gauche/à droite	a goash/a drwaht
Straight ahead	Tout droit	too drwah

Is it near/far?	C'est près/loin?	say pray/lwehn
I'd like . . .	Je voudrais . . .	zhuh voo-**dray**
a room	une chambre	ewn **shahm**-bruh
the key	la clé	la clay
a newspaper	un journal	uhn zhoor-**nahl**
a stamp	un timbre	uhn **tam**-bruh
I'd like to buy . . .	Je voudrais acheter . . .	zhuh voo-**dray** **ahsh**-tay
a cigar	un cigare	uhn see-**gar**
cigarettes	des cigarettes	day see-ga-**ret**
matches	des allumettes	days a-loo-**met**
dictionary	un dictionnaire	uhn deek-see-oh-**nare**
soap	du savon	dew sah-**vohn**
city map	un plan de ville	uhn plahn de **veel**
road map	une carte routière	ewn cart roo-tee-**air**
magazine	une revue	ewn reh-**vu**
envelopes	des enveloppes	dayz ahn-veh-**lope**
writing paper	du papier à lettres	dew pa-pee-**ay** a **let**-ruh
airmail writing paper	du papier avion	dew pa-pee-**ay** a-vee-**ohn**
postcard	une carte postale	ewn cart pos-**tal**
How much is it?	C'est combien?	say comb-bee-**ehn**
It's expensive/cheap	C'est cher/pas cher	say share/pa share
A little/a lot	Un peu/beaucoup	uhn peuh/bo-**koo**
More/less	Plus/moins	plu/mwehn
Enough/too (much)	Assez/trop	a-say/tro
I am ill/sick	Je suis malade	zhuh swee ma-**lahd**
Call a . . . doctor	Appelez un . . . médecin	a-play uhn mayd-**sehn**
Help!	Au secours!	o suh-**koor**
Stop!	Arrêtez!	a-reh-**tay**
Fire!	Au feu!	o fuh
Caution!/Look out!	Attention!	a-tahn-see-**ohn**

Dining Out

A bottle of . . .	une bouteille de . . .	ewn boo-**tay** duh
A cup of . . .	une tasse de . . .	ewn **tass** duh
A glass of . . .	un verre de . . .	uhn **vair** duh
Ashtray	un cendrier	uhn sahn-dree-**ay**
Bill/check	l'addition	la-dee-see-**ohn**
Bread	du pain	dew pan
Breakfast	le petit-déjeuner	luh puh-**tee** day-zhuh-**nay**
Butter	du beurre	dew burr
Cheers!	A votre santé!	ah vo-truh sahn-**tay**
Cocktail/aperitif	un apéritif	uhn ah-pay-ree-**teef**

Dinner	le dîner	luh dee-**nay**
Special of the day	le plat du jour	luh plah dew **zhoor**
Enjoy!	Bon appétit!	bohn a-pay-**tee**
Fixed-price menu	le menu	luh may-**new**
Fork	une fourchette	ewn four-**shet**
I am diabetic	Je suis diabétique	zhuh swee dee-ah-bay-**teek**
I am on a diet	Je suis au régime	zhuh sweez oray-**jeem**
I am vegetarian	Je suis végé-tarien(ne)	zhuh swee vay-zhay-ta-ree-**en**
I cannot eat . . .	Je ne peux pas manger de . . .	zhuh nuh **puh** pah mahn-**jay** deh
I'd like to order	Je voudrais commander	zhuh voo-**dray** ko-mahn-**day**
I'm hungry/thirsty	J'ai faim/soif	zhay fahm/swahf
Is service/the tip included?	Le service est-il compris?	luh sair-**veess** ay-teel com-**pree**
It's good/bad	C'est bon/mauvais	say bohn/mo-**vay**
It's hot/cold	C'est chaud/froid	say sho/frwah
Knife	un couteau	uhn koo-**toe**
Lunch	le déjeuner	luh day-zhuh-**nay**
Menu	la carte	la cart
Napkin	une serviette	ewn sair-vee-**et**
Pepper	du poivre	dew **pwah**-vruh
Plate	une assiette	ewn a-see-**et**
Please give me . . .	Merci de me donner . . .	Mair-**see** deh meh doe-**nay**
Salt	du sel	dew sell
Spoon	une cuillère	ewn kwee-**air**
Sugar	du sucre	dew **sook**-ruh
Waiter!/Waitress!	Monsieur!/ Mademoiselle!	muh-**syuh**/ mad-mwa-**zel**
Wine list	la carte des vins	la **cart** day van

MENU GUIDE

French	English
General Dining	
Entrée	Appetizer/Starter
Garniture au choix	Choice of vegetable side
Selon arrivage	When available
Supplément/En sus	Extra charge
Sur commande	Made to order
Appetizers/Starters	
Anchois	Anchovies
Andouille(tte)	Chitterling sausage
Assiette de charcuterie	Assorted pork products
Crudités	Mixed raw vegetable salad
Escargots	Snails
Jambon	Ham
Jambonneau	Cured pig's knuckle
Pâté	Liver puree blended with meat
Quenelles	Light dumplings
Saucisson	Dried sausage
Terrine	Pâté in an earthenware pot
Soups	
Bisque	Shellfish soup
Bouillabaisse	Fish and seafood stew
Julienne	Vegetable soup
Potage/Soupe	Soup
Potage parmentier	Thick potato soup
Pot-au-feu	Stew of meat and vegetables
Soupe du jour	Soup of the day
Soupe à l'oignon gratinée	French onion soup
Soupe au pistou	Provençal vegetable soup
Velouté de . . .	Cream of . . .
Vichyssoise	Cold leek and potato cream soup
Fish and Seafood	
Bar	Bass
Bourride	Fish stew from Marseilles
Brandade de morue	Creamed salt cod
Brochet	Pike
Cabillaud/Morue	Fresh cod
Calmar	Squid
Coquilles St-Jacques	Scallops
Crabe	Crab
Crevettes	Shrimp
Daurade	Sea bream
Écrevisses	Prawns/crayfish
Harengs	Herring
Homard	Lobster
Huîtres	Oysters
Langouste	Spiny lobster
Langoustine	Prawn/lobster
Lotte	Monkfish
Moules	Mussels
Palourdes	Clams

Rouget	Red mullet
Saumon	Salmon
Thon	Tuna
Truite	Trout

Meat

Agneau	Lamb
Ballotine	Boned, stuffed, and rolled
Blanquette de veau	Veal stew with a white-sauce base
Boeuf	Beef
Boeuf à la Bourguignonne	Beef stew
Boudin blanc	Sausage made with white meat
Boudin noir	Sausage made with pig's blood
Boulettes de viande	Meatballs
Brochette	Kabob
Cassoulet	Casserole of white beans, meat
Cervelle	Brains
Châteaubriand	Double fillet steak
Côtelettes	Chops
Choucroute garnie	Sausages and cured pork served with sauerkraut
Côte de boeuf	T-bone steak
Côte	Rib
Cuisses de grenouilles	Frogs' legs
Entrecôte	Rib or rib-eye steak
Épaule	Shoulder
Escalope	Cutlet
Foie	Liver
Gigot	Leg
Langue	Tongue
Médaillon	Tenderloin steak
Pavé	Thick slice of boned beef
Pieds de cochon	Pig's feet
Porc	Pork
Ragoût	Stew
Ris de veau	Veal sweetbreads
Rognons	Kidneys
Saucisses	Sausages
Selle	Saddle
Tournedos	Tenderloin of T-bone steak
Veau	Veal
Viande	Meat

Methods of Preparation

À point	Medium
À l'étouffée	Stewed
Au four	Baked
Bien cuit	Well-done
Bleu	Very rare
Bouilli	Boiled
Braisé	Braised
Frit	Fried
Grillé	Grilled
Rôti	Roast
Saignant	Rare
Sauté/poêlée	Sautéed

Game and Poultry

Blanc de volaille	Chicken breast
Caille	Quail
Canard/Caneton	Duck/duckling
Cerf/Chevreuil	Venison
Coq au vin	Chicken stewed in red wine
Dinde/Dindonneau	Turkey/Young turkey
Faisan	Pheasant
Lapin	Rabbit
Lièvre	Wild hare
Oie	Goose
Pigeon/Pigeonneau	Pigeon/Squab
Pintade/Pintadeau	Guinea fowl/Young guinea fowl
Poularde	Fattened pullet
Poulet/Poussin	Chicken/Spring chicken
Sanglier/Marcassin	Wild boar/Young wild boar
Volaille	Fowl

Vegetables

Artichaut	Artichoke
Asperge	Asparagus
Aubergine	Eggplant
Carottes	Carrots
Champignons	Mushrooms
Chou-fleur	Cauliflower
Chou (rouge)	Cabbage (red)
Choux de Bruxelles	Brussels sprouts
Courgette	Zucchini
Cresson	Watercress
Épinard	Spinach
Haricots blancs/verts	White kidney/green beans
Laitue	Lettuce
Lentilles	Lentils
Maïs	Corn
Oignons	Onions
Petits pois	Peas
Poireaux	Leeks
Poivrons	Peppers
Pomme de terre	Potato
Pommes frites	French fries
Tomates	Tomatoes

Desserts

Coupe (glacée)	Sundae
Crêpe	Thin pancake
Crème brûlée	Custard with caramelized topping
Crème caramel	Caramel-coated custard
Crème Chantilly	Whipped cream
Gâteau au chocolat	Chocolate cake
Glace	Ice cream
Mousse au chocolat	Chocolate mousse
Sabayon	Egg-and-wine-based custard
Tarte aux pommes	Apple pie
Tarte tatin	Caramelized apple tart
Tourte	Layer cake

Alcoholic Drinks

À l'eau	With water
Avec des glaçons	On the rocks
Kir	Chilled white wine mixed with black-currant syrup
Bière	Beer
blonde/brune	*light/dark*
Calvados	Apple brandy from Normandy
Eau-de-vie	Brandy
Liqueur	Cordial
Poire William	Pear brandy
Porto	Port
Vin	Wine
sec	*dry/neat*
brut	*very dry*
léger	*light*
doux	*sweet*
rouge	*red*
rosé	*rosé*
mousseux	*sparkling*
blanc	*white*

Nonalcoholic Drinks

Café	Coffee
noir	*black*
crème	*with steamed milk/cream*
au lait	*with steamed milk*
décaféiné	*caffeine-free*
Express	Espresso
Chocolat chaud	Hot chocolate
Eau minérale	Mineral water
gazeuse/non gazeuse	*carbonated/still*
Jus de . . .	. . . juice
Lait	Milk
Limonade	Lemonade
Thé	Tea
au lait/au citron	*with milk/lemon*
glacé	*Iced tea*
Tisane	Herb tea

INDEX

Icons and Symbols

★ Our special recommendations
✕ Restaurant
Lodging establishment
Lodging establishment whose restaurant warrants a special trip
Good for kids (rubber duck)
☞ Sends you to another section of the guide for more information
✉ Address
☏ Telephone number
Opening and closing times
Admission prices

Numbers in white and black circles ③ ❸ that appear on the maps, in the margins, and within the tours correspond to one another.

A

B

D